PHILIP'S

STREET ATLAS

Cheshire

irst published 1995 by
'hilip's, a division of
)ctopus Publishing Group Ltd
!–4 Heron Quays, London E14 4JP

econd colour edition 2002
irst impression 2002

SBN 0-540-08114-0

rinted and bound in Spain
y Cayfosa-Quebecor

Contents

III **Key to map symbols**

IV **Key to map pages**

VI **Route planning**

VIII **Administrative and Postcode boundaries**

1 **Street maps** at 2½ inches to 1 mile

237 **Street map of Chester city centre** at 5 inches to 1 mile

238 **Town maps** of Altrincham, Cheadle and Gatley, Stockport, Hyde, Romiley, Sale and Stalybridge

243 **Index** of towns and villages

244 **Index** of streets, hospitals, industrial estates, railway stations, schools, shopping centres, universities and places of interest

Digital Data

The exceptionally high-quality mapping found in this atlas is available as digital data in TIFF format, which is easily convertible to other bit mapped (raster) image formats.

The index is also available in digital form as a standard database table. It contains all the details found in the printed index together with the National Grid reference for the map square in which each entry is named.

For further information and to discuss your requirements, please contact Philip's on 020 7531 8439 or george.philip@philips-maps.co.uk

22a	**Motorway** with junction number
	Primary route – dual/single carriageway
	A road – dual/single carriageway
	B road – dual/single carriageway
	Minor road – dual/single carriageway
	Other minor road – dual/single carriageway
	Road under construction
	Pedestrianised area
DY7	**Postcode boundaries**
	County and unitary authority boundaries
	Railway
	Railway under construction
	Tramway, miniature railway
	Rural track, private road or narrow road in urban area
	Gate or obstruction to traffic (restrictions may not apply at all times or to all vehicles)
	Path, bridleway, byway open to all traffic, road used as a public path
	The representation in this atlas of a road, track or path is no evidence of the existence of a right of way
58 / 230	**Adjoining page indicators**
237	**The map area within the pink band is shown at a larger scale on the page indicated by the red block and arrow**

Abbreviation	Meaning	Abbreviation	Meaning
Acad	**Academy**	Mkt	**Market**
Allot Gdns	**Allotments**	Meml	**Memorial**
Cemy	**Cemetery**	Mon	**Monument**
C Ctr	**Civic Centre**	Mus	**Museum**
CH	**Club House**	Obsy	**Observatory**
Coll	**College**	Pal	**Royal Palace**
Crem	**Crematorium**	PH	**Public House**
Ent	**Enterprise**	Recn Gd	**Recreation Ground**
Ex H	**Exhibition Hall**	Resr	**Reservoir**
Ind Est	**Industrial Estate**	Ret Pk	**Retail Park**
IRB Sta	**Inshore Rescue Boat Station**	Sch	**School**
		Sh Ctr	**Shopping Centre**
Inst	**Institute**	TH	**Town Hall/House**
Ct	**Law Court**	Trad Est	**Trading Estate**
L Ctr	**Leisure Centre**	Univ	**University**
LC	**Level Crossing**	Wks	**Works**
Liby	**Library**	YH	**Youth Hostel**

Walsall	**Railway station**
	Private railway station
	Bus, coach station
	Ambulance station
	Coastguard station
	Fire station
	Police station
+	**Accident and Emergency entrance to hospital**
H	**Hospital**
+	**Place of worship**
i	**Information Centre** (open all year)
P	**Parking**
P&R	**Park and Ride**
PO	**Post Office**
	Camping site
	Caravan site
	Golf course
	Picnic site
Prim Sch	**Important buildings, schools, colleges, universities and hospitals**
River Medway	**Water name**
	River, stream
	Lock, weir
	Water
	Tidal water
	Woods
	Houses
Church	**Non-Roman antiquity**
ROMAN FORT	**Roman antiquity**

■ The small numbers around the edges of the maps identify the 1 kilometre National Grid lines ■ The dark grey border on the inside edge of some pages indicates that the mapping does not continue onto the adjacent page

'he scale of the maps on the pages numbered in blue
s 3.92 cm to 1 km • 2½ inches to 1 mile • 1: 25344

0 – ¼ – ½ – ¾ – 1 mile
0 – 250 m – 500 m – 750 m – 1 kilometre

'he scale of the maps on pages numbered in red
s 7.84 cm to 1 km • 5 inches to 1 mile • 1: 12672

0 – 220 yards – 440 yards – 660 yards – ½ mile
0 – 125 m – 250 m – 375 m – ½ kilometre

Key to map pages

122 Map pages at 2½ inches to 1 mile

237 Map pages at 5 inches to 1 mile

Scale

0 5 10 15 km

0 5 10 miles

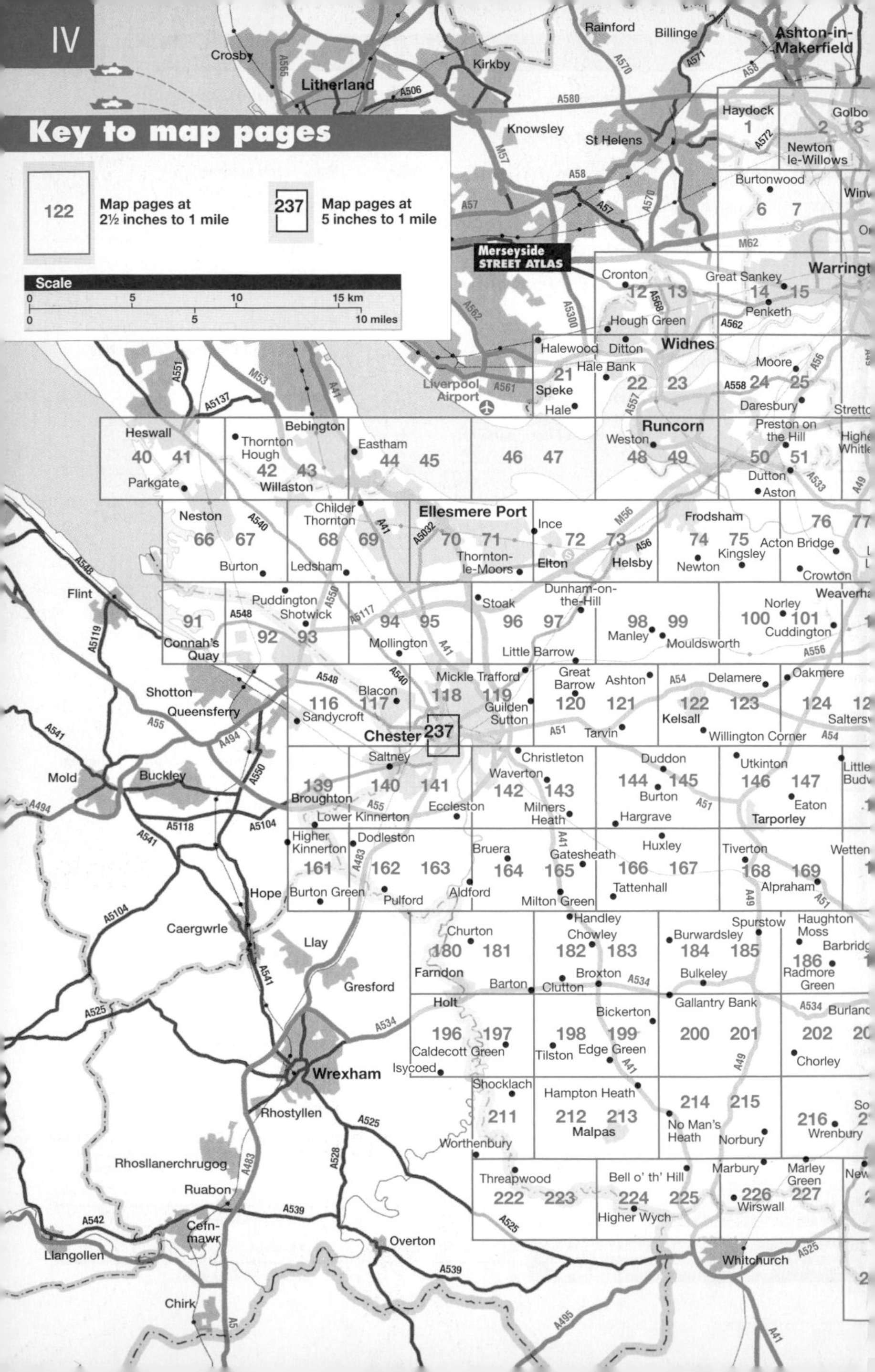

Crosby
Litherland
Kirkby
Rainford
Billinge
Ashton-in-Makerfield
Knowsley
St Helens
Haydock 1
Golborne 2 3
Newton le-Willows
Burtonwood 6 7
M62
Merseyside STREET ATLAS
Cronton 12 13
Hough Green
Great Sankey 14 15
Penketh
Warrington
Halewood
Ditton
Widnes
Hale Bank
21 22 23
Speke
Hale
Moore 24 25
Daresbury
Liverpool Airport
Heswall 40 41
Parkgate
Bebington
Thornton Hough 42 43
Willaston
Eastham 44 45
46 47
Runcorn
Weston 48 49
Preston on the Hill 50 51
Dutton
Aston
Neston 66 67
Burton
Childer Thornton 68 69
Ledsham
Ellesmere Port 70 71
Thornton-le-Moors
Ince 72 73
Elton
Helsby
Frodsham 74 75
Kingsley
Newton
Acton Bridge 76
Crowton
Flint
Connah's Quay 91
Puddington
Shotwick 92 93
Mollington 94 95
Stoak 96 97
Dunham-on-the-Hill
Little Barrow
Manley 98 99
Mouldsworth
Norley 100 101
Cuddington
Weaverham
Shotton
Queensferry
Sandycroft 116 117
Blacon
Mickle Trafford 118 119
Guilden Sutton
Great Barrow 120
Ashton 121
Tarvin
Delamere 122 123
Kelsall
Willington Corner
Oakmere 124
Chester 237
Mold
Buckley
Saltney
Broughton 139
140 141
Eccleston
Lower Kinnerton
Christleton
Waverton 142 143
Milners Heath
Duddon 144 145
Burton
Hargrave
Utkinton 146 147
Eaton
Tarporley
Higher Kinnerton 161
Dodleston 162 163
Burton Green
Pulford
Aldford
Bruera 164 165
Gatesheath
Milton Green
Huxley 166 167
Tattenhall
Tiverton 168 169
Alpraham
Wettenhall
Hope
Caergwrle
Llay
Gresford
Churton 180 181
Farndon
Barton
Handley
Chowley 182 183
Broxton
Clutton
Burwardsley 184 185
Spurstow
Bulkeley
Haughton Moss 186
Barbridge
Radmore Green
Holt
196 197
Caldecott Green
Isycoed
Wrexham
Bickerton
Tilston 198 199
Edge Green
Gallantry Bank
200 201
202
Burland
Chorley
Rhostyllen
Shocklach 211
Hampton Heath
212 213
Malpas
214 215
No Man's Heath
Norbury
216
Wrenbury
Worthenbury
Rhosllanerchrugog
Ruabon
Cefn-mawr
Llangollen
Threapwood 222 223
Bell o' th' Hill 224 225
Higher Wych
Marbury 226 227
Marley Green
Wirswall
Whitchurch
Overton
Chirk
A565 A506 A580 A570 A571 A58 A572 M57 A57 A5300 A562 A568 A56 A558 A551 M53 A5137 A41 A561 A557 A533 A49 A540 A5032 M56 A548 A5119 A550 A5117 A556 A54 A55 A494 A541 A51 A5118 A5104 A483 A525 A534 A528 A539 A542 A5 A495

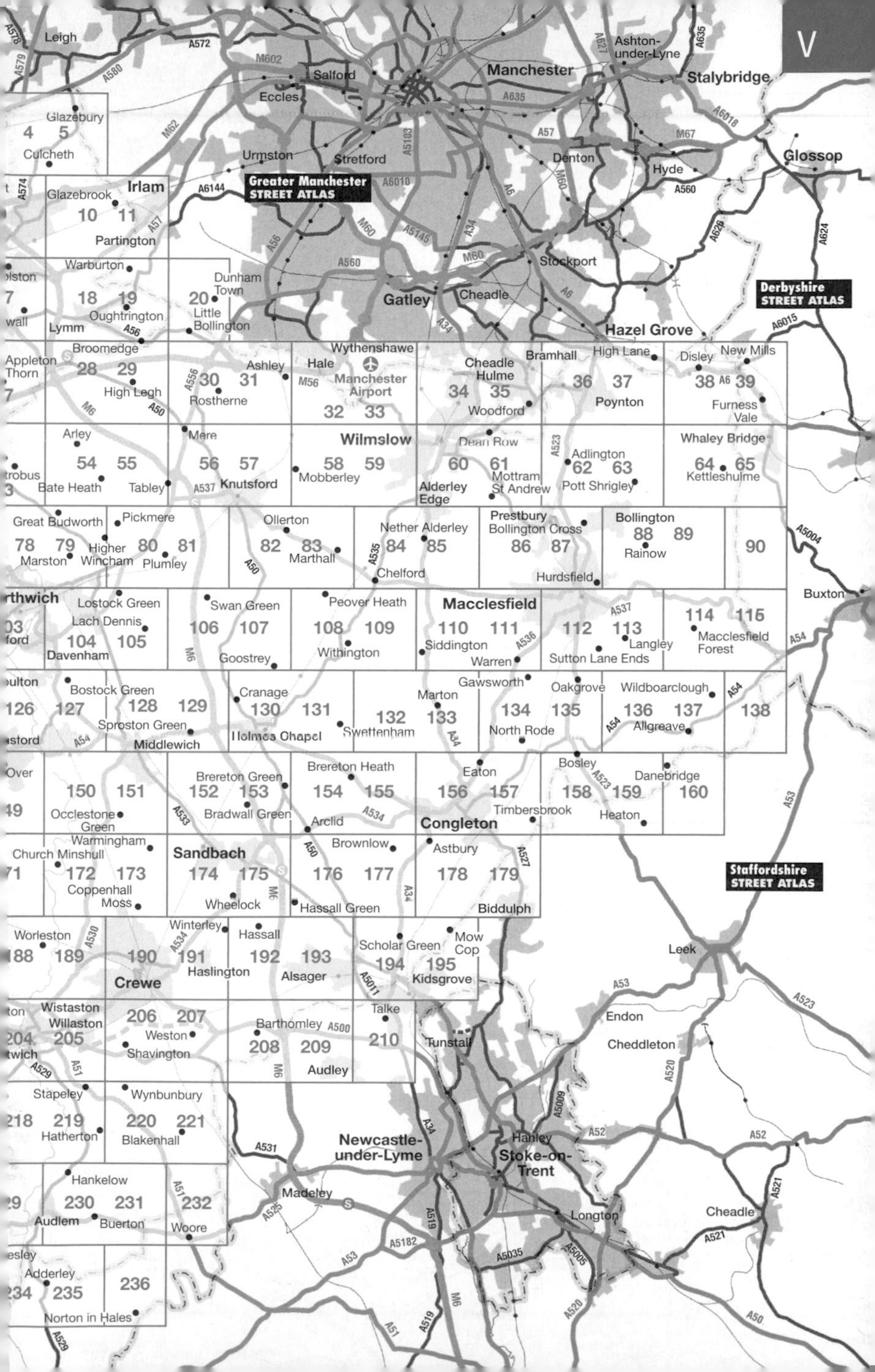
A578
Leigh
A572
M602
Ashton-under-Lyne
A627
A635
A579
A580
Salford
Manchester
Stalybridge
Eccles
A635
A6018
Glazebury
4 5
Culcheth
M62
A5103
A57
M67
Urmston
Stretford
Denton
Glossop
Hyde
A574
Irlam
Glazebrook
10 11
Partington
A57
A6144
Greater Manchester
STREET ATLAS
A6010
M60
A560
A626
A624
A56
M60
A5145
A34
A6
Warburton
18 19
Oughtrington
Lymm
A56
20
Dunham Town
Little Bollington
A560
M60
Stockport
Gatley
Cheadle
A6
A34
Derbyshire
STREET ATLAS
Hazel Grove
A6015
Appleton Thorn
Broomedge
28 29
High Legh
M6
A50
Wythenshawe
Hale
Manchester Airport
M56
32 33
Ashley
30 31
Rostherne
A556
Cheadle Hulme
34 35
Woodford
Bramhall
High Lane
36 37
Poynton
Disley
New Mills
38 A6 39
Furness Vale
Arley
54 55
Bate Heath
Tabley
Mere
56 57
A537
Knutsford
Wilmslow
58 59
Mobberley
Dean Row
60 61
Alderley Edge
Mottram St Andrew
A523
Adlington
62 63
Pott Shrigley
Whaley Bridge
64 65
Kettleshulme
Great Budworth
Pickmere
78 79
Marston
Higher Wincham
80 81
Plumley
Ollerton
82 83
Marthall
A50
A535
Nether Alderley
84 85
Chelford
Prestbury
Bollington Cross
86 87
Hurdsfield
Bollington
88 89
Rainow
90
A5004
Buxton
Northwich
Lostock Green
Lach Dennis
104 105
Davenham
Swan Green
106 107
Goostrey
M6
Peover Heath
108 109
Withington
Macclesfield
110 111
Siddington
A536
Warren
A537
112 113
Langley
Sutton Lane Ends
114 115
Macclesfield Forest
A54
Bostock Green
126 127
128 129
Sproston Green
A54
Middlewich
Cranage
130 131
Holmes Chapel
132
Swettenham
Marton
133
A34
Gawsworth
134 135
North Rode
Oakgrove
Wildboarclough
136 137
A54
Allgreave
A54
138
Over
150 151
Occlestone Green
Brereton Green
152 153
Bradwall Green
A533
Brereton Heath
154 155
Arclid
A534
Eaton
156 157
Congleton
Timbersbrook
Bosley
A523
158 159
Heaton
Danebridge
160
A53
Warmingham
Church Minshull
172 173
Coppenhall Moss
Sandbach
174 175
Wheelock
M6
A50
Brownlow
176 177
Hassall Green
A34
Astbury
178 179
A527
Biddulph
Staffordshire
STREET ATLAS
Worleston
188 189
A530
190
Crewe
Winterley
A534
191
Haslington
Hassall
192 193
Alsager
Scholar Green
194
A5011
Mow Cop
195
Kidsgrove
Leek
A53
A523
Wistaston
Willaston
204 205
206 207
Weston
Shavington
A529
A51
Barthomley
A500
208 209
Audley
M6
Talke
210
Tunstall
Endon
Cheddleton
A520
Stapeley
218 219
Hatherton
Wynbunbury
220 221
Blakenhall
A531
Newcastle-under-Lyme
A34
A5009
Hanley
Stoke-on-Trent
A52
A52
A521
Hankelow
230 231
Audlem
Buerton
A51
232
Woore
Madeley
A525
A519
Longton
Cheadle
A521
A5182
A53
A5035
A5005
Adderley
234 235
236
Norton in Hales
A529
M6
A51
A519
A520
A50

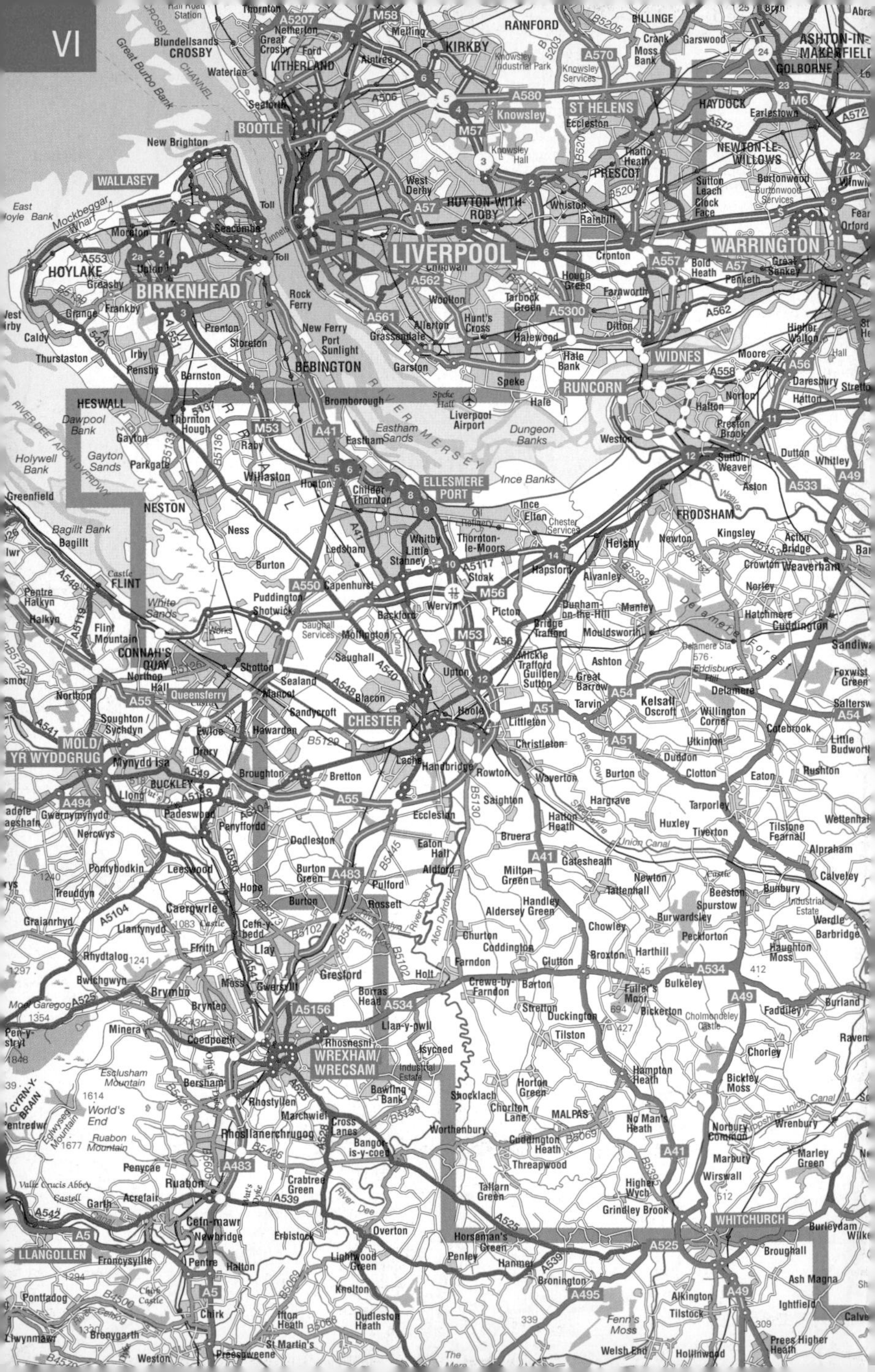

LIVERPOOL
BIRKENHEAD
BOOTLE
WALLASEY
CROSBY
LITHERLAND
KIRKBY
RAINFORD
ST HELENS
Knowsley
HAYDOCK
ASHTON-IN-MAKERFIELD
GOLBORNE
NEWTON-LE-WILLOWS
PRESCOT
HUYTON-WITH-ROBY
WARRINGTON
WIDNES
RUNCORN
HOYLAKE
BEBINGTON
HESWALL
NESTON
ELLESMERE PORT
Liverpool Airport
RIVER MERSEY
FRODSHAM
Helsby
FLINT
CONNAH'S QUAY
Queensferry
CHESTER
MOLD/ YR WYDDGRUG
BUCKLEY
Kelsall
Tarporley
WREXHAM/ WRECSAM
Ruabon
LLANGOLLEN
Chirk
MALPAS
WHITCHURCH
Bangor-is-y-coed
Overton
Hanmer
Delamere Forest
Shropshire Union Canal
M53
M56
M57
M58
M62
M6
A55
A41
A49
A51
A54
A534
A525
A483
A5
A539
A495

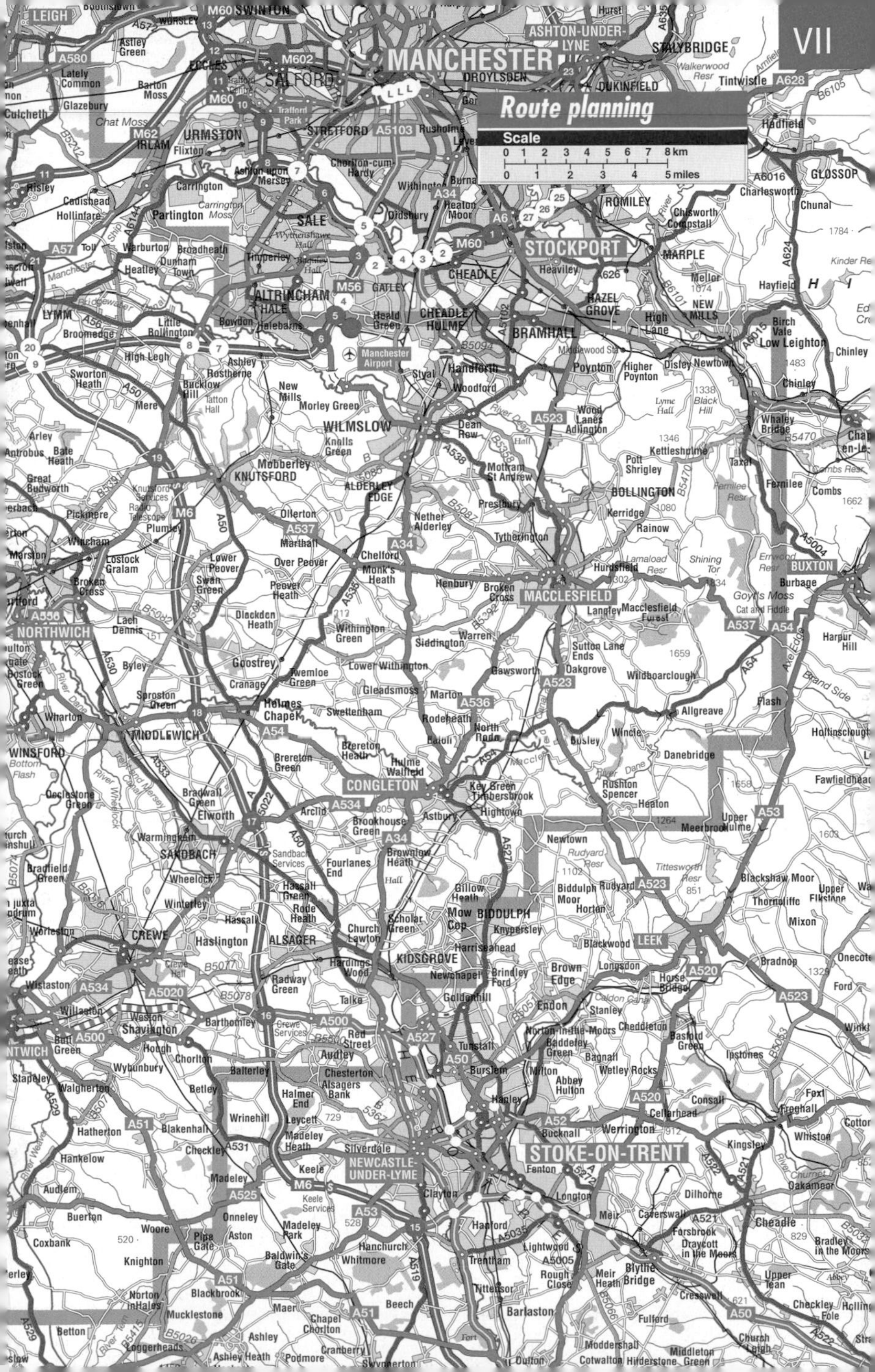

Route planning
Scale
0 1 2 3 4 5 6 7 8 km
0 1 2 3 4 5 miles
MANCHESTER
SALFORD
ASHTON-UNDER-LYNE
STALYBRIDGE
DROYLSDEN
DUKINFIELD
LEIGH
SWINTON
WORSLEY
ECCLES
Astley Green
Lately Common
Barton Moss
Glazebury
Culcheth
Chat Moss
URMSTON
IRLAM
Flixton
STRETFORD
Trafford Park
Rusholme
Chorlton-cum-Hardy
Ashton upon Mersey
Carrington
Carrington Moss
Risley
Cadishead
Hollinfare
Partington
SALE
Withington
Didsbury
Heaton Moor
Burnage
STOCKPORT
ROMILEY
Chisworth
Compstall
MARPLE
Mellor
NEW MILLS
HAZEL GROVE
High Lane
Hadfield
GLOSSOP
Charlesworth
Chunal
Hayfield
Tintwistle
Walkerwood Resr
Warburton
Broadheath
Heatley
Dunham Town
Timperley
ALTRINCHAM
HALE
Bowdon
Halebarns
Wythenshawe Hall
GATLEY
CHEADLE
Heaviley
CHEADLE HULME
Heald Green
BRAMHALL
Manchester Airport
LYMM
Broomedge
Little Bollington
High Legh
Ashley
Rostherne
Bucklow Hill
Tatton Hall
Mere
Swarton Heath
New Mills
Morley Green
Styal
Handforth
Woodford
Poynton
Middlewood Sta
Higher Poynton
Disley
Newtown
Birch Vale
Low Leighton
Chinley
Whaley Bridge
Lyme Hall
Black Hill
Wood Lanes
Adlington
WILMSLOW
Knolls Green
Dean Row
Mottram St Andrew
Pott Shrigley
Kettleshulme
Taxal
Fernilee
Fernilee Resr
Combs
Combs Resr
Arley
Antrobus
Bate Heath
Great Budworth
Mobberley
KNUTSFORD
Knutsford Services
ALDERLEY EDGE
Prestbury
BOLLINGTON
Kerridge
Rainow
Pickmere
Radio Telescope
Plumley
Ollerton
Nether Alderley
Tytherington
Wincham
Lostock Gralam
Marthall
Lower Peover
Over Peover
Chelford
Monk's Heath
Henbury
Broken Cross
MACCLESFIELD
Hurdsfield
Lamaload Resr
Shining Tor
Errwood Resr
BUXTON
Burbage
Goyt's Moss
Cat and Fiddle
Broken Cross
Swan Green
Peover Heath
NORTHWICH
Lach Dennis
Blackden Heath
Withington Green
Siddington
Warren
Langley
Macclesfield Forest
Sutton Lane Ends
Oakgrove
Wildboarclough
Harpur Hill
Axe Edge
Brand Side
Byley
Goostrey
Cranage
Twemloe Green
Lower Withington
Gleadsmoss
Marton
Gawsworth
Flash
Allgreave
Bostock Green
Wharton
Sproston Green
Holmes Chapel
Swettenham
Rodeheath
North Rode
Wincle
Bosley
Danebridge
Hollinsclough
WINSFORD
Bottom Flash
MIDDLEWICH
Brereton Heath
Brereton Green
Hulme Walfield
CONGLETON
Key Green
Timbersbrook
Rushton Spencer
Heaton
Fawfieldhead
Occlestone Green
Bradwall Green
Elworth
Arclid
Brookhouse Green
Astbury
Hightown
Meerbrook
Upper Hulme
Warmingham
SANDBACH
Sandbach Services
Fourlanes End
Brownlow Heath
Newtown
Rudyard Resr
Tittesworth Resr
Bradfield Green
Wheelock
Hassall Green
Rode Heath
Gillow Heath
Biddulph Moor
Rudyard
Horton
Blackshaw Moor
Upper Elkstone
Thorncliffe
Winterley
Hassall
Mow Cop
BIDDULPH
Knypersley
Mixon
Worleston
CREWE
Haslington
ALSAGER
Church Lawton
Scholar Green
KIDSGROVE
Harriseahead
Blackwood
LEEK
Crewe Hall
Hardings Wood
Newchapel
Brindley Ford
Brown Edge
Longsdon
Horse Bridge
Bradnop
Onecote
Wistaston
Radway Green
Talke
Goldenhill
Endon
Stanley
Ford
Willaston
Weston
Shavington
Barthomley
Crewe Services
Red Street
Tunstall
Norton-in-the-Moors
Baddeley Green
Cheddleton
Basford Green
Winkhill
Batt Green
Hough
Chorlton
Audley
Burslem
Bagnall
Wetley Rocks
Ipstones
Stapeley
Walgherton
Wybunbury
Balterley
Betley
Chesterton
Alsagers Bank
Halmer End
Milton
Abbey Hulton
Hanley
Consall
Cellarhead
Foxt
Froghall
Whiston
Cotton
Hatherton
Blakenhall
Wrinehill
Leycett
Madeley Heath
Silverdale
NEWCASTLE-UNDER-LYME
Bucknall
Werrington
STOKE-ON-TRENT
Kingsley
Hankelow
Checkley
Madeley
Keele
Keele Services
Fenton
Longton
Clayton
Dilhorne
Oakamoor
Audlem
Buerton
Onneley
Madeley Park
Hanford
Meir
Caverswall
Forsbrook
Draycott in the Moors
Cheadle
Bradley in the Moors
Coxbank
Woore
Pipe Gate
Aston
Hanchurch
Whitmore
Lightwood
Trentham
Rough Close
Meir Heath
Blythe Bridge
Upper Tean
Knighton
Baldwin's Gate
Tittensor
Cresswell
Checkley
Hollington
Fole
Norton in Hales
Blackbrook
Mucklestone
Maer
Beech
Barlaston
Fulford
Betton
Chapel Chorlton
Ashley
Cranberry
Moddershall
Church Leigh
Loggerheads
Ashley Heath
Podmore
Swynnerton
Cotwalton
Hilderstone
Middleton Green
Oulton
M60
M602
M62
M56
M6
A580
A57
A56
A50
A34
A6
A5103
A628
A6016
A624
A626
A523
A538
A537
A536
A535
A556
A530
A533
A54
A534
A53
A520
A527
A500
A5020
A51
A531
A525
A52
A5035
A5005
A521
A522
A5272
A529
A519
A5004
A5015
A5102
B5094
B5085
B5087
B5470
B6101
B6105
B5392
B5078
B5077
B5053
B5032
B5066
B5026
B5415
B5500
B5331
B5082

Major administrative and Postcode boundaries

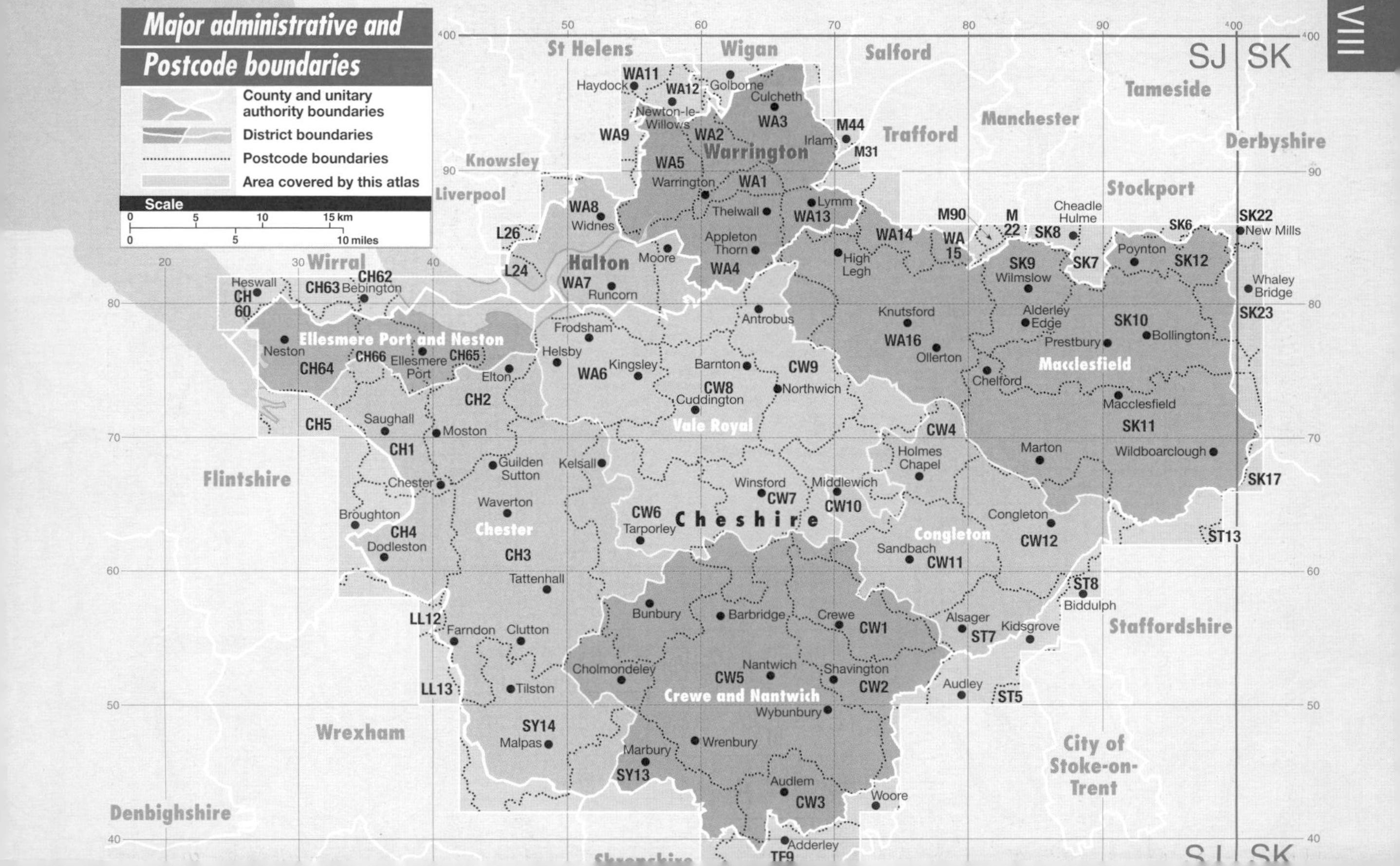

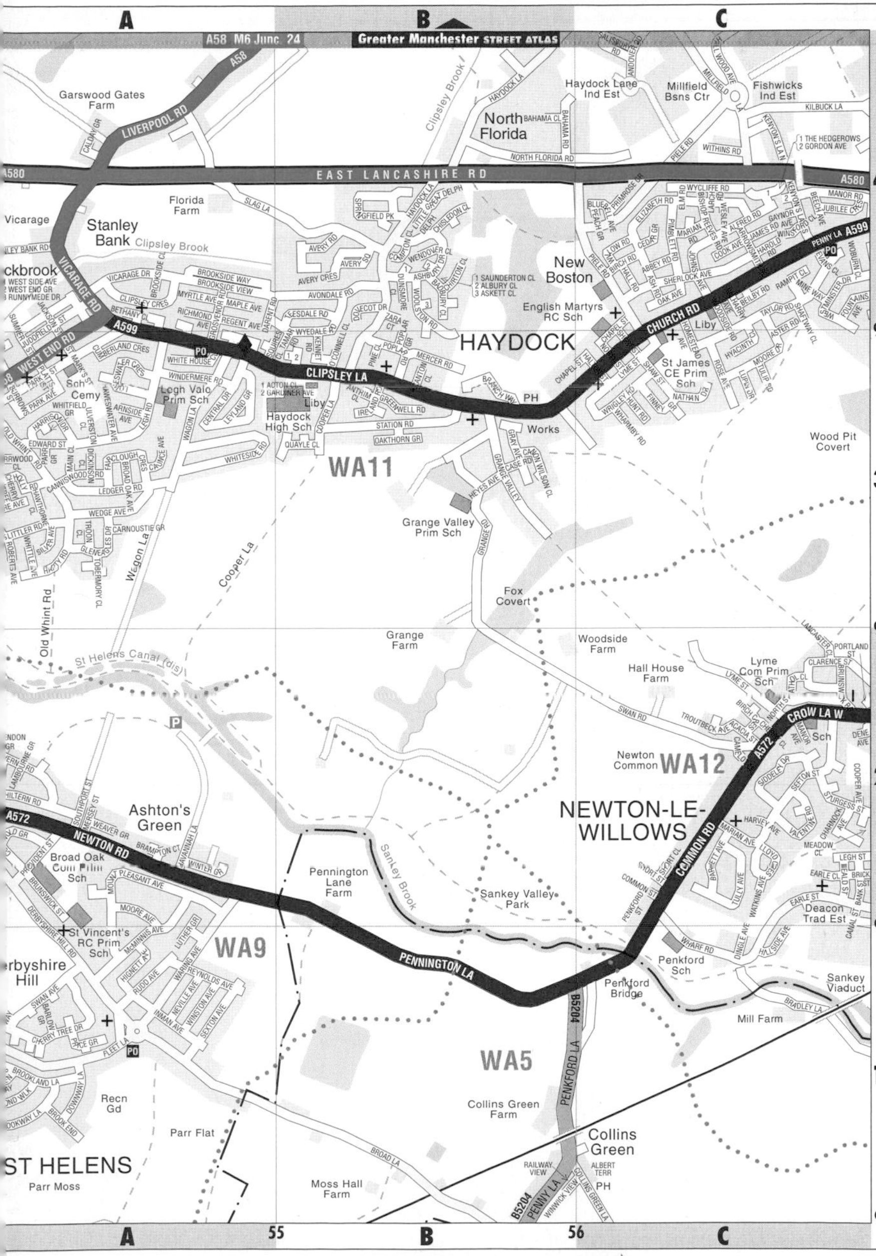

A
B
C
A58 M6 Junc. 24
Greater Manchester STREET ATLAS
Garswood Gates Farm
LIVERPOOL RD
A58
CALDAY GR
Haydock Lane Ind Est
Millfield Bsns Ctr
Fishwicks Ind Est
KILBUCK LA
North Florida
BAHAMA CL
BAHAMA RD
NORTH FLORIDA RD
HAYDOCK LA
Clipsley Brook
PIELE RD
WITHINS RD
1 THE HEDGEROWS
2 GORDON AVE
A580
EAST LANCASHIRE RD
A580
4
Florida Farm
SLAG LA
Vicarage
Stanley Bank
Clipsley Brook
VICARAGE RD
New Boston
English Martyrs RC Sch
CHURCH RD
PENNY LA
A599
1 SAUNDERTON CL
2 ALBURY CL
3 ASKETT CL
AVERY RD
AVERY SQ
AVERY CRES
AVONDALE RD
BROOKSIDE WAY
BROOKSIDE VIEW
VICARAGE DR
MYRTLE AVE
MAPLE AVE
RICHMOND AVE
REGENT AVE
CLIPSLEY CRES
BETHANY CL
A599
WEST END RD
1 WEST SIDE AVE
2 WEST END GR
3 RUNNYMEDE DR
HAYDOCK
Liby
St James CE Prim Sch
97
WHITE HOUSE
WINDERMERE RD
Legh Vale Prim Sch
Cemy
Sch
CLIPSLEY LA
1 ACTON CL
2 GARDINER AVE
Liby
Haydock High Sch
STATION RD
OAKTHORN GR
QUAYLE CL
PH
Works
WHITESIDE RD
WA11
Wood Pit Covert
3
Grange Valley Prim Sch
LEDGER RD
WEDGE AVE
CARNOUSTIE GR
Wagon La
Cooper La
Fox Covert
Old Whint Rd
96
Grange Farm
Woodside Farm
Hall House Farm
Lyme Com Prim Sch
St Helens Canal (dis)
SWAN RD
TROUTBECK AVE
CROW LA W
Sch
P
Newton Common
WA12
A572
2
Ashton's Green
NEWTON-LE-WILLOWS
A572
NEWTON RD
COMMON RD
Broad Oak Com Prim Sch
Sankey Brook
Pennington Lane Farm
Sankey Valley Park
Deacon Trad Est
St Vincent's RC Prim Sch
WA9
PENNINGTON LA
95
Derbyshire Hill
Penkford Sch
Penkford Bridge
Sankey Viaduct
Mill Farm
B5204
PO
WA5
1
PENKFORD LA
Recn Gd
Collins Green Farm
Parr Flat
Collins Green
BROAD LA
ST HELENS
Parr Moss
Moss Hall Farm
RAILWAY VIEW
ALBERT TERR
PH
B5204
PENNY LA
94
A
55
B
56
C

1

A
B
C
M6 Preston | A49 Wigan
Greater Manchester STREET ATLAS
Yew Tree Farm Trad Est
Old Boston Trad Est
Old Boston
Hotel
Haydock Park Race Course
White Door Covert
Haydock Park
WA3
White Door Dam
Lady Hill Plantation
SPRINGFIELD AVE 1
HIGHFIELD AVE 2
CLIFTONMILL MDWS 3
A580
A599
EAST LANCASHIRE RD
LODGE LA
PENNY LA
KILBUCK LA
23
Haydock Park Farm
Fox Covert
Dean Dam
Dean Dam Farm
WA11
Ellam's Brook
Ellam's Rough
Newton-Haydock Bridge
Woodlands Ind Est
Lawson's Farm
VISTA RD
B5209
NEWTON LA
Hollows Bridge
CH
ASHTON RD
Newton-le-Willows Com High Sch
1 LANGTON CL
2 GLADSTONE WAY
3 BROTHERTON WAY
4 ASSHETON CL
WA12
St Mary's RC Inf Sch
Newton Bank Prep Sch
HIGH ST
A572
CROW LA W
CROW LA E
Liby
PO
St Aelred's RC Tech Coll
St Peter's CE Prim Sch
CHURCH ST
Newton Lake
WATERWORKS DR
1 NORTHWOOD AVE
2 WOODLAND AVE
SOUTHWORTH RD
The District CE Prim Sch
St Helen's Coll Newton Campus
St Mary's RC Jun Sch
Newton-le-Willows Prim Sch
Newton-le-Willows
Stones Crossing
Mill Green Specl Sch
MILL LA
MARKET ST
Earlestown
Wargrave
Newton Park Farm
Deacon Trad Est
NEWTON-LE-WILLOWS
Mast
WELLINGTON GDNS 1
WELLINGTON CL 2
WOODS CT 3
GRAFTON ST 4
BACK BRIDGE ST 5
Earlestown
Sankey Valley Ind Est
Newton Community
H
P
Sch
Cemy
Newton Brook
WINWICK RD
Sankey Canal (dis)
Sankey Brook
Wargrave House Sch
Red Bank
HAVERTY PREC 1
NOON CT 2
CAUNCE AVE 3
LANGLEY AVE 4
SCOTT WLK 5
THOMPSON CL 6
INGHAM AVE 7
FEARNLEY WAY 8
KENT WAY 9
OLD HEY WLK 10
WA5
Vulcan Ind Est
Works
New Hey Farm
A49
4
97
3
96
2
95
1
94
57
58
59

1
7

A4
1 HEREFORD AVE
2 GLOUCESTER AVE
3 WORCESTER AVE

B4
1 SARSFIELD AVE
2 FOXGLOVE CL
3 GROSVENOR AVE
4 RIDGEWELL AVE

C4
1 TURRET HALL DR
2 ROYSTON CL
3 SANDFIELD CL
4 REDSTART CL
5 BUNTING CL
6 WILD ARUM CL
7 SPEEDWELL CL
8 STONECHAT CL
9 HUDSON GR
10 BALLANTYNE WAY
11 ARIEL WLK
12 SCOTIA WLK
13 TYLER WLK
14 ROBSON WAY
15 HORNCASTLE CL
16 HOPWOOD CL
17 BIRCH TREE RD
18 LUNEHURST

4

A B C

A 61 B 62 C

8
4

3
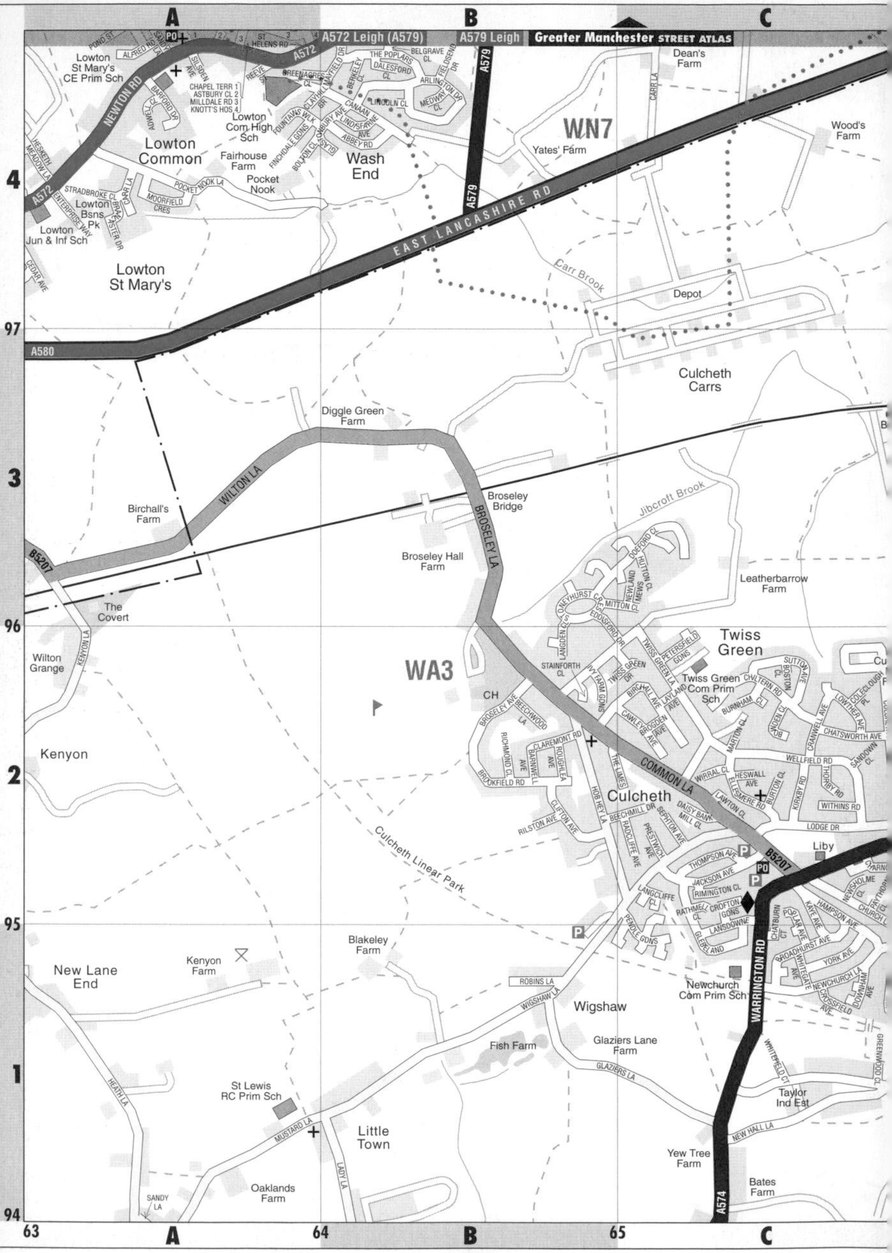
A
B
C
A572 Leigh (A579)
A579 Leigh
Greater Manchester STREET ATLAS
Lowton St Mary's CE Prim Sch
NEWTON RD
A572
Lowton Common
Lowton Com High Sch
Fairhouse Farm
Pocket Nook
POCKET NOOK LA
Wash End
Lowton Bsns Pk
Lowton Jun & Inf Sch
Lowton St Mary's
STRADBROKE CL
MOORFIELD CRES
CARR LA
ENTERPRISE WAY
CEDAR AVE
HESKETH MEADOW LA
ALFRED RD
POND ST
ST HELENS RD
SILSDEN AVE
BARFORD DR
ADWELL CL
CHAPEL TERR 1
ASTBURY CL 2
MILLDALE RD 3
KNOTT'S HOS 4
REEVE
GREENACRE CL
MAYFIELD DR
BERKELEY CL
THE POPLARS
DALESFORD CL
BELGRAVE CL
FIELDSEND DR
ARLINGTON DR
MEDWAY CL
LINCOLN CL
CANAAN
LINDISFARNE AVE
ABBEY RD
FOUNTAINS WLK
FINCHDALE GDNS
BOLTON CL
TINTERN AVE
Dean's Farm
WN7
Yates' Farm
Wood's Farm
EAST LANCASHIRE RD
A579
Carr Brook
Depot
Culcheth Carrs
A580
Diggle Green Farm
WILTON LA
Birchall's Farm
B5207
The Covert
Broseley Bridge
BROSELEY LA
Broseley Hall Farm
Jibcroft Brook
Leatherbarrow Farm
Twiss Green
Twiss Green Com Prim Sch
WA3
CH
Wilton Grange
KENYON LA
Kenyon
BROSELEY AVE
BEECHWOOD LA
RICHMOND CL
CLAREMONT RD
BARNWELL AVE
ROUGHLEA AVE
BROOKFIELD RD
HOB HEY LA
THE LIMES
COMMON LA
Culcheth
BEECHMILL DR
RADCLIFFE AVE
PRESTWICH AVE
SEPHTON AVE
DAISY BANK MILL CL
CLIFTON AVE
RILSTON AVE
STAINFORTH CL
LANGDEN CL
HONEYHURST CRES
MITTON CL
EDDISFORD DR
NEWLAND MEWS
HUTTON CL
DOEFORD CL
IVY FARM GDNS
TWISS GREEN DR
TWISS GREEN LA
PETERSFIELD GDNS
BIRCHALL AVE
CAWLEY AVE
BROGDEN AVE
LAYLAND AVE
CHILTERN RD
SUTTON AVE
BOSTON CL
BURNHAM CL
MARTON CL
BOWDEN CL
CRANWELL AVE
LOWTHER AVE
COLECLOUGH PL
CHATSWORTH AVE
SANDOWN CL
WELLFIELD RD
THORNBY RD
KIRKBY RD
BURTON CL
HESWALL AVE
WIRRAL CL
ELLESMERE RD
LAWTON CL
WITHINS RD
LODGE DR
Liby
Culcheth Linear Park
THOMPSON AVE
JACKSON AVE
RIMINGTON CL
CROFTON GDNS
RATHMELL CL
LANSDOWNE
GLEBELAND
LANGCLIFFE CL
PENDLE GDNS
B5207
WARRINGTON RD
CHATBURN CT
POPLAR AVE
HAMPSON AVE
NEWSHOLME CL
BROADHURST AVE
WHITEGATE AVE
YORK AVE
NEWCHURCH LA
DOWNHAM AVE
CROSSFIELD AVE
Newchurch Com Prim Sch
Blakeley Farm
Kenyon Farm
New Lane End
ROBINS LA
WIGSHAW LA
Wigshaw
Glaziers Lane Farm
GLAZIERS LA
Fish Farm
WHITEFIELD CT
GREENWOOD CL
Taylor Ind Est
NEW HALL LA
HEATH LA
St Lewis RC Prim Sch
MUSTARD LA
Little Town
LADY LA
Yew Tree Farm
Bates Farm
A574
Oaklands Farm
SANDY LA
4
97
3
96
2
95
1
94
63
64
65
A
B
C
3
9

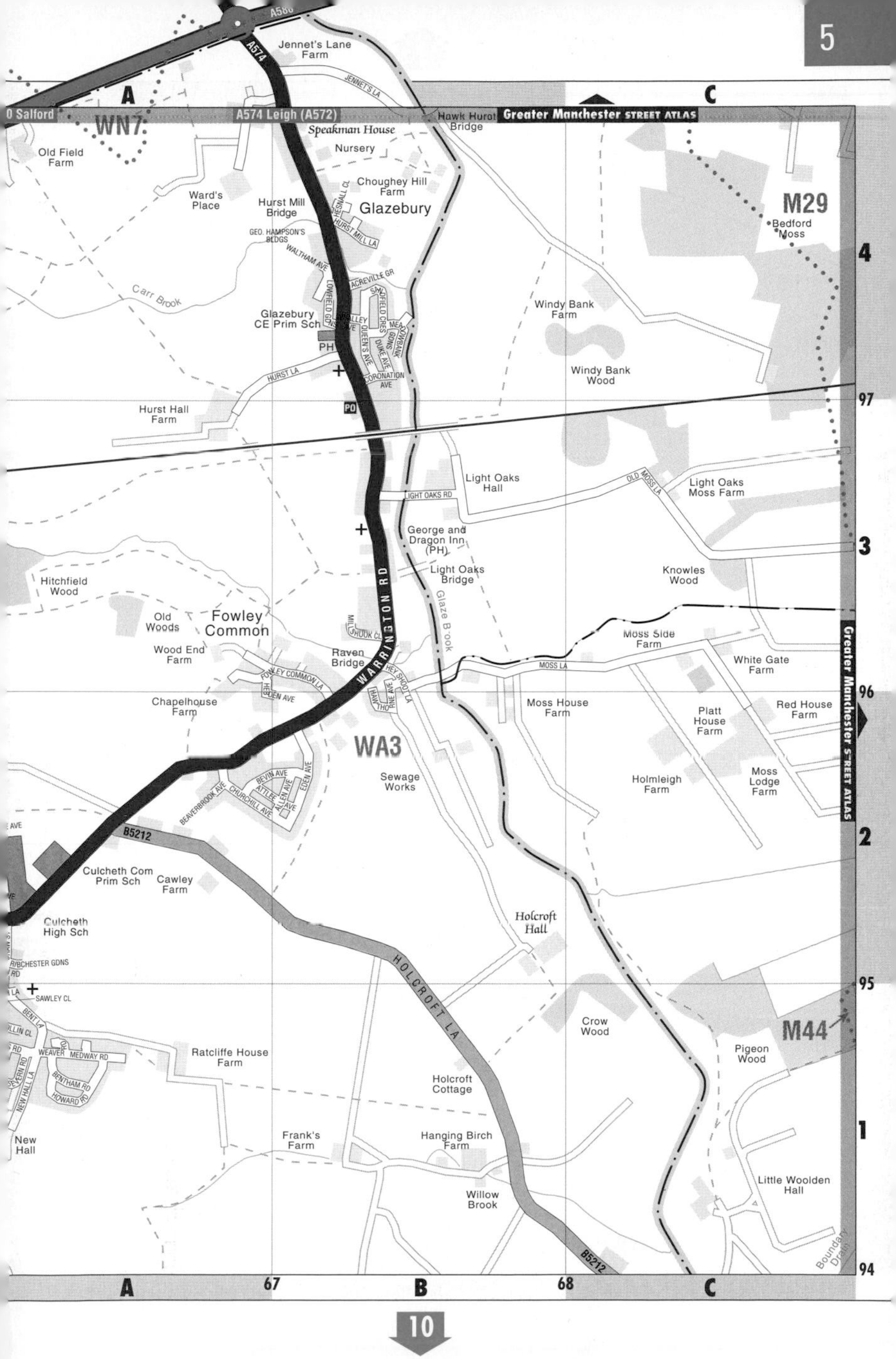
Greater Manchester STREET ATLAS
A574 Leigh (A572)
0 Salford
A580
A574
WN7
Jennet's Lane Farm
JENNET'S LA
Hawk Hurst Bridge
Speakman House
Nursery
Old Field Farm
Ward's Place
Hurst Mill Bridge
Choughey Hill Farm
Glazebury
GEO. HAMPSON'S BLDGS
WALTHAM AVE
HURST MILL LA
HESNALL CL
ACREVILLE GR
Carr Brook
Glazebury CE Prim Sch
PH
PO
HURST LA
CORONATION AVE
DUKE AVE
QUEEN'S AVE
LOWFIELD GDNS
Hurst Hall Farm
Windy Bank Farm
Windy Bank Wood
M29
Bedford Moss
Light Oaks Hall
LIGHT OAKS RD
OLD MOSS LA
Light Oaks Moss Farm
George and Dragon Inn (PH)
Light Oaks Bridge
Glaze Brook
Knowles Wood
Hitchfield Wood
Old Woods
Fowley Common
WARRINGTON RD
Wood End Farm
Raven Bridge
FOWLEY COMMON LA
HEBDEN AVE
HEY SHOOT LA
HAWTHORNE AVE
Moss Side Farm
MOSS LA
White Gate Farm
Chapelhouse Farm
Moss House Farm
Platt House Farm
Red House Farm
WA3
Sewage Works
Holmleigh Farm
Moss Lodge Farm
BEVIN AVE
ATTLEE AVE
ALLEN AVE
EDEN AVE
CHURCHILL AVE
BEAVERBROOK AVE
B5212
Culcheth Com Prim Sch
Cawley Farm
Culcheth High Sch
Holcroft Hall
HOLCROFT LA
RIBCHESTER GDNS
SAWLEY CL
BENT LA
Crow Wood
M44
Pigeon Wood
Ratcliffe House Farm
WEAVER
MEDWAY RD
BENTHAM RD
HOWARD RD
SEVERN RD
NEW HALL LA
Holcroft Cottage
New Hall
Frank's Farm
Hanging Birch Farm
Willow Brook
Little Woolden Hall
Boundary Drain
A
B
C
67
68
97
96
95
94
4
3
2
1

10

1

A B C

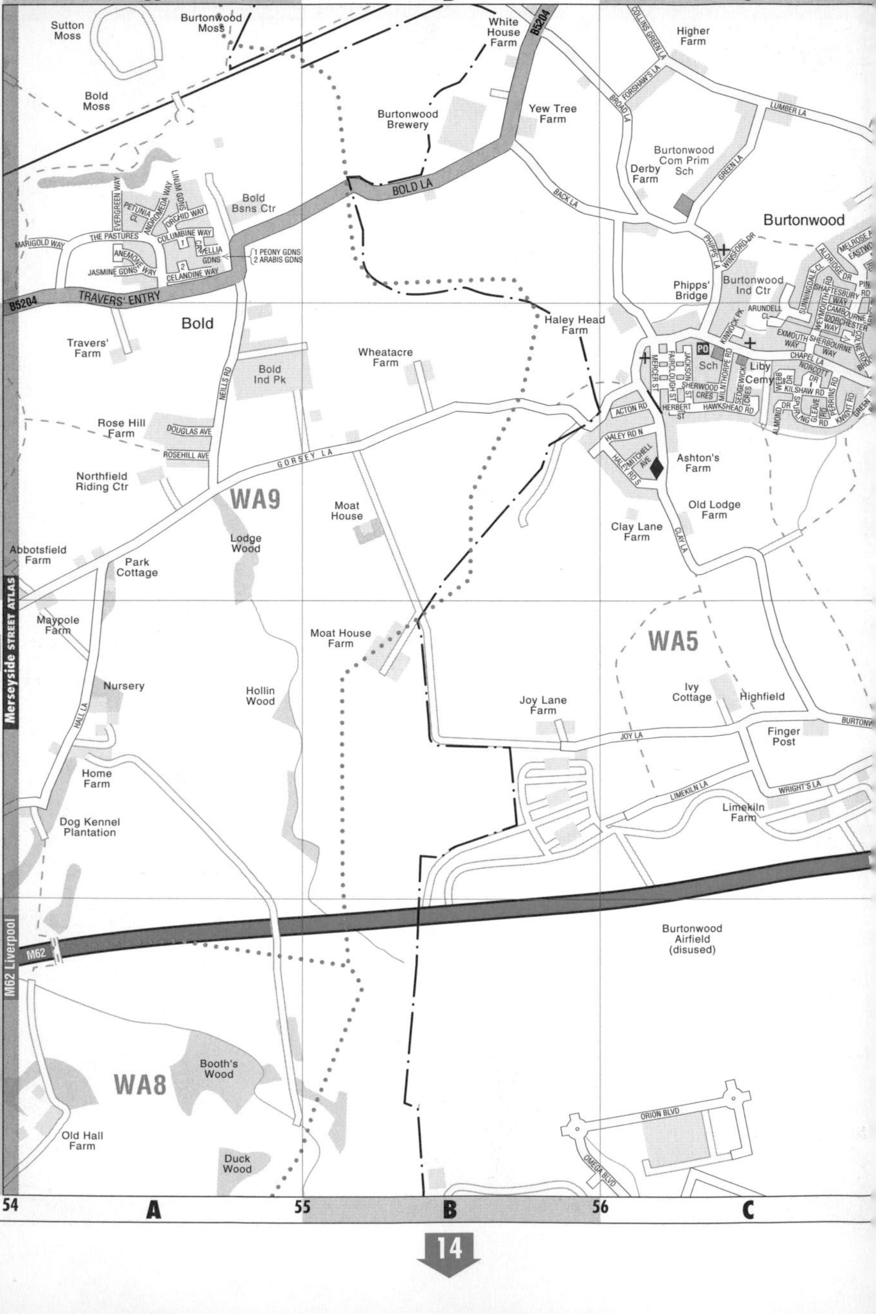
Sutton Moss
Burtonwood Moss
Bold Moss
White House Farm
B5204
Burtonwood Brewery
Yew Tree Farm
COLLINS GREEN LA
Higher Farm
FORSHAW'S LA
BROAD LA
LUMBER LA
Burtonwood Com Prim Sch
GREEN LA
Derby Farm
BACK LA
BOLD LA
Bold Bsns Ctr
EVERGREEN WAY
PETUNIA CL
ANDROMEDA WAY
LINUM GDNS
ORCHID WAY
THE PASTURES
COLUMBINE WAY
CAMELLIA GDNS
MARIGOLD WAY
ANEMONE WAY
JASMINE GDNS
CELANDINE WAY
1 PEONY GDNS
2 ARABIS GDNS
TRAVERS' ENTRY
Burtonwood
WINSFORD DR
PHIPPS LA
Phipps' Bridge
Burtonwood Ind Ctr
MELROSE AV
EASTWOOD
ALDRIDGE DR
SUNNINGDALE CL
SHAFTESBURY WAY
WEYMOUTH RD
CAMBOURNE WAY
DORCHESTER WAY
ARUNDELL CL
KINNOCK PK
EXMOUTH WAY
SHERBOURNE WAY
COLNE RD
Bold
Haley Head Farm
Travers' Farm
Wheatacre Farm
Bold Ind Pk
NEILLS RD
MERCER ST
FAIRCLOUGH ST
JACKSON ST
SHERWOOD CRES
MILNTHORPE RD
SEDGEWICK CRES
Sch
Liby
Cemy
CHAPEL LA
NORCOTT DR
WEBB DR
KILSHAW RD
HERBERT ST
HAWKSHEAD RD
ACTON RD
ALMOND DR
SPURLING RD
GLEAVE RD
PERRINS RD
KNIGHT RD
Rose Hill Farm
DOUGLAS AVE
ROSEHILL AVE
HALEY RD N
MITCHELL AVE
HALEY RD S
Ashton's Farm
GORSEY LA
Northfield Riding Ctr
WA9
Moat House
Old Lodge Farm
Clay Lane Farm
CLAY LA
Abbotsfield Farm
Lodge Wood
Park Cottage
Maypole Farm
Moat House Farm
WA5
Nursery
Hollin Wood
Ivy Cottage
Highfield
Joy Lane Farm
HALL LA
JOY LA
Finger Post
Home Farm
LIMEKILN LA
WRIGHT'S LA
Limekiln Farm
Dog Kennel Plantation
Burtonwood Airfield (disused)
M62
M62 Liverpool
Merseyside STREET ATLAS
Booth's Wood
WA8
ORION BLVD
Old Hall Farm
OMEGA BLVD
Duck Wood
4
93
3
92
2
91
1
90
54
55
56

A B C

14

2
8

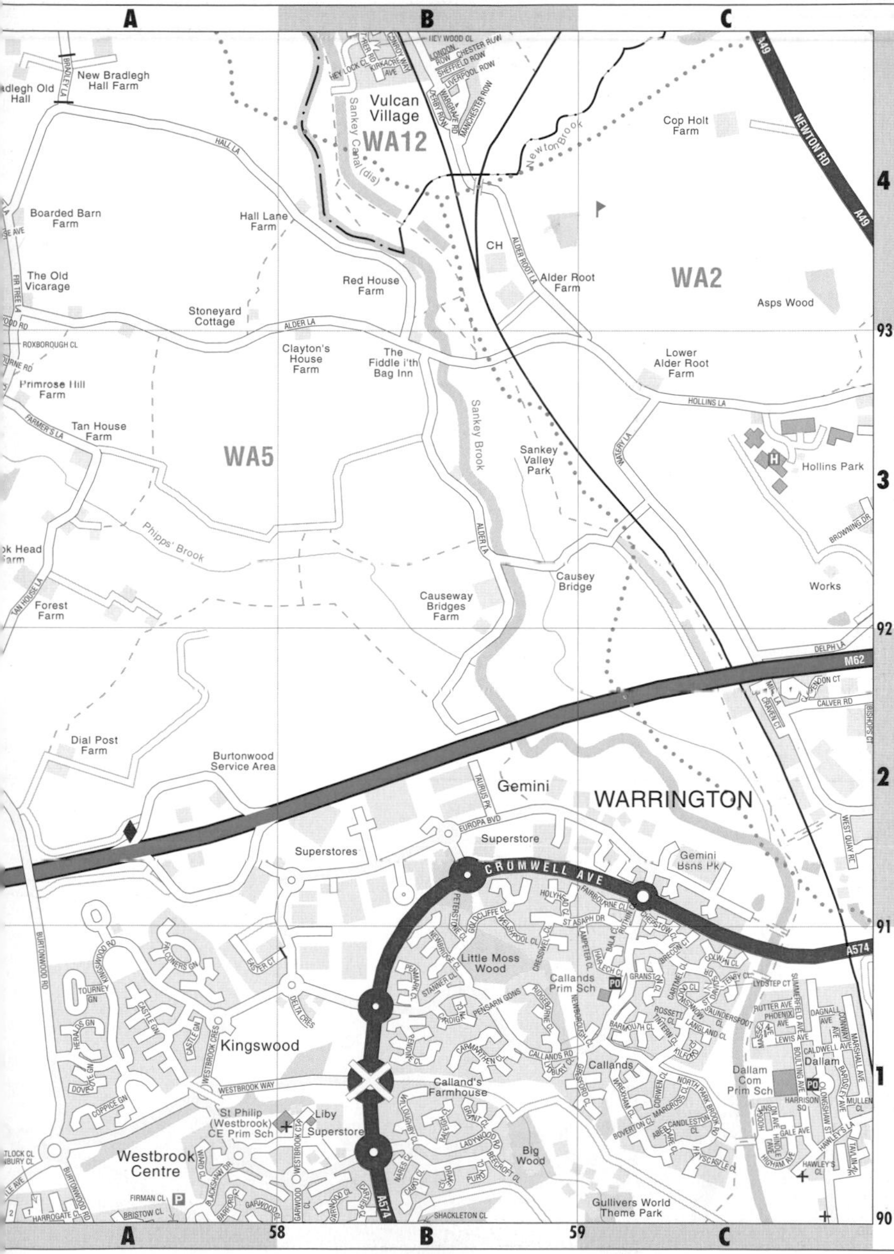
A
B
C
New Bradlegh Hall Farm
Bradlegh Old Hall
Vulcan Village
WA12
Sankey Canal (dis)
Cop Holt Farm
Newton Brook
NEWTON RD
A49
HALL LA
Boarded Barn Farm
Hall Lane Farm
CH
The Old Vicarage
Red House Farm
Alder Root Farm
WA2
Asps Wood
Stoneyard Cottage
ALDER LA
Clayton's House Farm
The Fiddle i'th Bag Inn
Lower Alder Root Farm
Primrose Hill Farm
HOLLINS LA
Tan House Farm
Sankey Brook
Sankey Valley Park
WA5
Hollins Park
Phipps' Brook
Forest Farm
Causeway Bridges Farm
Causey Bridge
Works
DELPH LA
M62
Dial Post Farm
Burtonwood Service Area
Gemini
WARRINGTON
EUROPA BVD
Superstore
Superstores
Gemini Bsns Pk
CROMWELL AVE
A574
Little Moss Wood
Callands Prim Sch
Kingswood
Callands
Dallam Com Prim Sch
Dallam
Calland's Farmhouse
St Philip (Westbrook) CE Prim Sch
Liby
Superstore
Westbrook Centre
Big Wood
Gullivers World Theme Park
WESTBROOK WAY
BURTONWOOD RD
4
3
2
1
93
92
91
90
58
59

15
8

7
3

A
B
C
4
93
3
92
2
91
1
90
60
61
62
Hermitage Green
The Hermit Inn (PH)
HERMITAGE GREEN LA
GEROSA AVE
A573
GOLBORNE RD
M6
A579
WINWICK LA
22
A49
Sand Pit
Island Plantation
Southworth Hall
Cockshot Farm
Smithy Br
SMITHY BROW
Cockshot Bridge
Cockshot Brook
DAM LA
WA3
Mill House Brow
SOUTHWORTH LA
Highfields
HIGHFIELD LA
WATERWORKS LA
OLD SCHOOL HOUSE LA
GREEN LANE CL
GREEN LA
THE PRIORY
SPIRES GDNS
Winwick
HOLLINS LA
CHURCH WLK
HORNBY LA
PILGRIM CL
ILEX AVE
ST OSWALDS CL
ASH RD
MAPLE RD
MYDDLETON LA
Winwick CE Prim Sch
Leisure Ctr
PH
PO
ST ANTHONY PL
FARINGDON RD
FALCONDALE RD
LINKSIDE AVE
WINWICK LINK RD
Arbury
ARBURY LA
Delph Farm
DELPH LA
HOLLINS DR
FLEMING DR
CROMPTON DR
ALCOTT PL
AUSTEN DR
BRONTE CL
RECTORY LA
RECTORY CL
WINWICK PARK AVE
CHESTERTON DR
BECKETT DR
SHERIDAN PL
BROWNING DR
Mainfield
Spa Well Farm
Midhops Farm
NEWTON RD
10
21
M62
9
Houghton Green
PH
MILL LA
WA2
Peel Hall
Radley Plantation
RADLEY LA
Recn Gd
WARRINGTON
ELM RD
BIRCH AVE
WOBURN RD
BISHOPS CT
TOLL BAR PL
POPLARS AVE
CAMERON CT
SEAFORD PL
LANCING AVE
COTSWOLD
ULVERSTON AVE
GRISEDALE AVE
ENNERDALE AVE
HASTINGS AVE
NEWHAVEN RD
CRAWLEY AVE
CHILTERN RD
KENTMERE PL
WANSFELL PL
OXENHAM RD
COTSWOLD RD
PENTLAND AVE
CLEVELAND RD
PETWORTH AVE
MILL LA
CALVER RD
TOLL BAR RD
BRENDON AVE
CHEVIOT AVE
ESWATER CL
ESKDALE AVE 1
BUTTERMERE CRES
THIRLMERE AVE
WINDERMERE AVE
RAVENSDALE CL
ULLSWATER AVE
Winwick Quay
St Andrew's CE Prim Sch
Hulme
St Stephen's RC Prim Sch
Leisure Ctr
CROMWELL AVE
A574
CROWE AVE
AJAX AVE
ACHILLES AVE
SINCLAIR AVE
COOPER AVE
POOLE CRES
POOLE AVE
BRANDWOOD AVE
MARRON AVE
DEAN CRES
ARMOUR AVE
DENSHAM AVE
CURRANS RD
GOUGH AVE
WINWICK RD
PATTERDALE AVE
KESWICK AVE
KIRKSTONE AVE
BOWNESS AVE
POPLARS AVE
STATHAM AVE
BYRON CT
THE COPPINS
SHAKESPEARE GR
KEATS GR
BURNS GR
SMALL CRES
SMALL AVE
TENNYSON DR
DRYDEN PL
RUSKIN AVE
KIPLING AVE
CLIVE AVE
MILVAIN DR
BEATTY AVE
MARINA DR
FIELDVIEW DR
SCHOOL RD
POVEY RD
Long Lane Com Prim
Longford
Sch
Dallam Brook
ANTRIM RD
Alaban Ret Pk
HAWLEY'S LA
EAGLE PARK DR
ATHLONE RD
WA5
A50
LONG LA
LONGFIELD RD
Winstanley Ind Est
Warrington Collegiate Inst
William Beamont Com High Sch
Warrington Bsns Pk
ORFORD GN
ST MARGARET'S AVE 1
VALE OWEN RD 2
HALLOWS AVE
MALCOLM AVE
FERGUSON DR
A50
MEREWOOD CL
QUAIL CL
LINNET CL
MALLARD CL
CANBERRA AVE
CONCORDE PL
HALIFAX CL
HUGHES PL
HUGHES AVE
FESTIVAL AVE
FESTIVAL CRES
PRIMROSE CL
Liby
PO
CAPESTHORNE RD
Orford
HORSESHOE CRES
GRASMERE AVE
SANDALWOOD
GREENWOOD CRES
MEDWAY CL
SEVERN CL
REDESDALE CL
TYNE CL
TROSSACH CL
MERRICK CL
LANGDALE CL
HUMBER RD
OSPREY CL
FOXFIELD CL
MORVEN CL
St Bridget's RC Prim Sch
WELLINGTON CL 1
LANCASTER CL 2
Blackbrook
BLACKBROOK AVE
VISCOUNT RD
ANSON CL
BLENHEIM CL
HARRIER RD
AVERY CL
Brook Acre Com Prim Sch
HARDING AVE
BOYLE AVE
DEREK AVE
MARTIN AVE
DARWEN GDNS
SEALAND CL
WOODVALE
ANDOVER CL
BAWTRY CT
DUXFORD CT
FINNINGLEY CT
HILDEN RD
CATFOSS CL
NORTHOLT CT
GOSPORT CL
RUISLIP CT
RUDLOE CT
VALLEY CT
WADDINGTON CL
BIRCHWOOD WAY
A574
Padgate
Recn Gd
1 POCKLINGTON CT
2 UNSWORTH CT
Liby
Padgate Com High Sch
DUNDEE CL
KINROSS CL
ENFIELD PARK RD
SHETLAND CL
BALLATER DR
LOCKERBIE CL
COLDSTREAM CL
MILL FARM CL
GAIRLOCH CL
Cinnamon Brow
MONTROSE CL
GABLES CL
CINNAMON LA N
PERTH CL
BRIERS CL
WELSBY CL
DELAFIELD CL
NEWTON GR
CROPPERS RD
ACKERLEY CL
ST BRIDGET'S CL
VULCAN CL
VALIANT CL
INSALL RD
PARK RD
OSBORNE AVE
BIRTLES RD
WARREN RD
BURTON RD
BRUCE AVE
NEVILLE AVE
HOLDEN PL

7
16

4
10

A
B
C
4
3
2
1
93
92
91
90
64
65
Sandy La
Wildings Old La
Heath La
Mustard Ave
Croft Heath Gdns
Croft Prim Sch
PH
Deacons Cl
Abbey Cl
Croft
Lord St
Kingsmead Ct
Oak St
Arkenshaw Rd
Round Thorn
Betsyfield Dr
Gerrard Rd
Birchall St
Browmere Dr
Pasture Dr
Eaves Brow Rd
Chadwick Ave
Churchfields
Wadeson Way
Gosling Rd
New La
Smithy La
Lady La
Brook House Farm
Laneside
Eaves Farm
Stone Platt
Eaves Brow
Eaves Brow Farm
Springfield Farm
Mill Houses
Spring La
Hop Pole Farm
Millhouse La
Mast
Hope Farm
Clares Farm
HM Remand Centre
Warrington Rd
A574
Rowe Farm
Hey Farm
Cross La
Silver La
M62
Cross Lane S
CH
Kelvin Cl
Risley
Trident Ind Est
Temple Ct
Daten Ave
Daten Pk
Clayton Rd
Melbury Ct
Raglan Ct
Heaton Ct
Adlington Ct
Maxwell St
The Quadrant
Reynold Ave
Griffith Ave
Kelvin St
Gawsworth Ct
Risley Rd
WA3
Smithills Cl
Birchwood Science Pk
Birchwood · Park Ave
Dunscar Cl
Cadshaw Cl
Turton Cl
Birchwood Tech Pk
Dalton St
The Beacons
1 Centurion Cl
2 Vanguard Ct
3 Renown Cl
4 Barham Ct
Chadwick Pl
Walton La
Stokes St
Dewar St
Faraday St
Cavendish Ave
Cavendish Pl
Davy Ave
Ravenhurst Ct
Trinity Ct
The Genesis Ctr
Newton Ave
Thompson St
Birchwood
Keyes Gdn
Aston Ave
Garrett Field
Delenty Dr
Fernbank Cl
Powell Ave
Marlow Cl
Havisham Cl
Sandycroft Cl
Moncliffe Cl
Copperfield Cl
Bracken Cl
Trefoil Cl
Norden Cl
Eccleston Cl
Holmes Ct
Lords La
Violet Cl
Campion Cl
Heather Cl
Locking Stumps Com Prim Sch
Fern Cl
Redvales Ct
Strawberry Cl
Sovereign Ct 1
Nuttall Ct 2
Windle St 3
Hawshaw Cl
Glover Rd
Stonechop Cl
PO
Armstrong Cl
Topping Ct
Locking Stumps La
Deanwater Cl
Picton Cl
Elton Cl
Carden Cl
Beeston Cl
Carrington Cl
Kinsale Dr
Warrington Rd
Hapsford Cl
Ledsham Cl
Kelsall Cl
Locking Stumps
Birchwood Ave
Pheasant Cl
Ordnance Ave
Redpoll La
Redshank La
Kingfisher Cl
Partridge Cl
Wren Cl
Swallow Cl
Woodpecker Cl
Fieldfare Cl
Admirals Rd
Dove Cl
Oakwood
Jay Cl
Chaffinch Cl
Sch
Oakwood Gate
Dunnock Gr
Goldfinch La
Kestrel La
Linnet Gr
Nightingale Cl
Whinchat Dr
Bickerton Cl
Fox Wood Sch
Forbes Cl
Noble Cl
Mallard La
Teal Gr
Halliday Cl
Talbot Cl
Chatfield Dr
Ramsey Cl
Layton Cl
Harcourt Cl
Whitworth Cl
Latham Cl
Curlew Gr
Pipit La
Admirals Rd
Miles Cl
Dyster Cl
Burrough Cl
Liby
Birchwood Com High Sch
Brock Rd
Sp Ctr
Hamnett Ct
Ainscough Rd
Patterson Cl
Woodhouse Cl
Rawlings Cl
Benson Rd
Birchwood Bvd
Birchwood Centre
Birchwood One Bsns Pk
Dewhurst Rd
Birchwood
Woolston Moss
Moss Lane Farm
Brookfield Farm
Moss La
Nicol Ave
St Andrews
Enfield Park Rd
Tweedsmuir Cl
Braemar Cl
Blackledge Cl
Oban Gr
Stonehaven Dr
Nairn Cl
Strumness Cl
Fyfield Cl
CH
Dig La
Birchwood Office Pk
Crab La
Rowland Cl
Aspinall Cl
Aviemore Dr
1 Waywell Cl
2 Cottam Dr
3 Libson Cl
4 Timmis Cl
5 Wasley Cl
Warrington Univ Coll (Padgate Campus)
WA2
College Cl
Long Barn La
Cinnamon Pk
Nook La
Arran Cl
Canada Cl
Fearnhead La
Ronald Dr
Barnes Ave
Cross Farm
Capenhurst Ave
Mere Rd
Chapel Cross Rd
Windscale Rd
Fearnhead
Meadow La
Dounrey Cl
Orchard St
Dell Dr
Winfrith Rd
Edgars Dr
B5210
Blackburne Cl
Longbarn Bvd
Anderson Cl
Harpers Rd
Fallowfield Gr
Sorrel Cl
Burtree Cl
Sage Cl
Lovage Cl
Freshfields Dr
Saffron Cl
Carpenter Gr
Peasley Cl
Pasture La
Oxmead Cl
Longbarn Prim Sch
Longbarn
Woolston Grange Ave
WA1
Station Road N
Padgate CE Prim Sch
Duckworth Gr
Guildford Cl
Mullion Gr
Maybery Gr
1 Shawbury Gr
2 Colemere Cl
Grosvenor Grange
Woolston Park
Aston Ct
Greys Ct
Kingsland Grange
Long Barn La
Poulton Cres
Totton Cl
Hardwick Grange
M6
Padgate
P

17
10

9
5

A
B
C
4
93
3
92
2
91
1
90
66
67
68
B5212
Keeper's Cottage
Glaze Brook
Aikin Knowle's Bridge
HOLCROFT LA
M62
B5212
Old Abbey Farm
Moss Side Farm
Ferndale Nurseries
Masts
Holcroft Moss
SILVER LA
11
M62
A574
PRESTWOOD CT
LEACROFT RD
Pestfurlong Hill
Ind Est
BIRCHWOOD WAY
SILVER LA
Pestfurlong Moss
Glazebrook Moss
A574
HAMSTERLEY CL
ALDEWOOD CL
ARDEN CL
GORSE COVERT RD
FALSTONE CL
DARNAWAY CL
STANMORE CL
APPLECROSS CL
BRAMSHILL CL
FISHERFIELD DR
RENDLESHAM CL
WOOLMER CL
ROCKINGHAM CL
Hoyle's Moss Farm
PO
Sch
HAZELBOROUGH CL
MOSS GATE
GORSE COVERT RD
WHITTLEWOOD CL
CHARNWOOD CL
RINGWOOD CL
BOWLAND CL
ASHDOWN LA
GILDERDALE CL
DALBY CL
LANGWELL CL
KILLINGWORTH LA
WESTWAY CRES 1
WIGMORE CL 2
DUNLEY CL 3
ROSENDALE DR 4
CULBIN CL 5
SCHOOL LA
New Hall Farm
Milverton Farm
MOSS LA
Gorse Covert
Birchwood Forest Park
ORDNANCE AVE
Visitors Ctr
Risley Moss
Omrod Farm
DAM LA
KEYES CL
Birchwood Brook
Bridge Farm
WA3
Risley Moss Local Nature Reserve
Moss Hall Farm
Hollingreave Farm
DANIEL CL
MANSFIELD CL
COLEBROOK CL
Land Fill Site
ADMIRALS RD
McCARTHY CL
PALLISER CL
PENNANT
ASHMORE CL
Moss Side
Prospect Farm
CHAFFINCH CL
PROSPECT LA
Ash Tree Farm
Moss Side Farm No.2
Moss Side Farm
MOSS SIDE LA
Rixton Moss
WOODEND LA
Brick Works
Woodend Farm
HOLLY BUSH LA
Woolston Moss
Rixton Clay Pits Nature Reserve
Works
MOAT LA
CHAPEL LA
CLAYDON GDNS
Works
Mast
Moss Head
Marshall's Farm
Rixton Firs
MANCHESTER RD
A57
BROOK LA
Moss Farm

9
18

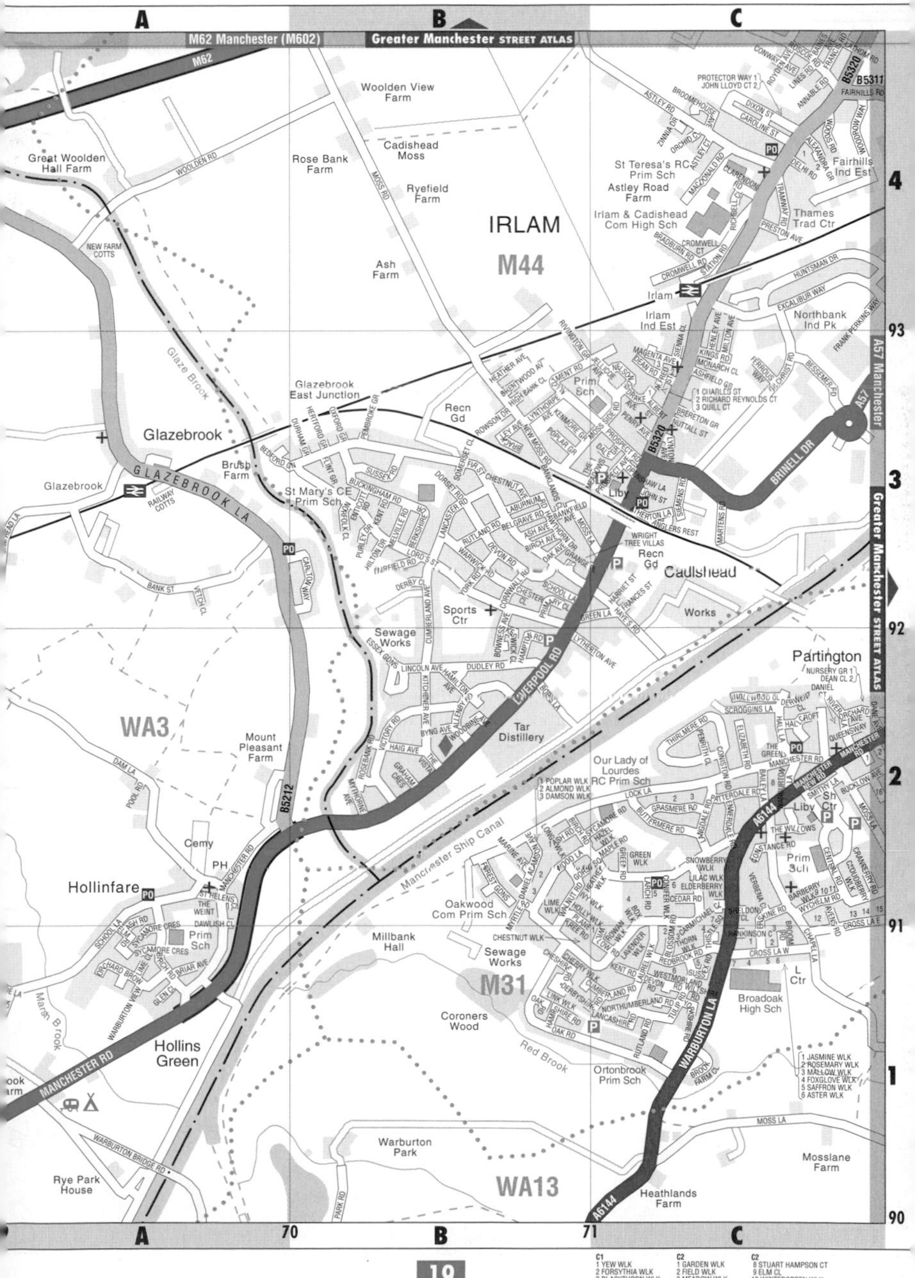

C1
1 YEW WLK
2 FORSYTHIA WLK
3 BLACKTHORN WLK
4 THISTLE WLK
5 MAGNOLIA CL
6 LOBELIA WLK
7 IRIS WLK

C2
1 GARDEN WLK
2 FIELD WLK
3 MEADOW WLK
4 HAWTHORN WLK
5 MAY WLK
6 PINE WLK
7 ROSE WLK

C2
8 STUART HAMPSON CT
9 ELM CL
10 WINTERGREEN WLK
11 BEECH CL
12 CAMOMILE WLK
13 CHARLOCK WLK
14 WOODRUFF WLK
15 COLUMBINE WLK
16 WORTHINGTON AVE

19

A
B
C
Merseyside STREET ATLAS
A57 Liverpool
M62 Manchest
Mill Wood
L35
M62
WARRINGTON RD 1
LOYOLA HEY 2
NORLAND'S LA 3
7
WARRINGTON RD
WATKINSON WAY
Sandhill Farm
NORLAND'S LA
M62 Liverpool
4
Higher Shaw Farm
SHAW ENTRY
Rough Head
Fox's Bank Brook
Cronton Wood
HALL LA
CRONTON LA
89
Visitor Ctr
Pex Hill
Norland's House
PENNY LA
Town End
L35
Penny Lane Farm
A5080 Liverpool (M62)
A5080
TUE LA
Nursery
THE RIDGEWAY
Cronton CE Prim Sch
Holy Family RC Prim Sch
MILL LA
3
Cronton Farm
Mast
Hotel
CRONTON LA
Smaller Gorse Farm
CRONTON RD
Cronton
Caxton Lodge
Widnes Sixth Form Coll
ALDER LA
SANDY LA
88
Merseyside STREET ATLAS
WA8
CHAPEL LA
LODGE LA
Rose Farm
Holly Farm
Upton
Ppg Sta
Stock's Well House
STOCKSWELL RD
CHERRYSUTTON MEWS
2
1 MARSDEN CT
2 KENNINGTON PK
DARLEY CL 1
BROXTON CL 2
FENTON CL 3
CAXTON CL 4
MADELINE McKENNA CT 5
All Saints Upton CE Prim Sch
HOUGH GREEN RD
GREAT ASHFIELD
PH
87
St Basil's RC Prim Sch
Rugby Football Ground
Ball o' Ditton
LANCASTER AVE
Hough Green
Our Lady of Perpetual Succour RC Inf Sch
Saints Peter & Paul RC High Sch
B5178
NETHERLEY RD
Hough Green
1
The Bankfield Sch
Ditton CE Prim Sch
LIVERPOOL RD
CH
B51
Ditton Prim Sch
Ashley Sch
1 CHESTNUT CT
2 ELIZABETH TERR
Chestnut Lodge Specl Sch
NEW BANK PL 1
MANOR PL 2
KENDAL RD 1
LUNE WAY 2
DERWENT RD 3
86
48
49
50
A
B
C

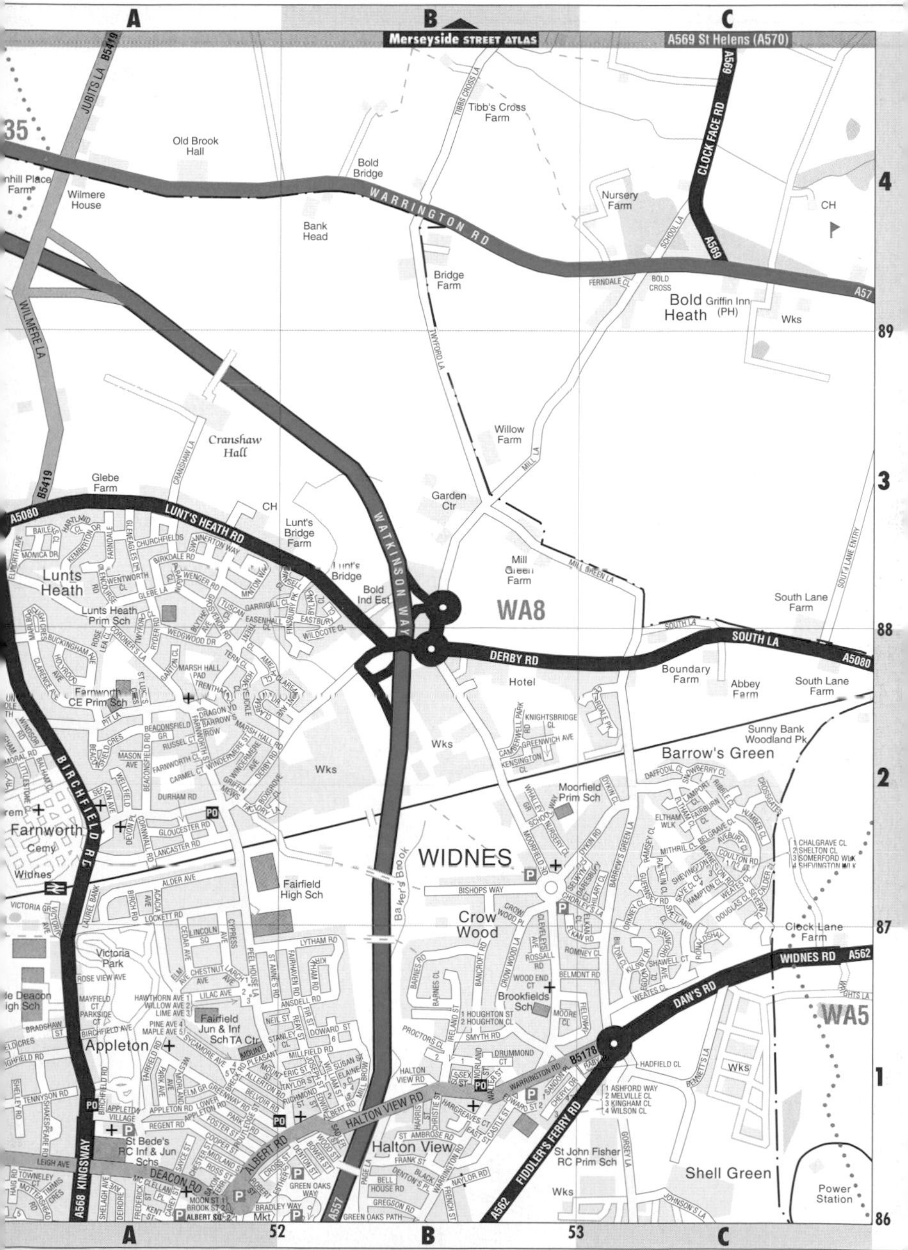
A
B
C
Merseyside STREET ATLAS
A569 St Helens (A570)
35
JUBITS LA
B5419
Old Brook Hall
Wilmere House
Bold Bridge
Tibb's Cross Farm
TIBBS CROSS LA
CLOCK FACE RD
A569
Nursery Farm
CH
4
WARRINGTON RD
Bank Head
Bridge Farm
SCHOOL LA
FERNDALE CL
BOLD CROSS
Bold Heath
Griffin Inn (PH)
Wks
A57
89
WILMERE LA
TWYFORD LA
Cranshaw Hall
CRANSHAW LA
Willow Farm
MILL LA
Glebe Farm
B5419
3
A5080
LUNT'S HEATH RD
CH
Lunt's Bridge Farm
Lunt's Bridge
Garden Ctr
Mill Green Farm
MILL GREEN LA
SOUTH LANE ENTRY
WATKINSON WAY
Lunts Heath
Lunts Heath Prim Sch
Bold Ind Est
WA8
South Lane Farm
SOUTH LA
88
DERBY RD
A5080
Hotel
Boundary Farm
Abbey Farm
South Lane Farm
Farnworth CE Prim Sch
Sunny Bank Woodland Pk
Wks
Barrow's Green
Wks
BIRCHFIELD RD
2
Moorfield Prim Sch
Farnworth
Cemy
Widnes
WIDNES
1 CHALGRAVE CL
2 SHELTON CL
3 SOMERFORD WLK
4 SHEVINGTON WLK
Fairfield High Sch
BISHOPS WAY
Baker's Brook
Crow Wood
87
Clock Lane Farm
WIDNES RD
A562
Victoria Park
DAN'S RD
WA5
Brookfields Sch
Fairfield Jun & Inf Sch
TA Ctr
Appleton
WARRINGTON RD
B5178
HADFIELD CL
1
Wks
HALTON VIEW RD
1 ASHFORD WAY
2 MELVILLE CL
3 KINGHAM CL
4 WILSON CL
FIDDLER'S FERRY RD
St Bede's RC Inf & Jun Schs
Halton View
St John Fisher RC Prim Sch
Shell Green
KINGSWAY
DEACON RD
ALBERT RD
GREEN OAKS WAY
Wks
Power Station
A568
A557
A562
Mkt
GREEN OAKS PATH
86
A
52
B
53
C

13
6

A
B
C
4
89
3
88
2
87
1
86
54
55
56
Eccles Plantation
Finch's Plantation
South Park Plantation
Lingley Mere
Lingley Green Ave
Great Sankey L Ctr
Great Sankey High Sch
Barrow Hall Com Prim Sch
Brow Farm
Whittle Brook
Park Farm
Bargyloo
Dawson House
Bancroft House
Lingley Green
A57
Warrington Rd
Hayfield Farm
South Lane Entry
Sandy La
The Trigger Pond (PH)
Laburnum Farm
Laburnum La
Greenside Farm
Sandy Lane Farm
WA8
Liverpool Rd
Park Road Com Prim Sch
Sankey
Sch
Liby
Recn Gd
Penk High
Camp (dis)
A5080
Sunny Bank Cotts
WA5
Four Top'd Oak
Brook Farm
Penketh Prim Sch
Penketh
South La
Farnworth Rd
Doe Green
Beech Ave
Cuerdley Rd
Widnes Rd
Fowl Farm
Mowcroft La
St Vincent's RC Prim Sch
Penketh South Com Prim Sch
Clifford Rd 1
Lyons Rd 2
Stanstead Ave 3
Hamble Dr 4
LC
Cuerdley Cross
Cuerdley Gn
A562
PH
Back La
Wrights La
Cross Lane Farm Cottages
Mersey Way
River Mersey
Ferry Inn (PH)
Swing Bridge
Marsh End Farm
Marsh La
Power Station
Trans Pennine Way
Fiddler's Ferry
Fiddler's Ferry Reach
St Helens Canal (disused)
WA5
WA4

13
24

7
16

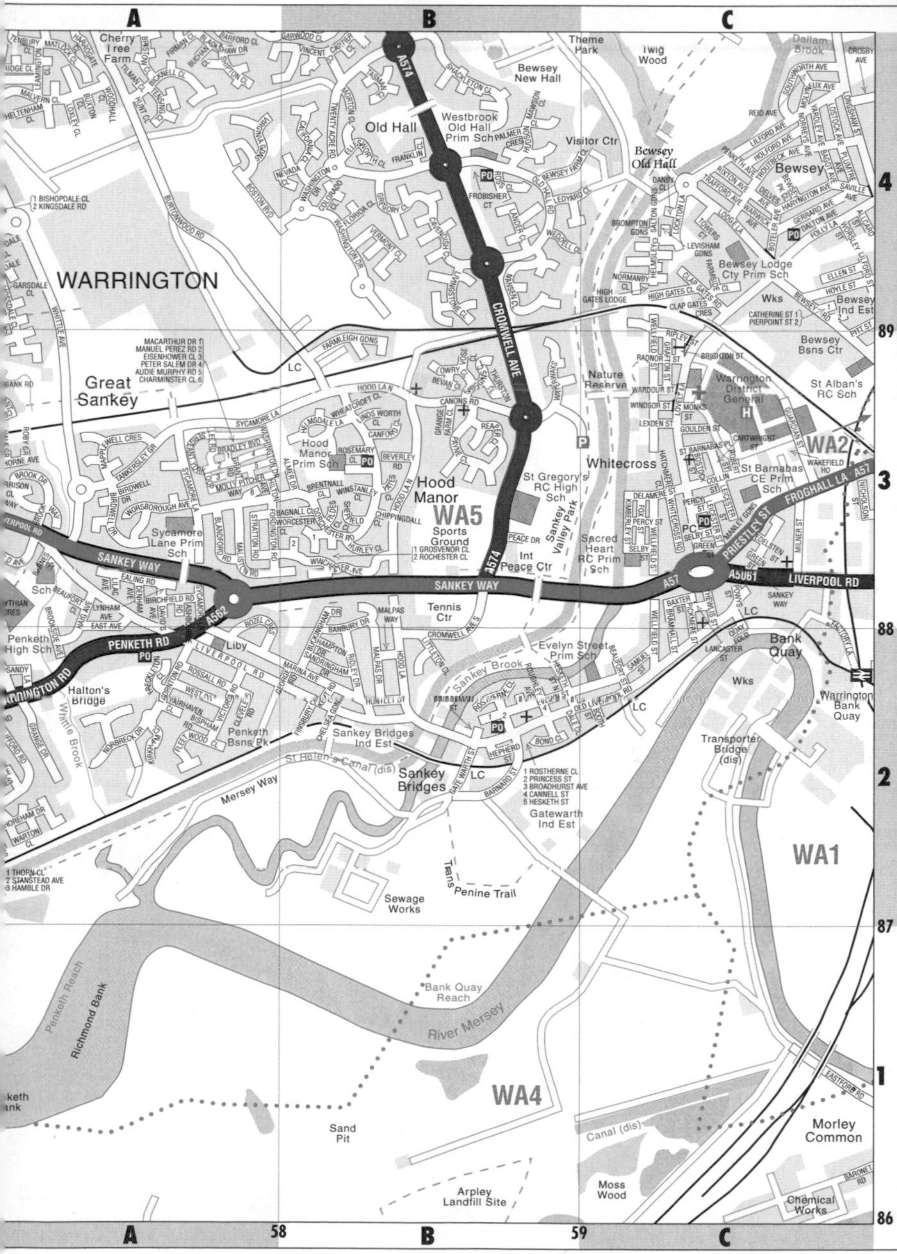
A
B
C
WARRINGTON
Great Sankey
Old Hall
Westbrook Old Hall Prim Sch
Bewsey New Hall
Theme Park
Twig Wood
Visitor Ctr
Bewsey Old Hall
Bewsey
Dallam Brook
Bewsey Lodge Cty Prim Sch
Wks
Bewsey Ind Est
Bewsey Bsns Ctr
St Alban's RC Sch
Nature Reserve
Warrington District General
WA2
Whitecross
St Barnabas CE Prim Sch
St Gregory's RC High Sch
Sankey Valley Park
Sacred Heart RC Prim Sch
Hood Manor
Hood Manor Prim Sch
WA5
Sports Ground
Int Peace Ctr
Tennis Ctr
Sycamore Lane Prim Sch
CROMWELL AVE
A574
SANKEY WAY
A57
A5061
LIVERPOOL RD
PRIESTLEY ST
FROGHALL LA
A562
PENKETH RD
WARRINGTON RD
Penketh High Sch
Halton's Bridge
Whittle Brook
Liby
Penketh Bsns Pk
Sankey Bridges Ind Est
Sankey Bridges
Evelyn Street Prim Sch
Sankey Brook
St Helen's Canal (dis)
Mersey Way
Gatewarth Ind Est
Bank Quay
Warrington Bank Quay
Transporter Bridge (dis)
WA1
Sewage Works
Trans Pennine Trail
Bank Quay Reach
River Mersey
Penketh Reach
Richmond Bank
WA4
Sand Pit
Canal (dis)
Arpley Landfill Site
Moss Wood
Morley Common
Chemical Works
4
3
2
1
89
88
87
86
58
59
1 BISHOPDALE CL
2 KINGSDALE RD
MACARTHUR DR 1
MANUEL PEREZ RD 2
EISENHOWER CL 3
PETER SALEM DR 4
AUDIE MURPHY RD 5
CHARMINSTER CL 6
1 GROSVENOR CL
2 ROCHESTER CL
1 ROSTHERNE CL
2 PRINCESS ST
3 BROADHURST AVE
4 CANNELL ST
5 HESKETH ST
1 THORN CL
2 STANSTEAD AVE
3 HAMBLE DR
CATHERINE ST 1
PIERPOINT ST 2

25
16

A3
1 NICHOLSON ST
2 PARK CT
3 LIVERPOOL RD
4 CROMWELL CT
5 EGYPT ST
6 JAMES ST
7 CROWN ST
8 BEWSEY ST
9 WESTMINSTER PL
10 PRINCE HENRY SQ
11 DOLMAS LA
12 NEWMARKET WLK
13 BANK ST
14 CHARLES FORBES CT

15

B3
1 JOHN MORRIS HO
2 BRANDWOOD HO
3 TANNING CT
4 WELLINGTON ST WRKSHPS

8

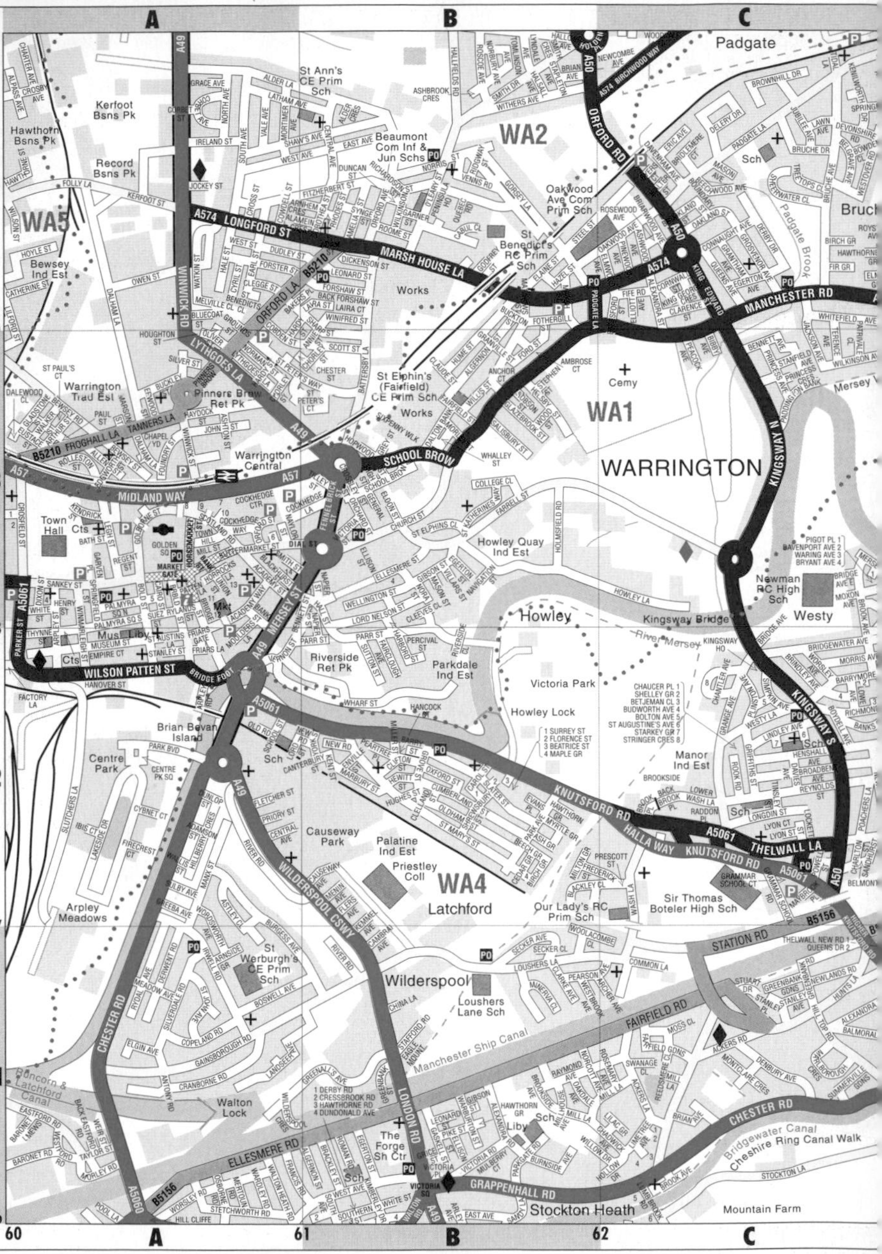

15

26

C1
1 WINDSOR CT
2 YORK CT
3 LANCASTER CT
4 TUDOR CT
5 LUMBROOK MEWS
6 WHARFSIDE CT

9
18

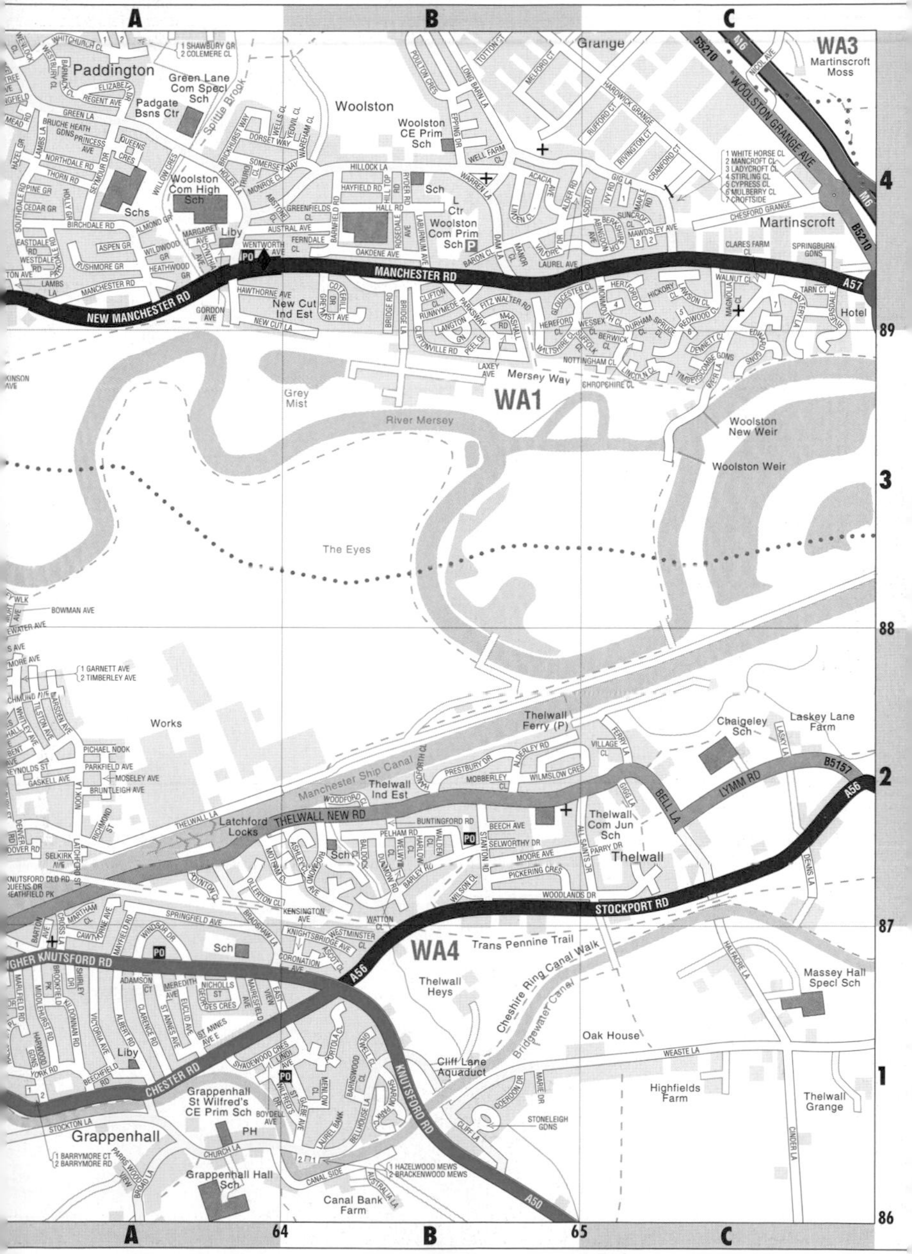
A
B
C
WA3
Martinscroft Moss
Grange
Paddington
Green Lane Com Specl Sch
Padgate Bsns Ctr
Spittle Brook
Woolston
Woolston CE Prim Sch
1 SHAWBURY GR
2 COLEMERE CL
WHITCHURCH CL
WESTBURY CL
BARNACK CL
ELIZABETH DR
REGENT AVE
GREEN LA
BRUCHE HEATH GDNS
PRINCESS AVE
QUEENS CRES
NORTHDALE RD
THORN RD
SEYMOUR DR
HOLLY GR
HAZEL GR
PINE GR
CEDAR GR
SOUTHDALE RD
LAMBS LA
BIRCHDALE RD
ALMOND GR
ASPEN GR
WILDWOOD GR
RUSHMORE GR
HEATHWOOD GR
EASTDALE RD
WESTDALE RD
LAMBS LA
MANCHESTER RD
Schs
Woolston Com High Sch
Liby
WILLOW CRES
HOLES LA
TRURO CL
BRICKHURST WAY
DORSET WAY
WELLS CL
YEOVIL CL
WAREHAM CL
SOMERSET WAY
MONROE CL
ABSTONE CL
MARGARET AVE
CYNTHIA AVE
WENTWORTH AVE
AUSTRAL AVE
GREENFIELDS CL
FERNDALE CL
HILLOCK LA
HAYFIELD RD
HALL RD
HILL TOP
RYDER RD
ROSEDALE AVE
BARNFIELD RD
OAKDENE AVE
LABURNUM AVE
Sch
L Ctr
Woolston Com Prim Sch
P
POULTON CRES
EPPING DR
LONG BARN LA
WELL FARM CL
WARREN LA
TOTTON CT
MELFORD CT
HARDWICK GRANGE
RUFFORD CT
RIVINGTON CT
CRANFORD CT
ACACIA AVE
ALDER RD
LINDEN CL
IVY RD
ASCOT CL
GIG LA
MAPLE RD
BERKSHIRE DR
SUNCROFT CL
MAWDSLEY AVE
ABINGDON AVE
VAUDREY DR
MANOR CL
DAM LA
BARON CL
LAUREL AVE
1 WHITE HORSE CL
2 MANCROFT CL
3 LADYCROFT CL
4 STIRLING CL
5 CYPRESS CL
6 MULBERRY CL
7 CROFTSIDE
CHESFORD GRANGE
Martinscroft
CLARES FARM CL
SPRINGBURN GDNS
WOOLSTON GRANGE AVE
B5210
M6
NICOL AVE
PO
NEW MANCHESTER RD
MANCHESTER RD
A57
GORDON AVE
HAWTHORNE AVE
New Cut Ind Est
NEW CUT LA
COTTERILL DR
GREYMIST AVE
BRIDGE RD
BRIDGE LA
CLIFTON CL
RUNNYMEDE
PARKSWAY
FITZ WALTER RD
LANGTON GN
MARSHALL RD
CLIFTONVILLE RD
PEEL CL
HEREFORD CL
GLOUCESTER CL
WESSEX CL
HERTFORD CL
MONMOUTH CL
HICKORY CL
LAWSON CL
DURHAM CL
SPRUCE CL
REDWOOD CL
BERWICK CL
WILTSHIRE CL
SUFFOLK CL
NOTTINGHAM CL
LINCOLN CL
TIMBERSCOMBE GDNS
DENNETT CL
WALNUT CL
MAGNOLIA CL
TARN CT
BATTERY LA
EDWARDS CL
RIVERSDALE
Hotel
LAXEY AVE
Mersey Way
CHROPSHIRE CL
WEIR LA
WA1
Grey Mist
River Mersey
Woolston New Weir
Woolston Weir
The Eyes
BOWMAN AVE
1 GARNETT AVE
2 TIMBERLEY AVE
Works
PICHAEL NOOK
PARKFIELD AVE
MOSELEY AVE
BRUNTLEIGH AVE
REYNOLDS ST
GASKELL AVE
NOOK LA
RICHMOND ST
DENVER RD
DOVER RD
SELKIRK AVE
LATCHFORD ST
KNUTSFORD OLD RD
QUEENS DR
HEATHFIELD PK
Manchester Ship Canal
THELWALL LA
Latchford Locks
Thelwall Ind Est
HAWORTH CL
WOODFORD CL
THELWALL NEW RD
BUNTINGFORD RD
PELHAM RD
HARLOW CL
WALDEN CL
WELWYN CL
BALDOCK CL
DUNMOW RD
BARLEY RD
ASHLEY CL
RICKMOND AVE
MOTTRAM CL
OLLERTON CL
Sch
PO
STANTON RD
WILSON CL
BEECH AVE
SELWORTHY DR
MOORE AVE
PICKERING CRES
PARRY DR
ALL SAINTS DR
WOODLANDS DR
Thelwall Ferry (P)
PRESTBURY DR
ALDERLEY RD
MOBBERLEY CL
WILMSLOW CRES
VILLAGE CL
FERRY LA
GIGG LA
BELL LA
Thelwall Com Jun Sch
Thelwall
Chaigeley Sch
Laskey Lane Farm
LASKY LA
LYMM RD
B5157
A56
STOCKPORT RD
DEWS LA
KENSINGTON AVE
WATTON CL
KNIGHTSBRIDGE AVE
WESTMINSTER CL
ASCOT CL
CORONATION AVE
WA4
Trans Pennine Trail
Cheshire Ring Canal Walk
Bridgewater Canal
Thelwall Heys
HALFACRE LA
Massey Hall Specl Sch
Oak House
WEASTE LA
Cliff Lane Aquaduct
Highfields Farm
Thelwall Grange
CINDER LA
COERDON DR
MARIE DR
STONELEIGH GDNS
CLIFF LA
BARTON AVE
CROSS LA
MARTHAM CL
CAWTHORNE AVE
MAYFIELD RD
SPRINGFIELD AVE
WINDSOR DR
BRADSHAW LA
PO
Sch
HIGHER KNUTSFORD RD
MARLFIELD RD
BROOKFIELD PK
SHIRLEY DR
KILDONNAN RD
MIDDLEHURST RD
VICTORIA AVE
ALBERT RD
CLARENCE RD
ADAMSON CT
MEREDITH AVE
ST ANNES AVE
EUCLID AVE
NICHOLLS ST
GEORGES CRES
ST ANNES AVE E
MAIRESFIELD AVE
EAST VIEW
HARWOOD GDNS
YORK RD
BEECHFIELD RD
Liby
CHESTER RD
Grappenhall St Wilfred's CE Prim Sch
PO
SHADEWOOD CRES
LINDI AVE
WINIFREDS DR
ST GLEBE AVE
BOYDELL AVE
MENLOW CL
ORTOLA CL
WELL CL
BARNSWOOD CL
BELLHOUSE LA
LAUREL BANK
SHARON PARK CL
KNUTSFORD RD
A50
STOCKTON LA
Grappenhall
PH
CHURCH LA
1 BARRYMORE CT
2 BARRYMORE RD
PARRS WOOD VIEW
BROAD LA
Grappenhall Hall Sch
CANAL SIDE
1 HAZELWOOD MEWS
2 BRACKENWOOD MEWS
AUSTRALIA LA
Canal Bank Farm
4
3
2
1
89
88
87
86
64
65
A
B
C

27
18

17
10

A
B
C
Green Alley Farm
Woodside Farm
Moss Side Farm
Nurseries
Green Valley Farm
MANCHESTER RD
BROOK LA
HOLLY BUSH LA
MOAT LA
A57
JUNIPER LA
M6
21
MANCHESTER RD
A57
WA3
Brookside Farm
Rixton Old Hall
Statham Lane
Mersey Way
Butchersfield Canal
River Mersey
Butchersfield
Bollin Point
Thelwall Eye
WA1
Manchester Ship Canal
River Bollin
Canal Deposit Ground
Thelwall Viaduct
C2
1 LYMM BROOK
2 HENRY ST
3 LEIGH ST
4 BRIDGEWATER ST
5 THIRLMERE LODGE
6 THE SQUARE
7 STAMFORD CT
8 DAIRY FARM CL
9 GRASMERE RD
10 LANGDALE AVE
B2
1 APPLETON MEWS
2 FIELDWAYS
3 THORNLEY CL
4 WATERBRIDGE CT
5 THE ANCHORAGE
6 BOOTH'S HILL HO
7 BROOKSIDE COTTS
STATHAM LA
CH
Sow Brook
Sewage Works
WA13
LYMM
Pool Farm
Hotel
POOL LA
BROOKSIDE AVE
Statham
MEADOW VIEW
WHITBARROW RD
Woodacre Farm
OLDFIELD RD
PO
WHITESANDS RD
THE POPLARS
WHITBARROW RD
BROOKLYN DR
YEW TREE CL
REDDISH LA
RUSHGREEN RD
WARRINGTON RD
STOCKPORT RD
Statham Com Prim Sch
ALBANY RD
ALBANY CRES
ALBANY GR
BROOK RD
DANEBANK RD
NEW RD
FLETCHERS
THIRLMERE DR
A56
Lymm Br
STATHAM AVE
STATHAM CL
CANAL BANK
MILLBANK
DE MEWS
CYRIL BELL CL
Trans Pennine Trail
LYMMINGTON AVE
Bridgewater Canal
MALTMANS RD
BROOK FIELD CL
DAVIES WAY
Liby
BOAT STAGE
ROSE BANK
Ravenba Com P
Ditchfield's Bridge
CAMSLEY LA
YEALD BROW
THORNLEY RD
PRINCESS RD
DAVID RD
JOHN RD
OAK RD
DAISY BANK RD
ASH RD
NEWFIELD
RIDGEWAY
MOSTON
EAGLE BROW
A6144
THE CROSS
PEPPER ST
THE PEPPERS
CHURCH WOOD VIEW
Camsley Grange Farm
BOOTH'S HILL RD
THE DINGLE
RECTORY LA
DOMVILLE CL
FAIRFIELD RD
ORCHARD AVE
DINGLE BANK CL
LONGBUTT LA
WYCHWOOD AVE
CHERRY TREE AVE
B5158
PARKWOOD CL
CHURCH RD
BEECH GR
MASSEY BROOK LA
OLD SMITHY LA
THE HATCHINGS
HAZEL DR
MAYFIELD VIEW
GREENWOOD RD
THE CRESCENT
MASSEY AVE
HEYES DR
ELM TREE RD
OAKLANDS DR
WAYSIDE CL
BAYCLIFFE
Lymm Dam
HIGHER LA
HARDY RD
Booth's Hill
Cherry Tree Prim Sch
HIGHFIELD RD
LADY ACRE CL
LAKESIDE RD
WEASTE LA
Massey brook Farm
HILLTOP RD
HIGHFIELD DR
MANOR RD
MANOR CL
Wr Twr
TOWER LA
Church Green
CHERRY LA
Cherrylane Farm
1 BOOTH'S HILL CL
2 HOLLY BANK
3 ELM TREE AVE
Booths Hill Farm
BOOTH'S LA
CROUCHLEY LA
CROUCHLEY HALL MEWS
Massey Brook
Higher House Farm
Kaylane Brook
WA4
Tanners Pool
THE AVENUE
Crosfield Bridge
Yewtree Farm
B5158
4
89
3
88
2
87
1
86
66
67
68

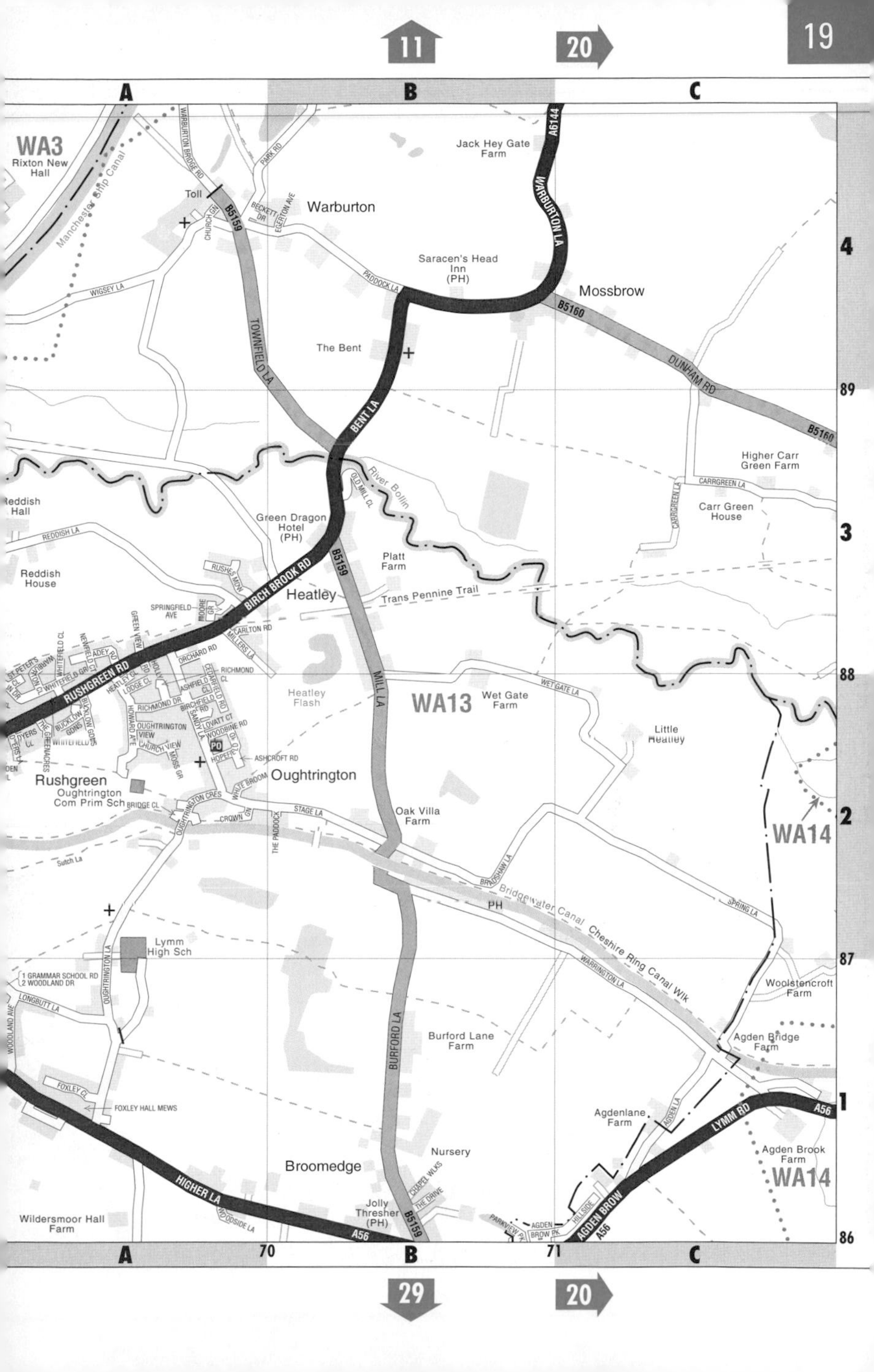
11
20
A
B
C
WA3
Rixton New Hall
Manchester Ship Canal
Toll
Warburton
Jack Hey Gate Farm
A6144
WARBURTON LA
WARBURTON BRIDGE RD
PARK RD
BECKETT DR
EGERTON AVE
CHURCH GN
B5159
Saracen's Head Inn (PH)
Mossbrow
B5160
PADDOCK LA
WIGSEY LA
TOWNFIELD LA
The Bent
DUNHAM RD
BENT LA
River Bollin
OLD MILL CL
Higher Carr Green Farm
CARRGREEN LA
Carr Green House
Reddish Hall
REDDISH LA
Green Dragon Hotel (PH)
Platt Farm
Reddish House
BIRCH BROOK RD
Heatley
Trans Pennine Trail
RUSHES MDW
SPRINGFIELD AVE
MOORE GR
CARLTON RD
MILLERS LA
ORCHARD RD
RICHMOND CL
RUSHGREEN RD
WA13
Wet Gate Farm
WET GATE LA
MILL LA
Heatley Flash
Little Heatley
ASHFIELD CL
CEDARFIELD RD
RICHMOND DR
BIRCHFIELD RD
LOVATT CT
WOODBINE RD
HOWARD AVE
OUGHTRINGTON VIEW
CHURCH VIEW
SANDY LA
HOPEFIELD
ASHCROFT RD
MOSS GR
PO
LODGE CL
HEATLEY CL
ADEY RD
WHITEFIELD GR
WHITEFIELD CL
NEWFIELD CT
GREEN VIEW
ST PETER'S CL
BUCKLOW GDNS
THE GREENACRES
DYERS CL
WHITEFIELD
Rushgreen
Oughtrington Com Prim Sch
Oughtrington
WHITE BROOM
BRIDGE CL
OUGHTRINGTON CRES
CROWN GN
STAGE LA
THE PADDOCK
Oak Villa Farm
WA14
Sutch La
BRADSHAW LA
Bridgewater Canal
Cheshire Ring Canal Wlk
PH
SPRING LA
Lymm High Sch
OUGHTRINGTON LA
1 GRAMMAR SCHOOL RD
2 WOODLAND DR
LONGBUTT LA
WOODLAND AVE
WARRINGTON LA
Woolstencroft Farm
Burford Lane Farm
BURFORD LA
Agden Bridge Farm
FOXLEY CL
FOXLEY HALL MEWS
Agdenlane Farm
AGDEN LA
LYMM RD
A56
Nursery
Agden Brook Farm
Broomedge
CHAPEL WLKS
THE DRIVE
HIGHER LA
Wildersmoor Hall Farm
WOODSIDE LA
Jolly Thresher (PH)
PARKVIEW PK
AGDEN BROW PK
HILLSIDE
AGDEN BROW
4
89
3
88
2
87
1
86
70
71
29

19

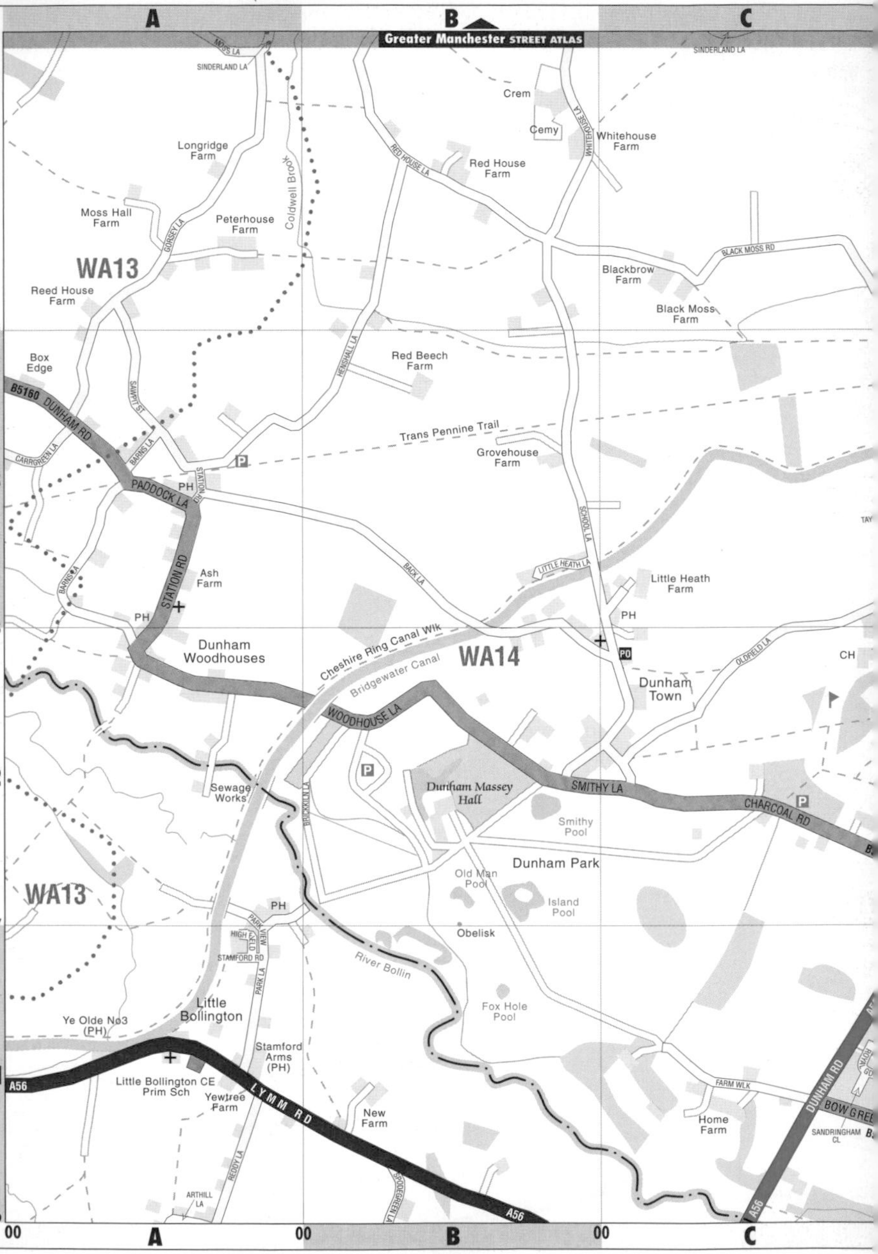

A
B
C
Greater Manchester STREET ATLAS
MOSS LA
SINDERLAND LA
Crem
Cemy
WHITEHOUSE LA
Whitehouse Farm
Longridge Farm
Coldwell Brook
RED HOUSE LA
Red House Farm
4
Moss Hall Farm
GORSEY LA
Peterhouse Farm
BLACK MOSS RD
WA13
Blackbrow Farm
Reed House Farm
Black Moss Farm
89
Box Edge
HENSHALL LA
Red Beech Farm
B5160 DUNHAM RD
SAWPIT ST
Trans Pennine Trail
Grovehouse Farm
CARRGREEN LA
BARNS LA
P
3
PADDOCK LA
PH
STATION RD
SCHOOL LA
TAY
LITTLE HEATH LA
BACK LA
BARNS LA
Ash Farm
STATION RD
Little Heath Farm
PH
PH
88
Cheshire Ring Canal Wlk
Dunham Woodhouses
WA14
PO
OLDFIELD LA
CH
Bridgewater Canal
Dunham Town
WOODHOUSE LA
P
2
Sewage Works
BRICKKILN LA
Dunham Massey Hall
SMITHY LA
CHARCOAL RD
P
Smithy Pool
Dunham Park
Old Man Pool
WA13
Island Pool
PH
PARK VIEW
87
HIGH FIELD
Obelisk
STAMFORD RD
River Bollin
PARK LA
Little Bollington
Fox Hole Pool
Ye Olde No3 (PH)
Stamford Arms (PH)
1
A56
Little Bollington CE Prim Sch
LYMM RD
Yewtree Farm
FARM WLK
DUNHAM RD
New Farm
Home Farm
BOW GREEN
SANDRINGHAM CL
REDDY LA
SPODEGREEN LA
ARTHILL LA
A56
A56
86
00
00
00

19
30

22

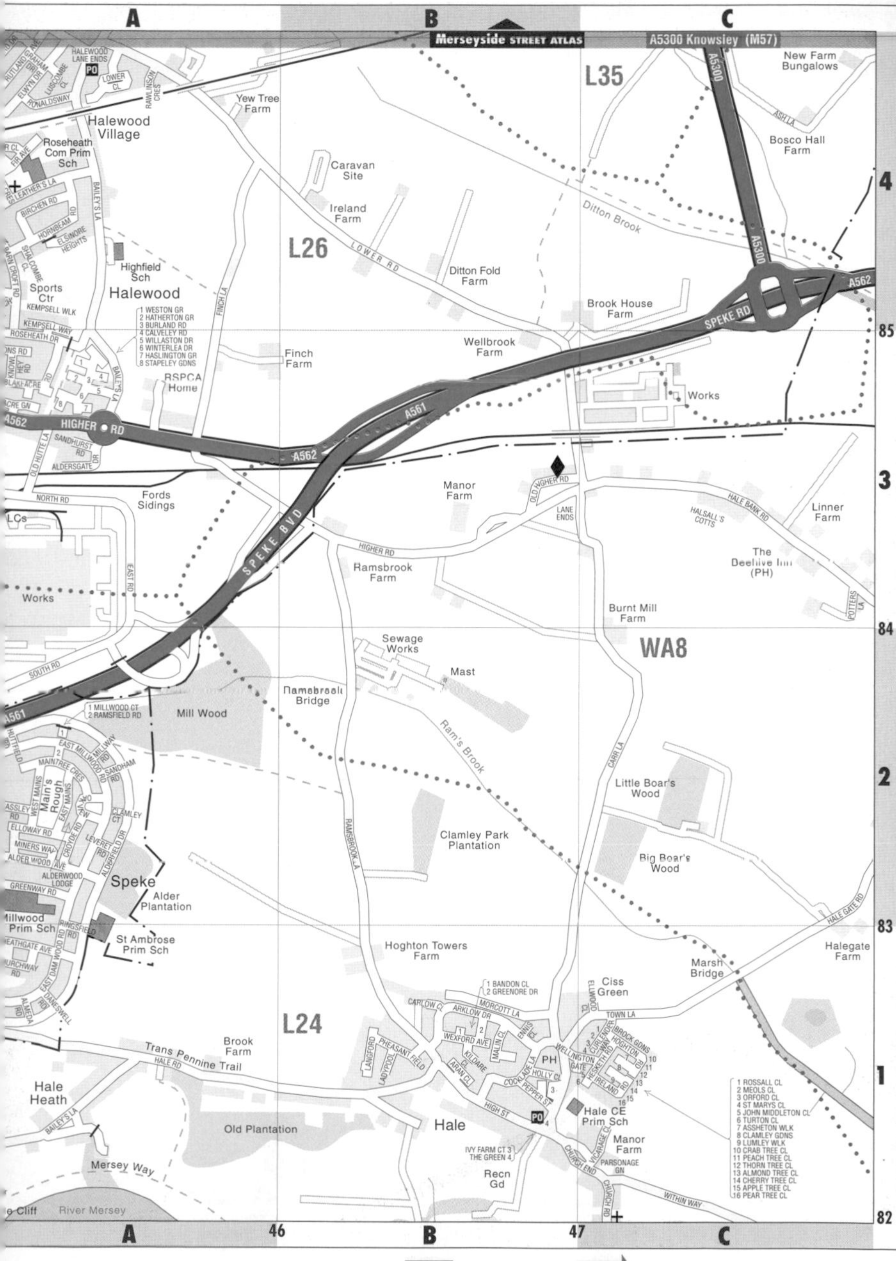

A
B
C
Merseyside STREET ATLAS
A5300 Knowsley (M57)
L35
L26
L24
WA8
Halewood Village
Halewood
Roseheath Com Prim Sch
Highfield Sch
Sports Ctr
RSPCA Home
Yew Tree Farm
Caravan Site
Ireland Farm
Ditton Fold Farm
Ditton Brook
New Farm Bungalows
Bosco Hall Farm
Brook House Farm
Wellbrook Farm
Finch Farm
Works
Manor Farm
Fords Sidings
Linner Farm
The Beehive Inn (PH)
Ramsbrook Farm
Burnt Mill Farm
Sewage Works
Mast
Ramsbrook Bridge
Ram's Brook
Mill Wood
Little Boar's Wood
Big Boar's Wood
Clamley Park Plantation
Speke
Alder Plantation
St Ambrose Prim Sch
Millwood Prim Sch
Hoghton Towers Farm
Marsh Bridge
Halegate Farm
Ciss Green
Brook Farm
Trans Pennine Trail
Hale Heath
Old Plantation
Hale
Hale CE Prim Sch
Manor Farm
Recn Gd
Mersey Way
River Mersey
LOWER RD
SPEKE RD
SPEKE BVD
HIGHER RD
A562
A561
A5300
HALE BANK RD
HALSALL'S COTTS
LANE ENDS
CARR LA
RAMSBROOK LA
HALE GATE RD
HALE RD
HIGH ST
TOWN LA
WITHIN WAY
CHURCH RD
CHURCH END
FINCH LA
NORTH RD
EAST RD
SOUTH RD
1 WESTON GR
2 HATHERTON GR
3 BURLAND RD
4 CALVELEY RD
5 WILLASTON DR
6 WINTERLEA DR
7 HASLINGTON GR
8 STAPELEY GDNS
1 MILLWOOD CT
2 RAMSFIELD RD
1 BANDON CL
2 GREENORE DR
IVY FARM CT 3
THE GREEN 4
1 ROSSALL CL
2 MEOLS CL
3 ORFORD CL
4 ST MARYS CL
5 JOHN MIDDLETON CL
6 TURTON CL
7 ASSHETON WLK
8 CLAMLEY GDNS
9 LUMLEY WLK
10 CRAB TREE CL
11 PEACH TREE CL
12 THORN TREE CL
13 ALMOND TREE CL
14 CHERRY TREE CL
15 APPLE TREE CL
16 PEAR TREE CL
4
85
3
84
2
83
1
82
46
47

47

22

21
12

B4
1 LEVENS WAY
2 RIDSDALE
3 LONSDALE CL
4 LEIGH GREEN CL
5 APPLEBY WLK
6 AYCLIFFE WLK

A
B
C
4
85
3
84
2
83
1
82
48
49
50
Oakfield Inf & Jun Schs
Ditton
Our Lady of Perpetual Succour RC Jun Sch
Clincton Wood
Express Ind Est
Works
St Michael's RC Prim Sch
Nazareth House
St Michael's Rd Ind Est
Lower House
WIDNES
Recn Gd
A562
SPEKE RD
WA8
Ditton Works
Ditton Brook
Steward's Brook
Timber Yd
Ditton Marsh
Gold Triangle Complex
Superstore
West Bank Dock Est
Halebank CE Prim Sch
Hale Road Ind Est
Sports Gd
Trans Pennine Trail
Hope Farm
Hale Bank
Visitor Ctr
Pickering Farm
Pickering's Pasture (Nature Reserve)
River Mersey
Runcorn Gap
Runcorn-Widnes Bridge
Dukesfield
WA7
Sewage Works
Manchester Ship Canal
Dock
Hale Gate Marsh
Decoy Marsh
Landing Stages
WESTON POINT EXPRESSWAY
Runcorn
Westfield Prim Sch
QUEENSWAY
A533
A557
L24
BRACKLEY ST 1
LEINSTER GDNS 2
MERSEY RD 3
SOUTH BANK TERR 4
CLARENCE ST 5
GREEK ST 6
GROVE ST 7
HANDLEY ST 8
SPEAKMAN ST 9
WATERLOO RD 10
EGERTON ST 11
CANON ST 12
PEEL ST 13
RUTLAND ST 14
HANKEY ST 15
WATERLOO RD 16
HIGH ST 17
DARESBURY EXPRESSWAY 18
LOWLANDS RD 19
CAVENDISH ST 20
ARTHUR ST 21

21
48

C1
1 PICOW ST
2 HAVERGAL ST
3 CURZON ST
4 LIGHTBURN ST
5 STANLEY VILLAS
6 SOUTHLANDS MEWS

BERT SQ
CKSON ST
UTH ST
LISBURY ST
LANDS ST
BBERT ST
7 DEAN CL
8 GLADSTONE ST
9 ELLIOT ST
10 TRAVIS ST
11 GRENFELL ST
12 ALFRED CL
13 TRINITY PL
14 EMILY ST
15 MAJOR CROSS ST
16 CHARLOTTE WLK
17 CLARKE GDNS
18 ELEANOR ST
19 DARLINGTON ST
20 THOMAS ST
21 OLLIER ST

13
24

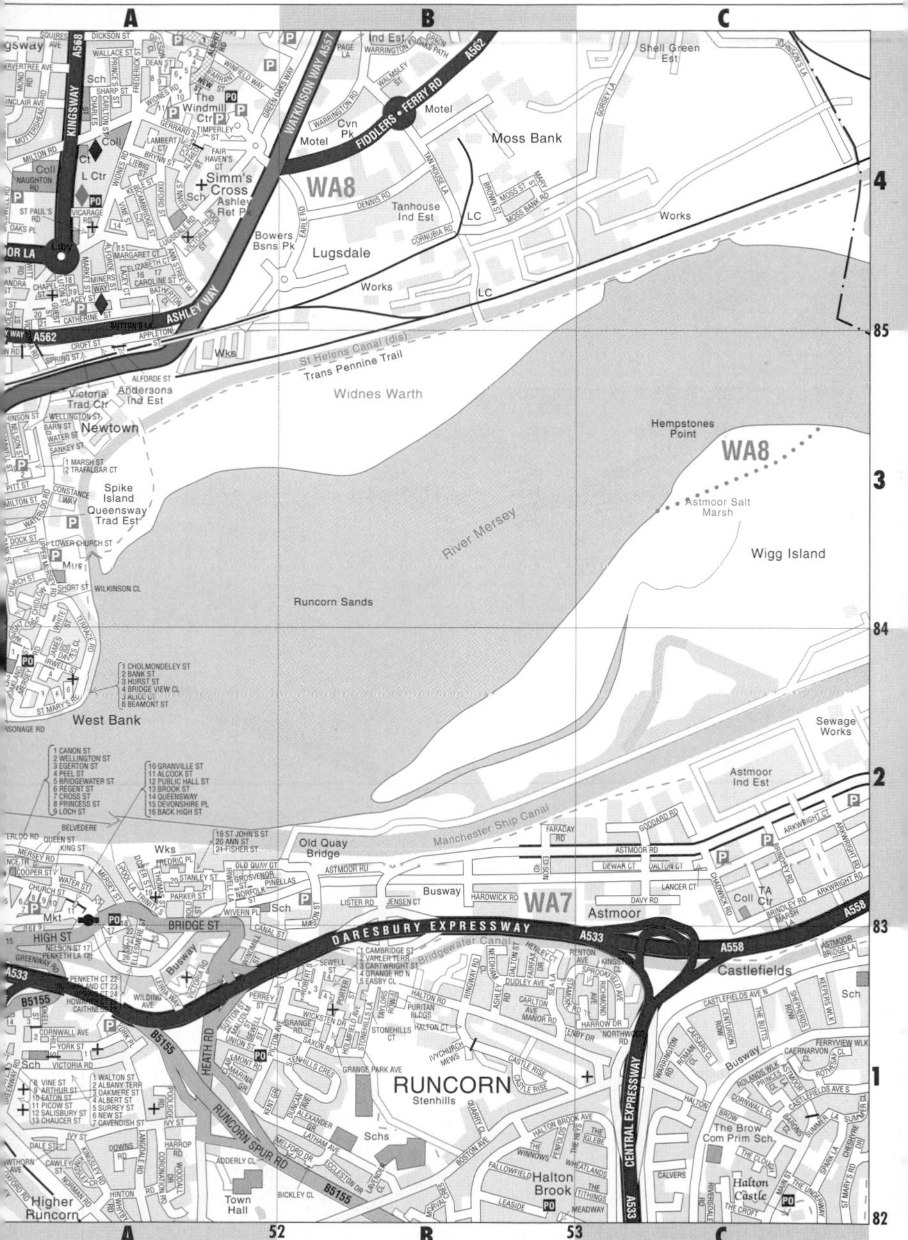

49
24

23
14

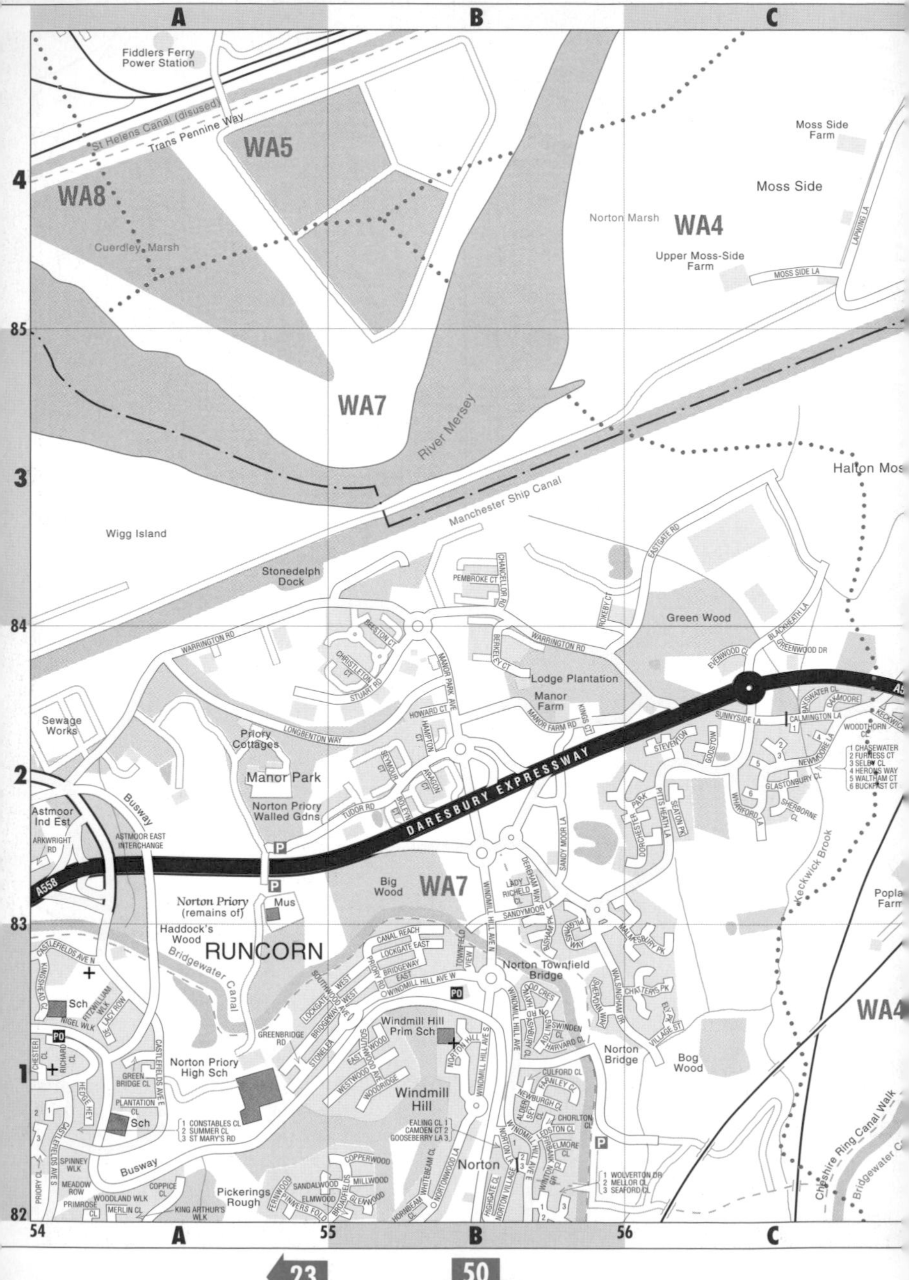
A
B
C
Fiddlers Ferry Power Station
St Helens Canal (disused)
Trans Pennine Way
WA5
WA8
Cuerdley Marsh
WA7
River Mersey
Moss Side Farm
Moss Side
Norton Marsh
WA4
Upper Moss-Side Farm
MOSS SIDE LA
LAPWING LA
Halton Moss
Manchester Ship Canal
Wigg Island
Stonedelph Dock
PEMBROKE CT
CHANCELLOR RD
EASTGATE RD
ROKEBY CT
Green Wood
BLACKHEATH LA
GREENWOOD DR
EVENWOOD CL
WARRINGTON RD
BEESTON CT
CHRISTLETON CT
STUART RD
MANOR PARK AVE
BERKELEY CT
Lodge Plantation
Manor Farm
MANOR FARM RD
KINGS CT
HOWARD CT
HAMPTON CT
LONGBENTON WAY
Sewage Works
Priory Cottages
Manor Park
Norton Priory Walled Gdns
SEYMOUR CT
ARAGON CT
TUDOR RD
BOLEYN CT
DARESBURY EXPRESSWAY
STEVENTON
GODSTOW
SUNNYSIDE LA
CALMINGTON LA
BAYSWATER CL
OAKMOORE
WOODTHORN CL
NEWMOORE LA
KECKWICK
1 CHASEWATER
2 FURNESS CT
3 SELBY CL
4 HERONS WAY
5 WALTHAM CT
6 BUCKFAST CT
GLASTONBURY CL
SHERBORNE CL
WHARFORD LA
PITTS HEATH LA
SEATON PK
DORCHESTER PARK
SANDY MOOR LA
Astmoor Ind Est
Busway
ARKWRIGHT RD
ASTMOOR EAST INTERCHANGE
A558
Big Wood
WA7
LADY RICHELD CL
DEREHAM WAY
SANDYMOOR LA
WINDMILL HILL AVE N
Keckwick Brook
Poplar Farm
Norton Priory (remains of)
Mus
Haddock's Wood
RUNCORN
Bridgewater Canal
CASTLEFIELDS AVE N
KINGSHEAD CL
Sch
FITZWILLIAM WLK
DE LACY ROW
NIGEL WLK
CANAL REACH
LOCKGATE EAST
PRIORY RD
BRIDGEWAY EAST
WINDMILL HILL AVE W
TOWNFIELD VIEW
LOCKGATE WEST
SOUTHWOOD AVE
BRIDGEWAY WEST
Norton Townfield Bridge
PILGRIMS WAY
MALMESBURY PK
CHATTERIS PK
SHERIDAN WAY
WALSINGHAM DR
ELY PK
VILLAGE ST
SWINDEN CL
HARVARD CL
ASHBURY CL
PO
CHESTER CL
RICHARD CL
GREENBRIDGE RD
STONELEA
EAST WOOD
SOUTHWOOD
Windmill Hill Prim Sch
NORTON HILL
WINDMILL HILL AVE S
WINDMILL HILL AVE
Norton Bridge
Bog Wood
WA4
GREEN BRIDGE CL
CASTLEFIELDS AVE E
HEDGE HEY
Norton Priory High Sch
WESTWOOD
WOODRIDGE
Windmill Hill
CULFORD CL
FARNLEY CL
NEWBURGH CL
ALDER SECT
CHORLTON CL
LEDSTON CL
ELMORE CL
PLANTATION CL
1 CONSTABLES CL
2 SUMMER CL
3 ST MARY'S RD
EALING CL 1
CAMDEN CT 2
GOOSEBERRY LA 3
Cheshire Ring Canal Walk
Bridgewater Canal
CASTLEFIELDS AVE S
SPINNEY WLK
MEADOW ROW
PRIMROSE CL
PRIORY CL
WOODLAND WLK
MERLIN CL
COPPICE CL
KING ARTHUR'S WLK
Pickerings Rough
COPPERWOOD
SANDALWOOD
MILLWOOD
ELMWOOD
GLENWOOD
FERNWOOD
PINNERS FOLD
BROADFIELDS
HORNBEAM CL
WHITEBEAM CL
NORTONWOOD LA
Norton
HIGHGATE CL
NORTON VILLAGE
NORTON LA
WINDMILL HILL AVE E
WINTON GR
1 WOLVERTON DR
2 MELLOR CL
3 SEAFORD CL
P
54
55
56
82
83
84
85
1
2
3
4

23
50

15
26

A
B
C
Works
Landfill Site
Birch Wood
Nature Reserve
Acton Grange Viaduct
Warehouses
Manchester Ship Canal
LAPWING LA
Moor Lane Bridge (Swing)
Sewage Works
Bellhouse Farm
Caravan Pk
MOORE LA
BELLHOUSE LA
MILL LA
GRANGE GREEN MANOR
Higher Walton
Church Park
CHESTER NEW RD
CHESTER RD
A56
LYCHGATE
OLD CHESTER RD
WALTON LEA RD
PH
CH
Walton Hall
Walton Bridge
Walton Hall Gardens
Porch-house Farm
RUNCORN RD
MOSS LA
Canal Farm
Acton Grange Bridge
HOLLY HEDGE LA
THOMASONS BRIDGE LA
UNDERBRIDGE LA
WARRINGTON RD
Bridgewater Canal
PO
Hollyhedge Farm
ROWSWOOD FARM
PARK LA
Moore
Moore Prim Sch
GIGG LA
CANAL SIDE
SIX ACRE LA
SIX ACRE GDNS
LINDFIELD CL
RUNCORN RD
Moore Bridge
Hall
HOBB LA
WA4
PH
HOLLYBANK
BEECHMOORE
Cheshire Ring Canal Walk
Norton House
Row's Wood
New Farm
Outer Wood
Hatton Lodge
Keckwick
Keckwick Bridge
DARESBURY EXPRESSWAY
KECKWICK LA
Daresbury Lodge
A558
Laboratory
Morts Wood
Bluecoat Farm
Common Side Farm
Hatton Cottage
Daresbury
B5356
PH
HALL LA
Hall Lane Farm
Hatton Hall
DELPH LA
DARESBURY LA
Daresbury Firs
Daresbury Prim Sch
CHESTER RD
Daresbury Hall
GOOSE LA
PH
B5356
HATTON LA 1
INNER GOSLING CL 2
Crow's Nest
SANKY LA
Daresbury Delph
A56
4
85
3
84
2
83
1
82
58
59
A
B
C

51
26

25
16

A
B
C
A56 WALTON NEW RD
A56 WALTON RD
CHESTER RD
Lower Walton
WARRINGTON
Crem
Hillcliffe
Cheshire Ring Canal Walk
Bridgewater Canal
Cobbs
The Cobbs Inf Sch
Witherwin Farm
Broomfields Jun Sch
Sch
Recn Ctr
Bridgewater High Sch (Upper Sch)
Hillfoot Farm
Cemy
Walton Hall
Bridgewater High Sch (Lower Sch)
High Warren
LONDON RD
Appleton Reservoir
Bellfield Farm
CH
Appleton Park
Dudlow's Green
WA4
Hurst Farm
Delamere Way
Hillside Farm
Pewterspear
Great Shepcroft Farm
St Matthews CE Prim Sch
STRETTON RD
Mosswood Hall
Goose Lane
Hatton
HATTON LA
Oaktree Farm
Stretton
Hotel
North Cheshire
TARPORLEY RD
Hatton Lane Farm
Fir Tree Farm
Mast
Stretton Fox (PH)
M56
4
85
3
84
2
83
1
82
60
61
62

25
52

A
B
C
Grappenhall Heys
Whitehouse Farm
Yew Tree Farm
KNUTSFORD RD
A50
CLIFF LA
CINDER LA
Massey Brook
HALL LA
BROAD LA
BOURCHIER WAY
CHICHESTER CL
DASHWOOD CL
LICHFIELD AVE
STRICKLAND CL
CROFT GDNS
CURZON DR
WITHERWIN AVE
STANSFIELD DR
KEEPER'S RD
Grappenhall Heys Com Prim Sch
Clifflane Farm
B5356
Reddish Hall Farm
CARTRIDGE LA
GRAPPENHALL LA
BRADLEY HALL COTTS
Bradley Hall
Appleton Thorn Trad Est
LUMB BROOK LA
NEW LA
B5356
WA4
ASHBERRY DR
THORNTREE GN
GREEN LA
YEW TREE LA
CROFTON CL
Booth's Farm
Barleycastle Farm
Tan House Farm
Thorn Inn (PH)
Greenlane Farm
SPINNEY GDNS
PARKLAND CL
HM Young Offender Institution
LYNCASTLE WAY
ASHER CT
BARLEYCASTLE LA
Barleycastle Trad Est
LYNCASTLE RD
LANGFORD WAY
M56
SWINE YARD LA
Appleton Thorn
BLACKCAP RD
STRETTON RD
Cross Farm
HATCHER CL
MARSH RD
CHAPEL LA
Appleton Thorn Prim Sch
BURLEY LA
Old Farm
AMBERLEIGH CL
BARLEY CASTLE CL
RED GABLES
PEPPER ST
Mast
ARLEY RD
Sewage Works
Airfield (disused)
Burleyheyes
Appleton Moss
New Farm
CW9
Stretton Moss
Fairbank Farm
NEW RD
REEDGATE LA
Reedgate Farm
Whitley Reed
Laurel Farm
MOSSHALL LA
Moss Hall
85
84
83
82
4
3
2
1
64
65

27
18

A
B
C
M6
B5158
Cherry Hall Farm
WA13
CHERRY LA
Yewtree Farm
Kaylane Bro
CROUCHLEY LA
Mag Brook
4
Oxheys Farm
Bradley Brook
Granthams
Great Oak Farm
OLD CHERRY LA
20
B5158
CHERRY CNR
85
A50
CLIFF LA
Service Area
Primrose Hill
Broad Heyes Farm
MAG LA
BROADHEYS LA
Motel
WITHER'S LA
Brook House Farm
Holly Farm
Little Oaks
3
WA4
Bears Inn (PH)
Sworton Heath
HEATH LA
9
FANNER'S LA
Rowlinson's Green
84
WA16
WITHER'S LA
Crows Nest Farm
M56
SWINEYARD LA
Mast
Swineyard Hall
MOSS BROW LA
Swineyard Hall
SWINEYARD LA
Badgers Croft
MOSS LA
2
INTACK LA
Crowley Brook
CROWLEY LA
Sink Moss
Moss Hall Farm
MOSS LA
MOSS LA
GOLDBORNE LA
83
Pennypleck House
Firtree Farm
PENNYPLECK LA
Sandilands Farm
CW9
1
Hobbs Hill Farm
HOBBS HILL LA
Arleyview Farm
REEDGATE LA
CAULDWELL'S GATE LA
Crowley Hall
Northwood House
Park Farm
M6
82
66
A
67
B
68
C

27
54

A
B
C
A56 HIGHER LA
LYMM RD A56
AGDEN BROW
PH
PO
B5159
Broomedge
PARK RD
PARKVIEW PK 1
AGDEN BROW PK 2
AGDEN PARK LA
Agden Park
Kaylane Brook
Deansgreen
KAY LA
WA13
HIGH LEGH RD
CROUCHLEY LA
CRABTREE LA
BEECHTREE LA
Agden Hall
FROGHALL LA
M56
4
AGDEN LA
Agden Lane Farm
BEECHTREE FARM CL
85
Mowpenbrow Farm
LIME TREE LA
Limetree Farm
MOSS LA
WA14
THOWLER LA
Crossroads Farm
Broad Oak Farm
MOWPEN BROW
WEST LA
PEACOCK LA
3
CRABTREE LA
High Legh Prim Sch
Lilac Farm
Moss Farm
High Legh
BACK LA
Crabtree Farm
BROADOAK LA
EGERTON
GLEBE
ROBERT MOFFAT
WEST HALL CT
THE AVENUE
84
PHEASANT WLK
WRENSHOT LA
VENABLES WAY
ARLEY END
KINDERTON CL
NORTH DR
SOMERVILLE CL
REPTON CL
HOLGRAVE CL
High Legh Park
CH
Woodside Farm
WOODLANDS CRES
SPURSTON CL
SHULDHAM CL
WHISTON CL
High Legh House
2
Wr Tw
WA16
Dairy Farm
HOLLIWELL'S BROW
LYCHFIELD LA
Bowden View Farm
Park Farm
83
BOWDEN VIEW LA
Leigh Oaks Farm
Holly House Farm
GOLBORNE LA
HULSEHEATH LA
PH
Hoo Green
A50
PO
OAK WOOD RD
1
ROWLEY BANK LA
Yew Tree Hall
Rowleybank Farm
WHITLEY LA
HOOGREEN LA
Goodiersgreen Farm
WOOD LA
WINTERBOTTOM LA
82
A
70
B
71
C

29
20

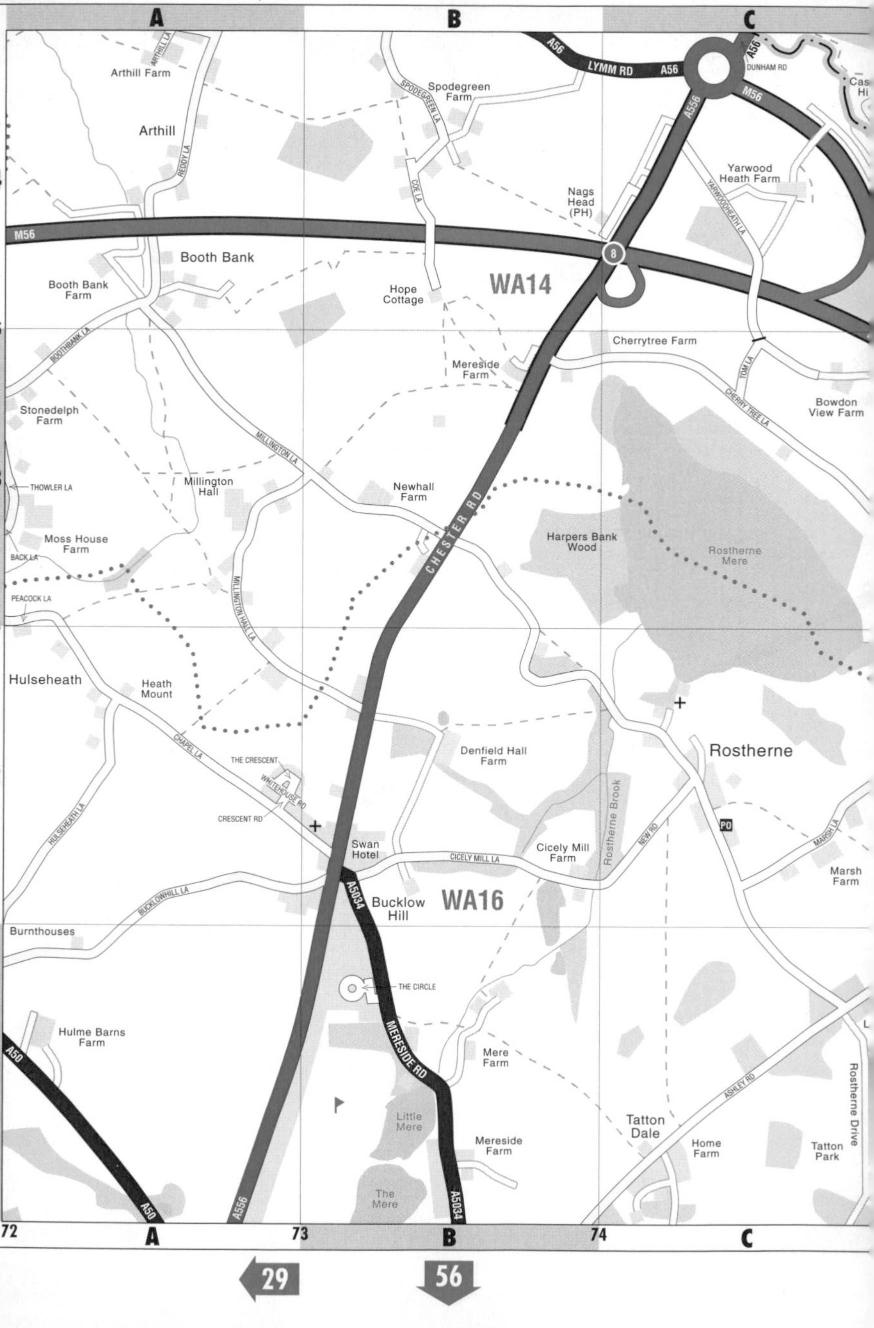
A
B
C
Arthill Farm
Arthill
Spodegreen Farm
LYMM RD
A56
DUNHAM RD
M56
A556
Yarwood Heath Farm
Nags Head (PH)
M56
Booth Bank
Booth Bank Farm
Hope Cottage
WA14
Cherrytree Farm
Mereside Farm
Bowdon View Farm
Stonedelph Farm
Millington Hall
Newhall Farm
THOWLER LA
Moss House Farm
BACK LA
Harpers Bank Wood
Rostherne Mere
CHESTER RD
PEACOCK LA
Hulseheath
Heath Mount
Rostherne
Denfield Hall Farm
THE CRESCENT
WHITEHOUSE RD
CRESCENT RD
CHAPEL LA
HULSEHEATH LA
Swan Hotel
CICELY MILL LA
Cicely Mill Farm
Rostherne Brook
NEW RD
MARSH LA
Marsh Farm
Bucklow Hill
WA16
BUCKLOWHILL LA
Burnthouses
A5034
THE CIRCLE
Hulme Barns Farm
MERESIDE RD
Mere Farm
Little Mere
Tatton Dale
ASHLEY RD
Rostherne Drive
Mereside Farm
Home Farm
Tatton Park
The Mere
A50
A556
4
85
3
84
2
83
1
82
72
73
74

29
56

32

A
B
C
Greater Manchester STREET ATLAS
ALTRINCHAM
MINSTER DR
CUMBERLAND DR
OAKWOOD LA
THE GORSE
BOLLIN AVE
PRIORY RD
PRIORY ST
SUNNY BANK RD
SOUTH DOWNS DR
SOUTH RD
BOW LA
1 ASHWOOD
2 WESTMORELAND CL
3 OAKWOOD CT
Bow Green Farm
The Priory
River Bollin
ASHLEY MILL LA N
NURSERY AVE
LABURNUM LA
AVON RD
TOLLAND LA
ARTHOG DR
ARTHOG RD
WYNGATE RD
WESTFIELDS
THE AVENUE
BANKHALL LA
BELGRAVIA GDNS
Ashley Heath
Coppice Farm
ASHLEYMILL LA
Sewage Works
ASHLEY RD
Dairy House Farm
Ryecroft Farm
Ashley Hall
CASTLE MILL LA
WA15
M56
WA14
Ashley
HOUGH GN
COW LA
EGERTON MOSS
PH
PO
BACK LA
Birkin House
Blackburn's Brook
DINTY LA
Birkin Farm
Stock Farm
Ashley CE Prim Sch
LAMB LA
BIRKINHEATH LA
Hough Green Farm
Shaw Green Farm
Birkinheath Covert
MARSH LA
ASHLEY RD
Arden House
Twiss's Wood
MOBBERLEY RD
Lower House Farm
Ward's Plantation
Birtles Farm
Sugar Brook Farm
Sugar Brook
Birkin Brook
Primrose Hill Farm
Rabbit Warren
BREACH HOUSE LA
Deer Enclosure
Tatton Park
Mobberley Brook
Kell House Farm
PEPPER ST
SMITH LA
WA16
4
85
3
84
2
83
1
82
76
77

57

32

31

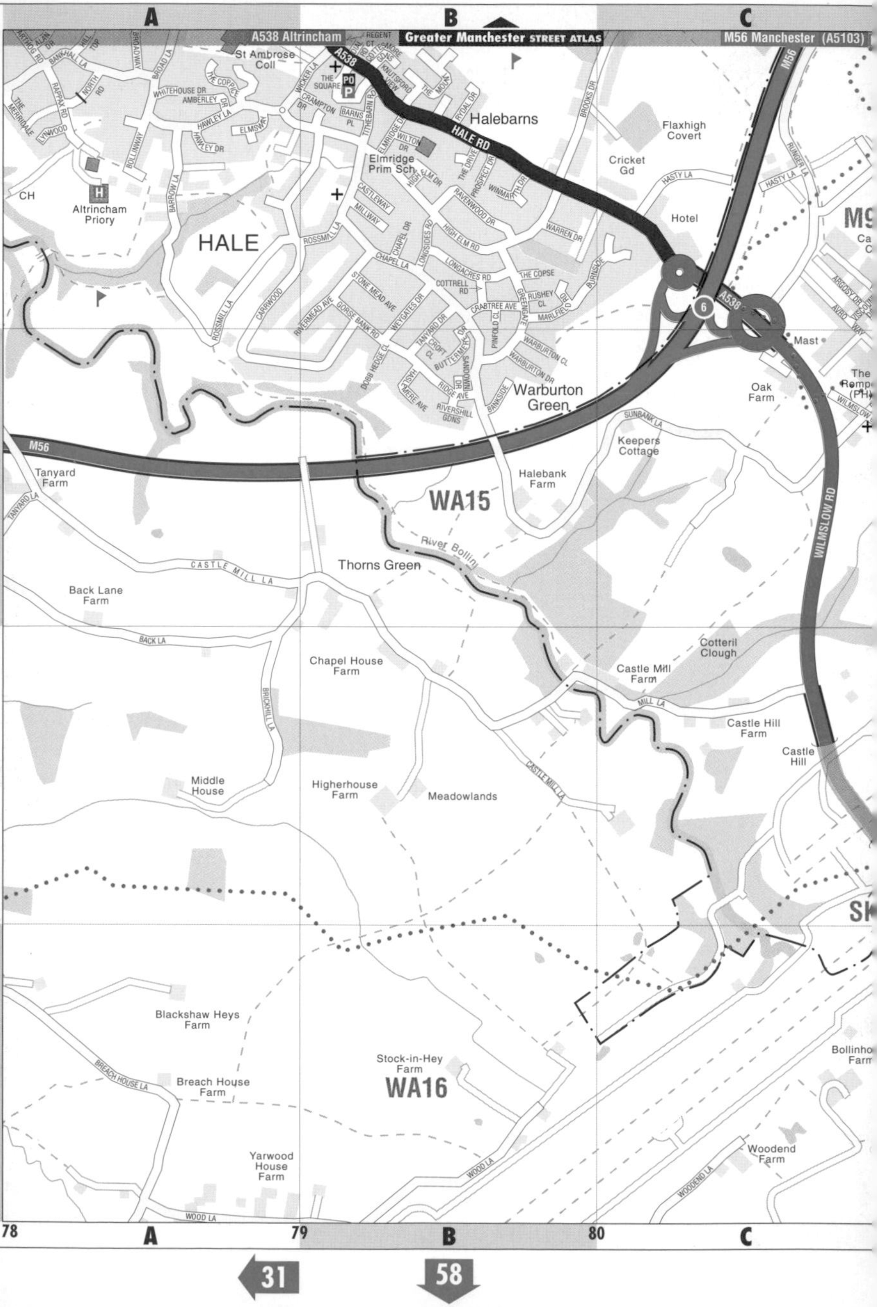
A538 Altrincham
Greater Manchester STREET ATLAS
M56 Manchester (A5103)
St Ambrose Coll
Halebarns
HALE RD
Flaxhigh Covert
Cricket Gd
Elmridge Prim Sch
Altrincham Priory
CH
HALE
Hotel
HASTY LA
WHITEHOUSE DR
AMBERLEY DR
HAWLEY LA
ELMSWAY
CRAMPTON DR
BARNS PL
THE SQUARE
ROSSMILL LA
CASTLEWAY
MILLWAY
CHAPEL LA
CHAPEL DR
LONGSIDES RD
LONGACRES RD
HIGH ELM RD
RAVENWOOD DR
WARREN DR
THE COPSE
RUSHEY CL
CRABTREE AVE
COTTRELL RD
PINFOLD CL
GREENGATE
MARLFIELD RD
BURNSIDE
STONE MEAD AVE
GORSE BANK RD
WEYGATES DR
TANYARD DR
CROFT CL
BUTTERMERE DR
SANDOWN DR
RIVERMEAD AVE
DOBB HEDGE CL
HASLEMERE AVE
RIDGE AVE
RIVERSHILL GDNS
BANKSIDE
WARBURTON CL
WARBURTON DR
Warburton Green
CARRWOOD
BARROW LA
BOLLINWAY
BROADWAY
ROSSMILL LA
Mast
Oak Farm
A538
M56
Tanyard Farm
TANYARD LA
Halebank Farm
WA15
Keepers Cottage
SUNBANK LA
River Bollin
Thorns Green
CASTLE MILL LA
Back Lane Farm
BACK LA
WILMSLOW RD
Cotteril Clough
Castle Mill Farm
MILL LA
Chapel House Farm
BRICKHILL LA
Castle Hill Farm
Castle Hill
Middle House
Higherhouse Farm
Meadowlands
Blackshaw Heys Farm
Breach House Farm
BREACH HOUSE LA
Stock-in-Hey Farm
WA16
Yarwood House Farm
WOOD LA
Woodend Farm
WOODEND LA
A
B
C
4
3
2
1
85
84
83
82
78
79
80

31

58

B4
1 ROSSETT AVE
2 WHITEFRIARS WLK
3 AUSTELL RD
4 CORNISHWAY IND EST
34

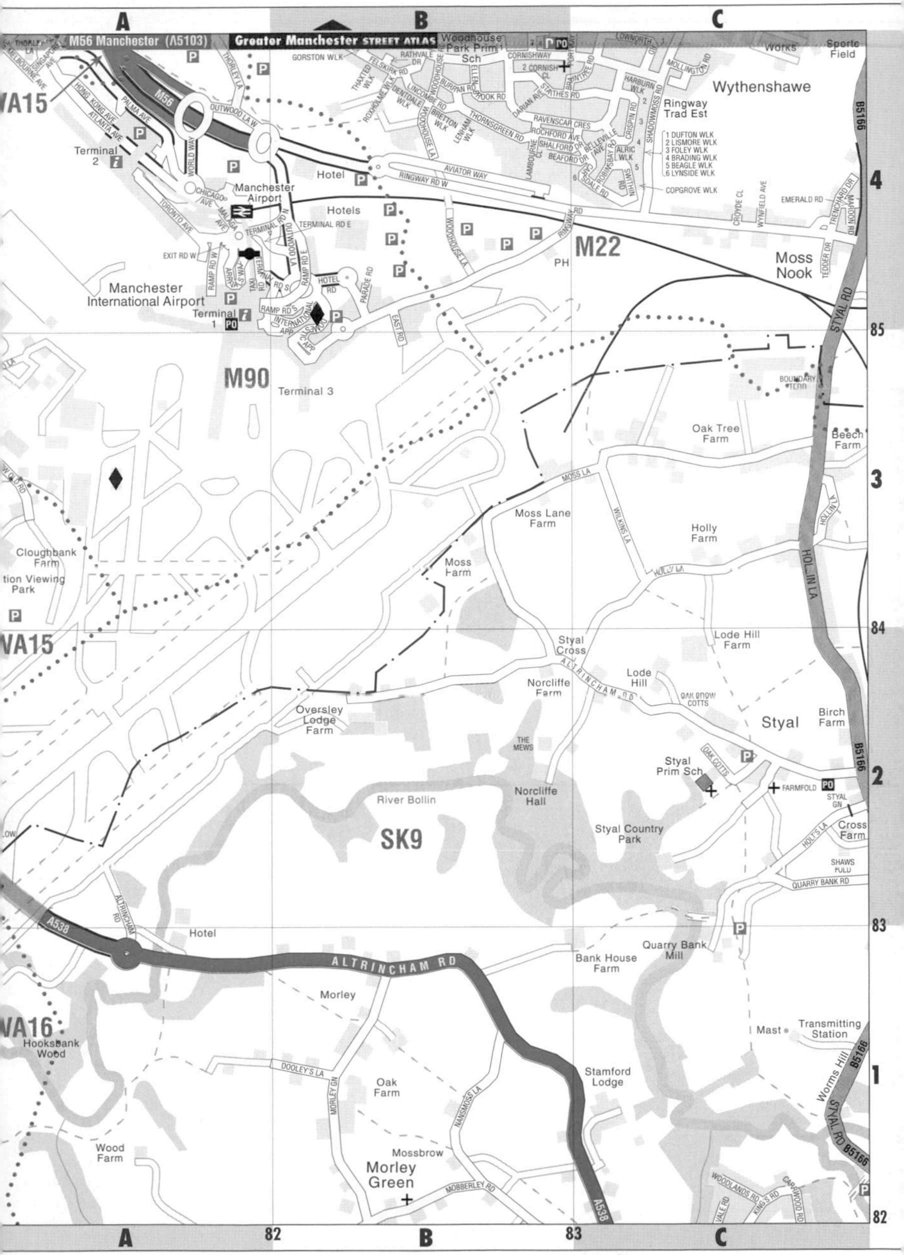
A
B
C
M56 Manchester (A5103)
Greater Manchester STREET ATLAS
Woodhouse Park Prim Sch
WA15
M56
Terminal 2
Manchester Airport
Hotel
Hotels
Manchester International Airport
Terminal 1
M22
PH
Wythenshawe
Ringway Trad Est
1 DUFTON WLK
2 LISMORE WLK
3 FOLEY WLK
4 BRADING WLK
5 BEAGLE WLK
6 LYNSIDE WLK
COPGROVE WLK
Works
Sports Field
Moss Nook
M90
Terminal 3
Oak Tree Farm
Beech Farm
Moss Lane Farm
Holly Farm
Moss Farm
Cloughbank Farm
tion Viewing Park
WA15
Styal Cross
Lode Hill Farm
Norcliffe Farm
Lode Hill
Oversley Lodge Farm
Styal
Birch Farm
THE MEWS
Styal Prim Sch
River Bollin
Norcliffe Hall
SK9
Styal Country Park
Cross Farm
Hotel
Quarry Bank Mill
Bank House Farm
Morley
ALTRINCHAM RD
WA16
Hooksbank Wood
Mast
Transmitting Station
Oak Farm
Stamford Lodge
Worms Hill
Wood Farm
Mossbrow
Morley Green
STYAL RD
HOLLIN LA
MOSS LA
A538
B5166
4
85
3
84
2
83
1
82
82
83

33

B3
1 TARVIN WAY
2 OVERTON WAY
3 STRETTON WAY
4 BIRTLES WAY
5 PEACOCK WAY
6 KELSALL WAY
7 CUDDINGTON WAY
8 WILLASTON WAY
9 NORBURY WAY
10 PICKMERE CT
11 EASTHAM WAY
12 UPTON WAY
13 ASTON WAY
14 HOOTON WAY
15 CHRISTLETON WAY
16 CRANAGE WAY

C3
1 SUTTON WAY
2 CHELFORD CT
3 SOMERFORD WAY
4 TATTON CT
5 MARTON WAY
6 NANTWICH WAY
7 HASSALL WAY
8 MARTHALL WAY

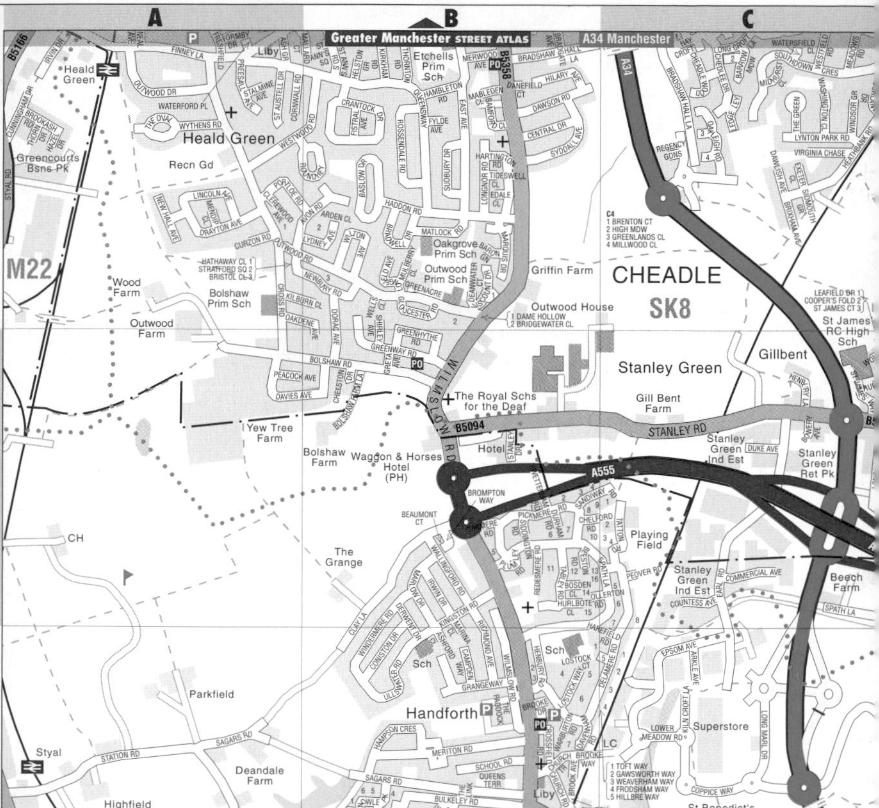

B1
1 TORBROOK GR
2 CLIFFBROOK GR
3 BENSON WLK
4 CARDENBROOK GR
5 TIMBERSBROOK GR
6 DE TRAFFORD MEWS
7 LADYBROOK GR
8 FODEN WLK
9 TAME WLK
10 MILLBROOK GR
11 REDBROOK GR
12 SHELLBROOK GR
13 TIVERTON DR
14 DEAN ROW CT
15 RINGSTEAD DR
16 DRAYTON CL
17 KNIGHTSBRIDGE CL
18 KINGSBURY DR
19 QUEENSBURY CL
20 CROWBROOK GR
21 LIME WLK
22 DINGLEBROOK GR
23 WADEBROOK GR

B2
1 HILLBRE WAY
2 SEALAND WAY
3 ECCLESTON WAY
4 HELSBY WAY
5 HEATLEY WAY
6 ELWORTH WAY
7 PARKGATE WAY

C1
1 BUDWORTH WLK
2 EDLESTONE GR
3 WOODCOTT GR
4 KETTLESHULME WLK
5 TILSTON WLK
6 SNAPEBROOK GR
7 DAIRYBROOK GR
8 APPLETON WLK
9 MOORSBROOK GR
10 RAINOW WA
11 PECKFORTON
12 SALTERSBRO
13 PINWOOD CT
14 KINGSTON C
15 MELROSE CT
16 SEYMOUR H
17 HAZELDEAN

33
60

36

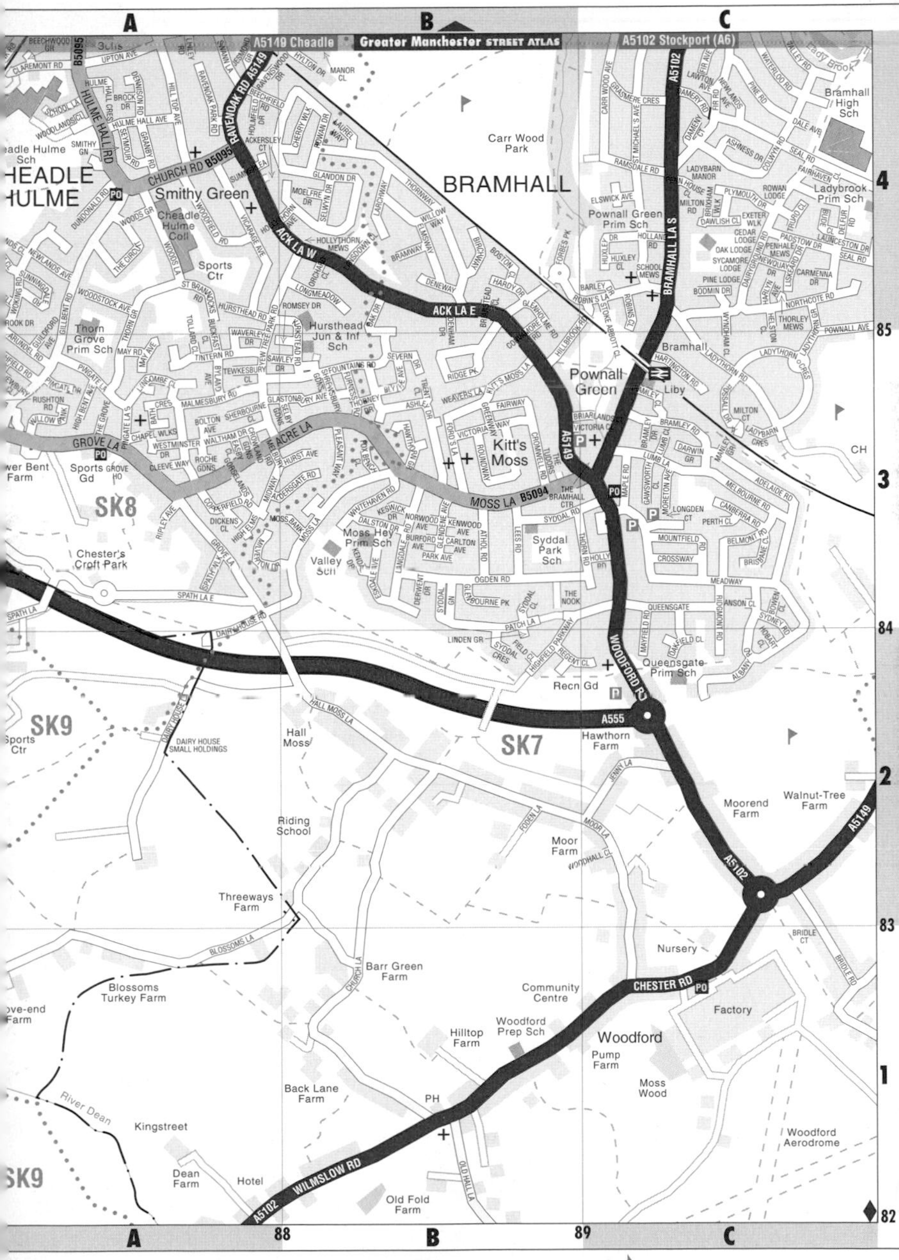
A5149 Cheadle
Greater Manchester STREET ATLAS
A5102 Stockport (A6)
A
B
C
4
85
3
84
2
83
1
82
88
89
CHEADLE HULME
Cheadle Hulme Sch
Smithy Green
Cheadle Hulme Coll
Sports Ctr
Thorn Grove Prim Sch
Sports Gd
SK8
Chester's Croft Park
SK9
BRAMHALL
Carr Wood Park
Hursthead Jun & Inf Sch
Kitt's Moss
Moss Hey Prim Sch
Valley Sch
Syddal Park Sch
Pownall Green
Pownall Green Prim Sch
Bramhall
Liby
Bramhall High Sch
Ladybrook Prim Sch
Ladybarn Manor
Queensgate Prim Sch
Recn Gd
Hawthorn Farm
SK7
Hall Moss
Dairy House Small Holdings
Riding School
Threeways Farm
Blossoms Turkey Farm
Barr Green Farm
Moor Farm
Moorend Farm
Walnut-Tree Farm
Nursery
Community Centre
Factory
Woodford
Woodford Prep Sch
Hilltop Farm
Pump Farm
Moss Wood
Back Lane Farm
PH
Kingstreet
River Dean
Dean Farm
Hotel
Old Fold Farm
Woodford Aerodrome
A5149
A5102
A555
B5094
B5095
CHURCH RD
HULME HALL RD
RAVENOAK RD
ACK LA W
ACK LA E
MOSS LA
GROVE LA
ACRE LA
BRAMHALL LA S
WOODFORD RD
CHESTER RD
WILMSLOW RD
HALL MOSS LA
SPATH LA E
DAIRYHOUSE RD
BLOSSOMS LA
CHURCH LA
OLD HALL LA
MOOR LA
FODEN LA
JENNY LA
BRIDLE RD
QUEENSGATE
MEADWAY
OGDEN RD

61

36

35

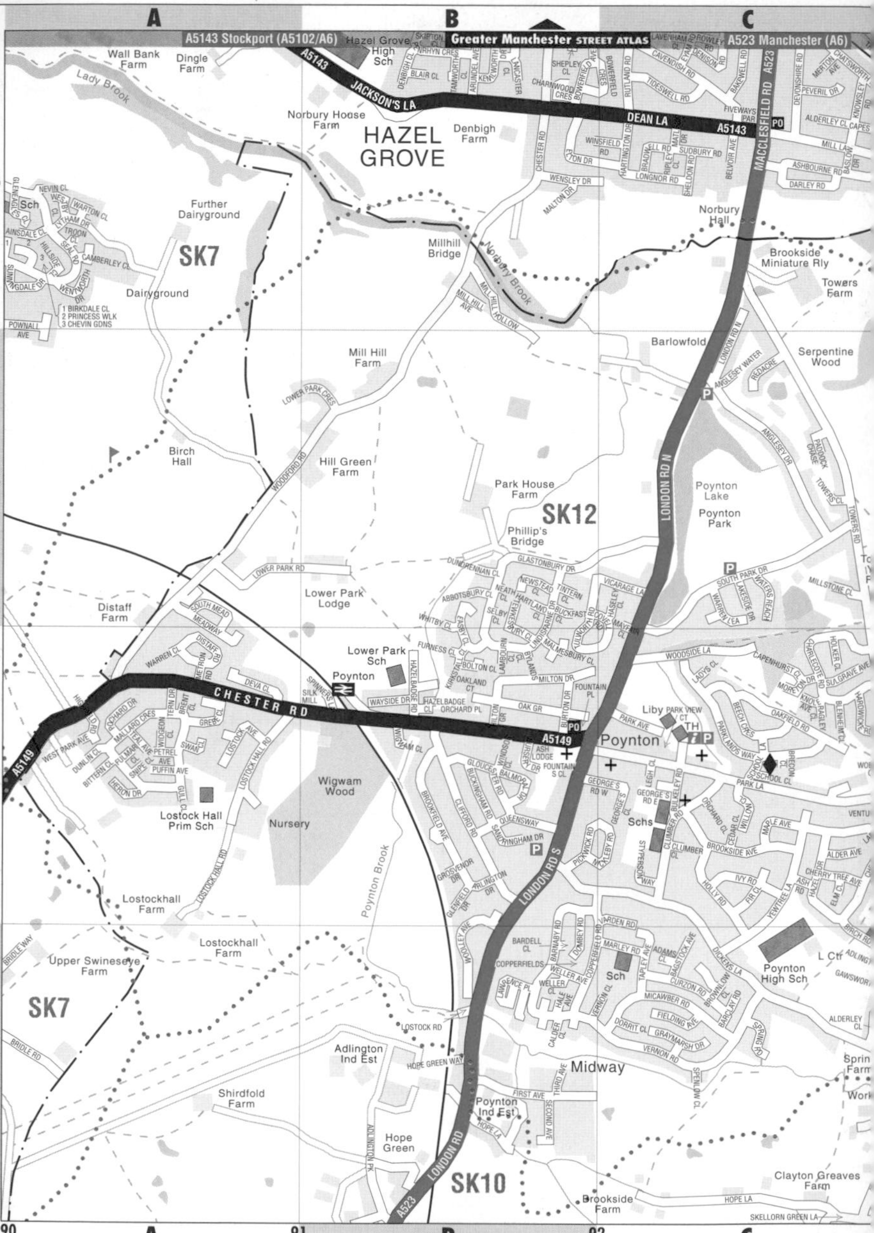

A
B
C
A5143 Stockport (A5102/A6)
Greater Manchester STREET ATLAS
A523 Manchester (A6)
Wall Bank Farm
Dingle Farm
Lady Brook
Hazel Grove High Sch
JACKSON'S LA
DEAN LA
A5143
MACCLESFIELD RD
A523
Norbury House Farm
HAZEL GROVE
Denbigh Farm
Further Dairyground
SK7
Dairyground
1 BIRKDALE CL
2 PRINCESS WLK
3 CHEVIN GDNS
Millhill Bridge
Norbury Brook
Norbury Hall
Brookside Miniature Rly
Towers Farm
Barlowfold
Serpentine Wood
Mill Hill Farm
Birch Hall
Hill Green Farm
Park House Farm
SK12
Phillip's Bridge
Poynton Lake
Poynton Park
LONDON RD N
Lower Park Lodge
Distaff Farm
Lower Park Sch
Poynton
CHESTER RD
A5149
Liby
TH
Poynton
Wigwam Wood
Nursery
Lostock Hall Prim Sch
Schs
Poynton Brook
LONDON RD S
Lostockhall Farm
Upper Swineseye Farm
Sch
L Ctr
Poynton High Sch
Adlington Ind Est
Midway
Shirdfold Farm
Poynton Ind Est
Hope Green
LONDON RD
SK10
Brookside Farm
Clayton Greaves Farm
HOPE LA
SKELLORN GREEN LA
4
85
3
84
2
83
1
82
90
91
92

35
62

38

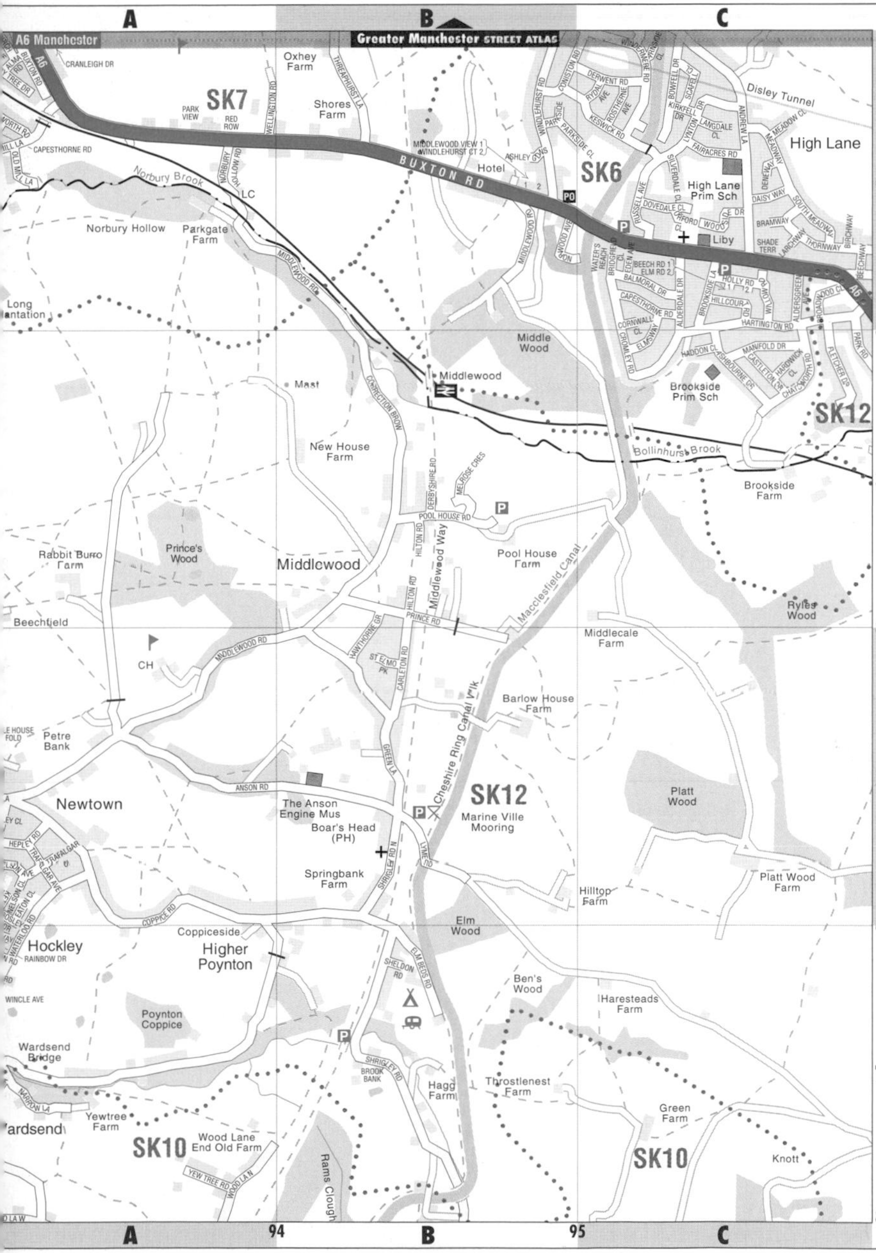
A6 Manchester
Greater Manchester STREET ATLAS
A
B
C
SK7
SK6
SK12
SK10
High Lane
Disley Tunnel
BUXTON RD
Oxhey Farm
Shores Farm
Hotel
High Lane Prim Sch
Liby
Norbury Brook
Norbury Hollow
Parkgate Farm
LC
Long Plantation
Middle Wood
Middlewood
Mast
New House Farm
Bollinhurst Brook
Brookside Prim Sch
Brookside Farm
Pool House Farm
Macclesfield Canal
Middlewood Way
Rabbit Burrow Farm
Prince's Wood
Middlewood
Beechfield
CH
Ryles Wood
Middlecale Farm
Barlow House Farm
Cheshire Ring Canal Wlk
Petre Bank
Newtown
The Anson Engine Mus
Boar's Head (PH)
Marine Ville Mooring
Platt Wood
Springbank Farm
Hilltop Farm
Platt Wood Farm
Elm Wood
Coppiceside
Hockley
Higher Poynton
Ben's Wood
Haresteads Farm
Poynton Coppice
Wardsend Bridge
Hagg Farm
Throstlenest Farm
Green Farm
Yewtree Farm
Wardsend
Wood Lane End Old Farm
Rams Clough
Knott
ANSON RD
MIDDLEWOOD RD
PRINCE RD
POOL HOUSE RD
COPPICE RD
SHRIGLEY RD
SHRIGLEY RD N
LYME RD
GREEN LA
ELM BEDS RD
YEW TREE RD
WOOD LA N
4
3
2
1
85
84
83
82
94
95

63

38

37

A B C

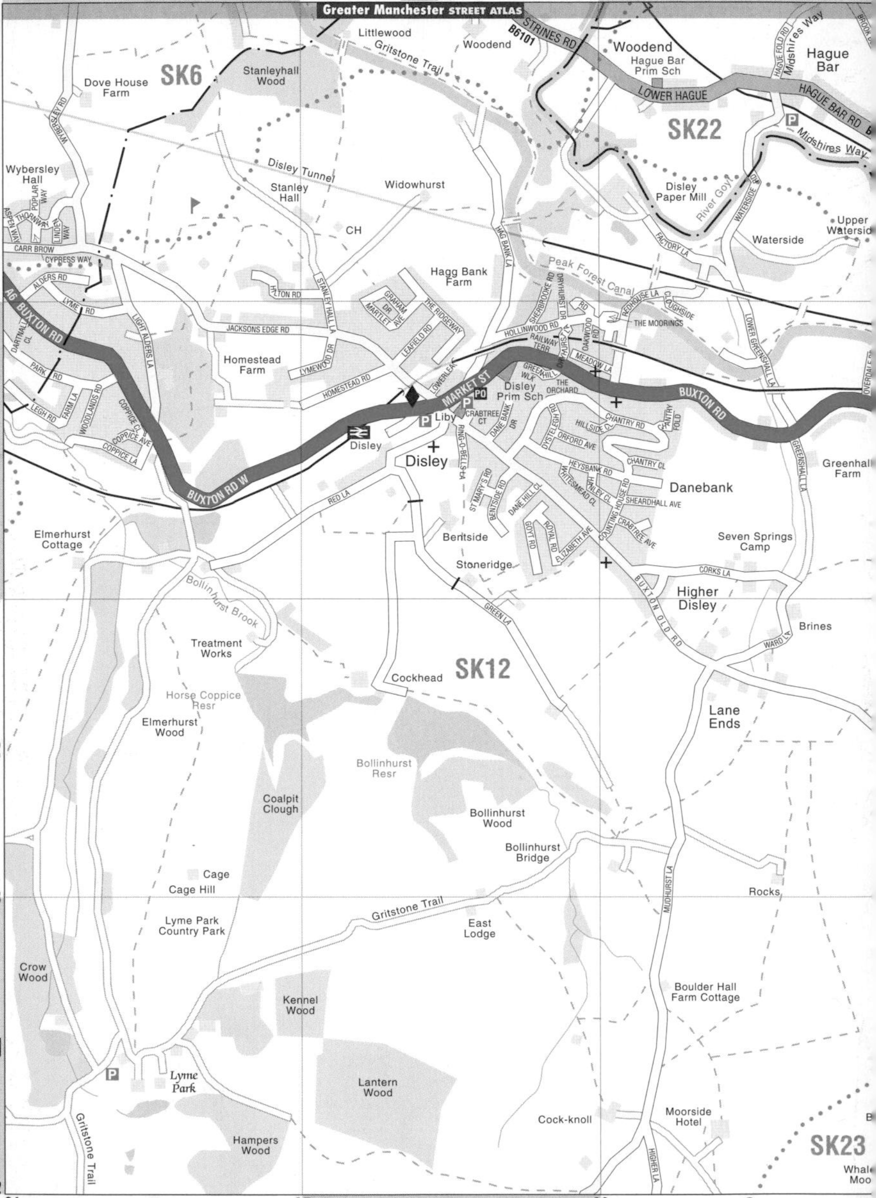
Greater Manchester STREET ATLAS
SK6
SK22
SK12
SK23
Littlewood
Gritstone Trail
Woodend
B6101
STRINES RD
Woodend
Hague Bar Prim Sch
LOWER HAGUE
Hague Bar
HAGUE BAR RD
HAGUE FOLD RD
Midshires Way
Dove House Farm
Stanleyhall Wood
Wybersley Hall
WYBERSLEY RD
POPLAR WAY
THORNWAY
ASPEN WAY
LINDEN WAY
CARR BROW
CYPRESS WAY
ALDERS RD
LYME RD
Disley Tunnel
Stanley Hall
Widowhurst
CH
Disley Paper Mill
River Goyt
WATERSIDE
Upper Waterside
Waterside
FACTORY LA
Peak Forest Canal
HAGG BANK LA
Hagg Bank Farm
HALTON RD
STANLEY HALL LA
GRAHAM DR
MARTLET AVE
THE RIDGEWAY
LEAFIELD RD
SHERBROOKE RD
DRYHURST DR
REDHOUSE LA
CLOUGHSIDE
THE MOORINGS
LOWER GREENSHALL LA
HOLLINWOOD RD
RAILWAY TERR
OAKWOOD RD
MEADOW LA
A6 BUXTON RD
DARTNALL CL
LIGHT ALDERS LA
JACKSONS EDGE RD
Homestead Farm
LYMEWOOD DR
HOMESTEAD RD
LOWERLEA
MARKET ST
PO
Disley Prim Sch
GREEN WLK
THE ORCHARD
BUXTON RD
PARK RD
LEGH RD
FARM LA
WOODLANDS RD
COPPICE CL
COPPICE AVE
COPPICE LA
Disley
Liby
CRABTREE CT
DANE BANK DR
RING-O-BELLS LA
DYSTELEGH RD
HILLSIDE CL
CHANTRY RD
CHANTRY FOLD
ORFORD AVE
CHANTRY CL
HEYSBANK RD
WHITESMEAD CL
HAWLEY CL
COUNTING HOUSE RD
SHEARDHALL AVE
CRABTREE AVE
Danebank
GREENSHALL LA
Greenhall Farm
OVERDALE
BROOK
BUXTON RD W
RED LA
ST MARY'S RD
BENTSIDE RD
DANE HILL CL
GOYT RD
ROYAL RD
ELIZABETH AVE
Elmerhurst Cottage
Bentside
Stoneridge
Seven Springs Camp
CORKS LA
Higher Disley
BUXTON OLD RD
Brines
WARD LA
Bollinhurst Brook
Treatment Works
GREEN LA
Cockhead
Lane Ends
Horse Coppice Resr
Elmerhurst Wood
Bollinhurst Resr
Coalpit Clough
Bollinhurst Wood
Bollinhurst Bridge
Cage
Cage Hill
MUDHURST LA
Rocks
Gritstone Trail
Lyme Park Country Park
East Lodge
Crow Wood
Kennel Wood
Boulder Hall Farm Cottage
Lyme Park
Lantern Wood
Moorside Hotel
Cock-knoll
Hampers Wood
HIGHER LA
Gritstone Trail
Whale Moo
4
85
3
84
2
83
1
82
96
97
98

A B C

37

64

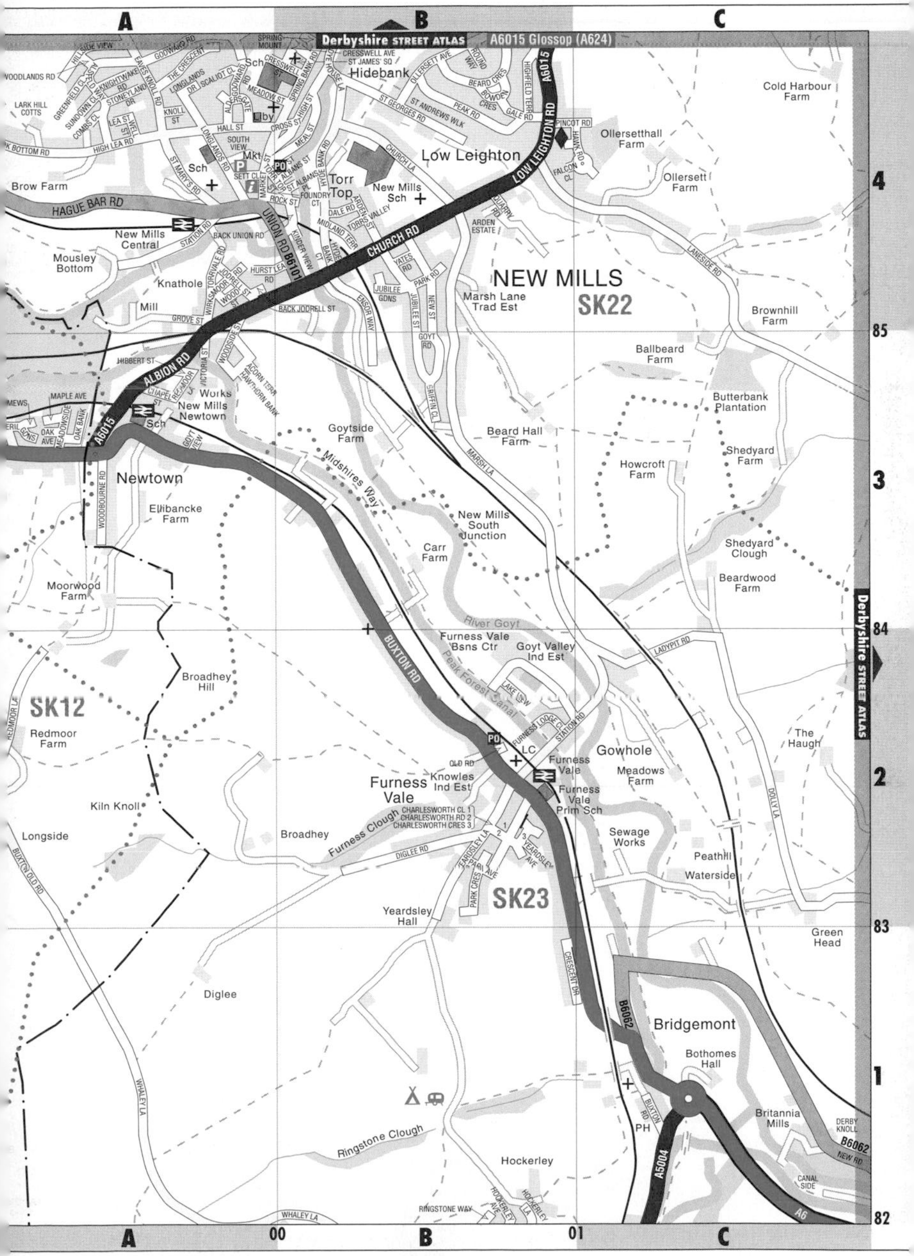

A
B
C
Derbyshire STREET ATLAS
A6015 Glossop (A624)
Hidebank
Low Leighton
Cold Harbour Farm
Ollersetthall Farm
Ollersett Farm
Brow Farm
HAGUE BAR RD
New Mills Central
Mousley Bottom
Knathole
Mill
Torr Top
New Mills Sch
CHURCH RD
LOW LEIGHTON RD
UNION RD B6101
ALBION RD
NEW MILLS
SK22
Marsh Lane Trad Est
Brownhill Farm
Ballbeard Farm
Butterbank Plantation
New Mills Newtown
Newtown
Goytside Farm
Beard Hall Farm
Howcroft Farm
Shedyard Farm
Midshires Way
Ellibancke Farm
New Mills South Junction
Carr Farm
Shedyard Clough
Beardwood Farm
Moorwood Farm
River Goyt
Furness Vale Bsns Ctr
Goyt Valley Ind Est
BUXTON RD
Peak Forest Canal
Broadhey Hill
SK12
Redmoor Farm
The Haugh
Gowhole
Furness Vale
Knowles Ind Est
Meadows Farm
Furness Vale Prim Sch
Kiln Knoll
Longside
Broadhey
Furness Clough
DIGLEE RD
Sewage Works
Peathill
Waterside
SK23
Yeardsley Hall
Green Head
Diglee
Bridgemont
Bothomes Hall
Britannia Mills
Ringstone Clough
Hockerley
B6062
A5004
A6
WHALEY LA
DOLLY LA
LADYPIT RD
LANESIDE RD
MARSH LA
4
85
3
84
2
83
1
82
00
01

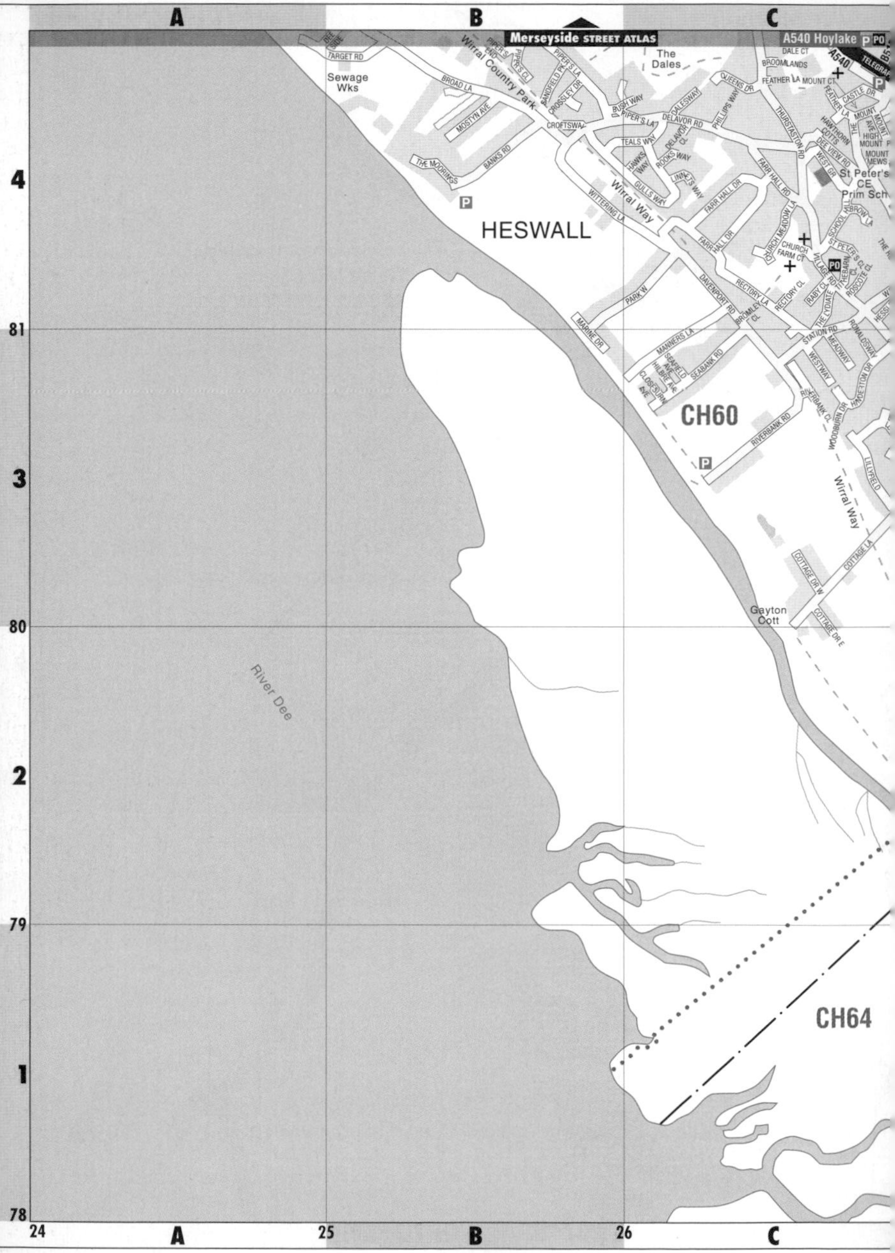
A
B
C
Merseyside STREET ATLAS
A540 Hoylake
TARGET RD
Sewage Wks
Wirral Country Park
The Dales
BROAD LA
MOSTYN AVE
THE MOORINGS
BANKS RD
CROFTSWAY
PIPER'S LA
BUSH WAY
DALESWAY
DELAVOR RD
TEALS WAY
HAWKS WAY
ROOKS WAY
GULLS WAY
QUEENS DR
PHILLIPS WAY
BROOMLANDS
DALE CT
FEATHER LA
MOUNT CT
THURSTASTON RD
FARR HALL RD
FARR HALL DR
CASTLE DR
DEE VIEW RD
WEST GR
St Peter's CE Prim Sch
SCHOOL LA
CHURCH MEADOW LA
CHURCH FARM CT
WITTERING LA
Wirral Way
HESWALL
PARK W
DAVENPORT RD
RECTORY LA
RECTORY CL
BROMLEY CL
MARINE DR
MANNERS LA
SEABANK RD
STATION RD
MEADWAY
WESTWAY
RONALDSWAY
HADDEN DR
WOODBURN DR
RIVERBANK RD
RIVERBANK CL
CH60
LILLYFIELD
COTTAGE LA
COTTAGE DR W
COTTAGE DR E
Gayton Cott
River Dee
CH64
4
81
3
80
2
79
1
78
24
25
26

42

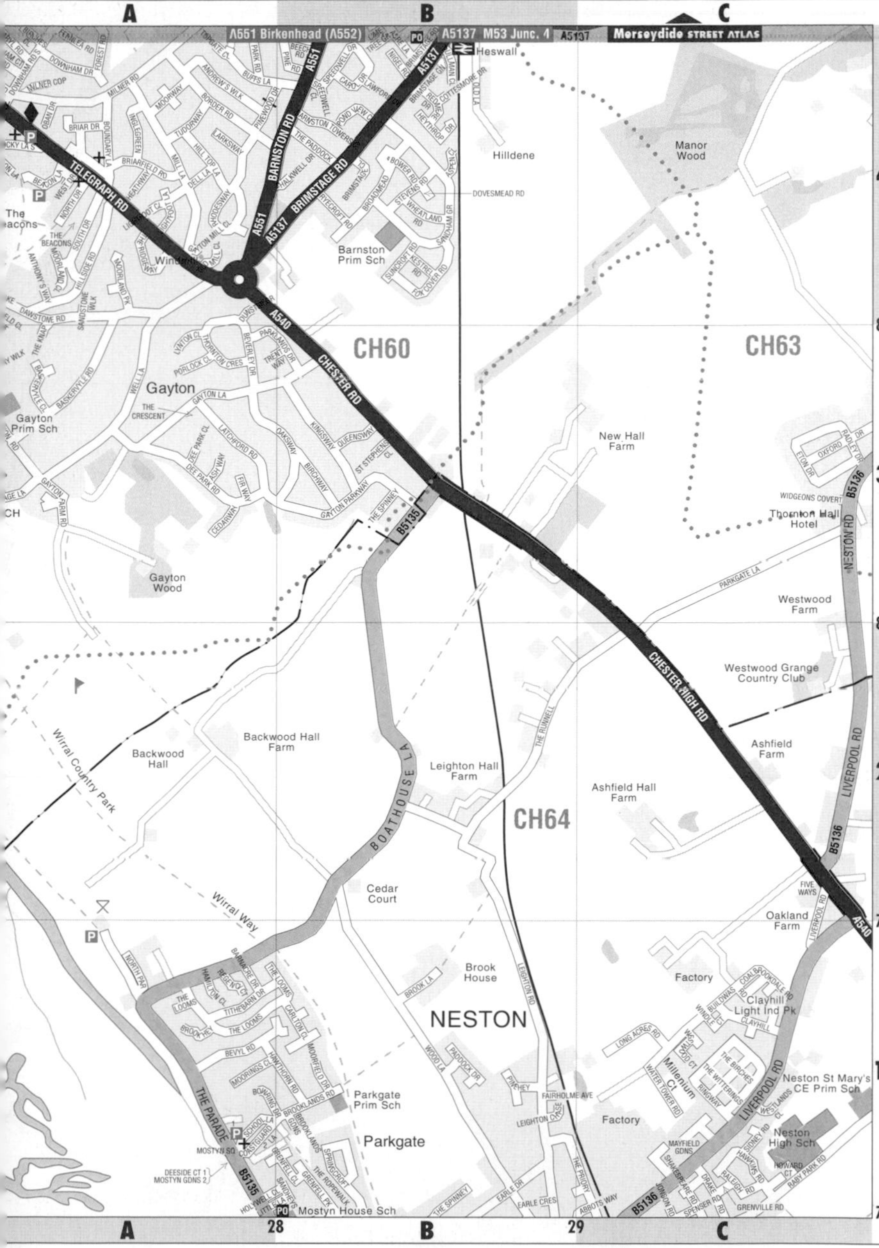
A
B
C
A551 Birkenhead (A552)
A5137 M53 Junc. 4
A5137
Merseyside STREET ATLAS
Heswall
Hilldene
Manor Wood
DOVESMEAD RD
Barnston Prim Sch
The Beacons
Windmill
TELEGRAPH RD
BARNSTON RD
BRIMSTAGE RD
A551
A5137
A540
CHESTER RD
CH60
CH63
Gayton
Gayton Prim Sch
THE CRESCENT
GAYTON LA
New Hall Farm
Thornton Hall Hotel
WIDGEONS COVERT
NESTON RD
B5136
B5135
Gayton Wood
PARKGATE LA
Westwood Farm
Westwood Grange Country Club
CHESTER HIGH RD
Backwood Hall Farm
Backwood Hall
Leighton Hall Farm
Ashfield Farm
Ashfield Hall Farm
LIVERPOOL RD
THE RUNNELL
BOATHOUSE LA
CH64
Wirral Country Park
Cedar Court
Wirral Way
FIVE WAYS
Oakland Farm
Brook House
Factory
Clayhill Light Ind Pk
NESTON
LEIGHTON RD
Millenium Ct
Neston St Mary's CE Prim Sch
Neston High Sch
Parkgate Prim Sch
Parkgate
THE PARADE
DEESIDE CT 1
MOSTYN GDNS 2
Mostyn House Sch
4
3
2
1
81
80
79
78
28
29

66

42

41

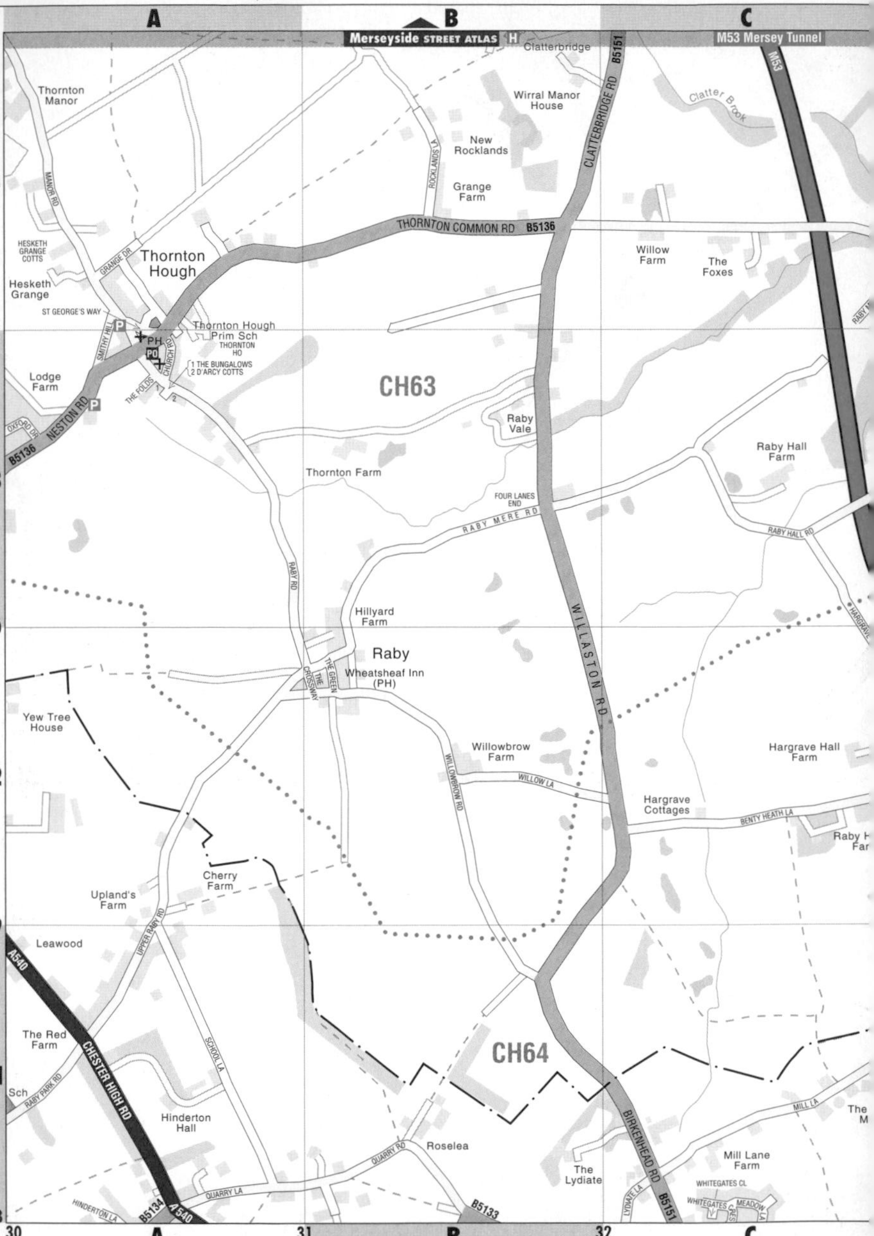
Merseyside STREET ATLAS
M53 Mersey Tunnel
Clatterbridge
Thornton Manor
Wirral Manor House
Clatter Brook
New Rocklands
Grange Farm
ROCKLANDS LA
CLATTERBRIDGE RD
B5151
M53
MANOR RD
THORNTON COMMON RD
B5136
HESKETH GRANGE COTTS
GRANGE DR
Thornton Hough
Willow Farm
The Foxes
Hesketh Grange
ST GEORGE'S WAY
Thornton Hough Prim Sch
THORNTON HO
SMITHY HILL
CHURCH RD
1 THE BUNGALOWS
2 D'ARCY COTTS
Lodge Farm
THE FOLDS
CH63
NESTON RD
OXFORD DR
Raby Vale
Raby Hall Farm
Thornton Farm
FOUR LANES END
RABY MERE RD
RABY HALL RD
RABY RD
Hillyard Farm
WILLASTON RD
Raby
Wheatsheaf Inn (PH)
THE CROSSWAY
THE GREEN
Yew Tree House
Willowbrow Farm
Hargrave Hall Farm
WILLOW LA
WILLOWBROW RD
Hargrave Cottages
BENTY HEATH LA
Cherry Farm
Upland's Farm
UPPER RABY RD
Leawood
A540
SCHOOL LA
The Red Farm
CH64
CHESTER HIGH RD
Sch
RABY PARK RD
Hinderton Hall
BIRKENHEAD RD
MILL LA
Roselea
QUARRY RD
The Lydiate
Mill Lane Farm
QUARRY LA
WHITEGATES CL
WHITEGATES CRES
MEADOW LA
LYDIATE LA
HINDERTON LA
B5134
B5133
30
31
32
A
B
C
1
2
3
4
78
79
80
81

41
67

44

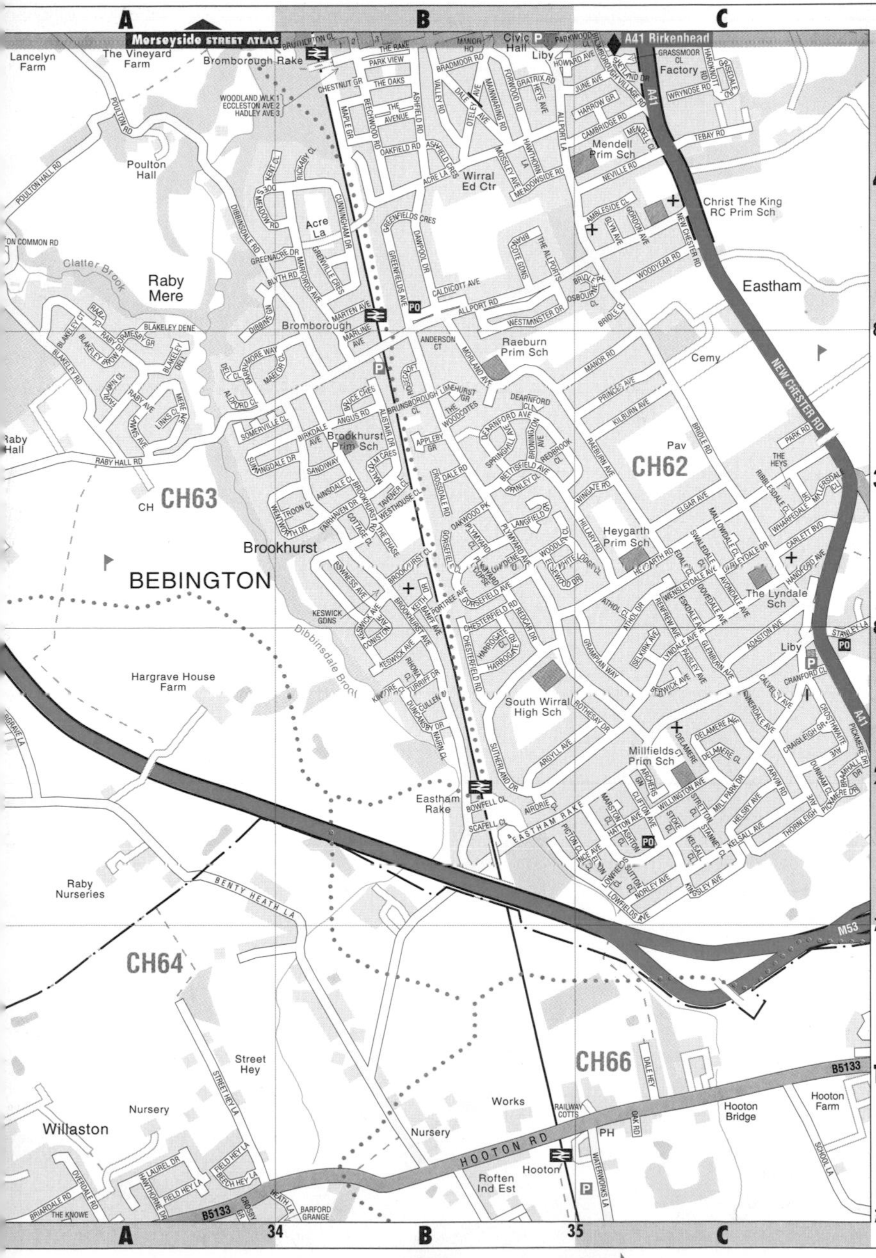
Merseyside STREET ATLAS
A41 Birkenhead
A
B
C
Lancelyn Farm
The Vineyard Farm
Bromborough Rake
Civic Hall
Liby
Factory
Poulton Hall
Wirral Ed Ctr
Mendell Prim Sch
Christ The King RC Prim Sch
Acre La
Raby Mere
Clatter Brook
Bromborough
Eastham
Raeburn Prim Sch
Cemy
NEW CHESTER RD
Brookhurst Prim Sch
Pav
CH62
Raby Hall
CH63
BEBINGTON
Brookhurst
Heygarth Prim Sch
The Lyndale Sch
Hargrave House Farm
Dibbinsdale Brook
South Wirral High Sch
Millfields Prim Sch
Eastham Rake
Raby Nurseries
BENTY HEATH LA
CH64
M53
Street Hey
CH66
Willaston
Nursery
Works
Hooton Bridge
Hooton Farm
HOOTON RD
Hooton
Roften Ind Est
B5133
PH
4
81
3
80
2
79
1
78
34
35

68
44

43

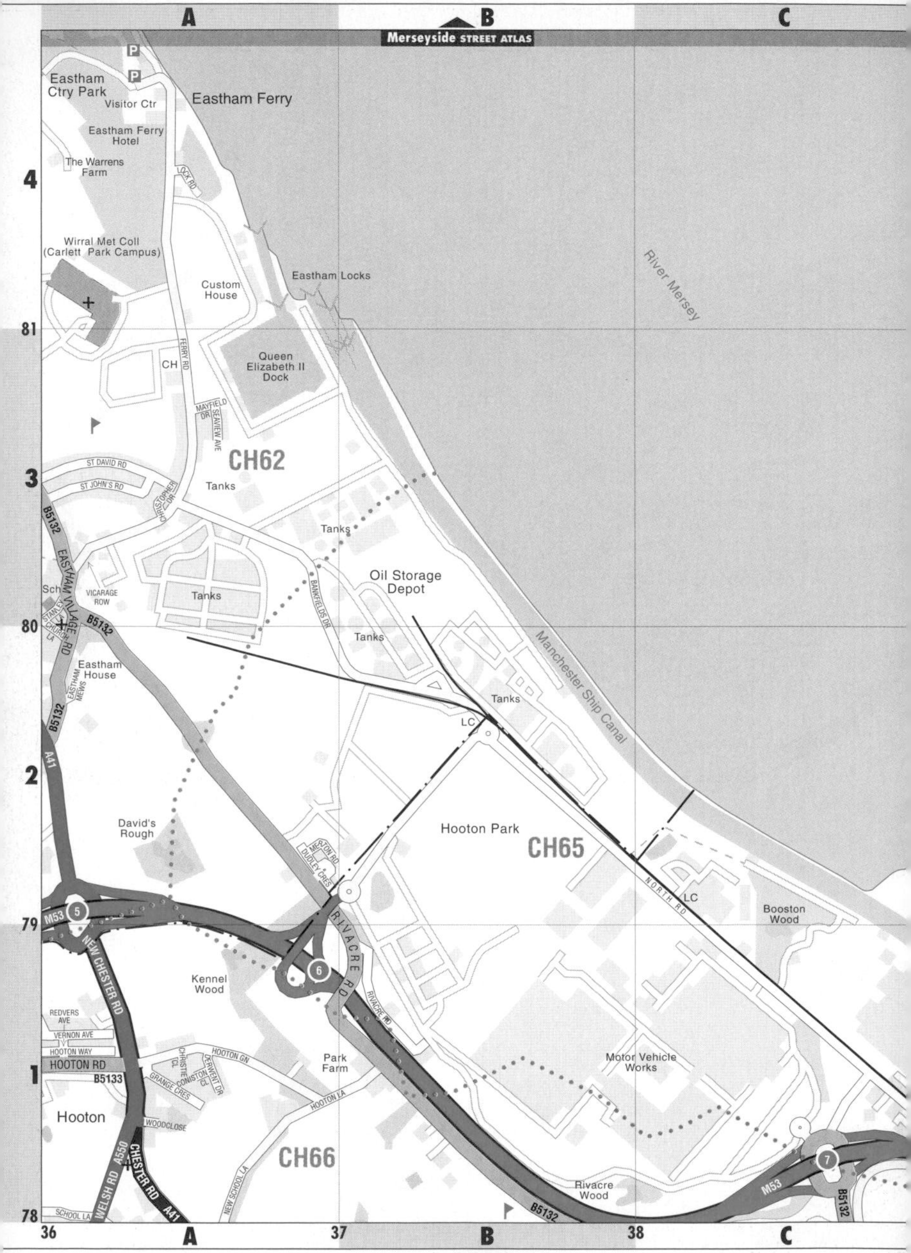
A
B
C
Merseyside STREET ATLAS
Eastham Ctry Park
Visitor Ctr
Eastham Ferry
Eastham Ferry Hotel
The Warrens Farm
LOCK RD
Wirral Met Coll (Carlett Park Campus)
Custom House
Eastham Locks
River Mersey
CH
FERRY RD
Queen Elizabeth II Dock
MAYFIELD DR
SEAVIEW AVE
CH62
ST DAVID RD
ST JOHN'S RD
CHRISTOPHER DR
Tanks
B5132
EASTHAM VILLAGE RD
Sch
VICARAGE ROW
STANLEY LA
CHURCH LA
BANKFIELDS DR
Oil Storage Depot
Manchester Ship Canal
Eastham House
EASTHAM MEWS
LC
A41
David's Rough
Hooton Park
CH65
MERTON RD
DUDLEY CRES
NORTH RD
Booston Wood
M53
5
6
NEW CHESTER RD
RIVACRE RD
Kennel Wood
REDVERS AVE
VERNON AVE
HOOTON WAY
HOOTON RD
B5133
HOOTON GN
CHRISTIE CL
CONISTON CL
DERWENT DR
GRANGE CRES
Park Farm
HOOTON LA
Motor Vehicle Works
Hooton
WOODCLOSE
A550
WELSH RD
CHESTER RD
CH66
NEW SCHOOL LA
Rivacre Wood
7
SCHOOL LA
4
81
3
80
2
79
1
78
36
37
38

43

69

46

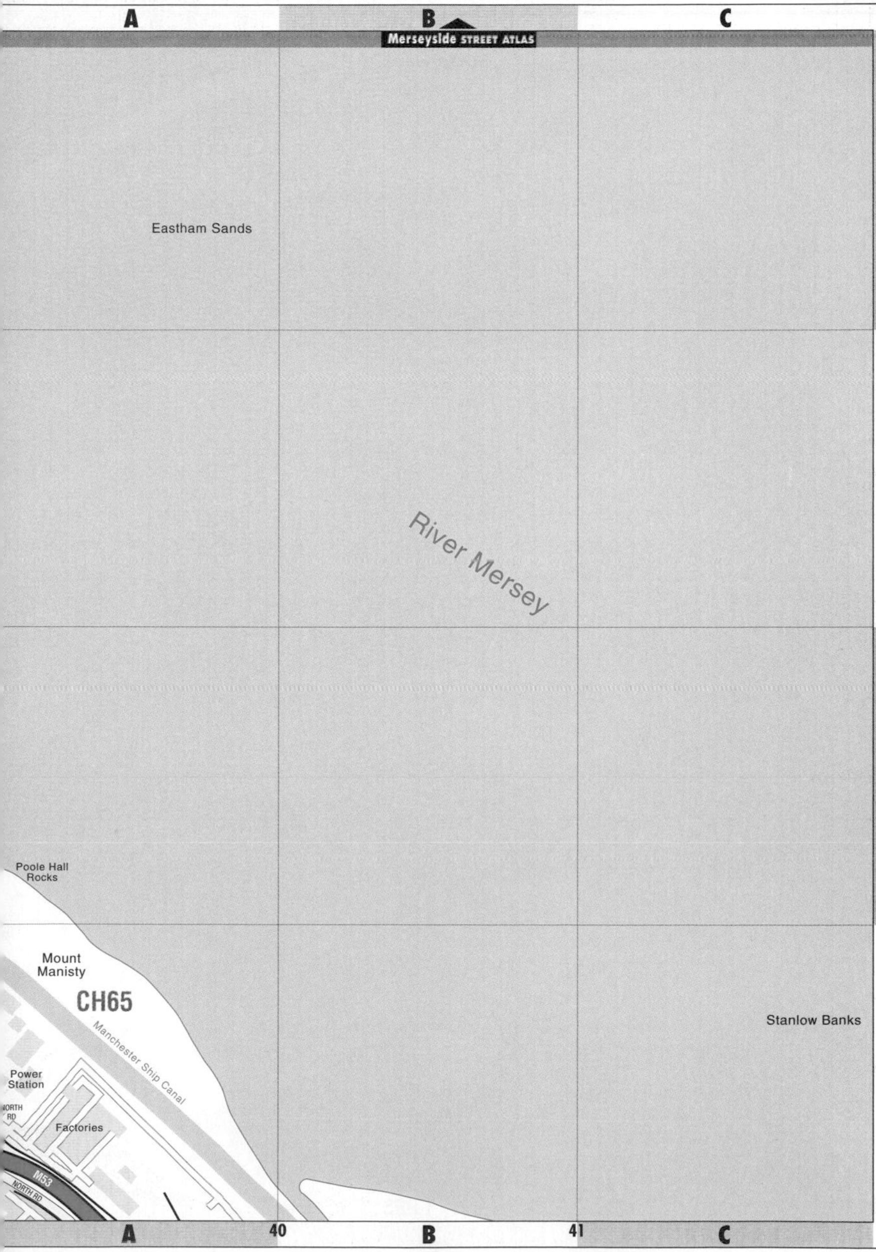
A
B
C
Merseyside STREET ATLAS
4
Eastham Sands
81
3
River Mersey
80
2
Poole Hall
Rocks
79
Mount
Manisty
CH65
Manchester Ship Canal
Stanlow Banks
Power
Station
1
Factories
M53
NORTH RD
78
40
41
A
B
C

70
46

45

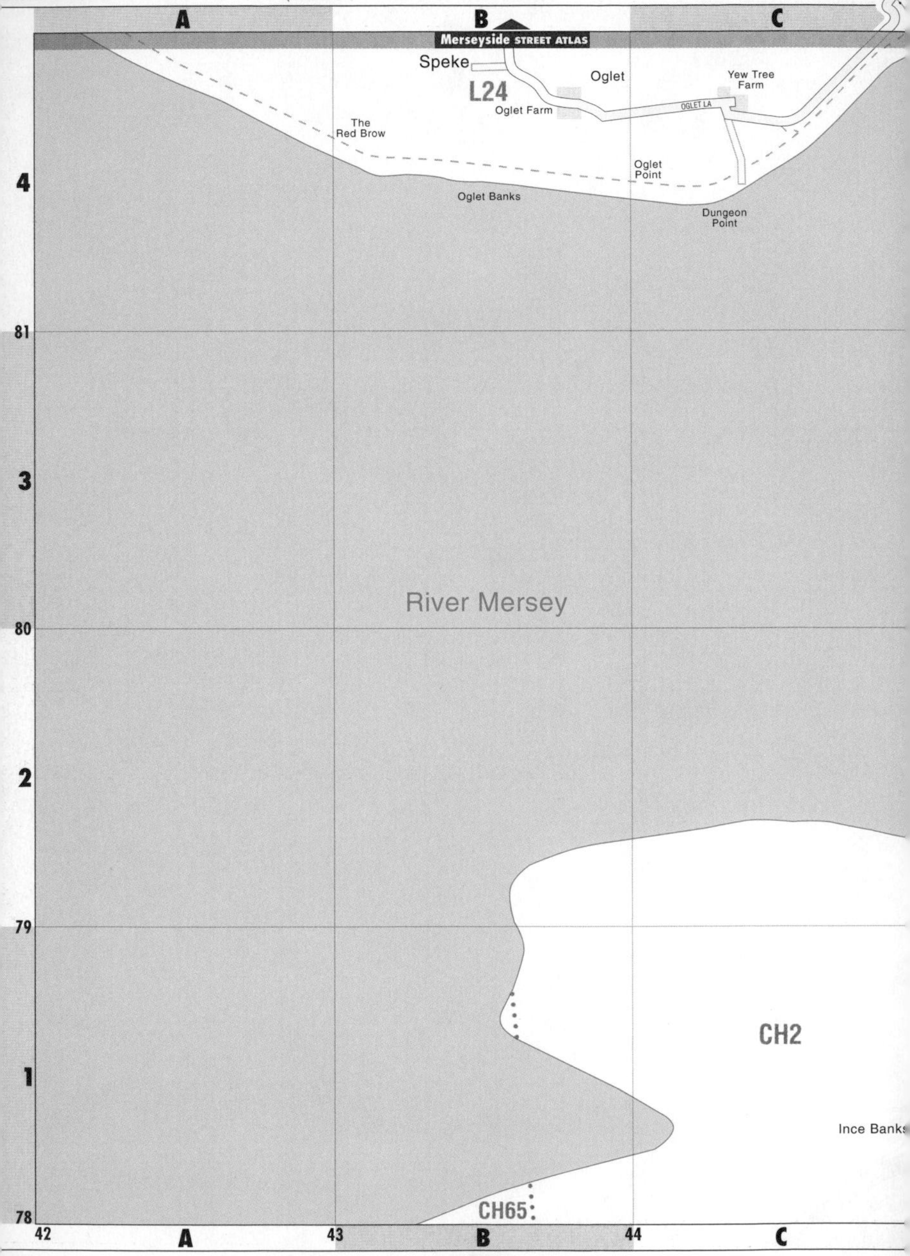
A
B
C
Merseyside STREET ATLAS
Speke
L24
Oglet
Yew Tree Farm
Oglet Farm
OGLET LA
The Red Brow
Oglet Point
Oglet Banks
Dungeon Point
4
81
3
River Mersey
80
2
79
CH2
1
78
CH65
42
43
44

45
71

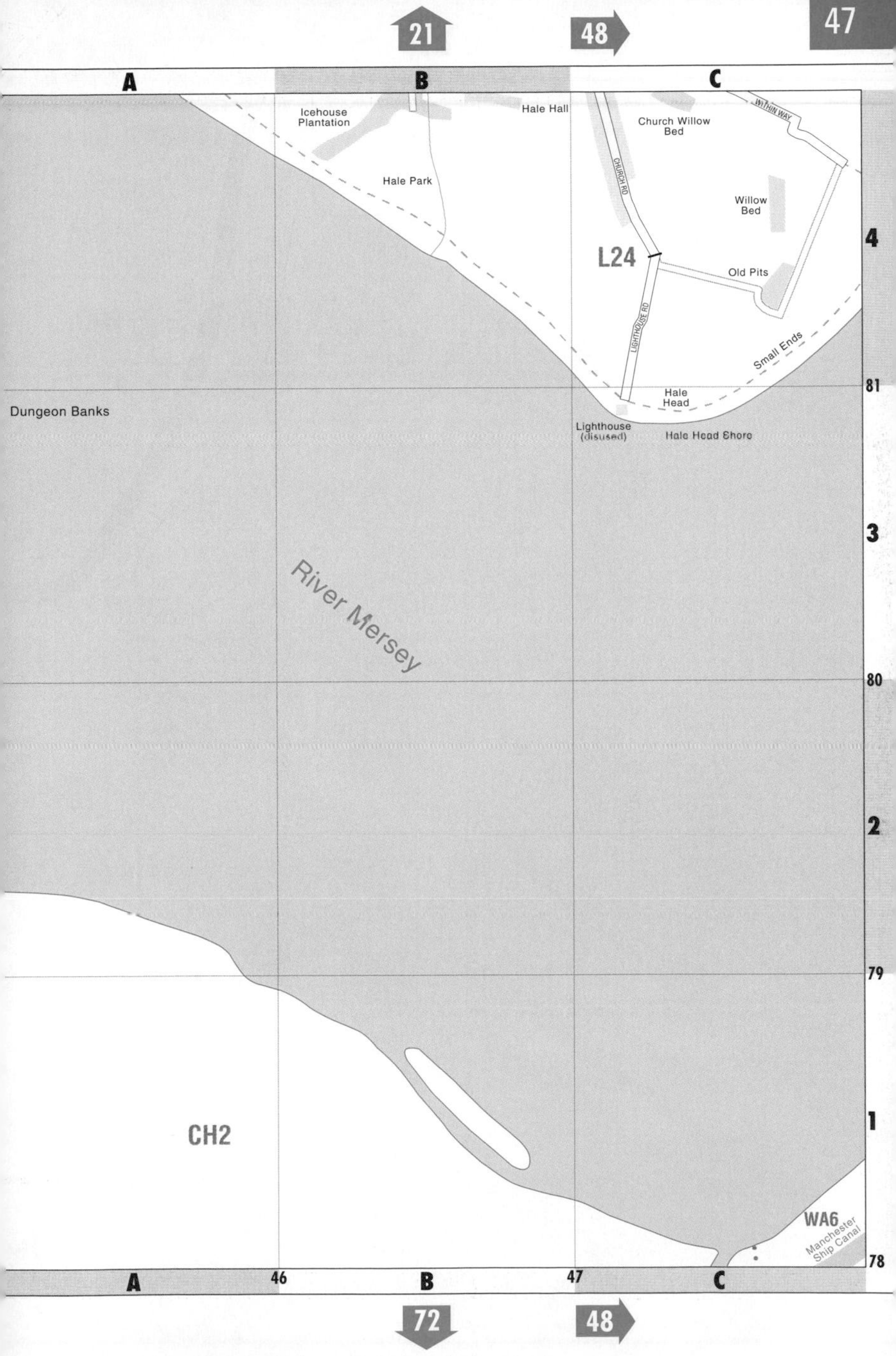
21
48
A
B
C
Icehouse Plantation
Hale Hall
Church Willow Bed
WITHIN WAY
Hale Park
CHURCH RD
Willow Bed
4
L24
Old Pits
LIGHTHOUSE RD
Small Ends
81
Hale Head
Dungeon Banks
Lighthouse (disused)
Hale Head Shore
3
River Mersey
80
2
79
1
CH2
WA6
Manchester Ship Canal
78
A
46
B
47
C
72
48

47
22

A
B
C
4
3
2
1
81
80
79
78
48
49
50
L24
River Mersey
Docks
Works
Runcorn & Western Canal (disused)
CLARKS TERR
MERSEY VIEW
PO
BEACON HILL VIEW
POST OFFICE LA
SOUTH RD
CANAL SIDE
WEST RD
Swing Bridge
Weston Mersey Locks
Manchester Ship Canal
Weston Point
BAKER RD
CULLEN RD
ALTA RD
SOUTH PAR
LEONARD ST
SYDNEY ST
LYDIATE LA
MATHER AVE
LC
SANDY LA
PICOW FARM RD
Recn Gd
ROSCOE CRES
CASTNER AVE
CHESHYRE'S LA
BANKES' LA
Works
Weaver Navigation
Weaver Sluices
A557
WESTON POINT EXPRESSWAY
RUSSELL RD
BEACONSFIELD RD
CUNNINGHAM DR
HALE VIEW
HILLSIDE AVE
CAMERON AVE
HAZEL AVE
PERRIN AVE
LANCASTER AVE
Weston Point Prim Sch
COLLIER'S ROW
WESTON RD
WESTON CT
PROSPECT ROW
MINSTER CT
Beacon Hill
SOUTHLANDS CT
Runcorn Hill (Public Park)
Nature Reserve
HIGHLANDS RD
WA7
COMPANY'S CL 1
MONTPELIER AVE 2
LAMBSICKLE CL 3
Mast
HEATH RD S
Weston
ASHTON CL
CRESTA DR
MARION DR
LAMBSICKLE
TILDSLEY
BANKES' LA
PO
Works
Weston Marsh Lock
River Weaver
ALDER LA
Frodsham Marsh Farm
Frodsham Marsh
Frodsham Score
Manchester Ship Canal
BROOK FURLONG
WA6
Canal Deposit Dump
Jetties
MOORDITCH LA
TADGERS LA
Canal Deposit Dump
MOORDITCH LA

47
73

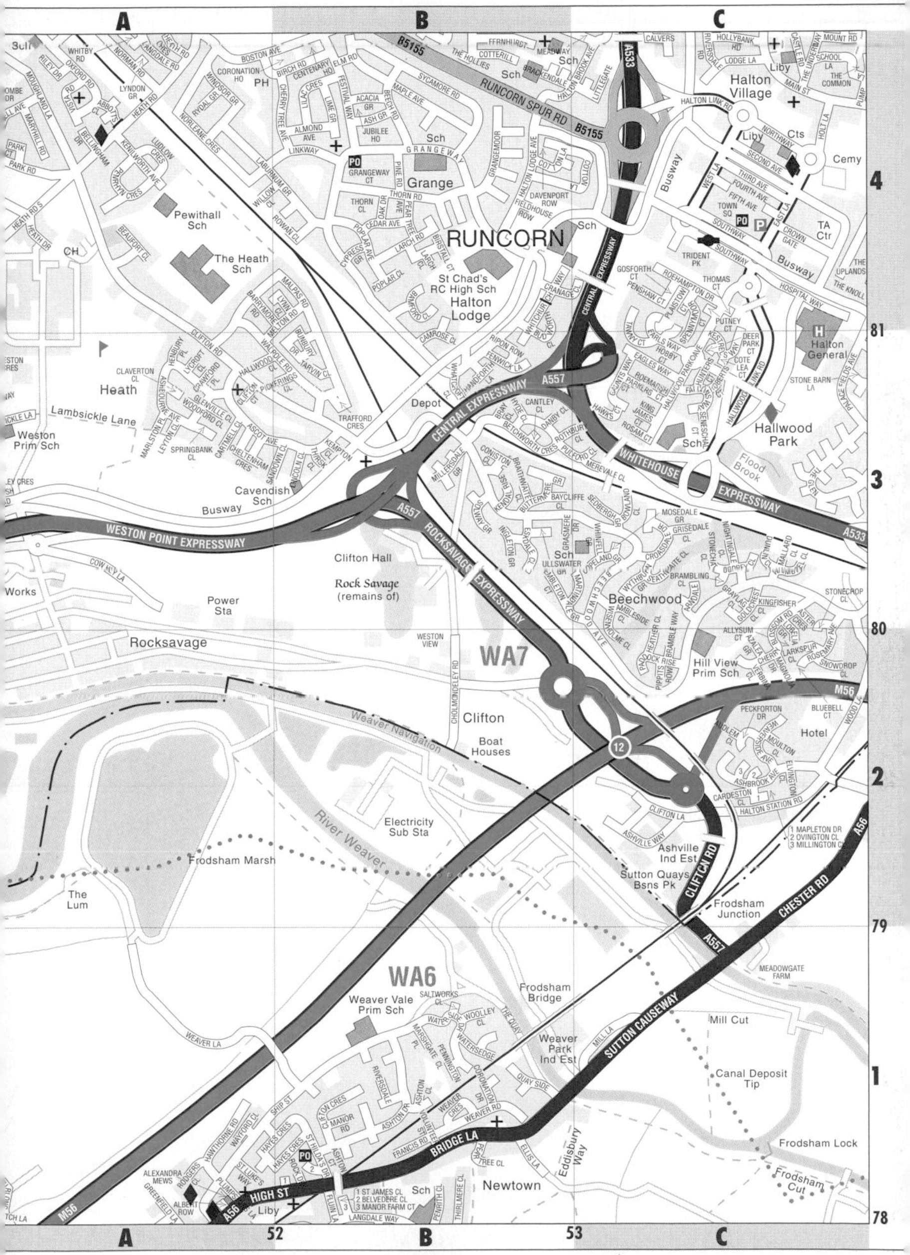
A
B
C
RUNCORN
Grange
Halton Village
Halton Lodge
St Chad's RC High Sch
Heath
Pewithall Sch
The Heath Sch
Weston Prim Sch
Cavendish Sch
Lambsickle Lane
Busway
WESTON POINT EXPRESSWAY
CENTRAL EXPRESSWAY
ROCKSAVAGE EXPRESSWAY
WHITEHOUSE EXPRESSWAY
RUNCORN SPUR RD
B5155
A533
A557
A56
M56
Depot
Clifton Hall
Rock Savage (remains of)
Power Sta
Rocksavage
Works
WESTON VIEW
WA7
Beechwood
Hill View Prim Sch
Hallwood Park
Halton General
Flood Brook
Cemy
TA Ctr
TOWN SQ
TRIDENT PK
HOSPITAL WAY
SOUTHWAY
HALTON LINK RD
Clifton
Boat Houses
Weaver Navigation
River Weaver
Electricity Sub Sta
Frodsham Marsh
The Lum
Ashville Ind Est
Sutton Quays Bsns Pk
CLIFTON RD
Frodsham Junction
CHESTER RD
MEADOWGATE FARM
WA6
Weaver Vale Prim Sch
Frodsham Bridge
Weaver Park Ind Est
SUTTON CAUSEWAY
Mill Cut
Canal Deposit Tip
Frodsham Lock
Frodsham Cut
BRIDGE LA
HIGH ST
Newtown
Eddisbury Way
WEAVER LA
Hotel
1 MAPLETON DR
2 OVINGTON CL
3 MILLINGTON CL
1 ST JAMES CL
2 BELVEDERE CL
3 MANOR FARM CT
81
80
79
78
4
3
2
1
52
53

49
24

A
B
C
4
81
3
80
2
79
1
78
54
55
56
RUNCORN
Town Park
Sch
Norton La
Main St
Primrose Cl
Merlin Cl
Rupert Row
Brereton Cl
Kiln Row
Castlefield Ave S
Village Cl
Camelot Way
Norton View
Stockham Cl
Briarwood
Crabtree Fold
Broadfields
Oxheys
Nortonwood La
Saddlers Rise
Long Spinney
Norton Gate
Abbey Hey
Kings Meadow
Green Coppice
Wr Twr
Stoney Holt
Fox Covert
Great Riding
Cloverfield
Busway
Norton Village
Windmill Hill Ave
Winslow Cl
Hillfield
Holbeck
Hilltop
Tower La
Warren Croft
Runcorn East
Norton Station Rd
Pochard Rise
Delphfield
Borrow's Bridge
1 Sabre Cl
2 Barton Cl
3 Sovereign Cl
4 Talisman Cl
5 Dorrington Cl
6 Ellerby Cl
7 Sawley Cl
8 Bayvil Cl
9 Woodend
10 Moresby Cl
Red Brow La
LC
Bankside
Portside
Marina
Marina Village
Keckwick Brook
Cheshire Ring Canal Walk
Norton Cotts
Dukes Wharf
The Uplands
Rawdon Cl
Worthington Cl
Cunliffe Cl
Charlton Cl
Dorset Ct
Badger Cl
Sparrowhawk Cl
Martin Cl
Palace Fields Ave
Palace Fields Local Centre
Sch
Manor Fell
Silkstone Cres
Stockham La
Greenhouse Farm Rd
Folkstone Way
Murdishaw
Wood Lane
Starling Cl
Robin Cl
Aldergate Ave
Micklegate
Hitchen's Cl
Schs
Southampton Way
Dalwood Cl
Littlebourne
Harbour Cl
Parkgate Way
Barnfield Ave
Woodfalls Farm
Fleetwood Wlk
Waterford Way
Newquay Cl
Tunnel
Camborne Cl
Launceston Cl
Truro Cl
Wood La
Brookvale Comp Sch
Busway
Busway
Palace Fields
Mullion Cl
Liskeard Cl
Saltash Cl
Stratton Cl
Brookvale Ave N
Brookvale Ave S
Bodmin Cl
Newlyn Cl
Tintagel Cl
Penare
Gorran Haven
Broome Ct
Padstow Sq
Sennen Cl
Hanover Ct
Kilncroft
Woodhatch Rd
Oxmoor Cl
Rushfield Cres
Brookvale
Goulders Ct
Backford Cl
Saltwood Dr
Stockham La
Murdishaw Ave
Sports Gd
1 Calverly Cl
2 Linwood Cl
3 Wellbrook Cl
4 Halsall Cl
5 Granby Cl
6 Abington Wlk
Heysham Cl
Hoylake Cl
The Ridgeway
Sch
The Hove
Schooner Cl
Navigation Cl
Mariner Cl
Chichester Cl
Spinnaker Cl
Compass Cl
Rose Cl
Quadrant Cl
Sextant Cl
Blyth Cl
Mooring Cl
Gorsewood Rd
Dover Cl
Plymouth Cl
Falmouth Pl
Portsmouth Pl
Tilbury Pl
Weymouth Cl
Bristol Cl
Exmouth Cres
The Wharf
Coronation Rd
Gorsey Wey
Sandy La
Aston Green
Canal Side Cotts
Preston Brook Bt
Waterfront
Canal Side
Bridgewater Grange
Lockwood View
Watermead Dr
Aston La
Preston Brook
Bridgewater
A533
WHITEHOUSE EXPRESSWAY
Northwich Rd
Portleven Rd
Mevagissey Rd
Fountains Cl
Helston Cl
Riding La
Ainley Cl
Hawkshead Cl
Troutbeck Cl
Kirkstone Cres
Skiddaw Cl
Wood La
Sycamore Dr
Cedar Ave
Beech Rd
Maple Ave
Station Terr
Station Rd
WA7
PH
A56
CHESTER RD
M56
A56
Aston Fields Rd
Aston La S
Aston La N
Whitehouse Ind Est
NORTHWICH RD
Rivington Rd
Fairoak Cl
Sutton Lodge Farm
Halton Station Rd
Sutton Weaver
Sutton Fields Farm
Stretche's Gorse
Aston Heath Farm
CH
Sutton Hall
Sutton
Lowe's Wood
Birdswood Farm
Aston Heath
Four Winds
Aston La
Aston by Sutton Prim Sch
Aston
Beckett's Wood
Chapel Wood
Weaver Navigation
WA6
Aston Lodge
Weaver View Cottages

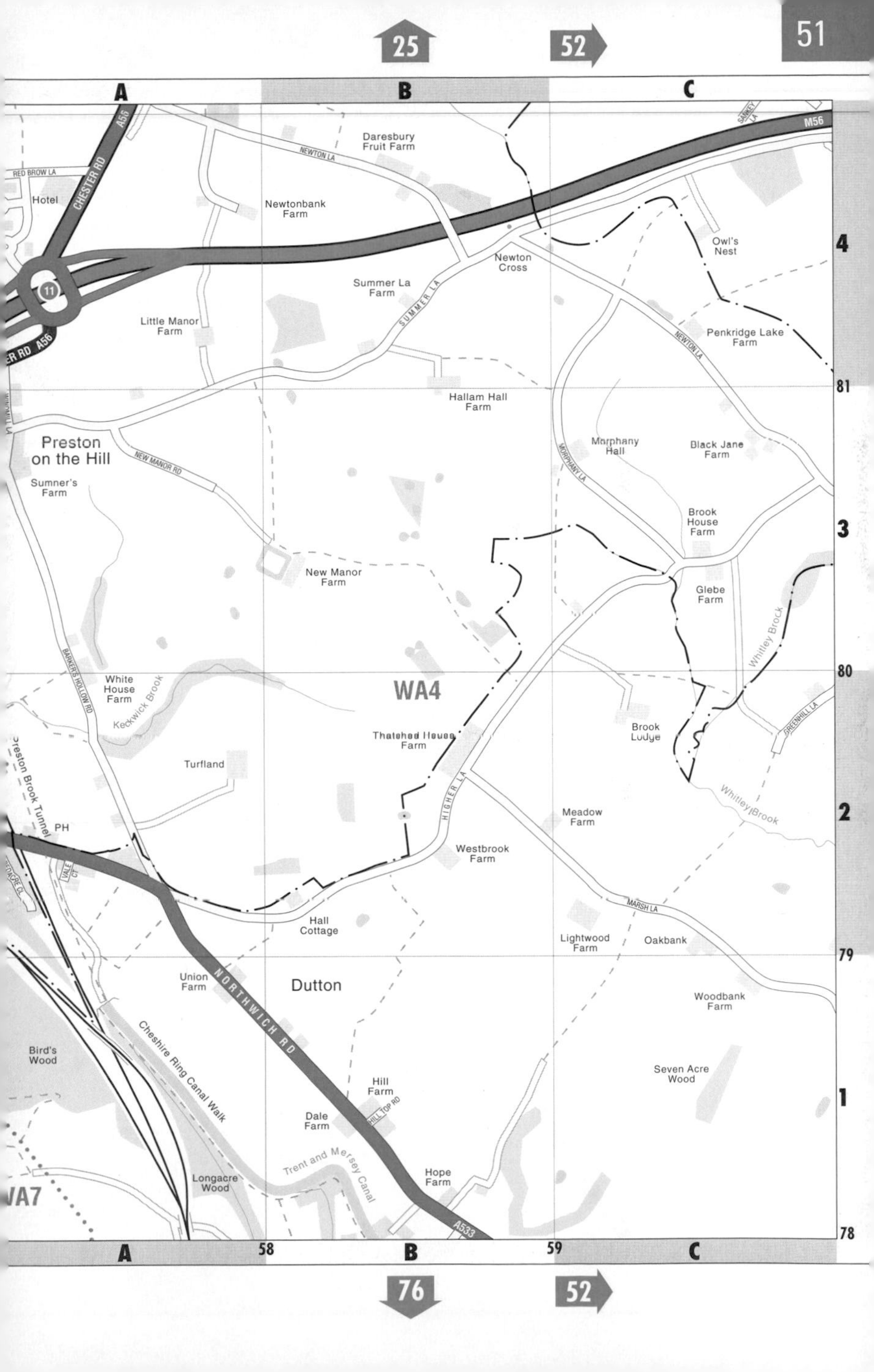
25
52
A
B
C
Daresbury Fruit Farm
NEWTON LA
SANKEY LA
M56
RED BROW LA
CHESTER RD
A56
Hotel
Newtonbank Farm
4
Owl's Nest
Newton Cross
11
Summer La Farm
SUMMER LA
Little Manor Farm
Penkridge Lake Farm
NEWTON LA
ER RD A56
81
Hallam Hall Farm
Preston on the Hill
NEW MANOR RD
Morphany Hall
MORPHANY LA
Black Jane Farm
Sumner's Farm
Brook House Farm
3
New Manor Farm
Glebe Farm
Whitley Brock
BARKER'S HOLLOW RD
80
White House Farm
Keckwick Brook
WA4
GREENHILL LA
Brook Lodge
Thatched House Farm
Preston Brook Tunnel
Turfland
HIGHER LA
Meadow Farm
2
Whitley Brook
PH
Westbrook Farm
VALE CT
MARSH LA
Hall Cottage
Lightwood Farm
Oakbank
79
Union Farm
Dutton
NORTHWICH RD
Woodbank Farm
Cheshire Ring Canal Walk
Bird's Wood
Seven Acre Wood
Hill Farm
1
HILL TOP RD
Dale Farm
Trent and Mersey Canal
Hope Farm
Longacre Wood
WA7
A533
78
A
58
B
59
C
76
52

51
26

A
B
C
M56
SUMMER LA
PH
A49
A559
SUMMIT CL
WELL LA
HALL LA
STRETTON HALL MEWS
COMMON LA
Lower Stretton
Lower Hall
Stretton House
Bradley Brook
PILLMOSS LA
Pillmoss Farm
Queastybirch Hall
4
NORTHWICH RD
Walnut Tree Farm
Pillmoss Farm
STOCKLEY LA
81
Cobbles
LIMES LA
Crowholt Farm
Greenbank
SCHOOL LA
BOOTHS LA
Norcott Brook
3
GRIMSDITCH LA
Whitley Brook
DARK LA
Grimsditch Hall
Higher Whitley
LAKE LA
BENTLEY'S FARM LA
Bentley's Farm
RADDEL LA
GREENHILL LA
THE TOWN GN
WA4
80
Manor Farm
NORMAN'S LA
Green Hill
Whitley Village Sch
Greenhills Farm
Whitley
TARPORLEY RD
Crimwellpool Farm
2
VILLAGE LA
BACK LA
The Grove
OLD MILL LA
Oldmill Farm
Marsh House Farm
Village Farm
STREET LA
Lower Whitley
79
Brookhouse Farm
CHETWODE MEWS
BROOKHOUSE LA
The Vicarage
Little Merryfall
GOOSEBROOK LA
Marsh Lane Farm
1
MARSH LA
Whitley Brook
Newholme Farm
Whitley Hall Cottages
RED LA
Whitley Hall
Big Merryfall
Merryfall Wood
Whitley House Farm
78
60
61
62

51
77

27
54

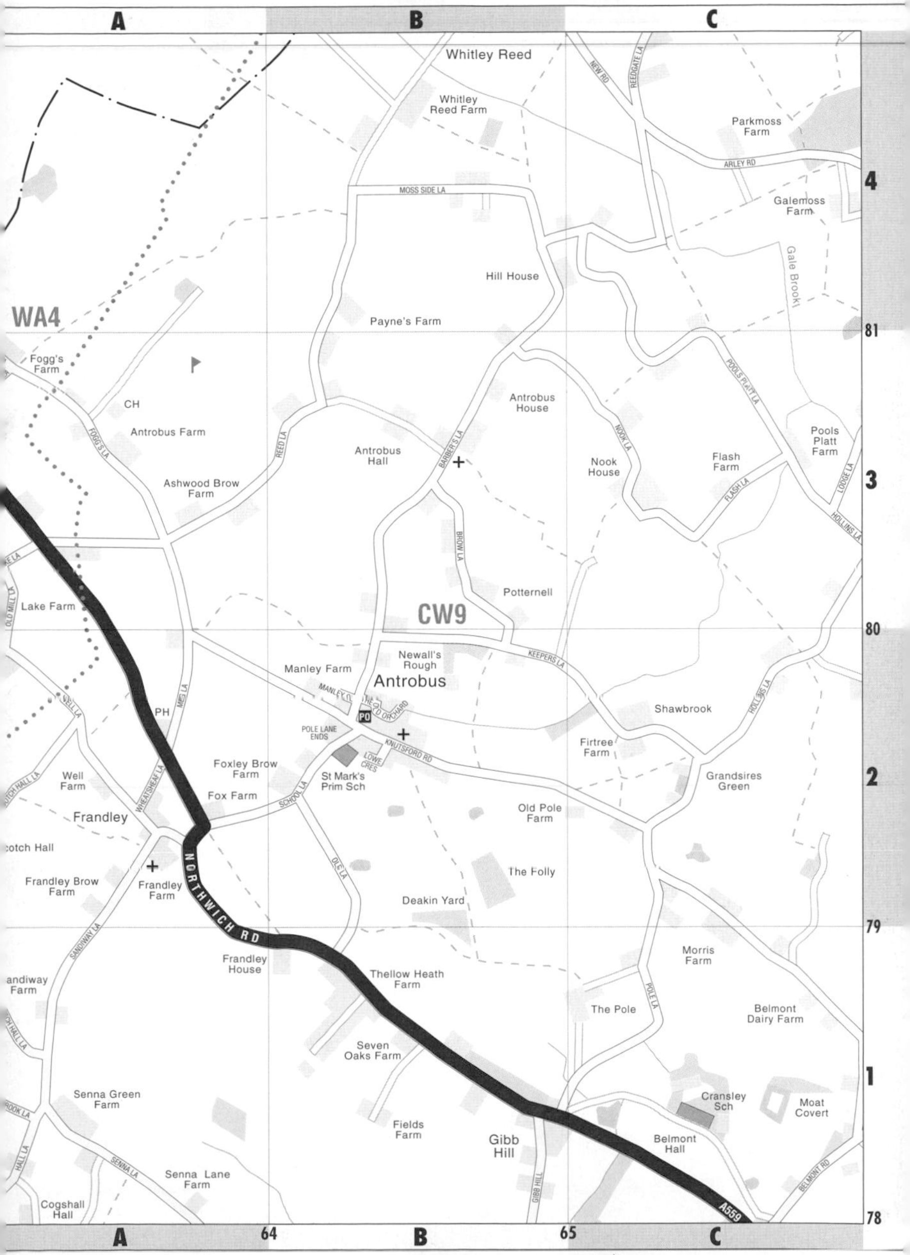
A
B
C
Whitley Reed
Whitley Reed Farm
NEW RD
REEDGATE LA
Parkmoss Farm
ARLEY RD
4
MOSS SIDE LA
Galemoss Farm
Gale Brook
Hill House
WA4
Payne's Farm
81
Fogg's Farm
CH
Antrobus Farm
FOGG'S LA
Antrobus House
POOLS PLATT LA
NOOK LA
Pools Platt Farm
REED LA
Antrobus Hall
BARBER'S LA
Nook House
Flash Farm
FLASH LA
LODGE LA
3
Ashwood Brow Farm
HOLLINS LA
BROW LA
OLD MILL LA
Lake Farm
Potternell
CW9
80
Newall's Rough
Manley Farm
Antrobus
KEEPERS LA
MANLEY LA
FIELD ORCHARD
WELL LA
MILL LA
PH
PO
Shawbrook
HOLLINS LA
POLE LANE ENDS
KNUTSFORD RD
Firtree Farm
LOWE CRES
Foxley Brow Farm
Well Farm
St Mark's Prim Sch
Grandsires Green
2
WHEATSHEAF LA
Fox Farm
SCHOOL LA
Old Pole Farm
Frandley
Scotch Hall
OLE LA
Frandley Brow Farm
Frandley Farm
NORTHWICH RD
The Folly
Deakin Yard
SANDIWAY LA
79
Frandley House
Morris Farm
Sandiway Farm
Thellow Heath Farm
POLE LA
The Pole
Belmont Dairy Farm
Seven Oaks Farm
1
Senna Green Farm
Cransley Sch
Moat Covert
Fields Farm
Gibb Hill
Belmont Hall
BELMONT RD
SENNA LA
Senna Lane Farm
GIBB HILL
Cogshall Hall
A559
78
64
65

78
54

53
28

A
B
C
4
3
2
1
81
80
79
78
66
67
68
M6
WA16
The Firs
Crowley Grange
CALDWELL'S GATE LA
Stockley Farm
Garland Hall
ARLEY RD
BACK LA
Arley
Home Farm
Arley Hall & Gardens
Lady Park
Arley Green
The As
LODGE LA
Crowley Lodge
SACK LA
Hollins Farm
HOLLINS LA
Big Wood
Arley Park
The Belts
CW9
Alderhedge Wood
Reed House Farm
The Kennels
CANN LA
Cann Fa
Arley Brook
New Farm
The Slacks
Willowbed Wood
Willow Lodge
Bate Heath
BUDWORTH RD
COLLIERS LA
ARLEY MOSSEND LA
Arley Moss Farm
Kays F
KNUTSFORD RD
Hilltop Farm
Moss End
Yewtree Farm
George's Lane Farm
Fields Farm
Budworth Heath
BUDWORTH HEATH LA
GEORGE'S LA
Wathall Farm
HEATH LA
Aston Park
Gravestones Farm

53
79

A
B
C
NORTHWOOD LA
Northwood Hall
Mere Heyes
Daisybank Farm
WINTERBOTTOM LA
Whitley Brook Farm
WHITLEY LA
4
uidepost Farm
Winterbottom
Bentleyhurst Farm
81
Litley Farm
CANN LA
3
Hollowood Farm
WA16
Gore Farm
80
Bongs Wood
CW9
Feldy Green
West Feldy
Bongs Rough
Heyrose Farm
Holehouses
OLD HALL LA
Pownall Green Farm
M6
2
CH
East Feldy Farm
HOLLY GR
Arley Brook
Tabley Brook
Tabley
Tableybrook Farm
B5391
Yew Tree Farm
efield rm
Feldy Oak Farm
79
Lower Feldy Green Farm
BUDWORTH RD
PICKMERE LA
Common Farm
Froglane Farm
Church Farm
1
School Farm
FROG LA
Black Clump
Flittogate Farm
The Grange
FLITTOGATE LA
HALL LA
Round Wood
Pickmerehall Farm
B5391
78
A
70
B
71
C

A
B
C
A50
A556
A5034
The Mere
CH
Mere Hall
MERE HOME FARM
WARRINGTON RD
MERESIDE RD
ASHLEY RD
Mere Lodge
Lady Mary's Walk
Rostherne Drive
Tatton Hall
Mereheath Drive
Mere
CLAMHUNGER LA
Knowlespit Farm
A5034
Lodge
The Temple
Melchett Mere
Tatton Park
CHESTER RD
Mere Platt Farm
Moss Plantation
Mereheath Plantation
Moss Cottage
MEREHEATH LA
Hotel
Church Farm
MOSS LA
Over Tabley
Roebuck Farm
Moss Farm
MANCHESTER RD
Garage
WA16
Over Tabley Hall
Bluebell Farm
OLD HALL LA
GREEN LA
Dairy House Farm
Swains Walk
M6
19
Cemy
Playing Fields
HOLLY GR
PH
PICKMERE LA
B5391
FRESHFIELDS
TABLEY CL
QUEENSWAY
SUGAR PIT LA
Tabley Hill Farm
Bank Farm
TABLEY RD
WILLOW GN
MEREHEATH
Tabley Hill
B5083
SPINNEY LA
Burnthouse Farm
TABLEY HILL LA
Tableyvale Farm
The Heath
WARREN AVE
WARREN CL
LADIES MILE
ELIZABETH GASKELL CT 1
WINDSOR WAY 2
ROYCE CT 3
HEATHLANDS HO 4
COUNTY TERR 5
MASTERS CT 6
Tableyvale Cottages
A5033
Yewtree House
CHESTER RD
GASKELL AVE
STANLEY RD
Villa Farm
NORTHWICH RD
LILAC AVE
ACACIA AVE
TABLEY GR
WESTFIELD DR
SANDILEIGH AVE
RACEFIELD RD
CRANFORD
A5033
WESTFIELD DR
Knutsford
L Ctr
SCHOOL CL
CRANFORD AVE
Belt Wood
Sudlow Farm
SUDLOW LA
Knutsford High Sch (Lower Sch)
MELLOR CRES
Knutsford High Sch (Upper Sch)
BEXTON RD
HAYTON ST
LEE CL
Knutsford Service Area
MEADOW DR
MEAD CL
A556
M6
4
81
3
80
2
79
1
78
72
73
74

31
58

A
B
C
4
3
2
1
81
80
79
78
76
77
Parkside Farm
Fourlane -ends
Mobberley Brook
Mobberley
STATION RD
PH
LC
HOBCROFT LA
LEYCESTER RD
SLADE LA
SMITH LA
PEPPER ST
SMALL LA
Tatton Mere Brook
Old Hall
Tatton Park
Hanging Bank
Park Farm
Square Wood
BROADOAK LA
BEECH AVE
Boathouse Plantation
Witchcote Wood
Broad Oak Farm
Smithlane Farm
Knutsford Drive
Shawheath Plantation
Birkin Brook
Tatton Mere
WA16
Sewage Works
Parkgate Farm
Tatton Mere Covert
Parkgate Trad Est
SUMMERFIELD RD
RAJAR COTTS
TOWN LA
B5085
MAYFIELD RD
RYECROFT LA
SPRINGFIELD RD
BERNISDALE RD
Oak Tree Farm
KNUTSFORD RD
MONTGOMERY CL
THE GROVE
WELLINGTON CL
MARLBOROUGH CL
HAIG CL
HAIG RD
PARKGATE LA
WOLFE CL
MARDON CL
BIRKIN CL
MILL KEEPERS CL
SPRINGWOOD AVE
MERRIMAN AVE
Dukenfield Hall
PAVEMENT LA
MEADOWSWEET RD
Dog Wood
MONTMORENCY RD
1 CHALFONT CT
2 SPRINGFIELDS
3 SUMMERFIELDS
4 SHAW HEATH VIEW
Longridge Trad Est
Pavement Lane Farm
KNUTSFORD
BRAIDWOOD AVE
PARKGATE
OAKFIELD AVE
LEIGH AVE
KESTREL AVE
HERON CL
LODGE RD
GREBE CL
MERLIN AVE
TEAL AVE
MALLARD CL
MOBBERLEY RD
NORBURY CL
NORTH FIELDS
SOUTHFIELDS
OVERFIELDS
Shaw Heath
LONGRIDGE
SHAW DR
HAYFIELDS
RUSKIN WAY
BRIAR CL
COPPICE GR
HILLSIDE RD
DRURY LA
RUSKIN CT
MOORSIDE
LOWE DR
CHURCHFIELDS
HELENA CL
ST JOHN'S CT
AUTUMN AVE
St John's Wood Com Sch
FORESTER AVE
MANOR CRES
Cross Town
TOWNFIELDS
BOOTHFIELDS
MANOR PARK N
KENILWORTH
Manor Park Sch
BROOKDALE AVE
MALT ST
MOORDALE RD
MIDDLE WLK
KING ST
WOODLANDS DR
MANSION DR
BEECH DR
ELLA GR
LICHFIELD CL
HIGHER DOWNS
BEECHWOOD
SANDIWAY
THORNEYHOLME DR
WOODSIDE
Sch
CHURCH MEWS
BRAMDEN DR
THE SHAMBLES
SHARSTON CRES
MANOR CT
MANOR PARK S
LINDOP CL
NORTH DOWNS
BIRCH GR
ASH GR
OAK VIEW
FOX GR
MOULTON CL
DOWNS END
DELMAR RD
LYNTON CL
ROCKFORD LODGE
LEWLANDS
Booths Mere
Springwood Farm
B5083
CHURCH HILL
MARCLIFFE GR
Civic Hall
Liby
TOFT RD
A537
BROOK ST
ADAMS HILL
HOLLOW LA
B5085
HOLFORD CRES
Knutsford
BROOK LA
GROVE PK
PARKHILL CT
PO
AYLESBY CL
SPARROW LA
Over Knutsford
Spring Wood
CHELFORD RD
TREVONE CL
A50
WOODVALE RD
LEGH RD
LEGH GDNS
BALMORAL CL
BUCKINGHAM DR
HALLSIDE PK
SOUTH DOWNS
FIR TREE AVE
CARRWOOD
WARWICK CL
Booths Hall

A1
1 TRINITY CT
2 TATTON CT
3 ROSCOES YD
4 MARBLE ARCH
5 MERE CT
6 EGERTON SQ
7 OLD MARKET PL
8 THE OLD COURT HO
9 ARGYLE CT
10 RED COW YD
11 GRANGE CT
12 WHITE BEAR YD
13 CHURCH VIEW
14 TATTON LODGE
15 SWINTON SQ
16 CORONATION SQ
17 RICHMOND HILL
18 WOODLANDS CT

82
58

57
32

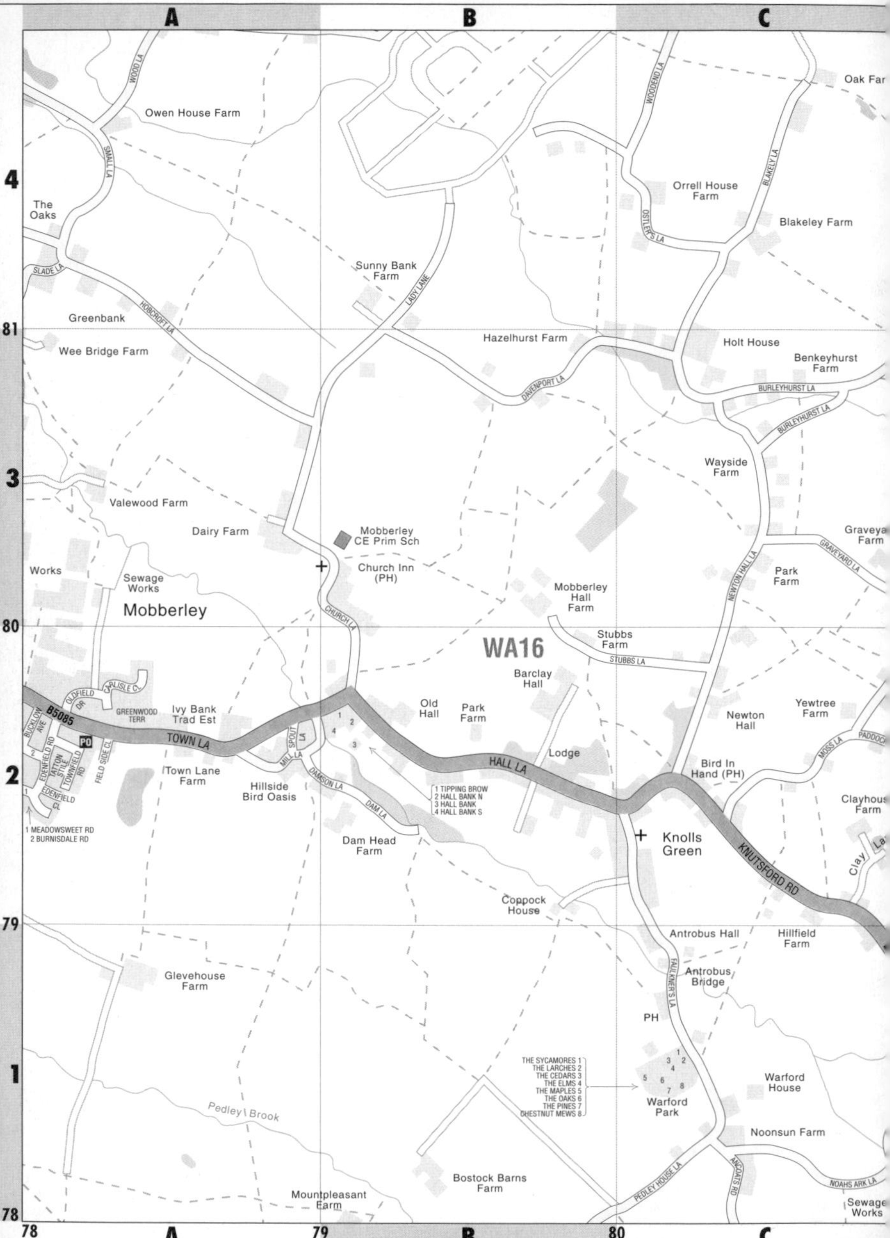
A
B
C
4
3
2
1
81
80
79
78
78
79
80
Oak Far
Owen House Farm
WOOD LA
SMALL LA
The Oaks
SLADE LA
HOBCROFT LA
Greenbank
Wee Bridge Farm
Orrell House Farm
WOODEND LA
BLAKELY LA
Blakeley Farm
OSTLERS LA
Sunny Bank Farm
LADY LANE
Hazelhurst Farm
DAVENPORT LA
Holt House
Benkeyhurst Farm
BURLEYHURST LA
Wayside Farm
Valewood Farm
Dairy Farm
Mobberley CE Prim Sch
Church Inn (PH)
Graveyard Farm
GRAVEYARD LA
Park Farm
NEWTON HALL LA
Works
Sewage Works
Mobberley
Mobberley Hall Farm
CHURCH LA
WA16
Stubbs Farm
STUBBS LA
Barclay Hall
OLDFIELD DR
CARLISLE CL
GREENWOOD TERR
Ivy Bank Trad Est
Old Hall
Park Farm
Yewtree Farm
Newton Hall
B5085
BUCKLOW AVE
PO
TOWN LA
SPOUT LA
MILL LA
Lodge
HALL LA
MOSS LA
PADDOCK
Bird In Hand (PH)
EDENFIELD RD
TATTON STILE
TOWNFIELD RD
FIELD SIDE CL
Town Lane Farm
Hillside Bird Oasis
DAMSON LA
DAM LA
1 TIPPING BROW
2 HALL BANK N
3 HALL BANK
4 HALL BANK S
Clayhouse Farm
EDENFIELD CL
1 MEADOWSWEET RD
2 BURNISDALE RD
Dam Head Farm
Knolls Green
KNUTSFORD RD
Clay La
Coppock House
Antrobus Hall
Hillfield Farm
Glevehouse Farm
Antrobus Bridge
FAULKNER'S LA
PH
THE SYCAMORES 1
THE LARCHES 2
THE CEDARS 3
THE ELMS 4
THE MAPLES 5
THE OAKS 6
THE PINES 7
CHESTNUT MEWS 8
Warford House
Warford Park
Pedley Brook
Noonsun Farm
Bostock Barns Farm
PEDLEY HOUSE LA
ANCOATS RD
NOAHS ARK LA
Mountpleasant Farm
Sewage Works

57
83

33
60

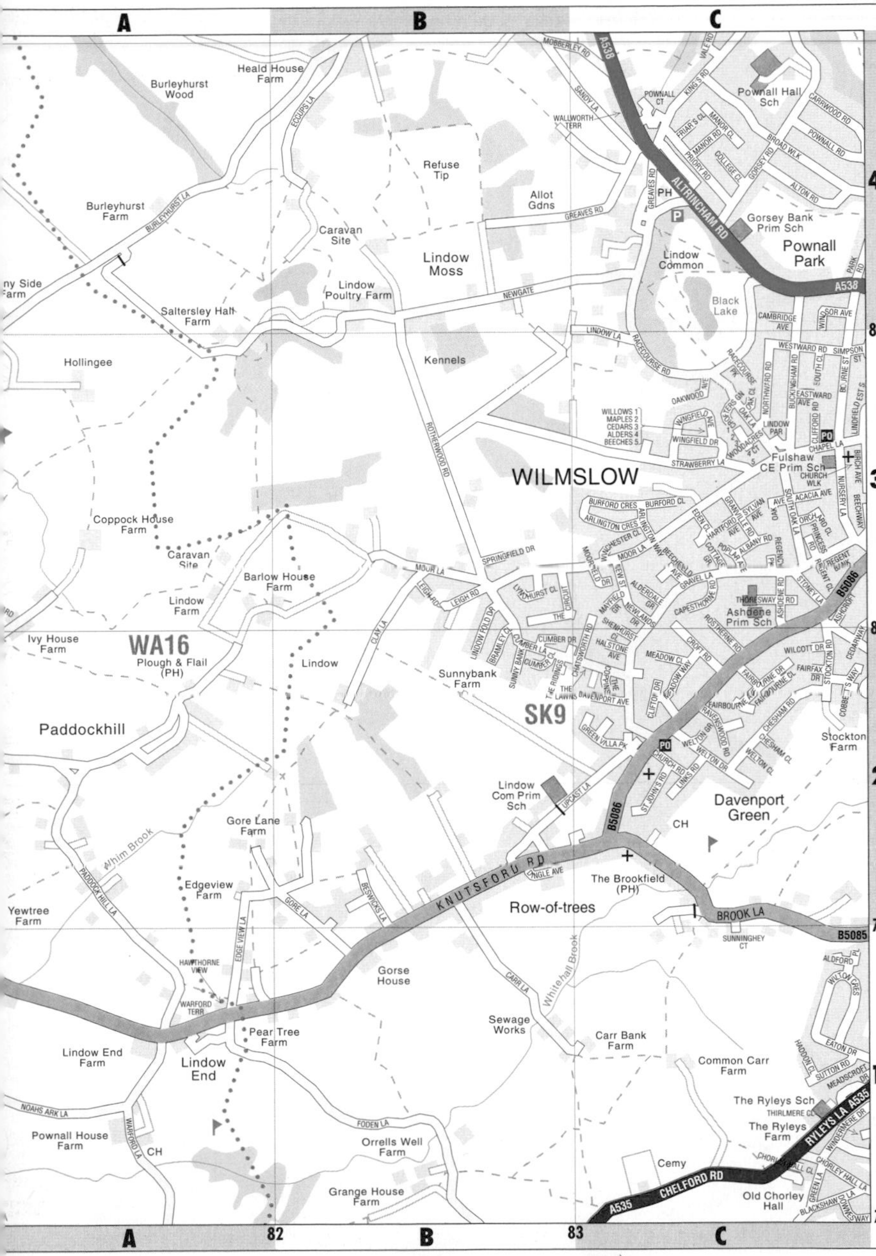
A
B
C
Heald House Farm
Burleyhurst Wood
Burleyhurst Farm
BURLEYHURST LA
ECCLIPS LA
Refuse Tip
Allot Gdns
GREAVES RD
Caravan Site
Lindow Moss
Lindow Poultry Farm
NEWGATE
Saltersley Hall Farm
Hollingee
Kennels
MOBBERLEY RD
SANDY LA
WALLWORTH TERR
POWNALL CT
A538
ALTRINCHAM RD
Pownall Hall Sch
KING'S RD
VALE RD
FRIAR'S CL
MANOR CL
MANOR RD
PRIORY RD
COLLEGE CL
GORSEY RD
BROAD WLK
CARRWOOD RD
POWNALL RD
ALTON RD
PH
Gorsey Bank Prim Sch
Pownall Park
PARK RD
Lindow Common
Black Lake
CAMBRIDGE AVE
WINDSOR AVE
LINDOW LA
RACECOURSE RD
WESTWARD RD
SIMPSON ST
OAKWOOD AVE
NORTHWARD RD
BUCKINGHAM RD
SOUTH CL
EASTWARD AVE
CLIFFORD RD
LINDFIELD EST S
WILLOWS 1
MAPLES 2
CEDARS 3
ALDERS 4
BEECHES 5
WINGFIELD AVE
WINGFIELD DR
LINDOW PAR
CHAPEL LA
PO
STRAWBERRY LA
Fulshaw CE Prim Sch
CHURCH WLK
BIRCH AVE
NURSERY LA
BEECHWAY
ACACIA AVE
SOUTH OAK LA
ROTHERWOOD RD
WILMSLOW
BURFORD CRES
BURFORD CL
ARLINGTON CRES
ARLINGTON WAY
WINCHESTER CL
MOOR LA
SPRINGFIELD DR
GRANVILLE RD
SYLVAN AVE
HARTFORD AVE
ALBANY RD
POPLAR AVE
REGENT PK
REGENT BANK
Coppock House Farm
Caravan Site
Barlow House Farm
Lindow Farm
LEIGH RD
CLAY LA
LYNDHURST CL
THE CIRCUIT
NEW ST
ALDERDALE GR
GRAVEL LA
CAPESTHORNE RD
THORESWAY RD
Ashdene Prim Sch
STONEY LA
ASHCROFT
B5086
Ivy House Farm
WA16
Plough & Flail (PH)
Lindow
LINDOW FOLD DR
BRAMLEY CL
CUMBER LA
CUMBER DR
CHATSWORTH RD
SHENHURST CL
HALSTONE AVE
MEADOW CL
CROFT RD
ROSTHERNE RD
WILCOTT DR
STOCKTON RD
CEDARWAY
FAIRFAX DR
Sunnybank Farm
SUNNY BANK
THE RIDINGS
THE LAWNS
DAVENPORT AVE
CLIFTON DR
MEADOW WAY
FAIRBOURNE DR
RAVENSWOOD RD
CHESHAM RD
COBBETT'S WAY
Paddockhill
SK9
GREEN VILLA PK
PO
WELTON GR
WELTON DR
WELTON CL
Stockton Farm
Lindow Com Prim Sch
UPCAST LA
CHURCH RD
ST JOHN'S RD
LINKS RD
Davenport Green
CH
Gore Lane Farm
Whim Brook
PADDOCK HILL LA
Edgeview Farm
GORE LA
BESWICKS LA
KNUTSFORD RD
INGLE AVE
The Brookfield (PH)
Row-of-trees
BROOK LA
B5085
SUNNINGHEY CT
Yewtree Farm
EDGE VIEW LA
HAWTHORNE VIEW
WARFORD TERR
Gorse House
CARR LA
Whitehall Brook
ALDFORD PL
WILTON CRES
Sewage Works
Carr Bank Farm
EATON DR
HADDON CL
SUTTON RD
MEADSCROFT DR
Lindow End Farm
Pear Tree Farm
Lindow End
Common Carr Farm
The Ryleys Sch
THIRLMERE CL
RYLEYS LA A535
NOAHS ARK LA
WARFORD LA
Pownall House Farm
CH
FODEN LA
Orrells Well Farm
The Ryleys Farm
WINDERMERE DR
Cemy
CHORLEY HALL CL
CHORLEY HALL LA
Grange House Farm
A535
CHELFORD RD
Old Chorley Hall
GREEN LA
BLACKSHAW LA
DOWNESWAY
4
81
3
80
2
79
1
78
82
83

84
60

59
34

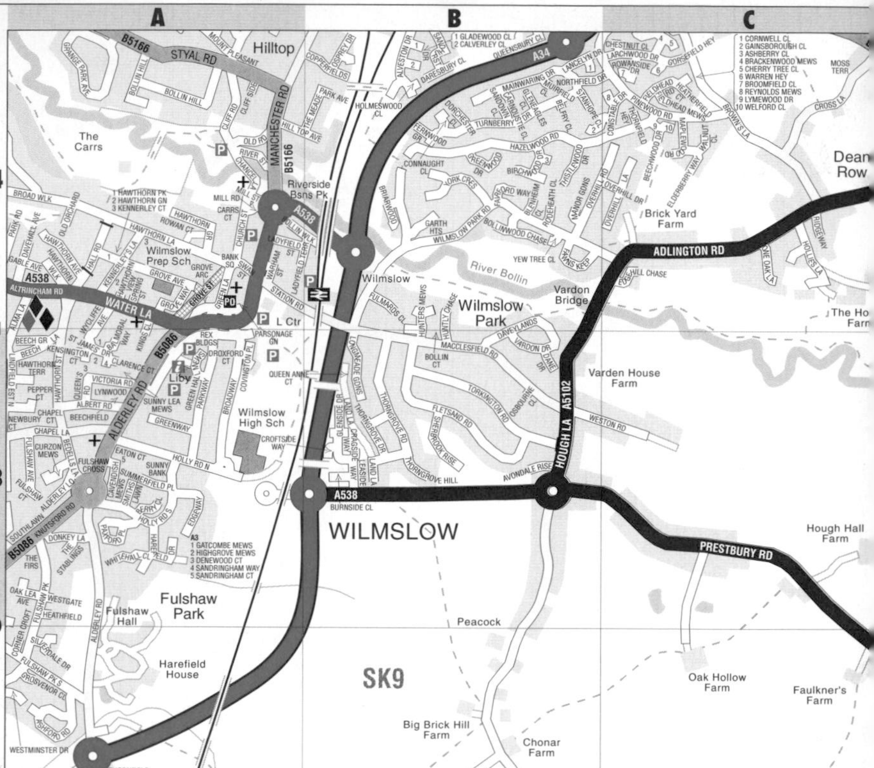

A1
1 THE PARADE
2 BROWN ST
3 GREEN ST
4 MASSEY ST
5 CHAPEL ST
6 ARDERNE PL
7 SOUTH GR
8 HUBERT WORTHINGTON HO
9 CARLISLE ST

59
85

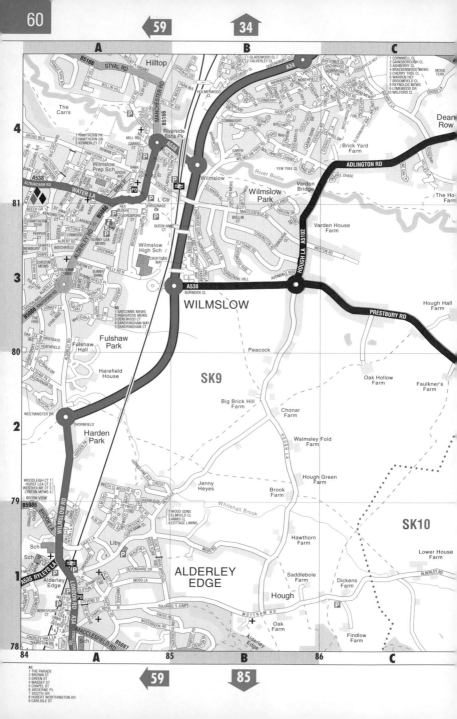

35
62

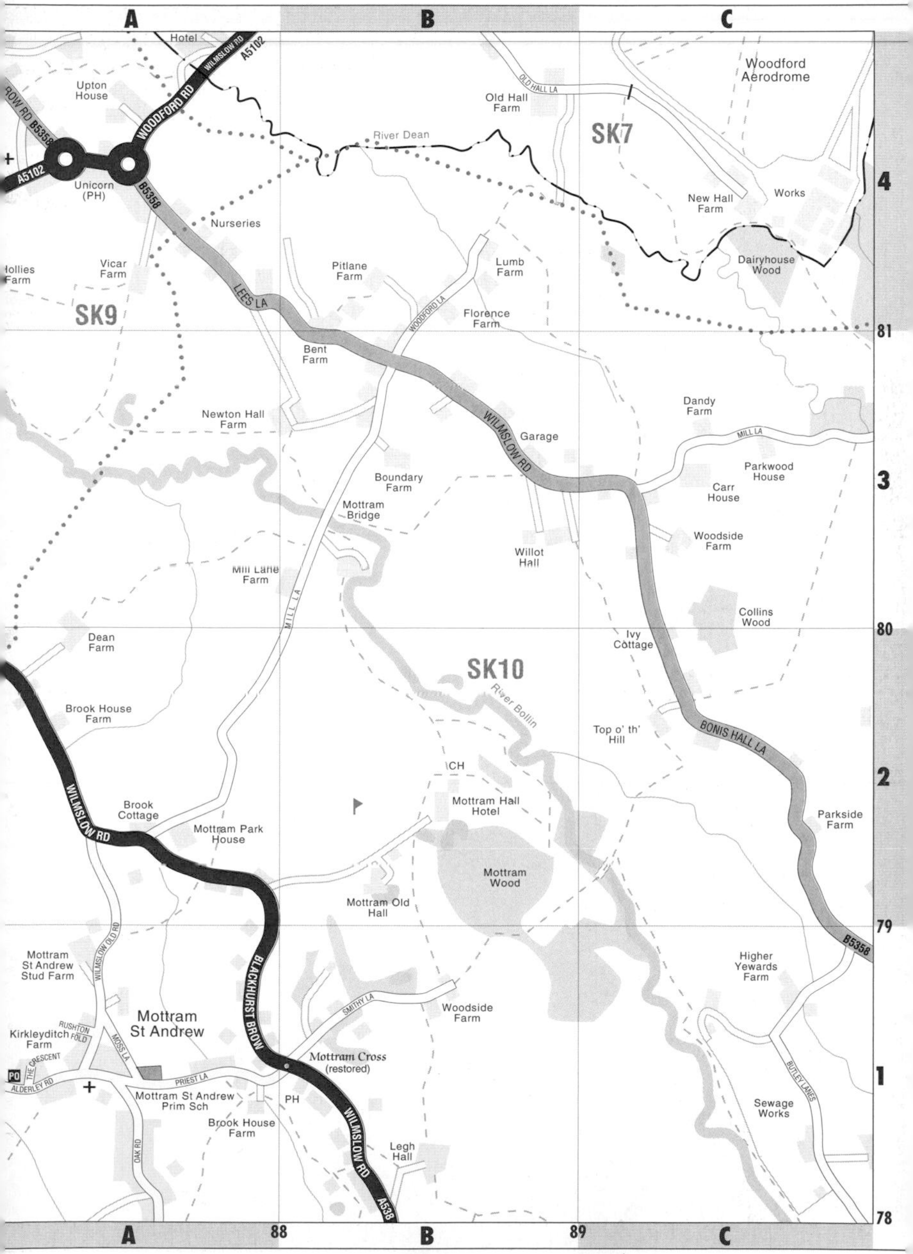
A
B
C
Hotel
WILMSLOW RD
A5102
Upton House
WOODFORD RD
B5358
A5102
Unicorn (PH)
B5358
Nurseries
Vicar Farm
Hollies Farm
SK9
Old Hall Farm
OLD HALL LA
River Dean
SK7
Woodford Aerodrome
New Hall Farm
Works
Dairyhouse Wood
Pitlane Farm
Lumb Farm
WOODFORD LA
Florence Farm
LEES LA
Bent Farm
Newton Hall Farm
WILMSLOW RD
Garage
Dandy Farm
MILL LA
Parkwood House
Carr House
Boundary Farm
Mottram Bridge
Woodside Farm
Willot Hall
Mill Lane Farm
MILL LA
Collins Wood
Dean Farm
Ivy Cottage
SK10
River Bollin
Brook House Farm
Top o' th' Hill
BONIS HALL LA
CH
Mottram Hall Hotel
Parkside Farm
Brook Cottage
WILMSLOW RD
Mottram Park House
Mottram Wood
Mottram Old Hall
B5358
Mottram St Andrew Stud Farm
WILMSLOW OLD RD
Higher Yewards Farm
BLACKHURST BROW
SMITHY LA
Woodside Farm
Mottram St Andrew
RUSHTON FOLD
Kirkleyditch Farm
MOSS LA
THE CRESCENT
PO
ALDERLEY RD
PRIEST LA
Mottram Cross (restored)
BUTLEY LANES
Mottram St Andrew Prim Sch
PH
Sewage Works
Brook House Farm
OAK RD
Legh Hall
WILMSLOW RD
A538
4
81
3
80
2
79
1
78
88
89

86
62

61
36

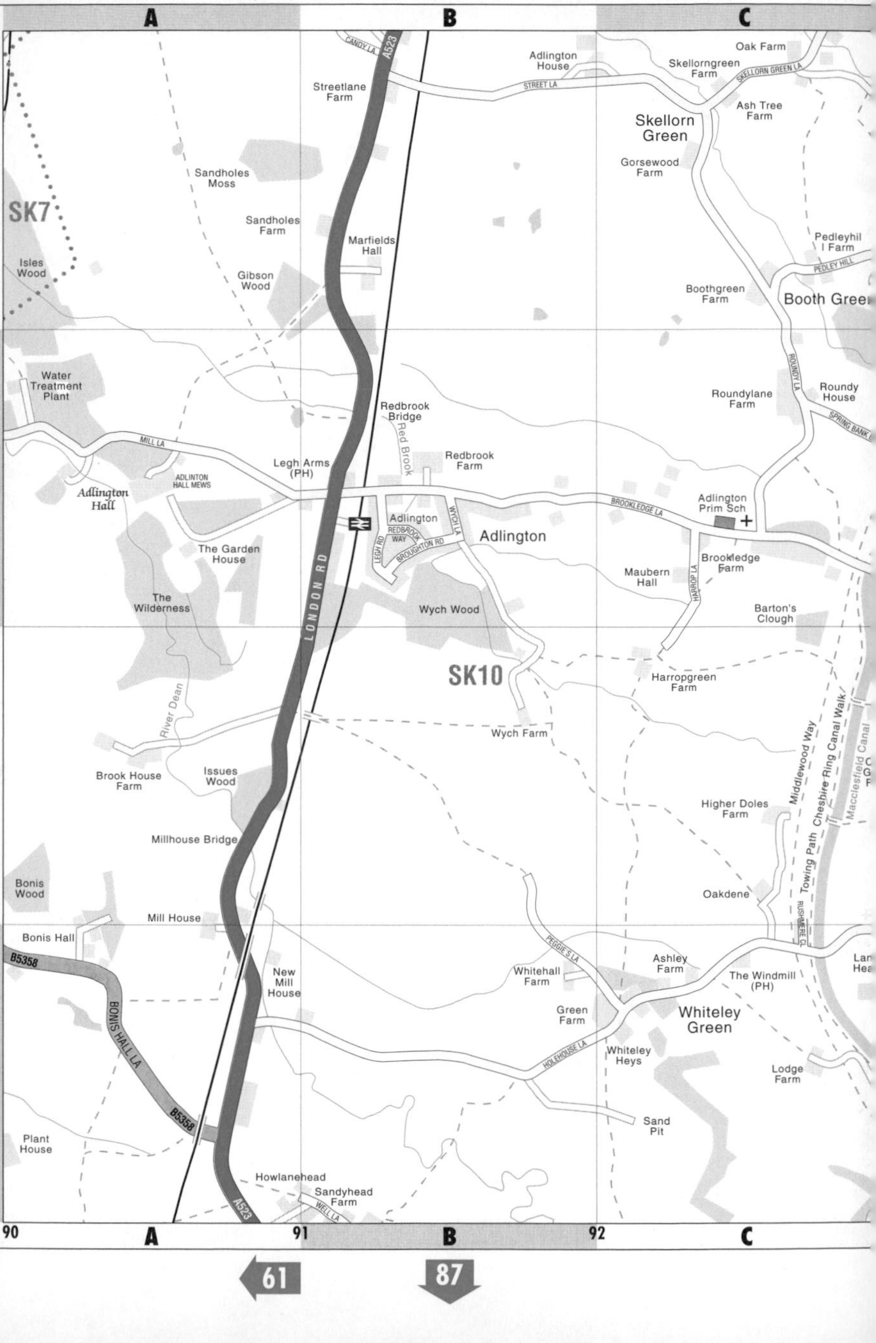
A
B
C
CANDY LA
A523
Adlington House
Oak Farm
Skellorngreen Farm
SKELLORN GREEN LA
STREET LA
Streetlane Farm
Skellorn Green
Ash Tree Farm
Gorsewood Farm
Sandholes Moss
4
SK7
Sandholes Farm
Marfields Hall
Pedleyhil l Farm
PEDLEY HILL
Isles Wood
Gibson Wood
Boothgreen Farm
Booth Gree
81
Water Treatment Plant
Redbrook Bridge
Red Brook
Roundylane Farm
ROUNDY LA
Roundy House
SPRING BANK
MILL LA
Redbrook Farm
Legh Arms (PH)
3
ADLINTON HALL MEWS
Adlington Hall
Adlington
WYCH LA
BROOKLEDGE LA
Adlington Prim Sch
REDBROOK WAY
LEGH RD
BROUGHTON RD
Adlington
The Garden House
Brookledge Farm
Maubern Hall
HARROP LA
LONDON RD
The Wilderness
Wych Wood
Barton's Clough
80
SK10
Harropgreen Farm
River Dean
Wych Farm
Middlewood Way
Cheshire Ring Canal Walk
Towing Path
Macclesfield Canal
2
Brook House Farm
Issues Wood
Higher Doles Farm
Millhouse Bridge
Bonis Wood
Oakdene
79
Mill House
Bonis Hall
RUSHMERE CL
B5358
PEGGIE'S LA
Ashley Farm
The Windmill (PH)
New Mill House
Whitehall Farm
BONIS HALL LA
Green Farm
Whiteley Green
1
Whiteley Heys
HOLEHOUSE LA
Lodge Farm
B5358
Sand Pit
Plant House
Howlanehead
Sandyhead Farm
WELL LA
A523
78
90
A
91
B
92
C

61
87

37
64

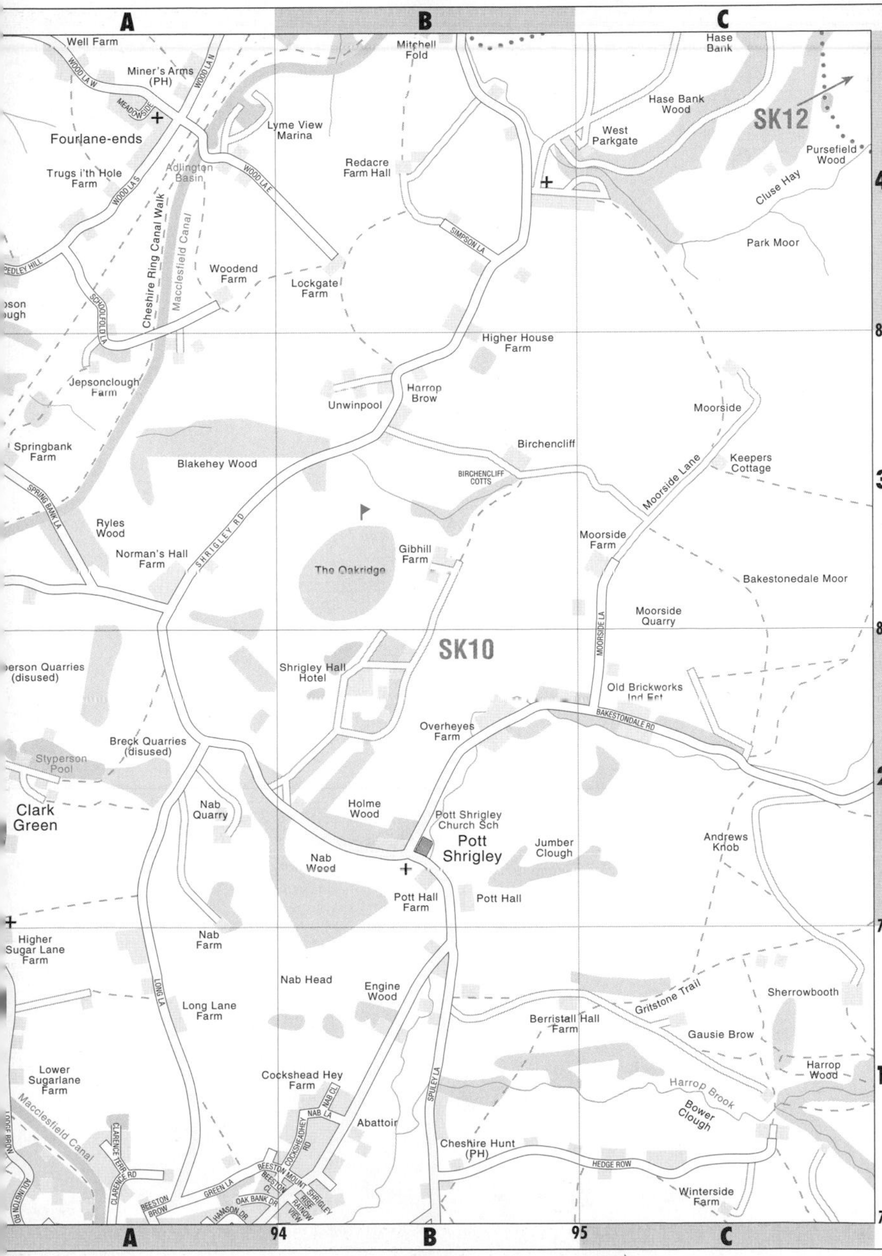
A
B
C
Well Farm
Miner's Arms (PH)
Fourlane-ends
Trugs i'th Hole Farm
Adlington Basin
Lyme View Marina
Mitchell Fold
Redacre Farm Hall
Hase Bank
Hase Bank Wood
West Parkgate
SK12
Pursefield Wood
Cluse Hay
Park Moor
Cheshire Ring Canal Walk
Macclesfield Canal
Woodend Farm
Lockgate Farm
Higher House Farm
Jepsonclough Farm
Harrop Brow
Unwinpool
Moorside
Springbank Farm
Blakehey Wood
Birchencliff
BIRCHENCLIFF COTTS
Keepers Cottage
Moorside Lane
Ryles Wood
Norman's Hall Farm
The Oakridge
Gibhill Farm
Moorside Farm
Bakestonedale Moor
Moorside Quarry
SK10
Shrigley Hall Hotel
Old Brickworks Ind Est
BAKESTONDALE RD
Overheyes Farm
Breck Quarries (disused)
Styperson Pool
Clark Green
Nab Quarry
Holme Wood
Pott Shrigley Church Sch
Pott Shrigley
Jumber Clough
Andrews Knob
Nab Wood
Pott Hall Farm
Pott Hall
Higher Sugar Lane Farm
Nab Farm
Nab Head
Engine Wood
Sherrowbooth
Long Lane Farm
Gritstone Trail
Berristall Hall Farm
Gausie Brow
Lower Sugarlane Farm
Cockshead Hey Farm
Harrop Wood
Harrop Brook
Bower Clough
Abattoir
Cheshire Hunt (PH)
HEDGE ROW
Winterside Farm
WOOD LA W
WOOD LA N
WOOD LA S
WOOD LA E
MEADOWSIDE
SIMPSON LA
PEDLEY HILL
SCHOOLFOLD LA
SPRING BANK LA
SHRIGLEY RD
MOORSIDE LA
LONG LA
SPULEY LA
GREEN LA
BEESTON BROW
CLARENCE TERR
CLARENCE RD
ADLINGTON RD
NAB CL
NAB LA
COCKSHEADHEY RD
BEESTON MOUNT
BEESTON CL
OAK BANK DR
HAMSON DR
SHRIGLEY RISE
RAINOW VIEW
81
80
79
78
1
2
3
4
94
95

88
64

63
38

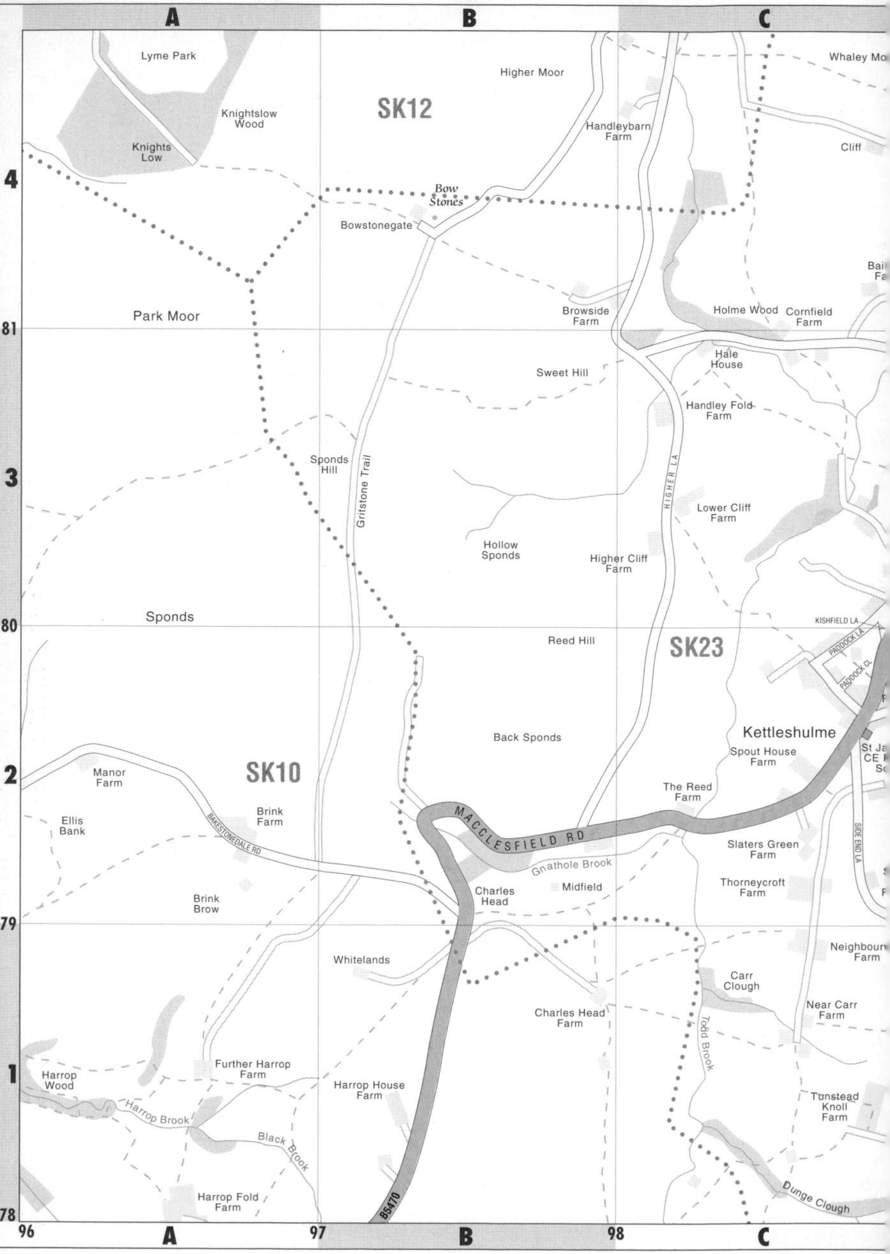
A
B
C
Lyme Park
Knightslow Wood
Knights Low
Higher Moor
SK12
Handleybarn Farm
Whaley Mo
Cliff
Bow Stones
Bowstonegate
Park Moor
Browside Farm
Holme Wood
Cornfield Farm
Sweet Hill
Hale House
Handley Fold Farm
Sponds Hill
Gritstone Trail
HIGHER LA
Lower Cliff Farm
Hollow Sponds
Higher Cliff Farm
Sponds
Reed Hill
SK23
KISHFIELD LA
PADDOCK LA
PADDOCK CL
Back Sponds
Kettleshulme
Spout House Farm
SK10
Manor Farm
The Reed Farm
MACCLESFIELD RD
Ellis Bank
Brink Farm
BAKESTONEDALE RD
Slaters Green Farm
SIDE END LA
Gnathole Brook
Charles Head
Midfield
Thorneycroft Farm
Brink Brow
Whitelands
Carr Clough
Neighbour Farm
Charles Head Farm
Near Carr Farm
Todd Brook
Further Harrop Farm
Harrop Wood
Harrop House Farm
Tunstead Knoll Farm
Harrop Brook
Black Brook
Harrop Fold Farm
Dunge Clough
B5470
4
81
3
80
2
79
1
78
96
97
98

63
89

39

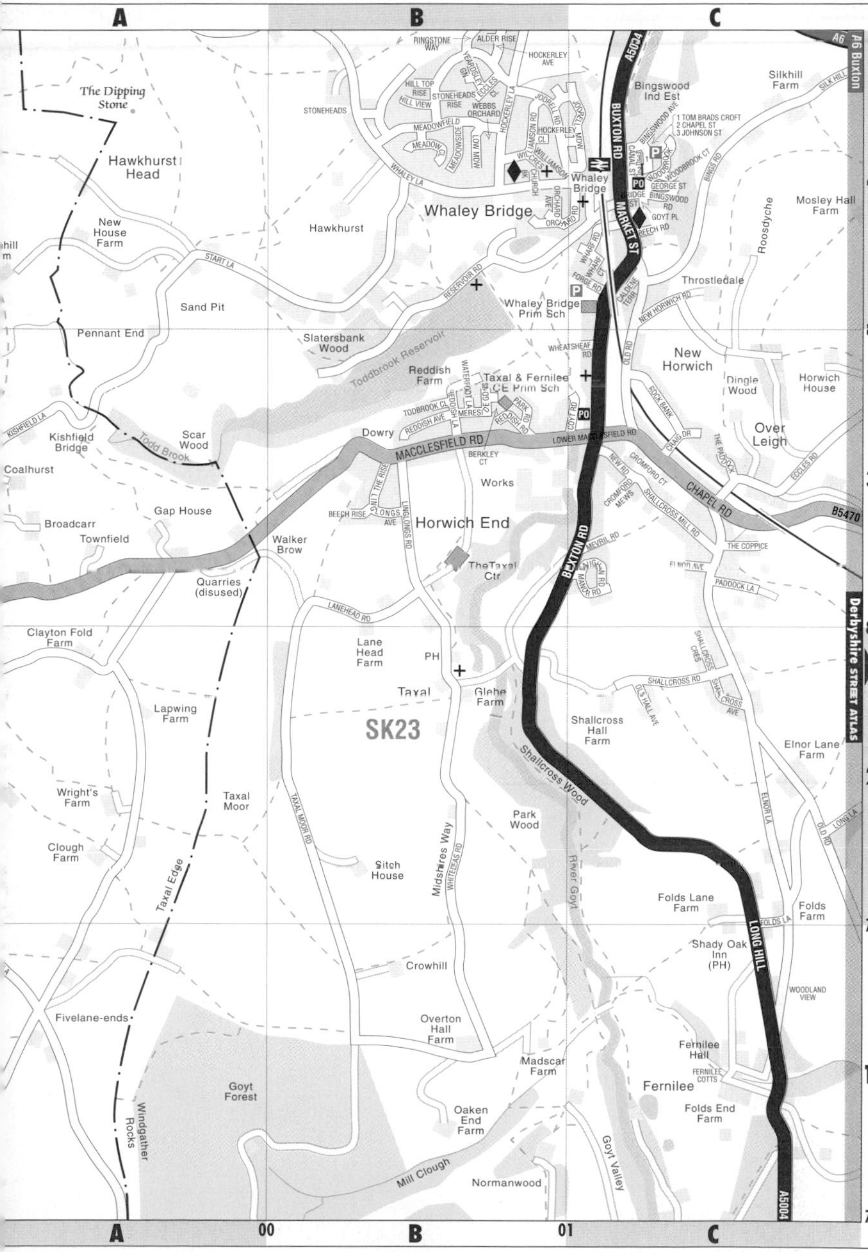
A
B
C
The Dipping Stone
Hawkhurst Head
New House Farm
Hawkhurst
Whaley Bridge
Bingswood Ind Est
Silkhill Farm
Mosley Hall Farm
Roosdyche
Throstledale
Sand Pit
Pennant End
Slatersbank Wood
Toddbrook Reservoir
Reddish Farm
Taxal & Fernilee CE Prim Sch
Whaley Bridge Prim Sch
New Horwich
Dingle Wood
Horwich House
Over Leigh
Kishfield Bridge
Scar Wood
Todd Brook
Dowry
Coalhurst
Gap House
Broadcarr
Townfield
Walker Brow
Horwich End
Works
The Taxal Ctr
Quarries (disused)
Clayton Fold Farm
Lane Head Farm
PH
Taxal
Glebe Farm
SK23
Lapwing Farm
Shallcross Hall Farm
Elnor Lane Farm
Shallcross Wood
Wright's Farm
Taxal Moor
Park Wood
Clough Farm
Sitch House
Midshires Way
River Goyt
Taxal Edge
Folds Lane Farm
Folds Farm
Shady Oak Inn (PH)
Crowhill
Fivelane-ends
Overton Hall Farm
Fernilee Hall
Madscar Farm
Fernilee
Goyt Forest
Oaken End Farm
Folds End Farm
Windgather Rocks
Mill Clough
Normanwood
Goyt Valley
BUXTON RD
MARKET ST
MACCLESFIELD RD
LOWER MACCLESFIELD RD
CHAPEL RD
LONG HILL
A5004
A6
A6 Buxton
B5470
1 TOM BRADS CROFT
2 CHAPEL ST
3 JOHNSON ST
Derbyshire STREET ATLAS
4
81
3
80
2
79
1
78
00
01

90

41

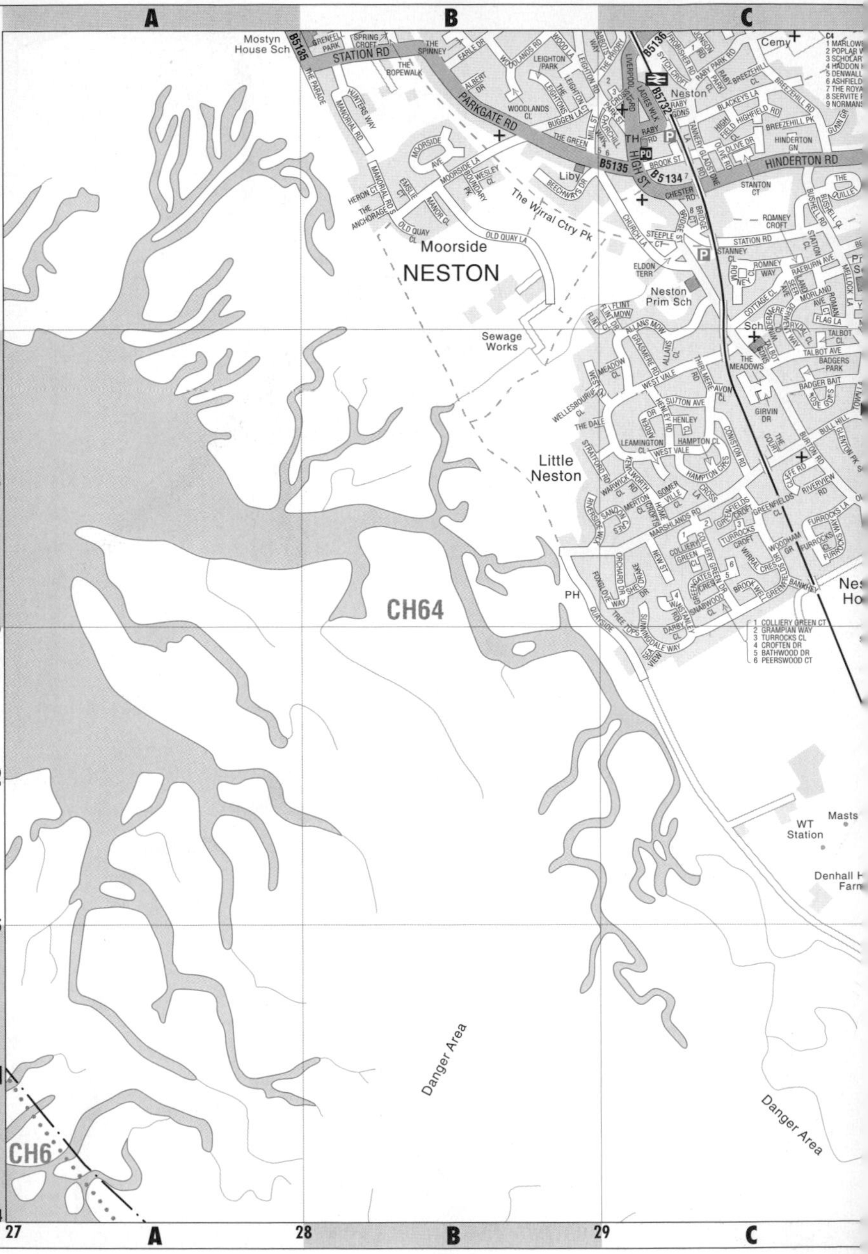
Mostyn House Sch
STATION RD
PARKGATE RD
HINDERTON RD
B5135
B5136
B5732
B5134
HIGH ST
Neston
Moorside
NESTON
The Wirral Ctry Pk
Neston Prim Sch
Sewage Works
Little Neston
CH64
PH
WT Station
Masts
Denhall H Farm
Danger Area
Danger Area
CH6
Cemy
C4
1 MARLOWE
2 POPLAR W
3 SCHOLAR
4 HADDON
5 DENWALL
6 ASHFIELD
7 THE ROYA
8 SERVITE
9 NORMANS
1 COLLIERY GREEN CT
2 GRAMPIAN WAY
3 TURROCKS CL
4 CROFTEN DR
5 BATHWOOD DR
6 PEERSWOOD CT
A
B
C
4
3
2
1
77
76
75
74
27
28
29

A
B
C
HINDERTON LA
HINDERTON RD
B5134
A540
HANNS HALL RD
WEATHERSTONE COTTS
HANNS HALL FARM
CHERRY CL
B5133
University of Liverpool, Faculty of Veterinary Science (Leahurst)
Wood Park
Windle Hill
Wirral Country Park
Wirral Way
CUCKOO LA
LEES LA
RAYMOND WAY
BENDEE AVE
DUNRAVEN RD
SANDY LA
HOWARDS WAY
ROCK FARM DR
ROCK FARM GR
WOODFALL GR
WOODFALL LA
Woodfall Inf & Jun Schs
MILL LA
Mill Farm
FLASHES LA
HILL TOP LA
HILL CL
MILL BANK
PALACE HEY
SHONES CROFT
CUMBERS LA
HOLT HEY
Ness
SMITHY CL 1
DIAL COTTS 3
SUNSET COTTS 4
SNAB LA 5
Orchard House
Haddon Hayes
HADDON LA
Visitor Ctr
Ness Botanic Gdns
Mickwell Brow
Friends Hall
Haddon Wood
Mast
Haddon Hall Farm
CH64
Hyfield
Ness Wood
Errington's Plantation
CHESTER HIGH RD
LYDIATE LA
DAMHEAD LA
B5151
WHITEGATES CRES
MEADOW CROFT
MEADOW LA
MEADOW CL
Willaston CE Prim Sch
NESTON RD
Liby
ELM RD
ELM GN
MILL GN
B5133
BROADLAKE
Ness Acre La
CHURCH FARM CT 1
WILLASTON FARM 2
WILLASTON GREEN MEWS 3
CHERRY BROW TERR 4
ATWORTH TERR 5
BUCKLEY LA
HADLOW LA
HADLOW RD
NEW HEY LA
FERNYESS LA
Willaston Grange
Shotwick Brook
WOOD END LA
DUNSTAN LA
Heath Farm
Dunstan Farm
Fiddleston Plantation
MUDHOUSE LA
DENHALL LA
NESTON RD
HADDON RD
WOOD LA
MILL LA
Burton Wood
VICARAGE LA
PRIESTWAY LA
STATION RD
THE RAKE
THE VILLAGE
PUDDINGTON LA
Burton
Bishop Wilson CE Prim Sch
Burton Manor Coll
Burton Marsh Farm
Burton Point Farm
4
77
3
76
2
75
1
74
31
32

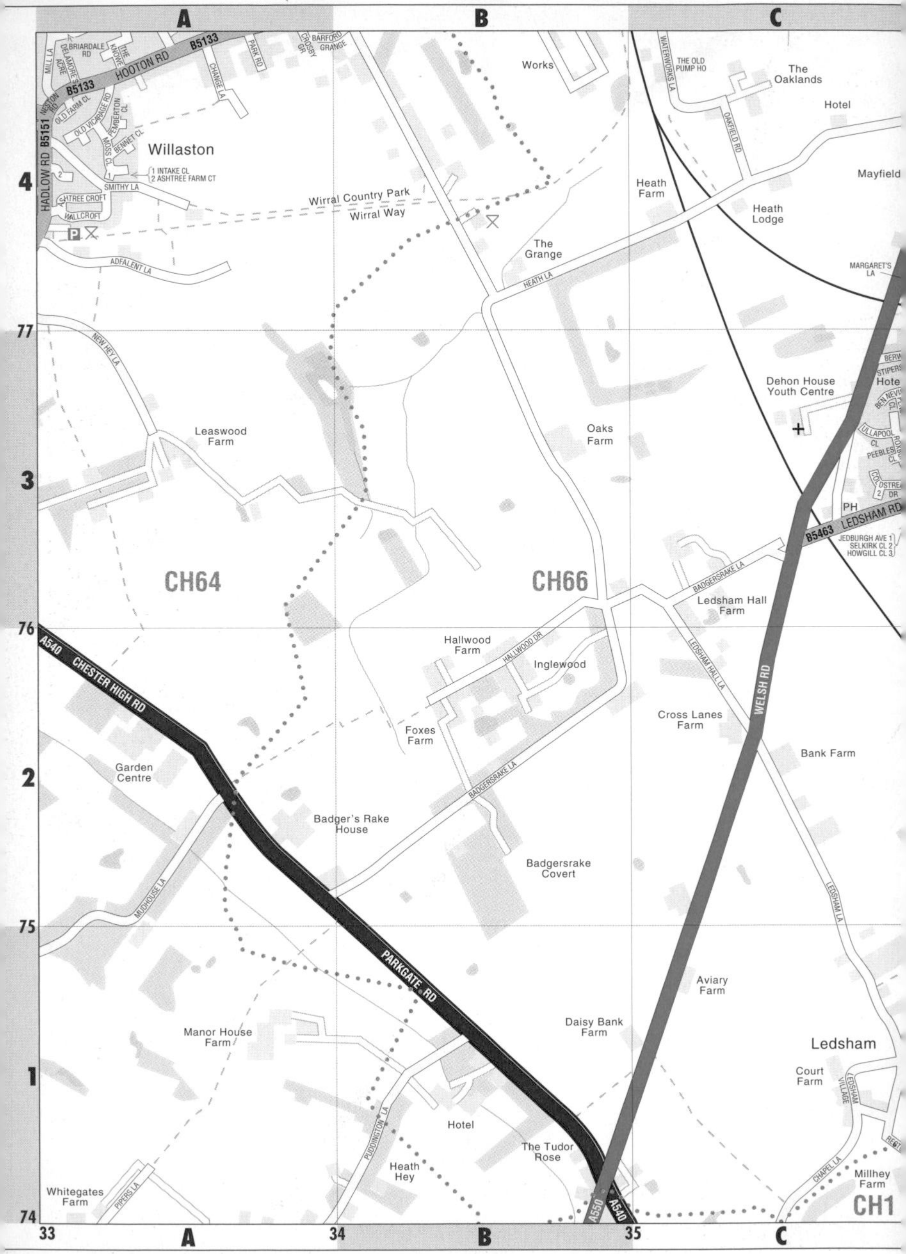
A
B
C
4
77
3
76
2
75
1
74
33
34
35
Willaston
HOOTON RD
B5133
HADLOW RD
B5151
NESTON RD
MILL LA
DELAMORE ACRE
BRIARDALE RD
THE KNOWE
CHANGE LA
PARK RD
CROSBY GR
BARFORD GRANGE
OLD FARM CL
OLD VICARAGE RD
PEMBERTON CL
MOSS CL
BENNET CL
1 INTAKE CL
2 ASHTREE FARM CT
SMITHY LA
ASHTREE CROFT
HALLCROFT
ADFALENT LA
Wirral Country Park
Wirral Way
Works
WATERWORKS LA
THE OLD PUMP HO
OAKFIELD RD
The Oaklands
Hotel
Mayfield
Heath Farm
Heath Lodge
The Grange
HEATH LA
MARGARET'S LA
NEW HEY LA
Dehon House Youth Centre
Leaswood Farm
Oaks Farm
ULLAPOOL CL
PEEBLES CL
PH
LEDSHAM RD
B5463
JEDBURGH AVE 1
SELKIRK CL 2
HOWGILL CL 3
CH64
CH66
BADGERSRAKE LA
Ledsham Hall Farm
LEDSHAM HALL LA
Hallwood Farm
HALLWOOD DR
Inglewood
A540
CHESTER HIGH RD
WELSH RD
Cross Lanes Farm
Foxes Farm
Bank Farm
Garden Centre
Badger's Rake House
Badgersrake Covert
MUDHOUSE LA
LEDSHAM LA
PARKGATE RD
Aviary Farm
Manor House Farm
Daisy Bank Farm
Ledsham
Court Farm
LEDSHAM VILLAGE
Hotel
PUDDINGTON LA
The Tudor Rose
Heath Hey
Whitegates Farm
PIPERS LA
A550
CHAPEL LA
Millhey Farm
CH1

B3
1 COOMBE PARK CT
2 SPRING AVE
3 GLENWOOD CL
4 BRIARDALE GDNS
5 SMITHY CT
6 CHALFIELD CL
7 CALDER WAY
8 LEAS CL
9 INNISFREE CL
10 EDEN CL
11 BRAESIDE CL

44
70

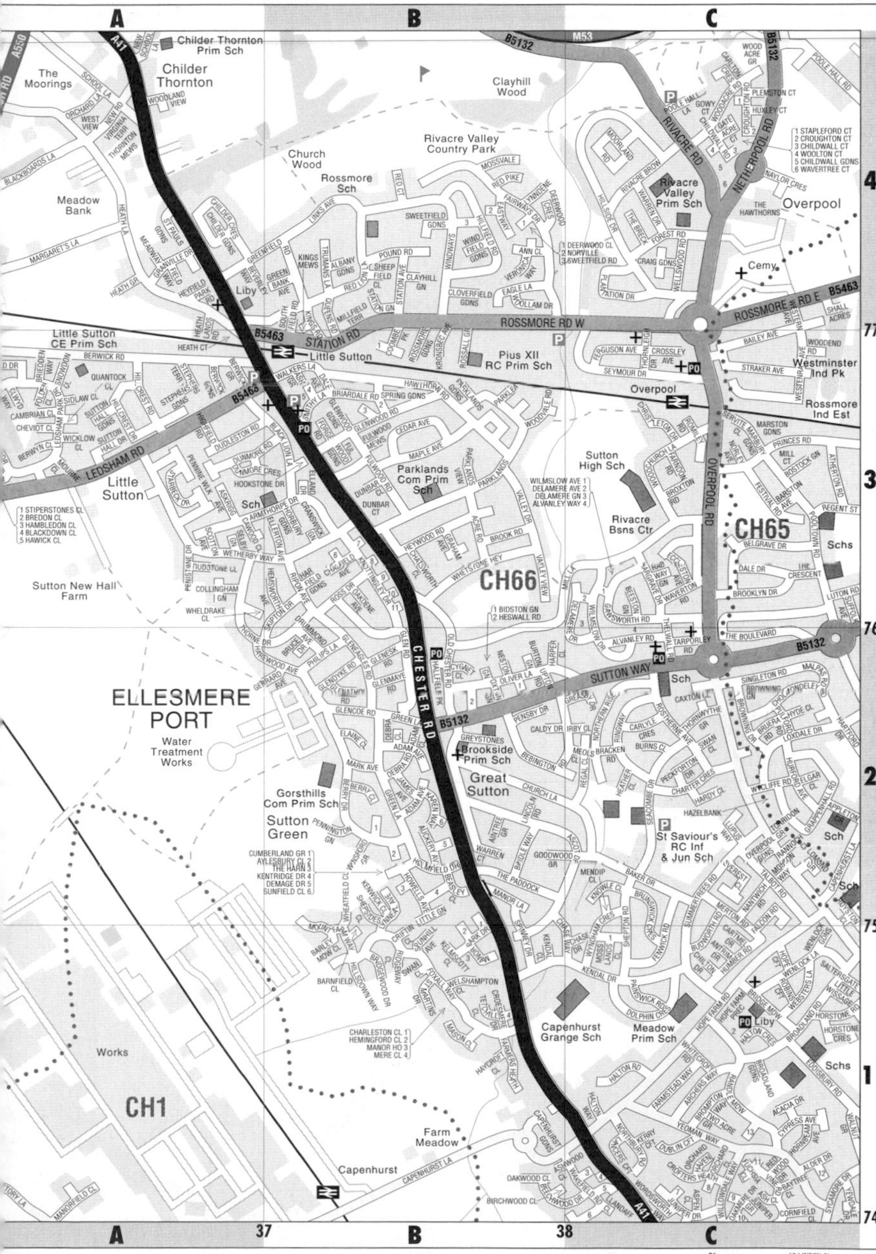

94
70

C1
1 BURDETT RD
2 RANDLE MEADOW CT
3 BRECON DR
4 CUMBRIA CL
5 BRISTOL DR
6 LAURELWOOD DR
7 PEAR TREE WAY
8 CROFTERS CL
9 HAZEL CL
10 LINDEN CL
11 MAGNOLIA CL
12 CHESTNUT AVE
13 WHITEBEAM AVE

69
B3
1 CHURCH WLK
2 CHURCH PAR
3 WORCESTER WLK
4 CRESSINGTON GDNS
5 CHARLES PRICE GDNS
6 THE COURT HO
45
B3
7 HIGHFIELD RD N
8 ASHFIELD RD N
9 WOODFIELD RD N
10 WELLINGTON CL
11 SHREWSBURY RD
12 WATERLOO CL
13 WELLESLEY WLK

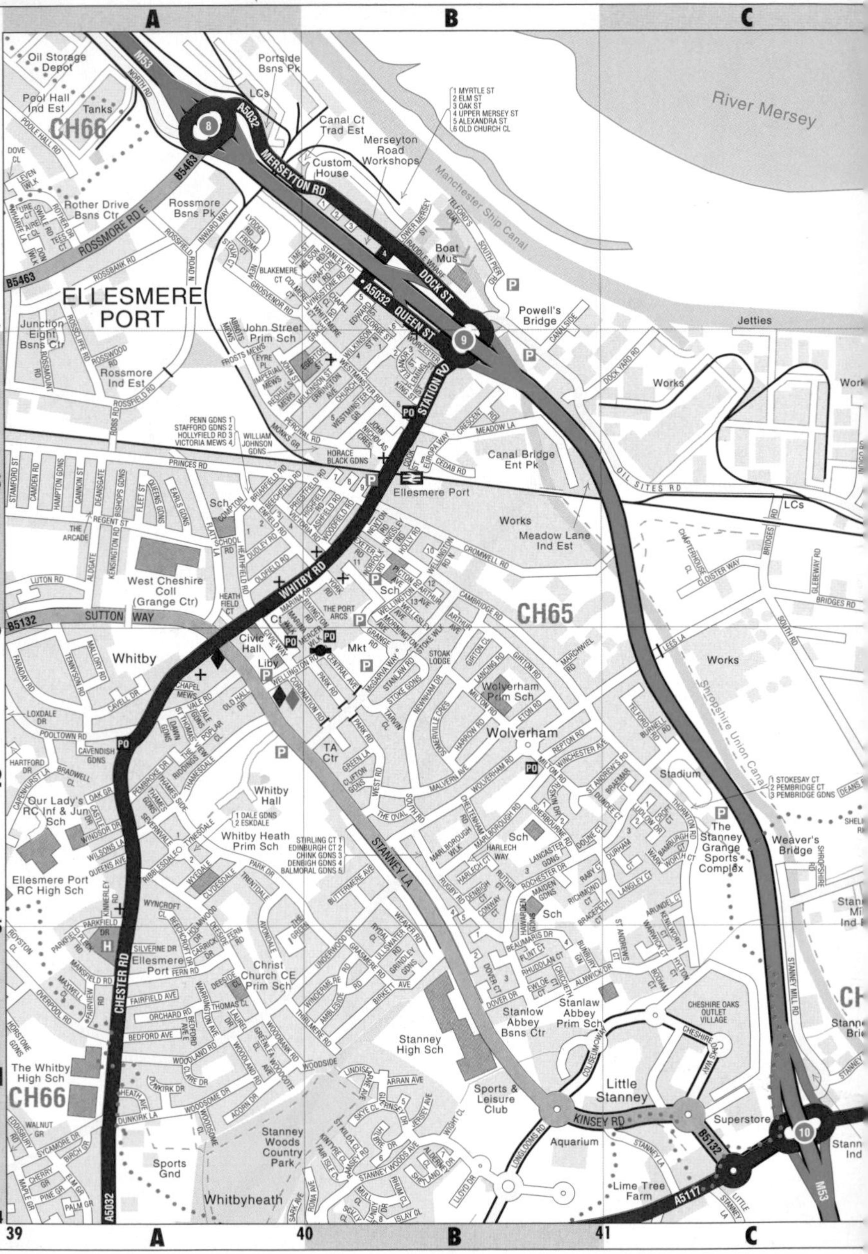
A
B
C
4
77
3
76
2
75
1
74
39
40
41
River Mersey
Manchester Ship Canal
Oil Storage Depot
Portside Bsns Pk
Pool Hall Ind Est
Tanks
CH66
LCs
Canal Ct Trad Est
Merseyton Road Workshops
Custom House
1 MYRTLE ST
2 ELM ST
3 OAK ST
4 UPPER MERSEY ST
5 ALEXANDRA ST
6 OLD CHURCH CL
Rother Drive Bsns Ctr
Rossmore Bsns Pk
Boat Mus
ELLESMERE PORT
Junction Eight Bsns Ctr
John Street Prim Sch
Powell's Bridge
Jetties
Works
Rossmore Ind Est
PENN GDNS 1
STAFFORD GDNS 2
HOLLYFIELD RD 3
VICTORIA MEWS 4
Canal Bridge Ent Pk
Ellesmere Port
Meadow Lane Ind Est
LCs
West Cheshire Coll (Grange Ctr)
CH65
Whitby
Civic Hall
Liby
Mkt
Wolverham Prim Sch
Wolverham
TA Ctr
Stadium
Our Lady's RC Inf & Jun Sch
Whitby Hall
1 DALE GDNS
2 ESKDALE
Whitby Heath Prim Sch
STIRLING CT 1
EDINBURGH CT 2
CHINK GDNS 3
DENBIGH GDNS 4
BALMORAL GDNS 5
The Stanney Grange Sports Complex
Weaver's Bridge
1 STOKESAY CT
2 PEMBRIDGE CT
3 PEMBRIDGE GDNS
Shropshire Union Canal
Ellesmere Port RC High Sch
Ellesmere Port
Christ Church CE Prim Sch
Stanlow Abbey Bsns Ctr
Stanlaw Abbey Prim Sch
CHESHIRE OAKS OUTLET VILLAGE
Stanney High Sch
The Whitby High Sch
CH66
Sports & Leisure Club
Little Stanney
Superstore
Aquarium
Stanney Woods Country Park
Sports Gnd
Whitbyheath
Lime Tree Farm
M53
A5032
B5463
B5132
A5117
CHESTER RD
WHITBY RD
STATION RD
QUEEN ST
DOCK ST
MERSEYTON RD
STANNEY LA
KINSEY RD
SUTTON WAY

69
95
B1
1 BUCKINGHAM RD
2 SANDRINGHAM GDNS
3 FOTHERINGAY CT
4 CAERNARVON CT
5 BARDSEY CL
6 ANGLESEY CL
7 ORKNEY CL
8 CUMBRAE DR

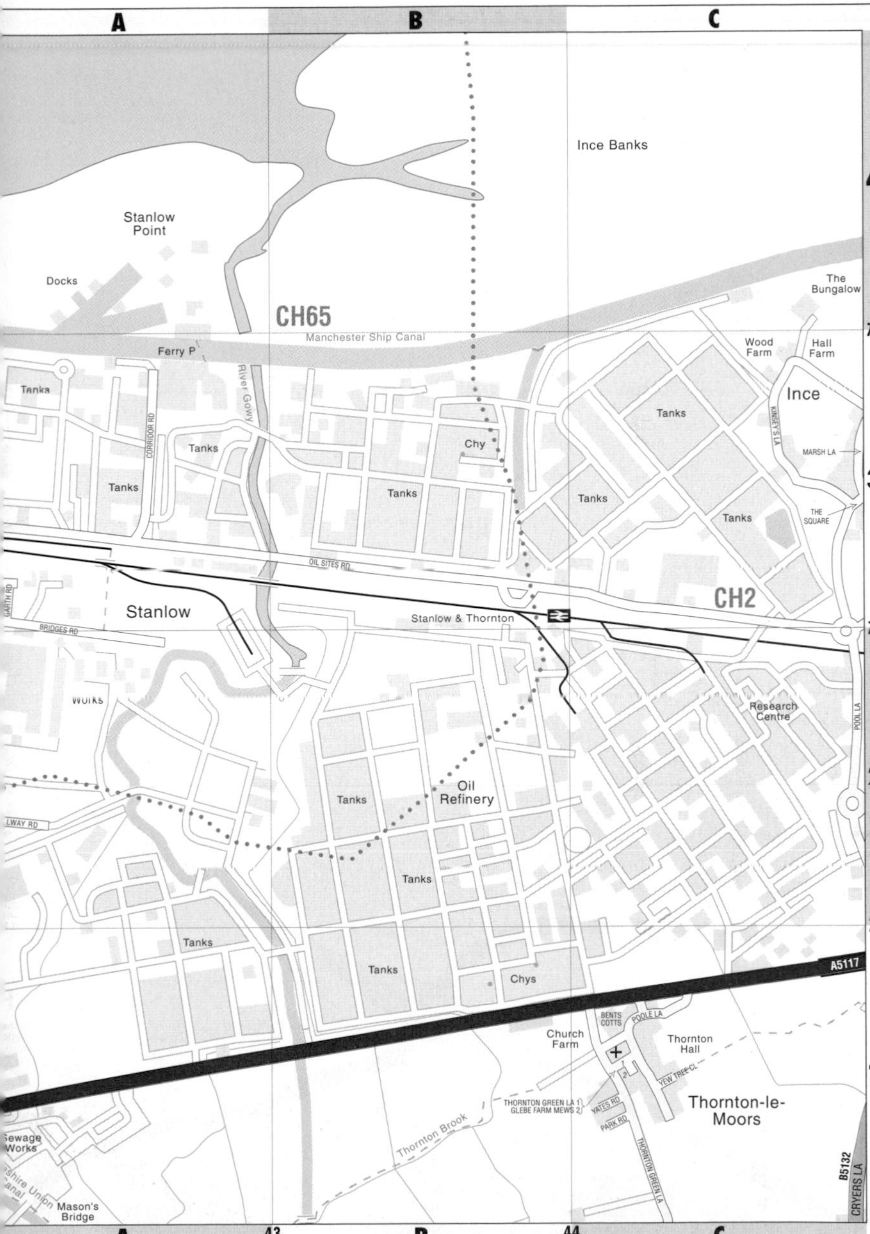
A
B
C
Ince Banks
Stanlow Point
Docks
CH65
Manchester Ship Canal
The Bungalow
Wood Farm
Hall Farm
Ince
Ferry P
River Gowy
Tanks
CORRIDOR RD
Chy
KINSEY'S LA
MARSH LA
THE SQUARE
OIL SITES RD
Stanlow
GARTH RD
BRIDGES RD
Stanlow & Thornton
CH2
Works
Research Centre
POOL LA
Oil Refinery
LWAY RD
Chys
A5117
BENTS COTTS
POOLE LA
Church Farm
Thornton Hall
YEW TREE CL
THORNTON GREEN LA 1
GLEBE FARM MEWS 2
YATES RD
PARK RD
Thornton-le-Moors
Thornton Brook
THORNTON GREEN LA
Sewage Works
shire Union Canal
Mason's Bridge
B5132
CRYERS LA
4
3
2
1
77
76
75
74
43
44

71
47

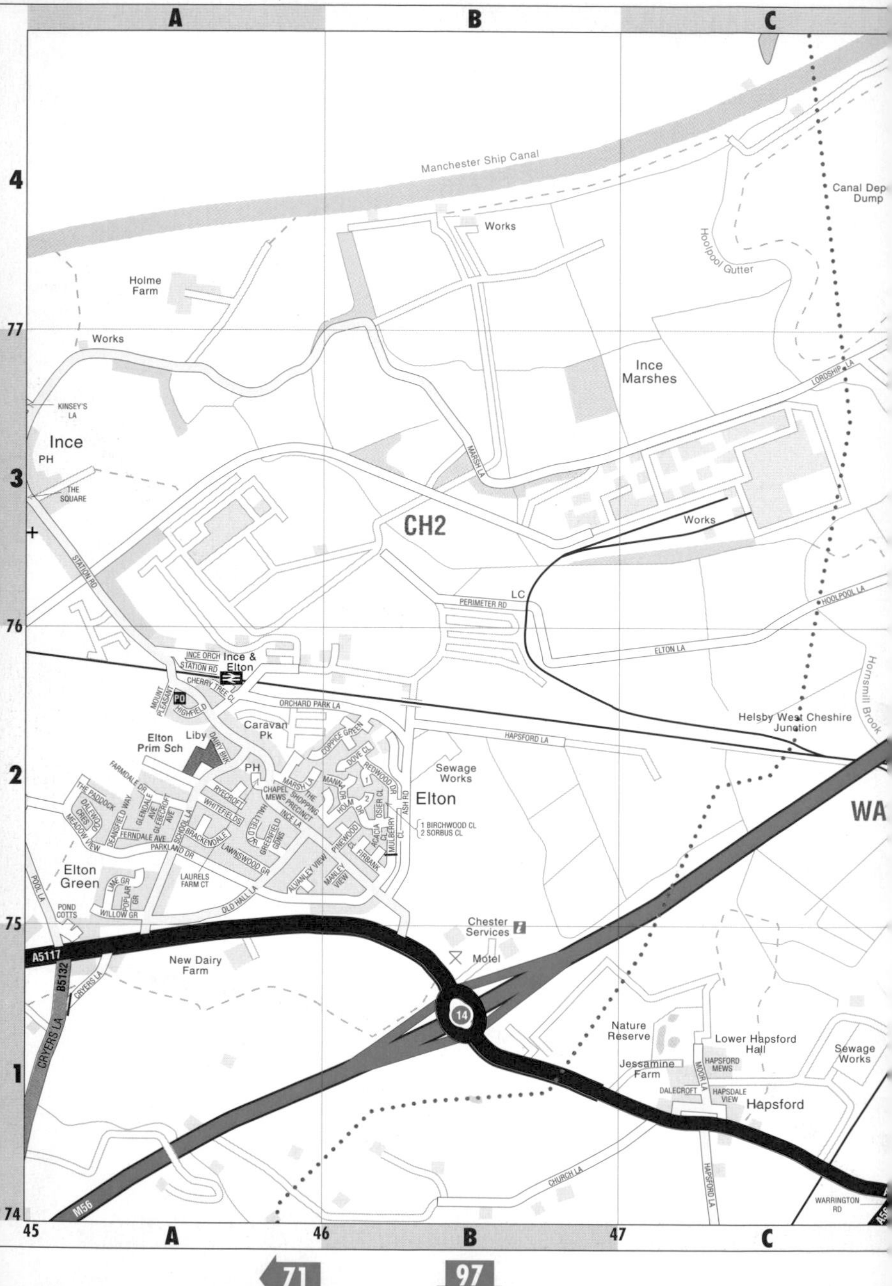
A
B
C
4
3
2
1
77
76
75
74
45
46
47
Manchester Ship Canal
Canal Dep
Dump
Works
Holme
Farm
Hoolpool Gutter
Works
Ince
Marshes
LORDSHIP LA
KINSEY'S
LA
Ince
PH
MARSH LA
THE
SQUARE
CH2
Works
STATION RD
LC
PERIMETER RD
HOOLPOOL LA
ELTON LA
Hornsmill Brook
INCE ORCH
STATION RD
Ince &
Elton
CHERRY TREE CL
MOUNT
PLEASANT
PO
HIGHFIELD
ORCHARD PARK LA
Caravan
Pk
COPPICE GREEN
Helsby West Cheshire
Junction
Elton
Prim Sch
Liby
DAIRY BANK
HAPSFORD LA
PH
Sewage
Works
DOVE CL
REDWOOD DR
FARMDALE DR
THE PADDOCK
DALEWOOD
CRES
MEADOW VIEW
DEANSFIELD WAY
GLENDALE
AVE
GLEBECROFT
AVE
RYECROFT
WHITEFIELDS
FERNDALE AVE
SCHOOL LA
BRACKENDALE
HALLFIELD DR
GREENFIELD
GDNS
CHAPEL
MEWS
MARSH LA
THE
SHOPPING
PRECINCT
INCE LA
MANNA DR
HOLM DR
OSIER CL
ACACIA CL
MULBERRY CL
ASH RD
Elton
1 BIRCHWOOD CL
2 SORBUS CL
WA
PARKLAND DR
LAWNSWOOD GR
PINEWOOD CL
FIRBANK
ALVANLEY VIEW
MANLEY VIEW
Elton
Green
LAURELS
FARM CT
POOL LA
LIME GR
POPLAR GR
POND
COTTS
WILLOW GR
OLD HALL LA
Chester
Services
Motel
A5117
New Dairy
Farm
B5132
CRYERS LA
GRYERS LA
14
Nature
Reserve
Lower Hapsford
Hall
Sewage
Works
Jessamine
Farm
HAPSFORD
MEWS
MOOR LA
DALECROFT
HAPSDALE
VIEW
Hapsford
CHURCH LA
HAPSFORD LA
M56
WARRINGTON
RD
A56

71
97

48
74

A
B
C
Canal Deposit Dump
Frodsham Marsh
Canal Deposit Dump
Lordship Marsh
Grassy Lane
Ppg Sta
Hatley Farm
Godscroft Hall
Hill View Farm
Helsby Marsh
WA6
Helsby High Sch
Spring Farm
Meadow Farm
Mast
Helsby
Woodhouses
Sch
CHESTER RD
Helsby
Helsby Hill
Covertside
Foxhill
Foxhill Wood
Wks
Libv
Firs Farm
Longster Trail
Alderhall
Ppg Sta
Works
Rock Farm
Poplar Tree Farm
Walnut Tree Farm
Commonside Farm
Bowlingalley Farm
Horns Mill Prim Sch
Alvanley
Alvanley Prim Sch
Cliff Farm
TARVIN RD
B5393 FRODSHAM RD
M56
A56
B5393
BALMORAL DR 1
RAKE HOUSE MEWS 2
VALE GDNS 3
WROXHAM CL 4
1 PYRUS GR
2 CHURCHFIELDS
3 GROVE TERR
1 CHAPEL VIEW
2 BRITANNIA RD
3 HOMEWAY
4 HEMLEGH VALE
5 MARLBOROUGH DR
6 BACK CROSLAND TERR
7 LONGSTER CL
8 THE ORCHARD
4
3
2
1
77
76
75
74
49
50
A
B
C

98
74

A4
1 MORETON TERR
2 GREENFIELD LA
3 COLLINSON CT
4 SANDFIELD CT
5 DERFEL TERR
6 WHITEHALL PL

73
49

73
99

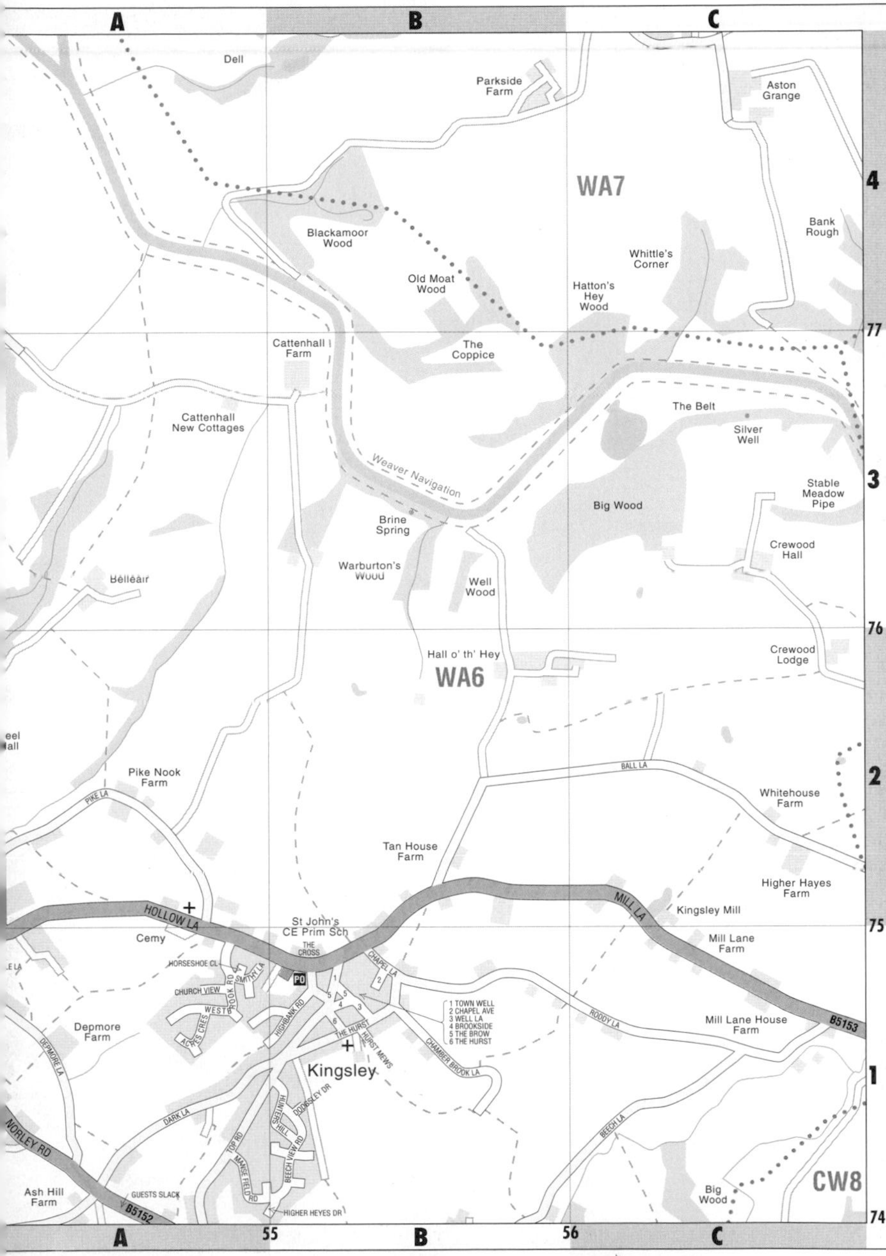
A
B
C
Dell
Parkside Farm
Aston Grange
WA7
Blackamoor Wood
Old Moat Wood
Whittle's Corner
Hatton's Hey Wood
Bank Rough
Cattenhall Farm
The Coppice
Cattenhall New Cottages
The Belt
Silver Well
Weaver Navigation
Stable Meadow Pipe
Big Wood
Brine Spring
Crewood Hall
Warburton's Wood
Well Wood
Belleair
Hall o' th' Hey
WA6
Crewood Lodge
Pike Nook Farm
BALL LA
Whitehouse Farm
PIKE LA
Tan House Farm
Higher Hayes Farm
HOLLOW LA
MILL LA
Kingsley Mill
St John's CE Prim Sch
Cemy
THE CROSS
Mill Lane Farm
HORSESHOE CL
SMITHY LA
CHAPEL LA
CHURCH VIEW
BROOK RD
WESTB
ACRES CRES
HIGHBANK RD
PO
1 TOWN WELL
2 CHAPEL AVE
3 WELL LA
4 BROOKSIDE
5 THE BROW
6 THE HURST
RODDY LA
Mill Lane House Farm
B5153
Depmore Farm
DEPMORE LA
THE HURST
HURST MEWS
CHAMBER BROOK LA
Kingsley
HUNTERS HILL
DODSLEY DR
DARK LA
NORLEY RD
TOP RD
MANSE FIELD RD
BEECH VIEW RD
BEECH LA
Ash Hill Farm
GUESTS SLACK
B5152
HIGHER HEYES DR
Big Wood
CW8
4
77
3
76
2
75
1
74
55
56

75 51

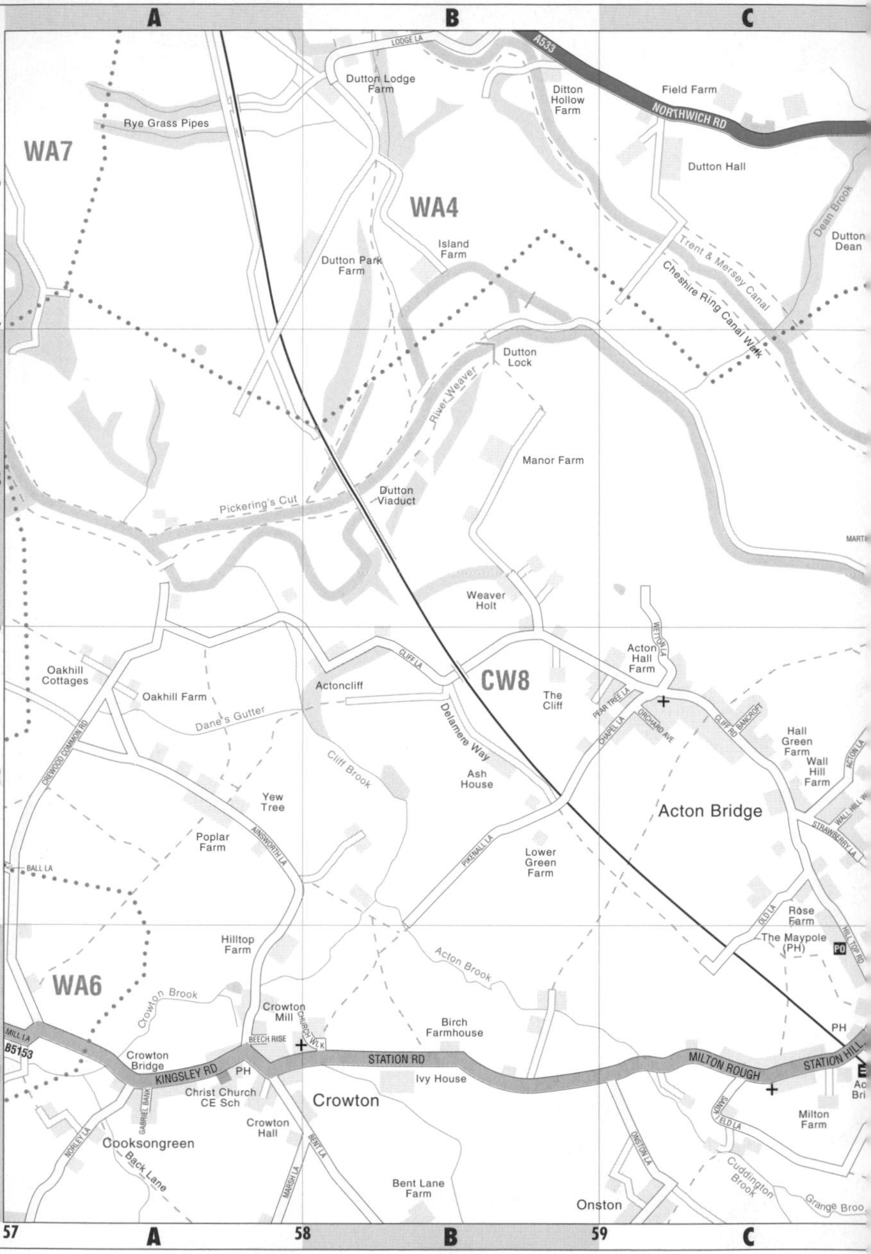
A
B
C
4
3
2
1
77
76
75
74
57
58
59
WA7
WA4
CW8
WA6
Rye Grass Pipes
Dutton Lodge Farm
LODGE LA
A533
Ditton Hollow Farm
Field Farm
NORTHWICH RD
Dutton Hall
Dean Brook
Dutton Dean
Island Farm
Dutton Park Farm
Trent & Mersey Canal
Cheshire Ring Canal Walk
Dutton Lock
River Weaver
Manor Farm
Dutton Viaduct
Pickering's Cut
Weaver Holt
Oakhill Cottages
Oakhill Farm
CLIFF LA
Actoncliff
The Cliff
Acton Hall Farm
WETTON LA
PEAR TREE LA
CHAPEL LA
ORCHARD AVE
CLIFF RD
BANCROFT
Hall Green Farm
Wall Hill Farm
Dane's Gutter
Delamere Way
CREWOOD COMMON RD
Cliff Brook
Ash House
Yew Tree
AINSWORTH LA
Acton Bridge
STRAWBERRY LA
Poplar Farm
PIKENALL LA
Lower Green Farm
BALL LA
OLD LA
Rose Farm
The Maypole (PH)
HILL TOP RD
Hilltop Farm
Acton Brook
Crowton Brook
Crowton Mill
CHURCH WLK
Birch Farmhouse
PH
MILL LA
B5153
BEECH RISE
STATION RD
MILTON ROUGH
STATION HILL
Crowton Bridge
KINGSLEY RD
Ivy House
Christ Church CE Sch
GABRIEL BANK
Crowton
Milton Farm
Crowton Hall
NORLEY LA
Cooksongreen
BENT LA
ONSTON LA
Cuddington Brook
Back Lane
MARSH LA
Bent Lane Farm
Onston
Grange Broo

52
78

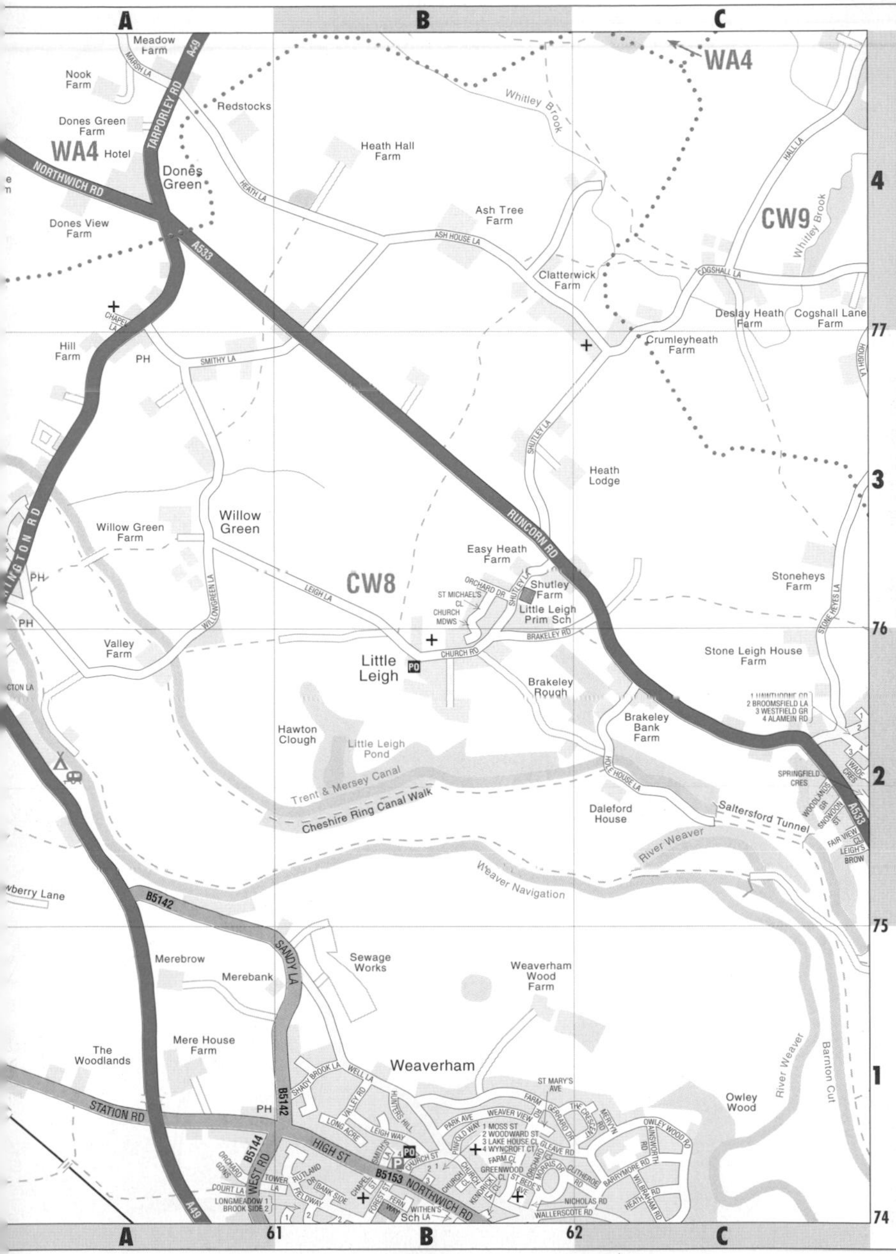
A
B
C
4
3
2
1
77
76
75
74
61
62
Meadow Farm
Nook Farm
Dones Green Farm
WA4
Hotel
NORTHWICH RD
Dones View Farm
TARPORLEY RD
A49
MARSH LA
Redstocks
Dones Green
HEATH LA
A533
Heath Hall Farm
Whitley Brook
WA4
ASH HOUSE LA
Ash Tree Farm
HALL LA
CW9
Whitley Brook
COGSHALL LA
Clatterwick Farm
Deslay Heath Farm
Cogshall Lane Farm
Crumleyheath Farm
HOUGH LA
CHAPEL LA
Hill Farm
PH
SMITHY LA
SHUTLEY LA
Heath Lodge
RUNCORN RD
Willow Green
Willow Green Farm
Easy Heath Farm
CW8
LEIGH LA
ORCHARD DR
ST MICHAEL'S CL
CHURCH MDWS
SHUTLEY LA
Shutley Farm
Little Leigh Prim Sch
Stoneheys Farm
STONE HEYES LA
BRAKELEY RD
WILLOWGREEN LA
PH
PH
Valley Farm
CHURCH RD
Little Leigh
Stone Leigh House Farm
Brakeley Rough
1 HAWTHORNE GR
2 BROOMSFIELD LA
3 WESTFIELD GR
4 ALAMEIN RD
Brakeley Bank Farm
Hawton Clough
Little Leigh Pond
HOLE HOUSE LA
SPRINGFIELD CRES
WADE CRES
Trent & Mersey Canal
Cheshire Ring Canal Walk
Daleford House
Saltersford Tunnel
WOODLANDS GR
SNOWDON ST
A533
FAIR VIEW CL
LEIGH'S BROW
River Weaver
Weaver Navigation
B5142
SANDY LA
Sewage Works
Merebrow
Merebank
Weaverham Wood Farm
The Woodlands
Mere House Farm
Weaverham
River Weaver
Barnton Cut
ST MARY'S AVE
Owley Wood
B5142
SHADY BROOK LA
WELL LA
VALLEY RD
HUNTERS HILL
STATION RD
PH
LONG ACRE
LEIGH WAY
PARK AVE
WEAVER VIEW
FARM
GERRARD DR
THE CRESCENT
MERVYN RD
OWLEY WOOD RD
1 MOSS ST
2 WOODWARD ST
3 LAKE HOUSE CL
4 WYNCROFT CT
PINFOLD WAY
GLEAVE RD
AINSWORTH RD
HIGH ST
SMITH'S LA
CHURCH ST
B5144
WEST RD
ORCHARD GDNS
RUTLAND DR
B5153
NORTHWICH RD
CHURCH CL
CHURCH
FARM CL
GREENWOOD CL
ORCHARD
MORRIS DR
CLITHEROE RD
BARRYMORE RD
WILBRAHAM RD
TOWER LA
COURT LA
BANK SIDE
CHAPEL ST
FOREST ST
KENDRICK CL
ST BEDE'S AVE
HEATH RD
NICHOLAS RD
LONGMEADOW 1
BROOK SIDE 2
FIELDWAY
FERN WAY
WITHEN'S LA
Sch
WALLERSCOTE RD
A49
wberry Lane
CTON LA
INGTON RD

102
78

77
53

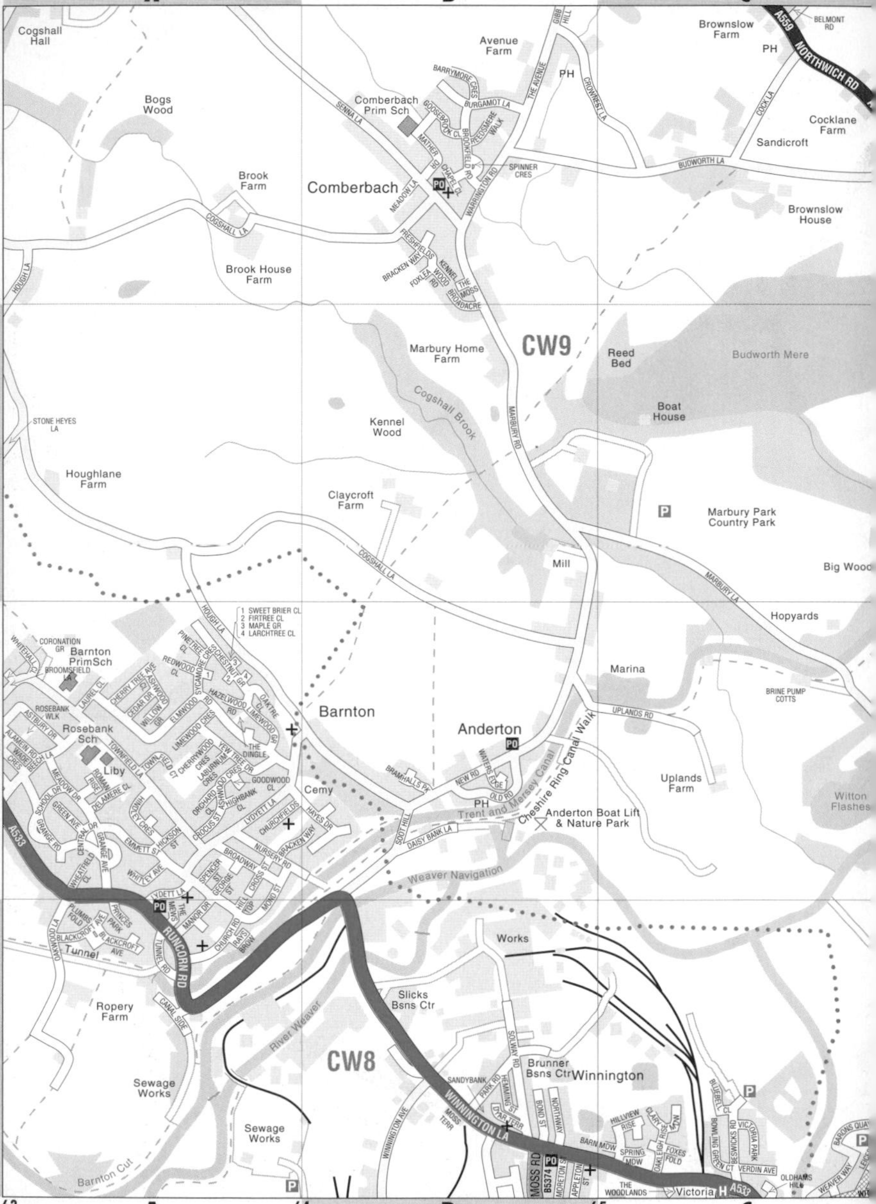
A
B
C
4
3
2
1
77
76
75
74
63
64
65
Cogshall Hall
Bogs Wood
Brook Farm
Comberbach
Comberbach Prim Sch
Avenue Farm
PH
Brownslow Farm
BELMONT RD
A559
NORTHWICH RD
COCK LA
Cocklane Farm
Sandicroft
BUDWORTH LA
Brownslow House
GIBB HILL
THE AVENUE
CROWNEST LA
BARRYMORE CRES
BURGAMOT LA
GOOSEBROOK CL
REEDSMERE WALK
BROOKFIELD RD
SPINNER CRES
WARRINGTON RD
SENNA LA
MATHER DR
CHAPEL CL
MEADOW LA
PO
COGSHALL LA
Brook House Farm
HOUGH LA
FRESHFIELDS
BRACKEN WAY
FOXLEA
KENNEL WOOD RD
THE MOSS
BROADACRE
CW9
Marbury Home Farm
Reed Bed
Budworth Mere
Cogshall Brook
Kennel Wood
Boat House
MARBURY RD
STONE HEYES LA
Houghlane Farm
Claycroft Farm
P
Marbury Park Country Park
Mill
Big Wood
MARBURY LA
Hopyards
1 SWEET BRIER CL
2 FIRTREE CL
3 MAPLE GR
4 LARCHTREE CL
Marina
BRINE PUMP COTTS
UPLANDS RD
CORONATION GR
Barnton PrimSch
BROOMSFIELD LA
WHITEHALL CL
PINETREE CL
CHERRY TREE AVE
ASHWOOD CL
REDWOOD CL
SYCAMORE CRES
CHESTNUT GR
LAUREL CL
CEDAR DR
WILLOW GR
ELMWOOD
HAZELWOOD RD
LIMEWOOD GR
OAKTREE CL
ROSEBANK WLK
ASTBURY DR
ALAMEIN RD
WADE CRES
BEECH LA
Rosebank Sch
Liby
TOWNFIELD LA
LIMEWOOD CRES
CHERRYWOOD CRES
YEW TREE DR
THE DINGLE
Barnton
Anderton
PO
WATERS EDGE
BRAMHALLS PK
NEW RD
OLD RD
PH
Trent and Mersey Canal
Cheshire Ring Canal Walk
Uplands Farm
Witton Flashes
Anderton Boat Lift & Nature Park
DAISY BANK LA
SOOT HILL
ROMAN RISE
DELAMERE CL
MEADOW DR
SCHOOL DR
GREEN AVE
LABURNUM CRES
ORCHARD CL
ASHWOOD CRES
GOODWOOD CL
HIGHBANK CL
Cemy
HAYES DR
CHURCHFIELDS
LYDYETT LA
CROCUS ST
HICKSON ST
EMMETT ST
WHITLEY AVE
GRANGE RD
CENTRAL DR
GRANGE AVE
WHEATFIELD CL
A533
BROADWAY
BRACKEN WAY
NURSERY RD
SPENCER ST
GEORGE ST
HILL TOP
CROSS ST
MOND ST
Weaver Navigation
LYDYETT LA
THE MEWS
MANOR DR
PO
PLUMBS FOLD
BLACKCROFT AVE
PRINCES PARK
OAKWOOD LA
Tunnel
TUNNEL RD
RUNCORN RD
CHURCH RD
RAYS BROW
Works
Slicks Bsns Ctr
Ropery Farm
CANAL SIDE
River Weaver
CW8
SOLWAY RD
Brunner Bsns Ctr
Winnington
Sewage Works
SANDYBANK
PARK RD
HEMMING ST
DYAR TERR
WINNINGTON LA
MOSS TERR
BOND ST
NORTHWAY
HILLVIEW RISE
CLARY MDW
BLUEBELL CL
P
BOWLING GREEN CT
BESWICKS RD
VICTORIA PARK
BARONS QUAY
WINNINGTON AVE
Sewage Works
BARN MDW
SPRING MDW
OAKLEIGH RISE
FOXES FOLD
VERDIN AVE
MOSS RD
B5374
PO
MORETON ST
APPLETON ST
THE WOODLANDS
Victoria
H
A533
OLDHAMS HILL
WEAVER WAY
Barnton Cut
P
A
B
C

77
103

54
80

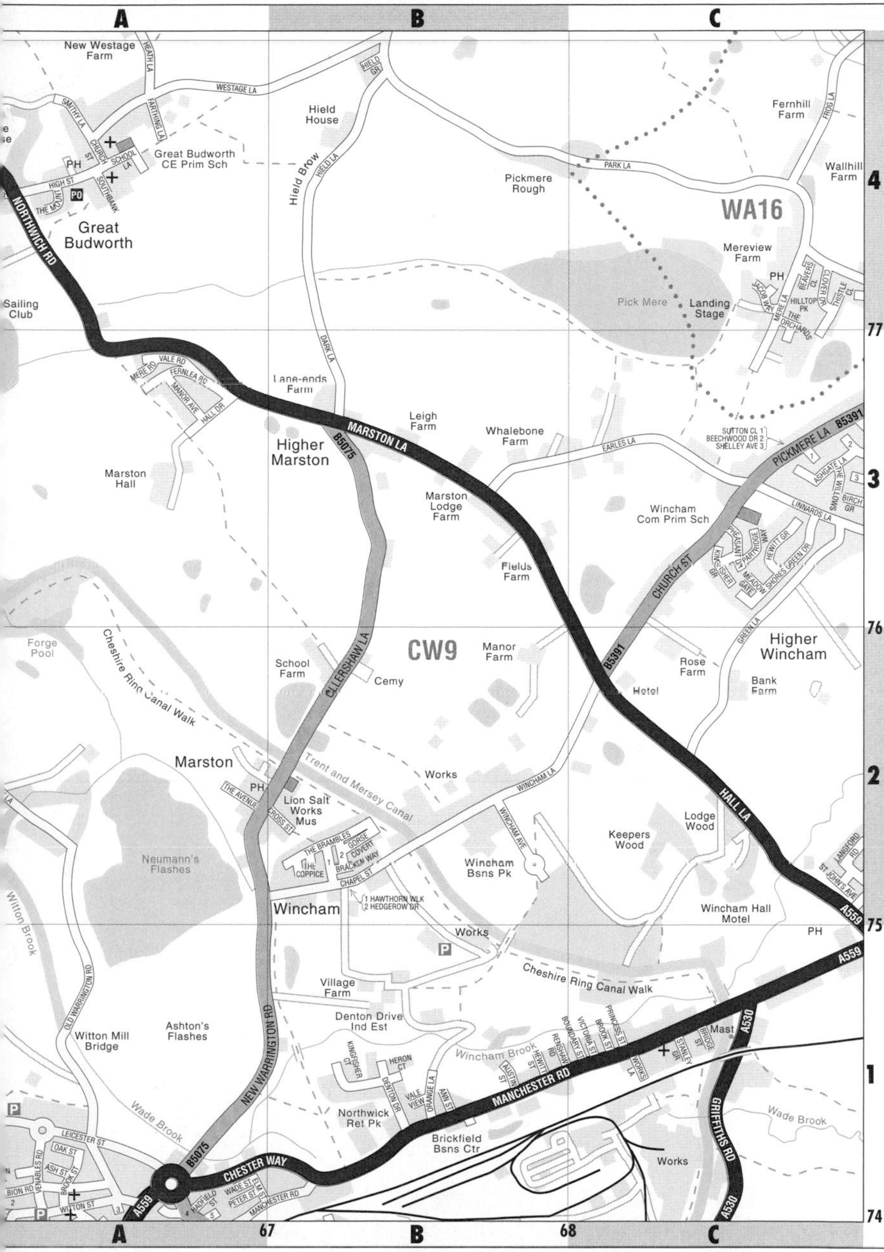
A
B
C
A
67
B
68
C
4
77
3
76
2
75
1
74
New Westage Farm
HEATH LA
WESTAGE LA
HIELD GR
SMITHY LA
FARTHING LA
CHURCH ST
SCHOOL LA
Great Budworth CE Prim Sch
PH
HIGH ST
SOUTHBANK
PO
THE MOUNT
Great Budworth
NORTHWICH RD
Hield House
Hield Brow
HIELD LA
Sailing Club
Fernhill Farm
FROG LA
PARK LA
Pickmere Rough
Wallhill Farm
WA16
Mereview Farm
PH
JACOB WAY
MERE LA
BEAVERS CL
CLOVER DR
THISTLE CL
HILLTOP PK
THE ORCHARDS
Pick Mere
Landing Stage
DARK LA
MERE RD
VALE RD
FERNLEA RD
MANOR AVE
HALL DR
Lane-ends Farm
Leigh Farm
MARSTON LA
B5075
Higher Marston
Whalebone Farm
EARLES LA
SUTTON CL 1
BEECHWOOD DR 2
SHELLEY AVE 3
PICKMERE LA
B5391
Marston Hall
Marston Lodge Farm
Wincham Com Prim Sch
ASHGATE LA
THE WILLOWS
BIRCH GR
LINNARDS LA
PHEASANT DR
PARTRIDGE WAY
HEWITT GR
GREEN DR
KINGFISHER GR
MEADOW GATE
SHORES
CHURCH ST
Fields Farm
Forge Pool
Cheshire Ring Canal Walk
School Farm
CLLERSHAW LA
Cemy
CW9
Manor Farm
B5391
Rose Farm
Hotel
GREEN LA
Higher Wincham
Bank Farm
Marston
PH
THE AVENUE
CROSS ST
Lion Salt Works Mus
Trent and Mersey Canal
Works
WINCHAM LA
WINCHAM AVE
HALL LA
Lodge Wood
Keepers Wood
THE BRAMBLES
GORSE COVERT
BRACKEN WAY
THE COPPICE
CHAPEL ST
Neumann's Flashes
Wincham Bsns Pk
LANGFORD RD
ST JOHN'S AVE
1 HAWTHORN WLK
2 HEDGEROW DR
Wincham
Wincham Hall Motel
A559
Witton Brook
Works
P
PH
A559
Cheshire Ring Canal Walk
Village Farm
OLD WARRINGTON RD
Denton Drive Ind Est
Mast
A530
Witton Mill Bridge
Ashton's Flashes
NEW WARRINGTON RD
KINGFISHER CT
HERON CT
DENTON DR
Wincham Brook
HEWITT RD
RENSHAW RD
BOUNDARY ST
VICTORIA ST
BROOK ST
PRINCESS ST
WORKS LA
STANLEY GR
BRIDGE ST
VALE VIEW
ORANGE LA
ANN ST
AUSTIN ST
MANCHESTER RD
GRIFFITHS RD
Wade Brook
Northwick Ret Pk
Brickfield Bsns Ctr
Wade Brook
LEICESTER ST
OAK ST
ASH ST
BROOK ST
VENABLES RD
WITTON ST
B5075
CHESTER WAY
WADE ST
ELM ST
PETER ST
HADFIELD ST
MANCHESTER RD
Works
A559
A530
P

104
80

OST OFFICE PL
PAUL'S PL
REST PL
ATION RD
RTON'S PL

79
55

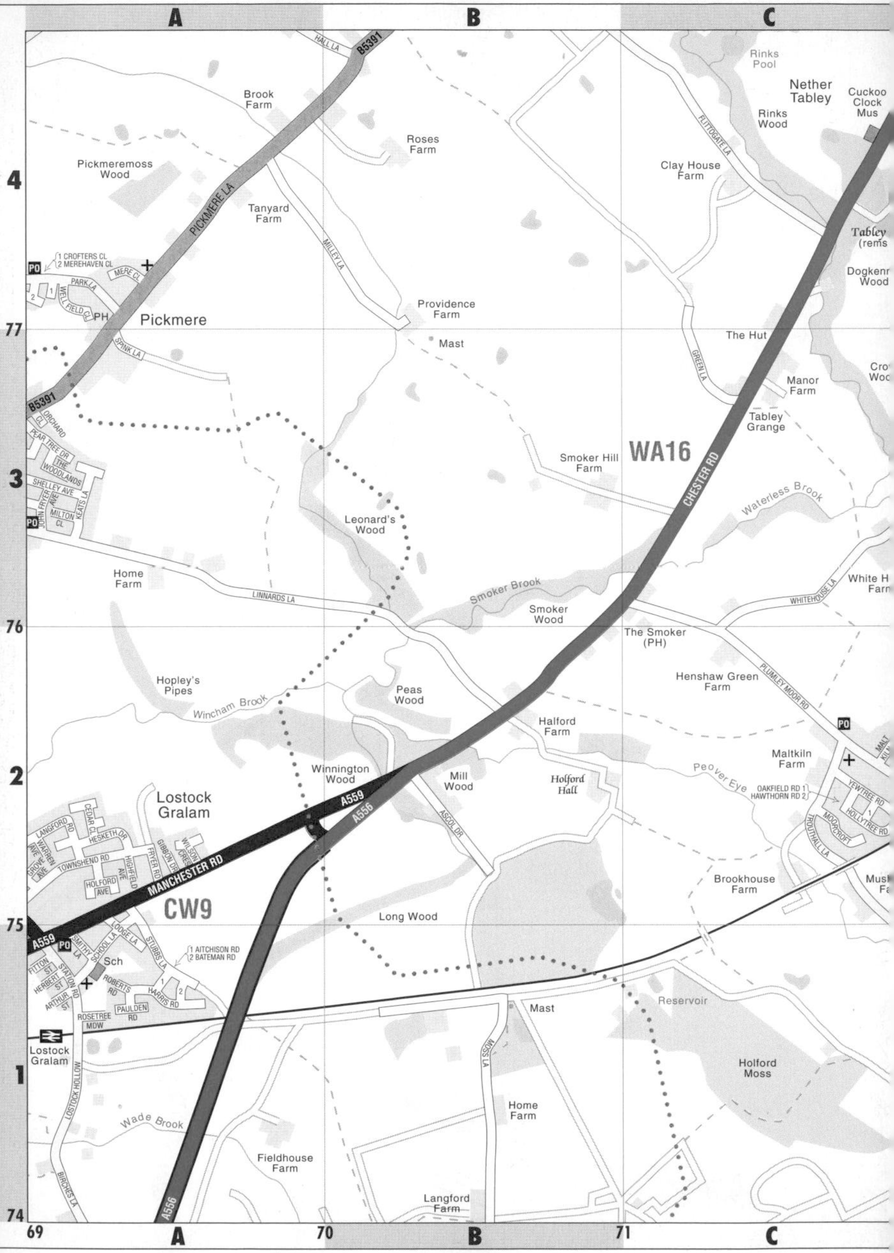
A
B
C
4
77
3
76
2
75
1
74
69
70
71
Brook Farm
HALL LA
B5391
Roses Farm
Rinks Pool
Nether Tabley
Cuckoo Clock Mus
Rinks Wood
FLITTOGATE LA
Clay House Farm
Pickmeremoss Wood
PICKMERE LA
Tanyard Farm
MILLEY LA
Tabley (rems
Dogkenn Wood
1 CROFTERS CL
2 MEREHAVEN CL
PO
MERE CL
PARK LA
WELL FIELD CL
PH
Pickmere
Providence Farm
Mast
The Hut
SPINK LA
GREEN LA
Manor Farm
B5391
ORCHARD CL
PEAR TREE DR
THE WOODLANDS
SHELLEY AVE
JOHN FRYER AVE
MILTON CL
KEATS LA
Tabley Grange
Smoker Hill Farm
WA16
CHESTER RD
Leonard's Wood
Waterless Brook
Home Farm
LINNARDS LA
Smoker Brook
Smoker Wood
WHITEHOUSE LA
White H Farm
The Smoker (PH)
Henshaw Green Farm
PLUMLEY MOOR RD
Hopley's Pipes
Peas Wood
Wincham Brook
Halford Farm
Maltkiln Farm
Winnington Wood
Mill Wood
Holford Hall
Peover Eye
OAKFIELD RD 1
HAWTHORN RD 2
YEWTREE RD
HOLLYTREE RD
MOORCROFT
TROUTHALL LA
Lostock Gralam
A559
A556
ASCOL DR
LANGFORD RD
CEDAR CL
HESKETH DR
WARREN AVE
GROVE AVE
TOWNSHEND RD
HIGHFIELD AVE
FRYER RD
GIBBON DR
WILSON CRES
HOLFORD AVE
MANCHESTER RD
CW9
Brookhouse Farm
Musk Fa
Long Wood
A559
SMITHY LA
SCHOOL LA
LODGE LA
STUBBS LA
1 AITCHISON RD
2 BATEMAN RD
Sch
FITTON ST
HERBERT ST
STATION RD
ARTHUR ST
ROBERTS RD
HARRIS RD
PAULDEN RD
ROSETREE MDW
Mast
Reservoir
Lostock Gralam
LOSTOCK HOLLOW
MOSS LA
Holford Moss
Wade Brook
Home Farm
Fieldhouse Farm
BIRCHES LA
Langford Farm
A556

79
105

56
82

A
B
C
A556
M6
Top Willowbed Wood
Tabley House
Blackhill Farm
BEXTON RD
GLOUCESTER RD
MALVERN RD
MEADOW DR
ASHWORTH PK
BLACKHILL LA
Serpentine Water
Bexton Prim Sch
Bexton House
BEXTON LA
Parkgate Farm
SUDLOW LA
Island Wood
Botany Bay Wood
Yewtree Farm
Bexton Hall Farm
Tabley Mere
Black Clump
Royd Wood
Parkside Farm
Bexton Wood
Parkside Cottage
Diamond Farm
Nursery
WA16
Ullardhall Farm
Ash Wood
Wash Farm
Wood's Tenement
Hucknall Farm
PINFOLD LA
Bucklow Farm
Victoria Wood
Plumley
Beech House Farm
PH
Pinfold Farm
Holly Tree Farm
The Grange
Plumleylane Farm
PLUMLEY MOOR RD
Beech Farm
Merry Farm
B5081
MIDDLEWICH RD
Heesom Green Farm
Smithy Green
TROUTHALL LA
Plumley Moor
Moss Farm
Lower Peover Hall
BROOM LA
Fields Farm
CH
Brookfield House
CHEADLE LA
BACK LA
Peover Eye
Lower Peover
CHURCH WLK
BARROW'S BROW
FREE GREEN LA
The Fields Farm
Red Brook
CROWN LA
THE COBBLES
Lower Peover CE Prim Sch
4
77
3
76
2
75
1
74
73

106
82

81
57
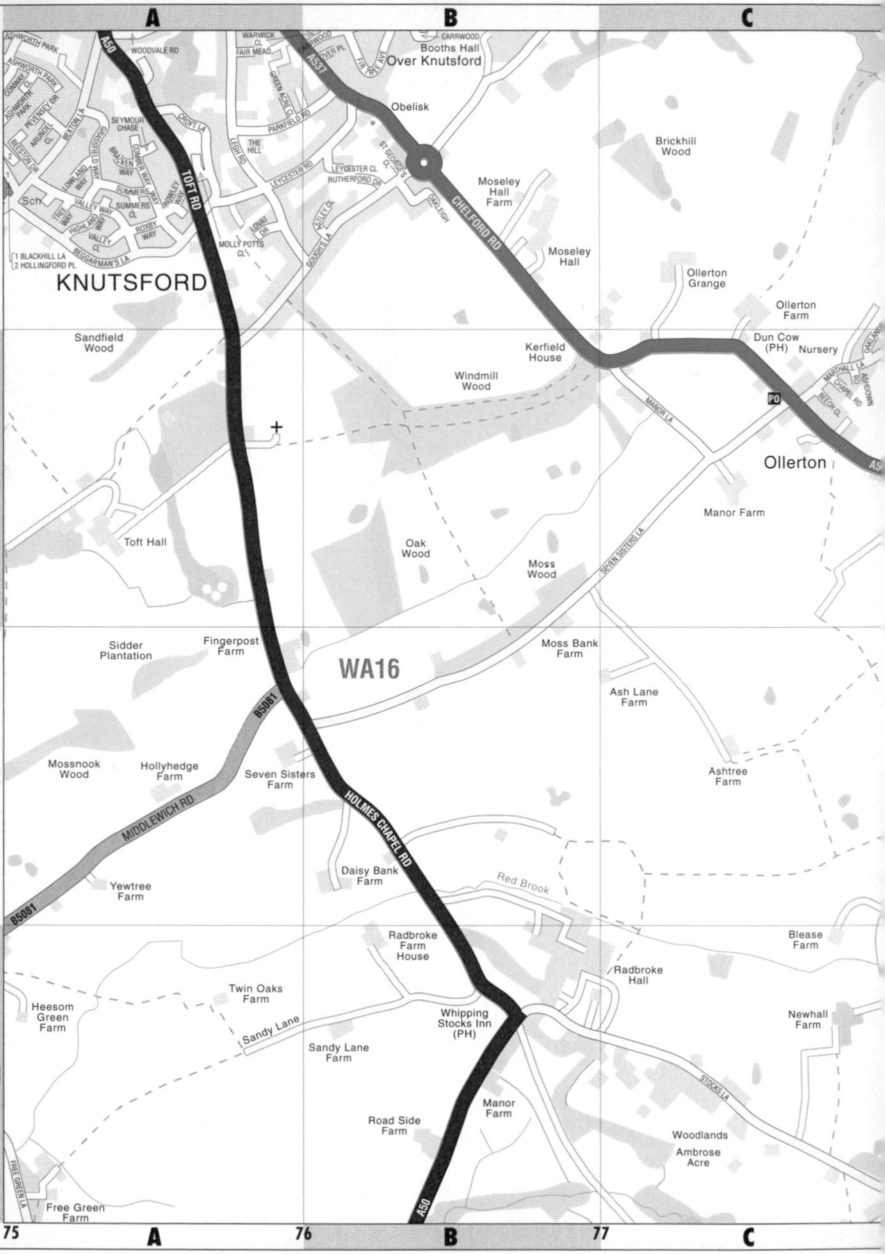
A
B
C
KNUTSFORD
Over Knutsford
Booths Hall
Obelisk
Brickhill Wood
Moseley Hall Farm
Moseley Hall
Ollerton Grange
Ollerton Farm
Dun Cow (PH)
Nursery
Kerfield House
Windmill Wood
Sandfield Wood
Ollerton
Manor Farm
Toft Hall
Oak Wood
Moss Wood
Sidder Plantation
Fingerpost Farm
WA16
Moss Bank Farm
Ash Lane Farm
Mossnook Wood
Hollyhedge Farm
Seven Sisters Farm
Ashtree Farm
Daisy Bank Farm
Yewtree Farm
Red Brook
Radbroke Farm House
Blease Farm
Radbroke Hall
Heesom Green Farm
Twin Oaks Farm
Whipping Stocks Inn (PH)
Newhall Farm
Sandy Lane
Sandy Lane Farm
Manor Farm
Road Side Farm
Woodlands
Ambrose Acre
Free Green Farm
TOFT RD
HOLMES CHAPEL RD
MIDDLEWICH RD
CHELFORD RD
SEVEN SISTERS LA
MANOR LA
STOCKS LA
A50
A537
B5081
1 BLACKHILL LA
2 HOLLINGFORD PL
75
76
77
74
1
2
3
4
81
107

A
B
C
Mountpleasant Farm
Pedley House Farm
PEDLEY HOUSE LA
Firtree Farm
Ryecroft Farm
PEDLEY LA
ANCOATS RD
High Grove Nursing Home
ULLSWATER DR
ENNERDALE CL
DERWENT WAY
BUTTERMERE DR
Oak Wood
MARTHALL LA
Brook Farm
Pedley Brook
SK9
Pinfold Stud
Kell Green Hall
Sandlebridge Farm
SANDLE BRIDGE RISE
MILL LA
David Lewis Sch
Alder Wood
PINFOLD LA
Kell Green Farm
Sandle Bridge
The David Lewis Centre
Baguley Fold
Brookhouse Farm
Marthall Brook
WA16
Sycamore Farm
Beech Farm
SANDLE BRIDGE LA
Holly Tree Farm
Ollerton Hall
CHELFORD RD
Marthall
Oak Farm
SCHOOL LA
Moss Farm
Cragg House Farm
Pear Tree Farm
Sandhole Farm
SANDHOLE LA
OldMoat Hall
PERCIVAL LA
MOSS LA
SNELSON LA
PH
GRANGEWOOD DR
DIXON DR
MIRFE CT
A537
KNUTSFORD RD
Bowden Bank Farm
Mere Hills Farm
Lower Moss Wood
Wr Twr
Greenways
Sunny Bank Farm
SK11
PEPPER ST
Colshaw Hall
CH
Snelson House
COMMON FARM LA
Heath Farm
CHELFORD LA
GREEN LA
MILL LA
COMMON LA
CINDER LA
ver Peover
ourlane-ends
STOCKS LA
Moss Farm
Snelson Covert
4
77
3
76
2
75
1
74
79
80

83
59

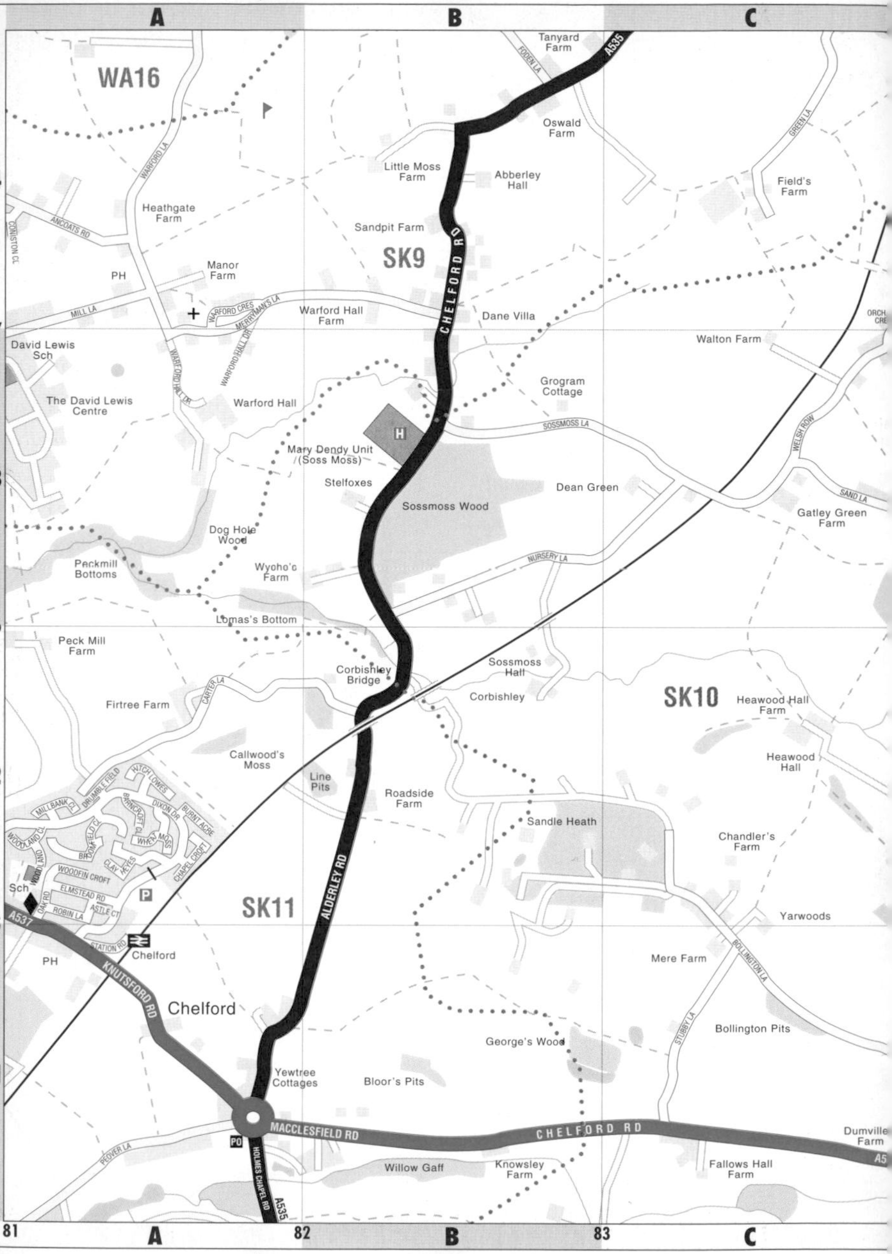
A
B
C
WA16
SK9
SK10
SK11
Tanyard Farm
Oswald Farm
Little Moss Farm
Abberley Hall
Field's Farm
Heathgate Farm
Sandpit Farm
Manor Farm
PH
Warford Hall Farm
Dane Villa
Walton Farm
David Lewis Sch
The David Lewis Centre
Warford Hall
Grogram Cottage
Mary Dendy Unit (Soss Moss)
Stelfoxes
Sossmoss Wood
Dean Green
Gatley Green Farm
Dog Hole Wood
Peckmill Bottoms
Wyoho's Farm
Lomas's Bottom
Peck Mill Farm
Corbishley Bridge
Sossmoss Hall
Corbishley
Heawood Hall Farm
Firtree Farm
Callwood's Moss
Line Pits
Roadside Farm
Heawood Hall
Sandle Heath
Chandler's Farm
Sch
Yarwoods
Chelford
Mere Farm
Bollington Pits
George's Wood
Yewtree Cottages
Bloor's Pits
Willow Gaff
Knowsley Farm
Fallows Hall Farm
Dumville Farm
A535
A537
CHELFORD RD
ALDERLEY RD
KNUTSFORD RD
MACCLESFIELD RD
HOLMES CHAPEL RD
MILL LA
WARFORD LA
ANCOATS RD
CONISTON CL
WARFORD CRES
MERRYMAN'S LA
WARFORD HALL DR
FODEN LA
GREEN LA
SOSSMOSS LA
NURSERY LA
WELSH ROW
SAND LA
CARTER LA
BOLLINGTON LA
STUBBY LA
PEOVER LA
STATION RD
ROBIN LA
ELMSTEAD RD
WOODFIN CROFT
ASTLE CT
CHAPEL CROFT
BURNT ACRE
DIXON DR
WITCH LOWES
DRUMBLE FIELD
MILLBANK CL
WOODLAND CL
PO
P
H
4
77
3
76
2
75
1
74
81
82
83

83
109

60
86

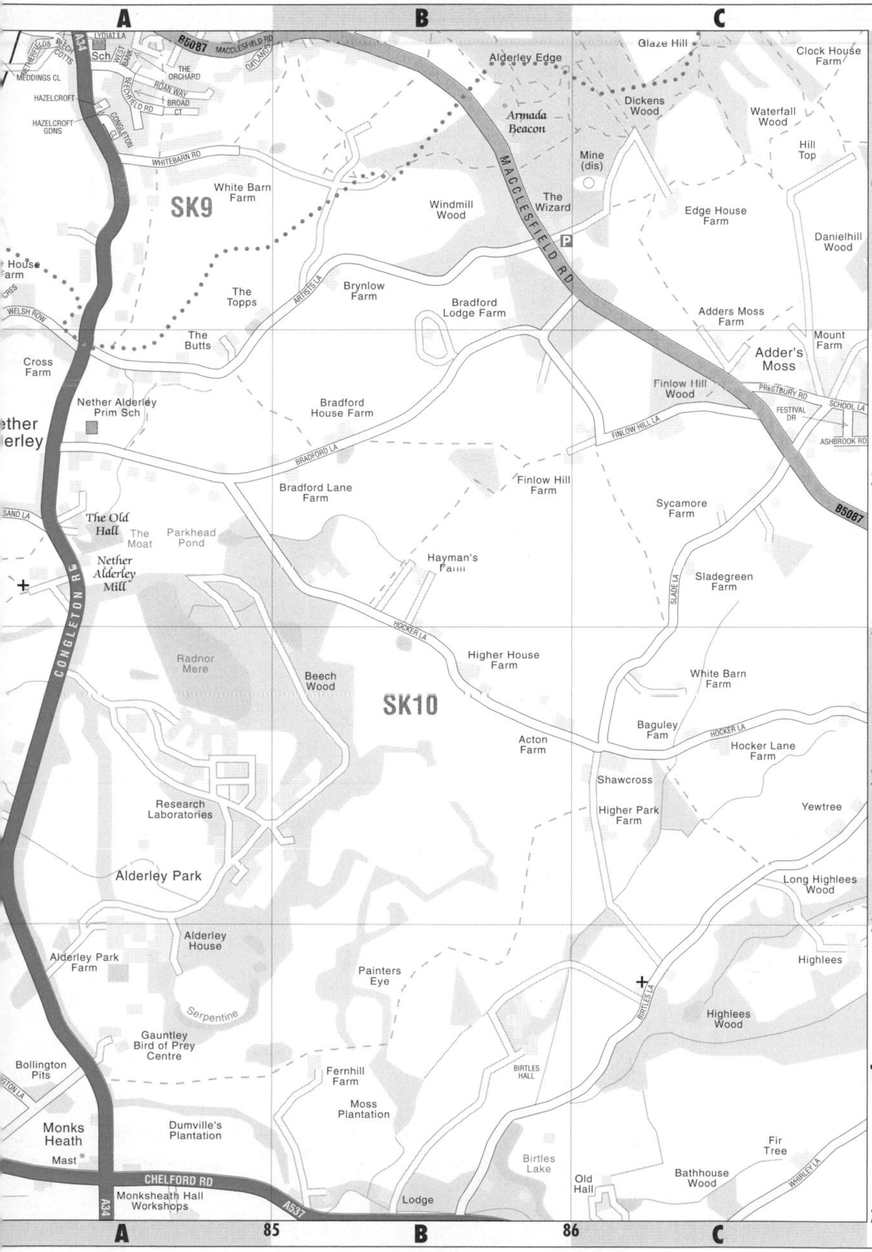
A
B
C
Alderley Edge
Glaze Hill
Clock House Farm
Dickens Wood
Waterfall Wood
Armada Beacon
Hill Top
Mine (dis)
The Wizard
White Barn Farm
SK9
Windmill Wood
Edge House Farm
Danielhill Wood
MACCLESFIELD RD
B5087
WHITEBARN RD
Brynlow Farm
The Topps
Bradford Lodge Farm
Adders Moss Farm
The Butts
Mount Farm
Adder's Moss
Cross Farm
Finlow Hill Wood
PRESTBURY RD
SCHOOL LA
FESTIVAL DR
ASHBROOK RD
Nether Alderley Prim Sch
Bradford House Farm
FINLOW HILL LA
BRADFORD LA
Bradford Lane Farm
Finlow Hill Farm
Sycamore Farm
The Old Hall
The Moat
Parkhead Pond
Hayman's Farm
Nether Alderley Mill
Sladegreen Farm
SLADE LA
HOCKER LA
CONGLETON RD
Radnor Mere
Beech Wood
Higher House Farm
White Barn Farm
SK10
Baguley Fam
Acton Farm
Hocker Lane Farm
Shawcross
Higher Park Farm
Yewtree
Research Laboratories
Alderley Park
Long Highlees Wood
Alderley House
Alderley Park Farm
Highlees
Painters Eye
BIRTLES LA
Serpentine
Highlees Wood
Gauntley Bird of Prey Centre
Bollington Pits
Fernhill Farm
BIRTLES HALL
Moss Plantation
Monks Heath
Dumville's Plantation
Fir Tree
Mast
Birtles Lake
Bathhouse Wood
WHIRLEY LA
CHELFORD RD
Old Hall
Monksheath Hall Workshops
Lodge
A34
A537
LYDIAT LA
Sch
MEDDINGS CL
HAZELCROFT
HAZELCROFT GDNS
THE ORCHARD
ROAN WAY
BROAD CT
BEECHFIELD RD
CONGLETON CL
WEST BANK
OATLANDS
WELSH ROW
SAND LA
ARTISTS LA
House Farm
Nether Alderley
4
77
3
76
2
75
1
74
85
86

110
86

85
61

A B C

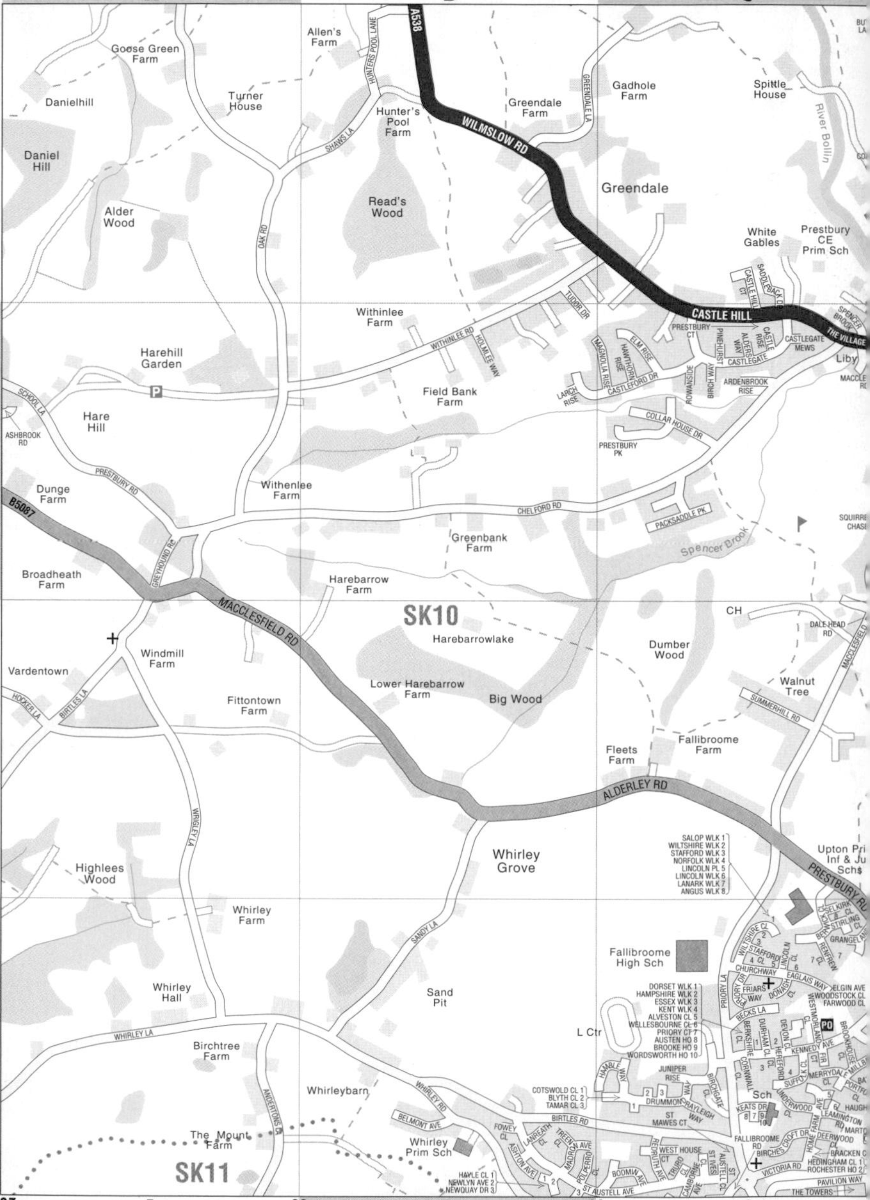
Goose Green Farm
Allen's Farm
HUNTERS POOL LANE
A538
Danielhill
Turner House
Hunter's Pool Farm
SHAWS LA
WILMSLOW RD
Greendale Farm
GREENDALE LA
Gadhole Farm
Spittle House
River Bollin
Daniel Hill
Read's Wood
Greendale
Alder Wood
OAK RD
White Gables
Prestbury CE Prim Sch
CASTLE HILL
SADDLEBACK DR
THE VILLAGE
SPENCER BROOK
TUDOR DR
Withinlee Farm
WITHINLEE RD
HOLMLEE WAY
PRESTBURY CT
MAGNOLIA RISE
ELM RISE
HAWTHORN RISE
ALDERS WAY
PINEHURST
CASTLE RISE
CASTLEGATE MEWS
CASTLEGATE
Liby
Harehill Garden
P
CASTLEFORD DR
ROWANSIDE
BIRCH WAY
ARDENBROOK RISE
LARCH RISE
SCHOOL LA
Field Bank Farm
Hare Hill
ASHBROOK RD
COLLAR HOUSE DR
PRESTBURY PK
PRESTBURY RD
Dunge Farm
Withenlee Farm
B5087
CHELFORD RD
PACKSADDLE PK
SQUIRREL CHASE
Greenbank Farm
GREYHOUND RD
Spencer Brook
Broadheath Farm
Harebarrow Farm
SK10
CH
MACCLESFIELD RD
DALE HEAD RD
Harebarrowlake
Windmill Farm
Vardentown
Dumber Wood
Lower Harebarrow Farm
Walnut Tree
HOCKER LA
BIRTLES LA
Fittontown Farm
Big Wood
SUMMERHILL RD
Fallibroome Farm
Fleets Farm
ALDERLEY RD
WRIGLEY LA
Whirley Grove
SALOP WLK 1
WILTSHIRE WLK 2
STAFFORD WLK 3
NORFOLK WLK 4
LINCOLN PL 5
LINCOLN WLK 6
LANARK WLK 7
ANGUS WLK 8
Upton Pri Inf & Ju Schs
PRESTBURY RD
Highlees Wood
Whirley Farm
SANDY LA
Fallibroome High Sch
Whirley Hall
Sand Pit
DORSET WLK 1
HAMPSHIRE WLK 2
ESSEX WLK 3
KENT WLK 4
ALVESTON CL 5
WELLESBOURNE CL 6
PRIORY CT 7
AUSTEN HO 8
BROOKE HO 9
WORDSWORTH HO 10
PRIORY LA
CHURCHWAY
EAGLAIS WAY
ELGIN AVE
WOODSTOCK CL
FARWOOD CL
BECKS LA
PO
WHIRLEY LA
L Ctr
Birchtree Farm
JUNIPER RISE
KENNEDY AVE
Whirleybarn
COTSWOLD CL 1
BLYTH CL 2
TAMAR CL 3
DRUMMOND WAY
RAYLEIGH WAY
Sch
ANDERTONS LA
WHIRLEY RD
BIRTLES RD
BELMONT AVE
ST MAWES CT
KEATS DR
FALLIBROOME RD
The Mount Farm
Whirley Prim Sch
FOWEY CL
WEST HOUSE CT
TRURO CL
ST IVES CL
AUSTELL CT
VICTORIA RD
SK11
HAYLE CL 1
NEWLYN AVE 2
NEWQUAY DR 3
ASHTON AVE
BODMIN AVE
REDRUTH AVE
ST AUSTELL AVE
PAVILION WAY
THE TOWERS

4
77
3
76
2
75
1
74

87 A 88 B 89 C

85
111

62
88

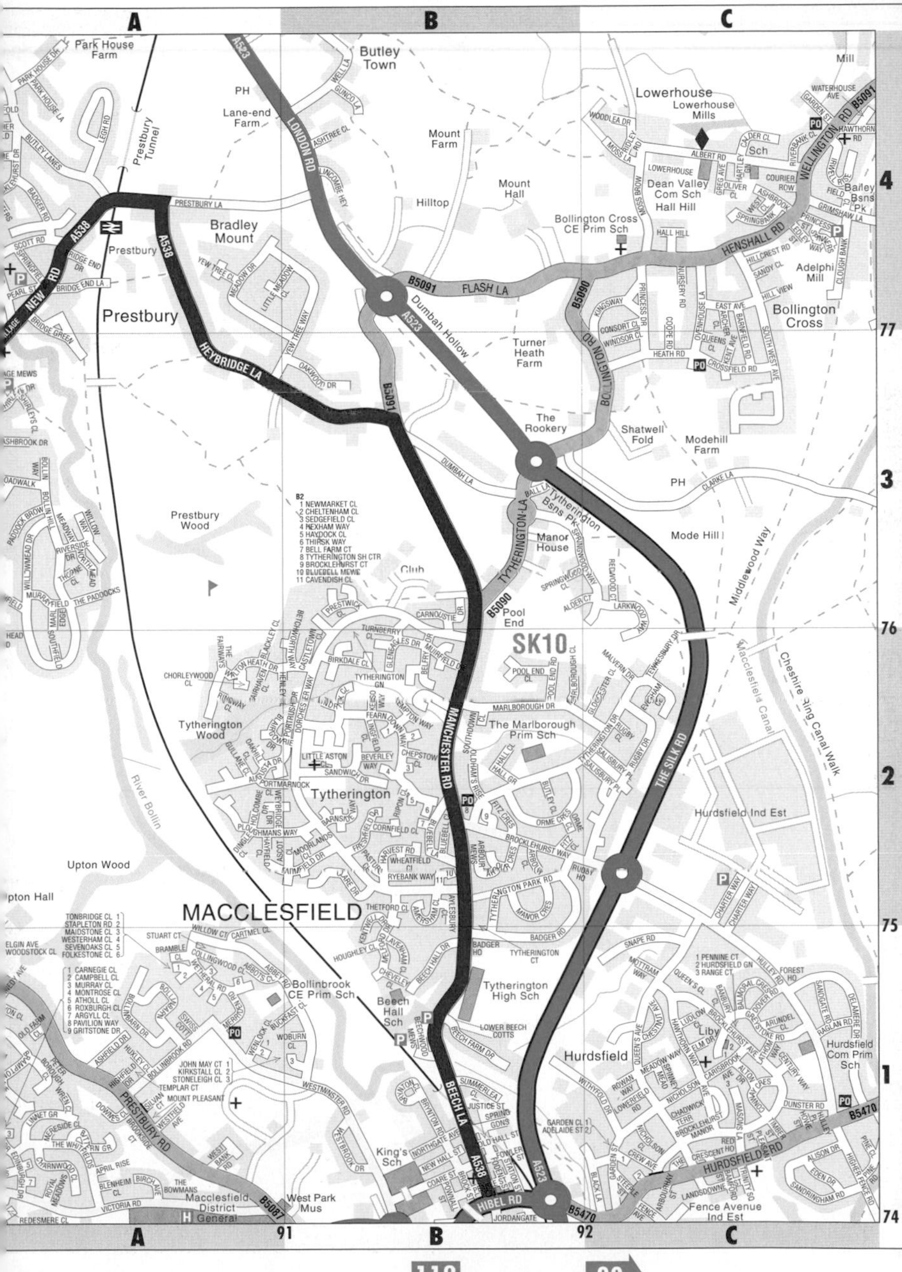
A
B
C
Park House Farm
Butley Town
PH
Lane-end Farm
Prestbury Tunnel
Mount Farm
Lowerhouse
Lowerhouse Mills
Mill
Mount Hall
Hilltop
Dean Valley Com Sch
Hall Hill
Bollington Cross CE Prim Sch
Sch
Bailey Bsns Pk
Bradley Mount
Prestbury
Adelphi Mill
Bollington Cross
Dumbah Hollow
Turner Heath Farm
The Rookery
Shatwell Fold
Modehill Farm
Prestbury Wood
Tytherington Bsns Pk
Manor House
Mode Hill
Middlewood Way
Club
Pool End
SK10
Macclesfield Canal
Cheshire Ring Canal Walk
Tytherington Wood
The Marlborough Prim Sch
Tytherington
River Bollin
Hurdsfield Ind Est
Upton Wood
Upton Hall
MACCLESFIELD
Bollinbrook CE Prim Sch
Beech Hall Sch
Tytherington High Sch
Hurdsfield
Hurdsfield Com Prim Sch
King's Sch
West Park Mus
Macclesfield District General
Fence Avenue Ind Est
Liby
A523
A538
B5091
B5090
B5087
B5470
LONDON RD
FLASH LA
HENSHALL RD
WELLINGTON RD
BOLLINGTON RD
HEYBRIDGE LA
PRESTBURY LA
TYTHERINGTON LA
MANCHESTER RD
THE SILK RD
BEECH LA
PRESTBURY RD
HURDSFIELD RD
HIBEL RD
DUMBAH LA
CLARKE LA
B2
1 NEWMARKET CL
2 CHELTENHAM CL
3 SEDGEFIELD CL
4 HEXHAM WAY
5 HAYDOCK CL
6 THIRSK WAY
7 BELL FARM CT
8 TYTHERINGTON SH CTR
9 BROCKLEHURST CT
10 BLUEBELL MEWS
11 CAVENDISH CL
TONBRIDGE CL 1
STAPLETON RD 2
MAIDSTONE CL 3
WESTERHAM CL 4
SEVENOAKS CL 5
FOLKESTONE CL 6
1 CARNEGIE CL
2 CAMPBELL CL
3 MURRAY CL
4 MONTROSE CL
5 ATHOLL CL
6 ROXBURGH CL
7 ARGYLL CL
8 PAVILION WAY
9 GRITSTONE DR
JOHN MAY CT 1
KIRKSTALL CL 2
STONELEIGH CL 3
1 PENNINE CT
2 HURDSFIELD GN
3 RANGE CT
GARDEN CL 1
ADELAIDE ST 2
4
77
3
76
2
75
1
74
91
92

87
63

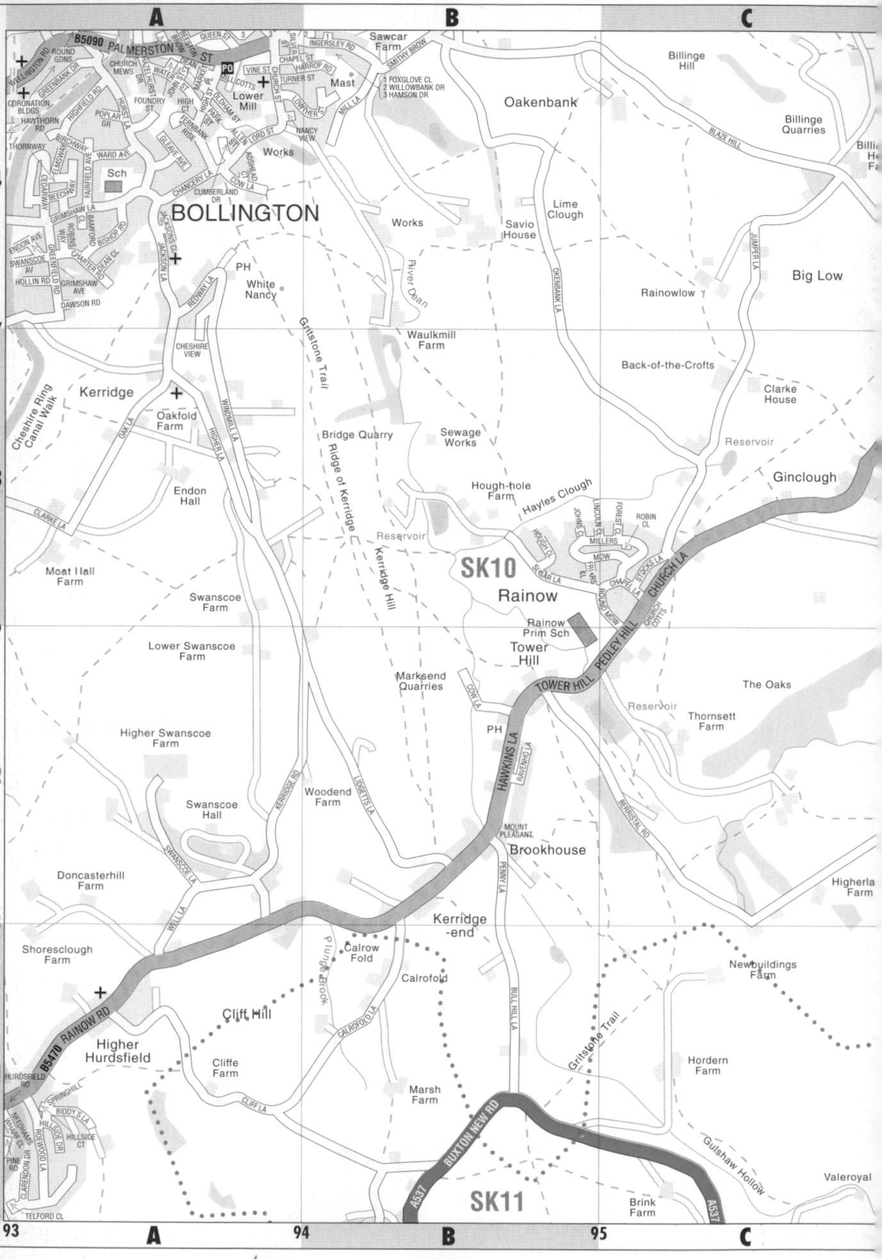
A
B
C
BOLLINGTON
B5090 PALMERSTON ST
Sawcar Farm
SMITHY BROW
Mast
Lower Mill
Works
Sch
PO
1 FOXGLOVE CL
2 WILLOWBANK DR
3 HAMSON DR
Oakenbank
Billinge Hill
Billinge Quarries
BLAZE HILL
Lime Clough
Savio House
OAKENBANK LA
JUMPER LA
Big Low
Rainowlow
River Dean
PH
White Nancy
REDWAY LA
JACKSON LA
Waulkmill Farm
Back-of-the-Crofts
Clarke House
Cheshire Ring Canal Walk
Kerridge
Oakfold Farm
CHESHIRE VIEW
WINDMILL LA
HIGHER LA
OAK LA
Gritstone Trail
Bridge Quarry
Ridge of Kerridge
Sewage Works
Reservoir
Ginclough
Endon Hall
CLARKE LA
Hough-hole Farm
Hayles Clough
Kerridge Hill
SK10
Rainow
Moat Hall Farm
Swanscoe Farm
Rainow Prim Sch
Tower Hill
TOWER HILL
PEDLEY HILL
CHURCH LA
Lower Swanscoe Farm
Marksend Quarries
The Oaks
Thornsett Farm
Higher Swanscoe Farm
HAWKINS LA
Woodend Farm
KERRIDGE RD
LIDGETTS LA
Swanscoe Hall
SWANSCOE LA
MOUNT PLEASANT
Brookhouse
BERRISTAL RD
Doncasterhill Farm
Higherla Farm
WELL LA
PENNY LA
Kerridge -end
Shoresclough Farm
Calrow Fold
Calrofold
Plunge Brook
Newbuildings Farm
B5470 RAINOW RD
Cliff Hill
BULL HILL LA
Higher Hurdsfield
Cliffe Farm
CALROFOLD LA
Hordern Farm
Marsh Farm
CLIFF LA
BUXTON NEW RD
A537
Gulshaw Hollow
Valeroyal
SK11
Brink Farm
TELFORD CL
93
94
95
77
76
75
74
1
2
3
4

87
113

A
B
C
Mellow Brook
New Hey Farm
B5470
Blackbrook Bridge
Summer Close
Hodgel Brook
Dunge Farm
SK23
Dunge Valley Gardens
Moss-side Brook
Hollowcowhey Farm
Withinlow Farm
MACCLESFIELD RD
Moss Brook
Broad Moss
4
PH
Saddle Cote
Green Booth
Paddock Knoll Farm
77
Green Stack
PIKE RD
Pike Low
BANK LA
Wimberry Moss
Cook Hill
Fox Hill
Blue Boar Farm
Jenkin Chapel
Dawson Barn Farm
3
SMITH LA
Jollycock Farm
Todd Brook
Saltersford Hall
EWRIN LA
Buxter Stoops Farm
Waggonshaw Brow
Common Barn
SK10
Howlersknowl
76
Nab End
Yearns Low
Redmoor Brow
Meml
Redmoor
HOOLEYHEY LA
Works
P
2
BERRISTALL RD
King's Clough
Lamaload Reservoir
Andrew's Edge
Ely Brow
75
Brock Low
Wickinford Farm
SK11
1
Higher Ballgreave Farm
ANKERS KNOWL LA
The Laches
74
A
97
B
98
C

89 65
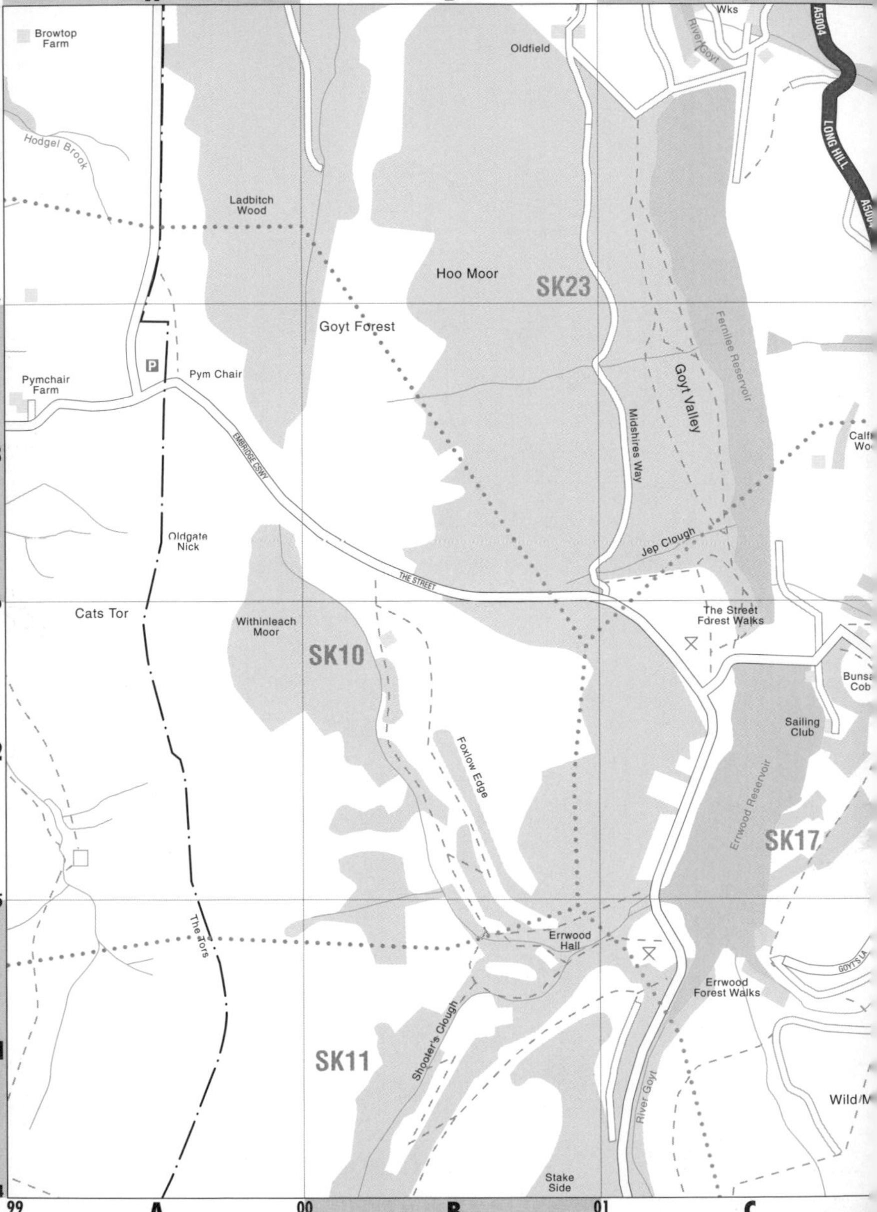
A
B
C
Browtop Farm
Hodgel Brook
Ladbitch Wood
Oldfield
Wks
River Goyt
A5004
LONG HILL
Hoo Moor
SK23
Goyt Forest
Pym Chair
Pymchair Farm
Fernilee Reservoir
Goyt Valley
Midshires Way
EMBRIDGE CSWY
Oldgate Nick
Jep Clough
THE STREET
Cats Tor
Withinleach Moor
SK10
The Street Forest Walks
Bunsa Cob
Sailing Club
Foxlow Edge
Errwood Reservoir
SK17
The Tors
Erring Hall
Errwood Hall
GOYT'S LA
Errwood Forest Walks
Shooter's Clough
SK11
River Goyt
Wild M
Stake Side
4
77
3
76
2
75
1
74
99
00
01
89 115

66
92

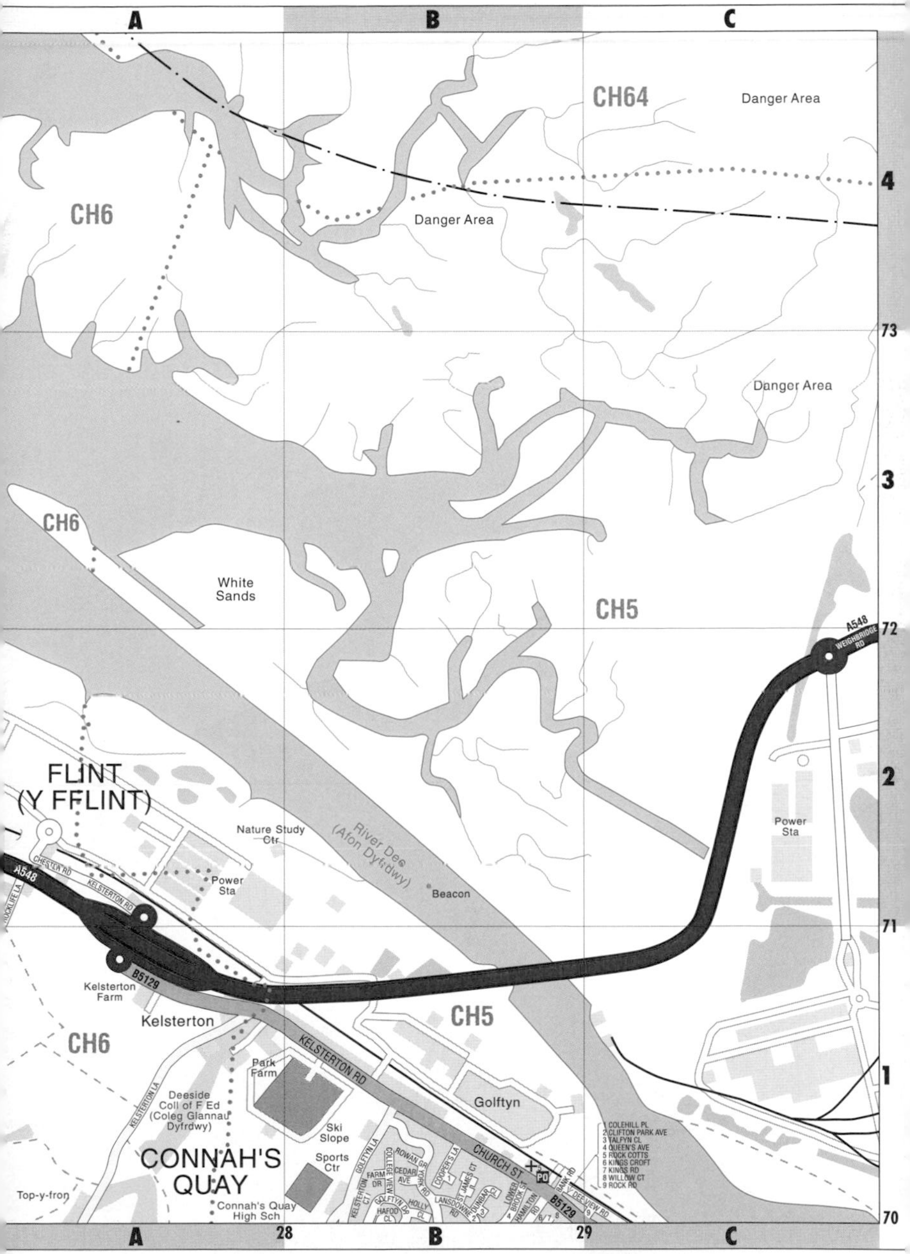

A
B
C
CH64
Danger Area
4
CH6
Danger Area
73
Danger Area
3
CH6
White Sands
CH5
72
A548
WEIGHBRIDGE RD
2
FLINT (Y FFLINT)
Power Sta
Nature Study Ctr
River Dee (Afon Dyfrdwy)
CHESTER RD
A548
KELSTERTON RD
Power Sta
Beacon
71
B5129
Kelsterton Farm
Kelsterton
CH5
CH6
KELSTERTON RD
1
Park Farm
Deeside Coll of F Ed (Coleg Glannau Dyfrdwy)
KELSTERTON LA
Golftyn
Ski Slope
Sports Ctr
CONNAH'S QUAY
Top-y-fron
Connah's Quay High Sch
GOLFTYN LA
COLLEGE VIEW
ROWAN GR
CEDAR AVE
YORK RD
FARM DR
KELSTERTON CT
GOLFTYN DR
HAFOD CL
HOLLY CL
COOPER'S LA
ST JAMES CT
LANSDOWNE RD
DUNBAR CL
CHURCH ST
LOWER BROOK ST
HAMILTON RD
PO
BANK RD
B5129
DEE VIEW RD
1 COLEHILL PL
2 CLIFTON PARK AVE
3 TALFYN CL
4 QUEEN'S AVE
5 ROCK COTTS
6 KINGS CROFT
7 KINGS RD
8 WILLOW CT
9 ROCK RD
70
A
28
B
29
C

92

91
67

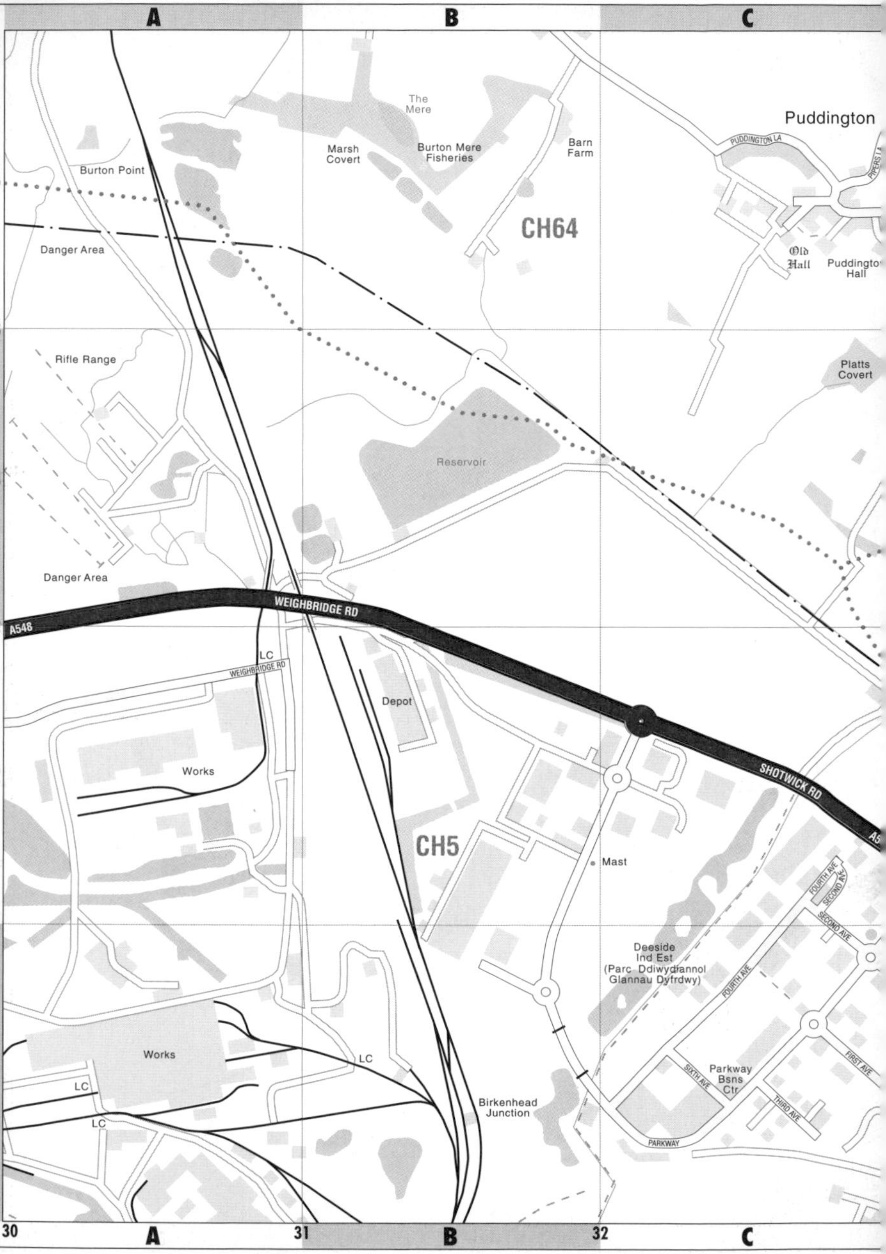
A
B
C
The Mere
Puddington
Marsh Covert
Burton Mere Fisheries
Barn Farm
PUDDINGTON LA
PIPERS LA
Burton Point
4
CH64
Danger Area
Old Hall
Puddington Hall
73
Rifle Range
Platts Covert
3
Reservoir
Danger Area
WEIGHBRIDGE RD
72
A548
LC
WEIGHBRIDGE RD
Depot
2
Works
SHOTWICK RD
CH5
Mast
FOURTH AVE
SECOND AVE
71
SECOND AVE
Deeside Ind Est (Parc Ddiwydiannol Glannau Dyfrdwy)
FOURTH AVE
Works
LC
1
LC
FIRST AVE
SIXTH AVE
Parkway Bsns Ctr
LC
Birkenhead Junction
THIRD AVE
PARKWAY
70
30
31
32

91

68
94

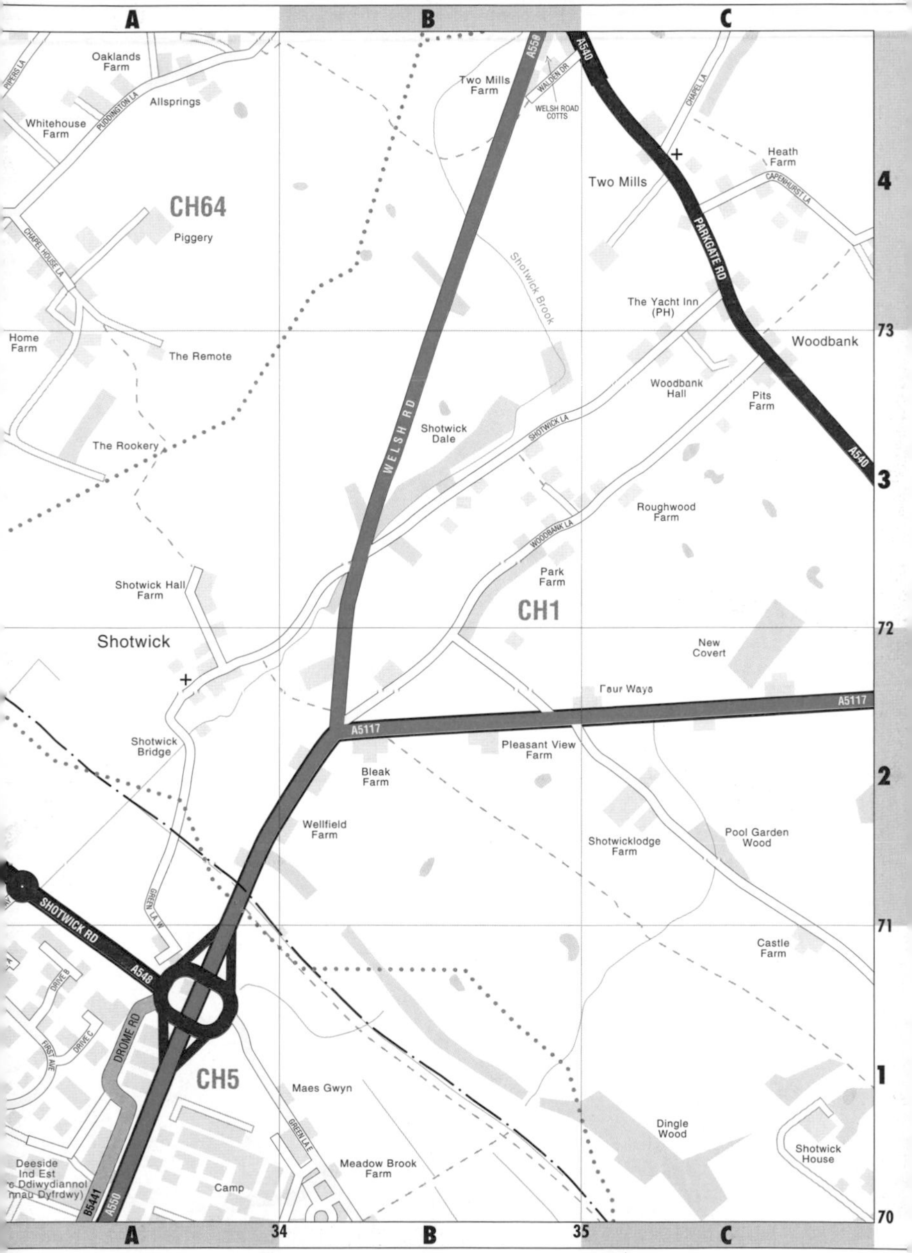
A
B
C
Oaklands Farm
Allsprings
Whitehouse Farm
PIPERS LA
PUDDINGTON LA
CH64
Piggery
CHAPEL HOUSE LA
Home Farm
The Remote
The Rookery
Shotwick Hall Farm
Shotwick
Shotwick Bridge
Two Mills Farm
A550
A540
WALDEN DR
WELSH ROAD COTTS
CHAPEL LA
Heath Farm
Two Mills
CAPENHURST LA
PARKGATE RD
Shotwick Brook
The Yacht Inn (PH)
Woodbank
Woodbank Hall
Pits Farm
WELSH RD
Shotwick Dale
SHOTWICK LA
Roughwood Farm
WOODBANK LA
Park Farm
CH1
New Covert
Four Ways
A5117
Pleasant View Farm
Bleak Farm
Wellfield Farm
Shotwicklodge Farm
Pool Garden Wood
Castle Farm
SHOTWICK RD
A548
GREEN LA W
DRIVE B
DRIVE C
FIRST AVE
DROME RD
CH5
Maes Gwyn
GREEN LA E
Meadow Brook Farm
Dingle Wood
Shotwick House
Deeside Ind Est
Camp
B5441
4
73
3
72
2
71
1
70
34
35

116
94

93
69

A
B
C
4
73
3
72
2
71
1
70
36
37
38
Capenhurst
Capenhurst CE Prim Sch
MANOR FARM CRES
RECTORY LA
CAPENHURST LA
PENFOLD CL
New Houses
Lower Brook Farm
DUNKIRK LA
Old Hall Farm
Big Wood
CH66
LAURELWOOD DR
BAKEWELL CL
ASHBOURNE CL
CANNOCK CL
LICHFIELD DR
ST ASAPH RD
OXFORD CL
CARDIFF CL
NORWICH DR
HOURD WAY
HEREFORD AVE
COVENTRY AVE
TEWKESBURY CL
CHESTER RD
A41
KEATS CL
LINDEN CL
VINE RD
HONEY SUCKLE CL
BRAMLEY CL
HOLM OAK WAY
APPLE TREE GR
LAMBOURNE CL
TUDOR CL
NORMAN CL
LAXTON CL
ARCHDALE CL
MELROSE DR
LINKSIDE WAY
WILLOWDALE WAY
MARKS CRES
PLOUGHMANS CL 1
THE FURROWS 2
PLOUGHMANS WAY 3
BADGERS CL 4
CANTERBURY CL 5
GLOUCESTER CL 6
SALISBURY CL 7
BANGOR CL 8
WELLS CL 9
SAXON WAY 10
WEST PARK DR 11
GREEN LAWNS DR 12
PARLIAMENT WAY 13
ST GEORGES AVE 14
ST DAVIDS DR 15
ROSEMERE DR 16
KINNINGTON WAY 17
BACKFORD GDNS 18
PETERBOROUGH CL 19
TRURO CL 20
LIVERPOOL
Acres Farm
Dunkirk Farm
Manor Farm
Dunkirk
Coalpit Lane
Depot
CHESTER GATES
A5117
M56
Acres Wood
A540
Ashcroft Farm
Gibbet Mill
Rendova Farm
POWEY LA
Lea Manor Farm
STRAWBERRY LA
Gebe Farm
Wood Farm
DEMAGE LA
GROVE RD
A5117
Saughall Nurseries
Hill Farm
COALPIT LA
CH1
Big Wood
PARKGATE RD
Nursery
Grove Farm
STATION RD
TOWNFIELD LA
LONG LA
Green Farm
Parkgate House
St Oswald's CE Prim Sch
PO
The Willows
Mollington
Warren Farm
LODGE LA
PARK AVE
PARK WAY
FIELDWAY
NEWCROFT
KINGSTON CT
MEADOWCROFT
The Thomas Wedge CE Jun Sch
PO
CHURCH RD
GREEN WAY
SAUGHALL HEY
Astbury House
FIDDLERS LA
Parkside Farm
MOLLINGTON CT
WILLOW LEA
WELL LA
FEILDEN CT
Wheatsheaf (PH)
KINGSWOOD AVE
OVERWOOD LA
MEADOW CT
Saughall
ALDERSEY CL
DARLINGTON CRES
ANVIL CL
RAKE WAY
The Ridings Com Inf Sch
THE CLOSE
FAIRHOLME CL
THE RIDINGS
SMITHY CL
CHAPEL CL
ROSEWOOD GR
KINGSWOOD LA
OVERWOOD AVE
HOME PARK
TARRANT CT
A540

93
117

70
96

A
B
C
Stanley Woods Country Park
THE GROVES
LABURNUM GR
STRAWBERRY DR
STRAWBERRY GN
CHESTER RD
A5032
ELM GR
LILAC GR
MAPLE GR
BEECH GR
PH
1 STAFFIN AVE
2 HANDA DR
3 SARK AVE
LUNDY RD
4 PUFFIN CL
5 BARRY CL
6 STANLEY WOODS AVE
7 FARNE CL
8 CUMBRIA DR
9 LEWIS CL
A5117
M53
LITTLE STANNEY LA
Rake Hall (PH)
Sunnydale
CH65
Strawberry Farm
1 APPLEDALE DR
2 PINEDALE CL
3 CONIFER CL
4 LIME TREE CL
4
HEATH LA
Rosscroft
Poplarhall
Heath Wood
WHITBY LA
11
M56
73
The Laurels
Mount Farm
RAKE LA
Axes Farm
Grove Farm
The Dungeon
CROUGHTON RD
WERVIN RD
3
Fairfield House Farm
Croughton
Top Farm
Croughton Cottage
CH2
Chorltonlodge Farm
GORDON LA
72
THE CHANNEL
CH1
CHURCH LA
Chorlton Hall
Backford Hall
LIVERPOOL RD
Backford
Backford Brook
Rockbank
LEA HALL PK
Lea Hall Farm
DEMAGE LA
2
Lea Hall
STATION RD
Collinge Farm
Friars Park
Croughall Bridge
Collinge Wood
Shropshire Union Canal
71
Towing Path
CAUGHALL RD
BADGERS WLK
Caughall Manor
Moston Hall
Butter Hill
Moston Hill Farm
Viaduct Wood
Moston
MALTA RD
1 CROOKENDEN CL
2 SIMPSON CL
3 BRODIE CL
1
WERVIN RD
NORMANDY RD
The Dale
P&R
Chester Zoological Gardens
ALAMEIN RD
PROSSER RD
A5116
MOSTON RD
A41
SALERNO RD
CROOKENDEN RD
SIMPSON RD
CHARLES RD
4 DAUNCEY CL
5 HARINGTON CL
6 HARINGTON RD
FLAG LA N
GREENACRES
ACRES LA
70
40
41

118
96

95
71

A
B
C
4
3
2
1
73
72
71
70
42
43
44
Stoak Grange
Shropshire Union Canal
LITTLE STANNEY LA
PH
CHURCH LA
Stoak
Densions's Bridge
HEATH LA
CROUGHTON RD
BUNBURY CL
Stoke Bridge
M56
15
M53
Ashwood House
Ash Wood
ASHWOOD LA
Wervin
Wervin New Hall
WERVIN RD
Woodside Farm
Ashton House
FOX COVERT LA
ACRES LA
CH2
PICTON LA
Picton
Hill Far
GREEN LA
Picton Hall
Green La
Ash Hey Farm
ASH HAY LA
New House Farm
Mill Brook
River Gowy
Sewage Works
Cryers Farm
THORNTON GREEN LA
Thornton Green Farm
CRYERS
Spring Farm
HALLSGREEN LA
HOB LA
Heath Farm
Wimbolds Trafford
INCE LA
Hall Farm
Park Farm
Landfill Site
MASSALS LA
PH
Trafford Bridge
Shrewsbury Arms Hotel (PH)
WARRINGTON RD
Saw Mill
1 HURLESTONE CL
2 WEAVER GR
3 DANE GR
4 ALYN RD
5 WOODLAND BANK
6 ST PETERS WAY
7 ST ANDREWS WLK
YORK DR
DEE RD
GOWY RD
A56
GLEBE MDWS
PLEMSTALL

95
119

72
98

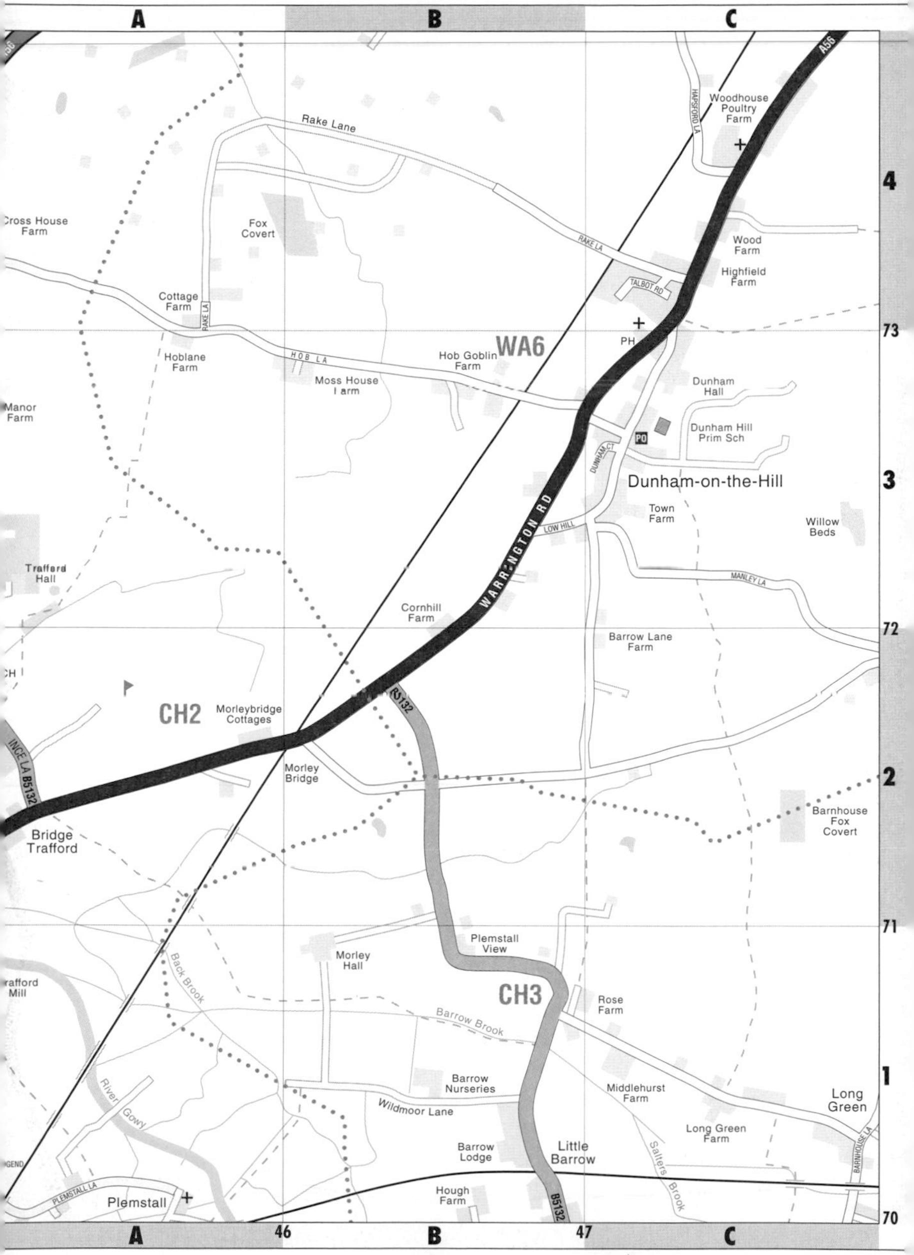
A
B
C
Woodhouse Poultry Farm
HAPSFORD LA
A56
Rake Lane
Cross House Farm
Fox Covert
RAKE LA
Wood Farm
Highfield Farm
TALBOT RD
Cottage Farm
RAKE LA
PH
WA6
Hoblane Farm
HOB LA
Hob Goblin Farm
Moss House Farm
Dunham Hall
Manor Farm
PO
Dunham Hill Prim Sch
DUNHAM CT
Dunham-on-the-Hill
Town Farm
Willow Beds
LOW HILL
WARRINGTON RD
Trafford Hall
MANLEY LA
Cornhill Farm
Barrow Lane Farm
CH2
Morleybridge Cottages
B5132
INCE LA B5132
Morley Bridge
Barnhouse Fox Covert
Bridge Trafford
Plemstall View
Morley Hall
Back Brook
Trafford Mill
CH3
Rose Farm
Barrow Brook
Barrow Nurseries
Middlehurst Farm
Long Green
River Gowy
Wildmoor Lane
Long Green Farm
Barrow Lodge
Little Barrow
Salters Brook
BARNHOUSE LA
PLEMSTALL LA
Plemstall
Hough Farm
B5132
4
73
3
72
2
71
1
70
46
47

120
98

97
73

A
B
C
4
3
2
1
73
72
71
70
48
49
50
Church-house Farm
B5393
Alvanley Hall
MANLEY RD
CH
Greengate Farm
The Green
TOWERS LA
PECK MILL LA
Peck Mill Farm
Crabtree Farm
Moor's Brook
Abbot's Clough Farm
Manley Old Hall
WA6
Windsurfing Ctr
Lowerhall Farm
Lower Farm
(dis)
Rose Farm
COB HALL LA
SUGAR LA
MANLEY LA
New House Farm
Manor Farm
Manley
Manley Hall
Dunham Heath
Manley House Farm
MOSS LA
MOSS DR
Siddall's Hill
CHAPEL LA
Rookery Farm
Peckmill Brook
Grange Farm
Swinford House
WELL LA
BARNHOUSE LA
Barnhouse Farm
NORTON'S LA
SMITHY LA
Mouldsworth Hall
Mouldsworth
CH3
Poplargrove Farm
Stone House Farm
Long Wood
Mouldsworth Motor Mus
GONGAR LA
The Rookery
Ashton Brook
CHURCH RD

97
121

74
100

A
B
C
Kingswood House
Maiden's Cross
Birch Hill
Birchdale Farm
Waterloo Farm
Waterloo
Hollins Farm
Castle Cob
Claim Farm
Kingswood Hall
Crossley Hospl East (dis)
Eddisbury Way
Delamere Way
Waterloo Gate
Simmond's Hill
Kingswood Cottage
New Pale Lodge
Handslough Farm
WA6
New Pale
Manley Knoll
Manley Village Sch
Buckoak
Intake
Ravelstone
The New Pale
Manley Common
Sandstone Trail
Rangeway Bank Farm
Delamere Forest Park
Ashton Brook
Ark Wood
Spy Hill
Battleaxe Rd
Mouldsworth
Brine's Brow
Spy Hill Farm
PH
Woodside
CH3
CW6
Ashton Brook Bridge
Baker Way
Forest Farm
Grey's Gate
CW8
The Grange
Eddisbury Farm
Lily Wood
Home Farm
BUSHELLS LA
BIRCH HILL
CROSSLEY PK
NEW COTTS
WATERLOO LA
NEW PALE RD
MANLEY RD
SCHOOL LA
PINGOT LA
MOSS LA
TARVIN RD
ASHTON RD
DARK ARK LA
STABLE LA
STATION RD
DELAMERE LA
GRANGE RD
CHURCH RD
YELD LA
4
73
3
72
2
71
1
70
52
53

122
100

99
75

A
B
C
B5152
GUESTS SLACK
TOP RD
Millfield Farm
Commonside
Beech Farm
Big Wood
CW8
Crofton Lodge
Dodsley Hall Farm
BEECH LA
Leigh Cottage
The Gorse
Foresthouse Farm
THE NURSERY
The Paddocks
Town Farm
New Pastures
NORLEY RD
TOWN FARM LA
Forestgate
Brownmoss Farm
Greenslade Farm
Norley Hall
FOREST LA
Forestgate Farm
Forestgate Farm
DELAMERE RD
NORLEY LA
WA6
HAMBLETTS HOLLOW
Pinewood Farm
Moy Park Farm
CRABMILL LA
THE SPINNEY
HIGH ST
Norley
MADDOCKS
Flaxmere
SCHOOL LA
POST OFFICE LA
Norley CE Prim Sch
Hatch Mere
PH
Low Farm
ASHTON RD
Hatchmere
Delamere Forest Sch
BLAKEMERE LA
GALLOWSCLOUGH LA
Forest Trail
Hunger Hill
Delamere Forest Inn (PH)
Harthill Bank
Barnsbridge Gates
Hart Hill
Sandstone Trail
Claims Farm
Blakemere Moss
Delamere Forest Park
Windyhowe Farm
Fir Brook
Linmere Moss
Delamere Way
Delamere Forest Visitor Ctr
Forest Trail
CW8
Eddisbury Lodge
Delamere
Station Cottages
B5152 STATION RD
Relicks Moss
CH
Burnt Wood
Sandstone Trail
Eddisbury Lodge Cottages
Works
4
73
3
72
2
71
1
70
54
55
56

76
102

A
B
C
A
58
B
59
C
4
73
3
72
2
71
1
70
Primrose Farm
Hollies Farm
Holly Bush Farm
Stanneybrook Farm
Vixen Cottage
Pingard's Lane
MARSH LA
SANDHOLE LA
PINGARD'S LA
BENT LA
Small Brook
Delamere Way
ONSTON LA
Willow Wood Farm
Barncroft Farm
SWAN CT
Cuddington Brook
Rydal Farm
BAG LA
Ruloe
Brook House
The Riddings
BARRASTITCH LA
Sewage Works
GORSE CL
STANNEYBROOK CL
SCHOOL BANK
BAG LA
WEST VIEW RD
WA6
DUTTON LA
BURGESS LA
Bratt's Bank
MOSS LA
Moss Farm
Delamere Way
Bratt's Lane
COW LA
Beechwood Farm
Camomile Lane
WOOD'S LA
The Home Farm
Delamere Park
Hunt's Hill Wood
Cuddington Hall Farm
CUDDINGTON LA
THE SPINNEY
THE CHINES
ORCHARD DENE
YEWLANDS
THE ASPENS
WESTREES
THE COPPICE
BADGERS SET
THE BURROWS
DELAMERE PARK WAY E
THE WARREN
LAWNS
FAWNS LEAP
COPPER WOOD
PARK WAY
THE STILES
DINGLE WAY
DENEHURST
FOXES HEY
PADDOCK WLK
THE DELL
THE DOWNS
DELAMERE PARK WAY W
CEDARWOOD
HOLLOW OAK LA
UPLANDS
THREEWAYS
CW8
Poplar Farm
Baycliffe
Cuddington
THE COBBLES 1
CUSEL NEST 2
SPRINGFIELDS
RAVENSFIELD
Royalty Covert
Camomile Farm
Foxey Hill
Ravenhead
CUDDINGTON LA
NORLEY RD
THE OLD ORCHARD
WARRINGTON RD
MILL LA
PARK CRES
PRIMROSE HILL
WINDSOR CL
MILLGATE
A49
Small Brook
CHEESE HILL LA
Wr Twr
Manor Farm
WASTE LA
BROOKSIDE
BRIDGE LA
MOSS LA
VALLEY LA
Beechfield
Newpool Farm
Gallowsclough Farm
GALLOWSCLOUGH LA
Delamere Manor
Ravensclough
FORGE CL
WEST LA
NIXON RD
MOSS LA
wsclough Hill
Forest View Inn (PH)
Manor Pool
Cuddington Brook
POPLAR CL
FOREST RD
CHERRY LA
GRANGE RD
MAPLE LA
MANOR RD
BOUNDARY LA N
BOUNDARY LA S
ACORN CL
OAK LA
ASH RD
LC
Whitegate Way
STONEYFORD LA
CRABTREE GREEN CT
Crabtreegreen Farm Ho
THE COURTYARD
CHESTNUT CL 1
BEECH CL 2
Golden Nook
Cuddington Prim Sch
Hornby's Rough
ABBOTSMERE CL 1
WHARBURTON CL 2
SANDWGTON DR
Lobslack Wood
OAKMERE HALL
A556
Crabtree Green
Delamere Nursery
Lob Slack
Craft Ctr
CHESTER RD
A49 TARPORLEY RD
Blakemere Hall Farm
Hole
Quarry
OVERDALE LA
A556
HOGSHEAD LA
Barry's Wood

124
102

101
77

101
125

A
B
C
NORTHWICH
(CONDATE)
Works
Moss Farm
Recn Ctr
Winnington Park
Com Prim Sch
Greenbank
Back
Wood
Weaverham
Grange
Hartfordbeach
CW8
Mid-Cheshire
Coll
Hartford
High Sch
Hartford
Campus
Hartford
Hartford Manor
Com Prim Sch
St Nicholas
RC High Sch
Greenbank
Residential
Sch
St Wilfrid's
RC Prim Sch
Marshall's
Arm
(Nature Reserve)
Cloughwood
Sch
The
Grange
Sch
Hartford
Prim Sch
Hotel
Poor's
Wood
Hartford
Bridge
Model
Farm
The Riddings
Hey's Wood
Eaton Hall
Farm
Valeroyal
Locks
Valeroyal
Park
Eaton
House
Farm
Davenham
CE Prim Sch
Greenlane
Farm
CW9
Dairy
Farm
Victoria
Mkt
Hall
Riverside
Trad
Est
Duttons
Bsns Ctr
Mus
Northwich
Salt Mus
Viaduct
Hunt's
Locks
Mid
Cheshire
Coll
Sir John
Deane's
Coll
Weaver Navigation
River Weaver
KINGSMEAD
LONDON RD
CHESTER RD
BEACH RD
CASTLE ST
MOSS RD
CHESTER WAY
WATLING ST
B5153
B5374
B5337
A559
A533
A556
4
3
2
1
73
72
71
70
64
65

C2
1 BICKERTON WAY
2 MOULDSWORTH CL
3 CHURTON CL
4 KNIGHTSBRIDGE AVE
5 BRIDGEMERE WAY
6 LITTLETON CL
7 PICTON CL
8 DUDDON CL
9 STYAL CL
10 HATHERTON CL
11 LAVISTER CL
12 ROWTON CL
13 PRESTBURY CL
14 HOUGHTON CL
15 CLAREMONT CL

A4
1 JOHN ST
2 CRUM HILL
3 MEADOW ST
4 WESLEY PL
5 ST HELEN'S RD
6 ALVINGHAM CL
7 KELSTERN CL
8 BIRKDALE CT
9 SLADE ST
10 WILLIAM ST
11 SIDDALL ST
12 SALKELD ST

103
79

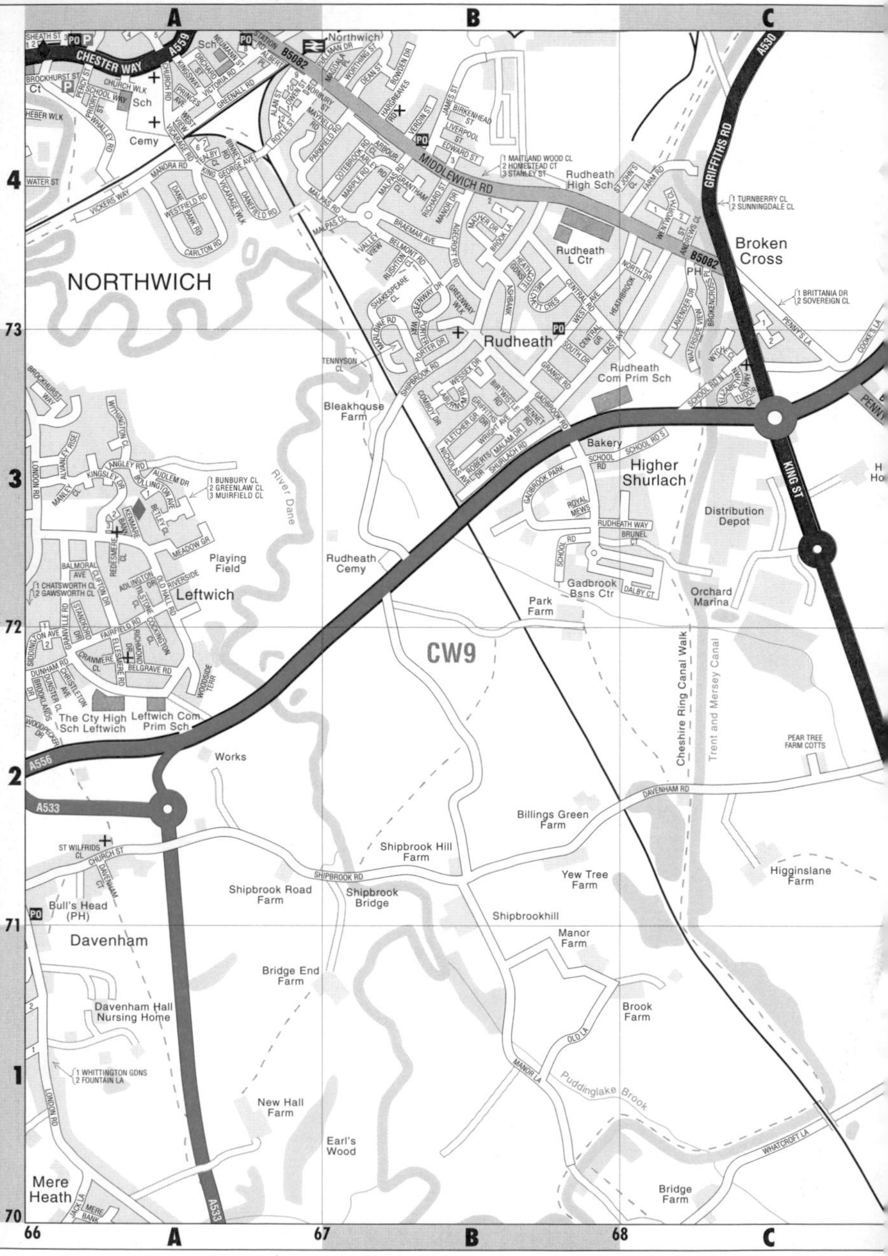

80
106

A
B
C
Lostock Green
Ridge Farm
Moss Side Farm
Mosslane Farm
Park Farm
Cape of Good Hope Farm
WA16
Crow Brook
Hulse Heath Farm
Hulse Farm
Portford Farm
Hulse House Farm
Melvin Holme
Birches Hall
CW9
Heath Farm
Ashbrook Farm
Yew Tree Farm
Lach Dennis
Snig Hall
Duke of Portland (PH)
New Hall Farm
Fir Tree Farm
Marsh Farm
WA16
Kingstreet Farm
Boundary Farm
Newall Farm
Stublach Grange
CW10
Drakelow Farm
Stublach Dairy Farm
Drakelow Hall Farm
Puddington Brook
BIRCHES LA
A556
GREENSIDE DR
VILLAGE CL
CINDER LA
BIRCH GR
MOSS LA
HANGMAN'S LA
HULSE LA
HULME LA
PATMOS LA
COMMON LA
PENNY'S LA
HOLMES CHAPEL RD
B5082
GREENSIDE CT
CROWDER'S LA
KING ST
A530
DRAKELOW LA
4
73
3
72
2
71
1
70
70
71

128
106

105
81

105
129

82
108

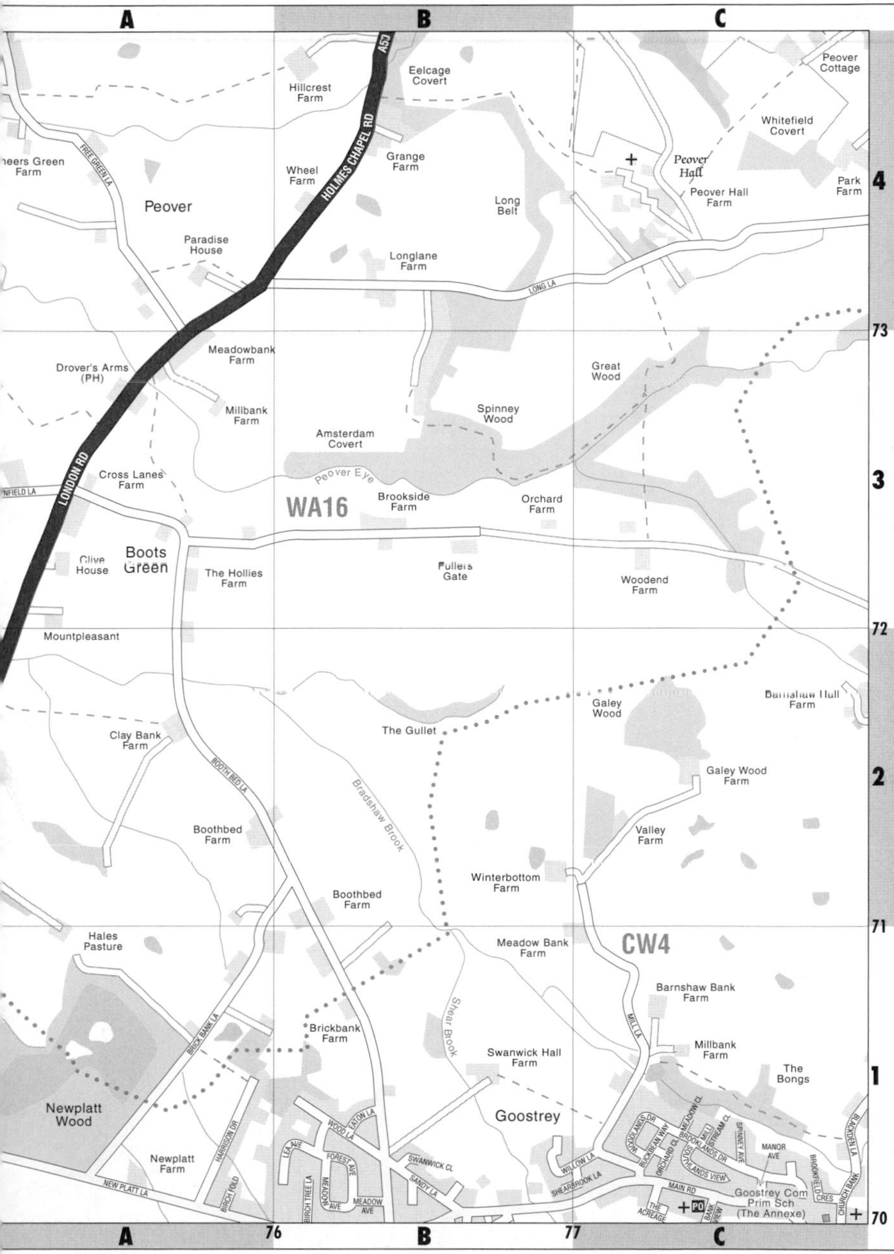
A
B
C
4
3
2
1
73
72
71
70
76
77
A5034
HOLMES CHAPEL RD
LONDON RD
Eelcage Covert
Hillcrest Farm
Peover Cottage
Whitefield Covert
Grange Farm
Wheel Farm
Peover Hall
Peover Hall Farm
Park Farm
Long Belt
FREE GREEN LA
Peover
Paradise House
Longlane Farm
LONG LA
Meadowbank Farm
Drover's Arms (PH)
Millbank Farm
Great Wood
Spinney Wood
Amsterdam Covert
Cross Lanes Farm
Peover Eye
WA16
Brookside Farm
Orchard Farm
Boots Green
Clive House
The Hollies Farm
Fullers Gate
Woodend Farm
Mountpleasant
Galey Wood
Barnshaw Hall Farm
The Gullet
Clay Bank Farm
BOOTH BED LA
Bradshaw Brook
Galey Wood Farm
Boothbed Farm
Valley Farm
Winterbottom Farm
Boothbed Farm
Hales Pasture
Meadow Bank Farm
CW4
Barnshaw Bank Farm
Shear Brook
MILL LA
BRICK BANK LA
Brickbank Farm
Swanwick Hall Farm
Millbank Farm
The Bongs
Newplatt Wood
HARRISON DR
Goostrey
Newplatt Farm
NEW PLATT LA
BIRCH FOLD
BIRCH TREE LA
LEA AVE
WOOD LA
EATON LA
FOREST AVE
MEADOW AVE
MEADOW AVE
SWANWICK CL
SANDY LA
WILLOW LA
SHEARBROOK LA
WOODLANDS DR
BUCKBEAN WAY
ORCHARD CL
MEADOW CL
BROOKLANDS DR
MILL STREAM CL
SPINNEY AVE
SOUTHLANDS VIEW
MANOR AVE
MAIN RD
THE ACREAGE
BANK VIEW
Goostrey Com Prim Sch (The Annexe)
BROOKFIELD CRES
BLACKDEN LA
CHURCH BANK
PO

130
108

107
83

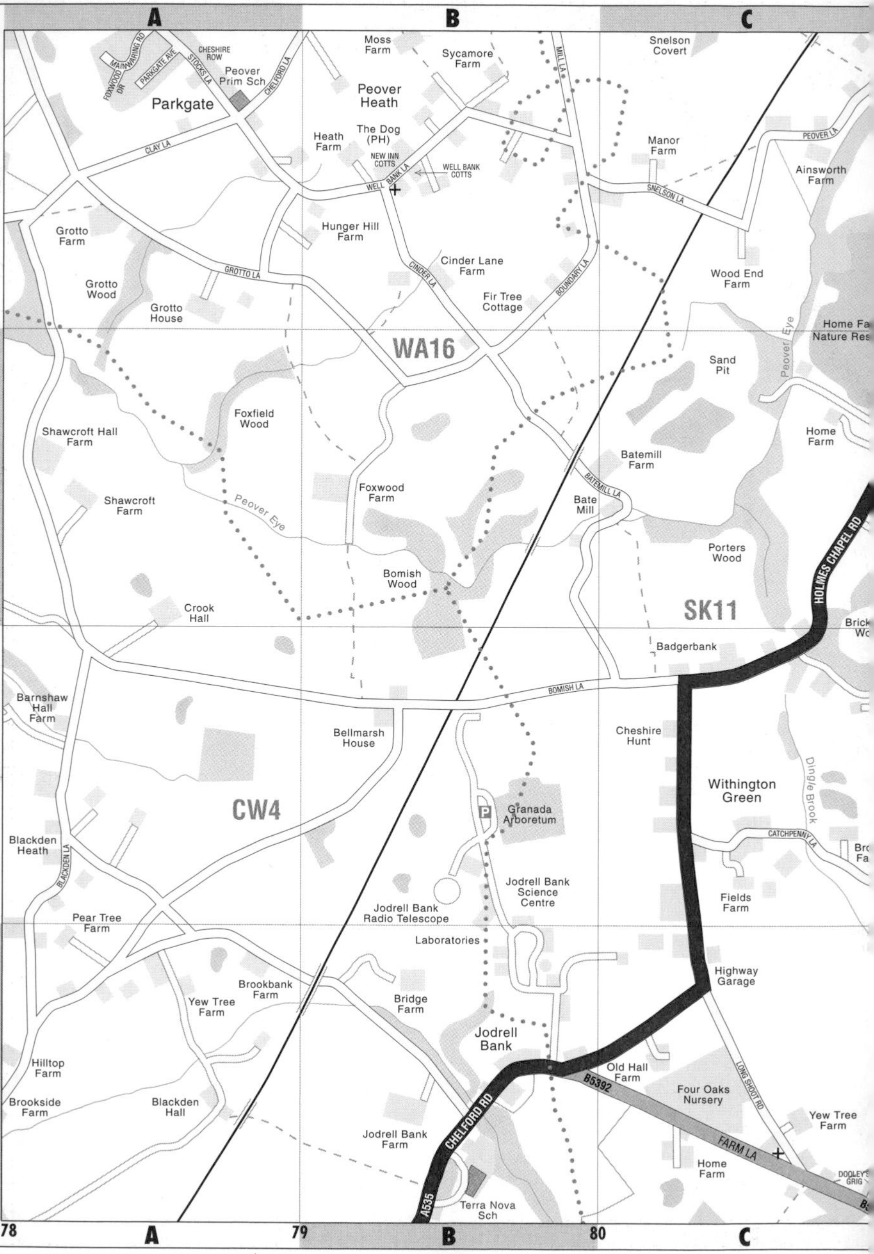
A
B
C
4
3
2
1
73
72
71
70
78
79
80
Moss Farm
Sycamore Farm
Snelson Covert
MILL LA
CHESHIRE ROW
Peover Prim Sch
CHELFORD LA
STOCKS LA
PARKGATE AVE
MAINWARING RD
FOXWOOD DR
Parkgate
Peover Heath
CLAY LA
Heath Farm
The Dog (PH)
NEW INN COTTS
WELL BANK COTTS
WELL BANK LA
Manor Farm
PEOVER LA
Ainsworth Farm
SNELSON LA
Grotto Farm
Hunger Hill Farm
Cinder Lane Farm
CINDER LA
BOUNDARY LA
Wood End Farm
Grotto Wood
GROTTO LA
Grotto House
Fir Tree Cottage
Home Fa
Nature Res
WA16
Sand Pit
Peover Eye
Foxfield Wood
Shawcroft Hall Farm
Home Farm
Batemill Farm
BATEMILL LA
Foxwood Farm
Bate Mill
Shawcroft Farm
Peover Eye
HOLMES CHAPEL RD
Porters Wood
Bomish Wood
Crook Hall
SK11
Brick
Badgerbank
BOMISH LA
Barnshaw Hall Farm
Bellmarsh House
Cheshire Hunt
Withington Green
Dingle Brook
CW4
P
Granada Arboretum
CATCHPENNY LA
Blackden Heath
BLACKDEN LA
Jodrell Bank Science Centre
Fields Farm
Jodrell Bank Radio Telescope
Pear Tree Farm
Laboratories
Highway Garage
Brookbank Farm
Yew Tree Farm
Bridge Farm
Jodrell Bank
Hilltop Farm
Old Hall Farm
B5392
Four Oaks Nursery
LONG SHOOT RD
Brookside Farm
Blackden Hall
CHELFORD RD
Yew Tree Farm
Jodrell Bank Farm
FARM LA
Home Farm
A535
Terra Nova Sch

107
131

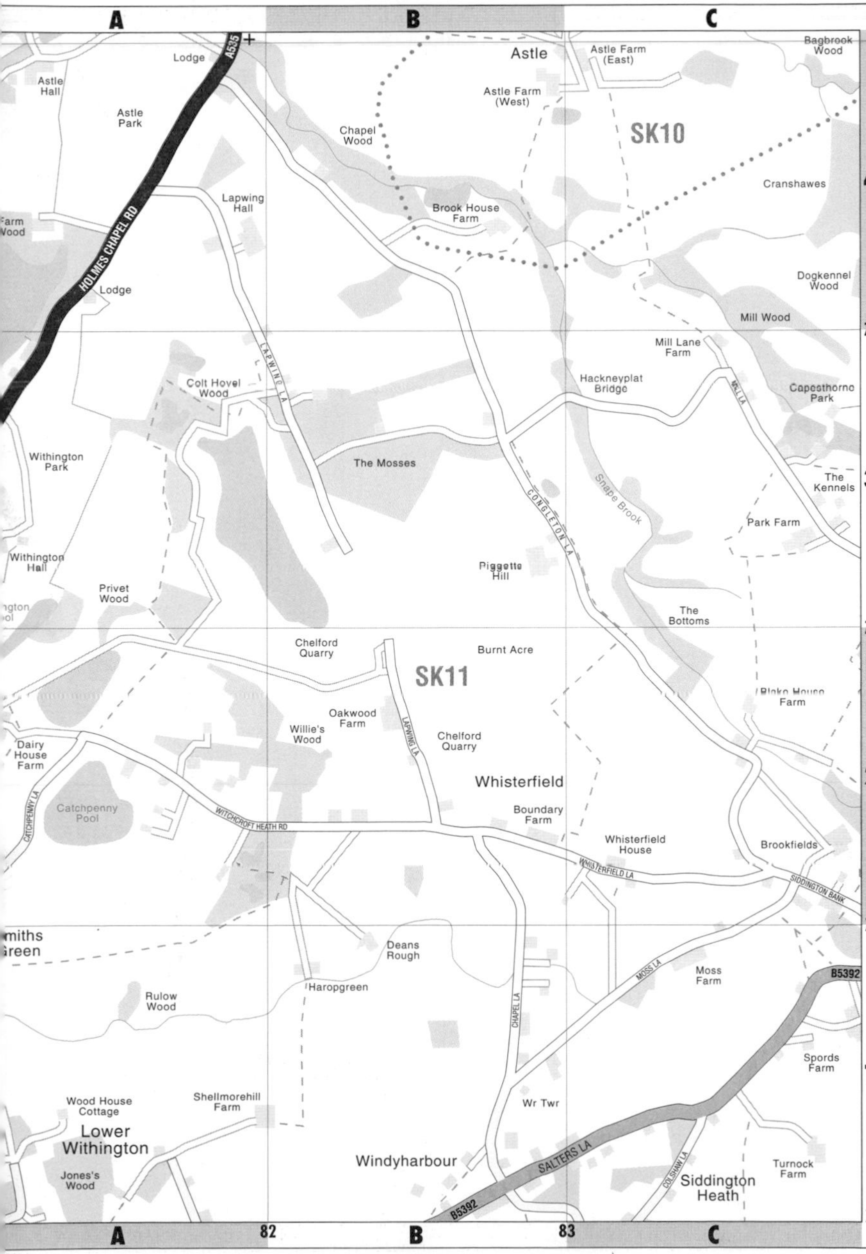
A
B
C
Astle
Astle Farm (East)
Bagbrook Wood
Lodge
A535
Astle Hall
Astle Park
Astle Farm (West)
SK10
Chapel Wood
Cranshawes
4
Lapwing Hall
Brook House Farm
Farm Wood
HOLMES CHAPEL RD
Lodge
Dogkennel Wood
Mill Wood
73
Mill Lane Farm
LAPWING LA
Colt Hovel Wood
Hackneyplat Bridge
MILL LA
Capesthorne Park
Withington Park
The Mosses
Snape Brook
CONGLETON LA
The Kennels
3
Park Farm
Withington Hall
Piggotts Hill
Privet Wood
The Bottoms
72
Chelford Quarry
Burnt Acre
SK11
Blake House Farm
Oakwood Farm
Dairy House Farm
Willie's Wood
LAPWING LA
Chelford Quarry
Whisterfield
2
CATCHPENNY LA
Catchpenny Pool
WITCHCROFT HEATH RD
Boundary Farm
Whisterfield House
Brookfields
WHISTERFIELD LA
SIDDINGTON BANK
71
Smiths Green
Deans Rough
MOSS LA
Moss Farm
B5392
Haropgreen
Rulow Wood
CHAPEL LA
Spords Farm
1
Wood House Cottage
Shellmorehill Farm
Wr Twr
Lower Withington
SALTERS LA
Windyharbour
Turnock Farm
Jones's Wood
COLSHAW LA
Siddington Heath
B5392
70
A
82
B
83
C

109
85

109
133

C4
1 ASHBOURNE MEWS
2 SHELBOURNE MEWS
3 ALDERNEY CL
4 BLANFORD DR
5 THE TOWERS
6 HEDINGHAM CL
7 MARLBOROUGH HO

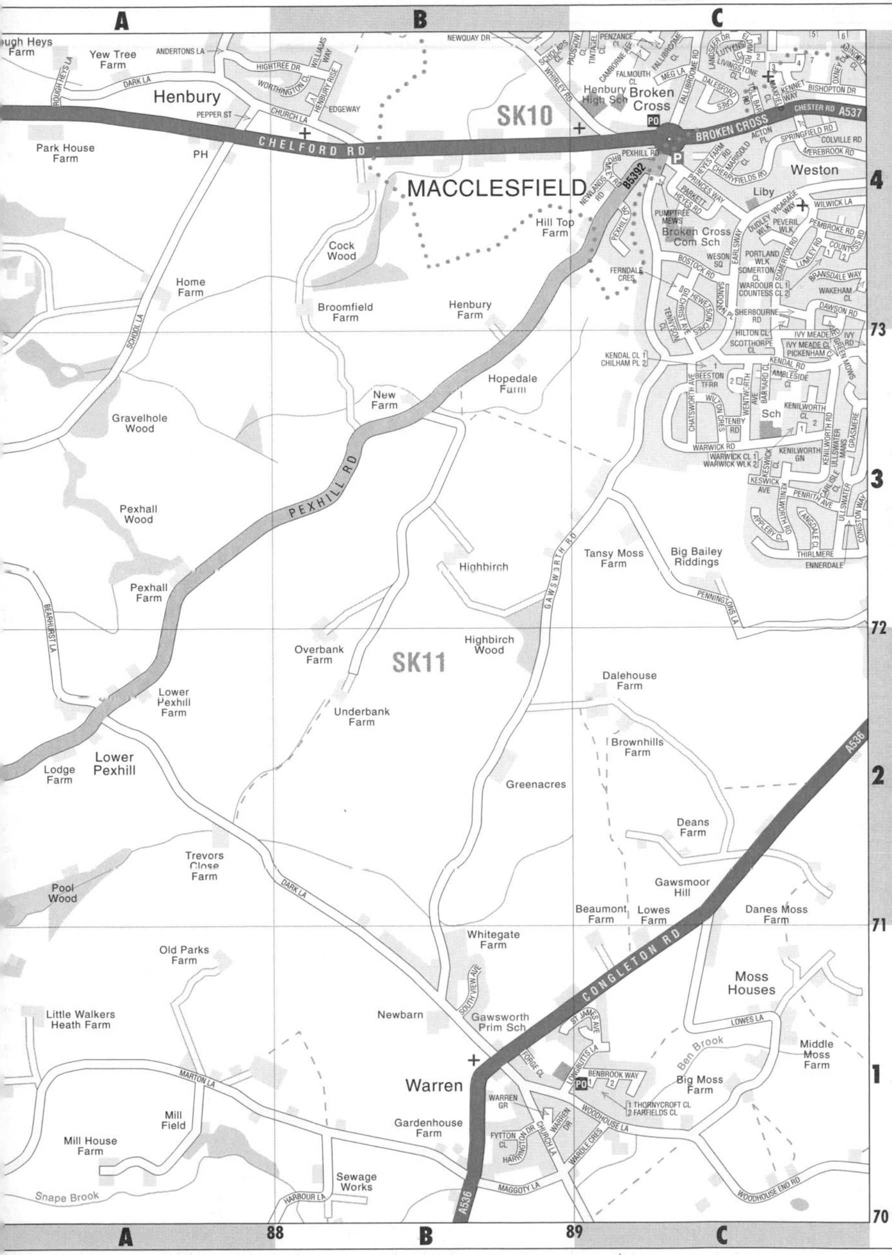

A3
1 QUEEN ANNE CT
2 HARRAPS PL
3 BARRACKS SQ
4 ARMOURY COURT MEWS
5 ARMOURY TWRS

111
87

C4
1 OXFORD CT
2 CANTERBURY CT
3 CUCKSTOOLPIT HILL
4 DAINTRY TERR
5 ST PAUL'S RD
6 HALLEFIELD DR
7 HALLEFIELD CRES
8 THORNYCROFT ST
9 CAWLEY ST
10 LOWER BANK ST
11 BUCKLOW WLK
12 KNUTSFORD ROAD WLK
13 WILMLOW WLK
14 ALDERLEY WLK
15 PEARSON ST
16 CAPESTHORNE WAY

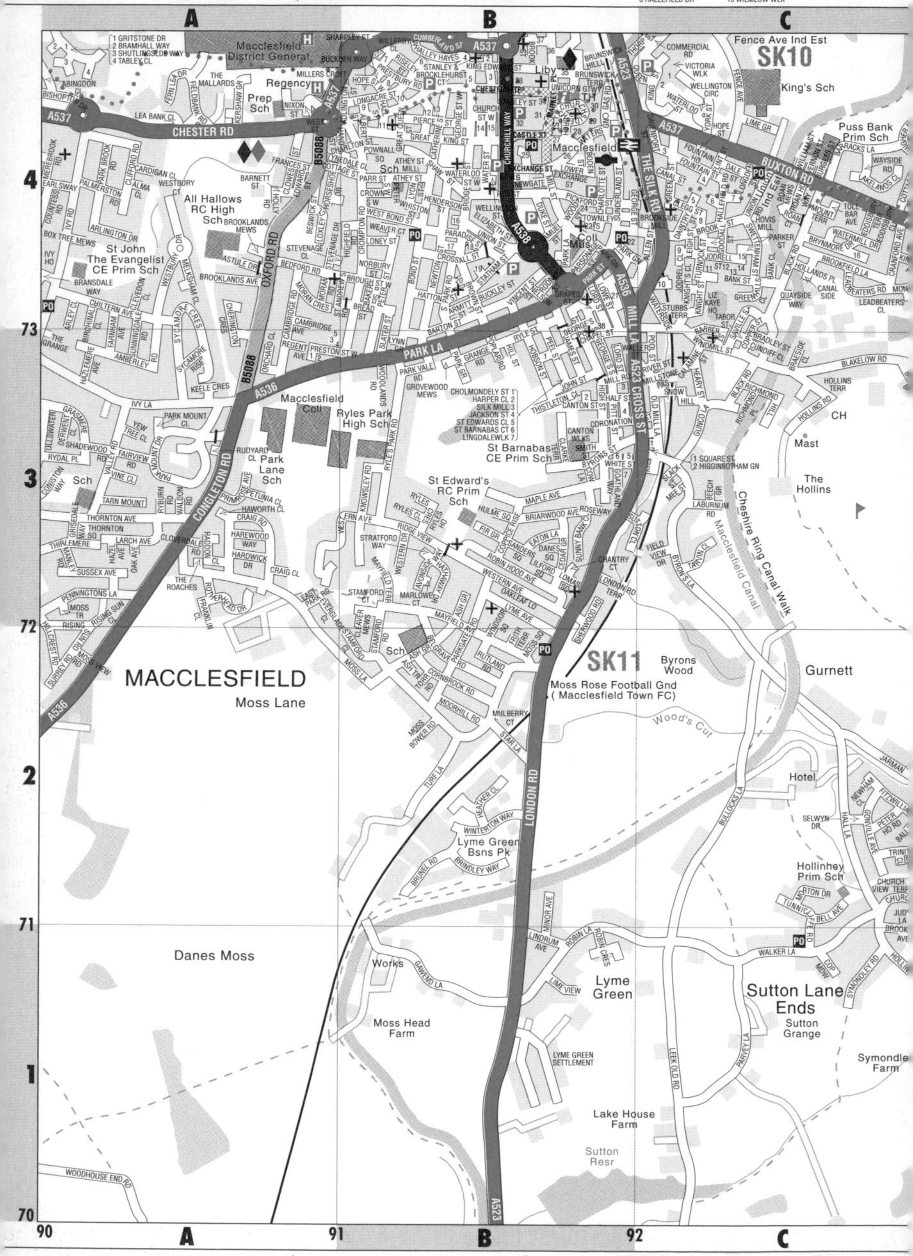
A
B
C
1 GRITSTONE DR
2 BRAMHALL WAY
3 SHUTLINGSLOE WAY
4 TABLEY CL
Macclesfield District General
Fence Ave Ind Est
SK10
King's Sch
Regency
Prep Sch
CHESTER RD
A537
B5088
Liby
Macclesfield
THE SILK RD
A523
Puss Bank Prim Sch
BUXTON RD
All Hallows RC High Sch
St John The Evangelist CE Prim Sch
OXFORD RD
Coll Mus
A538
PARK LA
A536
MILL LA
CROSS ST
Macclesfield Coll
Ryles Park High Sch
CHOLMONDELY ST 1
HARPER CL 2
SILK MILL 3
JACKSON ST 4
ST EDWARDS CL 5
ST BARNABAS CT 6
LINGDALEWLK 7
St Barnabas CE Prim Sch
Park Lane Sch
Sch
St Edward's RC Prim Sch
CONGLETON RD
1 SQUARE ST
2 HIGGINBOTHAM GN
CH
Mast
The Hollins
Cheshire Ring Canal Walk
Macclesfield Canal
SK11
Byrons Wood
Moss Rose Football Gnd (Macclesfield Town FC)
Gurnett
MACCLESFIELD
Moss Lane
Wood's Cut
LONDON RD
Hotel
Lyme Green Bsns Pk
Hollinhey Prim Sch
Danes Moss
Works
Lyme Green
Sutton Lane Ends
Sutton Grange
Moss Head Farm
LYME GREEN SETTLEMENT
Symondley Farm
Lake House Farm
Sutton Resr
WOODHOUSE END RD
4
73
3
72
2
71
1
70
90
91
92

111
135

B4
1 TUNNICLIFFE ST
2 KING EDWARD RD
3 LITTLE ST
4 WESTMINSTER ST
5 WESTMINSTER RD
6 GROSVENOR ST
7 WALKER ST
8 BOOTHBY ST
9 POYTON ST
10 ANDERSON ST
11 LANGFORD ST
12 PINFOLD ST
13 FOUNDRY CT
14 CHARLOTTE ST W
15 CHATHAM ST
16 MARSDEN TERR
17 BACK PARADISE ST
18 HOLLAND ST
19 ST JOHN'S RD
20 BLACKSHAW ST
21 BROKEN BANKS
22 MAYDEWS PAS
23 TOWNLEY PL
24 MARLBOROUGH CT
25 EXCHANGE CL
26 QUEEN VICTORIA ST
27 BACK WALLGATE
28 SHORT ST
29 108 STEPS
30 STEP HILL
31 MILL STREET MALL
32 CASTLE STREET MALL
33 RISELEY'S PAS
34 CHESTERGATE MALL
35 BRUNSWICK ST
36 JORDAN GATE
37 CUMBERLAND ST
38 BRUNSWICK CT

88
114

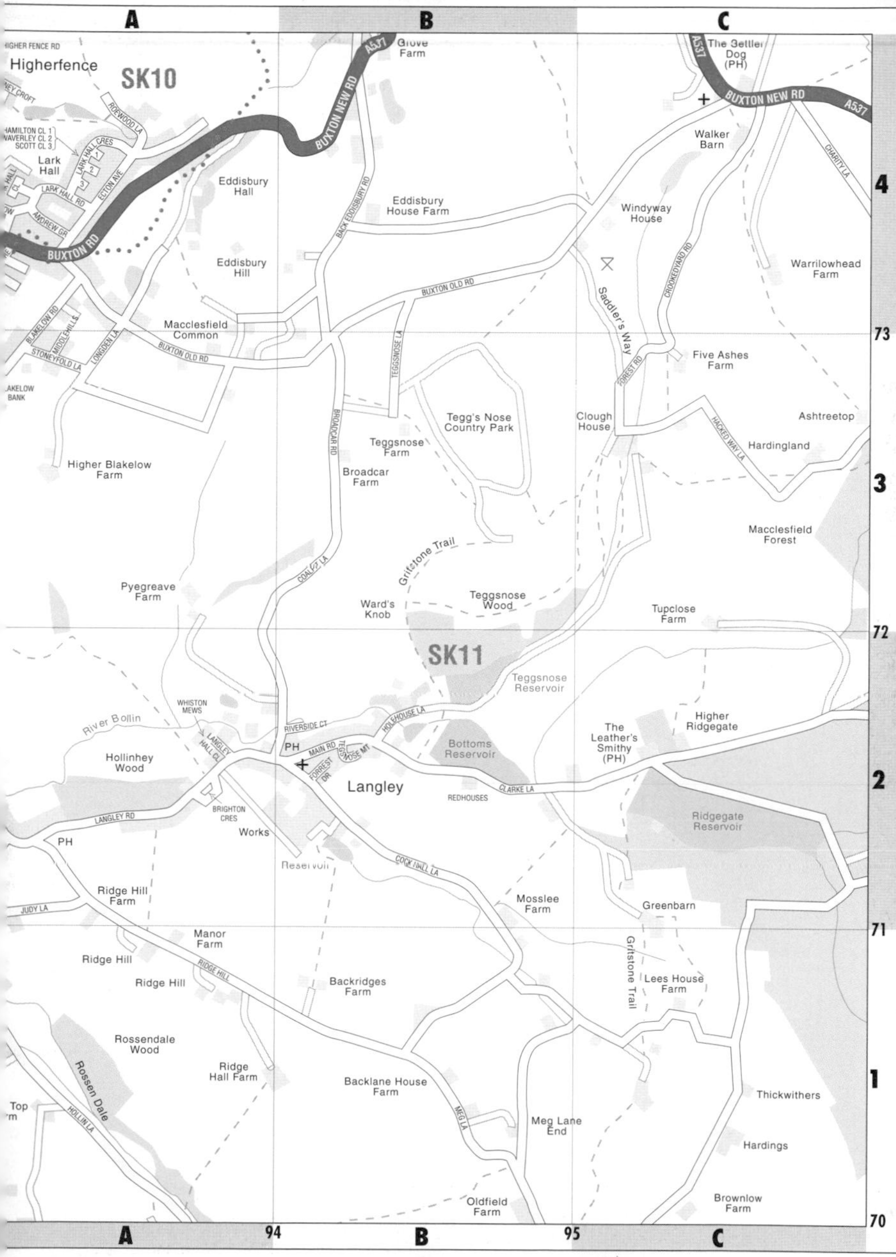

136
114

113
89

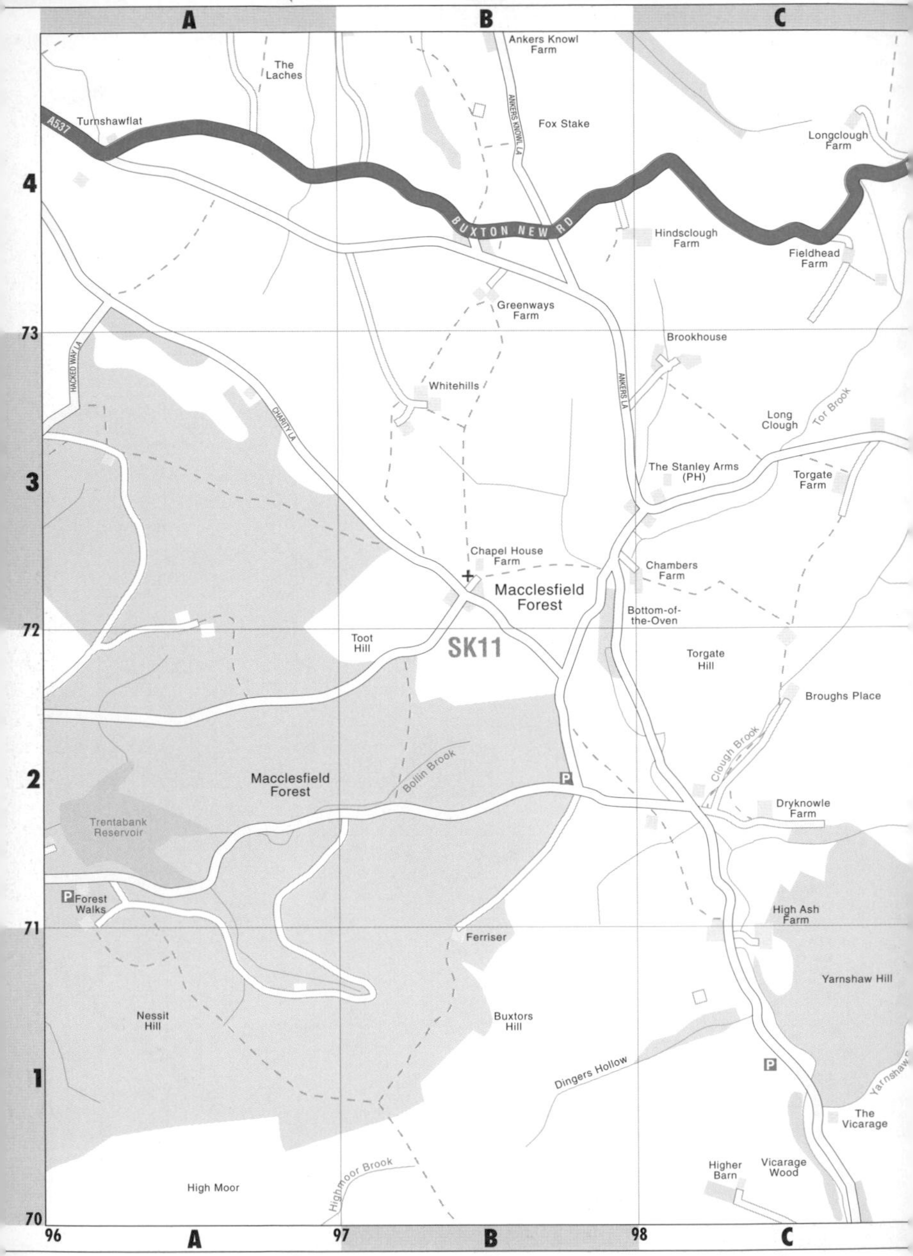
A
B
C
Ankers Knowl Farm
The Laches
Turnshawflat
A537
ANKERS KNOWL LA
Fox Stake
Longclough Farm
BUXTON NEW RD
Hindsclough Farm
Fieldhead Farm
Greenways Farm
Brookhouse
HACKED WAY LA
Whitehills
ANKERS LA
Long Clough
Tor Brook
CHARITY LA
The Stanley Arms (PH)
Torgate Farm
Chapel House Farm
Chambers Farm
Macclesfield Forest
Bottom-of-the-Oven
Toot Hill
SK11
Torgate Hill
Broughs Place
Clough Brook
Bollin Brook
Macclesfield Forest
Dryknowle Farm
Trentabank Reservoir
Forest Walks
High Ash Farm
Ferriser
Yarnshaw Hill
Nessit Hill
Buxtors Hill
Dingers Hollow
Yarnshaw
The Vicarage
Highmoor Brook
High Moor
Higher Barn
Vicarage Wood
4
73
3
72
2
71
1
70
96
97
98

113
137

90

A
B
C
Shining Tor
Stake Side
Goytsclough Quarry
P
River Goyt
Goyt's Moss
BUXTON NEW RD
Stake Farm
Stake Clough
Deep Clough
SK17
Goyt's Clough
Ravens Low
Foxhole Hollow
Jacob's Cabin
SK11
est Hollow
Mast
Cat and Fiddle (PH)
Derbyshire Bridge
The Scaurs
Cuckoo Rocks
A537
Tinkerspit Gutter
en Gutter
Correction Brook
A54
Whetstone Ridge
Danebower Hollow
Cheshire Knowl
Danethorn Hollow
Dane Bower
Danebower Quarries
4
73
3
72
2
71
1
70
00
01
Derbyshire STREET ATLAS
A537 Buxton (A54/A53)
A54 Buxton (A53)

138

93

A
B
C
Green Lane Est
Old Marsh Farm
Bridge Farm
Camp
Seahill Farm
Deva Bsns Pk
Brookfield Farm
Willow Farm
Station Cottages
Brook Farm
Home Farm
SEALAND RD
The Owl Ind Est
Waterloo Farm
Sealand
CH5
Sealand Manor
Church Farm
Shooting School
CH1
Deeside Cottages
Deeside House
Engineer Pk
River Row Cottages
St Ives Pk
Works
Glendale Bsns Pk
Sealand Nursery
Glendale Pk
River Dee (Afon Dyfrdwy)
Wood Farm
Sandycroft
CH5
Bridge Inn (PH)
Hawarden
CH4
The Beeches
Cop House Farm
Rake Cottages
A494 Queensferry
A550
B5441
A548
A494
WELSH RD
B5129
CHESTER RD
DEESIDE LA
GREEN LANE
4
3
2
1
69
68
67
66
33
34
35

139

94
118

140
118

117
95

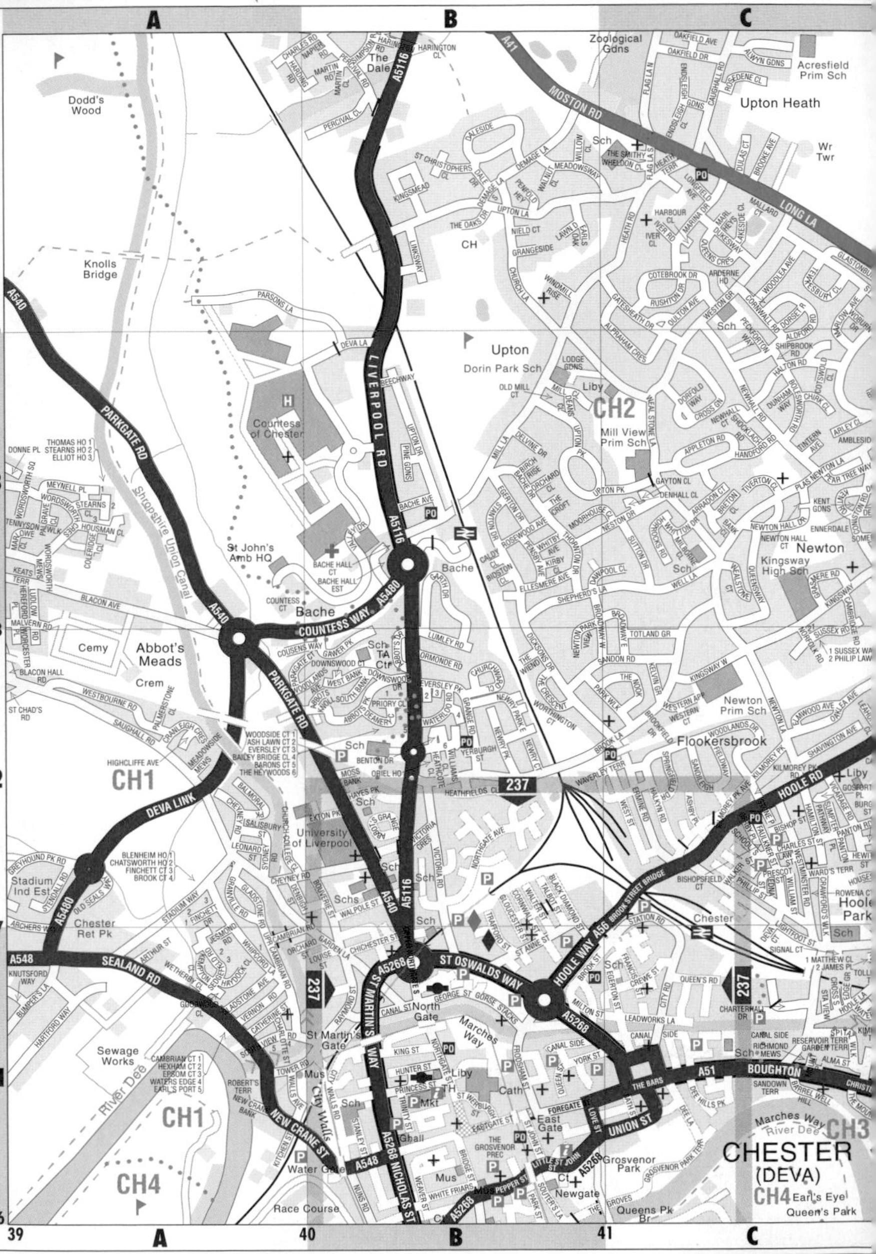
A
B
C
4
3
2
1
69
68
67
66
39
40
41
Dodd's Wood
Knolls Bridge
The Dale
Zoological Gdns
Acresfield Prim Sch
Upton Heath
Wr Twr
MOSTON RD
LONG LA
A41
A5116
A540
A5480
A548
A5268
A56
A51
LIVERPOOL RD
PARKGATE RD
COUNTESS WAY
DEVA LINK
SEALAND RD
ST OSWALDS WAY
HOOLE WAY
HOOLE RD
BOUGHTON
NEW CRANE ST
NICHOLAS ST
ST MARTIN'S WAY
UNION ST
Shropshire Union Canal
Countess of Chester
St John's Amb HQ
Bache
Upton
Dorin Park Sch
Mill View Prim Sch
CH2
Newton
Kingsway High Sch
Newton Prim Sch
Flookersbrook
Cemy
Abbot's Meads
Crem
CH1
Stadium Ind Est
Chester Ret Pk
University of Liverpool
North Gate
Marches Way
St Martin's Gate
City Walls
Cath
East Gate
Grosvenor Park
Water Gate
Race Course
Sewage Works
River Dee
CH4
CH3
CHESTER (DEVA)
Earl's Eye
Queen's Park
Queens Pk Br
Newgate
Hoole Park
Chester
237

117
141
For full street detail of the highlighted area see page 23

10 ARKLE CT

RLBOROUGH CT
ARS CROSS CT
RECROFT
UGHTON LODGE
CHARD CT
G EDWARD BLDGS
CKS AVE
STWARD RD
VILL DR

119
97

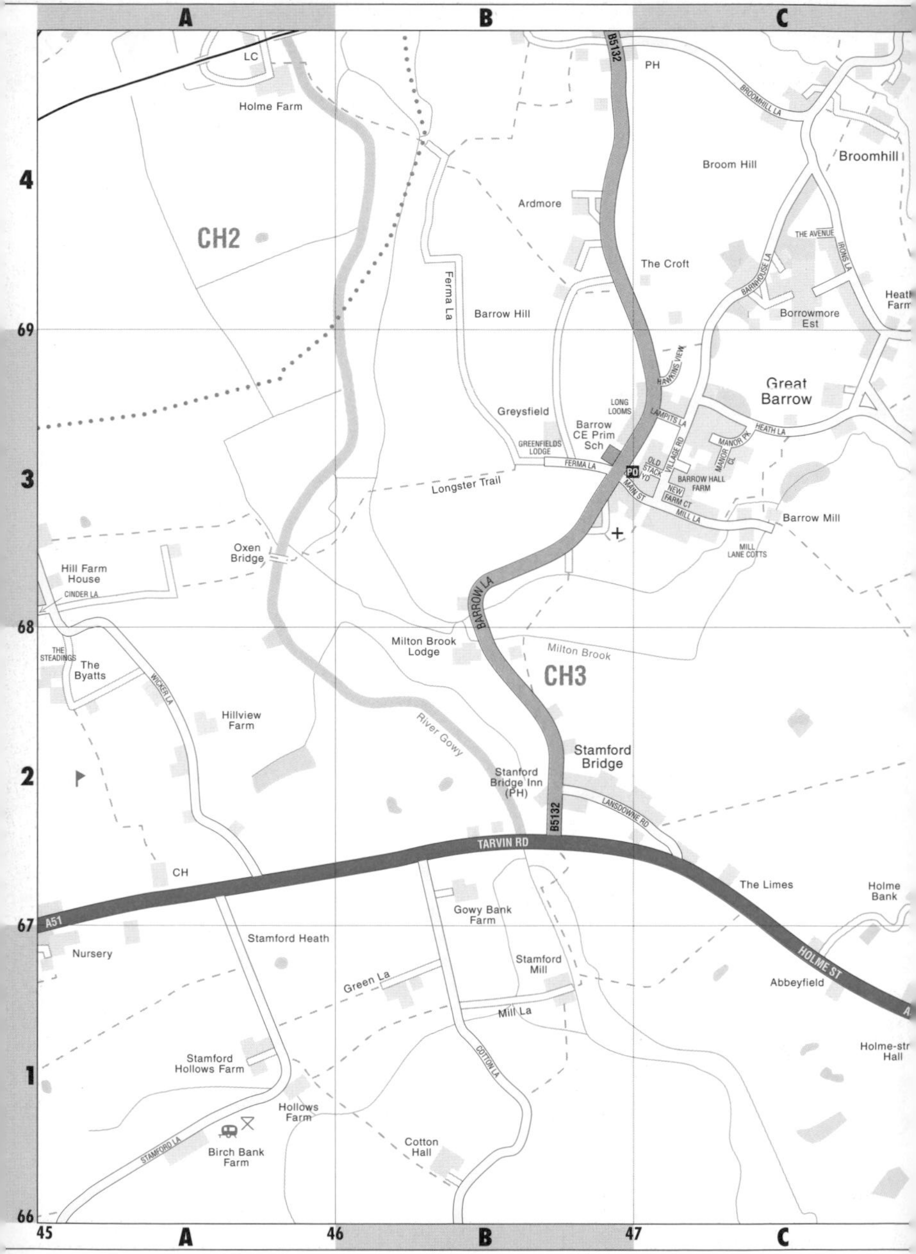
A
B
C
4
69
3
68
2
67
1
66
45
46
47
LC
Holme Farm
CH2
PH
B5132
BROOMHILL LA
Broom Hill
Broomhill
Ardmore
Ferma La
The Croft
THE AVENUE
IRONS LA
BARNHOUSE LA
Heath Farm
Barrow Hill
Borrowmore Est
HAWKINS VIEW
Great Barrow
LONG LOOMS
LAMPITS LA
Greysfield
Barrow CE Prim Sch
HEATH LA
MANOR PK
MANOR CL
VILLAGE RD
GREENFIELDS LODGE
FERMA LA
PO
OLD STACK YD
BARROW HALL FARM
MAIN ST
NEW FARM CT
Longster Trail
MILL LA
Barrow Mill
MILL LANE COTTS
Oxen Bridge
Hill Farm House
CINDER LA
BARROW LA
THE STEADINGS
The Byatts
Milton Brook Lodge
Milton Brook
CH3
WICKER LA
Hillview Farm
River Gowy
Stamford Bridge
Stanford Bridge Inn (PH)
LANSDOWNE RD
TARVIN RD
CH
The Limes
Holme Bank
A51
Gowy Bank Farm
Stamford Heath
Nursery
HOLME ST
Stamford Mill
Abbeyfield
Green La
Mill La
COTTON LA
Holme-str Hall
Stamford Hollows Farm
Hollows Farm
Cotton Hall
Birch Bank Farm
STAMFORD LA

119
143

98
122

A
B
C
Broomhill Farm
Swinfordmill Farm
Longster Trail
Peel Hall
Ashton Hayes Prim Sch
CHURCH CL
B5393
Hall
The Village Farm
THE MEADOWS
CHURCH RD
GONGAR LA
BROOKSIDE
Ashton
4
BOOTH AVE
PEEL CRES
FOXHUNTER CL
PEEL HALL LA
WEST END
PH
PENTRE LA
DUNN'S LA
WILLOW HAYES
SHAY LA
Brook Farm
Whitegate Farm
WHITEGATE
PO
VICKER'S CL
KELSALL RD
DUCK LA
PENTRE CL
OLD HALL CL
69
Hollowmoor Heath
IRONS LA
Horton Hall
ASHTON LA
Baker Way
Cheshire View Farm
Old Hall Farm
Kelvin View
3
Salters Brook
New Farm
Barrow Lane Farm
A54
Greenacres Farm
Park Hall Farm
Street Farm
CH3
68
Street Farm
Brook House Farm
BARROW LA
KELSALL RD
POOL LA
SANDY LA
Tarvin Sands Industries
MILL LA
Tarvin Sands
2
Tarvin Bridge
Pool Bank
PH
BYE PASS RD
1 RADCLIFFE CL
2 WOODWARD WLK
3 RIDGEWAY HO
SHAY LA
THE RIDGEWAY
THE PRYORS
THE BRUEN
Pool Bank Bsns Pk
Tarvin
ARDEN CL
67
Grosvenor Farm
PARK CL
HIGH ST
Church Farm
Oscroft Hall
Oscroft Farm
THE GREEN
PO
HOCKENHULL CRES
CHURCH ST
GROSVENOR RD
HOLME ST
A54
TOWNFIELD LA
FIELD LA
LANGFORD CT
Oscroft
Ash Farm
WILLINGTON RD
Liby
MEADOW CL
FIELD CL
HOCKENHULL LA
ANDREW'S CL
HALLFIELDS RD
A51
CROSSFIELDS
HOCKENHULL AVE
PITTS CL
SHEAF CL
DANE'S WAY
PLATTS LA
DEANS CL
GOWY CRES
HUNTER'S DR
HUNTER'S CRES
TARPORLEY RD
CROSS LANES
Oscroft House
1
HEATH CL
HEATH DR
BROOM CRES
BROOMHEATH LA
Tarvin Prim Sch
Brownheath Farm
Hockenhull Hall
HOCKENHULL LA
BROOMHEATH LA
A51
Moss Heyes
66
49
50

144
122

121
99

A
B
C
4
3
2
1
69
68
67
66
51
52
53
Park Farm
Ashton Hayes
Ash Wood
The Top Lodge
Dale Covert
Longley Wood
The Yeld Farm
Yeld Farm
Nettleford Wood
YELD LA
NORTONS LA
The Yeld
Sandstone Trail
Shay Lane
Lower Longley Farm
Longley Farm
FOREST GATE LA
SHAY LA
Nursery
MORREYS LA
King's Chair
Eddisbury Way
HALL LA
JINGLE LA
HILLCREST RD
CLEMLEY CL
Kelsall Hall
PRIMROSE HILL
LONGLEY AVE
BROOM'S LA
Northwood Hall
Weldon Farm
HOLLANDS LA
GRUB LA
DUTTON'S LA
OLD COACH RD
EDALE DR
CHESTER RD
A54
Holly Farm
REDHILL RD
FRODSHAM ST
CHAPEL GN
EARLE'S LA
CHURCH BANK
ORCHARD WAY
Primrose Hill
Childwall Farm
EGERTON CT
PH
CHURCH ST N
BRAMLEY CT
QUARRY LA
KINGSWOOD WLK
Delamere Farm
PO
P
THE DELL
ELIZABETH CL
CH3
PH
Lower Grange Farm
Kelsall
CHURCH ST
BROOK DR
KELSBORROW WAY
FOX HILL
Kelsall Com Sch
HALLOWS CL
HALLOWS DR
CARTER AVE
CASTLE CL
HILLSIDE RD
Kings Gate
Castle Hill
FLAT LA
HALLOWSGATE CT
WILLINGTON LA
WASTE LA
Hallowsgate
MEADOW BANK
Kelsborrow Castle
Forest House
PASTURE CL
THE WYND
BROOKSIDE
GREEN LA
CW6
Mast
The Commons
WILLINGTON RD
Boothsdale
Birch Hill
TIRLEY LA
PH
BOOTHSDALE
Roughlow Farm
Common Farm
COMMON LA
GOSEBERRY LA
Pearl Hole
Beeches Farm
CHAPEL LA
Sandstone Trail
Eddisbury Way
Manor Farm
Willington Corner
Weetwood Grange
Weetwood Common
LILAC CL
Willington Wood
WILLINGTON RD
MILL LA
WILLINGTON LA
CH
Pryors Hayes
Weetwood Farm
The Belt
Willington-mill Farm
Home Farm
Willington Hall
Rock Farm

100
124

146
124

A
B
C
A556
CHESTER RD
Crown Farm
FARM RD
CROWN COTTS
Delamere Lodge
Oakmere
Fourways Sand Quarry
Waste Farm
Keeper's Cottage
Oak Mere
Hogshead Wood
HOGSHEAD LA
Sand Pit
Massey's Lodge
CW8
OVERDALE LA
A49
Cheshire Kennels
Whitegate Way
Kennel Lane
Nunsmere
Reeking Hole
Shemmy Moss
Nunsmere Hall
Abbotsmoss Wood
Abbotsmoss Hall
Folly Farm
TARPORLEY RD
Horse Training Ground
Abbots Moss
Polo Ground
Corner Farm
Greenlands
SHAY'S LA
Spring Farm
Shaw's Farm
Shay's Farm
Shay's Lane Brook
A54
Cabbage Hall (PH)
Stonehouse Farm
CW6
Common Side
Sandymere Plantation
Sandybrow
Sandymere House
LONGSTONE LA
Shrewsbury Arms (PH)
Butts Farm
Moss Hall Farm
Oaktree Farm
SHOP LA
BEECH RD
Heathfield
Rosebank Farm
RACECOURSE LA
COACH RD
Sunnybank Farm
WHITEHALL LA
Burslem Cottage Farm
PARK RD
Sandiford Lodge
Polo Ground
Picnic Area
P
White hall
Poolhead Farm
SADLERS LA
B5152
STABLE LA
4
3
2
1
69
68
67
66
57
58
59

102
126

148
126

125
103

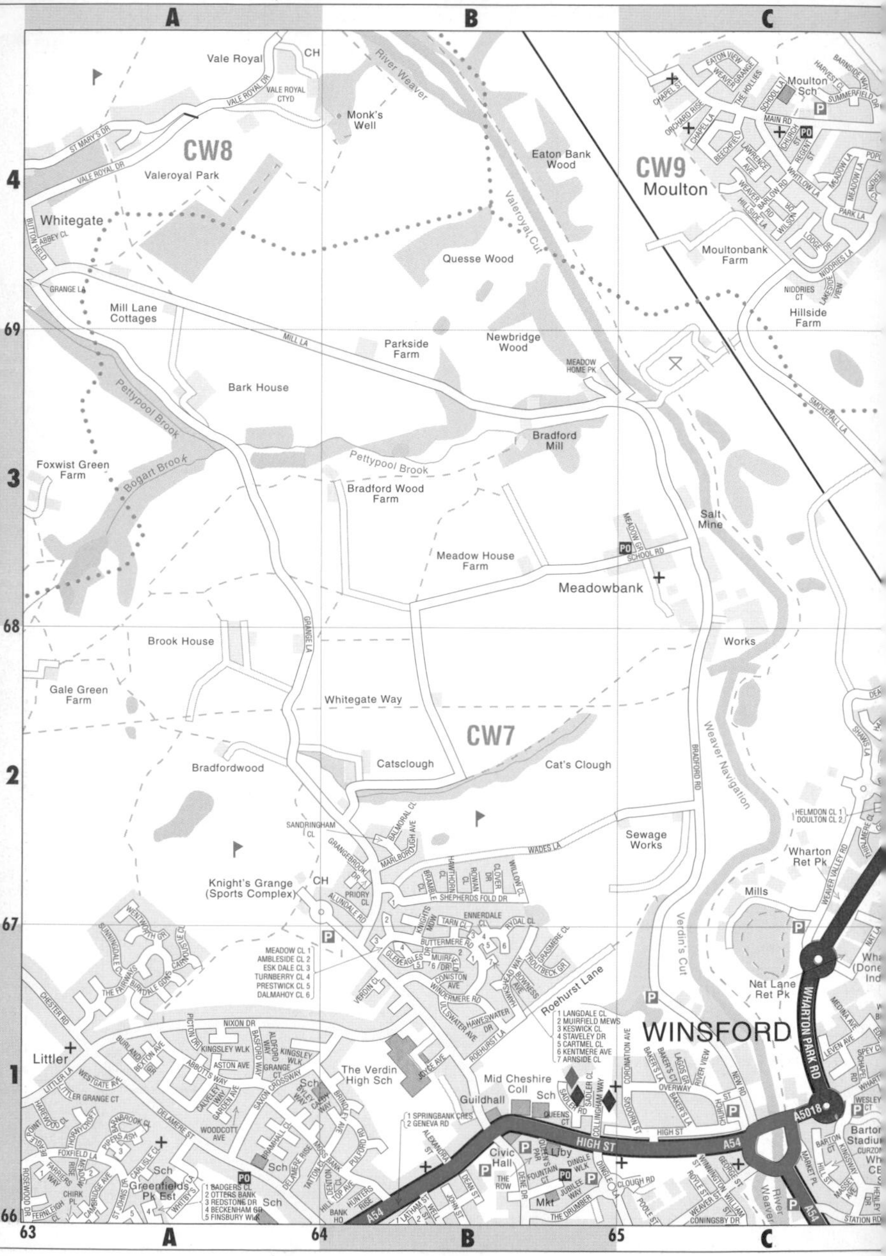

125
149

104
128

150
128

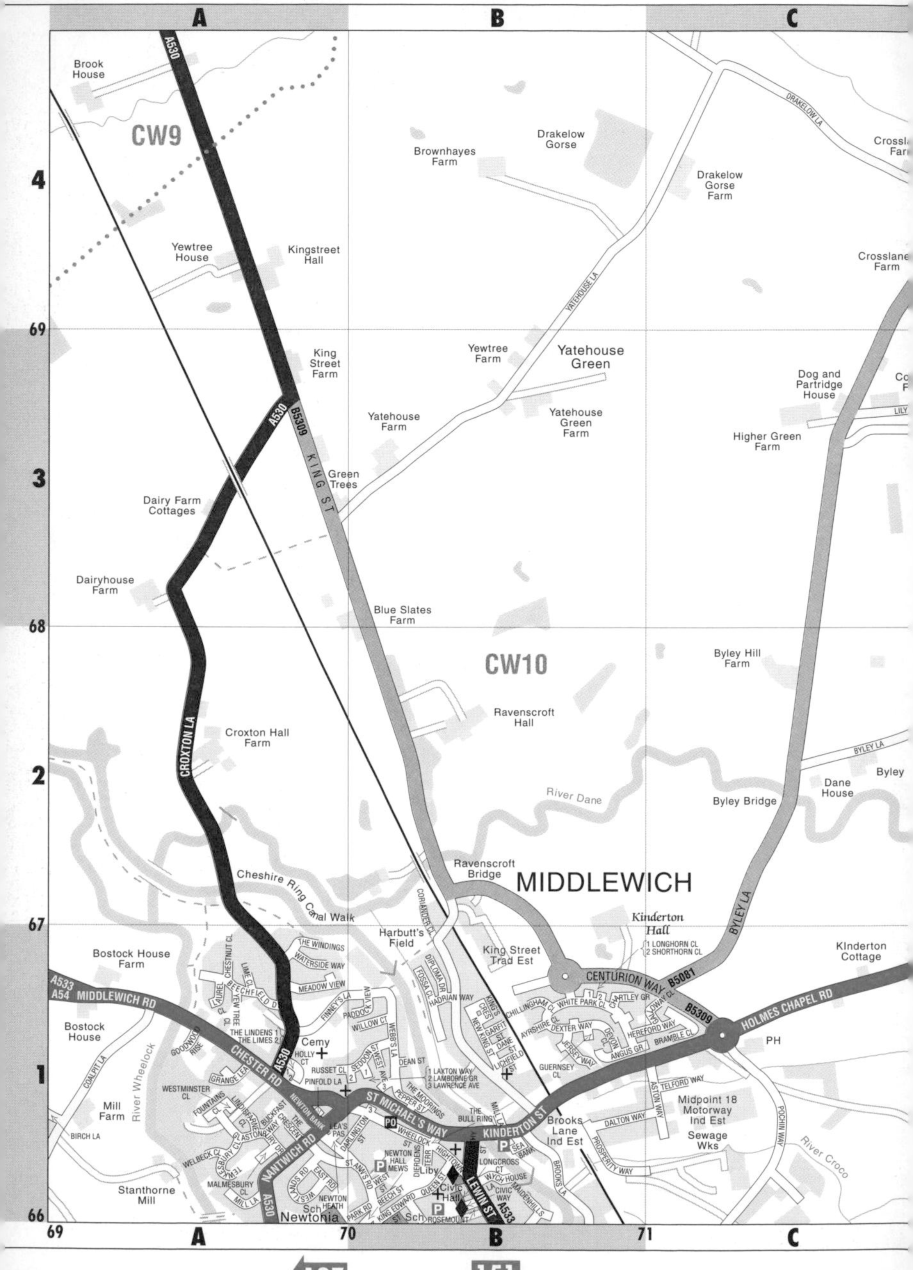
127
105
A
B
C
4
3
2
1
69
68
67
66
70
71
CW9
CW10
Brook House
Drakelow Gorse
Brownhayes Farm
Drakelow Gorse Farm
Yewtree House
Kingstreet Hall
King Street Farm
Yewtree Farm
Yatehouse Green
Yatehouse Farm
Yatehouse Green Farm
Dog and Partridge House
Higher Green Farm
Crosslane Farm
Green Trees
Dairy Farm Cottages
Dairyhouse Farm
Blue Slates Farm
Byley Hill Farm
Ravenscroft Hall
Croxton Hall Farm
River Dane
Byley Bridge
Dane House
Byley
Ravenscroft Bridge
MIDDLEWICH
Cheshire Ring Canal Walk
Kinderton Hall
Harbutt's Field
King Street Trad Est
Kinderton Cottage
Bostock House Farm
Bostock House
Mill Farm
River Wheelock
Stanthorne Mill
Cemy
Midpoint 18 Motorway Ind Est
Sewage Wks
Brooks Lane Ind Est
River Croco
Newtonia
Sch
Liby
Civic Hall
PH
A530
B5309
KING ST
CROXTON LA
YATEHOUSE LA
DRAKELOW LA
BYLEY LA
A533
A54 MIDDLEWICH RD
CHESTER RD
NANTWICH RD
ST MICHAEL'S WAY
KINDERTON ST
CENTURION WAY
B5081
HOLMES CHAPEL RD
LEWIN ST
1 LONGHORN CL
2 SHORTHORN CL
1 LAXTON WAY
2 LAMBORNE GR
3 LAWRENCE AVE
THE LINDENS 1
THE LIMES 2
BIRCH LA
COALPIT LA
POCHIN WAY
ASTON WAY
TELFORD WAY
DALTON WAY
PROSPERITY WAY
BROOKS LA
127
151

A
B
C
B5081
Puddinglake
DRAKELOW LA
Puddinglake Brook
Byley Prim Sch
Byley
Shanty Farm
MOSS LA
Nook Wood
M6
Warrington Common
B5082
A50
Rudheath Lodge Farm
KNUTSFORD RD
Chestnut Farm
Oak Tree Farm
KING'S LA
Mast
GOOSTREY LA
New Farm
OAK TREE LA
Holly House Farm
Holly House Est
MIDDLEWICH RD
Holly Bank
Lily Farm
LILY LA
CW10
BYLEY LA
Hall Farm
CRESCENT RD
Middlewich Road Ind Est
Mast
Pump House Farm
Peartree Farm
Mill Lane Farm
Cranage Hall
Keeper's Cottage
Cranage Cottage
Round House Farm
Manor Farm
Higher Farm
CW4
River Dane
Equestrian Training Centre
Sproston Wood
Cotton Hall
Cotton Farm
MIDDLEWICH RD
A54
LINGMELL GDNS
CONISTON DR
MIDDLEWICH RD
18
Daisy Bank Farm
Manor Farm
Holly Tree Farm
HOLMES CHAPEL RD
THE COTTAGES
The Limes
Brookfield Farm
Primrose Hall
Dairy House Farm
Sproston Green
WREN AVE
River Croco
POOLFORD LA
Hill Farm
BRERETON LA
Sproston Hall
Dockbank Farm
BROAD LA
Primrose Farm
Fender Wood
Spring Covert
CW10
Kinderton Lodge
Holly Farm
M6
4
69
3
68
2
67
1
66
73
74
A
B
C

129
107

129
153

108
132

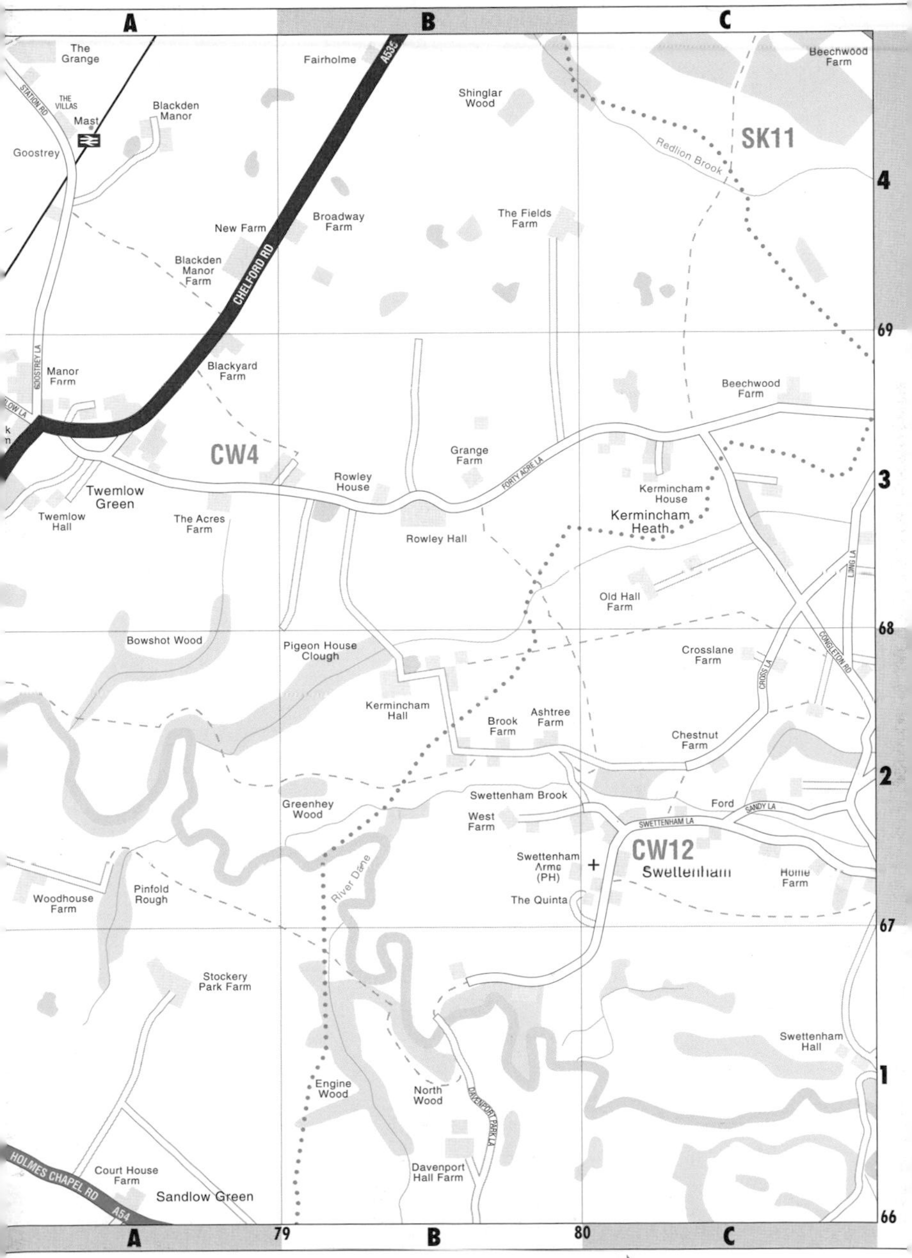

154
132

131
109

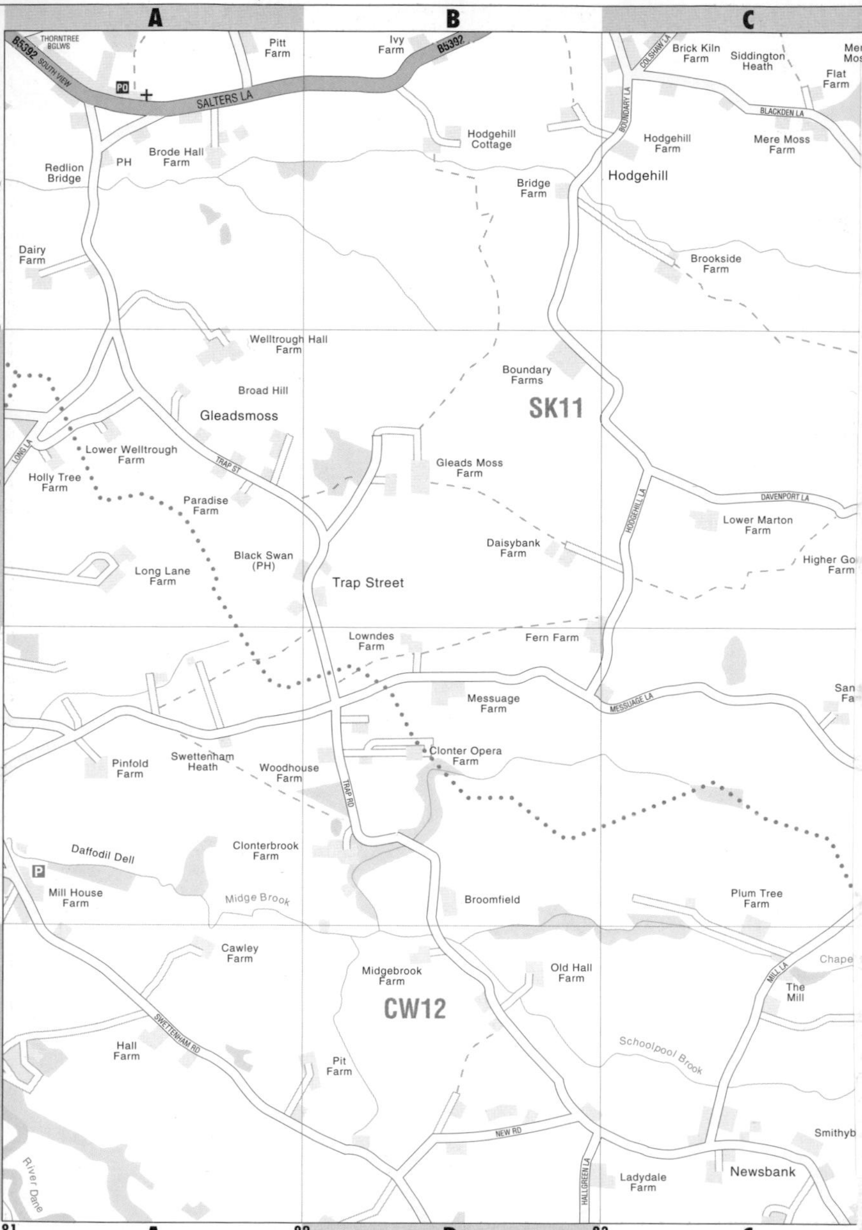
A
B
C
THORNTREE BGLWS
B5392
SOUTH VIEW
PO
Pitt Farm
Ivy Farm
B5392
SALTERS LA
Brick Kiln Farm
COLSHAW LA
Siddington Heath
Flat Farm
BLACKDEN LA
Hodgehill Cottage
BOUNDARY LA
Hodgehill Farm
Mere Moss Farm
Redlion Bridge
PH
Brode Hall Farm
4
Bridge Farm
Hodgehill
Dairy Farm
Brookside Farm
69
Welltrough Hall Farm
Boundary Farms
Broad Hill
Gleadsmoss
SK11
LONG LA
Lower Welltrough Farm
TRAP ST
Gleads Moss Farm
3
Holly Tree Farm
Paradise Farm
HODGEHILL LA
DAVENPORT LA
Lower Marton Farm
Daisybank Farm
Black Swan (PH)
Long Lane Farm
Trap Street
68
Lowndes Farm
Fern Farm
Messuage Farm
MESSUAGE LA
Clonter Opera Farm
Pinfold Farm
Swettenham Heath
Woodhouse Farm
2
TRAP RD
Daffodil Dell
Clonterbrook Farm
P
Mill House Farm
Midge Brook
Broomfield
Plum Tree Farm
67
Cawley Farm
Midgebrook Farm
Old Hall Farm
MILL LA
The Mill
CW12
SWETTENHAM RD
Hall Farm
Schoolpool Brook
1
Pit Farm
NEW RD
River Dane
HALLGREEN LA
Ladydale Farm
Newsbank
66
81
A
82
B
83
C

131
155

110
134

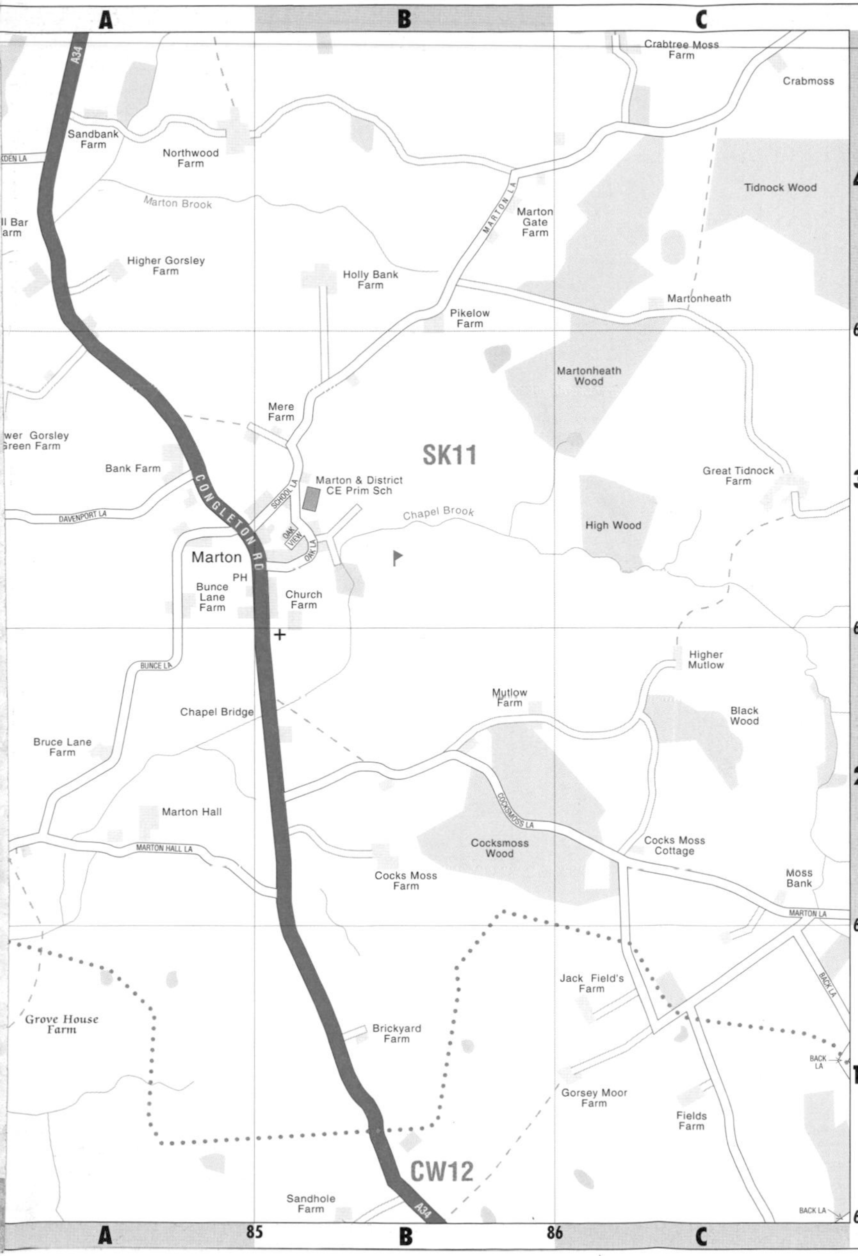

156
134

133
111
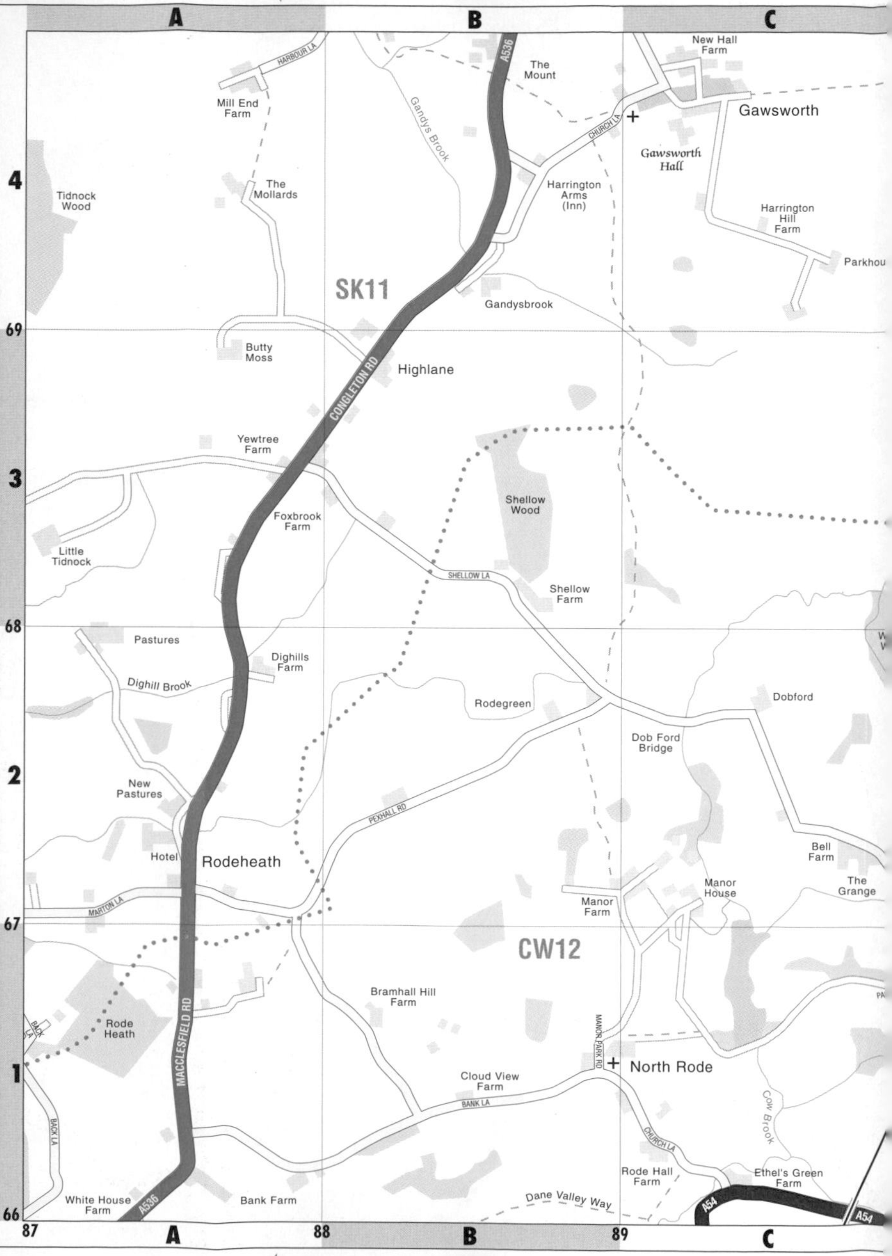
A
B
C
4
69
3
68
2
67
1
66
87
88
89
HARBOUR LA
Mill End Farm
A536
The Mount
New Hall Farm
Gawsworth
CHURCH LA
Gawsworth Hall
Gandys Brook
Tidnock Wood
The Mollards
Harrington Arms (Inn)
Harrington Hill Farm
Parkhou
SK11
Gandysbrook
Butty Moss
Highlane
CONGLETON RD
Yewtree Farm
Shellow Wood
Foxbrook Farm
Little Tidnock
SHELLOW LA
Shellow Farm
Pastures
Dighills Farm
Dighill Brook
Rodegreen
Dobford
Dob Ford Bridge
New Pastures
PEXHALL RD
Hotel
Rodeheath
Bell Farm
Manor House
The Grange
MARTON LA
Manor Farm
CW12
Bramhall Hill Farm
BACK LA
Rode Heath
MACCLESFIELD RD
MANOR PARK RD
North Rode
Cloud View Farm
BANK LA
Cow Brook
BACK LA
CHURCH LA
Rode Hall Farm
Ethel's Green Farm
White House Farm
A536
Bank Farm
Dane Valley Way
A54
A54
133
157

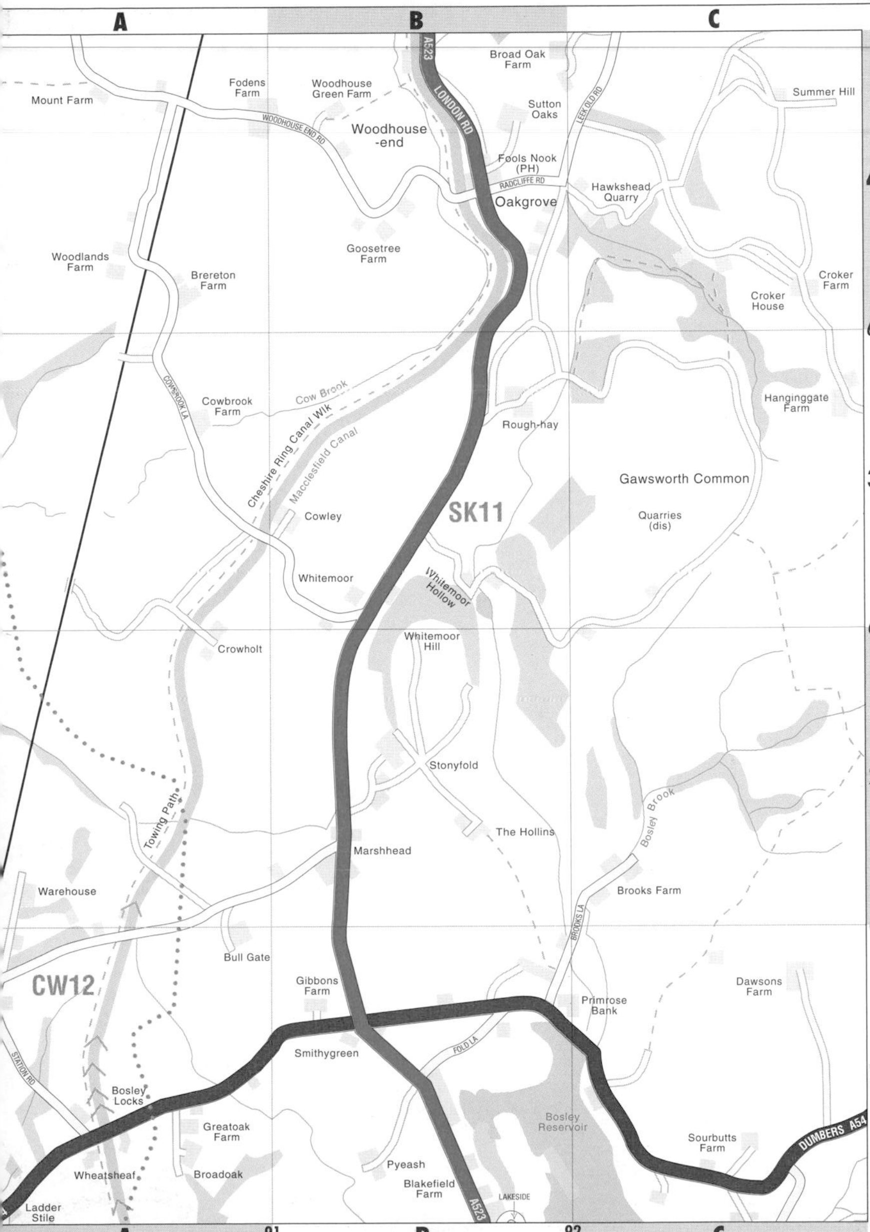
112
136
A
B
C
Mount Farm
Fodens Farm
Woodhouse Green Farm
WOODHOUSE END RD
Woodhouse -end
A523
LONDON RD
Broad Oak Farm
Sutton Oaks
LEEK OLD RD
Summer Hill
Fools Nook (PH)
RADCLIFFE RD
Oakgrove
Hawkshead Quarry
Woodlands Farm
Goosetree Farm
Brereton Farm
Croker House
Croker Farm
COWBROOK LA
Cow Brook
Cowbrook Farm
Cheshire Ring Canal Wlk
Macclesfield Canal
Rough-hay
Hanginggate Farm
Gawsworth Common
SK11
Cowley
Quarries (dis)
Whitemoor
Whitemoor Hollow
Crowholt
Whitemoor Hill
Stonyfold
Towing Path
The Hollins
Bosley Brook
Marshhead
Warehouse
Brooks Farm
BROOKS LA
Bull Gate
CW12
Gibbons Farm
Primrose Bank
Dawsons Farm
STATION RD
Smithygreen
FOLD LA
Bosley Locks
Greatoak Farm
Bosley Reservoir
Sourbutts Farm
DUMBERS A54
Pyeash
Wheatsheaf
Broadoak
Blakefield Farm
LAKESIDE
Ladder Stile
4
69
3
68
2
67
1
66
91
92
158
136

135
113

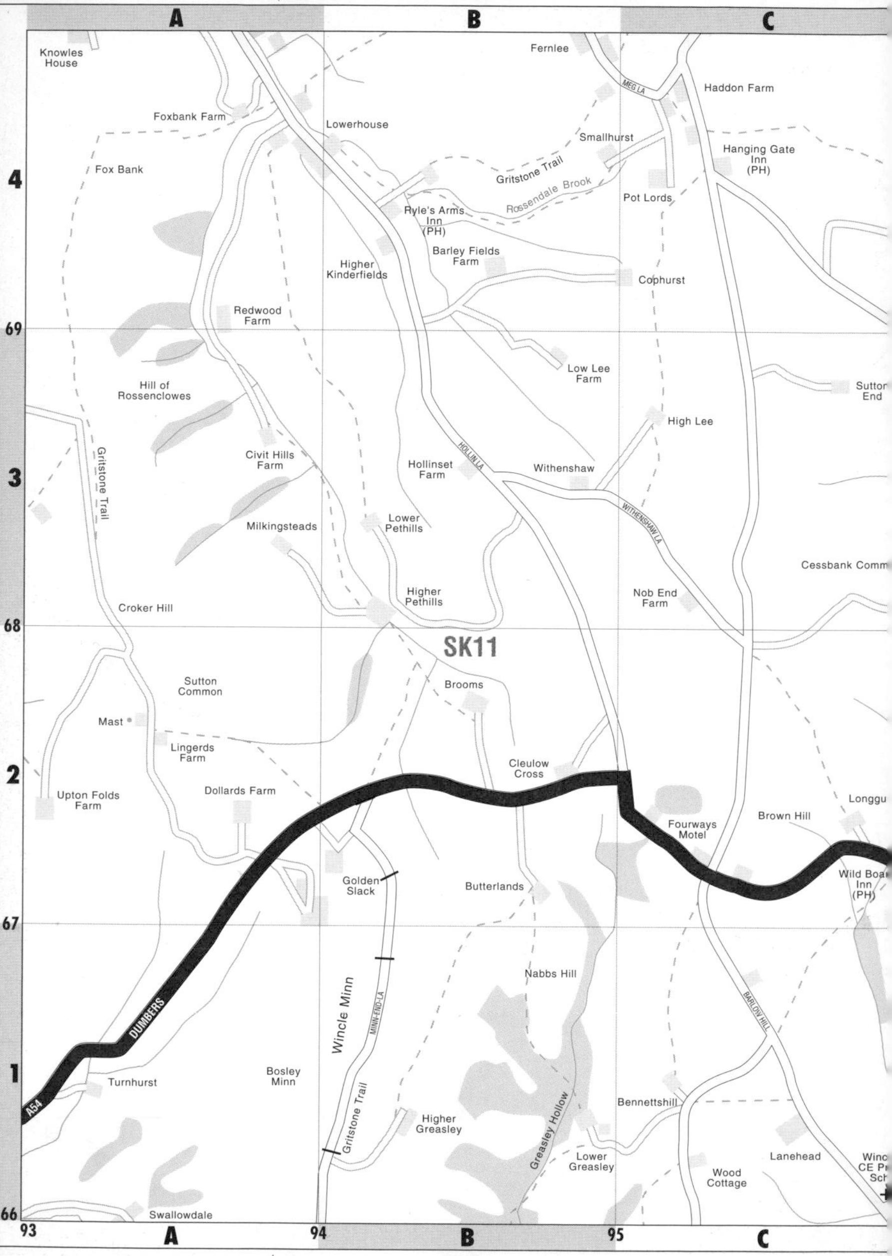
A
B
C
Knowles House
Fernlee
MEG LA
Haddon Farm
Foxbank Farm
Lowerhouse
Smallhurst
Hanging Gate Inn (PH)
Fox Bank
Gritstone Trail
Rossendale Brook
Pot Lords
Ryle's Arms Inn (PH)
Barley Fields Farm
Higher Kinderfields
Cophurst
Redwood Farm
Low Lee Farm
Hill of Rossenclowes
Sutton End
High Lee
Gritstone Trail
Civit Hills Farm
HOLLIN LA
Hollinset Farm
Withenshaw
WITHENSHAW LA
Lower Pethills
Milkingsteads
Cessbank Comm
Higher Pethills
Nob End Farm
Croker Hill
SK11
Sutton Common
Brooms
Mast
Lingerds Farm
Cleulow Cross
Upton Folds Farm
Dollards Farm
Longgu
Fourways Motel
Brown Hill
Golden Slack
Butterlands
Wild Boar Inn (PH)
Wincle Minn
MINN-END-LA
Nabbs Hill
BARLOW HILL
DUMBERS
Bosley Minn
Turnhurst
A54
Gritstone Trail
Greasley Hollow
Bennettshill
Higher Greasley
Lower Greasley
Lanehead
Wood Cottage
Swallowdale
4
69
3
68
2
67
1
66
93
94
95
A
B
C

135
159

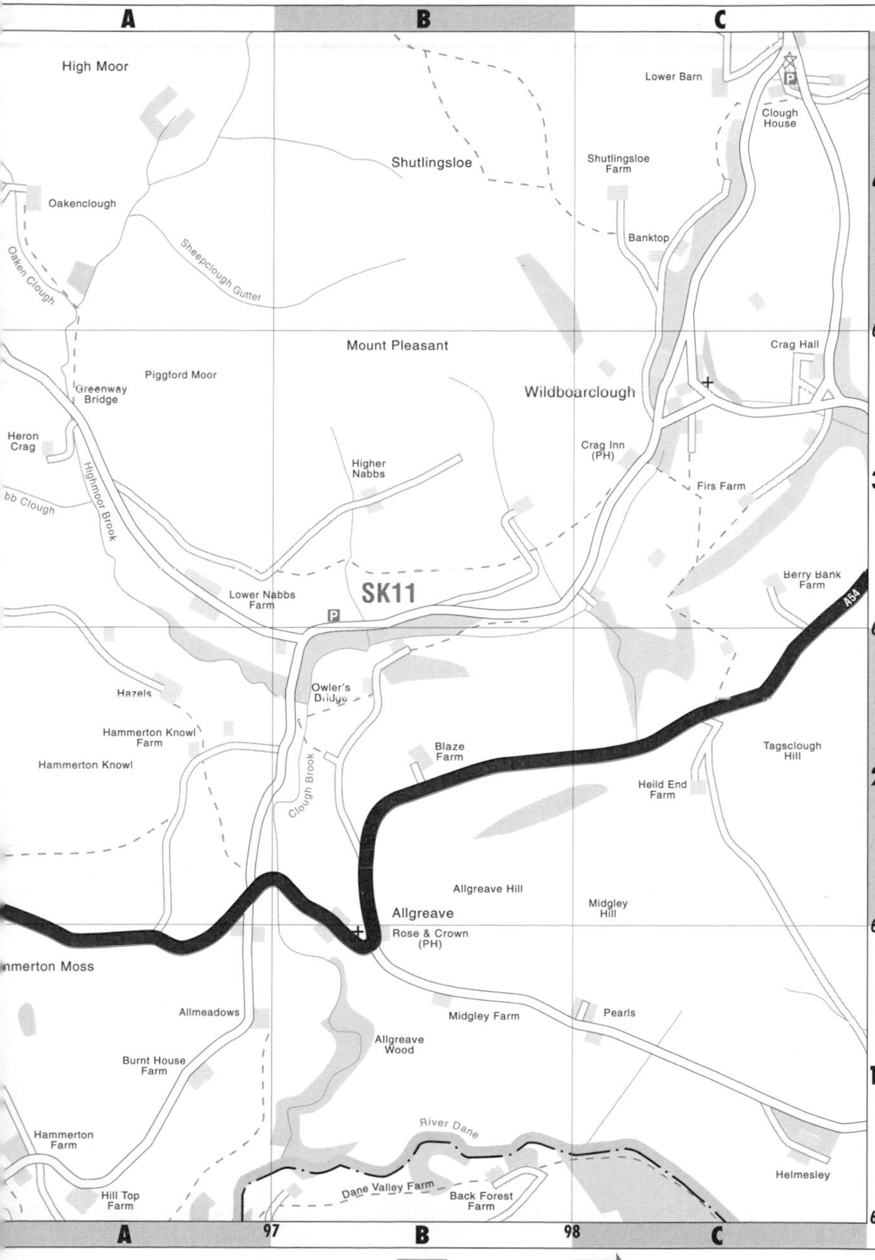
A
B
C
High Moor
Lower Barn
Clough House
Shutlingsloe
Shutlingsloe Farm
Oakenclough
Oaken Clough
Sheepclough Gutter
Banktop
4
69
Mount Pleasant
Crag Hall
Piggford Moor
Greenway Bridge
Wildboarclough
Heron Crag
Crag Inn (PH)
Higher Nabbs
Highmoor Brook
bb Clough
Firs Farm
3
Berry Bank Farm
Lower Nabbs Farm
SK11
A54
68
Owler's Bridge
Hazels
Hammerton Knowl Farm
Hammerton Knowl
Blaze Farm
Tagsclough Hill
Clough Brook
Heild End Farm
2
Allgreave Hill
Midgley Hill
Allgreave
Rose & Crown (PH)
67
nmerton Moss
Allmeadows
Midgley Farm
Pearls
Allgreave Wood
Burnt House Farm
1
River Dane
Hammerton Farm
Helmesley
Dane Valley Farm
Hill Top Farm
Back Forest Farm
66
97
98

137
115

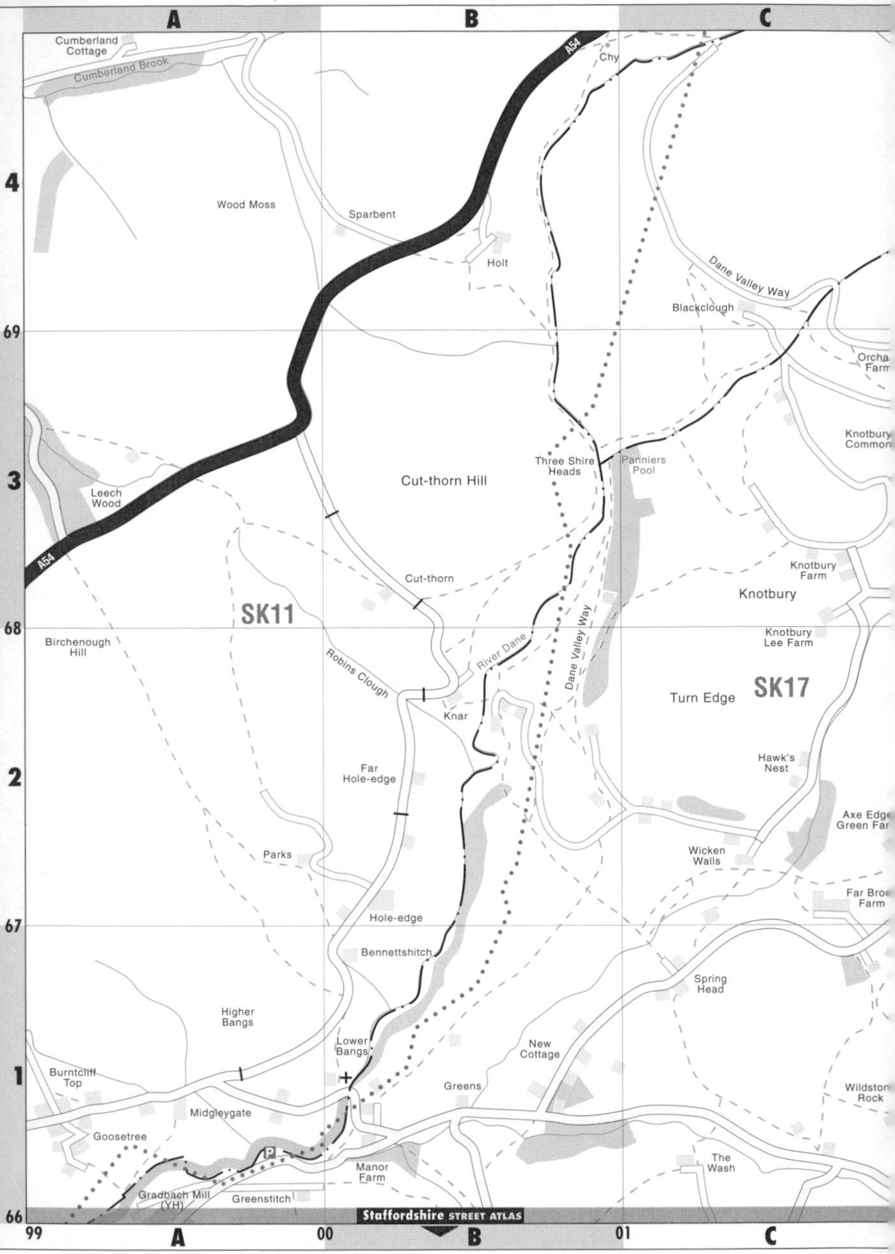
A
B
C
4
69
3
68
2
67
1
66
99
00
01
Cumberland Cottage
Cumberland Brook
A54
Chy
Wood Moss
Sparbent
Holt
Dane Valley Way
Blackclough
Orchard Farm
Knotbury Common
Three Shire Heads
Panniers Pool
Leech Wood
Cut-thorn Hill
Cut-thorn
Knotbury Farm
Knotbury
SK11
Birchenough Hill
Robins Clough
River Dane
Knotbury Lee Farm
Turn Edge
SK17
Knar
Far Hole-edge
Hawk's Nest
Axe Edge Green Farm
Parks
Wicken Walls
Far Broo Farm
Hole-edge
Bennettshitch
Spring Head
Higher Bangs
Lower Bangs
New Cottage
Burntcliff Top
Greens
Wildstone Rock
Midgleygate
Goosetree
P
The Wash
Manor Farm
Gradbach Mill (YH)
Greenstitch

116
140

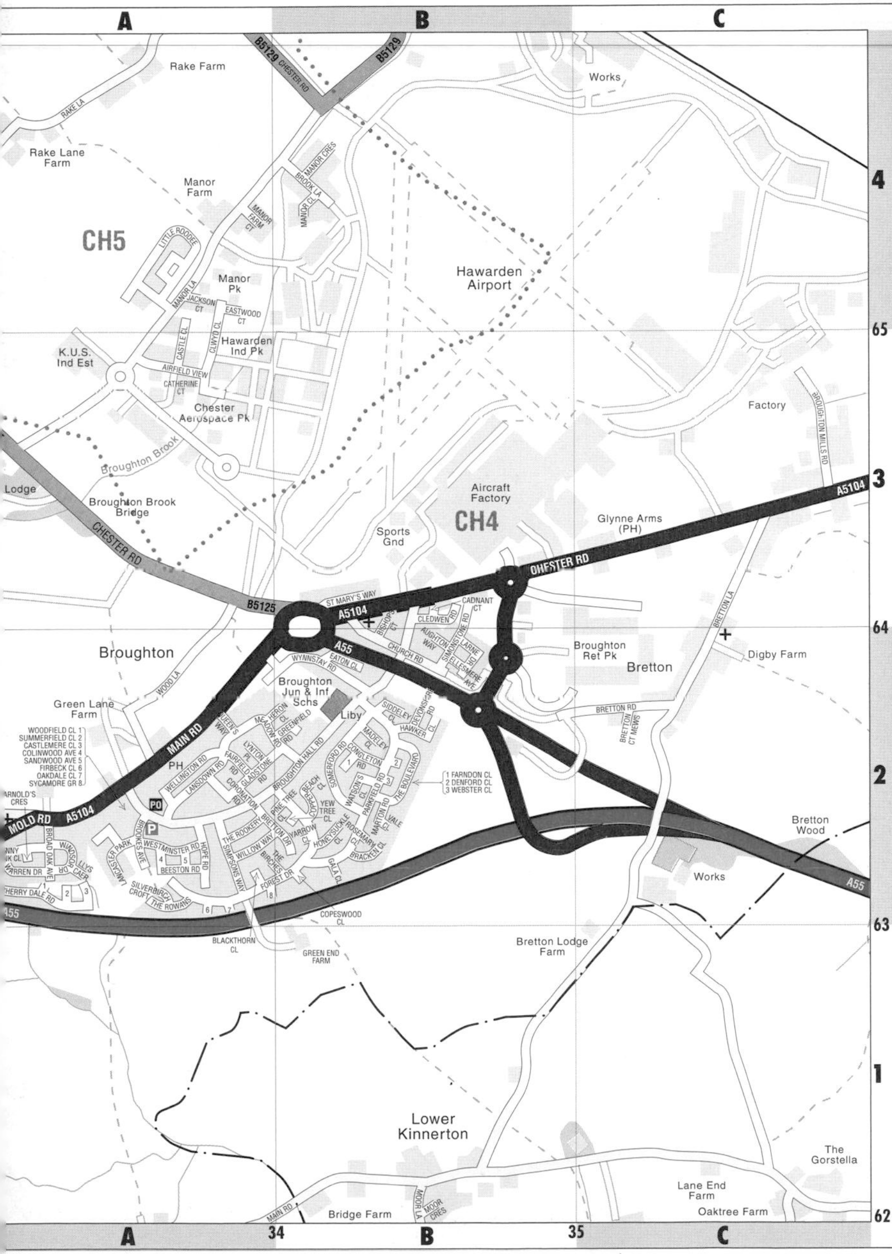
A
B
C
4
3
2
1
65
64
63
62
34
35
Rake Farm
Works
RAKE LA
Rake Lane Farm
Manor Farm
CH5
B5129 CHESTER RD
B5129
MANOR CRES
BROOK LA
MANOR CL
MANOR FARM CT
LITTLE ROODEE
MANOR LA
JACKSON CT
EASTWOOD CT
Manor Pk
Hawarden Airport
CLWYD CL
CASTLE CL
Hawarden Ind Pk
K.U.S. Ind Est
AIRFIELD VIEW
CATHERINE CT
Chester Aerospace Pk
Factory
BROUGHTON MILLS RD
Broughton Brook
Lodge
Broughton Brook Bridge
CHESTER RD
Aircraft Factory
CH4
Sports Gnd
Glynne Arms (PH)
A5104
CHESTER RD
B5125
ST MARY'S WAY
A5104
CADNANT CT
CLEDWEN RD
BISHOPS CT
AUGHTON WAY
SIMONSTONE RD
LARNE CL
ELLESMERE AVE
CHURCH RD
BRETTON LA
Broughton
Broughton Ret Pk
Bretton
Digby Farm
A55
WYNNSTAY RD
EATON CL
Broughton Jun & Inf Schs
Liby
WOOD LA
Green Lane Farm
QUEEN'S WAY
MEADOW RD
HERON CL
GREENFIELD RD
SIDDELEY CL
DEVONSHIRE RD
HAWKER CL
BRETTON RD
BRETTON CT MEWS
MAIN RD
WOODFIELD CL 1
SUMMERFIELD CL 2
CASTLEMERE CL 3
COLINWOOD AVE 4
SANDWOOD AVE 5
FIRBECK CL 6
OAKDALE CL 7
SYCAMORE GR 8
PH
WELLINGTON RD
LANSDOWN RD
FAIRFIELD RD
LYNTON PL
GLADSTONE RD
CORONATION RD
BROUGHTON HALL RD
SOMERFORD RD
CONGLETON RD
MADELEY CL
BEECH CL
COPPER BEECH
YEW TREE CL
WATSON'S CL
PARKFIELD RD
MARTON RD
THE BOULEVARD
1 FARNDON CL
2 DENFORD CL
3 WEBSTER CL
ARNOLD'S CRES
MOLD RD
A5104
PO
P
BROAD OAK AVE
WINDSOR DR
LLYS CAER
WARREN DR
CHERRY DALE RD
LANCASTER PARK
BROOKES AVE
WESTMINSTER RD
HOPE RD
BEESTON RD
SILVERBIRCH CROFT
THE ROWANS
THE ROOKERY
SIMPSONS WAY
WILLOW WAY
BRETTON DR
PINE TREE CL
THE BIRCHES
YARROW CL
HONEYSUCKLE CL
ROSEMARY CL
BRACKEN CL
VALE CL
FOREST DR
GALA CL
Bretton Wood
Works
A55
COPESWOOD CL
BLACKTHORN CL
GREEN END FARM
Bretton Lodge Farm
Lower Kinnerton
The Gorstella
Lane End Farm
Oaktree Farm
MAIN RD
Bridge Farm
MOOR LA
MOOR CRES

161
140

139
117

139
162

or full street detail of the
ighlighted area see page 237.

118
142

163
142

Boughton Heath
Sch
Hotel
College of Law (Christleton Hall)
Christleton
Christleton Prim Sch
Christleton Sports Ctr
Christleton High Sch
The Bishops' Blue Coat CE High Sch
Recn Ctr & Liby
Supermarket
Manor Farm
Dee Banks Sch
Shropshire Union Canal
WHITCHURCH RD
Rowton Grange
Grange Farm
Rowton Moor
Caldy Brook
Gorse Hall New Farm
Huntington Com Prim Sch
Saighton Camp
Rowton
Hotel
Promisedland Farm
Huntington
CHESTER RD
CH3
Claypits Farm
Ridges Lane
Portersheath Farm
Old Hall
Churton Heyes Farm
Heathcroft Farm
Ridgeway Farm
Ridges Lane
Saighton Lane Farm
SANDY LA
Rose Farm House
Huntington Hall
The Grange
Henlake Brook
Saighton Hall Farm
Saighton
Saighton CE Prim Sch
CHAPEL LA
MILLFIELD LA
SAIGHTON LA
A41
A55
B5130
A
B
C
42
43
44
62
1
63
2
64
3
65
4

120
144

165
144

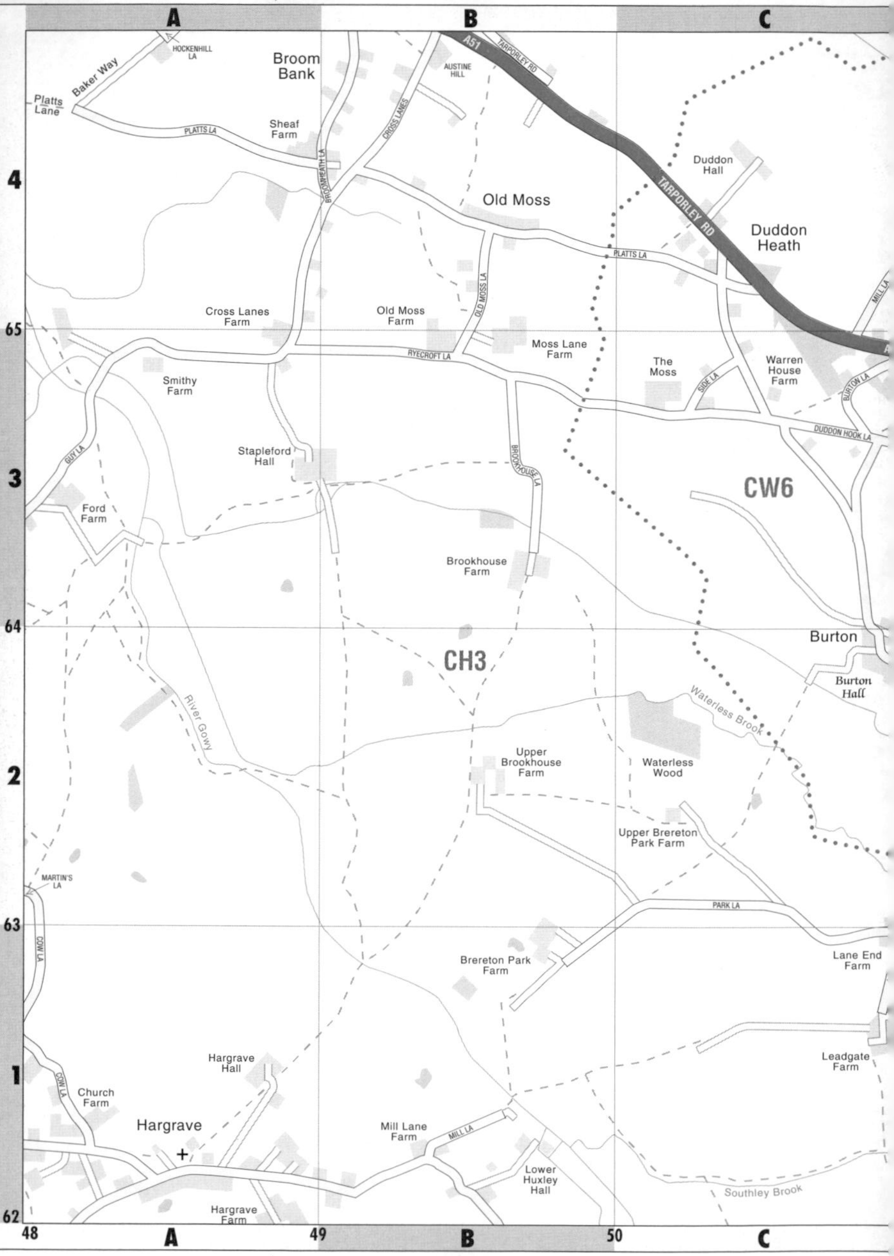
A
B
C
4
3
2
1
65
64
63
62
48
49
50
HOCKENHILL LA
Baker Way
Platts Lane
PLATTS LA
Broom Bank
Sheaf Farm
BROOMHEATH LA
CROSS LANES
AUSTINE HILL
A51
TARPORLEY RD
Old Moss
Duddon Hall
Duddon Heath
PLATTS LA
OLD MOSS LA
MILL LA
Cross Lanes Farm
Old Moss Farm
Moss Lane Farm
RYECROFT LA
The Moss
SIDE LA
Warren House Farm
BURTON LA
DUDDON HOOK LA
Smithy Farm
Stapleford Hall
BROOKHOUSE LA
GUY LA
Ford Farm
CW6
Brookhouse Farm
CH3
Burton
Burton Hall
Waterless Brook
River Gowy
Upper Brookhouse Farm
Waterless Wood
Upper Brereton Park Farm
MARTIN'S LA
PARK LA
COW LA
Brereton Park Farm
Lane End Farm
Leadgate Farm
Hargrave Hall
COW LA
Church Farm
Hargrave
Mill Lane Farm
MILL LA
Lower Huxley Hall
Hargrave Farm
Southley Brook

A
B
C
Duddon Mill
Eddisbury Way
MILL LA
Fir Tree Farm
Brook Farm
The Rookery
Willington Hall
The Glen
Jone's Wood
Duddon Common
COMMON LA
Dickinson's Wood
Sandstone Trail
Oak Tree Farm
WOOD LA
CROSSKEYS CL
GREENACRES
NEW RD
FIELDSIDE
DUDDON CL
LAUREL PK
TARPORLEY RD
Duddon Old Hall
Duddon
Clotton Common
Tethe Bank Farm
St Peter's CE Prim Sch
YEW TREE BANK
DUDDON RD
Brookhouse Farm
Yew Tree Farm
CW6
Burton Farm
Clotton
The Dulla Head (PH)
HIGH ST
Lower House
Eddisbury Way
CROOKED LA
ROAD ST
A51
The Spinney
Castle View
Iddinshall Grange
Hoofield
Hoofield Hall
CH3
Waterless Brook
Iddinshall Rough
HOOFIELD LA
Holborn Hill Farm
Brook Lodge
Hoofield Covert
Sandstone Trail
4
65
3
64
2
63
1
62
52
53

145
123

A
B
C
Grove House
Hillside Farm
TIRLEY LA
High Billings House
Hollins Hill Farm
Holbitch Slack
Bentley Wood
St Paul's CE Prim Sch
QUARRY BANK
Rowley Farm
HOLLINS HILL
Hollins House
Quarrybank
4
JOHN ST
THE CRESCENT
N BROOK RD
CROFT CL
NORTHGATE
Utkinton
BIG FIELD LA
PO
ROWLANDS VIEW
Rose Cottage
UTKINTON LA
65
Shaw House
WOOD LA
Woodlane Farm
SMITHY LA
Bank House
Lime Tree Farm
The Smithy
TARPORLEY RD
Oxpasture Wood
Yewtree Farm
HALL LA
Utkinton Hall
Luddington Hill
3
Fishersgreen Farm
FISHERS GN
Hall Wood
RIDGE HILL
UTKINTON RD
Ridgehill Farm
Summerhouse Bank
Eatonhill Farm
Lightfoot Lane
64
CW6
CH
Hill House
Platts Wood
Ash Wood
HEATH GN
Hill Farm
2
Road Street House
SAPLING LA
A51
ROAD ST
A51
Ash Hill
Sandstone Trail
Ash Hill House
Salterswell House
BURTON AVE
HEATHERWAYS
Portal
FOREST RD
CEDARWOOD CL
THE BLYTHINGS
COBBLERS CROSS LA
63
BACK LANES
Back Lanes
LIME CL
WOODLANDS FIR CL
THE GROVE
ELM WAY CL
CH
Arderne Hall
THE CLOSE
CHESTNUT CT
CHESTNUT CL
Cobblers Cross
MILLFIELD LA
SOUTH CL
HENRY ST
ASH CL
OAKTREE CL
P
BELL MEADOW CT
PO
H
PARK RD
Flaxyard Farm
MARKET CT
Taporley War Memorial
Hotels
RATHBONE PARK
COPPERFIELDS
FLAXYARDS
1
HIGH ST
Tarporley CE Prim Sch
BIRDS LA
P
TORR RISE
PEARWOOD CL
FOXHILL CT
EATON LA
CORONATION TERR
OATHILLS CL
Tarporley
GREENLAND CL
THE AVENUE
OATHILLS DR
Arderne Home Farm
CHURCHILL DR
Poultry Farm
BANBURY CT
COOPER TERR
MEADOWFIELD
BRIDGEDOWN
Tarporley Com High Sch
EATON RD
ORCHARD COTTS
HONEY FIELDS
BIRCH HEATH RD
NANTWICH RD
WINDSOR AVE
THE PADDOCK
BOWMERE RD
WALKERS LA
Rhuddall Heath
THE HAWTHORNS
BOWMERE CL
A49
62
54
55
56
A
B
C

145
168

A
B
C
Cotebrook
PH
Tom's Hole
WOODLANDS CL
TARPORLEY RD
A49
OULTON MILL LA
Mill Pond
Alvanley Arms (PH)
Little Budworth Country Park
Mast
WHITEHALL LA
COACH RD
Mill Covert
Hill Top Farm
Park Place Farm
PARK RD
Egerton Arms (PH)
Budworth Pool
Little Budworth
PINFOLD LA
VICARAGE LA
MILL LA
WELL LA
BOOTH AVE
ST PETER'S DR
TOWNSFIELD DR
YEW TREE CL
PO
P
Home Farm
Jackie Stewart Bsns Ctr
RUSHTON LA
BROWNHILLS RD
BEECH LA
Brownhill
Beechlane Farm
EATON LA
Garner House
Oulton House
Oulton Park
Lower Farm
Motor Racing Circuit
Hazelhurst Covert
Rushton
CW6
Oulton Lake
Moss Hall Farm
DOGMORE LA
Red Lion (PH)
Parkwall Farm
KINGS LA
Withey Bed
Eaton
Eaton Farm
LOWER LA
ELM TREE CT
EDGEWELL LA
Eaton Prim Sch
WHALLEY DR
Hunt's Hill
Old Lanes
HICKHURST LA
Oak Tree Farm
Oultonlowe Farm
Philo House
Boothouse Farm
MILL LA
WINTERFORD LA
Winterford Farm
THE HALL LA
Oxheys
Philo Gorse
4
65
3
64
2
63
1
62
58
59

147
125
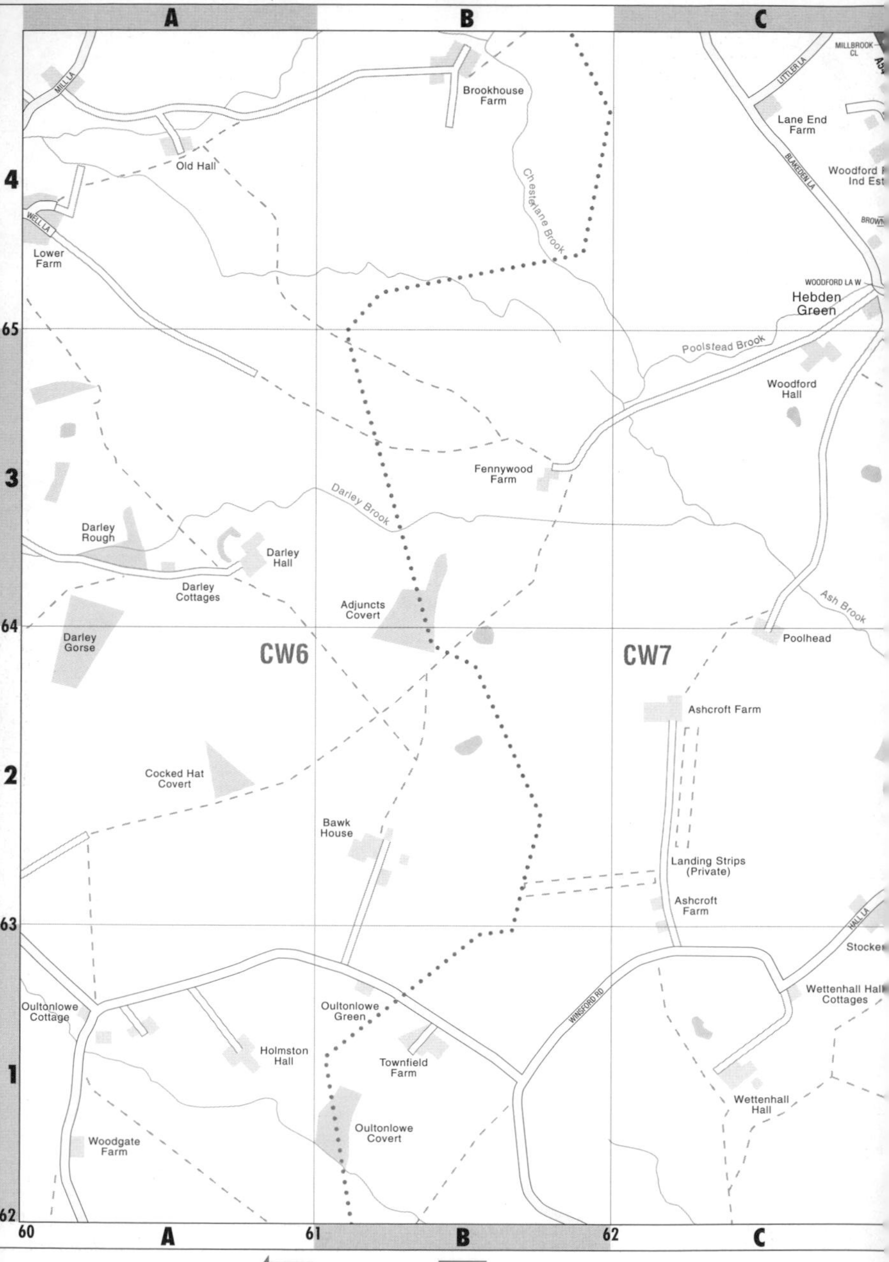

147
170

126 150

DHOLE COTTS
KENHAM GR
CKWELL CL
TMAN PL
ENTS WAY
BURY AVE

7 ALEXANDRA SQ
8 HAMPSTEAD CT
9 WESTMINSTER GR
10 ST JAMES TERR
11 CROFTWOOD CL
12 BRACKENFIELD WAY
13 FAIROAK CL

14 BROOMFIELD CL
15 INNOVATION HO
16 CHEVIOT CT

B4
1 DELAMERE ST
2 HIGH ST
3 CHEPSTOW CL
4 CALDICOTT CL
5 CARMARTHEN CL
6 CLIFFORD PL

7 BLENHEIM GDNS
8 TOWNFIELDS COTTS
9 TOWNFIELDS GDNS
10 NORMANDY AVE
11 DENESGATE
12 LOWER HAIGH ST

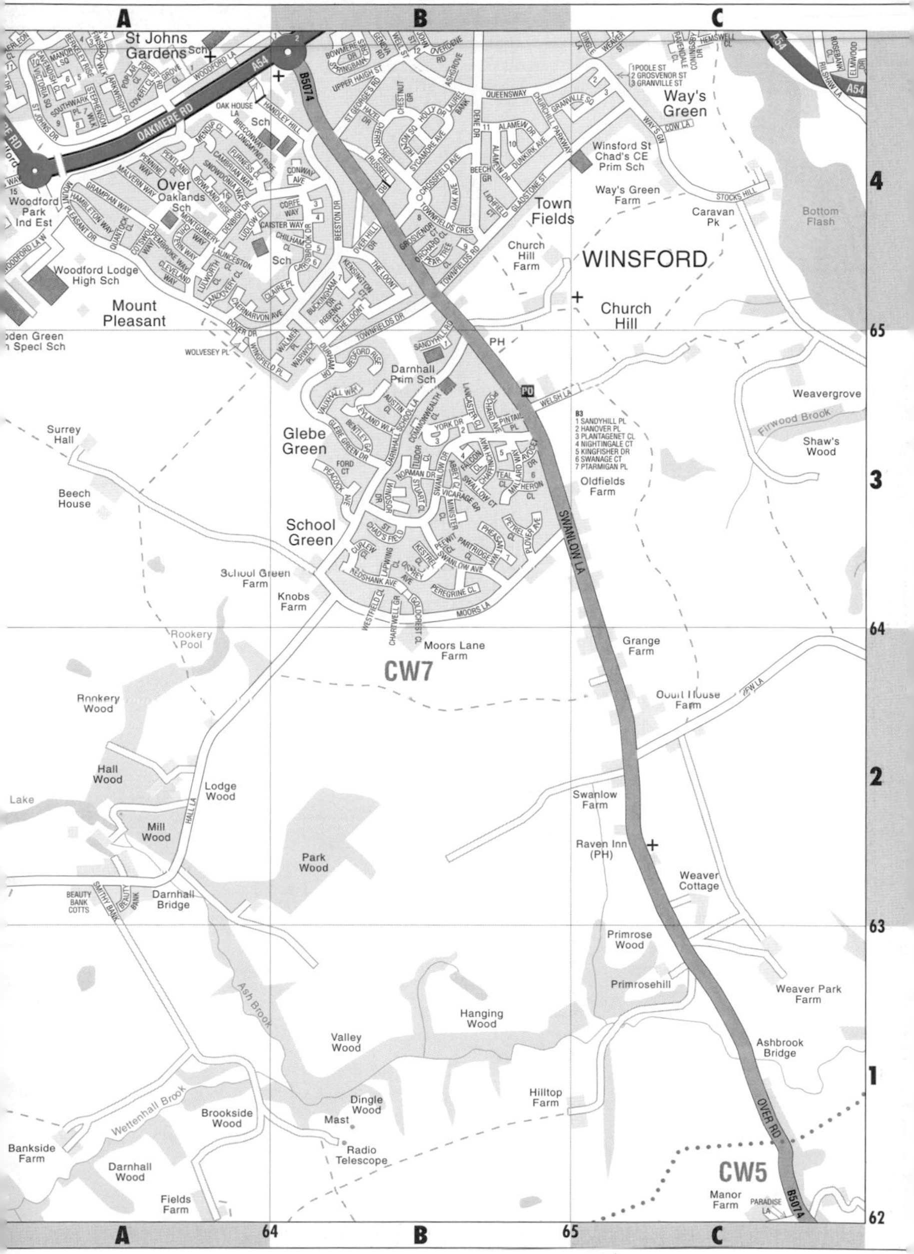

149
127

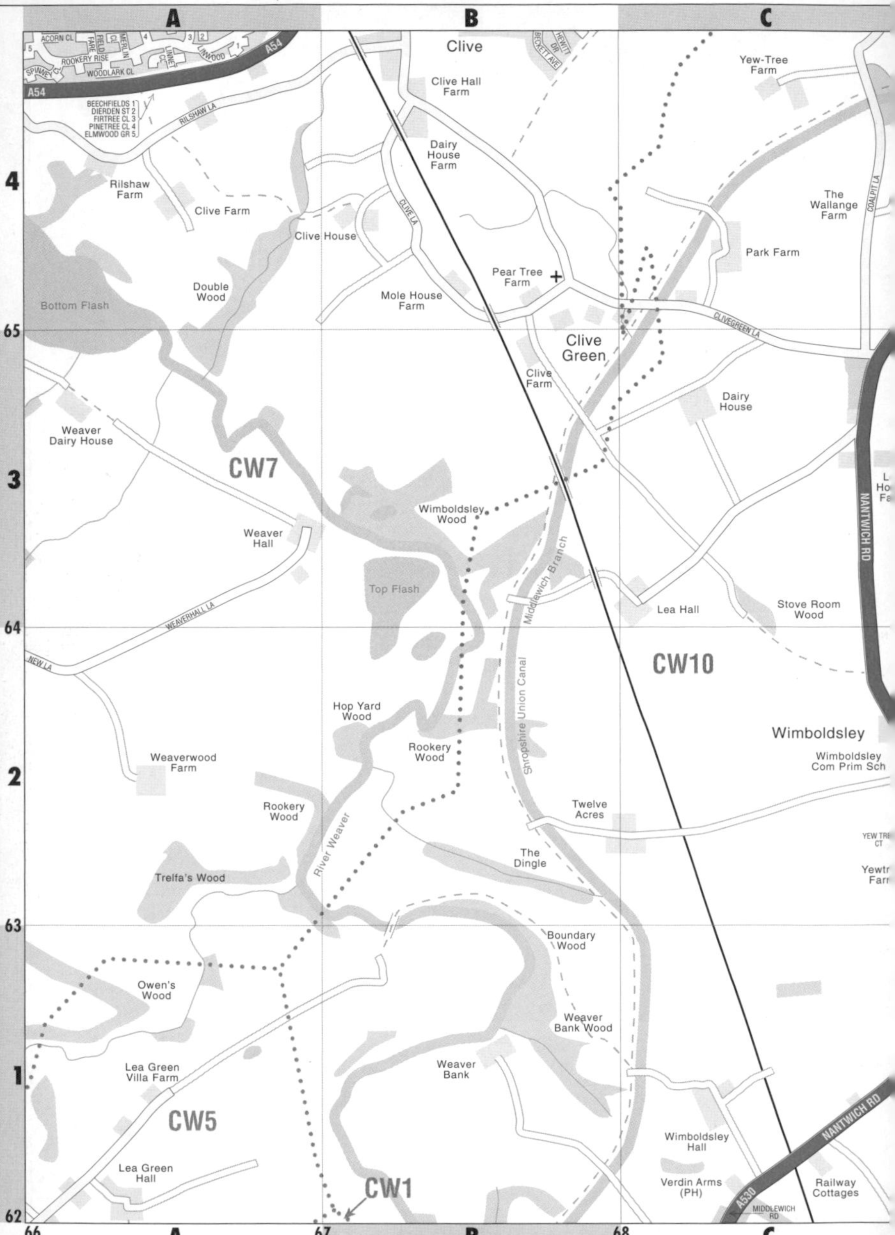
A
B
C
4
3
2
1
65
64
63
62
66
67
68
ACORN CL
ROOKERY RISE
SPINNEY
WOODLARK CL
LINWOOD
MERLIN CL
LINNET CL
FIELD FARE
A54
BEECHFIELDS 1
DIERDEN ST 2
FIRTREE CL 3
PINETREE CL 4
ELMWOOD GR 5
RILSHAW LA
Clive
BECKETT AVE
HEWITT DR
Clive Hall Farm
Yew-Tree Farm
Dairy House Farm
Rilshaw Farm
Clive Farm
Clive House
CLIVE LA
The Wallange Farm
COALPIT LA
Park Farm
Double Wood
Bottom Flash
Pear Tree Farm
Mole House Farm
CLIVEGREEN LA
Clive Green
Clive Farm
Dairy House
Weaver Dairy House
CW7
Wimboldsley Wood
Weaver Hall
Middlewich Branch
NANTWICH RD
Top Flash
WEAVERHALL LA
Lea Hall
Stove Room Wood
NEW LA
CW10
Shropshire Union Canal
Hop Yard Wood
Rookery Wood
Wimboldsley
Weaverwood Farm
Wimboldsley Com Prim Sch
Rookery Wood
Twelve Acres
River Weaver
YEW TREE CT
The Dingle
Trelfa's Wood
Boundary Wood
Owen's Wood
Weaver Bank Wood
Lea Green Villa Farm
Weaver Bank
CW5
NANTWICH RD
Wimboldsley Hall
Lea Green Hall
CW1
Verdin Arms (PH)
Railway Cottages
A530
MIDDLEWICH RD

149
172

B4
1 NEWTON HALL MEWS
2 HANNAH'S WLK
3 MANOR LA
4 ASHFIELD ST
5 SMALLWOOD CL
6 CRESANNE CL

128

B4
7 WARMINGHAM CT

152

A
B
C
4
65
3
64
2
63
1
62
70
71
MIDDLEWICH
CW10
CW11
Shropshire Union Canal
Middlewich Branch
anthorne Lock
A530
NANTWICH RD
Middlewich Prim Sch
Sch
L Ctr
A533
LEWIN ST
MAIDENHILLS
CANAL TERR
BROOKS LA
ROAD BETA
POCHIN WAY
Sanderson's Brook
Depot
ERF WAY
WESTBURY CL 1
SWANSCOE CL 2
SHROPSHIRE CL
Flea La
ROYLANDS DR
STALLARD WAY
ST ANN'S RD
HUBERT DR
WARDLE MEWS
Brooks Lane Ind Est
ST ANN'S AVE
HAYHURST AVE
KITFIELD AVE
MANOR FIELDS
RUTLAND DR
FALLOW CT
ORCHARD CL
ELM RD
ASH GR
POPLAR DR
OAK DR
DENBIGH CRES
PIPPIN CL
DUNMORE CL
BARRINGTON DR
MANOR CRES
LONGMOSS CL
KERRIDGE CL
BRYNLOW DR
SIMONSWOOD CL
BRADLEY CL
BLAKELOW CL
WAVERTREE DR
ROLT CRES
LONGWOOD CL
LONG LA
OLD GATE CL
GREENDALE DR
WARREN CL
RYECROFT CL
WESTON CL
HURDSFIELD CL
Manor Park
WHITLEY CL
RAINOW CL
WHIRLEY CL
MOTTRAM CL
RUSHTON DR
ASTLE CL
BUTLEY CL
HENBURY CL
SUTTON LA
WHITEGATE CL
Schs
LONG LA S
DALE CT
CHADWICK CT
QUEEN'S DR
Ind Est
Works
Cledford Hall
Norcroft Farm
HEATON CL
MOSLEY CL
HANKELOW CL
WORLESTON CL
WHITEMORE RD
GEORGE VI AVE
GEORGE VI CL
CORONATION RD
CHADWICK FIELDS ORCH
PRINCESS CRES
ALEXANDRA RD
CLEDFORD LA
Works
Trent & Mersey Canal
FALKNER DR
Keepers Cottage
MOSS DR
REDSHAW CL
CROSS LA
HUTCHINS CL
CLEDFORD CRES
TELFER CL
FERNLEIGH CL
ROWAN CL
COPPICE DR
BOOTH LA
ASHMORE CL
GORSLEY CL
CHADWICK RD
EARDSWICK RD
Old Gorse
THE GREEN
GSTONE WAY
LISTER CL
ALDINGTON DR
FAIRACRE DR
CEDAR CL
VENABLES WAY
SHILTON CL
ALLGREAVE CL 1
TYTHERINGTON CL 2
WOODEND CL 3
NIGHTINGALE CL 4
BLACKWELL CL 5
TARVIN CL 6
KESTREL CL
FALCON CL
BEESTON CL
BUNBURY CL
DAVENHAM WAY
OSPREY CL
MILTON CL
STEELE RD
BYRON CL
KINGSWOOD CRES
PH
Works
Sutton Hall Farm
ASHTON CL
SYCAMORE DR
NORTHWOOD AVE
INGLEWOOD AVE
1 WOODSTOCK DR
2 CHESTERTON CL
3 SHELLY CL
Cheshire Ring Canal Walk
Sutton Mill
WARMINGHAM LA
A533
Newfield Farm
Sutton Lane
Saunders Field
Pettywood Farm
Field's Farm
Tetton Hall Cottages
River Wheelock
estonegreen Farm
Tetton Hall
TETTON LA
Manor Farm
West Farm
Occlestone Green
pley House
Home Farm
New Farm
Withinstreet Farm
mithy
Forge Mill Farm
Forge Cottages
Sparrowgrove
FORGE MILL LA
Denmar
Oldhough Manor
Oldhough Cottage
DRAGON'S LA
The Bungalow
Fields Farm

173

152

151
129

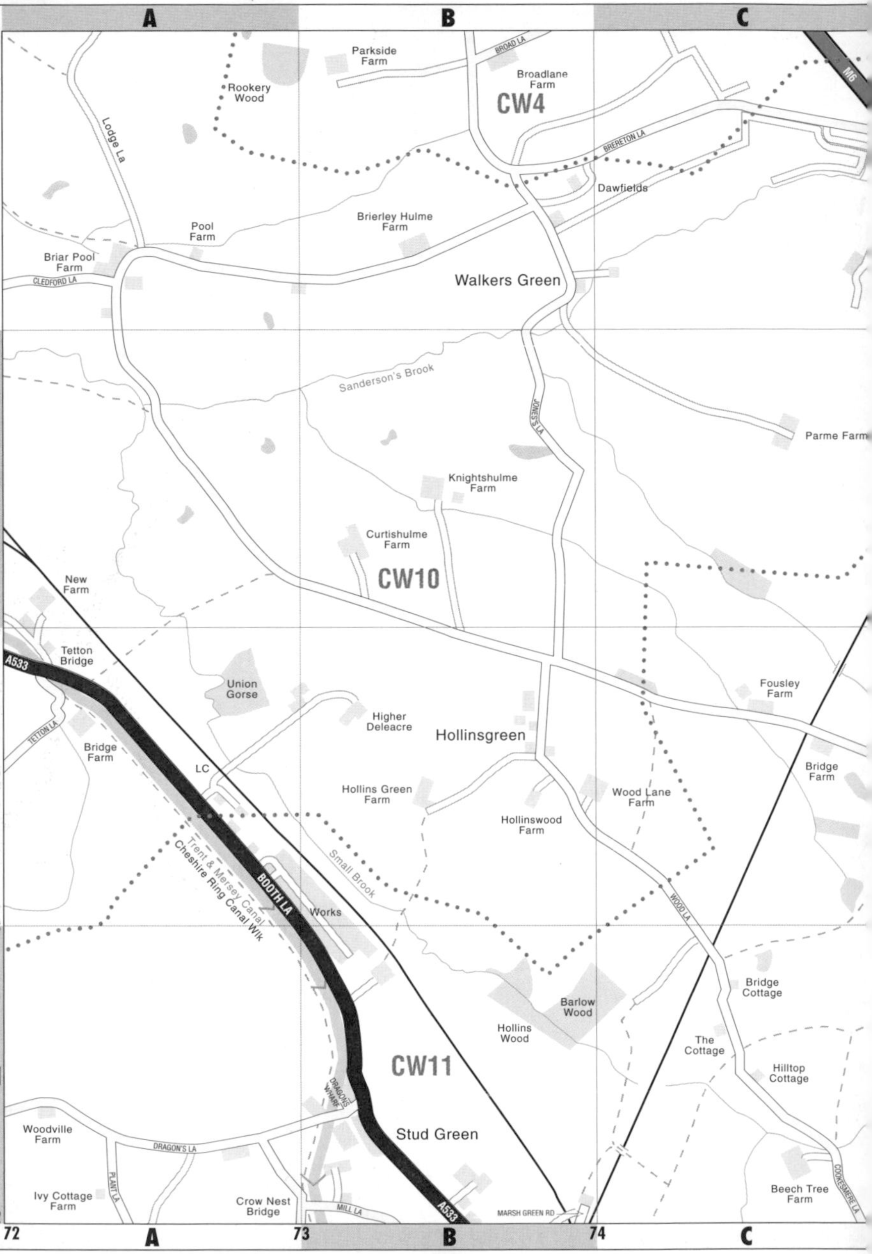

151
174

130
154

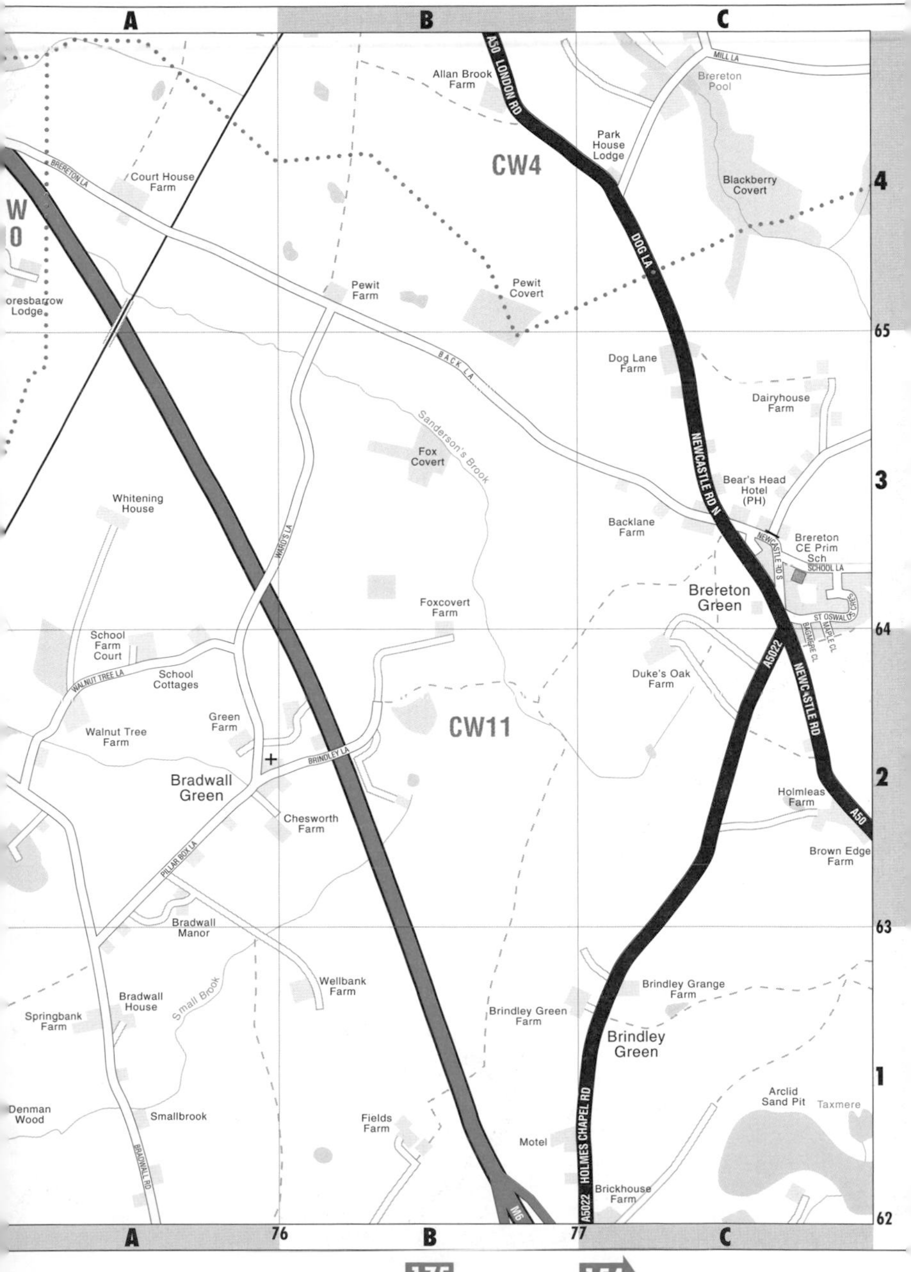
A
B
C
Allan Brook Farm
A50 LONDON RD
MILL LA
Brereton Pool
Park House Lodge
CW4
Court House Farm
BRERETON LA
Blackberry Covert
DOG LA
Pewit Farm
Pewit Covert
oresbarrow Lodge
BACK LA
Dog Lane Farm
Dairyhouse Farm
Sanderson's Brook
Fox Covert
NEWCASTLE RD N
Bear's Head Hotel (PH)
Whitening House
Backlane Farm
WARD'S LA
NEWCASTLE RD S
Brereton CE Prim Sch
SCHOOL LA
Brereton Green
Foxcovert Farm
ST OSWALDS CRES
BAGMERE CL
MAPLE CL
School Farm Court
A5022
NEWCASTLE RD
WALNUT TREE LA
School Cottages
Duke's Oak Farm
Green Farm
CW11
Walnut Tree Farm
BRINDLEY LA
Bradwall Green
Holmleas Farm
A50
Chesworth Farm
PILLAR BOX LA
Brown Edge Farm
Bradwall Manor
Brindley Grange Farm
Wellbank Farm
Small Brook
Bradwall House
Springbank Farm
Brindley Green Farm
Brindley Green
HOLMES CHAPEL RD
Arclid Sand Pit
Taxmere
Denman Wood
Smallbrook
Fields Farm
Motel
BRADWALL RD
Brickhouse Farm
M6
A5022
4
65
3
64
2
63
1
62
76
77

175
154

153 131

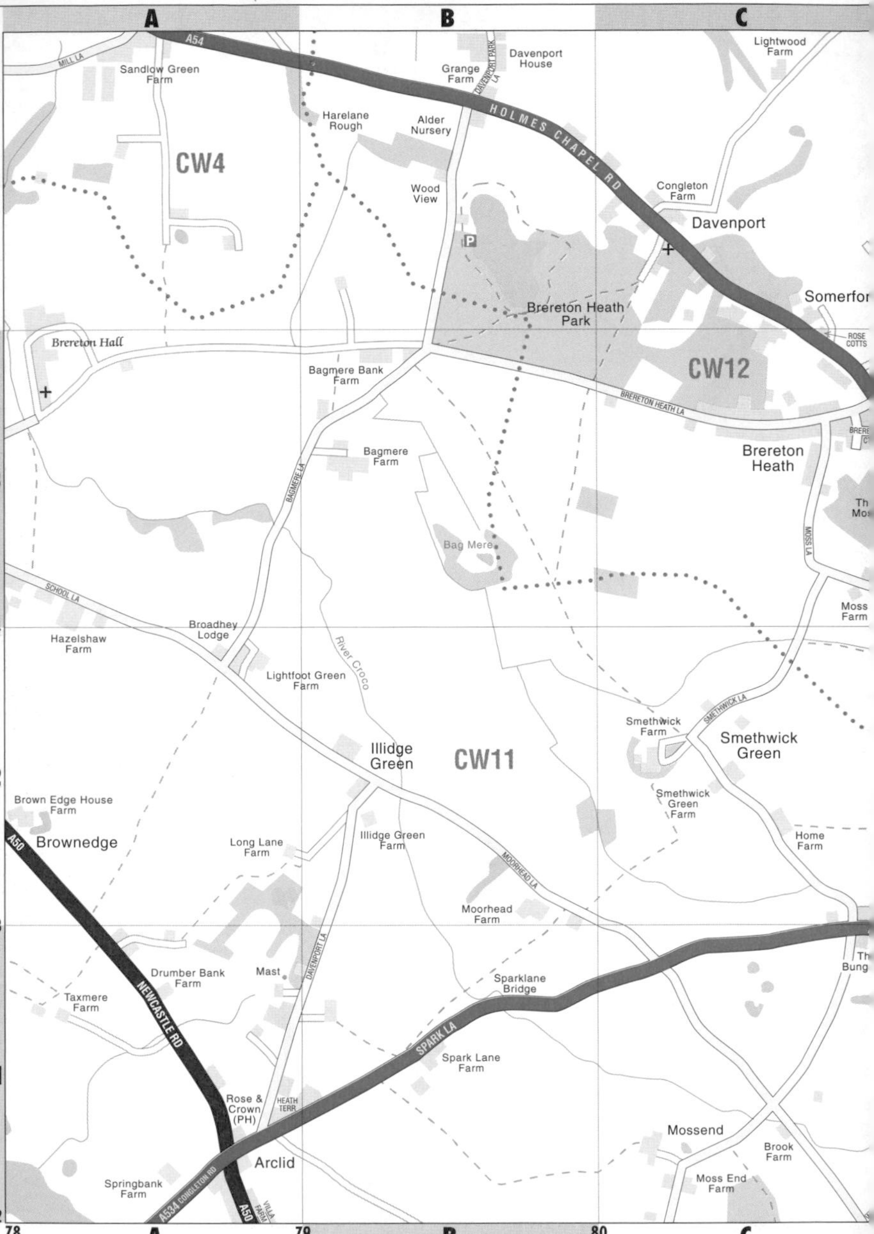

153 176

132
156

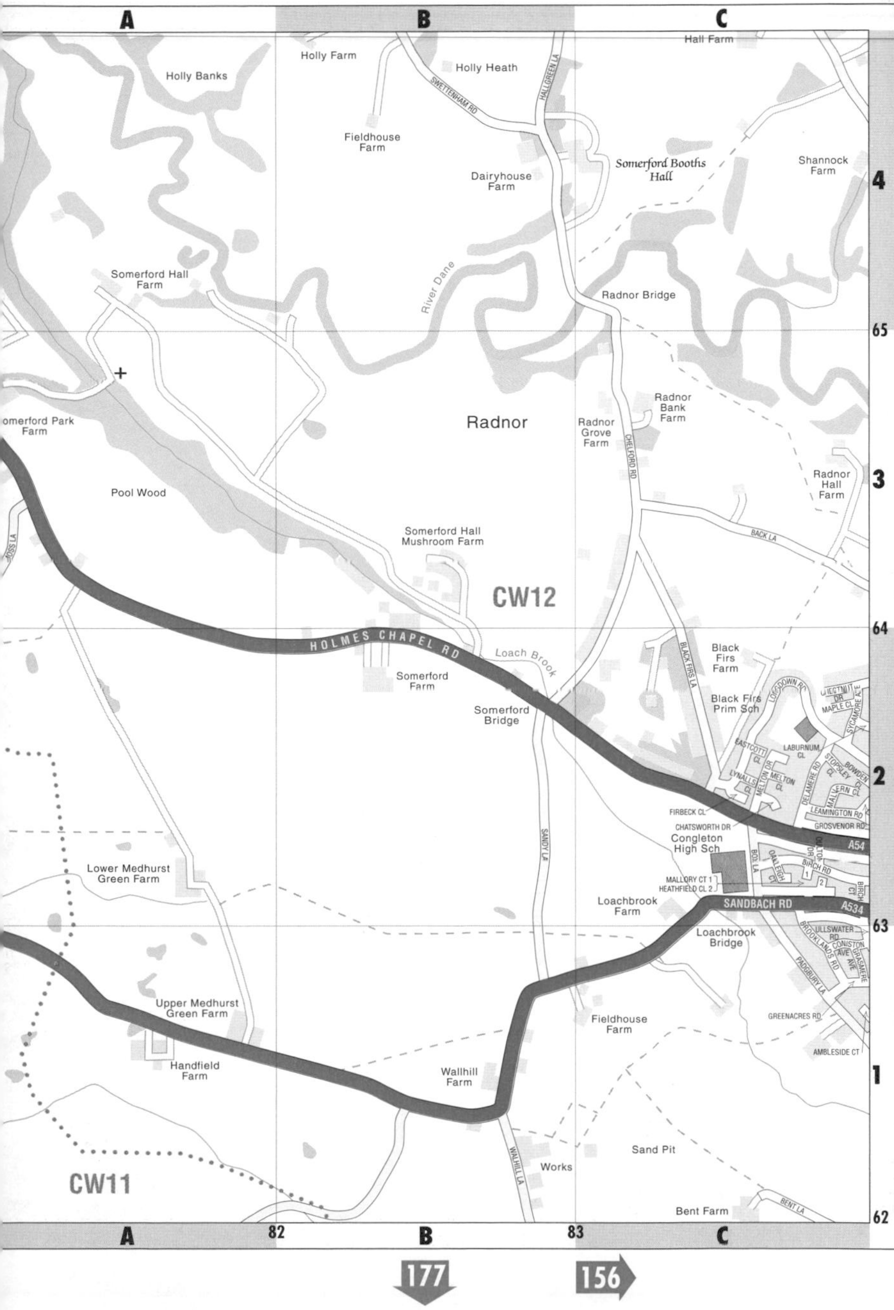

177
156

155
133

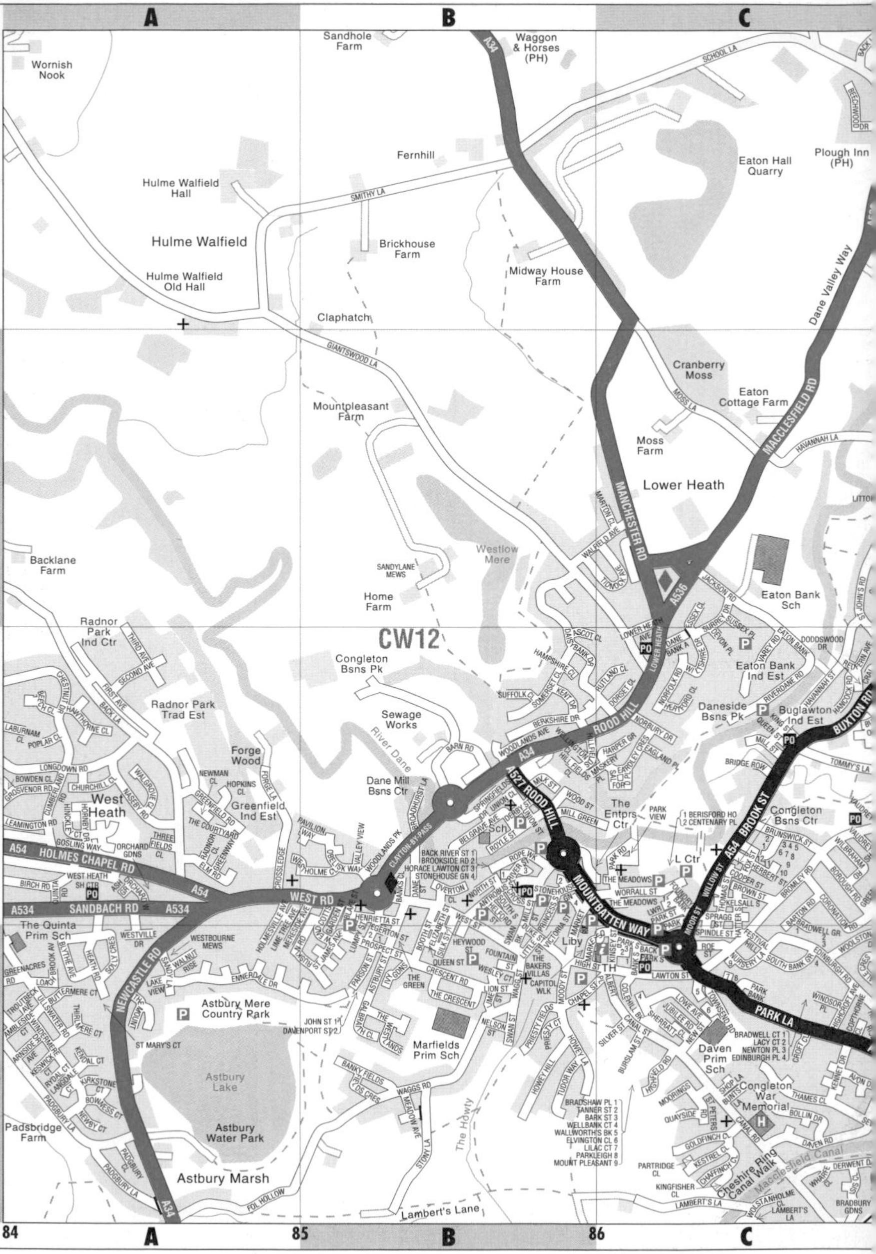
A
B
C
4
65
3
64
2
63
1
62
84
85
86
Sandhole Farm
Waggon & Horses (PH)
Wornish Nook
Fernhill
Hulme Walfield Hall
Hulme Walfield
Hulme Walfield Old Hall
Brickhouse Farm
Midway House Farm
Eaton Hall Quarry
Plough Inn (PH)
Dane Valley Way
Claphatch
GIANTSWOOD LA
SMITHY LA
SCHOOL LA
Cranberry Moss
Eaton Cottage Farm
MACCLESFIELD RD
MOSS LA
Moss Farm
HAVANNAH LA
Mountpleasant Farm
Lower Heath
MANCHESTER RD
Westlow Mere
Backlane Farm
SANDYLANE MEWS
Home Farm
CW12
Radnor Park Ind Ctr
Congleton Bsns Pk
Eaton Bank Sch
Eaton Bank Ind Est
Daneside Bsns Pk
Buglawton Ind Est
Radnor Park Trad Est
Sewage Works
River Dane
ROOD HILL
BUXTON RD
Forge Wood
Dane Mill Bsns Ctr
West Heath
Greenfield Ind Est
A527 ROOD HILL
The Entprs Ctr
Congleton Bsns Ctr
MOUNTBATTEN WAY
BROOK ST
L Ctr
A54 HOLMES CHAPEL RD
WEST RD
CLAYTON-BY-PASS
A534 SANDBACH RD
The Quinta Prim Sch
Liby
TH
PARK LA
NEWCASTLE RD
Astbury Mere Country Park
Marfields Prim Sch
Daven Prim Sch
Congleton War Memorial
Astbury Lake
Astbury Water Park
Padsbridge Farm
Astbury Marsh
The Howty
Cheshire Ring Canal Walk
Macclesfield Canal
Lambert's Lane
FOL HOLLOW
A34
A536
BACK RIVER ST 1
BROOKSIDE RD 2
HORACE LAWTON CT 3
STONEHOUSE GN 4
1 BERISFORD HO
2 CENTENARY PL
JOHN ST 1
DAVENPORT ST 2
BRADSHAW PL 1
TANNER ST 2
BARK ST 3
WELLBANK CT 4
WALLWORTH'S BK 5
ELVINGTON CL 6
LILAC CT 7
PARKLEIGH 8
MOUNT PLEASANT 9
BRADWELL CT 1
LACY CT 2
NEWTON PL 3
EDINBURGH PL 4

155
178

C2
1 SMALLWOOD CT
2 SOMERFORD CT
3 CRANAGE CT
4 GOOSTREY CT
5 MOSTON CT
6 BETCHTON CT
7 RODE CT
8 TETTON CT
9 NEWBOLD CT
10 ARCLID CT
11 ST STEPHENS CT
12 ELWORTH CT

134
158

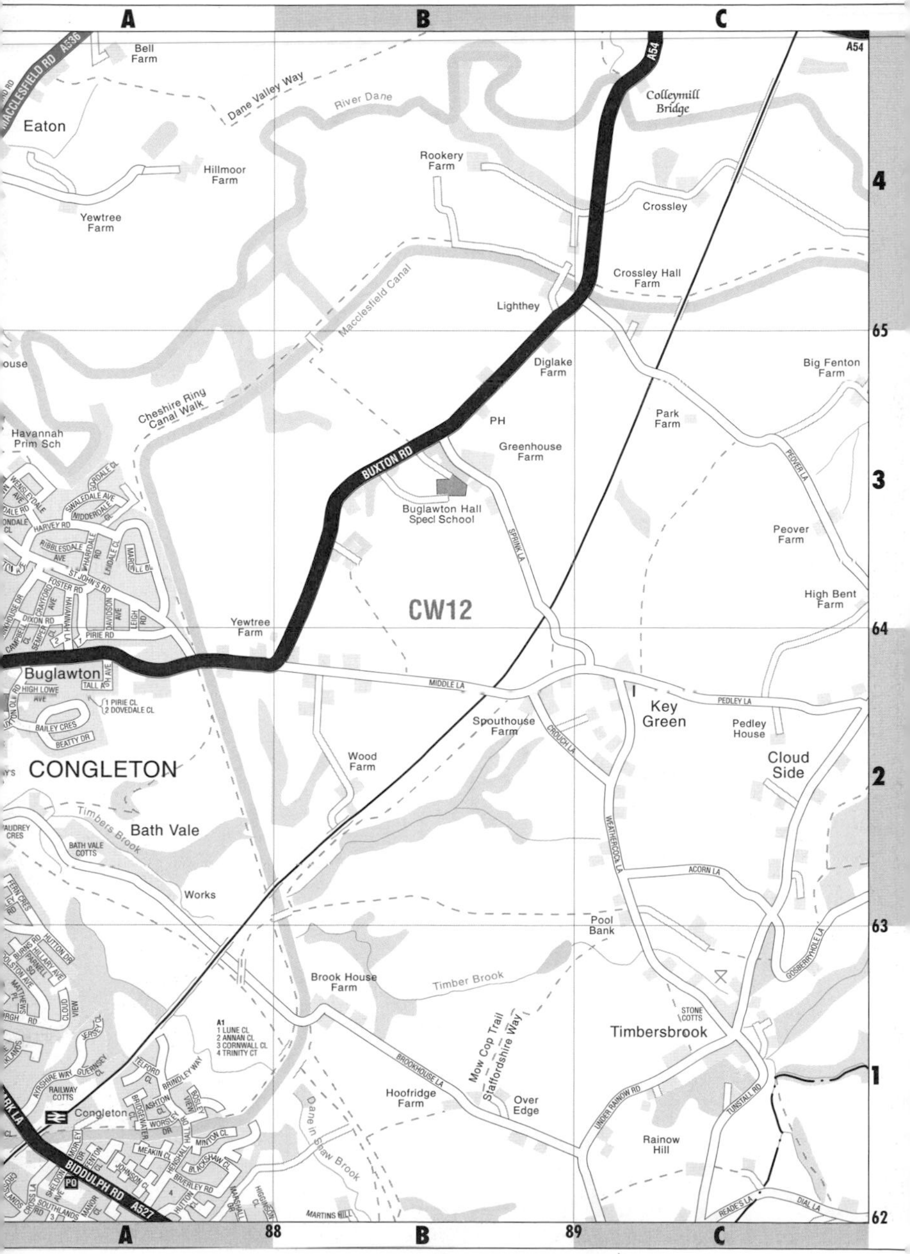
A
B
C
4
3
2
1
65
64
63
62
88
89
A54
A536
MACCLESFIELD RD
Bell Farm
Eaton
Dane Valley Way
River Dane
Colleymill Bridge
Rookery Farm
Hillmoor Farm
Yewtree Farm
Crossley
Crossley Hall Farm
Lighthey
Macclesfield Canal
Diglake Farm
Big Fenton Farm
Cheshire Ring Canal Walk
Havannah Prim Sch
PH
Park Farm
Greenhouse Farm
BUXTON RD
PEOVER LA
Buglawton Hall Specl School
Peover Farm
SPRINK LA
High Bent Farm
CW12
Yewtree Farm
Buglawton
MIDDLE LA
PEDLEY LA
Key Green
Pedley House
Spouthouse Farm
CROUCH LA
Cloud Side
Wood Farm
CONGLETON
Bath Vale
Timbers Brook
BATH VALE COTTS
WEATHERCOCK LA
ACORN LA
Works
Pool Bank
GOSBERRYHOLE LA
Brook House Farm
Timber Brook
STONE COTTS
Timbersbrook
Mow Cop Trail
Staffordshire Way
BROOKHOUSE LA
Hoofridge Farm
Over Edge
UNDER RAINOW RD
TUNSTALL RD
Rainow Hill
Dane in Shaw Brook
MARTINS HILL
READE'S LA
DIAL LA
Congleton
RAILWAY COTTS
PO
BIDDULPH RD
A527
A1
1 LUNE CL
2 ANNAN CL
3 CORNWALL CL
4 TRINITY CT
1 PIRIE CL
2 DOVEDALE CL
HARVEY RD
RIBBLESDALE AVE
ST JOHN'S RD
FOSTER RD
DIXON RD
PIRIE RD
HIGH LOWE AVE
BAILEY CRES
BEATTY DR
SWALEDALE AVE
NIDDERDALE
WENSLEYDALE AVE
HAVANNAH LA
DAVIDSON AVE
LEIGH RD
AYRSHIRE WAY
GUERNSEY
JERSEY
TELFORD CL
BRINDLEY WAY
ASHTON CL
WORSLEY DR
BOSLEY VIEW
MINTON CL
MEAKIN CL
JOHNSON CL
BLACKSHAW CL
BRIERLEY RD
HUTTON DR
HILLARY AVE
PARNELL
CLOUD VIEW
MATTHEWS
SOUTHLANDS
MANOR CL
CROSS LA
HIGGINSON CL
MARSHALL

179
158

157
135

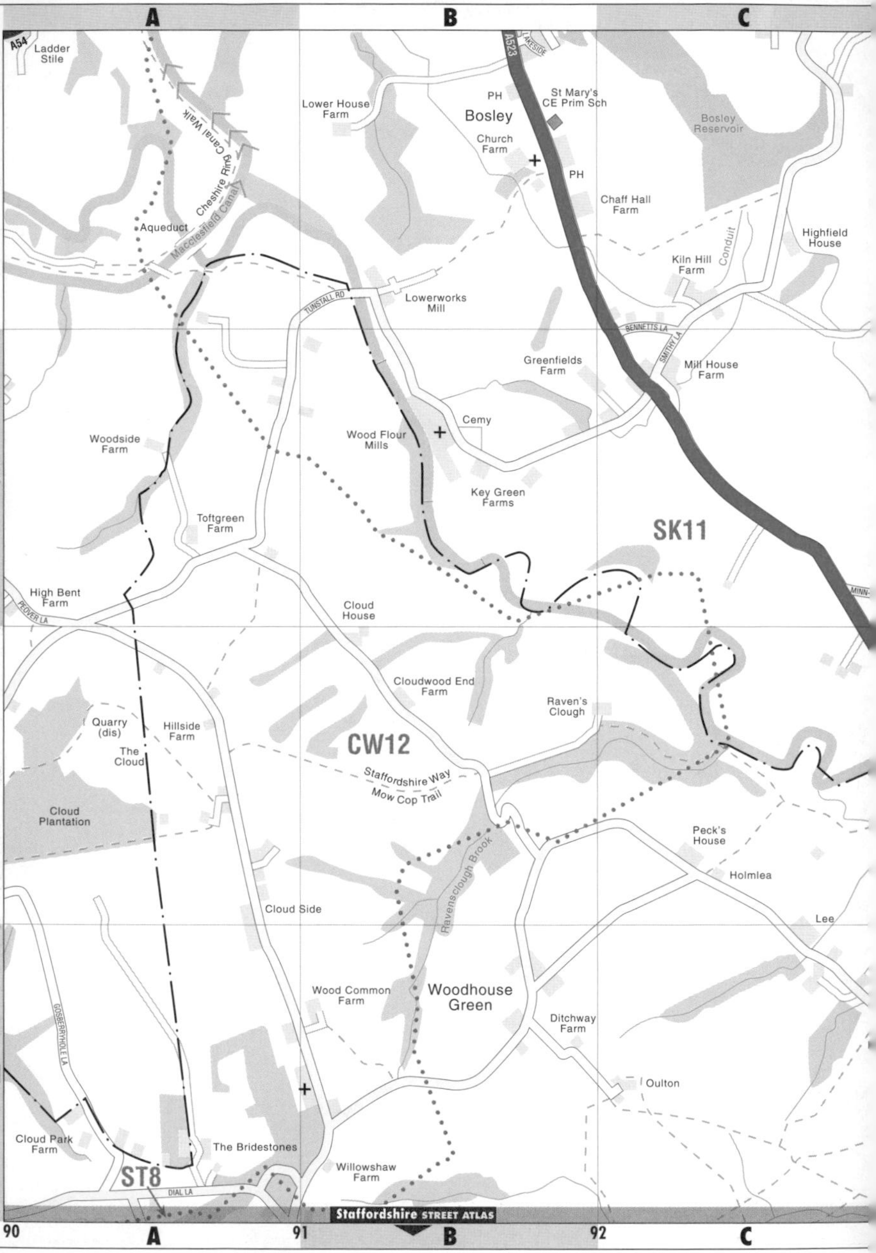
A
B
C
4
65
3
64
2
63
1
62
90
91
92
A54
Ladder Stile
Cheshire Ring Canal Walk
Macclesfield Canal
Aqueduct
Lower House Farm
PH
Bosley
St Mary's CE Prim Sch
Church Farm
PH
A523
LAKESIDE
Bosley Reservoir
Chaff Hall Farm
Highfield House
Kiln Hill Farm
Conduit
TUNSTALL RD
Lowerworks Mill
BENNETTS LA
SMITHY LA
Mill House Farm
Greenfields Farm
Cemy
Wood Flour Mills
Woodside Farm
Key Green Farms
SK11
Toftgreen Farm
High Bent Farm
PEOVER LA
Cloud House
Cloudwood End Farm
Raven's Clough
Quarry (dis)
Hillside Farm
The Cloud
CW12
Staffordshire Way
Mow Cop Trail
Cloud Plantation
Peck's House
Holmlea
Ravensclough Brook
Cloud Side
Lee
Wood Common Farm
Woodhouse Green
Ditchway Farm
GOSBERRYHOLE LA
Oulton
Cloud Park Farm
The Bridestones
Willowshaw Farm
ST8
DIAL LA
Staffordshire STREET ATLAS

157

A
B
C
Mareknowles
Gritstone Trail
Rookery Wood
Nettlebeds
Wincle Grange
Shell Brook
Hawkslee
Kiss Wood
MINN-END-LA
Dumkins
Lower Minnend
Higher Minnend
Whitelee
Whitelee Wood
Cartlidge Wood
Barleighford Farm
SK11
Hammond's Hole
Hugbridge Farm
River Dane
Hollinhall
Barleigh Ford Bridge
Dane Valley Way
Gritstone Trail
Hug Bridge
Thompson
Wormhill
Heatonlow
Wallhill
Brandy-Lea
Haddon
Rushton Inn
Staffordshire Way
Rushton Spencer
Heaton
Heaton Hall
Tofthall
Rushton CE Prim Sch
SUGAR ST
Weathercock Farm
Tythebarn
STATION LA
PH
PH
Rushton Bank
P
ASKERBANK
A523
Heaton House Farm
Axstones Spring
Overhouses Farm
4
65
3
64
2
63
1
62
94
95

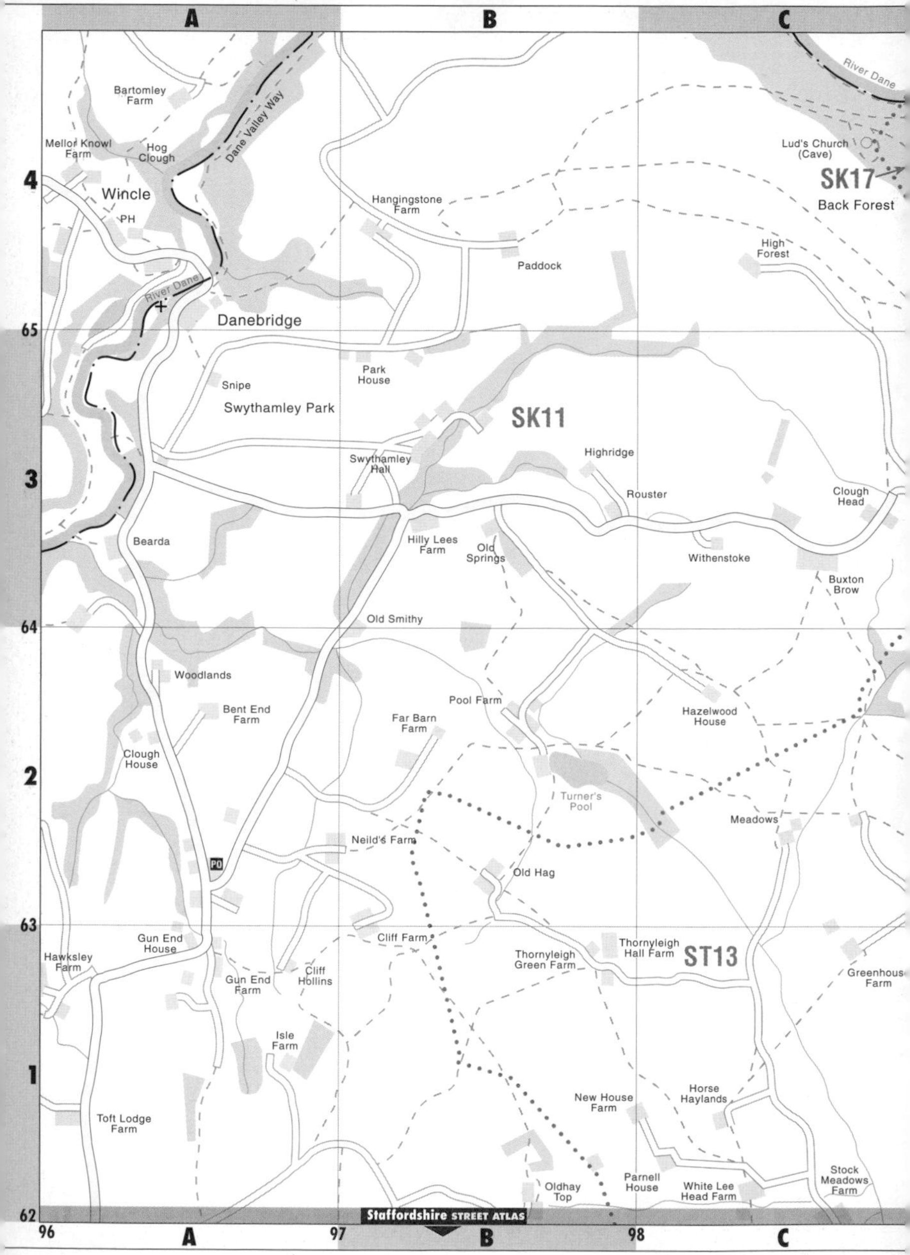
A
B
C
4
3
2
1
65
64
63
62
96
97
98
River Dane
Bartomley Farm
Mellor Knowl Farm
Hog Clough
Dane Valley Way
Wincle
PH
Lud's Church (Cave)
SK17
Back Forest
Hangingstone Farm
High Forest
Paddock
Danebridge
Park House
Snipe
Swythamley Park
SK11
Highridge
Swythamley Hall
Rouster
Clough Head
Bearda
Hilly Lees Farm
Old Springs
Withenstoke
Buxton Brow
Old Smithy
Woodlands
Bent End Farm
Pool Farm
Far Barn Farm
Hazelwood House
Clough House
Turner's Pool
Meadows
Neild's Farm
PO
Old Hag
Cliff Farm
Gun End House
Hawksley Farm
Thornyleigh Green Farm
Thornyleigh Hall Farm
ST13
Greenhouse Farm
Gun End Farm
Cliff Hollins
Isle Farm
New House Farm
Horse Haylands
Toft Lodge Farm
Oldhay Top
Parnell House
White Lee Head Farm
Stock Meadows Farm

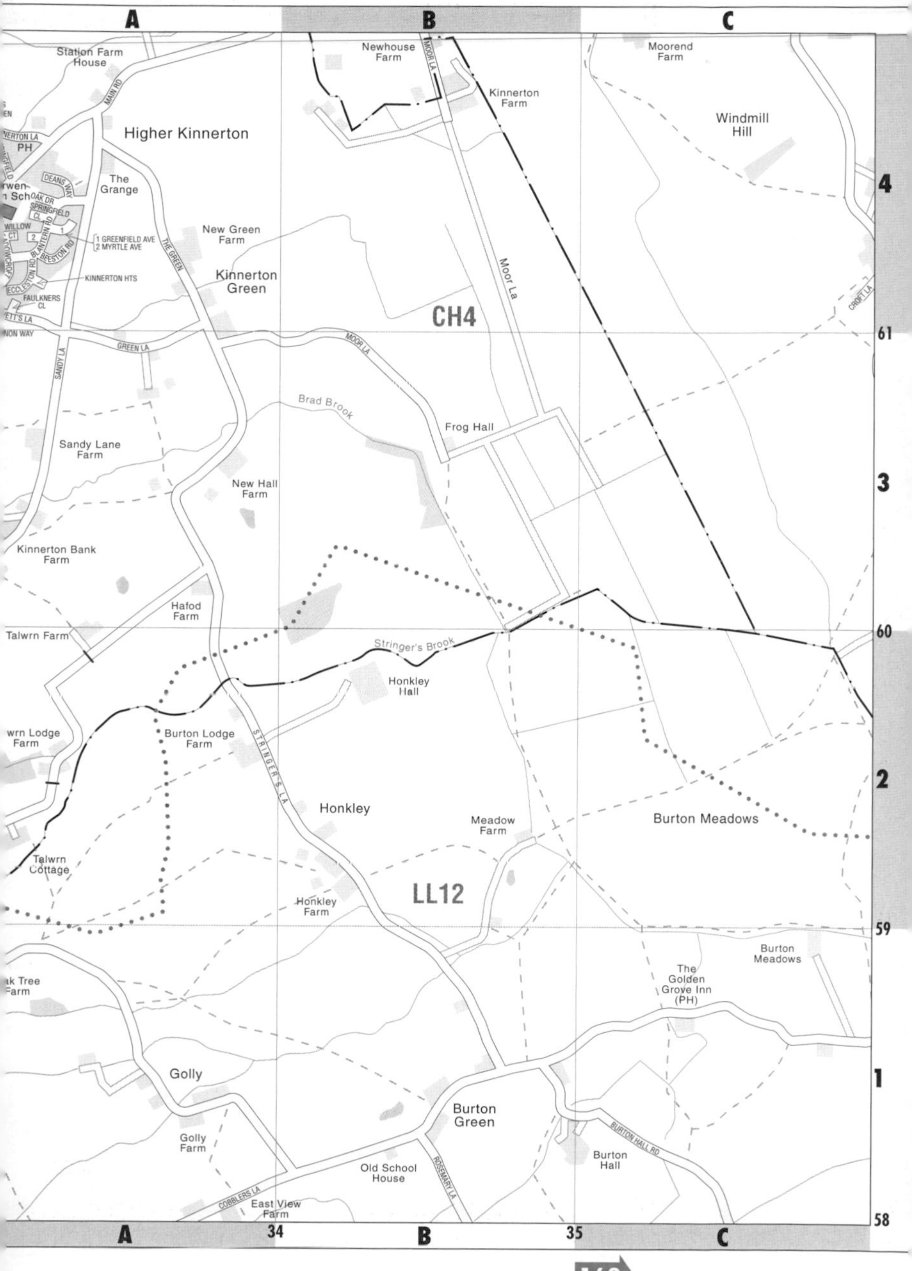
A
B
C
Station Farm House
Newhouse Farm
MOOR LA
Moorend Farm
Kinnerton Farm
Windmill Hill
MAIN RD
Higher Kinnerton
PH
The Grange
DEANS WAY
OAK DR
SPRINGFIELD CL
WILLOW CT
BLANTERN RD
BEESTON RD
1 GREENFIELD AVE
2 MYRTLE AVE
New Green Farm
THE GREEN
Moor La
KINNERTON HTS
Kinnerton Green
FAULKNERS CL
CH4
CROFT LA
GREEN LA
MOOR LA
SANDY LA
Brad Brook
Frog Hall
Sandy Lane Farm
New Hall Farm
Kinnerton Bank Farm
Hafod Farm
Talwrn Farm
Stringer's Brook
Honkley Hall
Burton Lodge Farm
STRINGER'S LA
Honkley
Meadow Farm
Burton Meadows
Talwrn Cottage
LL12
Honkley Farm
Burton Meadows
The Golden Grove Inn (PH)
Golly
Burton Green
Golly Farm
BURTON HALL RD
ROSEMARY LA
Burton Hall
Old School House
COBBLERS LA
East View Farm
4
61
3
60
2
59
1
58
34
35
A
B
C

161
140

A
B
C
Black Wood
Belgrave Bridge
Rake La
A483
B5445
Balderton Dr
Greenwalls
Dodleston Hall
Dodleston CE Prim Sch
Dodleston
St Mary's Rd
Mallory Wlk
Penfold Way
Boydell Way
Egerton Wlk
Croft
Church
Croft La
PO
Castle Way
Belgrave Cl
Balderton Dr
Belgrave Av
Belgrave Cottages
Belgrave Lodge
Belgrave
Moat Farm
Pulford La
Oldfields Farm
Works
Straight Mile
Dodleston Lane Farm
CH4
Wrexham Rd
Cuckoo's Nest
The Elms
The Elms
Meadow House Farm
Moorfield Cottages
Lyndale Farm
The Manor
LC
Dodleston La
Pulford
Fairmeadow
Burganey Ct
Castle Cl
Pulford Ct
Old La
Castle Hill Hotel
Pulford App
Pulford Brook
Broadoak
Pulford Bridge
Broadoak Farm
LC
Brookside Farm
Rossett Bsns Village
Collynie
Cam-yr-Alyn Farm
Chester Rd
Sewage Works
LL12
Drift Cotts
Roselands Ct
Lavister
Lavister Wlks
B5445
Llyndir Hall Hotel
Llyndir La
Darland La
Rossett Pk
A483 Wrexham
4
61
3
60
2
59
1
58
36
37
38

161

141
164

A
B
C
RAKE LA
Rake Lane Cottages
The Gullet
Eaton Lodge
River Dee
CH3
Eaton Estate Office
Eaton Stud
Chester Approach
Johnson's Rough
Lodge
Belgrave Avenue
Lodge
Kennel Wood
Kennels Farm
Mon
Eaton Hall
CH3
elgrave Moat Farm
Airfield (disused)
Iron Bridge
Lodge
CH4
Duck Wood
Blobb Hill
Park Plantation
Poultonhall Farm
Pulford Approach
STRAIGHT MILE
The Old chool House
Far Acre
Oxleisure Pool
Aldford
CHURCH LA
PO
Abbey Gate Coll (The Jun Dept)
MIDDLE LA
RUSHMERE LA
GREEN LAKE LA
OLD LA
Black and White Cottages
GREEN FARM
Poulton
CH3
SCHOOL LA
Yew Tree Farm
Townfield Lands
Jones Wood
B5130
Chapelhouse Farm
Old Pulford Brook
CHESTER RD
Alford Hall
Speed's Plantation
B5130
4
61
3
60
2
59
1
58
40
41

180
164

163
142

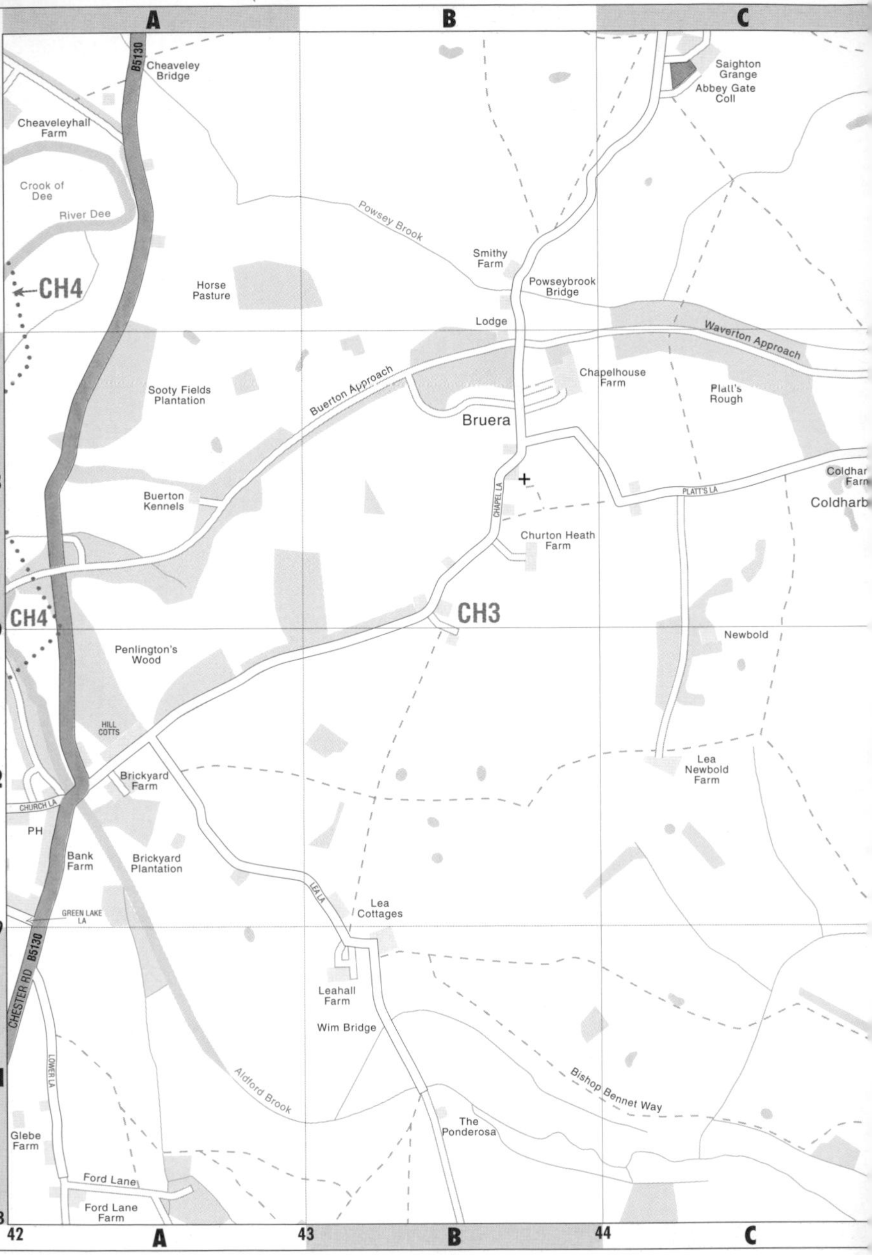
A
B
C
B5130
Cheaveley Bridge
Saighton Grange
Abbey Gate Coll
Cheaveleyhall Farm
4
Crook of Dee
River Dee
Powsey Brook
Smithy Farm
CH4
Horse Pasture
Powseybrook Bridge
Lodge
61
Waverton Approach
Sooty Fields Plantation
Buerton Approach
Chapelhouse Farm
Plall's Rough
Bruera
3
CHAPEL LA
Coldhar Farn
Buerton Kennels
PLATT'S LA
Coldharb
Churton Heath Farm
CH4
CH3
60
Penlington's Wood
Newbold
HILL COTTS
2
Brickyard Farm
Lea Newbold Farm
CHURCH LA
PH
Bank Farm
Brickyard Plantation
LEA LA
Lea Cottages
GREEN LAKE LA
59
B5130
CHESTER RD
Leahall Farm
Wim Bridge
LOWER LA
1
Aldford Brook
Bishop Bennet Way
The Ponderosa
Glebe Farm
Ford Lane
Ford Lane Farm
58
42
A
43
B
44
C

163
181

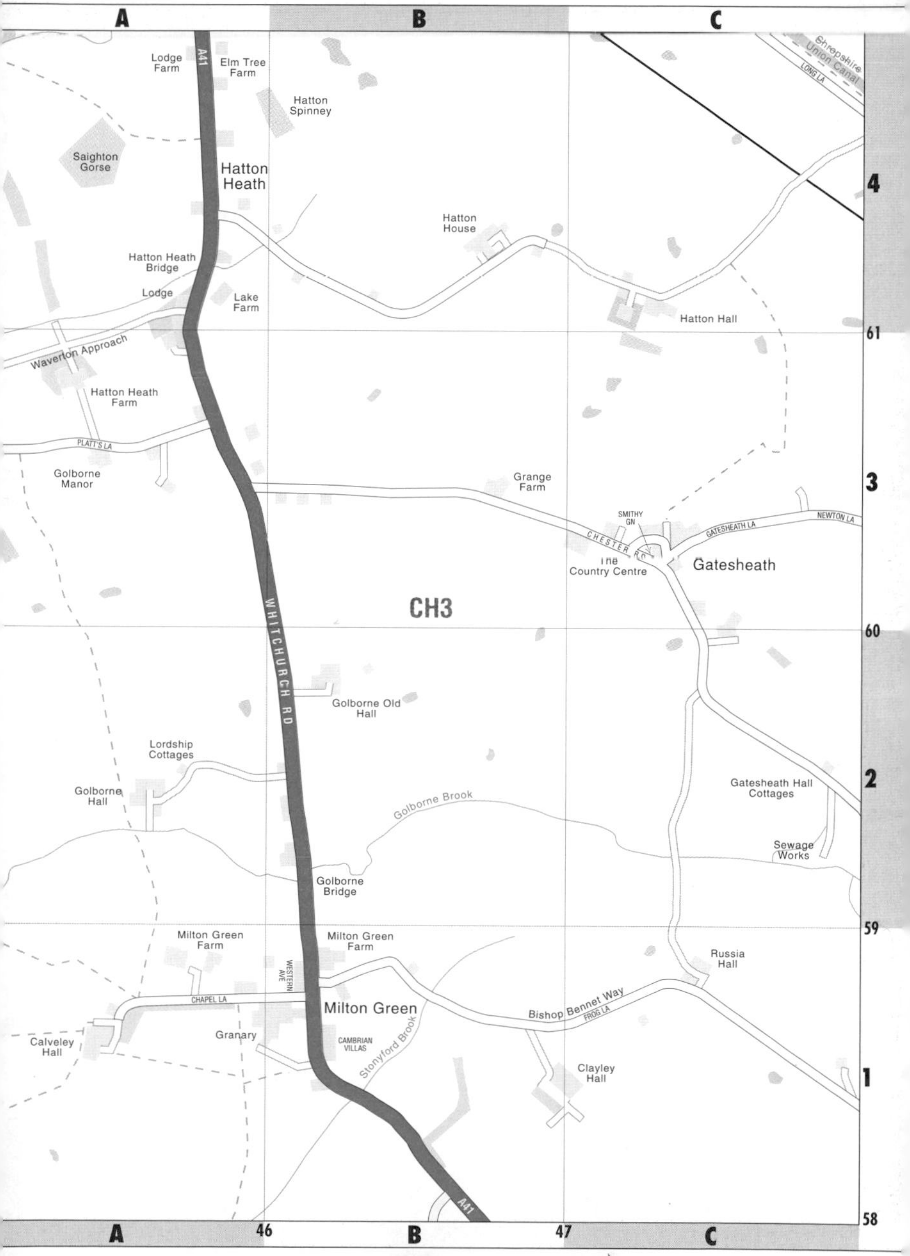
A
B
C
Lodge Farm
Elm Tree Farm
A41
Hatton Spinney
Shropshire Union Canal
LONG LA
Saighton Gorse
Hatton Heath
Hatton House
Hatton Heath Bridge
Lodge
Lake Farm
Hatton Hall
Waverton Approach
Hatton Heath Farm
PLATT'S LA
Golborne Manor
Grange Farm
SMITHY GN
CHESTER RD
GATESHEATH LA
NEWTON LA
The Country Centre
Gatesheath
CH3
WHITCHURCH RD
Golborne Old Hall
Lordship Cottages
Golborne Hall
Golborne Brook
Gatesheath Hall Cottages
Sewage Works
Golborne Bridge
Milton Green Farm
Milton Green Farm
WESTERN AVE
CHAPEL LA
Milton Green
Russia Hall
Bishop Bennet Way
FROG LA
Calveley Hall
Granary
CAMBRIAN VILLAS
Stonyford Brook
Clayley Hall
A41
4
61
3
60
2
59
1
58
46
47
A
B
C

165
144

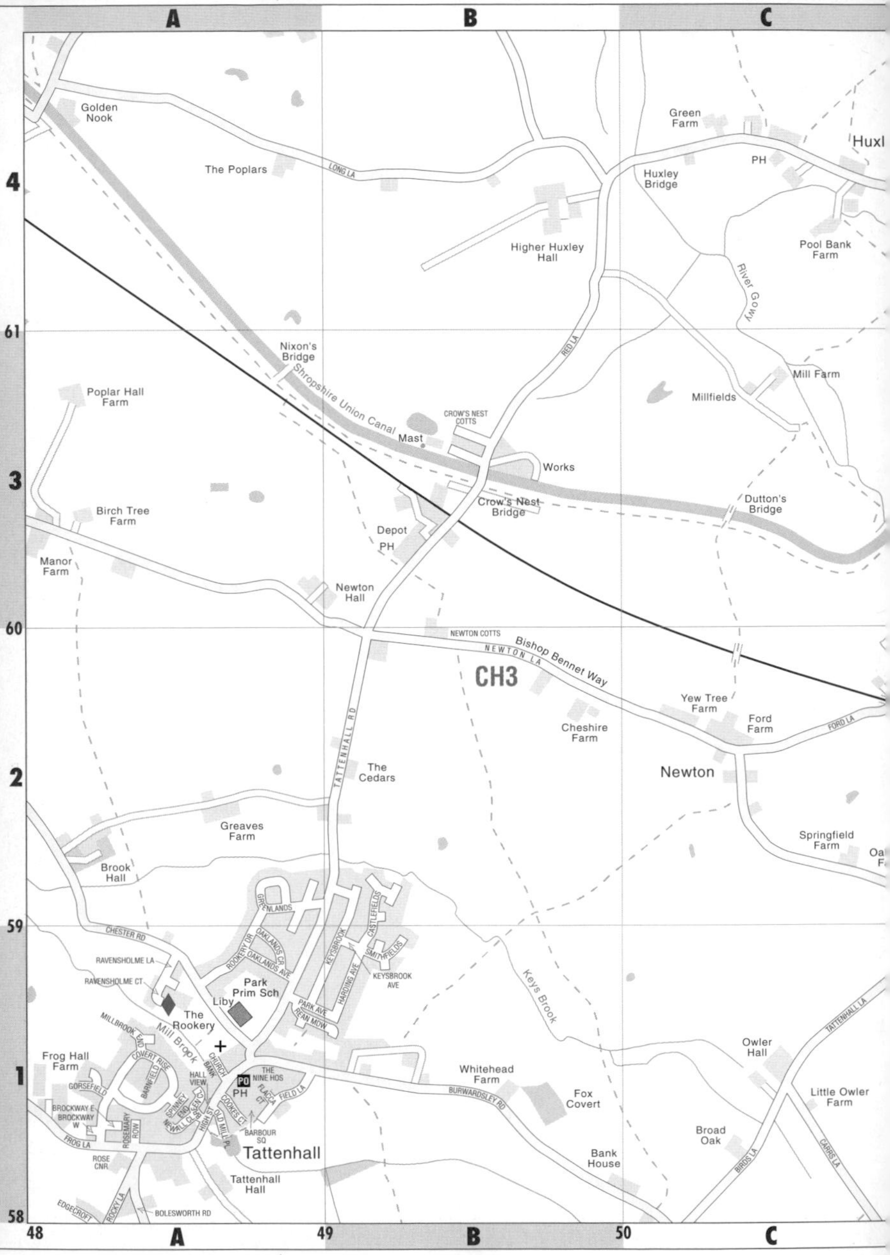
A
B
C
4
61
3
60
2
59
1
58
48
49
50
Golden Nook
The Poplars
LONG LA
Green Farm
Huxl
PH
Huxley Bridge
Pool Bank Farm
Higher Huxley Hall
River Gowy
RED LA
Nixon's Bridge
Shropshire Union Canal
Poplar Hall Farm
CROW'S NEST COTTS
Mast
Mill Farm
Millfields
Works
Crow's Nest Bridge
Dutton's Bridge
Birch Tree Farm
Depot
PH
Manor Farm
Newton Hall
NEWTON COTTS
NEWTON LA
Bishop Bennet Way
CH3
Yew Tree Farm
Ford Farm
FORD LA
Cheshire Farm
TATTENHALL RD
The Cedars
Newton
Greaves Farm
Springfield Farm
Brook Hall
GREENLANDS
CASTLEFIELDS
CHESTER RD
ROOKERY DR
OAKLANDS CR
OAKLANDS AVE
KEYSBROOK
SMITHFIELDS
HARDING AVE
KEYSBROOK AVE
RAVENSHOLME LA
RAVENSHOLME CT
Park Prim Sch
Liby
Keys Brook
The Rookery
PARK AVE
REAN MDW
MILLBROOK END
Mill Brook
TATTENHALL LA
Frog Hall Farm
COVERT RISE
BARNFIELD
CHURCH BANK
THE NINE HOS
HALL VIEW
PO
PH
FLACCA CT
FIELD LA
Whitehead Farm
Owler Hall
GORSEFIELD
SPINNEY END
GREEN CL
BURWARDSLEY RD
Fox Covert
Little Owler Farm
BROCKWAY E
BROCKWAY W
ROSEMARY ROW
NEWALL CL
HIGH ST
OLD MILL PL
COOKES CT
BARBOUR SQ
FROG LA
Broad Oak
ROSE CNR
Tattenhall
Bank House
BIRDS LA
CARRS LA
Tattenhall Hall
EDGECROFT
ROCKY LA
BOLESWORTH RD

165
183

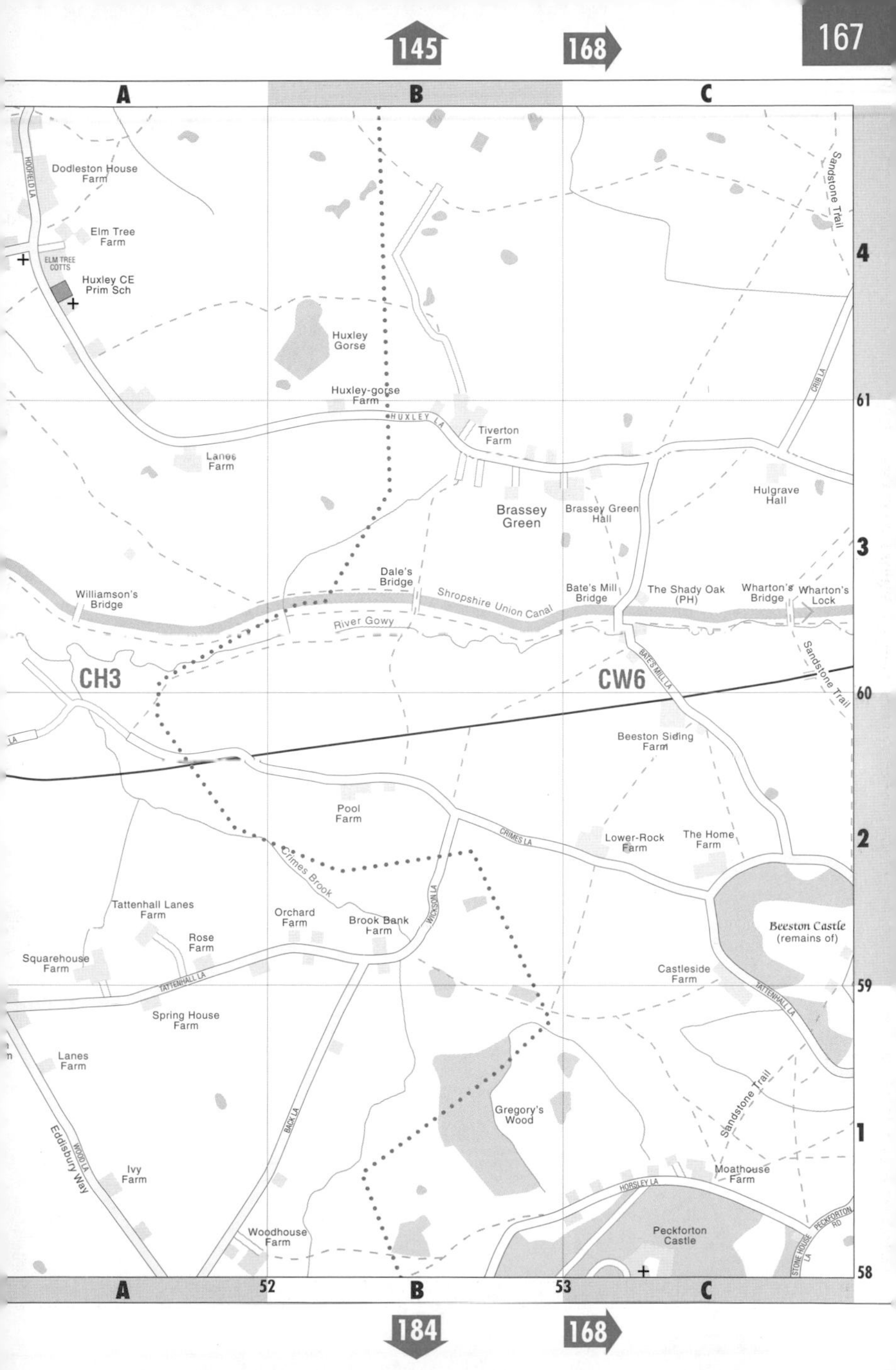
145
168
A
B
C
Dodleston House Farm
HOOFIELD LA
Elm Tree Farm
ELM TREE COTTS
Huxley CE Prim Sch
Huxley Gorse
Huxley-gorse Farm
HUXLEY LA
Tiverton Farm
Lanes Farm
Brassey Green
Brassey Green Hall
Hulgrave Hall
CRIB LA
Sandstone Trail
4
61
3
Williamson's Bridge
Dale's Bridge
Shropshire Union Canal
River Gowy
Bate's Mill Bridge
The Shady Oak (PH)
Wharton's Bridge
Wharton's Lock
CH3
CW6
BATE'S MILL LA
60
Beeston Siding Farm
Pool Farm
CRIMES LA
Lower-Rock Farm
The Home Farm
2
Crimes Brook
Tattenhall Lanes Farm
Orchard Farm
Brook Bank Farm
WICKSON LA
Beeston Castle (remains of)
Rose Farm
Squarehouse Farm
TATTENHALL LA
Castleside Farm
59
Spring House Farm
Lanes Farm
Gregory's Wood
1
Eddisbury Way
WOOD LA
BACK LA
Ivy Farm
Moathouse Farm
HORSLEY LA
PECKFORTON RD
Woodhouse Farm
Peckforton Castle
STONE HOUSE LA
58
52
53
184
168

167
146

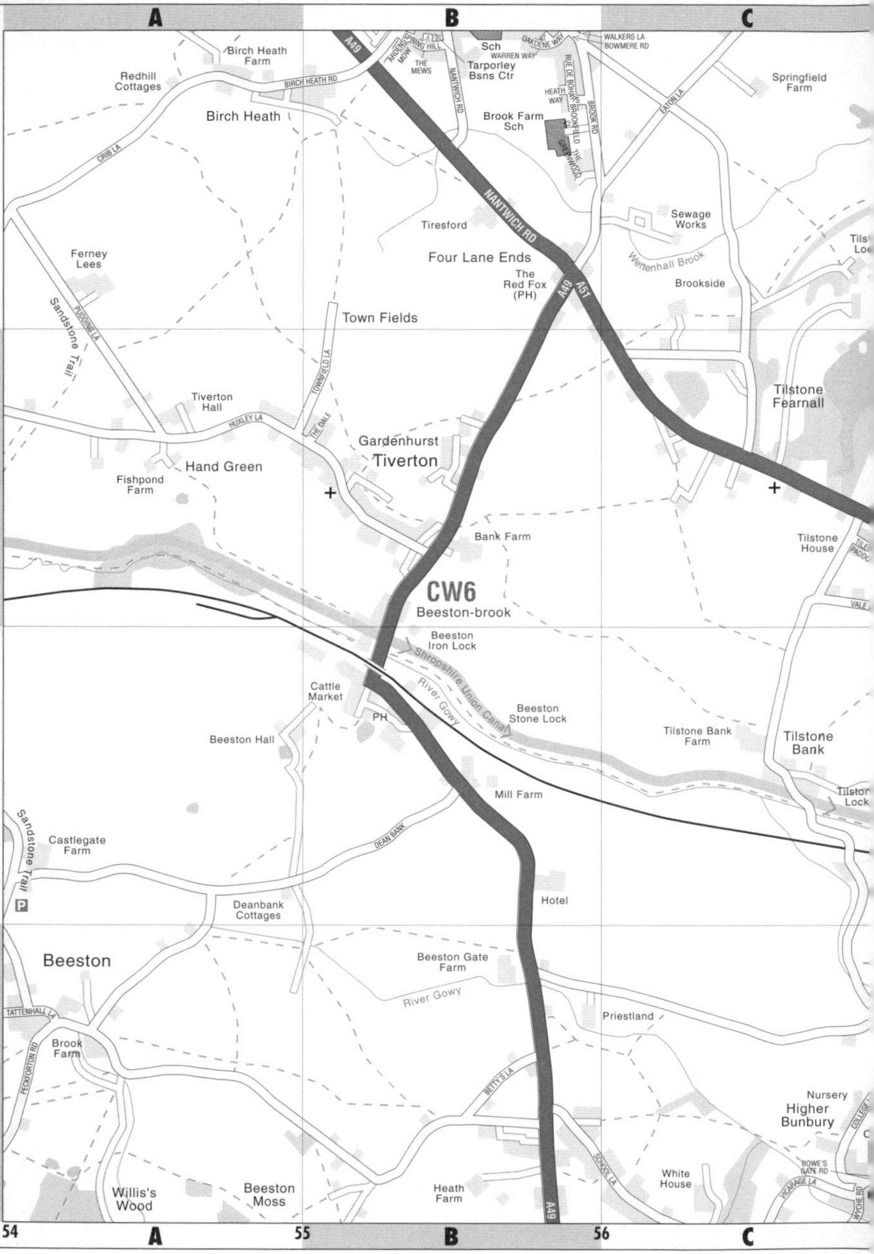
A
B
C
Birch Heath Farm
Redhill Cottages
BIRCH HEATH RD
Birch Heath
A49
Sch
Tarporley Bsns Ctr
NANTWICH RD
Brook Farm Sch
BROOK RD
EATON LA
Springfield Farm
CRIB LA
4
Tiresford
Four Lane Ends
Sewage Works
Wettenhall Brook
Ferney Lees
The Red Fox (PH)
A51
Brookside
Town Fields
Sandstone Trail
PUDDING LA
61
TOWNFIELD LA
Tilstone Fearnall
Tiverton Hall
HUXLEY LA
THE DALE
Gardenhurst
Tiverton
Hand Green
Fishpond Farm
3
Bank Farm
Tilstone House
CW6
Beeston-brook
60
Beeston Iron Lock
Shropshire Union Canal
River Gowy
Cattle Market
PH
Beeston Stone Lock
Tilstone Bank Farm
Tilstone Bank
Beeston Hall
2
Mill Farm
Castlegate Farm
DEAN BANK
Hotel
Deanbank Cottages
59
Beeston
Beeston Gate Farm
River Gowy
Priestland
TATTENHALL LA
Brook Farm
PECKFORTON RD
1
BETTY'S LA
Nursery
Higher Bunbury
SCHOOL LA
White House
VICARAGE LA
Willis's Wood
Beeston Moss
Heath Farm
58
54
55
56

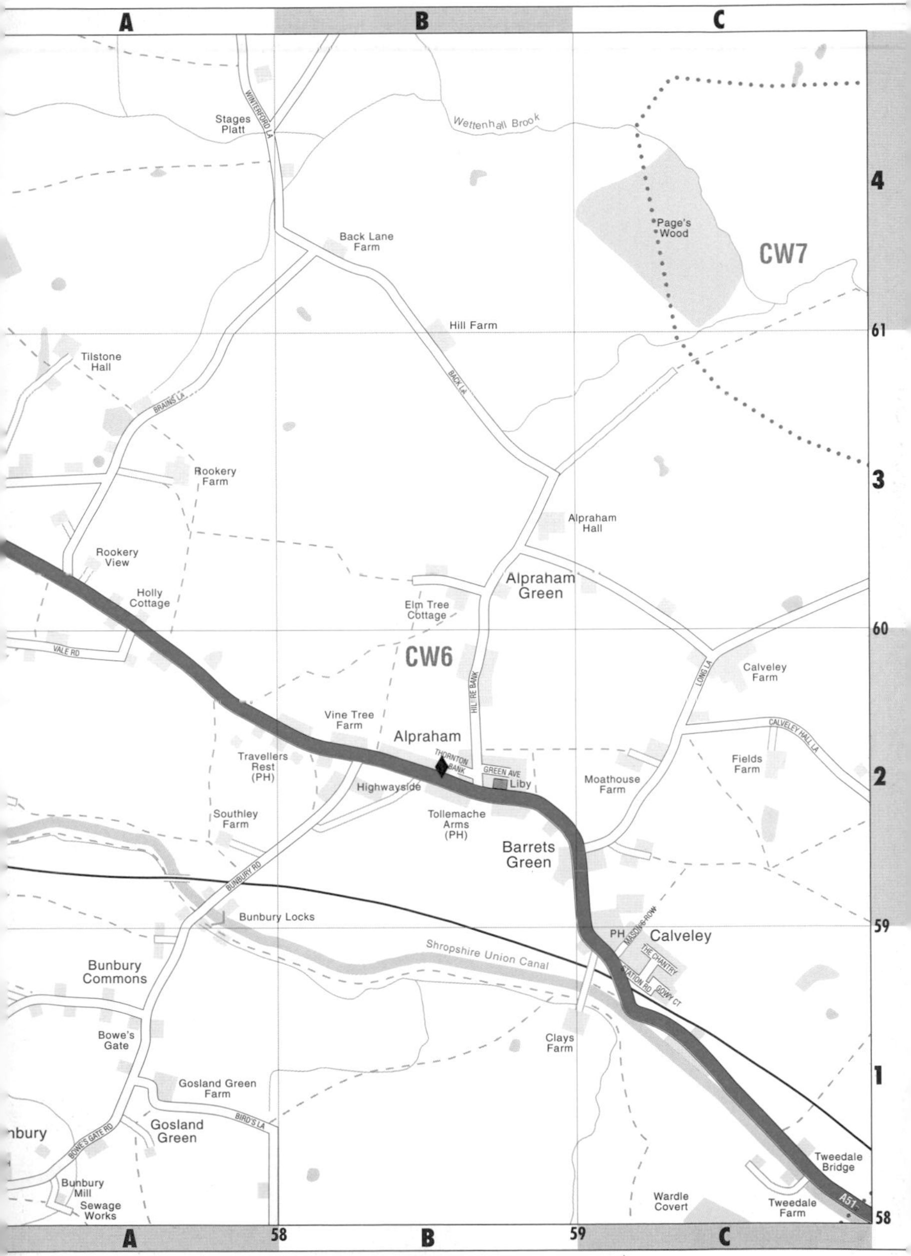
A
B
C
Stages Platt
WINTERFORD LA
Wettenhall Brook
Page's Wood
CW7
Back Lane Farm
Hill Farm
Tilstone Hall
BRAINS LA
BACK LA
Rookery Farm
Alpraham Hall
Rookery View
Holly Cottage
Alpraham Green
Elm Tree Cottage
VALE RD
CW6
LONG LA
Calveley Farm
HILL RE BANK
Vine Tree Farm
Alpraham
CALVELEY HALL LA
Travellers Rest (PH)
THORNTON BANK
GREEN AVE
Liby
Fields Farm
Highwayside
Moathouse Farm
Southley Farm
Tollemache Arms (PH)
Barrets Green
BUNBURY RD
Bunbury Locks
MASONS ROW
PH
Calveley
Shropshire Union Canal
THE CHANTRY
STATION RD
GOWY CT
Bunbury Commons
Bowe's Gate
Clays Farm
Gosland Green Farm
BIRD'S LA
Gosland Green
BOWE'S GATE RD
nbury
Bunbury Mill
Sewage Works
Wardle Covert
Tweedale Bridge
Tweedale Farm
A51
4
61
3
60
2
59
1
58
58
59
A
B
C

169
148

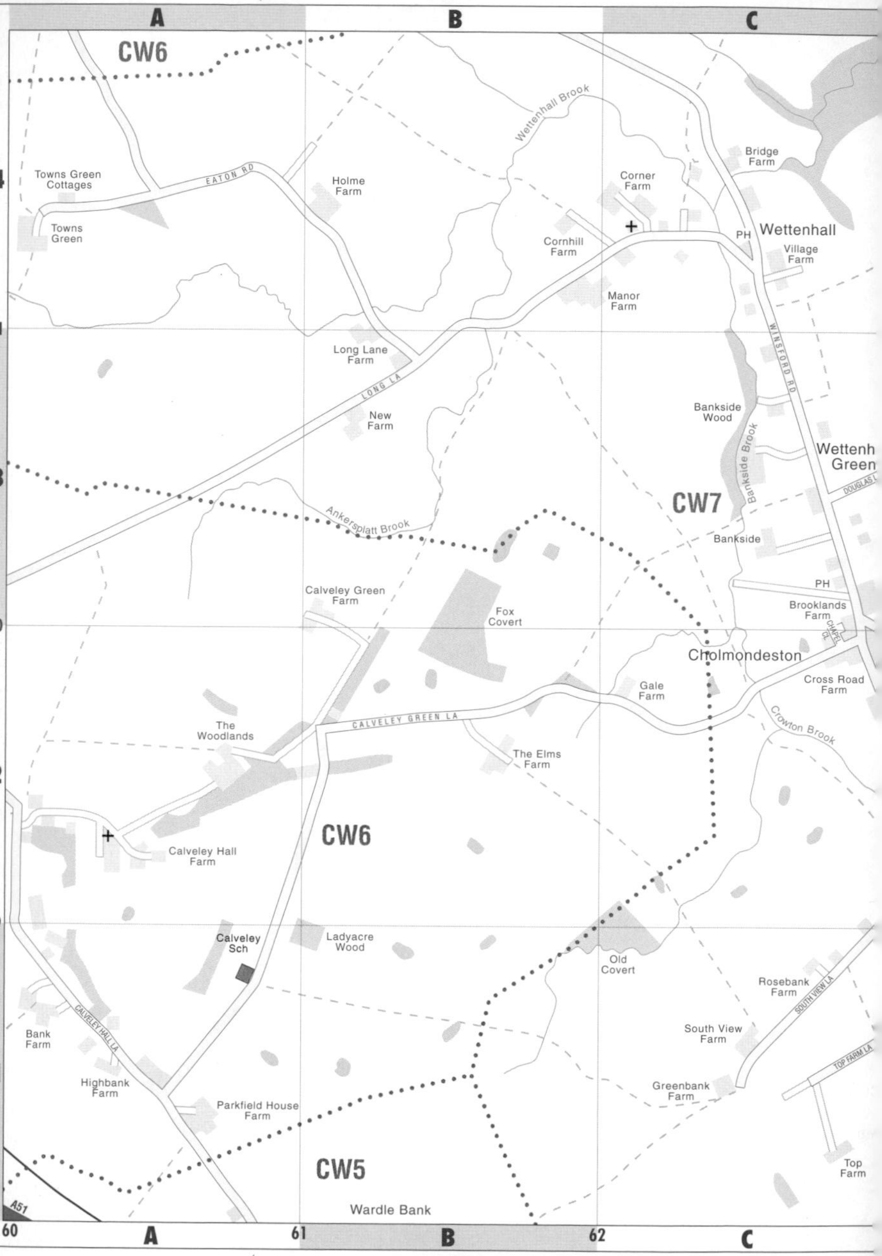
A
B
C
CW6
Wettenhall Brook
Towns Green Cottages
EATON RD
Holme Farm
Corner Farm
Bridge Farm
Towns Green
Cornhill Farm
PH
Wettenhall
Village Farm
Manor Farm
4
61
Long Lane Farm
LONG LA
WINSFORD RD
New Farm
Bankside Wood
Bankside Brook
Wettenh Green
3
DOUGLAS L
CW7
Ankersplatt Brook
Bankside
PH
Calveley Green Farm
Fox Covert
Brooklands Farm
60
CHAPEL CL
Cholmondeston
Gale Farm
Cross Road Farm
CALVELEY GREEN LA
Crowton Brook
The Woodlands
The Elms Farm
2
Calveley Hall Farm
CW6
59
Calveley Sch
Ladyacre Wood
Old Covert
Rosebank Farm
SOUTH VIEW LA
CALVELEY HALL LA
Bank Farm
South View Farm
1
TOP FARM LA
Highbank Farm
Greenbank Farm
Parkfield House Farm
CW5
Top Farm
A51
58
Wardle Bank
60
A
61
B
62
C

169
187

A
B
C
Fields Farm
Wettenhall Wood
Home Farm
B5074 OVER RD
PARADISE LA
Minshull Hall Farm
Paradise Farm
Woodside
Paradise Green
Whitegate Cottage
Poolfield Wood
DOUGLAS LA
Paradise Green Farm
Eel Brook
Paradise Wood
WOODGREEN LA
Woodgreen Farm
Poplar Farm
Wades Green
B5074
CW5
Wades Green Farm
River Weaver
CW7
Willow Tree Farmhouse
MINSHULL LA
Wade's Green Hall
Mast
Rosalie Farm
Paradise Covert
Brook Farm
Outlanes Farm
Hawthorn Farm
Cholmondeston Hall
WINSFORD RD
Crewe & Nantwich Circular Wlk
Shropshire Union Canal
Middlewich Branch
Nanney's Bridge
Cholmondeston
Bottom House Farm
Brickyard Bridge
Out Lanes
Daisy Bank Farm
Highfield Farm
Aston Gorse
CW5
Bridge Farm
Aston Grove Farm
4
61
3
60
2
59
1
58
64
65

171
150

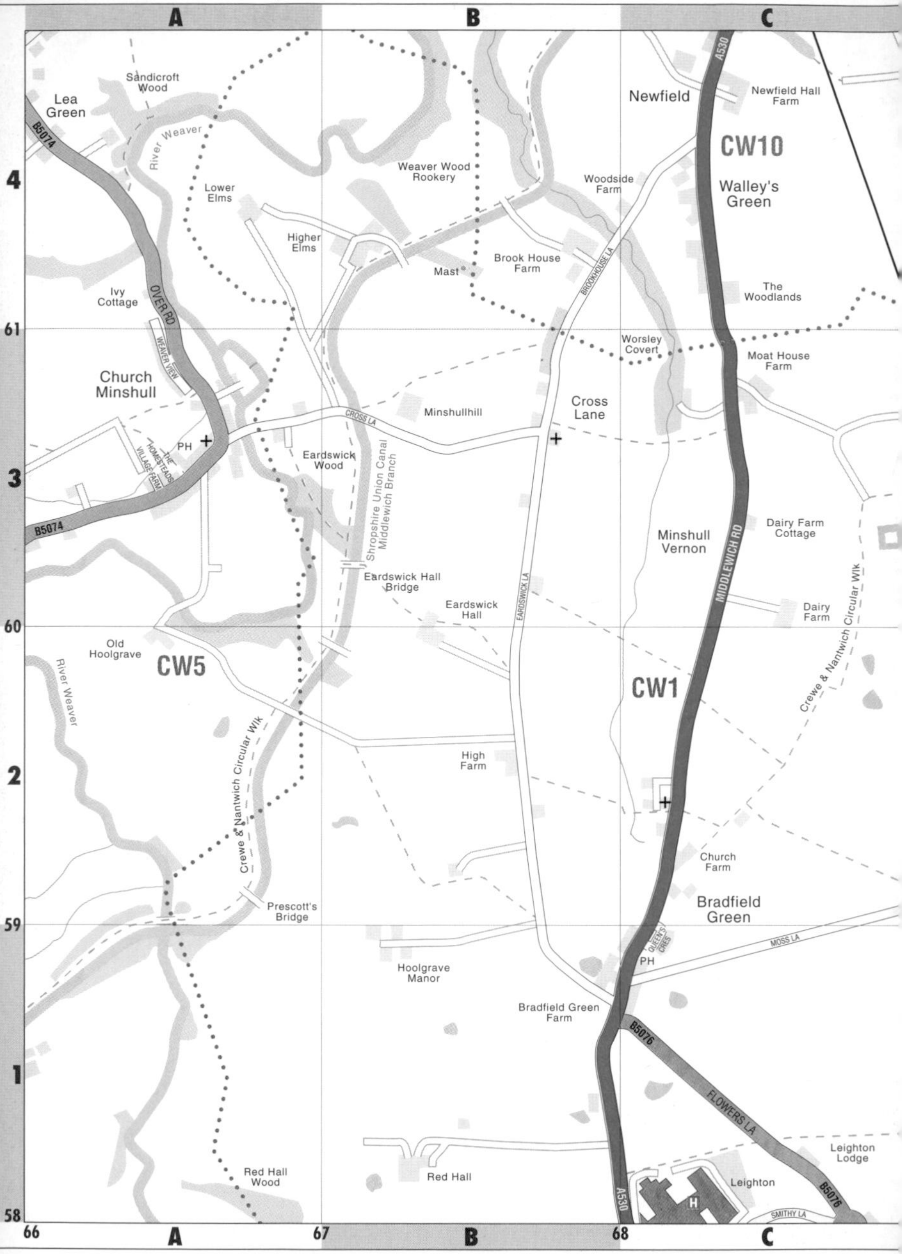

171
189

151
174

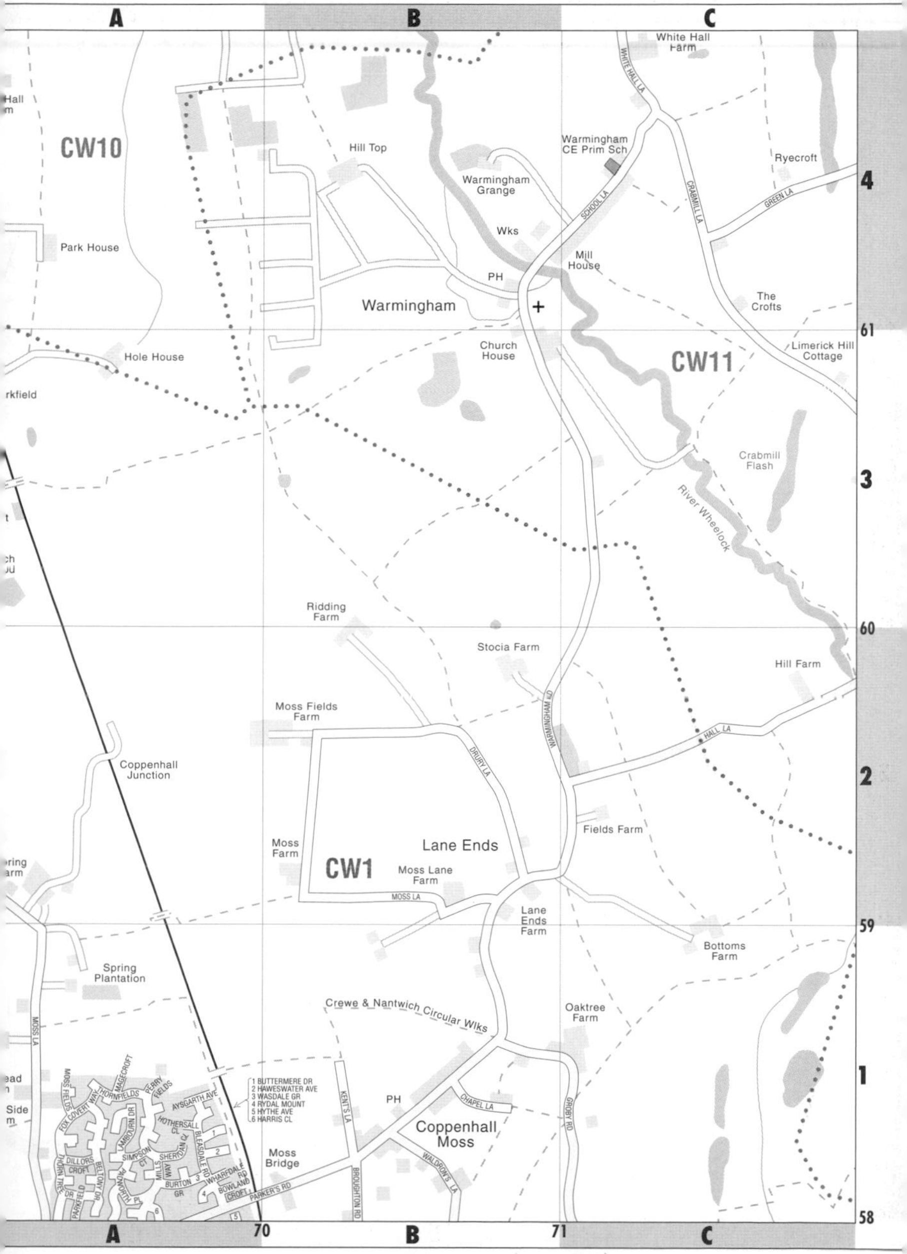
A
B
C
CW10
Hall
Park House
Hole House
rkfield
Hill Top
Warmingham Grange
Wks
PH
Warmingham
Church House
White Hall Farm
WHITE HALL LA
Warmingham CE Prim Sch
SCHOOL LA
Mill House
Ryecroft
GREEN LA
CRABMILL LA
The Crofts
Limerick Hill Cottage
CW11
Crabmill Flash
River Wheelock
4
61
3
60
2
59
1
58
Ridding Farm
Stocia Farm
Hill Farm
Moss Fields Farm
WARMINGHAM RD
HALL LA
DRURY LA
Coppenhall Junction
Fields Farm
Moss Farm
Lane Ends
CW1
Moss Lane Farm
MOSS LA
Lane Ends Farm
Bottoms Farm
Spring Plantation
Crewe & Nantwich Circular Wlks
Oaktree Farm
MOSS LA
1 BUTTERMERE DR
2 HAWESWATER AVE
3 WASDALE GR
4 RYDAL MOUNT
5 HYTHE AVE
6 HARRIS CL
KENT'S LA
PH
CHAPEL LA
GROBY RD
Coppenhall Moss
Moss Bridge
BROUGHTON RD
WALDRON'S LA
PARKER'S RD
MOSS FIELDS
FOX COVERT WAY
THORNFIELDS
MAGECROFT
PERRY FIELDS
AYSGARTH AVE
HOTHERSALL CL
BLEASDALE RD
LAMBOURN DR
SIMPSON CT
SHERIDAN CL
MILLS WAY
DILLORS CROFT
BELTONY DR
THORN TREE DR
PARKFIELD
BURTON GR
WHARFDALE RD
BOWLAND CROFT
70
71

190
174

173
152

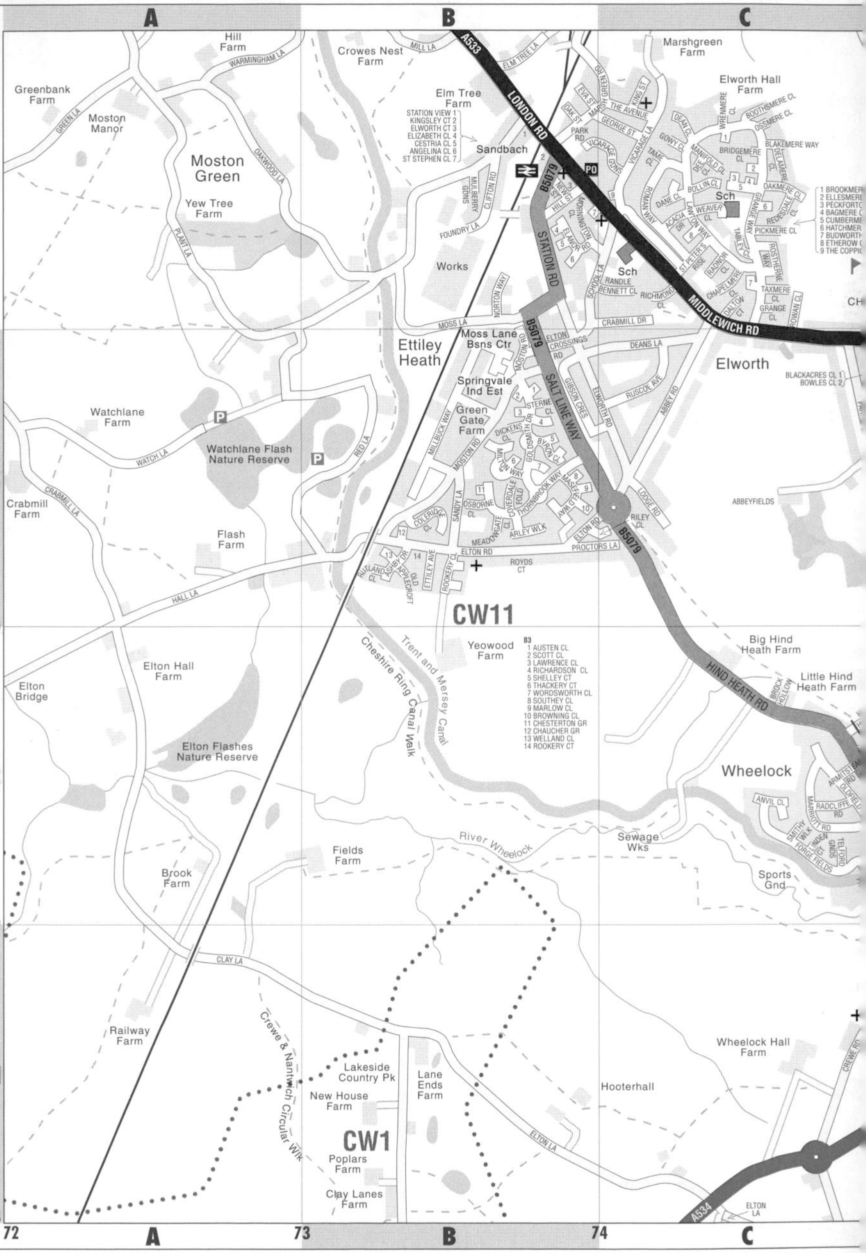
A
B
C
4
61
3
60
2
59
1
58
72
73
74
Hill Farm
Warmingham La
Greenbank Farm
Green La
Moston Manor
Moston Green
Oakwood La
Yew Tree Farm
Plant La
Crowes Nest Farm
Mill La
A533
Elm Tree La
London Rd
Elm Tree Farm
STATION VIEW 1
KINGSLEY CT 2
ELWORTH CT 3
ELIZABETH CL 4
CESTRIA CL 5
ANGELINA CL 6
ST STEPHEN CL 7
Sandbach
Mulberry Gdns
Clifton Rd
Foundry La
Works
Norton Way
Moss La
Marshgreen Farm
Elworth Hall Farm
Eva St
Marsh Green Rd
King St
The Avenue
Oak St
George St
Park Rd
Vicarage Gdns
Vicarage La
PO
B5079
Hill St
Wornington Rd
Station Rd
Tame Cl
Roman Way
Dane Cl
Gowy Cl
Manifold Cl
Dee Cl
Bollin Cl
Weaver Cl
Acacia Dr
Lawton Way
St Peter's Rise
Radnor Cl
Chapelmere Cl
Dalton Ct
Taxmere Cl
Grange Cl
Rowan Cl
Wrenmere Cl
Boothsmere Cl
Ossmere Cl
Blakemere Way
Bridgemere Cl
Delamere Cl
Oakmere Cl
Redesdale Cl
Grange Way
Tabley Cl
Pickmere Cl
Rostherne Way
Sch
School La
Randle Bennett Cl
Richmond Cl
Middlewich Rd
Crabmill Dr
1 BROOKMERE
2 ELLESMERE
3 PECKFORTON
4 BAGMERE
5 CUMBERMERE
6 HATCHMERE
7 BUDWORTH
8 ETHEROW
9 THE COPPICE
Ettiley Heath
Moss Lane Bsns Ctr
Moston Rd
Elton Crossings Rd
Deans La
Elworth
BLACKACRES CL 1
BOWLES CL 2
Springvale Ind Est
Green Gate Farm
Millbuck Way
Salt Line Way
Gibson Cres
Elworth Rd
Ruscoe Ave
Abbey Rd
Sterne Cl
Dickens Cl
Goldsmith Dr
Byron Cl
Milton Way
Thornbrook Way
Masefield Way
Avon Cl
Lodge Rd
Abbeyfields
Watchlane Farm
Watchlane Flash Nature Reserve
Watch La
P
Red La
Crabmill La
Crabmill Farm
Sandy La
Osborne Cl
Coverdale Fold
Coleridge Cl
Meadowgate
Arley Wlk
Elton Rd
Riley Cl
Proctors La
Flash Farm
Rutland Cl
Ashby Dr
Old Applecroft
Ettiley Ave
Rookery Cl
Royds Ct
Hall La
CW11
B3
1 AUSTEN CL
2 SCOTT CL
3 LAWRENCE CL
4 RICHARDSON CL
5 SHELLEY CT
6 THACKERY CT
7 WORDSWORTH CL
8 SOUTHEY CL
9 MARLOW CL
10 BROWNING CL
11 CHESTERTON GR
12 CHAUCHER GR
13 WELLAND CL
14 ROOKERY CT
Yeowood Farm
Cheshire Ring Canal Walk
Trent and Mersey Canal
Big Hind Heath Farm
Hind Heath Rd
Brock Hollow
Little Hind Heath Farm
Elton Hall Farm
Elton Bridge
Elton Flashes Nature Reserve
Wheelock
Anvil Cl
Armitstead Rd
Oldfield
Radcliffe Rd
Marriott Rd
Smithy Wlk
Linden Ct
Forge Fields
Telford Gdns
River Wheelock
Sewage Wks
Sports Gnd
Fields Farm
Brook Farm
Clay La
Railway Farm
Crewe & Nantwich Circular Wlk
Lakeside Country Pk
New House Farm
Lane Ends Farm
Hooterhall
Wheelock Hall Farm
Crewe Rd
CW1
Poplars Farm
Clay Lanes Farm
Elton La
A534
ELTON LA

A3
1 CECIL RIGBY CL
2 WESLEY AVE
3 CROWN BANK
4 MARKET SQ
5 BROOKHOUSE RD
6 CHESTNUT HO
7 OAK HO
8 ASH HO
9 ELM HO

153
176

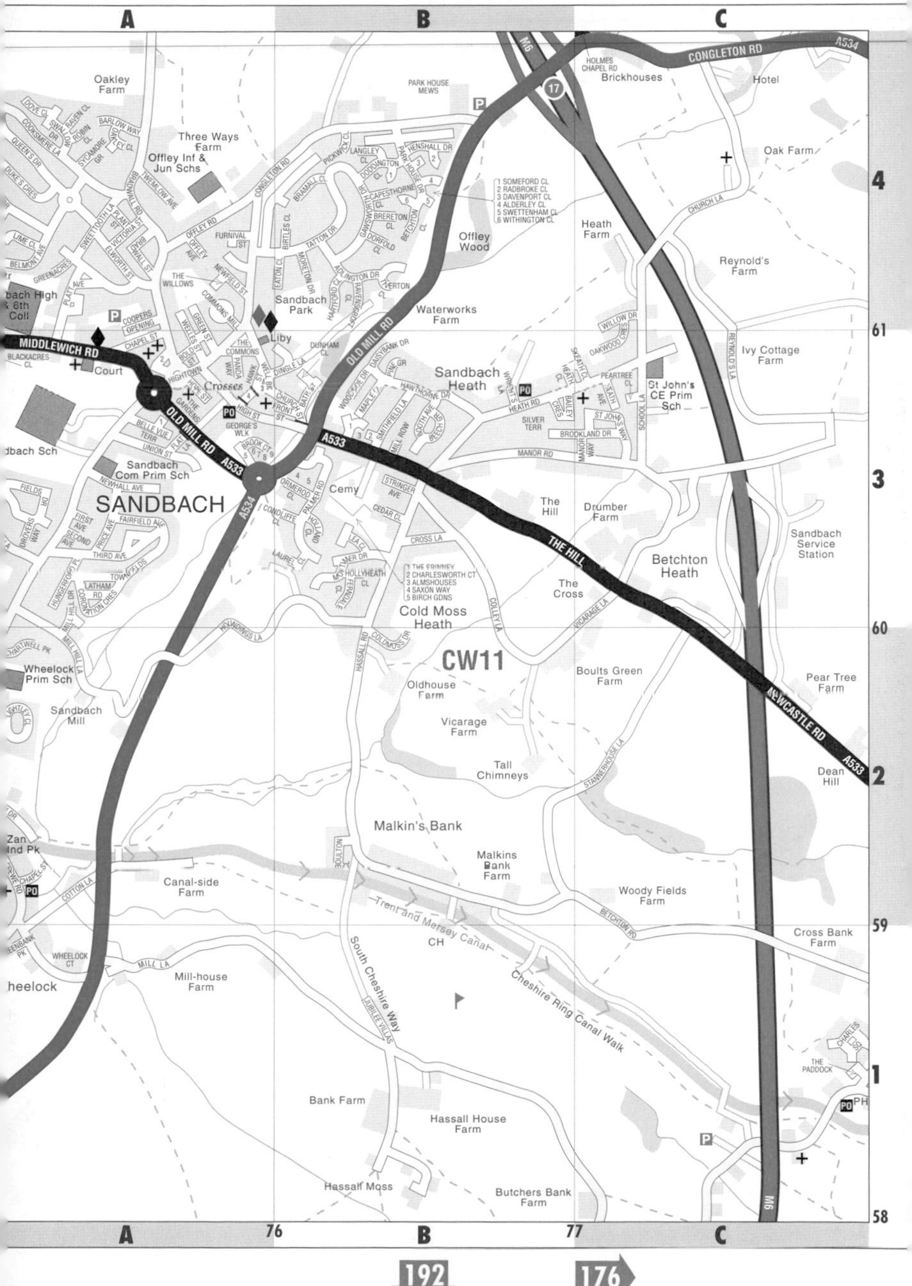

192
176

175
154

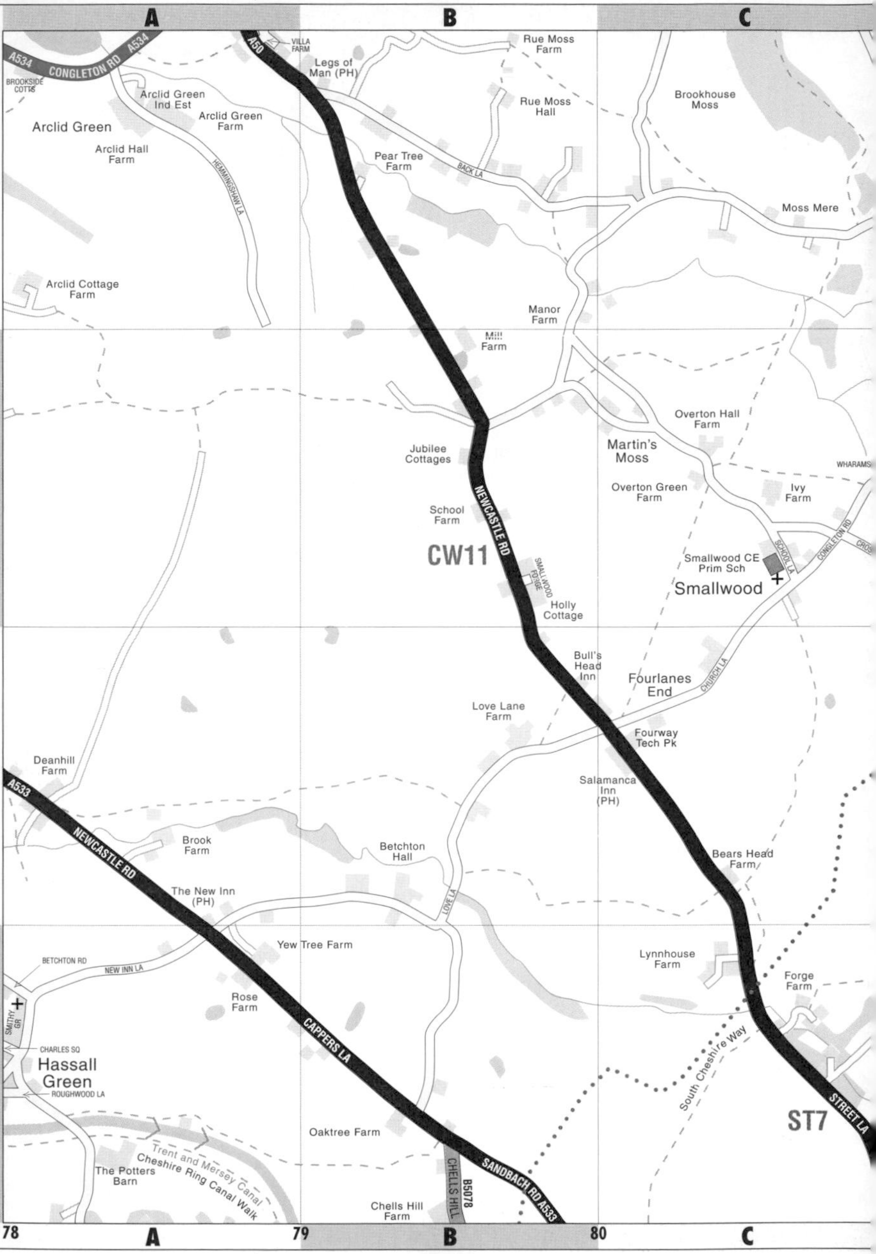
A
B
C
4
3
2
1
61
60
59
58
78
79
80
A534
CONGLETON RD
A534
BROOKSIDE COTTS
A50
VILLA FARM
Legs of Man (PH)
Rue Moss Farm
Arclid Green Ind Est
Arclid Green
Arclid Green Farm
Arclid Hall Farm
HEMMINGSHAW LA
Rue Moss Hall
Brookhouse Moss
Pear Tree Farm
BACK LA
Moss Mere
Arclid Cottage Farm
Manor Farm
Mill Farm
Overton Hall Farm
Jubilee Cottages
Martin's Moss
WHARAMS
Overton Green Farm
Ivy Farm
School Farm
NEWCASTLE RD
CW11
SMALLWOOD FORGE
SCHOOL LA
CONGLETON RD
CROS
Smallwood CE Prim Sch
Smallwood
Holly Cottage
Bull's Head Inn
Fourlanes End
CHURCH LA
Love Lane Farm
Fourway Tech Pk
Deanhill Farm
Salamanca Inn (PH)
A533
NEWCASTLE RD
Brook Farm
Betchton Hall
Bears Head Farm
The New Inn (PH)
LOVE LA
Yew Tree Farm
BETCHTON RD
NEW INN LA
Lynnhouse Farm
Forge Farm
SMITHY GR
Rose Farm
CAPPERS LA
CHARLES SQ
Hassall Green
ROUGHWOOD LA
South Cheshire Way
STREET LA
ST7
Oaktree Farm
Trent and Mersey Canal
Cheshire Ring Canal Walk
The Potters Barn
CHELLS HILL
B5078
SANDBACH RD A533
Chells Hill Farm

175
193

155
178

194
178

177
156

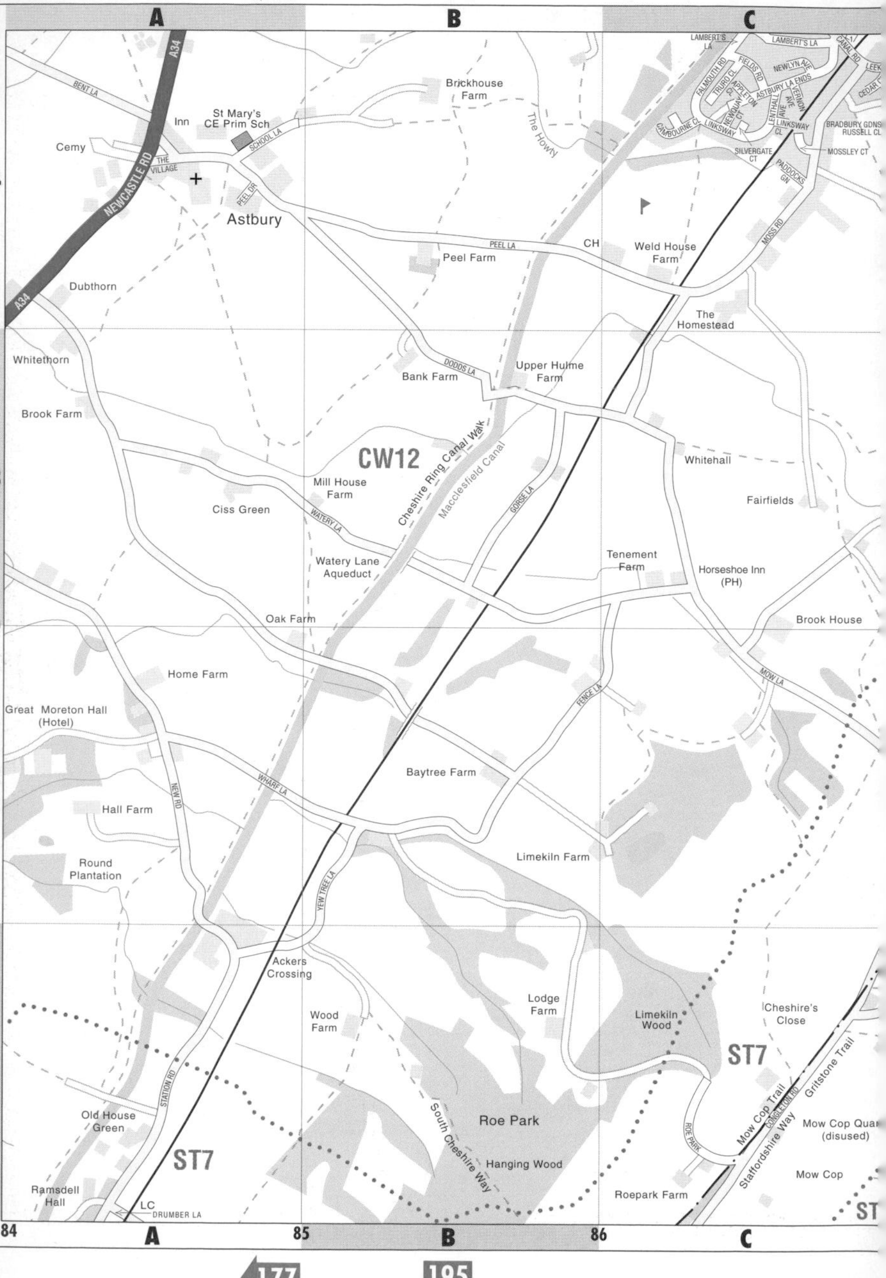

177
195

157

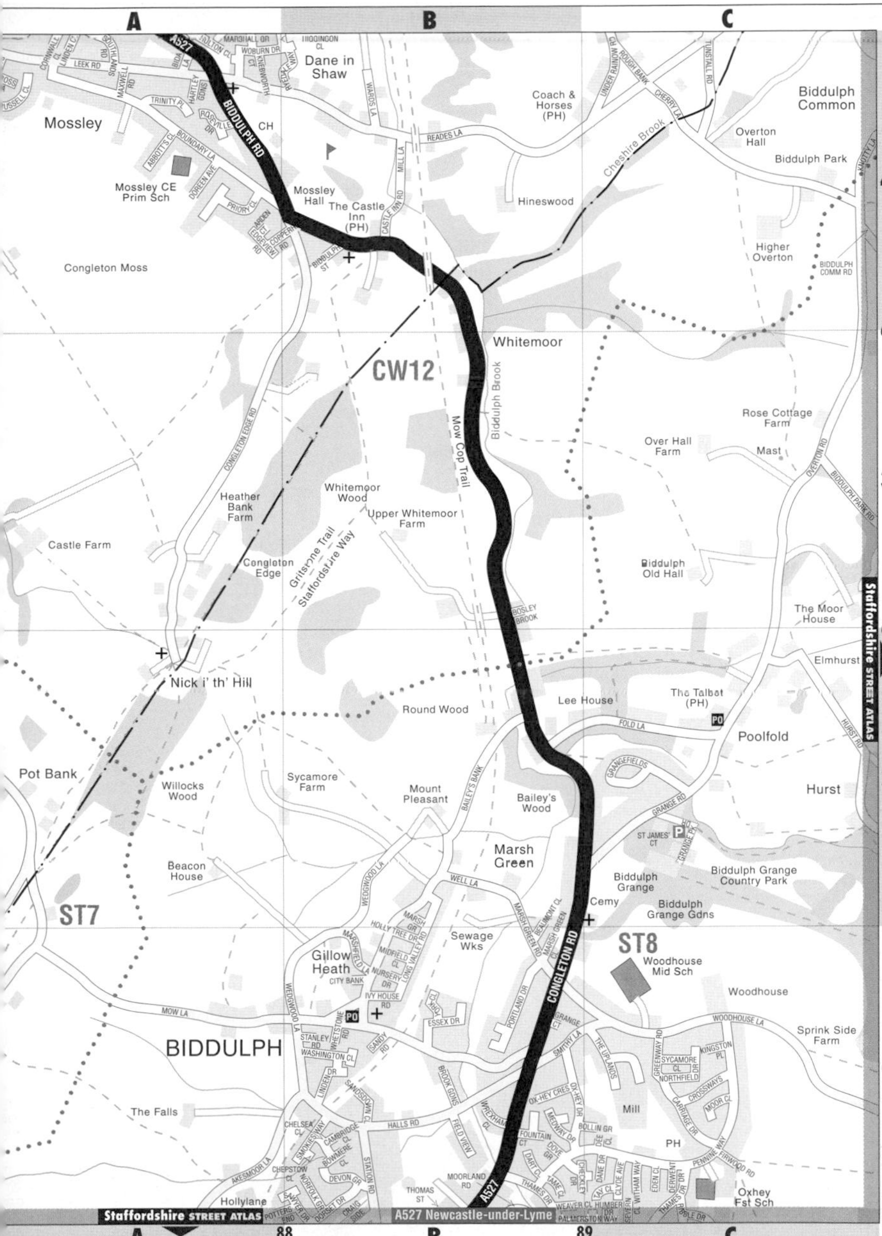
A
B
C
A
88
B
89
C
4
61
3
60
2
59
1
58
Mossley
Dane in Shaw
Coach & Horses (PH)
Biddulph Common
Overton Hall
Biddulph Park
Mossley CE Prim Sch
CH
Mossley Hall
The Castle Inn (PH)
Hineswood
Cheshire Brook
Higher Overton
BIDDULPH COMM RD
Congleton Moss
Whitemoor
CW12
Biddulph Brook
Mow Cop Trail
Rose Cottage Farm
Over Hall Farm
Mast
Heather Bank Farm
Whitemoor Wood
Upper Whitemoor Farm
Castle Farm
Congleton Edge
Gritstone Trail
Staffordshire Way
Biddulph Old Hall
The Moor House
Elmhurst
BOSLEY BROOK
Nick i' th' Hill
Round Wood
Lee House
The Talbot (PH)
PO
FOLD LA
Poolfold
Pot Bank
Willocks Wood
Sycamore Farm
Mount Pleasant
Bailey's Wood
Hurst
GRANGEFIELDS
GRANGE RD
ST JAMES' CT
P
GRANGE PK
Marsh Green
Beacon House
Biddulph Grange
Biddulph Grange Country Park
Cemy
Biddulph Grange Gdns
ST7
ST8
Woodhouse Mid Sch
Gillow Heath
Sewage Wks
CONGLETON RD
Woodhouse
MOW LA
BIDDULPH
WOODHOUSE LA
Sprink Side Farm
Mill
The Falls
HALLS RD
PH
Hollylane
Oxhey Fst Sch
A527
BIDDULPH RD
LEEK RD
TRINITY PL
BOUNDARY LA
READES LA
MILL LA
CASTLE INN RD
WARDS LA
ROUGH BANK
CHERRY LA
TUNSTALL RD
CONGLETON EDGE RD
OVERTON RD
BIDDULPH PARK RD
HURST RD
BAILEY'S BANK
WELL LA
WEDGWOOD LA
MARSH GREEN RD
PORTLAND DR
ESSEX DR
BROOK GDNS
FIELD VIEW
SMITHY LA
THE UPLANDS
GREENWAY RD
SYCAMORE CL
NORTHFIELD
CROSSWAYS
MOOR CL
CARRIAGE DR
PENNINE WAY
FIRWOOD RD
WASHINGTON CL
STANLEY RD
SANDY RD
CITY BANK
IVY HOUSE RD
AKESMOOR LA
CHEPSTOW CL
STATION RD
MOORLAND RD
THOMAS ST
FOUNTAIN CT
THAMES DR
WEAVER CL
HUMBER DR
PALMERSTON WAY
RIBBLE DR
Staffordshire STREET ATLAS
A527 Newcastle-under-Lyme
Staffordshire STREET ATLAS

163

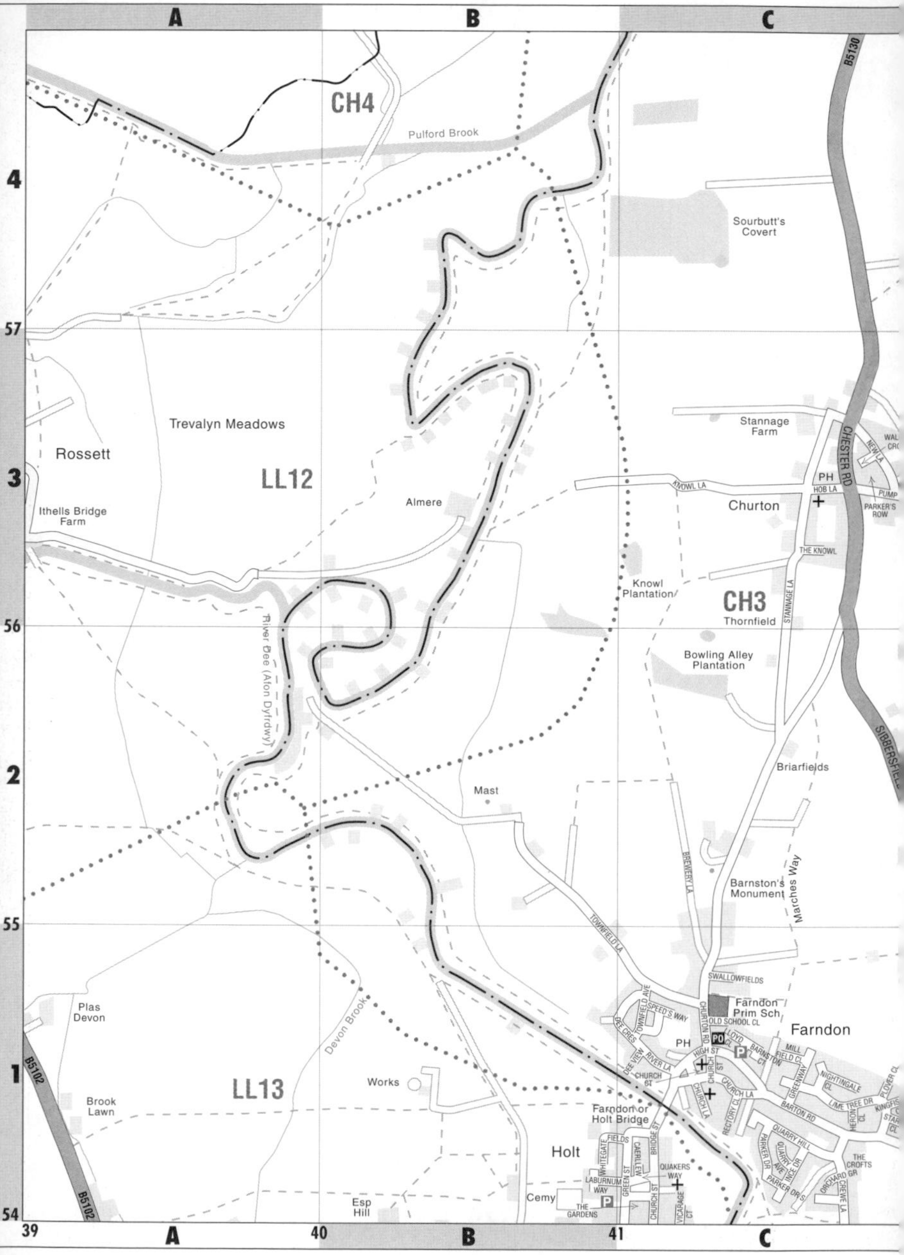
A
B
C
4
3
2
1
57
56
55
54
39
40
41
CH4
Pulford Brook
Sourbutt's Covert
B5130
Trevalyn Meadows
Rossett
LL12
Almere
Ithells Bridge Farm
Stannage Farm
CHESTER RD
KNOWL LA
PH
HOB LA
PUMP
PARKER'S ROW
Churton
THE KNOWL
Knowl Plantation
CH3
Thornfield
STANNAGE LA
Bowling Alley Plantation
River Dee (Afon Dyfrdwy)
SIBBERSFIELD
Briarfields
Mast
BREWERY LA
Barnston's Monument
Marches Way
TOWNFIELD LA
SWALLOWFIELDS
Farndon Prim Sch
OLD SCHOOL CL
Farndon
PO
PH
HIGH ST
CHURTON RD
SPEED'S WAY
TOWNFIELD AVE
DEE CRES
DEE VIEW
RIVER LA
CHURCH ST
CHURCH LA
CHURCH LA
RECTORY CL
LLOYD CL
BARNSTON CT
MILL FIELD CL
GREENWAY
NIGHTINGALE CL
LIME TREE DR
BARTON RD
HERON CL
QUARRY HILL
PARKER DR
QUARRY AVE
INCE DR
PARKER DR S
ORCHARD GR
CREWE LA
THE CROFTS
Plas Devon
Devon Brook
B5102
LL13
Works
Brook Lawn
Farndon or Holt Bridge
Holt
WHITEGATE FIELDS
CAERLLEW
BRIDGE ST
GREEN ST
QUAKERS WAY
LABURNUM WAY
CHURCH ST
VICARAGE CT
Cemy
THE GARDENS
P
Esp Hill
B5102

196

164
182
A
B
C
Lea Farm
Beachin Wood
Marches Way
Lower Lane
Grange Fox Covert
Grange Farm
Coddington Brook
Bishop Bennert Way
Old Beachin Farm
4
57
Edgerley Farm
Churton Stud Farm
EDGERLEY LA
SPRING LA
Middle Beachin Farm
CHURCH MEAD
PUMP LA
MARSH LA
Edgerley Covert
3
BEACHIN LA
Beachin Cottages
Plowley Brook
CH3
56
Highfield Farm
Royalty Cottage
The Royalty
HIGHFIELD LA
Rose Cottage
Bishop Bennert Way
Sibbersfield Hall
2
SIBBERSFIELD LA
MARSH LA
55
Marsh House
The Starling's Wood
Springfield Stud Farm
1
SY14
Higher Farm
BARTON RD
Barton
A534
BARTON RD
Hardley Farm
Rowleyhill
BARTON RD
B5130
A534
Morrislake Bridge
Cock Inn (PH)
54
43
44
A
B
C
197
182

181
165

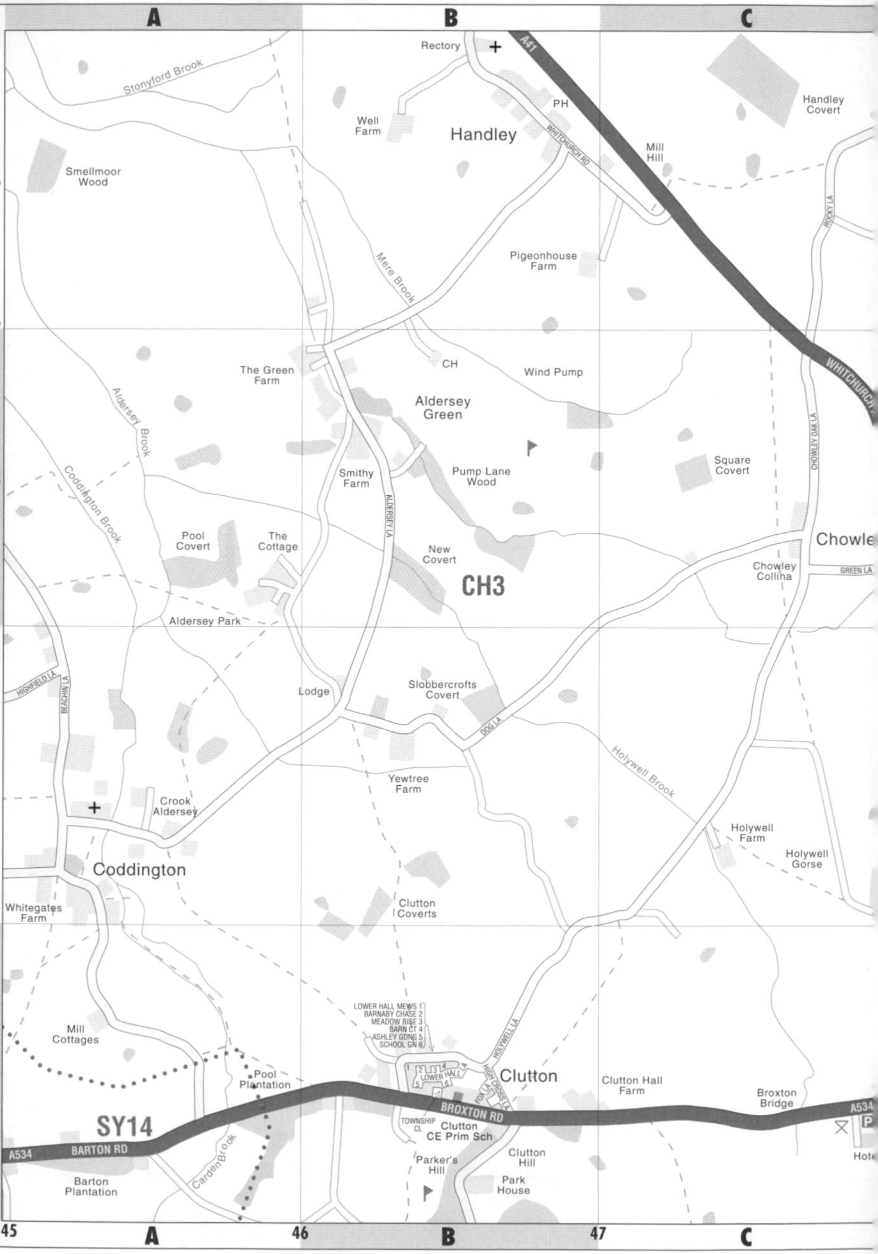
A
B
C
4
57
3
56
2
55
1
54
45
46
47
Rectory
A41
PH
Handley
Covert
Well
Farm
Handley
WHITCHURCH RD
Mill
Hill
Stonyford Brook
Smellmoor
Wood
ROCKY LA
Pigeonhouse
Farm
Mere Brook
The Green
Farm
CH
Wind Pump
WHITCHURCH
Aldersey
Green
Aldersey
Brook
CHOWLEY OAK LA
Coddington Brook
Smithy
Farm
Pump Lane
Wood
Square
Covert
ALDERSEY LA
Pool
Covert
The
Cottage
New
Covert
Chowle
Chowley
Collina
GREEN LA
CH3
Aldersey Park
HIGHFIELD LA
BEACHIN LA
Lodge
Slobbercrofts
Covert
DOG LA
Holywell Brook
Yewtree
Farm
Crook
Aldersey
Holywell
Farm
Holywell
Gorse
Coddington
Whitegates
Farm
Clutton
Coverts
LOWER HALL MEWS 1
BARNABY CHASE 2
MEADOW RISE 3
BARN CT 4
ASHLEY GDNS 5
SCHOOL GN 6
Mill
Cottages
HOLYWELL LA
LOWER HALL
Clutton
HIGH CROSS LA
FOX LA
Clutton Hall
Farm
Pool
Plantation
Broxton
Bridge
BROXTON RD
A534
SY14
TOWNSHIP
CL
Clutton
CE Prim Sch
P
A534
BARTON RD
Carden Brook
Parker's
Hill
Clutton
Hill
Hote
Barton
Plantation
Park
House

181
198

166
184

199
184

183
167

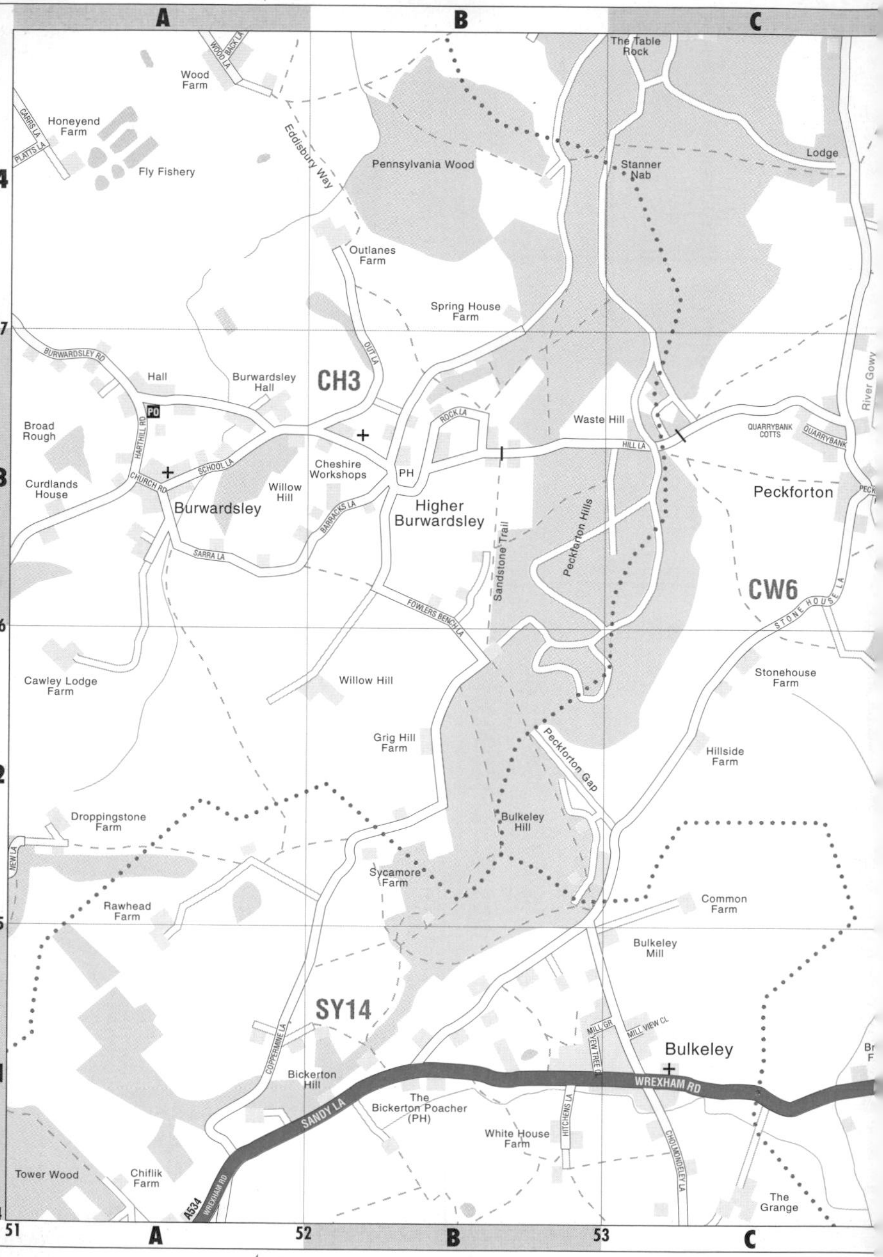

183
200

168
186

201
186

185
169

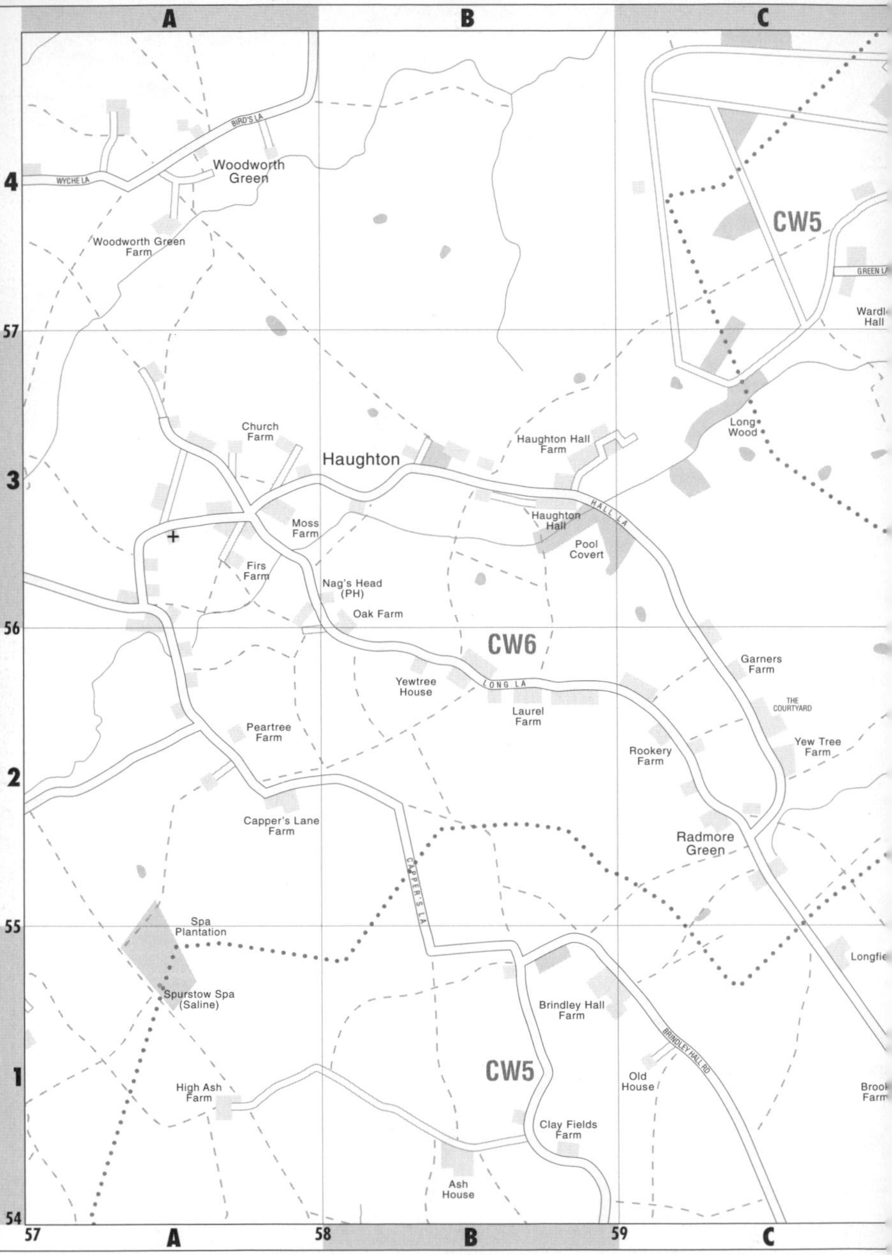
A
B
C
4
3
2
1
57
56
55
54
57
58
59
BIRD'S LA
WYCHE LA
Woodworth Green
Woodworth Green Farm
CW5
GREEN LA
Wardl Hall
Church Farm
Haughton
Haughton Hall Farm
Long Wood
Moss Farm
Haughton Hall
HALL LA
Pool Covert
Firs Farm
Nag's Head (PH)
Oak Farm
CW6
Garners Farm
Yewtree House
LONG LA
Laurel Farm
THE COURTYARD
Peartree Farm
Rookery Farm
Yew Tree Farm
Capper's Lane Farm
Radmore Green
CAPPER'S LA
Spa Plantation
Longfie
Spurstow Spa (Saline)
Brindley Hall Farm
BRINDLEY HALL RD
CW5
Old House
High Ash Farm
Brook Farm
Clay Fields Farm
Ash House

185
202

170
188

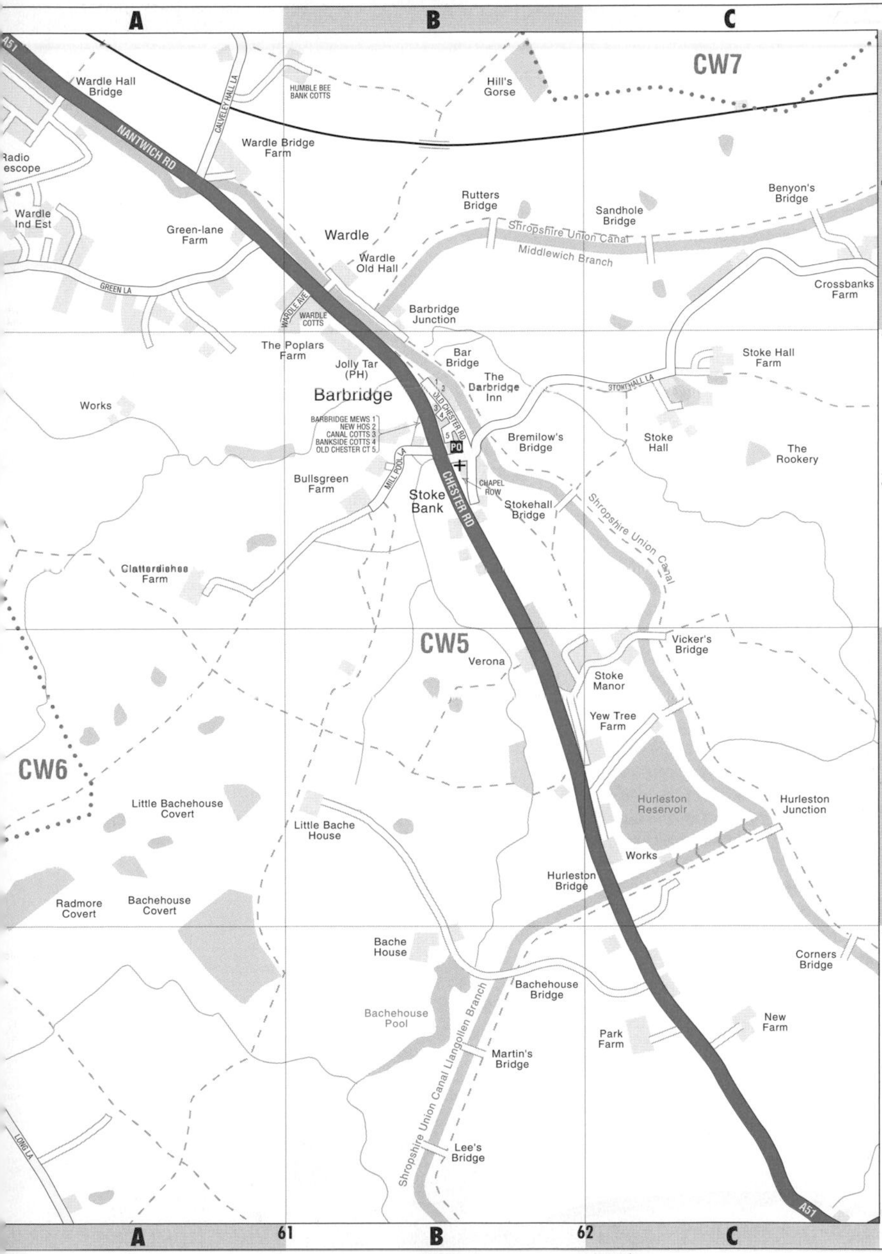
A
B
C
CW7
Wardle Hall Bridge
HUMBLE BEE BANK COTTS
CALVELEY HALL LA
Hill's Gorse
NANTWICH RD
Wardle Bridge Farm
Radio escope
Wardle Ind Est
Rutters Bridge
Sandhole Bridge
Benyon's Bridge
4
Green-lane Farm
Wardle
Shropshire Union Canal
Middlewich Branch
Wardle Old Hall
GREEN LA
Crossbanks Farm
WARDLE AVE
WARDLE COTTS
Barbridge Junction
57
The Poplars Farm
Bar Bridge
Stoke Hall Farm
Jolly Tar (PH)
The Barbridge Inn
STOKE HALL LA
Works
Barbridge
OLD CHESTER RD
BARBRIDGE MEWS 1
NEW HOS 2
CANAL COTTS 3
BANKSIDE COTTS 4
OLD CHESTER CT 5
Bremilow's Bridge
Stoke Hall
The Rookery
PO
Bullsgreen Farm
MILL POOL LA
CHAPEL ROW
3
Stoke Bank
CHESTER RD
Stokehall Bridge
Shropshire Union Canal
Clatterdishes Farm
56
CW5
Vicker's Bridge
Verona
Stoke Manor
Yew Tree Farm
CW6
2
Little Bachehouse Covert
Hurleston Reservoir
Hurleston Junction
Little Bache House
Works
Hurleston Bridge
Radmore Covert
Bachehouse Covert
55
Bache House
Corners Bridge
Bachehouse Bridge
Bachehouse Pool
Shropshire Union Canal Llangollen Branch
New Farm
Park Farm
Martin's Bridge
1
LONG LA
Lee's Bridge
A51
54
61
62

203
188

187
171

187
204

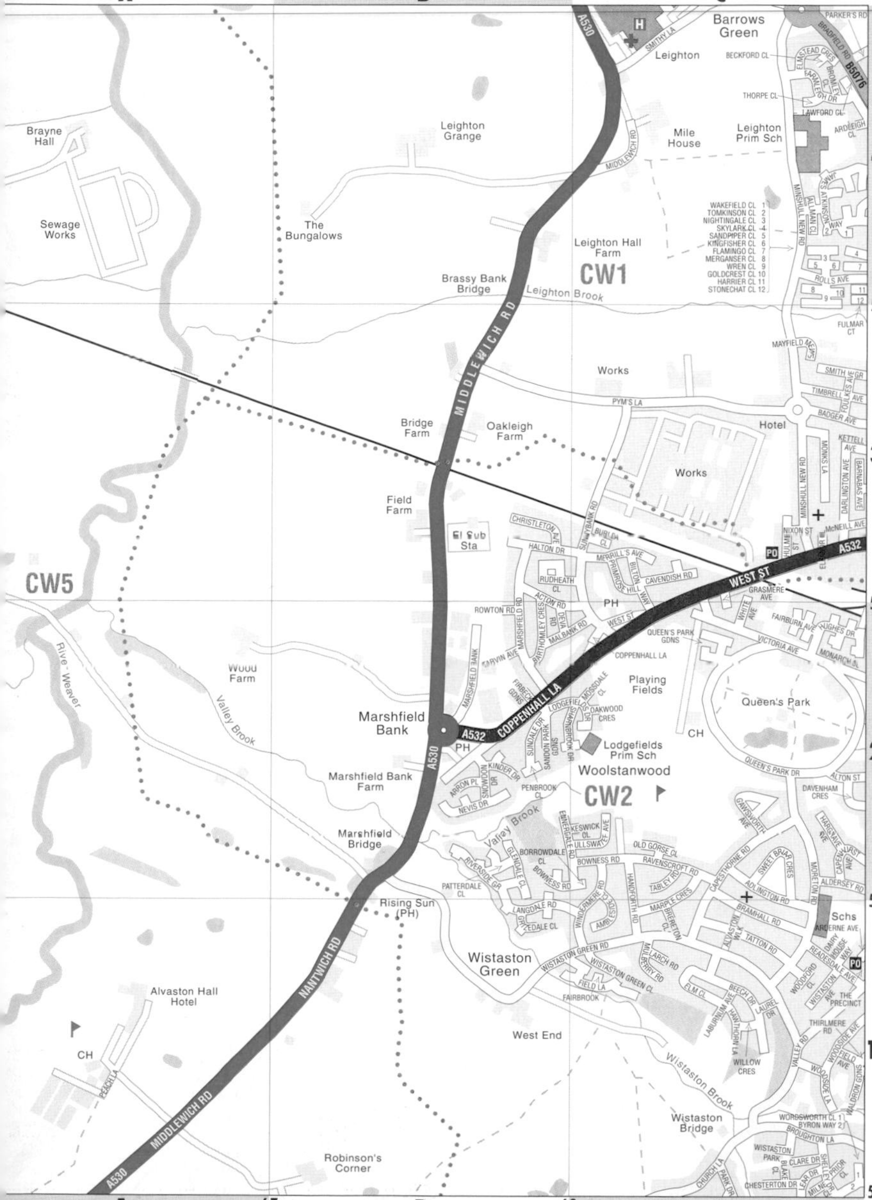
A
B
C
Barrows Green
Leighton
Brayne Hall
Leighton Grange
Mile House
Leighton Prim Sch
Sewage Works
The Bungalows
Leighton Hall Farm
CW1
Brassy Bank Bridge
Leighton Brook
WAKEFIELD CL 1
TOMKINSON CL 2
NIGHTINGALE CL 3
SKYLARK CL 4
SANDPIPER CL 5
KINGFISHER CL 6
FLAMINGO CL 7
MERGANSER CL 8
WREN CL 9
GOLDCREST CL 10
HARRIER CL 11
STONECHAT CL 12
MIDDLEWICH RD
A530
Works
PYM'S LA
Hotel
Bridge Farm
Oakleigh Farm
Field Farm
El Sub Sta
CW5
WEST ST
A532
COPPENHALL LA
Wood Farm
Valley Brook
River Weaver
Playing Fields
Queen's Park
Marshfield Bank
Lodgefields Prim Sch
Woolstanwood
CW2
Marshfield Bank Farm
Marshfield Bridge
Rising Sun (PH)
Wistaston Green
Schs
Alvaston Hall Hotel
NANTWICH RD
West End
Wistaston Brook
Wistaston Bridge
Robinson's Corner
4
57
3
56
2
55
1
54
67
68

189
173

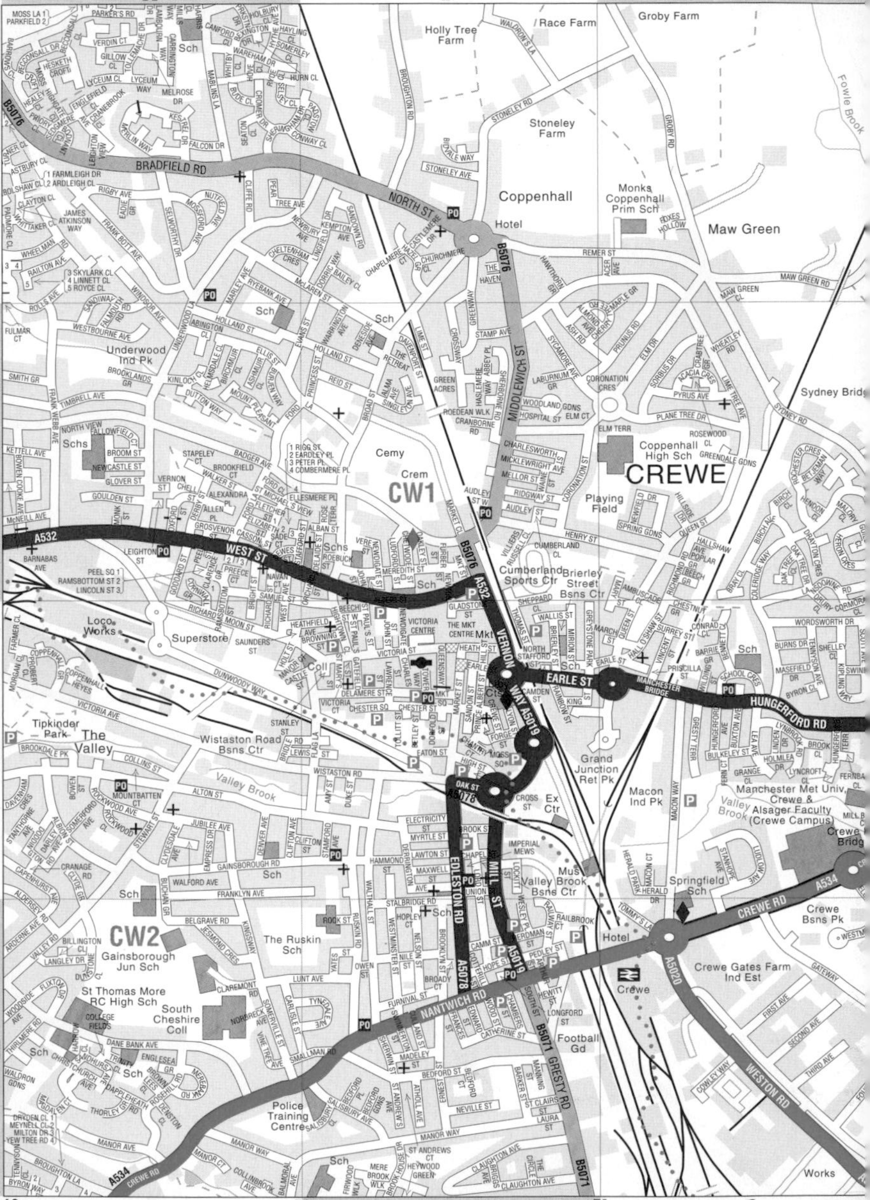
A
B
C
4
3
2
1
57
56
55
54
69
70
71
Holly Tree Farm
Race Farm
Groby Farm
Stoneley Farm
Coppenhall
Hotel
Monks Coppenhall Prim Sch
Maw Green
Fowle Brook
Sydney Bridge
BRADFIELD RD
NORTH ST
B5076
MIDDLEWICH ST
REMER ST
MAW GREEN RD
Underwood Ind Pk
Schs
Cemy
Crem
CW1
Coppenhall High Sch
CREWE
Playing Field
A532
WEST ST
VERNON WAY A5019
EARLE ST
HUNGERFORD RD
MANCHESTER BRIDGE
Cumberland Sports Ctr
Brierley Street Bsns Ctr
Loco Works
Superstore
VICTORIA CENTRE
THE MKT CENTRE
Mkt
Coll
DUNWOODY WAY
Tipkinder Park
The Valley
Wistaston Road Bsns Ctr
Valley Brook
Grand Junction Ret Pk
Macon Ind Pk
Manchester Met Univ, Crewe & Alsager Faculty (Crewe Campus)
Ex Ctr
Mus
Valley Brook Bsns Ctr
Springfield Sch
EDLESTON RD
A5078
MILL ST
A5019
Hotel
Crewe
CREWE RD
A534
A5020
Crewe Bsns Pk
Crewe Gates Farm Ind Est
WESTON RD
CW2
Gainsborough Jun Sch
The Ruskin Sch
St Thomas More RC High Sch
South Cheshire Coll
NANTWICH RD
B5071
GRESTY RD
Football Gd
Police Training Centre
Works

189
206

174
192

A B C

A534
ELTON LA
Hooter Hall Farm
HOLLYFIELDS
PH
WESTERN PK 1
HILL CROFT 2
COPPICE RD 3
ALSAGER RD
CW11
BOWKERS CROFT
CROSS LA
WOODCOTE PL
HASSALL RD
Crewe & Nantwich Circular Wlk
Foxholme Farm
MAW LA
CLAY LA
Yew Tree Farm
Clayhanger Hall Farm
Brook House Farm
Winterley
NEWTONS LA
NESFIELD CL
NESFIELD DR
NEWTONS GR
NEWTONS CRES
FISHERMANS CL
POOL LA
POOL VIEW
Holly Bush Farm
KENT'S GREEN LA
Kent's Green Farm
Winterley Pool
Thorney Fields Farm
Fox Covert
Winterley House
Fowle Brook
The Dingle Prim Sch
Works
RHODEN ST
HERBERT ST
ENDLE CL
AVON DR
Bradeley Hall
THE DINGLE
VICARAGE RD
CARTWRIGHT RD
REPTON DR
LYNTON GR
Sandfield House Farm
DELVES BROUGHTON CT 1
PALMERSTON CL 2
WELLS AVE
CREWE RD
BROOKFIELD
Haslington
Sydney
BRADELEY RD
Bradeley Abattoir
ASQUITH CL
PELHAM CL
ASHLEY MDW
HOLMSHAW LA
Park Farm
GUTTERSCROFT
MULCASTER CT
WALPOLE CL
SHELBURNE DR
GRENVILLE CL
PORTLAND GR
BATTERBEE CT
Hall Farm
CHATHAM WAY
MELBOURNE GR
PELICAN CL
BRADELEY HALL RD
PRIMROSE AVE
CHAMBERLAIN CT
WEST ST
NEW ST
ORCHARD
SCHOOL ST
CHURCH VIEW
PARK RD
THE BRAMBLES
CAMPBELL CL
RUSSELL DR
BRADELEY RD
ST MATTHEWS CL
P
ROSEBERRY WAY
HENRY ST
MERE ST
MERE CL
WATERLOO RD
Haslington Hall
Field Farm
POOL MEADOWS RD
KINGSLEY RD
HAMILTON
BALFOUR CL
BARNES CL
1 TREVITHICK CL
2 RENAISSANCE CT
CLIFFORD GR
OAKLAND AVE
LEYLAND GR
CROSSLAND
MOUNT PLEASANT
STANIER CL
VICTORIA AVE
VICTORIA CT
BOLD ST
HOBBS CL
WALKER CL
GRESLEY CL
NIGEL
CLOVERFIELDS
JESSOP WAY
TATE DR
CROSS RD
VERITY CL
PO
WELLESLEY AVE
GRACE CL
RHODES CL
CROSS ST
FIELDS RD
SOUTH AVE
CREWE GREEN AVE
HEATH VIEW
WALDRON RD
Haslington Prim Sch
A534
B5077
CW1
The Bank
Clapgates Farm
South Cheshire Way
Springfield Specl Sch
Tollgate Farm
Crewe Green
Slaughter Hill
Valley Brook
CH
ELECTRA WAY
MALLARD WAY
Park Farm
Crewe Bsns Pk
Temple of Peace Wood
QUAKERS COPPICE
Quaker's Coppice Nature Reserve
Rookery Wood
Crewe Gates Farm Ind Est
Englesea Brook
BUTTERTON LA
B5077
OLD PARK RD
Englesea House
BARTHOMLEY RD
Crewe Hall (Hotel)

4
57
3
56
2
55
1
54

A 73 B 74 C

207
192

191
175

191
208

A B C

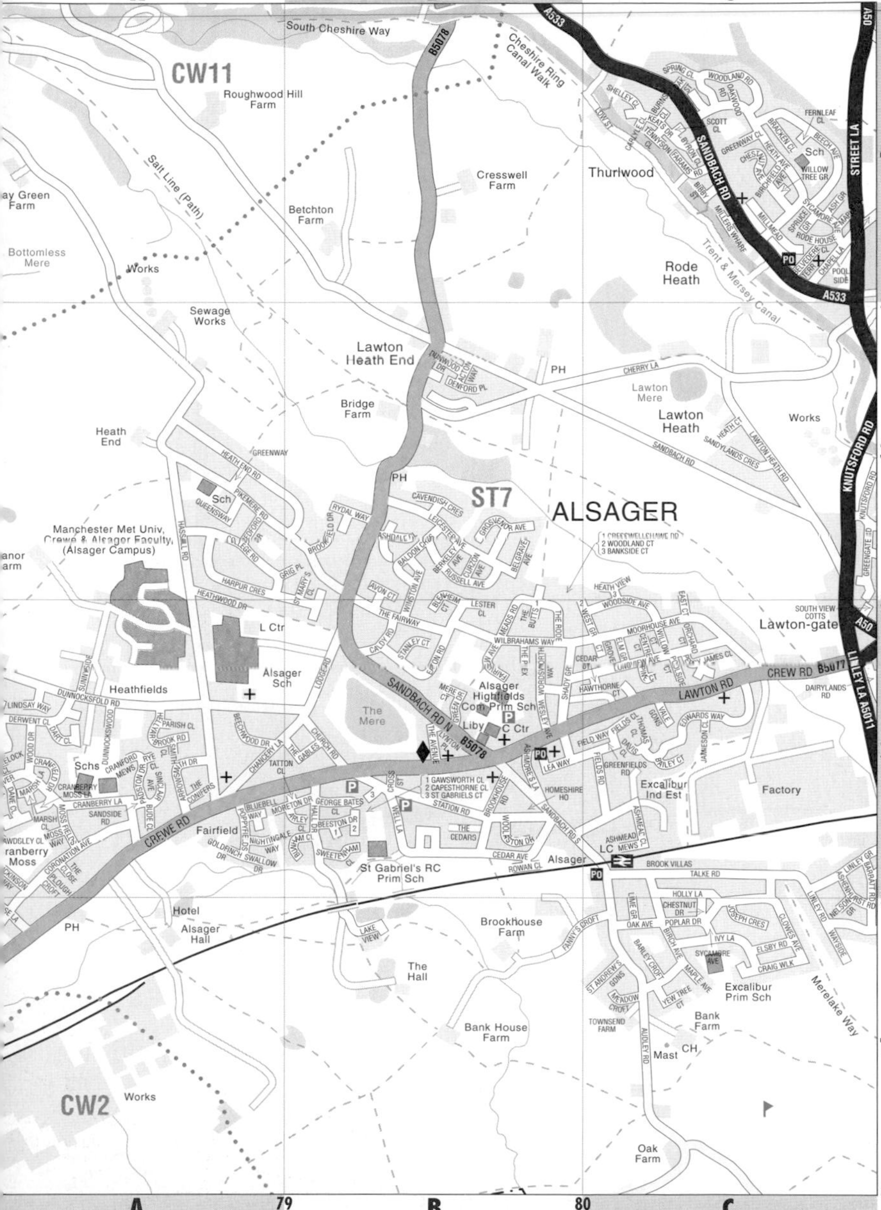
South Cheshire Way
Cheshire Ring Canal Walk
CW11
Roughwood Hill Farm
B5078
A533
A50
Salt Line (Path)
ay Green Farm
Bottomless Mere
Works
Sewage Works
Betchton Farm
Cresswell Farm
Thurlwood
SPRING CL
WOODLAND RD
OAKWOOD
SHELLEY CL
BURNS
KEATS DR
TENNYSON
BYRON CL
FARAMS RD
BIBBY ST
SCOTT CL
GREENWAY CL
BRACKEN CL
FERNLEAF CL
BEECH AVE
HEATH AVE
BIRCHFIELD AVE
Sch
WILLOW TREE GR
STREET LA
SANDBACH RD
MILLERS WHARF
MILLMEAD
SYCAMORE AVE
SPRUCE GR
RODE HOUSE
BELVEDERE CL
CHAPEL LA
POOL SIDE
PO
Rode Heath
Trent & Mersey Canal
Lawton Heath End
DENFORD PL
PH
CHERRY LA
Lawton Mere
Lawton Heath
Works
Bridge Farm
Heath End
HEATH END RD
GREENWAY
SANDBACH RD
HEATH CT
SANDYLANDS CRES
LAWTON HEATH RD
KNUTSFORD RD
PH
ST7
ALSAGER
Sch
PIKEMERE RD
QUEENSWAY
CAVENDISH CRES
RYDAL WAY
LEICESTER AVE
GROSVENOR AVE
BELGRAVE AVE
1 CRESSWELLSHAWE RD
2 WOODLAND CT
3 BANKSIDE CT
Manchester Met Univ, Crewe & Alsager Faculty (Alsager Campus)
anor arm
HASSALL RD
HARPUR CRES
GRIG PL
ST MARY'S CL
BALDON CL
BERKELEY AVE
CURZON AVE
RUSSELL AVE
AVON CT
WINSTON AVE
BLENHEIM CT
LESTER CL
HEATHWOOD DR
THE FAIRWAY
MEADS RD
THE BUTTS
THE RODE
HEATH VIEW
WOODSIDE AVE
EAST CT
GREENGATE RD
SOUTH VIEW COTTS
Lawton-gate
L Ctr
STANLEY CT
WILBRAHAMS WAY
MOORHOUSE AVE
ORCHARD CL
JAMES CL
CEDAR CT
HAWTHORNE CT
SHADY GR
CREW RD B5077
LINLEY LA A5011
DAIRYLANDS RD
LAWTON RD
Alsager Sch
LODGE RD
SUNNYSIDE
DUNNOCKSFOLD RD
Heathfields
LINDSAY WAY
DERWENT CL
PARISH CL
BROOK RD
BEECHWOOD DR
The Mere
SANDBACH RD N
Alsager Highfields Com Prim Sch
Liby
C Ctr
P
EDWARDS WAY
FIELD WAY
FIELDS CL
THOMAS CL
DAVIS CL
BAILEY CT
JAMESON CL
CRANFORD MEWS
CRANBERRY MOSS LA
CRANBERRY LA
SANDSIDE RD
Schs
THE CONIFERS
CHANCERY LA
TATTON CL
THE GABLES
CHURCH RD
THE AVENUE
B5078
1 GAWSWORTH CL
2 CAPESTHORNE CL
3 ST GABRIELS CT
ASHMORE'S LA
LEA WAY
FIELDS RD
GREENFIELDS RD
Excalibur Ind Est
Factory
CREWE RD
Fairfield
BLUEBELL WAY
MORETON DR
GEORGE BATES CL
BEESTON DR
STATION RD
BROOKHOUSE RD
HOMESHIRE HO
SANDBACH RD S
ASHMEAD CL
ASHMEAD MEWS
NIGHTINGALE WAY
GOLDFINCH DR
SWALLOW DR
SWEETENHAM CL
THE CEDARS
WOOLSTON DR
CEDAR AVE
ROWAN CL
Alsager
LC
BROOK VILLAS
TALKE RD
CORONATION AVE
ranberry Moss
St Gabriel's RC Prim Sch
PO
HOLLY LA
CHESTNUT DR
POPLAR DR
JOSEPH CRES
CLOWES AVE
LINLEY GR
LINLEY RD
WAYSIDE
OAK AVE
LIME GR
IVY LA
ELSBY RD
CRAIG WLK
PH
Hotel
Alsager Hall
LAKE VIEW
Brookhouse Farm
FANNY'S CROFT
BARLEY CROFT
BIRCH AVE
MAPLE AVE
SYCAMORE AVE
Excalibur Prim Sch
Merelake Way
The Hall
ST ANDREW'S GDNS
MEADOW CROFT
YEW TREE CT
Bank Farm
Bank House Farm
TOWNSEND FARM
AUDLEY RD
Mast
CH
CW2
Works
Oak Farm
4
57
3
56
2
55
1
54
79
80

A 79 B 80 C

193
177

193
210

178

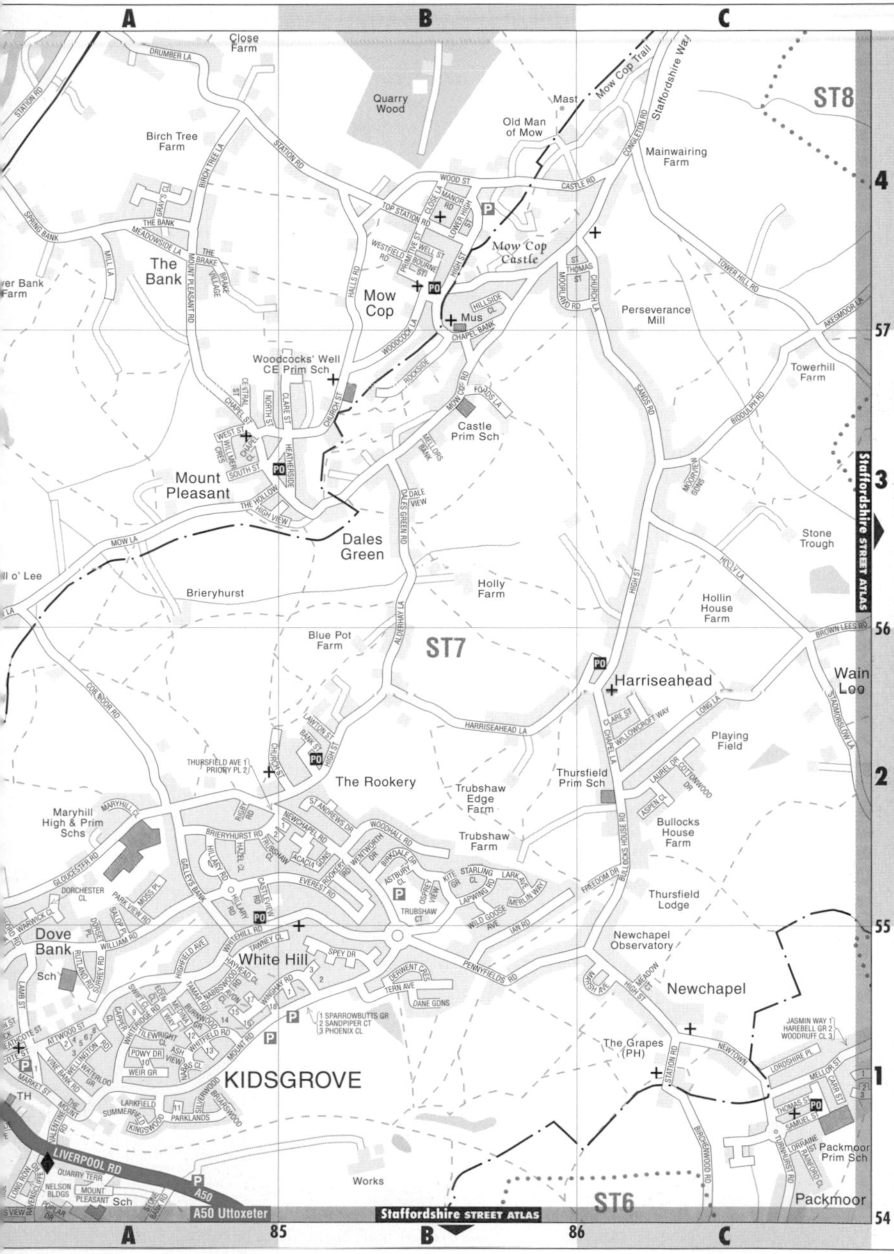

A1
1 KINNERSLEY ST
2 GILBERT CL
3 NAPIER GDNS
4 PEEL CT
5 BANK CT
6 HIGHERLAND CT
7 WESLEY GDNS
8 VICTORIA CT
9 SWALLOW CL
10 WHEELOCK WAY
11 CHARNWOOD
12 DIAMOND AVE
13 MOSSFIELD CRES
14 LITTLE ROW
15 BRIGHTS AVE
16 BIRCHES WAY
17 SILVERMINE CL
18 MAGPIE CRES

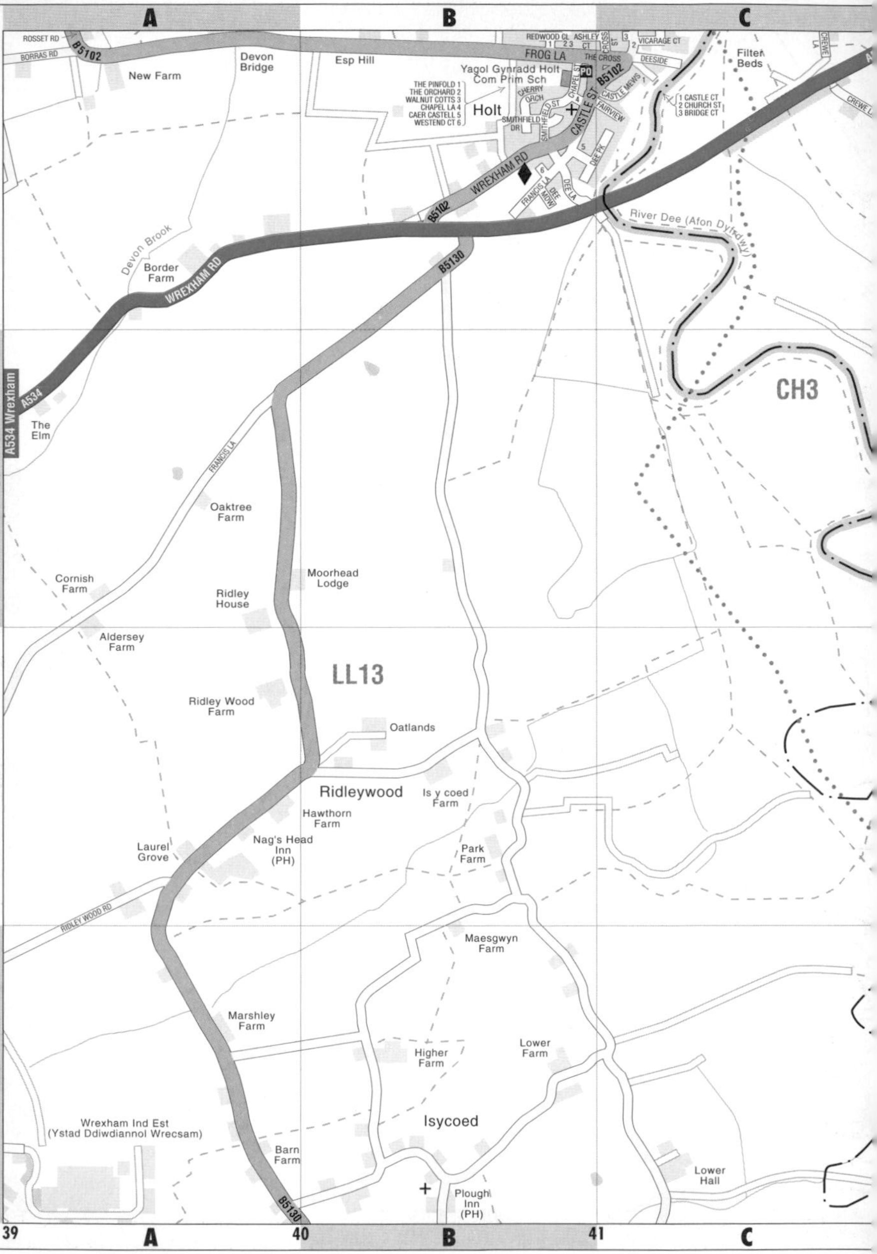
180
A
B
C
4
3
2
1
53
52
51
50
39
40
41
New Farm
Devon Bridge
Esp Hill
Holt
Yagol Gynradd Holt Com Prim Sch
Filter Beds
Devon Brook
Border Farm
WREXHAM RD
B5130
B5102
FROG LA
CASTLE ST
River Dee (Afon Dyfrdwy)
CH3
LL13
A534 Wrexham
The Elm
FRANCIS LA
Oaktree Farm
Cornish Farm
Moorhead Lodge
Ridley House
Aldersey Farm
Ridley Wood Farm
Oatlands
Ridleywood
Is y coed Farm
Hawthorn Farm
Nag's Head Inn (PH)
Laurel Grove
Park Farm
RIDLEY WOOD RD
Maesgwyn Farm
Marshley Farm
Higher Farm
Lower Farm
Isycoed
Wrexham Ind Est (Ystad Ddiwdiannol Wrecsam)
Barn Farm
Plough Inn (PH)
Lower Hall

181
198

A
B
C
Rowley Hill Farm
Tom Irons' Rough
eadow View
Crewe-by-Farndon
CREWE LAS
Lodge Farm
Wetreins Green Farm
Crewe Hall
Kingslee
Wetreins Green
Stretton Lower Hall
WETREINS LA
The Wetreins
rewe Hill
CREWE HILL LA
Mrs Leche's Gorse
Stretton Hall
Stretton Old Hall
Stretton
Crewe Gorse
Bishop Bennet Way
The Wetreins
SY14
Crewe Farm
Caldecott Farm
Caldecott Green
CH3
River Dee (Afon Dyfrdwy)
Caldecott Hall
Grafton New Covert
Marches Way
Castletown
Caldecott Farm
Castletown Bridge
Castletown Rough
CASTLETOWN LA
River Dee (Afon Dyfrdwy)
Lords Fields
LL13
Chestnuts
CHURCH RD
SY14
4
53
3
52
2
51
1
50
43
44
211
198

197
182

197
212

183
200

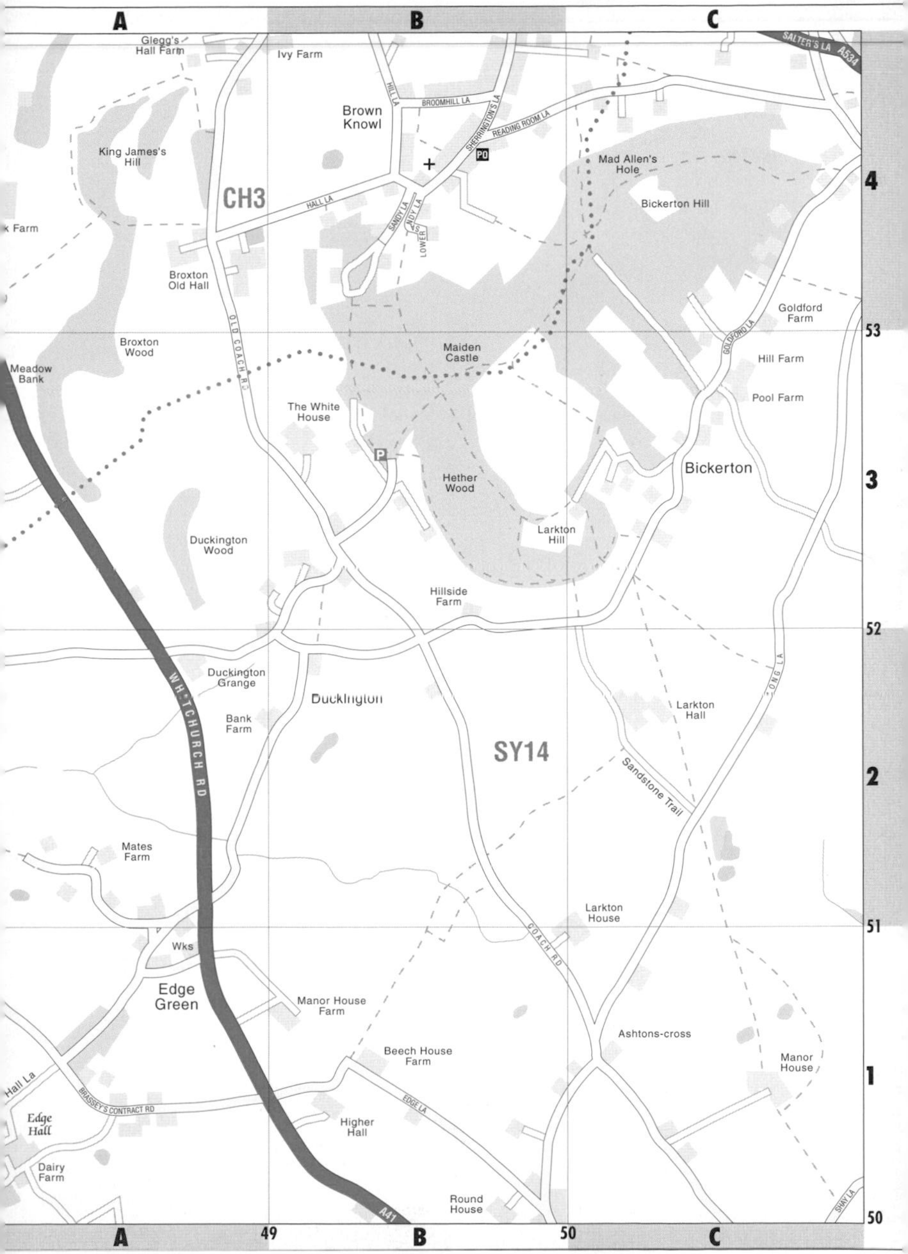

213
200

199
184

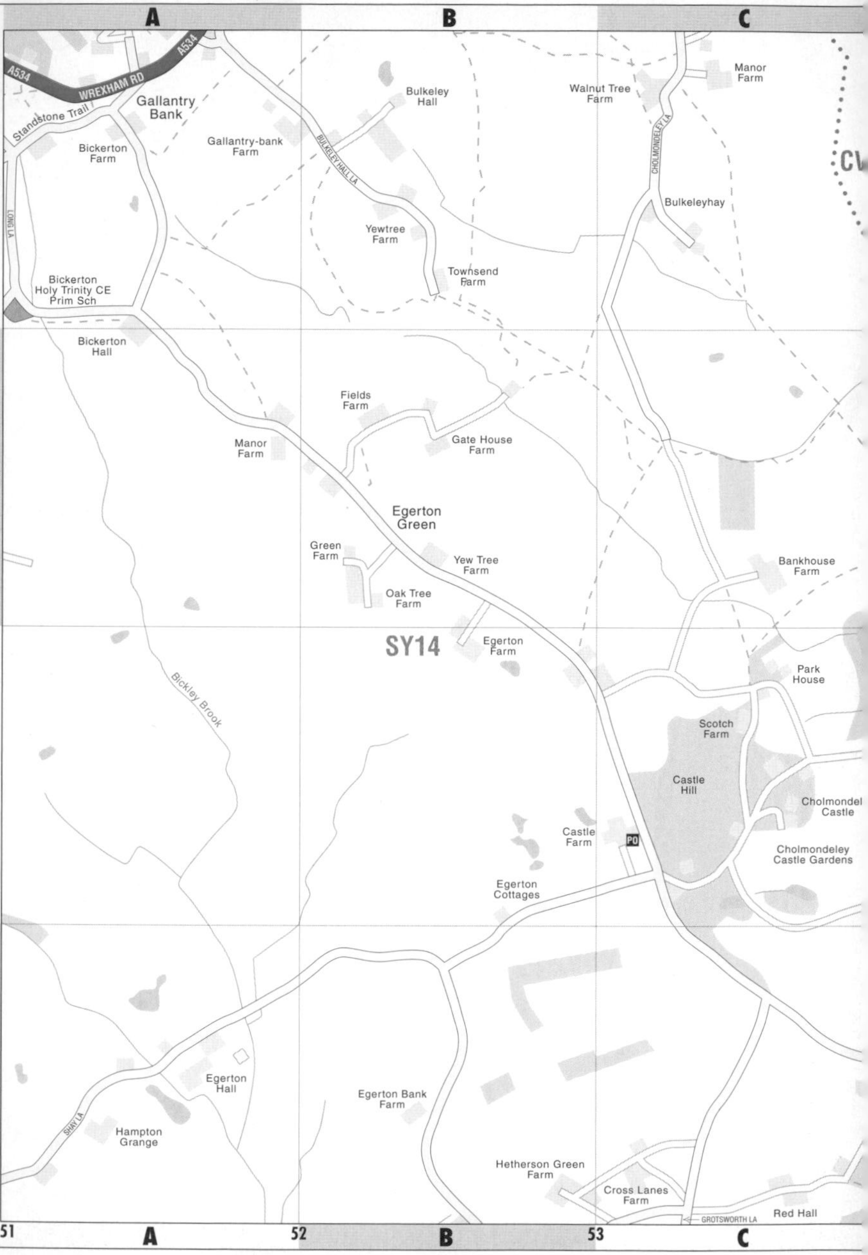
A
B
C
A534
WREXHAM RD
Gallantry Bank
Standstone Trail
Bickerton Farm
Gallantry-bank Farm
Bulkeley Hall
BULKELEY HALL LA
Walnut Tree Farm
Manor Farm
CHOLMONDELEY LA
Bulkeleyhay
LONG LA
Yewtree Farm
Townsend Farm
Bickerton Holy Trinity CE Prim Sch
Bickerton Hall
Fields Farm
Manor Farm
Gate House Farm
Egerton Green
Green Farm
Yew Tree Farm
Oak Tree Farm
Bankhouse Farm
SY14
Egerton Farm
Park House
Bickley Brook
Scotch Farm
Castle Hill
Cholmondel Castle
Castle Farm
PO
Cholmondeley Castle Gardens
Egerton Cottages
Egerton Hall
Egerton Bank Farm
SHAY LA
Hampton Grange
Hetherson Green Farm
Cross Lanes Farm
GROTSWORTH LA
Red Hall
4
53
3
52
2
51
1
50
51
52
53

199
214

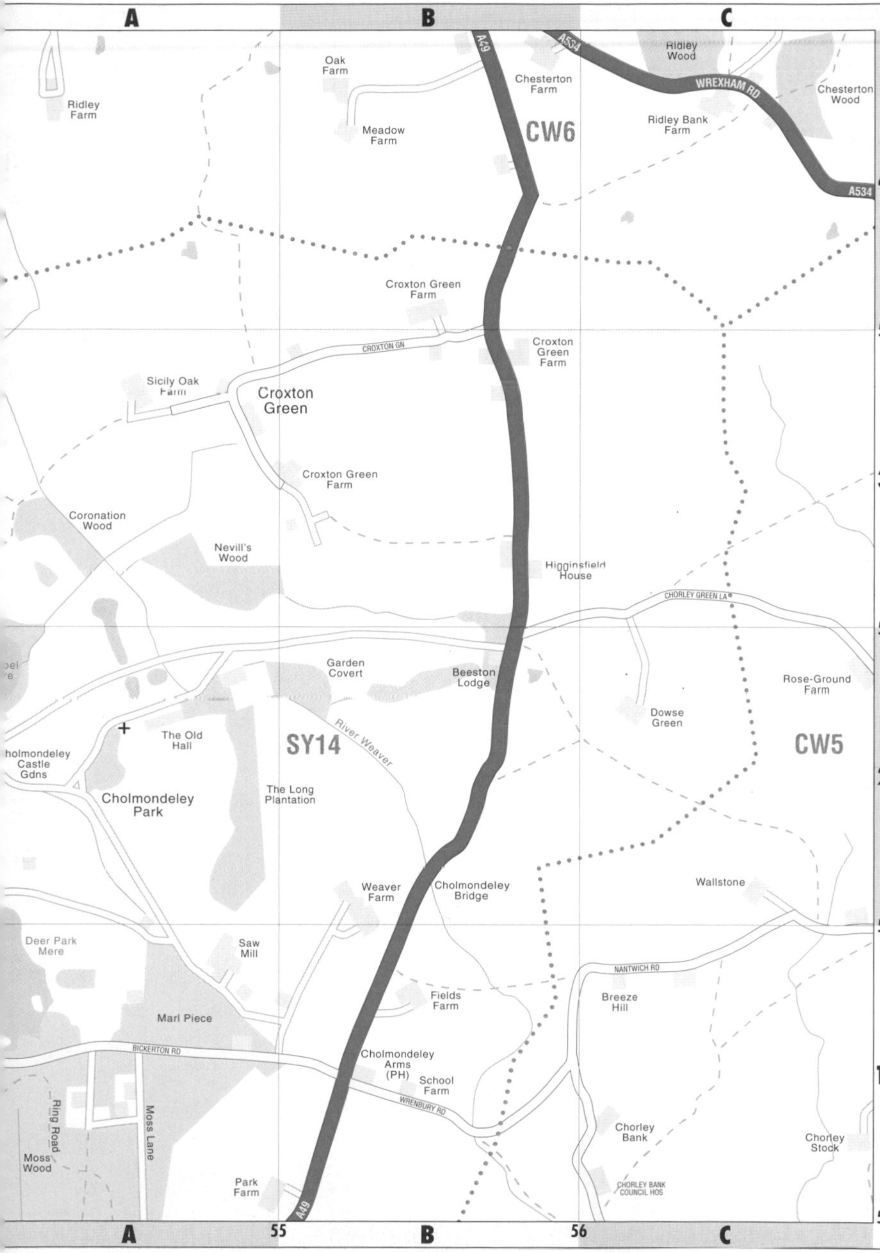
A
B
C
Ridley Farm
Oak Farm
Meadow Farm
A49
A534
Chesterton Farm
CW6
Ridley Wood
WREXHAM RD
Ridley Bank Farm
Chesterton Wood
4
Croxton Green Farm
53
Croxton Green Farm
CROXTON GN
Sicily Oak Farm
Croxton Green
Croxton Green Farm
3
Coronation Wood
Nevill's Wood
Higginsfield House
CHORLEY GREEN LA
52
Garden Covert
Beeston Lodge
Rose-Ground Farm
The Old Hall
SY14
River Weaver
Dowse Green
CW5
Cholmondeley Castle Gdns
Cholmondeley Park
The Long Plantation
2
Weaver Farm
Cholmondeley Bridge
Wallstone
51
Deer Park Mere
Saw Mill
NANTWICH RD
Fields Farm
Breeze Hill
Marl Piece
BICKERTON RD
Cholmondeley Arms (PH)
School Farm
WRENBURY RD
1
Ring Road
Moss Lane
Moss Wood
Chorley Bank
Chorley Stock
Park Farm
CHORLEY BANK COUNCIL HOS
50
55
56

201
186

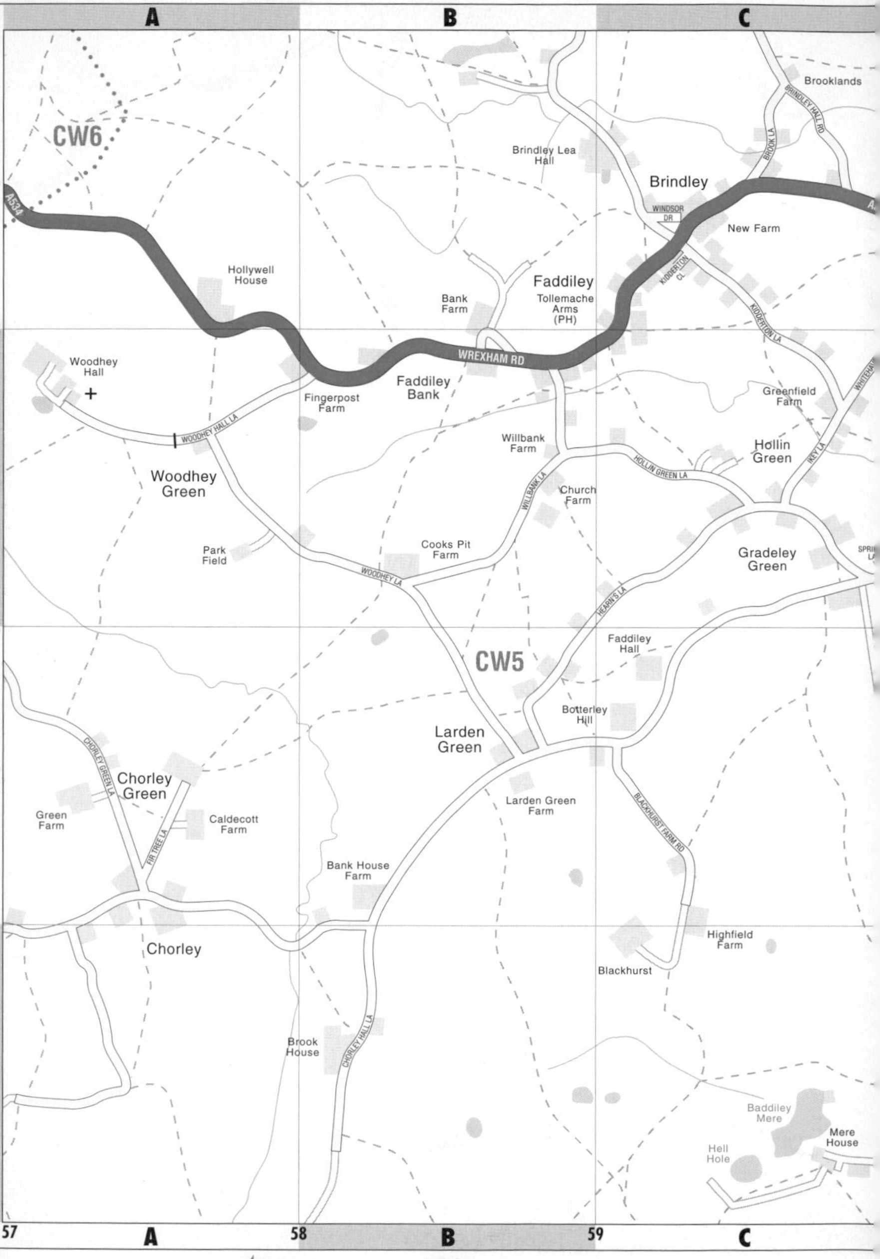
A
B
C
4
53
3
52
2
51
1
50
57
58
59
CW6
A534
Brookland
BRINDLEY HALL RD
BROOK LA
Brindley Lea Hall
Brindley
WINDSOR DR
New Farm
KIDDERTON CL
Hollywell House
Faddiley
Bank Farm
Tollemache Arms (PH)
KIDDERTON LA
WREXHAM RD
Woodhey Hall
Fingerpost Farm
Faddiley Bank
Greenfield Farm
WOODHEY HALL LA
Willbank Farm
Hollin Green
HOLLIN GREEN LA
IKEY LA
Woodhey Green
WILLBANK LA
Church Farm
Park Field
Cooks Pit Farm
Gradeley Green
WOODHEY LA
HEARN'S LA
Faddiley Hall
CW5
Botterley Hill
Larden Green
CHORLEY GREEN LA
Chorley Green
Larden Green Farm
Green Farm
Caldecott Farm
FIR TREE LA
BLACKHURST FARM RD
Bank House Farm
Highfield Farm
Chorley
Blackhurst
Brook House
CHORLEY HALL LA
Baddiley Mere
Mere House
Hell Hole

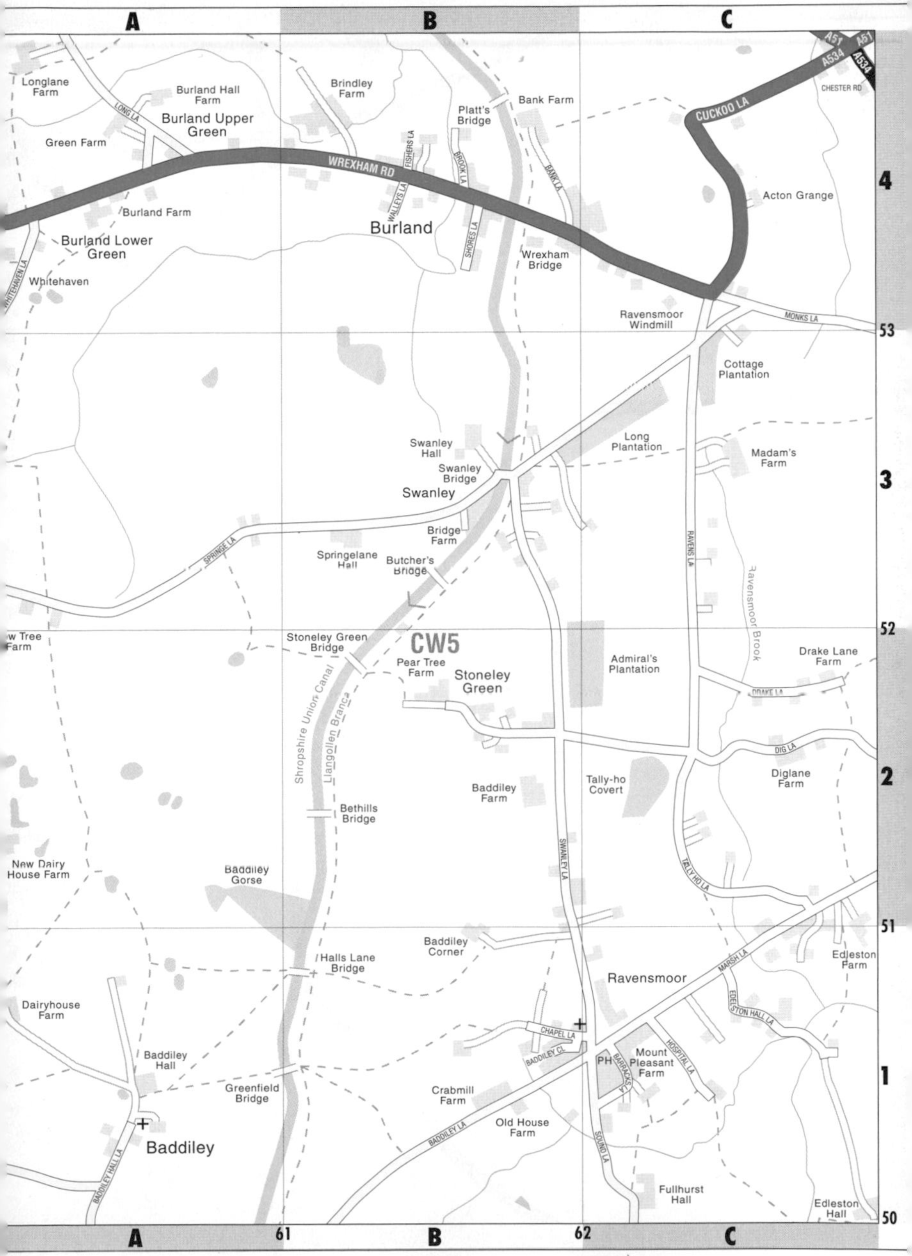
A
B
C
Longlane Farm
Burland Hall Farm
Burland Upper Green
Green Farm
LONG LA
Brindley Farm
Platt's Bridge
Bank Farm
FISHERS LA
BROOK LA
BANK LA
WREXHAM RD
WALLEYS LA
Burland Farm
Burland
SHORES LA
Burland Lower Green
WHITEHAVEN LA
Whitehaven
Wrexham Bridge
CUCKOO LA
A51
A534
CHESTER RD
Acton Grange
Ravensmoor Windmill
MONKS LA
Cottage Plantation
Swanley Hall
Long Plantation
Madam's Farm
Swanley Bridge
Swanley
SPRINGE LA
Bridge Farm
Springelane Hall
Butcher's Bridge
RAVENS LA
Ravensmoor Brook
Stoneley Green Bridge
CW5
Pear Tree Farm
Stoneley Green
Admiral's Plantation
Drake Lane Farm
DRAKE LA
DIG LA
Shropshire Union Canal
Llangollen Branch
Baddiley Farm
Tally-ho Covert
Diglane Farm
Bethills Bridge
SWANLEY LA
New Dairy House Farm
Baddiley Gorse
TALLY HO LA
Baddiley Corner
Halls Lane Bridge
Ravensmoor
MARSH LA
Edleston Farm
Dairyhouse Farm
EDELSTON HALL LA
CHAPEL LA
BADDILEY CL
PH
BARRACKS LA
Mount Pleasant Farm
HOSPITAL LA
Baddiley Hall
Greenfield Bridge
Crabmill Farm
Old House Farm
BADDILEY LA
SOUND LA
Baddiley
BADDILEY HALL LA
Fullhurst Hall
Edleston Hall
4
53
3
52
2
51
1
50
61
62

203
188

C3
1 BARONY BLDGS
2 BARONIA PL
3 VOLUNTEER AVE
4 BOWYER AVE
5 SCHOOL LA
6 CHAPEL MEWS
7 SWINE MARKET
8 OAT MARKET
9 CASTLE ST
10 CROMWELL CT
11 MAISTERSON CT
12 RECTORY CL
13 BOWLING GREEN CT
14 ROOKERY CL
15 LABURNUM AVE
16 HAWTHORN AVE
17 NUTHURST GDNS
18 MANSION CT
19 CHURCHE'S CT

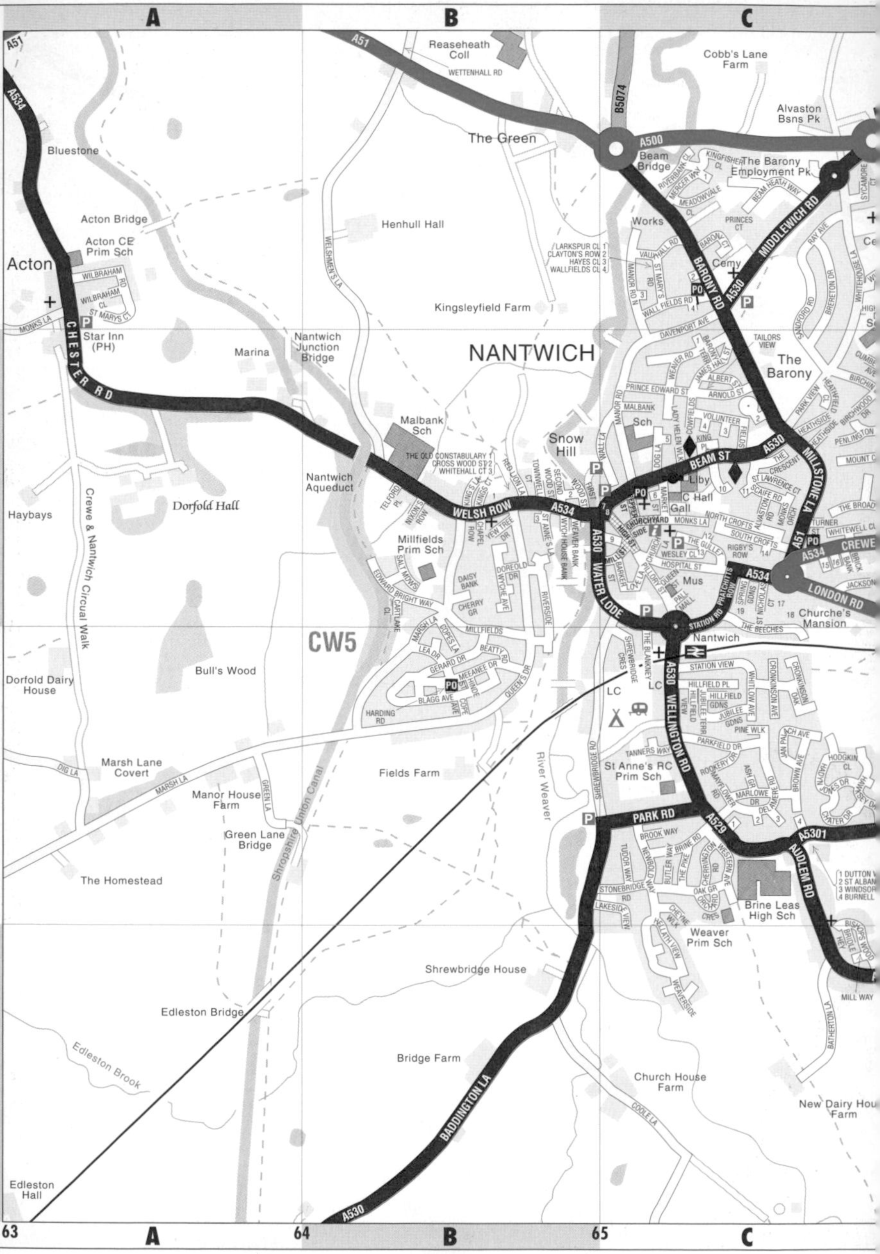

203
218

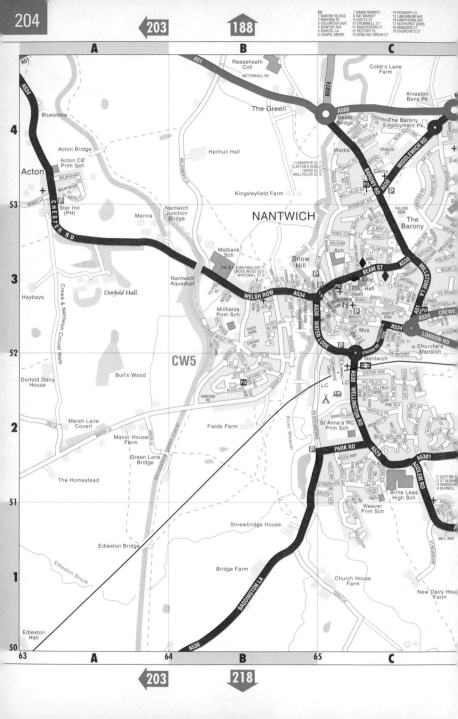

189 206

219 206

205
190

205
220

191
208

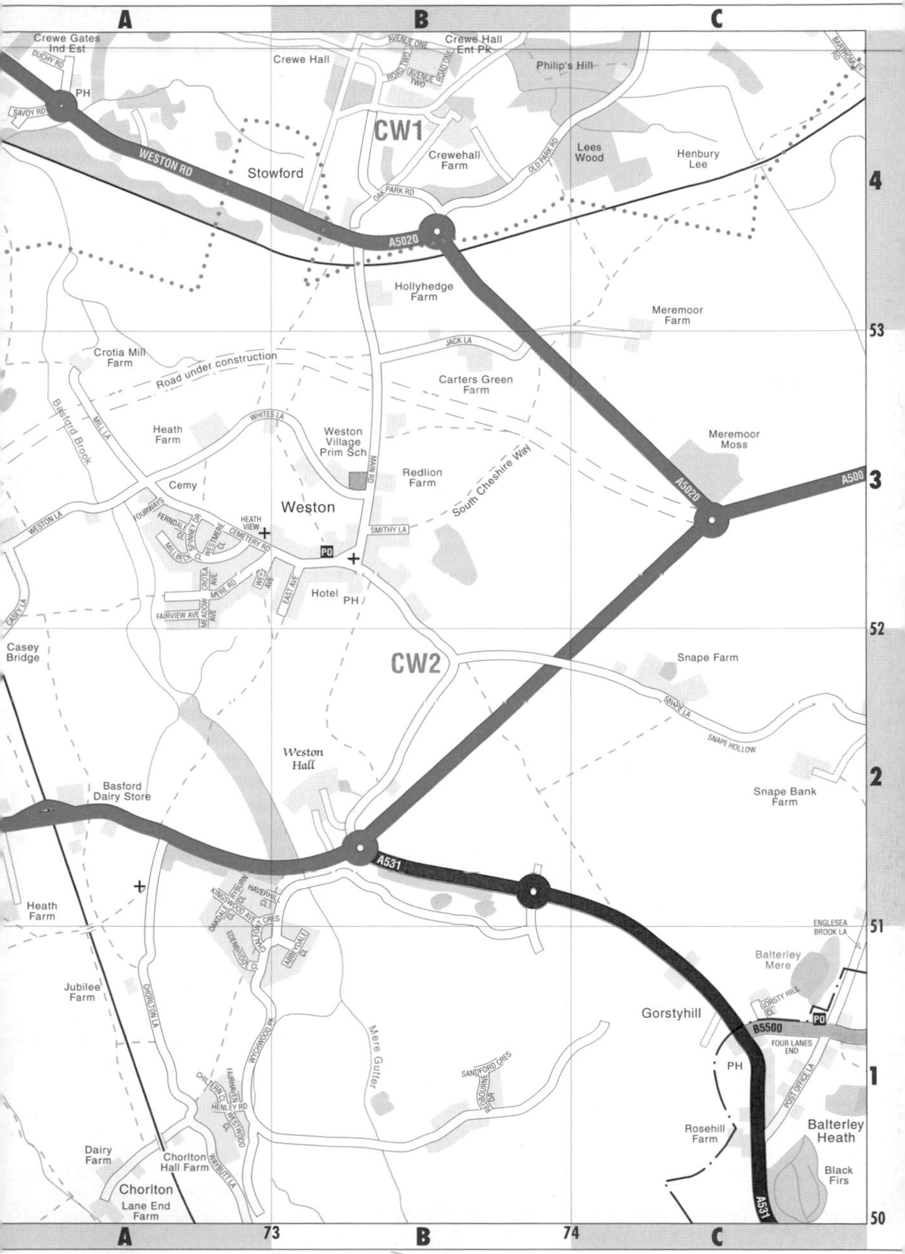

221
208

A
B
C
4
53
3
52
2
51
1
50
75
76
77
Valley Brook
LC
Top End Farm
Bridge House Farm
Walnut Tree Farm
Mill Farm
MILL LA
M6
B5078
RADWAY GREEN RD
Fox Fa
Toad Hole Farm
Smith Green Farm
Smith's Green
Daisy Bank Farm
Flas Hou
BARTHOMLEY RD
SMITHY LA
New Farm
Monneley Farm
Cherrytree Farm
Churchfield Farm
Bluemire Farm
SMITHY LA
A500
RADWAY GREEN RD
Barthomley
White Lion (PH)
Motel
B5078
16
A5
Town House Farm
HUNGERFORD PL
Glebe Farm
Englesea Brook
Old Hall Farm
CW2
Valley Farm
AUDLEY RD
Domvilles Wood
Bayley-Lane Farm
SNAPE LA
Basford Coppice
DEANS LA
Manor Farm
Englesea-brook
Mus
Domvilles Farm
Dean Rough
The Limes Farm
ENGLESEA BROOK LA
Dean Brook
Knowl End
BARTHOMLEY RD
Balterley Green Farm
ST7
Spring Farm
Balterley Green
Mill Dale Farm
B5500
Mill Dale
Pear Tree Lake Farm
Shortfields Farm
Pear Tree Farm
Hall o' th' Wood
Black Mere
Balterley
Bell Farm
NANTWICH RD
BACK LA
LIMBRICK RD
Waggon and Horses (PH)
M6 Staf

193
210

A
B
C
Bank Top
CW2
AUDLEY RD
4
Lower Foxley
Foxley
Mosshouse
Foxley Drumble
Foxley Gorse
Foxley Farm
EARDLEYEND RD
53
Brockwood Hill Farm
High Foxley Farm
Wrench's Coppice
Eardleyend
Park Manor Farm
3
Eardley Hall
ALSAGER RD
rockwood Hill
The Fields
Millend
MILLEND LA
HULLOCK'S POOL RD
CROSS LA
A500
Cross Farm
52
Brook Farm
ST7
Poole House
Hullock's Pool
Park Lane Farm
Sewage Wks
Great Oak Farm
GREATOAK RD
Yewtree Farm
Park End
PARK LA
New Farm
2
Park Farm
Townhouse
Moat Farm
Ravensmead Prim Sch
Pear Tree Farm
EDWARD ST
BIGNALL END RD
Bignall End
TIBB ST
Firs Farm
MOAT LA
Community Ctr
OLD RD
RAVENS CL
WOOD ST
ALBERT ST
DIGLAKE ST
CHAPEL ST
HOPE ST
NEW RD
RAVEN'S LA
PO
51
B5500
New Peel Farm
WILBRAHAM'S WLK
CHURCH BANK
WATLANDS RD
RILEYS WAY
GEORGES WAY
BENJAMINS WAY
IKINS DR
MCKELLIN CL
AARONS DR
BRIDGE CL
Kent Hill Farm
P
ST JAMES CT
BOYLES HALL RD
GRESLEY WAY
BOUGHEY RD
Liby
WESTLANDS
GREENWAYS
BRINDLEYS WAY
MONUMENT VIEW
Audley
BARLEYFIELDS
DEAN HOLLOW
CHESTER RD
CHAPEL LA
HALL ST
HILL TERR
FAIRFIELDS
DELPHSIDE
STEPHENS WAY
BARTHOMLEY RD
CHURCH ST
The Quarry
VERNON AVE
VERNON CL
PO
CHERRY TREE RD 1
CEDAR CRES 2
WEDGEWOOD AVE 3
1
PEEL HOLLOW
WESTFIELD AVE
MEADOWSIDE AVE
NANTWICH RD
Wereton
KELSALL WAY
BOOTH ST
DURBER CL
KING ST
MELLARD ST
GEORGE ST
HOUGHER WALL RD
GRASSYGREEN LA
BOON HILL RD
BIRCH RD
ELM TREE DR
Old Peel Farm
NEW KING ST
QUEEN ST
PRINCESS AVE
MADDOCK ST
HAWTHORNE AVE
PEAR TREE RD
WERETON RD
Quarry New Farm
Rye Hills
Grange Farm
Boon Hill
CARR LA
Shraleybrook
Greenbutts House
RYEHILLS
Ryehill Farm
Wood Lane Prim Sch
TOM FIELDS
50
Staffordshire STREET ATLAS
79
80

210

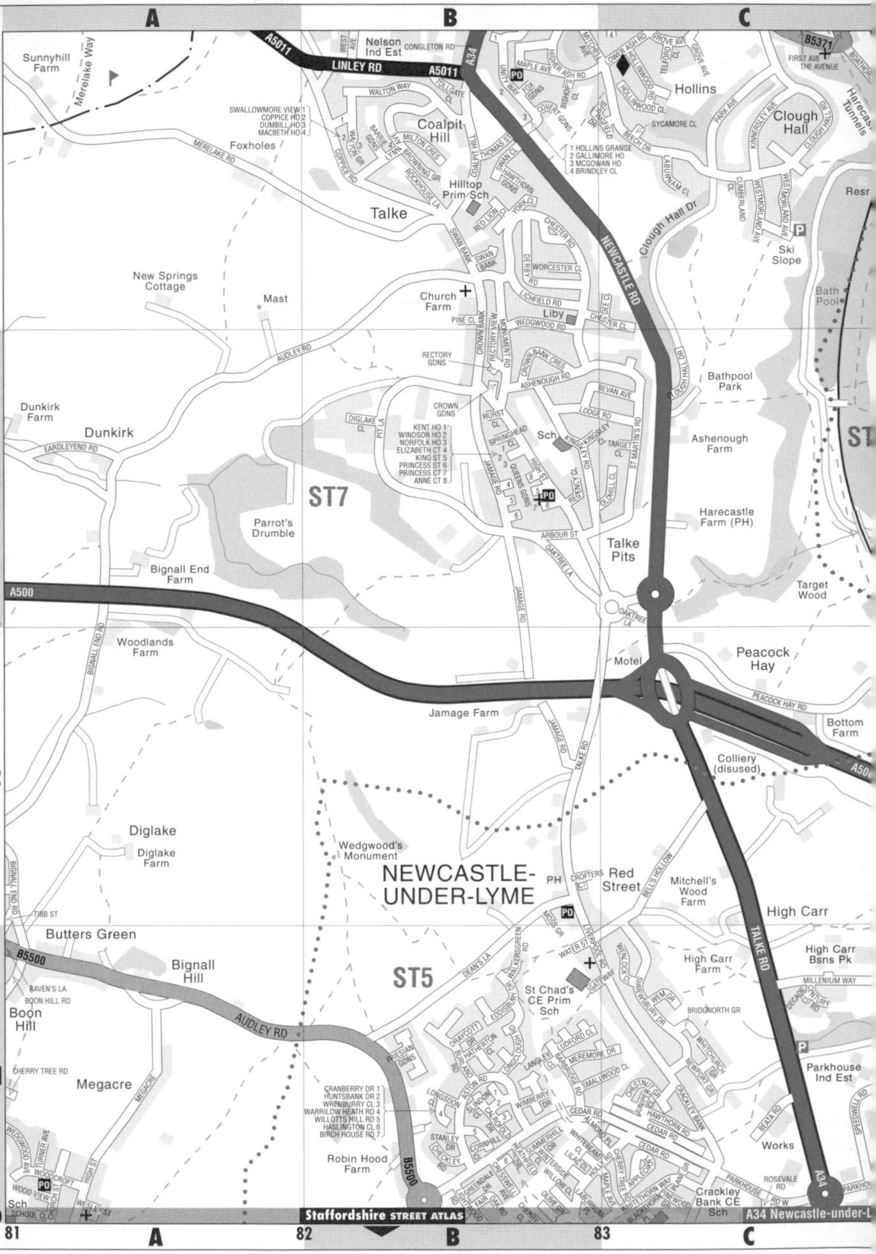
A
B
C
Sunnyhill Farm
Merelake Way
A5011
LINLEY RD
Nelson Ind Est
CONGLETON RD
A34
WALTON WAY
TOLLGATE CL
SWALLOWMORE VIEW 1
COPPICE HO 2
DUMBILL HO 3
MACBETH HO 4
Coalpit Hill
Foxholes
MERELAKE RD
COPPICE RD
MILTON CRES
BROWNING GR
ROCKHOUSE LA
COALPIT HILL
THOMAS ST
Hilltop Prim Sch
Talke
SWAN BANK
RED LION CL
YORK CL
HAWTHORN GDNS
UNITY WAY
MAPLE AVE
HIGHER ASH RD
FOX GDNS
COVERT GDNS
BISHOP'S CL
MITCHELL AVE
SPRINGFIELD DR
LOWER ASH RD
HOLLINWOOD RD
HOLLINWOOD CL
GROVE AVE
TELFORD CL
Hollins
SYCAMORE CL
BEECH DR
LABURNAM CL
1 HOLLINS GRANGE
2 GALLIMORE HO
3 MCGOWAN HO
4 BRINDLEY CL
PARK AVE
KINNERSLEY AVE
Clough Hall
CLOUGH HALL DR
B5371
FIRST AVE
THE AVENUE
Harecastle Tunnels
CUMBERLAND CL
WESTMORLAND AVE
Clough Hall Dr
Ski Slope
Resr
Bath Pool
NEWCASTLE RD
CHESTER RD
DERBY RD
WORCESTER CL
LICHFIELD RD
Liby
CHESTER CL
WEDGWOOD RD
PINE CL
Church Farm
New Springs Cottage
Mast
53
4
AUDLEY RD
CROWN BANK
RECTORY VIEW
MONUMENT RD
RECTORY GDNS
CROWN BANK CRES
ASHENOUGH RD
BEVAN AVE
LODGE RD
Bathpool Park
CROWN GDNS
HURST CL
DIGLAKE CL
PIT LA
KENT HO 1
WINDSOR HO 2
NORFOLK HO 3
ELIZABETH CT 4
KING ST 5
PRINCESS ST 6
PRINCESS CT 7
ANNE CT 8
SPRINGHEAD CL
Sch
KINGSLEY CL
TARGET CL
ST MARTIN'S RD
Ashenough Farm
Dunkirk Farm
Dunkirk
EARDLEYEND RD
3
ST7
JAMAGE RD
QUEENS GDNS
HIGH ST
REGENCY CL
OLDHILL CL
Parrot's Drumble
ARBOUR ST
OAKTREE LA
Talke Pits
Harecastle Farm (PH)
Bignall End Farm
A500
Target Wood
52
Woodlands Farm
BIGNALL END RD
Motel
Peacock Hay
PEACOCK HAY RD
Jamage Farm
Bottom Farm
Colliery (disused)
2
TALKE RD
Diglake
Diglake Farm
Wedgwood's Monument
NEWCASTLE-UNDER-LYME
PH
CROFTERS CT
Red Street
BELL'S HOLLOW
Mitchell's Wood Farm
High Carr
51
TIBB ST
Butters Green
MOSS GR
WATER ST
B5500
Bignall Hill
ST5
DEAN'S LA
WALKERSGREEN RD
LIVERPOOL RD
GATEWAY
WENLOCK CL
High Carr Farm
High Carr Bsns Pk
MILLENIUM WAY
St Chad's CE Prim Sch
RAVEN'S LA
BOON HILL RD
Boon Hill
SHREWSBURY DR
WEM GR
BRIDGNORTH GR
AUDLEY RD
DRAYCOTT DR
EDDISBURY DR
HATHERTON CL
LONGCLOUGH RD
LUDFORD CL
MEREMORE DR
FRIESIAN GDNS
BURLAND RD
LANGLEY CL
BARBRIDGE RD
SMALLWOOD CL
WHITCHURCH GR
NEWPORT GR
1
CHERRY TREE RD
Megacre
MEGACRE
CRANBERRY DR 1
HUNTSBANK DR 2
WRENBURY CL 3
WARRILOW HEATH RD 4
WILLOTTS HILL RD 5
HASLINGTON CL 6
BIRCH HOUSE RD 7
ASTON RD
LONGSDON CL
WIMBERRY DR
CHESTNUT GR
JUNIPER CL
CRACKLEY BANK
HAWTHORN RD
CEDAR RD
Parkhouse Ind Est
Works
BEATA RD
SPEEDWELL RD
WEDGWOOD AVE
TURNER AVE
WOODCROFT
WOOD VIEW
HIGH ST
Robin Hood Farm
B5500
STANLEY DR
CHECKLEY RD
CORNHILL CL
SUMMERHILL DR
WINTERSIDE CL
WILLOW CL
WHITEBEAM CL
LILAC CL
HOLLY RD
MAPLE AVE
CHERRY TREE RD
APPLECROFT
LABURNUM PL
OLIVE GR
CEDAR RD
PARKHOUSE RD W
ROSEVALE RD
Crackley Bank CE Sch
A34
Sch
SCHOOL CL
CHURCH ST
WESLEY ST
50
81
82
83
A34 Newcastle-under-L

197
212

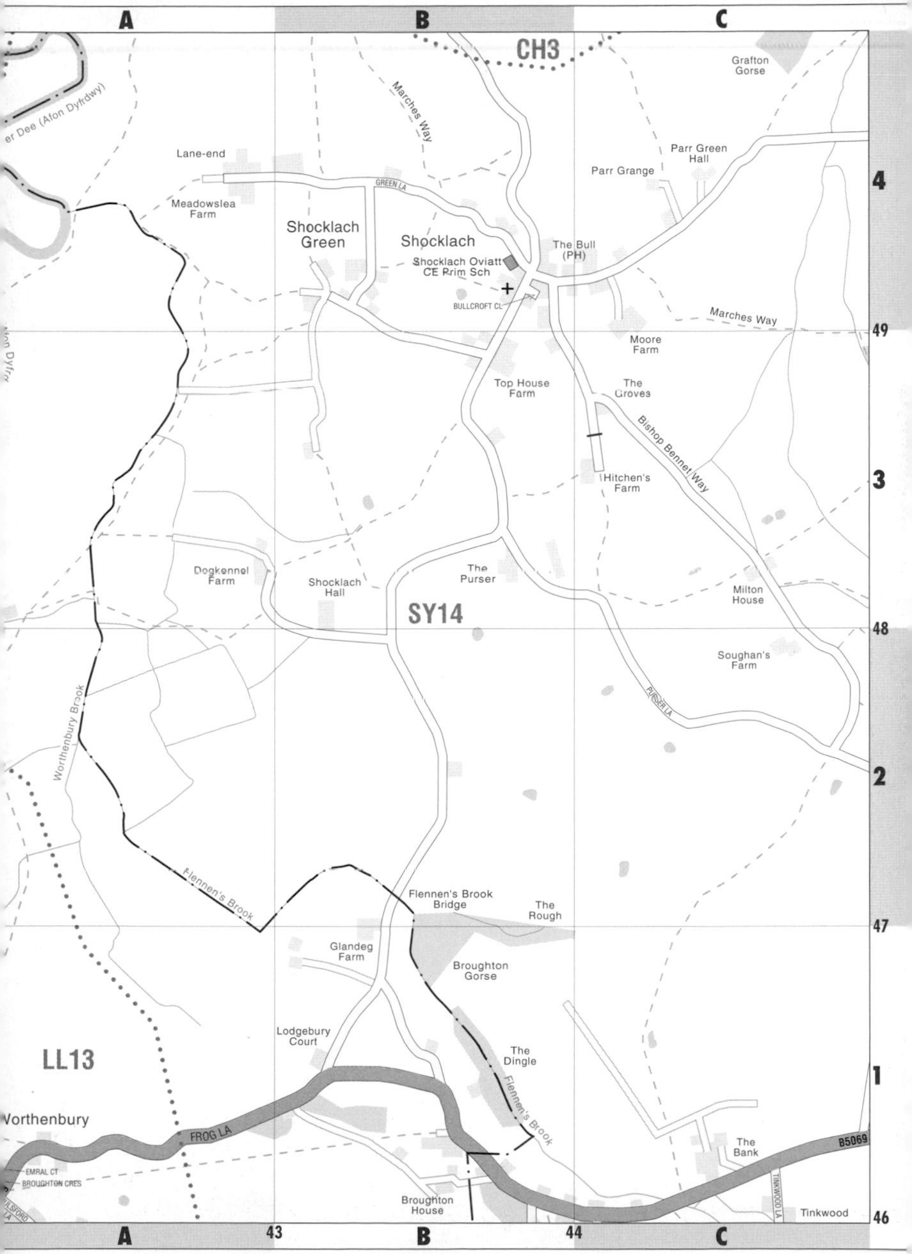
A
B
C
CH3
Grafton Gorse
Marches Way
er Dee (Afon Dyfrdwy)
Lane-end
Parr Green Hall
Parr Grange
GREEN LA
4
Meadowslea Farm
Shocklach Green
Shocklach
The Bull (PH)
Shocklach Oviatt CE Prim Sch
BULLCROFT CL
Marches Way
49
Moore Farm
Top House Farm
The Groves
Bishop Bennet Way
Hitchen's Farm
3
Dogkennel Farm
Shocklach Hall
The Purser
Milton House
SY14
48
Soughan's Farm
PURSER LA
Worthenbury Brook
2
Flennen's Brook
Flennen's Brook Bridge
The Rough
47
Glandeg Farm
Broughton Gorse
Lodgebury Court
The Dingle
LL13
1
Flennen's Brook
Worthenbury
FROG LA
The Bank
B5069
EMRAL CT
BROUGHTON CRES
TINKWOOD LA
Broughton House
Tinkwood
46
A
43
B
44
C

222
212

211
198

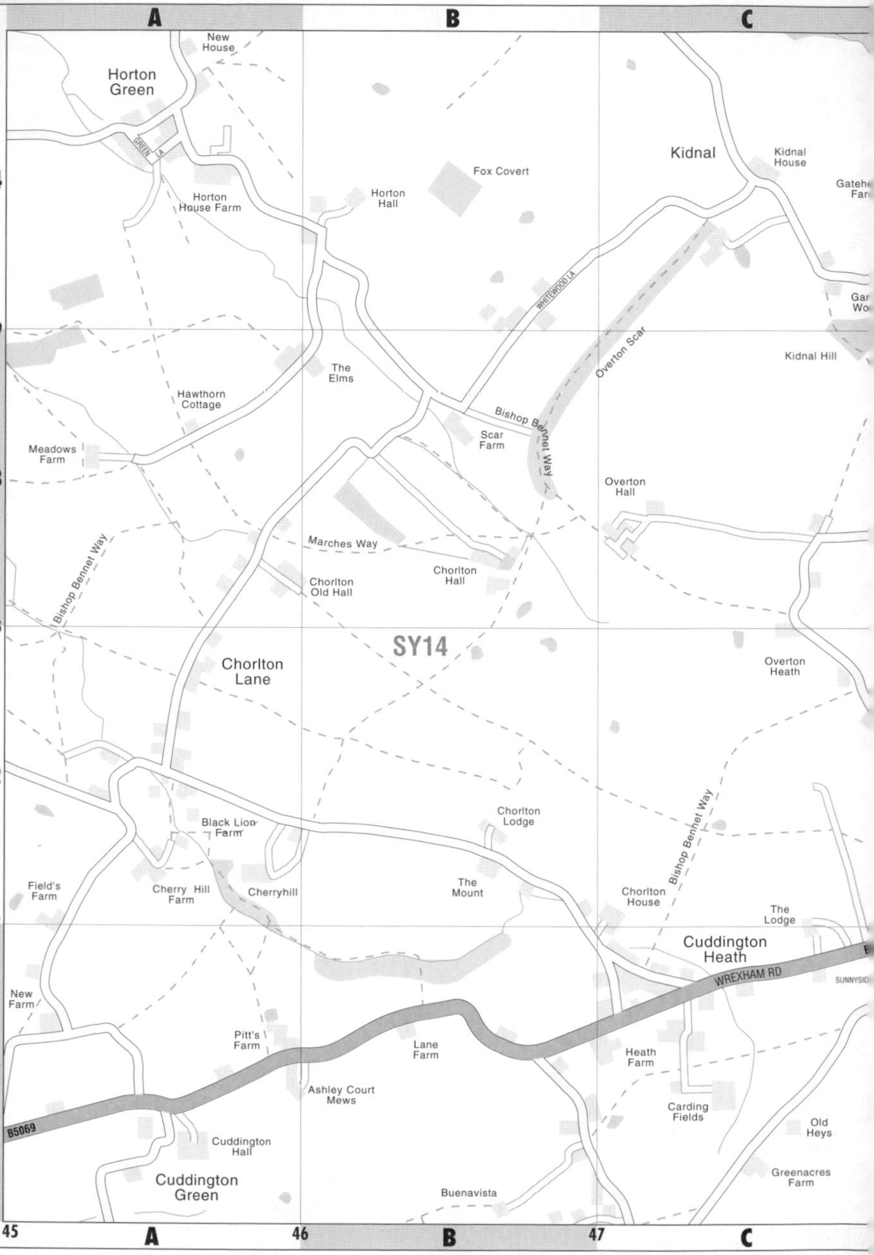

211
223

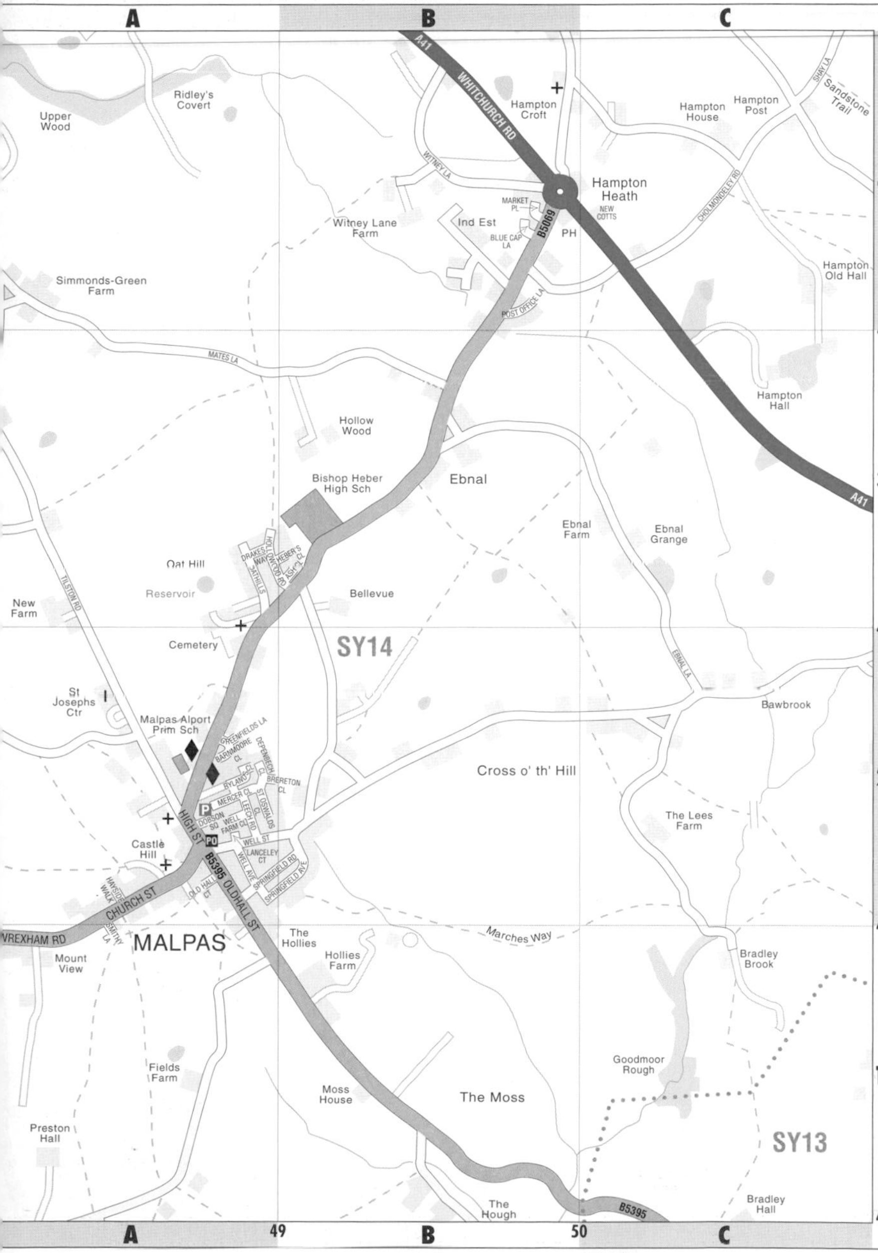
A
B
C
Upper Wood
Ridley's Covert
A41
WHITCHURCH RD
Hampton Croft
Hampton House
Hampton Post
SHAY LA
Sandstone Trail
WITNEY LA
Hampton Heath
MARKET PL
NEW COTTS
CHOLMONDELEY RD
Witney Lane Farm
Ind Est
BLUE CAP LA
B5069
PH
Hampton Old Hall
Simmonds-Green Farm
POST OFFICE LA
MATES LA
Hampton Hall
Hollow Wood
Bishop Heber High Sch
Ebnal
Ebnal Farm
Ebnal Grange
Oat Hill
DRAKES
HOLLOWOOD RD
OATHILLS
HEBER'S
ASH CL
TILSTON RD
New Farm
Reservoir
Bellevue
Cemetery
SY14
EBNAL LA
St Josephs Ctr
Bawbrook
Malpas Alport Prim Sch
GREENFIELDS LA
BARNMOORE CL
DEPENBECH
BYLAND
BRERETON CL
Cross o' th' Hill
MERCER CL
ST OSWALDS
DOBSON SQ
WELL FARM CL
LEECH RD
HIGH ST
WELL ST
The Lees Farm
Castle Hill
PO
B5395
LANCELEY CT
WELL AVE
SPRINGFIELD RD
SPRINGFIELD AVE
HAYSIDE WALK
CHURCH ST
OLD HALL CT
OLDHALL ST
WREXHAM RD
SMITHY LA
MALPAS
The Hollies
Marches Way
Hollies Farm
Mount View
Bradley Brook
Fields Farm
Goodmoor Rough
Moss House
The Moss
Preston Hall
SY13
The Hough
B5395
Bradley Hall
4
49
3
48
2
47
1
46
49
50

213
200

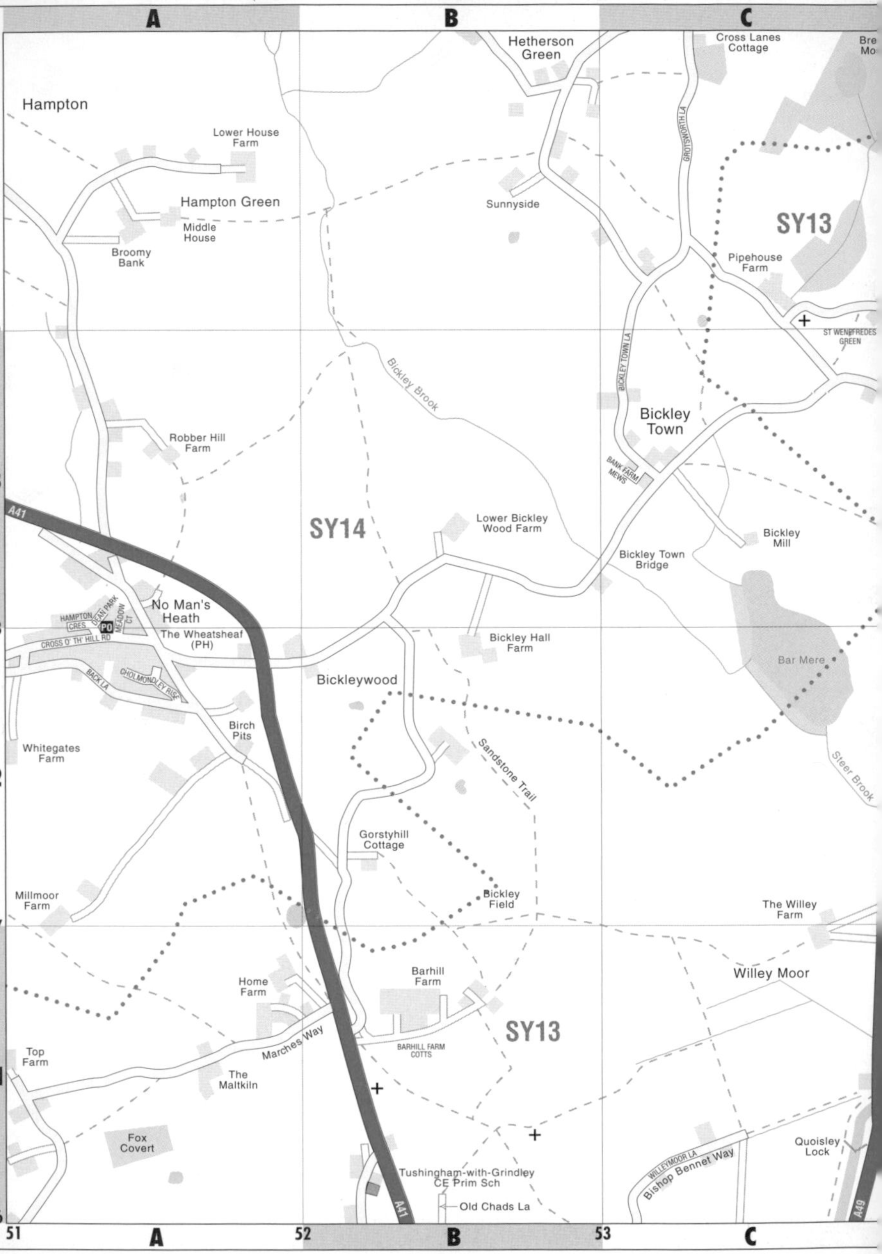
A
B
C
Hetherson Green
Cross Lanes Cottage
Hampton
Lower House Farm
GROTSWORTH LA
Hampton Green
Sunnyside
SY13
Middle House
Broomy Bank
Pipehouse Farm
ST WENEFREDES GREEN
Bickley Brook
BICKLEY TOWN LA
Bickley Town
Robber Hill Farm
BANK FARM MEWS
A41
SY14
Lower Bickley Wood Farm
Bickley Mill
Bickley Town Bridge
No Man's Heath
HAMPTON CRES
DEAN PARK
MEADOW CT
PO
The Wheatsheaf (PH)
CROSS O' TH' HILL RD
Bickley Hall Farm
Bar Mere
BACK LA
CHOLMONDLEY RISE
Bickleywood
Birch Pits
Sandstone Trail
Whitegates Farm
Steer Brook
Gorstyhill Cottage
Millmoor Farm
Bickley Field
The Willey Farm
Willey Moor
Home Farm
Barhill Farm
SY13
Marches Way
BARHILL FARM COTTS
Top Farm
The Maltkiln
Fox Covert
WILLEYMOOR LA
Bishop Bennet Way
Quoisley Lock
Tushingham-with-Grindley CE Prim Sch
Old Chads La
A49
4
49
3
48
2
47
1
46
51
52
53

213
225

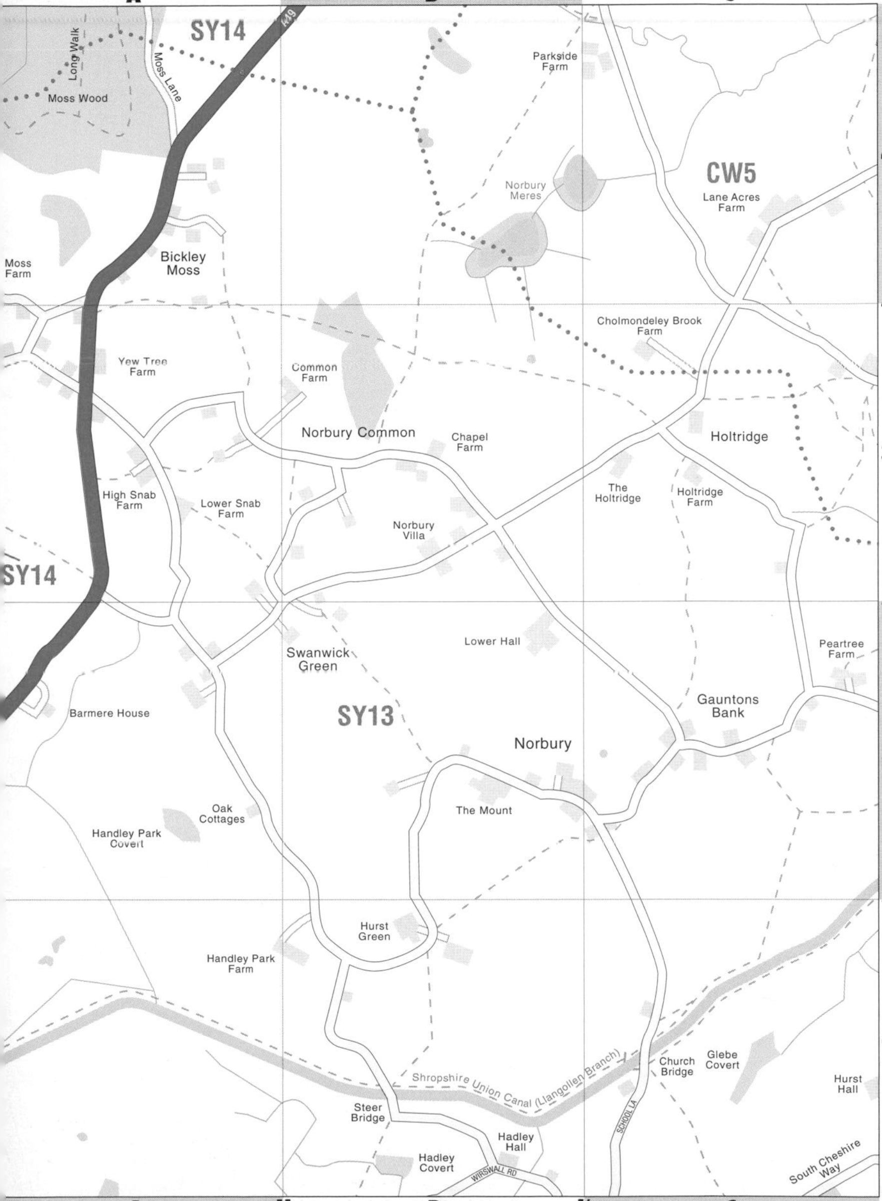
A
B
C
SY14
A49
Long Walk
Moss Wood
Moss Lane
Parkside Farm
Norbury Meres
CW5
Lane Acres Farm
Moss Farm
Bickley Moss
Cholmondeley Brook Farm
Yew Tree Farm
Common Farm
Norbury Common
Chapel Farm
Holtridge
The Holtridge
Holtridge Farm
High Snab Farm
Lower Snab Farm
Norbury Villa
SY14
Lower Hall
Peartree Farm
Swanwick Green
SY13
Gauntons Bank
Barmere House
Norbury
The Mount
Oak Cottages
Handley Park Covert
Hurst Green
Handley Park Farm
Shropshire Union Canal (Llangollen Branch)
School La
Church Bridge
Glebe Covert
Hurst Hall
Steer Bridge
Hadley Hall
Hadley Covert
Wirswall Rd
South Cheshire Way
4
49
3
48
2
47
1
46
55
56

215
202

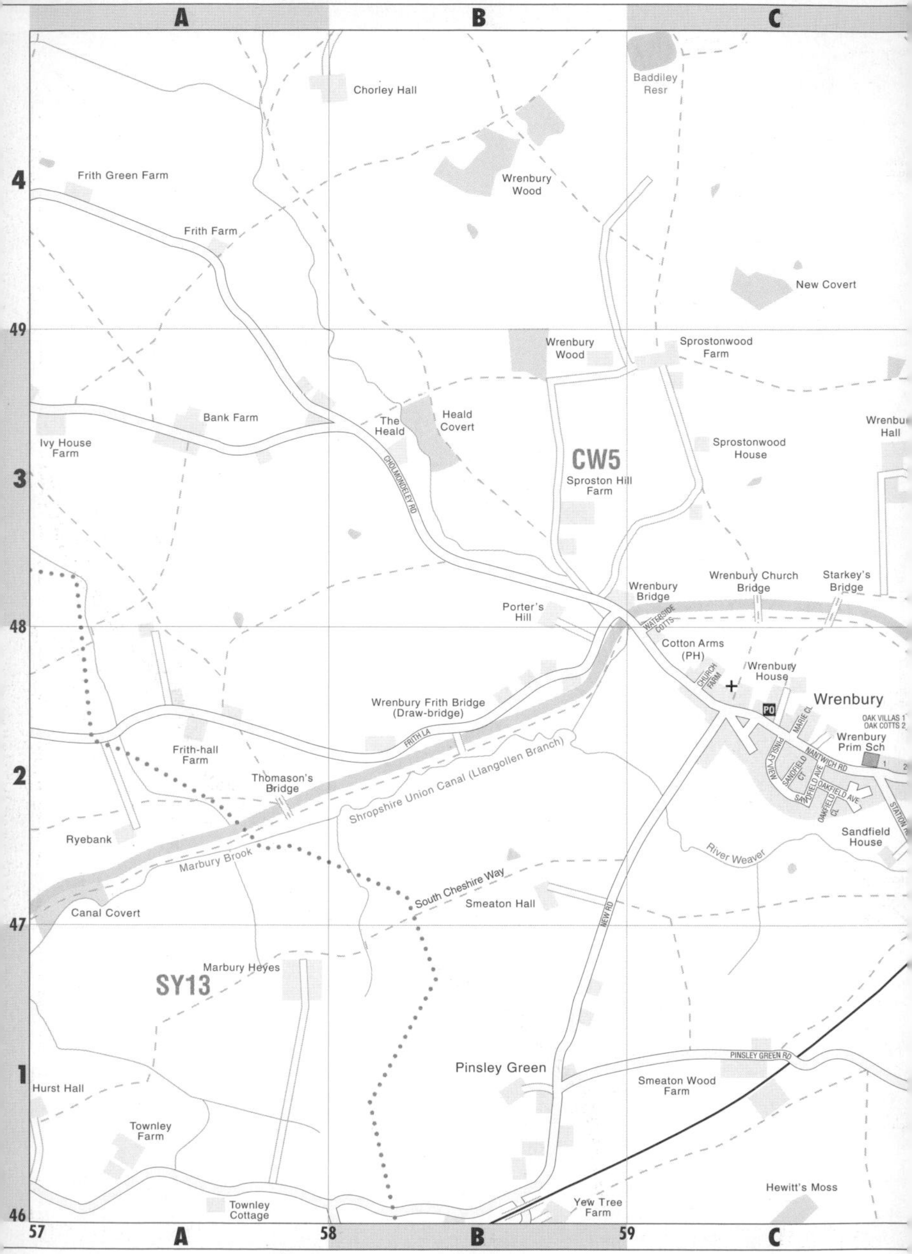
A
B
C
4
49
3
48
2
47
1
46
57
58
59
Chorley Hall
Baddiley Resr
Frith Green Farm
Wrenbury Wood
Frith Farm
New Covert
Wrenbury Wood
Sprostonwood Farm
Bank Farm
The Heald
Heald Covert
Ivy House Farm
CW5
Sproston Hill Farm
Sprostonwood House
Wrenbury Hall
CHOLMONDELEY RD
Wrenbury Bridge
Wrenbury Church Bridge
Starkey's Bridge
Porter's Hill
WATERSIDE COTTS
Cotton Arms (PH)
CHURCH FARM
Wrenbury House
Wrenbury
PO
MARIE CL
OAK VILLAS
OAK COTTS
Wrenbury Prim Sch
NANTWICH RD
PINSLEY VIEW
SANDFIELD CT
SANDFIELD AVE
OAKFIELD AVE
OAKFIELD CL
STATION RD
Wrenbury Frith Bridge (Draw-bridge)
FRITH LA
Frith-hall Farm
Thomason's Bridge
Shropshire Union Canal (Llangollen Branch)
Ryebank
Marbury Brook
River Weaver
Sandfield House
South Cheshire Way
Smeaton Hall
Canal Covert
NEW RD
SY13
Marbury Heyes
Pinsley Green
PINSLEY GREEN RD
Smeaton Wood Farm
Hurst Hall
Townley Farm
Hewitt's Moss
Townley Cottage
Yew Tree Farm

215
227

203
218

228
218

217
204

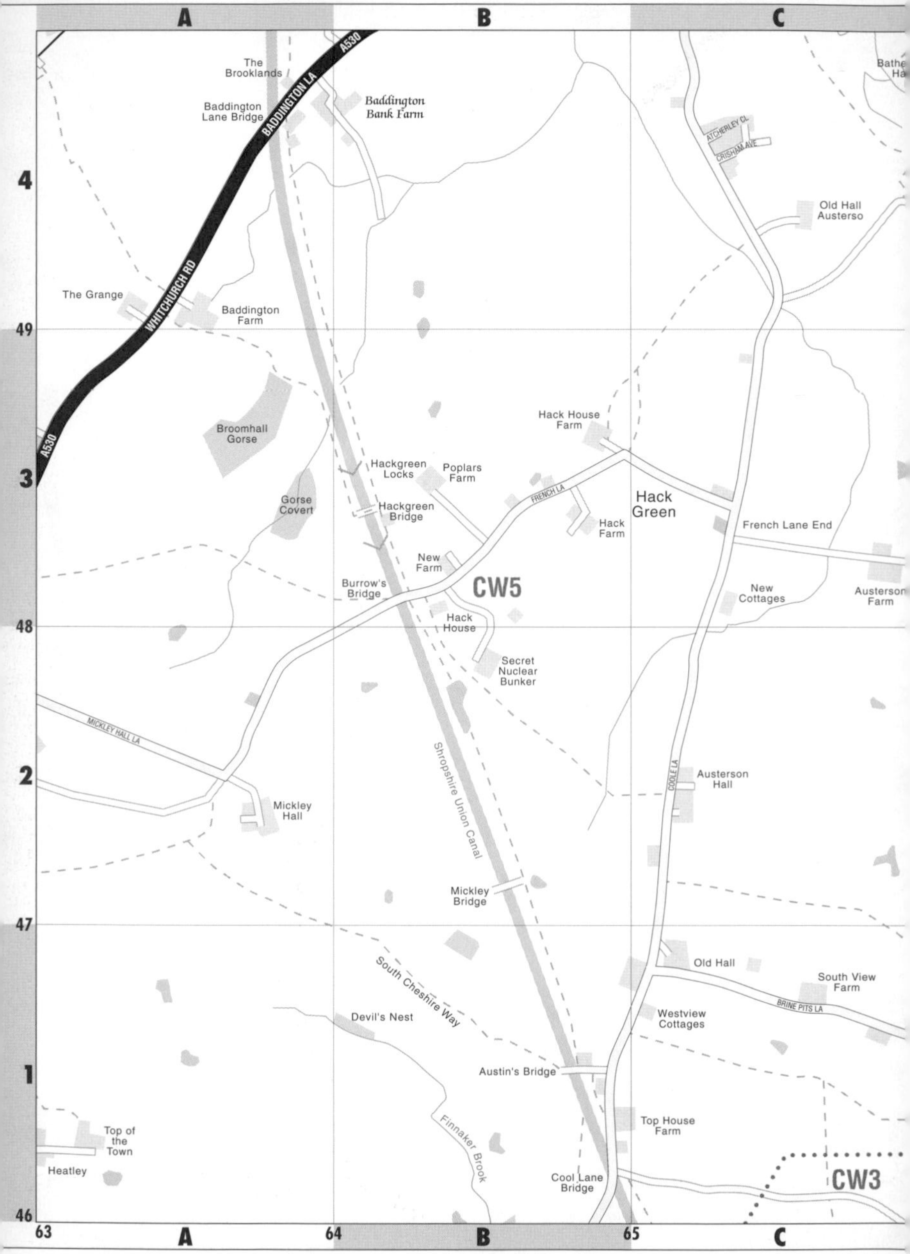
A
B
C
4
3
2
1
49
48
47
46
63
64
65
The Brooklands
Baddington Lane Bridge
BADDINGTON LA
A530
Baddington Bank Farm
ATCHERLEY CL
CRISHAM AVE
Old Hall Austerso
Bathe
Ha
The Grange
WHITCHURCH RD
Baddington Farm
Broomhall Gorse
Hack House Farm
Hackgreen Locks
Poplars Farm
Gorse Covert
Hackgreen Bridge
FRENCH LA
Hack Farm
Hack Green
French Lane End
New Farm
Burrow's Bridge
CW5
New Cottages
Austerson Farm
Hack House
Secret Nuclear Bunker
MICKLEY HALL LA
Shropshire Union Canal
COOLE LA
Austerson Hall
Mickley Hall
Mickley Bridge
Old Hall
South View Farm
South Cheshire Way
BRINE PITS LA
Devil's Nest
Westview Cottages
Austin's Bridge
Finnaker Brook
Top House Farm
Top of the Town
Heatley
Cool Lane Bridge
CW3

217
229

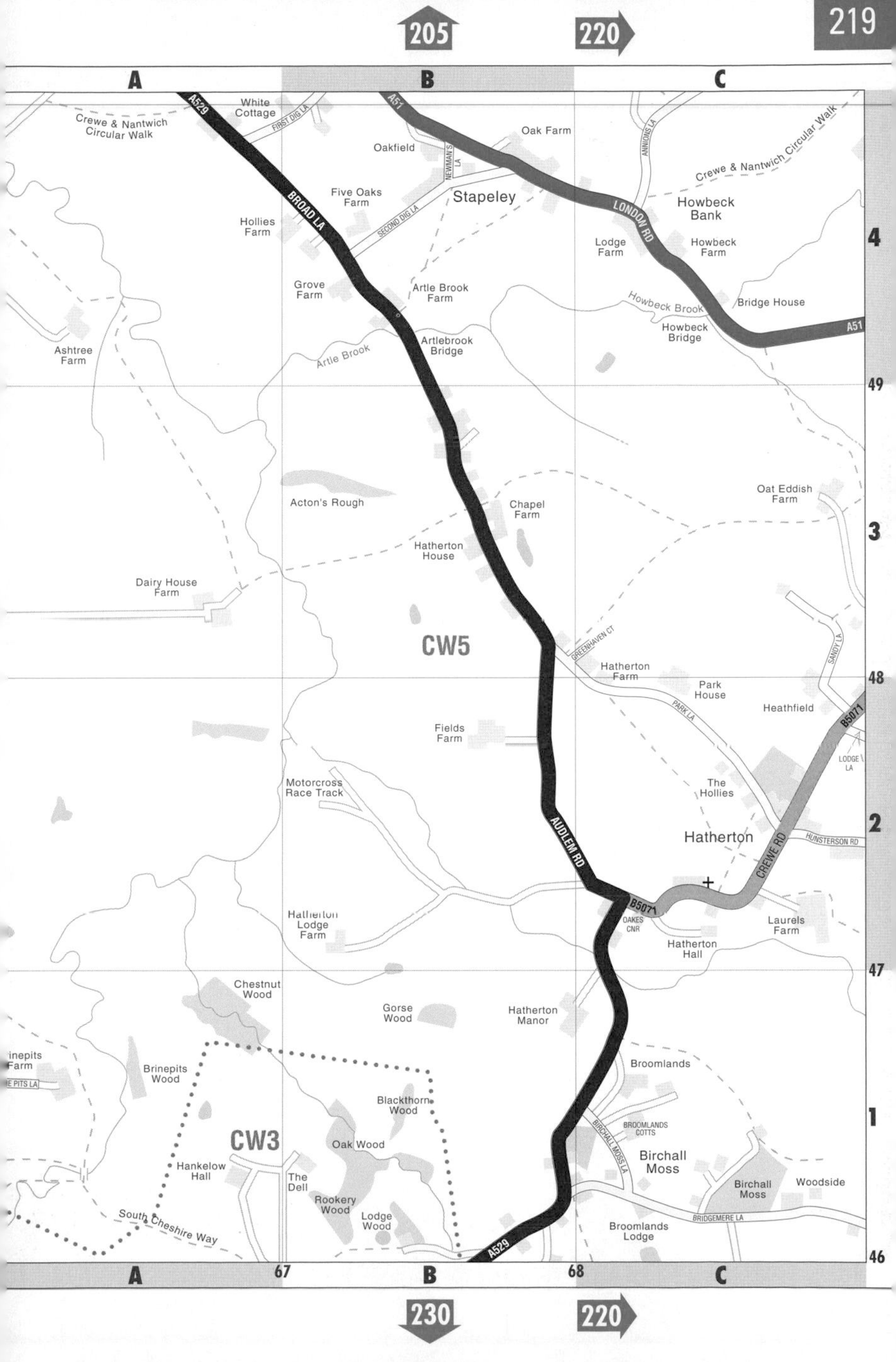
205
220
A
B
C
A529
A51
White Cottage
Crewe & Nantwich Circular Walk
FIRST DIG LA
Oak Farm
ANNIONS LA
Oakfield
NEWMAN'S LA
Five Oaks Farm
Stapeley
Howbeck Bank
BROAD LA
SECOND DIG LA
LONDON RD
Hollies Farm
Lodge Farm
Howbeck Farm
4
Grove Farm
Artle Brook Farm
Howbeck Brook
Bridge House
Howbeck Bridge
Ashtree Farm
Artlebrook Bridge
Artle Brook
49
Oat Eddish Farm
Acton's Rough
Chapel Farm
3
Hatherton House
Dairy House Farm
CW5
GREENHAVEN CT
SANDY LA
Hatherton Farm
48
Park House
PARK LA
Heathfield
B5071
Fields Farm
LODGE LA
Motorcross Race Track
The Hollies
2
AUDLEM RD
Hatherton
CREWE RD
HUNSTERSON RD
OAKES CNR
Hatherton Lodge Farm
Laurels Farm
Hatherton Hall
47
Chestnut Wood
Gorse Wood
Hatherton Manor
Brinepits Farm
Brinepits Wood
Broomlands
Blackthorn Wood
1
BIRCHALL MOSS LA
BROOMLANDS COTTS
CW3
Oak Wood
Birchall Moss
Hankelow Hall
The Dell
Birchall Moss
Woodside
Rookery Wood
Lodge Wood
South Cheshire Way
BRIDGEMERE LA
Broomlands Lodge
46
67
68
230
220

A
B
C
4
49
3
48
2
47
1
46
69
70
71
CW2
CW5
B5071
MAIN RD
RIDDINGS LA
KILN LA
CHURCH WAY
CHURCHFIELDS
GLEBE CL
FIELDS VIEW CL
1 ST CHADS CL
2 SOUTHFIELDS CL
3 MOORLANS DR
PO
Red Lion (PH)
The Riddings
Wybunbury
Cemy
BRIDGE ST
Brook House
Wybunbury Delves CE Prim Sch
Hall Bank
Vicarage
Cobb's Moss
COBBS LA
Ellesmere Farm
WRINEHILL RD
A51
Hough Mill Farm
The Cliffe
Sand Pit
Jerusalem
Manor Farm
WYBUNBURY RD
PH
Walgherton
BACK LA
Jericho
Lea Hall
Lea Farm
Lea Forge Farm
Lodge Farm
The Oaks
Hunter's Hill
Forge Bank
CREWE RD
Poolbank
Trout Farm
Lea Park
Whispey Hill
George's Wood
Dagfields Craft Centre
Perry's Rough
Doddington Mill Farm
MILL LA
LONDON RD
South Cheshire Way
Speakman's Moss
Northwood
LODGE LA
Hatherton Lodge
Mill Covert
George's Wood
Birchenhill Wood
Black Mere
Robin Knight's Rough
Demesne House
Sewage Works
Doddington Park
HUNSTERSON RD
Black Covert
The Castle
Doddington Park House
Hatherton Lodge Farm
Glover's Moss
Ridley's Pool
Wilbraham's Walk
Lake Lodge
Doddington Hall
Chapel Wood
Pepperstreet Moss
Doddington Pool
Bearcat Fields
Manor Farm
Hunsterson
The Duckery
BRIDGEMERE LA
PEWIT LA
Doddington Park Farm

207

A
B
C
CW2
CW3
CW5
West Heath
The Anchorage
Swill Brook
WAYBUTT LA
The Elms
A531
MAIN RD A531
Betley
Doddlespool Hall
DODDLESPOOL BARNS
Doddlespool Farm
Buddileigh
Elmer Riddings
The Slum
A531 Newcastle-under-Lyme (A525)
WRINEHILL RD
Half Moon Farm
Gonsley Green Farm
Betley Common
Mere Gutter
Oak Tree Farm
COMMON LA
Green Valley Farm
Gonsley Cottages
akenhall Moss
Coppice Bank
Lower Den Farm
Manor Farm
Staffordshire STREET ATLAS
Betley Mere
DEN LA
Higher Den Farm
Den Bridge
Cracow Moss
Fog Cottages
West View
Blakenhall
MILL LA
Ash Tree Farm
Yew Tree Farm
New Farm
Hayes Farm
Blakenhall Farm
Dairy Farm
Bunkers Hill
Randilow Farmhouse
Ash Coppice
Shaw's Rough
Grange Farm
Checkley Brook
Checkley Bridge
Checkley Brook Farm
The Coppice
CHECKLEY LA
Checkley Hall
Checkley
Little Meadow
4
49
3
48
2
47
1
46
73
74

232

211

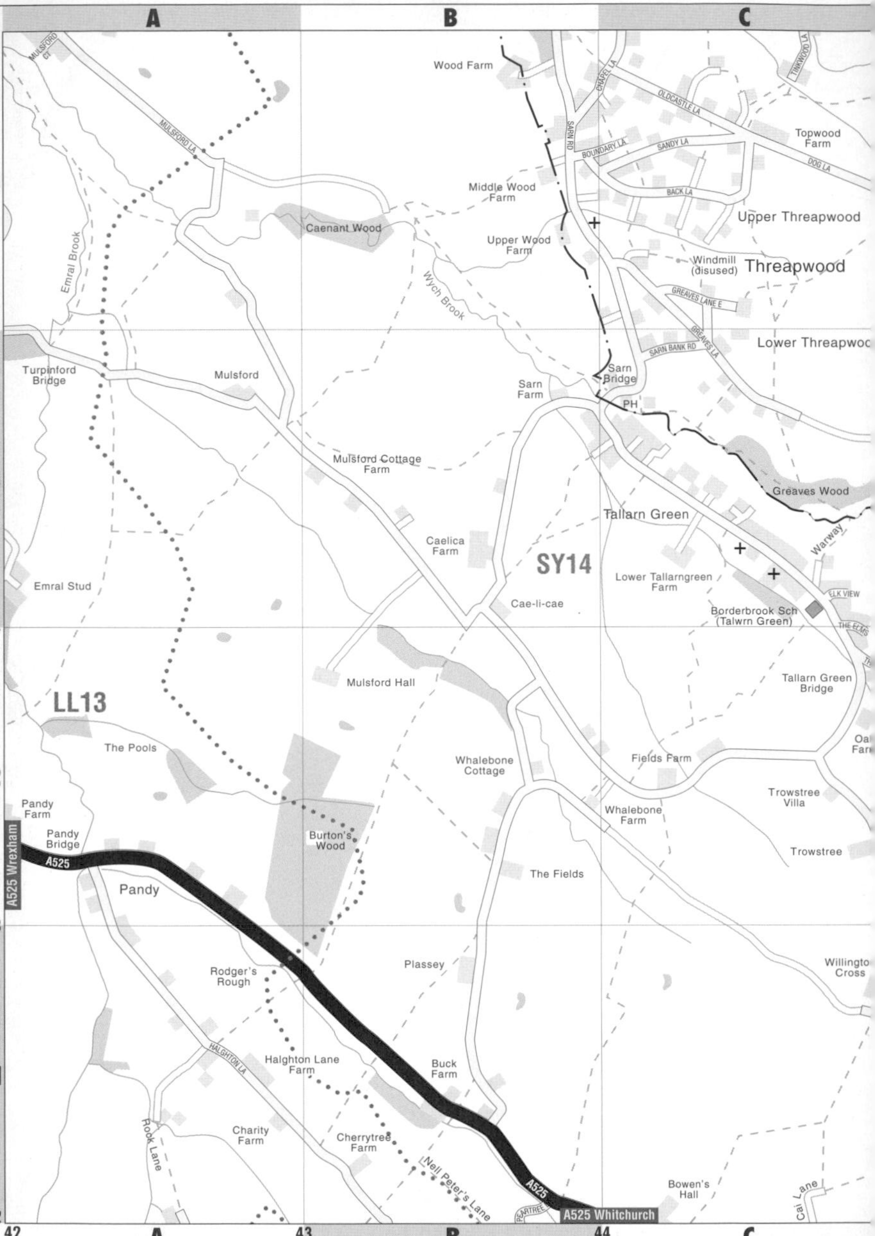
A
B
C
4
45
3
44
2
43
1
42
42
43
44
Wood Farm
Mulsford Ct
Mulsford La
Chapel La
Oldcastle La
Tinkwood La
Sarn Rd
Boundary La
Sandy La
Topwood Farm
Dog La
Back La
Middle Wood Farm
Upper Threapwood
Caenant Wood
Upper Wood Farm
Windmill (disused)
Threapwood
Emral Brook
Wych Brook
Greaves Lane E
Greaves La
Sarn Bank Rd
Lower Threapwoo
Turpinford Bridge
Mulsford
Sarn Farm
Sarn Bridge
PH
Mulsford Cottage Farm
Greaves Wood
Tallarn Green
Caelica Farm
SY14
Warway
Emral Stud
Lower Tallarngreen Farm
Cae-li-cae
Elk View
Borderbrook Sch (Talwrn Green)
The Elms
Mulsford Hall
Tallarn Green Bridge
LL13
The Pools
Whalebone Cottage
Fields Farm
Oa Far
Pandy Farm
Trowstree Villa
Whalebone Farm
Pandy Bridge
Burton's Wood
A525 Wrexham
A525
Trowstree
Pandy
The Fields
Willingto Cross
Rodger's Rough
Plassey
Halghton La
Halghton Lane Farm
Buck Farm
Rock Lane
Charity Farm
Cherrytree Farm
Nell Peter's Lane
Peartree
A525 Whitchurch
Bowen's Hall
Cai Lane
A
B
C

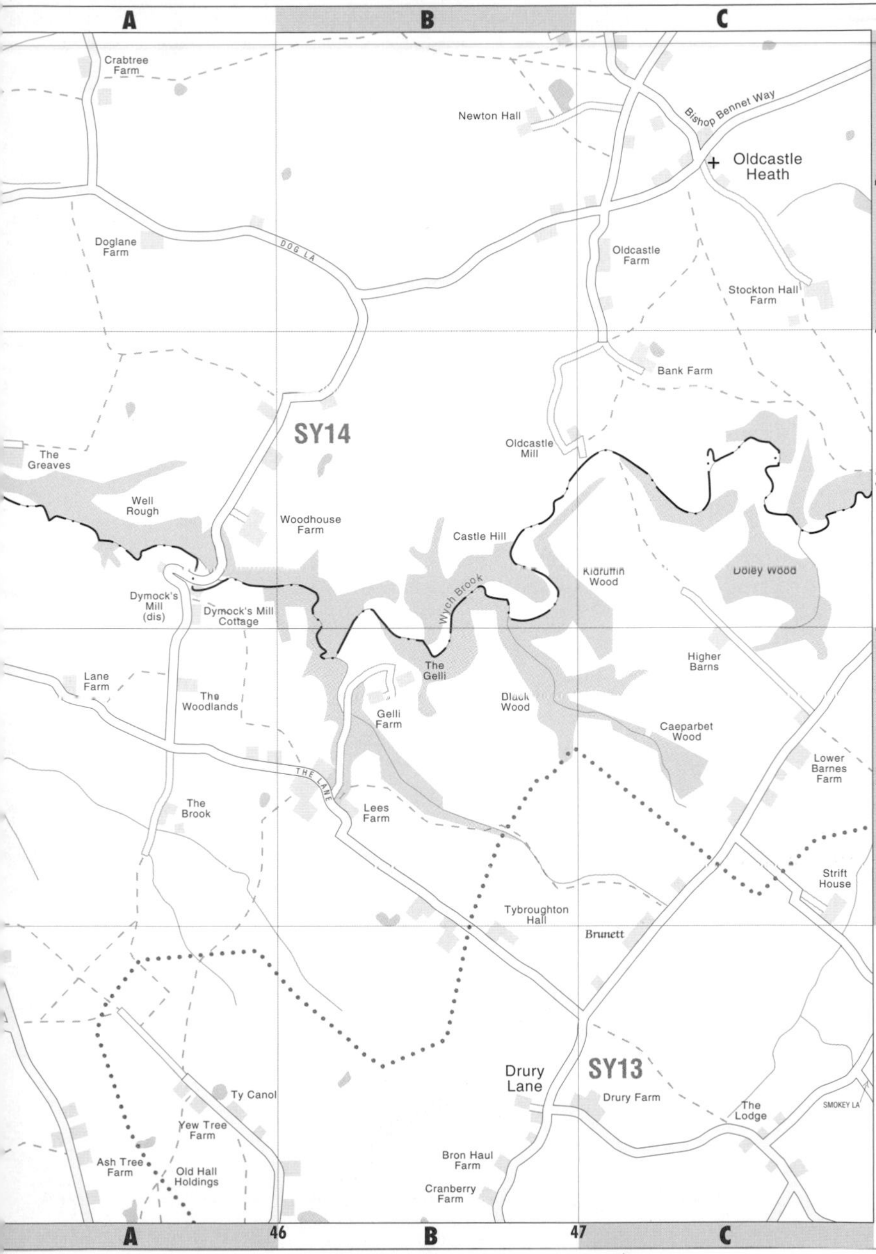
A
B
C
Crabtree Farm
Newton Hall
Bishop Bennet Way
Oldcastle Heath
4
Doglane Farm
DOG LA
Oldcastle Farm
Stockton Hall Farm
45
Bank Farm
SY14
Oldcastle Mill
The Greaves
3
Well Rough
Woodhouse Farm
Castle Hill
Kidruffin Wood
Doley Wood
Wych Brook
Dymock's Mill (dis)
Dymock's Mill Cottage
44
The Gelli
Higher Barns
Lane Farm
The Woodlands
Black Wood
Gelli Farm
Caeparbet Wood
Lower Barnes Farm
2
THE LANE
The Brook
Lees Farm
Strift House
Tybroughton Hall
Brunett
43
Drury Lane
SY13
1
Ty Canol
Drury Farm
The Lodge
SMOKEY LA
Yew Tree Farm
Ash Tree Farm
Old Hall Holdings
Bron Haul Farm
Cranberry Farm
42
A
46
B
47
C

223
213

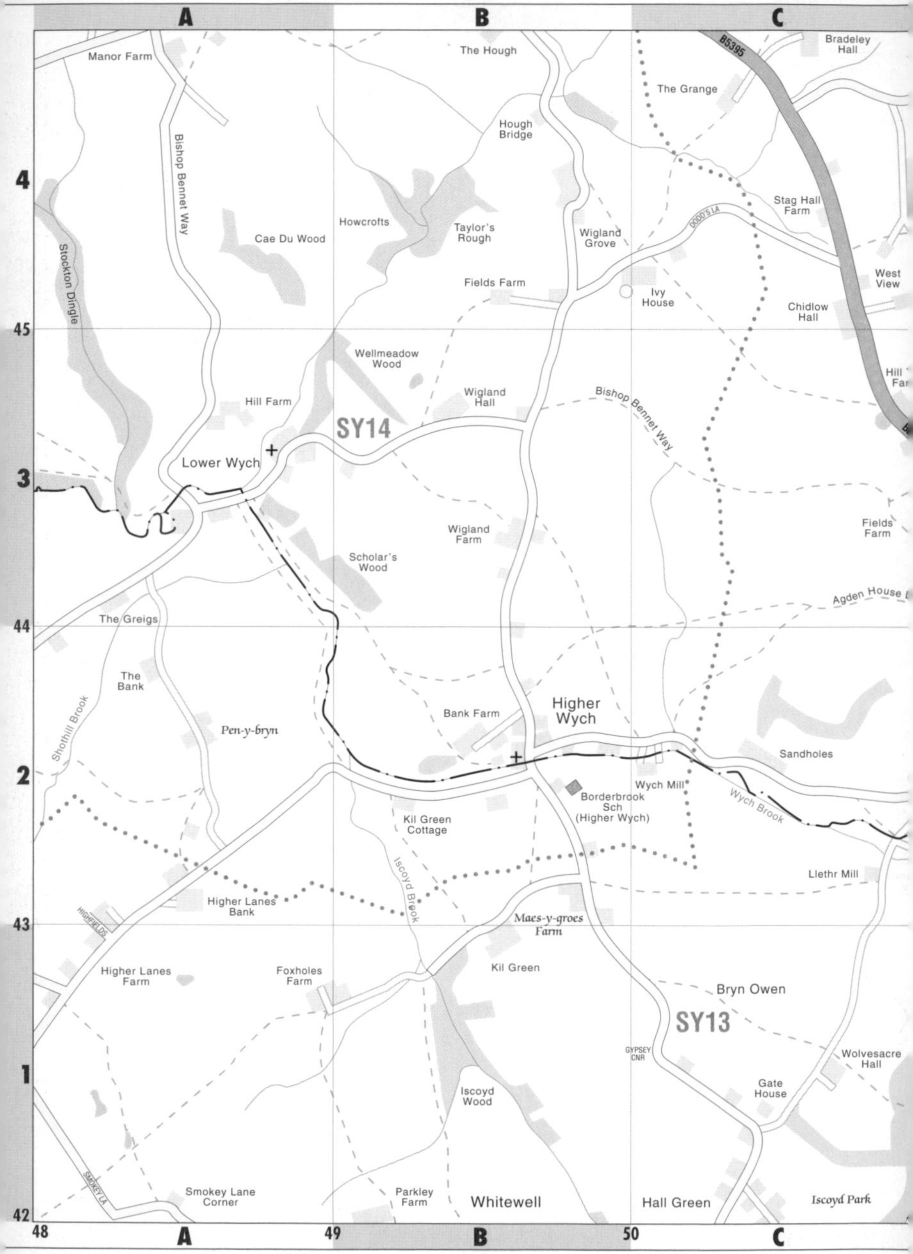
A
B
C
Manor Farm
The Hough
B5395
Bradeley Hall
The Grange
Bishop Bennet Way
Hough Bridge
4
Stockton Dingle
Cae Du Wood
Howcrofts
Taylor's Rough
Wigland Grove
DODD'S LA
Stag Hall Farm
Fields Farm
Ivy House
West View
Chidlow Hall
45
Wellmeadow Wood
Wigland Hall
Hill Farm
SY14
Bishop Bennet Way
Lower Wych
3
Wigland Farm
Fields Farm
Scholar's Wood
Agden House
The Greigs
44
The Bank
Shothill Brook
Pen-y-bryn
Bank Farm
Higher Wych
Sandholes
2
Wych Mill
Borderbrook Sch (Higher Wych)
Wych Brook
Kil Green Cottage
Iscoyd Brook
Llethr Mill
Higher Lanes Bank
HIGHFIELDS
43
Maes-y-groes Farm
Higher Lanes Farm
Foxholes Farm
Kil Green
Bryn Owen
SY13
GYPSEY CNR
Wolvesacre Hall
1
Iscoyd Wood
Gate House
SMOKEY LA
Smokey Lane Corner
Parkley Farm
Whitewell
Hall Green
Iscoyd Park
42
48
49
50

223

214
226

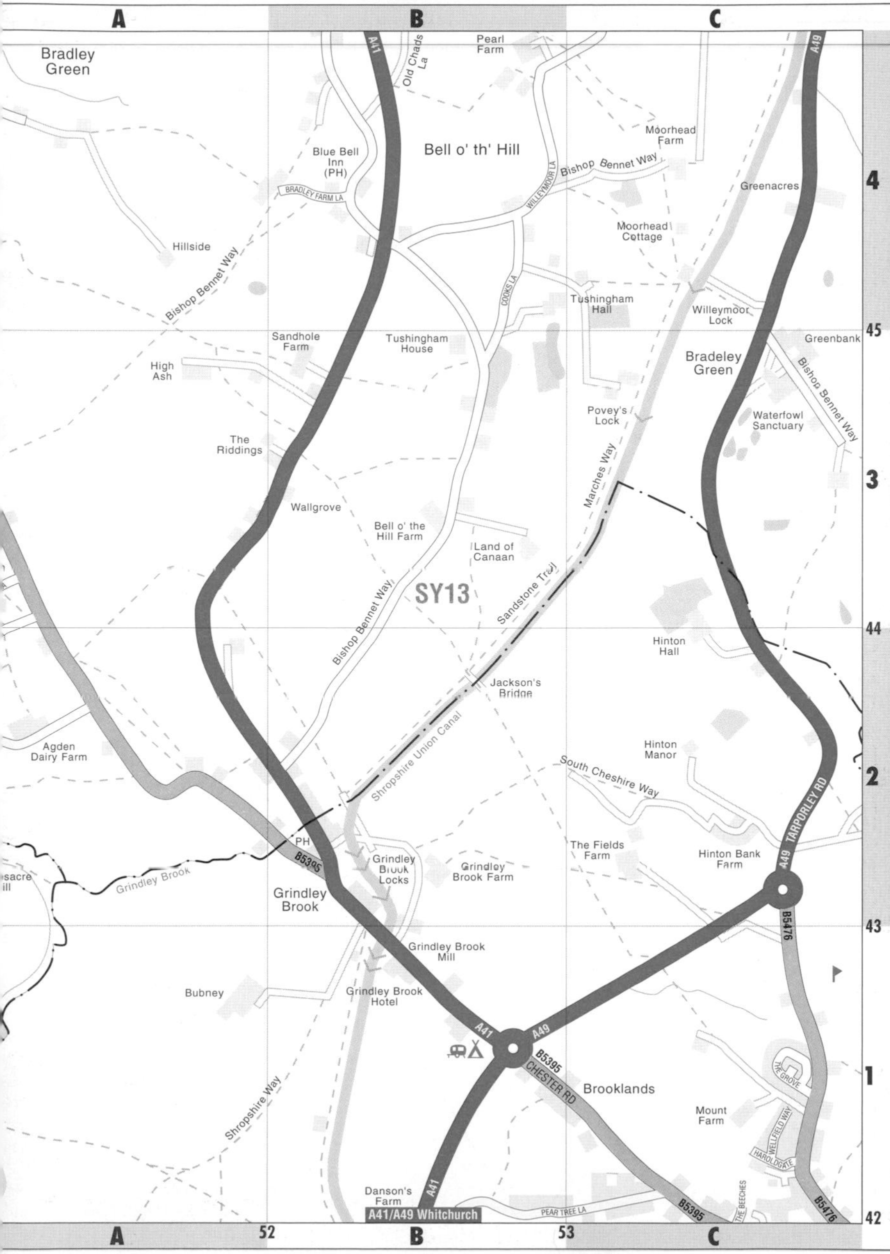
A
B
C
Bradley Green
Pearl Farm
Old Chads La
A41
A49
Bell o' th' Hill
Blue Bell Inn (PH)
BRADLEY FARM LA
Moorhead Farm
Bishop Bennet Way
WILLEYMOOR LA
Greenacres
4
Moorhead Cottage
Hillside
Bishop Bennet Way
COOKS LA
Tushingham Hall
Willeymoor Lock
Greenbank
45
Sandhole Farm
Tushingham House
High Ash
Bradeley Green
Bishop Bennet Way
Povey's Lock
Waterfowl Sanctuary
The Riddings
Marches Way
3
Wallgrove
Bell o' the Hill Farm
Land of Canaan
SY13
Sandstone Trail
Bishop Bennet Way
44
Hinton Hall
Jackson's Bridge
Agden Dairy Farm
Hinton Manor
Shropshire Union Canal
South Cheshire Way
2
TARPORLEY RD
PH
B5395
Grindley Brook
Grindley Brook Locks
Grindley Brook Farm
The Fields Farm
Hinton Bank Farm
A49
Grindley Brook
B5476
43
Grindley Brook Mill
Bubney
Grindley Brook Hotel
A41
A49
B5395
CHESTER RD
Brooklands
THE GROVE
1
Shropshire Way
Mount Farm
WELLFIELD WAY
HAROLDGATE
Danson's Farm
A41
THE BEECHES
A41/A49 Whitchurch
PEAR TREE LA
B5395
B5476
42
52
53

226

225
215

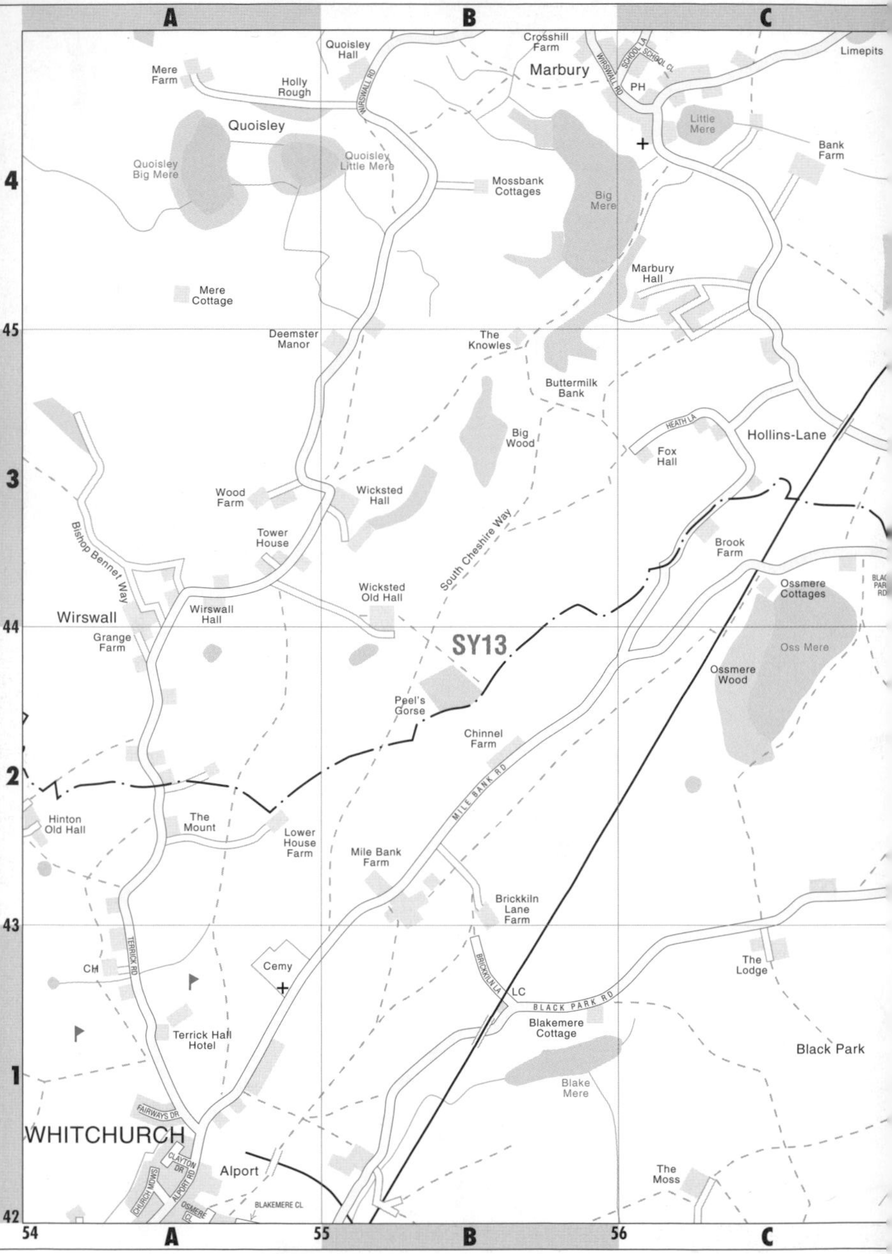
A
B
C
Quoisley Hall
Crosshill Farm
Marbury
Limepits
Mere Farm
Holly Rough
WIRSWALL RD
SCHOOL LA
SCHOOL CL
PH
Quoisley
Little Mere
Bank Farm
Quoisley Big Mere
Quoisley Little Mere
Mossbank Cottages
Big Mere
4
Marbury Hall
Mere Cottage
45
Deemster Manor
The Knowles
Buttermilk Bank
HEATH LA
Big Wood
Hollins-Lane
Fox Hall
3
Wood Farm
Wicksted Hall
Tower House
Bishop Bennet Way
South Cheshire Way
Brook Farm
Wicksted Old Hall
Ossmere Cottages
Wirswall
Wirswall Hall
44
Grange Farm
SY13
Oss Mere
Ossmere Wood
Peel's Gorse
Chinnel Farm
2
MILE BANK RD
Hinton Old Hall
The Mount
Lower House Farm
Mile Bank Farm
Brickkiln Lane Farm
43
TERRICK RD
Cemy
The Lodge
CH
BRICKKILN LA
LC
BLACK PARK RD
Blakemere Cottage
Terrick Hall Hotel
Black Park
1
Blake Mere
FAIRWAYS DR
WHITCHURCH
CLAYTON DR
Alport
The Moss
CHURCH MDWS
ALPORT RD
OSMERE CL
BLAKEMERE CL
42
54
55
56

225

216
228

A
B
C
Marley Moss
LC
Poole
Hook
Marley
Green
Marley
Hall
Adamley
Pool
CW5
4
Marley Hall
Covert
Poole
Gorse
45
Big Wood
Poole's Hiding Wood
Duckbay
Island
Monument
Summerhouse
Island
Comber Mere
3
Hollyhurst
Brankelow
Moss
Long Walk
Covert
Combermere
Abbey
Brankelow
Folly
Combermere Park
Hollyhurst
Wood
Larder
Wood
44
Cocked Hat
SY13
BLACK PARK RD
The Stews
A530
2
Bridge
Plantation
Stonelodge
Wood
WHITCHURCH RD
Steel's
Rough
Plantation
A525
Combermere
Cottage
43
Shropshire Gate
Farm
Wood Farm
Bank Acres
Farm
Old Woodhouses
Lower Lodge
Martin's
Ash
Shropshire Lane
Farm
1
SHROPSHIRE LA
Ancient
Briton
(PH)
Broadoak
Farm
DARK LA
New Woodhouses
Bank
Farm
A525
A525 Whitchurch
42
58
59
A
B
C

228

A
B
C
4
45
3
44
2
43
1
42
60
61
62
A530
Rose Mount
Flag Lane
Royals Wood Farm
COUNCIL HOS
Mill Farm
Newhall
MAIDEN EST
Sheppenhall Hall
Hollinlane Farm
HOLLIN LA
HEATLEY LA
Hall o' Coole
Court's Gorse
Newbridge Farm
Moor Hall Farm
CW5
SALESBROOK LA
New Cottages
WHITCHURCH RD
Brickbank Wood
New Lodge
Moorfields
Sales Brook
Mount Pleasant Farm
BANK COOLE LA
The Hollies
Kingswoodgreen Farm
Salesbrook Farm
River Weaver
SHEPPENHALL LA
Dodds Green Farm
Barnett Brook
Home Farm
Barnettbrook Bridge
Springfield
DODD'S GREEN LA
Grindley Green
A525
Goldsmith House Farm
The Rookery
Ferneybank
Blue Bache Farm
Walkmill Covert
SY13
The Woodlands
Walkmill Bridge
Rookery Farm
Walkmill Farm
Burleydam Nurseries
Walkmill Brook
Royal's Green
The Old Vicarage
Royal's Green Farm
Combermere Arms (PH)
Burleydam
Elm House Farm
Lower Farm
Fingerpost Cottages
LODMORE LA
Chapel Covert
FIELDS VIEW

A
B
C
CW5
Hollin Green
HOLLINGREEN LA
Oak Farm
Pinnacle Farm
Coole Hall Farm
Monks Hall Farm
Bennett's Bridge
The Laurels
Shropshire Union Canal
Cherry Tree Farm
Park House Farm
Coole Lane Farm
Coos Farm
Manor Farm
COOLE LA
Moss Hall Aqueduct
Daisy Bank House
Moss Hall
Moss Hall Bridge
Lower House Farm
BACK COOLE LA
A529
CHESHIRE ST
BROADWAYS
CHURCHFIELDS
ALDELYME
Oomy
Ty-Gwy
Brickwall Farm
Copthorne
PH
A525
SHROPSHIRE ST
A529
CW3
Sewage Works
Lower Lightwood Green Farm
Lightwood Green
Oldmill Bridge
WHITCHURCH RD
Browns Bank Farm
Audlem Bridge
1 OLD VICARAGE GDNS
2 CHAPEL CL
3 TELFORD WAY
Grey's Bridge
Brown's Bank
Works
LIGHTWOOD GREEN AVE
WOODAVENS GR
Weaver Bank Farm
Newtown Cottages
West View
Hillside
COUNCIL HOS
MILL LA
GREEN LA
River Weaver
htwood Green Farm
Swanbach Grange
Swanbach
Newtown Farm
Swanbach Farm
Bridge Farm
BAGLEY LA
HEYWOOD LA
A529
4
45
3
44
2
43
1
42
64
65

229
219

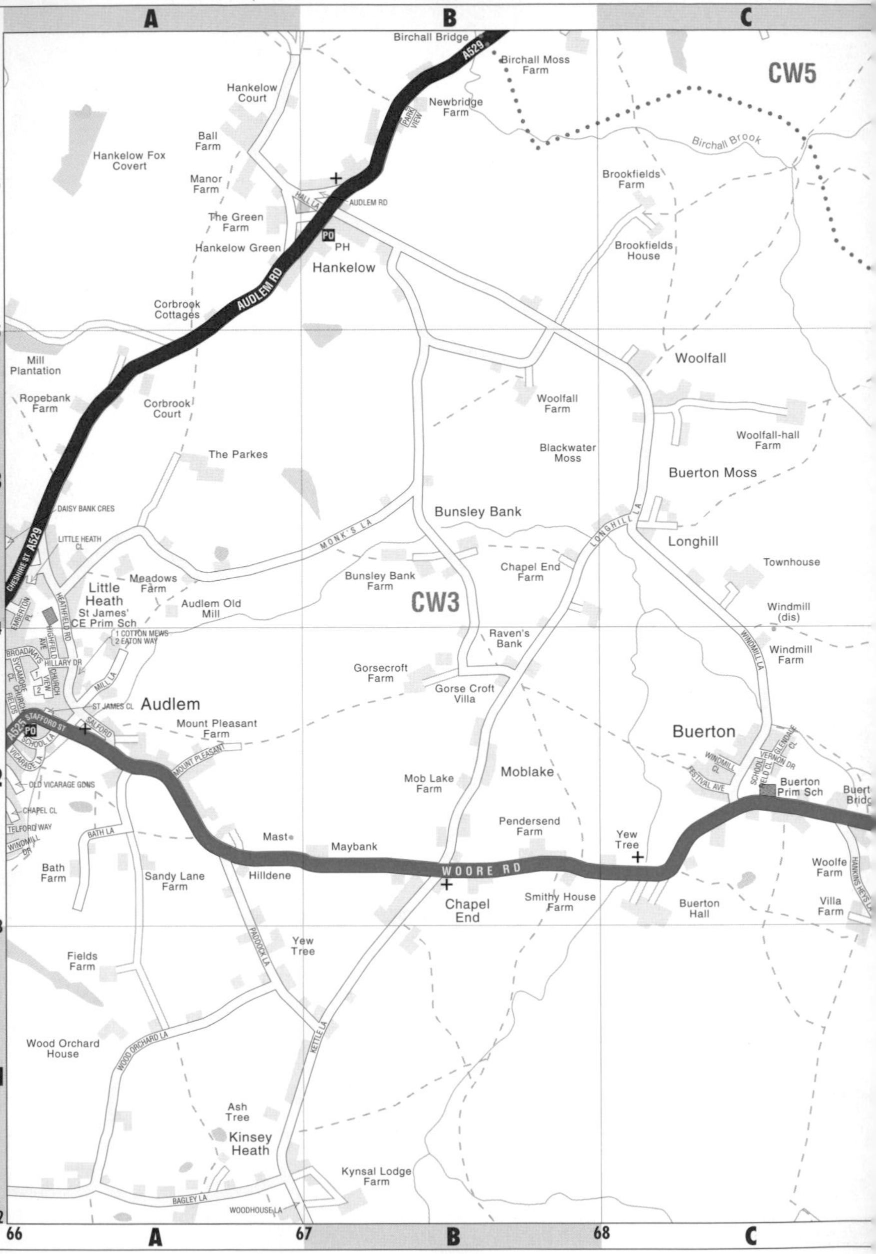
A
B
C
4
3
2
1
45
44
43
42
66
67
68
CW5
CW3
A529
A525
Birchall Bridge
Birchall Moss Farm
Newbridge Farm
PARK VIEW
Birchall Brook
Hankelow Court
Ball Farm
Hankelow Fox Covert
Manor Farm
HALL LA
AUDLEM RD
The Green Farm
Hankelow Green
PO
PH
Hankelow
Brookfields Farm
Brookfields House
Corbrook Cottages
Mill Plantation
Ropebank Farm
Corbrook Court
Woolfall
Woolfall Farm
Blackwater Moss
Woolfall-hall Farm
The Parkes
Buerton Moss
DAISY BANK CRES
Bunsley Bank
LONGHILL LA
Longhill
LITTLE HEATH CL
MONK'S LA
CHESHIRE ST
Meadows Farm
Bunsley Bank Farm
Chapel End Farm
Townhouse
Little Heath
Audlem Old Mill
St James' CE Prim Sch
Windmill (dis)
EMBERTON PL
HEATHFIELD RD
1 COTTON MEWS
2 EATON WAY
Raven's Bank
Windmill Farm
WINDMILL LA
BROADWAYS
SYCAMORE CL
HIGHFIELD AVE
HILLARY DR
CHURCH VIEW
CHURCH FIELDS
MILL LA
Gorsecroft Farm
Gorse Croft Villa
ST JAMES CL
Audlem
STAFFORD ST
SALFORD
SCHOOL LA
Mount Pleasant Farm
MOUNT PLEASANT
Buerton
WINDMILL CL
VERNON DR
GLENDALE CL
FESTIVAL AVE
SCHOOL FIELD CL
Buerton Prim Sch
VICARAGE LA
OLD VICARAGE GDNS
Mob Lake Farm
Moblake
CHAPEL CL
TELFORD WAY
WINDMILL DR
BATH LA
Mast
Maybank
Pendersend Farm
Yew Tree
Bath Farm
Sandy Lane Farm
Hilldene
WOORE RD
Chapel End
Smithy House Farm
Buerton Hall
Woolfe Farm
Villa Farm
HANKINS HEYS LA
PADDOCK LA
Yew Tree
Fields Farm
Wood Orchard House
WOOD ORCHARD LA
KETTLE LA
Ash Tree
Kinsey Heath
Kynsal Lodge Farm
BAGLEY LA
WOODHOUSE LA

229
235

A B C

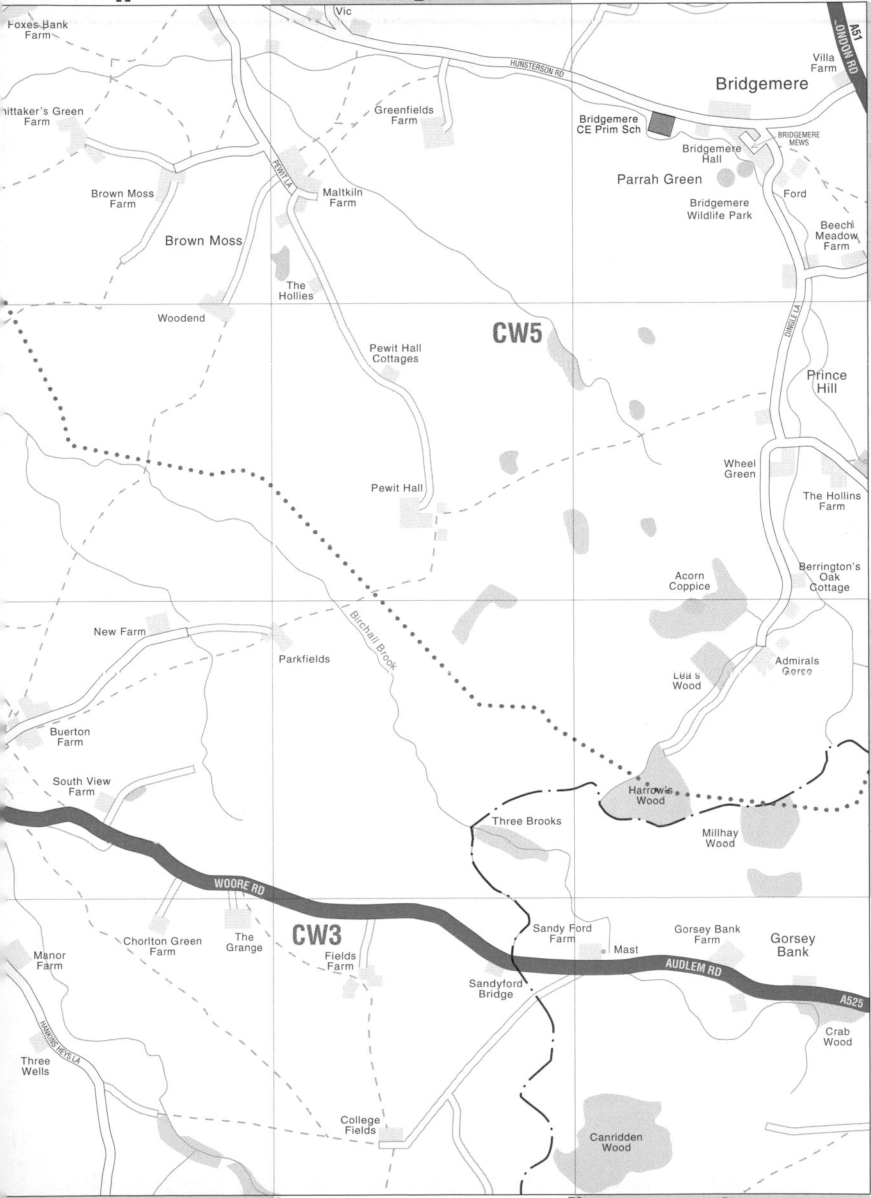

4
45
3
44
2
43
1
42

A 70 B 71 C

231
221

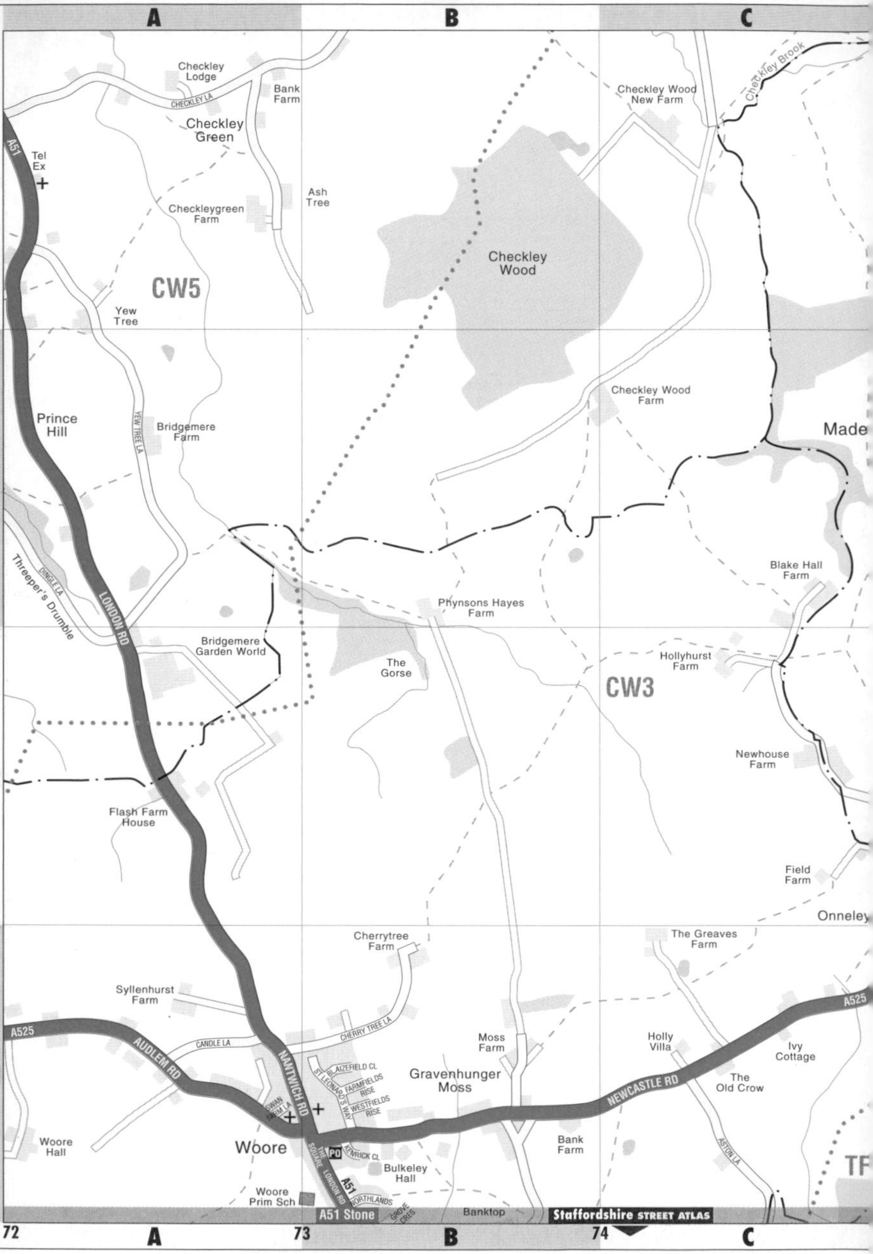
A
B
C
4
3
2
1
45
44
43
42
72
73
74
Checkley Lodge
Bank Farm
CHECKLEY LA
Checkley Green
Checkley Wood New Farm
Checkley Brook
A51
Tel Ex
Ash Tree
Checkleygreen Farm
Checkley Wood
CW5
Yew Tree
Checkley Wood Farm
Prince Hill
YEW TREE LA
Bridgemere Farm
Made
DINGLE LA
Threeper's Drumble
LONDON RD
Blake Hall Farm
Phynsons Hayes Farm
Bridgemere Garden World
The Gorse
Hollyhurst Farm
CW3
Newhouse Farm
Flash Farm House
Field Farm
Onneley
Cherrytree Farm
The Greaves Farm
Syllenhurst Farm
A525
AUDLEM RD
CANDLE LA
CHERRY TREE LA
NANTWICH RD
Moss Farm
Holly Villa
Ivy Cottage
AIZEFIELD CL
ST LEONARD'S WAY
FARMFIELDS RISE
WESTFIELDS RISE
SWAN FARM LA
Gravenhunger Moss
NEWCASTLE RD
The Old Crow
Woore Hall
Woore
PO
KENRICK CL
Bank Farm
ASTON LA
THE SQUARE
Bulkeley Hall
Woore Prim Sch
NORTHLANDS
GROVE CRES
A51 Stone
Banktop
TF

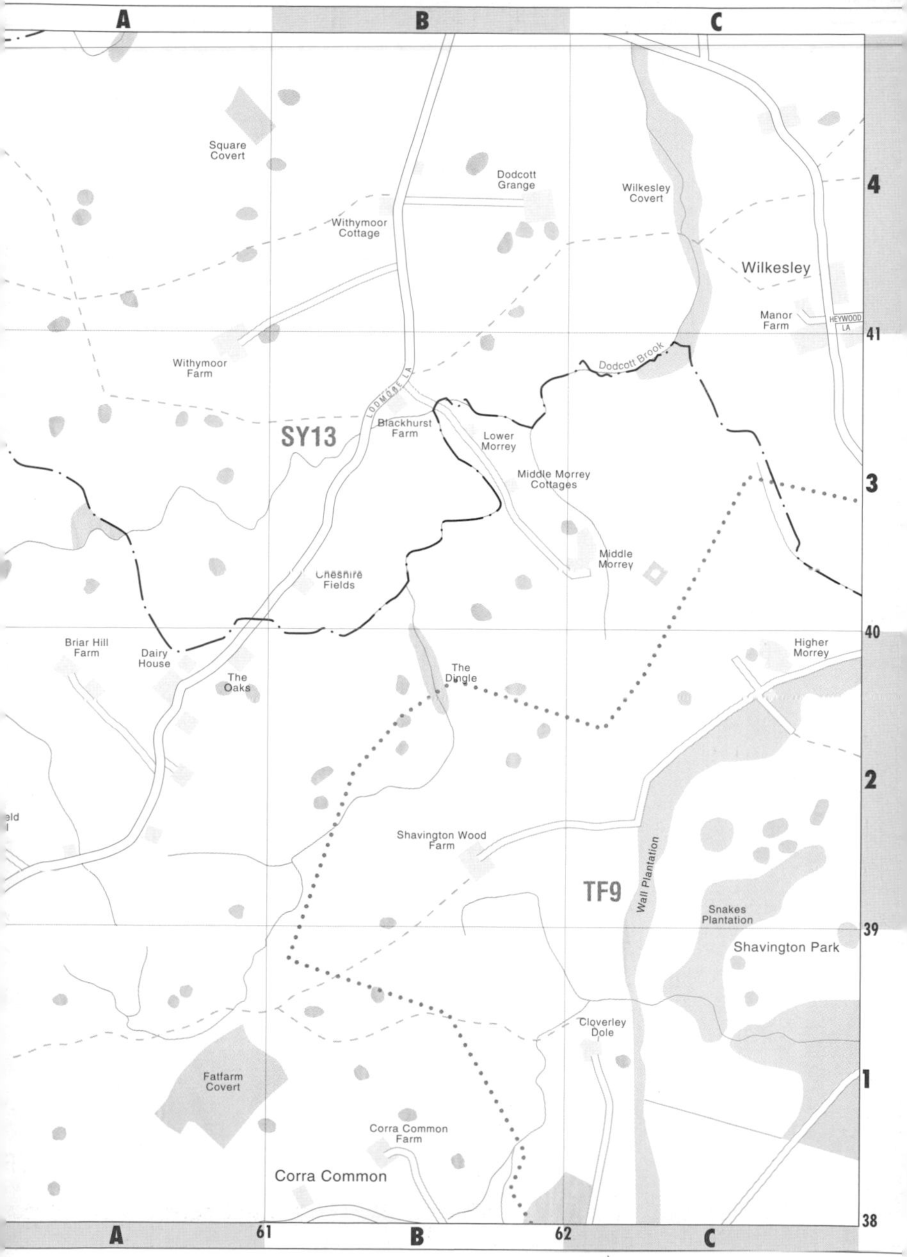
A
B
C
Square Covert
Dodcott Grange
Wilkesley Covert
Withymoor Cottage
Wilkesley
Manor Farm
HEYWOOD LA
Withymoor Farm
LODMORE LA
Dodcott Brook
SY13
Blackhurst Farm
Lower Morrey
Middle Morrey Cottages
Middle Morrey
Cheshire Fields
Briar Hill Farm
Dairy House
The Oaks
The Dingle
Higher Morrey
Shavington Wood Farm
Wall Plantation
TF9
Snakes Plantation
Shavington Park
Cloverley Dole
Fatfarm Covert
Corra Common Farm
Corra Common
4
41
3
40
2
39
1
38
61
62

233
229

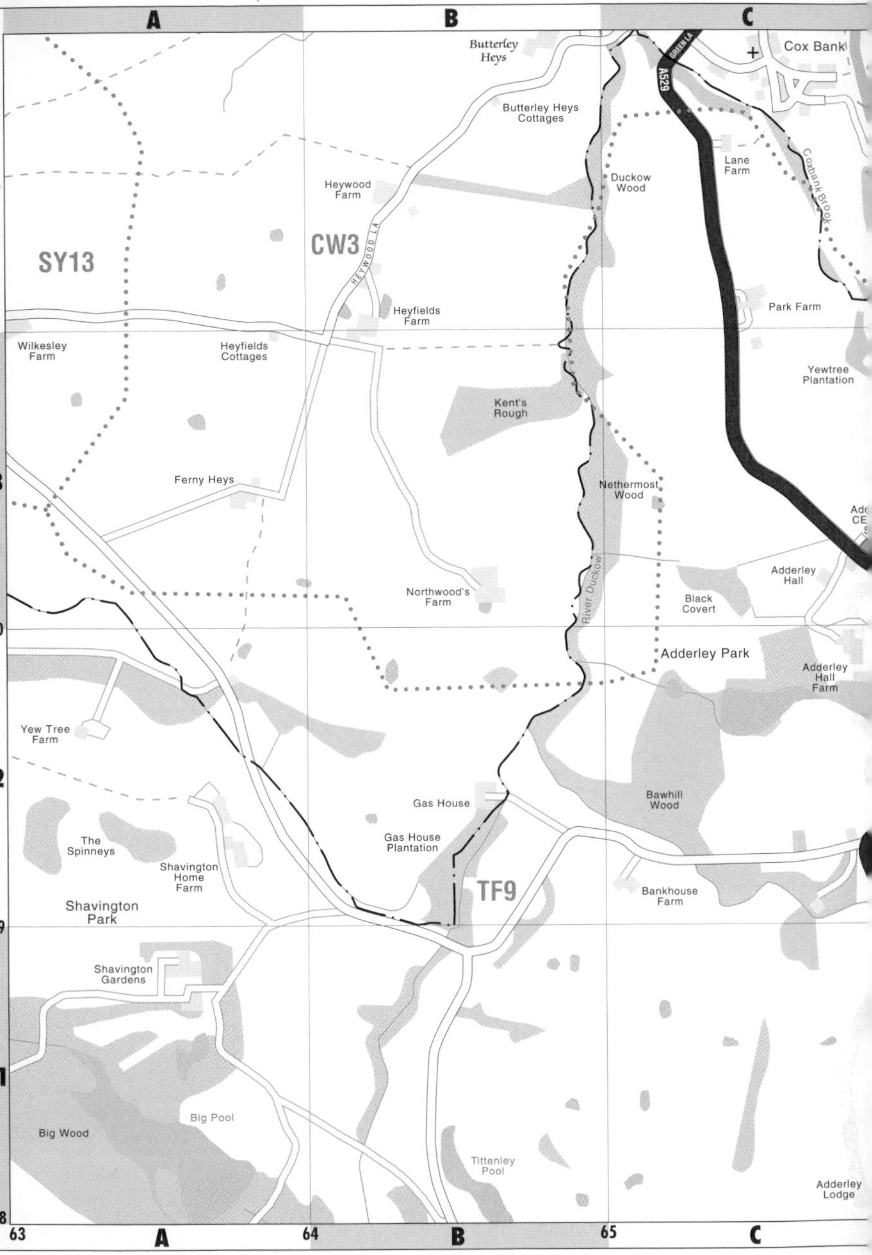
A
B
C
Butterley Heys
Cox Bank
GREEN LA
A529
Butterley Heys Cottages
Lane Farm
Coxbank Brook
Duckow Wood
Heywood Farm
4
SY13
CW3
HEYWOOD LA
Heyfields Farm
Park Farm
41
Wilkesley Farm
Heyfields Cottages
Yewtree Plantation
Kent's Rough
3
Ferny Heys
Nethermost Wood
Adderley Hall
River Duckow
Northwood's Farm
Black Covert
40
Adderley Park
Adderley Hall Farm
Yew Tree Farm
2
Gas House
Bawhill Wood
Gas House Plantation
The Spinneys
Shavington Home Farm
TF9
Bankhouse Farm
Shavington Park
39
Shavington Gardens
1
Big Pool
Big Wood
Tittenley Pool
Adderley Lodge
38
63
64
65

230
236

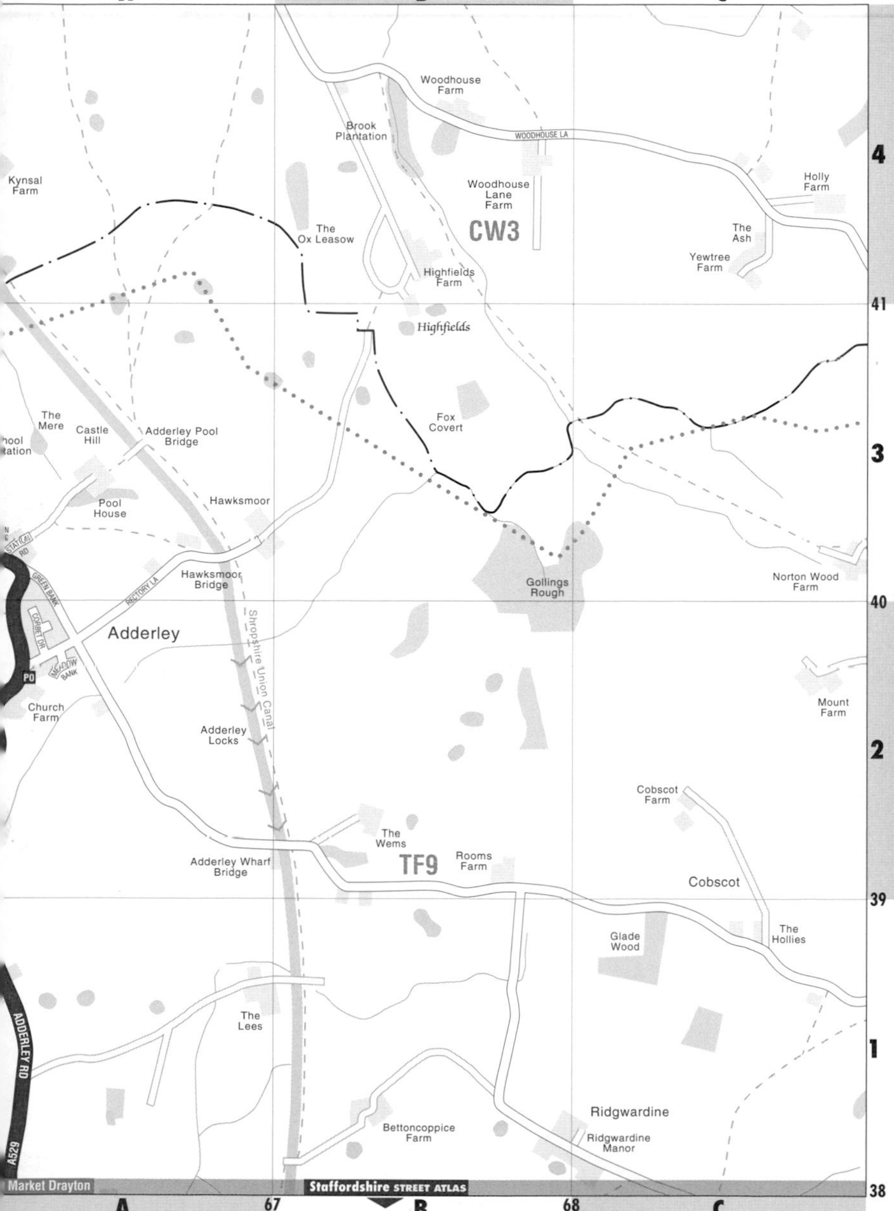
A
B
C
Woodhouse Farm
WOODHOUSE LA
Brook Plantation
Kynsal Farm
Woodhouse Lane Farm
CW3
Holly Farm
The Ox Leasow
The Ash
Yewtree Farm
Highfields Farm
Highfields
Fox Covert
The Mere
Castle Hill
Adderley Pool Bridge
Pool House
Hawksmoor
STATION RD
GREEN BANK
RECTORY LA
Hawksmoor Bridge
Gollings Rough
Norton Wood Farm
CORBET DR
Adderley
MEADOW BANK
PO
Shropshire Union Canal
Mount Farm
Church Farm
Adderley Locks
Cobscot Farm
The Wems
Rooms Farm
TF9
Adderley Wharf Bridge
Cobscot
The Hollies
Glade Wood
The Lees
ADDERLEY RD
Ridgwardine
Bettoncoppice Farm
Ridgwardine Manor
A529
4
41
3
40
2
39
1
38
67
68

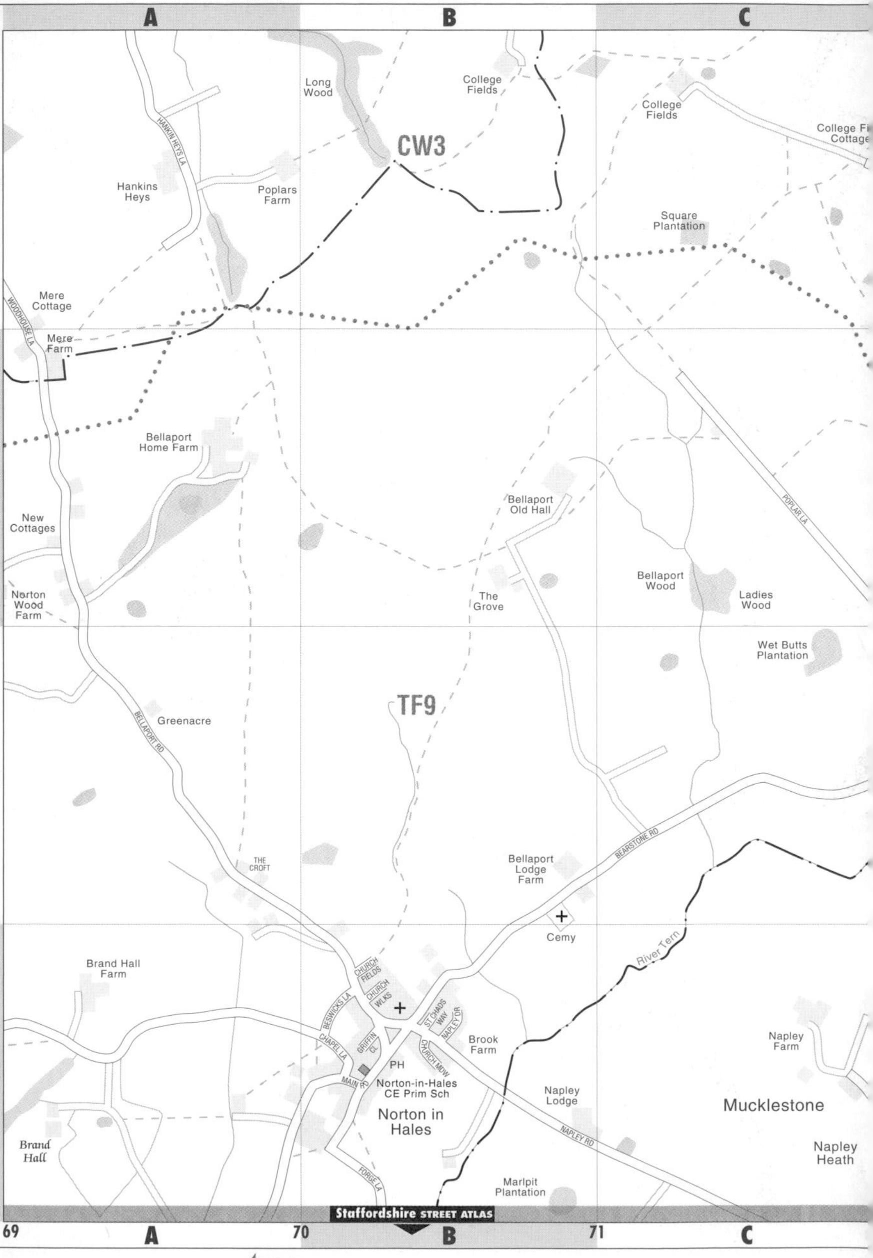
A
B
C
4
3
2
1
41
40
39
38
69
70
71
Long Wood
College Fields
CW3
College Fields
College Fi
Cottage
HANKIN HEYS LA
Hankins Heys
Poplars Farm
Square Plantation
Mere Cottage
WOODHOUSE LA
Mere Farm
Bellaport Home Farm
New Cottages
Bellaport Old Hall
POPLAR LA
Norton Wood Farm
Bellaport Wood
Ladies Wood
The Grove
Wet Butts Plantation
TF9
BELLAPORT RD
Greenacre
BEARSTONE RD
THE CROFT
Bellaport Lodge Farm
Cemy
River Tern
Brand Hall Farm
CHURCH FIELDS
CHURCH WLKS
BESWICKS LA
ST CHADS WAY
NAPLEY DR
CHAPEL LA
GRIFFIN CL
CHURCH MDW
Brook Farm
Napley Farm
PH
MAIN RD
Norton-in-Hales CE Prim Sch
Napley Lodge
Mucklestone
Norton in Hales
NAPLEY RD
Brand Hall
Napley Heath
FORGE LA
Marlpit Plantation
Staffordshire STREET ATLAS

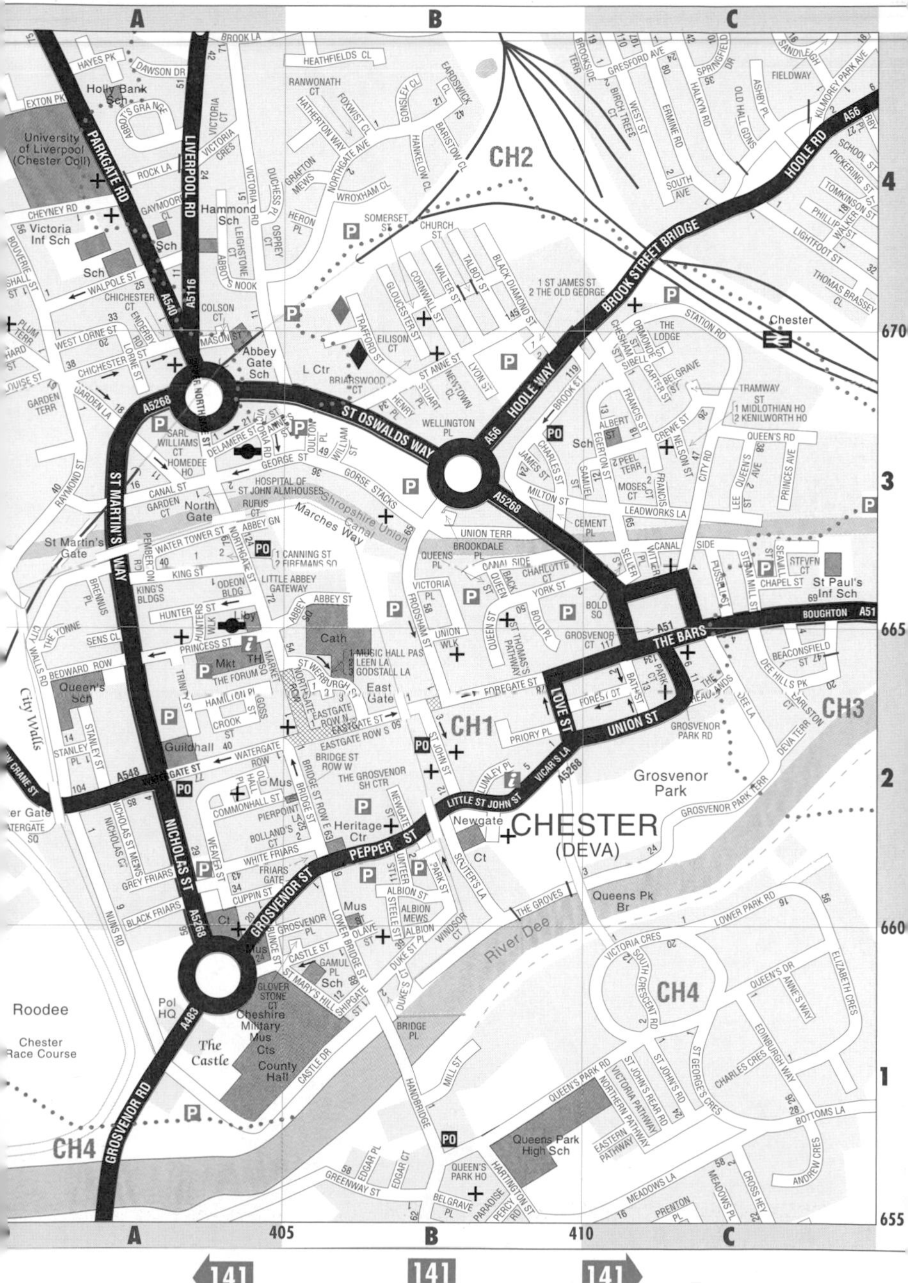
A
B
C
CH2
CH1
CH3
CH4
CHESTER
(DEVA)
PARKGATE RD
LIVERPOOL RD
A540
A5116
A5268
ST OSWALDS WAY
HOOLE WAY
A56
BROOK STREET BRIDGE
HOOLE RD
ST MARTIN'S WAY
NICHOLAS ST
GROSVENOR RD
A483
GROSVENOR ST
PEPPER ST
LITTLE ST JOHN ST
VICAR'S LA
THE BARS
A51
BOUGHTON
LOVE ST
UNION ST
FOREGATE ST
FROSTHAM ST
BROOK LA
HEATHFIELDS CL
HAYES PK
DAWSON DR
Holly Bank Sch
EXTON PK
University of Liverpool (Chester Coll)
ROCK LA
CHEYNEY RD
Victoria Inf Sch
Hammond Sch
WALPOLE ST
CHICHESTER ST
WEST LORNE ST
GARDEN LA
GARDEN TERR
RAYMOND ST
Abbey Gate Sch
North Gate
St Martin's Gate
WATER TOWER ST
KING ST
HUNTER ST
PRINCESS ST
Mkt
THE FORUM
Liby
Cath
East Gate
EASTGATE ST
Guildhall
WATERGATE ST
A548
CRANE ST
City Walls
Queen's Sch
STANLEY PL
Heritage Ctr
WHITE FRIARS
GREY FRIARS
BLACK FRIARS
CUPPIN ST
NUNS RD
Roodee
Chester Race Course
The Castle
Cheshire Military Mus
County Hall
Pol HQ
CASTLE DR
BRIDGE PL
HANDBRIDGE
MILL ST
River Dee
Queens Pk Br
THE GROVES
Grosvenor Park
GROSVENOR PARK RD
GROSVENOR PARK TERR
Newgate
Ct
ST JOHN ST
Queens Park High Sch
QUEEN'S PARK RD
VICTORIA CRES
SOUTH CRESCENT RD
LOWER PARK RD
ELIZABETH CRES
QUEEN'S DR
EDINBURGH WAY
CHARLES CRES
BOTTOMS LA
ANDREW CRES
MEADOWS LA
GREENWAY ST
EDGAR PL
PARADISE
HARTINGTON ST
Chester
STATION RD
CITY RD
QUEEN'S RD
PRINCES AVE
LEADWORKS LA
MILTON ST
CHARLES ST
UNION TERR
BROOKDALE PL
Shropshire Union Canal
Marches Way
GORSE STACKS
GEORGE ST
CANAL ST
FRODSHAM ST
St Paul's Inf Sch
BEACONSFIELD ST
DEE HILLS PK
DEVA TERR
SANDILEIGH
FIELDWAY
KILMOREY PARK AVE
SCHOOL ST
PICKERING ST
TOMKINSON ST
PHILLIP ST
LIGHTFOOT ST
THOMAS BRASSEY CL
GRESFORD AVE
WEST ST
ERMINE RD
HALKYN RD
OLD HALL GDNS
SOUTH AVE
SPRINGFIELD DR
NORTHGATE AVE
WROXHAM CL
GRAFTON MEWS
HERON PL
SOMERSET ST
CHURCH ST
CORNWALL ST
WALTER ST
TALBOT ST
BLACK DIAMOND ST
GLOUCESTER ST
TRAFFORD ST
L Ctr
WELLINGTON PL
1 ST JAMES ST
2 THE OLD GEORGE
1 MIDLOTHIAN HO
2 KENILWORTH HO
1 CANNING ST
2 FIREMANS SQ
1 MUSIC HALL PAS
2 LEEN LA
3 GODSTALL LA
405
410
670
665
660
655
4
3
2
1

D5
1 POLICE ST
2 STAMFORD WAY
3 STAMFORD SQ
4 OLD MARKET PL

E6
1 LYNGARTH HO
2 ASTBURY CL
3 THELWALL CL
4 THE WOODS
5 SELWORTH CL

C4
1 STAMFORD GRANGE
2 EASINGWOLD

D3
1 ROSTHERNE ST
2 WILLIAM WLK

D4
1 GREENWOOD ST
2 THE CAUSEWAY
3 CROSS ST
4 BREWERY ST
5 GRAFTON MALL
6 LLOYD SQ
7 OSBOURNE PL

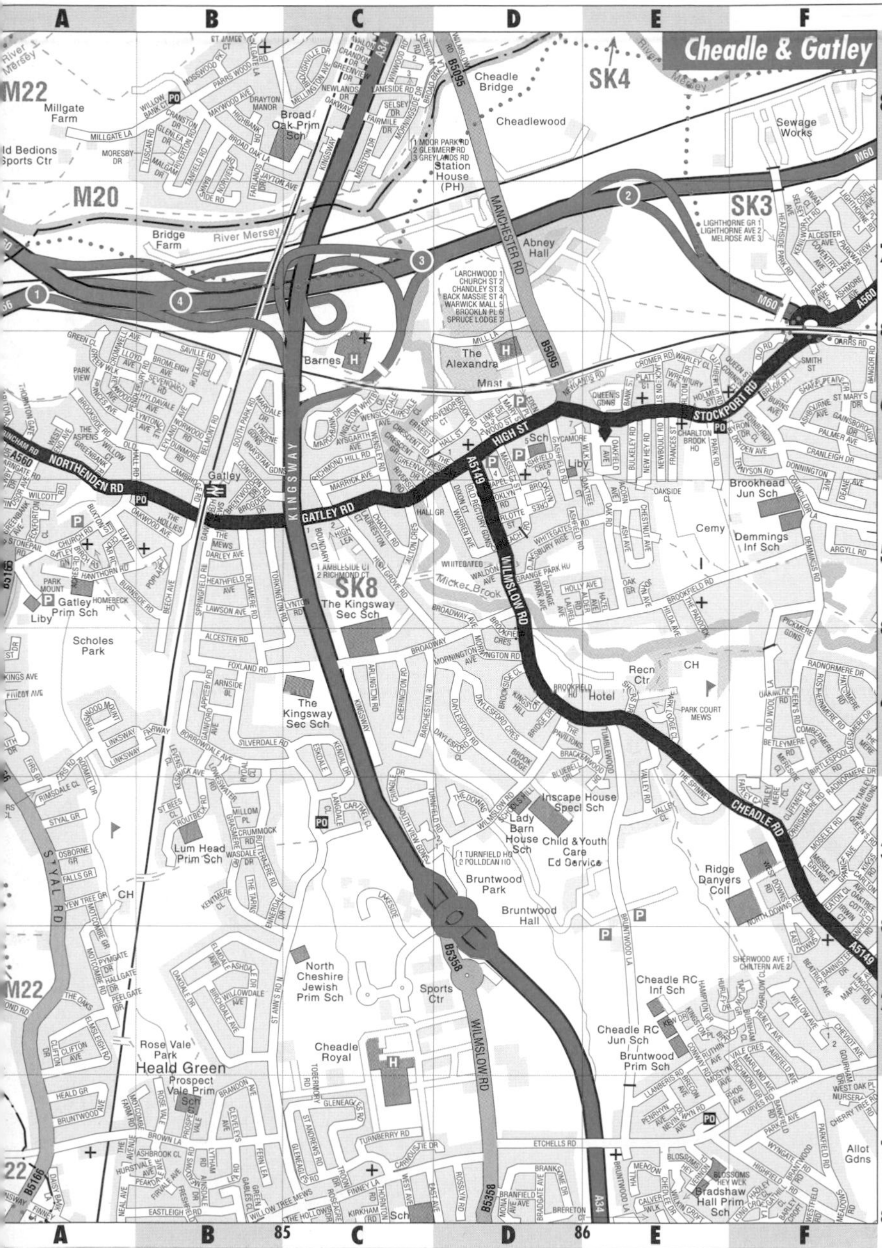
Cheadle & Gatley
A
B
C
D
E
F
8
7
6
5
4
3
2
1
89
88
87
86
85
86
M22
M20
SK4
SK3
SK8
Millgate Farm
Bridge Farm
River Mersey
Broad Oak Prim Sch
Cheadle Bridge
Cheadlewood
Station House (PH)
Abney Hall
Sewage Works
Barnes
The Alexandra
Moat
Gatley
NORTHENDEN RD
GATLEY RD
HIGH ST
STOCKPORT RD
KINGSWAY
WILMSLOW RD
MANCHESTER RD
CHEADLE RD
STYAL RD
Gatley Prim Sch
Liby
Scholes Park
The Kingsway Sec Sch
Micker Brook
Brookhead Jun Sch
Demmings Inf Sch
Cemy
Recn Ctr
Hotel
Lum Head Prim Sch
Lady Barn House Sch
Inscape House Specl Sch
Child & Youth Care Ed Service
Bruntwood Park
Bruntwood Hall
Ridge Danyers Coll
North Cheshire Jewish Prim Sch
Sports Ctr
Cheadle Royal
Cheadle RC Inf Sch
Cheadle RC Jun Sch
Bruntwood Prim Sch
Rose Vale Park
Heald Green
Prospect Vale Prim Sch
Bradshaw Hall Prim Sch
Allot Gdns
A34
A560
A5149
B5095
B5358
B5166
M60

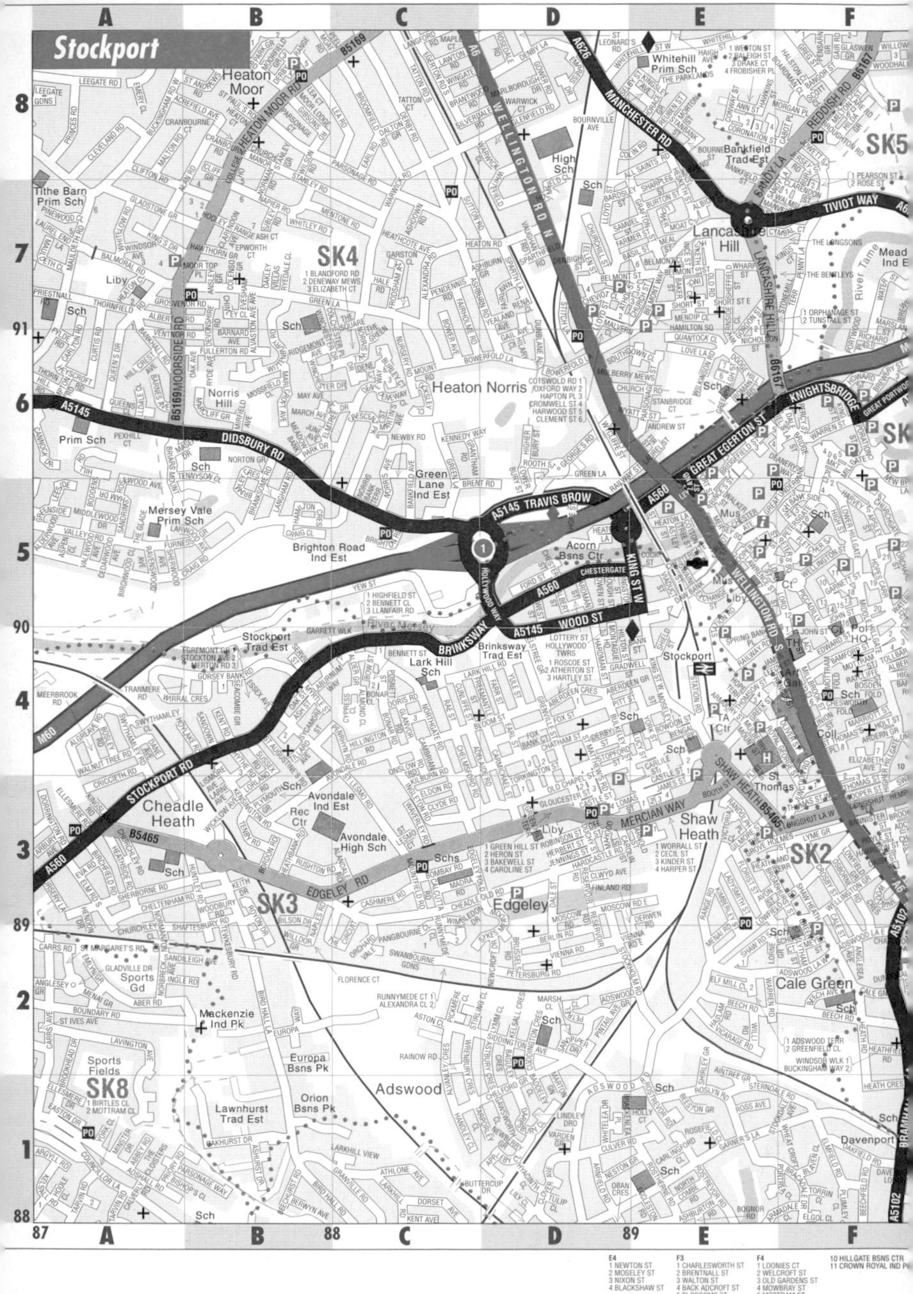

A
B
C
D
E
F
Stockport
Heaton Moor
SK4
SK5
SK3
SK2
SK8
Heaton Norris
Norris Hill
Lancashire Hill
Cheadle Heath
Shaw Heath
Edgeley
Adswood
Cale Green
Davenport
Stockport
Tithe Barn Prim Sch
Whitehill Prim Sch
Mersey Vale Prim Sch
Green Lane Ind Est
Brighton Road Ind Est
Bankfield Trad Est
Stockport Trad Est
Brinksway Trad Est
Acorn Bsns Ctr
Lark Hill Sch
Avondale Ind Est
Avondale High Sch
Mackenzie Ind Pk
Europa Bsns Pk
Orion Bsns Pk
Lawnhurst Trad Est
Sports Gd
Sports Fields
Mead Ind Est
River Mersey
River Tame
DIDSBURY RD
WELLINGTON RD N
WELLINGTON RD S
MANCHESTER RD
LANCASHIRE HILL
TIVIOT WAY
KNIGHTSBRIDGE
GREAT EGERTON ST
A5145 TRAVIS BROW
BRINKSWAY
KING ST W
WOOD ST
CHESTERGATE
STOCKPORT RD
EDGELEY RD
MERCIAN WAY
SHAW HEATH
HEATON MOOR RD
MOORSIDE RD
A5145
A560
A6
A626
B5169
B5465
B6167
M60
A5102
8
7
91
6
5
90
4
3
89
2
1
88
87
88
89

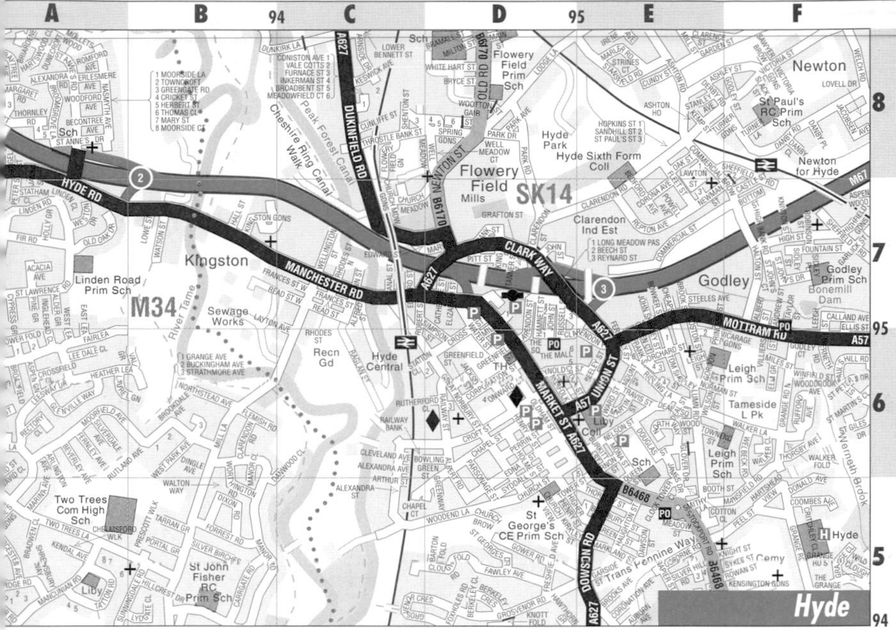

A
B
94
C
D
95
E
F
8
7
95
6
5
94
Newton
Flowery Field Prim Sch
Flowery Field Mills
SK14
Hyde Park
Hyde Sixth Form Coll
St Paul's RC Prim Sch
Newton for Hyde
M67
Clarendon Ind Est
Kingston
Linden Road Prim Sch
M34
Sewage Works
Godley
Godley Prim Sch
Bonemill Dam
HYDE RD
MANCHESTER RD
DUKINFIELD RD
NEWTON ST
CLARK WAY
MARKET ST
UNION ST
MOTTRAM RD
A57
A627
B6170
B6468
Hyde Central
Recn Gd
Leigh Prim Sch
Tameside L Pk
Leigh Prim Sch
Peak Forest Canal
Cheshire Ring Canal Walk
River Tame
Two Trees Com High Sch
St John Fisher RC Prim Sch
St George's CE Prim Sch
Trans Pennine Way
Cemy
Hyde
Wernteth Brook
DOWSON RD
Hyde

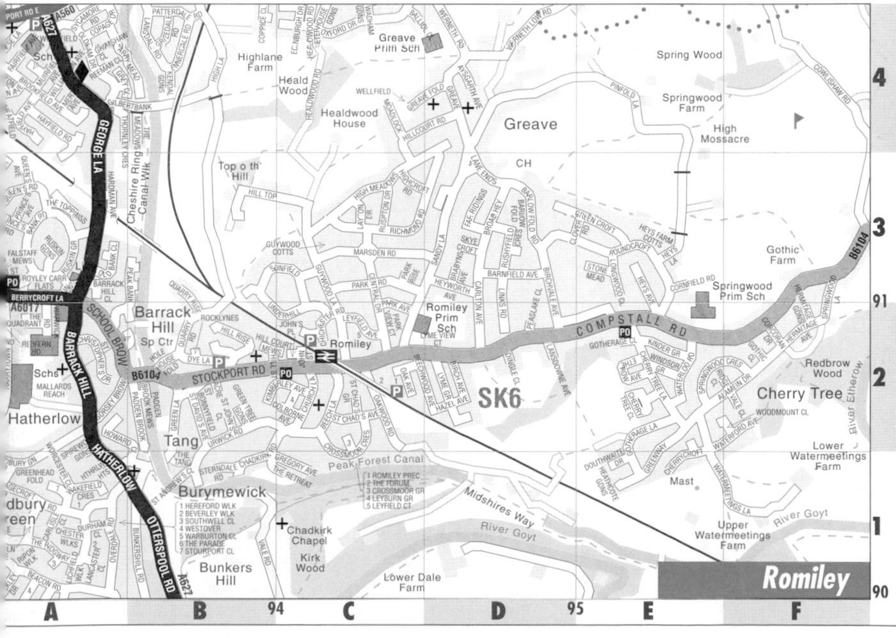

4
3
91
2
1
90
A
B
94
C
D
95
E
F
Greave Prim Sch
Highlane Farm
Heald Wood
Healdwood House
Greave
CH
Spring Wood
Springwood Farm
High Mossacre
Top o th' Hill
Gothic Farm
Springwood Prim Sch
GEORGE LA
Cheshire Ring Canal Walk
Barrack Hill
Sp Ctr
BARRACK HILL
SCHOOL BROW
STOCKPORT RD
B6104
Romiley
Romiley Prim Sch
COMPSTALL RD
SK6
Redbrow Wood
Cherry Tree
Hatherlow
Schs
Tang
Burymewick
HATHERLOW
OTTERSPOOL RD
Peak Forest Canal
Midshires Way
River Goyt
Chadkirk Chapel
Kirk Wood
Bunkers Hill
Lower Dale Farm
Mast
Lower Watermeetings Farm
Upper Watermeetings Farm
River Etherow
Romiley

B7
1 YORK HO
2 ATKINSON HO
3 WILSON ST
4 PARTINGTON PL
5 ORCHARD PL
6 CURZON RD
7 BENBOW ST

D6
1 NORFOLK HO
2 ROWSON CT
3 WARWICK HO
4 WILKINSON ST
5 HOLLY HEYS

F5
1 PASTUREFIELD CL
2 CORNFIELD CL
3 THRESHER CL
4 ROSEWOOD GDNS
5 WOODCHURCH WLK

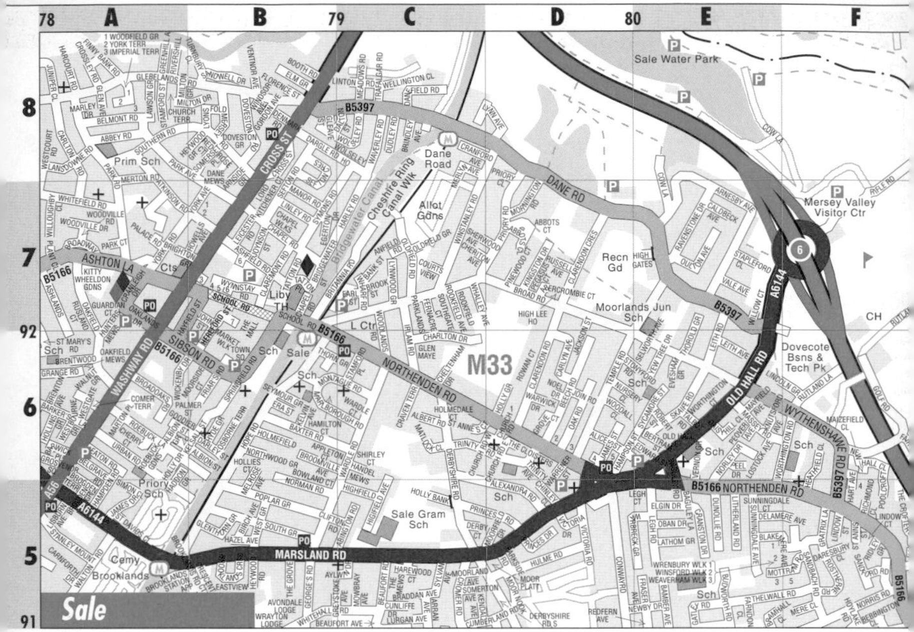

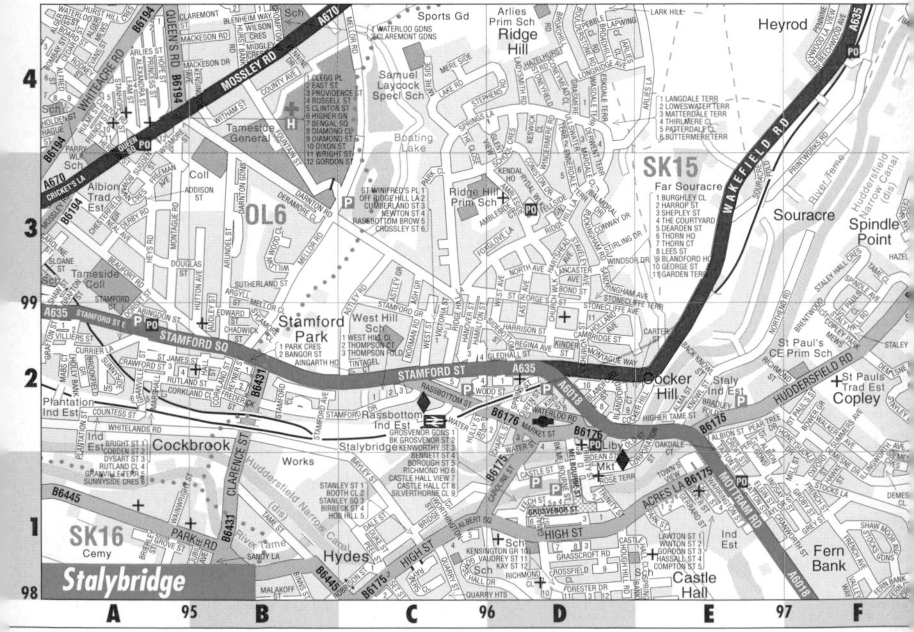

Index

Church Rd **6** Beckenham BR2..........**53** C6

Place name
May be abbreviated on the map

Location number
Present when a number indicates the place's position in a crowded area of mapping

Locality, town or village
Shown when more than one place has the same name

Postcode district
District for the indexed place

Page and grid square
Page number and grid reference for the standard mapping

Public and commercial buildings are highlighted in magenta. Places of interest are highlighted in blue with a star★

Abbreviations used in the index

Acad	**Academy**	Comm	**Common**	Gd	**Ground**	L	**Leisure**	Prom	**Prom**
App	**Approach**	Cott	**Cottage**	Gdn	**Garden**	La	**Lane**	Rd	**Road**
Arc	**Arcade**	Cres	**Crescent**	Gn	**Green**	Liby	**Library**	Recn	**Recreation**
Ave	**Avenue**	Cswy	**Causeway**	Gr	**Grove**	Mdw	**Meadow**	Ret	**Retail**
Bglw	**Bungalow**	Ct	**Court**	H	**Hall**	Meml	**Memorial**	Sh	**Shopping**
Bldg	**Building**	Ctr	**Centre**	Ho	**House**	Mkt	**Market**	Sq	**Square**
Bsns, Bus	**Business**	Ctry	**Country**	Hospl	**Hospital**	Mus	**Museum**	St	**Street**
Bvd	**Boulevard**	Cty	**County**	HQ	**Headquarters**	Orch	**Orchard**	Sta	**Station**
Cath	**Cathedral**	Dr	**Drive**	Hts	**Heights**	Pal	**Palace**	Terr	**Terrace**
Cir	**Circus**	Dro	**Drove**	Ind	**Industrial**	Par	**Parade**	TH	**Town Hall**
Cl	**Close**	Ed	**Education**	Inst	**Institute**	Pas	**Passage**	Univ	**University**
Cnr	**Corner**	Emb	**Embankment**	Int	**International**	Pk	**Park**	Wk, Wlk	**Walk**
Coll	**College**	Est	**Estate**	Intc	**Interchange**	Pl	**Place**	Wr	**Water**
Com	**Community**	Ex	**Exhibition**	Junc	**Junction**	Prec	**Precinct**	Yd	**Yard**

Index of localities, towns and villages

Acton 204 A4
Acton Bridge 76 C2
Adderley 235 A2
Adlington 62 B3
Alderley Edge 60 B1
Aldford 163 C2
Allostock 106 C2
Alpraham 169 B2
Alsager 193 C3
Altrincham 31 B4
Altrincham 238
Alvanley 73 B1
Anderton 78 B2
Antrobus 53 B2
Appleton Thorn 27 A2
Ashley 31 C3
Ashton 121 C4
Astbury 178 A4
Aston 217 B1
Audlem 230 A2
Audley 209 B1
Backford 95 A2
Barbridge 187 B3
Barnton 78 B2
Barthomley 208 B3
Barton 181 C1
Bate Heath 54 C2
Bebington 43 A3
Beeston 168 A1
Bell o' th' Hill 225 B4
Betley 221 C4
Bickerton 199 C3
Bickley Town 214 C3
Biddulph 179 A1
Blacon 117 C2
Blakenhall 221 A2
Bold Heath 13 C4
Bollington 88 A4
Bosley 158 B4
Bradwall Green 153 A2
Bramhall 35 B4
Brereton Green 153 C3
Bridgemere 231 C4
Broomedge 19 B1
Broughton 139 A2
Brown Knowl 199 B4
Broxton 183 A1
Buerton 230 C2
Bulkeley 184 C1
Bunbury 185 C4
Burland 203 B4
Burton 67 B1
Burton Green 161 B1
Burtonwood 6 C4
Burwardsley 184 A3
Capenhurst 94 A4
Cheadle 34 C4
Cheadle 239
Chelford 84 A1
Chester 118 C1
Cholmondeston 170 C2
Chorlton 207 A1
Christleton 142 C4
Church Minshull 172 A3
Churton 180 C3
Clutton 182 B1
Coddington 182 A2
Collins Green 1 C1
Comberbach 78 B4
Congleton 157 A2
Connah's Quay 91 A1
Cranage 130 A3
Crewe 190 C3
Crewe-by-Farndon 197 A4
Croft 9 A4
Cronton 12 B3
Crowton 76 B1
Cuddington 101 C2
Culcheth 4 C2
Daresbury 25 A1
Davenham 104 A1
Delamere 123 B3
Disley 38 B3
Dodleston 162 A4
Duddon 145 A3
Dunham-on-the-Hill 97 C3
Dutton 51 B1
Eaton 147 A2
Eaton (nr Congleton) 157 A4
Eccleston 141 B1
Edge Green 199 A1
Ellesmere Port 70 A4
Elton 72 B2
Faddiley 202 B4
Farndon 180 C1
Fowley Common 5 A3
Frodsham 74 B4
Gatesheath 165 C3
Gatley 239
Glazebury 5 B4
Golborne 3 A4
Goostrey 107 B1
Gorstyhill 207 C1
Grappenhall Heys 27 A4
Great Barrow 120 C3
Great Budworth 79 A4
Guilden Sutton 119 C3
Hale 21 B1
Halewood 21 A4
Hampton 214 A4
Handforth 34 B2
Hargrave 144 A1
Hartford 103 B3
Harthill 183 C2
Haslington 191 C3
Hassall Green 176 A1
Hatherton 219 C2
Hatton 26 A1
Haughton 186 B3
Hawarden 116 A1
Haydock 1 B3
Haymoor Green 205 C1
Hazel Grove 36 B4
Helsby 73 B2
Henbury 111 A4
Heswall 40 B4
High Lane 37 C4
High Legh 29 A3
Higher Kinnerton 161 A4
Higher Walton 25 C4
Higher Wincham 79 C2
Hollinfare 11 A2
Hollins Green 11 A1
Holmes Chapel 130 B2
Holt 196 B4
Hooton 44 A1
Hough Common 206 C1
Huntington 142 A3
Huxley 166 C4
Hyde 241
Irlam 11 B4
Isycoed 196 B1
Kelsall 122 B2
Kettleshulme 64 C2
Kidsgrove 195 A1
Kingsley 75 B1
Knutsford 57 A2
Lach Dennis 105 B3
Langley 113 B2
Lavister 162 B1
Lawton Heath 193 C3
Lawton Heath End 193 B3
Lawton-gate 194 A2
Ledsham 68 C1
Lindow End 59 A1
Little Bollington 20 A1
Little Budworth 147 C4
Little Leigh 77 B2
Lostock Gralam 80 A2
Lostock Green 105 A4
Lower Kinnerton 139 B1
Lower Peover 81 C1
Lymm 18 C2
Macclesfield 112 A2
Macclesfield Forest 114 B3
Madeley 232 C3
Malpas 213 A1
Manley 99 A2
Marbury 226 B4
Marston 79 A2
Marton 133 A3
Mere 56 B4
Mickle Trafford 119 C4
Middlewich 128 B2
Milton Green 165 B1
Mobberley 57 C4
Mollington 94 C1
Moore 25 A3
Mottram St Andrew 61 A1
Mouldsworth 98 C1
Moulton 126 C4
Mount Pleasant 195 A3
Mow Cop 195 B4
Nantwich 204 B3
Neston 66 B4
Nether Alderley 85 A3
New Mills 39 B4
Newcastle-under-Lyme 210 B2
Newhall 228 B4
Newton-le-Willows 2 A1
No Man's Heath 214 A3
Norley 100 C3
Northwich 103 B4
Norton in Hales 236 B1
Oakmere 124 A4
Ollerton 82 C3
Packmoor 195 C1
Partington 11 C2
Peckforton 184 C3
Peover 107 A4
Pickmere 80 A4
Picton 96 B2
Plumley 81 A2
Pott Shrigley 63 B2
Poynton 36 C2
Prestbury 87 A4
Preston on the Hill 51 A3
Puddington 92 C4
Pulford 162 B2
Rainow 88 B3
Ravensmoor 203 C1
Rode Heath 193 C4
Romiley 241
Rostherne 30 C2
Royal's Green 228 C1
Runcorn 23 B1
Rushton Spencer 159 A1
Saighton 142 C1
Sale 242
Sandbach 175 A3
Saughall 94 A1
Scholar Green 194 C4
Sealand 116 C3
Shavington 206 B3
Shocklach 211 B4
Shotwick 93 A2
Siddington 110 A2
Smallwood 176 C3
Sound 217 C3
Speke 21 A2
Sproston Green 129 B1
Spurstow 185 B3
St Helens 1 A1
Stalybridge 242
Stanlow 71 A3
Stapeley 219 B4
Stoak 96 A4
Stockport 240
Stretton 26 C1
Styal 33 C2
Sutton 50 A1
Sutton Lane Ends 112 C1
Swettenham 131 C2
Tabley 55 C2
Talke 210 B4
Tarporley 146 B1
Tarvin 121 B2
Tattenhall 166 A1
The Bank 195 A4
Thornton Hough 42 A4
Thornton-le-Moors 71 C1
Threapwood 222 C4
Tilston 198 A2
Tiverton 168 B3
Utkinton 146 A4
Warmingham 173 B4
Warren 111 B1
Warrington 16 C3
Waverton 143 A2
Weaverham 77 B1
Weston 207 B3
Wettenhall 170 C4
Whaley Bridge 65 B4
Whitchurch 226 A1
Whitegate 126 A4
Whitewell 224 B1
Whitley 52 B2
Widnes 22 C4
Willaston 68 A4
Willaston (nr Nantwich) 205 B3
Wilmslow 60 B3
Wimbolds Trafford 96 C3
Wimboldsley 150 C2
Wincle 160 A4
Winsford 126 C1
Winwick 8 A3
Wistaston 205 B4
Withington Green 108 C2
Woodford 35 C1
Woore 232 A1
Worleston 188 C3
Worthenbury 211 A1
Wrenbury 216 C2
Wybunbury 220 A4
Wythenshawe 33 C4

1

108 Steps 29 SK11 112 B4

A

Aarons Dr ST7 209 C1
Abbey Cl
Altrincham WA14 238 B1
Croft WA3 9 A4
Whitegate CW8 126 A4
Widnes WA8 22 B4
Abbey Fields CW2 205 B4
Abbey Gate Coll CH3 164 C4
Abbey Gate Coll (The Jun Dept) CH3 163 C2
Abbey Gate Sch CH2 237 A4
Abbey Gn CH1 237 A3
Abbey Hey WA7 50 B4
Abbey La Delamere CW8 123 C3
Hartford CW8 103 A2
Abbey Pl CW1 190 B3
Abbey Rd Golborne WA3 4 B4
Haydock WA11 1 C4
Macclesfield SK10 87 A1
Sale M33 242 A8
Sandbach CW11 174 C3
Stockport SK8 240 A1
Widnes WA8 22 B4
Abbey Sq CH1 237 B3
Abbey St CH1 237 B3
Abbey Way CW8 103 A2
Abbeydale Cl CW2 207 B1
Abbeyfields CW11 174 C3
Abbeyway N WA11 2 A4
Abbeyway S WA11 2 A4
Abbot's Dr CH2 118 B2
Abbot's Grange CH2 237 A4
Abbot's Nook CH2 237 A4
Abbots Cl
Macclesfield SK10 87 A1
Sale M33 242 D7
Abbots Ct M33 242 D7
Abbots Knoll CH2 118 B2
Abbots Mews CH65 70 A3
Abbots Pk CH2 118 B2
Abbots Way
Hartford CW8 103 A2
Neston CH64 41 C1
Abbotsbury Cl
Poynton SK12 36 B3
Wistaston CW2 206 A4
Abbotsfield Cl WA4 26 C3
Abbotsford Gr WA14 238 E8
Abbotsmere Cl CW8 101 C1
Abbott's Cl CW12 179 A4
Abbotts Cl Runcorn WA7 49 A4
Waverton CH3 143 A3
Abbotts Rd CH3 143 A3
Abbotts Way CW7 126 A1
Aber Rd SK8 240 A2
Abercrombie Ct M33 242 D7
Aberdare Cl WA5 7 C1
Aberdaron Dr CH1 117 C2
Aberdeen Cres SK3 240 D4
Aberdeen Gr SK3 240 D4
Aberfeldy Cl CW4 130 A1
Abingdon Ave WA1 17 C4
Abingdon Cl SK11 111 C4
Abingdon Cres CH4 140 C3
Abingdon St OL6 242 A2
Abington Cl CW1 190 A3
Abington Rd M33 242 C5
Abington Wlk WA7 50 B3
Abstone Cl WA1 17 A4
Acacia Ave
Altrincham WA15 238 F3
Denton M34 241 A7
Knutsford WA16 56 C1
Warrington WA1 17 B4
Widnes WA8 13 A2
Wilmslow SK9 59 C3
Acacia Cl CH2 72 B2
Acacia Cres CW1 190 C3
Acacia Dr
Altrincham WA15 238 F3
Ellesmere Port CH66 69 C1
Sandbach CW11 174 C4
Acacia Gdns ST7 195 B2
Acacia Gr Runcorn WA7 49 B4
4 Stockport SK5 240 F8
Acacia St WA12 1 C2
Academy St WA1 16 A3
Academy Way WA1 16 A3
Acer Ave CW1 190 C4
Achilles Ave WA2 8 A1
Ack La E SK7 35 B4
Ack La W SK7,SK8 35 B4
Ackerley Cl WA2 8 C2
Ackers La WA4 16 C1
Ackers Rd WA4 16 C1
Ackersley Ct SK8 35 A4
Acorn Ave SK8 239 E5
Acorn Bank Cl CW2 206 A4
Acorn Bsns Ctr SK4 240 D5
Acorn Cl Cuddington CW8 101 C1
Winsford CW7 150 A4
Acorn Dr CH65 70 A1
Acorn La CW12 157 C2
Acorn St WA12 2 B2
Acorn Terr SK22 39 A3
Acre Gn L26 21 A3
Acre La Bebington CH62 43 B4
Bramhall SK7,SK8 35 B3
Heswall CH60 41 B4
Acre Rd CH66 69 B3
Acre St SK6 241 B2
Acreage The
Bunbury CW6 185 C4
Goostrey CW4 107 C1
Acrefield Ave SK4 240 B8
Acrefield Rd WA8 12 A1
Acres Cres WA6 75 A1
Acres La Chester CH2 118 B4
Stalybridge SK15 242 E1
Acres Rd SK8 239 A5
Acresfield Prim Sch CH2 118 C4
Acreville Gr WA3 5 B4
Acton Ave WA4 26 B2
Acton Bridge Sta CW8 76 C1
Acton CE Prim Sch CW5 204 A4
Acton Cl WA11 1 B3
Acton La CW8 76 C2
Acton Pl SK11 111 C4
Acton Rd Burtonwood WA5 6 C3
Crewe CW2 189 B3
Acton Way ST7 193 B3
Adam Ave CH66 69 B2
Adam Cl CH66 69 B2
Adam St WA2 16 B4
Adams Cl
Newton-le-W WA12 2 B1
Poynton SK12 36 C1
Adams Hill WA16 57 A1
Adamson Cl WA4 17 A1
Adamson St WA4 16 A2
Adaston Ave CH62 43 C2
Adcroft St SK1 240 F3
Adder Hill CH3 142 A4
Adderley CE Prim Sch TF9 234 C3
Adderly Cl WA7 23 B1
Addingham Ave WA8 22 B4
Addison Ave OL6 242 A3
Addison Cl CW2 205 C4
Addison Rd WA15 238 E2
Addison Sq WA8 13 A1
Adela Rd WA7 22 C1
Adelaide Rd Blacon CH1 117 B2
Bramhall SK7 35 C3
Stockport SK3 240 D4
Adelaide Sch CW1 190 B3
Adelaide St Crewe CW1 190 B3
Macclesfield SK10 87 C1
Adey Rd WA13 19 A3
Adfalent La CH64 68 A4
Adlington Cl SK12 36 C1
Adlington Ct WA3 9 C3
Adlington Dr
Northwich CW9 104 A3
Sandbach CW11 175 B4
Adlington Ind Est SK10 36 B1
Adlington Pk SK10 36 B1
Adlington Prim Sch SK10 62 C3
Adlington Rd
Bollington SK10 63 A1
Crewe CW2 189 C2
Runcorn WA7 24 B1
Wilmslow SK9 60 C4
Adlington St SK11 112 B4
Adlington Sta SK10 62 B3
Adlington Way 8 M34 241 A5
Adlinton Hall Mews SK10 62 A3
Admirals Rd WA3 9 C2
Adshall Rd SK8 240 A1
Adshead Ct SK10 88 A4
Adswood Gr SK3 240 D2
Adswood La E SK2 240 F2
Adswood La W SK3 240 F2
Adswood Prim Sch SK3 240 E1
Adswood Rd SK3 240 D1
Adswood Terr SK3 240 E2
Adwell Cl WA3 4 A4
Aegean Rd WA14 238 A6
Afton WA8 12 A1
Agden Brow WA13 19 C1
Agden Brow Pk WA13 29 B4
Agden House La SY13 225 A3
Agden La
Broomedge WA13 19 C1
Little Bollington WA13 29 C4
Agden Park La WA13 29 B4
Agecroft Rd
Northwich CW9 104 B4
Romiley SK6 241 A1
Aingarth Ho SK15 242 C2
Ainley Cl WA7 50 A3
Ainscough Rd WA3 9 C2
Ainsdale Cl
Bebington CH63 43 B3
Bramhall SK7 36 A4
Warrington WA5 14 C2
Ainsdale Dr SK8 239 B1
Ainsworth La CW8 76 A2
Ainsworth Rd CW8 77 C1
Aintree Gr
Ellesmere Port CH66 69 B2
Stockport SK3 240 E1
Airdrie Cl CH62 43 B2
Aire WA8 12 A1
Aire Cl CH65 70 A4
Aire Pl CW7 127 A1
Airedale Cl Gatley SK8 239 C6
Warrington WA5 14 C4
Airedale Ct WA14 238 E5
Airfield View CH4 139 A3
Aitchison Rd CW9 80 A1
Ajax Ave WA2 8 A1
Akesmoor La
Biddulph ST8 179 A1
Kidsgrove ST7 195 C4
Alamein Cres WA2 16 B4
Alamein Dr Romiley SK6 241 F2
Winsford CW7 149 B4
Alamein Rd Barnton CW8 78 A2
Chester CH2 95 A1
Alan Dr WA15 32 A4
Alan Rd SK4 240 B8
Alan St CW9 104 A4
Alandale Rd SK3 240 C3
Alban Ret Pk WA2 8 A1
Alban St CW1 190 B3
Albany Cres WA13 18 B2
Albany Gdns CH66 69 B4
Albany Gr WA13 18 B2
Albany Rd Bramhall SK7 35 C2
Lymm WA13 18 B2
Wilmslow SK9 59 C3
Albany Terr WA7 23 A1
Albert Ct WA14 238 D4
Albert Dr Neston CH64 66 B4
Warrington WA5 14 B3
Albert Pl
Altrincham WA14 238 D5
Congleton CW12 156 C1
Northwich CW9 104 A4
Albert Rd
Altrincham WA15 238 E3
Bollington SK10 87 C4
Hyde SK14 241 D6
Sale M33 242 C6
Stockport SK4 240 A7
Warrington WA4 17 A1
Widnes WA8 13 A1
Wilmslow SK9 60 A3
Albert Rd E WA15 238 E3
Albert Row WA6 49 A1
Albert Sq
Altrincham WA14 238 D3
Stalybridge SK15 242 C1
1 Widnes WA8 23 A4
Albert St Audley ST7 209 C2
Chester CH2 237 C3
Crewe CW1 190 B3
Hyde SK14 241 F7
Irlam M44 11 C3
Knutsford WA16 56 C1
Macclesfield SK11 112 B4
Nantwich CW5 204 C3
Runcorn WA7 23 A1
Stockport SK3 240 D5
Albert Terr WA5 1 C1
Alberta St SK1 240 F4
Albion Cl SK4 240 E7
Albion Gdns SK15 242 E1
Albion Gr M33 242 A6
Albion Ho SK15 242 F2
Albion Mews CH1 237 B2
Albion Pl CH4 237 B1
Albion Rd New Mills SK22 39 A3
Northwich CW9 79 A1
Albion St Chester CH1 237 B2
Crewe CW2 190 A2
Sale M33 242 B6
Stalybridge SK15 242 E2
Albion Trad Est OL6 242 A3
Albion Wlk CW9 79 A1
Albury Cl WA11 1 B4
Alcester Ave SK3 239 F7
Alcester Rd SK8 239 B4
Alcock St WA7 23 A2
Alcott Pl WA2 8 A3
Aldcliffe WA3 3 C4
Aldelyme CW3 229 C2
Alder Ave Poynton SK12 36 C2
Widnes WA8 13 A2
Alder Cres WA2 16 B4
Alder Ct SK10 87 B3
Alder Dr
Ellesmere Port CH66 69 C1
Stalybridge SK15 242 F3
Alder Gr Chester CH2 119 A2
Denton M34 241 A7
Stockport SK3 240 C4
Alder La
Burtonwood WA2,WA5 7 B4
Cronton WA8 12 A3
Frodsham WA6,WA7 48 B2
Warrington WA2 16 A4
Alder Rd Cheadle SK8 239 E5
Golborne WA3 3 C4
Warrington WA1 17 B4
Weaverham CW8 102 B4
Alder Rise SK23 65 B4
Alder Root La WA2 7 B4
Alder St WA12 2 B2
Alder Wood Ave L24 21 A2
Alderbank Rd WA5 15 A3
Alderdale Dr SK6 37 C4
Alderdale Gr SK9 59 C3
Alderfield Dr L24 21 A2
Aldergate Ave WA7 50 B4
Alderhay La ST7 195 B3
Alderley Ave WA3 3 B4
Alderley Cl
Hazel Grove SK7 36 C4
Poynton SK12 36 C1
Sandbach CW11 175 B4
Alderley Edge* SK9 60 B1
Alderley Edge Com Prim Sch SK9 60 A1
Alderley Edge Sch for Girls SK9 60 A1
Alderley Edge Sta SK9 60 A1
Alderley Lodge SK9 60 A3
Alderley Rd
Alderley Edge SK10,SK9 60 C1
Chelford SK10 84 B2
Northwich CW8 103 C4
Prestbury SK10 86 C2
Warrington WA4 17 B2
Wilmslow SK9 60 A3
Alderley Wlk 14 SK11 112 C4
Alderly Pl CH1 117 C3
Alderman Bolton Inf & Jun Sch WA4 16 C2
Alderney Cl
Ellesmere Port CH65 70 B1
3 Macclesfield SK11 111 C4
Alderney Ho CH2 119 A2
Alders SK9 59 C3
Alders Rd SK12 38 A4
Alders Way SK10 86 C3
Aldersey CE Prim Sch CW6 185 C4
Aldersey Cl Runcorn WA7 24 B1
Saughall CH1 94 A1
Aldersey La CH3 182 B3
Aldersey Rd CW2 190 A1
Aldersgate SK22 39 A4
Aldersgate Dr L26 21 A3
Aldersgate Rd SK7,SK8 35 B3
Aldersgreen Ave SK6 37 C4
Alderton Gr CW7 127 A2
Alderwood Ave SK4 240 A5
Alderwood Lo L24 21 A2
Aldewood Cl WA3 10 A3
Aldford Cl Bebington CH63 43 A3
Hough Common CW2 206 C1
Aldford Pl SK9 59 C1
Aldford Rd CH2 118 C3
Aldford Way CW7 126 A1
Aldgate CH65 70 A3
Aldington Dr CW10 151 B3
Aldridge Dr WA5 6 C4
Aled Way CH4 140 B3
Alexander Dr WA8 22 B4
Alexander Gr WA7 23 B1
Alexandra Ave SK14 241 C6
Alexandra Cl SK3 240 C2
Alexandra Gr M44 11 C4
Alexandra Hospl The SK8 239 D6
Alexandra Ind Est WA8 22 C4
Alexandra Mews WA6 49 A1
Alexandra Park Inf Sch SK3 240 C3
Alexandra Park Jun Sch SK3 240 C3
Alexandra Pl CW1 190 A3
Alexandra Rd
Dukinfield M34 241 A8
Middlewich CW10 151 B3
Sale M33 242 D5
Stockport SK4 240 C7
Warrington WA4 16 C1
Warrington, Stockton Heath WA4 16 B1
Alexandra Sq 7 CW7 149 A4
Alexandra St
Ashton-u-Lyne OL6 242 A4
Ellesmere Port CH65 70 B4
Hyde SK14 241 C5
Warrington WA1 16 C4
Widnes WA8 23 A4
Winsford CW7 126 B1
Alforde St WA8 23 A4
Alfred Cl 12 WA8 23 A4
Alfred Rd Golborne WA3 4 A4
Haydock WA11 1 C4
Alfred St
Ashton-u-Lyne OL6 242 A4
Dukinfield SK14 241 C7
Irlam M44 11 C3
Newton-le-W WA12 2 C2
Northwich CW8 103 C3
Widnes WA8 23 A4
Alger Mews OL6 242 A4
Alger St OL6 242 A4
Algernon St Runcorn WA7 22 C2
Warrington WA1 16 B3
Warrington, Stockton Heath WA4 16 B1
Algreave Rd SK3 240 A4
Alice Ct WA8 23 A2
Alice St M33 242 D6
Alison Ct 4 SK4 240 B7
Alison Dr Goostrey CW4 130 B4
Macclesfield SK10 87 C1
Alistair Dr CH63 43 B3
All Hallows RC High Sch SK11 112 A4
All Saints CE Prim Sch
Runcorn WA7 23 A2
Stockport SK4 240 D7
All Saints Dr WA4 17 C2
All Saints RC Prim Sch WA3 3 A4
All Saints Upton CE Prim Sch WA8 12 A2
All Saints' CE Inf Sch CH2 119 A2
All Saints' Rd SK4 240 E8
Allandale WA14 238 B4
Allans Cl CH64 66 C3
Allans Mdw CH64 66 C4
Allansford Ave CH3 143 A2
Allcard St WA5 15 C4
Allen Ave WA3 5 B2
Allen Dr CW9 103 C1
Allen Pl CW1 190 A3
Allen Rd WA7 48 B4
Allen St Bollington SK10 88 A4
Allen St *continued*
Macclesfield SK11 112 C4
Warrington WA2 16 A3
Allenby Rd M44 11 B2
Allendale WA7 50 A3
Allerby Way WA3 3 C4
Allerton Rd WA8 13 A1
Allgreave Cl CW10 151 B3
Allington Pl CH4 141 C4
Allman Cl CW1 189 C4
Allotment Rd M44 11 B3
Allport La CH62 43 B4
Allport Rd CH62,CH63 43 B4
Allports The CH62 43 B4
Allumbrook Ave CW4 130 B2
Allysum Ct WA7 49 C2
Alma Ave CW1 190 B3
Alma Cl
Macclesfield SK11 112 A4
Scholar Green ST7 194 C4
Alma La SK9 60 A4
Alma Rd SK7 37 A4
Alma St Chester CH2 118 C1
Newton-le-W WA12 2 A2
Stalybridge SK15 242 E2
Almeda Rd L24 21 A1
Almer Dr WA5 15 B3
Almond Ave Crewe CW1 190 C3
Runcorn WA7 49 B4
Almond Cl SK3 240 C4
Almond Dr WA5 6 C3
Almond Gr
Warrington WA1 17 A4
Weaverham CW8 102 C4
Widnes WA8 22 B4
Almond Pl ST5 210 C1
Almond Tree Cl L24 21 C1
Almond Wlk M31 11 B2
Almshouses CW11 175 B3
Alnwick Dr CH65 70 B1
Alpass Ave WA5 16 A4
Alpine St WA12 2 A2
Alport Rd SY13 226 A1
Alpraham Cres CH2 118 C3
Alric Wlk M22 33 C4
Alsager Highfields Com Prim Sch ST7 193 B2
Alsager Rd Audley ST7 209 B3
Haslington CW11 192 B4
Alsager Sch ST7 193 A2
Alsager Sta ST7 193 C2
Alsfeld Way SK22 39 A4
Alstone Dr WA14 238 A6
Alt WA8 12 A1
Alt Wlk CW7 127 A1
Alton Dr SK10 87 C1
Alton Rd SK9 59 C4
Alton St CW2 190 A2
Altrincham Bsns Pk WA14 238 B7
Altrincham CE Prim Sch WA14 238 D5
Altrincham General Hospl WA14 238 D4
Altrincham Gram Sch for Boys WA14 238 D2
Altrincham Gram Sch for Girls
Altrincham WA14 238 B3
Altrincham WA14 238 C3
Altrincham Prep Sch WA14 238 D1
Altrincham Priory Hospl WA15 32 A4
Altrincham Rd Styal SK9 33 C2
Wilmslow SK9 33 B1
Altrincham Sta WA15 238 E4
Altringham Ret Pk WA14 238 C7
Alum Ct CW4 130 B1
Alun Cres CH4 141 A3
Alundale Rd CW7 126 B2
Alvanley Cres SK3 240 C2
Alvanley Dr WA6 73 B1
Alvanley Prim Sch WA6 73 B1
Alvanley Rd
Ellesmere Port CH66 69 C2
Helsby WA6 73 B1
Alvanley Rise CW9 104 A3
Alvanley Terr WA6 74 A4
Alvanley View CH2 72 A2
Alvanley Way CH66 69 C2
Alvaston Ave SK4 240 B6
Alvaston Bsns Pk CW5 204 C4
Alvaston Rd CW5 204 C3
Alvaston Wlk CW2 189 C1
Alverstone Cl WA5 14 B4
Alverton Cl WA8 22 B4
Alveston Cl SK10 86 C1
Alveston Dr SK9 60 B4
Alvingham Cl 6 CW9 104 A4
Alvis Rd CH5 116 A2
Alwyn Gdns CH2 118 C4
Alyn Rd CH2 96 C1
Alyndale Rd CH4 140 B3
Ambassador Pl WA15 238 E5
Amberleigh Cl WA4 27 A2
Amberley Dr WA15 32 A4
Amberley Rd SK11 112 A3
Ambleside Chester CH2 119 A3
Stalybridge SK15 242 D3
Ambleside Cl
Bebington CH62 43 C4
Macclesfield SK11 111 C3
Runcorn WA7 49 C3
Winsford CW7 126 B2
Wistaston CW2 189 C1
Ambleside Cres WA2 8 B2

Ambleside Ct
Congleton CW12 ....155 C1
Gatley SK8 ....239 C5
Stalybridge SK15 ....242 D3
Ambleside Rd CH65 ....70 B1
Ambrose Ct WA1 ....16 B3
Ambuscade Cl CW1 ....190 C3
Amelia Cl WA8 ....13 A2
Amelia St 3 Hyde SK14 ..241 E6
Warrington WA2 ....16 B4
Amersham Cl SK10 ....87 B2
Amis Gr WA3 ....3 C4
Amy St CW2 ....190 B2
Anchor Cl WA7 ....50 B3
Anchor Ct WA1 ....16 B3
Anchorage The
5 Lymm WA13 ....18 B2
Neston CH64 ....66 B4
Waverton CH3 ....143 A3
Ancoats Rd WA16,SK9 ....83 C4
Anderson Cl Crewe CW1 .191 A2
Warrington WA2 ....9 A1
Anderson Ct CH62 ....43 B3
Anderson St 10 SK11 ....112 B4
Andersons Ind Est WA8 ..23 A3
Anderton Boat Lift & Nature Park* CW9 ....78 B2
Anderton Way SK9 ....34 B2
Andertons La SK10,SK11 ..86 A1
Andover Cl WA2 ....8 C1
Andover Rd WA11 ....1 C4
Andrew Cl WA8 ....22 B4
Andrew Cres CH4 ....237 C1
Andrew Gr SK10 ....113 A4
Andrew La SK6 ....37 C4
Andrew St Hyde SK14 ....241 F7
Stockport SK4 ....240 D6
Andrew's Cl CH3 ....121 A1
Andrew's Wlk CH60 ....41 A4
Andromeda Way WA9 ....6 A4
Anemone Way WA9 ....6 A4
Anfield Rd Cheadle SK8 ...239 F3
Sale M33 ....242 C7
Angel St M34 ....241 A8
Angelina Cl CW11 ....174 B4
Anglers Rest M44 ....11 C3
Anglesea Ave SK2 ....240 F2
Anglesey Cl 6 CH65 ....70 B1
Anglesey Dr SK12 ....36 C3
Anglesey Gr SK8 ....240 A2
Anglesey Water SK12 ....36 C3
Angus Gr CW10 ....128 B1
Angus Rd CH63 ....43 B3
Angus Wlk SK10 ....86 C1
Ankers Knowl La SK11 ..114 B4
Ankers La SK11 ....114 B3
Ann Cl CH66 ....69 B4
Ann St Dukinfield SK14 ...241 C7
Northwich CW9 ....79 B1
Runcorn WA7 ....23 A2
Stockport SK5 ....240 E8
Ann St W WA8 ....23 A4
Annable Rd M44 ....11 C4
Annan Cl 2 CW12 ....157 A1
Anne Ct ST7 ....210 D3
Anne's Way CH4 ....237 C1
Annette Ave WA12 ....2 A3
Annie St WA2 ....16 B3
Annions La CW5 ....205 C1
Annis Cl SK9 ....60 A1
Annis Rd SK9 ....60 A1
Ansdell Rd WA8 ....13 B1
Ansley Gr SK4 ....240 B7
Anson Cl Bramhall SK7 ....35 C3
Warrington WA2 ....8 C1
Anson Engine Mus The* SK12 ....37 B2
Anson Rd Handforth SK9 ...34 C1
Poynton SK12 ....37 A2
Anthony Dr CW9 ....126 C4
Anthony's Way CH60 ....41 A4
Antons Rd L26 ....21 A3
Antony Rd WA4 ....16 A1
Antrim Cl WA11 ....1 B3
Antrim Dr CH66 ....69 C1
Antrim Rd WA2 ....8 A1
Antrobus St CW12 ....156 B2
Anvil Cl Haslington CW11 .174 C2
Saughall CH1 ....94 A1
Apple Market St 10 CW9 ....103 C4
Apple Tree Cl L24 ....21 C1
Apple Tree Gr CH66 ....94 C4
Appleby Cl
Macclesfield SK11 ....111 C3
Stockport SK3 ....240 D1
Widnes WA8 ....22 B4
Appleby Gr CH62 ....43 B3
Appleby Rd Gatley SK8 ...239 B4
Warrington WA2 ....8 B2
Appleby Wlk 5 WA8 ....22 B4
Applecroft ST5 ....210 C1
Applecross Cl WA3 ....10 A3
Appledale Dr CH1 ....95 A4
Applefield CW8 ....103 B4
Appleford Cl WA4 ....26 C4
Appleton Cl CW12 ....178 C4
Appleton Ct M33 ....242 B6
Appleton Dr CH65 ....69 C2
Appleton Hall Gdns WA4 .26 C3
Appleton Mews 1 WA13 .18 B2
Appleton Rd
Altrincham WA15 ....238 F1
Chester CH2 ....118 C3
Widnes WA8 ....13 A1
Appleton St
Northwich CW8 ....78 B1
Widnes WA8 ....23 A4
Appleton Thorn Prim Sch WA4 ....27 B2
Appleton Thorn Trad Est WA4 ....27 B3
Appleton Village WA8 ....13 A1
Appleton Wlk 8 SK9 ....34 C1
Appletree Gr WA2 ....8 C1
Appleyards La CH4 ....141 C4
April Rise SK10 ....87 A1
Apsley Cl WA14 ....238 B1
Apsley Gr WA14 ....238 B1
Apsley St SK1 ....240 F5
Arabis Gdns WA9 ....6 A4
Aragon Ct WA7 ....24 B2
Aragon Gn CH1 ....117 C3
Aran Cl L24 ....21 B1
Arbour Cl
Macclesfield SK10 ....87 B2
Northwich CW9 ....104 B4
Arbour Cres SK10 ....87 B2
Arbour Mews SK10 ....87 B2
Arbour St ST7 ....210 B3
Arbourhay St SK10 ....87 C1
Arbury Ave SK3 ....240 A3
Arbury La WA2 ....8 B3
Arcade The
Ellesmere Port CH65 ....70 A3
3 Northwich CW9 ....103 C4
Archer Ave WA4 ....16 C1
Archer Cl SK10 ....87 C4
Archers Gn CH62 ....43 C2
Archers Way Blacon CH1 .118 A2
Ellesmere Port CH66 ....69 C1
Arclid Cl SK9 ....34 C1
Arclid Ct 10 CW12 ....156 C2
Arclid Green Ind Est CW11 ....176 A4
Arcon Pl WA14 ....238 A6
Arden WA8 ....12 A1
Arden Cl Gatley SK8 ....34 B4
Tarvin CH3 ....121 B2
Warrington WA3 ....10 A3
Arden Ct CW12 ....179 A4
Arden Dr CH64 ....66 C3
Arden Est SK22 ....39 B4
Arden St SK22 ....39 B4
Ardenbrook Rise SK10 ....86 C3
Ardens Mdw CW6 ....168 B4
Ardern Gr SK1 ....240 F4
Ardern Lea WA6 ....73 B1
Arderne Ave CW2 ....190 A1
Arderne Ho CH2 ....118 C4
Arderne Pl 6 SK9 ....60 A1
Ardleigh Cl CW1 ....189 C4
Argosy Dr M90 ....32 C4
Argyle Ct 9 WA16 ....57 A1
Argyll Ave Bebington CH62 .43 B2
Chester CH4 ....141 A4
Argyll Cl SK10 ....87 A1
Argyll Rd SK8 ....239 F5
Argyll St OL6 ....242 B3
Ariel Wlk 11 WA3 ....3 C4
Arkenshaw Rd WA3 ....9 A4
Arkenstone Cl WA8 ....12 B1
Arkle Ave SK8,SK9 ....34 C2
Arkle Ct 10 CH3 ....119 A1
Arklow Dr L24 ....21 B1
Arkwright Cl CW7 ....149 A4
Arkwright Ct WA7 ....23 C2
Arkwright Rd WA7 ....23 C2
Arley Ave WA4 ....26 B4
Arley Cl Alsager ST7 ....193 B2
Altrincham WA14 ....238 D8
Chester CH2 ....118 C3
Macclesfield SK11 ....112 A4
Arley Dr WA8 ....12 A1
Arley End WA16 ....29 B2
Arley Hall & Gdns* CW9 ..54 B3
Arley Mere Cl SK8 ....239 F3
Arley Mossend La CW9 ...54 B1
Arley Pl CW2 ....206 A4
Arley Rd Antrobus CW9 ....54 A4
Appleton Thorn WA4 ....27 B2
Northwich CW9 ....104 B4
Arley Wlk CW11 ....174 B3
Arlies Cl SK15 ....242 D4
Arlies La SK15 ....242 E4
Arlies Prim Sch SK15 ...242 D4
Arlies St OL6 ....242 A4
Arlington Ave M34 ....241 A6
Arlington Cl CW2 ....206 B4
Arlington Cres SK9 ....59 C3
Arlington Dr
Golborne WA3,WN7 ....4 B4
Macclesfield SK11 ....112 A4
Poynton SK12 ....36 B2
Warrington WA5 ....14 C2
Arlington Rd SK8 ....239 C4
Arlington Way SK9 ....59 C3
Armadale Cl SK3 ....240 F1
Armentieres SK15 ....242 D1
Armistead Way CW4 ....130 A3
Armitage Rd WA14 ....238 D3
Armitstead Rd CW11 ....174 C2
Armitt St SK11 ....112 B4
Armour Ave WA2 ....8 A1
Armoury Court Mews 4 SK11 ....112 A3
Armoury St SK3 ....240 E4
Armoury Twrs 5 SK11 ...112 A3
Armstrong Cl
Audlem CW3 ....229 C2
Warrington WA3 ....9 B2
Armthorpe Dr CH66 ....69 B3
Arncliffe Dr WA5 ....6 C3
Arndale WA7 ....49 C3
Arnesby Ave M33 ....242 E7
Arnfield Rd SK3 ....240 D1
Arnhem Cres WA2 ....16 B4
Arnhem Way CH3 ....142 A3
Arnold Pl WA8 ....22 B4
Arnold St Nantwich CW5 ..204 C3
Stockport SK3 ....240 E3
Arnold's Cres CH4 ....139 A2
Arnolds Yd WA14 ....238 D5
Arnside Ave
Congleton CW12 ....156 A1
Haydock WA11 ....1 A3
Arnside Cl Gatley SK8 ....239 B4
High Lane SK6 ....37 C4
Winsford CW7 ....126 B1
Arnside Dr SK14 ....241 C8
Arnside Gr Sale M33 ....242 B8
Warrington WA4 ....16 A1
Arpley Rd WA1 ....16 A2
Arpley St WA1 ....16 A2
Arradon Ct CH2 ....118 C3
Arran Ave
Ellesmere Port CH65 ....70 B1
Sale M33 ....242 C5
Arran Cl
Holmes Chapel CW4 ....130 B1
Warrington WA2 ....9 A1
Arran Dr WA6 ....74 B3
Arrivals Way M90 ....33 A4
Arron Pl CW2 ....189 B2
Arrowcroft Rd CH3 ....119 C3
Arrowsmith Dr ST7 ....193 A2
Arrowsmith Rd WA11 ....1 C4
Arthill La WA14 ....30 A4
Arthog Dr WA15 ....31 C4
Arthog Rd WA15 ....31 C4
Arthur Ave CH65 ....70 B3
Arthur St Blacon CH1 ....118 A1
Crewe CW2 ....190 B1
Hyde SK14 ....241 C5
Lostock Gralam CW9 ....80 A1
Runcorn WA7 ....23 A1
Warrington WA2 ....16 A3
Artists La SK10 ....85 B4
Artle Rd CW2 ....206 B4
Arundel Ave SK7 ....36 B4
Arundel Cl
Knutsford WA16 ....82 A4
Macclesfield SK10 ....87 C1
Wistaston CW2 ....205 C4
Arundel Ct CH65 ....70 C2
Arundel Rd SK8 ....35 A3
Arundel St OL6 ....242 B3
Arundell Cl WA5 ....6 C3
Ascol Dr WA16 ....80 B2
Ascot Ave WA7 ....49 A3
Ascot Cl Congleton CW12 .156 B2
Macclesfield SK10 ....87 B2
Warrington WA4 ....17 B1
Warrington, Martinscroft WA1 ....17 C4
Ascot Dr CH66 ....69 C2
Ash Ave Altrincham WA14 .238 A5
Cheadle SK8 ....239 E5
Irlam M44 ....11 B3
Newton-le-W WA12 ....2 B1
Ash Cl Ellesmere Port CH66 .69 C1
Holmes Chapel CW4 ....130 B2
Malpas SY14 ....213 B3
Tarporley CW6 ....146 B1
Ash Ct SK4 ....240 B7
Ash Gr
Altrincham, Bowdon WA14 .238 C1
Altrincham, Timperley WA15 ....238 F7
Chester CH4 ....141 A3
Congleton CW12 ....156 A2
Ellesmere Port CH66 ....69 B3
Gatley SK8 ....34 A4
Golborne WA3 ....3 A4
Handforth SK9 ....34 B2
Knutsford WA16 ....57 B1
Macclesfield SK11 ....112 B2
Middlewich CW10 ....151 B4
Nantwich CW5 ....204 C2
Rode Heath ST7 ....193 C4
Runcorn WA7 ....49 B4
Stalybridge SK15 ....242 C3
Warrington WA4 ....16 B2
Weaverham CW8 ....102 C4
Widnes WA8 ....22 B4
Ash Grove Sch SK11 ....112 B2
Ash Hay La CH2 ....96 B1
Ash Ho 8 CW11 ....175 A3
Ash House La CW8 ....77 B4
Ash La Warrington WA4 ....26 C4
Widnes WA8 ....22 A4
Ash Lawn Ct CH2 ....118 B2
Ash Lo SK12 ....36 B2
Ash Priors WA8 ....12 B2
Ash Rd Crewe CW1 ....190 B3
Cuddington CW8 ....101 C1
Elton CH2 ....72 B2
Haydock WA11 ....1 C4
Hollinfare WA3 ....11 A1
Lymm WA13 ....18 B2
Partington M31 ....11 B2
Poynton SK12 ....36 C2
Warrington WA5 ....14 C2
Winwick WA2 ....8 A3
Ash St Northwich CW9 ....79 A1
Stockport SK3 ....240 B4
Ash Terr SK11 ....112 B2
Ash View ST7 ....195 A1
Ash Way CH60 ....41 A3
Ashbank CW9 ....104 B4
Ashberry Cl SK9 ....60 B4
Ashberry Dr WA4 ....27 A3
Ashbourne Ave
Cheadle SK8 ....239 F6
Ashbourne Ave continued
Runcorn WA7 ....49 A3
Ashbourne Cl CH66 ....94 C4
Ashbourne Dr SK6 ....37 C3
Ashbourne Mews 1 SK11 ....111 C4
Ashbourne Rd
Hazel Grove SK7 ....36 C4
Warrington WA5 ....15 A3
Ashbrook Ave WA7 ....49 C2
Ashbrook Cl SK8 ....239 B1
Ashbrook Cres WA2 ....16 B4
Ashbrook Dr SK10 ....87 A3
Ashbrook Rd
Bollington SK10 ....87 C4
Nether Alderley SK10 ....85 C3
Ashburn Gr SK4 ....240 D7
Ashburn Rd SK4 ....240 D7
Ashburton Rd SK3 ....240 E1
Ashbury Cl WA7 ....24 B1
Ashbury Dr WA11 ....1 B4
Ashby Dr CW11 ....174 B3
Ashby Pl CH2 ....237 C4
Ashcroft SK9 ....59 C3
Ashcroft Ave CW2 ....206 A2
Ashcroft Rd WA13 ....19 A2
Ashdale Cl ST7 ....193 B3
Ashdale Dr SK8 ....239 B2
Ashdene Prim Sch SK9 ...59 C3
Ashdene Rd SK9 ....59 C3
Ashdown La WA3 ....10 A3
Ashdown Rd
Ollerton WA16 ....82 C3
Stockport SK4 ....240 C7
Ashenhurst Rd ST7 ....193 C2
Ashenough Rd ST7 ....210 B3
Asher Ct WA4 ....27 B2
Ashfield Cl WA13 ....19 A2
Ashfield Cres
Bebington CH62 ....43 B4
Blacon CH1 ....117 B3
Cheadle SK8 ....239 D6
Ashfield Dr SK10 ....87 A1
Ashfield Gr M44 ....11 C3
Ashfield Ho 6 CH64 ....66 C4
Ashfield Rd
Altrincham WA15 ....238 E3
Bebington CH62 ....43 B4
Cheadle SK8 ....239 D6
Ellesmere Port CH65 ....70 B3
Sale M33 ....242 B7
Ashfield Rd N 8 CH65 ....70 B3
Ashfield St 4 CW10 ....151 B4
Ashford Cl SK9 ....34 B2
Ashford Rd SK9 ....60 A2
Ashford Way WA8 ....13 B1
Ashgate La CW9 ....79 C3
Ashgrove CW7 ....149 B4
Ashlands Frodsham WA6 ...74 B4
Sale M33 ....242 A7
Ashlea Dr CW5 ....205 C3
Ashleigh Cl CH4 ....140 C3
Ashley CE Prim Sch WA15 ....31 C3
Ashley Cl WA4 ....17 B2
Ashley Ct
Altrincham WA15 ....238 E1
Frodsham WA6 ....74 A4
Holt LL13 ....196 B4
Ashley Dr Bramhall SK7 ....35 B3
Hartford CW8 ....103 A3
Ashley Gdns Clutton CH3 .182 B1
High Lane SK6 ....37 B4
3 Hyde SK14 ....241 E5
Ashley Gn WA8 ....22 B4
Ashley Grange CW9 ....103 C2
Ashley Mdw CW1 ....191 B3
Ashley Mews 2 SK14 ....241 E5
Ashley Mill La N WA14 ....31 C4
Ashley Rd
Altrincham WA15 ....238 E2
Ashley WA14,WA15 ....31 C4
Handforth SK9 ....34 A1
Mere WA16 ....56 B4
Runcorn WA7 ....23 B1
Ashley Ret Pk WA8 ....23 A4
Ashley Sch WA8 ....12 B1
Ashley St SK14 ....241 E8
Ashley Sta WA15 ....31 C3
Ashley Way WA8 ....23 A4
Ashley Way W WA8 ....22 C4
Ashleymill La WA14 ....31 B4
Ashleys The 6 SK4 ....240 B7
Ashmead Cl ST7 ....193 C2
Ashmead Mews ST7 ....193 C2
Ashmore Ave SK3 ....239 F7
Ashmore Cl
Middlewich CW10 ....151 B3
Warrington WA3 ....10 A2
Ashmore's La ST7 ....193 B2
Ashmuir Cl Blacon CH1 ...117 C2
Crewe CW1 ....190 A3
Ashness Dr SK7 ....35 C4
Ashridge St WA7 ....22 C2
Ashton Ave
Altrincham WA14 ....238 E6
Macclesfield SK10 ....86 B1
Ashton Cl Bebington CH62 .43 C2
Congleton CW12 ....157 A1
Frodsham WA6 ....49 B1
Middlewich CW10 ....151 B3
Northwich CW9 ....103 C2
Runcorn WA7 ....48 C3
Ashton Ct WA6 ....49 B1
Ashton Dr WA6 ....49 B1
Ashton Hayes Prim Sch CH3 ....121 C4
Ashton Ho SK14 ....241 E8
Ashton House SK14 ....241 E8
Ashton La CH3 ....121 C3
Ashton Rd Manley WA6 ....99 C2
Newton-le-W WA12 ....2 B3
Norley WA6 ....100 A2
Ashton Sixth Form Coll OL6 ....242 B3
Ashton St WA2 ....16 A3
Ashtree Cl Neston CH64 ...67 A4
Prestbury SK10 ....87 B4
Ashtree Croft CH64 ....68 A4
Ashtree Dr CH64 ....67 A4
Ashtree Farm Ct CH64 ....68 A4
Ashurst Dr SK3 ....240 B1
Ashville Ct CW2 ....206 A4
Ashville Ind Est WA7 ....49 C2
Ashville Way WA7 ....49 C2
Ashwood WA14 ....31 A4
Ashwood Ave
Golborne WA3 ....3 B4
Warrington WA1 ....16 C4
Ashwood Cl Barnton CW8 ..78 A2
Ellesmere Port CH66 ....69 B1
Ashwood Cres CW8 ....78 A2
Ashwood Ct CH2 ....119 A2
Ashwood La CH2 ....96 A3
Ashwood Rd SK12 ....38 B3
Ashworth Cl WA14 ....238 B1
Ashworth Pk WA16 ....81 C4
Asiatic Cotts CH5 ....116 A2
Askerbank La SK11 ....159 A1
Askett Cl WA11 ....1 B4
Askrigg Ave CH66 ....69 A3
Aspen Cl
Ellesmere Port CH66 ....69 C1
Heswall CH60 ....41 B4
Kidsgrove ST7 ....195 C2
Stockport SK4 ....240 A5
Aspen Gn M34 ....241 A6
Aspen Gr Saughall CH1 ....117 A4
Warrington WA1 ....17 A4
Aspen Way Chester CH2 ..119 A2
High Lane SK6 ....38 A4
Aspen Wood SK14 ....241 F7
Aspens The
Cuddington CW8 ....101 B3
Gatley SK8 ....239 A6
Aspinall Cl WA2 ....9 A2
Aspull Cl WA3 ....9 B2
Asquith Cl CW1 ....191 B3
Assheton Cl WA12 ....2 A2
Assheton Wlk L24 ....21 C1
Astbury Cl
2 Altrincham WA15 ....238 E6
Crewe CW1 ....190 A4
Golborne WA3 ....4 A4
Kidsgrove ST7 ....195 B2
Astbury Cres SK3 ....240 D2
Astbury Dr CW8 ....78 A2
Astbury Lane Ends CW12 ....178 C4
Astbury Mere Ctry Pk* CW12 ....156 A1
Astbury St CW12 ....156 B1
Aster Cres WA7 ....49 C3
Aster Rd WA11 ....1 C4
Aster Wlk M31 ....11 C1
Astle Cl CW10 ....151 B4
Astle Ct SK11 ....84 A2
Astley Cl Knutsford WA16 ..82 B4
Warrington WA4 ....16 A2
Widnes WA8 ....12 B2
Astley Ct M44 ....11 C4
Astley Gr SK15 ....242 C3
Astley Rd Irlam M44 ....11 C4
Stalybridge SK15 ....242 C2
Astley St SK4 ....240 E5
Astmoor Bridge La WA7 ..23 C1
Astmoor East Intc WA7 ...24 A2
Astmoor Ind Est WA7 ....23 C2
Astmoor La WA7 ....23 C1
Astmoor Prim Sch WA7 ..23 C1
Aston Ave CW7 ....126 A1
Aston by Sutton Prim Sch WA7 ....50 B1
Aston Cl SK3 ....240 C2
Aston Ct WA1 ....9 B1
Aston Fields Rd WA7 ....50 C2
Aston Gn WA7 ....50 C3
Aston La Runcorn WA7 .....50 C3
Sutton WA7 ....50 B1
Woore CW3 ....232 C1
Aston La N WA7 ....50 C2
Aston La S WA7 ....50 C2
Aston Rd ST5 ....210 B1
Aston Way
Middlewich CW10 ....128 C1
13 Wilmslow SK9 ....34 B3
Astor Dr WA4 ....26 C4
Astule Dr SK11 ....112 A4
Atcherley Cl CW5 ....218 C4
Athelbrae Cl CW8 ....103 C4
Atherton Inf Sch CH65 ....69 C3
Atherton La M44 ....11 C3
Atherton Rd CH65 ....69 C3
Atherton St SK3 ....240 D4
Athey St SK11 ....112 B4
Athey St Mill SK11 ....112 B4
Athlone Ave SK8 ....240 C1
Athlone Rd WA2 ....8 A1
Athol Cl Bebington CH62 ...43 C3
Newton-le-W WA12 ....1 C2
Athol Dr CH62 ....43 C3
Athol Rd SK7 ....35 B3
Athol St SK4 ....240 D7

Atholl Ave CW2 190 B1
Atholl Cl SK10 87 A1
Atkinson Ho 2 M33 242 B7
Atkinson Rd M33 242 A7
Atlanta Ave M90 33 A4
Atlantic Bsns Ctr WA14 238 C7
Atlantic St WA14 238 B6
Attenbury's La WA14 238 E8
Attenbury's Park Est WA14 238 E8
Atterbury Cl WA8 12 B1
Attlee Ave WA3 5 B2
Attwood Cl CW1 191 B2
Attwood St ST7 195 A1
Atworth Terr CH64 67 C4
Aubourn Cl WA8 12 B2
Auburn Ave SK14 241 E5
Auckery Ave CH66 69 B2
Auckland Rd CH1 117 B2
Audie Murphy Rd WA5 15 A3
Audlem Cl WA7 49 C2
Audlem Dr CW9 104 A3
Audlem Rd Audlem CW3 230 A4
Hatherton CW5 219 B2
Nantwich CW5 204 C2
Woore CW3 232 A1
Audley Cres CH4 141 C3
Audley Rd Alsager ST7 193 C1
Barthomley CW2,ST7 208 C3
Newcastle-u-L ST7,ST5 210 A1
Talke ST7 210 A3
Audley St
Ashton-u-Lyne OL6 242 B2
Crewe CW1 190 B3
Audley St W CW1 190 B3
Audre Cl WA5 14 B3
Aughton Way CH4 139 B2
Augusta Dr SK10 87 A2
Austell Rd 3 M22 33 B4
Austen Cl 1 CW11 174 B3
Austen Dr WA2 8 A3
Austen Ho SK10 86 C1
Austin Cl CW7 149 B3
Austin St CW9 79 B1
Austine Hill CH3 144 B4
Austral Ave WA1 17 B4
Australia La WA4 17 B1
Autumn Ave WA16 57 B1
Avalon Dr M20 239 C8
Avebury Cl Golborne WA3 3 C4
Widnes WA8 13 C2
Avens Rd M31 11 C2
Avenue One CW1 207 B4
Avenue St 3 SK1 240 F6
Avenue The
Alderley Edge SK9 60 A1
Alsager ST7 193 B2
Altrincham WA15 31 C4
Bebington CH62 43 B4
Comberbach CW9 78 B4
Gatley SK8 239 A1
Great Barrow CH3 120 C4
High Legh WA16 29 B3
Kidsgrove ST7 194 C1
Lymm WA13 18 B1
Marston CW9 79 A2
Newton-le-W WA12 2 B2
Sandbach CW11 174 C4
Tarporley CW6 146 B1
Avenue Two CW1 207 B4
Avery Cl WA2 8 C1
Avery Cres WA11 1 B4
Avery Rd WA11 1 B4
Avery Sq WA11 1 B4
Aviator Way SK9 33 B4
Aviemore Dr WA2 9 A2
Avocet Cl
Newton-le-W WA12 2 B2
Warrington WA2 8 B2
Avocet Dr
Altrincham WA14 238 B8
Winsford CW7 149 B3
Avon WA8 12 A1
Avon Ave WA5 14 C2
Avon Cl Kidsgrove ST7 195 A1
Macclesfield SK10 87 A1
Neston CH64 66 C3
Avon Ct ST7 193 B3
Avon Dr Congleton CW12 156 C1
Crewe CW1 191 A3
Avon Rd Altrincham WA15 31 C4
Culcheth WA3 5 A1
Gatley SK8 34 B4
Avon St SK3 240 E3
Avon Wlk CW7 127 A1
Avondale CH65 70 A1
Avondale Ave CH62 43 C3
Avondale Dr WA8 12 A1
Avondale High Sch SK3 240 B3
Avondale Ind Est SK3 240 B3
Avondale Lodge M33 242 B5
Avondale Rd Haydock WA11 1 B4
Stockport SK3 240 C4
Avondale Rise SK9 60 B3
Avonlea Cl CH4 140 C3
Avonside Way SK11 112 B3
Avro Way M90 32 C4
Aycliffe Wlk 6 WA8 22 B4
Aylesbury Cl
Ellesmere Port CH66 69 B2
Macclesfield SK10 87 B2
Aylesby Cl WA16 57 A1
Aylsham Cl WA8 12 B2
Aylwin Dr M33 242 C5
Ayrshire Cl CW10 128 B1
Ayrshire Way CW12 157 A1
Aysgarth Ave
Cheadle SK8 239 C6
Crewe CW1 173 A1
Romiley SK6 241 D4
Ayshford Cl WA14 238 B6
Azalea Gr WA7 49 C2

B

Babbacombe Rd WA5 14 C2
Babbage Rd CH5 116 A2
Bache Ave CH2 118 B3
Bache Dr CH2 118 B3
Bache Hall Ct CH2 118 B3
Bache Hall Est CH2 118 B3
Bache St CH2 118 B3
Bachefield Ave CH3 142 A3
Bachelor's Ct CH3 142 A4
Bachelor's La CH3 142 A4
Back Bridge St WA12 2 A2
Back Brook Pl WA4 16 C2
Back Crosland Terr WA6 73 A1
Back Cross La
Congleton CW12 179 A4
Newton-le-W WA12 2 A2
Back Eastford Rd WA4 16 A1
Back Eddisbury Rd SK11 113 B4
Back Forshaw St WA2 16 B4
Back Heathcote St ST7 195 A1
Back High St WA7 23 A1
Back Jodrell St SK22 39 A4
Back Knowl St SK15 242 E2
Back La Alpraham CW6 169 B3
Altrincham WA15 32 A2
Alvanley WA6 73 B1
Bate Heath CW9 54 B4
Beeston CH3 167 B1
Betley CW2 208 B1
Brereton Green CW11 153 B3
Burtonwood WA5 6 B4
Congleton CW12 156 A2
Duddon CW6 145 A3
Eaton (nr Congleton) CW12 156 C4
High Legh WA14 29 C3
Lower Peover WA16 106 A4
Marton CW12,SK11 133 C1
No Man's Heath SY14 214 A2
Partington WA14 20 B3
Plumley WA16 81 A1
Shavington CW2 206 C2
Smallwood CW11 176 B4
Threapwood SY14 222 C4
Warrington WA5 14 A2
Whitley WA4 52 C2
Wybunbury CW5 220 B3
Back Lanes CW6 146 A1
Back Legh St WA12 2 A2
Back Market St WA12 2 A2
Back Massie St SK8 239 D6
Back Paradise St 17 SK11 112 B4
Back Park St CW12 156 C1
Back Queen St CH1 237 B3
Back River St CW12 156 B2
Back Union Rd SK22 39 B4
Back Wallgate 27 SK11 112 B4
Back Water St 2 SK1 240 F6
Backford Cl WA7 50 B3
Backford Gdns CH1 94 C4
Badbury Cl WA11 1 B4
Badcock's La CW6 185 C2
Baddeley Cl SK3 240 D1
Baddiley Cl CW5 203 B1
Baddiley Hall La CW5 217 A4
Baddiley La CW5 203 B1
Baddington La CW5 204 B1
Badger Ave CW1 190 A3
Badger Bait CH64 66 C3
Badger Cl WA7 50 A3
Badger Ho SK10 87 B1
Badger Rd
Macclesfield SK10 87 B1
Prestbury SK10 87 A4
Badgers Cl
Christleton CH3 142 C4
Ellesmere Port CH66 94 C4
Winsford CW7 126 A1
Badgers Pk CH64 66 C3
Badgers Set CW8 101 B3
Badgers Wlk CH2 95 C1
Badgers Wood CW2 205 C4
Badgersrake La
Ellesmere Port CH66 68 C3
Ledsham CH66 68 B2
Bag La
Cuddington CW8,WA6 101 C4
Norley WA6 101 A3
Bagley La CW3 230 A1
Bagmere Cl
Brereton Green CW11 153 C2
Sandbach CW11 174 C4
Bagmere La CW11 154 A3
Bagnall Cl WA5 15 B3
Bagot Ave WA5 15 C4
Bagstock Ave SK12 36 C1
Baguley Ave WA8 22 A3
Baguley Cres SK3 240 D2
Baguley La M33 242 E5
Baguley Rd M33 242 E6
Bahama Cl WA11 1 B4
Bahama Rd WA11 1 B4
Bailey Ave CH65 69 C3
Bailey Bridge Cl CH2 118 B2
Bailey Bsns Pk SK10 87 C4
Bailey Cl CW1 190 B4
Bailey Cres
Congleton CW12 157 A2
Sandbach CW11 175 B3
Bailey Ct ST7 193 C2
Bailey La M31 11 C2
Bailey Wlk WA14 31 B4
Bailey's Bank ST8 179 B2
Bailey's La Hale L24 21 A1
Halewood L26 21 A4
Baileys Cl WA8 13 A3
Bainbridge Ave WA3 3 C4
Baines Ave M44 11 C4
Baker Dr CH66 69 C2
Baker Rd WA7 48 B4
Baker St
Macclesfield SK11 112 B4
Stalybridge SK15 242 E1
Stockport SK4 240 E7
Baker's Ct CW7 126 C1
Baker's La CW7 126 C1
Bakers Pl WA2 16 A4
Bakers Villas The CW12 156 B1
Bakestondale Rd SK10 63 C2
Bakewell Cl CH66 94 C4
Bakewell Rd
Burtonwood WA5 7 A4
Hazel Grove SK7 36 C4
Bakewell St SK3 240 D3
Bala Cl WA5 7 C1
Baldock Cl WA4 17 B2
Baldon Cres ST7 193 B3
Balfour Cl CW1 191 B2
Balfour Rd WA14 238 D7
Balfour St WA7 22 C1
Balham Cl WA8 13 A2
Balharry Ave WA11 1 C4
Ball La Bollington SK10 87 B3
Kingsley WA6 75 C2
Ball Pathway WA8 12 C1
Ballantyne Way 10 WA3 3 C4
Ballater Cres CH3 119 A1
Ballater Dr WA2 8 C2
Balliol Cl Romiley SK6 241 C4
Sutton Lane Ends SK11 112 C2
Balmoral Ave
Crewe CW2 190 A1
Northwich CW9 104 A3
Balmoral Cl
Knutsford WA16 57 A1
Willaston (nr Nantwich) CW5 205 B2
Winsford CW7 126 B2
Balmoral Cres SK10 87 C1
Balmoral Ct 3 SK4 240 A7
Balmoral Dr Helsby WA6 73 A2
High Lane SK6 37 C4
Holmes Chapel CW4 130 A1
Poynton SK12 36 B2
Sale WA14 238 F8
Stalybridge SK15 242 D3
Balmoral Gdns CH65 70 B2
Balmoral Pk CH1 118 A2
Balmoral Rd
Altrincham WA15 238 E4
Stockport SK4 240 A7
Warrington WA4 16 C1
Widnes WA8 13 A2
Balmoral Way SK9 60 A3
Baltic Rd WA14 238 A6
Bamber Ave M33 242 E5
Bamburgh Ct CH65 70 C2
Bamford Cl Gatley SK8 34 B4
Runcorn WA7 49 B4
Bamford St
Macclesfield SK10 87 C1
Stockport SK1 240 F4
Banastre Dr WA12 2 C2
Banbury Cl SK10 87 C1
Banbury Ct CW6 146 B1
Banbury Dr
Altrincham WA14 238 E8
Warrington WA5 15 B3
Banbury St
Kidsgrove ST7 194 B1
11 Stockport SK1 240 F5
Bancroft CW8 76 C2
Bancroft Rd WA8 13 B1
Bandon Cl L24 21 B1
Banff Ave CH63 43 B3
Bangor Cl CH66 94 C4
Bangor Rd SK8 239 F6
Bangor St
Ashton-u-Lyne OL6,SK15 242 B2
Stockport SK5 240 F8
Bank Cl Chester CH2 118 C3
Macclesfield SK11 112 C4
Neston CH64 67 A3
Bank Coole La CW5 228 C3
Bank Ct 5 ST7 195 A1
Bank Farm Mews SY14 214 C3
Bank Gdns WA5 14 C2
Bank Ho CW7 126 B1
Bank House La
Helsby WA6 73 B2
Smallwood CW11 177 A3
Bank La Burland CW5 203 B4
Congleton CW12 134 B1
Rainow SK10 89 B3
Bank Mews WA6 73 B2
Bank Rd
Connah's Quay CH5 91 B1
Romiley SK6 241 A3
Bank Side CW8 77 B1
Bank Sq SK9 60 A4
Bank St Cheadle SK8 239 E6
Congleton CW12 156 C1
Hollinfare WA3 11 A3
Bank St *continued*
Hyde SK14 241 D7
Kidsgrove ST7 195 B2
Newton-le-W WA12 1 C2
Sale M33 242 C7
18 Warrington WA1 16 A3
Widnes WA8 23 A2
Bank The ST7 195 A4
Bank View CW4 107 C1
Bankes' La WA7 48 C3
Bankfield Ave Irlam M44 11 B3
Stockport SK4 240 C5
Wistaston CW2 206 A4
Bankfield Rd
Cheadle SK8 239 F1
Widnes WA8 12 B1
Bankfield Sch The WA8 12 B1
Bankfield St SK5 240 E7
Bankfield Trad Est SK5 240 E8
Bankfields Dr CH65,CH62 44 A3
Bankhall La WA14,WA15 31 C4
Bankhall Rd SK4 240 A6
Bankhey CH64 66 C3
Bankhouse Dr CW12 157 A3
Banklands Cl M44 11 B3
Banks Cl CW12 156 B2
Banks Cres WA4 16 C2
Banks Rd CH60 40 B4
Bankside Altrincham WA15 32 B3
Runcorn WA7 50 C4
Bankside Cl
Barbridge CW5 187 B3
Handforth SK9 34 B1
Bankside Ct ST7 193 C3
Bankside Rd M20 239 B7
Banky Fields CW12 156 B1
Bann St SK3 240 E4
Bannacks Cl CW5 205 B3
Bannister Dr SK8 239 F2
Bannister St SK1 240 F3
Barbauld St WA1 16 A3
Barber Dr ST7 194 C4
Barber St SK11 112 C3
Barber's La Antrobus CW9 53 B3
Northwich CW8 103 C4
Barberry Cl WA14 238 B7
Barberry Wlk M31 11 C2
Barbondale Cl WA5 14 C4
Barbour Sq CH3 166 A1
Barbridge Mews CW5 187 B3
Barbridge Rd ST5 210 B1
Barcheston Rd SK8 239 C4
Barclay Rd SK12 36 C1
Bardell Cl SK12 36 B1
Bardsey Cl 5 CH65 70 B1
Bardsley Ave WA5 7 C1
Bardsley St SK4 240 D7
Barford Cl WA5 7 A1
Barford Dr Golborne WA3 4 A4
Handforth SK9 34 B1
Barford Grange CH66 68 B4
Barham Ct WA3 9 B2
Barhill Farm Cotts SY13 214 B1
Barington Dr WA7 50 C4
Baristow Cl CH2 237 B4
Bark St CW12 156 C1
Barker St Crewe CW2 190 B1
Nantwich CW5 204 C3
Barker's Hollow Rd WA4 51 B4
Barkhill Rd CH2 119 A4
Barley Castle Cl WA4 27 A2
Barley Croft Alsager ST7 193 C1
Cheadle SK8 239 F1
Chester CH3 142 A4
Barley Dr SK7 35 C4
Barley Mow Cl CH66 69 B1
Barley Rd WA4 17 B2
Barleycastle La WA4,CW9 27 B2
Barleycastle Trad Est WA4 27 B2
Barleycroft Terr ST7 194 C4
Barleyfields ST7 209 B1
Barleywood Cl CW2 206 A4
Barlow Dr CW7 148 C4
Barlow Fold SK6 241 D3
Barlow Fold Rd SK6 241 D3
Barlow Gr WA9 1 A1
Barlow Hill SK11 136 C1
Barlow Rd
Altrincham WA14 238 B7
Handforth SK9 34 A1
Moulton CW9 126 C4
Barlow Way CW11 175 A4
Barmouth Cl WA5 7 C1
Barn Croft WA6 73 B2
Barn Croft Rd L26 21 A4
Barn Ct CH3 182 B1
Barn La WA3 2 C4
Barn Mdw CW8 78 C1
Barn Rd CW12 156 B2
Barn St WA8 23 A3
Barn Way WA12 2 A2
Barnabas Ave CW1 189 C3
Barnaby Chase CH3 182 B1
Barnaby Rd SK12 36 B1
Barnack Cl WA1 17 A4
Barnacre Dr CH64 41 A1
Barnard Ave SK4 240 B6
Barnard Cl SK11 111 C3
Barnard St WA5 15 B2
Barnbridge Cl ST7 194 C4
Barnbrook Cl CW7 126 A1
Barncroft WA7 50 B4
Barncroft Cl SK11 84 A2
Barnes Ave
Stockport SK4 240 A6
Warrington WA2 9 A1
Barnes Cl Blacon CH1 117 C3
Barnes Cl *continued*
Haslington CW1 191 B2
Warrington WA5 15 A3
Widnes WA8 13 B1
Barnes Hospl SK8 239 C6
Barnes Rd WA8 13 B1
Barneston Rd WA8 13 C2
Barnett Ave WA12 1 C2
Barnett St SK11 112 A4
Barnett Wlk CW2 206 B4
Barnfield CH3 166 A1
Barnfield Ave
Romiley SK6 241 D3
Runcorn WA7 50 B3
Barnfield Cl CH66 69 B1
Barnfield Rd
Bollington SK10 87 C3
Warrington WA1 17 B4
Barngate Rd SK8 239 A6
Barnham Cl WA3 3 A4
Barnhill Grange CH3 183 A2
Barnhill Rd CH3 183 A1
Barnhouse La
Great Barrow CH3 120 C4
Mouldsworth CH3 98 A2
Barnmoore Cl SY14 213 A2
Barns La WA14 20 A3
Barns Pl WA15 32 B4
Barns The CW10 127 B3
Barnside Way
Macclesfield SK10 87 B2
Moulton CW9 126 C4
Barnstaple Way WA5 14 C2
Barnston Ct CH3 180 C1
Barnston Prim Sch CH60 41 B4
Barnston Rd CH60 41 B4
Barnston Towers Cl CH60 41 B4
Barnswood Cl WA4 17 B1
Barnton Cl WA3 3 B4
Barnton Prim Sch CW8 78 A2
Barnwell Ave WA3 4 B2
Barnwell Cl CW2 206 A4
Barnwood Dr CH4 140 C3
Baron Cl WA1 17 B4
Baron Gn SK8 34 B4
Baron's Cl WA8 22 B4
Baronet Mews WA4 16 A1
Baronet Rd WA4 16 A1
Baronia Pl 2 CW5 204 C3
Barons Cl WA7 23 C1
Barons Ct CH2 118 B2
Barons Quay Rd CW9 78 C1
Barons Rd
Shavington CW2 206 A2
Worleston CW5 188 C3
Barony Bldgs 1 CW5 204 C3
Barony Ct CW5 204 C3
Barony Employment Pk The CW5 204 C4
Barony Rd CW5 204 C4
Barony Terr CW5 204 C3
Barony Way CH4 140 C3
Barrack Hill SK6 241 A2
Barrack Hill Cl SK6 241 A3
Barrack Hill Prim Sch SK6 241 A2
Barracks La
Burwardsley CH3 184 B3
Macclesfield SK10 112 C4
Ravensmoor CW5 203 C1
Barracks Sq 3 SK11 112 A3
Barrastitch La CW8 101 C3
Barratt Rd ST7 193 C2
Barrel Well Hill CH2 118 C1
Barrie Gdns ST7 210 B4
Barrie Gr CW1 190 C2
Barrington Cl WA14 238 D6
Barrington Dr CW10 151 B4
Barrington Rd WA14 238 D5
Barrow Ave WA2 8 C1
Barrow CE Prim Sch CH3 120 B3
Barrow Hall Com Prim Sch WA5 14 C4
Barrow Hall Farm CH3 120 C3
Barrow Hall La WA5 14 C4
Barrow La
Altrincham WA15 32 A4
Culcheth WA2,WA3 3 B1
Great Barrow CH3 120 B3
Tarvin CH3 121 B2
Barrow Mdw SK8 34 C4
Barrow's Brow WA16 81 C1
Barrow's Green La WA8 13 C2
Barrow's Row WA8 13 A2
Barrowdale Rd WA3 3 A4
Barrows Cl CW1 190 A4
Barrule Cl WA4 26 B4
Barry Cl CH65 95 B4
Barry Rise WA14 238 A2
Barry St WA4 16 B2
Barrymore Ave WA4 16 C2
Barrymore Cres CW9 78 B4
Barrymore Ct WA4 17 A1
Barrymore Rd
Runcorn WA7 49 A4
Warrington WA4 17 A1
Weaverham CW8 77 C1
Barrymore Way CH63 43 A3
Bars The CH2 237 C2
Barsbank Cl WA13 18 B2
Barsbank La WA13 18 B2
Barshaw Gdns WA4 26 B2
Barston Ave CH65 69 C3
Bartegate WA7 50 A3
Bartholomew Way CH4 141 B3
Bartholomews Ct CH5 116 C3

Barthomley Cres CW2 ...189 B2
Barthomley Rd
Audley ST7 ...209 A1
Barthomley CW2 ...208 A4
Betley ST7 ...208 C2
Barton Ave WA4 ...17 A1
Barton Cl Runcorn WA7 ...50 B4
Wilmslow SK9 ...34 B1
Barton Ct CW7 ...126 C1
Barton Fold SK14 ...241 D5
Barton Rd
Barton CH3,SY14 ...181 B1
Congleton CW12 ...156 C2
Farndon CH3 ...180 C1
Barton St SK11 ...112 B3
Barton Stad CW7 ...126 C1
Bartons Pl 5 CW9 ...79 A1
Barwick Pl M33 ...242 A6
Barwood Ave ST7 ...194 A3
Basford Rd CW2 ...206 B4
Basford Way CW7 ...126 A1
Basil St SK4 ...240 E7
Baskervyle Cl CH60 ...41 A3
Baskervyle Rd CH60 ...41 A3
Baslow Dr Gatley SK8 ...34 B4
Hazel Grove SK7 ...36 C4
Basssett Cl CW5 ...205 B3
Batchelors Wing The CW10 ...127 B3
Bate's Mill La CW6 ...167 C3
Bateman Rd CW9 ...80 A1
Batemans Cl CW2 ...206 A4
Batemill Cl SK10 ...86 C1
Batemill La WA16,SK11 ...108 B3
Bates La WA6 ...73 B2
Bath Cres SK8 ...35 A3
Bath La CW3 ...230 A2
Bath Pl WA14 ...238 D2
Bath St Altrincham WA14 ...238 D2
Chester CH1 ...237 C2
Sandbach CW11 ...175 B3
Warrington WA1 ...16 A3
Bath Vale Cotts CW12 ...157 A2
Batherton Cl WA8 ...23 A4
Batherton La CW5 ...204 C1
Bathwood Dr CH64 ...66 C3
Batterbee Ct CW1 ...191 B3
Battersby La WA2 ...16 B3
Battersea Ct WA8 ...12 C2
Battery La WA1 ...17 C4
Bawtry Ct WA2 ...8 C1
Baxter Cl WA7 ...50 B4
Baxter Rd M33 ...242 B6
Baxter St WA5 ...15 C3
Baycliffe WA13 ...18 B1
Baycliffe Cl WA7 ...49 B3
Bayley Rd CW5 ...205 B3
Bayley St SK15 ...242 C1
Bayswater Cl WA7 ...24 C2
Baytree Ave M34 ...241 A8
Baytree Cl CH66 ...69 C1
Bayvil Cl WA7 ...50 C4
Beach Gr CW8 ...103 B3
Beach Rd CW8 ...103 A3
Beachin La CH3 ...102 A2
Beacon Hill View WA7 ...48 B4
Beacon La CH60 ...41 A4
Beacon Rd SK6 ...241 A1
Beacons The
Heswall CH60 ...41 A4
Warrington WA3 ...9 C3
Beaconsfield Cres WA8 ...13 A2
Beaconsfield Gr WA8 ...13 A2
Beaconsfield Rd
Altrincham WA14 ...238 D7
Runcorn WA7 ...22 C1
Widnes WA8 ...13 A2
Beaconsfield St CH2 ...237 C2
Beadnell Dr WA5 ...14 C2
Beaford Dr M22 ...33 C4
Beagle Point CW7 ...126 A1
Beagle Wlk M22 ...33 C4
Beam Heath Way CW5 ...204 C4
Beam St CW5 ...204 C3
Beamish Cl WA4 ...26 B2
Beamont Com Inf & Jun Schs WA2 ...16 B4
Beamont St WA8 ...23 A2
Beard Cres SK22 ...39 B4
Beardsmore Dr WA3 ...3 C4
Bearhurst La SK11 ...111 A2
Bearstone Rd TF9 ...236 C2
Beasley Cl CH66 ...69 B2
Beata Rd ST5 ...210 C1
Beatrice Ave SK8 ...239 F2
Beatrice St WA4 ...16 B2
Beatty Ave WA2 ...8 B1
Beatty Dr CW12 ...157 A2
Beatty Rd CW5 ...204 B2
Beaufort Ave M33 ...242 C5
Beaufort Chase SK9 ...34 C1
Beaufort Cl
Alderley Edge SK9 ...60 A1
Runcorn WA7 ...49 A4
Warrington WA5 ...15 A3
Widnes WA8 ...22 A4
Beaufort Rd
Ashton-u-Lyne OL6 ...242 A3
Sale M33 ...242 C5
Beaufort St WA5 ...15 C2
Beaulieu WA15 ...238 F2
Beaulieu Ave CW7 ...126 C1
Beaumaris Dr CH65 ...70 B1
Beaumont Cl
Biddulph ST8 ...179 B2
Chester CH4 ...140 C3
Wistaston CW2 ...205 C4
Beaumont Ct SK9 ...34 B3
Beauty Bank
Whitegate CW7 ...125 C3
Winsford CW7 ...149 A2
Beauty Bank Cotts CW7 ...149 A2
Beauxfields WA4 ...26 B4
Beaver Cl CH4 ...140 C3
Beaver Ctr The CW9 ...103 C4
Beaverbrook Ave WA3 ...5 A2
Beavers Cl WA16 ...79 C4
Bebbington Cl M33 ...242 F5
Bebington Rd CH66 ...69 B2
Becconsall Cl CW1 ...190 A4
Becconsall Dr CW1 ...190 A4
Bechers WA8 ...12 A2
Beckenham Gr CW7 ...126 A1
Beckett Ave CW7 ...150 B4
Beckett Dr Lymm WA13 ...19 A4
Winwick WA2 ...8 A3
Beckett's La CH3 ...142 A4
Beckford Cl CW1 ...189 C4
Becks La SK10 ...86 C1
Becontree Ave M34 ...241 A8
Bedells La SK9 ...60 A3
Bedford Ave
Ellesmere Port CH65 ...70 A1
Hyde SK14 ...241 E7
Bedford Ave E CH65 ...70 A1
Bedford Ct CW2 ...190 B1
Bedford Gdns CW2 ...190 B1
Bedford Gn M44 ...11 A3
Bedford Gr ST7 ...193 A3
Bedford Pl CW2 ...190 B1
Bedford Rd
Kidsgrove ST7 ...195 A2
Macclesfield SK11 ...112 A4
Bedford Rise CW7 ...149 B3
Bedford St Crewe CW2 ...190 B1
Warrington WA4 ...26 B4
Bedward Row CH1 ...237 A2
Beech Ave Culcheth WA3 ...5 A2
Frodsham WA6 ...74 B4
Gatley SK8 ...239 B5
Golborne WA3 ...3 C4
Haydock WA11 ...1 C4
Mobberley WA16 ...57 C3
Rode Heath ST7 ...193 C4
Stockport SK3 ...240 F2
Warrington, Penketh WA5 ...14 B2
Warrington, Thelwall WA4 ...17 B2
Beech Cl
Alderley Edge SK9 ...60 A2
Congleton CW12 ...156 A2
Cuddington CW8 ...101 C1
Holmes Chapel CW4 ...130 B2
Newton-le-W WA12 ...2 B1
Ollerton WA16 ...82 C3
11 Partington M31 ...11 C2
Beech Cotts
Alderley Edge SK9 ...85 A4
Stretton WA4 ...26 C1
Beech Cres SK12 ...36 C2
Beech Dr Knutsford WA16 ...57 B1
Talke ST7 ...210 C4
Wistaston CW2 ...189 C1
Beech Farm Dr SK10 ...87 D1
Beech Gr Chester CH2 ...119 A2
Crewe CW1 ...190 C3
Ellesmere Port CH1 ...95 A4
Lymm WA13 ...18 A1
Macclesfield SK11 ...112 C3
Sandbach CW11 ...175 B3
Warrington WA1 ...17 A4
Warrington, Latchford WA4 ...16 B2
Weaverham CW8 ...102 B4
Wilmslow SK9 ...60 A3
Winsford CW7 ...149 B4
Beech Hall Dr SK10 ...87 B1
Beech Hall Sch SK10 ...87 B1
Beech Hey La CH64 ...43 A1
Beech Heyes Cl CW8 ...102 C4
Beech Heyes Dr CW8 ...102 C4
Beech La Barnton CW8 ...78 A2
Eaton CW6 ...147 A3
Macclesfield SK10 ...87 B1
Norley WA6 ...75 C1
Romiley SK6 ...241 C2
Wilmslow SK9 ...60 A3
Beech Lawn WA14 ...238 C4
Beech Mount WA14 ...238 D2
Beech Rd
Alderley Edge SK9 ...60 A2
Altrincham WA15 ...238 E3
Heswall CH60 ...41 B4
High Lane SK6 ...37 C4
Little Budworth CW6 ...124 B1
Runcorn WA7 ...49 B4
Sale M33 ...242 D6
Stockport SK2,SK3 ...240 F2
Sutton WA7 ...50 A2
Warrington WA4 ...26 B4
Whaley Bridge SK23 ...65 C4
Beech Rise Crowton CW8 ...76 A1
Whaley Bridge SK23 ...65 B3
Beech St Hyde SK14 ...241 D7
Middlewich CW10 ...128 B1
Beech St W CW1 ...190 B2
Beech Tree Cl CW5 ...205 B3
Beech View Rd WA6 ...75 B1
Beechcroft Ave CW2 ...206 A4
Beechcroft Dr CH65 ...70 A1
Beeches SK9 ...59 C3
Beeches The
Altrincham WA14 ...238 C2
Chester CH2 ...119 A3
Helsby WA6 ...73 B2
Nantwich CW5 ...204 C3
Whitchurch SY13 ...225 C1
Beechfield
Altrincham WA14 ...238 C3
Moulton CW9 ...126 C4
Wilmslow SK9 ...60 A3
Beechfield Ave SK9 ...59 C3
Beechfield Cl CH60 ...41 A4
Beechfield Dr CW10 ...128 A1
Beechfield Gdns CW8 ...103 A3
Beechfield Rd
Alderley Edge SK9 ...85 A4
Cheadle SK8 ...35 A4
Ellesmere Port CH65 ...70 A3
Stockport SK3 ...240 F1
Warrington WA4 ...17 A1
Beechfields CW7 ...150 A4
Beechlands Ave CH3 ...119 A1
Beechmill Dr WA3 ...4 C2
Beechmoore WA4 ...25 A3
Beechmuir CH1 ...117 C2
Beechtree Farm Cl WA16 ...29 B4
Beechtree La WA13 ...29 A4
Beechurst Rd SK8 ...240 B1
Beechway Bollington SK10 ...88 A4
Chester CH2 ...118 B3
High Lane SK6 ...37 C4
Wilmslow SK9 ...59 C3
Beechways WA4 ...26 B3
Beechways Dr CH64 ...66 B4
Beechwood
Altrincham WA14 ...238 B1
Knutsford WA16 ...57 B1
Beechwood Ave
Hartford CW8 ...103 A3
Newton-le-W WA12 ...2 B2
Romiley SK6 ...241 D2
Runcorn WA7 ...49 C3
Stalybridge SK15 ...242 F4
3 Stockport SK5 ...240 F8
Warrington, Great Sankey WA5 ...14 C3
Warrington, Padgate WA1 ...16 C4
Beechwood Dr
Alsager ST7 ...193 A2
Eaton (nr Congleton) CW12 ...156 C4
Ellesmere Port CH66 ...69 B1
Higher Wincham CW9 ...79 C3
Wilmslow SK9 ...60 C4
Beechwood Gr SK8 ...35 A4
Beechwood La
Culcheth WA3 ...4 B2
Stalybridge SK15 ...242 F4
Beechwood Mews SK10 ...87 B1
Beechwood Prim Sch WA7 ...49 C3
Beechwood Rd
Bebington CH62 ...43 B4
Broughton CH4 ...140 C3
Beechwood Sch CW1 ...190 B3
Beecroft Cl WA5 ...7 B1
Beeley St SK14 ...241 E6
Beeston Ave WA15 ...238 F6
Beeston Brow SK10 ...88 A4
Beeston Castle* CW6 ...167 C2
Beeston Cl Bollington SK10 ...63 D1
Holmes Chapel CW4 ...130 A2
Middlewich CW10 ...151 B3
Warrington WA3 ...9 B2
Beeston Ct WA7 ...24 B2
Beeston Dr Alsager ST7 ...193 B2
Knutsford WA16 ...82 A4
Winsford CW7 ...149 B4
Beeston Gn CH66 ...69 C3
Beeston Gr SK3 ...240 E1
Beeston Mount SK10 ...63 B1
Beeston Rd
Broughton CH4 ...139 A2
Handforth SK9 ...34 B3
Higher Kinnerton CH4 ...161 A4
Beeston St CW8 ...103 C4
Beeston Terr SK11 ...111 C3
Beeston View CH4 ...141 C4
Beggarman's La WA16 ...82 A4
Beilby Rd WA11 ...1 C4
Belfry Cl SK9 ...60 B4
Belfry Dr SK10 ...87 B2
Belgrave Ave
Alsager ST7 ...193 B3
Broughton CH4 ...140 C3
Congleton CW12 ...156 B2
Warrington WA1 ...16 C4
Belgrave Cl
Dodleston CH4 ...162 A3
Golborne WN7 ...4 B4
Widnes WA8 ...13 C2
Belgrave Dr CH65 ...69 C3
Belgrave Inf Sch CH4 ...141 A3
Belgrave Pl CH4 ...237 B1
Belgrave Rd
Altrincham WA14 ...238 C3
Chester CH3 ...142 A4
Crewe CW2 ...190 A1
Irlam M44 ...11 B3
Macclesfield SK11 ...112 B2
Northwich CW9 ...104 A2
Sale M33 ...242 A6
Belgrave St CH2 ...237 C3
Belgravia Ct WA8 ...12 C2
Belgravia Gdns WA15 ...31 C4
Bell Ave SK11 ...112 C2
Bell Farm Ct 7 SK10 ...87 B2
Bell House Rd WA8 ...13 B1
Bell La WA4 ...17 C2
Bell Meadow Ct CW6 ...146 B1
Bell's Hollow ST5 ...210 C2
Bellaport Rd TF9 ...236 A2
Bellard Dr CH2 ...119 A2
Bellcast Cl WA4 ...26 B3
Belldale Cl SK4 ...240 A6
Belle Vue Terr CW11 ...175 A3
Bellemonte Rd WA6 ...74 B4
Belleville Ave M22 ...33 C4
Bellhouse La
Higher Walton WA4 ...25 B4
Warrington WA4 ...17 B1
Bellingham Dr WA7 ...49 A4
Bellsfield Cl WA13 ...18 C1
Bellvue La CH3 ...119 C2
Belmont Ave
Macclesfield SK10 ...86 B1
Sandbach CW11 ...175 A4
Warrington WA4 ...16 C2
Belmont Cl SK4 ...240 E7
Belmont Cres WA5 ...15 A3
Belmont Rd
Altrincham WA15 ...238 E2
Bramhall SK7 ...35 C3
Gatley SK8 ...239 B6
Great Budworth CW9 ...53 C1
Northwich CW9 ...104 B4
Sale M33 ...242 A8
Widnes WA8 ...13 C1
Belmont St SK4 ...240 E7
Belmont Way SK4 ...240 E7
Beltony Dr CW1 ...173 A1
Belvedere WA7 ...23 A2
Belvedere Cl WA6 ...49 B1
Belvedere Dr CH1 ...117 C2
Belvedere Rd WA12 ...2 A3
Belvedere Terr ST7 ...193 C4
Belvoir Ave SK7 ...36 C4
Belvoir Rd
Warrington WA4 ...26 A4
Widnes WA8 ...13 A1
Bembridge Cl
Widnes WA8 ...12 C2
Warrington WA5 ...14 B4
Bembridge Ct CW10 ...151 B4
Bemrose Ave WA14 ...238 C6
Ben Nevis Dr CH66 ...68 C3
Benbow St 7 M33 ...242 B7
Benbrook Gr SK9 ...34 C1
Benbrook Way SK11 ...111 C1
Bendee Ave CH64 ...67 A4
Bendee Rd CH64 ...67 A4
Bengal Sq OL6 ...242 A4
Bengal St SK3 ...240 E4
Benjamins Way ST7 ...209 C1
Bennet Cl CH64 ...68 A4
Bennet Rd CW9 ...104 B3
Bennett Ave WA1 ...16 C3
Bennett Cl Crewe CW1 ...190 C2
4 Stockport SK3 ...240 C4
Bennett St
Stalybridge SK15 ...242 D1
3 Stockport SK3 ...240 C4
Warrington WA1 ...16 A3
Bennett's La
Higher Kinnerton CH4 ...161 A4
Widnes WA8 ...13 C1
Bennetts La SK11 ...158 C3
Benson Rd WA3 ...9 B2
Benson Wlk 10 SK9 ...34 D1
Bent La Astbury CW12 ...178 A4
Crowton CW8 ...101 B4
Culcheth WA3 ...5 A1
Lymm WA13 ...19 B3
Bentham Ave WA2 ...8 B2
Bentham Rd WA3 ...5 A1
Bentinck Cl WA14 ...238 C4
Bentinck Rd WA14 ...238 C4
Bentinck St WA7 ...22 C2
Bentley Dr CW1 ...191 A3
Bentley Gr CW7 ...149 B3
Bentley's Farm La WA4 ...52 C3
Bentleys The SK5 ...240 F7
Benton Dr CH2 ...118 B2
Bents Cotts CH2 ...71 C1
Bentside Rd SK12 ...38 B3
Benty Heath La CH64, CH66 ...43 A2
Beresford Ct SK9 ...60 A1
Beresford St WA1 ...16 C4
Berisford Cl WA15 ...238 E7
Berisford Ho CW12 ...156 C2
Berkeley Ave ST7 ...193 B3
Berkeley Cl Golborne WN7 ...4 B4
Hyde SK14 ...241 D5
Berkeley Cres
Hyde SK14 ...241 D5
Wistaston CW2 ...206 A4
Berkeley Ct WA7 ...24 B2
Berkeley Prim Sch The CW2 ...206 A4
Berkeley Rise CW7 ...149 A4
Berkley Ct SK23 ...65 B3
Berkley Dr CH4 ...141 B3
Berkshire Cl SK10 ...86 C1
Berkshire Dr
Congleton CW12 ...156 B2
Irlam M44 ...11 B3
Warrington WA1 ...17 C4
Berlin Rd SK3 ...240 D2
Bernard Ave WA4 ...26 B4
Bernisdale Rd WA16 ...57 C2
Bernsdale Cl CH5 ...116 A2
Berristal Rd SK10 ...88 C2
Berry Cl
Ellesmere Port CH66 ...69 B2
Wilmslow SK9 ...60 A3
Berry Dr CH66 ...69 B2
Berry Rd WA8 ...12 B1
Berrycroft La SK6 ...241 A3
Berrystead CW8 ...103 A2
Bertram St
Newton-le-W WA12 ...2 A2
Bertram St *continued*
Sale M33 ...242 E6
Berwick Ave CH62 ...43 C2
Berwick Cl
Macclesfield SK10 ...86 C1
Warrington WA1 ...17 C3
Berwick Ct CW4 ...130 A1
Berwick Gdns CH66 ...69 A3
Berwick Gr CH66 ...69 A3
Berwick Rd CH66 ...69 A3
Berwyn Ave SK8 ...240 B1
Berwyn Cl CH66 ...69 A3
Bessancourt CW4 ...130 B2
Bessemer Rd M44 ...11 C3
Beswick St SK11 ...112 A4
Beswicks La
Lindow End SK9 ...59 B2
Norton in Hales TF9 ...236 B1
Beswicks Rd CW8 ...78 C1
Betchton Cl CW11 ...175 B4
Betchton Ct 6 CW12 ...156 C2
Betchton Rd CW11 ...175 C1
Betchworth Cres WA7 ...49 B3
Betchworth Way SK10 ...87 B2
Bethany Cl WA11 ...1 A4
Betjeman Cl WA4 ...16 C2
Betjeman Way CW1 ...190 C3
Betley Cl CW9 ...104 A3
Betley St CW1 ...190 B2
Betleymere Rd SK8 ...239 F4
Betsyfield Dr WA3 ...9 A4
Bettisfield Ave CH62 ...43 B3
Betty's La CW6 ...168 B1
Bevan Ave ST7 ...210 C3
Bevan Cl WA5 ...15 B3
Beverley Ave
Denton M34 ...241 A6
Warrington WA4 ...26 B4
Beverley Dr CH60 ...41 A3
Beverley Rd WA5 ...15 B3
Beverley Way
Ellesmere Port CH66 ...69 A4
Macclesfield SK10 ...87 B2
Beverley Wlk SK6 ...241 A1
Bevin Ave WA3 ...5 A2
Bevyl Rd CH64 ...41 A1
Bewley Ct CH3 ...142 A4
Bewsey Bsns Ctr WA5 ...15 C3
Bewsey Farm Cl WA5 ...15 B4
Bewsey Ind Est WA5 ...16 A4
Bewsey Lodge Cty Prim Sch WA5 ...15 C4
Bewsey Pk Cl WA5 ...15 C4
Bewsey Rd WA2,WA5 ...16 A3
Bewsey St 8 WA2 ...16 A3
Bexhill Ave
Altrincham WA15 ...238 F6
Warrington WA2 ...8 A2
Bexington Dr CW1 ...190 A4
Bexton Ave CW7 ...126 A1
Bexton La WA16 ...82 A4
Bexton Prim Sch WA16 ...81 C4
Bexton Rd WA16 ...56 C1
Bibby Ave WA1 ...16 C3
Bibby St ST7 ...193 C4
Bickerton Ave WA6 ...74 B4
Bickerton Cl WA3 ...9 B2
Bickerton Holy Trinity CE Prim Sch SY14 ...200 A4
Bickerton Rd
Altrincham WA14 ...238 B6
Bickley Town SY14 ...201 A1
Bickerton Way 1 CW9 ...103 C2
Bickley Cl
Hough Common CW2 ...206 C1
Runcorn WA7 ...23 B1
Warrington WA2 ...8 C2
Bickley Town La SY14 ...214 C3
Bicknell Cl WA5 ...15 A4
Bida La CW12 ...179 A4
Biddulph Common Rd ST8 ...179 C4
Biddulph Grange Ctry Pk* ST8 ...179 C2
Biddulph Grange Gdn* ST8 ...179 C2
Biddulph Park Rd ST8 ...179 C3
Biddulph Rd
Biddulph ST7 ...195 C3
Congleton CW12 ...179 A4
Biddulph St CW12 ...179 B4
Biddy's La SK10 ...88 A1
Bideford Rd WA5 ...14 C2
Bidston Cl CH2 ...118 B3
Bidston Dr SK9 ...34 C1
Bidston Gn CH66 ...69 B2
Bidvale Way CW1 ...190 B4
Big Field La CW6 ...146 A4
Biggin Ct WA2 ...8 C1
Bignall End Rd
Audley ST7 ...210 A2
Newcastle-u-L ST7 ...210 A2
Billington Ave WA12 ...2 B3
Billington Cl Crewe CW2 ...190 A1
Warrington WA5 ...14 C4
Billington Rd WA8 ...12 A2
Bilson Dr SK3 ...240 B3
Bilton Cl WA8 ...13 C1
Bilton Way CW2 ...189 C3
Bings Rd SK23 ...65 C4
Bingswood Ave SK23 ...65 C4
Bingswood Ind Est SK23 ...65 C4
Bingswood Rd SK23 ...65 C4
Binney Rd CW9 ...104 A4
Binns St SK15 ...242 B1

Binyon Way CW1 191 A2
Birbeck St SK15 242 C1
Birch Ave Alsager ST7 193 C1
Crewe CW1 190 C3
Irlam M44 11 B3
Macclesfield SK10 87 A1
Romiley SK6 241 D2
Sale M33 242 B5
3 Stockport SK4 240 B8
Warrington WA2 8 A2
Wilmslow SK9 59 C3
Winsford CW7 127 A1
Birch Brook Rd WA13 19 B3
Birch Cl Crewe CW1 190 C3
Holmes Chapel CW4 130 B2
Birch Cres WA12 1 C2
Birch Ct CW12 155 C2
Birch Fold CW4 107 A1
Birch Gdns CW11 175 B3
Birch Gr
Ellesmere Port CH66 70 A1
Higher Wincham CW9 79 C3
Knutsford WA16 57 B1
Lostock Green CW9 105 A4
Warrington, Bruche WA1 16 C4
Warrington, Latchford WA4 16 B2
Birch Heath La CH3 142 C4
Birch Heath Rd CW6 168 B4
Birch Hill WA6 99 B4
Birch House Rd ST5 210 B1
Birch La
Hough Common CW2 206 C1
Winsford CW10 127 C1
Birch Rd Audley ST7 209 C1
Chester CH4 140 C3
Congleton CW12 155 C2
Gatley SK8 239 A5
Haydock WA11 1 C4
Hollinfare WA3 11 A1
Partington M31 11 B2
Poynton SK12 36 C1
Runcorn WA7 49 B4
Widnes WA8 13 A2
Birch Rise CH2 118 B3
Birch Tree Ave SK7 37 A4
Birch Tree Cl WA14 238 C1
Birch Tree Ct CH2 237 C4
Birch Tree La
Antrobus WA4 53 A3
Goostrey CW4 107 B1
The Bank ST7 195 A4
Birch Tree Rd 17 WA3 3 C4
Birch Way SK10 86 C3
Birchall Ave WA3 4 C2
Birchall Moss La CW5 219 C1
Birchall St WA3 9 A4
Birchall Wlk CW2 206 B4
Birchdale WA14 238 C2
Birchdale Ave SK8 239 B2
Birchdale Cres WA4 26 B4
Birchdale Rd
Warrington, Appleton WA4 26 B4
Warrington, Paddington WA1 17 A4
Birchen Rd L26 21 A4
Birchencliff Cotts SK10 63 B3
Birchenwood Rd ST6, ST7 195 C1
Birches Cl CH60 41 A4
Birches Croft Dr SK10 86 C1
Birches La CW9 105 A4
Birches The
Broughton CH4 139 A2
Crewe CW2 206 B4
Neston CH64 41 C1
Birches Way 16 ST7 195 A1
Birchfield Ave
Rode Heath ST7 193 C4
Widnes WA8 13 A1
Birchfield Mews 3 SK14 241 D6
Birchfield Rd Lymm WA13 19 A2
Stockport SK3 240 A3
Warrington WA5 15 A3
Widnes, Appleton WA8 13 A1
Widnes, Farnworth WA8 13 A2
Birchfields WA15 238 F1
Birchgate Cl SK10 86 C1
Birchin Cl CW5 205 A3
Birchin La CW5 205 A3
Birchinall Cl SK11 112 A4
Birchmuir CH1 117 C2
Birchmuir Cl CW1 190 A3
Birchvale Ave SK6 241 D3
Birchway Bollington SK10 88 A4
Bramhall SK7 35 B4
Heswall CH60 41 B3
High Lane SK6 37 C4
Birchways WA4 26 C3
Birchwood Ave WA2,WA3 9 B2
Birchwood Bvd WA3 9 B1
Birchwood CE Prim Sch WA3 9 C2
Birchwood Cl
Ellesmere Port CH66 69 B1
Elton CH2 72 B2
Stockport SK4 240 A5
Birchwood Com High Sch WA3 9 B2
Birchwood Dr
Lower Peover WA16 106 B4
Nantwich CW5 204 C3
Wilmslow SK9 60 B4
Birchwood Office Pk WA2 9 A2
Birchwood One Bsns Pk WA3 9 C1
Birchwood Park Ave WA3 9 B3
Birchwood Science Pk WA3 9 B3
Birchwood Sta WA3 9 C1
Birchwood Tech Pk WA3 9 C3
Birchwood Way WA2 8 C1
Bird Hall La SK3 240 B2
Bird Hall Rd SK8 240 C1
Bird's La CW6 186 A4
Birds La Tarporley CW6 146 B1
Tattenhall CH3 166 C1
Birdwell Dr WA5 15 A3
Birkdale Ave CH63 43 B3
Birkdale Cl Bramhall SK7 36 A4
Macclesfield SK10 87 B2
Birkdale Ct 8 CW9 104 A4
Birkdale Dr ST7 195 B2
Birkdale Gdns CW7 126 A1
Birkdale Rd
Warrington WA5 14 C2
Widnes WA8 13 A3
Birkenhead Rd CH64 42 C1
Birkenhead St CW9 104 B4
Birkett Ave CH65 70 B1
Birkin Cl WA16 57 B2
Birkinheath La WA14 31 A2
Birley Cl WA15 238 F7
Birley St WA12 2 B2
Birstall Ct WA7 49 B4
Birtles Cl
Sandbach CW11 175 B4
Stockport SK8 240 A1
Birtles Hall SK10 85 B1
Birtles La SK10 85 C1
Birtles Rd
Macclesfield SK10 86 B1
Warrington WA2 8 B1
Birtles Way 4 SK9 34 B3
Birtlespool Rd SK8 239 F4
Birtley Ct WA8 12 A1
Birtwistle Rd CW9 104 B3
Bisham Pk WA7 24 B1
Bishop Heber High Sch SY14 213 B3
Bishop Rd SK10 88 A4
Bishop Reeves Rd WA11 1 C4
Bishop St CH2 118 C2
Bishop Wilson CE Prim Sch CH64 67 B1
Bishop's Cl
Stockport SK8 240 A1
Talke ST7 210 B4
Bishopdale Cl WA5 14 C4
Bishopgates Dr CW9 103 C2
Bishops Cl WA14 238 B1
Bishops Ct
Broughton CH4 139 B2
Warrington WA2 8 A2
Bishops Gdns CH65 70 A3
Bishops Way WA8 13 B2
Bishops Wood CW5 204 C1
Bishops' Blue Coat CE High Sch The CH3 142 A4
Bishopsfield Ct CH2 118 C2
Bishopton Dr SK11 111 C4
Bispham Rd WA5 15 A2
Bittern Cl Poynton SK12 36 A2
Runcorn WA7 50 B4
Warrington WA2 8 B2
Bittern Gr SK10 87 A1
Bk Adcroft St 4 SK1 240 F3
Bk Grosvenor St SK15 242 D1
Bk Melbourne St SK15 242 D1
Black Denton's Pl WA8 13 B1
Black Diamond St CH2 237 B4
Black Firs La CW12 155 C2
Black Firs Prim Sch CW12 155 C2
Black Friars CH1 237 A2
Black La SK10 87 C1
Black Lion La CH66 69 B3
Black Moss Rd WA14 20 C4
Black Park Rd SY13 226 B1
Black Rd SK11 112 C4
Blackacres Cl CW11 174 C3
Blackberry Cl WA14 238 B8
Blackboards La CH66 69 A4
Blackbrook Ave WA2 8 C1
Blackbrook Cl WA8 12 B2
Blackburn Cl WA3 3 C4
Blackburne Ave WA8 22 A3
Blackburne Cl WA2 9 B1
Blackcap Rd WA4 27 A2
Blackcroft Ave CW8 78 A1
Blackden La
Goostrey CW4 108 A2
Siddington SK11 132 C4
Blackdown Cl CH66 69 A3
Blackeys La CH64 66 C4
Blackheath La WA7 24 C3
Blackhill La WA16 81 C4
Blackhurst Brow SK10 61 A1
Blackhurst Farm Rd CW5 202 C2
Blackhurst St WA1 16 A3
Blackledge Cl WA2 9 A2
Blackley Cl
Macclesfield SK10 87 A2
Warrington WA4 16 B2
Blackshaw Cl CW12 157 A1
Blackshaw Dr WA5 7 A1
Blackshaw La SK9 59 C1
Blackshaw St
20 Macclesfield SK11 112 B4
4 Stockport SK3 240 E4
Blackthorn Cl
Broughton CH4 139 A2
Huntington CH3 142 A3
Wistaston CW2 206 A4
Blackthorn Pl ST5 210 C1
Blackthorn Wlk 3 M31 11 C1
Blackthorne Ave CH1 95 A4
Blackwell Cl CW10 151 B3
Blacon Ave CH1 118 A3
Blacon Hall Jun Sch CH1 117 C3
Blacon Hall Rd CH1 117 C3
Blacon High Sch CH1 117 B2
Blacon Inf Sch CH1 117 C3
Blacon Point Rd CH1 117 C2
Blagg Ave CW5 204 B2
Blair Cl SK7 36 B4
Blair Dr WA8 12 B2
Blairgowrie Dr SK10 87 A2
Blaizefield Cl CW3 232 B1
Blake Cl Blacon CH1 117 C3
Wistaston CW2 189 C1
Blake La CW8 102 A1
Blake St CW12 156 B2
Blakeacre Rd L26 21 A3
Blakeden La CW7 148 C4
Blakeley Brow CH63 43 A3
Blakeley Ct CH63 43 A4
Blakeley Dell CH63 43 A3
Blakeley Dene CH63 43 A4
Blakeley Rd CH63 43 A3
Blakelow Bank SK11 112 C3
Blakelow Cl CW10 151 A4
Blakelow Cres CW5 205 C2
Blakelow Rd SK11 112 C3
Blakely La WA16 58 C4
Blakemere Ave M33 242 E5
Blakemere Cl SY13 226 A1
Blakemere Ct CH65 70 B4
Blakemere Dr CW9 103 C3
Blakemere La WA6 100 B2
Blakemere Way CW11 174 C4
Blakeswood WA14 238 B5
Blandford Ct SK15 242 D2
Blandford Dr
4 Macclesfield SK11 111 C4
Northwich CW9 103 C2
Blandford Ho SK15 242 D2
Blandford Rd
Stockport SK4 240 C6
Warrington WA5 15 A3
Blandford St SK15 242 D2
Blankney The CW5 204 C2
Blantern Rd CH4 161 A4
Blantyre St WA7 22 C2
Blaven Cl SK3 240 F1
Blaze Hill SK10 88 C4
Bleasdale Rd
Crewe CW1 173 A1
Newton-le-W WA12 2 B2
Bleeding Wolf La ST7 194 C3
Blenheim Cl
Altrincham WA14 238 D2
Davenham CW9 103 C2
Macclesfield SK10 87 A1
Poynton SK12 36 C2
Warrington WA2 8 C1
Wilmslow SK9 60 B4
Wistaston CW2 205 C4
Blenheim Ct ST7 193 B3
Blenheim Gdns 7 CW7 149 B4
Blenheim Ho CH1 118 A2
Blenheim Way OL6 242 B4
Blessed Thomas Holford RC High Sch WA15 238 E4
Bloom St SK3 240 D4
Bloomsbury Way WA8 12 B2
Blossom Hts CW8 103 B4
Blossom Rd M31 11 C1
Blossoms Hey SK8 239 E1
Blossoms Hey Wlk SK8 239 E1
Blossoms La SK7 35 A1
Blossoms St 5 SK2 240 F3
Blounts La SY14 213 B4
Blue Chip Bsns Pk WA14 238 C7
Blue Hatch WA6 74 B4
Blue Planet Aquarium The* CH65 70 B1
Blue Ridge Cl WA5 14 C4
Bluebell Ave WA11 1 C4
Bluebell Cl
Huntington CH3 142 A3
Macclesfield SK10 87 B2
Northwich CW8 78 C1
Bluebell Ct WA7 49 C2
Bluebell Gr SK8 239 D4
Bluebell La SK10 87 B2
Bluebell Mews 10 SK10 87 B2
Bluebell Way
Alsager ST7 193 A2
Handforth SK9 34 B1
Blueberry Rd WA14 238 A2
Bluecoat St WA2 16 A4
Blundell Rd WA8 22 B4
Blyth Cl Macclesfield SK10 86 C1
Runcorn WA7 50 B3
Blyth Rd CH63 43 B4
Blythe Ave Bramhall SK7 35 B3
Congleton CW12 156 A1
Widnes WA8 13 A3
Blythe Pl CW7 127 A1
Blythings The CW6 146 B2
Board St OL6 242 A4
Boardman Cl SK5 240 F8
Boat Mus* CH65 70 B4
Boat Stage WA13 18 C2
Boathorse Rd ST7 210 C4
Boathouse La CH64 41 B2
Bob's La M44 11 B2
Boddens Hill Rd SK4 240 A6
Boden Dr CW5 205 B2
Boden St SK11 112 B4
Bodiam Ct CH65 70 C1
Bodmin Ave SK10 86 C1
Bodmin Cl WA7 50 A3
Bodmin Dr SK7 35 C4
Bodnant Cl CW1 190 A4
Bold Bsns Ctr WA9 6 A4
Bold Cross WA8 13 C4
Bold Ind Est WA8 13 B3
Bold Ind Park WA9 6 A3
Bold La WA5,WA9 6 B4
Bold Pl CH1 237 B3
Bold Sq CH2 237 C3
Bold St Altrincham WA14 238 D3
Haslington CW1 191 B2
Runcorn WA7 23 A2
Sandbach CW11 175 A3
Warrington WA1 16 A3
Widnes WA8 23 A4
Bolesworth Hill Rd CH3 183 B2
Bolesworth Rd
Chester CH2 118 C3
Tattenhall CH3 183 B4
Boleyn Cl CH1 117 C3
Boleyn Ct WA7 24 B2
Bolland's Ct CH1 237 A2
Bolleyn Wood Ct SK9 34 A1
Bollin Ave
Altrincham WA14 238 B1
Winsford CW7 127 A1
Bollin Cl Alsager ST7 192 C2
Culcheth WA3 5 A1
Lymm WA13 19 A2
Sandbach CW11 174 C4
Winsford CW7 127 A1
Bollin Ct
Altrincham WA14 238 B1
Wilmslow SK9 60 B3
Bollin Dr
Altrincham WA14 238 E8
Congleton CW12 156 C1
Lymm WA13 19 A2
Bollin Gr ST8 179 C1
Bollin Hill Prestbury SK10 87 A3
Wilmslow SK9 60 A4
Bollin Mews SK10 86 C4
Bollin Prim Sch WA14 238 B1
Bollin Sq WA14 238 B1
Bollin Way SK10 87 A3
Bollin Wlk SK9 60 B4
Bollinbarn SK10 87 A1
Bollinbarn Dr SK10 87 A1
Bollinbrook CE Prim Sch SK10 87 A1
Bollinbrook Rd SK10 87 A1
Bollington Ave CW9 104 A3
Bollington Cross CE Prim Sch SK10 87 C4
Bollington La SK10 84 C1
Bollington Rd SK10 87 C3
Bollinway WA15 32 A4
Bollinwood Chase SK9 60 B4
Bolshaw Cl CW1 190 A4
Bolshaw Farm La SK8 34 B3
Bolshaw Prim Sch SK8 34 A4
Bolshaw Rd SK8 34 B3
Bolton Ave Bramhall SK8 35 A3
Warrington WA4 16 C2
Bolton Cl Golborne WA3 4 A4
Poynton SK12 36 B2
Bombay Rd SK3 240 C3
Bombay St OL6 242 A4
Bomish La CW4,SK11 108 B2
Bonar Cl SK3 240 C4
Bonar Rd 5 SK3 240 C4
Bond Cl WA5 15 B2
Bond St
Macclesfield SK11 112 B4
Northwich CW8 78 B1
Stalybridge SK15 242 D3
Bonis Hall La SK10 61 C2
Bonnyfield SK6 241 B2
Bonville Chase WA14 238 A4
Bonville Rd WA14 238 A4
Boon Hill Rd ST7 209 C1
Booth Ave Ashton CH3 121 C4
Little Budworth CW6 147 C4
Sandbach CW11 175 B3
Booth Bed La WA16, CW4 107 A2
Booth Cl SK15 242 C1
Booth La CW10 151 C3
Booth Rd
Altrincham WA14 238 C4
Handforth SK9 34 A1
Hartford CW8 103 A2
Sale M33 242 B8
Booth St Audley ST7 209 B1
Congleton CW12 156 B1
Hyde SK14 241 E5
Stockport SK3 240 E3
Warrington WA5 15 C2
Booth's Hill Cl WA13 18 B1
Booth's Hill Ho 6 WA13 18 B2
Booth's Hill Rd WA13 18 B2
Booth's La WA13 18 A1
Boothbank La WA14 30 A3
Boothby St 8 SK11 112 B4
Boothfields WA16 57 B1
Booths La WA4 52 C3
Boothsdale CW6 122 B2
Boothsmere Cl CW11 174 C4
Border Rd CH60 41 A4
Border Way CH3 119 B1
Borderbrook Sch (Higher Wych) SY14 224 B
Borderbrook Sch (Talwrn Green) SY14 222 C
Borders Ind Pk The CH4 140 B
Bordon Rd SK3 240 B
Borough Arc SK14 241 D
Borough Rd
Altrincham WA15 238 E
Congleton CW12 156 C
Borough St SK15 242 D
Borras Rd LL13 196 A
Borron Rd WA12 2 A
Borrowdale Ave
Gatley SK8 239 B
Warrington WA2 8 B
Borrowdale Cl
Crewe CW2 189 C
Frodsham WA6 74 B
Borrowdale Rd WA8 22 B
Borrowdale Terr SK15 242 D
Borrowmore Est CH3 120 C
Bosden Cl SK9 34 B
Bosden Fold SK1 240 F
Bosley Brook CW12 179 B
Bosley Cl
Middlewich CW10 151 B
Wilmslow SK9 34 B
Bosley Dr SK12 37 A
Bosley Rd SK3 240 A
Bosley View CW12 157 A
Bostock Gn CH65 69 C
Bostock Hall CW10 127 B
Bostock Rd
Macclesfield SK11 111 C
Moulton CW7,CW10 127 B
Bostock St WA5 15 C
Boston Ave WA7 23 B
Boston Bvd WA5 15 A
Boston Cl Bramhall SK7 35 B
Culcheth WA3 4 C
Boston St SK14 241 E
Boswell Ave WA4 16 A
Boteler Ave WA5 15 C
Bottom St SK14 241 F
Bottoms La CH4 237 C
Boughey Rd ST7 209 C
Boughton CH2 118 C
Boughton Heath Prim Sch CH3 142 A
Boughton Hill Ave CH3 119 A
Boughton Hill Dr CH3 119 A
Boughton Lodge 4 CH3 119 A
Boulderstone Rd SK15 242 D
Boulevard The
Broughton CH4 139 B
Ellesmere Port CH65 69 C
Boulting Ave WA5 7 C
Boulton Cl CW11 175 B
Boundary Ct SK8 239 C
Boundary La
Chester CH4 140 C
Congleton CW12 179 A
Heswall CH60 41 A
Peover WA16,SK11 108 B
Siddington SK11 132 C
Threapwood SY14 222 C
Boundary La N CW8 101 C
Boundary La S CW8 101 C
Boundary Pk CH64 66 B
Boundary Rd SK8 240 A
Boundary St
Northwich CW9 79 C
Warrington WA1 16 C
Boundary Terr SK9 33 C
Bourchier Way WA4 27 A
Bourne Ave WA3 3 B
Bourne Cl CW8 102 C
Bourne Rd ST7 194 C
Bourne St Mow Cop ST7 195 B
Stockport SK4 240 E
Wilmslow SK9 59 C
Bournemouth Cl WA7 50 B
Bournville Ave SK4 240 E
Bouverie St CH2 237 A
Boverton Cl WA5 7 C
Bow Green Mews WA14 238 B
Bow Green Rd WA14 238 A
Bow La WA14 31 A
Bow St SK3 240 C
Bowden Cl
Congleton CW12 156 A
Culcheth WA3 4 C
Warrington WA1 16 C
Bowden Cres SK22 39 B
Bowden Dr CW9 104 B
Bowden View La WA16 29 C
Bowdon CE Prim Sch WA14 238 C
Bowdon Prep Sch WA14 238 C
Bowdon Rd WA14 238 C
Bowdon Rise WA14 238 D
Bowdon St SK3 240 E
Bowe's Gate Rd CW6 169 A
Bowen Cl Bramhall SK7 35 C
Widnes WA8 12 B
Bowen Cooke Ave CW1 190 A
Bowen St CW2 190 A
Bower Ave SK4 240 C
Bower Cres WA4 26 B
Bower Gr SK15 242 F
Bower Rd
Altrincham WA15 238 F
Heswall CH60 41 B
Bower St WA8 13 B

owerfield Ave SK7 ....36 B4
owerfield Cres SK7 ....36 C4
owerfold La SK4 ....240 D6
owers Bsns Pk WA8 ....23 A4
owery Ave SK8 ....34 C3
owfell Cl CH62 ....43 B2
owfell Dr SK6 ....37 C4
owker St SK14 ....241 E7
owkers Croft CW11 ....191 C4
owland Cl Runcorn WA7 ..49 C3
Warrington WA3 ....10 A3
owland Croft CW1 ....173 A1
owland Ct M33 ....242 B6
owland Rise CW7 ....149 A4
owles Cl CW11 ....175 A3
owling Green Ct
3 Nantwich CW5 ....204 C3
Northwich CW8 ....78 C1
owling Green St SK14 .241 D6
owman Ave WA4 ....17 A3
owman Cres OL6 ....242 A3
owmans The SK10 ....87 A1
owmere Cl
Biddulph ST8 ....179 B1
arporley CW6 ....146 B1
owmere Dr CW7 ....149 B4
owmere Rd CW6 ....146 B1
owness Ave
ebington CH63 ....43 B3
rlam M44 ....11 B2
Warrington WA2 ....8 B1
Winsford CW7 ....126 B1
owness Cl CW4 ....130 A2
owness Ct CW12 ....156 A1
owness Rd CW2 ....189 B2
owood Ct WA2 ....8 A2
owring Dr CH64 ....41 A1
owyer Ave 4 CW5 ....204 C3
ox La CW12 ....156 C2
ox Tree Mews SK11 ....112 A4
ox Wlk M31 ....11 C2
oxgrove Cl WA8 ....13 A2
oxmoor Cl CH4 ....141 A3
oydell Ave
Warrington WA4 ....17 A1
Warrington, Westy WA4 ....16 C2
oydell Way CH4 ....162 A3
oyle Ave WA2 ....8 C1
oyles Hall Rd ST7 ....209 C1
rabyns Ave SK6 ....241 D3
racadale Dr SK3 ....240 F1
racepeth Ct CH65 ....70 B2
racken Cl
roughton CH4 ....139 B2
Macclesfield SK10 ....86 C1
ode Heath ST7 ....193 C4
Warrington WA3 ....9 B3
racken Rd CH66 ....69 C2
racken Way
arnton CW8 ....78 A2
omberbach CW9 ....78 B4
rodsham WA6 ....74 B3
igher Wincham CW9 ....79 B2
nutsford WA16 ....82 A4
rackendale Elton CH2 ....72 A2
uncorn WA7 ....49 B4
rackenfield Way 12
CW7 ....149 A4
rackenlea Pl SK3 ....240 D1
rackenwood Cl CW2 ....206 A4
rackenwood Dr SK8 ..239 E4
rackenwood Mews
Warrington WA4 ....17 B1
Wilmslow SK9 ....60 C4
rackley Ave M44 ....11 B3
rackley St Runcorn WA7 ..22 C2
Warrington WA4 ....16 B1
radburn Rd M44 ....11 C4
radburns La CW8 ....103 A3
radbury Ave WA14 ....238 A5
radbury Gdns CW12 ....156 C1
radbury Rd CW7 ....127 A1
radbury St SK14 ....241 E5
raddan Ave M33 ....242 C5
raddon Cl CW9 ....103 C2
radeley Hall Rd CW1 ....191 A3
radeley Rd CW1 ....191 B2
radfield Rd CW1 ....190 A4
radford La SK10 ....85 B3
radford Rd CW7 ....126 C2
radford St CH4 ....141 B4
radgate Ave SK8 ....239 D1
radgate Rd WA14 ....238 A5
rading Wlk M22 ....33 C4
radlegh Rd WA12 ....2 A1
radley Bvd WA5 ....15 A3
radley Cl
Altrincham WA15 ....238 E7
Middlewich CW10 ....151 A4
radley Farm La SY13 ....225 B4
radley Fold SK15 ....242 E2
radley Hall Cotts WA4 ..27 C3
radley La Frodsham WA6 ..74 B3
Newton-le-W WA5,WA12 ....2 A1
radley St SK11 ....112 C3
radley Way WA8 ....13 A1
radmoor Rd CH62 ....43 B4
radshaw Ave CH4 ....140 A4
radshaw Com Prim Sch
WA4 ....17 A1
radshaw Hall La
Cheadle SK8 ....34 C4
Gatley SK8 ....34 B4
radshaw Hall Prim Sch
SK8 ....239 E1
radshaw La Lymm WA13 ..19 B2
Warrington WA4 ....17 A2
radshaw Pl CW12 ....156 C1

Bradshaw St WA8 ....13 A1
Bradwall Rd CW11 ....175 A4
Bradwall St CW11 ....175 A4
Bradwell Cl CH65 ....70 A2
Bradwell Ct CW12 ....156 C1
Bradwell Rd SK8 ....34 B4
Bradwell Gr CW12 ....156 C2
Bradwell Rd Golborne WA3 ..3 C4
Hazel Grove SK7 ....36 C4
Bradwen Cl M34 ....241 A5
Braemar Ave CW9 ....104 B4
Braemar Cl
Holmes Chapel CW4 ....130 B1
Warrington WA2 ....9 A2
Wistaston CW2 ....205 C4
Braemar Ct CH65 ....70 C2
Braeside Cl
11 Ellesmere Port CH66 ....69 B3
Macclesfield SK11 ....112 C3
Braidwood Ave WA16 ....57 B2
Brains La CW6 ....169 A3
Braintree Rd M22 ....33 C4
Braithwaite Cl WA7 ....49 B3
Braithwaite Rd WA3 ....3 B4
Brake The ST7 ....195 A4
Brake Village ST7 ....195 A4
Brakeley Rd CW8 ....77 B2
Bramall Cl CW11 ....175 B4
Bramall St SK14 ....241 D8
Bramble Cl Chester CH3 ..142 A4
Macclesfield SK10 ....87 A1
Warrington WA5 ....14 C2
Winsford CW7 ....126 B2
Bramble Way WA7 ....49 C2
Brambles The
Haslington CW1 ....191 A2
Higher Wincham CW9 ....79 B2
Brambling Cl WA7 ....49 C3
Brambling Way WA3 ....3 C4
Bramhall Cl Sale M33 ....242 E5
Winsford CW7 ....126 A1
Bramhall Ctr The SK7 ....35 C3
Bramhall Dr
Bebington CH62 ....43 C2
Holmes Chapel CW4 ....130 A2
Bramhall High Sch SK7 ..35 C4
Bramhall La SK2,SK3 ....240 F1
Bramhall La S SK7 ....35 C4
Bramhall Rd CW2 ....189 C1
Bramhall St WA5 ....15 C3
Bramhall Sta SK7 ....35 C3
Bramhall Way SK11 ....112 A4
Bramhalls Pk CW9 ....78 B2
Bramley Cl Bramhall SK7 ..35 C3
Ellesmere Port CH66 ....94 C4
Wilmslow SK9 ....59 B2
Bramley Cres SK4 ....240 B5
Bramley Ct CW6 ....122 B3
Bramley Dr SK7 ....35 C3
Bramley Mews WA4 ....26 B4
Bramley Rd SK7 ....35 C3
Bramley Wlk WA6 ....73 A1
Brampton Ave SK10 ....87 A1
Brampton Ct WA9 ....1 A2
Bramshill Cl WA3 ....10 A3
Bramway Bramhall SK7 ....35 B4
High Lane SK6 ....37 C4
Brancaster Dr WA3 ....4 A4
Branch Way WA11 ....1 B3
Brancote Gdns CH62 ....43 B4
Branden Dr WA16 ....57 A1
Brandon WA8 ....12 A1
Brandon Ave SK8 ....239 B1
Brandon Cl SK9 ....34 B1
Brandwood Ave WA2 ....8 A1
Brandwood Ho 2 WA1 ....16 B3
Branfield Ave SK8 ....239 D1
Branksome Dr SK8 ....239 D1
Branksome Rd SK4 ....240 B5
Bransdale Cl WA5 ....14 C4
Bransdale Way SK11 ....111 C4
Brantfield Ct WA2 ....8 C1
Brantwood Rd
Cheadle SK8 ....239 F1
Stockport SK4 ....240 C8
Brassey St CH3 ....118 C1
Brassey Way CW5 ....205 B3
Brassey's Contract Rd
SY14 ....199 A1
Brathay Cl WA2 ....8 B2
Brattswood Dr ST7 ....194 A3
Bray Cl Cheadle SK8 ....239 E2
Crewe CW1 ....190 C3
Runcorn WA7 ....49 B3
Bray Rd CH4 ....140 C3
Braystan Gdns SK8 ....239 B6
Breach House La WA16 ..32 A1
Bread St SK11 ....112 B4
Breamar Cl CH3 ....119 B2
Breck Rd WA8 ....13 A1
Breck The CH66 ....69 C4
Brecon Ave SK8 ....239 E1
Brecon Cl SK12 ....36 C2
Brecon Ct WA5 ....7 C1
Brecon Dr 3 CH66 ....69 C1
Brecon Way CW2 ....206 A4
Breconway CW7 ....149 A4
Bredbury Gn SK6 ....241 A1
Bredon Cl CH66 ....69 A3
Breen Cl CH3 ....166 A1
Breezehill Cl CH64 ....66 C4
Breezehill Pk CH64 ....66 C4
Breezehill Rd CH64 ....66 C4
Brendon Ave WA2 ....8 A2
Brendon Gr WA9 ....1 A2
Brennus Pl CH1 ....237 A3
Brent Cl SK12 ....36 A2
Brent Rd SK4 ....240 C5

Brentfield WA8 ....12 B1
Brentnall Cl WA5 ....15 B3
Brentnall St 2 SK1 ....240 F3
Brenton Ave M33 ....242 A6
Brenton Ct 1 SK8 ....34 C4
Brentwood M33 ....242 A6
Brentwood Ave
Altrincham WA14 ....238 E7
Irlam M44 ....11 B3
Brentwood Cl SK15 ....242 F2
Brentwood Cres WA14 ..238 E6
Brentwood Dr SK8 ....239 B5
Brentwood Rd CH1 ....117 C3
Brentwood Specl Sch
WA14 ....238 E7
Brereton CE Prim Sch
CW11 ....153 C3
Brereton Cl
Altrincham WA14 ....238 C1
Crewe CW2 ....189 C1
Malpas SY14 ....213 A2
Runcorn WA7 ....50 A4
Sandbach CW11 ....175 B4
Brereton Ct
Brereton Green CW12 ....154 C3
Cheadle SK8 ....239 E1
Brereton Dr CW5 ....204 C4
Brereton Gr M44 ....11 C3
Brereton Heath La
CW11,CW12 ....154 C3
Brereton Heath Pk*
CW12 ....154 B4
Brereton La
Brereton Green CW10,
CW11 ....153 A4
Sproston Green CW4 ....152 C4
Brereton Rd
Handforth SK9 ....34 C2
Hartford CW8 ....103 A2
Breton Cl CH2 ....118 C3
Bretton Ct Mews CH4 ....139 C2
Bretton Dr CH4 ....139 A2
Bretton La CH4 ....139 C3
Bretton Rd CH4 ....139 C2
Bretton Wlk M22 ....33 B4
Brewery La CH3 ....180 C2
Brewery St
4 Altrincham WA14 ....238 D4
Stockport SK1 ....240 F7
Brian Ave Warrington WA2 .16 B4
Warrington, Stockton Heath
WA4 ....16 C1
Briar Ave WA3 ....11 A1
Briar Cl WA16 ....57 A2
Briar Dr CH60 ....41 A4
Briar La CW8 ....102 C4
Briar Rd WA3 ....3 A4
Briardale Cl CW2 ....205 C4
Briardale Gdns 4 CH66 ..69 B3
Briardale Rd
Ellesmere Port CH66 ....69 B3
Willaston CH64 ....43 A1
Briardene M34 ....241 A8
Briarfield Ave WA8 ....12 A1
Briarfield Rd
Ellesmere Port CH65 ....70 A3
Heswall CH60 ....41 A4
Briarlands Cl SK7 ....35 B3
Briars Mount SK4 ....240 A6
Briarstead Cl SK7 ....35 B4
Briarswood ST7 ....195 A1
Briarswood Ct CH2 ....237 B3
Briarwood Runcorn WA7 ...50 A4
Wilmslow SK9 ....60 B4
Briarwood Ave
Macclesfield SK11 ....112 B3
Warrington WA1 ....16 C4
Brick Bank CW5 ....204 C3
Brick Bank La WA16,
CW4 ....107 A1
Brick Kiln La CW10 ....127 A4
Brick St Newton-le-W WA12 ..1 C2
Newton-le-W WA12 ....2 A2
Warrington WA1 ....16 B3
Brickfield Bsns Ctr CW9 ..79 B1
Brickfield La CH3 ....119 C1
Brickhill La WA15 ....32 A2
Brickhurst Way WA1 ....17 A4
Brickkiln La
Little Bollington WA14 ....20 B2
Whitchurch SY13 ....226 B1
Brickkiln Row WA14 ....238 C1
Bridge Ave WA4 ....16 C2
Bridge Ave E WA4 ....16 C3
Bridge Cl Audley ST7 ....209 C1
Cuddington CW8 ....102 A2
Lymm WA13 ....19 A2
Wistaston CW2 ....206 A4
Bridge Ct Chester CH2 ....119 A1
Holt LL13 ....196 C4
Neston CH64 ....66 C4
Bridge Dr Cheadle SK8 ..239 D4
Christleton CH3 ....142 B4
Handforth SK9 ....34 B2
Bridge End Dr SK10 ....87 A4
Bridge End La SK10 ....87 A4
Bridge Foot WA1 ....16 A2
Bridge Gn SK10 ....87 A4
Bridge Gr WA15 ....238 F7
Bridge Hall Prim Sch
SK3 ....240 D2
Bridge La
Cuddington CW8 ....101 C2
Frodsham WA6 ....49 B1
Warrington, Appleton WA4 ..26 C4
Warrington, Woolston WA1 ..17 B4
Bridge Mdw CH66 ....69 C1
Bridge Pl CH4 ....237 B1

Bridge Rd WA1 ....17 B4
Bridge Row CW12 ....156 C2
Bridge St Broughton CH4 .140 B4
Chester CH1 ....237 B2
Golborne WA3 ....3 A4
Holt LL13 ....180 C1
Macclesfield SK11 ....112 B4
Neston CH64 ....66 C4
Newton-le-W WA12 ....2 A2
Northwich CW9 ....79 C1
Runcorn WA7 ....23 A2
Stalybridge SK15 ....242 C1
Stockport SK1 ....240 F6
Warrington WA1 ....16 A3
Whaley Bridge SK23 ....65 C4
Wybunbury CW5 ....220 A4
Bridge St Row E CH1 ....237 B2
Bridge St Row W CH1 ....237 B2
Bridge Terr CH3 ....119 A1
Bridge View Cl WA8 ....23 A2
Bridgedown CW6 ....146 B1
Bridgefield Ave SK9 ....34 B1
Bridgefield St SK1 ....240 E6
Bridgeman Rd CH1 ....117 C2
Bridgeman St WA5 ....15 B2
Bridgemere CE Prim Sch
CW5 ....231 C4
Bridgemere Cl CW11 ....174 C4
Bridgemere Garden World*
CW5 ....232 A2
Bridgemere La CW5 ....220 A1
Bridgemere Mews CW5 .231 C4
Bridgemere Way 5
CW9 ....103 C2
Bridgend CH2 ....97 A1
Bridgend Cl WA8 ....12 B2
Bridges Rd CH65 ....70 C3
Bridgeside Dr WA6 ....73 A2
Bridgewater Ave WA4 ....16 C2
Bridgewater Cl
Cheadle SK8 ....34 B4
Congleton CW12 ....157 A1
Bridgewater Dr CH3 ....119 B1
Bridgewater Grange
WA7 ....50 C3
Bridgewater High Sch (Lower
Sch) WA4 ....26 B3
Bridgewater High Sch (Upper
Sch) WA4 ....26 B4
Bridgewater Mews WA4 ..26 B4
Bridgewater Rd WA14 ..238 D7
Bridgewater St
4 Lymm WA13 ....18 C2
Runcorn WA7 ....23 A1
Sale M33 ....242 B7
Bridgeway E WA7 ....24 B1
Bridgeway W WA7 ....24 B1
Bridgewood Dr CH66 ....69 B1
Bridgfield Cl SK6 ....37 C4
Bridgnorth Gr ST5 ....210 C1
Bridle Cl CH62 ....43 C4
Bridle Ct SK7 ....35 C1
Bridle Hey CW5 ....204 C1
Bridle Pk CH62 ....43 C4
Bridle Rd Bebington CH62 ..43 C3
Crewe CW2 ....190 A2
Woodford SK7,SK10 ....35 C1
Bridle Way
Ellesmere Port CH66 ....69 B2
Woodford SK7 ....36 A1
Bridlemere Ct WA1 ....16 C4
Briedden Way CH66 ....69 A3
Brien Ave WA14 ....238 E7
Brierley Prim Sch CW1 ..190 B2
Brierley Rd CW12 ....157 A1
Brierley St Crewe CW1 ..190 B2
Stalybridge SK16 ....242 A1
Briers Cl WA2 ....8 C2
Brieryhurst Rd ST7 ....195 A2
Briggs Ave CW2 ....190 B1
Bright St
Ashton-u-Lyne OL6 ....242 A2
Crewe CW1 ....190 A3
Brighton Cres SK11 ....113 A2
Brighton Gr
1 Hyde SK14 ....241 E5
Sale M33 ....242 B7
Brighton Rd SK4 ....240 C5
Brighton Road Ind Est
SK4 ....240 B5
Brighton St WA5 ....15 C3
Brights Ave 15 ST7 ....195 A1
Brightwell Cl WA5 ....14 C3
Brimelow Cres WA5 ....14 C2
Brimstage Cl CH60 ....41 B4
Brimstage Gn CH60 ....41 B4
Brimstage Rd CH60 ....41 B4
Brindley Ave Sale M33 ..242 C8
Warrington WA4 ....16 C2
Winsford CW7 ....126 B1
Brindley Cl
Kidsgrove ST7 ....194 C1
Talke ST7 ....210 B4
Brindley Gr SK9 ....34 C1
Brindley Hall Rd
Burland CW5 ....186 C1
Faddiley CW5 ....202 C4
Brindley La CW11 ....153 B2
Brindley Pk CW11 ....174 C2
Brindley Rd WA7 ....23 C2
Brindley St WA7 ....22 C2
Brindley Way
Congleton CW12 ....157 A1
Macclesfield SK11 ....112 B2
Brindley Wharf WA7 ....50 C3
Brindleys Way ST7 ....209 C1
Brine Leas High Sch
CW5 ....204 C2

Brine Pits La CW5 ....218 C1
Brine Pump Cotts CW9 ..78 C2
Brine Rd CW5 ....204 C2
Brinell Dr M44 ....11 C3
Brinksway SK3 ....240 C4
Brinksway Trad Est 1
SK3 ....240 C4
Brinley Cl CH62 ....43 B3
Brinton Cl WA8 ....22 C4
Brisbane Cl SK7 ....35 C3
Brisbane Rd CH1 ....117 B2
Bristol Ave WA7 ....50 C3
Bristol Cl Blacon CH1 ....117 C3
Cheadle SK8 ....34 B4
Bristol Dr 5 CH66 ....69 C1
Bristow Cl WA5 ....15 A4
Britannia Gdns WA6 ....73 A1
Britannia Rd Helsby WA6 ..73 A1
Sale M33 ....242 C7
Brittania Dr CW9 ....104 C4
Brixham Ave SK8 ....34 C4
Brixham Wlk SK7 ....35 C4
Broad Ct SK9 ....85 A4
Broad Hey SK6 ....241 D3
Broad La Altrincham WA15 ..32 A4
Appleton Thorn WA4 ....27 B4
Burtonwood WA5 ....6 C4
Haydock WA5,WA9 ....1 B1
Heswall CH60 ....40 B4
Sproston Green CW4 ....129 C1
Stapeley CW5 ....205 A1
Broad Oak Ave
Broughton CH4 ....139 A2
Haydock WA11 ....1 A3
Warrington WA5 ....14 C2
Broad Oak Com Prim Sch
WA9 ....1 A2
Broad Oak La M20 ....239 B8
Broad Oak Prim Sch
M20 ....239 C8
Broad Rd M33 ....242 D7
Broad St CW1 ....190 B3
Broad Street Inf Sch
CW1 ....190 B3
Broad Wlk SK9 ....59 C4
Broadacre CW9 ....78 B3
Broadacres CW5 ....217 C2
Broadbent Ave WA4 ....16 C2
Broadbent St SK14 ....241 D8
Broadcar Rd SK11 ....113 B3
Broadfield Cl M34 ....241 A6
Broadfields WA7 ....50 B4
Broadheath Prim Sch
WA14 ....238 C8
Broadheath Terr WA8 ....12 B1
Broadheys La WA16 ....28 B3
Broadhurst Ave
Culcheth WA3 ....4 C1
Warrington WA5 ....15 B2
Broadhurst La CW12 ....156 B2
Broadhurst St SK3 ....240 F3
Broadlake CH64 ....67 C4
Broadland Gdns CH66 ....69 C1
Broadland Rd CH66 ....69 C1
Broadleigh Way CW2 ....206 B4
Broadley Ave WA3 ....3 B4
Broadmead Chester CH3 .119 B1
Heswall CH60 ....41 B4
Broadoak High Sch M31 ..11 C1
Broadoak La
High Legh WA16 ....29 B3
Mobberley WA16 ....57 C3
Broadoaks Rd M33 ....242 A6
Broadwalk SK10 ....87 A3
Broadway
Altrincham WA15 ....32 A4
Barnton CW8 ....78 A2
Cheadle SK8 ....239 C4
Sale M33 ....242 A7
Widnes WA8 ....12 A1
Wilmslow SK9 ....60 A3
Broadway Ave SK8 ....239 D5
Broadway E CH2 ....118 C3
Broadway The CW5 ....204 C3
Broadway W CH2 ....118 B3
Broadways CW3 ....230 A2
Broadwood Cl SK6 ....37 C4
Broady Ct CW2 ....190 B1
Brock Dr SK8 ....35 A4
Brock Gdns L24 ....21 C1
Brock Hollow CW11 ....174 C2
Brock Rd WA3 ....9 B2
Brock St SK10 ....87 B1
Brockhurst St CW9 ....104 A4
Brockhurst Way CW9 ....104 A3
Brocklebank Dr CW8 ....103 C4
Brocklehurst Ave SK10 ..87 C1
Brocklehurst Ct 9 SK10 ..87 B2
Brocklehurst Dr SK10 ....87 A4
Brocklehurst Manor
SK10 ....87 C1
Brocklehurst Way SK10 ..87 B2
Brockway E CH3 ....166 A1
Brockway W CH3 ....166 A1
Brockwell Cl 3 CW7 ....149 A4
Brodie Cl CH2 ....95 B1
Brogden Ave WA3 ....4 C2
Brogden Dr SK8 ....239 B5
Brogden Gr M33 ....242 A5
Brogden Terr M33 ....242 A5
Broken Banks 21 SK11 ....112 B4
Broken Cross SK11 ....111 C4
Broken Cross Com Sch
SK11 ....111 C4
Brokencross Pl CW9 ....104 C4

Bromborough Rake Sta CH62 ... 43 B4
Bromborough Sta CH63 ... 43 B4
Bromborough Village Rd CH62 ... 43 C4
Bromleigh Ave SK8 ... 239 B6
Bromley Ave WA3 ... 3 B4
Bromley Cl Crewe CW1 ... 189 C4
Heswall CH60 ... 40 C4
Warrington WA2 ... 8 C2
Bromley Dr CW4 ... 130 B1
Bromley Rd
Congleton CW12 ... 156 C2
Macclesfield SK10 ... 111 C4
Brompton Gdns WA5 ... 15 C4
Brompton Rd SK4 ... 240 A6
Brompton Way
Ellesmere Port CH66 ... 69 C1
Handforth SK9 ... 34 B3
Bronington Ave CH62 ... 43 B3
Bronte Cl WA2 ... 8 A3
Brook Acre Com Prim Sch WA2 ... 8 C1
Brook Ave
Altrincham WA15 ... 238 E6
Handforth SK9 ... 34 B2
Shavington CW2 ... 206 B3
Warrington, Stockton Heath WA4 ... 16 C1
Warrington, Westy WA4 ... 16 C3
Brook Bank SK12 ... 37 B1
Brook Bottom Rd SK22 ... 39 A4
Brook Cl
Altrincham WA15 ... 238 E6
Crewe CW1 ... 190 C2
Cronton WA8 ... 12 B3
Brook Ct Chester CH1 ... 118 A2
Sandbach CW11 ... 175 A3
Brook Dr Kelsall CW6 ... 122 B2
Warrington WA5 ... 15 A3
Brook End WA9 ... 1 A1
Brook Farm Sch CW6 ... 168 B4
Brook Fm Cl M31 ... 11 C1
Brook Furlong WA6 ... 48 C1
Brook Gdns ST8 ... 179 B1
Brook Hey CH64 ... 41 A1
Brook House Dr CW2 ... 206 B4
Brook La
Alderley Edge SK9 ... 59 C2
Altrincham WA15 ... 238 F6
Astbury CW12 ... 177 C3
Broughton CH5 ... 139 B4
Burland CW5 ... 203 B4
Chester CH2 ... 118 C2
Faddiley CW5 ... 202 C4
Knutsford WA16 ... 57 A1
Neston CH64 ... 41 B1
Northwich CW9 ... 104 B4
Warrington WA3 ... 18 A4
Brook Lodge SK8 ... 239 D4
Brook Pl WA4 ... 16 C2
Brook Rd Cheadle SK8 ... 239 D6
Ellesmere Port CH66 ... 69 B3
Lymm WA13 ... 18 B2
Tarporley CW6 ... 168 B4
Brook Side CW8 ... 102 B4
Brook St Cheadle SK8 ... 239 F6
Chester CH2 ... 237 B3
Congleton CW12 ... 156 C2
Crewe CW2 ... 190 B2
Golborne WA3 ... 3 A4
Hyde SK14 ... 241 E7
Knutsford WA16 ... 57 A1
Macclesfield SK11 ... 112 C4
Neston CH64 ... 66 C4
Northwich CW9 ... 79 A1
Northwich, Lostock Gralam CW9 ... 79 C1
Runcorn WA7 ... 23 A1
Sale M33 ... 242 C7
Widnes WA8 ... 13 A1
Brook Street Bridge CH2 ... 237 C4
Brook Terr CW11 ... 175 A2
Brook View
Alderley Edge SK9 ... 60 A2
Allostock WA16 ... 106 C2
Brook Villas ST7 ... 193 C2
Brook Way
Nantwich CW5 ... 204 C2
Warrington WA5 ... 15 A3
Brook Well CH64 ... 66 C3
Brookash Rd M22 ... 34 A4
Brookdale WA8 ... 12 A2
Brookdale Ave
Denton M34 ... 241 B6
Knutsford WA16 ... 57 B1
Brookdale Ct CH3 ... 143 B3
Brookdale Pk CW2 ... 190 A2
Brookdale Pl CH1 ... 237 B3
Brookdale Way CH3 ... 143 A3
Brooke Ave CH2 ... 118 C4
Brooke Dean Com Sch SK9 ... 34 B2
Brooke Dr SK9 ... 34 B2
Brooke Ho SK10 ... 86 C1
Brooke Way SK9 ... 34 B2
Brookes Ave CH4 ... 139 A2
Brookfield CW1 ... 191 B3
Brookfield Ave
Altrincham WA15 ... 238 F8
Poynton SK12 ... 36 B2
Romiley SK6 ... 241 A4
Runcorn WA7 ... 23 C1
Brookfield Cl Lymm WA13 ... 18 B2
Brookfield Cl *continued*
Tarporley CW6 ... 168 B4
Brookfield Cres
Cheadle SK8 ... 239 D4
Goostrey CW4 ... 107 C1
Brookfield Ct CW1 ... 190 A3
Brookfield Dr
Alsager ST7 ... 193 B3
Chester CH2 ... 118 C2
Holmes Chapel CW4 ... 130 A2
Brookfield Gr OL6 ... 242 A2
Brookfield Ho SK8 ... 239 D4
Brookfield La SK11 ... 112 C4
Brookfield Pk WA4 ... 17 A1
Brookfield Rd
Cheadle SK8 ... 239 E5
Comberbach CW9 ... 78 B4
Culcheth WA3 ... 4 B2
Lymm WA13 ... 18 B2
Brookfield St WA12 ... 2 A2
Brookfields Sch WA8 ... 13 B1
Brookhead Dr SK8 ... 240 A2
Brookhead Jun Sch SK8 ... 239 F5
Brookhouse Cl SK10 ... 86 C1
Brookhouse La
Church Minshull CW1, CW10 ... 172 B4
Congleton CW12 ... 157 B1
Duddon CH3 ... 144 B3
Whitley WA4 ... 52 A1
Brookhouse Rd
Alsager ST7 ... 193 B2
5 Sandbach CW11 ... 175 A3
Brookhurst Ave CH63 ... 43 B3
Brookhurst Cl CH63 ... 43 B3
Brookhurst Prim Sch CH63 ... 43 B3
Brookhurst Rd CH63 ... 43 B3
Brookland Ave CW2 ... 205 C4
Brookland Dr CW11 ... 175 C3
Brookland La WA9 ... 1 A1
Brookland St WA1 ... 16 C4
Brooklands Ave SK11 ... 112 A4
Brooklands Cres M33 ... 242 B5
Brooklands Ct M33 ... 242 B5
Brooklands Dr
Goostrey CW4 ... 107 C1
Northwich CW9 ... 104 A2
Brooklands Gdns CH64 ... 41 B1
Brooklands Gr CW1 ... 190 A3
Brooklands Mews SK11 ... 112 A4
Brooklands Pl M33 ... 242 A5
Brooklands Rd
Congleton CW12 ... 155 C1
Neston CH64 ... 41 B1
Brooklands Sta M33 ... 242 A5
Brooklands Station App M33 ... 242 A5
Brookledge La SK10 ... 62 C3
Brookln Pl SK8 ... 239 D6
Brooklyn Cres SK8 ... 239 D5
Brooklyn Dr
Ellesmere Port CH65 ... 69 C3
Lymm WA13 ... 18 C2
Brooklyn Rd SK8 ... 239 D5
Brooklyn St CW2 ... 190 B1
Brookmere Cl CW11 ... 174 C4
Brooks Ave SK14 ... 241 E5
Brooks Dr WA15 ... 32 B4
Brooks La Bosley SK11 ... 135 C1
Middlewich CW10 ... 128 B1
Brooks Lane Ind Est CW10 ... 151 B4
Brooks St SK1 ... 240 F3
Brookside Ashton CH3 ... 121 C4
Chester CH3 ... 142 A4
Cuddington CW8 ... 101 C2
Kelsall CW6 ... 122 B2
Kingsley WA6 ... 75 B1
Warrington WA4 ... 16 C2
Brookside Ave
Lymm WA13 ... 18 B2
Poynton SK12 ... 36 C2
Sutton Lane Ends SK11 ... 112 C1
Warrington, Great Sankey WA5 ... 15 A2
Warrington, Stockton Heath WA4 ... 16 B1
Brookside Cl
Cheadle SK8 ... 239 D4
Haydock WA11 ... 1 A4
Brookside Cotts
7 Lymm WA13 ... 18 B2
Sandbach CW11 ... 176 A4
Brookside Ct SK10 ... 87 A1
Brookside Gn CW2 ... 206 B4
Brookside La SK6 ... 37 C4
Brookside Mill SK11 ... 112 C4
Brookside Miniature Rly* SK12 ... 36 C4
Brookside Prim Sch
Ellesmere Port CH66 ... 69 B2
Ellesmere Port CH66 ... 69 C2
High Lane SK6 ... 37 C3
Brookside Rd
Congleton CW12 ... 156 B2
Frodsham WA6 ... 74 A4
Gatley SK8 ... 239 A6
Brookside Terr CH2 ... 237 C4
Brookside View WA11 ... 1 A4
Brookside Way WA11 ... 1 A4
Brookvale Ave N WA7 ... 50 A3
Brookvale Ave S WA7 ... 50 A3
Brookvale Cl WA5 ... 6 C3
Brookvale Comp Sch WA7 ... 50 B3
Brookvale Prim Sch WA7 ... 50 A3
Brookway WA15 ... 238 F7
Brookway La WA9 ... 1 A1
Brookwood Cl WA4 ... 26 A4
Broom Ave WA4 ... 26 C3
Broom Cres CH3 ... 121 A1
Broom La WA16 ... 81 C1
Broom Rd
Altrincham WA15 ... 238 E3
Partington M31 ... 11 C1
Broom St CW1 ... 190 A3
Broom's La CW6 ... 122 B3
Broome Ct WA7 ... 50 A3
Broomehouse Ave M44 ... 11 C4
Broomfield Cl
Chelford SK11 ... 84 A2
Wilmslow SK9 ... 60 C4
14 Winsford CW7 ... 149 A4
Broomfield La WA15 ... 238 E3
Broomfield Rd SK4 ... 240 C8
Broomfields Jun Sch WA4 ... 26 C4
Broomfields Rd WA4 ... 26 B4
Broomgrove La M34 ... 241 A8
Broomheath La CH3 ... 144 B4
Broomhill La
Brown Knowl CH3 ... 199 B4
Great Barrow CH3 ... 120 C4
Broomlands CH60 ... 40 C4
Broomlands Cotts CW5 ... 219 C1
Broomsfield La CW8 ... 78 A2
Broomville Ave M33 ... 242 B6
Broseley Ave WA3 ... 4 B2
Broseley La WA3 ... 4 B3
Brotherton Cl CH62 ... 43 B4
Brotherton Way WA12 ... 2 A2
Brough St W SK11 ... 112 B4
Broughton Ave WA3 ... 3 B4
Broughton Cl WA4 ... 26 C4
Broughton Cres SY14 ... 211 A1
Broughton Hall Rd CH4 ... 139 B2
Broughton Inf Sch CH4 ... 139 B2
Broughton Jun Sch CH4 ... 139 B2
Broughton La CW2 ... 189 C1
Broughton Mills Rd CH4 ... 139 C3
Broughton Rd
Adlington SK10 ... 62 B3
Crewe CW1 ... 190 B4
Stockport SK5 ... 240 F8
Broughton Ret Pk CH4 ... 139 C2
Broughton Way WA8 ... 22 A3
Broughville Dr M20 ... 239 C8
Brow Com Prim Sch The WA7 ... 23 C1
Brow La Antrobus CW9 ... 53 B3
Heswall CH60 ... 40 C4
Brow The WA6 ... 75 B1
Browmere Dr WA3 ... 9 A4
Brown Ave
Lawton-gate ST7 ... 194 A3
Nantwich CW5 ... 204 C2
Brown Heath Rd CH3 ... 143 A3
Brown La SK8 ... 239 B1
Brown Lees Cl CW2 ... 190 A1
Brown Lees Rd ST7 ... 195 C2
Brown St
2 Alderley Edge SK9 ... 60 A1
Altrincham WA14 ... 238 D3
Congleton CW12 ... 156 C2
Macclesfield SK11 ... 112 B4
1 Stockport SK1 ... 240 E6
Widnes WA8 ... 23 B4
Brown's La Chester CH4 ... 141 B4
Wilmslow SK9 ... 60 C4
Brownhill Dr WA1 ... 16 C4
Brownhills Rd CW6 ... 147 B3
Browning Ave WA8 ... 22 C4
Browning Cl Blacon CH1 ... 117 C3
10 Sandbach CW11 ... 174 B3
Browning Dr
Ellesmere Port CH65 ... 69 C2
Winwick WA2 ... 8 A3
Browning Gn CH65 ... 69 C2
Browning Gr ST7 ... 210 B4
Browning St CW1 ... 190 B2
Browning Way CW7 ... 149 A4
Brownlow Cl SK12 ... 36 C1
Broxton Ave CW10 ... 151 B3
Broxton Cl WA8 ... 12 B2
Broxton Rd Clutton CH3 ... 182 B1
Ellesmere Port CH66 ... 69 C3
Bruce Ave WA2 ... 8 B1
Bruce Cres CH63 ... 43 B3
Bruce Dr CH66 ... 69 B2
Bruche Ave WA1 ... 16 C4
Bruche Com Inf Sch WA1 ... 17 A4
Bruche Com Jun Sch WA1 ... 17 A4
Bruche Dr WA1 ... 16 C4
Bruche Heath Gdns WA1 ... 17 A4
Bruen The CH3 ... 121 B2
Bruera Rd CH65 ... 69 C2
Brunel Ct CW9 ... 104 C3
Brunel Rd SK11 ... 112 B2
Brunner Bsns Ctr CW8 ... 78 B1
Brunner Gr CW5 ... 205 A3
Brunner Rd WA8 ... 23 A4
Brunsborough Cl CH62 ... 43 B3
Brunswick Cres CH66 ... 69 C2
Brunswick Ct 3 SK11 ... 112 B4
Brunswick Hill SK11 ... 112 B4
Brunswick Rd
Altrincham WA14 ... 238 D7
Newton-le-W WA12 ... 1 C2
Brunswick St
Congleton CW12 ... 156 C2
Brunswick St *continued*
35 Macclesfield SK11 ... 112 B4
St Helens WA9 ... 1 A2
Brunswick Terr SK11 ... 112 B4
Bruntleigh Ave WA4 ... 17 A2
Bruntwood Ave SK8 ... 239 A1
Bruntwood La SK8 ... 239 E2
Bruntwood Prim Sch SK8 ... 239 E2
Brussels Rd SK3 ... 240 D2
Bryant Ave WA4 ... 16 C3
Bryce St SK14 ... 241 D8
Brymau Five Est CH4 ... 140 B4
Brymau Four Est CH4 ... 140 B4
Brymau One Est CH4 ... 140 C4
Brymau Three Est CH4 ... 140 B4
Brymau Two Est CH4 ... 140 C4
Brynlow Dr CW10 ... 151 A4
Brynmore Dr SK11 ... 112 C4
Brynn St WA8 ... 23 A4
Brynton Cl SK10 ... 87 B1
Brynton Rd SK10 ... 87 B1
Buchan Cl WA5 ... 15 A4
Buchan Gr CW2 ... 190 A2
Buck La CW2 ... 206 C2
Buckbean Way CW4 ... 107 C1
Buckden Way SK11 ... 112 B4
Buckfast Ave WA11 ... 2 A4
Buckfast Cl Bramhall SK8 ... 35 A3
Macclesfield SK10 ... 87 B1
Poynton SK12 ... 36 B3
Warrington WA5 ... 14 C2
Buckfast Ct WA7 ... 24 C2
Buckfast Way CW10 ... 128 A1
Buckingham Ave
Chester CH3 ... 119 A1
Denton M34 ... 241 B6
Widnes WA8 ... 13 A2
Buckingham Cl CW2 ... 205 C4
Buckingham Dr
Davenham CW9 ... 103 C2
Knutsford WA16 ... 57 A1
Warrington WA5 ... 15 B2
Winsford CW7 ... 149 B4
Buckingham Rd
1 Ellesmere Port CH65 ... 70 B1
Irlam M44 ... 11 B3
Poynton SK12 ... 36 B2
Stalybridge SK15 ... 242 D3
Wilmslow SK9 ... 59 C3
Buckingham Rd W SK4 ... 240 A8
Buckingham Way SK2 ... 240 F2
Buckland Cl WA8 ... 22 B4
Buckley Ave CW10 ... 128 C4
Buckley Cl CW10 ... 151 A4
Buckley Dr SK6 ... 241 A1
Buckley St
Macclesfield SK11 ... 112 B4
Warrington WA2 ... 16 A3
Bucklow Ave
Mobberley WA16 ... 58 A2
Partington M31 ... 11 C2
Bucklow Gdns WA13 ... 19 A2
Bucklow View WA14 ... 238 A3
Bucklow Wlk 11 SK11 ... 112 C4
Bucklowhill La WA16 ... 30 A2
Buckton St WA1 ... 16 B4
Bude Cl Alsager ST7 ... 193 A2
Bramhall SK7 ... 35 C4
Crewe CW1 ... 190 A4
Bude Rd WA8 ... 12 C1
Budworth Ave
Warrington WA4 ... 16 C2
Widnes WA8 ... 12 B1
Budworth Cl Runcorn WA7 ... 49 B4
Sandbach CW11 ... 174 C4
Budworth Heath La CW9 ... 54 B1
Budworth La CW9 ... 78 C4
Budworth Rd
Bate Heath CW9 ... 54 C1
Ellesmere Port CH66 ... 69 C1
Sale M33 ... 242 E5
Tabley WA16 ... 55 B1
Budworth Wlk 1 SK9 ... 34 C1
Buerton Prim Sch CW3 ... 230 C2
Buffs La CH60 ... 41 A4
Buggen La CH64 ... 66 B4
Buglawton Hall Specl Sch CW12 ... 157 B3
Buglawton Ind Est CW12 ... 156 C2
Buglawton Prim Sch CW12 ... 157 A2
Buildwas Rd CH64 ... 41 C1
Bulkeley Hall La SY14 ... 200 B4
Bulkeley Rd Cheadle SK8 ... 239 E6
Handforth SK9 ... 34 B2
Poynton SK12 ... 36 C2
Bulkeley St Chester CH3 ... 119 A1
Stockport SK3 ... 240 D4
Bull Hill CH64 ... 66 C3
Bull Hill La SK10 ... 88 B1
Bull Ring CW9 ... 103 C4
Bull Ring The CW10 ... 128 B1
Bullcroft Cl SY14 ... 211 B4
Bullock St SK2 ... 240 F3
Bullocks House Rd ST7 ... 195 C2
Bullocks La SK11 ... 112 C2
Bumper's La CH1 ... 117 C1
Bunbury Cl
Middlewich CW10 ... 151 B3
Northwich CW9 ... 104 A3
Stoak CH2 ... 96 A4
Bunbury Dr WA7 ... 49 B3
Bunbury Gn CH65 ... 70 B1
Bunbury La CW6 ... 185 C4
Bunbury Rd CW6 ... 169 B2
Bunce La SK11 ... 133 A2
Bunce St CH4 ... 237
Bungalow Rd WA12 ... 2
Bungalows The CH63 ... 42
Bunham Cl ST7 ... 193
Bunkershill Rd SK6 ... 241
Bunting Cl 5 WA3 ... 3
Buntingford Rd WA4 ... 17
Bunts La CW12 ... 156
Burdett Rd 1 CH66 ... 69
Burfield Dr WA4 ... 26
Burford Ave SK7 ... 35
Burford Cl SK9 ... 59
Burford Cres SK9 ... 59
Burford La WA13 ... 19
Burgamot La CW9 ... 78
Burganey Ct CH4 ... 162
Burges St CH2 ... 118
Burgess Ave WA4 ... 16
Burgess Cl CW5 ... 205
Burgess Dr CH1 ... 117
Burgess La WA6 ... 101
Burgess Pl 18 CW8 ... 103
Burgess St SK10 ... 112
Burghley Cl SK15 ... 242
Burjen Way CW1 ... 190
Burkhardt Dr WA12 ... 2
Burkitt St SK14 ... 241
Burland Cl WA7 ... 22
Burland Gr CW7 ... 126
Burland Rd Halewood L26 ... 21
Newcastle-u-L ST5 ... 210
Burlea Cl CW2 ... 189
Burlea Dr CW2 ... 206
Burlescombe Cl WA14 ... 238
Burley Ct SK4 ... 240
Burley La WA4 ... 27
Burleyhurst La SK9,WA16 ... 59
Burlington Ct WA14 ... 238
Burlington Rd WA14 ... 238
Burnell Cl CW5 ... 204
Burnell Rd CH65 ... 70
Burnet Cl WA2 ... 9
Burnfell WA3 ... 3
Burnham Cl Cheadle SK8 ... 239
Culcheth WA3 ... 4
Warrington WA5 ... 14
Widnes WA8 ... 12
Burnham Rd CH4 ... 140
Burns Ave SK8 ... 239
Burns Cl
Ellesmere Port CH66 ... 69
Rode Heath ST7 ... 193
Burns Cres WA8 ... 22
Burns Dr CW1 ... 190
Burns Gr WA2 ... 8
Burns Rd CW12 ... 157
Burns Way CH1 ... 117
Burnsall Ave WA3 ... 3
Burnsall Dr WA8 ... 12
Burnside WA15 ... 32
Burnside Ave WA4 ... 16
Burnside Cl SK9 ... 60
Burnside Rd SK8 ... 239
Burnt Acre SK11 ... 84
Burnwood Gr ST7 ... 195
Burran Rd M22 ... 33
Burrough Cl WA3 ... 9
Burrows Hill CW8 ... 103
Burrows La WA6 ... 73
Burrows St WA11 ... 1
Burrows The CW8 ... 101
Bursar Cl WA12 ... 2
Burslam St CW12 ... 156
Burton Ave CW6 ... 146
Burton Cl Culcheth WA3 ... 4
Widnes WA8 ... 12
Burton Dr SK12 ... 36
Burton Gn CH66 ... 69
Burton Gr CW1 ... 173
Burton Hall Rd LL12 ... 161
Burton La CW6 ... 144
Burton Manor Coll CH64 ... 67
Burton Rd Blacon CH1 ... 117
Neston CH64 ... 66
Warrington WA2 ... 8
Burton St SK4 ... 240
Burtonwood Com Prim Sch WA5 ... 6
Burtonwood Ind Ctr WA5 ... 6
Burtonwood Rd WA5 ... 7
Burtonwood Service Area WA5 ... 7
Burwardsley Rd CH3 ... 166
Burwardsley Way CW9 ... 103
Bury St SK5 ... 240
Bush Rd Christleton CH3 ... 142
Widnes WA8 ... 22
Bush Way CH60 ... 40
Bushell Cl CH64 ... 66
Bushell Rd CH64 ... 66
Bushells La WA6 ... 99
Butler Way CW5 ... 204
Butley Cl
Macclesfield SK10 ... 87
Middlewich CW10 ... 151
Butley Lanes SK10 ... 61
Butterbache Rd CH3 ... 142
Butterbur Cl CH3 ... 142
Buttercup Dr SK3 ... 240
Buttermarket St WA1 ... 16
Buttermere Ave
Ellesmere Port CH65 ... 70
Warrington WA2 ... 8
Buttermere Cl WA6 ... 74
Buttermere Cres WA2 ... 8
Buttermere Ct CW12 ... 156
Buttermere Dr
Alderley Edge SK9 ... 83

ttermere Dr *continued*
trincham WA15 32 B3
ewe CW1 173 A1
ttermere Gr WA7 49 B3
ttermere Rd
tley SK8 239 B3
rtington M31 11 C2
nsford CW7 126 B1
ttermere Terr SK15 242 D3
tterton La CW1 192 B1
tton Field CW8 126 A4
tts The Alsager ST7 193 B2
ncorn WA7 23 C1
xton Ave CW1 190 C2
xton Cl WA5 15 A4
xton New Rd
acclesfield Forest SK11 114 B4
inow SK10 88 B1
xton Old Rd
ngleton CW12 157 A2
sley SK12 38 C2
acclesfield SK11 113 B4
xton Rd
ngleton CW12 157 B3
sley SK12 38 C3
zel Grove SK7 37 A4
gh Lane SK12,SK6,SK7 37 B4
acclesfield SK10,SK11 112 C4
w Mills SK22,SK23 39 B2
haley Bridge SK23 39 C1
haley Bridge, New Horwich
23 65 C3
xton Rd W SK12 38 A3
xton St SK8 239 A5
e Pass Rd CH3 121 A2
e Pass The CH3 119 C1
and Ave SK8 35 A3
and Cl WA8 13 B3
ands Cl SK12 36 B2
ey La Cranage CW10 129 B3
iddlewich CW10 128 C2
ley Prim Sch CW10 129 A4
ley Way CW7 126 A1
ng Ave M44 11 B2
rom St WA14 238 D3
ron Cl Blacon CH1 117 C3
ewe CW1 190 C2
iddlewich CW10 151 B3
de Heath ST7 193 C4
ndbach CW11 174 B3
ron Ct
trincham WA14 238 D6
arrington WA2 8 B1
ron Dr SK8 239 F6
ron St WA7 23 A1
ron Way CW2 190 A1
ron's La SK11 112 C3
rons St SK11 112 B3
thom Cl CH3 142 C4

bot Cl WA5 7 B1
bot Pl SK5 240 F8
bul Cl WA2 16 B4
dishead Prim Sch M44 11 C3
dnant Cl CH1 117 B2
dnant Ct CH4 139 B3
dshaw Cl WA3 9 B3
er Castell LL13 196 B4
erleon Cl CW7 149 A4
erllew LL13 180 C1
ernarvon Ave CW7 149 A4
ernarvon Cl WA7 23 C1
ernarvon Ct 4 CH65 70 B1
ernarvon Rd CW2 205 C4
esars Cl WA7 23 C1
irns Cres CH1 117 B2
iro St WA1 16 A3
ister Way CW7 149 B4
ithness Ct WA7 23 A1
lamine St SK11 112 C3
lcutta Rd SK3 240 C3
lday Gr WA11 1 A4
ldbeck Ave Sale M33 242 E7
arrington WA2 8 B1
ldene Terr SK23 65 C4
lder Ave CW1 191 A3
lder Cl Bollington SK10 87 C4
ynton SK12 36 B1
idnes WA8 13 C2
lder Way 7 CH66 69 B3
lderfield Cl WA4 26 A4
ldicott Ave CH62 43 B4
ldicott Cl 4 CW7 149 B4
ldwell Ave WA5 7 C1
ldwell Cl CW5 205 A2
ldwell Rd WA8 23 A4
ldwell's Gate La CW9 54 A4
ldy Cl CH2 118 B3
ldy Dr CH66 69 B2
ldy Rd Alsager ST7 193 B2
andforth SK9 34 B2
ldy Valley Rd CH3 142 A4
ldy Way CW7 126 A1
le Gn SK2 240 F2
le Green Prim Sch
3 240 F2
le St SK2 240 F2
lifornia Cl WA5 15 B4
lland Ave SK14 241 F7
llands Prim Sch WA5 7 C1
llands Rd WA5 7 B1
lmington La WA7 24 C2
lrofold Dr ST5 210 B1
lrofold La SK10 88 B1
lstock Cl WA5 14 C2

Calveley Ave CH62 43 C2
Calveley Cl CW9 103 C3
Calveley Green La CW6, CW7 170 B2
Calveley Hall La CW5, CW6 170 A1
Calveley Rd Halewood L26 21 A3
Macclesfield SK10 86 C1
Calveley Sch CW6 170 A1
Calveley Way CW7 126 A1
Calver Rd WA2 8 A2
Calver Wlk SK8 239 E1
Calverley Cl SK9 60 B4
Calverly Cl WA7 50 B3
Calverly Rd SK8 240 A1
Calvers WA7 23 C1
Camberley Cl SK7 36 A4
Camberwell Park Rd WA8 13 B2
Camborne Ave SK10 111 C4
Camborne Cl WA7 50 B3
Cambourne Cl CW12 178 C4
Cambourne Rd WA5 6 C3
Cambrai Ave WA4 16 B1
Cambrian Ave CH3 119 A1
Cambrian Cl CH66 69 A3
Cambrian Rd SK3 240 C4
Cambrian Villas CH3 165 B1
Cambrian Way CW7 149 A4
Cambridge Ave
Macclesfield SK11 112 A4
Wilmslow SK9 59 C4
Winsford CW7 126 A1
Cambridge Cl
Biddulph ST8 179 B1
Warrington WA4 26 A4
Cambridge Gdns
Helsby WA6 73 B2
Warrington WA4 26 B3
Cambridge Rd
Altrincham WA15 238 E2
Bebington CH62 43 C4
Chester CH2 118 C3
Ellesmere Port CH65 70 B3
Gatley SK8 239 B5
Macclesfield SK11 112 A4
Cambridge Road Com Prim Sch CH65 70 B3
Cambridge St
Runcorn WA7 23 B1
Stalybridge SK15 242 D2
Widnes WA8 23 A4
Camden Ct WA7 24 B1
Camden Rd CH65 70 A3
Camden St CW1 190 B2
Camellia Gdns WA9 6 A4
Camelot Cl WA12 1 C2
Camelot Gr CW2 206 B2
Camelot Way WA7 50 A4
Cameron Ave
Runcorn WA7 48 C4
Shavington CW2 206 A2
Cameron Ct WA2 8 A2
Cameron Rd WA8 23 A4
Camm St CW2 190 D1
Camomile Wlk 12 M31 11 C2
Campbell Ave WA7 49 A4
Campbell Cl
Congleton CW12 157 A2
Haslington CW1 191 B2
Macclesfield SK10 87 A1
Northwich CW9 103 C2
Campbell Cres WA5 14 C3
Campden Way SK9 34 B2
Campion Cl
Huntington CH3 142 A3
Warrington WA3 9 B3
Campsey Ash WA8 12 C2
Camrose Cl WA7 49 B3
Camsley La WA13 18 A2
Canaan WA3 4 B4
Canada Cl WA2 9 A1
Canadian Ave CH2 119 A2
Canal Bank WA13 18 B2
Canal Bridge Ent Pk CH65 70 B3
Canal Cotts CW5 187 B3
Canal Ct Trad Est CH65 70 B4
Canal Rd
Altrincham WA14 238 E8
Congleton CW12 156 C1
Canal Reach WA7 24 B1
Canal Side Barnton CW8 78 A1
Chester CH2 237 C3
Macclesfield SK11 112 C4
Moore WA4 25 B3
Preston on the Hill WA4 50 C3
Runcorn WA7 48 B4
Warrington WA4 17 B1
Whaley Bridge SK23 39 C1
Canal Side Cotts WA7 50 C3
Canal St Chester CH1 237 A3
Congleton CW12 156 C1
Dukinfield SK14 241 C7
Macclesfield SK11 112 C4
Newton-le-W WA12 1 C2
Runcorn WA7 23 A1
Stalybridge SK15 242 D1
Stockport SK1 240 F4
Whaley Bridge SK23 65 C4
Canal Terr CW10 151 B4
Canalside CH65 70 B3
Canberra Ave WA2 8 B2
Canberra Rd SK7 35 C3
Canberra Sq WA2 8 B1
Canberra Way CH1 117 B2
Candelan Way WA16 29 B2
Candle La CW3 232 A1

Candleston Cl WA5 7 C1
Candy La SK10 62 B4
Canford Cl Crewe CW1 190 A4
Warrington WA5 15 B3
Canley Cl 7 SK1 240 F4
Cann La CW9 55 A3
Cann La N WA4 26 C3
Cann La S WA4 26 C2
Cannell Ct WA7 50 A3
Cannell St WA5 15 B2
Canning St Chester CH1 237 A3
7 Stockport SK4 240 E6
Canniswood Rd WA11 1 A3
Cannock Cl CH66 94 C4
Cannock Dr SK4 240 A6
Cannon St CH65 70 A3
Cannon Way CH4 161 A4
Canon Dr WA14 238 B1
Canon St WA7 22 C2
Canon Wilson Cl WA11 1 B3
Canons Rd WA5 15 B3
Canterbury Cl CH66 94 C4
Canterbury Ct 2 SK10 112 C4
Canterbury Rd
Blacon CH1 117 C3
Widnes WA8 22 B4
Canterbury St WA4 16 B2
Cantley Cl WA7 49 B3
Canton Pl CW8 103 B4
Canton St SK11 112 B3
Canton Wlks SK11 112 B3
Canute Pl WA16 57 A1
Capeland Cl CH4 140 C3
Capenhurst Ave
Crewe CW2 190 A2
Warrington WA2 9 A1
Capenhurst CE Prim Sch CH1 94 A4
Capenhurst Cl SK12 36 C2
Capenhurst Gdns CH66 69 B1
Capenhurst Grange Sch CH66 69 C1
Capenhurst La
Capenhurst CH1 94 A4
Ellesmere Port CH65 70 A2
Capenhurst Sta CH1 69 B1
Capesthorne Cl
Alsager ST7 193 B2
Davenham CW9 103 C2
Hazel Grove SK7 36 C4
Holmes Chapel CW4 130 A2
Sandbach CW11 175 B4
Widnes WA8 22 C4
Capesthorne Hall* SK11 110 A3
Capesthorne Rd
Crewe CW2 189 C2
Hazel Grove SK7 36 C4
High Lane SK6 37 C4
Warrington WA2 8 B1
Waverton CH3 143 A3
Wilmslow SK9 59 C3
Capesthorne Way 16 SK11 112 C4
Capitol Wlk CW12 156 D1
Capper Cl ST7 195 A1
Capper's La CW5,CW6 186 B2
Cappers La CW11 176 B1
Carden Cl WA3 9 B2
Cardenbrook Gr 4 SK9 34 B1
Cardeston Cl WA7 49 C2
Cardiff Cl CH66 94 C4
Cardigan Cl
Macclesfield SK11 112 A4
Warrington WA5 7 B1
Carey St WA8 13 A1
Carisbrook Ave SK10 87 C1
Carisbrook Dr CW7 149 B4
Carisbrooke Cl CW2 205 C4
Carleton Rd SK12 37 B2
Carlett Bvd CH62 43 C3
Carlile St SK3 240 E4
Carlingford Cl SK3 240 E1
Carlingford Rd WA4 26 A4
Carlisle Cl
Macclesfield SK11 111 C3
Mobberley WA16 58 A2
Romiley SK6 241 A1
Winsford CW7 126 A1
Carlisle Dr WA14 238 E8
Carlisle Rd CH1 117 C3
Carlisle St
9 Alderley Edge SK9 60 A1
Crewe CW2 190 A1
Warrington WA4 26 B4
Carlow Cl L24 21 B1
Carlton Ave Bramhall SK7 35 B3
Broughton CH4 140 B3
Cheadle SK8 239 F3
Handforth SK9 34 B1
Romiley SK6 241 D2
Runcorn WA7 23 B1
Carlton Cl
Mickle Trafford CH2 119 C4
Neston CH64 41 B1
Carlton Cres CH66 69 C4
Carlton Dr SK8 239 A6
Carlton Pl CH2 119 A2
Carlton Rd Lymm WA13 19 A3
Northwich CW9 104 A4
Sale M33 242 A8
Stockport SK4 240 A6
Carlton St
Warrington WA4 26 B4
Widnes WA8 23 A4
Carlton Way M44 11 B3
Carlyle Cl ST7 193 C4
Carlyle Cres CH66 69 C2

Carlyn Ave M33 242 D6
Carmarthen Cl
Warrington WA5 7 B1
5 Winsford CW7 149 B4
Carmel Cl CH1 117 B2
Carmel Ct WA8 13 A2
Carmenna Dr SK7 35 C4
Carmichael Cl M31 11 C2
Carmichael St SK3 240 D4
Carnegie Cl SK10 87 A1
Carnforth Dr M33 242 A5
Carnoustie Cl
Wilmslow SK9 60 B4
Winsford CW7 126 A1
Carnoustie Dr
Gatley SK8 239 C1
Macclesfield SK10 87 B3
Carnoustie Gr WA11 1 A3
Carol Dr CH60 41 B4
Carol St WA4 16 B2
Caroline St Irlam M44 11 C4
Stalybridge SK15 242 D1
Stockport SK3 240 D3
Widnes WA8 23 A4
Carpenter Gr WA2 9 A1
Carr Brow SK6 38 A4
Carr La Alderley Edge SK9 59 B1
Audley ST7 209 A1
Golborne WN7 4 C4
Hale L24,WA8 21 C2
Carr Mill Mews SK9 34 A1
Carr St ST7 195 C1
Carr Wood Ave SK7 35 C4
Carrgate Rd M34 241 B5
Carrgreen La WA13 19 C3
Carriage Dr Biddulph ST8 179 C1
Frodsham WA6 74 A3
Carriages The WA14 238 C4
Carrick Dr CH65 70 A1
Carrick Rd CH4 141 A4
Carrington Cl WA3 9 B2
Carrington Way CW1 190 A4
Carroll Dr CW2 205 C4
Carrs Ave SK8 240 A2
Carrs Ct SK9 60 A4
Carrs La CH3 166 C1
Carrs Rd SK8 239 F6
Carrwood
Altrincham WA15 32 A4
Knutsford WA16 57 B1
Carrwood Cl WA11 1 A3
Carrwood Rd SK9 59 C4
Carsdale Rd M22 33 C4
Carter Ave CW6 122 B2
Carter La SK11 84 A2
Carter St Chester CH2 237 C3
Stalybridge SK15 242 E2
Cartier Cl WA5 15 B4
Cartlake Cl CW5 204 B3
Cartledge Cl CW8 102 A2
Cartmel Ave WA2 8 B2
Cartmel Cl Gatley SK8 239 C3
Holmes Chapel CW4 130 A2
Macclesfield SK10 87 A1
Warrington WA5 7 C1
Winsford CW7 126 B1
Cartmel Dr CH66 69 C1
Cartmell Cl WA7 49 A3
Cartridge La WA4 27 C3
Cartwright Rd CW1 191 B3
Cartwright St
Runcorn WA7 23 B1
Warrington WA5 15 C3
Carver Ave CW4 130 A3
Carver Cl CW7 127 A2
Carver Rd WA15 238 E2
Case Rd WA11 1 B3
Casey La CW2 206 C2
Cashmere Rd SK3 240 C3
Caspian Rd WA14 238 A6
Cassia Green La CW7 125 B3
Cassley Rd L24 21 A2
Casson St CW1 190 A3
Castle Bank CW8 103 C4
Castle Cl Broughton CH4 139 A3
Kelsall CW6 122 B2
Pulford CH4 162 B1
Castle Croft Rd CH4 141 A3
Castle Ct Holt LL13 196 C4
Northwich CW8 103 C4
Castle Dr Chester CH4 237 B1
Ellesmere Port CH65 70 A2
Heswall CH60 40 C4
Castle Gn WA5 7 A1
Castle Hall Cl SK15 242 E1
Castle Hall Ct SK15 242 D1
Castle Hall View SK15 242 D1
Castle Hill
Newton-le-W WA12 2 C2
Prestbury SK10 86 C3
Pulford CH4 162 B1
Castle Hill Ct SK10 86 C4
Castle Hill Farm 16 CW8 103 C4
Castle Inn Rd CW12 179 B4
Castle Mews LL13 196 C4
Castle Mill La WA15 32 A3
Castle Prim Sch ST7 195 B3
Castle Rd Kidsgrove ST7 195 B4
Runcorn WA7 49 C4
Castle Rise
Prestbury SK10 86 C3
Runcorn WA7 23 B1
Castle St Chester CH4 237 B1
Crewe CW1 190 B2
Holt LL13 196 B4
Hyde SK14 241 F7
Macclesfield SK11 112 B4

Castle St *continued*
9 Nantwich CW5 204 C3
Northwich CW8 103 C4
Stalybridge SK15 242 D1
Stockport SK3 240 D3
Widnes WA8 13 B1
Castle St Mall 32 SK11 112 B4
Castle View Prim Sch WA7 49 B4
Castle Way CH4 162 A3
Castle Yd SK1 240 F6
Castlefields CH3 166 B2
Castlefields Ave E WA7 24 A1
Castlefields Ave N WA7 23 C1
Castlefields Ave S WA7 24 A1
Castleford Dr SK10 86 C3
Castlegate SK10 86 C3
Castlegate Mews SK10 86 C3
Castlemead Wlk CW9 103 C2
Castlemere Cl CH4 139 A2
Castlemere Dr CW1 190 B4
Castleton Dr SK6 37 C3
Castleton St WA14 238 C7
Castletown Cl SK10 87 B2
Castletown La CH3 197 B1
Castleview Rd ST7 195 A2
Castleway WA15 32 B4
Catalan Cl CW7 127 A1
Catalyst Mus* WA8 23 A3
Catchpenny La SK11 108 C2
Catford Cl WA8 12 B1
Catfoss Cl WA2 8 C1
Cathcart Gn CH3 119 C3
Cathedral Church of Christ & the Blessed Virgin Mary CH1 237 B2
Catherine Ct CH5 139 A3
Catherine Rd WA14 238 C3
Catherine St
Chester CH1 118 A1
Crewe CW2 190 B1
Hyde SK14 241 D7
Macclesfield SK11 112 B4
Warrington WA5 15 C4
Warrington WA5 16 A4
Widnes WA8 23 A4
Catherine Way WA12 2 A1
Catterall Ave WA2 8 B1
Caughall Rd CH2 95 C1
Caunce Ave Golborne WA3 3 A4
Haydock WA11 1 A3
Newton-le-W WA12 2 B1
Causeway Ave WA4 16 B2
Causeway Pk WA4 16 B2
Causeway The 2 WA14 238 D4
Cavalier Dr CH1 117 C3
Cavan Cl SK3 239 F7
Cavell Dr CH65 70 A2
Cavendish Ave WA3 9 C3
Cavendish Cl
11 Macclesfield SK10 87 B2
Warrington WA5 15 B4
Winsford CW7 149 A4
Cavendish Cres ST7 193 B3
Cavendish Farm Rd WA7 49 A3
Cavendish Gdns CH65 70 A2
Cavendish Mews SK9 60 A3
Cavendish Pl WA3 9 C3
Cavendish Rd
Altrincham WA14 238 C3
Chester CH4 141 A3
Crewe CW2 189 C3
Hazel Grove SK7 36 C4
Cavendish Sch WA7 49 B3
Cavendish St WA7 22 C1
Cavendish Way CW4 130 A2
Caversham Cl WA4 26 C3
Cawdor Dr CH3 119 A1
Cawdor St Runcorn WA7 22 C2
Warrington WA4 26 B4
Cawfield Ave WA8 12 B1
Cawley Ave WA3 4 C2
Cawley St
9 Macclesfield SK11 112 C4
Runcorn WA7 23 A1
Cawood Cl CH66 69 A3
Cawthorne Ave WA4 17 A1
Caxton Cl
Ellesmere Port CH66 69 C2
Widnes WA8 12 B2
Cecil Rd WA15 238 E2
Cecil Rigby Cl 1 CW11 175 A3
Cecil St Chester CH3 119 A1
Stalybridge SK15 242 E1
Stockport SK3 240 E3
Cedab Rd CH65 70 B3
Cedar Ave Alsager ST7 193 B2
Altrincham WA14 238 C4
Connah's Quay CH5 116 A4
Connah's Quay CH5 91 B1
Ellesmere Port CH66 69 B3
Golborne WA3 4 A4
Kidsgrove ST7 194 B1
Runcorn WA7 49 B4
Stalybridge SK15 242 F3
Sutton WA7 50 A2
Widnes WA8 13 A1
Cedar Cl
Connah's Quay CH5 116 A4
Holmes Chapel CW4 130 B2
Lostock Gralam CW9 80 A2
Middlewich CW10 151 C3
Poynton SK12 36 C2
Sandbach CW11 175 B3
Cedar Cres Audley ST7 209 C1

Cedar Cres *continued*
Newton-le-W WA12 .... 2 B1
Cedar Ct Alsager ST7 .... 193 C2
Congleton CW12 .... 178 C4
Culcheth WA3 .... 4 C1
Willaston (nr Nantwich) CW5 .... 205 B3
Cedar Dr Barnton CW8 .... 78 A2
Chester CH2 .... 119 A2
Cedar Gr Chester CH2 .... 119 A2
Haydock WA11 .... 1 C4
Macclesfield SK11 .... 112 B3
Nantwich CW5 .... 205 A3
Neston CH64 .... 66 C4
Warrington WA1 .... 17 A4
Warrington, Latchford WA4 .... 16 B2
Winsford CW7 .... 127 A1
Cedar Lo SK7 .... 35 C4
Cedar Mews CH1 .... 117 C2
Cedar Pk CH3 .... 119 B1
Cedar Rd
Altrincham WA15 .... 238 E3
Gatley SK8 .... 239 A5
Newcastle-u-L ST5 .... 210 B1
Partington M31 .... 11 C2
Warrington WA5 .... 14 C3
Weaverham CW8 .... 102 B4
Cedar St
Ashton-u-Lyne OL6 .... 242 A4
Newton-le-W WA12 .... 2 B1
Cedar Way CW2 .... 206 A4
Cedardale Dr CH66 .... 94 C4
Cedardale Pk WA8 .... 13 C2
Cedarfield Rd WA13 .... 19 A2
Cedars SK9 .... 59 C3
Cedars The Alsager ST7 .... 193 B2
Mobberley WA16 .... 58 C1
Cedarway Heswall CH60 .... 41 A3
Wilmslow SK9 .... 59 C3
Cedarways WA4 .... 26 B3
Cedarwood CW8 .... 101 B3
Cedarwood Ave SK4 .... 240 A5
Cedarwood Cl CW6 .... 146 B2
Celandine Cl CH3 .... 142 A4
Celandine Way WA9 .... 6 A4
Celyn Cres CH4 .... 140 B3
Cement Pl CH2 .... 237 B3
Cemetery Rd CW2 .... 207 A3
Cemlyn Cl CH1 .... 117 C2
Centenary Ho WA7 .... 49 B4
Centenary Pl CW12 .... 156 C2
Central Ave Alsager CW2 .... 192 C1
Ellesmere Port CH65 .... 70 B2
Warrington WA2 .... 16 B4
Warrington, Latchford WA4 .... 16 A2
Central Dr Barnton CW8 .... 78 A2
Gatley SK8 .... 34 B4
Haydock WA11 .... 1 A3
Romiley SK6 .... 241 C3
Central Expressway WA7 .... 49 C4
Central Gr CW9 .... 104 B4
Central Rd
Northwich CW9 .... 104 B4
Partington M31 .... 11 C2
Central St ST7 .... 195 A3
Central Trad Est CH4 .... 140 C4
Central Way
Altrincham WA14 .... 238 D4
Newton-le-W WA12 .... 2 C1
Centre Ct ST7 .... 193 C2
Centre Park Sq WA1 .... 16 A2
Centre Pk WA2 .... 16 A2
Centurion Cl WA3 .... 9 B2
Centurion Row WA7 .... 23 C1
Centurion Way CW10 .... 128 B1
Century Park Ind Area WA14 .... 238 A6
Century Rd ST5 .... 210 C1
Century Way SK10 .... 87 C1
Cestria Cl CW11 .... 174 B4
Chadkirk Chapel* SK6 .... 241 C1
Chadkirk Rd SK6 .... 241 B1
Chads Gn CW5 .... 206 A1
Chadvil Rd SK8 .... 239 C5
Chadwick Ave Croft WA3 .... 9 A4
Warrington WA4 .... 16 C1
Chadwick Cl SK9 .... 34 B1
Chadwick Ct CW10 .... 151 B4
Chadwick Fields Orch CW10 .... 151 B3
Chadwick Pl WA3 .... 9 C3
Chadwick Rd
Middlewich CW10 .... 151 B3
Runcorn WA7 .... 23 C2
Chadwick St
Ashton-u-Lyne OL6 .... 242 B2
8 Stockport SK1 .... 240 F4
Chadwick Terr SK10 .... 87 C1
Chaffinch Cl
Congleton CW12 .... 156 C1
Warrington WA3 .... 9 C2
Chaffinch Way CW7 .... 149 B3
Chaigeley Sch WA4 .... 17 C2
Chain Maker's Row CH4 .... 140 C4
Chalfield Ave CH66 .... 69 B3
Chalfield Cl
6 Ellesmere Port CH66 .... 69 B3
Wistaston CW2 .... 206 A4
Chalfont Cl WA4 .... 26 C3
Chalfont Cres CW2 .... 207 A1
Chalfont Ct WA16 .... 57 B2
Chalgrave Cl WA8 .... 13 C2
Chalkwell Dr CH60 .... 41 B4
Challinor St CH3 .... 119 A1
Chamber Brook La WA6 .... 75 B1
Chamberlain Ct CW1 .... 191 B3
Chambers St CW2 .... 190 B1
Chance Hall La CW12, ST7 .... 177 B2
Chancel La SK9 .... 60 A4
Chancellor Rd WA7 .... 24 B3
Chancery La Alsager ST7 .... 193 A2
Bollington SK10 .... 88 A4
Chandler Way WA3 .... 3 C4
Chandlers Ct WA7 .... 22 C1
Chandley St SK8 .... 239 D6
Chandos Cl CH4 .... 141 C3
Change La CH64 .... 68 A4
Channel The CH1 .... 95 A2
Chantler Ave WA4 .... 16 C2
Chantry Ave CW8 .... 103 A2
Chantry Cl SK12 .... 38 C3
Chantry Ct Blacon CH1 .... 117 C1
Crewe CW1 .... 190 B2
Macclesfield SK11 .... 112 B3
Chantry Fold SK12 .... 38 C3
Chantry Rd SK12 .... 38 C3
Chantry The CW6 .... 169 C1
Chantry Wlk CH60 .... 41 A3
Chapel Ave WA6 .... 75 B1
Chapel Bank ST7 .... 195 B3
Chapel Cl Audlem CW3 .... 229 C2
Cholmondeston CW7 .... 170 C2
Comberbach CW9 .... 78 B4
Ellesmere Port CH65 .... 70 B2
Mount Pleasant ST7 .... 195 A3
Saughall CH1 .... 94 A1
Waverton CH3 .... 143 A3
Chapel Cotts CH3 .... 143 A3
Chapel Croft SK11 .... 84 A2
Chapel Cross Rd WA2 .... 9 A1
Chapel Ct
Altrincham WA14 .... 238 D4
Hyde SK14 .... 241 C5
Northwich CW9 .... 103 C4
Wilmslow SK9 .... 60 A3
Chapel Dr WA15 .... 32 B4
Chapel Gn CW6 .... 122 B3
Chapel House La CH64 .... 93 A4
Chapel La
Acton Bridge CW8 .... 76 C2
Alldford CH3 .... 164 B3
Allostock WA16 .... 106 C2
Altrincham WA15 .... 32 B4
Appleton Thorn WA4 .... 27 A2
Audley ST7 .... 209 B1
Burtonwood WA5 .... 6 C3
Chester CH3 .... 119 A1
Crewe CW1 .... 173 B1
Dutton WA4 .... 77 A4
Ellesmere Port CH66 .... 68 C1
Hollins Green WA3 .... 10 C1
Holt LL13 .... 196 B4
Kelsall CW6 .... 122 C1
Kidsgrove ST7 .... 195 C2
Kingsley WA6 .... 75 B1
Manley WA6,CH3 .... 98 C2
Mere WA16 .... 30 A2
Milton Green CH3 .... 165 A1
Moulton CW9 .... 126 C4
Norton in Hales TF9 .... 236 B1
Partington M31 .... 11 C1
Rainow SK10 .... 88 C3
Ravensmoor CW5 .... 203 B1
Rode Heath ST7 .... 193 C4
Threapwood SY14 .... 222 C4
Warrington WA4 .... 26 B4
Widnes WA8 .... 12 B2
Wilmslow SK9 .... 60 A3
Withington Green SK11 .... 109 B1
Chapel Mews
Ellesmere Port CH65 .... 70 A2
Elton CH2 .... 72 A2
6 Nantwich CW5 .... 204 C3
Chapel Mus Mow Cop* ST7 .... 195 B4
Chapel Rd
Alderley Edge SK9 .... 60 A1
Ollerton WA16 .... 82 C3
Sale M33 .... 242 B7
Warrington WA5 .... 14 C2
Whaley Bridge SK23 .... 65 C3
Winsford CW7 .... 126 C1
Chapel Row
Barbridge CW5 .... 187 B3
Nantwich CW5 .... 204 B3
Chapel St
5 Alderley Edge SK9 .... 60 A1
Audley ST7 .... 209 C2
Bollington SK10 .... 88 A4
Cheadle SK8 .... 239 D5
Chester CH2 .... 237 C3
Congleton CW12 .... 156 B1
Crewe CW2 .... 190 B2
Haydock WA11 .... 1 C3
Higher Wincham CW9 .... 79 B2
Holt LL13 .... 196 B4
Hyde SK14 .... 241 D6
Kidsgrove ST7 .... 194 B1
Macclesfield SK11 .... 112 B3
Moulton CW9 .... 126 C4
Mount Pleasant ST7 .... 195 A3
New Mills SK22 .... 39 A3
Newton-le-W WA12 .... 2 A2
Northwich CW8 .... 103 C4
Sandbach CW11 .... 175 A3
Sandbach, Wheelock CW11 .... 175 A2
Stalybridge SK15 .... 242 D2
Weaverham CW8 .... 77 B1
Whaley Bridge SK23 .... 65 C4
Widnes WA8 .... 23 A4
Chapel Terr WA3 .... 4 A4
Chapel View WA6 .... 73 A1
Chapel Wlks Bramhall SK8 .... 35 A3
Broomedge WA13 .... 19 B1
Sale M33 .... 242 B7
Chapel Yd WA2 .... 16 A3
Chapelfields WA6 .... 74 A4
Chapelmere Cl CW11 .... 174 C4
Chapelmere Ct CW1 .... 190 B4
Chapman Cl WA8 .... 12 B2
Chapterhouse Cl CH65 .... 70 C3
Charcoal Rd WA14 .... 20 C2
Charcoal Woods WA14 .... 238 A3
Charity La SK11 .... 114 A3
Charlcote Cres CW2 .... 206 B4
Charlecote Rd SK12 .... 36 C2
Charles Ave
Davenham CW9 .... 103 C1
Warrington WA5 .... 14 C3
Charles Cres CH4 .... 237 C1
Charles Darwin Prim Sch CW8 .... 103 C4
Charles Forbes Ct 14 WA1 .... 16 A3
Charles Price Gdns 5 CH65 .... 70 B3
Charles Rd CH2 .... 95 B1
Charles Sq CW11 .... 175 C1
Charles St Chester CH2 .... 237 B3
Chester, Hoole Pk CH2 .... 118 C2
Crewe CW1 .... 190 B2
Irlam M44 .... 11 C3
Widnes WA8 .... 23 A4
Charleston Cl CH66 .... 69 B1
Charlesworth Cl SK23 .... 39 B2
Charlesworth Cres SK23 .... 39 B2
Charlesworth Ct CW11 .... 175 B3
Charlesworth Rd SK23 .... 39 B2
Charlesworth St
Crewe CW1 .... 190 B3
1 Stockport SK1 .... 240 F3
Charlock Sq WA14 .... 238 B8
Charlock Wlk 13 M31 .... 11 C2
Charlotte Ct CH1 .... 237 B3
Charlotte St Cheadle SK8 .... 239 D5
Chester CH1 .... 118 A1
Macclesfield SK11 .... 112 B4
Charlotte St W 14 SK11 .... 112 B4
Charlotte Wlk 16 WA8 .... 23 A4
Charlton Brook Ho SK8 .... 239 E6
Charlton Cl WA7 .... 50 A4
Charlton Dr M33 .... 242 C6
Charlton St
Macclesfield SK11 .... 112 B4
Warrington WA4 .... 16 C2
Charminster Cl WA5 .... 15 A3
Charnock Ave WA12 .... 1 C2
Charnock Rd WA3 .... 4 C2
Charnwood 11 ST7 .... 195 A1
Charnwood Cl
Macclesfield SK10 .... 87 A1
Warrington WA3 .... 10 A3
Charnwood Cres SK7 .... 36 B4
Charter Ave WA5 .... 16 A4
Charter Cres CH66 .... 69 C2
Charter Rd
Altrincham WA15 .... 238 E4
Bollington SK10 .... 88 A4
Charter Way SK10 .... 87 C2
Charterhall Dr CH2 .... 118 C1
Chartist Ho SK14 .... 241 E6
Chartley Gr CW10 .... 128 B1
Chartwell Gr CW7 .... 149 B3
Chartwell Pk CW11 .... 175 A2
Chase Dr CH66 .... 69 C1
Chase The CH63 .... 43 B3
Chase Way CH66 .... 69 C1
Chasefield WA14 .... 238 A2
Chaser Ct CH1 .... 117 C2
Chasewater WA7 .... 24 C2
Chatburn Ct WA3 .... 4 C1
Chater Dr CW5 .... 204 C2
Chatfield Dr WA3 .... 9 C2
Chatham St
15 Macclesfield SK11 .... 112 B4
Stockport SK3 .... 240 D4
Chatham Way CW1 .... 191 B3
Chatswood Ave SK2 .... 240 F2
Chatsworth Ave
Culcheth WA3 .... 4 C2
Macclesfield SK11 .... 111 C3
Chatsworth Cl
Ellesmere Port CH66 .... 69 B3
Northwich CW9 .... 104 A3
Wistaston CW2 .... 206 A4
Chatsworth Dr
Chester CH2 .... 119 A3
Congleton CW12 .... 155 C2
Widnes WA8 .... 12 B2
Chatsworth Ho CH1 .... 118 A2
Chatsworth Rd
Hazel Grove SK7 .... 36 C4
High Lane SK6 .... 37 C3
Wilmslow SK9 .... 59 C2
Chatteris Pk WA7 .... 24 C1
Chatterton Dr WA7 .... 50 C4
Chatwell Gdns WA4 .... 26 C3
Chaucer Cl CH1 .... 117 C3
Chaucer Pl WA4 .... 16 C2
Chaucer St WA7 .... 23 A1
Chaucher Gr 12 CW11 .... 174 B3
Cheadle Heath Prim Sch SK3 .... 240 A3
Cheadle Hulme Coll SK8 .... 35 A4
Cheadle Hulme Sch SK8 .... 35 A4
Cheadle La
Lower Peover WA16 .... 106 A4
Plumley WA16 .... 81 A1
Cheadle Old Rd SK3 .... 240 C3
Cheadle Prim Sch SK8 .... 239 D6
Cheadle RC Inf Sch SK8 .... 239 E2
Cheadle RC Jun Sch SK8 .... 239 E2
Cheadle Rd SK8 .... 239 F3
Cheadle Royal Hospl SK8 .... 239 C2
Cheadle Wood SK8 .... 34 C4
Cheam Rd WA15 .... 238 F8
Cheapside SK14 .... 241 E7
Checkley Dr ST8 .... 179 B1
Checkley La CW3 .... 221 C1
Checkley Rd ST5 .... 210 B1
Cheddar Gr WA5 .... 6 C4
Chedlee Dr SK8 .... 34 C4
Chedworth Dr WA8 .... 12 B2
Cheerbrook Rd CW5 .... 205 B2
Cheese Hill La WA6, CW8 .... 101 A2
Cheetham Gdns SK15 .... 242 E1
Chelford Ave WA3 .... 3 B4
Chelford CE Prim Sch SK11 .... 84 A2
Chelford Cl
Altrincham WA15 .... 238 E6
Blacon CH1 .... 117 C1
Warrington WA4 .... 26 B4
Chelford Ct 2 SK9 .... 34 C3
Chelford Gr SK3 .... 240 D1
Chelford La WA16 .... 83 B1
Chelford Rd
Chelford SK10,SK11 .... 84 B1
Chelford, Marthall WA16, SK11 .... 83 B2
Congleton CW12 .... 155 C3
Goostrey CW4 .... 131 A4
Handforth SK9 .... 34 B3
Henbury SK10 .... 110 C4
Knutsford WA16 .... 82 B4
Macclesfield SK10,SK11 .... 111 B4
Nether Alderley SK9 .... 84 B4
Nether Alderley, Monks Heath SK10 .... 85 A1
Prestbury SK10 .... 86 B3
Chelford Sta SK11 .... 84 A1
Chell St CW1 .... 190 A3
Chells Hill CW11 .... 176 B1
Chelmsford Rd SK3 .... 240 C4
Chelsea Cl ST8 .... 179 B1
Chelsea Gdns WA5 .... 15 B2
Chelston Dr SK8 .... 34 B3
Cheltenham Cl
2 Macclesfield SK10 .... 87 B2
Warrington WA5 .... 15 A4
Cheltenham Cres
Crewe CW1 .... 190 A4
Runcorn WA7 .... 49 A3
Cheltenham Dr
Newton-le-W WA12 .... 2 B3
Sale M33 .... 242 C6
Cheltenham Rd
Ellesmere Port CH65 .... 70 B2
Stockport SK3 .... 240 A3
Chemical St WA12 .... 2 A2
Cheney Wlk CW2 .... 206 B4
Chepstow Cl
Biddulph ST8 .... 179 B1
Macclesfield SK10 .... 87 B2
Warrington WA5 .... 7 C1
3 Winsford CW7 .... 149 B4
Cherington Cl SK9 .... 34 C2
Cherington Cres SK11 .... 112 A4
Cherington Rd SK8 .... 239 C4
Cheriton Ave M33 .... 242 C7
Cheriton Way CW2 .... 206 A4
Cherrington Rd CW5 .... 204 C2
Cherry Blossom Rd WA7 .... 49 C2
Cherry Brow Terr CH64 .... 67 C4
Cherry Cl
Newcastle-u-L ST5 .... 210 B1
Newton-le-W WA12 .... 1 C2
Willaston CH64 .... 67 B4
Cherry Cnr WA13 .... 28 A4
Cherry Cres CW7 .... 149 B4
Cherry Ct M33 .... 242 A6
Cherry Dale Rd CH4 .... 139 A2
Cherry Gr
Ellesmere Port CH66 .... 70 A1
Nantwich CW5 .... 204 B3
Cherry Grove Prim Sch CH3 .... 119 A1
Cherry Grove Rd CH3 .... 119 A1
Cherry La
Congleton CW12 .... 179 C4
Cuddington CW8 .... 101 C1
Lawton Heath ST7 .... 193 C3
Lymm WA13 .... 28 A4
Weaverham CW8 .... 102 B4
Cherry Orch LL13 .... 196 B4
Cherry Rd CH3 .... 119 A1
Cherry Tree Ave
Barnton CW8 .... 78 A2
Lawton-gate ST7 .... 194 A3
Lymm WA13 .... 18 B1
Poynton SK12 .... 36 C2
Runcorn WA7 .... 49 B4
Warrington WA5 .... 14 C2
Cherry Tree Cl Elton CH2 .... 72 A2
Hale L24 .... 21 C1
Haydock WA11 .... 1 A3
Romiley SK6 .... 241 E2
Wilmslow SK9 .... 60 C4
Cherry Tree Dr
Hazel Grove SK7 .... 37 A4
St Helens WA9 .... 1 A1
Cherry Tree La
Romiley SK6 .... 241 E2
Rostherne WA16 .... 30 C3
Cherry Tree La *continued*
Woore CW3 232
Cherry Tree Prim Sch WA13 18
Cherry Tree Rd
Audley ST7 209
Crewe CW1 190
Golborne WA3 3
Newcastle-u-L ST5 210
Cherry Wlk Cheadle SK8 35
Lower Peover WA16 106
Partington M31 11
Cherrycroft SK6 241
Cherryfields Rd SK11 111
Cherrysutton WA8 12
Cherrysutton Mews WA8 12
Cherrywood Cres CW8 78
Cherwell Cl Cheadle SK8 35
Warrington WA2 8
Cheryl Ct CW8 102
Cheryl Dr WA8 13
Chesford Grange WA1 17
Chesham Cl SK9 59
Chesham Pl WA14 238
Chesham Rd SK9 59
Chesham St CH2 237
Cheshire Cl WA12 2
Cheshire Farm* CH3 166
Cheshire Military Mus* CH4 237
Cheshire Oaks Outlet Village CH65 70
Cheshire Oaks Way CH65 70
Cheshire Rd M31 11
Cheshire Row WA16 108
Cheshire St CW3 229
Cheshire View
Bollington SK10 88
Chester CH4 141
Cheshire Workshops* CH3 184
Cheshyre Dr WA7 23
Cheshyre's La WA7 48
Chessington Cl WA4 26
Chester Aerospace Pk CH4 139
Chester Ave
Altrincham WA15 238
Golborne WA3 3
Chester Bsns Pk CH4 141
Chester Cl Handforth SK9 34
Irlam M44 11
Runcorn WA7 24
Talke ST7 210
Chester Gates CH1 94
Chester High Rd
Neston CH64 41
Willaston CH64 67
Chester La CW7 125
Chester New Rd WA4 25
Chester Rd Acton CW5 204
Audley ST7 209
Barbridge CW5 187
Broughton CH4 139
Churton CH3 180
Connah's Quay CH6 91
Daresbury WA4 25
Delamere CW6,CW8 123
Ellesmere Port, Great Sutton CH66 69
Ellesmere Port, Whitby CH65,CH66 70
Frodsham WA6 74
Gatesheath CH3 165
Hartford CW8 102
Hartford, Greenbank CW8 103
Hawarden CH5 116
Hazel Grove SK7 36
Helsby WA6 73
Heswall CH60,CH64 41
Higher Walton WA4 25
Holmes Chapel CW4 130
Huntington CH3 142
Kelsall CW6 122
Knutsford WA16 56
Lavister LL12,CH4 162
Macclesfield SK11 112
Middlewich CW10 128
Neston CH64 66
Oakmere CW8 124
Plumley WA16 80
Poynton SK12 36
Rostherne WA14 30
Runcorn WA7 50
Sutton WA7 50
Tabley WA16 56
Talke ST7 210
Tattenhall CH3 166
Warrington WA4 17
Whitchurch SY13 225
Winsford CW7 125
Woodford SK7 35
Chester Ret Pk CH1 118
Chester Row WA12 7
Chester Sq CW1 190
Chester St Chester CH4 140
Stockport SK3 240
Warrington WA1 16
Widnes WA8 13
Chester Sta CH2 237
Chester Toy & Doll Mus* CH1 237
Chester Way CW9 104
Chester West Employment Pk CH1 117
Chester Wlks SK6 241
Chester Zoological Gdns* CH2 95

hesterbank Bsns Pk
CH4 .140 B4
hesterfield Cl CW7 .125 C1
hesterfield Gr OL6 .242 A3
hesterfield Rd CH62 .43 B2
hestergate
Macclesfield SK11 .112 B4
Stockport SK3 .240 E5
hestergate Mall 34
SK11 .112 B4
hesterton Cl CW10 .151 C3
hesterton Dr
Winwick WA2 .8 A3
Wistaston CW2 .189 C1
hesterton Gr 11 CW11 .174 B3
hestnut Ave
Cheadle SK8 .239 E5
12 Ellesmere Port CH66 .69 C1
Irlam M44 .11 B3
Macclesfield SK10 .87 C1
Rode Heath ST7 .193 C4
Shavington CW2 .206 B3
Warrington WA5 .14 C3
Widnes WA8 .13 A1
hestnut Cl Chester CH2 .119 A2
Cuddington CW8 .101 C1
Middlewich CW10 .128 A1
Tarporley CW6 .146 B1
Wilmslow SK9 .60 C4
hestnut Ct
Tarporley CW6 .146 B1
Widnes WA8 .12 B1
hestnut Dr Alsager ST7 .193 C1
Congleton CW12 .156 A2
Holmes Chapel CW4 .130 B2
Poynton SK12 .36 C2
hestnut Gr Barnton CW8 .78 A2
Bebington CH62 .43 B4
Crewe CW1 .190 C3
Golborne WA3 .3 C4
Newcastle-u-L ST5 .210 C1
Winsford CW7 .149 B4
hestnut Ho 6 CW11 .175 A3
hestnut La WA6 .73 C2
hestnut Lodge Specl Sch
WA8 .12 C1
hestnut Mews WA16 .58 C1
hestnut Villas SK4 .240 B5
hestnut Wlk M31 .11 B1
hesworth Cl SK1 .240 F4
hesworth Fold SK1 .240 F4
hetham Ct WA2 .8 A2
hetton Dr WA7 .50 C4
hetwode Mews WA4 .52 D1
hetwode St CW1 .190 B3
hetwood Dr WA8 .12 C2
heveley Cl SK10 .87 B1
hevin Gdns SK7 .36 A4
heviot Ave Cheadle SK8 .239 F2
Warrington WA2 .8 A2
heviot Cl
Ellesmere Port CH66 .69 A3
Stockport SK4 .240 D7
heviot Ct 16 CW7 .149 A4
hevithorne Cl WA14 .238 B5
hevron Cl CH1 .117 C2
hevron Hey CH1 .117 C2
hevron Pl WA14 .238 D7
heyne Wlk CW5 .204 C2
heyney Rd Blacon CH1 .118 A2
Chester CH1 .118 A2
hicago Ave M90 .33 A4
hichester Cl
Grappenhall Heys WA4 .27 A4
Runcorn WA7 .50 B3
hichester Ct CH1 .237 A3
hichester Rd SK6 .241 C2
hichester St CH1 .237 A3
hidlow Cl
Hough Common CW2 .206 C2
Widnes WA8 .23 A3
hild's La CW12 .177 C3
hilder Cres CH66 .69 A4
hilder Gdns CH66 .69 A4
hilder Thornton Prim Sch
CH66 .69 A4
hildwall Ct CH66 .69 C4
hildwall Gdns CH66 .69 C4
hildwall Rd CH66 .69 C4
hilham Cl CW7 .149 B4
hilham Pl SK11 .111 C3
hilington Ave WA8 .22 B4
hillingham Cl CW10 .128 B1
hiltern Ave Cheadle SK8 .239 F2
Macclesfield SK11 .112 A4
hiltern Cl Chester CH4 .141 A3
Cuddington CW8 .102 A1
Hough Common CW2 .207 A1
hiltern Cres WA2 .8 A2
hiltern Dr WA15 .238 F2
hiltern Pl WA2 .8 A2
hiltern Rd Culcheth WA3 .4 C2
St Helens WA9 .1 A2
Warrington WA2 .8 A2
hiltern Way CW7 .149 A4
hilton Dr CH66 .69 C1
hilwell Cl WA8 .12 B2
hilworth Cl CW2 .206 B4
hina La WA4 .16 B1
hines The CW8 .101 B3
hink Gdns CH65 .70 B2
hinley Cl Sale M33 .242 D5
Stockport SK4 .240 B7
hippingdall Cl WA5 .15 B3
hipstead Cl CW8 .103 A2
hirk Cl CH2 .118 C3
hirk Pl CW7 .126 A1
hirton Cl WA11 .1 B4
Chisledon Cl WA11 .1 B4
Chislet Ct WA8 .12 C2
Chiswick Cl WA7 .50 B4
Chiswick Gdns WA4 .26 C3
Chokeberry Cl WA14 .238 B8
Chollerton Cl WA16 .29 B2
Cholmley Dr WA12 .2 C1
Cholmondeley Ave
WA14 .238 E8
Cholmondeley Castle Gdns*
SY14 .201 A2
Cholmondeley La SY14 .200 C4
Cholmondeley Rd
Ellesmere Port CH65 .69 C2
Hampton SY14 .213 C4
Runcorn WA7 .49 B2
Wrenbury CW5 .216 B3
Cholmondeley St WA8 .23 A2
Cholmondely St SK11 .112 B3
Cholmondley Rise SY14 .214 A2
Chomlea WA14 .238 B4
Chorley Bank Council Hos
CW5 .201 C1
Chorley Green La CW5,
SY14 .201 C3
Chorley Hall Cl SK9 .59 C1
Chorley Hall La
Alderley Edge SK9 .60 A1
Faddiley CW5 .202 B1
Chorley St WA2 .16 A3
Chorley's La WA8 .13 C2
Chorleywood Cl SK10 .87 A2
Chorlton Cl WA7 .24 B1
Chorlton Dr SK8 .239 E6
Chorlton La CW2 .207 A1
Chowley Oak La CH3 .182 C3
Chrimes Dr CW8 .123 C3
Christ Church CE Prim Sch
CH65 .70 A1
Christ Church CE Sch
CW8 .76 A1
Christ The King RC Prim Sch
CH62 .43 C4
Christchurch Ave CW2 .190 A1
Christie Cl CH66 .44 A1
Christie St WA8 .13 B1
Christleton Ave
Crewe CW2 .189 B3
Northwich CW9 .104 A2
Christleton Ct WA7 .24 B2
Christleton Dr CH66 .69 C3
Christleton High Sch
CH3 .142 C4
Christleton Prim Sch
CH3 .142 C4
Christleton Rd CH3 .119 A1
Christleton Sports Ctr
CH3 .142 C4
Christleton Way 15 SK9 .34 B3
Christopher Dr CH62 .44 A3
Chudleigh Cl WA14 .238 B6
Church Ave SK9 .34 A1
Church Bank
Altrincham WA14 .238 B2
Audley ST7 .209 B1
Goostrey CW4 .107 C1
Kelsall CW6 .122 B3
Tattenhall CH3 .166 A1
Church Bk SK23 .65 B4
Church Brow
Altrincham WA14 .238 B2
Hyde SK14 .241 D5
Church Cl Handforth SK9 .34 B2
Weaverham CW8 .77 B1
Church College Cl CH1 .118 A2
Church Coppenhall Jun Sch
CW1 .190 A3
Church Cotts
Rainow SK10 .88 C3
Waverton CH3 .143 B2
Church Croft CH4 .162 A3
Church Ct
Altrincham WA15 .238 E1
Ashton CH3 .121 C4
Farndon CH3 .180 C1
Church Dr
Newton-le-W WA12 .2 B1
Warrington WA2 .9 A1
Church End L24 .21 B1
Church Farm CW5 .216 C2
Church Farm Ct
Heswall CH60 .40 C4
Willaston CH64 .67 C4
Church Fields TF9 .236 B1
Church Gn WA13 .19 A4
Church Hall Cl CH1 .117 C2
Church Hill WA16 .57 A1
Church La
Alderley Edge SK9 .60 A1
Alford CH3 .163 C2
Backford CH1 .95 A2
Bebington CH62 .44 A2
Chester CH2 .118 B4
Congleton CW12 .134 C1
Culcheth WA3 .4 C2
Ellesmere Port CH66 .69 B2
Elton WA6 .72 B1
Farndon CH3 .180 C1
Golborne WA3 .3 B4
Guilden Sutton CH3 .119 C3
Henbury SK11 .111 B4
Lawton-gate ST7 .194 B2
Mobberley WA16 .58 B3
Mow Cop ST7 .195 C4
Nantwich CW5 .204 C3
Neston CH64 .66 C4
New Mills SK22 .39 B4
Rainow SK10 .88 C3
Church La *continued*
Romiley SK6 .241 C2
Sandbach CW11 .175 C4
Scholar Green ST7 .194 B4
Smallwood CW11 .176 C2
Stoak CH2 .96 A4
Sutton Lane Ends SK11 .112 C2
Warren SK11 .134 B4
Warrington WA4 .17 A1
Weaverham CW8 .77 B1
Wistaston CW2 .205 C4
Woodford SK7 .35 B1
Church Lawton Prim Sch
ST7 .194 A3
Church Manor SK4 .240 B8
Church Mdw
Dukinfield SK14 .241 C7
Norton in Hales TF9 .236 B1
Church Mdws
Little Leigh CW8 .77 B3
Whitchurch SY13 .226 A1
Church Mead CH3 .181 A3
Church Meadow Gdns
SK14 .241 C7
Church Meadow La CH60 .40 C4
Church Meadow Wlk
WA8 .22 A3
Church Mews
Bollington SK10 .88 A4
Knutsford WA16 .57 A1
Church Par 2 CH65 .70 B3
Church Rd Alsager ST7 .193 B2
Ashton CH3 .121 C4
Barnton CW8 .78 A1
Broughton CH4 .139 B2
Burwardsley CH3 .184 A3
Cheadle SK8 .35 A4
Eccleston CH4 .141 C1
Frodsham WA6 .74 B4
Gatley SK8 .239 A5
Hale L24 .47 C4
Handforth SK9 .34 B2
Haydock WA11 .1 C4
Little Leigh CW8 .77 B2
Lymm WA13 .18 C1
New Mills SK22 .39 B4
Northwich CW9 .104 A4
Sale M33 .242 D6
Saughall CH1 .94 A1
Shocklach CH3 .197 B1
Stockport SK4 .240 E6
Thornton Hough CH63 .42 A3
Tilston SY14 .198 A2
Wilmslow SK9 .59 C2
Worleston CW5 .188 B3
Church Rd E M33 .242 D6
Church Rd W M33 .242 D6
Church Rise CW8 .102 A1
Church Row CW6 .168 C1
Church St
Altrincham WA14 .238 D5
Audley ST7 .209 B1
Audley ST7 .210 A1
Bollington SK10 .88 A4
Cheadle SK8 .239 D6
Chester CH2 .237 B4
Connah's Quay CH5 .91 B1
Davenham CW9 .104 A2
Ellesmere Port CH65 .70 B3
Farndon CH3 .180 C1
Frodsham WA6 .74 A4
Great Budworth CW9 .79 A4
Higher Wincham CW9 .79 C3
Holt LL13 .180 C1
Hyde SK14 .241 D5
Kelsall CW6 .122 B2
Kidsgrove, Butt Lane ST7 .194 B1
Kidsgrove, The Rookery
ST7 .195 A2
Macclesfield SK11 .112 B4
Malpas SY14 .213 A2
Moulton CW9 .126 C4
Mount Pleasant ST7 .195 B3
Newton-le-W WA12 .2 C2
Runcorn WA7 .23 A2
Sandbach CW11 .175 B3
Stalybridge SK15 .242 D2
Stockport SK4 .240 E7
Tarvin CH3 .121 B1
Warrington WA1 .16 B3
Weaverham CW8 .77 B1
Widnes WA8 .23 A3
Wilmslow SK9 .60 A4
Winsford CW7 .126 C1
Church St N CW6 .122 B3
Church St W SK11 .112 B4
Church Steadings CH3 .143 B2
Church Terr
Handforth SK9 .34 B2
Sale M33 .242 A8
Church View
Audlem CW3 .230 A2
Handforth SK9 .34 A1
Haslington CW1 .191 B3
Hyde SK14 .241 D5
Kingsley WA6 .75 A1
13 Knutsford WA16 .57 A1
Lymm WA13 .19 A2
Church View Terr SK11 .112 C2
Church View Wlk CW2 .205 C4
Church Way Blacon CH1 .117 C3
Wybunbury CW5 .220 A4
Church Wlk Crowton CW8 .76 B1
1 Ellesmere Port CH65 .70 B3
Holmes Chapel CW4 .130 B2
Knutsford WA16 .57 A1
Lower Peover WA16 .81 C1
Northwich CW9 .104 A4
Church Wlk *continued*
Stalybridge SK15 .242 D3
Wilmslow SK9 .59 C3
Winwick WA2 .8 A3
Church Wlks
Christleton CH3 .142 C4
Norton in Hales TF9 .236 B1
Church Wood View
WA13 .18 C2
Churche's Ct 19 CW5 .204 C3
Churche's Mansion*
CW5 .204 C3
Churchfield Rd WA6 .74 B4
Churchfields
Altrincham WA14 .238 B1
Audlem CW3 .230 A2
Barnton CW8 .78 A2
Croft WA3 .9 A4
Cuddington CW8 .102 A1
Helsby WA6 .73 B2
Knutsford WA16 .57 B1
Widnes WA8 .13 A3
Wybunbury CW5 .220 A4
Churchgate SK1 .240 F5
Churchill Ave WA3 .5 A2
Churchill Cl CW12 .156 A2
Churchill Dr CW6 .146 B1
Churchill Parkway CW7 .149 B4
Churchill Rd WA14 .238 D7
Churchill St SK4 .240 D7
Churchill Way
Macclesfield SK11 .112 B4
Neston CH64 .66 C4
Churchley Cl SK3 .240 A2
Churchley Rd SK3 .240 A3
Churchmere Cl CW1 .190 B4
Churchside SK11 .112 B4
Churchside Wlk CH4 .140 C4
Churchward Cl CH2 .118 B2
Churchway Alvanley WA6 .73 B1
Macclesfield SK10 .86 C1
Churchway Rd L24 .21 A1
Churchyard Side CW5 .204 C3
Churton Cl
3 Davenham CW9 .103 C2
Hough Common CW2 .206 C2
Churton Rd Chester CH3 .119 A1
Farndon CH3 .180 C1
Churton St CH3 .119 A1
Cicely Mill La WA16 .30 B2
Cinder Cl CH3 .119 C3
Cinder Hill CW7 .125 C3
Cinder Hill La ST7 .194 C4
Cinder La Chelford SK11 .83 C1
Guilden Sutton CH3 .119 C3
Lostock Green CW9 .105 A4
Peover WA16 .108 B4
Warrington WA4 .17 C1
Worleston CW5 .188 B1
Cinnamon Brow CE Prim Sch
WA2 .8 C2
Cinnamon La WA2 .8 C1
Cinnamon La N WA2 .8 C2
Cinnamon Pk WA2 .9 A2
Circle Ave CW5 .205 C2
Circle The Crewe CW2 .190 B1
Mere WA16 .30 B1
Circuit The
Alderley Edge SK9 .60 A2
Bramhall SK8 .35 A4
Stockport SK3 .240 C2
Wilmslow SK9 .59 B3
Circular Dr CH4 .140 C2
City Bank ST8 .179 B1
City Rd CH2 .237 C3
City Walls Rd CH1 .237 A2
Civic Way
Ellesmere Port CH65 .70 A2
Middlewich CW10 .128 B1
Clair Ave CH5 .116 A2
Claire Pl CW7 .149 B4
Clamhunger La WA16 .56 B4
Clamley Ct L24 .21 A2
Clamley Gdns L24 .21 C1
Clanfield Ave WA8 .12 B2
Clap Gate Cres WA8 .22 A3
Clap Gates Cres WA5 .15 C4
Clap Gates Rd WA5 .15 C4
Clare Ave Chester CH2 .119 A2
Wilmslow SK9 .34 B2
Clare Dr
Ellesmere Port CH65 .70 A1
Macclesfield SK10 .87 B2
Wistaston CW2 .189 C1
Clare Rd SK5 .240 F8
Clare St Kidsgrove ST7 .195 C2
Mount Pleasant ST7 .195 B3
Claremont Ave
Altrincham WA14 .238 E8
Widnes WA8 .13 B2
Claremont Cl 15 CW9 .103 C2
Claremont Dr
Altrincham WA14 .238 E8
Widnes WA8 .13 A2
Claremont Gdns OL6 .242 B4
Claremont Gr WA15 .238 E3
Claremont Rd
Cheadle SK8 .35 A4
Crewe CW2 .190 A1
Culcheth WA3 .4 B2
Runcorn WA7 .23 A1
Sale M33 .242 B7
Claremont St OL6 .242 B4
Clarence Ave
Chester CH3 .119 A1
Warrington WA5 .14 B3
Widnes WA8 .13 A2
Clarence Ct
Newton-le-W WA12 .2 A2
Wilmslow SK9 .60 A3
Clarence Gr CW1 .190 A3
Clarence Rd
Altrincham WA15 .238 F3
Bollington SK10 .63 A1
Warrington WA4 .17 A1
Clarence St Hyde SK14 .241 E8
Newton-le-W WA12 .1 C2
Runcorn WA7 .22 C2
Stalybridge OL6,SK15,
SK16 .242 B1
Warrington WA1 .16 C4
Clarence Terr
Bollington SK10 .63 A1
Runcorn WA7 .23 A2
Clarendon Ave
Altrincham WA15 .238 E5
Stockport SK4 .240 B7
Clarendon Cl
Chester CH4 .141 C3
Runcorn WA7 .50 B4
Clarendon Cres M33 .242 D7
Clarendon Ct WA2 .7 C2
Clarendon Dr SK10 .88 A1
Clarendon Ind Est SK14 .241 E7
Clarendon Pl SK14 .241 E6
Clarendon Rd
Denton M34 .241 B6
Hyde SK14 .241 E7
Irlam M44 .11 C4
Sale M33 .242 D6
Clarendon St Hyde SK14 .241 D7
Stockport SK5 .240 F7
Clares Farm Cl WA1 .17 C4
Clark Way SK14 .241 D7
Clarke Ave Culcheth WA3 .5 A2
Warrington WA4 .16 B1
Clarke Gdns 17 WA8 .23 A4
Clarke La Bollington SK10 .87 C3
Langley SK11 .113 B2
Clarke St WA14 .238 D7
Clarke Terr SK11 .112 B3
Clarks Terr WA7 .48 B4
Clary Mdw CW8 .78 C1
Clatterbridge Hospl
CH63 .42 B4
Clatterbridge Rd CH63 .42 B4
Claude St WA1 .16 B3
Claughton Ave CW2 .190 B1
Claverton Cl WA7 .49 A3
Clay Heyes SK11 .84 A2
Clay La Burtonwood WA5 .6 C3
Handforth SK9 .34 B3
Peover WA16 .108 A4
Sandbach CW11 .174 A1
Wilmslow SK9 .59 B2
Winsford CW7 .125 A2
Claydon Gdns WA3 .10 C1
Clayhill CH64 .41 C1
Clayhill Gn CH66 .69 B4
Clayhill Gr WA3 .4 A4
Clayhill Light Ind Pk
CH64 .41 C1
Claypit Rd CH4 .141 A3
Claypitts La CH3 .142 C3
Clayton Ave
Congleton CW12 .157 A3
Golborne WA3 .3 C4
Clayton Cl CW1 .190 A4
Clayton Cres
Runcorn WA7 .22 C1
Widnes WA8 .12 C1
Clayton Dr SY13 .226 A1
Clayton Rd WA3 .9 C3
Clayton's Row CW5 .204 C4
Clayton-by-pass CW12 .156 B2
Cleaver Mews SK11 .112 B3
Cleaver Rd CH1 .117 C2
Cledford Cres CW10 .151 C3
Cledford Inf Sch CW10 .151 B4
Cledford Jun Sch CW10 .151 B4
Cledford La CW10 .151 C4
Cledwen Rd CH4 .139 B3
Cleethorpes Rd WA7 .50 B4
Cleeve Way SK8 .35 A3
Cleeves Cl WA1 .16 B3
Clegg Pl OL6 .242 A4
Clegg St SK11 .112 C4
Clegge St WA2 .16 A4
Cleggs Cl CH3 .142 A4
Clelland St WA4 .16 B2
Clement St SK4 .240 E7
Clemley Cl CW6 .122 B3
Clerewood Ave SK8 .34 A4
Clevedon Cl SK11 .112 A4
Cleveland Ave SK14 .241 C6
Cleveland Dr CH66 .69 A3
Cleveland Rd
Altrincham WA15 .238 F3
Stockport SK4 .240 A8
Warrington WA2 .8 A2
Cleveland Way CW7 .149 A4
Cleveleys Ave Gatley SK8 .239 B1
Widnes WA8 .13 B1
Cleveleys Rd WA5 .15 A2
Cleves Cl CH1 .117 B3
Cliff Gr SK4 .240 B8
Cliff La Acton Bridge CW8 .76 B2
Lymm WA13 .28 A3
Macclesfield SK10 .88 A1
Rainow SK10 .88 A1
Warrington WA4 .17 B1
Cliff Rd Acton Bridge CW8 .76 C2

Cliff Rd *continued*
Wilmslow SK9 .....60 A4
Cliff Side SK9 .....60 A4
Cliff View WA6 .....74 A4
Cliffbrook Gr 2 SK9 .....34 B1
Cliffe Rd Crewe CW1 .....190 A4
Neston CH64 .....66 C3
Warrington WA4 .....26 B4
Cliffe St 3 WA8 .....13 B1
Cliffmere Cl SK8 .....239 F3
Clifford Dr CH4 .....140 C3
Clifford Gr CW1 .....191 B2
Clifford Pl 6 CW7 .....149 B4
Clifford Rd
Macclesfield SK11 .....112 A4
Poynton SK12 .....36 B2
Warrington WA5 .....15 A2
Wilmslow SK9 .....59 C3
Clifton Ave
Altrincham WA15 .....238 E5
Bebington CH62 .....43 C2
Crewe CW2 .....190 A2
Culcheth WA3 .....4 B2
Gatley SK8 .....239 A2
Clifton Cl WA1 .....17 B4
Clifton Cres WA6 .....49 B1
Clifton Ct WA7 .....49 A3
Clifton Dr Blacon CH1 .....117 C2
Cheadle, Heald Green SK8 .....239 A2
Cheadle,Gatley SK8 .....239 A6
Northwich CW9 .....104 A3
Wilmslow SK9 .....59 C2
Clifton Gdns CH65 .....70 B2
Clifton La WA7 .....49 C2
Clifton Park Ave CH5 .....91 B1
Clifton Rd Runcorn WA7 .....49 C2
Runcorn, Heath WA7 .....49 A3
Sale M33 .....242 B5
Sandbach CW11 .....174 B4
Stockport SK4 .....240 A8
Clifton St
Alderley Edge SK9 .....60 A1
Crewe CW2 .....190 A2
Warrington WA4 .....16 B2
Cliftonmill Mdws WA3 .....2 C4
Cliftonville Rd WA1 .....17 B3
Clincton Cl WA8 .....22 A4
Clincton View WA8 .....22 A4
Clinton St OL6 .....242 A4
Clipsley Cres WA11 .....1 A4
Clipsley La WA11 .....1 B3
Clitheroe Rd CW8 .....77 C1
Clive Ave WA2 .....8 B1
Clive La CW7 .....150 B4
Cliveden Rd CH4 .....140 C3
Clivegreen La CW10 .....150 C4
Clock Face Rd WA8 .....13 C4
Clock Tower Cl SK14 .....241 E5
Cloister Way CH65 .....70 C3
Cloisters The Sale M33 .....242 D6
Stockport SK8 .....240 A1
Clonners Field CW5 .....205 A2
Close La Alsager ST7 .....192 C2
Mow Cop ST7 .....195 B4
Close The Alsager ST7 .....193 A2
Altrincham WA14 .....238 C5
Blacon CH1 .....117 B2
Newton-le-W WA12 .....2 C1
Northwich CW8 .....103 B3
Saughall CH1 .....94 A1
Stalybridge SK15 .....242 C4
Tarporley CW6 .....146 B1
Closeburn Ave CH60 .....40 C3
Cloud The* CW12 .....158 A2
Cloud View CW12 .....157 A1
Cloudberry Wlk M31 .....11 C2
Clough Ave Handforth SK9 .....34 A1
Warrington WA2 .....8 A1
Clough Bank SK10 .....87 C4
Clough Fold Rd SK14 .....241 D5
Clough Hall Dr ST7 .....210 C3
Clough Hall Rd ST7 .....210 C4
Clough Hall Tech Sch
ST7 .....194 C1
Clough La CW8 .....103 B3
Clough Rd CW7 .....126 C1
Clough The WA7 .....23 C1
Clough Wlk CW2 .....206 B4
Cloughside SK12 .....38 C3
Cloughwood Sch CW8 .....103 B3
Clovelly Ave WA5 .....14 C4
Clovelly Gr WA7 .....50 B3
Clover Ave Frodsham WA6 .....74 B4
Stockport SK3 .....240 D1
Clover Ct WA7 .....50 A3
Clover Dr Pickmere WA16 .....79 C4
Winsford CW7 .....126 B2
Clover La CH4 .....140 C3
Clover Pl CH4 .....140 C3
Clover Rd SK6 .....241 E3
Cloverdale CW8 .....103 B4
Cloverdale Rd SK11 .....112 A3
Cloverfield WA7 .....50 B4
Cloverfield Gdns CH66 .....69 B4
Cloverfields CW1 .....191 A2
Clowes Ave ST7 .....193 C1
Clowes St SK11 .....112 A4
Clumber Cl SK12 .....36 C2
Clumber Rd SK12 .....36 C2
Clutton CE Prim Sch
CH3 .....182 B1
Clwyd Ave SK3 .....240 D3
Clwyd Cl CH4 .....139 A3
Clwyd Way CH66 .....69 A3
Clyde Ave ST8 .....179 C1
Clyde Cres CW7 .....127 A1
Clyde Gr CW2 .....190 A2
Clyde Rd SK3 .....240 C3
Clydesdale CH65 .....70 A2
Clydesdale Ave CW2 .....190 A2
Clydesdale Rd WA4 .....26 B4
Coach Rd Broxton CH3 .....183 A2
Edge Green SY14 .....199 B1
Little Budworth CW6 .....147 B4
Coachway SK10 .....86 C4
Coalbrookdale Rd CH64 .....41 C1
Coalpit Hill ST7 .....210 B4
Coalpit La Langley SK11 .....113 B3
Mollington CH1 .....94 B2
Winsford CW10 .....127 C1
Coalport Dr CW7 .....126 C2
Coare St SK10 .....87 B1
Coastguard La CH64 .....41 A1
Cob Hall La WA6 .....98 B3
Cob Moor Rd ST7 .....195 A2
Cobal Ct WA6 .....74 A4
Cobbett's Way SK9 .....59 C2
Cobblers Cross La CW6 .....146 C1
Cobblers La LL12 .....161 A1
Cobbles The
Chester CH4 .....141 B4
Cuddington CW8 .....101 B2
Lower Peover WA16 .....81 C1
Cobblestone Ct CH2 .....119 C4
Cobbs Inf Sch The WA4 .....26 C4
Cobbs La
Hough Common CW2 .....206 C1
Warrington WA4 .....26 C4
Cobden St
Ashton-u-Lyne OL6 .....242 A2
Newton-le-W WA12 .....2 B2
Warrington WA2 .....16 A3
Cock Hall La SK11 .....113 B2
Cock La CW9 .....78 C4
Cock Lane Ends WA8 .....22 A2
Cocker Hill SK15 .....242 E2
Cockhedge Ctr WA1 .....16 A3
Cockhedge La WA1 .....16 B3
Cockhedge Way WA1 .....16 A3
Cockington Cl CW9 .....104 A2
Cocklade La L24 .....21 B1
Cockpit La CW8 .....102 A1
Cocksheadhey Rd SK10 .....63 B1
Cocksmoss La SK11 .....133 B2
Coe La WA14 .....30 B4
Coerdon Dr WA4 .....17 B1
Cogshall La
Comberbach CW9 .....78 A4
Little Leigh CW8,CW9 .....77 C4
Northwich CW9 .....78 B3
Colborne Ave SK6 .....241 C2
Colchester Pl SK4 .....240 C7
Colchester Sq CH4 .....140 C3
Coldmoss Dr CW11 .....175 B2
Coldstream Cl WA2 .....8 C2
Coldstream Dr CH66 .....68 C3
Cole Ave WA12 .....2 B2
Colebrook Cl WA3 .....10 A2
Coleclough Pl WA3 .....4 C2
Colehill Bank CW12 .....156 C1
Colehill Pl CH5 .....91 B1
Colemere Cl WA1 .....17 A4
Colenso Gr SK4 .....240 B7
Coleridge Cl Blacon CH1 .....118 A3
Sandbach CW11 .....174 B3
Coleridge Gr WA8 .....12 C1
Coleridge Way CW1 .....190 C3
Colin Rd SK4 .....240 E8
Colinwood Ave CH4 .....139 A2
Coliseum Way CH65 .....70 B1
Collar House Dr SK10 .....86 C3
College Cl
Warrington WA1 .....16 B3
Warrington, Fearnhead WA2 .....9 A1
Wilmslow SK9 .....59 C4
College Fields CW2 .....190 A1
College Gn CH4 .....141 B4
College Ho
Altrincham WA14 .....238 C1
Stockport SK4 .....240 B8
College La CW6 .....168 C1
College of Law (Christleton
Hall) CH3 .....142 B4
College Rd ST7 .....193 A3
College View CH5 .....91 B1
Colley La CW11 .....175 B3
Colleys La Nantwich CW2 .....205 B4
Willaston (nr Nantwich)
CW2 .....205 B4
Collier St WA7 .....22 C2
Collier's Row WA7 .....48 C4
Colliers La CW9 .....54 C1
Colliery Green Cl CH64 .....66 C3
Colliery Green Ct CH64 .....66 C3
Colliery Green Dr CH64 .....66 C3
Collin St WA5 .....15 C3
Collinbrook Ave CW2 .....190 A1
Collingham Gn CH66 .....69 A3
Collingham Way CW7 .....126 B1
Collingtree Ave CW7 .....127 A2
Collingwood Cl
Macclesfield SK10 .....87 A1
Poynton SK12 .....37 A2
Collingwood Rd WA12 .....2 A2
Collins Green La WA5 .....1 C1
Collins St CW2 .....190 A2
Collinson Ct 3 WA6 .....74 A4
Colmere Cl WA2 .....9 A1
Colmere Ct CH65 .....70 B4
Colne Rd WA5 .....6 C3
Colorado Cl WA5 .....15 B4
Colshaw Dr SK9 .....34 B1
Colshaw La SK11 .....109 C1
Colson Ct CH1 .....237 A4
Coltsfoot Dr WA14 .....238 B8
Columbine Cl
Huntington CH3 .....142 A3
Widnes WA8 .....12 A2
Columbine Way WA9 .....6 A4
Columbine Wlk 15 M31 .....11 C2
Colville Ct WA2 .....8 A2
Colville Rd SK11 .....111 C4
Colwick Ave WA14 .....238 E6
Colwyn Cl WA5 .....7 C1
Colwyn Rd Bramhall SK7 .....35 C4
Cheadle SK8 .....239 E1
Comber Way WA16 .....82 A4
Comberbach Dr CW5 .....205 A2
Comberbach Prim Sch
CW9 .....78 B4
Combermere Cl SK8 .....239 F4
Combermere Pl CW1 .....190 A3
Comboy Dr CW9 .....104 B3
Combs Cl SK22 .....39 A4
Comer Terr M33 .....242 A6
Commercial Ave SK8 .....34 C3
Commercial Brow SK14 .....241 E8
Commercial Rd SK10 .....112 C4
Commercial St SK14 .....241 E7
Common Farm La SK11 .....83 C1
Common La Betley CW3 .....221 C3
Chelford SK11 .....83 C1
Culcheth WA3 .....4 C2
Duddon CW6 .....145 A4
Kelsall CW6 .....122 B2
Lach Dennis CW9 .....105 C3
Stretton WA4 .....52 C4
Warrington WA4 .....16 C1
Waverton CH3 .....143 A2
Winsford CW7 .....125 A3
Common Rd WA12,WA5 .....1 C2
Common St WA12 .....1 C2
Common The WA7 .....49 C4
Commonhall St CH1 .....237 A2
Commons Mill CW11 .....175 A4
Commons The CW11 .....175 A3
Commonside WA6 .....73 C1
Commonwealth Cl CW7 .....149 B3
Company's Cl WA7 .....48 C3
Compass Cl WA7 .....50 B3
Compstall Rd SK6 .....241 E2
Compton Cl WA11 .....1 B4
Compton Pl Chester CH4 .....141 A3
Ellesmere Port CH65 .....70 A3
Compton St SK15 .....242 E1
Concorde Pl WA2 .....8 B1
Concourse Way WA9 .....1 A1
Condliffe Cl CW11 .....175 B3
Conery Cl WA6 .....73 B2
Coney Gr WA7 .....50 A3
Coneymead SK15 .....242 D4
Congleton Bsns Ctr
CW12 .....156 C2
Congleton Bsns Pk
CW12 .....156 B2
Congleton Cl SK9 .....85 A4
Congleton Edge Rd
CW12 .....179 A3
Congleton High Sch
CW12 .....155 C2
Congleton La SK11 .....109 B3
Congleton Rd
Alderley Edge SK9 .....60 A1
Biddulph ST7 .....178 C1
Biddulph ST8 .....179 B1
Broughton CH4 .....139 B2
Kidsgrove ST7 .....194 B1
Macclesfield SK11 .....112 A3
Marton SK11 .....133 A3
Nether Alderley SK10 .....85 A3
Sandbach CW11 .....175 A4
Sandbach CW11 .....175 C4
Scholar Green CW12,ST7 .....177 C2
Siddington SK11 .....110 A3
Smallwood CW11 .....177 A3
Swettenham CW4,CW12 .....131 C2
Talke ST7 .....210 B4
Warren SK11 .....111 C1
Congleton Rd N ST7 .....194 C3
Congleton Rd S ST7 .....194 B2
Congleton Sta CW12 .....157 A1
Congleton War Meml Hospl
CW12 .....156 C1
Conifer Cl CH1 .....95 A4
Conifer Gr WA5 .....14 C4
Conifer Wlk M31 .....11 C2
Conifers The ST7 .....193 A2
Coningsby Dr CW7 .....126 C1
Coniston Ave
Bebington CH63 .....43 B2
Congleton CW12 .....155 C1
Dukinfield SK14 .....241 C8
Warrington WA5 .....14 B2
Winsford CW7 .....126 B1
Coniston Cl
Alderley Edge SK9 .....84 A4
Hooton CH66 .....44 A1
Nantwich CW5 .....205 A3
Runcorn WA7 .....49 B3
Coniston Dr
Frodsham WA6 .....74 B4
Handforth SK9 .....34 B2
Holmes Chapel CW4 .....130 A2
Stalybridge SK15 .....242 D3
Coniston Rd
Chester CH2 .....118 C3
Gatley SK8 .....239 B5
High Lane SK6 .....37 B4
Neston CH64 .....66 C3
Partington M31 .....11 C2
Coniston Way SK11 .....111 C3
Connah's Quay High Sch
CH5 .....91 B1
Connaught Ave WA1 .....16 C4
Connaught Cl SK9 .....60 B4
Connaught Dr WA12 .....2 B1
Conrad Cl CW1 .....190 C2
Conroy Way WA12 .....7 B4
Consort Cl SK10 .....87 C4
Consort Pl WA14 .....238 B3
Constable Dr SK9 .....60 C4
Constables Cl WA7 .....24 A1
Constance Rd M31 .....11 C2
Constance Way WA8 .....23 A3
Convamore Rd SK7 .....35 B4
Conway Ave Irlam M44 .....11 C4
Warrington WA5 .....7 C1
Winsford CW7 .....149 B4
Conway Cl
Broughton CH4 .....140 B3
Crewe CW1 .....190 B4
Knutsford WA16 .....82 A4
Warrington WA5 .....14 C3
Conway Cres SK10 .....87 C1
Conway Ct CH65 .....70 B2
Conway Dr
Newton-le-W WA12 .....2 C2
Stalybridge SK15 .....242 D3
Conway Rd Cheadle SK8 .....239 E2
Sale M33 .....242 D5
Conway St SK5 .....240 E8
Coogee Ave WA5 .....14 C4
Cook Ave WA11 .....1 C4
Cook St
Ellesmere Port CH65 .....70 B3
Stockport SK3 .....240 E5
Cooke's La CW9 .....104 C3
Cookes Ct CH3 .....166 A1
Cooks La SY13 .....225 B4
Cooksmere La CW11 .....175 A4
Coole La Nantwich CW5 .....218 C2
Newhall CW3 .....229 B3
Coombe Dr WA7 .....49 A4
Coombe Park Ct 1 CH66 .....69 B3
Coombe Pk CH66 .....69 B3
Coombes Ave SK14 .....241 F5
Coope Rd SK10 .....87 C3
Cooper Ave
Newton-le-W WA12 .....1 C2
Warrington WA2 .....8 A1
Cooper La WA11 .....1 B3
Cooper St
Congleton CW12 .....156 C2
Runcorn WA7 .....23 A2
Stockport SK1 .....240 F3
Widnes WA8 .....13 A1
Cooper Terr CW6 .....146 B1
Cooper's Croft CH3 .....142 A4
Cooper's Fold SK8 .....34 C3
Cooper's La CH5 .....91 B1
Coopers Opening CW11 .....175 A4
Cop Mdw SK11 .....112 C1
Copage Dr SK6 .....241 A4
Cope Ave CW5 .....204 B2
Copeland Gr WA7 .....49 C3
Copeland Rd WA4 .....16 A1
Copes La CW5 .....204 B2
Copeswood Cl CH4 .....139 B2
Copgrove Wlk M22 .....33 C4
Copley Ave SK15 .....242 F2
Copley High Sch SK15 .....242 F2
Copley Park Mews SK15 .....242 F2
Coppenhall Gr CW2 .....190 A2
Coppenhall Heyes CW2 .....190 A2
Coppenhall High Sch
CW1 .....190 C3
Coppenhall La CW2 .....189 B2
Copper Beach Cl CH4 .....139 B2
Copper St SK11 .....112 C3
Copper Wood CW8 .....101 C3
Copperfield Cl WA3 .....9 B3
Copperfield Rd
Bramhall SK8 .....35 A3
Poynton SK12 .....36 B1
Copperfields
Poynton SK12 .....36 B1
Tarporley CW6 .....146 B1
Wilmslow SK9 .....60 B4
Copperhill Rd CW12 .....179 A4
Coppermine La SY14 .....184 A1
Copperwood WA7 .....24 B1
Coppice Ave SK12 .....38 A3
Coppice Cl High Lane SK12 .....38 A3
Romiley SK6 .....241 B4
Runcorn WA7 .....24 A1
Willaston (nr Nantwich)
CW5 .....205 B3
Coppice Dr CW10 .....151 C3
Coppice Gn WA5 .....7 A1
Coppice Gr WA16 .....57 A2
Coppice Ho ST7 .....210 B4
Coppice La SK12 .....38 A3
Coppice Rd
Haslington CW11 .....192 A4
Poynton SK12 .....37 A2
Talke ST7 .....210 B4
Willaston (nr Nantwich)
CW5 .....205 B3
Coppice Rise SK11 .....112 B3
Coppice The
Altrincham WA15 .....32 A4
Cuddington CW8 .....101 B3
Higher Wincham CW9 .....79 B2
Sandbach CW11 .....174 C4
Whaley Bridge SK23 .....65 C3
Coppice Way SK9 .....34 C2
Coppins Cl Chester CH3 .....119 A1
Helsby WA6 .....73 A2
Coppins The
Warrington WA2 .....8 B
Wilmslow SK9 .....59 C
Copse The
Altrincham WA15 .....32 B
Newton-le-W WA12 .....2 A
Runcorn WA7 .....50 A
Copthorne Cl CW12 .....156 C
Copthorne Dr CW3 .....229 C
Copyhold CW8 .....102 B
Corbet Ave WA2 .....16 A
Corbet Dr TF9 .....235 A
Corbet St WA2 .....16 A
Corcoran Dr SK6 .....241 F
Corfe Way CW7 .....149 B
Coriander Cl CW10 .....128 B
Corkland Cl OL6 .....242 B
Corkland St OL6 .....242 B
Corks La SK12 .....38 C
Corley Ave SK3 .....239 F
Cormorant Cl CW1 .....190 C
Cormorant Dr WA7 .....22 C
Cornbrook Rd SK11 .....112 B
Corner Croft SK9 .....60 A
Corner Ct SK8 .....239 F
Cornerhouse La WA8 .....12 B
Corners The CW8 .....102 C
Cornfield Cl
Ellesmere Port CH66 .....69 C
Macclesfield SK10 .....87 B
2 Sale M33 .....242 F
Cornfield Rd SK6 .....241 E
Cornforth Way WA8 .....12 C
Cornhill Cl ST5 .....210 B
Cornish Cl M22 .....33 B
Cornishway M22 .....33 B
Cornishway Ind Est 4
M22 .....33 B
Cornubia Rd WA8 .....23 B
Cornwall Ave WA7 .....23 A
Cornwall Cl
3 Congleton CW12 .....157 A
High Lane SK6 .....37 C
Macclesfield SK10 .....86 C
Runcorn WA7 .....23 C
Cornwall Gr CW1 .....190 A
Cornwall Rd
Chester CH2 .....118 C
Gatley SK8 .....34 A
Irlam M44 .....11 B
Widnes WA8 .....13 A
Cornwall St Chester CH2 .....237 B
Warrington WA1 .....16 C
Cornwell Cl SK9 .....60 B
Corona Ave SK14 .....241 E
Coronation Ave
Alsager ST7 .....193 A
Glazebury WA3 .....5 B
Hyde SK14 .....241 E
Warrington WA4 .....17 B
Winsford CW7 .....126 C
Coronation Bldgs SK10 .....88 A
Coronation Cres
Crewe CW1 .....190 C
Kidsgrove ST7 .....194 C
Sandbach CW11 .....175 A
Coronation Dr
Frodsham WA6 .....49 B
Haydock WA11 .....2 A
Newton-le-W WA12 .....2 C
Warrington WA5 .....14 C
Widnes WA8 .....22 B
Coronation Gr CW8 .....78 A
Coronation Ho WA7 .....49 B
Coronation Rd
Broughton CH4 .....139 A
Congleton CW12 .....156 C
Ellesmere Port CH65 .....70 B
Middlewich CW10 .....151 B
Runcorn, Higher Runcorn
WA7 .....23 A
Runcorn, Preston Brook
WA7 .....50 C
Coronation Sq 16 WA16 .....57 A
Coronation St
Chester CH4 .....140 C
Crewe CW1 .....190 B
Macclesfield SK11 .....112 B
Stockport SK5 .....240 E
Coronation Terr CW6 .....146 B
Coroner's La WA8 .....13 A
Coronet Ave CW9 .....103 C
Coronet Way WA8 .....22 A
Corporation St
Hyde SK14 .....241 D
Stalybridge SK15 .....242 D
Stockport SK1 .....240 F
Correction Brow SK12 .....37 B
Corridor Rd CH65 .....71 A
Corstons La CH64 .....67 A
Corwen Cl WA5 .....7 C
Cossack Ave WA2 .....8 B
Cote Lea Ct WA7 .....49 C
Cotebrook Dr CH2 .....118 C
Cotebrook Rd CW9 .....104 B
Cotes Pl CH1 .....117 C
Cotgreaves Cl CH4 .....141 A
Cotswold Ave WA3 .....3 B
Cotswold Cl Chester CH2 .....118 C
Cuddington CW8 .....102 A
Macclesfield SK10 .....86 C
Cotswold Gr WA9 .....1 A
Cotswold Pl WA2 .....8 A
Cotswold Rd
Stockport SK4 .....240 D
Warrington WA2 .....8 A
Cotswold Way CW7 .....149 A
Cottage Cl Bebington CH63 .....43 B

Cottage Cl *continued*
Neston CH64 .66 C4
Cottage Dr E CH60 .40 C3
Cottage Dr W CH60 .40 C3
Cottage Gr SK9 .59 C3
Cottage La Heswall CH60 .40 C3
Macclesfield SK10 .112 C4
Cottage Lawns SK9 .60 A1
Cottage Rd CH4 .141 A3
Cottage St SK11 .112 A4
Cottages The CW4 .129 B1
Cottam Dr WA2 .9 A2
Cotterdale Cl WA5 .14 C4
Cotterill WA7 .49 B4
Cotterill Dr WA1 .17 B4
Cotterill St CW2 .190 B1
Cottesmore Dr CH60 .41 B4
Cottesmore Gdns WA15 .32 B4
Cotton Cl SK14 .241 E5
Cotton La Duddon CW6 .145 B4
Runcorn WA7 .49 B4
Sandbach CW11 .175 A2
Cotton Mews CW3 .230 A2
Cotton Tree St SK4 .240 E5
Cottons Bridge WA7 .50 C3
Cottonwood Dr ST7 .195 C2
Cottrell Rd WA15 .32 B4
Coulton Rd WA8 .13 C2
Council Hos
Audlem CW3 .229 C1
Newhall CW5 .228 A4
Countess Ave SK8 .34 C3
Countess Cl SK11 .111 C4
Countess Ct CH1 .118 A3
Countess of Chester Hospl
CH2 .118 A3
Countess Rd SK11 .112 A4
Countess St OL6 .242 A2
Countess Way CH2 .118 B2
Counting House Rd SK12 .38 C3
Country Ctr The★ CH3 .165 C3
County Ave OL6 .242 B4
County Terr WA16 .56 C1
Courier Row SK10 .87 C4
Court Ho The [6] CH65 .70 B3
Court La CW8 .77 A1
Court The CH64 .66 C3
Courtney Gn SK9 .34 B1
Courtney Pl WA14 .238 A1
Courtney Rd CH4 .140 C2
Courts View M33 .242 C7
Courtyard The
Congleton CW12 .156 A2
Cuddington CW8 .101 C1
Haughton CW6 .186 C2
Middlewich CW10 .127 B3
Newton-le-W WA12 .2 C2
Stalybridge SK15 .242 D2
Weaverham CW8 .102 A4
Cousens Way CH1 .118 A2
Cove The WA15 .238 F3
Covell Rd SK12 .36 B3
Covent Gdn [18] SK1 .240 F5
Coventry Ave
Ellesmere Port CH66 .94 C4
Gatley SK3 .239 F7
Coverdale Cl WA5 .14 C4
Coverdale Fold CW11 .174 B3
Covert Cl CW7 .149 A4
Covert Gdns ST7 .210 B4
Covert Rise CH3 .166 A1
Covington Pl SK9 .60 A3
Cow Hey La WA7 .49 A3
Cow La Ashley WA15 .31 C3
Bollington SK10 .88 A4
Hargrave CH3 .144 A1
Macclesfield SK11 .112 B3
Norley WA6 .101 A3
Rainow SK10 .88 B2
Sale M33 .242 E7
Winsford CW7 .149 C4
Cowanway WA8 .12 C3
Cowbrook La SK11 .135 A3
Cowdell St WA2 .16 A4
Cowfields CW5 .204 C3
Cowhey Cl CH4 .141 A3
Cowley Way CW1 .190 C1
Cowlishaw Rd SK14,SK6 .241 F4
Cowper Cl CW2 .206 A4
Cowthorne Dr CH3 .143 A2
Coyt Rd SK23 .65 C3
Crab La WA2 .9 A2
Crab Tree Cl L24 .21 C1
Crabmill Dr CW11 .174 C4
Crabmill La Norley WA6 .100 C3
Sandbach CW11 .174 A3
Warmingham CW11 .173 C4
Crabtree Ave
Altrincham WA15 .32 B4
Disley SK12 .38 C3
Crabtree Cl WA12 .2 C2
Crabtree Ct SK12 .38 B3
Crabtree Fold WA7 .50 B4
Crabtree Gr CW1 .190 C3
Crabtree Green Ct CW8 .101 B1
Crabtree La WA16 .29 A3
Crabwall Pl CH1 .117 C3
Crackley Bank ST5 .210 C1
Crackley Bank CE Prim Sch
ST5 .210 C1
Cradley WA8 .12 B1
Cragside Way SK9 .60 B3
Craig Cl
Macclesfield SK11 .112 A3
Stockport SK4 .240 B5
Craig Dr SK23 .65 C3
Craig Gdns CH66 .69 C4
Craig Rd Congleton CW12 .156 C2
Craig Rd *continued*
Macclesfield SK11 .112 A3
Stockport SK4 .240 B5
Craig Wlk ST7 .193 C1
Craigleigh Gr CH62 .43 C2
Craigside ST8 .179 B1
Craithe Rd CH3 .119 A1
Crampton Dr WA15 .32 B4
Cranage Cl WA7 .49 B4
Cranage Ct [3] CW12 .156 C2
Cranage Rd CW2 .190 A2
Cranage Way [16] SK9 .34 B3
Cranberry Cl WA14 .238 B8
Cranberry Dr ST5 .210 B1
Cranberry Inf Sch ST7 .193 A2
Cranberry Jun Sch ST7 .193 A2
Cranberry La ST7 .193 A2
Cranberry Moss La ST7 .193 A2
Cranberry Rd M31 .11 C2
Cranborne Rd
Crewe CW1 .190 B3
Warrington WA4 .16 A1
Cranbourne Ct SK4 .240 B8
Cranbourne Rd SK4 .240 B8
Crandon Dr M20 .239 C8
Cranebrook Cl CW1 .190 A4
Cranfield Dr ST7 .193 A2
Cranford Ave
Knutsford WA16 .56 C1
Macclesfield SK11 .112 C4
Sale M33 .242 C8
Cranford Cl CH62 .43 C2
Cranford Ct Chester CH4 .141 A3
Warrington WA1 .17 C4
Cranford Mews ST7 .193 A2
Cranford Rd SK9 .34 A1
Cranham Ave WA3 .3 C4
Cranleigh Cl WA4 .26 A4
Cranleigh Cres CH1 .118 A2
Cranleigh Dr
Cheadle SK8 .239 F6
Hazel Grove SK7 .37 A4
Sale M33 .242 A7
Cranmere Cl CW9 .104 A2
Cranshaw La WA8 .13 A3
Cransley Sch CW9 .53 C1
Cranston Dr
Manchester M20 .239 B8
Sale M33 .242 E5
Cranswick Gn CH66 .69 B3
Crantock Dr SK8 .34 B4
Cranwell Ave WA3 .4 C2
Cranworth St SK15 .242 E1
Crauford Rd CW12 .157 A4
Craven Ave WA3 .3 C4
Craven Ct WA2 .7 C2
Craven Dr WA14 .238 C8
Craven Rd WA14 .238 C7
Craven Terr M33 .242 C6
Crawford Ave WA8 .12 A1
Crawford Pl WA7 .49 A3
Crawford St OL6 .242 A2
Crawford's Wlk CH2 .118 C2
Crawley Ave WA2 .8 A2
Crayford Ave CW12 .157 A3
Crediton Cl WA14 .238 B6
Cresanne Cl [6] CW10 .151 B4
Crescent Ct M33 .242 B5
Crescent Dr Helsby WA6 .73 A2
Whaley Bridge SK23 .39 B1
Crescent Gr SK8 .239 C6
Crescent Pk SK4 .240 C6
Crescent Rd
Alderley Edge SK9 .60 A1
Altrincham WA14 .238 A6
Altrincham, Hale WA15 .238 E1
Cheadle SK8 .239 C6
Congleton CW12 .156 B1
Cranage CW4 .129 C3
Ellesmere Port CH65 .70 B3
Rostherne WA16 .30 A2
Crescent The
Altrincham WA14 .238 A5
Altrincham, Timperley
WA15 .238 F7
Cheadle SK8 .239 D6
Chester CH2 .118 B2
Congleton CW12 .156 B1
Ellesmere Port CH65 .69 C3
Hartford CW8 .103 A3
Heswall, Gayton CH60 .41 A3
Lymm WA13 .18 C1
Macclesfield SK10 .87 C1
Middlewich CW10 .128 A1
Mottram St Andrew SK10 .61 A1
Nantwich CW5 .204 C3
New Mills SK22 .39 A4
Northwich CW9 .103 C3
Rostherne WA16 .30 A2
Utkinton CW6 .146 A4
Weaverham CW8 .77 C1
Cressbrook Rd WA4 .16 B1
Cressington Gdns [4]
CH65 .70 B3
Cresswell Ave
New Mills SK22 .39 B4
Newcastle-u-L ST5 .210 B1
Cresswell Cl WA5 .7 B1
Cresswell St SK22 .39 B4
Cresswellshawe Rd ST7 .193 B2
Cresta Dr WA7 .48 C3
Crestwood Cl CW2 .206 A4
Crew Ave SK10 .87 C1
Crew Rd ST7 .193 C2
Crewe Bsns Pk CW1 .190 C1
Crewe Gates Farm Ind Est
CW1 .190 C1
Crewe Gates Ind Est
CW1 .207 A4
Crewe Green Ave CW1 .191 A2
Crewe Green Rd CW1 .191 A2
Crewe Hall Ent Pk CW1 .207 B4
Crewe Hill La CH3 .197 A3
Crewe La CH3 .180 C1
Crewe La S CH3 .197 A4
Crewe Rd Alsager ST7 .193 A2
Crewe CW1 .190 C1
Haslington CW1,CW11 .191 B3
Hatherton CW5 .219 C2
Nantwich CW2,CW5 .205 B3
Sandbach CW11 .175 A2
Shavington CW2 .206 B3
Crewe St Chester CH2 .237 C3
Crewe CW1 .190 B2
Crewe Sta CW1 .190 C1
Crewood Common Rd
CW8 .76 A2
Crib La CW6 .168 A4
Criccieth Ct CH65 .70 B1
Criccieth Rd SK3 .240 A3
Cricket St M34 .241 A8
Cricket's La OL6 .242 A3
Criftin Cl CH66 .69 B1
Crimes La CH3,CW6 .167 B2
Cringle Dr SK8 .239 C3
Crisham Ave CW5 .218 C4
Crispin Rd M22 .33 C4
Critchley Cl SK14 .241 F5
Critchley Rd L24 .21 A2
Croasdale Dr WA7 .49 C3
Crocus St CW8 .78 A2
Croesmere Dr CH66 .69 B1
Croft Cl Altrincham WA15 .32 B3
Congleton CW12 .156 C1
Utkinton CW6 .146 A4
Waverton CH3 .143 A3
Croft Ct CH65 .70 C2
Croft Gdns WA4 .27 A4
Croft Heath Gdns WA3 .9 A4
Croft La Dodleston CH4 .162 A4
Knutsford WA16 .82 A4
Croft Prim Sch WA3 .9 A4
Croft Rd SK9 .59 C2
Croft St Golborne WA3 .3 A4
Hyde SK14 .241 D6
Stalybridge SK15 .242 E2
Widnes WA8 .23 A3
Croft The Chester CH2 .118 B3
Norton in Hales TF9 .236 A2
Runcorn WA7 .23 C1
Croften Dr CH64 .66 C3
Crofters Cl
[8] Ellesmere Port CH66 .69 C1
Pickmere WA16 .80 A4
Wistaston CW2 .206 A4
Crofters Ct
Holmes Chapel CW4 .130 B2
Newcastle-u-L ST5 .210 B2
Crofters Gn SK9 .59 C3
Crofters Heath CH66 .69 C1
Crofters Lea CW8 .103 B4
Crofters Pk CH5 .116 A2
Crofters The M33 .242 F5
Crofters Way CH1 .116 C4
Crofton Cl WA4 .27 B3
Crofton Gdns WA3 .4 C2
Crofton Rd WA7 .22 C1
Crofts The CH3 .180 C1
Croftside WA1 .17 C4
Croftside Way SK9 .60 B3
Croftsway CH60 .40 B4
Croftwood Cl [11] CW7 .149 A4
Cromdale Way WA5 .14 C3
Cromer Dr CW1 .190 A4
Cromer Rd Cheadle SK8 .239 E6
Sale M33 .242 C5
Cromford Ct SK23 .65 C3
Cromford Mews SK23 .65 C3
Cromley Rd SK6 .37 C3
Crompton Dr WA2 .8 A3
Crompton Rd SK11 .112 B4
Crompton St OL6 .242 B4
Cromwell Ave
Gatley SK8 .239 A6
Warrington WA5 .15 B4
Cromwell Ave S WA5 .15 B2
Cromwell Cl WA12 .2 A2
Cromwell Ct Irlam M44 .11 C4
[10] Nantwich CW5 .204 C3
[4] Warrington WA1 .16 A3
Cromwell Dr CW2 .206 B2
Cromwell Rd
Bramhall SK7 .35 B3
Ellesmere Port CH65 .70 B3
Irlam M44 .11 C4
Northwich CW8 .103 C4
Cromwell St
Stockport SK4 .240 D7
Widnes WA8 .23 A3
Cronkinson Ave CW5 .204 C2
Cronkinson Oak CW5 .204 C2
Cronton CE Prim Sch
WA8 .12 B3
Cronton La
Cronton WA8,L35 .12 A4
Widnes WA8 .12 C3
Cronton Park Ave WA8 .12 B3
Cronton Park Cl WA8 .12 B3
Cronton Rd WA8 .12 B3
Cronulla Dr WA5 .14 C4
Crook La CW7 .127 A1
Crook St Chester CH1 .237 A2
Hyde SK14 .241 E6
Crooked La CH3,CW6 .145 B2
Crookedyard Rd SK11 .113 C4
Crookenden Cl CH2 .95 B1
Crookenden Rd CH2 .95 B1
Croppers Rd WA2 .8 C2
Crosby Ave WA5 .16 A4
Crosby Gr CH64 .68 A4
Crosby St SK2 .240 F3
Crosfield St WA1 .16 A3
Cross Farm WA2 .9 A1
Cross Gn CH2 .118 C3
Cross Gr WA15 .238 F8
Cross Hey CH4 .237 C1
Cross La Audley ST7 .209 C3
Church Minshull CW1,CW5 .172 B3
Congleton CW12 .157 A1
Croft WA3 .9 B4
Frodsham WA6 .73 A4
Haslington CW11 .191 C4
Middlewich CW10 .151 B3
Neston CH64 .66 C3
Newton-le-W WA12 .2 A2
Sandbach CW11 .175 B3
Smallwood CW11 .176 C3
Swettenham CW12 .131 C2
Warrington WA4 .17 A2
Wilmslow SK9 .60 C4
Cross La E M31 .11 C2
Cross La W M31 .11 C1
Cross Lane S WA3 .9 B3
Cross Lanes Tarvin CH3 .121 B1
Tarvin, Old Moss CH3 .144 B4
Cross O' Th' Hill Rd
SY14 .214 A2
Cross Rd Gatley SK8 .34 A4
Haslington CW1 .191 B2
Cross St Alsager ST7 .193 B2
[3] Altrincham WA14 .238 D4
Barnton CW8 .78 A2
Chester CH2 .118 C1
Congleton CW12 .156 B2
Crewe CW1 .190 B2
Golborne WA3 .3 A4
Haslington CW1 .191 B2
Holt LL13 .196 C4
Hyde SK14 .241 D6
Macclesfield SK11 .112 C3
Marston CW9 .79 B2
Neston CH64 .66 C4
New Mills SK22 .39 B4
Runcorn WA7 .23 A2
Sale M32,M33 .242 B8
Warrington WA2 .16 A4
Widnes WA8 .13 B1
Cross The Holt LL13 .196 C4
Kingsley WA6 .75 B1
Lymm WA13 .18 C2
Cross Wood St CW5 .204 B3
Crossall St SK11 .112 B4
Crossdale Rd CH62 .43 B3
Crossfield Ave
Culcheth WA3 .4 C1
Winsford CW7 .149 B4
Crossfield Cl
Denton M34 .241 A6
Stalybridge SK15 .242 D1
Crossfield Rd
Bollington SK10 .87 C3
Handforth SK9 .34 B2
Crossfields CH3 .121 A1
Crossgates WA8 .13 C2
Crossings The WA12 .2 B2
Crosskeys Cl CW6 .145 A3
Crossland Terr WA6 .73 A1
Crosslands
Congleton CW12 .157 A1
Haslington CW1 .191 B2
Crossledge CW12 .156 A2
Crossley Ave CH66 .69 C3
Crossley Cres CH2 .119 A3
Crossley Dr CH60 .40 B4
Crossley Pk WA6 .99 B4
Crossley Rd M33 .242 A8
Crossley St
Stalybridge SK15 .242 C2
Warrington WA1 .16 B3
Crossmoor Cres SK6 .241 C1
Crossmoor Gr SK6 .241 C2
Crossway Bramhall SK7 .35 C3
Crewe CW1 .190 B3
Widnes WA8 .22 B4
Crossway The CH63 .42 B2
Crossways ST8 .179 C1
Crossways Rd ST7 .194 A2
Crosthwaite Ave CH62 .43 C2
Croston Cl
Alderley Edge SK9 .60 B1
Widnes WA8 .12 B2
Crotia Ave CW2 .207 A3
Crouch La CW12 .157 B2
Crouchley Hall Mews
WA13 .18 C1
Crouchley La WA13 .18 C1
Croughton Ct CH66 .69 C4
Croughton Rd
Ellesmere Port CH66 .69 C4
Stoak CH2 .96 A4
Stoak, Croughton CH2 .95 C3
Crow La E WA12 .2 B2
Crow La W WA12 .2 A2
Crow Wood La WA8 .13 B1
Crow Wood Pl WA8 .13 B2
Crow's Nest Cotts CH3 .166 B3
Crowbrook Gr [20] SK9 .34 B1
Crowder's La CW9 .105 A2
Crowe Ave WA2 .8 A1
Crowland Gdns SK8 .35 A3
Crowley La CW9,WA16 .28 A2
Crown Ave WA8 .22 A4
Crown Bank
[3] Sandbach CW11 .175 A3
Talke ST7 .210 B3
Crown Bank Cres ST7 .210 B3
Crown Cotts CW8 .124 A4
Crown Ctyd CW3 .229 C2
Crown Fields Cl WA12 .2 A3
Crown Gate WA7 .49 C4
Crown Gdns
Newton-le-W WA12 .2 A2
Talke ST7 .210 B3
Crown Gn WA13 .19 A2
Crown Ind Est WA14 .238 E7
Crown La WA16 .106 B4
Crown Mews CW3 .229 C2
Crown Park Dr WA12 .2 A3
Crown Pasages WA15 .238 E2
Crown Royal Ind Pk [11]
SK1 .240 F4
Crown St
Newton-le-W WA12 .2 A2
[8] Northwich CW8 .103 C4
[7] Warrington WA1 .16 A3
Crown St W SK11 .112 B4
Crownest La CW9 .78 C4
Crowther Ct [6] SK4 .240 A7
Croxton Gn SY14 .201 B3
Croxton La CW10 .128 A2
Croxton Way CW8 .103 A2
Croyde Cl M22 .33 C4
Croyde Rd L24 .21 A2
Crum Hill [2] CW9 .104 A4
Crummock Rd SK8 .239 B3
Cryers La Elton CH2 .72 A1
Thornton-le-M CH2 .96 C4
Cty High Sch Leftwich The
CW9 .104 A2
Cuckoo Clock Mus★
WA16 .80 C4
Cuckoo La Acton CW5 .203 C4
Neston CH64 .67 B4
Cuckstoolpit Hill [3]
SK11 .112 C4
Cuddington Cres SK3 .240 D2
Cuddington La CW8 .101 B2
Cuddington Prim Sch
CW8 .101 C1
Cuddington Sta CW8 .102 A2
Cuddington Way [7] SK9 .34 B3
Cuerdley Gn WA5 .14 A1
Cuerdley Rd WA5 .14 B2
Culbin Cl WA3 .10 A3
Culcheth Com Prim Sch
WA3 .5 A2
Culcheth Hall Dr WA3 .4 C2
Culcheth Hall Prep Sch
WA14 .238 D3
Culcheth High Sch WA3 .5 A2
Culcheth Rd WA14 .238 D3
Culford Cl WA7 .24 B1
Culland St CW2 .190 B1
Cullen Cl CH63 .43 B2
Cullen Rd WA7 .48 B4
Culver Rd SK3 .240 D1
Cumber Cl SK9 .59 B2
Cumber Dr SK9 .59 B2
Cumber La SK9 .59 B2
Cumberland Ave
Irlam M44 .11 B3
Nantwich CW5 .204 C3
Cumberland Cl
Crewe CW1 .190 B3
Talke ST7 .210 C4
Cumberland Cres WA11 .1 A3
Cumberland Dr
Altrincham WA14 .31 A4
Bollington SK10 .88 A4
Cumberland Gr CH66 .69 B2
Cumberland Rd
Congleton CW12 .156 A2
Partington M31 .11 C1
Sale M33 .242 C5
Cumberland Sports Ctr
CW1 .190 B3
Cumberland St
[37] Macclesfield SK11 .112 B4
Stalybridge SK15 .242 C2
Warrington WA4 .16 B2
Cumbermere Dr CW11 .174 C4
Cumbers Dr CH64 .67 A3
Cumbers La CH64 .67 A3
Cumbrae Dr [8] CH65 .70 B1
Cumbria Cl [4] CH66 .69 C1
Cuncliffe Cl WA7 .50 A4
Cundiff Cl SK11 .112 C3
Cundy St SK14 .241 E8
Cunliffe Ave WA12 .2 A3
Cunliffe Dr M33 .242 C5
Cunliffe St
Dukinfield SK14 .241 C8
Stockport SK3 .240 C4
Cunningham Cl WA5 .14 C3
Cunningham Dr
Bebington CH63 .43 B4
Gatley M22 .34 A4
Runcorn WA7 .22 C1
Cunningham Rd WA8 .22 B4
Cuppin St CH1 .237 A2
Curlender Way L24 .21 C1
Curlew Cl Golborne WA3 .3 B4
Winsford CW7 .149 B3
Curlew Gr WA3 .9 C2
Currans Rd WA2 .8 A1
Currier La OL6 .242 A2
Curtis Rd SK4 .240 A6

Curzon Ave ST7 193 B3
Curzon Cl CH4 141 A4
Curzon Dr WA4 27 A4
Curzon Gr CW7 126 C1
Curzon Mews SK9 60 A3
Curzon Pk N CH4 141 A4
Curzon Pk S CH4 141 A4
Curzon Rd
Ashton-u-Lyne OL6 242 A4
Gatley SK8 34 A4
Poynton SK12 36 C1
6 Sale M33 242 B7
Curzon St Chester CH4 140 C4
3 Runcorn WA7 22 C1
Cuthbert Rd SK8 239 E6
Cybnet Ct WA1 16 A2
Cygnet Cl CH66 69 B2
Cyman Cl CH1 117 B2
Cymbal Ct SK5 240 F7
Cynthia Ave WA1 17 A4
Cynthia Rd WA7 22 C1
Cypress Ave
Ellesmere Port CH66 69 C1
Widnes WA8 13 A1
Cypress Cl Stockport SK3 240 C4
Warrington WA1 17 C4
Cypress Gr Denton M34 241 A7
Runcorn WA7 49 B4
Cypress Mews CW8 102 C4
Cypress Way SK6 38 A4
Cyril Bell Cl WA13 18 C2
Cyril St WA2 16 A4

D

D'Arcy Cotts CH63 42 A3
Daffodil Cl WA8 13 C2
Dagfields Craft & Antiques Ctr* CW5 220 A2
Dagnall Ave WA5 7 C1
Daintry St SK11 112 C4
Daintry Terr 4 SK11 112 C4
Dairy Farm Cl 8 WA13 18 C2
Dairy House La SK7 35 A2
Dairy House Rd SK7,SK8 35 A3
Dairy House Small Holdings SK7 35 A2
Dairy House Way CW2 189 C1
Dairy La CW5 188 B3
Dairyground Rd SK7 35 C4
Dairyhouse La WA14 238 B7
Dairylands Rd ST7 193 C2
Daisy Ave WA12 2 B1
Daisy Bank Culcheth WA3 4 C2
Nantwich CW5 204 B3
Daisy Bank Cres CW3 229 C3
Daisy Bank La
Anderton CW9 78 B2
Cheadle SK8 239 A1
Daisy Bank Rd
Lymm WA13 18 B2
Warrington WA5 14 C2
Daisy St SK1,SK2 240 F3
Daisy Way SK6 37 C4
Daisybank Dr
Congleton CW12 156 B2
Sandbach CW11 175 B3
Daisyhill Cl M33 242 E6
Dalby Cl WA3 10 A3
Dalby Ct CW9 104 C3
Dale Ave Bebington CH62 43 B4
Bramhall SK7 35 C4
Ellesmere Port CH66 69 B3
Dale Cl Warrington WA5 15 B2
Widnes WA8 22 A4
Dale Cres CW12 156 C1
Dale Ct Heswall CH60 40 C4
Middlewich CW10 151 B4
Dale Dr Chester CH2 118 B4
Ellesmere Port CH65 69 C3
Dale Gdns CH65 70 A2
Dale Gr Altrincham WA15 238 F7
Congleton CW12 157 A1
Irlam M44 11 C3
Dale Head Rd SK10 86 C2
Dale Hey CH66 43 C1
Dale House Fold SK12 37 A2
Dale La WA4 26 C4
Dale Rd Bebington CH62 43 B3
Golborne WA3 3 A4
New Mills SK22 39 B4
Dale St Chester CH3 119 A1
Macclesfield SK11 112 C4
Runcorn WA7 23 A1
Stalybridge SK15 242 C1
Stockport SK3 240 D3
Dale The Neston CH64 66 C3
Tiverton CW6 168 B3
Warrington WA5 14 C3
Dale View Kidsgrove ST7 195 B3
Newton-le-W WA12 2 C2
Dale's Sq CW9 103 C3
Dalebrook Ct SK4 240 C6
Dalecroft WA6 72 C1
Dalefords La
Cuddington CW8 102 A1
Whitegate CW8 125 B4
Dales Green Rd ST7 195 B3
Dalesford Cl WN7 4 B4
Dalesford Cres SK11 111 C4
Daleside CH2 118 B4
Dalesway CH60 40 C4
Dalewood Cl WA2 16 A3
Dalewood Cres CH2 72 A2
Dalham La WA2 16 A4
Dallam Com Prim Sch WA5 7 C1
Dalmahoy Cl CW7 126 B1
Dalrybrook Gr 7 SK9 34 C1
Dalston Dr SK7 35 B3
Dalton Ave WA5 15 C4
Dalton Bank WA1 16 B3
Dalton Cl CH1 117 C2
Dalton Ct Runcorn WA7 23 C2
Sandbach CW11 174 C4
Dalton Gr SK4 240 C8
Dalton St Runcorn WA7 23 B1
Sale M33 242 C8
Warrington WA3 9 C3
Dalton Way CW10 128 B1
Dalveen Dr WA15 238 F7
Dalwood Cl WA7 50 C4
Dam Head La WA3 11 A3
Dam La Hollinfare WA3 11 A2
Mobberley WA16 58 B2
Warrington WA1 17 B4
Winwick WA3 8 C4
Dame Hollow SK8 34 B4
Dameny Ct SK7 35 C4
Damery Rd SK7 35 C4
Damhead La CH64 67 C4
Damian Dr WA12 2 A3
Dams La WA16 106 B3
Damson La WA16 58 A2
Damson Wlk M31 11 B2
Dan's Rd WA8 13 C1
Danby Cl Hyde SK14 241 F8
Runcorn WA7 49 B3
Warrington WA5 15 C4
Danby Pl SK14 241 F8
Danby Rd SK14 241 F8
Dane Ave Partington M31 11 C2
Stockport SK3 240 A4
Dane Bank Ave
Congleton CW12 156 C2
Crewe CW2 190 A1
Dane Bank Dr SK12 38 B3
Dane Bank Rd CW9 104 A4
Dane Cl Alsager ST7 193 A2
Sandbach CW11 174 C4
Dane Dr Biddulph ST8 179 C1
Wilmslow SK9 60 B3
Dane Gdns ST7 195 B1
Dane Gr CH2 119 C4
Dane Hill Cl SK12 38 B3
Dane Mews M33 242 B6
Dane Mill Bsns Ctr CW12 156 B2
Dane Pl CW7 127 A1
Dane Rd M33 242 D7
Dane Road Sta M33 242 C8
Dane St Congleton CW12 156 B2
Middlewich CW10 128 B1
Northwich CW9 103 C4
Danebank Rd WA13 18 C2
Danebank Rd E WA13 18 C2
Danefield Ct SK8 34 B4
Danefield Rd
Holmes Chapel CW4 130 B2
Northwich CW9 104 A4
Sale M33 242 C8
Danes Sq SK11 112 B3
Danesbury Rise SK8 239 D5
Danescroft WA8 12 A2
Daneside Bsns Pk CW12 156 C2
Daneswell Rd L24 21 A1
Daniel Adamson Ave M31 11 B2
Daniel Cl WA3 10 A2
Daniel Ct M31 11 C2
Daniel's La SK1 240 E6
Daniell Way CH3 142 A4
Danwood Cl M34 241 B5
Dappleheath Rd CW2 190 A1
Darby Cl CH64 66 C2
Darent Rd WA11 1 A4
Daresbury Ave WA15 238 E5
Daresbury Cl
Holmes Chapel CW4 130 A2
Sale M33 242 F5
Stockport SK3 240 D1
Wilmslow SK9 60 B4
Daresbury Ct WA8 13 C2
Daresbury Expressway
Daresbury WA4 25 A2
Runcorn WA7 24 B2
Daresbury La WA4 25 B1
Daresbury Prim Sch WA4 25 A1
Dargle Rd M33 242 B8
Darian Ave M22 33 B4
Dark Ark La CH3,WA6 99 A2
Dark La Henbury SK11 111 A4
Kingsley WA6 75 A1
Marston CW9 79 B3
Tattenhall CH3 183 C4
Warren SK11 111 B2
Whitchurch SY13 227 A1
Whitley WA4 52 B3
Darkie Mdw CW6 185 C4
Darland La LL12 162 B1
Darley Ave Crewe CW2 190 A2
Gatley SK8 239 B5
Warrington WA2 8 C2
Darley Cl WA8 12 A2
Darley Rd SK7 36 C4
Darley St M33 242 B6
Darleydale Dr CH62 43 C3
Darlington Ave CW1 189 C3
Darlington Cres CH1 94 A1
Darlington Ct 19 WA8 23 A4
Darlington St CW10 128 B1
Darnaway Cl WA3 10 A3
Darnhall Prim Sch CW7 149 B3
Darnhall School La CW7 149 B3
Darnton Gdns OL6 242 B3
Darnton Rd OL6,SK15 242 B3
Dart Cl Alsager ST7 193 A2
Biddulph ST8 179 B1
Dart Wlk CW7 127 A1
Dartnall Cl SK12 38 A3
Darwen Gdns WA2 8 C1
Darwin Gr SK7 35 C3
Darwin Rd CH1 117 B2
Darwin St CW8 103 C4
Daryl Rd CH60 41 A4
Dashwood Cl WA4 27 A4
Daten Ave WA3 9 C3
Daten Pk WA3 9 C3
Dauncey Cl CH2 95 B1
Davehall Ave SK9 60 A4
Daven Prim Sch CW12 156 C1
Daven Rd CW12 156 C1
Davenham Ave WA1 16 C4
Davenham CE Prim Sch CW9 103 C1
Davenham Cres CW2 190 A2
Davenham Ct CW9 104 A2
Davenham Rd
Davenham CW9 104 C2
Handforth SK9 34 B2
Davenham Way CW10 151 B3
Davenport Ave
Crewe CW2 206 B4
Nantwich CW5 204 C4
Warrington WA4 16 C3
Wilmslow SK9 59 C2
Davenport Cl CW11 175 B4
Davenport La
Altrincham WA14 238 C7
Brereton Green CW11 154 B1
Marton SK11 132 C3
Mobberley WA16 58 B3
Davenport Lodge SK3 240 F1
Davenport Park La
Brereton Green CW12 154 B4
Swettenham CW12 131 B1
Davenport Rd CH60 40 C4
Davenport Row WA7 49 B4
Davenport St
Congleton CW12 156 B1
Crewe CW1 190 B3
Macclesfield SK11 112 C4
Davenport Sta SK3 240 F1
Davey La SK9 60 A1
Daveylands SK9 60 B4
David Cl M34 241 A5
David Lewis Sch SK9 83 C3
David Rd WA13 18 B2
David St Denton M34 241 A6
Northwich CW8 103 C4
David's Ave WA5 15 A3
Davidson Ave CW12 157 A3
Davies Ave Gatley SK8 34 A3
Newton-le-W WA12 2 B2
Warrington WA4 16 C2
Davies Cl WA8 23 A2
Davies Way WA13 18 C2
Davis Cl ST7 193 C2
Davy Ave WA3 9 C3
Davy Rd WA7 23 C2
Daw Bank SK3 240 E5
Dawlish Ave SK8 34 C4
Dawlish Cl Bramhall SK7 35 C4
Hollinfare WA3 11 A2
Dawn Cl CH64 67 A3
Dawn Gdns CH65 70 A2
Dawpool Cl CH2 118 B3
Dawpool Dr CH62 43 B4
Dawson Dr CH2 237 A4
Dawson Rd
Altrincham WA14 238 D8
Bollington SK10 88 A4
Gatley SK8 34 B4
Macclesfield SK11 111 C4
Dawson St SK14 241 E5
Dawstone Rd CH60 41 A4
Dawstone Rise CH60 40 C4
Daylesford Cl SK8 239 D4
Daylesford Cres SK8 239 D4
Daylesford Rd SK8 239 D4
Day Lacy Row WA7 24 A1
De Trafford Mews 6 SK9 34 B1
Deacon Cl WA14 238 B1
Deacon Rd WA8 13 A1
Deacon Trad Est WA12 2 A1
Deacons Cl WA3 9 A4
Deadman's La CW5 205 A1
Deakin's Rd CW7 127 A2
Deal Sq SK14 241 E6
Deal St SK14 241 E6
Dean Bank CW6 168 B2
Dean Cl Bollington SK10 88 A4
Handforth SK9 34 B1
Partington M31 11 C2
Sandbach CW11 174 C4
7 Widnes WA8 23 A4
Dean Cres WA2 8 A1
Dean Ct Bollington SK10 88 A4
Golborne WA3 3 A4
Dean Dr Altrincham WA14 238 B1
Handforth SK9 34 B1
Dean Hollow ST7 209 B1
Dean La SK7 36 C4
Dean Meadow WA12 2 B2
Dean Pk SY14 214 A3
Dean Rd Golborne WA3 3 A4
Dean Rd continued
Handforth SK9 34 C2
Irlam M44 11 C3
Dean Row Ct 14 SK9 34 B1
Dean Row Jun Sch SK9 34 C1
Dean Row Rd SK9 61 A4
Dean St Middlewich CW10 128 B1
Northwich CW9 104 B4
Stalybridge SK15 242 D1
Widnes WA8 23 A4
Winsford CW7 126 B1
Dean Valley Com Sch SK10 87 C4
Dean's La ST5 210 B1
Deane Ave SK8 239 F5
Deane Ct CW5 205 A2
Deanery Cl CH2 118 B2
Deanery Way SK1 240 F6
Deans Cl Chester CH2 118 B3
Tarvin CH3 121 A1
Deans La
Barthomley CW2 208 B2
Sandbach CW11 174 C3
Warrington WA4 17 C2
Deans Rd CH65 70 C2
Deans Way
Higher Kinnerton CH4 161 A4
Tarvin CH3 121 A1
Deansgate CH65 70 A3
Deansgate La WA14, WA15 238 E7
Deansway WA8 22 B4
Deanwater Cl WA3 9 B2
Deanwater Ct SK8 34 B4
Deanway SK9 34 B1
Deanway Trad Est SK9 34 B2
Dearden St SK15 242 D2
Dearnford Ave CH62 43 B3
Dearnford Cl CH62 43 B3
Debra Cl CH66 69 B2
Debra Rd CH66 69 B2
Decade Cl ST5 210 C1
Dee Banks CH4 141 C4
Dee Banks Sch CH3 142 A4
Dee Cl Biddulph ST8 179 C1
Sandbach CW11 174 C4
Talke ST7 210 C4
Dee Cres CH3 180 C1
Dee Fords Ave CH3 119 A1
Dee Hills Pk CH2 237 C2
Dee La Chester CH2 237 C2
Holt LL13 196 B4
Dee Mdws LL13 196 B4
Dee Park Cl CH60 41 A3
Dee Park Rd CH60 41 A3
Dee Pk LL13 196 B4
Dee Point Prim Sch CH1 117 B2
Dee Side CH60 40 B4
Dee View CH3 180 C1
Dee View Rd
Connah's Quay CH5 91 B1
Heswall CH60 40 C4
Dee Way CW7 127 A1
Deep Dale WA5 14 C3
Deepdale WA8 12 B2
Deer Park Ct WA7 49 C3
Deerwood Cl
Ellesmere Port CH66 69 B4
Macclesfield SK10 86 C1
Deerwood Cres CH66 69 B4
Deeside
Ellesmere Port CH65 70 A2
Holt LL13 196 C4
Deeside Cl CH65 70 A1
Deeside Coll of F Ed (Coleg Glannau Dyfrdwy) CH5 91 B1
Deeside Cres CH1 116 C3
Deeside Ct CH64 41 A1
Deeside Ind Est (Parc Ddiwydiannol Glannau Dyfrdwy) CH5 93 A1
Deeside La CH1 116 B2
Deirdre Ave WA8 13 A1
Delafield Cl WA2 8 C2
Delamer Rd WA14 238 C3
Delamere Ave
Bebington CH62 43 C2
Ellesmere Port CH66 69 C3
Golborne WA3 3 C3
Sale M33 242 E5
Widnes WA8 12 B1
Delamere CE Prim Sch CW6 123 B3
Delamere Cl Barnton CW8 78 A2
Bebington CH62 43 C2
Sandbach CW11 174 C4
Delamere Ct Alsager ST7 192 C2
Bebington CH62 43 C2
Delamere Dr
Ellesmere Port CH66 69 C3
Macclesfield SK10 87 C1
Delamere Forest Sch WA6 100 B2
Delamere Forest Visitor Ctr* CW8 100 A1
Delamere Gn CH66 69 C3
Delamere La CH3 99 A1
Delamere Park Way E CW8 101 B3
Delamere Park Way W CW8 101 B3
Delamere Rd
Congleton CW12 155 C2
Gatley SK8 239 B5
Handforth SK9 34 C2
Nantwich CW5 204 C2
Norley WA6 100 A3
Delamere Rise CW7 126 A
Delamere St
Chester CH1 237 A
Crewe CW1 190 B2
Warrington WA5 15 C
Winsford CW7 126 A
Delamere Sta CW8 100 B
Delamore's Acre CH64 68 A4
Delavor Cl CH60 40 C4
Delavor Rd CH60 40 C4
Delenty Dr WA3 9 C2
Delery Dr WA1 16 C4
Delfur Rd SK7 35 C4
Delhi Rd M44 11 C4
Dell Cl CH63 43 A
Dell Dr WA2 9 A
Dell La CH60 41 A4
Dell The Cuddington CW8 101 B
Guilden Sutton CH3 119 C
Kelsall CW6 122 B2
Delmar Rd WA16 57 B
Delph La Daresbury WA4 25 A
Winwick WA2 8 C
Delphfield WA7 50 B4
Delphfields Rd WA4 26 B4
Delphside ST7 209 C
Delta Cres WA5 7 B
Delta Ct CH4 140 A
Delves Ave WA5 15 C4
Delves Broughton Ct CW1 191 B
Delves Cl CW2 206 A2
Delves Wlk CH3 142 A4
Delvine Dr CH2 118 B
Demage Dr CH66 69 B2
Demage La Backford CH1 94 C2
Chester CH2 118 B4
Demage La S CH2 118 B4
Demesne Cl SK15 242 F
Demesne Cres SK15 242 F
Demesne Dr SK15 242 F
Demmings Inf Sch SK8 239 F5
Demmings Rd SK8 239 F5
Den La CW3,CW5 221 B2
Denbigh Cl
Hazel Grove SK7 36 B4
Helsby WA6 73 A
Denbigh Cres CW10 151 B4
Denbigh Ct CH65 70 B2
Denbigh Dr CW7 149 A4
Denbigh Gdns CH65 70 B2
Denbigh St Chester CH1 118 A2
Stockport SK4 240 D7
Denbury Ave WA4 16 C
Denbury Dr WA14 238 B5
Denby La SK4 240 D8
Dene Ave WA12 1 C2
Dene Ct SK4 240 C6
Dene Dr CW7 149 B4
Denehurst Cl WA5 14 C2
Denehurst Park Way CW8 101 B
Denesgate 11 CW7 149 B4
Deneside Ave CW1 190 B
Deneway Bramhall SK7 35 B4
High Lane SK6 37 C4
Stockport SK4 240 C6
Deneway Cl SK4 240 C6
Deneway Mews SK4 240 C6
Denewood Ct 3 SK9 60 A
Denford Cl CH4 139 B2
Denford Pl ST7 193 B
Denhall Cl CH2 118 C
Denhall La CH64 67 A2
Denham Ave WA5 15 A
Denham Dr SK7 35 B4
Denholm Rd M20 239 C8
Denise Ave WA5 14 C
Denison Rd SK7 36 C4
Denmark Rd M33 242 B8
Denmark St WA14 238 D4
Dennett Cl WA1 17 C
Dennis Dr CH4 141 A
Dennis Rd WA8 23 B4
Dennison Rd SK8 35 A4
Densham Ave WA2 8 A1
Denston Cl CW2 190 A1
Denstone Dr CH4 141 A2
Dentdale Wlk M22 33 B4
Dentith Dr CH1 117 C3
Denton Cl CW7 126 B1
Denton Dr CW9 79 B1
Denton Drive Ind Est CW9 79 B1
Denton St WA8 13 B1
Denver Ave CW2 190 A2
Denver Rd WA4 17 A2
Denwall Ho 5 CH64 66 C4
Depenbech Cl SY14 213 A2
Depleach Rd SK8 239 D5
Depmore La WA6 75 A1
Deramore Cl OL6 242 B3
Derby Cl Irlam M44 11 B3
Newton-le-W WA12 2 A2
Derby Ct M33 242 C5
Derby Dr WA1 16 C4
Derby Knoll SK23 39 C1
Derby Pl CH2 118 C2
Derby Range SK4 240 B8
Derby Rd
Ashton-u-Lyne OL6 242 A3
Golborne WA3 3 B4
Hyde SK14 241 E8
Stockport SK4 240 C8
Talke ST7 210 B4
Warrington WA4 16 B1
Widnes, Barrow's Green WA8 13 B2

Derby Rd *continued*
Widnes, Lunts Heath WA8 13 A2
Derby Row WA12 7 B4
Derby St
Altrincham WA14 238 E5
Congleton CW12 156 B2
Crewe CW1 190 A3
Newton-le-W WA12 2 A2
Stockport SK3 240 D4
Derbyshire Hill Rd WA9 1 A1
Derbyshire Rd
High Lane SK12 37 B3
Partington M31 11 C1
Sale M33 242 C6
Dereham Way WA7 24 B2
Derek Ave WA2 8 C1
Derfel Terr 5 WA6 74 A4
Derrington Ave CW2 190 B2
Derwen Prim Sch CH4 161 A4
Derwen Rd SK3 240 E3
Derwent Ave CW7 127 A1
Derwent Cl Alsager ST7 193 A2
Culcheth WA3 5 A1
Holmes Chapel CW4 130 A2
Macclesfield SK11 112 A3
Partington M31 11 C2
Willaston (nr Nantwich) CW5 205 B3
Derwent Cres ST7 195 B1
Derwent Dr Biddulph ST8 179 C1
Bramhall SK7 35 B3
Congleton CW12 156 C1
Handforth SK9 34 B3
Hooton CH66 44 A1
Derwent Rd Chester CH2 118 C3
High Lane SK6 37 C4
Warrington WA4 16 A1
Widnes WA8 12 B1
Derwent Terr SK15 242 D4
Derwent Way
Neston CH64 66 C4
Alderley Edge SK9 83 C4
Desoto Rd WA8 22 C3
Desoto Rd E WA8 22 C3
Desoto Rd W WA8 22 C3
Deva Ave CH4 140 B3
Deva Bsns Pk CH5 116 A4
Deva Cl SK12 36 A2
Deva Ct CH2 118 C1
Deva La CH2 118 B3
Deva Link CH1 118 A2
Deva Rd CW2 189 B2
Deva Stad (Chester City FC) CH1 117 C1
Deva Terr CH2 237 C2
Devisdale Grange WA14 238 B3
Devisdale Rd WA14 238 B4
Devon Cl
Macclesfield SK10 86 C1
Middlewich CW10 128 B1
Devon Gr ST8 179 B1
Devon Pl
Congleton CW12 156 C2
Widnes WA8 13 A2
Devon Rd Chester CH2 118 C3
Irlam M44 11 B3
Partington M31 11 C1
Devonshire Dr SK9 60 A1
Devonshire Gdns WA12 2 B1
Devonshire Pl
Chester CH4 141 C4
Runcorn WA7 23 A1
Devonshire Rd
Altrincham WA14 238 D6
Broughton CH4 139 B2
Hazel Grove SK7 36 C4
Stockport SK4 240 B7
Warrington WA1 16 C4
Dewar Ct WA7 23 C2
Dewar St WA3 9 C3
Dewes St CW1 190 A3
Dewhurst Rd WA3 9 B1
Dexter Way CW10 128 B1
Dial Cotts CH64 67 A3
Dial La CW12 158 A1
Dial Rd WA15 32 B4
Dial St WA1 16 B3
Diamond Ave 12 ST7 195 A1
Diamond Cl OL6 242 A4
Diamond St OL6 242 A4
Dibbins Gn CH63 43 A4
Dibbinsdale Rd CH63 43 A4
Dickens Cl Cheadle SK8 35 A4
Sandbach CW11 174 B3
Dickens La SK12 36 C1
Dickenson St WA2 16 B4
Dickinson Cl WA11 1 A3
Dickinson Way ST7 193 A2
Dickson Cl WA8 23 A4
Dickson St 2 WA8 23 A4
Dicksons Dr CH2 118 B2
Didsbury Rd SK4 240 B6
Dierden St CW7 127 A1
Dierdens Terr CW10 128 B1
Dig La Acton CW5 203 C2
Frodsham WA6 74 A4
Shavington CW2 206 A2
Diglake Cl ST7 210 B3
Diglake St ST7 209 C2
Diglee Rd SK23 39 B2
Dillors Croft CW1 173 A1
Dinas Cl CH1 117 B2
Dingle Ave
Alderley Edge SK9 59 B2
Denton M34 241 B6
Newton-le-W WA12 1 C1
Dingle Bank CH4 141 B4
Dingle Bank Cl WA13 18 C2
Dingle Cl
Macclesfield SK10 87 A2
Romiley SK6 241 D2
Dingle La
Bridgemere CW5 231 C3
Kelsall CW6 122 C3
Sandbach CW11 175 B3
Warrington WA4 26 C3
Winsford CW7 126 B1
Dingle Prim Sch The CW1 191 B3
Dingle The Barnton CW8 78 A2
Haslington CW1 191 B3
Lymm WA13 18 C2
Dingle Way CW8 101 C3
Dingle Wlk CW7 126 B1
Dinglebrook Gr 22 SK9 34 B1
Dingleway WA4 26 B4
Dinnington Ct WA8 12 C2
Diploma Dr CW10 128 B1
Dipping Brook Ave WA4 26 C2
Dirty La WA14 31 A3
Disley Prim Sch SK12 38 B3
Disley Sta SK12 38 B3
Disley Wlk M34 241 A5
Distaff Rd SK12 36 A2
District CE Prim Sch The WA12 2 A2
Ditchfield La WA16 29 B2
Ditchfield Pl WA8 22 A4
Ditchfield Rd
Warrington WA5 14 C2
Widnes WA8 22 A4
Ditton CE Prim Sch WA8 12 A1
Ditton Prim Sch WA8 12 C1
Ditton Rd WA8 22 B3
Dixon Ave WA12 2 B3
Dixon Cl WA11 2 A4
Dixon Ct SK8 239 D5
Dixon Dr SK11 84 A2
Dixon Rd
Congleton CW12 157 A3
Hyde M34 241 B5
Dixon St
Ashton-u-Lyne OL6 242 A4
Irlam M44 11 C4
Warrington WA1 16 A3
Dixon's Ho CH3 142 C4
Dobb Hedge Cl WA15 32 B3
Dobell's Rd CW9 103 C3
Dobers La WA6 74 B2
Dobson Sq SY14 213 A2
Dock Rd Northwich CW9 103 C4
Widnes WA8 22 C3
Dock Road Edwardian Pumping Station The* CW9 103 C4
Dock St
Ellesmere Port CH65 70 B4
Widnes WA8 23 A3
Dock Yard Rd CH65 70 C3
Dodd's Green La SY13 228 B2
Dodd's La
Appleton Thorn WA4 27 A3
Bell o 'th' Hill SY13,SY14 224 C4
Warrington WA4 17 A2
Doddington Cl CW11 175 B4
Doddington Rd CW2 190 A2
Doddlespool Barns CW3 221 C4
Dodds La CW12 178 B3
Doddswood Dr CW12 156 C2
Dodge Hill SK4 240 E6
Dodgsley Dr WA6 75 B1
Dodleston CE Prim Sch CH4 162 A4
Dodleston La CH4 162 B2
Doe's Meadow Rd CH63 43 A4
Doeford Cl WA3 4 C3
Dog La
Brereton Green CW4, CW11 153 C4
Nantwich CW5 204 C3
Tattenhall CH3 182 B2
Threapwood SY14 223 B4
Dogmore La CW6 147 B2
Dolly La SK23 39 C2
Dolmas La 11 WA1 16 A3
Dolphin Cres CH66 69 C1
Dolphin Ct CH4 141 A4
Dombey Rd SK12 36 B1
Domestic App M90 33 B3
Domville Cl WA13 18 C2
Don Wlk CH65 70 A4
Donagh Cl SK10 86 C1
Donald Ave SK14 241 F5
Donkey La SK9 60 A3
Donne Pl CH1 117 C3
Donnington Ave SK8 239 F6
Donnington Way CH4 140 C4
Dooley's Grig SK11 108 C1
Dooley's La SK9 33 B1
Dorac Ave SK8 34 B4
Dorchester Cl
Kidsgrove ST7 195 A2
Wilmslow SK9 60 B4
Dorchester Pk WA7 24 C2
Dorchester Rd
Chester CH4 140 C3
Warrington WA5 15 B3
Dorchester Way
Burtonwood WA5 6 C3
Macclesfield SK10 87 B2
Doreen Ave CW12 179 A4
Doreold Dr CW5 204 B3
Dorfold Cl CW11 175 B4
Dorfold Hall* CW5 204 A3
Dorfold St CW1 190 B2
Dorfold Way CH2 118 C3
Doric Ave WA6 74 B4
Dorin Park Sch CH2 118 B3
Doris Rd SK3 240 C4
Dormer Cl CH3 143 A3
Dorney Cl WA4 26 C3
Dornoch Ct CW4 130 A1
Dorothea St WA2 16 B4
Dorric Way CW1 190 B4
Dorrington Cl WA7 50 B4
Dorrington Rd SK3 240 A3
Dorrit Cl SK12 36 C1
Dorset Ave SK8 240 C1
Dorset Cl CW12 156 C2
Dorset Ct WA7 50 A3
Dorset Dr ST8 179 B1
Dorset Pl Chester CH2 119 A3
Kidsgrove ST7 195 A1
Dorset Rd
Altrincham WA14 238 B5
Chester CH2 118 C4
Irlam M44 11 B3
Dorset St OL6 242 A2
Dorset Way WA1 17 A4
Dorset Wlk SK10 86 C1
Douglas Ave WA9 6 A3
Douglas Cl Hartford CW8 103 B3
Widnes WA8 13 C2
Douglas La CW7 171 A3
Douglas Pl CH4 140 C3
Douglas St
Ashton-u-Lyne OL6 242 A3
Hyde SK14 241 E6
Doulton Cl CW7 126 C2
Doune Ct CH65 70 B2
Dounrey Cl WA2 9 A1
Douthwaite Dr SK6 241 E1
Dove Bank Prim Sch ST7 195 A1
Dove Cl
Ellesmere Port CH66 70 A4
Elton CH2 72 B2
Helsby WA6 73 B3
Sandbach CW11 175 A4
Warrington WA3 9 C2
Dove Gr ST8 179 B1
Dove Pl CW7 127 A1
Dovecot Dr WA11 1 B4
Dovecote Bsns & Tech Pk M33 242 F6
Dovecote Cl CW2 206 A4
Dovecote Gn WA5 7 A1
Dovedale Ave CH62 43 C3
Dovedale Cl
Congleton CW12 157 A2
High Lane SK6 37 C4
Warrington WA2 8 C2
Dovedale Ct WA8 12 A2
Dover Cl WA7 50 C3
Dover Ct CH65 70 B1
Dover Dr
Ellesmere Port CH65 70 B1
Winsford CW7 149 A4
Dover Rd Chester CH4 141 A3
Macclesfield SK10 87 C1
Warrington WA4 17 A2
Dover St WA7 23 A2
Dovesmead Rd CH60 41 B4
Doveston Gr M33 242 B8
Doveston Rd M33 242 B8
Doward St WA8 13 B1
Downes Cl SK10 87 A1
Downesway SK9 59 C1
Downham Ave WA3 4 C1
Downham Ct CH60 41 A4
Downham Dr CH60 41 A4
Downham Pl CH1 117 C2
Downham Rd S CH60 41 A4
Downing Cl SK11 112 C2
Downs Dr WA14 238 E8
Downs End WA16 57 B1
Downs Rd WA7 23 A1
Downs The
Altrincham WA14 238 D3
Cheadle SK8 239 D3
Cuddington CW8 101 B3
Downsfield Rd CH4 141 A3
Downside WA8 12 A2
Downswood Ct CH2 118 B2
Downswood Dr CH2 118 B2
Downway La WA9 1 A1
Dragon Yd WA8 13 A2
Dragon's La CW11 152 A1
Dragons Wharf CW11 152 B1
Drake Ave M44 11 C3
Drake Cl WA5 7 B1
Drake Ct SK5 240 E8
Drake La CW5 203 C2
Drake Rd
Altrincham WA14 238 B8
Neston CH64 41 C1
Drakelow La CW10 128 C4
Drakes Way SY14 213 A3
Draycott Dr ST5 210 B1
Drayton Ave SK8 34 A4
Drayton Cl Runcorn WA7 22 C1
16 Handforth SK9 34 B1
Drayton Cres CW1 190 C3
Drayton Manor M20 239 B8
Drenfell Rd ST7 194 C4
Drift Cotts LL12 162 B1
Drill Field Rd CW9 103 C4
Drive A CH5 93 A1
Drive B CH5 93 A1
Drive C CH5 93 A1
Drive The
Altrincham WA15 32 B4
Broomedge WA13 19 B1
Holmes Chapel CW4 130 B1
Drome Rd CH5 93 A1
Drovers Way CW11 175 A3
Droxford Ct SK9 60 A3
Drs Green & Slater Rest Hos 4 SK4 240 A7
Drumber La ST7 195 A4
Drumber The CW7 126 B1
Drumble Field SK11 84 A2
Drummond Ave CH66 69 B2
Drummond Ct WA8 13 B1
Drummond Way SK10 86 C1
Druridge Dr WA5 14 C2
Drury Cl CW1 190 C3
Drury La Knutsford WA16 57 A1
Warmingham CW1 173 B2
Dryden Ave SK8 239 F6
Dryden Cl CW2 190 A1
Dryden Pl WA2 8 B1
Dryhurst Dr SK12 38 B3
Dryhurst La SK12 38 B3
Dublin Croft CH66 69 C1
Duchess Pl CH2 237 A4
Duchy Rd CW1 207 A4
Duchy St SK3 240 D3
Duck La CH3 121 C4
Duckworth Gr WA2 9 A1
Duddon Cl
8 Davenham CW9 103 C2
Duddon CW6 145 A3
Duddon Hook La CW6 144 C3
Duddon Rd CW6 145 A3
Dudleston Rd CH66 69 A3
Dudley Ave WA7 23 B1
Dudley Cres CH65 44 A2
Dudley Rd
Ellesmere Port CH65 70 A3
Irlam M44 11 B2
Sale M33 242 C8
Dudley St WA2 16 A4
Dudley Wlk SK11 111 C4
Dudlow Green Rd WA4 26 C3
Dufton Wlk M22 33 C4
Duke Ave Cheadle SK8 34 C3
Glazebury WA3 5 B4
Duke Cl WA7 22 C1
Duke St Alderley Edge SK9 60 A1
Chester CH4 237 B1
Congleton CW12 156 B1
Crewe CW2 190 B2
Macclesfield SK11 112 B4
Newton-le-W WA12 2 A2
Stalybridge SK15 242 C1
9 Stockport SK1 240 F5
Duke's Cres CW11 175 A4
Duke's Ct CH4 237 B1
Dukes Way CW9 103 C3
Dukes Wharf WA7 50 C4
Dukesway CH2 118 C4
Dukinfield Rd SK14 241 C8
Dulas Ct CH2 118 C4
Dulverton Ave CH3 119 B1
Dumbah La SK10 87 B3
Dumbers SK11 136 A1
Dumbill Ho ST7 210 B4
Dunbar Cl
Connah's Quay CH5 91 B1
Ellesmere Port CH66 69 B3
Holmes Chapel CW4 130 B1
Dunbar Ct CH66 69 B3
Dunblane Ave SK4 240 D6
Duncan Ave
Newton-le-W WA12 2 B3
Runcorn WA7 23 B1
Duncan St WA2 16 B4
Duncansby Cres WA5 14 C3
Duncansby Dr CH63 43 B2
Dundalk La WA8 22 B4
Dundalk Rd WA8 22 C4
Dundee Cl WA2 8 C2
Dundee Ct CH65 70 C2
Dundonald Ave WA4 16 B1
Dundonald Rd SK8 35 A4
Dundonald St SK2 240 F2
Dundrennan Cl SK12 36 B3
Dunecroft M34 241 A8
Dunge Valley Gdns* SK23 89 C4
Dunham Cl
Bebington CH62 43 C2
Sandbach CW11 175 B3
Dunham Cres CW2 206 A4
Dunham Ct WA6 97 C3
Dunham Hill Prim Sch WA6 97 C3
Dunham Lawn WA14 238 B4
Dunham Massey Hall* WA14 20 B2
Dunham Pk* WA14 20 B2
Dunham Rd
Altrincham WA14 238 B4
Northwich CW9 104 A2
Partington WA13 19 C4
Dunham Rise WA14 238 C4
Dunham Way CH2 118 C3
Dunkirk Ave CW7 149 B4
Dunkirk Dr CH65 70 A1
Dunkirk La
Capenhurst CH1 94 B4
Ellesmere Port CH65 70 A1
Hyde SK14 241 B8
Dunley Cl WA3 10 A3
Dunlin Ave WA12 2 B2
Dunlin Cl Poynton SK12 36 A2
Runcorn WA7 49 C3
Warrington WA2 8 C2
Dunlin Wlk WA14 238 B8
Dunlop St WA4 16 A2
Dunmore Cl CW10 151 B4
Dunmore Cres CH66 69 A3
Dunmore Rd
Ellesmere Port CH66 69 A3
Gatley SK8 239 B6
Dunmow Rd WA4 17 B2
Dunn's La CH3 121 C4
Dunnillow Field CW5 205 A2
Dunnock Cl WA2 8 C2
Dunnock Gr WA3 9 C2
Dunnocksfold Rd ST7 193 A2
Dunnockswood ST7 193 A2
Dunollie Rd M33 242 E5
Dunoon Cl CW4 130 A1
Dunraven Rd CH64 67 A4
Dunscar Cl WA3 9 B3
Dunsford WA8 12 A2
Dunsmore Cl WA11 1 B4
Dunstan La CH64 67 C2
Dunster Cl CW9 104 A2
Dunster Gr CH60 41 A4
Dunster Rd SK10 87 C1
Dunstone Cl CW2 190 A1
Dunwood Dr ST7 193 B3
Dunwoody Way CW1, CW2 190 A2
Durban Ave CH3 142 B4
Durber Cl ST7 209 B1
Durham Cl
Macclesfield SK10 86 C1
Romiley SK6 241 A1
Warrington WA1 17 C4
Durham Ct CH65 70 C2
Durham Dr CW7 149 B3
Durham Gr M44 11 B3
Durham Rd Blacon CH1 117 C3
Handforth SK9 34 B3
Widnes WA8 13 A2
Durlston Cl WA8 12 B1
Durrell Way WA3 3 C4
Dutton Gn CH2 70 C2
Dutton La CW8,WA6 101 B3
Dutton Way CW5 204 C2
Dutton's La CW6 122 B3
Duttons Bsns Ctr CW9 103 C4
Duxford Ct WA2 8 C1
Dyar Terr CW8 78 B1
Dye House La SK22 39 B4
Dye La SK6 241 B2
Dyers Cl WA13 19 A2
Dyers La WA13 19 A2
Dykin Cl WA8 13 C2
Dykin Rd WA8 13 C2
Dysart St OL6 242 A2
Dyserth Gr 2 SK5 240 F8
Dyserth Rd CH1 117 B2
Dystelegh Rd SK12 38 B3

E

Eadie Gr CW1 190 A4
Eaglais Way SK10 86 C1
Eagland Pl CW12 156 C2
Eagle Brow WA13 18 B2
Eagle La CH66 69 B4
Eagle Lodge WA15 238 F2
Eagle Mount WA4 16 B1
Eagle Park Dr WA2 8 A1
Eagles Way WA7 49 C3
Eaglesfield CW8 103 B2
Ealing Cl WA7 24 B1
Ealing Rd WA5 15 A3
Eanlewood La WA7 50 B4
Eardley Cres CW12 156 C2
Eardley Pl CW1 190 A3
Eardleyend Rd ST7 209 C4
Eardswick Cl CH2 237 B4
Eardswick La CW1 172 B3
Eardswick Rd CW10 151 B3
Earl Rd Handforth SK8,SK9 34 C3
Stockport SK4 240 C8
Earl St Sale M33 242 C7
Stockport SK3 240 D4
Warrington WA2 16 A4
Earl's Port CH1 118 A1
Earle Cl WA12 1 C2
Earle Cres CH64 41 B1
Earle Dr CH64 41 B1
Earle Rd WA8 23 B4
Earle St Crewe CW1 190 B2
Newton-le-W WA12 2 A2
Earle's La CW6 122 B3
Earles La CW9 79 C3
Earlestown Sta WA12 2 A2
Earls Gdns CH65 70 A3
Earls Oak CH2 118 B4
Earls Rd CW2 206 A2
Earls Way
Davenham CW9 103 C2
Runcorn WA7 49 C3
Earlscliffe Ct WA14 238 B4
Earlston Ct CH2 237 C2
Earlsway Chester CH4 141 A4
Macclesfield SK11 111 C4
Earlswood Mews CW9 103 C2
Easby Cl Bramhall SK8 35 A3
Poynton SK12 36 B2
Runcorn WA7 23 B1
Easenhall Cl WA8 13 B3
Easingwold 2 WA14 238 C4
East Ave Bollington SK10 87 C4
Gatley SK8 34 B4
Northwich CW9 104 B3
Stalybridge SK15 242 D3
Warrington WA2 16 B4

East Ave *continued*
Warrington, Great Sankey WA5 ... 15 A2
Warrington, Stockton Heath WA4 ... 16 B1
Weston CW2 ... 207 B3
East Ct ST7 ... 193 C2
East Dam Wood Rd L24 ... 21 A1
East Downs Rd
Altrincham WA14 ... 238 C2
Cheadle SK8 ... 239 F2
East Dudley St CW7 ... 126 C1
East Gn CH5 ... 116 A3
East La Cuddington CW8 ... 102 A2
Runcorn WA7 ... 49 C4
East Lancashire Rd
Ashton-u-Lyne WA11,WA12, WA3 ... 2 B4
Haydock WA11 ... 1 B4
East Lea M34 ... 241 A6
East Mains L24 ... 21 A2
East Millwood Rd L24 ... 21 A2
East Park Rd SK11 ... 112 A3
East Rd Halewood L24,L26 ... 21 A3
Middlewich CW10 ... 128 A1
Wythenshawe M90 ... 33 B4
East St Ashton-u-Lyne OL6 ... 242 A4
Widnes WA8 ... 13 B1
East View WA4 ... 17 A1
Eastbury Cl WA8 ... 13 B3
Eastcott Cl CW12 ... 155 C2
Eastdale Pl WA14 ... 238 D7
Eastdale Rd WA1 ... 17 A4
Easter Ct WA5 ... 7 A1
Eastern Pathway CH4 ... 237 C1
Eastern Rd
Shavington CW5 ... 205 C3
Willaston (nr Nantwich) CW5 ... 205 C3
Eastfields Gr CH1 ... 117 A4
Eastford Rd WA4 ... 16 A1
Eastgate Rd
Holmes Chapel CW4 ... 130 B2
Runcorn WA7 ... 24 C3
Eastgate Row N CH1 ... 237 B2
Eastgate Row S CH1 ... 237 B2
Eastgate St CH1 ... 237 B2
Eastham Ctry Pk* CH62 ... 44 A4
Eastham Mews CH62 ... 44 A2
Eastham Rake CH62,CH64 ... 43 B2
Eastham Rake Sta CH63 ... 43 B2
Eastham Village Rd CH62 ... 44 A3
Eastham Way 11 SK9 ... 34 B3
Eastleigh Rd SK8 ... 239 B1
Easton Dr SK8 ... 240 A1
Eastview M33 ... 242 B5
Eastward Ave SK9 ... 59 C3
Eastway
Ellesmere Port CH66 ... 69 B4
Widnes WA8 ... 12 B1
Eastwood WA7 ... 24 B1
Eastwood Ave WA12 ... 2 C2
Eastwood Ct CH4 ... 139 A3
Eastwood Rd WA5 ... 6 A4
Eaton Ave CH4 ... 141 B4
Eaton Bank CW12 ... 156 C2
Eaton Bank Ind Est CW12 ... 156 C2
Eaton Bank Sch CW12 ... 156 C3
Eaton Cl Broughton CH4 ... 139 B2
Cheadle SK8 ... 239 F3
Poynton SK12 ... 37 A2
Sandbach CW11 ... 175 B4
Eaton Cres CW9 ... 103 C1
Eaton Ct
Altrincham WA14 ... 238 C1
Wilmslow SK9 ... 60 A3
Eaton Dr
Alderley Edge SK9 ... 59 C1
Middlewich CW10 ... 151 A4
Eaton Gr CH4 ... 140 C3
Eaton La Davenham CW9 ... 103 C1
Eaton CW6 ... 147 A3
Goostrey CW4 ... 107 B1
Macclesfield SK11 ... 112 B3
Tarporley CW6 ... 168 C4
Eaton Mews CH4 ... 141 B4
Eaton Pl CW8 ... 102 C2
Eaton Prim Sch CW6 ... 147 A2
Eaton Rd Alsager ST7 ... 193 B2
Altrincham WA14 ... 238 C1
Chester CH4 ... 141 C2
Sale M33 ... 242 A6
Tarporley CW6 ... 146 B1
Wettenhall CW7 ... 170 B4
Eaton St Crewe CW2 ... 190 B2
Runcorn WA7 ... 23 A1
Eaton View CW9 ... 126 C4
Eaton Way CW3 ... 230 A2
Eaves Brow Rd WA3 ... 9 A4
Eaves Knoll Rd SK22 ... 39 A4
Ebnal La SY14 ... 213 C2
Ebury Pl CH4 ... 141 B4
Eccles Cl SK23 ... 65 B4
Eccles Rd SK23 ... 65 C3
Eccleston Ave
Bebington CH62 ... 43 B4
Chester CH4 ... 141 B3
Ellesmere Port CH66 ... 69 C3
Eccleston CE Prim Sch CH4 ... 141 C1
Eccleston Cl WA3 ... 9 B3
Eccleston Dr WA7 ... 23 B1
Eccleston Rd CH4 ... 161 A4
Eccleston Way 3 SK9 ... 34 B2
Eccups La SK9 ... 59 B4
Echo Cl CH4 ... 140 C3
Ecton Ave SK10 ... 113 A4
Ecton Cl CW7 ... 127 A2
Edale Cl
Altrincham WA14 ... 238 C1
Bebington CH62 ... 43 C3
Gatley SK8 ... 34 B4
Edale Dr CW6 ... 122 B3
Edburton Ct WA3 ... 3 A4
Eddisbury Cl SK11 ... 112 C4
Eddisbury Dr ST5 ... 210 B1
Eddisbury Hill CW6,CW8 ... 123 B4
Eddisbury Rd CH66 ... 69 C1
Eddisbury Sq WA6 ... 74 A4
Eddisbury Terr SK11 ... 112 C4
Eddisbury Way CW9 ... 103 C2
Eddisford Dr WA3 ... 4 B3
Edelsten St WA5 ... 15 C3
Edelston Hall La CW5 ... 203 C1
Eden Ave
Fowley Common WA3 ... 5 B2
High Lane SK6 ... 37 C4
Winsford CW7 ... 126 C1
Eden Cl Biddulph ST8 ... 179 C1
10 Ellesmere Port CH66 ... 69 B3
Kidsgrove ST7 ... 195 A1
Wilmslow SK9 ... 59 C3
Eden Dr SK10 ... 87 C1
Eden Pl SK8 ... 239 D6
Edenbridge Gdns WA4 ... 26 C2
Edendale WA8 ... 12 A1
Edenfield Cl WA16 ... 58 A2
Edenfield Rd WA16 ... 58 A2
Edenhall Cl CW4 ... 130 A2
Edgar Ct CH4 ... 237 B1
Edgar Pl CH4 ... 237 B1
Edgars Dr WA2 ... 9 A1
Edge Gr CH2 ... 118 C1
Edge La SY14 ... 199 B1
Edge View La SK9 ... 59 A1
Edgecroft CH3 ... 166 A1
Edgehill Chase SK9 ... 60 C4
Edgeley Fold SK3 ... 240 C3
Edgeley Rd SK3 ... 240 B3
Edgemoor WA14 ... 238 A2
Edgerley La CH3 ... 181 A3
Edgerton Rd WA3 ... 3 C4
Edgeview Rd CW12 ... 179 A4
Edgeway Henbury SK11 ... 111 B4
Wilmslow SK9 ... 60 A3
Edgewell La CW6 ... 147 A2
Edgewood CH3 ... 142 A4
Edgewood Dr
Bebington CH62 ... 43 B3
Wistaston CW2 ... 206 A4
Edgworth St WA2 ... 16 A3
Edinbridge Cl CW2 ... 207 A1
Edinburgh Cl SK8 ... 239 F6
Edinburgh Ct CH65 ... 70 B2
Edinburgh Dr
Macclesfield SK10 ... 87 A1
Romiley SK6 ... 241 C4
Edinburgh Pl CW12 ... 156 C1
Edinburgh Rd
Congleton CW12 ... 156 C1
Widnes WA8 ... 22 A4
Wistaston CW2 ... 205 C4
Edinburgh Way CH4 ... 237 C1
Edison Rd WA7 ... 23 B2
Edith St WA7 ... 22 C2
Edleston Prim Sch CW2 ... 190 B2
Edleston Rd CW2 ... 190 B2
Edlestone Gr 2 SK9 ... 34 C1
Edmund Cl SK4 ... 240 E8
Edna St Chester CH2 ... 118 C2
Hyde SK14 ... 241 D6
Edward Bright Way CW5 ... 204 B3
Edward Ct WA14 ... 238 B7
Edward Gdns WA1 ... 17 C3
Edward Rd WA5 ... 14 B3
Edward St
Ashton-u-Lyne OL6 ... 242 B2
Audley ST7 ... 209 C2
Crewe CW2 ... 190 B1
Dukinfield SK14 ... 241 C7
Ellesmere Port CH65 ... 70 B4
Haydock WA11 ... 1 A3
Macclesfield SK11 ... 112 A4
Northwich CW9 ... 104 B4
Sale M33 ... 242 E6
Stockport SK1 ... 240 F4
Widnes WA8 ... 13 B1
Edwards Ave CW2 ... 206 B3
Edwards Cl CW2 ... 206 B3
Edwards Rd CH4 ... 141 A3
Edwards Way
Alsager ST7 ... 193 C2
Widnes WA8 ... 22 B4
Edwin St WA8 ... 13 B1
Egdon Cl WA8 ... 13 C1
Egerton WA16 ... 29 B3
Egerton Ave
Hartford CW8 ... 103 A2
Partington WA13 ... 19 B4
Warrington WA1 ... 16 C4
Egerton Ct
Dukinfield M34 ... 241 A8
Kelsall CW6 ... 122 A3
Egerton Dr Chester CH2 ... 118 B3
Sale M33 ... 242 B7
Egerton Lodge M34 ... 241 A8
Egerton Moss WA15 ... 31 C3
Egerton Prim Sch WA16 ... 56 C1
Egerton Rd Blacon CH1 ... 117 B3
Handforth SK9 ... 34 A1
Egerton Rd *continued*
Lymm WA13 ... 18 B1
Egerton Rd S SK4 ... 240 C8
Egerton Sq 6 WA16 ... 57 A1
Egerton St Chester CH2 ... 237 C3
Congleton CW12 ... 156 B1
Ellesmere Port CH65 ... 70 B3
Runcorn WA7 ... 22 C2
Warrington, Howley WA1 ... 16 B3
Warrington, Stockton Heath WA4 ... 16 B1
Egerton Street Sch CH2 ... 237 C3
Egerton Wlk CH4 ... 162 A4
Eggbridge La CH3 ... 143 A3
Egremont Gr 2 SK3 ... 240 B4
Egypt St
5 Warrington WA1 ... 16 A3
Widnes WA8 ... 22 C4
Eilison Ct CH2 ... 237 B3
Eisenhower Cl WA5 ... 15 A3
Elaine Cl
Ellesmere Port CH66 ... 69 B2
Widnes WA8 ... 13 B1
Elaine St WA1 ... 16 B4
Elanor Rd CW11 ... 174 B4
Elcho Rd WA14 ... 238 B3
Elcombe Ave WA3 ... 3 C4
Elder Dr CH4 ... 140 C3
Elderberry Way SK9 ... 60 C4
Elderberry Wlk M31 ... 11 C2
Eldon Rd
Macclesfield SK11 ... 111 C4
Stockport SK3 ... 240 C3
Eldon St WA1 ... 16 B3
Eldon Terr CH64 ... 66 C4
Eleanor Cl CW1 ... 189 C3
Eleanor St
Ellesmere Port CH65 ... 70 B3
13 Widnes WA8 ... 23 A4
Electra Way CW1 ... 191 A1
Electricity St CW2 ... 190 B2
Elf Mill Cl SK3 ... 240 E2
Elgar Ave CH62 ... 43 C3
Elgar Cl CH65 ... 69 C2
Elgin Ave
Holmes Chapel CW4 ... 130 A1
Macclesfield SK10 ... 87 A1
Warrington WA4 ... 16 A1
Elgin Cl CH3 ... 119 A2
Elgin Dr M33 ... 242 E5
Elgin St SK15 ... 242 E1
Elgol Cl SK3 ... 240 F1
Eliot Cl CW1 ... 191 A2
Elizabeth Ave Disley SK12 ... 38 B3
Stalybridge SK15 ... 242 D2
Stockport SK1 ... 240 F4
Elizabeth Cl Kelsall CW6 ... 122 B3
Sandbach CW11 ... 174 B4
Elizabeth Cres CH4 ... 237 C1
Elizabeth Ct
Stockport SK4 ... 240 C6
Talke ST7 ... 210 B3
Widnes WA8 ... 23 A4
Elizabeth Dr WA1 ... 17 A4
Elizabeth Gaskell Ct WA16 ... 56 C1
Elizabeth Rd Haydock WA11 ... 1 C4
Partington M31 ... 11 C2
Elizabeth St
Congleton CW12 ... 156 B1
Crewe CW1 ... 190 A3
Hyde SK14 ... 241 D7
Macclesfield SK11 ... 112 B4
Elizabeth Terr WA8 ... 12 B1
Elizabethan Way CW9 ... 104 C3
Elk View SY14 ... 222 C3
Elkan Cl WA8 ... 13 C1
Elkan Rd WA8 ... 13 C1
Ella Gr WA16 ... 57 A1
Elland Dr CH66 ... 69 B3
Ellen Brook Rd M22 ... 33 B4
Ellen St Stockport SK4 ... 240 D7
Warrington WA5 ... 15 C4
Ellerby Cl WA7 ... 50 C4
Ellerton Ave CH66 ... 69 B3
Ellerton Cl WA8 ... 12 B2
Ellesmere Ave
Broughton CH4 ... 139 B2
Chester CH2 ... 118 B3
Ellesmere Cl CW11 ... 174 C4
Ellesmere Dr SK8 ... 240 A1
Ellesmere Pl CW1 ... 190 A3
Ellesmere Port Hospl CH65 ... 70 A1
Ellesmere Port RC High Sch CH65 ... 70 A2
Ellesmere Port Sta CH65 ... 70 B3
Ellesmere Port Stadium The CH65 ... 70 C2
Ellesmere Rd
Altrincham WA14 ... 238 E6
Culcheth WA3 ... 4 C2
Northwich CW9 ... 104 A2
Stockport SK3 ... 240 A3
Warrington WA4 ... 16 A1
Ellesmere St
Runcorn WA7 ... 23 A1
Warrington WA1 ... 16 B3
Ellesworth Cl WA5 ... 15 B4
Ellingham Way CW9 ... 103 C2
Elliot Ave WA1 ... 16 C4
Elliot Ho CH1 ... 118 A3
Elliot St 9 WA8 ... 23 A4
Ellis La WA6 ... 49 B1
Ellis St Crewe CW1 ... 190 A3
Hyde SK14 ... 241 F6
Widnes WA8 ... 22 C4
Ellison St
Warrington, Howley WA1 ... 16 B3
Warrington, Stockton Heath WA4 ... 16 B1
Elloway Rd L24 ... 21 A2
Ellwood Cl L24 ... 21 C1
Ellwood Gn CW2 ... 206 C2
Elm Ave Newton-le-W WA12 ... 2 B1
Widnes WA8 ... 13 A1
Elm Beds Rd SK12 ... 37 B1
Elm Cl 9 Partington M31 ... 11 C2
Poynton SK12 ... 36 C2
Tarporley CW6 ... 146 B1
Wistaston CW2 ... 189 C1
Elm Cres SK9 ... 60 A2
Elm Ct CW1 ... 190 B3
Elm Dr Crewe CW1 ... 190 C3
Holmes Chapel CW4 ... 130 B2
Macclesfield SK10 ... 87 C1
Elm Gn CH64 ... 67 C4
Elm Gr Alderley Edge SK9 ... 60 A1
Alsager ST7 ... 193 C2
Broughton CH4 ... 140 C3
Ellesmere Port CH66 ... 70 A1
Handforth SK9 ... 34 B2
Hyde SK14 ... 241 F6
Sale M33 ... 242 B8
Warrington WA1 ... 16 C4
Widnes WA8 ... 13 A1
Winsford CW7 ... 127 A1
Elm Ho 9 CW11 ... 175 A3
Elm Rd Altrincham WA15 ... 238 E3
Congleton CW12 ... 156 A2
Gatley SK8 ... 239 A5
Haydock WA11 ... 1 C4
High Lane SK6 ... 37 C4
Hollinfare WA3 ... 11 A1
Middlewich CW10 ... 151 B4
Runcorn WA7 ... 49 B4
Warrington, Cinnamon Brow WA5 ... 14 C2
Warrington, Winwick Quay WA2 ... 8 A2
Weaverham CW8 ... 102 B4
Willaston CH64 ... 67 C4
Elm Rd S SK3 ... 240 A3
Elm Rise Frodsham WA6 ... 74 B4
Prestbury SK10 ... 86 C3
Elm Sq CH4 ... 140 C3
Elm St Ellesmere Port CH65 ... 70 B4
Northwich CW9 ... 79 A1
Elm Terr CW1 ... 190 C3
Elm Tree Ave Lymm WA13 ... 18 B1
Warrington WA1 ... 16 C4
Elm Tree Cotts CH3 ... 167 A4
Elm Tree Ct CW6 ... 147 A2
Elm Tree Dr ST7 ... 209 C1
Elm Tree La CW11 ... 174 B4
Elm Tree Rd Golborne WA3 ... 3 C4
Lymm WA13 ... 18 B1
Elmdale Ave SK8 ... 239 B2
Elmfield Cl SK9 ... 60 A1
Elmfield Rd
Alderley Edge SK9 ... 60 A1
Stockport SK3 ... 240 F1
Elmir CH1 ... 117 C2
Elmore Cl
Holmes Chapel CW4 ... 130 A2
Runcorn WA7 ... 24 B1
Elmridge Ct WA3 ... 3 C4
Elmridge Dr WA15 ... 32 B4
Elmridge Prim Sch WA15 ... 32 B4
Elms The Golborne WA3 ... 3 C4
Mobberley WA16 ... 58 C1
Runcorn WA7 ... 22 C1
Threapwood SY14 ... 222 C2
Elmsett Cl WA5 ... 14 C3
Elmsleigh Rd SK8 ... 239 A2
Elmstead Cres CW1 ... 189 C4
Elmstead Rd SK11 ... 84 A2
Elmsway Altrincham WA15 ... 32 A4
Bollington SK10 ... 88 A4
Bramhall SK7 ... 35 B4
High Lane SK6 ... 37 C3
Elmtree Dr SK4 ... 240 C6
Elmwood WA7 ... 24 B1
Elmwood Ave
Chester CH2 ... 118 C2
Warrington WA1 ... 16 C4
Elmwood Cl ST7 ... 194 A2
Elmwood Gr CW7 ... 149 C4
Elmwood Rd CW8 ... 78 A2
Elnor Ave SK23 ... 65 C3
Elnor La SK23 ... 65 C2
Elsby Rd ST7 ... 193 C1
Elsinore Hts L26 ... 21 A4
Elston Ave WA12 ... 2 B3
Elstree Ave CH3 ... 119 A2
Elstree Gr SK3 ... 240 D4
Elswick Ave SK7 ... 35 C4
Eltham Cl WA8 ... 13 C2
Eltham Wlk WA8 ... 13 C2
Elton Cl Bebington CH62 ... 43 C2
Golborne WA3 ... 3 C4
Handforth SK9 ... 34 C1
Warrington WA3 ... 9 B2
Elton Crossings Rd CW11 ... 174 B3
Elton Dr SK7 ... 36 B4
Elton La Elton CH2 ... 72 C2
Haslington CW11 ... 174 B1
Elton Lordship La WA6 ... 73 A4
Elton Prim Sch CH2 ... 72 A2
Elton Rd CW11 ... 174 B3
Elvington Cl
Congleton CW12 ... 156 C1
Runcorn WA7 ... 49 C2
Elwood Way CW5 ... 205 A2
Elworth Ave WA8 ... 13 A
Elworth CE Prim Sch CW11 ... 174 C
Elworth Ct
12 Congleton CW12 ... 156 C
Sandbach CW11 ... 174 B
Elworth Hall Prim Sch CW11 ... 174 C
Elworth Rd CW11 ... 174 C
Elworth St CW11 ... 175 A
Elworth Way 6 SK9 ... 34 B
Elwyn Dr L26 ... 21 A
Ely Cl CH66 ... 94 C
Ely Pk WA7 ... 24 C
Embassy Cl CH1 ... 117 B
Emberton Pl CW3 ... 230 A
Embleton Ct WA7 ... 49 B
Embridge Cswy SK10, SK17 ... 90 A
Emerald Rd M22 ... 33 C
Emery Cl
Altrincham WA14 ... 238 D
Stockport SK4 ... 240 A
Emily St 14 WA8 ... 23 A
Emlyn Gr SK8 ... 240 A
Emmett St CW8 ... 78 A
Empire Ct WA1 ... 16 A
Empress Dr Crewe CW2 ... 190 A
Stockport SK4 ... 240 D
Emral Ct SY14 ... 211 A
Emslie Ct CH64 ... 66 B
Enderby Rd CH1 ... 237 A
Endon Av SK10 ... 88 A
Endsleigh Cl CH2 ... 118 C
Endsleigh Gdns CH2 ... 118 C
Enfield Cl CW2 ... 206 A
Enfield Park Rd WA2 ... 8 C
Enfield Rd CH65 ... 70 A
Engelsea Brook La CW2 ... 208 A
Engineer Pk CH5 ... 116 A
Englefield Ave CH4 ... 140 B
Englefield Cl CW1 ... 190 A
Englesea Brook Mus of Primitive Methodism* CW2 ... 208 A
Englesea Gr CW2 ... 190 A
English Martyrs RC Sch WA11 ... 1 C
Ennerdale Chester CH2 ... 118 C
Macclesfield SK11 ... 111 C
Ennerdale Ave
Bebington CH62 ... 43 C
Warrington WA2 ... 8 A
Ennerdale Cl
Alderley Edge SK9 ... 83 C
Winsford CW7 ... 126 B
Ennerdale Dr
Congleton CW12 ... 156 A
Frodsham WA6 ... 74 B
Gatley SK8 ... 239 B
Ennerdale Rd
Crewe CW2 ... 189 B
Partington M31 ... 11 C
Romiley SK6 ... 241 B
Ennerdale Terr SK15 ... 242 D
Ennis Cl L24 ... 21 B
Ensor Way SK22 ... 39 B
Enterprise Ctr The CW12 ... 156 C
Enterprise Way WA3 ... 4 A
Enticott Rd M44 ... 11
Enville Rd WA14 ... 238
Enville St WA4 ... 16
Epping Dr WA1 ... 17
Epsom Ave SK8,SK9 ... 34
Epsom Gdns WA4 ... 26
Epworth Cl WA5 ... 6
Epworth Ct SK4 ... 240
Era St M33 ... 242
ERF Way CW10 ... 151
Eric Ave WA1 ... 16
Eric St WA8 ... 13
Erindale Cres WA6 ... 74
Erlesmere Ave M34 ... 241
Ermine Rd CH2 ... 237
Ernest St Cheadle SK8 ... 239
Crewe CW2 ... 190
Errington Ave CH65 ... 70
Errwood Forest Walks* SK17 ... 90
Erskine Rd M31 ... 11
Erwood St WA2 ... 16
Esk Dale Cl CW7 ... 126
Esk Rd CW7 ... 127
Eskdale Cheadle SK8 ... 239
Ellesmere Port CH65 ... 70
Eskdale Ave
Bebington CH62 ... 43
Bramhall SK7 ... 35
Warrington WA2 ... 8
Eskdale Cl WA7 ... 49
Eskdale Terr SK15 ... 242
Essex Ave SK3 ... 240
Essex Cl CW12 ... 156
Essex Dr Biddulph ST8 ... 179
Kidsgrove ST7 ... 194
Essex Gdns M44 ... 11
Essex Rd CH2 ... 119
Essex Wlk SK10 ... 86
Esther St WA8 ... 13
Esthers La CW8 ... 102
Etchells Prim Sch SK8 ... 239
Etchells Rd SK8 ... 239
Etchells St 6 SK1 ... 240
Etharow Ct 6 SK14 ... 241
Ethelda Dr CH2 ... 119
Etherow Ave SK6 ... 241
Etherow Cl CW11 ... 174

ton Dr CH63 .41 C3
ton Rd CH65 .70 B2
tterick Pk CH3 .119 A1
ttiley Ave CW11 .174 B3
uclid Ave WA4 .17 A1
uropa Bsns Pk SK3 .240 B2
uropa Bvd WA5 .7 B2
uropa Way
Ellesmere Port CH65 .70 B3
Stockport SK3 .240 B2
ustace St WA2 .16 A3
va Rd SK3 .240 A3
va St CW11 .174 B4
vans Cl WA11 .1 C4
vans Pl WA4 .16 B2
vans St
Ashton-u-Lyne OL6 .242 A4
Crewe CW1 .190 B3
vansleigh Dr CH5 .116 A2
velyn St WA5 .15 B2
velyn Street Prim Sch
WA5 .15 C2
venholme WA14 .238 B2
venwood Cl WA7 .24 C2
verdon Cl CW7 .126 C2
verest Cl CH66 .69 C2
verest Rd ST7 .195 B2
verglade Cl SK11 .112 A3
vergreen Way WA9 .6 A4
verite Rd WA8 .22 A4
versley WA8 .12 A1
versley Cl Frodsham WA6 .74 B3
Warrington WA4 .26 C3
versley Ct CH2 .118 B2
versley Pk CH2 .118 B2
vesham Ave SK4 .240 B7
vesham Cl
Macclesfield SK10 .87 C2
Warrington WA4 .26 B4
vesham Dr SK9 .34 B1
vesham Gr M33 .242 E6
wart St CH4 .140 A4
wloe Ct CH65 .70 B1
wrin La SK10 .89 B3
xcalibur Ind Est ST7 .193 C2
xcalibur Prim Sch ST7 .193 C1
xcalibur Way M44 .11 C4
xchange Cl 25 SK11 .112 B4
xchange St
Macclesfield SK11 .112 B4
Stockport SK3 .240 E5
xeter Cl SK8 .34 C4
xeter Pl CH1 .117 C3
xeter Rd CH65 .70 B3
xeter Wlk SK7 .35 C4
xit Rd W M90 .33 A4
xmouth Cres WA7 .50 C3
xmouth Way WA5 .6 C3
xpress Ind Est WA8 .22 A4
xton Pk CH2 .237 A4
yam Rd SK7 .36 C4
yebrook Rd WA14 .238 A2
yre Pl CH65 .70 A3
yston Cl CW9 .103 C3

F

actory La Disley SK12 .38 C4
Warrington WA1,WA5 .15 C2
Widnes WA8 .13 A2
actory Rd CH5 .116 A2
air Haven's Ct WA8 .23 A4
air Isle Cl CH65 .70 B1
air Mead WA16 .82 A4
air Oak Rd ST5 .210 B1
air View Cl CW8 .77 C2
airacre Dr CW10 .151 C3
airacres Rd SK6 .37 C4
airbourne Ave
Alderley Edge SK9 .60 A2
Wilmslow SK9 .59 C2
airbourne Cl
Warrington WA5 .7 C2
Wilmslow SK9 .59 C2
airbourne Dr SK9 .59 C2
airbrook CW2 .189 C1
airbrother Cres WA2 .8 B1
airburn Ave CW2 .189 C2
airburn Cl WA8 .13 C2
airclough Ave WA1 .16 B2
airclough Cres WA11 .1 A3
airclough St
Burtonwood WA5 .6 C3
Newton-le-W WA12 .2 A2
airfax Dr Runcorn WA7 .23 B1
Wilmslow SK9 .59 C2
airfield Ave
Cheadle SK8 .239 F2
Ellesmere Port CH65 .70 A1
Romiley SK6 .241 A4
Sandbach CW11 .175 A3
airfield Gdns WA4 .16 C1
airfield High Sch WA8 .13 A2
airfield Jun & Inf Sch
WA8 .13 A1
airfield Rd
Broughton CH4 .139 A2
Chester CH2 .119 A2
Irlam M44 .11 B3
Lymm WA13 .18 C2
Northwich CW9 .104 A2
Warrington WA4 .16 C1
Widnes WA8 .13 A1
airfield St WA1 .16 B3
airfields ST7 .209 C1
airford Rd CH4 .140 C3
airford Way SK9 .60 B4
Fairhaven CW2 .207 A1
Fairhaven Cl Bramhall SK7 .35 C4
Macclesfield SK10 .87 A2
Warrington WA5 .15 A2
Fairhaven Dr CH63 .43 B3
Fairhaven Rd WA8 .13 B1
Fairhills Ind Est M44 .11 C4
Fairhills Rd M44 .11 C4
Fairholm Rd CW9 .127 A4
Fairholme Ave CH64 .41 B1
Fairholme Cl CH1 .94 A1
Fairholme Rd SK4 .240 C7
Fairlawn SK4 .240 D7
Fairlawn Cl CH63 .43 A3
Fairlea M34 .241 A6
Fairmeadow CH4 .162 B1
Fairmile Dr M20 .239 C8
Fairoak Cl 18 CW7 .149 A4
Fairoak Ct WA7 .50 C2
Fairoak La WA7 .50 C2
Fairview LL13 .196 C4
Fairview Ave
Alsager ST7 .193 B2
Weston CW2 .207 A3
Fairview Rd
Ellesmere Port CH65 .70 A1
Macclesfield SK11 .112 A3
Fairway Bramhall SK7 .35 B3
Gatley SK8 .239 B4
Hawarden CH5 .116 A1
Fairway The ST7 .193 B2
Fairways Frodsham WA6 .74 B4
Warrington WA4 .26 B3
Fairways Dr
Ellesmere Port CH66 .69 B4
Whitchurch SY13 .226 A1
Fairways The
Macclesfield SK10 .87 A2
Winsford CW7 .126 A1
Fairywell Cl SK9 .34 B1
Falcon Cl
Middlewich CW10 .151 B3
New Mills SK22 .39 B4
Winsford CW7 .149 B3
Falcon Dr CW1 .190 A4
Falcon Rd CH66 .69 C2
Falcondale Rd WA2 .8 A3
Falconers Gn WA5 .7 A1
Falcons Way WA7 .49 C3
Fallibroome Cl SK11 .111 C4
Fallibroome High Sch
SK10 .86 C1
Fallibroome Rd SK11 .111 C4
Fallow Ct CW10 .151 B4
Fallowfield WA7 .23 B1
Fallowfield Cl CW7 .125 C1
Fallowfield Ct CW1 .190 A3
Fallowfield Gr WA2 .9 A1
Falls Gr SK8 .239 A3
Falmouth Cl SK10 .111 C4
Falmouth Dr WA5 .14 C2
Falmouth Pl WA7 .50 C3
Falmouth Rd
Congleton CW12 .178 C4
Crewe CW1 .190 A3
Falstaff Mews SK6 .241 A3
Falstone Cl WA3 .10 A3
Falstone Dr WA7 .50 C4
Fanner's La WA16 .28 B3
Fanny's Croft ST7 .193 B1
Fanshawe La SK11 .110 C3
Fanshawe Wlk CW2 .206 B4
Far Ridings SK6 .241 D3
Faraday Rd
Ellesmere Port CH65 .70 A2
Runcorn WA7 .23 B2
Faraday St WA3 .9 C2
Farams Rd ST7 .193 C4
Farbailey Cl CH4 .141 A3
Farfields Cl SK11 .111 C1
Faringdon Rd WA2 .8 A3
Farlands Dr M20 .239 B7
Farley Cl CW10 .151 A4
Farley Ct SK8 .239 F3
Farm Cl CW8 .77 B1
Farm Dr CH5 .91 B1
Farm La High Lane SK12 .38 A3
Warrington WA4 .26 C4
Withington Green SK11 .108 C1
Farm Rd Northwich CW9 .104 C4
Oakmere CW8 .124 A4
Weaverham CW8 .77 B1
Farm Way WA12 .2 C1
Farm Wlk WA14 .20 C1
Farmdale Dr CH2 .72 A2
Farmer Cl CW2 .190 A2
Farmer St SK4 .240 E7
Farmer's La WA5 .7 A3
Farmers Heath CH66 .69 B1
Farmfield Dr SK10 .87 B2
Farmfields Rise CW3 .232 B1
Farmfold SK9 .33 C2
Farmleigh Dr CW1 .189 C4
Farmleigh Gdns WA5 .15 B3
Farmside Cl WA5 .15 C4
Farmstead Way CH66 .69 C1
Farndale WA8 .13 A3
Farndale Cl
Warrington WA5 .14 C4
Wistaston CW2 .206 A3
Farndon Cl
Broughton CH4 .139 B2
Cuddington CW8 .102 A2
Sale M33 .242 E5
Farndon Prim Sch CH3 .180 C1
Farndon Rd CH66 .69 C3
Farne Cl CH2 .95 B4
Farnham Ave SK11 .112 A3
Farnham Cl Cheadle SK8 .35 A4
Warrington WA4 .26 C4
Farnhill Cl WA7 .50 B4
Farnley Cl WA7 .24 B1
Farnworth CE Prim Sch
WA8 .13 A2
Farnworth Cl WA8 .13 A2
Farnworth Rd WA5 .14 B2
Farnworth St WA8 .13 A2
Farr Hall Dr CH60 .40 C4
Farr Hall Rd CH60 .40 C4
Farr St SK3 .240 D4
Farrant St WA8 .23 A4
Farrell Rd WA4 .26 B4
Farrell St WA1 .16 B3
Farriers Way CW7 .126 A1
Farthing La CW9 .79 A4
Farwood Cl SK10 .86 C1
Faulkner Dr CW10 .151 C3
Faulkner St CH2 .118 C2
Faulkner's La WA16 .58 C1
Faulkners Cl CH4 .161 A4
Faulkners La CH3 .142 B4
Fawley Ave SK14 .241 D5
Fawns Keep SK9 .60 B4
Fawns Leap CW8 .101 C3
Fearndown Way SK10 .87 B2
Fearnhead Cross WA2 .8 C1
Fearnhead La WA2 .9 A1
Fearnley Way WA12 .2 B1
Feather La CH60 .40 C4
Feilden Ct CH1 .94 C1
Felix Rd CW8 .103 C4
Fellside Gn SK15 .242 D3
Felskirk Rd M22 .33 B4
Fence Ave SK10 .112 C4
Fence Ave Ind Est SK10 .112 C4
Fence La CW12 .178 B2
Fenham Dr WA5 .14 C2
Fennel St WA1 .16 B3
Fenton Cl
Congleton CW12 .157 A1
Widnes WA8 .12 B2
Fenwick La WA7 .49 B3
Fenwick Rd CH66 .69 C1
Ferguson Ave CH66 .69 C3
Ferguson Dr WA2 .8 B1
Ferma La CH3 .120 B3
Fern Ave WA12 .2 B1
Fern Bank SK15 .242 F1
Fern Cl WA3 .9 B2
Fern Cres
Congleton CW12 .157 A2
Stalybridge SK15 .242 F1
Fern Ct CW1 .190 C2
Fern Lea SK8 .239 B1
Fern Lea Dr SK11 .112 A4
Fern Rd CH65 .70 A1
Fern Way CW8 .77 B1
Fernacre M33 .242 C7
Fernally St SK14 .241 E6
Fernbank Cl Crewe CW1 .190 C2
Warrington WA3 .9 C2
Winsford CW7 .127 A1
Fernbank Rise SK10 .88 A4
Ferndale Ave CH2 .72 A2
Ferndale Cl
Bold Heath WA8 .13 C4
Sandbach CW11 .175 B3
Warrington WA1 .17 B4
Weston CW2 .207 A3
Ferndale Cres SK11 .111 C4
Fernhill Rd CH1 .117 C3
Fernhurst WA7 .49 B4
Fernilee Cotts SK23 .65 C1
Fernlea WA15 .238 F1
Fernlea Rd Heswall CH60 .41 A4
Marston CW9 .79 A3
Fernleaf Cl ST7 .193 C4
Fernleigh CW8 .103 B4
Fernleigh Cl
Middlewich CW10 .151 C3
Winsford CW7 .126 A1
Fernley Ave M34 .241 A6
Fernway CW7 .127 A1
Fernwood WA7 .24 A1
Fernwood Gr SK9 .60 B4
Fernyess La CH64 .67 C4
Ferrous Way M44 .11 C3
Ferry Cl CH5 .116 A3
Ferry La Sealand CH1 .117 B1
Warrington WA4 .17 C2
Ferry Rd CH62 .44 A3
Ferryview Wlk WA7 .23 C1
Festival Ave
Buerton CW3 .230 C2
Warrington WA2 .8 B1
Festival Cres WA2 .8 B1
Festival Dr SK10 .85 C3
Festival Hill CW12 .156 C1
Festival Rd CH65 .69 C3
Festival Way WA7 .49 B4
Fiddler's Ferry Rd WA8 .13 B1
Fiddlers La CH1 .94 B1
Field Ave CW2 .189 C1
Field Cl Bollington SK10 .87 C4
Bramhall SK7 .35 B2
Northwich CW8 .103 B4
Tarvin CH3 .121 A1
Field Hey La CH64 .43 A1
Field La Tarvin CH3 .121 A1
Tattenhall CH3 .166 A1
Warrington WA4 .26 B3
Wistaston CW2 .189 C1
Field Side Cl WA16 .58 A2
Field St SK6 .241 A3
Field View ST8 .179 B1
Field View Dr SK11 .112 C3
Field Way ST7 .193 C2
Field Wlk 2 M31 .11 C2
Fieldbank Rd SK11 .112 A4
Fieldfare CW7 .150 A4
Fieldfare Cl Golborne WA3 .3 B4
Warrington WA3 .9 C2
Fieldgate WA8 .22 A3
Fieldhead Mews SK9 .60 C4
Fieldhead Rd SK9 .60 C4
Fieldhouse Row WA7 .49 B4
Fielding Ave SK12 .36 C1
Fields Cl ST7 .193 C2
Fields Cres CW12 .156 B1
Fields Dr CW11 .175 A3
Fields Rd Alsager ST7 .193 C2
Congleton CW12 .178 C4
Haslington CW1 .191 B2
Fields The CW5 .205 B3
Fields View SY13 .228 B1
Fields View Cl CW5 .220 A4
Fieldsend Dr WN7 .4 B4
Fieldside CW6 .145 A3
Fieldsway WA7 .49 A3
Fieldview Dr WA2 .8 B1
Fieldway Chester CH2 .118 C2
Ellesmere Port CH66 .69 A4
Frodsham WA6 .74 B4
Saughall CH1 .94 A1
Weaverham CW8 .77 B1
Widnes WA8 .13 C1
Fieldways 2 WA13 .18 B2
Fife Rd WA1 .16 C4
Fifth Ave Kidsgrove ST7 .194 C1
Runcorn WA7 .49 C4
Fildes Cl WA5 .15 B3
Filkin's La CH3 .119 A1
Finch La L26 .21 A4
Finchdale Gdns WA3 .4 A4
Finchett Ct CH1 .118 A2
Finchett Dr CH1 .118 A2
Finchley Rd WA15 .238 E3
Findlay Cl WA12 .2 B1
Finlan Rd WA8 .22 C4
Finland Rd SK3 .240 D3
Finlay Ave WA5 .14 C2
Finlow Hill La SK10 .85 C3
Finney Cl SK9 .34 B1
Finney Dr SK9 .34 B1
Finney Gr WA11 .1 C3
Finney La SK8 .239 C1
Finney's La CW10 .128 A1
Finningley Ct WA2 .8 C1
Finny Bank Rd M33 .242 A8
Finsbury Cl WA5 .15 B2
Finsbury Pk WA8 .13 B3
Finsbury Way SK9 .34 C1
Finsbury Wlk CW7 .149 A4
Fir Ave Bramhall SK7 .35 C4
Halewood L26 .21 A4
Fir Cl Halewood L26 .21 A4
Poynton SK12 .36 C2
Tarporley CW6 .146 B1
Fir Ct SK10 .86 C1
Fir Gr Macclesfield SK11 .112 B3
Warrington WA1 .16 C4
Weaverham CW8 .102 C4
Fir La CW8 .102 A1
Fir Rd Bramhall SK7 .35 C4
Denton M34 .241 A7
Fir St Irlam M44 .11 B3
Stockport SK4 .240 E6
Widnes WA8 .13 B1
Fir Tree Ave
Chester CH4 .141 A3
Golborne WA3 .3 C4
Knutsford WA16 .82 B4
Fir Tree Cl WA4 .26 B1
Fir Tree La
Burtonwood WA5 .7 A4
Chester CH3 .119 C1
Faddiley CW5 .202 A2
Fir Tree Wlk WA3 .3 C4
Fir Way CH60 .41 A3
Firbank CH2 .72 B2
Firbank Cl WA7 .24 B1
Firbeck Cl
Broughton CH4 .139 A2
Congleton CW12 .155 C2
Firbeck Gdns CW2 .189 B2
Firdale Rd CW8 .103 B4
Firecrest Ct WA1 .16 A2
Firemans Sq CH1 .237 A3
Firman Cl WA5 .15 A4
Firs Cl SK8 .239 A3
Firs Gr SK8 .239 A4
Firs La WA4 .26 A3
Firs Pottery The* CW5 .217 B1
Firs Rd SK8 .239 A4
Firs Sch The CH2 .118 C3
Firs The Altrincham WA14 .238 B3
Wilmslow SK9 .60 A3
Firs View WA6 .73 B2
First Ave
Congleton CW12 .156 A2
Connah's Quay CH5 .93 A1
Crewe CW1 .190 C1
Kidsgrove ST7 .194 C1
Poynton SK12 .36 B1
Sandbach CW11 .175 A3
First Dig La CW5 .219 B4
First Wood St CW5 .204 B3
Firswood Mount SK8 .239 A4
Firthfields Cl CW9 .103 C1
Firths Fields CW9 .103 C1
Firtree Ave WA1 .17 A4
Firtree Cl Barnton CW8 .78 A2
Winsford CW7 .127 A1
Firtree Gr CH1 .95 A4
Firvale Ave SK8 .239 B1
Firwood Rd ST8 .179 C1
Firwood Wlk CW2 .190 B1
Fisher Ave WA2 .8 A1
Fisher Rd CH1 .117 C2
Fisher St WA7 .23 A2
Fisherfield Dr WA3 .10 A3
Fishermans Cl CW11 .191 C4
Fishers Gn CW6 .146 A3
Fishers La CW5 .203 B4
Fishpool Rd CW8 .123 C2
Fishwicks Ind Est WA11 .1 C4
Fistral Ave SK8 .34 B4
Fitton St CW9 .80 A1
Fitton's Cl CW5 .217 C3
Fitz Cl SK10 .87 B2
Fitz Cres SK10 .87 B2
Fitz Walter Rd WA1 .17 B4
Fitzherbert St WA2 .16 B4
Fitzwilliam Ave SK11 .112 C2
Fitzwilliam Wlk WA7 .24 A1
Five Ashes Rd CH4 .141 A3
Five Ways CH64 .41 C2
Fivelanes End WA6 .74 B3
Fiveways Par SK7 .36 C4
Flacca Ct CH3 .166 A1
Flag La Crewe CW1,CW2 .190 B2
Neston CH64 .66 C4
Flag La N CH2 .118 C4
Flag La S CH2 .118 C4
Flamingo Cl CW1 .189 C4
Flander Cl WA8 .12 B1
Flash La Antrobus CW9 .53 C3
Bollington SK10 .87 B4
Flashes La CH64 .67 A3
Flat La Kelsall CW6 .122 B2
Sandbach CW11 .175 A3
Flatt La CH65 .70 A3
Flatts La SK23 .64 C2
Flaxley Cl WA3 .10 A3
Flaxmere Dr CH3 .142 A4
Flaxyards CW6 .146 C1
Fleet La WA9 .1 A1
Fleet St
Ellesmere Port CH65 .70 A3
Hyde SK14 .241 E7
Fleetwood Cl WA5 .15 A2
Fleetwood Dr WA12 .2 A2
Fleetwood Wlk WA7 .50 B3
Fleming Dr WA2 .8 A3
Fleming St CH65 .70 B3
Flemish Rd M34 .241 B6
Flers Ave WA4 .16 B2
Fletcher Dr
Altrincham WA14 .238 C1
High Lane SK12 .37 C3
Fletcher Gr CW9 .104 B3
Fletcher St Crewe CW1 .190 A3
Stockport SK1 .240 F5
Warrington WA4 .16 A2
Fletchers La WA13 .18 C2
Fletsand Rd SK9 .60 D3
Flint Cl CH64 .66 C3
Flint Ct CH65 .70 B1
Flint Dr CH64 .66 C3
Flint Gr M44 .11 B3
Flint Mdw CH64 .66 C4
Flint St Macclesfield SK11 .112 C4
Stockport SK3 .240 E3
Flittogate La WA16 .80 C4
Flixton Dr CW2 .190 A1
Florence Ct SK3 .240 B2
Florence St Sale M33 .242 B8
6 Stockport SK4 .240 E6
Warrington WA4 .16 B2
Florida Cl WA5 .15 B4
Florist St SK3 .240 E3
Flower St CW8 .103 C4
Flowers La CW1 .172 C1
Flowerscroft CW5 .205 A2
Flowery Field Gn SK14 .241 C8
Flowery Field Prim Sch
SK14 .241 D8
Fluin La WA6 .74 B4
Foden Ave ST7 .194 A2
Foden La
Alderley Edge SK9 .59 B1
Woodford SK7 .35 B2
Foden St SK10 .87 B1
Foden Wlk 8 SK9 .34 B1
Fogg's La CW9,WA4 .53 A3
Fol Hollow CW12 .156 A1
Fold La Biddulph ST8 .179 C2
Bosley SK11 .135 B1
Fold The SK10 .87 A4
Folden Cl CH66 .69 A3
Folds La SK23 .65 C2
Folds The CH63 .42 A3
Foley Wlk M22 .33 C4
Folkestone Cl SK10 .87 A1
Folkstone Way WA7 .50 B4
Folly La WA5 .15 C4
Forbes Cl WA3 .9 C2
Forbes Pk SK7 .35 B4
Ford Cl CW1 .190 A3
Ford Ct CW7 .149 B3
Ford La Crewe CW1 .190 A3
Tattenhall CH3 .166 C2
Ford St Stockport SK3 .240 D5
Warrington WA1 .16 B3
Ford's La SK7 .35 B3
Fordington Rd WA5 .15 A3
Fords La ST7 .195 B3
Fordton Leisure Ctr WA2 .8 A2
Foregate St CH1 .237 B2

Foreland Cl WA5 14 B4
Forest Ave CW4 107 B1
Forest Cl
Cuddington CW8 101 C2
Rainow SK10 88 C3
Forest Dr
Altrincham WA15 238 F6
Broughton CH4 139 A2
Forest Gate La CW6 122 C4
Forest Gdns M31 11 B2
Forest Ho SK10 87 C1
Forest La WA6 100 B3
Forest Pl 3 CW9 79 A1
Forest Rd
Cuddington CW8 101 C2
Ellesmere Port CH66 69 C4
Heswall CH60 41 A4
Macclesfield SK11 113 C3
Tarporley CW6 146 B2
Winsford CW7 149 A4
Forest Sch WA15 238 F6
Forest St Chester CH1 237 C2
Weaverham CW8 102 B4
Forester Ave WA16 57 B1
Forester Dr SK15 242 D1
Foresters Cl WA6 101 A3
Forge Cl Cronton WA8 12 B3
Warren SK11 111 B1
Forge Fields CW11 174 C2
Forge La
Congleton CW12 156 A2
Norton in Hales TF9 236 B1
Forge Mill La CW10 151 B1
Forge Rd
Ellesmere Port CH66 69 B3
Warrington WA5 14 C3
Whaley Bridge SK23 65 C4
Forge Sh Ctr The WA4 16 B1
Forge St CW1 190 B2
Forge Way CH4 140 C2
Formby Cl WA5 14 C2
Formby Dr SK8 34 A4
Forrest Dr SK11 113 B2
Forrest Rd M34 241 B5
Forshaw St WA2 16 B4
Forshaw's La WA5 6 C4
Forster Ave CW8 102 C4
Forster St WA2 16 A4
Forsythia Wlk 2 M31 11 C1
Forty Acre La CW4, CW12 131 B3
Forum The Chester CH1 237 A2
Romiley SK6 241 C2
Forwood Rd CH62 43 B4
Fossa Cl CW10 128 B1
Foster Rd CW12 157 A3
Foster St WA8 13 A1
Fothergill St WA1 16 B4
Fotheringay Ct 3 CH65 70 B1
Foulkes Ave CW1 189 C3
Foundry Bank CW12 156 C2
Foundry Ct
13 Macclesfield SK11 112 B4
New Mills SK22 39 B4
Foundry La
Sandbach CW11 174 B4
Scholar Green ST7 194 C4
Widnes WA8 22 B3
Foundry St
Bollington SK10 88 A4
Newton-le-W WA12 2 A2
Warrington WA2 16 A3
Fountain Ct Biddulph ST8 179 B1
Winsford CW7 126 B1
Fountain Ho SK11 112 C4
Fountain La
Davenham CW9 103 C1
Frodsham WA6 74 A4
Fountain Pl SK12 36 B2
Fountain St
Ashton-u-Lyne OL6 242 B4
Congleton CW12 156 B1
Hyde SK14 241 F7
Macclesfield SK11 112 C4
Fountains Ave WA11 1 C4
Fountains Cl
Middlewich CW10 128 A1
Poynton SK12 36 B2
Runcorn WA7 50 B3
Fountains Rd SK7,SK8 35 B3
Fountains Wlk WA3 4 A4
Four Lane Ends WA6 74 A1
Four Lanes End
Betley CW2 207 C1
Thornton Hough CH63 42 B3
Fourseasons Cl CW2 206 A4
Fourth Ave
Connah's Quay CH5 92 C1
Crewe CW1 190 C1
Kidsgrove ST7 194 C1
Runcorn WA7 49 C4
Fourway Tech Pk CW11 176 C2
Fourways CW2 207 A3
Fowey Cl SK10 86 B1
Fowler Rd CH1 117 B2
Fowler St SK10 87 B1
Fowlers Bench La CH3 184 B3
Fowley Common La WA3 5 B3
Fox Bank Ct SK3 240 D4
Fox Bench Cl SK7,SK8 35 B3
Fox Cl WA15 238 F6
Fox Cover CH3 119 C3
Fox Cover Rd CH60 41 B4
Fox Covert WA7 50 B4
Fox Covert La CH2 96 A1
Fox Covert Way CW1 173 A1
Fox Gdns Lymm WA13 18 B2
Talke ST7 210 B4
Fox Gr WA16 57 B1
Fox Hill CW6 122 B2
Fox La Clutton CH3 182 B1
Waverton CH3 143 A3
Fox Lea CH1 117 A4
Fox St Congleton CW12 156 C2
Runcorn WA7 23 A1
Stockport SK3 240 D4
Warrington WA5 15 C3
Fox Wood Sch WA3 9 C2
Fox's Dr CH5 116 A3
Foxall Way CH66 69 B1
Foxcote WA8 12 A1
Foxcote Cl CH1 117 B3
Foxcovert La WA16 106 C4
Foxdale Ct WA4 26 B4
Foxendale Cl CW8 103 B4
Foxes Fold CW8 78 C1
Foxes Hey CW8 101 B3
Foxes Hollow CW1 190 C4
Foxes Wlk CH3 142 A4
Foxfield La CW7 126 A1
Foxglove Cl
Bollington SK10 88 B4
2 Golborne WA3 3 B4
Huntington CH3 142 A3
Wistaston CW2 206 A4
Foxglove Ct WA6 74 B4
Foxglove Dr WA14 238 C8
Foxglove La SK15 242 D3
Foxglove Way CH64 66 C3
Foxglove Wlk M31 11 C1
Foxhall Rd WA15 238 F6
Foxhill WA14 238 A5
Foxhill Ct CW6 146 C1
Foxhill Gr WA6 73 B2
Foxhills Cl WA4 26 B2
Foxhunter Cl CH3 121 C4
Foxland Rd SK8 239 B4
Foxlea CW9 78 B4
Foxley Cl WA13 19 A1
Foxley Hall Mews WA13 19 A1
Foxley Heath WA8 22 C4
Foxwist Cl CH2 237 B4
Foxwist Gr CW7 125 C3
Foxwood Dr WA16 108 A4
Frances Ave SK8 239 A6
Frances St Cheadle SK8 239 E6
Crewe CW2 190 B1
Dukinfield SK14 241 C7
Irlam M44 11 C3
Macclesfield SK11 112 A4
Stockport SK1,SK3 240 E4
Frances St W SK14 241 C7
Francis Cl WA8 22 B4
Francis Ct CH2 237 C3
Francis La LL13 196 A3
Francis Rd Frodsham WA6 49 B1
Irlam M44 11 C4
Warrington WA4 16 B1
Francis St CH2 237 C3
Frank Bott Ave CW1 190 A4
Frank Perkins Way M44 11 C4
Frank St Hyde SK14 241 E6
Widnes WA8 13 B1
Frank Webb Ave CW1 190 A3
Franklin Cl
Macclesfield SK11 112 A3
Warrington WA5 15 B4
Fraser Ave M33 242 E5
Fraser Ct CH4 141 B4
Fraser Rd WA5 14 B3
Frawley Ave WA12 2 B3
Freckleton Cl WA5 15 A2
Frederick St
Ashton-u-Lyne OL6,SK15 242 B2
Warrington WA4 16 C2
Widnes WA8 23 A4
Frederick Terr WA8 22 A2
Fredric Pl WA7 23 A2
Free Green La WA16 107 A4
Freedom Dr ST7 195 C2
Freeman Ave OL6 242 A3
Freemantle St SK3 240 D4
French Ave SK15 242 F1
French La CW5 218 B3
French St
Ashton-u-Lyne OL6 242 A4
Stalybridge SK15 242 F1
Widnes WA8 13 B1
Freshfield SK8 34 A4
Freshfield Ave SK14 241 D5
Freshfield Dr SK10 87 B2
Freshfields
Comberbach CW9 78 B4
Wistaston CW2 206 A4
Freshfields Dr WA2 9 B2
Freshmeadow La WA6 73 A1
Freshwater Cl WA5 14 B4
Friar's Cl SK9 59 C4
Friar's Rd M33 242 B6
Friars Ave WA5 14 C3
Friars Cl
Altrincham WA14 238 B1
Rainow SK10 88 B3
Friars Gate Chester CH1 237 B2
Warrington WA1 16 A2
Friars La WA1 16 A2
Friars Way SK10 86 C1
Frida Cres CW8 103 C3
Friends La WA5 14 B3
Friesian Gdns ST5 210 B1
Frieston Rd WA14 238 E8
Frith Ave CW8 123 B4
Frith La CW5 216 B2
Frith Terr SK11 112 B2
Frobisher Ct WA5 15 B4
Frobisher Pl SK5 240 E8
Frobisher Rd CH64 66 C4
Froda Ave WA6 74 A4
Frodsham Ave SK4 240 C7
Frodsham CE Prim Sch WA6 74 B4
Frodsham Rd WA6 73 B1
Frodsham Sch WA6 74 A4
Frodsham St
Chester CH1 237 B3
Kelsall CW6 122 A3
Frodsham Sta WA6 74 A4
Frodsham Way SK9 34 C2
Frog La Holt LL13 196 B4
Milton Green CH3 165 C1
Pickmere WA16 55 A1
Tattenhall CH3 166 A1
Worthenbury SY14 211 A1
Froghall La
High Legh WA16 29 B4
Warrington WA2,WA5 15 C3
Frome Ct CH65 70 A4
Front St CW11 175 B3
Frosts Mews CH65 70 A3
Fryer Rd CW9 80 A2
Fuchsia Cl CH66 69 C1
Fulbeck WA8 12 B1
Fulbeck Cl CW2 206 A4
Fulbrook Dr SK8 35 A3
Fuller Dr CW2 206 A4
Fullerton Rd
Hartford CW8 103 A2
Stockport SK4 240 B6
Fulmar Cl SK12 36 A2
Fulmar Ct CW1 189 C4
Fulmards Cl SK9 60 B4
Fulshaw Ave SK9 60 A3
Fulshaw CE Prim Sch SK9 59 C3
Fulshaw Cross SK9 60 A3
Fulshaw Ct SK9 60 A3
Fulshaw Pk SK9 60 A3
Fulshaw Pk S SK9 60 A2
Fulton Gr CW9 103 C1
Fulwood Gdns CH66 69 B3
Fulwood Mews CH66 69 B3
Fulwood Rd
Ellesmere Port CH66 69 B3
Golborne WA3 3 C4
Furber St CW1 190 B3
Furnace St SK14 241 C8
Furne Rd CH1 117 C2
Furness Cl
Holmes Chapel CW4 130 A2
Poynton SK12 36 B2
Winsford CW7 149 A4
Furness Ct WA7 24 C2
Furness Gr SK4 240 A5
Furness Lodge Cl SK23 39 B2
Furness Rd SK8 35 B3
Furness Vale Bsns Ctr SK23 39 B2
Furness Vale Prim Sch SK23 39 B2
Furness Vale Sta SK23 39 B2
Furnival St Crewe CW2 190 B1
Sandbach CW11 175 A4
Furrocks Cl CH64 66 C3
Furrocks La CH64 66 C3
Furrocks Way CH64 66 C3
Furrows The CH66 94 C4
Fylde Ave SK8 34 B4
Fylde Rd SK4 240 A6
Fytton Cl SK11 111 B1

G

Gable Ave SK9 60 A4
Gable St WA12 2 A2
Gables Cl WA2 8 C2
Gables The ST7 193 B2
Gabriel Bank CW8 76 A1
Gadbrook Bsns Ctr CW9 104 B3
Gadbrook Pk CW9 104 B3
Gadbrook Rd CW9 104 B3
Gaddum Rd WA14 238 B1
Gail Ave SK4 240 D6
Gail Cl SK9 60 A1
Gainford Ave SK8 239 B4
Gainford Cl WA8 12 B2
Gainsborough Cl SK9 60 B4
Gainsborough Ct WA8 12 A1
Gainsborough Dr SK8 239 F6
Gainsborough Inf Sch CW2 190 A2
Gainsborough Jun Sch CW2 190 A1
Gainsborough Rd
Crewe CW2 190 A2
Warrington WA4 16 A1
Gair Rd SK5 240 F8
Gair St SK14 241 D8
Gairloch Cl WA2 8 C2
Gaisgill Ct WA8 12 B1
Gala Cl CH4 139 B2
Galbraith Cl CW12 156 B1
Gale Ave WA5 7 C1
Gale Rd SK22 39 B4
Galion Way WA8 12 C2
Galleys Bank ST7 195 A2
Gallimore Ho ST7 210 B4
Galloway Cl CW4 130 B1
Gallowsclough La WA6 100 C2
Galway Gr CW2 206 A2
Game St CW11 175 A2
Gamul Pl CH4 237 B1
Ganton Cl WA8 13 A2
Garden Ave CW7 126 A1
Garden Cl SK10 87 C1
Garden Ct CH1 237 A3
Garden La
Altrincham WA14 238 D5
Chester CH1 237 A3
Harthill CH3 183 C2
Garden Rd WA16 56 C2
Garden St Bollington SK10 87 C4
Congleton CW12 156 B2
Hyde SK14 241 E8
Macclesfield SK10 87 C1
Garden Terr
Chester CH1 237 A3
Chester, Hoole Park CH2 118 C1
Stalybridge SK15 242 D2
Garden Wlk 1 M31 11 C2
Gardens The Holt LL13 180 C1
Sandbach CW11 175 A3
Gardiner Ave WA11 1 B3
Garfit St CW10 128 B1
Garlick St SK14 241 F7
Garner Cl WA14 238 D2
Garner St WA2 16 B4
Garner's La SK3 240 E1
Garnett Ave WA4 17 A2
Garnett St SK1 240 F5
Garnetts La WA8 22 A2
Garrett Field WA3 9 B3
Garrett Wlk SK3 240 C4
Garrigill Cl WA8 13 B3
Garsdale Cl WA5 15 A4
Garside Ave WA3 3 B4
Garside St SK14 241 E5
Garston Cl SK4 240 C7
Garth Ave WA15 238 E6
Garth Dr CH2 118 B3
Garth Hts SK9 60 B4
Garth Rd CH65 71 A3
Garven Pl WA1 16 A3
Garwood Cl WA5 15 B4
Gas Rd SK11 112 B4
Gas St SK4 240 E5
Gaskell Ave
Knutsford WA16 56 C1
Warrington WA4 17 A2
Gaskell Rd WA14 238 D6
Gaskell St WA4 16 B1
Gatcombe Mews 1 SK9 60 A3
Gate Warth St WA5 15 B2
Gateacre Ct CH66 69 C4
Gatefield St CW1 190 B2
Gatesheath Dr CH2 118 C4
Gatesheath La CH3 165 C3
Gatewarth Ind Est WA5 15 B2
Gateway Crewe CW1 190 C1
Newcastle-u-L ST5 210 B1
Gathill Cl SK8 239 F1
Gathurst Ct WA8 22 B4
Gatley Gn SK8 239 A5
Gatley Prim Sch SK8 239 A5
Gatley Rd Cheadle SK8 239 C5
Sale M33 242 E5
Gatley Sta SK8 239 B5
Gauntley Bird of Prey Ctr* SK10 85 A1
Gaunts Way WA7 49 C3
Gavin Rd WA8 22 A4
Gawend La SK11 112 B1
Gawer Pk CH2 118 B2
Gawsworth Ave CW2 189 C2
Gawsworth Cl
Alsager ST7 193 B2
Bramhall SK7 35 C3
Holmes Chapel CW4 130 A2
Northwich CW9 104 A2
Poynton SK12 36 C1
Stockport SK3 240 D1
Gawsworth Ct WA3 9 C3
Gawsworth Dr CW11 175 B4
Gawsworth Hall* SK11 134 C4
Gawsworth Mews SK8 239 B5
Gawsworth Prim Sch SK11 111 B1
Gawsworth Rd
Ellesmere Port CH66 69 C3
Macclesfield SK11 111 B3
Gawsworth Way
4 Denton M34 241 A5
Handforth SK9 34 C2
Gayhurst Ave WA2 8 C1
Gaymoore Cl CH2 237 A4
Gaynor Ave WA11 1 C4
Gayton Cl CH2 118 C3
Gayton Farm Rd CH60 41 A3
Gayton La CH60 41 A3
Gayton Mill Cl CH60 41 A4
Gayton Parkway CH60 41 B3
Gayton Prim Sch CH60 41 A3
Gayton Rd CH60 41 A3
Gee St SK3 240 D3
Gemini Bsns Pk WA5 7 C2
Gemmull Cl CW3 229 C2
General St WA1 16 B3
Genesis Ctr The WA3 9 C3
Geneva Rd CW7 126 B1
Geo Hampson's Bldgs WA3 5 B4
George Bates Cl ST7 193 B2
George Kenyon Mews CH4 140 C3
George La SK6 241 A4
George Rd WA5 15 B2
George Richards Way WA14 238 C7
George St
Alderley Edge SK9 60 A
Altrincham WA14 238 D
Audley ST7 209 B
Barnton CW8 78 A
Chester CH1 237 A
Denton M34 241 A
Ellesmere Port CH65 70 B
Knutsford WA16 57 A
Macclesfield SK11 112 B
Newton-le-W WA12 2 A
Sandbach CW11 174 C
Stalybridge SK15 242 D
Whaley Bridge SK23 65 C
Winsford CW7 126 C
George St W SK11 112 B
George VI Ave CW10 151 B
George VI Cl CW10 151 B
George's Cl SK12 36 C
George's La CW9 54 B
George's Prec WA5 14 B
George's Rd Sale M33 242 B
Stockport SK4 240 D
George's Rd E SK12 36 C
George's Rd W SK12 36 C
George's Wlk CW11 175 A
Georges Cres WA4 17 A
Georges Way ST7 209 C
Gerard Dr CW5 204 B
Gerosa Ave WA2 8 A
Gerrard Ave
Ellesmere Port CH66 69 B
Warrington WA5 15 C
Gerrard Dr CW8 77 B
Gerrard Rd WA3 9 A
Gerrard St
Stalybridge SK15 242 E
Widnes WA8 23 A
Gerrards Ave CH3 119 A
Giantswood La CW12 156 B
Gibb Hill CW9 53 B
Gibbon Dr CW9 80 A
Gibson Cres CW11 174 B
Gibson St
Warrington, Howley WA1 16 B
Warrington, Stockton Heath WA4 16 B
Gibson Way WA14 238 C
Gibsons Rd SK4 240 B
Gig La WA1 17 C
Gigg La Moore WA4 25 A
Warrington WA4 17 C
Gilbert Cl 2 ST7 195 A
Gilbert Rd WA15 238 E
Gilbertbank SK6 241 B
Gilchrist Ave SK11 111 C
Gilchrist Rd M44 11 C
Gilderdale Cl WA3 10 A
Gillan Cl WA7 50 B
Gillbent Rd SK8 35 A
Gillow Cl CW1 190 A
Gilmore St SK3 240 E
Giltbrook Cl WA8 12 C
Gilwell Cl WA4 17 B
Gingerbread La CW5 205 A
Girton Cl CH65 70 B
Girton Rd CH65 70 B
Girvin Dr CH64 66 C
Glade The SK4 240 A
Gladewood Cl SK9 60 B
Gladstone Ave CH1 118 A
Gladstone Ct 1 SK4 240 B
Gladstone Gr SK4 240 A
Gladstone Rd
Altrincham WA14 238 D
Broughton CH4 139 A
Chester CH1 118 A
Neston CH64 66 C
Gladstone St Crewe CW1 190 E
Northwich CW8 103 C
Warrington WA2 16 A
8 Widnes WA8 23 A
Willaston (nr Nantwich) CW5 205 E
Winsford CW7 149 E
Gladstone Way WA12 2 A
Gladville Dr SK8 240 A
Glaisdale Cl CW2 206 A
Glamis Cl Chester CH3 119 A
Wistaston CW2 205 C
Glan Aber Pk CH4 141 A
Glanaber Ct CH4 141 A
Glandon Dr SK8 35 E
Glanvor Rd SK3 240 C
Glastonbury Ave
Bramhall SK8 35 E
Chester CH2 118 C
Golborne WA3 4 E
Glastonbury Cl WA7 24 C
Glastonbury Dr
Middlewich CW10 128 A
Poynton SK12 36 E
Glaswen Gr SK5 240
Glazebrook La WA3 11 A
Glazebrook St WA1 16
Glazebrook Sta WA3 11 A
Glazebury CE Prim Sch WA3 5
Glaziers La WA3 4
Gleadmere WA8 12
Gleave Av SK10 88 A
Gleave Rd Burtonwood WA5 6 C
Weaverham CW8 77
Gleave St M33 242
Glebe Ave WA4 17
Glebe Cl CW5 220 A
Glebe Farm Mews CH2 71 C
Glebe Green Dr CW7 149

Glebe La WA8 13 A3
Glebe Mdws CH2 96 C1
Glebe Rd CW8 102 A2
Glebe St ST7 194 B1
Glebe The WA7 23 C1
Glebecroft Ave CH2 72 A2
Glebeland WA3 4 C1
Glebelands Rd
Knutsford WA16 57 A1
Sale M33 242 A8
Glebeway Rd CH65 70 C3
Gledhall St SK15 242 D2
Glen Aber Dr CH4 140 C4
Glen Ave M33 242 A8
Glen Cl WA3 11 A1
Glen Maye M33 242 C6
Glen Rd CH66 69 B2
Glen The Blacon CH1 117 C3
Runcorn WA7 49 C3
Glenathol Rd CH66 69 B2
Glenbourne Pk SK7 35 B3
Glenburn Ave CH62 43 C2
Glencoe Cl CW4 130 B1
Glencoe Rd CH66 69 B2
Glencourse Rd WA8 13 A3
Glendale Ave Elton CH2 72 A2
Hawarden CH5 116 A2
Glendale Bsns Pk CH5 116 A2
Glendale Cl
Buerton CW3 230 C2
Wistaston CW2 189 B2
Glendale Pk CH5 116 A2
Glendene Ave SK7 35 B3
Glendyke Rd CH66 69 B2
Gleneagles Cl
Bramhall SK7 36 A4
Chester CH3 119 A2
Wilmslow SK9 60 B4
Gleneagles Dr
Haydock WA11 1 A3
Holmes Chapel CW4 130 A1
Macclesfield SK10 87 B2
Widnes WA8 13 A3
Winsford CW7 126 B1
Gleneagles Rd
Ellesmere Port CH66 69 B2
Gatley SK8 239 C1
Glenesk Rd CH66 69 B2
Glenfield WA14 238 B4
Glenfield Dr SK12 36 B2
Glenfield Rd SK4 240 D8
Glenholme Rd SK7 35 B4
Glenlea Dr M20 239 B8
Glenmaye Rd CH66 69 B2
Glenmere Rd M20 239 C8
Glenn Pl WA8 12 C1
Glenorchy Cl CW4 130 B1
Glenside Cl CH1 117 B3
Glenside Dr SK9 60 B3
Glent View SK15 242 D4
Glenthorn Gr M33 242 B5
Glenton Pk CH64 66 C3
Glenville Cl WA7 49 A3
Glenville Way M34 241 A6
Glenville Wlk SK15 242 D1
Glenwood WA7 24 B1
Glenwood Cl 3 CH66 69 B3
Glenwood Gdns CH66 69 B3
Glenwood Rd CH66 69 B3
Gleyve WA16 29 B3
Gloucester Ave 2 WA3 3 A4
Gloucester Cl
Ellesmere Port CH66 94 C4
Macclesfield SK10 87 C2
Warrington WA1 17 B4
Gloucester Rd Gatley SK8 34 B4
Kidsgrove ST7 194 C1
Knutsford WA16 81 C4
Poynton SK12 36 B2
Widnes WA8 13 A2
Gloucester St
Chester CH2 237 B4
Stockport SK3 240 D3
Glover Dr SK14 241 E6
Glover Rd WA3 9 B2
Glover St Crewe CW1 190 A3
Newton-le-W WA12 2 B2
Glovers Loom CH3 142 A4
Gloverstone Ct CH4 237 B1
Glyn Ave CH62 43 C4
Goathland Way SK11 112 B3
Goddard Rd WA7 23 C2
Goddard St CW1 190 A3
Godfrey St WA2 16 B4
Godley Ct SK14 241 F6
Godley Prim Sch SK14 241 F7
Godley St SK14 241 F8
Godscroft La WA6 73 C3
Godshill Cl WA5 14 B4
Godstall La CH1 237 B2
Godstow WA7 24 C2
Godward Rd SK22 39 A4
Golborne Cty Prim Sch
WA3 3 A4
Golborne Dale Rd WA12 3 A3
Golborne Rd Golborne WA3 3 B4
Winwick WA12,WA2 8 A4
Golborne St
Newton-le-W WA12 2 C2
Warrington WA1 16 A3
Gold Triangle Complex
WA8 22 B3
Goldborne La WA16 28 C1
Goldcliffe Cl WA5 7 B2
Goldcrest Cl Crewe CW1 189 C4
Runcorn WA7 49 C3
Winsford CW7 149 B3
Golden Sq WA1 16 A3
Goldfinch Cl CW12 156 C1
Goldfinch Dr ST7 193 A2
Goldfinch La WA3 9 C2
Goldford La SY14 199 C3
Goldsmith Dr CW11 174 B3
Golf Rd Altrincham WA15 238 F3
Sale M33 242 F6
Golftyn Dr CH5 91 B1
Golftyn La CH5 91 B1
Gongar La CH3 98 C1
Gonsley Cl CH2 237 B4
Gonville Ave SK11 112 C2
Gooch Dr WA12 2 B1
Goodall St SK11 112 C4
Goodall's Cnr CW2 206 B2
Goodier St M33 242 A6
Goodrington Rd SK9 34 C2
Goodwood Cl
Barnton CW8 78 A2
Chester CH1 118 A1
Goodwood Gr CH66 69 B2
Goodwood Rise CW10 128 A1
Goose Gn WA14 238 D4
Goose La WA4 26 A1
Gooseberry La
Kelsall CW6 122 C2
Runcorn WA7 24 B1
Goosebrook Cl CW9 78 B4
Goosebrook La WA4,CW9 52 C1
Goosetrey Cl SK9 34 C1
Goostrey Com Prim Sch
CW4 130 C4
Goostrey Com Prim Sch (The
Annexe) CW4 107 C1
Goostrey Ct 4 CW12 156 C2
Goostrey La CW4 130 A4
Goostrey Sta CW4 131 A4
Gordale Cl
Congleton CW12 157 A3
Warrington WA5 14 C4
Gordon Ave
Bebington CH62 43 C4
Haydock WA11 1 C4
Sale M33 242 B8
Warrington WA1 17 A4
Gordon La CH1 95 A3
Gordon St
Ashton-u-Lyne OL6 242 A4
Hyde SK14 241 E6
Stalybridge SK15 242 E1
Stockport SK4 240 E7
Gordon Terr SK15 242 D2
Gore La SK9 59 B2
Gorse Bank Rd WA15 32 B4
Gorse Cl WA6 101 A3
Gorse Covert CW9 79 B2
Gorse Covert Prim Sch
WA3 10 A3
Gorse Covert Rd WA3 10 A3
Gorse Hall Dr SK15 242 C1
Gorse Hall Prim Sch
SK15 242 D1
Gorse La CW12 178 B3
Gorse Sq M31 11 B2
Gorse Stacks CH1 237 B3
Gorse The WA14 31 A4
Gorse Way CH3 142 A3
Gorsefield CH3 166 A1
Gorsefield Ave CH62 43 B3
Gorsefield Cl CH62 43 B3
Gorsefield Hey SK9 60 C4
Gorselands SK8 35 A3
Gorsewood Prim Sch
WA7 50 B4
Gorsewood Rd WA7 50 B3
Gorsey Bank Cres CW5 220 A4
Gorsey Bank Prim Sch
SK9 59 C4
Gorsey Bank Rd SK3 240 B4
Gorsey Brow SK6 241 A2
Gorsey La
Altrincham WA14 238 B5
Partington WA13 20 A4
St Helens WA5,WA9 6 B3
Warrington WA1,WA2 16 B4
Widnes WA8 13 C1
Gorsey Rd SK9 59 C4
Gorseywell La WA7 50 C3
Gorsley Cl CW10 151 B3
Gorstage La CW8 102 B4
Gorsthills Com Prim Sch
CH66 69 B2
Gorston Wlk M22 33 B4
Gorsty Hill Cl CW2 207 C1
Gosberryhole La CW12 158 A1
Gosforth Ct WA7 49 C4
Gosforth Pl CH2 118 C2
Gosling Cl WA4 26 A1
Gosling Rd WA3 9 A4
Gosling Way CW12 156 A2
Gosport Cl WA2 8 C1
Goss St CH1 237 A2
Gotherage Cl SK6 241 E2
Gotherage La SK6 241 E2
Gothic Cl SK6 241 F2
Gough Ave WA2 8 A1
Gough St SK3 240 D5
Gough's La WA16 82 B4
Goulden St Crewe CW1 190 A3
Warrington WA5 15 C3
Goulders Ct WA7 50 A3
Gourham Dr SK8 239 F2
Gower Rd Hyde SK14 241 D5
Stockport SK4 240 D8
Gowy Cl Alsager ST7 192 C2
Sandbach CW11 174 C4
Wilmslow SK9 34 C1
Gowy Cres CH3 121 A1
Gowy Ct Alpraham CW6 169 C1
Ellesmere Port CH66 69 C4
Gowy Rd CH2 96 C1
Gowy Wlk CW7 127 A2
Goyt Pl SK23 65 C4
Goyt Rd Disley SK12 38 B3
New Mills SK22 39 B3
Goyt Valley Ind Est SK23 39 B2
Goyt View SK22 39 A3
Grace Ave WA2 16 A4
Grace Cl CW1 191 B2
Gradbach Mill* SK17 138 A1
Gradwell St SK3 240 D4
Grafton Mall 5 WA14 238 D4
Grafton Mews CH2 237 B4
Grafton Rd CH65 70 B4
Grafton St
Altrincham WA14 238 D4
Ashton-u-Lyne OL6 242 A2
Hyde SK14 241 D7
Newton-le-W WA12 2 A2
Stockport SK4 240 E7
Warrington WA5 15 C3
Graham Ave CH66 69 B3
Graham Cl WA8 12 B1
Graham Cres M44 11 B2
Graham Dr Disley SK12 38 B3
Halewood L26 21 A4
Graham Rd Blacon CH1 117 C2
Widnes WA8 22 B4
Grainger's Rd CW9 103 C3
Grammar School Ct WA4 16 C2
Grammar School Rd
Lymm WA13 18 C1
Warrington WA4 16 C2
Grampian Way
Bebington CH62 43 C2
Neston CH64 66 C3
Winsford CW7 149 A4
Granby Cl WA7 50 B3
Granby Rd Cheadle SK8 35 A4
Warrington WA4 26 A4
Grand Junction Ret Pk
CW1 190 B2
Grandford La CW5 217 B1
Granford Cl WA14 238 D7
Grange Ave Barnton CW8 78 A2
Cheadle SK8 239 F3
Denton M34 241 B6
Warrington WA4 16 C2
Grange Cl Crewe CW1 190 C2
Golborne WA3 3 B3
Hyde SK14 241 F5
Sandbach CW11 174 C4
Grange Comp Sch The
WA7 23 B1
Grange Cres CH66 44 A1
Grange Ct
Altrincham WA14 238 C1
Biddulph ST8 179 B1
11 Knutsford WA16 57 A1
Winsford CW7 126 A1
Grange Dr Hartford CW8 103 A3
Thornton Hough CH63 42 A4
Warrington WA5 15 A2
Widnes WA8 12 B1
Grange Farm Cl WA5 15 B3
Grange Green Manor
WA4 25 C4
Grange Inf Sch The WA7 23 B1
Grange Jun Sch The
Hartford CW8 103 A3
Runcorn WA7 23 B1
Grange La Tilston SY14 198 C2
Weaverham CW8 102 A4
Whitegate CW8 125 C4
Winsford CW7 126 A2
Grange Lea CW10 128 A1
Grange Park Ave
Cheadle SK8 239 D5
Runcorn WA7 23 B1
Wilmslow SK9 60 A4
Grange Park Rd SK8 239 D5
Grange Pk Dr ST8 179 C2
Grange Pl M44 11 B3
Grange Prim Sch CW7 126 A1
Grange Rd
Altrincham WA14 238 C1
Ashton CH3 99 A1
Barnton CW8 78 A2
Biddulph ST8 179 C2
Chester CH3 119 B1
Chester, Bache CH2 118 B2
Cuddington CW8 101 C1
Ellesmere Port CH65 70 B2
Haydock WA11 1 B3
Macclesfield SK11 112 B3
Northwich, Rudheath CW9 104 B3
Runcorn WA7 23 B1
Sale M33 242 A6
Grange Rd N Hyde SK14 241 F6
Runcorn WA7 23 B1
Grange Rd W CH3 119 B1
Grange Sch The CW8 103 A3
Grange The
Hartford CW8 103 A3
Hyde SK14 241 F5
Macclesfield SK11 112 A3
Grange Valley WA11 1 B3
Grange Valley Prim Sch
WA11 1 B3
Grange Villas CH3 142 C3
Grange Way CW11 174 C4
Grangebrook Dr CW7 126 B2
Grangefields ST8 179 C2
Grangelands SK10 86 C1
Grangemoor WA7 49 B4
Grangeside CH2 118 B4
Grangeway Runcorn WA7 49 B4
Wilmslow SK9 34 B2
Grangeway Ct WA7 49 B4
Grangewood Dr SK11 83 C2
Granston Cl WA5 7 C1
Grant Cl WA5 7 B1
Grant Rd WA5 15 A3
Grantham Ave
Warrington WA1 16 C4
Warrington, Walton WA4 26 A4
Grantham Cl CW9 104 B4
Grantham Rd SK4 240 C6
Granville Dr CH66 69 A4
Granville Rd
Chester CH1 118 A2
Northwich CW9 104 A3
Stockport SK8 240 C1
Wilmslow SK9 59 C3
Granville Sq CW7 149 C4
Granville St
Ashton-u-Lyne OL6 242 A2
Runcorn WA7 23 A2
Warrington WA1 16 B3
Winsford CW7 149 C4
Grapes St SK11 112 B4
Grappenhall Hall Sch
WA4 17 A1
Grappenhall Heys Com Prim
Sch WA4 27 A4
Grappenhall La WA4 27 C3
Grappenhall Rd
Ellesmere Port CH65 69 C2
Warrington WA4 16 B1
Grappenhall St Wilfred's CE
Prim Sch WA4 17 A1
Grasmere SK11 111 C3
Grasmere Ave
Congleton CW12 155 C1
Crewe CW2 189 C3
Warrington WA2 8 C2
Grasmere Cl
Stalybridge SK15 242 D4
Winsford CW7 126 B1
Grasmere Cres SK7 35 C4
Grasmere Dr
Holmes Chapel CW4 130 A2
Runcorn WA7 49 B3
Grasmere Rd
Alderley Edge SK9 60 A1
Chester CH2 118 C3
Ellesmere Port CH65 70 B1
Frodsham WA6 74 B4
Gatley SK8 239 B3
9 Lymm WA13 18 C2
Neston CH64 66 C3
Partington M31 11 C2
Grason Ave SK9 34 B1
Grasscroft Rd SK15 242 D1
Grassfield Way WA16 82 A4
Grassmoor Cl CH62 43 C4
Grassygreen La ST7 209 C1
Gratrix La M33 242 F5
Gratrix Rd CH62 43 B4
Gravel La SK9 59 C3
Graveyard La WA16 58 C3
Gray Ave WA11 1 B3
Gray's Cl ST7 195 A4
Graylag Cl WA7 49 C3
Graymarsh Dr SK12 36 C1
Graysands Rd WA15 238 F3
Greasby Dr CH66 69 C2
Great Ashfield WA8 12 B2
Great Budworth CE Prim Sch
CW9 79 A4
Great Delph WA11 1 B4
Great Egerton St SK1 240 E6
Great King St SK11 112 B4
Great Norbury St SK14 241 D6
Great Portwood St SK1 240 F6
Great Queen St SK11 112 B4
Great Riding WA7 50 B4
Great Sankey High Sch
WA5 14 C4
Great Sankey L Ctr WA5 14 C4
Great Sankey Prim Sch
WA5 15 A3
Great Underbank SK1 240 F5
Greatoak Rd ST7 209 C2
Greave SK6 241 D4
Greave Fold SK6 241 D4
Greave Prim Sch SK6 241 D4
Greaves La SY14 222 C3
Greaves Lane E SY14 222 C4
Greaves Rd SK9 59 C4
Grebe Cl Knutsford WA16 57 A2
Poynton SK12 36 A2
Greeba Ave WA4 16 A2
Greek St Runcorn WA7 22 C2
Stockport SK3 240 E4
Green Acre Cl WA16 82 A4
Green Ave
Alpraham CW6 169 B2
Barnton CW8 78 A2
Davenham CW9 103 C2
Green Bank
Adderley TF9 235 A3
Chester CH4 141 C3
Green Bridge Cl WA7 24 A1
Green Cl SK8 239 A6
Green Coppice WA7 50 B4
Green Courts WA14 238 B3
Green Croft SK6 241 E3
Green Dr Alsager ST7 193 B2
Handforth SK9 34 B1
Green End Farm CH4 139 B1
Green Farm CH4 163 A1
Green Gables Cl SK8 239 B1
Green Hall Mews SK9 60 A3
Green Hill St SK3 240 D3
Green Hill Terr SK3 240 D3
Green Jones Brow WA5 6 C3
Green La Acton CW5 204 A2
Appleton Thorn WA4 27 A3
Audlem CW3 229 C1
Barbridge CW5 187 A4
Bollington SK10 63 A1
Burtonwood WA5 6 C4
Chester CH3 119 A2
Chester, Lache CH4 140 C2
Davenham CW9 103 C2
Disley SK12 38 B2
Ellesmere Port CH65 70 B2
Ellesmere Port, Great Sutton
CH66 69 B2
High Lane SK12 37 B2
Higher Kinnerton CH4 161 A3
Higher Wincham CW9 79 C2
Irlam M44 11 C3
Kelsall CW6 122 B2
Knutsford WA16 56 B2
Lindow End SK9 84 C4
Peover WA16 83 B1
Picton CH2 96 B2
Plumley WA16 80 C3
Romiley SK6 241 B2
Sandbach CW11 173 C4
Saughall CH1 117 B4
Shocklach SY14 211 B4
Stockport SK4 240 B7
Stockport SK4 240 C6
Stockport SK4 240 D5
Tattenhall CH3 182 C3
Tilston SY14 212 A4
Warrington WA1 17 A4
Widnes WA8 12 C1
Willaston (nr Nantwich)
CW5 205 C3
Wilmslow SK9 60 A4
Winwick WA2 8 A4
Green La E CH5 116 B4
Green La W CH5 93 A2
Green Lake La CH3 163 C2
Green Lane Cl WA2 8 A4
Green Lane Com Specl Sch
WA1 17 A4
Green Lane Est CH5 116 B4
Green Lane Ind Est SK4 240 C5
Green Lawns Dr CH66 94 C4
Green Mdws Golborne WA3 3 C3
Macclesfield SK11 111 C3
Green Oaks Path WA8 23 B4
Green Oaks Way WA8 23 B4
Green Pk CW8 102 C4
Green Rd M31 11 C2
Green St
3 Alderley Edge SK9 60 A1
Holt LL13 180 C1
Hyde SK14 241 E5
Knutsford WA16 57 A1
Macclesfield SK11 112 C4
Sandbach CW11 175 A4
Stockport SK3 240 F2
Warrington WA5 15 C3
Green The Cheadle SK8 34 C4
Congleton CW12 156 B1
Ellesmere Port CH65 70 A1
Hale L24 21 B1
Handforth SK9 34 C2
Hartford CW8 103 A3
Harthill CH3 183 C2
Higher Kinnerton CH4 161 A4
Lawton-gate ST7 194 A2
Middlewich CW10 151 B3
Neston CH64 66 B4
Neston, Little Neston CH64 66 C3
Partington M31 11 C2
Stockport SK4 240 C6
Tarvin CH3 121 C1
Thornton Hough CH63 42 B2
Green Tree Gdns SK6 241 B2
Green View WA13 19 A3
Green Villa Pk SK9 59 C2
Green Way CH1 94 A1
Green Wlk
Altrincham WA14 238 B3
Cuddington CW8 102 A2
Gatley SK8 239 A6
Partington M31 11 C2
Greenacre SK8 34 B4
Greenacre Dr CH63 43 B4
Greenacre Rd CH4 140 C2
Greenacres Crewe CW1 190 B3
Duddon CW6 145 A3
Frodsham WA6 74 B3
Sandbach CW11 175 A4
Chester CH2 95 C1
Greenacres Cl WA3,WN7 4 A4
Greenacres Rd CW12 155 C1
Greenacres The WA13 19 A2
Greenall Ave WA5 14 B2
Greenall Rd CW9 104 A4
Greenall's Ave WA4 16 B1
Greenbank Ave
Ellesmere Port CH66 69 B4
Gatley SK8 239 A5
Greenbank Cl CW5 205 B3
Greenbank Dr SK10 88 A4
Greenbank Gdns WA4 16 C1
Greenbank La CW8 103 B3
Greenbank Pk CW11 175 A1
Greenbank Rd
Chester CH2 119 A2
Gatley SK8 239 A6

Greenbank Rd *continued*
Warrington WA4 16 C1
Greenbank Residential Sch CW8 103 B3
Greenbank St WA4 16 B1
Greenbank Sta CW8 103 B3
Greenbridge Rd WA7 24 A1
Greencourts Bsns Pk M22 34 A4
Greendale Dr
Middlewich CW10 151 A4
Newcastle-u-L ST5 210 B1
Greendale Gdns CW1 190 C3
Greendale La SK10 86 B4
Greenfield Ave CH4 161 A4
Greenfield Cl
New Mills SK22 39 A4
Newton-le-W WA12 2 B2
Stockport SK3 240 E2
Greenfield Cres
Chester CH2 119 A3
Waverton CH3 143 A3
Greenfield Gdns CH2 72 A2
Greenfield Ind Est CW12 156 A2
Greenfield La
Chester CH2 119 A3
Frodsham WA6 49 A1
Greenfield Prim Sch SK14 241 E6
Greenfield Rd
Bollington SK10 88 A4
Broughton CH4 139 B2
Congleton CW12 156 A2
Ellesmere Port CH66 69 A4
Waverton CH3 143 A3
Greenfield St SK14 241 D6
Greenfield Way CW8 102 A2
Greenfields Chester CH2 95 C1
Winsford CW7 127 A1
Greenfields Ave
Bebington CH62 43 B4
Shavington CW2 206 A2
Warrington WA4 26 B4
Greenfields Cl
Neston CH64 66 C3
Warrington WA1 17 B4
Greenfields Cres CH62 43 B4
Greenfields Croft CH64 66 C3
Greenfields Dr CH64 66 C3
Greenfields La SY14 213 A2
Greenfields Lodge CH3 120 B3
Greenfields Prim Sch CW7 126 A1
Greenfields Rd ST7 193 C2
Greengate WA15 32 B4
Greengate Rd Hyde M34 241 A8
Lawton-gate ST7 193 C3
Greengates Cres CH64 66 C3
Greenhalgh St SK4 240 E6
Greenhaven Ct CW5 219 C3
Greenhead Fold SK6 241 A1
Greenhill Ave M33 242 A8
Greenhill La WA4 52 A3
Greenhill Wlk SK12 38 B3
Greenhills Cl SK11 112 C4
Greenhouse Farm Rd WA7 50 A4
Greenhythe Rd SK8 34 B3
Greenland Cl CW6 146 B1
Greenlands CH3 166 A2
Greenlands Cl 3 SK8 34 C4
Greenlaw Cl CW9 104 A3
Greenlea Cl CH65 70 A1
Greenoaks Farm Ind Est WA8 23 B4
Greenore Dr L24 21 B1
Greenshall La SK12 38 C3
Greenshank Cl WA12 2 B2
Greenside SK4 240 A5
Greenside Ave WA6 74 B4
Greenside Ct CW9 105 B3
Greenside Dr
Altrincham WA14 238 E1
Lostock Green CW9 105 A4
Greensway CH4 141 A4
Greenvale Dr SK8 239 C6
Greenview Dr M20 239 C8
Greenway Alsager ST7 193 A3
Altrincham WA14 238 A5
Bramhall SK7 35 B3
Congleton CW12 156 A2
Crewe CW1 190 B4
Farndon CH3 180 C1
Hyde SK14 241 D5
Romiley SK6 241 E1
Tilston SY14 198 B2
Warrington WA4 26 B4
Warrington, Great Sankey WA5 14 C4
Warrington, Paddington WA1 16 C4
Wilmslow SK9 60 A3
Greenway Cl Helsby WA6 73 A2
Rode Heath ST7 193 C4
Greenway Dr CW9 104 B4
Greenway Rd
Biddulph ST8 179 C1
Gatley SK8 34 B3
Runcorn WA7 23 A1
Sale WA15 238 F8
Speke L24 21 A2
Widnes WA8 13 A1
Greenway St CH4 237 B1
Greenway Wlk CW9 104 B4
Greenways ST7 209 C1
Greenwell Rd WA11 1 B3
Greenwich Ave WA8 13 B2
Greenwood Ave
Chester CH4 141 B4
Congleton CW12 156 C2
Greenwood Cl
Culcheth WA3 4 C1
Weaverham CW8 77 B1
Greenwood Cres WA2 8 C1
Greenwood Dr
Newton-le-W WA12 2 B1
Runcorn WA7 24 C2
Wilmslow SK9 60 B4
Greenwood Rd WA13 18 C1
Greenwood St 1 WA14 238 D4
Greenwood Terr WA16 58 A2
Greg Ave SK10 87 C4
Greg Mews SK9 34 A1
Gregory Ave SK6 241 C1
Gregory Cl WA5 15 B4
Gregson Rd WA8 13 B1
Grenfell Cl CH64 41 B1
Grenfell Pk CH64 41 B1
Grenfell St 11 WA8 23 A4
Grenville Cl CW1 191 B3
Grenville Cres CH63 43 B4
Grenville Rd CH64 41 C1
Grenville St SK3 240 D4
Grenville Terr OL6 242 A2
Gresford Ave CH2 237 C4
Gresford Cl WA5 7 C1
Gresley Way ST7 209 C1
Gresty Green Rd CW2 206 B4
Gresty La CW2 206 A4
Gresty Rd CW2 190 B1
Gresty Road Football Gd (Crewe Alexandra FC) CW2 190 B1
Gresty Terr CW1 190 C2
Greta Ave SK8 34 B3
Greville Dr CW7 127 A1
Grey Cl SK6 241 A4
Grey Friars CH1 237 A2
Grey Rd WA14 238 C5
Grey St Stalybridge SK15 242 F1
Warrington WA1 16 B3
Greyhound Park Rd CH1 117 C2
Greyhound Pk CH1 118 A1
Greyhound Rd SK10 86 A3
Greylands Rd M20 239 C8
Greymist Ave WA1 17 B4
Greys Ct WA1 9 B1
Greystoke Ave M33 242 B5
Greystoke Dr SK9 60 A1
Greystoke Rd SK10 87 C1
Greystone Pk CW1 190 B2
Greystone Rd WA5 14 C2
Greystones CH66 69 B2
Greystones Rd CH3 119 B1
Grice St WA4 16 B1
Griffin Cl Blacon CH1 117 C3
New Mills SK22 39 B3
Norton in Hales TF9 236 B1
Griffin Mews WA8 13 A2
Griffith Ave WA3 9 C3
Griffiths Dr CW9 104 B3
Griffiths Rd
Lostock Gralam CW9 79 C1
Northwich CW9 104 C4
Griffiths St WA4 16 C2
Grig Pl ST7 193 B3
Grimsditch La WA4 52 A3
Grimshaw Ave SK10 88 A4
Grimshaw Cl SK6 241 A4
Grimshaw La SK10 88 A4
Grindley Bank CH2 119 C4
Grindley Gdns CH65 70 B1
Grisedale Ave WA2 8 A2
Grisedale Cl WA7 49 C3
Grisedale Rd CH62 43 C4
Grisedale Way SK11 112 A3
Gritstone Dr SK11 112 A4
Grizedale WA8 12 A1
Grizedale Cl CW2 189 B1
Grizedale Rd SK6 241 B4
Groarke Dr WA5 14 B3
Groby Ct WA14 238 C4
Groby Pl WA14 238 D5
Groby Rd
Altrincham WA14 238 C4
Crewe CW1 190 C4
Groby St SK15 242 F1
Grosvenor Ave
Alsager ST7 193 B3
3 Golborne WA3 3 B4
Hartford CW8 103 A2
Warrington WA1 16 C4
Grosvenor Cl
Warrington WA5 15 B3
Wilmslow SK9 60 A2
Grosvenor Cres SK14 241 C5
Grosvenor Ct
Cheadle SK8 239 D6
Chester CH1 237 C2
Winsford CW7 149 B4
Grosvenor Dr SK12 36 B2
Grosvenor Gdns
Newton-le-W WA12 2 B1
Stalybridge SK15 242 D1
Grosvenor Grange WA1 9 A1
Grosvenor Ho SK15 242 D1
Grosvenor Mus* CH4 237 A1
Grosvenor Nuffield Hospl CH4 141 B3
Grosvenor Pk Rd CH2 237 C2
Grosvenor Pk Terr CH2 237 C2
Grosvenor Pl CH4 237 B1
Grosvenor Rd
Altrincham WA14 238 E5
Chester CH4 141 B4
Congleton CW12 156 A2
Haydock WA11 1 A4
Hyde SK14 241 D5
Stockport SK4 240 B7
Tarvin CH3 121 A1
Widnes WA8 13 A3
Grosvenor Sh Ctr The CH1 237 B2
Grosvenor Sq M33 242 A6
Grosvenor St
Chester CH1 237 A2
Crewe CW1 190 A3
6 Macclesfield SK11 112 B4
Runcorn WA7 23 A2
Stalybridge SK15 242 D1
9 Stockport SK1 240 F4
Winsford CW7 149 C4
Grotsworth La SY14 214 C4
Grotto La WA16 108 A4
Grounds St WA2 16 A4
Grove Arc SK9 60 A1
Grove Ave Chester CH3 119 A2
Kidsgrove ST7 194 C1
Lawton-gate ST7 194 A2
Lostock Gralam CW9 80 A2
Lymm WA13 18 B2
Wilmslow SK9 60 A4
Grove Cl CW7 149 A4
Grove Cres CW3 232 B1
Grove Ct Alsager ST7 193 C2
Lymm WA13 18 B2
Sale M33 242 D6
Grove Gdns CH3 119 C1
Grove Ho SK8 35 A3
Grove La SK7,SK8 35 A3
Grove Park Ave ST7 194 A2
Grove Pk WA16 57 A1
Grove Rd
Altrincham WA15 238 E3
Backford CH1 94 C2
Grove Rise WA13 18 C2
Grove St New Mills SK22 39 A4
Runcorn WA7 22 C2
Stalybridge SK16 242 A1
Warrington WA4 16 B2
Wilmslow SK9 60 A4
Grove Terr WA6 73 B2
Grove The Bramhall SK8 35 A3
Knutsford WA16 57 B2
Lawton-gate ST7 194 A2
Lymm WA13 18 C2
Sale M33 242 B5
Stockport SK3 240 E3
Warrington WA5 14 C2
Grove Way SK9 60 A4
Grovemount CW9 103 C1
Groves The Chester CH1 237 B2
Ellesmere Port CH1 95 A4
Tarporley CW6 146 B1
GroveThe SY13 225 C1
Grovewood Mews SK11 112 B3
Grub La CW6 122 B3
Grundy Cl WA8 12 C2
Grundy St WA3 3 A4
Guardian Ct M33 242 A7
Guardian St WA5 15 C3
Guernsey Cl
Congleton CW12 157 A1
Middlewich CW10 128 B1
Warrington WA4 26 B4
Guernsey Dr CH65 70 B1
Guernsey Ho CH2 119 A3
Guernsey Rd WA8 13 C2
Guest St WA8 23 A4
Guests Slack WA6 100 A4
Guilden Gn CH3 119 C2
Guilden Sutton CE Prim Sch CH3 119 C3
Guilden Sutton La CH3 119 B3
Guildford Ave SK8 35 A3
Guildford Cl WA2 9 A1
Guildford Rd CH4 140 C3
Guillemot Cl CW1 190 C3
Gull Cl SK12 36 A2
Gullane Cl SK10 87 A2
Gullet The CW5 204 C3
Gullivers World Theme Pk* WA5 7 C1
Gulls Way CH60 40 C4
Gunco La
Macclesfield SK11 112 C3
Prestbury SK10 87 B4
Gunn Gr CH64 66 C4
Gutterscroft CW1 191 B3
Gutticar Rd WA8 12 A1
Guy La CH3 143 B3
Guywood Cotts SK6 241 C3
Guywood La SK6 241 C3
Gypsey Cnr SY13 224 C1

H

Hack Green Secret Nuclear Bunker* CW5 218 B2
Hackberry Cl WA14 238 B8
Hacked Way La SK11 113 C3
Haddon Cl
Alderley Edge SK9 59 C1
High Lane SK6 37 C3
Holmes Chapel CW4 130 A2
Macclesfield SK11 112 A3
Wistaston CW2 206 A4
Haddon Dr WA8 12 B2
Haddon Gr
Altrincham WA15 238 F7
Sale M33 242 A6
Haddon Ho 4 CH64 66 C4
Haddon La CH64 67 B2
Haddon Rd Burton CH64 67 B1
Gatley SK8 34 B4
Hadfield Cl WA8 13 C1
Hadfield St CW9 79 A1
Hadleigh Cl WA5 14 C3
Hadley Ave CH62 43 B4
Hadley Cl SK8 239 F1
Hadlow La CH64 67 C4
Hadlow Rd CH64 67 C3
Hadrian Dr CH1 117 C3
Hadrian Way
Cuddington CW8 102 A1
Middlewich CW10 128 B1
Hafod Cl Blacon CH1 117 B2
Connah's Quay CH5 91 B1
Hag Bank La SK12 38 B4
Hague Bar Prim Sch SK22 38 C4
Hague Bar Rd SK22 39 A4
Hague Fold Rd SK22 38 C4
Hague Pl SK15 242 D2
Hague St OL6 242 A4
Haig Ave Irlam M44 11 B2
Warrington WA5 15 A3
Haig Ct WA16 57 B2
Haig Rd Knutsford WA16 57 B2
Widnes WA8 13 A1
Haigh Lawn WA14 238 B3
Hale Ave SK12 36 B1
Hale Bank Rd WA8 21 C3
Hale Bank Terr WA8 22 A2
Hale CE Prim Sch L24 21 C1
Hale Ct WA14 238 D2
Hale Gate Rd Hale WA8 21 C2
Widnes WA8 22 A2
Hale Gr WA5 15 A3
Hale Low Rd WA15 238 F3
Hale Prep Sch WA15 238 E3
Hale Rd Altrincham WA15 32 B4
Hale L24 21 A1
Stockport SK4 240 C7
Widnes WA8 22 B4
Widnes, Ditton WA8 22 B4
Hale Road Ind Est WA8 22 A2
Hale St WA2 16 A4
Hale Sta WA14 238 D2
Hale View WA7 48 C4
Hale View Rd WA6 73 B2
Halebank CE Prim Sch WA8 22 A3
Halewood Lane Ends L26 21 A4
Haley Rd N WA5 6 C3
Haley Rd S WA5 6 C3
Half St SK11 112 B3
Halfacre La WA4 17 C1
Halghton La LL13 222 A1
Halifax Cl WA2 8 B1
Halkett Cl CH4 140 C3
Halkyn Rd CH2 237 C4
Hall Ave Altrincham WA15 238 F7
Widnes WA8 12 A1
Hall Bank WA16 58 B2
Hall Bank N WA16 58 B2
Hall Bank S WA16 58 B2
Hall Cl SK10 87 B2
Hall Dr Alsager ST7 193 B2
Marston CW9 79 A3
Warrington WA4 26 B3
Willaston (nr Nantwich) CW5 205 B3
Hall Gr Cheadle SK8 239 C6
Macclesfield SK10 87 B2
Hall Hill SK10 87 C4
Hall La Antrobus CW9 53 A1
Appleton Thorn WA4 27 A4
Audlem CW3 230 B4
Brown Knowl CH3 199 B4
Cronton WA8,L35 12 B4
Daresbury WA4 25 B1
Haughton CW6 186 B3
Higher Wincham CW9 79 C2
Kelsall CW6 122 B3
Little Leigh CW9 77 C4
Mobberley WA16 58 B2
Newton-le-W WA5 7 A4
Partington M31 11 C2
Pickmere WA16 55 A1
Sandbach CW11 174 A3
St Helens WA9 6 A2
Stretton WA4 52 C4
Sutton Lane Ends SK11 112 C2
Utkinton CW6 146 B3
Warmingham CW11 173 C2
Winsford CW7 149 A2
Hall La The CW6 147 B1
Hall Mdw SK8 239 E1
Hall Moss La SK7 35 B2
Hall Nook WA5 14 C2
Hall O'shaw St CW1 190 C2
Hall Rd Altrincham WA14 238 C1
Handforth SK9 34 C2
Haydock WA11 1 C4
Warrington WA1 17 B4
Wilmslow SK9 60 A4
Hall St Ashton-u-Lyne OL6 242 B2
Audley ST7 209 B1
Cheadle SK8 239 D6
Denton SK14 241 B7
Macclesfield SK11 112 B4
New Mills SK22 39 A4
Warrington WA1 16 B3
Hall Terr WA5 14 C4
Hall View CH3 166 A1
Hall View Cl CW8 102 A4
Hall Wood Ave WA11 1 C4
Halla Way WA4 16 C2
Hallastone Rd WA6 73 A2
Hallcroft M31 11 C2
Hallcroft Pl WA4 17 A1
Hallefield Cres SK11 112 C4
Hallefield Dr 6 SK11 112 C4
Hallefield Rd 7 SK11 112 C4
Hallfield Dr CH2 72 A2
Hallfield Pk CH66 69 B2
Hallfields Rd Tarvin CH3 121 B1
Warrington WA2 8 B1
Hallgate Dr SK8 239 A2
Hallgreen La CW12 155 B4
Halliday Cl WA3 9 C2
Halliwell's Brow WA16 29 A2
Hallows Ave WA2 16 B4
Hallows Cl CW6 122 B2
Hallows Dr CW6 122 B2
Hallowsgate Ct CW6 122 B2
Halls Rd Biddulph ST8 179 B1
Mow Cop ST7 195 B4
Hallsgreen La CH2 96 C4
Hallshaw Ave CW1 190 C3
Hallside Pk WA16 57 B1
Hallwood Cl WA7 49 A3
Hallwood Dr CH66 68 B2
Hallwood Link Rd WA7 49 C3
Hallwood Park Ave WA7 49 C3
Hallwood Park Prim Sch WA7 49 C3
Hallwood Rd SK9 34 B1
Halsall Ave WA2 16 B4
Halsall Cl WA7 50 B3
Halsall's Cotts WA8 21 C3
Halston Cl SK5 240 F8
Halstone Ave SK9 59 C2
Halton Brook Ave WA7 23 B1
Halton Castle* WA7 23 C1
Halton Coll of F Ed WA8 23 A4
Halton Coll of F Ed (Annexe)
Runcorn WA7 23 C2
Widnes WA8 23 A4
Halton Cres CH66 69 C1
Halton Ct WA7 23 B1
Halton Dr CW2 189 B3
Halton General Hospl WA7 49 C3
Halton Link Rd WA7 49 C4
Halton Lodge Ave WA7 49 B4
Halton Lodge Prim Sch WA7 49 B4
Halton Rd Chester CH2 118 C3
Ellesmere Port CH66 69 C1
Runcorn WA7 23 B1
Warrington WA5 14 C3
Halton St Haydock WA11 1 C3
Hyde SK14 241 F7
Halton Station Rd WA7 49 C2
Halton View Rd WA8 13 B1
Halton Way CH66 69 C1
Hamble Dr WA5 14 C2
Hamble Way SK10 86 C1
Hambledon Cl CH66 69 A3
Hambleton Cl WA8 12 B2
Hambleton Rd SK8 34 B4
Hambleton Way CW7 149 A4
Hambletts Hollow WA6 100 C3
Hamilton Ave
Hawarden CH5 116 A2
Irlam M44 11 B2
Hamilton Cl
Haslington CW1 191 B2
Macclesfield SK10 113 A4
Neston CH64 41 A1
Hamilton Cres SK4 240 B5
Hamilton Ct M33 242 B6
Hamilton Pl CH1 237 A2
Hamilton Rd
Connah's Quay CH5 91 B1
Lymm WA13 18 B2
Hamilton Sq SK4 240 E7
Hamilton St Chester CH2 118 C2
Stalybridge SK15 242 C2
Hammond Sch
Chester CH2 119 A4
Chester CH2 237 A4
Hammond St CW2 190 B2
Hamnett Ct WA3 9 C2
Hamnett St SK14 241 D7
Hamon Rd WA15 238 E4
Hampden Rd M33 242 A5
Hampshire Cl CW12 156 B2
Hampshire Rd M31 11 B1
Hampshire Wlk SK10 86 C1
Hampson Ave WA3 4 C2
Hampson Cres SK9 34 B2
Hampson St M33 242 D6
Hampstead Ct 8 CW7 149 A4
Hampton Cl Neston CH64 66 C3
Widnes WA8 13 C2
Hampton Cres
Neston CH64 66 C3
No Man's Heath SY14 214 A2
Hampton Ct WA7 24 B2
Hampton Dr Cronton WA8 12 B3
Warrington WA5 15 B2
Hampton Gdns CH65 70 A3
Hampton Gr SK8 239 E2
Hampton Rd
Chester CH4 140 C3
Irlam M44 11 B2
Hamson Dr SK10 63 A1
Hamsterley Cl WA3 10 A3
Hanbury Cl CW2 206 A4
Hancock Ct WA4 16 B2

Hancock Rd CW12 156 C2
Hand St SK11 112 A4
Handa Dr CH65 95 A4
Handbridge CH4 237 B1
Handel Mews M33 242 C6
Handford Ave CH62 43 C3
Handford Rd CH2 118 C3
Handforth Cl WA4 17 B2
Handforth La WA7 49 B3
Handforth Rd
Crewe CW2 189 C2
Handforth SK9 34 C1
Handforth Sta SK9 34 B2
Handley Cl SK3 240 C1
Handley Hill CW7 149 B4
Handley Hill Prim Sch CW7 149 A4
Handley St WA7 22 C2
Hangman's La CW9 105 B4
Hankelow Cl
Chester CH2 237 B4
Middlewich CW10 151 B3
Hankey St WA7 22 C1
Hankins Heys La CW3 231 A1
Hankinson Cl M31 11 C1
Hanley Cl Disley SK12 38 B3
Widnes WA8 12 B1
Hanley Rd WA8 12 B1
Hannah's Wlk 2 CW10 151 B4
Hanns Hall Farm CH64 67 B4
Hanns Hall Rd CH64 67 B4
Hanover Bsns Pk WA14 238 B7
Hanover Ct WA7 50 A3
Hanover Dr 2 CW7 149 B3
Hanover Rd WA14 238 B7
Hanover St
Stalybridge SK15 242 C2
Warrington WA1 16 A2
Hapsdale View WA6 72 C1
Hapsford Cl WA3 9 B2
Hapsford La
Dunham-on-t-H WA6 97 C4
Elton CH2 72 B2
Elton, Hapsford WA6 72 C1
Hapton Pl SK4 240 E7
Harbord St WA1 16 B2
Harbour Cl Chester CH2 118 C4
Runcorn WA7 50 B3
Harbour La SK11 111 B1
Harburn Wlk M22 33 C4
Harcourt Cl WA3 9 C2
Harcourt Rd
Altrincham WA14 238 D6
Sale M33 242 A8
Hardcastle Rd SK3 240 D3
Harden Pk SK9 60 A2
Harding Ave
Tattenhall CH3 166 B1
Warrington WA2 8 C1
Harding Rd Chester CH2 118 A4
Nantwich CW5 204 B2
Hardings Mdw ST7 194 C1
Hardingswood Rd ST7 194 C1
Hardknott Rd CH62 43 C4
Hardman Ave SK6 241 A3
Hardman St SK3 240 D4
Hardwick Cl SK6 37 C3
Hardwick Dr SK11 112 A3
Hardwick Grange WA1 17 C4
Hardwick Rd WA7 23 B2
Hardwicke Rd SK12 36 C2
Hardy Cl
Ellesmere Port CH66 69 C2
Wistaston CW2 205 C4
Hardy Dr
Altrincham WA15 238 F7
Bramhall SK7 35 B4
Hardy Rd WA13 18 B1
Hardy St WA2 16 A3
Hare La CH3 119 B2
Hare's La WA6 73 C4
Harebell Cl CH3 142 A3
Harebell Gr ST7 195 C1
Harecastle Ave ST7 194 C1
Harefield Dr SK9 60 A3
Harefield Rd SK9 34 C2
Harehill Gdn* SK10 86 A3
Harewood Ave CH66 69 B2
Harewood Cl
Northwich CW9 103 C2
Winsford CW7 126 A1
Harewood Ct M33 242 C5
Harewood Way SK11 112 A3
Harewood Wlk 6 M34 241 A5
Harfield Gdns CH66 69 B3
Harford Cl WA5 14 C2
Hargrave Ave CW2 189 C2
Hargrave Dr CH66 69 C3
Hargrave La
Bebington CH64 43 A2
Thornton Hough CH63,CH64 42 C3
Hargreaves Ct WA8 13 B1
Hargreaves Rd CW9 104 B4
Harington Cl CH2 95 B1
Harington Rd CH2 118 B4
Harlech Cl WA5 7 C1
Harlech Ct CH65 70 B2
Harlech Way CH65 70 B2
Harley Rd M33 242 C7
Harlow Cl WA4 17 B2
Harlyn Ave SK7 35 C4
Harlyn Gdns WA5 14 B2
Harn The CH66 69 B2
Harold Rd WA11 1 C4
Haroldgate SY13 225 C1
Harper Cl
Ellesmere Port CH66 69 B2
Macclesfield SK11 112 B3
Harper Gr CW12 156 C2
Harpers Rd WA2 9 A1
Harpur Cres ST7 193 A3
Harraps Pl 2 SK11 112 A3
Harrier Cl CW1 189 C4
Harrier Rd WA2 8 C1
Harriet St M44 11 C3
Harrington Dr SK11 111 B1
Harrington Rd WA14 238 B5
Harris Cl CW1 173 A1
Harris Rd CW9 80 A1
Harris St WA8 13 B1
Harriseahead La ST7 195 B2
Harrison Dr
Allostock CW4 107 A1
Haydock WA11 1 A3
Harrison Gr CH5 116 A2
Harrison Sq WA5 7 C1
Harrison St
Stalybridge SK15 242 D2
Stockport SK1,SK2 240 F3
Widnes WA8 22 A3
Harrison Way WA12 2 B2
Harrisons Pl 17 CW8 103 C4
Harrogate Cl
Bebington CH62 43 B2
Warrington WA5 7 A1
Harrogate Rd CH62 43 B2
Harrop La SK10 62 C3
Harrop Rd
Altrincham WA15 238 F2
Bollington SK10 88 B4
Runcorn WA7 23 A1
Harrop St SK15 242 D2
Harrow Cl Crewe CW2 190 A1
Warrington WA4 26 C3
Harrow Dr WA7 23 C1
Harrow Gr CH62 43 C4
Harrow Rd CH65 70 B2
Harrow Way CW9 103 C2
Harrytown SK6 241 A2
Harrytown RC High Sch SK6 241 A2
Hart Ave M33 242 F5
Hart St WA14 238 E5
Hartford Ave SK9 59 C3
Hartford Bsns Ctr CW8 102 C2
Hartford Cl CW11 175 B4
Hartford Dr CH65 69 C2
Hartford High Sch CW8 103 B3
Hartford Manor Com Prim Sch CW8 103 B3
Hartford Prim Sch CW8 103 A2
Hartford Rd CW9 103 C1
Hartford Sta CW8 103 A2
Hartford Way CH1 118 A1
Harthill Cl CW9 103 C3
Harthill La CH3 183 C2
Harthill Prim Sch CH3 183 C2
Harthill Rd Blacon CH1 117 C3
Burwardsley CH3 184 A3
Hartington Dr SK7 36 C4
Hartington Rd
Altrincham WA14 238 D8
Bramhall SK7 35 C3
Gatley SK8 34 B4
High Lane SK12,SK6 37 C4
Hartington St CH4 141 C4
Hartland Cl Poynton SK12 36 B3
Widnes WA8 13 A3
Hartley Cl WA13 18 C2
Hartley Gdns CW12 179 A4
Hartley Gn SK10 87 C4
Hartley Rd WA14 238 C5
Hartley St SK3 240 D4
Hartshead Ave SK15 242 D3
Hartshead View SK14 241 F5
Hartswood Cl Hyde M34 241 A8
Warrington WA4 26 C2
Hartwell Gr CW7 126 C2
Harty Rd WA11 1 A3
Harvard Cl WA7 24 B1
Harvard Ct WA2 8 A2
Harvest Cl CW9 126 C4
Harvest Rd SK10 87 B2
Harvey Ave
Nantwich CW5 205 A3
Newton-le-W WA12 1 C2
Harvey Ct WA2 8 A2
Harvey Rd CW12 157 A3
Harvey St SK1 240 F5
Harvin Gr M34 241 A6
Harwood Gdns WA4 17 A1
Harwood St SK4 240 E7
Haryngton Ave WA5 15 C4
Haseley Cl SK12 36 C3
Haslam Rd SK3 240 E2
Haslemere Ave WA15 32 B3
Haslemere Dr WA5 14 B2
Haslemere Way CW1 190 B3
Haslin Cres CH3 142 B4
Haslington Cl ST5 210 B1
Haslington Gr L26 21 A3
Haslington Prim Sch CW1 191 B2
Hassall Rd Alsager ST7 193 A3
Haslington CW11 192 A4
Sandbach CW11 175 B2
Hassall St SK15 242 E1
Hassall Way 7 SK9 34 C3
Hastings Ave WA2 8 A2
Hasty La Altrincham WA15 32 C4
Wythenshawe M90 33 A4
Hatch Mere* WA6 100 B3
Hatchery Cl WA4 27 A2
Hatchings The WA13 18 C1
Hatchmere Cl
Sandbach CW11 174 C4
Hatchmere Cl *continued*
Warrington WA5 15 C3
Hatchmere Dr CH3 142 A4
Hatchmere Rd SK8 239 F4
Hatfield Ct CW4 130 A2
Hatfield Gdns WA4 26 C2
Hathaway Cl SK8 34 A4
Hathaway Dr SK11 112 B3
Hatherlow SK6 241 A1
Hatherlow Hts SK6 241 A1
Hatherton Cl
10 Davenham CW9 103 C2
Newcastle-u-L ST5 210 B1
Hatherton Gr L26 21 A3
Hatherton Way CH2 237 B4
Hatley La WA6 73 C4
Hatter St CW12 156 C2
Hatton Ave CH62 43 C2
Hatton La Northwich CW8 103 B3
Stretton WA4 26 A1
Hatton Rd CH1 117 C3
Hatton St
Macclesfield SK11 112 B4
3 Stockport SK1 240 E6
Haughton Cl SK10 86 C1
Haughton Hall Rd M34 241 A7
Haughton St SK14 241 E5
Havannah La
Congleton CW12 156 C3
St Helens WA9 1 A2
Havannah Prim Sch CW12 157 A3
Havannah St CW12 156 C2
Haven The
Altrincham WA15 238 F3
Crewe CW1 190 B4
Havergal St 2 WA7 22 C1
Haverhill Cl CW2 207 A2
Havisham Cl WA3 9 B3
Hawarde Cl WA12 2 A2
Hawarden Airport CH4, CH5 139 B4
Hawarden Gdns CH65 70 B1
Hawarden Ind Pk CH4 139 A3
Hawarden Rd WA14 238 D6
Haweswater Ave
Crewe CW1 173 A1
Haydock WA11 1 A3
Haweswater Cl WA7 50 A3
Haweswater Dr CW7 126 B1
Hawick Cl CH66 69 A3
Hawk Rd SK22 39 C4
Hawk St CW11 175 A3
Hawke St SK15 242 F1
Hawker Cl CH4 139 B2
Hawkins La SK10 88 B2
Hawkins Rd CH64 41 C1
Hawkins St SK5 240 E8
Hawkins View CH3 120 C3
Hawks Ct WA7 49 C3
Hawks Way CH60 40 C4
Hawksey Dr CW5 204 C2
Hawkshaw Cl WA3 9 B2
Hawkshead Rd WA5 6 C3
Hawkshead Way CW7 126 B1
Hawkstone Gr WA6 73 B2
Hawley Dr WA15 32 A4
Hawley La WA15 32 A4
Hawley's Cl WA5 7 C1
Hawley's La WA2,WA5 8 A1
Haworth Ave CW12 157 A3
Haworth Cl SK11 112 A3
Hawthorn Ave
Altrincham WA15 238 F8
16 Nantwich CW5 204 C3
Newton-le-W WA12 2 B2
Runcorn WA7 23 A1
Widnes WA8 13 A1
Wilmslow SK9 60 A4
Hawthorn Bank SK22 39 A3
Hawthorn Bsns Pk WA5 16 A4
Hawthorn Cl
Altrincham WA15 238 F7
Holmes Chapel CW4 130 B2
Winsford CW7 126 B2
Hawthorn Cotts CH60 40 C4
Hawthorn Dr M44 11 B3
Hawthorn Gdns ST7 210 B4
Hawthorn Gn SK9 60 A4
Hawthorn Gr
Bramhall SK7 35 B3
Crewe CW1 190 B4
Hyde SK14 241 D5
Stockport SK4 240 B7
Warrington WA4 16 B2
Wilmslow SK9 60 A4
Hawthorn La
Bebington CH62 43 B4
Wilmslow SK9 60 A4
Wistaston CW2 189 C1
Hawthorn Pk SK9 60 A4
Hawthorn Rd
Altrincham WA15 238 E3
Bollington SK10 87 C4
Chester CH4 140 C3
Christleton CH3 142 C4
Ellesmere Port CH66 69 B3
Gatley SK8 239 A5
Neston CH64 41 B1
Newcastle-u-L ST5 210 C1
Plumley WA16 80 C2
Weaverham CW8 102 B4
Hawthorn Rise SK10 86 C3
Hawthorn St SK9 60 A3
Hawthorn Terr
Stockport SK4 240 B7
Wilmslow SK9 60 A3
Hawthorn View
Connah's Quay CH5 116 A4
Wilmslow SK9 60 A4
Hawthorn Villas CW4 130 B2
Hawthorn Way SK10 87 C1
Hawthorn Wlk
Higher Wincham CW9 79 B2
4 Partington M31 11 C2
Wilmslow SK9 60 A4
Hawthorne Ave
Audley ST7 209 C1
Fowley Common WA3 5 B3
Warrington, Great Sankey WA5 15 A3
Warrington, Woolston WA1 17 A4
Hawthorne Cl
Congleton CW12 156 A2
Haydock WA11 1 A3
Hawthorne Ct ST7 193 C2
Hawthorne Dr
Sandbach CW11 175 B3
Willaston CH64 43 A1
Hawthorne Gr
Barnton CW8 77 C2
High Lane SK12 37 B2
Warrington WA1 16 C4
Winsford CW7 127 A1
Hawthorne Rd WA4 26 B4
Hawthorne St WA5 16 A4
Hawthorne View WA16 59 A1
Hawthorns The
Bunbury CW6 185 C4
Ellesmere Port CH66 69 C4
Northwich CW8 103 B4
Tarporley CW6 146 B1
Hay Croft SK8 34 C4
Haycroft Cl CH66 69 B1
Haydan Mews WA6 73 C3
Haydn Jones Dr CW5 204 C2
Haydock Cl Chester CH1 118 A1
5 Macclesfield SK10 87 B2
Haydock High Sch WA11 1 A3
Haydock La WA11 1 B4
Haydock La Ind Est WA11 1 C4
Haydock St
Newton-le-W WA12 2 A2
Warrington WA2 16 A3
Haye's Rd M44 11 C3
Hayes Cl CW5 204 C4
Hayes Cres WA6 49 B1
Hayes Dr CW8 78 B2
Hayes Pk CH2 237 A4
Hayfield Ave SK6 241 A4
Hayfield Cl SK10 87 A2
Hayfield Rd Romiley SK6 241 A4
Warrington WA1 17 B4
Hayfield St M33 242 B7
Hayfields WA16 57 B2
Hayfields Gr CW3 229 C2
Hayhead Cl ST7 195 A1
Hayhurst Ave CW10 151 B4
Hayhurst Cl CW9 103 C4
Hayle Cl SK10 86 B1
Hayling Cl CW1 190 A4
Haymakers Cl CH4 140 C2
Haymakers Way CH1 117 A4
Haymoor Green Rd CW5 205 C2
Hayscastle Cl WA5 7 C1
Hayside Wlk SY14 213 A2
Hayton St WA16 56 C1
Haywood Cres WA7 24 B1
Hazel Ave Cheadle SK8 239 E5
Macclesfield SK11 112 A3
Romiley SK6 241 D2
Runcorn WA7 48 C4
Sale M33 242 B5
Hazel Cl
9 Ellesmere Port CH66 69 C1
Kidsgrove ST7 195 A2
Hazel Dr Gatley M22 34 A4
Lymm WA13 18 C1
Poynton SK12 36 C2
Weaverham CW8 102 B4
Winsford CW7 149 B4
Hazel Gr Alsager ST7 194 A2
Crewe CW1 190 B4
Golborne WA3 3 A4
Warrington WA1 17 A4
Hazel Grove High Sch SK7 36 B4
Hazel Rd
Altrincham WA14 238 D6
Chester CH4 140 C3
Stalybridge SK15 242 F3
Hazel St WA1 16 B4
Hazel Wlk M31 11 C2
Hazelbadge Cl SK12 36 B2
Hazelbadge Rd SK12 36 B2
Hazelbank CH65 69 C2
Hazelborough Cl WA3 10 A3
Hazelcroft SK9 85 A4
Hazelcroft Gdns SK9 85 A4
Hazeldean Ct 17 SK9 34 C1
Hazelehurst Rd WA6 74 B3
Hazelhurst Dr SK10 88 A4
Hazelhurst Rd SK15 242 D4
Hazelmere Cl CW8 103 B3
Hazelwood Mews WA4 17 B1
Hazelwood Rd
Altrincham WA15 238 E2
Barnton CW8 78 A2
Wilmslow SK9 60 B4
Hazlemere Ave SK11 112 A3
Headland Cl WA3 3 C3
Headlands The CH2 237 C2
Headworth Cl CW9 103 C2
Heald Cl WA14 238 C2
Heald Dr WA14 238 C2
Heald Gr SK8 239 A1
Heald Green Sta M22 34 A4
Heald Rd WA14 238 C2
Heald St WA12 1 C2
Healdwood Rd SK6 241 C4
Healey Cl CW1 190 A4
Hearn's La CW5 202 C3
Heary St SK11 112 C3
Heath Ave
Ellesmere Port CH65 70 A1
Rode Heath ST7 193 C4
Sandbach CW11 175 C3
Heath Bank CH3 119 B3
Heath Cl Chester CH3 142 A4
Sandbach CW11 175 B3
Tarvin CH3 121 A1
Heath Cres SK2 240 F1
Heath Ct Alsager ST7 193 C3
Ellesmere Port CH66 69 A3
Heath Dr Runcorn WA7 49 A4
Tarvin CH3 121 A1
Heath End Rd ST7 193 A3
Heath Gn CW6 146 B2
Heath Gr CH66 69 A4
Heath La Chester CH3 142 A4
Culcheth WA3 4 A1
Golborne WA3 3 B3
Great Barrow CH3 120 C3
Great Budworth CW9 54 A1
High Legh WA16 28 B3
Little Leigh WA4,CW8 77 A4
Lower Peover WA16 106 C3
Marbury SY13 226 C3
Stoak CH2 95 C4
Willaston CH66 68 B4
Heath Park Gr WA7 48 C4
Heath Rd
Altrincham WA14 238 D2
Bollington SK10 87 C3
Chester CH2 118 C4
Congleton CW12 156 A1
Runcorn WA7 23 A1
Sale WA15 238 F8
Sandbach CW11 175 B3
Stockport SK2 240 F2
Warrington WA5 14 C3
Weaverham CW8 77 C1
Widnes WA8 12 B1
Heath Rd S WA7 48 C3
Heath Sch The WA7 49 A4
Heath St Crewe CW1 190 B2
Golborne WA3 3 A4
Warrington WA4 26 B4
Heath Terr Chester CH2 118 C4
Smallwood CW11 154 A1
Heath View Alsager ST7 193 C3
Weston CW2 207 A3
Heath Way CW6 168 B4
Heathbank Rd
Cheadle SK8 34 C4
Stockport SK3 240 B3
Heathbrook CW9 104 C4
Heathcote Ave SK4 240 C7
Heathcote Cl CH2 118 B2
Heathcote Gdns
Northwich CW9 104 B4
Romiley SK6 241 E1
Heathcote St ST7 195 A1
Heather Ave M44 11 B3
Heather Brae WA12 2 A2
Heather Cl
Ellesmere Port CH66 69 C2
Macclesfield SK11 112 B2
Runcorn WA7 49 C2
Warrington WA3 9 B3
Heather Ct CH3 142 A4
Heather Lea M34 241 A6
Heather Rd WA14,WA15 238 E1
Heather Wlk M31 11 C2
Heatherfield Ct SK9 60 C4
Heathergate Pl CW2 206 A4
Heatherside ST7 195 B3
Heatherways CW6 146 B2
Heathfield SK9 60 A3
Heathfield Ave
Crewe CW1 190 B2
Gatley SK8 239 B5
Heathfield Cl
Congleton CW12 155 C2
Nantwich CW5 204 C3
Sale M33 242 F6
Heathfield Ct CH65 70 A3
Heathfield Dr ST5 210 B1
Heathfield Pk
Warrington WA4 17 A1
Widnes WA8 12 B2
Heathfield Rd
Audlem CW3 230 A3
Ellesmere Port CH65 70 A3
Stockport SK2 240 F2
Heathfield Sq WA16 56 C1
Heathfields WA14 238 C3
Heathfields Cl CH2 237 B4
Heathgate Ave L24 21 A1
Heathland Terr SK3 240 E3
Heathlands Ho WA16 56 C1
Heathlands Rd CH66 69 A4
Heathmoor Ave WA3 3 B3
Heaths La CW6 123 B1
Heathside CW5 204 C3
Heathside Park Rd SK3 239 F7
Heathside Rd SK3 240 A3
Heathview CW1 191 B2
Heathview Cl WA8 22 A3

Heathview Rd WA8 .22 A3
Heathway CH60 .41 A4
Heathwood Dr ST7 .193 A3
Heathwood Gr WA1 .17 A4
Heatley Cl WA13 .19 A2
Heatley La CW5 .217 C2
Heatley Way 5 SK9 .34 B2
Heaton Cl
Middlewich CW10 .151 B3
Stockport SK4 .240 A7
Heaton Ct Stockport SK4 .240 B8
Warrington WA3 .9 C3
Heaton La SK4 .240 E5
Heaton Moor Rd SK4 .240 B8
Heaton Rd SK4 .240 C7
Heaton Sq CW7 .149 B4
Heaward Cl CW2 .206 A2
Hebden Ave
Fowley Common WA3 .5 A3
Romiley SK6 .241 A4
Hebden Green Com Specl Sch CW7 .149 A4
Heber Wlk CW9 .104 A4
Heber's Cl SY14 .213 B3
Hedge Hey WA7 .24 A1
Hedge Row SK10 .63 C1
Hedgerow Dr CW9 .79 B2
Hedgerows The WA11 .1 C4
Hedingham Cl 6 SK10 .111 C4
Hefferston Grange Dr CW8 .102 A4
Hefferston Rise CW8 .102 A4
Heights The WA6 .73 B2
Helena Cl WA16 .57 B1
Helford St CW12 .156 B2
Hellath View CW5 .204 C1
Hellyar-Brook Rd ST7 .193 A2
Helmsdale Cl CW1 .190 A3
Helmsdale La WA5 .15 B3
Helmsley Cl WA5 .15 C4
Helsby Ave CH62 .43 C2
Helsby High Sch WA6 .73 B3
Helsby Rd WA6 .73 B1
Helsby St WA1 .16 B3
Helsby Sta WA6 .73 A2
Helsby Way 4 SK9 .34 B2
Helston Cl Bramhall SK7 .35 C4
Runcorn WA7 .50 A3
Warrington WA5 .14 C3
Helston Gr SK8 .34 B4
Helton Cl CW4 .130 A2
Hemingford Cl CH66 .69 B3
Hemlegh Vale WA6 .73 A1
Hemming St CW8 .78 B1
Hemmingshaw La CW11 .176 A4
Hemswell Cl CW7 .149 C4
Hemsworth Ave CH66 .69 B3
Henbury Cl CW10 .151 B4
Henbury High Sch SK10 .111 C4
Henbury La SK8 .34 C3
Henbury Pl WA7 .49 A3
Henbury Rd SK9 .34 B2
Henbury Rise SK11 .111 B4
Henderson Cl WA5 .14 B3
Henderson Rd
2 Widnes WA8 .13 A1
Widnes, Lower House WA8 .22 C4
Henderson St SK11 .112 B4
Hendham Dr WA14 .238 B5
Hendon Cl CW1 .190 C3
Hendon Dr SK3 .240 A3
Henley Ave Cheadle SK8 .239 F2
Irlam M44 .11 C3
Henley Cl
Macclesfield SK10 .87 A2
Neston CH64 .66 C3
Warrington WA4 .26 C3
Henley Ct WA7 .23 B1
Henley Dr
Altrincham WA15 .238 F7
Winsford CW7 .126 C1
Henley Rd Chester CH4 .140 C3
Hough Common CW2 .207 A1
Neston CH64 .66 C3
Henrietta St CW12 .156 B2
Henry Pl CH2 .237 B3
Henry St Crewe CW1 .190 B3
Haslington CW1 .191 B2
Hyde SK14 .241 D6
2 Lymm WA13 .18 C2
Tarporley CW6 .146 B1
Warrington WA1 .16 A3
4 Widnes WA8 .13 B1
Henry Wood Ct CH4 .140 C3
Henshall Ave WA4 .16 C2
Henshall Dr CW11 .175 B4
Henshall Hall Dr CW12 .157 A1
Henshall La WA14 .20 B3
Henshall Rd SK10 .87 C4
Henshall St CH2 .237 A4
Henshaw La SK11 .110 C1
Hepherd St WA5 .15 B2
Hepley Rd SK12 .37 A2
Herald Dr CW1 .190 C2
Herald Pk CW1 .190 C2
Heralds Cl WA8 .22 B4
Heralds Gn WA5 .7 A1
Herbert St Burtonwood WA5 .6 C3
Congleton CW12 .156 C2
Crewe CW1 .191 A3
Dukinfield M34 .241 A8
Lostock Gralam CW9 .80 A1
Stockport SK3 .240 D3
Herdman St CW2 .190 B1
Hereford Ave
Ellesmere Port CH66 .94 C4
1 Golborne WA3 .3 A4
Hereford Cl
Macclesfield SK10 .86 C1
Warrington WA1 .17 B4
Hereford Dr SK9 .34 C2
Hereford Pl CH1 .118 A3
Hereford St M33 .242 B6
Hereford Way CW10 .128 B1
Hereford Wlk SK6 .241 A1
Hereward Rd CH3 .119 A1
Hermitage Ave SK6 .241 F2
Hermitage Ct
Holmes Chapel CW4 .130 B2
Saughall CH1 .117 A4
Hermitage Dr CW4 .130 B2
Hermitage Gdns SK6 .241 F2
Hermitage Green La WA2, WA12 .8 A4
Hermitage La CW4 .130 B4
Hermitage Prim Sch CW4 .130 B2
Hermitage Rd CH1 .117 A4
Heron Cl Broughton CH4 .139 A2
Farndon CH3 .180 C1
Knutsford WA16 .57 A2
Runcorn WA7 .50 B4
Winsford CW7 .149 B3
Heron Cres CW1 .190 C3
Heron Ct Neston CH64 .66 B4
Northwich CW9 .79 B1
Stockport SK3 .240 E3
Heron Dr SK12 .36 A2
Heron Pl CH2 .237 B4
Heron St SK3 .240 D3
Herons Way Chester CH4 .141 A2
Runcorn WA7 .24 C2
Herrick Cl CW2 .206 A4
Herries St OL6 .242 A4
Hertford Cl
Congleton CW12 .156 C2
Warrington WA1 .17 C4
Hertford Gr M44 .11 B3
Hesketh Cl WA5 .14 C2
Hesketh Croft CW1 .190 A4
Hesketh Dr CW9 .80 A2
Hesketh Grange Cotts CH63 .42 A4
Hesketh Meadow La WA3 .4 A4
Hesketh Rd L24 .21 C1
Hesketh St Stockport SK4 .240 E7
Warrington WA5 .15 B2
Hesketh St N WA5 .15 B2
Hesnall Cl WA3 .5 B4
Hessle Dr CH60 .40 C4
Heswall Ave WA3 .4 C2
Heswall Rd CH66 .69 B2
Heswall Sta CH60 .41 B4
Hewitt Dr CW7 .150 B4
Hewitt Gr CW9 .79 C3
Hewitt St Chester CH2 .118 C2
Crewe CW2 .190 B1
Northwich CW9 .79 B1
Warrington WA4 .16 B2
Hexham Way 4 SK10 .87 B2
Hey Lock Cl WA12 .7 A4
Hey Shoot La WA3 .5 B3
Hey Wood Cl WA12 .7 B4
Heybridge La SK10 .87 A3
Heyes Ave WA11 .1 B3
Heyes Dr WA13 .18 B1
Heyes Farm Rd SK11 .111 C4
Heyes La
Alderley Edge SK9 .60 A2
Warrington WA4 .26 C4
Heyes Pk CW8 .102 C2
Heyes Rd WA8 .22 B4
Heyeswood La CW8 .103 A2
Heyfield Park Rd CH66 .69 A4
Heygarth Prim Sch CH62 .43 C3
Heygarth Rd CH62 .43 C3
Heys Ave Bebington CH62 .43 B4
Romiley SK6 .241 E3
Heys Farm Cotts SK6 .241 E3
Heys La SK6 .241 E3
Heys Prim Sch The OL6 .242 A3
Heys Rd OL6 .242 A3
Heys The Bebington CH62 .43 C3
Runcorn WA7 .23 C1
Heysbank Rd SK12 .38 B3
Heyscroft Rd SK4 .240 A6
Heysham Cl WA7 .50 B3
Heysoms Ave CW8 .103 B4
Heysoms Cl CW8 .103 B4
Heythrop Dr CH60 .41 B4
Heywood Cl SK9 .60 A1
Heywood Gn CW2 .206 B4
Heywood Gr M33 .242 B8
Heywood La CW3,SY13 .234 B4
Heywood Rd
Alderley Edge SK9 .60 A1
Ellesmere Port CH66 .69 B3
Sale M33 .242 B5
Heywood St CW12 .156 B1
Heywoods Ridge CW3 .229 C2
Heywoods The CH2 .118 B2
Heyworth Ave SK6 .241 D3
Hibbert Ave 5 SK14 .241 E5
Hibbert St New Mills SK22 .39 A3
6 Widnes WA8 .23 A4
Hibel Rd SK10 .87 B1
Hickhurst La CW6 .147 B2
Hickmore Heys CH3 .119 C3
Hickory Cl WA1 .17 C4
Hickson St CW8 .78 A2
Hickton Dr WA14 .238 B6
Hidcote Cl CW2 .206 A4
Hield Gr CW9 .79 B4
Hield La CW9 .79 B4
Higginbotham Gn SK11 .112 C3
Higginson Cl CW12 .179 B4
High Bank WA14 .238 D5
High Bank Cl M44 .11 B3
High Bank Rd SK14 .241 F7
High Bank Side SK1 .240 F5
High Bent Ave SK8 .35 A3
High Carr Bsns Pk ST5 .210 C1
High Cross La CH3 .182 B1
High Ct SK10 .88 A4
High Elm Dr WA15 .32 B4
High Elm Rd WA15 .32 B4
High Elms SK8 .35 A3
High Field WA14 .20 A1
High Gates M33 .242 E7
High Gates Cl WA5 .15 C4
High Gates Lodge WA5 .15 C4
High Grove Rd SK8 .239 C5
High La SK6 .241 B4
High Lane Prim Sch SK6 .37 C4
High Lea SK8 .239 C5
High Lea Rd SK22 .39 A4
High Lee Ho M33 .242 D6
High Legh Prim Sch WA16 .29 B3
High Legh Rd WA13 .29 B4
High Lowe Ave CW12 .157 A2
High Mdw 2 SK8 .34 C4
High Mdws SK6 .241 C3
High Mount CH60 .40 C4
High St Altrincham WA14 .238 D4
Audley ST7 .210 A1
Bollington SK10 .88 A4
Broughton CH4 .140 C4
Cheadle SK8 .239 D6
Congleton CW12 .156 B1
Crewe CW2 .190 B2
Duddon CW6 .145 B2
Farndon CH3 .180 C1
Frodsham WA6 .49 A1
Golborne WA3 .3 A4
Great Budworth CW9 .79 A4
Hale L24 .21 B1
Hyde SK14 .241 F7
Kidsgrove, Harriseahead ST7 .195 C3
Kidsgrove, Newchapel ST7 .195 C1
Kidsgrove, The Rookery ST7 .195 B2
Macclesfield SK11 .112 B3
Malpas SY14 .213 A2
Mow Cop ST7 .195 B4
Nantwich CW5 .204 C3
Neston CH64 .66 C4
New Mills SK22 .39 B4
Newton-le-W WA12 .2 B2
Norley WA6 .100 C3
Northwich CW9 .103 C4
Runcorn WA7 .23 A1
Sandbach CW11 .175 A3
Stalybridge SK15 .242 D1
Stockport SK1 .240 F5
Talke ST7 .210 B3
Tarporley CW6 .146 B1
Tarvin CH3 .121 A1
Tattenhall CH3 .166 A1
Warrington WA1 .16 B3
Weaverham CW8 .77 B1
Winsford CW7 .126 B1
High View Helsby WA6 .73 B2
Mount Pleasant ST7 .195 A3
High Warren Cl WA4 .26 B3
Higham Ave WA5 .7 C1
Highbank Cl CW8 .78 A2
Highbank Dr M20 .239 B8
Highbank Rd
Kingsley WA6 .75 B1
Northwich CW8 .103 B4
Highcliffe Ave CH1 .118 A2
Highcroft Ave CW12 .156 C1
Highcroft Rd SK6 .241 C3
Higher Ash Rd ST7 .210 B4
Higher Ashton WA8 .12 C2
Higher Barlow Row SK1 .240 F4
Higher Bents La SK6 .241 A3
Higher Bury St SK4 .240 D6
Higher Carden La SY14 .198 B3
Higher Downs
Altrincham WA14 .238 C3
Knutsford WA16 .57 B1
Higher Fence Rd SK10 .87 C1
Higher Ferry CH1 .140 A4
Higher Gn OL6 .242 A4
Higher Henry St SK14 .241 E5
Higher Heyes Dr WA6 .75 B1
Higher Hillgate SK1 .240 F4
Higher Knutsford Rd WA4 .16 C1
Higher La Bollington SK10 .88 A3
Dutton WA4 .51 B2
Kettleshulme SK23 .64 C3
Lymm WA13 .19 A1
Higher Rd Hale L26,WA8 .21 B3
Halewood L26 .21 A3
Higher Tame St SK15 .242 E2
Higherland Ct 6 ST7 .195 A1
Highfield Elton CH2 .72 A2
Prestbury SK10 .87 A3
Sale M33 .242 C5
Highfield Ave
Audlem CW3 .230 A2
Golborne WA3 .2 C4
Kidsgrove ST7 .195 A1
Lostock Gralam CW9 .80 A2
Warrington, Appleton WA4 .26 B2
Highfield Ave *continued*
Warrington, Great Sankey WA5 .15 A3
Highfield Cl CH64 .66 C4
Highfield Com Prim Sch CH1 .117 C2
Highfield Cres
Widnes WA8 .13 A1
Wilmslow SK9 .34 B1
Highfield Dr Lymm WA13 .18 B1
Macclesfield SK10 .87 A1
Nantwich CW5 .205 A3
Highfield Est SK9 .34 B1
Highfield Gdns SK14 .241 F7
Highfield La
Coddington CH3 .181 C2
Golborne WA3 .3 B3
Winwick WA2 .8 B4
Highfield Parkway SK7 .35 B2
Highfield Pl 14 CW8 .103 C4
Highfield Rd Blacon CH1 .117 B3
Bollington SK10 .88 A4
Cheadle SK8 .239 F1
Congleton CW12 .156 C1
Ellesmere Port CH65 .70 B3
Ellesmere Port, Little Sutton CH66 .69 A3
Lymm WA13 .18 B1
Macclesfield SK11 .112 B4
Neston CH64 .66 C4
Northwich CW8 .103 C4
Poynton SK12 .36 A2
Widnes WA8 .13 A1
Highfield Rd N 7 CH65 .70 B3
Highfield Sch L26 .21 A4
Highfield St 2 SK3 .240 C4
Highfield Terr SK22 .39 B4
Highfields SY13 .224 A1
Highfields Com Prim Sch CW5 .204 C3
Highgate Cl Crewe CW1 .190 A4
Runcorn WA7 .24 B1
Highgate Rd WA14 .238 B4
Highgrove Mews 2 SK9 .60 A3
Highland Ave SK6 .241 A2
Highland Way WA16 .82 A4
Highlands Rd WA7 .48 C4
Highlands The CW6 .185 C4
Highmarsh Cres WA12 .2 A2
Hightown Crewe CW1 .190 B2
Middlewich CW10 .128 B1
Sandbach CW11 .175 A3
Hightree Dr SK11 .111 B4
Highwood Rd WA4 .26 B4
Higifield Ave M33 .242 C5
Hignett Ave WA9 .1 A1
Hilary Ave SK8 .34 B4
Hilary Cl Chester CH3 .119 A1
Stockport SK4 .240 D6
Warrington WA5 .14 B3
Widnes WA8 .13 C2
Hilbre Ave CH60 .40 C3
Hilbre Bank CW6 .169 B2
Hilbre Dr CH65 .70 B1
Hilda Ave SK8 .239 E5
Hilda Gr SK5 .240 F8
Hilda St 5 SK5 .240 F8
Hilden Pl WA2 .8 C1
Hilden Rd WA2 .8 C1
Hill Cl CH64 .67 A3
Hill Cliffe Rd WA4 .26 A4
Hill Cotts CH3 .164 A2
Hill Court Mews SK6 .241 B2
Hill Crest Ave SK4 .240 A6
Hill Croft CW11 .191 C4
Hill Ct CH64 .67 A3
Hill Dr SK9 .34 C2
Hill Fields Cl CW12 .156 B2
Hill La Brown Knowl CH3 .199 B4
Burwardsley CW6 .184 C3
Hill Rd CH4 .141 C1
Hill Rd N WA6 .73 B2
Hill Rd S WA6 .73 B2
Hill Rise
Altrincham WA14 .238 A5
Romiley SK6 .241 B2
Hill St Altrincham WA14 .238 C8
Crewe CW1 .190 B2
Macclesfield SK11 .112 B3
Romiley SK6 .241 B2
Runcorn WA7 .23 A1
Sandbach CW11 .174 B4
Winsford CW7 .126 C1
Hill Terr ST7 .209 B1
Hill The Knutsford WA16 .82 A4
Sandbach CW11 .175 B3
Hill Top Altrincham WA15 .32 A4
Barnton CW8 .78 A1
Romiley SK6 .241 B3
Hill Top Ave Cheadle SK8 .35 A4
Wilmslow SK9 .60 A4
Winsford CW7 .126 B1
Hill Top La Heswall CH60 .41 A4
Neston CH64 .67 A3
Hill Top Rd
Acton Bridge CW8 .76 C1
Dutton WA4 .51 B1
Warrington, Stockton Heath WA4 .16 C1
Warrington, Woolston WA1 .17 B4
Hill Top Rise SK23 .65 B4
Hill View Bollington SK10 .87 C4
Whaley Bridge SK23 .65 B4
Widnes WA8 .12 C3
Hill View Ave WA6 .73 A1
Hill View Prim Sch WA7 .49 C2
Hillary Ave CW12 .157 A1
Hillary Dr CW3 .230 A2
Hillary Rd Bebington CH62 .43 C3
Kidsgrove ST7 .195 A2
Hillberry Cres WA4 .16 A2
Hillbre Way Handforth SK9 .34 C2
1 Wilmslow SK9 .34 B2
Hillbrook Rd SK7 .35 B3
Hillcourt Rd
High Lane SK6 .37 C4
Romiley SK6 .241 C4
Hillcrest Ave CW4 .130 A2
Hillcrest Dr Denton M34 .241 B5
Ellesmere Port CH66 .69 A3
Hillcrest Gram Sch SK3 .240 F2
Hillcrest Rd
Bollington SK10 .87 C4
Ellesmere Port CH66 .69 A3
Kelsall CW6 .122 C3
Warren SK11 .112 A2
Hillcroft Rd WA14 .238 A5
Hillesden Rise CW12 .156 C1
Hillfield Frodsham WA6 .74 A4
Runcorn WA7 .50 B4
Hillfield Gdns CW5 .204 C2
Hillfield Pl CW5 .204 C2
Hillfield Rd CH66 .69 B4
Hillfield View CW5 .204 C2
Hillfields CW12 .156 B2
Hillfoot Cres WA4 .26 A4
Hillfoot La WA6 .74 C2
Hillgate Bsns Ctr 10 SK1 .240 F4
Hillington Rd SK3 .240 C4
Hillock La WA1 .17 B4
Hillsboro Ave WA6 .74 B4
Hillsdown Way CH66 .69 B1
Hillside Broomedge WA13 .19 C1
Northwich CW8 .103 B4
Hillside Ave
Newton-le-W WA12 .1 C1
Runcorn WA7 .48 C4
Hillside Bird Oasis* WA16 .58 A2
Hillside Cl Bramhall SK7 .36 A4
Disley SK12 .38 C3
Kidsgrove ST7 .195 B4
Hillside Ct SK10 .88 A1
Hillside Dr Crewe CW1 .190 C3
Ellesmere Port CH66 .69 C4
Macclesfield SK10 .88 A1
Hillside Gr WA5 .14 C2
Hillside La CW9 .126 C4
Hillside Prim Sch WA6 .73 B2
Hillside Rd Blacon CH1 .117 C2
Frodsham WA6 .74 B4
Heswall CH60 .41 A4
Kelsall CW6 .122 B2
Knutsford WA16 .57 A1
Warrington WA4 .26 B2
Hillside View SK22 .39 A4
Hilltop WA7 .50 B4
Hilltop Pk WA16 .79 C4
Hilltop Prim Sch ST7 .210 B4
Hilltop Rd
Guilden Sutton CH3 .119 C3
Lymm WA13 .18 B1
Hillview Cl WA6 .74 B4
Hillview Rise CW8 .78 C1
Hilton Ave WA5 .15 A3
Hilton Cl
Macclesfield SK11 .111 C4
Middlewich CW10 .151 A4
Hilton Dr M44 .11 B3
Hilton Gr SK12 .36 B2
Hilton Rd Disley SK12 .38 A4
High Lane SK12 .37 B3
Hilton St SK3 .240 D4
Hinchley Cl CW8 .103 A2
Hinckley Ct CW12 .156 A2
Hind Heath La CW11 .174 C2
Hind Heath Rd CW11 .174 C2
Hinde St CW5 .204 B2
Hinderton Dr CH60 .40 C3
Hinderton Gn CH64 .66 C4
Hinderton La CH64 .67 A4
Hinderton Rd CH64 .66 C4
Hinderton Sch CH65 .69 C2
Hindle Ave WA5 .7 C1
Hindley Cres CW8 .78 A2
Hindley St SK1 .240 F4
Hinton Cres WA4 .26 C4
Hinton Rd Crewe CW2 .206 B4
Runcorn WA7 .23 A1
Hitch Lowes SK11 .84 A2
Hitchen's Cl WA7 .50 B4
Hitchens La SY14 .184 B1
Hob Hey La WA3 .4 B2
Hob Hill SK15 .242 C1
Hob La Churton CH3 .180 C3
Dunham-on-t-H WA6 .97 B3
Hobart Cl SK7 .35 C2
Hobart Way CH1 .117 B2
Hobb La WA4 .25 B3
Hobbs Cl CW1 .191 B2
Hobbs Hill La WA16 .28 C1
Hobby Ct WA7 .49 C3
Hobcroft La WA16 .58 A4
Hobson St SK11 .112 B3
Hockenhull Ave CH3 .121 A1
Hockenhull Cres CH3 .121 B1
Hockenhull La CH3 .121 A1
Hocker La SK10 .85 B2
Hockerley Ave SK23 .65 B4
Hockerley Cl SK23 .65 B4
Hockerley La SK23 .65 B4
Hockley Cl SK12 .37 A2
Hockley Rd SK12 .37 A2
Hodge La Hartford CW8 .103 A3
Weaverham CW8 .102 B3

Hodgehill La SK11 ....132 C3
Hodgkin Cl CW5 ....204 C2
Hodgkinson Ave WA5 ....7 C1
Hoghton Rd L24 ....21 C1
Hogshead La CW8 ....124 B4
Holbeck WA7 ....50 B4
Holbein Cl CH4 ....141 C3
Holborn Ct WA8 ....12 C2
Holborn St 14 SK1 ....240 F5
Holbrook Cl WA5 ....14 C3
Holbury Cl CW1 ....190 A4
Holcombe Ave WA3 ....3 B4
Holcombe Cl WA14 ....238 B6
Holcombe Dr SK10 ....87 A2
Holcroft La WA3 ....5 B1
Holden Pl WA2 ....16 B4
Hole House Fold SK6 ....241 B2
Hole House La CW8 ....77 C2
Holehouse La
Adlington SK10 ....62 B1
Langley SK11 ....113 B2
Scholar Green ST7 ....194 B4
Holes La WA1 ....17 A4
Holford Ave
Lostock Gralam CW9 ....80 A2
Warrington WA5 ....15 C4
Holford Cres WA16 ....57 A1
Holford Way WA12 ....2 C2
Holgrave Cl WA16 ....29 B2
Holker Cl SK12 ....36 C2
Holkham Cl WA8 ....12 C1
Holkham The CH3 ....119 A1
Holland Ave SK15 ....242 D2
Holland Cl CW11 ....175 B3
Holland Rd SK7 ....35 C4
Holland St Crewe CW1 ....190 A3
18 Macclesfield SK11 ....112 B4
Hollands La CW6 ....122 B3
Hollands Pl SK11 ....112 C4
Hollands Rd CW9 ....103 C4
Hollies Ct M33 ....242 B6
Hollies La SK9 ....60 C4
Hollies The Gatley SK8 ....239 B5
Moulton CW9 ....126 C4
Runcorn WA7 ....49 B4
Shavington CW2 ....206 A2
3 Stockport SK4 ....240 B7
Hollin Green La CW5 ....202 C3
Hollin La Newhall CW5 ....228 B4
Styal SK9 ....33 C3
Sutton Lane Ends SK11 ....136 B3
Hollin Rd SK10 ....88 A4
Hollingford Pl WA16 ....82 A4
Hollingreen La CW5 ....229 A4
Hollinhey Prim Sch
SK11 ....112 C2
Hollins Cres ST7 ....194 C1
Hollins Dr WA2 ....8 A3
Hollins Gr M33 ....242 A6
Hollins Grange ST7 ....210 B4
Hollins Hill CW6 ....146 C4
Hollins La Antrobus CW9 ....53 C2
Winwick WA2 ....7 C3
Hollins Park Hospl WA2 ....7 C3
Hollins Rd SK11 ....112 C3
Hollins Terr SK11 ....112 C3
Hollins Way WA8 ....22 A3
Hollinshead Cl ST7 ....194 C4
Hollinwood Cl ST7 ....210 C4
Hollinwood Rd
Disley SK12 ....38 B3
Talke ST7 ....210 C4
Hollow Dr WA4 ....16 C1
Hollow La Kingsley WA6 ....75 A2
Knutsford WA16 ....57 A1
Hollow Oak La CW8 ....101 B2
Hollow The Cheadle SK8 ....239 C1
Mount Pleasant ST7 ....195 A3
Holloway WA7 ....22 C1
Hollowood Rd SY14 ....213 A3
Hollows The SK8 ....239 C1
Holly Ave Cheadle SK8 ....239 D5
Newton-le-W WA12 ....2 B2
Holly Bank Frodsham WA6 ....74 B4
Helsby WA6 ....73 B1
Lymm WA13 ....18 B1
Sale M33 ....242 C5
Stalybridge OL6 ....242 A2
Holly Bank Rd SK9 ....34 A1
Holly Bank Sch CH2 ....237 A4
Holly Bush La WA3 ....10 B1
Holly Cl Connah's Quay CH5 ....91 B1
Hale L24 ....21 B1
Mickle Trafford CH2 ....119 C4
Holly Ct Helsby WA6 ....73 B3
Middlewich CW10 ....128 A1
Stockport SK3 ....240 E1
Holly Dr Sale M33 ....242 A6
Winsford CW7 ....149 B4
Holly Gr Denton M34 ....241 A7
Sale M33 ....242 D6
Tabley WA16 ....56 A2
Warrington WA1 ....17 A4
Holly Grange WA14 ....238 D2
Holly Hedge La WA4 ....25 B3
Holly Heys 5 M33 ....242 D6
Holly House Est CW10 ....129 B3
Holly La Alsager ST7 ....193 C2
Kidsgrove ST7 ....195 C3
Styal SK9 ....33 C3
Holly Mount CW2 ....206 C3
Holly Rd Bramhall SK7 ....35 C3
Chester CH4 ....140 C3
Ellesmere Port CH65 ....70 B3
Golborne WA3 ....3 B4
Haydock WA11 ....1 A3
High Lane SK6 ....37 C4
Lymm WA13 ....19 A3
Holly Rd *continued*
Macclesfield SK11 ....112 A4
Newcastle-u-L ST5 ....210 C1
Poynton SK12 ....36 C2
Warrington WA5 ....14 C3
Weaverham CW8 ....102 B4
Holly Rd N SK9 ....60 A3
Holly Rd S SK9 ....60 A3
Holly Terr Tilston SY14 ....198 B2
Warrington WA5 ....14 C3
Holly Tree Dr
Biddulph ST8 ....179 B1
Lower Peover WA16 ....106 B4
Holly Wlk Northwich CW8 ....103 B4
Partington M31 ....11 B2
Hollybank Audlem CW3 ....229 C2
Moore WA4 ....25 A3
Hollybank Rd WA7 ....49 C4
Hollybush Cres CW5 ....205 B3
Hollyfield Rd CH65 ....70 A3
Hollyfields CW11 ....191 C4
Hollyheath Cl CW11 ....175 B3
Hollythorn Ave SK8 ....35 B4
Hollythorn Mews SK8 ....35 B4
Hollytree Rd WA16 ....80 C2
Hollywood WA14 ....238 D2
Hollywood Twrs SK3 ....240 D4
Hollywood Way SK3 ....240 D5
Holm Cl CH3 ....142 C4
Holm Dr CH2 ....72 B2
Holm Oak Way CH66 ....94 C4
Holme St Hyde SK14 ....241 D6
Tarvin CH3 ....120 C1
Holmedale Ct M33 ....242 C6
Holmefield M33 ....242 B6
Holmes Chapel Comp Sch
CW4 ....130 A1
Holmes Chapel Prim Sch
CW4 ....130 A2
Holmes Chapel Rd
Allostock WA16 ....106 A2
Brereton Green CW4,
CW12 ....154 B4
Congleton CW12 ....155 B2
Knutsford WA16 ....82 B2
Lach Dennis CW9 ....105 C2
Middlewich CW10 ....128 C1
Ollerton WA16 ....82 B2
Sandbach CW11 ....153 C1
Sproston Green CW4 ....129 B1
Withington Green SK11 ....109 A4
Holmes Chapel Sta
CW4 ....130 B2
Holmes Ct WA3 ....9 B2
Holmes St Cheadle SK8 ....239 E6
Stockport SK2 ....240 E3
Holmesville Ave CW12 ....156 A2
Holmeswood Cl SK9 ....60 B4
Holmfield Ave WA7 ....23 B1
Holmfield Cl SK4 ....240 D7
Holmfield Dr Cheadle SK8 ....35 A4
Ellesmere Port CH66 ....69 B2
Holmlea Dr CW1 ....190 C2
Holmlee Way SK10 ....86 B3
Holmrook WA14 ....238 B5
Holmsfield Rd WA1 ....16 B3
Holmshaw La CW1 ....192 A2
Holmwood WA14 ....238 A3
Holmwood Dr CH65 ....70 A1
Holset Dr WA14 ....238 B5
Holt Hey CH64 ....67 A3
Holt La WA7 ....49 C4
Holt St Altrincham WA14 ....238 C8
Crewe CW1 ....190 A2
Stockport SK1 ....240 F4
Holt's La SK9 ....33 C2
Holy Family RC Prim Sch
Cronton WA8 ....12 B3
Sale M33 ....242 E6
Holy Spirit RC Prim Sch The
WA7 ....49 B4
Holyhead Cl WA5 ....7 B2
Holyrood Ave WA8 ....13 A2
Holyrood Dr CW2 ....205 C4
Holyrood Way CH3 ....119 A1
Holywell Cl CH64 ....41 A1
Holywell La CH3 ....182 B1
Home Farm Ave SK10 ....86 C1
Home Pk CH1 ....94 C1
Homebeck Ho SK8 ....239 A5
Homecrofts CH64 ....66 C3
Homedee Ho CH1 ....237 A3
Homeshire Ho ST7 ....193 B2
Homestead Ave WA11 ....1 C3
Homestead Ct CW9 ....104 B4
Homestead Rd SK12 ....38 B3
Homesteads The CW5 ....172 A3
Homeway WA6 ....73 A1
Homewood Cres CW8 ....103 A3
Honey Fields CW6 ....146 B1
Honey Suckle Cl CH66 ....94 C4
Honeysuckle Cl
Broughton CH4 ....139 B2
Widnes WA8 ....13 A2
Honeysuckle Dr SK15 ....242 F2
Hong Kong Ave M90 ....33 A4
Honister Ave WA2 ....8 B1
Honiton Way
Altrincham WA14 ....238 B6
Warrington WA5 ....14 C2
Hood La WA5 ....15 B2
Hood La N WA5 ....15 B3
Hood Manor Prim Sch
WA5 ....15 B3
Hood Rd WA8 ....12 C1
Hoofield La Duddon CH3 ....145 A1
Huxley CH3 ....167 A4
Hoogreen La WA16 ....29 C1
Hooker St CW8 ....103 C4
Hookstone Dr CH66 ....69 B3
Hoole Cl SK8 ....240 A1
Hoole Gdns CH2 ....119 A2
Hoole Ho CH2 ....119 A2
Hoole La CH2 ....119 A2
Hoole Rd CH2 ....119 A2
Hoole Way CH2 ....237 B3
Hooley Range SK4 ....240 B7
Hooleyhey La SK10,SK11 ....89 B2
Hoolpool La WA6 ....72 C3
Hooper St SK1 ....240 E5
Hooton Gn CH66 ....44 A1
Hooton La CH66 ....44 A1
Hooton Rd CH64,CH66 ....43 B1
Hooton Sta CH66 ....43 B1
Hooton Way Hooton CH66 ....44 A1
14 Warrington SK9 ....34 B3
Hope Ave SK9 ....34 B2
Hope Croft CH66 ....69 C1
Hope Farm Prec CH66 ....69 C1
Hope Farm Rd CH66 ....69 C1
Hope Green Way SK10 ....36 B1
Hope La SK10 ....36 C1
Hope Rd Broughton CH4 ....139 A2
Sale M33 ....242 B6
Hope St
Ashton-u-Lyne OL6 ....242 A4
Audley ST7 ....209 C2
Chester CH4 ....140 C4
Crewe CW2 ....190 B1
Macclesfield SK11 ....112 C4
Newton-le-W WA12 ....2 A2
Northwich CW8 ....103 C4
Sandbach CW11 ....175 A3
Stockport SK4 ....240 D5
Hope St W SK11 ....112 B4
Hope Terr SK3 ....240 E4
Hopefield Rd WA13 ....19 A2
Hopes Carr SK1 ....240 F5
Hopkins Cl CW12 ....156 A2
Hopkins Field WA14 ....238 B1
Hopkins St SK14 ....241 E8
Hopley Ct CW2 ....190 A2
Hopwood Cl 16 WA3 ....3 C4
Hopwood St WA1 ....16 B3
Horace Black Gdns CH65 ....70 B3
Horace Gr SK4 ....240 E8
Horace Lawton Ct
CW12 ....156 B2
Horbury Gdns CH66 ....69 B3
Hornbeam Ave CH66 ....69 C1
Hornbeam Cl WA7 ....24 B1
Hornbeam Rd L26 ....21 A4
Hornby Dr
Congleton CW12 ....156 A2
Nantwich CW5 ....205 A3
Hornby La WA2 ....8 A3
Horncastle Cl 15 WA3 ....3 C4
Horns Mill Prim Sch
WA6 ....73 A1
Horridge Ave WA12 ....2 B3
Horrocks La WA1 ....16 A3
Horrocks Rd CH2 ....118 C3
Horsemarket St WA1 ....16 A3
Horseshoe Cl WA6 ....75 A1
Horseshoe Cres WA2 ....8 C2
Horseshoe Dr SK11 ....112 A4
Horseshoe La SK9 ....60 A1
Horsley La CW6 ....167 C1
Horstone Cres CH66 ....69 C1
Horstone Gdns CH66 ....70 A1
Horstone Rd CH66 ....69 C1
Hospital La CW5 ....203 C1
Hospital Of St John
Almhouses CH1 ....237 A3
Hospital St Crewe CW1 ....190 B3
Nantwich CW5 ....204 C3
Hospital Way WA7 ....49 C4
Hotel Rd M90 ....33 B4
Hotel St WA12 ....2 A2
Hothersall Cl CW1 ....173 A1
Hough Cl SK10 ....88 B3
Hough Gn Ashley WA15 ....31 C3
Chester CH4 ....141 A4
Hough Green Rd WA8 ....12 A2
Hough Green Sta WA8 ....12 A1
Hough La
Barnton CW8,CW9 ....78 A2
Norley WA6 ....100 C3
Wilmslow SK9 ....60 B2
Hough's La WA4 ....26 A3
Hougher Wall Rd ST7 ....209 B1
Houghley Cl SK10 ....87 B1
Houghton Cl
Chester CH2 ....118 C2
Newton-le-W WA12 ....2 A2
13 Northwich CW9 ....103 C2
Widnes WA8 ....13 B1
Houghton Croft WA8 ....12 B3
Houghton St
Newton-le-W WA12 ....2 A2
Warrington WA2 ....16 A3
Widnes WA8 ....13 B1
Houldsworth Ave WA14 ....238 E7
Houndings La CW11 ....175 A3
Hourd Way CH66 ....94 C4
Housesteads Dr CH2 ....118 C2
Housman Cl CH1 ....118 A3
Hove Cl CW1 ....190 A4
Hove The WA7 ....50 B3
Hoverty Prec WA12 ....2 A1
Hovis Mill SK11 ....112 C4
Howard Ave
Bebington CH62 ....43 B4
Lymm WA13 ....19 A2
Howard Cl SK6 ....241 A2
Howard Ct Neston CH64 ....41 C1
Howard Ct *continued*
Runcorn WA7 ....24 B2
Howard Pl 5 SK14 ....241 D6
Howard Rd
Broughton CH4 ....140 B3
Culcheth WA3 ....5 A1
Howard St Crewe CW1 ....191 A3
Stockport SK1 ....240 F6
Howards Way CH64 ....67 A3
Howarth Ct WA7 ....23 A1
Howbeck Cres CW5 ....220 A4
Howbeck Wlk CW2 ....206 B4
Howe Rd CH4 ....141 A4
Howe St SK10 ....87 C1
Howells Ave
Ellesmere Port CH66 ....69 B2
Sale M33 ....242 B7
Howey Hill CW12 ....156 B1
Howey La
Congleton CW12 ....156 B1
Frodsham WA6 ....74 A4
Howey Rise WA6 ....74 A4
Howgill Cl CH66 ....68 C3
Howley La WA1 ....16 C3
Howley Quay Ind Est
WA1 ....16 B3
Howson Rd WA2 ....8 B2
Howty Cl SK9 ....34 B1
Hoxton Cl SK6 ....241 A4
Hoylake Cl WA7 ....50 B3
Hoylake Rd Sale M33 ....242 F5
Stockport SK3 ....240 B4
Hoyle St WA5 ....15 C4
Hubert Dr CW10 ....151 B4
Hubert Worthington Ho 8
SK9 ....60 A1
Hudson Cl WA5 ....15 B4
Hudson Gr 9 WA3 ....3 C4
Hugh St CH4 ....141 B4
Hughes Ave WA2 ....8 B1
Hughes Dr CW2 ....189 C2
Hughes Pl WA2 ....8 B1
Hughes St WA4 ....16 B2
Hulley Pl SK10 ....87 C1
Hulley Rd SK10 ....87 C1
Hullock's Pool Rd ST7 ....209 C3
Hully St SK15 ....242 C2
Hulme Hall Ave SK8 ....35 A4
Hulme Hall Cres SK8 ....35 A4
Hulme Hall La WA16 ....106 A2
Hulme Hall Rd SK8 ....35 A4
Hulme Hall Schs SK8 ....35 A4
Hulme La WA16 ....106 B4
Hulme Rd M33 ....242 D5
Hulme Sq SK11 ....112 B3
Hulme St
Ashton-u-Lyne OL6 ....242 A4
Crewe CW1 ....189 C3
Hulse La CW9 ....105 B3
Hulseheath La WA16 ....30 A2
Humber Cl WA8 ....13 C2
Humber Dr ST8 ....179 C1
Humber Rd
Ellesmere Port CH66 ....69 C1
Warrington WA2 ....8 C1
Humble Bee Bank Cotts
CW5 ....187 B4
Hume St WA1 ....16 B3
Humphrey's Cl WA7 ....50 B4
Hungerford Ave CW1 ....190 C2
Hungerford Pl
Barthomley CW2 ....208 B3
Sandbach CW11 ....175 A3
Hungerford Prim Sch
CW1 ....190 C2
Hungerford Rd CW1 ....190 C2
Hungerford Terr CW1 ....190 C2
Hunsterson Rd
Bridgemere CW5 ....231 B4
Hatherton CW5 ....220 A2
Hunt Cl WA5 ....15 A4
Hunt Rd WA11 ....1 C3
Hunter Ave
Shavington CW2 ....206 B4
Warrington WA2 ....8 A2
Hunter St CH1 ....237 A3
Hunter's Cres CH3 ....121 B1
Hunter's Dr CH3 ....121 B1
Hunter's View SK9 ....34 B2
Hunters Cl SK9 ....34 C1
Hunters Ct Helsby WA6 ....73 B2
Runcorn WA7 ....49 C3
Hunters Field CW8 ....103 B4
Hunters Hill Kingsley WA6 ....75 B1
Weaverham CW8 ....77 B1
Hunters Lo SK9 ....34 C1
Hunters Mews Sale M33 ....242 A7
Wilmslow SK9 ....60 B4
Hunters Pool La SK10 ....86 B4
Hunters Rise CW7 ....126 B1
Hunters Way CH64 ....66 B4
Hunters Wlk CH1 ....237 A3
Huntersfield CW2 ....206 A2
Huntington Com Prim Sch
CH3 ....142 A3
Huntley Rd SK3 ....240 B3
Huntley St WA5 ....15 B2
Huntly Chase SK9 ....60 B4
Hunts Cl CH3 ....119 A1
Hunts Field Cl WA13 ....18 B1
Hunts La WA4 ....16 C1
Huntsbank Bsns Pk
CW2 ....205 C4
Huntsbank Dr ST5 ....210 B1
Huntsham Cl WA14 ....238 B6
Huntsman Dr M44 ....11 C4
Hurdsfield Cl CW10 ....151 B4
Hurdsfield Com Prim Sch
SK10 ....87 C1
Hurdsfield Gn SK10 ....87 C1
Hurdsfield Ho SK10 ....87 C1
Hurdsfield Ind Est SK10 ....87 C2
Hurdsfield Rd SK10 ....87 C1
Hurford Ave CH65 ....69 C2
Hurlbote Cl SK9 ....34 B3
Hurlestone Cl CH2 ....96 C1
Hurley Cl WA5 ....15 B3
Hurley Dr SK8 ....239 E2
Hurn Cl CW1 ....190 A4
Hurst Ave SK8 ....35 B3
Hurst Bank Rd OL6 ....242 B4
Hurst Cl ST7 ....210 B3
Hurst Ct CW6 ....185 C4
Hurst Hill Cres OL6 ....242 A4
Hurst La Bollington SK10 ....88 A4
Glazebury WA3 ....5 B4
Hurst Lea Ct SK9 ....60 A1
Hurst Lea Rd SK22 ....39 B4
Hurst Mews WA6 ....75 B1
Hurst Mill La WA3 ....5 B4
Hurst Rd ST8 ....179 C2
Hurst St WA8 ....23 A2
Hurst The WA6 ....75 B1
Hursthead Inf Sch SK8 ....35 B3
Hursthead Jun Sch SK8 ....35 B4
Hursthead Rd SK8 ....35 A4
Hurstvale Ave SK8 ....239 B1
Hurstwood CH3 ....143 A2
Huskisson Way WA12 ....2 A2
Hutchins' Cl CW10 ....151 C3
Hutchinson St WA8 ....22 C3
Huttfield Rd L24 ....21 A2
Hutton Ave OL6 ....242 B3
Hutton Cl
Congleton CW12 ....157 A1
Culcheth WA3 ....4 C3
Hutton Dr CW12 ....157 A1
Huxley CE Prim Sch
CH3 ....167 A4
Huxley Cl Bramhall SK7 ....35 C4
Macclesfield SK10 ....87 A1
Huxley Ct CH66 ....69 C4
Huxley Dr SK7 ....35 C4
Huxley La CH3,CW6 ....167 B3
Huxley St
Altrincham WA14 ....238 D7
Northwich CW8 ....103 C4
Huxley Terr WA14 ....238 C1
Hyacinth Cl Haydock WA11 ....1 C3
Stockport SK3 ....240 D1
Hyde Bank Ct SK22 ....39 B4
Hyde Bank Rd SK22 ....39 B4
Hyde Central Sta SK14 ....241 C6
Hyde Cl
Ellesmere Port CH65 ....69 C2
Runcorn WA7 ....49 B3
Hyde Gr M33 ....242 B6
Hyde Hospl SK14 ....241 F5
Hyde Rd M34,SK14 ....241 A7
Hyde Sixth Form Coll
SK14 ....241 E8
Hyde Tech Sch SK14 ....241 D8
Hydes Terr SK15 ....242 E2
Hyldavale Ave SK8 ....239 B6
Hylton Ct CH65 ....70 C1
Hylton Dr SK8 ....35 B4
Hythe Ave CW1 ....190 A4
Hythe Rd SK3 ....240 B4

I

Ian Rd ST7 ....195 B1
Ibis Ct WA1 ....16 A2
Ikey La CW5 ....202 C3
Ikins Dr ST7 ....209 C1
Ilex Ave WA2 ....8 A4
Ilford Gdns WA4 ....26 B2
Illingworth Ave SK15 ....242 F2
Imperial Ave CH1 ....117 B2
Imperial Mews
Crewe CW2 ....190 B2
Ellesmere Port CH65 ....70 A3
Imperial Terr M33 ....242 A6
Ince & Elton Sta CH2 ....72 A2
Ince Ave CH62 ....43 C2
Ince Cl SK4 ....240 E7
Ince Dr CH3 ....180 C1
Ince La Elton CH2 ....72 A2
Wimbolds Trafford CH2 ....96 C3
Ince Orch CH2 ....72 A2
Ince St SK4 ....240 E7
Indigo Rd CH65 ....70 C3
Ingersley Rd SK10 ....88 B4
Ingham Ave WA12 ....2 B1
Ingham Cl CH3 ....119 A1
Ingham Rd WA8 ....12 C2
Ingle Rd SK8 ....240 A2
Inglegreen CH60 ....41 A4
Inglehead Cl M34 ....241 A6
Inglenook Rd WA5 ....14 C2
Ingleton Cl Cheadle SK8 ....239 C6
Holmes Chapel CW4 ....130 A2
Newton-le-W WA12 ....2 A2
Ingleton Gr WA7 ....49 B3
Ingleton Rd SK3 ....240 C3
Inglewood WA14 ....238 B3
Inglewood Ave CW10 ....151 B3
Inglewood Cl
Partington M31 ....11 C2
Warrington WA3 ....10 A3
Inkerman St SK14 ....241 D8

Inman Ave WA9 1 A1
Inner Gosling Cl WA4 25 C1
Innisfree Cl 9 CH66 69 B3
Innovation Ho 15 CW7 149 A4
Insall Rd WA2 8 C1
Inscape House Specl Sch SK8 239 D3
Int Peace Ctr WA5 15 B3
Intack La WA16 28 A2
Intake Cl CH64 68 A4
International App M90 33 B4
Inveresk Rd SY14 198 B2
Inward Way CH65 70 A4
Ion Path CW7 127 B1
Ipswich Way 1 M34 241 A5
Irby Cl CH66 69 C2
Ireland Rd Hale L24 21 C1
Haydock WA11 1 B3
Ireland St Warrington WA2 16 A4
Widnes WA8 13 B1
Iris Cl WA8 12 B1
Iris Wlk 7 M31 11 C1
Irlam & Cadishead Com High Sch M44 11 C4
Irlam Rd M33 242 C6
Irlam Sta M44 11 C4
Ironbridge Dr CW4 130 B1
Irons La CH3 120 C4
Irvin Dr M22,SK8 34 A4
Irving's Cres CH4 140 C3
Irwell Gr WA4 16 A1
Irwell La WA7 23 A2
Irwell Rise SK10 87 C4
Irwell St WA8 23 A2
Irwin Ct SK8 239 F3
Irwin Dr SK9 34 B3
Irwin Rd WA14 238 D8
Isabella Ct CH4 140 C3
Isherwood Cl WA2 8 C2
Isis Cl CW12 156 C1
Islay Cl CH65 70 B1
Iveagh Cl WA7 50 A4
Iver Cl Chester CH2 118 C4
Cronton WA8 12 B3
Iver Rd CH2 118 C4
Ivy Ave WA12 2 B1
Ivy Bank Prim Sch SK11 112 A3
Ivy Bank Trad Est WA16 58 A2
Ivy Ct CH4 162 B1
Ivy Dr CW8 102 A1
Ivy Farm Ct L24 21 B1
Ivy Farm Dr CH64 66 C3
Ivy Farm Gdns WA3 4 B2
Ivy Farm Rd CH3 183 B1
Ivy Gdns CW12 156 B1
Ivy Ho SK11 112 A4
Ivy House Rd ST8 179 B1
Ivy La Alsager ST7 193 C1
Macclesfield SK11 112 A3
Ivy Meade Cl SK11 111 C4
Ivy Meade Rd SK11 111 C3
Ivy Mews CH2 119 A3
Ivy Rd Golborne WA3 3 A4
Macclesfield SK11 112 A4
Poynton SK12 36 C2
Warrington WA1 17 C4
Ivy St WA7 23 A1
Ivy Wlk M31 11 B2
Ivychurch Mews WA7 23 B1

J

Jack La
Moulton CW9,CW10 127 A3
Weston CW2 207 B3
Jackie Stewart Bsns Ctr CW6 147 B3
Jackson Ave Culcheth WA3 4 C2
Nantwich CW5 204 C3
Warrington WA1 16 C3
Jackson Ct CH4 139 A3
Jackson La SK10 88 A4
Jackson Rd CW12 156 C3
Jackson St
Burtonwood WA5 6 C3
Cheadle SK8 239 E6
Haydock WA11 1 A4
Hyde SK14 241 D6
Macclesfield SK11 112 B3
Sale M33 242 D7
Jackson's La SK7 36 B4
Jacksons Cl SK10 88 A4
Jacksons Edge Rd SK12 38 A3
Jacob Way WA16 79 C4
Jacobsen Ave SK14 241 F8
Jamage Rd ST7 210 B3
James Atkinson Way CW1 189 C4
James Ave CH66 69 B2
James Cl WA8 23 A2
James Dr SK14 241 E6
James Hall St CW5 204 C3
James Leech St SK1 240 E4
James Pl CH2 118 C1
James Rd WA11 1 C4
James St Chester CH2 237 B3
Dukinfield M34 241 A8
Macclesfield SK11 112 B3
Northwich CW9 104 B4
Sale M33 242 D6
Stockport SK3 240 E3
6 Warrington WA1 16 A3
Jamieson Cl Alsager ST7 193 C2
Chester CH3 119 A1
Jan Palach Ave CW5 204 C2
Jarman SK11 112 C2
Jasmin Way ST7 195 C1
Jasmine Gdns WA9 6 A4
Jasmine Gr WA8 22 B4
Jasmine Wlk M31 11 C1
Jay Cl WA3 10 A2
Jays Cl WA7 50 C4
Jayton Ave M20 239 B8
Jedburgh Ave CH66 69 A3
Jellicoe Ave M44 11 C3
Jennet's La WA3 5 B4
Jennings St SK3 240 D3
Jenny La SK7 35 C2
Jensen Ct WA7 23 B2
Jersey Ave CH65 70 B1
Jersey Cl CW12 157 A1
Jersey Rd SK5 240 F8
Jersey Way CW10 128 B1
Jervis Cl WA2 9 A2
Jesmond Cres CW2 190 A1
Jesmond Gr SK8 35 A4
Jesmond Rd CH1 118 A1
Jessop Way CW1 191 B2
JH Godwin Prim Sch CH1 117 B2
Jockey St WA2 16 A4
Jodrell Bank Science Ctr* SK11 108 B2
Jodrell Cl
Holmes Chapel CW4 130 A2
Macclesfield SK11 112 C4
Jodrell Mdw SK23 65 C4
Jodrell Rd SK23 65 B4
Jodrell St
Macclesfield SK11 112 C4
New Mills SK22 39 A4
John Ave SK8 239 E5
John Brunner Cres CW8 103 C3
John Fryer Ave CW9 80 A3
John Gresty Dr CW5 205 B3
John Lloyd Ct M44 11 C4
John May Ct SK10 87 B1
John Middleton Cl L24 21 C1
John Morris Ho 1 WA1 16 B3
John Nicholas Cres CH65 70 B3
John Rd WA13 18 B2
John Shepley St SK14 241 E6
John St Altrincham WA14 238 D4
Bollington SK10 88 A4
Congleton CW12 156 B1
Crewe CW1 190 B2
Ellesmere Port CH65 70 A3
Golborne WA3 3 A4
Hyde SK14 241 D7
Irlam M44 11 C3
Macclesfield SK11 112 B3
1 Northwich CW9 104 A4
Romiley SK6 241 C2
Sale M33 242 B7
Stockport SK1 240 F5
Utkinton CW6 146 A4
Warrington WA2 16 A3
Winsford CW7 126 B1
John Street Prim Sch CH65 70 A3
John's Pl SK6 241 C2
Johns Ave Haydock WA11 1 C4
Runcorn WA7 48 C4
Johns Cl SK10 88 B3
Johnson Ave WA12 2 A3
Johnson Cl CW12 157 A1
Johnson St SK23 65 C4
Johnson's La WA8 23 C4
Johnsons Cl CH4 141 A3
Join Rd M33 242 D6
Jonathan's Way CH1 117 C3
Jones Sq SK1 240 F3
Jones's La CW10 152 B3
Jonson Rd CH64 66 C4
Jordangate 36 SK11 112 B4
Joseph Cres ST7 193 C1
Joseph St WA8 13 B1
Joules Ct SK1 240 F4
Jowett St SK5 240 F8
Joy La WA5 6 C2
Joyce Ave CW7 126 B1
Joynson St M33 242 B7
Jubilee Ave Crewe CW2 190 A2
Stalybridge SK16 242 B1
Warrington, Padgate WA1 16 C4
Warrington, Penketh WA5 14 C2
Jubilee Cres WA11 1 C4
Jubilee Ct CW4 130 A2
Jubilee Gdns
Nantwich CW5 204 C2
New Mills SK22 39 B4
Jubilee Gr WA13 18 B2
Jubilee Ho WA7 49 B4
Jubilee Rd CW12 156 C1
Jubilee St SK22 39 B4
Jubilee Terr CW5 204 C2
Jubilee Villas CW11 175 B1
Jubilee Way Widnes WA8 12 C1
Winsford CW7 126 B1
Jubit's La WA8 13 A4
Juddfield St WA11 1 A4
Judy La SK11 113 A2
Julian Way WA8 12 C2
July Cotts CW4 141 C1
Jumper La SK10 88 C4
Junction Eight Bsns Ctr CH65 70 A4
Junction La WA12 2 A2
Junction Rd SK1,SK2 240 F3
June Ave Bebington CH62 43 C4
Stockport SK4 240 B6
Juniper Cl
Newcastle-u-L ST5 210 C1
Sale M33 242 A6
Juniper Dr CH66 69 C1
Juniper Gr CH66 69 C1
Juniper La WA3 18 A4
Juniper Rise SK10 86 C1
Jupiter Dr CH1 117 C1
Jurby Ct WA2 8 C1
Justice St SK10 87 B1

K

Karen Cl WA5 7 A3
Karen Way CH66 69 B2
Kay La WA13 29 A4
Kay St SK15 242 D1
Kaye Ave WA3 4 C2
Keats Cl
Ellesmere Port CH66 94 C4
Widnes WA8 22 C4
Keats Dr Macclesfield SK10 86 C1
Rode Heath ST7 193 C4
Wistaston CW2 206 A4
Keats Gr WA2 8 B1
Keats La CW9 80 A3
Keats Terr CH1 118 A3
Keble St WA8 23 A4
Keckwick La
Daresbury WA4 25 A2
Runcorn WA4 24 C2
Keele Cres SK11 112 A3
Keeper's La CW8 102 C4
Keeper's Rd WA4 27 A4
Keepers Cl WA16 57 B2
Keepers La CW9 53 B2
Keepers Wlk WA7 23 C1
Keith Ave WA5 14 C3
Keith Dr Bebington CH63 43 B3
Stockport SK3 240 B3
Kelburn Ct WA3 9 C3
Kelmscott Cl CH66 69 B1
Kelsall Ave CH62 43 C2
Kelsall Cl Bebington CH62 43 C2
Warrington WA3 9 B2
Widnes WA8 12 B1
Kelsall Com Prim Sch CW6 122 B2
Kelsall Cres SK3 240 D2
Kelsall Rd Ashton CH3 121 C4
Stockport SK8 240 A1
Tarvin CH3 121 B2
Kelsall St
Congleton CW12 156 C2
Sale M33 242 B6
Kelsall Way Audley ST7 209 B1
6 Wilmslow SK9 34 B3
Kelsborrow Cl CW9 103 C2
Kelsborrow Way CW6 122 B2
Kelso Way SK10 87 B2
Kelstern Cl 7 CW9 104 A4
Kelsterton Ct CH5 91 B1
Kelsterton La CH6 91 A1
Kelsterton Rd CH6,CH5 91 A1
Kelvin Ave M33 242 B6
Kelvin Cl WA3 9 B3
Kelvin Gr CH2 118 C2
Kelvin St WA3 9 C3
Kemberton Dr WA8 13 A3
Kemble Cl CW2 206 A4
Kemmel Ave WA4 16 B2
Kemp St SK14 241 E8
Kempsell Way L26 21 A4
Kempsell Wlk L26 21 A4
Kempton Ave CW1 190 B4
Kempton Cl Chester CH1 118 A1
Newton-le-W WA12 2 B3
Runcorn WA7 49 B3
Kempton Way SK10 87 B2
Kendal Ave Denton M34 241 A5
Sale M33 242 C5
Warrington WA2 8 B1
Kendal Cl Chester CH2 119 A3
Ellesmere Port CH66 69 B1
Macclesfield SK11 111 C3
Kendal Ct CW12 156 A1
Kendal Dr Bramhall SK7 35 B3
Ellesmere Port CH66 69 C1
Gatley SK8 239 C4
Kendal Gdns SK6 241 B4
Kendal Ho SK15 242 D3
Kendal Rd
Macclesfield SK11 111 C3
Widnes WA8 12 B1
Kendal Rise WA7 49 B3
Kendrick Cl CW8 77 B1
Kendrick St WA1 16 A3
Kenilworth Ave
Handforth SK9 34 B2
Knutsford WA16 57 B1
Runcorn WA7 49 A4
Kenilworth Cl
Macclesfield SK11 111 C3
Wistaston CW2 206 A4
Kenilworth Ct CH65 70 C1
Kenilworth Dr
Hazel Grove SK7 36 B4
Warrington WA1 16 C4
Kenilworth Gdns WA12 2 B1
Kenilworth Gn SK11 111 C3
Kenilworth Ho CH2 237 C3
Kenilworth Rd
Cheadle SK3 239 F7
Golborne WA3 3 C4
Macclesfield SK11 111 C3
Neston CH64 66 C3
Kenley Ave WA8 12 B3
Kenmare Bank CW9 104 A3
Kenmore Gr M44 11 B3
Kennard Pl WA14 238 E6
Kennedy Ave SK10 86 C1
Kennedy Cl CH2 119 A3
Kennedy Way SK4 240 C6
Kennel La CW8 102 A1
Kennelwood Rd CW9 78 B4
Kennerley Ct SK9 60 A4
Kennerley's La SK9 60 A4
Kennet Cl SK9 34 B1
Kennet Dr CW12 156 C1
Kennet Rd WA11 1 B3
Kennet Way SK11 111 C4
Kenneth Rd WA8 22 B4
Kennington Pk WA8 12 C2
Kenrick Cl CW3 232 B1
Kensington Ave
Ashton-u-Lyne OL6 242 B4
Warrington WA4 17 B1
Kensington Cl
Chester CH4 141 A3
Widnes WA8 13 B2
Kensington Ct
Alsager ST7 192 C2
Wilmslow SK9 60 A3
Winsford CW7 149 B4
Kensington Dr CW5 205 B2
Kensington Gdns
Altrincham WA15 238 F1
Hyde SK14 241 F5
Kensington Gn CH4 140 C3
Kensington Gr
Sale WA14 238 E8
Stalybridge SK15 242 D1
Kensington Rd
Chester CH4 141 A3
Ellesmere Port CH65 70 A3
Stockport SK3 240 B3
Kensington Way CW9 103 C2
Kent Ave Bollington SK10 87 C3
Stockport SK8 240 C1
Kent Cl CH63 43 A4
Kent Dr CW12 156 B2
Kent Gdns CH2 118 C3
Kent Gr WA7 23 A1
Kent Ho ST7 210 B3
Kent Rd Chester CH2 118 C3
Irlam M44 11 B3
Partington M31 11 C1
Stockport SK3 240 B4
Warrington WA5 15 B2
Kent St Warrington WA4 16 B2
Widnes WA8 13 A1
Kent Way WA12 2 B1
Kent Wlk SK10 86 C1
Kent's Green La CW1, CW11 191 C4
Kent's La CW1 173 B1
Kentmere Ave CW7 126 B1
Kentmere Cl SK8 239 B3
Kentmere Pl WA2 8 A2
Kenton Rd L26 21 A4
Kentridge Dr CH66 69 B2
Kentwell Dr SK10 87 B2
Kenview Cl WA8 22 A2
Kenwick Cl CH66 69 B2
Kenwood Ave
Altrincham WA15 238 F2
Bramhall SK7 35 B3
Gatley SK8 239 A6
Kenworthy St SK15 242 D1
Kenyon Ave WA5 14 C3
Kenyon La WA3 4 A2
Kenyon's La N WA11 1 C4
Kenyon's La S WA11 1 C4
Kerfoot Bsns Pk WA2 16 A4
Kerfoot St WA2 16 A4
Keristal Ave CH3 142 A4
Kerridge Cl CW10 151 A4
Kerridge Rd SK10 88 A2
Kerry Cft CH66 69 C1
Kershaw Gr SK11 112 A4
Kershaw St WA8 12 B1
Kershaw Way WA12 2 B3
Kestrel Ave WA16 57 A2
Kestrel Cl
Congleton CW12 156 C1
Middlewich CW10 151 B3
Winsford CW7 149 B3
Kestrel Dr CW1 190 A4
Kestrel La WA3 9 C2
Kestrel Rd Heswall CH60 41 B4
Northwich CW8 103 B4
Kestrels Way WA7 49 C3
Keswick Ave
Bebington CH63 43 B2
Dukinfield SK14 241 C8
Gatley SK8 239 B4
Macclesfield SK11 111 C3
Warrington WA2 8 B1
Keswick Cl Chester CH2 119 A3
Crewe CW2 189 C2
Irlam M44 11 B2
Macclesfield SK11 111 C3
Stalybridge SK15 242 D4
Widnes WA8 12 B1
Winsford CW7 126 B1
Keswick Cres WA2 8 B1
Keswick Ct CW12 156 A1
Keswick Dr Bramhall SK7 35 B3
Frodsham WA6 74 B4
Keswick Gdns CH63 43 B3
Keswick Rd SK6 37 C4
Ketlan Ct CH4 140 C4
Kettell Ave CW1 190 A3
Kettle La CW3 230 B1
Kettleshulme Way SK12 37 A2
Kettleshulme Wlk 4 SK9 34 C1
Kew Dr SK8 239 E2
Keyes Cl WA3 9 C2
Keyes Gdn WA3 9 C2
Keysbrook CH3 166 B1
Keysbrook Ave CH3 166 B1
Kidderton Cl CW5 202 C4
Kidderton La CW5 202 C4
Kidsgrove Sta ST7 194 C1
Kilbuck La WA11 2 A4
Kilburn Ave CH62 43 C3
Kilburn Cl SK8 34 A4
Kilburn Rd SK3 240 C3
Kildare Cl L24 21 B1
Kildonnan Rd WA4 17 A1
Kilford Cl WA5 7 C1
Killingworth La WA3 10 A3
Kilmorey Park Rd CH2 118 C2
Kilmorey Pk CH2 118 C2
Kilmorey Pk Ave CH2 237 C4
Kiln Croft La SK9 34 C2
Kiln La CW5 220 A4
Kilncroft WA7 50 A3
Kilsby Dr WA8 13 C1
Kilshaw Rd WA5 6 C3
Kilsyth Cl WA2 8 C2
Kimberley Ave SK6 241 C2
Kimberley Dr WA4 16 B1
Kimberley St
Stockport SK3 240 E3
Warrington WA5 15 C3
Kimberley Terr CH2 118 C1
Kinder Dr CW2 189 B2
Kinder Gr SK6 241 E2
Kinder St
Stalybridge SK15 242 D2
Stockport SK3 240 E3
Kinder View SK22 39 B4
Kinderton Cl WA16 29 B2
Kinderton St CW10 128 B1
King Arthur's Wlk WA7 24 A1
King Edward Bldgs 6 CH3 119 A1
King Edward Cl CW9 103 C3
King Edward Rd
Knutsford WA16 57 A1
2 Macclesfield SK11 112 B4
King Edward St
Macclesfield SK11 112 B4
Middlewich CW10 128 B1
Warrington WA1 16 C4
King George Ave CW9 104 A4
King George Cres WA1 16 C4
King George Rd WA11 2 A4
King James Ct WA7 49 C3
King Pl CW5 204 C3
King St Audley ST7 209 B1
Chester CH1 237 A3
Congleton CW12 156 C2
Crewe CW1 190 B2
Ellesmere Port CH65 70 B3
Hartford CW8 103 A3
Hyde SK14 241 D7
Kidsgrove ST7 195 A1
Knutsford WA16 57 A1
Macclesfield SK10 112 C4
Middlewich CW10 128 A3
Newton-le-W WA12 2 A2
Northwich CW9 104 C3
Runcorn WA7 23 A2
Sandbach CW11 174 C4
Stalybridge SK15 242 D2
Talke ST7 210 B3
King St E SK1 240 F6
King Street Trad Est CW10 128 B1
King's Ave WA3 3 C4
King's Bldgs CH1 237 A3
King's Cres CW10 128 B1
King's Cres E CH3 119 A1
King's Cres W CH3 119 A1
King's Dr SK4 240 A7
King's La Allostock CW10 106 B1
Nantwich CW5 204 B3
King's Rd Romiley SK6 241 A3
Wilmslow SK9 59 C4
King's Sch Chester CH4 141 A2
Macclesfield SK10 112 C4
Macclesfield SK10 87 B1
Kingfisher Cl
Congleton CW12 156 C1
Crewe CW1 189 C4
Farndon CH3 180 C1
Nantwich CW5 204 C4
Runcorn WA7 49 C3
Warrington WA3 9 C2
Kingfisher Ct CW9 79 B1
Kingfisher Dr 5 CW7 149 B3
Kingfisher Gr CW9 79 C3
Kingham Cl WA8 13 B1
Kinglsey Ct CW11 174 B4
Kings Acre WA14 238 A1
Kings Ave SK8 239 A4
Kings Cl Chester CH4 140 C3
Wilmslow SK9 60 A3
Kings Croft CH5 91 B1
Kings Ct Nantwich CW5 204 B3
Runcorn WA7 24 B2
Stockport SK5 240 F7
Kings Dr Helsby WA6 73 A2
Wistaston CW2 205 C4
Kings Gate CW8 102 A1
Kings Grove Sch CW2 190 A2
Kings La CW6 147 B2
Kings Lea Ho CH3 142 A4
Kings Mdw Runcorn WA7 50 B4
Shavington CW2 206 C1
Kings Mews CH66 69 B4

Kings Rd
Connah's Quay CH5 91 B1
Ellesmere Port CH66 69 B4
Golborne WA3 3 A4
Irlam M44 11 C3
Warrington WA2 9 A1
Kingsbury Cl WA4 26 B2
Kingsbury Dr 18 SK9 34 B1
Kingsdale Rd WA5 14 C4
Kingsfield Ct CH4 141 B2
Kingshead Cl WA7 24 A1
Kingsland Grange WA1 9 B1
Kingsland Rd SK3 240 A3
Kingsley Ave
Bebington CH62 43 C2
Handforth SK9 34 B1
Stockport SK4 240 E8
Kingsley Cl Hartford CW8 103 B3
Talke ST7 210 B3
Kingsley Com Prim Sch WA6 74 C1
Kingsley Cres WA7 23 A1
Kingsley Dr
Northwich CW9 104 A3
Warrington WA4 26 B4
Kingsley Gdns CH3 142 A4
Kingsley Gn WA6 74 C3
Kingsley Rd Chester CH3 142 A4
Congleton CW12 157 A2
Crowton CW8 76 A1
Ellesmere Port CH65 70 B3
Frodsham WA6 74 C2
Haslington CW1 191 B2
Runcorn WA7 23 A1
Talke ST7 210 B3
Kingsley Wlk CW7 126 A1
Kingsmead Chester CH2 118 B4
Davenham CW9 103 C2
Northwich CW9 103 C3
Kingsmead Ct WA3 9 A4
Kingsmead Sq CW9 103 C2
Kingston Ave
Macclesfield SK11 112 C4
Warrington WA5 14 C3
Kingston Cl WA7 23 C1
Kingston Ct
14 Handforth SK9 34 C1
Saughall CH1 94 A1
Kingston Dr M33 242 D7
Kingston Gdns SK14 241 B7
Kingston Hill SK8 239 D4
Kingston Pl Biddulph ST8 179 C1
Cheadle SK8 239 E2
Kingston Rd SK9 34 D3
Kingston St SK3 240 D5
Kingsway
Altrincham WA14 238 D5
Bollington SK10 87 C4
Cheadle M20,SK8 239 C6
Chester CH2 118 C3
Crewe CW2 190 A1
Frodsham WA6 74 A4
Heswall CH60 41 B3
Newton-le-W WA12 2 B1
Northwich CW9 104 A4
Widnes WA8 13 A1
Winsford CW7 126 C1
Kingsway High Sch CH2 118 C3
Kingsway Ho WA4 16 C2
Kingsway N WA1 16 C3
Kingsway S WA1,WA4 16 C2
Kingsway Sec Sch The SK8 239 C4
Kingsway W CH2 118 C2
Kingswood ST7 195 A1
Kingswood Ave
Chorlton CW2 207 A2
Saughall CH1 94 B1
Kingswood Cres CW10 151 C3
Kingswood La CH1 94 B1
Kingswood Rd WA5 7 A1
Kingswood Wlk CW6 122 B3
Kinloch Cl Crewe CW1 190 A3
Halewood L26 21 A4
Kinnerley Rd CH65 70 A2
Kinnersley Ave ST7 210 C4
Kinnersley St 1 ST7 195 A1
Kinnerton Cl CH4 140 C3
Kinnerton Hts CH4 161 A4
Kinnerton La CH4 161 A4
Kinnington Way CH1 94 C4
Kinnock Pk WA5 6 C3
Kinross Cl WA2 8 C2
Kinsale Dr WA3 9 B2
Kinsey Rd CH65 70 B1
Kinsey St CW12 156 C1
Kinsey's La CH2 71 C3
Kintore Cl Bebington CH63 43 B2
Winsford CW7 127 A2
Kintore Dr WA5 14 B3
Kintyre Cl CH65 70 B1
Kipling Ave WA2 8 B1
Kipling Cres WA8 22 C4
Kipling Rd CH1 117 C3
Kipling Way CW1 190 C2
Kirby Cl CH2 118 B3
Kirkacre Ave WA12 7 B4
Kirkby Rd WA3 4 C2
Kirkcaldy Ave WA5 14 B3
Kirkfell Dr SK6 37 C4
Kirkham Ave WA3 3 C3
Kirkham Cl WA5 15 A2
Kirkham Rd Gatley SK8 34 B4
Widnes WA8 13 B1
Kirkley St SK14 241 E5
Kirkstall Cl
Macclesfield SK10 87 A1

Kirkstall Cl *continued*
Poynton SK12 36 B2
Kirkstead Rd SK8 35 B3
Kirkstead Way WA3 3 A4
Kirkstone Ave WA2 8 B1
Kirkstone Cres WA7 50 A2
Kirkstone Ct CW12 156 A1
Kirkwall Dr WA5 15 A2
Kirkwood Cl CH3 119 A1
Kishfield La SK23 65 A3
Kitchen St CH1 118 A1
Kitchener Ave M44 11 B2
Kite Gr ST7 195 B2
Kitfield Ave CW10 151 B4
Kitt's Moss La SK7 35 B3
Kitty Wheeldon Gdns M33 242 A7
Knap The CH60 41 A3
Knebworth Ct CW12 179 A4
Knight Rd WA5 6 C3
Knight St Hyde SK14 241 E5
Macclesfield SK11 112 C4
Knight's Cl SK11 112 C4
Knight's Grange (Sports Complex) CW7 126 B2
Knights La CW6 123 C1
Knights Mdw CW7 126 B2
Knights Way CW2 206 A2
Knightsbridge SK1 240 F6
Knightsbridge Ave
4 Davenham CW9 103 C2
Warrington WA4 17 B1
Knightsbridge Cl
17 Handforth SK9 34 B1
Widnes WA8 13 B2
Knightwake Rd SK22 39 A4
Knivton St SK14 241 F7
Knole Ave SK12 36 C2
Knoll St SK22 39 A4
Knoll The WA7 49 C4
Knott Fold SK14 241 D5
Knott's Hos WN7 4 A4
Knottingley Dr CH66 69 B3
Knotty La CW12 179 C4
Knowe The CH64 68 A4
Knowl Hey Rd L26 21 A3
Knowl La CH3 180 C3
Knowl St SK15 242 E2
Knowl The CH3 180 C3
Knowle Cl CH66 69 C2
Knowle Gn SK9 34 B2
Knowle Pk SK9 34 B2
Knowles Ind Est SK23 39 B2
Knowles St 6 WA8 13 B1
Knowsley Ave WA3 3 A4
Knowsley La ST7 194 C2
Knowsley Rd
Chester CH2 118 C2
Hazel Grove SK7 36 C4
Macclesfield SK11 112 B3
Knutsford & Dist Hospl WA16 56 C1
Knutsford Ave M33 242 E6
Knutsford High Sch (Lower Sch) WA16 56 C1
Knutsford High Sch (Upper Sch) WA16 56 C1
Knutsford Rd
Antrobus CW9 53 B2
Appleton Thorn WA4 27 C4
Chelford SK11 84 A1
Great Budworth CW9 54 A1
Holmes Chapel CW4 130 A3
Lawton-gate ST7 193 C3
Mobberley WA16 57 C2
Warrington WA4 16 B2
Wilmslow SK9,WA16 59 B2
Knutsford Road Wlk 12 SK11 112 C4
Knutsford Sta WA16 57 A1
Knutsford View WA15 32 B4
Knutsford Way CH1 117 C1
Kohima Cres CH3 142 A3
Kronsbec Ave CH66 69 B3
KUS Ind Est CH5 139 A3
Kynaston Dr CH4 140 B4

L

Laburnam Cl
Congleton CW12 156 A2
Talke ST7 210 C4
Laburnham Farm Cl CH64 67 A3
Laburnum Ave
15 Nantwich CW5 204 C3
Warrington WA1 17 B4
Wistaston CW2 189 C1
Laburnum Cres CW8 78 A2
Laburnum Gr
Broughton CH4 140 C3
Crewe CW1 190 B3
Ellesmere Port CH1 95 A4
Runcorn WA7 49 B4
Weaverham CW8 102 B4
Laburnum La
Altrincham WA15 31 C4
Warrington WA5,WA8 14 B3
Laburnum Pl ST5 210 B1
Laburnum Rd
Davenham CW9 103 C2
Golborne WA3 3 C4
Irlam M44 11 B3
Macclesfield SK11 112 C3
Northwich CW9 104 B3
Laburnum Way
Holt LL13 180 B1

Laburnum Way *continued*
Stockport SK3 240 B4
Lacey Ave SK9 34 A1
Lacey Ct Widnes WA8 23 A4
Wilmslow SK9 34 A1
Lacey Gn SK9 34 A1
Lacey Gr SK9 34 B1
Lacey Green Prim Sch SK9 34 A1
Lacey St WA8 23 A4
Lache Hall Cres CH4 140 C2
Lache La Chester CH4 141 A3
Dodleston CH4 140 C2
Lache Park Ave CH4 141 A3
Lache Prim Sch CH4 141 A3
Lacy Ct CW12 156 C1
Lacy St SK1 240 F4
Ladies Mile WA16 56 C1
Ladies Wlk CH64 66 C4
Lady Acre Cl WA13 18 B1
Lady Barn House Sch SK8 239 D3
Lady Helen Wlk CW5 204 C3
Lady Kelvin Rd WA14 238 C6
Lady La Croft WA3 9 B4
Mobberley WA16 58 B4
Lady Richeld Cl WA7 24 B2
Ladybarn Ave WA3 2 C4
Ladybarn Cres SK7 35 C3
Ladybarn Manor SK7 35 C4
Ladybridge Prim Sch SK8 240 B1
Ladybrook Gr 7 SK9 34 B1
Ladybrook Prim Sch SK7 35 C4
Ladycroft Cl WA1 17 C4
Ladyfield St SK9 60 A4
Ladyfield Terr SK9 60 B4
Ladypit Rd SK23 39 C2
Ladypool L24 21 B1
Ladys Cl SK12 36 C2
Ladysmith Rd SK15 242 D4
Ladysmith St SK3 240 E3
Ladythorn Cres SK7 35 C3
Ladythorn Gr SK7 35 C3
Ladythorn Rd SK7 35 C3
Ladywood Rd WA5 7 B1
Lagos Gr CW7 126 C1
Laira Ct WA2 16 B4
Laira St WA2 16 B4
Lake House Cl CW8 77 B1
Lake La WA4 52 C3
Lake Rd SK15 242 C4
Lake View Alsager ST7 193 B1
Congleton CW12 156 A1
Whaley Bridge SK23 39 B2
Lakelands Cl SK10 112 C4
Lakeside Bosley SK11 158 B4
Chester CH4 141 B1
Gatley SK8 239 C3
Lakeside Cl Chester CH2 118 C4
Widnes WA8 22 A4
Lakeside Ctry Pk* CW1 174 B1
Lakeside Dr Poynton SK12 36 C3
Warrington WA1 16 A2
Lakeside Rd WA13 18 B1
Lakeside View
Moulton CW7 126 C4
Nantwich CW5 204 C2
Lakewood CH4 141 A1
Laleston Cl WA8 22 C4
Lamb La WA14 31 B2
Lamb St ST7 195 A1
Lambert Ct WA8 23 A4
Lambert Way CW8 103 A2
Lambert's La CW12 156 C1
Lamborne Gr CW10 128 B1
Lambourn Ave WA8 12 B3
Lambourn Cl SK12 36 B2
Lambourn Dr CW1 173 A1
Lambourne Cl
Ellesmere Port CH66 94 C4
Wythenshawe M22 33 B4
Lambourne Gr WA9 1 A2
Lambs La WA1 17 A4
Lambsickle Cl WA7 48 C3
Lambsickle La WA7 49 A3
Lamerton Cl WA5 14 B2
Lamerton Way SK9 34 C1
Lampeter Cl WA5 7 C1
Lampits La CH3 120 C3
Lamport Cl WA8 13 C2
Lampton Cl WA14 238 D7
Lanark Wlk SK10 86 C1
Lancashire Hill SK4,SK5 240 E7
Lancashire Rd M31 11 C1
Lancaster Ave
Golborne WA3 3 B4
Runcorn WA7 48 C4
Stalybridge SK15 242 D3
Widnes WA8 12 A1
Lancaster Cl
Hazel Grove SK7 36 B4
Newton-le-W WA12 1 C2
Romiley SK6 241 A1
Warrington WA2 8 C1
Winsford CW7 149 B3
Lancaster Ct 3 WA4 16 C1
Lancaster Dr CH3 119 A1
Lancaster Fields CW1 191 A1
Lancaster Gdns CH65 70 B2
Lancaster Pk CH4 139 A2
Lancaster Rd
Handforth SK9 34 C1
Irlam M44 11 B3
Widnes WA8 13 A2
Lancaster St WA5 15 C3
Lanceley Ct SY14 213 A2
Lancelyn Dr SK9 60 B4

Lancer Ct WA7 23 C2
Lancers Cft CH66 69 C1
Lancing Ave WA2 8 A2
Lancing Rd CH65 70 B2
Land Cut La WA3 9 B2
Land La SK9 60 B3
Lander Cl WA5 15 B4
Landor Cl WA3 3 C4
Landscape Dean WA6 73 B2
Landsdowne St SK10 87 C1
Landseer Ave
Neston CH64 66 C4
Warrington WA4 16 A1
Landseer Dr SK11 111 C4
Landswood Pk CW8 103 A2
Lane Ends Hale WA8 21 B3
Romiley SK6 241 D3
Lane Head Ave WA3 3 C4
Lane Head Rd SK23 65 B3
Lane The SY13,SY14 223 B2
Laneside Rd
Manchester M20 239 C8
New Mills SK22 39 C4
Langcliffe Cl WA3 4 C2
Langdale Ave 10 WA13 18 C2
Langdale Cl
Altrincham WA15 238 E5
Gatley SK8 239 C3
High Lane SK6 37 C4
Macclesfield SK11 111 C3
Warrington WA2 8 C1
Widnes WA8 22 B4
Winsford CW7 126 B1
Langdale Ct CW12 156 A1
Langdale Rd Bramhall SK7 35 B3
Partington M31 11 C2
Romiley SK6 241 B4
Runcorn WA7 23 A1
Wistaston CW2 189 B1
Langdale Terr SK15 242 D4
Langdale Way WA6 49 B1
Langden Cl WA3 4 B2
Langdon Ho CH4 141 A4
Langfield WA3 3 C4
Langfield Gr CH62 43 B3
Langford L24 21 B1
Langford Ct CH3 121 B1
Langford Rd
Lostock Gralam CW9 80 A2
Stockport SK4 240 C8
Langford St 11 SK11 112 B4
Langford Way WA4 27 B2
Langham Rd
Altrincham WA14 238 C2
Stockport SK4 240 B5
Langland Cl WA5 7 C1
Langley Ave WA12 2 B1
Langley Cl
Newcastle-u-L ST5 210 B1
Sandbach CW11 175 B4
Langley Ct CH65 70 C2
Langley Dr Chester CW2 190 A1
Handforth SK9 34 C2
Langley Hall Cl SK11 113 A2
Langley Rd
Northwich CW9 104 A3
Sutton Lane Ends SK11 113 A2
Langport Dr CH3 119 B1
Langton Cl
Newton-le-W WA12 2 A2
Widnes WA8 12 A2
Langton Gn WA1 17 B4
Langwell Cl WA3 10 A3
Lanreath Cl SK10 86 B1
Lansdown Cl SK7,SK8 35 B4
Lansdown Rd CH4 139 A2
Lansdowne Culcheth WA3 4 C1
Frodsham WA6 74 B3
Lansdowne Ave SK6 241 D2
Lansdowne Gr CH4 141 A4
Lansdowne Rd
Altrincham WA14 238 D6
Connah's Quay CH5 91 B1
Crewe CW1 190 C3
Great Barrow CH3 120 B2
Sale M33 242 A8
Lapwing Cl Golborne WA3 3 B4
Newton-le-W WA12 2 B2
Stalybridge SK15 242 D4
Winsford CW7 149 B3
Lapwing Gr WA7 50 A3
Lapwing La Moore WA4 25 A4
Withington Green SK11 109 B2
Withington Green SK11 109 B3
Lapwing Rd ST7 195 B2
Larch Ave
Macclesfield SK11 112 A3
Newton-le-W WA12 2 B1
Shavington CW2 206 C3
Warrington WA5 14 C3
Widnes WA8 13 A1
Larch Cl Golborne WA3 3 C3
Poynton SK12 36 C2
Runcorn WA7 49 B4
Weaverham CW8 102 B4
Larch Rd Denton M34 241 A7
Haydock WA11 1 C4
Partington M31 11 C2
Runcorn WA7 49 B4
Wistaston CW2 189 C1
Larch Rise SK10 86 B3
Larch Way CH4 140 C3
Larchdale Cl CH66 94 C4
Larches The WA16 58 C1
Larchfields CH1 117 A4
Larchtree Cl CW8 78 A2
Larchway Bramhall SK7 35 B4
High Lane SK6 37 C4

Larchways WA4 26 B3
Larchwood SK8 239 D6
Larchwood Dr SK9 60 C4
Lark Ave ST7 195 B2
Lark Hall Cl SK10 113 A4
Lark Hall Cres SK10 113 A4
Lark Hall Rd SK10 113 A4
Lark Hill SK15 242 D4
Lark Hill Cotts SK22 39 A4
Lark Hill Prim Sch SK3 240 C4
Lark Hill Rd SK3 240 D4
Larkfield ST7 195 A1
Larkfield Ave WA1 17 A3
Larkhill Rd SK8 240 C1
Larkhill View SK8 240 C1
Larkspur Cl Chester CH4 140 C2
Nantwich CW5 204 C4
Runcorn WA7 49 C2
Larkstoke Cl WA4 26 C3
Larksway CH60 41 A4
Larkwood Way SK10 87 C3
Larne Ave SK3 240 B3
Larwood Ave SK4 240 B5
Lasky La WA4 17 C2
Latchford CE Prim Sch WA4 16 A2
Latchford Rd CH60 41 A3
Latchford St WA4 17 A2
Latham Ave Helsby WA6 73 A1
Newton-le-W WA12 2 B2
Runcorn WA7 23 B1
Warrington WA2 16 A4
Latham Ho WA12 2 A2
Latham Rd CW11 175 A3
Latham St CW7 126 B1
Lathom Gr M33 242 E5
Lathom Rd M44 11 C4
Lathom Way SK10 87 C1
Launceston Cl
Runcorn WA7 50 B3
Winsford CW7 149 A4
Launceston Dr
Bramhall SK7 35 C4
Warrington WA5 14 C2
Laura St CW2 190 B1
Laurel Ave Cheadle SK8 239 D5
Newton-le-W WA12 2 B2
Warrington WA1 17 B4
Laurel Bank
Warrington WA4 17 B1
Widnes WA8 13 A2
Winsford CW7 149 B4
Laurel Cl Barnton CW8 78 A2
Middlewich CW10 128 A1
Sandbach CW11 175 B3
Laurel Dr
Ellesmere Port CH65 70 A1
Kidsgrove ST7 195 C2
Willaston CH64 43 A1
Wistaston CW2 189 C1
Laurel End La SK4 240 A7
Laurel Gn M34 241 A6
Laurel Gr Chester CH2 119 A2
Golborne WA3 3 B4
Laurel Pk CW6 145 A3
Laurel Rd 1 SK4 240 B8
Laurel St SK4 240 E6
Laurel Way SK8 35 B4
Laurel Wlk M31 11 C1
Laurels Farm Ct CH2 72 A2
Laurelwood Dr 6 CH66 69 C1
Laureston Ave CW1 190 C2
Laurieston Ct SK8 239 C5
Lavender Cl WA7 23 B1
Lavender Dr CW9 104 C4
Lavender Wlk M31 11 C1
Lavenders Brow 22 SK1 240 F5
Lavenham Cl
Hazel Grove SK7 36 C4
Macclesfield SK10 87 B1
Lavington Ave SK8 240 A2
Lavister Cl 11 CW9 103 C2
Lavister Wlks LL12 162 B1
Law St CH2 118 C2
Lawford Cl CW1 189 C4
Lawford Dr CH60 41 B4
Lawn Ave WA1 16 C4
Lawn Dr
Altrincham WA15 238 E6
Chester CH2 118 B4
Lawnhurst Trad Est SK8 240 B1
Lawns Ave CH63 43 A3
Lawns The
Altrincham WA14 238 C3
Wilmslow SK9 59 C2
Lawnsdale CW8 101 B3
Lawnswood Gr CH2 72 A2
Lawrence Ave CW9 126 C4
Lawrence Ave E CW10 128 B1
Lawrence Cl
Cranage CW4 130 A3
3 Sandbach CW11 174 B3
Lawrence Pl SK12 36 B1
Lawrence Rd WA14 238 C6
Lawrence St Crewe CW1 190 B2
Hawarden CH5 116 A2
Stockport SK1 240 E5
Laws Gdns CH3 142 A4
Lawson Ave SK8 239 B5
Lawson Cl WA1 17 C4
Lawson Gr M33 242 A8
Lawton Ave Bramhall SK7 35 C4
Lawton-gate ST7 194 B2
Lawton Cl WA3 4 C2
Lawton Coppice ST7 194 C2

Lawton Heath Rd ST7 193 C3
Lawton Rd Alsager ST7 193 C2
Stockport SK4 240 C8
Lawton St
Congleton CW12 156 C1
Crewe CW2 190 B2
Hyde SK14 241 E7
Kidsgrove ST7 195 B2
Stalybridge SK15 242 E1
Lawton Way CW11 174 C4
Lawtongate Est ST7 194 A2
Laxey Ave WA1 17 B3
Laxton Cl CH66 94 C4
Laxton Way CW10 128 B1
Layland Ave WA3 4 C2
Layton Ave SK14 241 C6
Layton Cl WA3 9 C2
Layton Dr SK6 241 C3
Lea Ave Crewe CW1 190 C2
Goostrey CW4 107 B1
Lea Bank Cl SK11 112 A4
Lea Cl CW11 175 B3
Lea Cross Gr WA8 12 B2
Lea Ct SK4 240 B8
Lea Dr Nantwich CW5 204 B2
Wimboldsley CW10 151 A2
Lea Hall Pk CH1 95 A2
Lea La CH3 164 B2
Lea Rd Gatley SK8 239 B1
Stockport SK4 240 C8
Lea St SK22 39 A4
Lea Way ST7 193 B2
Lea's Pas CW10 128 A1
Leacroft Rd WA3 10 A4
Leadbeaters Cl SK11 112 C4
Leadbeaters Rd SK11 112 C4
Leadgate La CH3 144 C1
Leadsmithy St CW10 128 B1
Leadworks La CH2 237 C3
Leaf La CW7 127 A1
Leaf Lane Inf Sch CW7 127 A1
Leafield Dr SK8 34 C3
Leafield Rd SK12 38 B3
Leafy Way CW8 102 B4
Leahurst Cl CH2 118 C2
Leam St OL6 242 A4
Leamington Ave WA12 2 B1
Leamington Cl
Neston CH64 66 C3
Warrington WA5 15 A4
Leamington Rd
Congleton CW12 155 C2
Macclesfield SK10 86 C1
Lear Dr CW2 205 C4
Leas Cl 8 CH66 69 B3
Leaside WA7 23 B1
Leaside Rd CH1 117 C3
Leaside Way SK9 60 B3
Leatham Cl WA3 9 C2
Leather's La L26 21 A4
Leawood Cl CW8 103 A3
Ledbury Dr CW2 206 A4
Ledge Ley SK8 34 C4
Ledger Rd WA11 1 A3
Ledley St SK10 87 C4
Ledsham Cl WA3 9 B2
Ledsham Hall La CH66 68 C2
Ledsham La CH66 68 C2
Ledsham Park Dr CH66 69 A3
Ledsham Rd CH66 69 A3
Ledsham Village CH66 68 C1
Ledston Cl WA7 24 B1
Ledward La WA14 238 B2
Ledward St CW7 127 A1
Ledyard Cl WA5 15 B4
Lee Ave WA14 238 C7
Lee Cl WA16 56 C1
Lee Dale Cl M34 241 A6
Lee Dr CW8 103 C4
Lee Rd WA5 15 A3
Lee St Chester CH2 237 C3
16 Stockport SK1 240 F5
Leech Rd SY14 213 A2
Leech St Hyde SK14 241 F6
Stalybridge SK15 242 D1
Leegate Gdns SK4 240 A8
Leegate Rd SK4 240 A8
Leek Old Rd SK11 112 C1
Leek Rd CW12 179 A4
Leen La CH1 237 B2
Lees La
Ellesmere Port CH65 70 C2
Mottram St Andrew SK10 61 A4
Neston CH64 67 A4
Lees Rd SK7 35 B3
Lees St SK15 242 D2
Leeside SK4 240 A5
Leesway Dr M34 241 A6
Leewood Ct 7 SK4 240 B7
Leftwich Com Prim Sch
CW9 104 A2
Legh Cl SK12 36 C2
Legh Ct M33 242 E5
Legh Gdns WA16 57 A1
Legh Rd Adlington SK10 62 B3
Haydock WA11 1 A3
High Lane SK12 38 A3
Knutsford WA16 82 A4
Prestbury SK10 87 A4
Sale M33 242 E5
Legh St Golborne WA3 3 A4
Newton-le-W WA12 2 A2
Warrington WA1 16 A3
Legh Vale Prim Sch WA11 1 A3
Leicester Ave ST7 193 B3
Leicester Rd
Altrincham WA15 238 F2
Sale M33 242 B7
Leicester St
Northwich CW9 79 A1
Warrington WA5 15 C3
Leigh Ave Knutsford WA16 57 B2
Widnes WA8 13 A1
Leigh Green Cl 4 WA8 22 B4
Leigh La CW8 77 B3
Leigh Prim Sch
Hyde SK14 241 E6
Hyde SK14 241 F6
Leigh Rd
Altrincham WA15 238 E2
Congleton CW12 157 A3
Wilmslow SK9 59 B3
Leigh St Hyde SK14 241 E6
3 Lymm WA13 18 C2
Macclesfield SK11 112 C4
Leigh Way CW8 77 B1
Leigh's Brow CW8 77 C2
Leighstone Ct CH2 237 A4
Leighton Chase CH64 41 B1
Leighton Ct CH64 66 B4
Leighton Hospl CW1 172 C1
Leighton Pk CH64 66 B4
Leighton Prim Sch CW1 189 C4
Leighton Rd CH64 41 B1
Leighton St CW1 190 A3
Leighton View CW1 190 A4
Leightons The CH64 66 B4
Leinster Gdns WA7 22 C2
Leinster St WA7 22 C2
Leiria Way WA7 23 A1
Leith Ave M33 242 E6
Leith Rd M33 242 E6
Lenham Wlk M22 33 B4
Lenthall Ave CW12 178 C4
Leon Cl WA5 14 B4
Leonard St Blacon CH1 118 A2
Runcorn WA7 48 B4
Warrington WA2 16 B4
Warrington, Stockton Heath
WA4 16 B1
Leslie Rd CW7 149 A4
Lessingham Rd WA8 12 C2
Lester Cl ST7 193 B2
Leven Ave CW7 126 C1
Leven Wlk CH66 70 A4
Levens Cl SK8 239 B4
Levens Way 1 WA8 22 B4
Leveret Rd L24 21 A2
Leverett Cl WA14 238 A5
Levisham Gdns WA5 15 C4
Lewin St CW10 128 B1
Lewis Ave WA5 7 C1
Lewis Cl
Ellesmere Port CH65 95 B4
Nantwich CW5 205 A3
Lewis Cres WA8 23 A4
Lewis Gr WA8 12 B1
Lewis St CW1 190 B2
Lexden St WA5 15 C3
Leyburn Gr SK6 241 C2
Leycester Cl WA16 82 B4
Leycester Rd
Knutsford WA16 82 A4
Mobberley WA16 57 C4
Leyfield Ave SK6 241 C2
Leyfield Ct Chester CH4 140 C3
Romiley SK6 241 C2
Leygate View SK22 39 A4
Leyland Ave SK8 239 B6
Leyland Dr CH4 140 B3
Leyland Gr
Haslington CW1 191 B2
Haydock WA11 1 A3
Leyland St SK1 240 E5
Leyland Wlk CW7 149 B3
Leys Rd WA14 238 E8
Leyton Cl WA7 49 A3
Libson Cl WA2 9 A2
Lichfield Ave WA3 3 B4
Lichfield Cl WA16 57 B1
Lichfield Ct CW7 149 B4
Lichfield Dr CH66 94 C4
Lichfield Rd Blacon CH1 117 C3
Talke ST7 210 B4
Lichfield St CW10 128 B1
Lichfield Wlk SK6 241 A1
Lidgetts La SK10 88 B2
Liebig St WA8 23 A4
Light Alders La SK12 38 A3
Light Oaks Rd WA3 5 B3
Lightburn St 4 WA7 22 C1
Lightfoot Cl CH60 41 A4
Lightfoot La Eaton CW6 147 A2
Heswall CH60 41 A4
Lightfoot St CH2 118 C1
Lighthorne Ave SK3 239 F7
Lighthorne Gr SK3 239 F7
Lighthorne Rd SK3 239 F7
Lighthouse Rd L24 47 C4
Lightley Cl CW11 175 A2
Lightwood Green Ave
CW3 229 A1
Lightwood Rd ST5 210 B1
Lilac Ave Knutsford WA16 56 C1
Warrington WA5 15 A3
Widnes WA8 13 A1
Lilac Cl Kelsall CW6 122 C1
Newcastle-u-L ST5 210 B1
Lilac Cres WA7 49 B4
Lilac Ct CW12 156 C1
Lilac Dr CW8 103 B3
Lilac Gr
Ellesmere Port CH1 95 A4
Lilac Gr *continued*
Warrington WA4 16 C1
Lilac St SK2 240 F2
Lilac Wlk M31 11 C2
Lilford Ave WA5 15 C4
Lilford Dr WA5 14 C3
Lilford Sq SK11 112 B3
Lilford St WA5 15 C4
Lillyfield CH60 40 C3
Lily Ave WA12 2 B1
Lily Cl SK3 240 D1
Lily La CW10 129 A3
Lime Ave Frodsham WA6 74 B4
Northwich CW9 103 C3
Weaverham CW8 102 B4
Widnes WA8 13 A1
Lime Cl Hollinfare WA3 11 A1
Middlewich CW10 128 A1
Sandbach CW11 175 A4
Tarporley CW6 146 B1
Lime Ct CW9 103 C3
Lime Gr Alsager ST7 193 C1
Broughton CH4 140 B3
Cheadle SK8 239 D6
Chester CH2 119 A2
Elton CH2 72 A2
Golborne WA3 3 C3
Macclesfield SK10 112 C4
Runcorn WA7 49 B4
Shavington CW2 206 B2
Winsford CW7 127 A1
Lime Kiln La ST7 194 C1
Lime St Congleton CW12 156 B1
Crewe CW1 190 B3
Ellesmere Port CH65 70 B4
Lime Tree Ave
Congleton CW12 156 A2
Crewe CW1 190 C3
Lime Tree Cl CH1 95 A4
Lime Tree Dr CH3 180 C1
Lime Tree Gr CH60 41 B4
Lime Tree La WA16 29 B3
Lime Tree Prim Sch
M33 242 E5
Lime View SK11 112 B1
Lime Wlk
21 Handforth SK9 34 B1
Partington M31 11 B2
Limefield Ave WA13 18 C1
Limehurst Gr CH62 43 B3
Limekiln La WA5 6 C2
Limekiln Row WA7 50 A4
Limes La WA4 52 B3
Limes The Culcheth WA3 4 B2
Golborne WA3 3 B3
Middlewich CW10 128 A1
Limetree Ave
Warrington WA1 17 A4
Warrington, Stockton Heath
WA4 16 C1
Limeways WA4 26 C3
Limewood Cres CW8 78 A2
Limewood Gr CW8 78 A2
Lincoln Ave Gatley SK8 34 A4
Irlam M44 11 B2
Lincoln Cl Golborne WN7 4 B4
Macclesfield SK10 86 C1
Rainow SK10 88 C3
Runcorn WA7 49 B3
Warrington WA1 17 C3
Lincoln Ct WA6 73 A2
Lincoln Dr CH2 119 A3
Lincoln Gr M33 242 F6
Lincoln Pl SK10 86 C1
Lincoln Rd Blacon CH1 117 C3
Ellesmere Port CH66 69 B2
Handforth SK9 34 C1
Kidsgrove ST7 194 C1
Lincoln Rise SK6 241 A1
Lincoln Sq WA8 13 A1
Lincoln St CW1 190 A3
Lincoln Wlk SK10 86 C1
Lincombe Hey SK10 87 B4
Lincombe Rd M22 33 B4
Lindale Cl CW12 157 A3
Linden Ave WA15 238 E5
Linden Cl
Congleton CW12 179 A4
Denton M34 241 A7
Ellesmere Port CH66 94 C4
Lymm WA13 19 A2
Warrington WA1 17 B4
Linden Ct
Sandbach CW11 174 C2
Widnes WA8 12 C2
Linden Dr Biddulph ST8 179 B1
Crewe CW1 190 C2
Helsby WA6 73 A1
Mickle Trafford CH2 96 C1
Linden Gr Bramhall SK7 35 B2
Broughton CH4 140 B3
Chester CH2 119 A2
Linden Rd M34 241 A7
Linden Road Prim Sch
M34 241 A7
Linden Way High Lane SK6 38 A4
Widnes WA8 12 C2
Lindens The CW10 128 A1
Lindfield Cl WA4 25 A3
Lindfield Est N SK9 60 A3
Lindfield Est S SK9 59 C3
Lindi Ave WA4 17 B1
Lindisfarne Ave
Ellesmere Port CH65 70 B1
Golborne WA3 4 B4
Lindisfarne Cl CW10 128 A1
Lindisfarne Dr SK12 36 B2
Lindley Ave WA4 16 C2
Lindley Dro SK3 240 D1
Lindop Cl WA16 57 B1
Lindop Rd WA15 238 F1
Lindow Com Prim Sch
SK9 59 B2
Lindow Ct M33 242 F5
Lindow Fold Dr SK9 59 B3
Lindow La SK9 59 C3
Lindow Par SK9 59 C3
Lindow St M33 242 F5
Lindrick Cl SK10 87 B2
Lindrum Ave SK11 112 B1
Linds Worth Cl WA5 15 B3
Lindsay St SK15 242 E1
Lindsay Way ST7 193 A2
Lindsay Wlk CW8 102 A2
Lindsell Rd WA14 238 C8
Linear View WA12 2 B1
Lines Rd M44 11 C4
Linfields CH4 140 C3
Lingdale Rd SK8 239 F2
Lingdale Wlk SK11 112 B3
Lingfield Cl SK10 87 B2
Lingfield Dr CW1 190 B4
Lingfield Rd WA7 22 C1
Lingley Green Ave WA5 14 B4
Lingley Rd WA5 14 B3
Linglongs Ave SK23 65 B3
Linglongs Rd SK23 65 B3
Lingmell Gdns CW4 129 C2
Lingwell Ave WA8 12 B1
Lingwood Rd WA5 14 C3
Link The SK9 34 B2
Link Wlk M31 11 B1
Links Ave CH66 69 B4
Links Cl CH63 43 A3
Links Rd Romiley SK6 241 D2
Wilmslow SK9 59 C2
Linkside Ave WA2 8 A3
Linkside Way CH66 94 C4
Linksway Chester CH2 118 B4
Congleton CW12 178 C4
Gatley SK8 239 A4
Linksway Cl CW12 178 C4
Linkway WA7 49 B4
Linley Gr Alsager ST7 193 C2
Stockport SK3 240 D1
Linley La ST7 194 A1
Linley Rd Alsager ST7 193 C1
Cheadle SK8 35 A4
Sale M33 242 B7
Talke ST7 210 B4
Linley Trad Est ST7 194 B1
Linnards La CW9,WA16 80 A3
Linnet Cl
Newton-le-W WA12 2 B2
Warrington WA2 8 B2
Winsford CW7 150 A4
Linnet Gr
Macclesfield SK10 87 A1
Warrington WA3 9 C2
Linnets Way CH60 40 C4
Linnett Cl CW1 190 A4
Linton Rd M33 242 C8
Linum Gdns WA9 6 A4
Linwood Cl WA7 50 B3
Lion Salt Works Mus*
CW9 79 B2
Lion St CW12 156 B1
Lisburn Ave M33 242 A5
Liskeard Cl WA7 50 A3
Liskeard Dr SK7 35 C4
Lismore WA15 238 F2
Lismore Ave SK3 240 B4
Lismore Wlk M22 33 C4
Lisson Gr WA15 238 E2
Lister Cl CW10 151 B3
Lister Rd WA7 23 B2
Litherland Rd M33 242 E5
Little Abbey Gateway
CH1 237 A3
Little Aston Cl SK10 87 B2
Little Bollington CE Prim Sch
WA14 20 A1
Little Budworth Ctry Pk
CW6 147 B4
Little Delph WA11 1 B4
Little Egerton St 5 SK1 240 E6
Little Gn CH66 69 B2
Little Heath Cl CW3 230 A3
Little Heath La WA14 20 B3
Little Heath Rd
Chester CH3 119 C1
Christleton CH3 142 C4
Little La CH64 41 B1
Little Leigh Prim Sch
CW8 77 B3
Little Meadow Cl SK10 87 A4
Little Meadow Rd WA14 238 B1
Little Moreton Hall*
CW12 177 C1
Little Moss Cl ST7 194 C3
Little Moss La ST7 194 C3
Little Roodee CH5 139 A4
Little Row 14 ST7 195 A1
Little St Congleton CW12 156 B1
3 Macclesfield SK11 112 B4
Little St John St CH1 237 B2
Little Stanney La CH2 95 C4
Little Sutton CE Prim Sch
CH66 69 A3
Little Sutton Sta CH66 69 B3
Little Underbank 1
SK1 240 F5
Little Wissage CH66 69 C1
Littlebourne WA7 50 C4
Littlecote Ave WA4 26 B2
Littledale Rd WA5 14 C4
Littledales La CW8 102 C2
Littlegate WA7 49 C4
Littler Grange Ct CW7 126 A1
Littler La CW7 125 C1
Littler Rd WA11 1 A3
Littlestone Cl WA8 13 A2
Littleton Cl
6 Davenham CW9 103 C2
Warrington WA5 15 B2
Littleton La CH3 119 C1
Littondale Cl CW12 157 A3
Liverpool Pl WA8 12 B1
Liverpool Rd
Backford CH1,CH2 95 A2
Chester CH2 118 B3
Haydock WA11 1 A4
Irlam M44,WA3 11 B2
Kidsgrove ST7 195 A1
Neston CH64 41 C1
Newcastle-u-L ST5 210 B1
Warrington WA5,WA1 15 C3
Warrington, Great Sankey
WA5,WA8 14 C3
Widnes WA8 12 B1
Liverpool Rd E ST7 194 C1
Liverpool Rd W ST7 194 A2
Liverpool Row WA12 7 B4
Liverpool St CW9 104 B4
Livingstone Cl
Macclesfield SK11 111 C4
Warrington WA5 15 B4
Livingstone Rd CH65 70 B4
Livingstone Way CW10 151 B3
Liz Kaye Ho SK11 112 C4
Llanberis Rd SK8 239 E1
Llandaff Cl CH66 69 C1
Llandovery Cl CW7 149 A4
Llanfair Rd 7 SK3 240 C4
Lloyd Ave SK8 239 A6
Lloyd Cl CH3 180 C1
Lloyd Cres WA12 1 C2
Lloyd Dr CH65 70 B1
Lloyd Gdns WA14 238 D3
Lloyd Pl CH1 117 C2
Lloyd Sq 6 WA14 238 D4
Lloyd St
Altrincham WA14,WA15 238 D4
Stockport SK4 240 D7
Lloyd's Ct WA14 238 D4
Llyndir La LL12 162 A1
Llys Caer CH4 139 A2
Llys Derwen CH4 161 A4
Loachbrook Ave CW12 156 A1
Lobelia Gr WA7 49 C3
Lobelia Wlk 6 M31 11 C1
Loch St WA7 23 A2
Lochinvar Ave CH66 68 C3
Lochleven Rd CW2 206 A4
Lochmaben Cl CW4 130 A1
Lock La M31 11 C2
Lock Rd Altrincham WA14 238 C6
Bebington CH62 44 A4
Warrington WA1 16 C3
Locker Ave WA2 8 A1
Lockerbie Cl
Holmes Chapel CW4 130 B1
Warrington WA2 8 C2
Lockett Rd WA8 13 A2
Lockett St WA4 16 C2
Lockgate E WA7 24 B1
Lockgate W WA7 24 A1
Locking Stumps Com Prim
Sch WA3 9 B2
Locking Stumps La WA3 9 A2
Lockitt St CW2 190 B2
Locksley Cl SK4 240 C6
Lockton La WA5 15 C4
Lockwood View WA7 50 C3
Lodge Brow SK10 63 A1
Lodge Cl WA13 19 A2
Lodge Dr Culcheth WA3 4 C2
Moulton CW9 126 C4
Winsford CW7 127 A1
Lodge Gdns CH2 118 B3
Lodge Hollow WA6 73 A2
Lodge La Antrobus CW9 54 A3
Dutton WA4 76 B4
Hartford CW8 103 A2
Hatherton CW5 220 A2
Hyde SK14 241 D8
Lostock Gralam CW9 80 A1
Newton-le-W WA12 2 A4
Runcorn WA7 49 C4
Saughall CH1 94 A1
Warrington WA5 15 C4
Widnes WA8 12 A2
Lodge Rd Alsager ST7 193 B2
Knutsford WA16 57 B2
Sandbach CW11 174 C3
Talke ST7 210 B3
Widnes WA8 22 A4
Lodge The CH2 237 C3
Lodgefields Dr CW2 189 C2
Lodgefields Prim Sch
CW2 189 C2
Lodmore La SY13 233 B3
Lofthouse Gate WA8 12 C2
Lomas Sq SK11 112 B3
Lomas St SK3 240 D3
Lomax Rd CW5 205 B3
Lomond Gr CH66 69 C2
London Pl 13 SK1 240 F5
London Rd Adlington SK10 62 B3
Alderley Edge SK9 60 A1
Allostock WA16 107 A3
Bridgemere CW5 232 A3
Davenham CW9 104 A1
Frodsham WA6 74 A4

ondon Rd *continued*
Hatherton CW5 .220 B2
Holmes Chapel CW4 .130 B1
Macclesfield SK11 .112 B2
Nantwich CW5 .204 C3
Northwich CW9 .103 C4
Sandbach CW11 .174 B4
Stapeley CW5 .205 A2
Warrington WA4 .26 B3
ondon Rd N SK12 .36 C3
ondon Rd S SK12 .36 B2
ondon Rd Terr SK11 .112 B3
ondon Row WA12 .7 B4
ondon Sq 10 SK1 .240 F5
oney St SK11 .112 B4
ong Acre CW8 .77 B1
ong Acres Rd CH64 .41 C1
ong Barn La WA1 .17 B4
ong Croft La SK8 .239 F1
ong Hill SK23 .65 C1
ong La Alpraham CW6 .169 C2
Bickerton SY14 .199 C2
Bollington SK10 .63 A1
Burland CW5 .203 A4
Chester CH2 .119 A3
Hargrave CH3 .143 B1
Haughton CW6 .186 B2
Huxley CH3 .166 B4
Kidsgrove ST7 .195 C2
Lower Peover WA16 .107 B4
Middlewich CW10 .151 B4
Saughall CH1 .94 A1
Swettenham CW12 .131 C3
Tilston SY14 .198 A2
Warrington WA2 .8 A1
Wettenhall CW6,CW7 .170 B3
Whaley Bridge SK23 .65 C2
ong La S CW10 .151 B4
ong Lane Com Prim Sch
WA2 .8 A1
ong Looms CH3 .120 C3
ong Marl Dr SK9 .34 C2
ong Mdw CH60 .40 C3
ong Meadow Pas
SK14 .241 D7
ong Row ST7 .195 A1
ong Shoot CW4 .130 B4
ong Shoot Rd SK11 .108 C1
ong Spinney WA7 .50 B4
ong Valley Rd ST8 .179 B1
ng Wlk M31 .11 B2
ngacre St SK11 .112 B4
ngacres Rd WA15 .32 B4
ngbarn Bvd WA2 .9 B1
ngbarn Com Prim Sch
WA3 .9 A1
ngbenton Way WA7 .24 A2
ngburgh Cl CH2 .118 C2
ngbutt La WA13 .19 A1
ngbutts La SK11 .111 C1
ngclough Rd ST5 .210 B1
ngcroft Dr WA14 .238 B4
ngcross Ct CW10 .128 B1
ngdale Dr CH1 .117 B3
ngden Ct SK7 .35 C3
ngden La SK11 .113 A3
ngden St SK11 .112 C4
ngdin St WA4 .16 C2
ngdown Rd CW12 .155 C2
ngfield Ave
Chester CH2 .118 C4
Hatley SK8 .34 B4
ngfield Rd WA2 .8 B1
ngford St Crewe CW2 .190 B1
Warrington WA2 .16 A4
nghill La CW3 .230 C3
nghorn Cl CW10 .128 B1
nglands Dr SK22 .39 A4
nglands Rd SK22 .39 A4
ngley Ave CW6 .122 D3
nglooms Rd CH65 .70 B1
ngmeade Gdns SK9 .60 B3
ngmeadow Cheadle SK8 .35 B4
Weaverham CW8 .102 B4
ngmoss Cl CW10 .151 A4
ngmynd Rise CW7 .149 A4
ngnor Rd Gatley SK8 .34 B4
Hazel Grove SK7 .36 C4
ngridge WA16 .57 B2
ngridge Ave SK15 .242 D4
ngridge Trad Est
WA16 .57 B2
ngsdon Cl ST5 .210 B1
ngshaw St WA5 .15 C4
ngshut La SK1,SK2 .240 F3
ngshut La W SK2 .240 F3
ngsides Rd WA15 .32 B4
ngsight La SK8 .34 C3
ngsons The SK5 .240 F7
ngster Cl WA6 .73 A1
ngstone La CW6 .124 C2
ngton Ave WA3 .3 B4
ngview Ave ST7 .193 C2
ngwood Cl
Middlewich CW10 .151 B4
Romiley SK6 .241 E3
ngwood Rd
Stretton WA4 .26 C3
Warrington WA4 .26 C3
nsdale Cl
Warrington WA5 .14 C4
3 Widnes WA8 .22 B4
nsdale Ct CH4 .140 C2
oe Cl WA8 .12 C1
oms The CH64 .41 A1
onies Ct 1 SK1 .240 F4
ont The CW7 .149 B4
rd Kitchener Ct M33 .242 B7
Lord Nelson St WA1 .16 B3
Lord St Bollington SK10 .88 A4
Chester CH3 .118 C1
Crewe CW2 .190 B2
Croft WA3 .9 A4
Macclesfield SK11 .112 B4
Newton-le-W WA12 .2 A2
Runcorn WA7 .22 C2
Stockport SK1 .240 F5
Warrington WA4 .16 A2
Lord's St M44 .11 B3
Lords La WA3 .9 B2
Lords Mill Rd CW2 .206 A2
Lordship La WA6 .73 A4
Lordshire Pl ST7 .195 C1
Loreto Convent Gram Sch
WA14 .238 C5
Loreto Convent Prep Sch
WA14 .238 C5
Lorland Rd SK3 .240 B3
Lorne Gr SK3 .240 E2
Lorne St CH1 .237 A3
Lorraine St ST7 .195 C1
Lostock Ave Poynton SK12 .36 A2
Sale M33 .242 E6
Warrington WA5 .15 C4
Lostock Ct SK9 .34 B2
Lostock Gralam CE Prim Sch
CW9 .80 A1
Lostock Gralam Sta CW9 .80 A1
Lostock Hall Prim Sch
SK12 .36 A2
Lostock Hall Rd SK12 .36 A2
Lostock Hollow CW9 .80 A1
Lostock Rd SK12 .36 B1
Lostock Way SK9 .34 B2
Lottery St SK3 .240 D5
Louise St CH1 .237 A3
Loushers La WA4 .16 B1
Loushers Lane Sch WA4 .16 B1
Lovage Cl WA2 .9 B1
Lovat Dr WA16 .82 A4
Lovatt Ct WA13 .19 A2
Love La
Hassall Green CW11 .176 B2
Nantwich CW5 .204 C3
Stockport SK4 .240 E6
Love St CH1 .237 B2
Lovel Terr WA8 .22 A3
Lovell Dr SK14 .241 F8
Lovely La WA5 .15 C3
Low Hill WA6 .97 B3
Low Leighton Rd SK22 .39 B4
Low Mdw SK23 .65 B4
Low St ST7 .193 C4
Lowcross La SY14 .198 B2
Lowe Ave
Congleton CW12 .156 C1
Warrington WA4 .16 C2
Lowe Cres CW9 .53 B2
Lowe Dr WA16 .57 A1
Lowe St Denton M34 .241 B7
Golborne WA3 .3 A4
Macclesfield SK11 .112 B4
16 Stockport SK1 .240 F6
Lower Appleton Rd WA8 .13 A1
Lower Ash Rd ST7 .194 C1
Lower Bank St 10 SK11 .112 C4
Lower Beech Cotts SK10 .87 B1
Lower Bridge St CH4 .237 B1
Lower Brook St CH5 .91 B1
Lower Bury St SK4 .240 D6
Lower Carrs 21 SK1 .240 F5
Lower Church St WA8 .23 A3
Lower Cl L26 .21 A4
Lower Darwin St CW8 .103 C3
Lower Exchange St
SK11 .112 B4
Lower Field Rd CH4 .141 A3
Lower Fold M34 .241 A6
Lower Greenshall La
SK12 .38 C3
Lower Hague SK22 .38 C4
Lower Haigh St 12 CW7 .149 B4
Lower Hall La CH3 .182 B1
Lower Hall Mews CH3 .182 B1
Lower Heath CW12 .156 C2
Lower Heath Ave CW12 .156 C2
Lower High St ST7 .195 B4
Lower Hillgate SK1 .240 F5
Lower House La WA8 .22 C4
Lower La CW6 .147 A2
Lower Macclesfield Rd
SK23 .65 C3
Lower Meadow Rd SK9 .34 C2
Lower Mersey St CH65 .70 B4
Lower Moat Cl SK4 .240 E7
Lower Park Cres SK12 .36 B3
Lower Park Rd
Chester CH4 .237 C2
Poynton SK12 .36 A3
Lower Park Sch SK12 .36 B2
Lower Park St CW12 .156 C2
Lower Peover CE Prim Sch
WA16 .81 C1
Lower Rake La WA6 .73 A2
Lower Rd L26,WA8 .21 B4
Lower Robin Hood La
WA6 .73 A2
Lower Sandy La CH3 .199 B4
Lower Wash La WA4 .16 C2
Lowerfield Rd SK10 .87 C1
Lowerhouse SK10 .87 C4
Lowerlea SK12 .38 B3
Lowes La SK11 .111 C1
Lowes The WA14 .238 B1
Loweswater Cl WA2 .8 A2
Loweswater Cres WA11 .1 A3
Loweswater Rd SK8 .239 B3
Loweswater Terr SK15 .242 D4
Lowfield Gdns WA3 .5 B4
Lowfield Gr SK2 .240 F3
Lowfield Rd SK2,SK3 .240 E3
Lowfields Ave CH62 .43 C2
Lowfields Cl CH62 .43 C2
Lowland Way WA16 .82 A4
Lowlands Rd WA7 .22 C1
Lownorth Rd M22 .33 C4
Lowry Cl WA5 .15 B3
Lowther Ave WA3 .4 C2
Lowther St SK10 .88 B4
Lowton Bsns Pk WA3 .4 A4
Lowton Com High Sch
WA3 .4 A4
Lowton Gdns WA3 .3 A3
Lowton Jun & Inf Sch
WA3 .4 A4
Lowton Rd WA3 .3 B4
Lowton St Mary's CE Prim
Sch WA3 .4 A4
Lowton West Prim Sch
WA3 .3 B4
Loxdale Dr CH65 .69 C2
Loxley Cl
Macclesfield SK11 .112 A4
Warrington WA5 .15 A4
Loyola Hey L35 .12 C4
Lucerne Cl CH3 .142 A3
Lucy St SK3 .240 E4
Ludford Cl ST5 .210 B1
Ludford St CW1 .190 B3
Ludlow Ave CW1 .190 C2
Ludlow Cl
Macclesfield SK10 .87 C1
Winsford CW7 .149 A4
Ludlow Cres WA7 .49 A4
Ludlow Dr CH65 .70 C2
Ludlow Rd CH1 .118 A3
Ludwell Cl CH4 .141 A3
Lugsdale Rd WA8 .23 A4
Lulworth Cl CW7 .149 A4
Lum Head Prim Sch
SK8 .239 B3
Lumb Brook La WA4 .27 A3
Lumb Brook Rd WA4 .26 C4
Lumb Cl SK7 .35 C3
Lumb La SK7 .35 C3
Lumber La WA5 .6 C4
Lumbrook Mews 5 WA4 .16 C1
Lumley Pl CH1 .237 B2
Lumley Rd Chester CH2 .118 B2
Macclesfield SK11 .111 C4
Lumley Wlk L24 .21 C1
Lumn Hollow 4 SK14 .241 E6
Lumn Rd SK14 .241 E6
Lumpy St CW12 .156 B2
Lundy Dr CH2 .95 B4
Lune Cl 1 CW12 .157 A1
Lune Way WA8 .12 B1
Lunehurst 18 WA3 .3 C4
Lunt Ave CW2 .190 B1
Lunt's Heath Rd WA8 .13 A3
Lunts Heath Prim Sch
WA8 .13 A3
Lupin Dr Haydock WA11 .1 C3
Huntington CH3 .142 A3
Lupus Way CH66 .69 C2
Lurgan Ave M33 .242 C5
Luscombe Cl L26 .21 A4
Lutener Ave WA14 .238 C8
Luther Gr WA9 .1 A1
Luton Rd CH65 .70 A3
Luton St WA8 .23 A4
Lutyens Cl SK11 .111 C4
Lyceum Cl CW1 .190 A4
Lyceum Way CW1 .190 A4
Lychgate WA4 .25 C4
Lycroft Cl WA7 .49 A3
Lydbury Cl WA5 .7 B1
Lydden Rd CH65 .70 A4
Lydgate Cl Denton M34 .241 B5
Wistaston CW2 .205 C4
Lydiat La SK9 .60 A1
Lydiate La Runcorn WA7 .48 B4
Willaston CH64 .42 C1
Lydiate The CH60 .40 C4
Lydney Ave SK8 .34 B4
Lydstep Ct WA5 .7 C1
Lydyett La CW8 .78 A2
Lymcote Dr CW8 .103 A2
Lyme Ave
Macclesfield SK11 .112 B3
Wilmslow SK9 .34 A1
Lyme Com Prim Sch
WA12 .1 C2
Lyme Gr
Altrincham WA14 .238 C4
Lymm WA13 .18 B1
Romiley SK6 .241 D2
Stockport SK2 .240 F3
Lyme Green Bsns Pk
SK11 .112 B2
Lyme Green Settlement
SK11 .112 B1
Lyme Park* SK12 .38 A1
Lyme Park Ctry Pk SK12 .38 A1
Lyme Rd Disley SK12 .37 B2
High Lane SK12 .38 A3
Lyme St Haydock WA11 .1 C3
Newton-le-W WA12 .1 C2
Lyme View Ct SK6 .241 D2
Lymewood Dr Disley SK12 .38 B3
Wilmslow SK9 .60 C4
Lymm Brook 1 WA13 .18 C2
Lymm Cl SK3 .240 D2
Lymm High Sch WA13 .19 A2
Lymm Rd
Little Bollington WA14 .20 A1
Warrington WA4 .17 C2
Lymmhay La WA13 .18 C2
Lymmington Ave WA13 .18 B2
Lynalls Cl CW12 .155 C2
Lynbrook Rd CW1 .190 C2
Lyncastle Rd WA4 .27 B2
Lyncastle Way WA4 .27 B2
Lyncombe Cl SK8 .35 A3
Lyncroft Cl CW1 .190 C2
Lyndale Ave
Bebington CH62 .43 C2
Warrington WA2 .16 B4
Warrington, Fearnhead WA2 .8 C1
Lyndale Ct CW7 .127 A2
Lyndale Sch The CH62 .43 C3
Lyndene Gdns SK8 .239 B6
Lyndhurst Cl SK9 .59 B3
Lyndon Gr WA7 .49 A4
Lyngard Cl SK9 .34 C1
Lyngarth Ho 1 WA14 .238 E6
Lynham Ave WA5 .15 A3
Lynn Ave Sale M33 .242 D8
Talke ST7 .210 B4
Lynn Cl WA7 .49 B4
Lynn Gr SK11 .112 B3
Lynndene CH66 .69 B4
Lynneal Ave CH66 .69 B2
Lynside Wlk M22 .33 C4
Lynthorpe Ave M44 .11 B3
Lynton Ave M44 .11 C3
Lynton Cl Heswall CH60 .41 A3
Knutsford WA16 .57 B1
Warrington WA5 .14 C2
Lynton Cres WA8 .12 C1
Lynton Dr SK6 .37 C4
Lynton Gdns WA4 .26 B2
Lynton Gr
Altrincham WA15 .238 F5
Haslington CW1 .191 B3
Lynton La SK9 .60 A1
Lynton Mews SK9 .60 A1
Lynton Park Rd SK8 .34 C4
Lynton Pl Alsager ST7 .193 B2
Broughton CH4 .139 A2
Lynton Rd SK8 .239 C5
Lynton Way CW2 .206 A4
Lyntonvale Ave SK8 .239 B6
Lynwood Altrincham WA15 .32 A4
Wilmslow SK9 .60 A3
Lynwood Ave
Golborne WA3 .3 C3
Warrington WA4 .26 B1
Lynwood Gr M33 .242 C7
Lynwood Rd CH1 .117 C3
Lyon Ct WA4 .16 C2
Lyon Ind Est WA14 .238 B7
Lyon Rd WA14 .238 C7
Lyon St Chester CH2 .237 B3
Crewe CW1 .190 B2
Macclesfield SK11 .112 B4
Warrington WA4 .16 C2
Lyon's La WA4 .26 C3
Lyons Fold M33 .242 B8
Lyons Rd WA5 .15 A2
Lyster Cl WA3 .9 C2
Lytham Dr SK7 .36 A4
Lytham Rd Gatley SK8 .239 B1
Widnes WA8 .13 B1
Lytham St SK3 .240 F2
Lytherton Ave M44 .11 B2
Lythgoes La WA2 .16 A3

M

Mableden Cl SK8 .34 B4
Mablins La CW1 .190 A4
Mablins Lane Com Prim Sch
CW1 .190 A4
Mabs Ct OL6 .242 A2
Macarthur Dr WA5 .15 A3
Macbeth Ho ST7 .210 B4
Macclesfield Coll
Macclesfield SK11 .112 A3
Macclesfield SK11 .112 B4
Macclesfield District General
Hospl SK11 .112 A4
Macclesfield Rd
Alderley Edge SK9 .85 B4
Chelford SK11 .84 A1
Congleton CW12 .156 C3
Hazel Grove SK7 .36 C4
Holmes Chapel CW4 .130 C2
Kettleshulme SK23,SK10 .64 B2
Prestbury SK10 .86 C2
Rainow SK10 .89 A4
Whaley Bridge SK23 .65 B3
Wilmslow SK9 .60 B3
Macclesfield Sta SK11 .112 B4
Macdermott Rd WA8 .22 C3
Macdonald Rd M44 .11 C4
Mackenzie Ind Pk SK3,
SK8 .240 B2
Mackeson Dr OL6 .242 B4
Mackeson Rd OL6 .242 B4
Macon Ct CW1 .190 C2
Macon Ind Pk CW1 .190 C2
Macon Way CW1 .190 C2
Maddock St ST7 .209 B1
Maddocks Hill WA6 .100 C3
Madeley Cl
Altrincham WA14 .31 C4
Broughton CH4 .139 B2
Madeley St CW2 .190 B1
Madeline McKenna Ct
WA8 .12 B2
Madras Rd SK3 .240 C3
Madron Ave SK10 .86 B1
Maelor Cl CH63 .43 B3
Maes-y-coed CH4 .140 C3
Mag La WA13,WA16 .28 C3
Magdala Pl CW9 .104 B4
Magdalen Ct CW2 .190 A1
Magecroft CW1 .173 A1
Magenta Ave M44 .11 C3
Maggoty La SK11 .111 B1
Magnolia Cl
11 Ellesmere Port CH66 .69 C1
5 Partington M31 .11 C1
Warrington WA1 .17 C4
Magnolia Dr WA7 .49 C2
Magnolia Rise SK10 .86 C3
Magpie Cres 18 ST7 .195 A1
Mahood St SK3 .240 D3
Maiden Est CW5 .228 B4
Maiden Gdns CH65 .70 B2
Maidenhills CW10 .128 B1
Maidstone Cl SK10 .87 A1
Maidstone Wlk M34 .241 A5
Maidwell Cl CW7 .127 A2
Main Cl WA11 .1 A3
Main La WA3 .3 C2
Main Rd Betley CW2,CW3 .221 C4
Broughton CH4 .139 A2
Goostrey CW4 .107 C1
Higher Kinnerton CH4 .161 A4
Langley SK11 .113 B2
Moulton CW9 .126 C4
Norton in Hales TF9 .236 B1
Shavington CW2 .206 A2
Weston CW2 .207 B3
Worleston CW5 .188 C3
Wybunbury CW5 .220 A4
Main St Frodsham WA6 .74 A4
Great Barrow CH3 .120 C3
Hyde SK14 .241 D8
Runcorn WA7 .49 C4
Maintree Cres L24 .21 A2
Mainwaring Cl CW5 .205 A2
Mainwaring Dr
Broughton CH4 .140 B4
Wilmslow SK9 .60 B4
Mainwaring Rd
Bebington CH62 .43 B4
Peover WA16 .108 A4
Mairesfield Ave WA4 .17 A1
Maisterson Ct 11 CW5 .204 C3
Maitland Way CH1 .117 B2
Maitland Wood Cl CW9 .104 B4
Maizefield Cl M33 .242 F6
Major Cross St 15 WA8 .23 A4
Makepeace Cl CH3 .119 B2
Malaga Ave M90 .33 A4
Malakoff St SK15 .242 B1
Malam Dr CW9 .104 B3
Malbank CW5 .204 C3
Malbank Rd CW2 .189 C2
Malbank Sch CW5 .204 B3
Malcolm Ave WA2 .8 B1
Malcolm Cres CH63 .43 B3
Malcolm St WA7 .23 A1
Malgam Dr M20 .239 B8
Malhamdale Rd CW12 .157 A3
Malin Cl L24 .21 B1
Maliston Rd WA5 .15 A3
Mall The Hyde SK14 .241 D6
Sale M33 .242 B7
Mallaig Cl CW4 .130 B1
Mallard Cl
Knutsford WA16 .57 A1
Runcorn WA7 .49 C3
Warrington WA2 .8 B2
Mallard Cres SK12 .36 A2
Mallard Ct Cheadle SK8 .34 B4
Chester CH2 .118 C4
Mallard Gn WA14 .238 B8
Mallard La WA3 .9 C2
Mallard Way Crewe CW1 .191 A1
Winsford CW7 .149 B3
Mallards Reach SK6 .241 A2
Mallards The SK11 .112 A4
Mallory Ct
Altrincham WA14 .238 C3
Congleton CW12 .155 C2
Mallory Rd CH65 .70 A2
Mallory Wlk CH4 .162 A4
Mallow Cl CH3 .142 A3
Mallow Wlk M31 .11 C1
Mallowdale Cl CH62 .43 C3
Malmesbury Cl
Middlewich CW10 .128 A1
Poynton SK12 .36 B2
Malmesbury Pk WA7 .24 C1
Malmesbury Rd SK8 .35 A3
Malory Cl CW1 .190 C3
Malpas Alport Prim Sch
SY14 .213 A2
Malpas Cl Handforth SK9 .34 C1
Northwich CW9 .104 B4
Malpas Dr WA5 .15 B2
Malpas Rd
Ellesmere Port CH65 .69 C2
Northwich CW9 .104 B4
Runcorn WA7 .49 B4
Malpas Way WA5 .15 B2
Malrae WA15 .238 E1
Malt Kiln Rd WA16 .80 C2
Malt St WA16 .57 A1
Malta Rd CH2 .95 A1
Maltmans Rd WA13 .18 B2
Malton Ave WA3 .3 C4

Malton Cl WA8 .....12 B3
Malton Dr
Altrincham WA14 .....238 A6
Hazel Grove SK7 .....36 B4
Malton Rd SK4 .....240 A8
Malvern Ave CH65 .....70 B2
Malvern Cl
Congleton CW12 .....155 C2
Shavington CW2 .....206 A2
Stockport SK4 .....240 D7
Warrington WA5 .....15 A4
Malvern Dr
Altrincham WA14 .....238 B5
Macclesfield SK10 .....87 C2
Malvern Rd Blacon CH1 ..118 A3
Haydock WA9 .....1 A2
Knutsford WA16 .....81 C4
Malvern Way CW7 .....149 A4
Manchester Airport Sta
M90 .....33 A4
Manchester Bridge
CW1 .....190 C2
Manchester International Airport M90 .....33 A4
Manchester Met Univ, Crewe & Alsager Faculty, (Alsager Campus) ST7 .....193 A3
Manchester Met Univ, Crewe & Alsager Faculty, (Crewe Campus) CW1 .....190 C2
Manchester New Rd M31 .11 C2
Manchester Rd
Altrincham WA14 .....238 D7
Cheadle M20,SK8 .....239 D7
Congleton CW12 .....156 C3
Dukinfield SK14 .....241 C7
Handforth SK9 .....34 B1
Hollinfare WA3 .....11 A1
Knutsford WA16 .....56 C2
Macclesfield SK10 .....87 B2
Northwich CW9 .....79 B1
Partington M31 .....11 C2
Stockport SK4 .....240 E8
Warrington WA3 .....18 A4
Warrington, Bruche WA1 ..16 C4
Manchester Row WA12 ....7 B4
Mancroft Cl WA1 .....17 C4
Mandarin Gn WA14 .....238 B8
Manifold Cl CW11 .....174 C4
Manifold Dr SK6 .....37 C3
Manley Cl Antrobus CW9 ...53 B2
Holmes Chapel CW4 .....130 A2
Northwich CW9 .....104 A3
Manley Gdns WA5 .....15 C3
Manley Gr SK7 .....35 C3
Manley La
Dunham-on-t-H WA6 .....97 C3
Manley WA6 .....98 B2
Manley Rd Frodsham WA6 .74 A2
Manley WA6 .....98 C4
Warren SK11 .....112 A3
Manley View CH2 .....72 B2
Manley Village Sch WA6 ..99 A3
Manna Dr CH2 .....72 B2
Manners La CH60 .....40 C3
Manning La S CH2 .....119 A3
Manning St CW2 .....190 B1
Mannings La CH2 .....119 A3
Manor Ave Crewe CW2 ...190 A1
Golborne WA3 .....3 B4
Goostrey CW4 .....107 C1
Marston CW9 .....79 A3
Newton-le-W WA12 .....1 C2
Manor CE Jun Sch The
WA12 .....1 C2
Manor Cl Broughton CH5 ..139 B4
Cheadle SK8 .....35 B4
Congleton CW12 .....157 A1
Denton M34 .....241 B6
Great Barrow CH3 .....120 C3
Lymm WA13 .....18 C1
Neston CH64 .....66 B4
Warrington WA1 .....17 B4
Wilmslow SK9 .....59 C4
Manor Cres
Broughton CH4 .....139 B4
Knutsford WA16 .....57 A1
Macclesfield SK10 .....87 B2
Middlewich CW10 .....151 B4
Manor Ct Crewe CW2 .....190 A1
Golborne WA3 .....3 B4
Knutsford WA16 .....57 A1
Manor Dr Barnton CW8 ....78 A1
Chester CH3 .....119 B1
Northwich, Rudheath CW9 .104 B4
Manor Farm Cl CH2 .....119 C4
Manor Farm Cres CH1 .....94 A4
Manor Farm Ct
Broughton CH5 .....139 A4
Frodsham WA6 .....49 B1
Manor Farm Rd WA7 .....24 B2
Manor Fell WA7 .....50 A4
Manor Fields CW10 .....151 B4
Manor Gdns SK9 .....60 B4
Manor Gr CW8 .....103 B3
Manor Ho Bebington CH62 .43 B4
Ellesmere Port CH66 .....69 B1
Manor House Prim Sch
WA6 .....49 B1
Manor Ind Est WA4 .....16 C2
Manor La Broughton CH5 .139 A4
Davenham CW9 .....104 B1
Ellesmere Port CH66 .....69 B2
Holmes Chapel CW4 .....130 B2
3 Middlewich CW10 .....151 B4
Manor La *continued*
Ollerton WA16 .....82 C3
Manor Park Ave WA7 .....24 B2
Manor Park Dr CH66 .....69 B1
Manor Park N WA16 .....57 B1
Manor Park Rd CW12 .....134 B1
Manor Park S WA16 .....57 B1
Manor Park Sch WA16 ...57 B1
Manor Pk
Great Barrow CH3 .....120 C3
Hawarden CH4 .....139 A4
Manor Pl WA8 .....12 A1
Manor Rd
Altrincham WA15 .....238 E4
Bebington CH62 .....43 C3
Chester CH4 .....141 A3
Cuddington CW8 .....101 C1
Denton M34 .....241 B5
Frodsham WA6 .....49 B1
Haydock WA11 .....1 C4
Lymm WA13 .....18 C1
Mow Cop ST7 .....195 B4
Nantwich CW5 .....204 C3
Runcorn WA7 .....23 B1
Sale M33 .....242 B7
Sandbach CW11 .....175 B3
Sealand CH5 .....116 A3
Thornton Hough CH63 .....42 A4
Whaley Bridge SK23 .....65 C3
Widnes WA8 .....12 A1
Wilmslow SK9 .....59 C4
Manor Rd N CW5 .....204 C4
Manor Sq CW7 .....149 A4
Manor St CW8 .....103 B3
Manor Way Crewe CW2 ..190 B1
Sandbach CW11 .....175 C3
Manora Rd CW9 .....104 A4
Manorfield Cl CH1 .....69 A1
Manorial Rd S CH64 .....66 B4
Manse Field Rd WA6 .....75 A1
Manse Gdns WA12 .....2 B2
Mansell Cl WA8 .....13 B3
Mansfield Cl WA3 .....10 A2
Mansfield Prim Sch
CH65 .....69 C2
Mansfield Rd
Ellesmere Port CH65 .....70 A1
Hyde SK14 .....241 F5
Mansion Ct 18 CW5 .....204 C3
Mansion Dr WA16 .....57 A1
Manston Rd WA5 .....14 C2
Manuel Perez Rd WA5 .....15 A3
Manvers St SK5 .....240 E7
Manx St WA4 .....16 A2
Maori Dr WA6 .....74 A4
Maple Ave Alsager ST7 ...193 C1
Cheadle SK8 .....239 F2
Disley SK12 .....39 A3
Ellesmere Port CH66 .....69 B3
Golborne WA3 .....3 C4
Haydock WA11 .....1 A4
Macclesfield SK11 .....112 B3
Newcastle-u-L ST5 .....210 C1
Newton-le-W WA12 .....2 B1
Poynton SK12 .....36 C2
Runcorn WA7 .....49 B4
Sutton WA7 .....50 A2
Talke ST7 .....210 B4
Widnes WA8 .....13 A1
Maple Cl
Brereton Green CW11 ...153 C2
Congleton CW12 .....155 C2
Holmes Chapel CW4 .....130 B2
Sandbach CW11 .....175 B3
Maple Cres WA5 .....14 C2
Maple Ct SK4 .....240 C8
Maple Gr Barnton CW8 ....78 A2
Bebington CH62 .....43 B4
Broughton CH4 .....140 B3
Chester CH2 .....119 A2
Crewe CW1 .....190 C4
Ellesmere Port CH1 .....95 A4
Northwich, Greenbank
CW8 .....103 B4
Warrington WA4 .....16 B2
Winsford CW7 .....127 A1
Maple La CW8 .....101 C1
Maple Pl ST7 .....193 C4
Maple Rd
Alderley Edge SK9 .....60 A2
Bramhall SK7 .....35 C3
Partington M31 .....11 C2
Warrington WA1 .....17 C4
Winwick WA2 .....8 A3
Maples SK9 .....59 C3
Maples The
Mobberley WA16 .....58 C1
Winsford CW7 .....127 A2
Mapleton Dr WA7 .....49 C2
Maplewood Gr CH1 .....117 A4
Maplewood Rd SK9 .....60 C4
Mapplewell Cres WA5 .....15 A3
Marble Arch 4 WA16 .....57 A1
Marbury Gdns CH65 .....69 C3
Marbury La CW9 .....78 C3
Marbury Pk Ctry Pk*
CW9 .....78 C3
Marbury Rd Chester CH3 .119 B1
Comberbach CW9 .....78 B3
Handforth SK9 .....34 A1
Marbury St WA4 .....16 B2
March Ave SK4 .....240 B6
March St CW1 .....190 C2
Marchbank Dr SK8 .....239 C6
Marchwiel Rd CH65 .....70 B2
Marcien Way WA8 .....12 C2
Marcliff Gr
Knutsford WA16 .....57 A1
Marcliff Gr *continued*
Stockport SK4 .....240 B6
Marcross Cl WA5 .....7 C1
Mardale Ave WA2 .....8 B2
Mardale Cl
Congleton CW12 .....157 A3
Stalybridge SK15 .....242 D3
Mardale Cres WA13 .....18 C2
Mardale Ct CW4 .....130 A1
Mardale Dr SK8 .....239 B6
Mardon Cl WA16 .....57 B2
Marfields Prim Sch
CW12 .....156 B1
Marford Cl CW9 .....103 C3
Marfords Ave CH63 .....43 B4
Margaret Ave WA1 .....17 A4
Margaret Ct WA8 .....23 A4
Margaret Rd M34 .....241 A8
Margaret's La CH66 .....69 A4
Margery Ave ST7 .....194 C4
Marian Ave WA12 .....1 C2
Marian Dr CH3 .....142 A4
Marian Rd WA11 .....1 C4
Marie Cl CW5 .....216 C2
Marie Dr WA4 .....17 B1
Marigold Cl SK11 .....111 C4
Marigold Way WA9 .....6 A4
Marina Ave Hyde M34 ...241 A5
Warrington WA5 .....15 B2
Marina Cl SK9 .....34 B3
Marina Dr Chester CH2 ..118 C4
Ellesmere Port CH65 .....70 A3
Warrington WA2 .....8 B1
Marina Gr WA7 .....23 A1
Marina La WA7 .....50 C4
Marina Village WA7 .....50 C4
Marina Wlk CH65 .....70 A3
Marine Ave M31 .....11 B2
Marine Dr CH60 .....40 B3
Marine Flats CH3 .....142 C4
Mariner Cl WA7 .....50 B3
Marion Dr WA7 .....48 C3
Maritime Cl WA12 .....2 B3
Mark Ave CH66 .....69 B2
Mark Cl CH2 .....118 C1
Market Cl CW1 .....190 B3
Market Ct CW6 .....146 B1
Market Ctr The CW1 ....190 B2
Market Gate WA1 .....16 A3
Market Pl Bollington SK10 .88 A4
Hampton SY14 .....213 B4
1 Hyde SK14 .....241 D6
Macclesfield SK11 .....112 B4
Stockport SK1 .....240 F6
Winsford CW7 .....126 C1
Market Sq Chester CH1 ..237 A2
Congleton CW12 .....156 C1
Crewe CW1 .....190 B2
4 Sandbach CW11 .....175 A3
Market St
Altrincham WA14 .....238 D4
Congleton CW12 .....156 B1
Crewe CW1 .....190 B2
Crewe CW1 .....190 B3
Disley SK12 .....38 B3
Hyde SK14 .....241 D6
Kidsgrove ST7 .....195 A1
Nantwich CW5 .....204 C3
New Mills SK22 .....39 A4
Newton-le-W WA12 .....2 A2
9 Northwich CW9 .....103 C4
Stalybridge SK15 .....242 D2
Whaley Bridge SK23 .....65 C4
Widnes WA8 .....23 A4
Market Way 7 CW9 .....103 C4
Market Wlk M33 .....242 B6
Markland St SK14 .....241 E5
Marl Croft CH3 .....142 A4
Marl Edge SK10 .....87 A3
Marl Heys CH2 .....118 C4
Marland Ave SK8 .....239 F2
Marlborough Ave
Alderley Edge SK9 .....60 A1
Winsford CW7 .....126 B2
Marlborough Cl
Knutsford WA16 .....57 B2
Macclesfield SK10 .....87 B2
Wistaston CW2 .....205 C4
Marlborough Cres
Warrington WA4 .....16 C1
Widnes WA8 .....13 A3
Marlborough Ct
1 Chester CH3 .....119 A1
24 Macclesfield SK11 .....112 B4
Marlborough Dr
Helsby WA6 .....73 A1
Macclesfield SK10 .....87 B2
Stockport SK4 .....240 D8
Marlborough Ho 7
SK11 .....111 C4
Marlborough Prim Sch The
SK10 .....87 B2
Marlborough Rd
Altrincham WA14 .....238 D2
Ellesmere Port CH65 .....70 B2
Sale M33 .....242 B6
Marlborough Wlk CH65 ...70 B2
Marlcroft Ave SK4 .....240 B6
Marler Rd SK14 .....241 E8
Marleston Ct CH4 .....140 C1
Marley Ave CW1 .....190 A4
Marley Cl WA15 .....238 F7
Marley Dr M33 .....242 A8
Marley Rd SK12 .....36 C1
Marley Way CH4 .....140 C4
Marlfield Rd
Altrincham WA15 .....32 B4
Warrington WA4 .....17 A1
Marline Ave CH63 .....43 B3
Marling Cl WA6 .....74 B3
Marling Pk WA8 .....12 A1
Marloes WA14 .....238 B2
Marlow Ave CH2 .....118 C4
Marlow Cl Cheadle SK8 ..239 F2
9 Sandbach CW11 .....174 B3
Warrington WA3 .....9 B3
Marlow Dr
Altrincham WA14 .....20 C1
Handforth SK9 .....34 B3
Marlowe Cl Blacon CH1 ..118 A3
Widnes WA8 .....12 C1
Marlowe Ct SK11 .....112 B3
Marlowe Dr CW5 .....204 C2
Marlowe Rd
1 Neston CH64 .....66 C4
Northwich CW9 .....104 B3
Marlston Ave CH4 .....141 A3
Marlston Pl WA7 .....49 A3
Maroon Rd M22 .....33 C4
Marple Cres CW2 .....189 C2
Marple Rd CW9 .....104 B4
Marquis Dr SK8 .....34 B4
Marrick Ave SK8 .....239 C5
Marriott Rd CW11 .....174 C2
Marriott St SK1 .....240 F4
Marron Ave WA2 .....8 A1
Marsden Ave WA4 .....17 A2
Marsden Ct WA8 .....12 C2
Marsden Rd SK6 .....241 C3
Marsden Terr 16 SK11 ....112 B4
Marsh Ave ST7 .....195 C1
Marsh Cl Alsager ST7 ....193 A2
Stockport SK3 .....240 D2
Marsh Gr ST8 .....179 B2
Marsh Green Cl ST8 ....179 B1
Marsh Green Rd
Biddulph ST8 .....179 B1
Sandbach CW11 .....174 C4
Marsh Hall Pad WA8 .....13 A2
Marsh Hall Rd WA8 .....13 A2
Marsh House La WA1,
WA2 .....16 B4
Marsh La Acton CW5 .....204 A2
Alsager ST7 .....193 A2
Barton CH3,SY14 .....181 C2
Churton CH3 .....181 A3
Crowton CW8,WA6 .....101 A4
Dutton WA4 .....51 C2
Elton CH2 .....72 A2
Elton CH2 .....72 B3
Frodsham WA6 .....74 A4
Holmes Chapel CW4 .....130 C1
Mere WA14 .....30 C2
Nantwich CW5 .....204 B3
New Mills SK22,SK23 .....39 B3
Ravensmoor CW5 .....203 C1
Runcorn WA7 .....23 C2
Warrington WA5 .....14 B1
Marsh Lane Trad Est
SK22 .....39 B4
Marsh Rd WA4 .....27 A2
Marsh St Warrington WA1 ..16 B4
Widnes WA8 .....23 A3
Marshall Ave WA5 .....7 C1
Marshall Ct OL6 .....242 A2
Marshall Gr CW12 .....179 A4
Marshall La CW8 .....103 B3
Marshall Rd WA1 .....17 B4
Marshalls Ct CW8 .....103 B3
Marshfield Bank CW2 ...189 B2
Marshfield La ST8 .....179 B1
Marshfield Rd CW2 .....189 B2
Marshgate WA8 .....22 A3
Marshgate Pl WA6 .....49 B1
Marshlands Rd CH64 .....66 C3
Marshway Dr WA12 .....2 A3
Marsland Rd M33 .....242 B5
Marsland St SK1 .....240 F6
Marson St WA2 .....16 A3
Marston Cl CH62 .....43 C2
Marston Gdns CH65 .....69 C3
Marston La CW9 .....79 B3
Marten Ave CH63 .....43 B4
Martens Rd M44 .....11 C3
Marthall La
Chelford WA16 .....83 A4
Ollerton WA16 .....82 C3
Marthall Way 8 SK9 .....34 C3
Martham Cl WA4 .....17 A2
Martin Ave
Newton-le-W WA12 .....2 B3
Warrington WA2 .....8 C1
Martin Cl Chester CH2 ...118 B4
Runcorn WA7 .....50 A4
Martin Rd Chester CH2 ...118 B4
Frodsham WA6 .....74 A4
Martin St SK14 .....241 E6
Martin's La CH3 .....143 C2
Martindale Gr WA7 .....49 B3
Martins Fields CW8 .....77 A3
Martins Hill CW12 .....157 B1
Martland Ave WA3 .....3 C4
Martlet Ave SK12 .....38 B3
Marton & District CE Prim Sch SK11 .....133 B3
Marton Cl
Congleton CW12 .....156 C3
Culcheth WA3 .....4 C2
Hough Common CW2 .....206 C2
Macclesfield SK10 .....86 C1
Marton Gn SK3 .....240 D1
Marton Hall La SK11 ....133 A2
Marton La
Congleton SK11 .....134 A2
Marton SK11 .....133 B4
Warren SK11 .....111 A1
Marton Pl M33 .....242 A
Marton Rd CH4 .....139 B
Marton Way 5 SK9 .....34 C
Marwood Cl WA14 .....238 B
Mary Dendy Unit (Soss Moss)
SK10 .....84 B
Mary St Cheadle SK8 .....239 D
Crewe CW1 .....190 C
Dukinfield M34 .....241 A
Hyde SK14 .....241 D
Widnes WA8 .....23 B
Maryfield Cl WA3 .....3 A
Maryhill Cl ST7 .....195 A
Maryhill High Sch ST7 ..195 A
Maryhill Prim Sch ST7 ..195 A
Maryhill Rd WA7 .....49 A
Marys Gate CW2 .....205 C
Masefield Ave WA8 .....22 C
Masefield Dr Blacon CH1 .117 C
Crewe CW1 .....190 C
Stockport SK4 .....240 A
Maskery Pl CW12 .....156 B
Mason Ave
Warrington WA1 .....16 C
Widnes WA8 .....13 A
Mason Cl CH66 69
Mason St Chester CH2 ...237 A
Runcorn WA7 .....23 B
Warrington WA1 16
Mason's Row CW6 .....169 C
Masons La SK10 .....87 C
Massals La CH2 .....96 C
Massey Ave
Hartford CW8 .....103 A
Lymm WA13 .....18 A
Warrington WA5 .....7 C
Winsford CW7 .....126 C
Massey Brook La WA13 ...18 A
Massey Hall Specl Sch
WA4 .....17 C
Massey Rd
Altrincham WA15 238
Sale M33 242
Massey St
4 Alderley Edge SK9 60
17 Stockport SK1 240
Masseyfield Rd WA7 50
Massie St SK8 239
Masters Ct WA16 56
Mates La SY14 213
Mather Ave Golborne WA3 ..3
Runcorn WA7 48
Mather Cl CW10 151
Mather Dr
Comberbach CW9 78
Northwich CW9 104
Mathers Cl WA2 9
Mathieson Rd WA8 22
Matlock Cl Sale M33 242
Warrington WA5 15
Matlock Dr SK7 36
Matlock Mews WA14 238
Matlock Rd SK8 34
Matterdale Cl WA6 74
Matterdale Terr SK15 ...242
Matthew Cl CH2 118
Matthews Pl CW12 157
Matthews St WA1 16
Matty's La WA6 74
Mauldeth Cl SK4 240
Mauldeth Rd SK4 240
Mavor Ct CW1 190
Maw Green Cl CW1 190
Maw Green Rd CW1 190
Maw La CW1 191
Mawdsley Ave WA1 17
Mawdsley Cl ST7 193
Mawson Cl WA5 15
Maxfield Cl SK11 111
Maxwell Cl CH65 70
Maxwell Rd CW12 179
Maxwell St Crewe CW2 ..190
Warrington WA3 9
May Ave Bramhall SK8 35
Stockport SK4 240
May Rd Bramhall SK8 35
Heswall CH60 41
May Wlk 5 M31 11
Mayberry Gr WA2 9
Maybrook Pl WA4 16
Maydews Pas 22 SK11 ...112
Maydor Ave CH4 140
Mayfair Cl Poynton SK12 ..36
Warrington WA5 14
Mayfair Dr CW9 103
Mayfair Gr WA8 12
Mayfield Ave
Macclesfield SK11 112
Sale M33 242
Widnes WA8 12
Mayfield Cl CW4 130
Mayfield Ct WA8 13
Mayfield Dr
Bebington CH62 44
Cuddington CW8 102
Golborne WA3,WN7 4
Mayfield Gdns CH64 41
Mayfield Gr
Cuddington CW8 102
Wilmslow SK9 59
Mayfield Mews CW1 189
Mayfield Rd Blacon CH1 ..117
Bramhall SK7 35
Mobberley WA16 57
Northwich CW9 104
Warrington WA4 17
Mayfield Terr SK11 112
Mayfield View WA13 18

Mayflower Rd CW5 .....204 C2
Mayor's Rd WA15 .....238 E4
Maythorn Ave WA3 ....9 A4
Maytree Ave CH3 ....119 A1
Maywood Ave M20 ....239 B8
Mc Clellan Pl WA8 ....13 A1
McCarthy Cl WA3 ....10 A2
McGarva Way CH65 ....70 B2
Mcgowan Ho ST7 ....210 B4
McKee Ave WA2 ....8 A1
Mckellin Cl ST7 ....209 C1
McLaren St CW1 ....190 B4
McMinnis Ave WA9 ....1 A1
McNeill Ave CW1 ....190 A3
Mead Ave ST7 ....194 C4
Mead Cl WA16 ....56 C1
Mead Rd WA1 ....17 A4
Meade The SK9 ....60 B4
Meadow Ave
Congleton CW12 ....156 B1
Goostrey CW4 ....107 B1
Warrington WA4 ....16 A1
Weston CW2 ....207 A3
Meadow Bank
Adderley TF9 ....235 A2
Kelsall CW6 ....122 B2
Stockport SK4 ....240 B6
Meadow Brow SK9 ....60 A1
Meadow Cl
Cuddington CW8 ....102 A2
Goostrey CW4 ....107 C1
Helsby WA6 ....73 A2
High Lane SK6 ....37 C4
Neston CH64 ....66 C3
Newton-le-W WA12 ....1 C2
Shavington CW2 ....206 B3
Tarvin CH3 ....121 A1
Whaley Bridge SK23 ......65 B4
Widnes WA8 ....12 B2
Willaston CH64 ....67 C4
Wilmslow SK9 ....59 C2
Winsford CW7 ....126 B2
Meadow Croft
Alsager ST7 ....193 C1
Willaston CH64 ....67 C4
Meadow Ct
Mollington CH1 ....94 C1
No Man's Heath SY14 .....214 A2
Packmoor ST7 ....195 C1
Meadow Dr Barnton CW8 ..78 A2
Knutsford WA16 ....81 C4
Prestbury SK10 ....87 A4
Wistaston CW2 ....205 C4
Meadow Field Rd CH4 ....141 A2
Meadow Gate CW9 ....79 C3
Meadow Gr
Northwich CW9 ....104 A3
Winsford CW7 ....126 C3
Meadow Home Pk CW7 ..126 B3
Meadow Ind Est SK5 ....240 F7
Meadow La
Comberbach CW9 ....78 B4
Disley SK12 ....38 B3
Ellesmere Port CH65 ......70 B3
Huntington CH3 ....142 A3
Moulton CW9 ....126 C4
Warrington WA2 ....9 A1
Willaston CH64 ....67 C4
Meadow Lane Ind Est
CH65 ....70 B3
Meadow Prim Sch CH66 ..69 C1
Meadow Rd
Broughton CH4 ....139 B2
Weaverham CW8 ....102 C4
Meadow Rise
Clutton CH3 ....182 B1
Winsford CW7 ....126 A1
Meadow Row WA7 ....24 A1
Meadow St Hyde SK14 ...241 E5
New Mills SK22 ....39 B4
3 Northwich CW9 ....104 A4
Meadow The CW4 ....130 B4
Meadow View Elton CH2 ..72 A2
Lymm WA13 ....18 B2
Middlewich CW10 ......128 A1
Sealand CH5 ....116 A3
Meadow View Dr WA6 ....74 A4
Meadow Way
Lawton-gate ST7 ....194 A3
Macclesfield SK10 ....87 C1
Wilmslow SK9 ....59 C2
Meadow Wlk 3 M31 .....11 C2
Meadowbank Gdns WA3 ...5 B4
Meadowcroft
Higher Kinnerton CH4 ....161 A4
Saughall CH1 ....94 A1
Meadowfield
Tarporley CW6 ....146 B1
Whaley Bridge SK23 ......65 B4
Meadowfield Ct SK14 ...241 D8
Meadowgate Cl CW11 ...174 B3
Meadowgate Farm WA6 ..49 C1
Meadows La
Chester CH4 ....237 C1
Saughall CH1 ....117 A4
Meadows Pl CH4 ....141 C4
Meadows Rd Cheadle SK8 .34 C4
Gatley SK8 ....239 B1
Kidsgrove ST7 ....194 C1
Sale M33 ....242 C8
Meadows The
Ashton CH3 ....121 C4
Congleton CW12 ....156 C2
Hale M44 ....11 C3
Neston CH64 ....66 C3
Romiley SK6 ....241 B4
Meadowside
Adlington SK10 ....63 A4

Meadowside continued
Disley SK12 ....39 A3
Northwich CW8 ....103 B4
Whaley Bridge SK23 ......65 B4
Meadowside Ave ST7 ...209 B1
Meadowside La ST7 ....195 A4
Meadowside Mews CH1 .118 A2
Meadowside Rd CH62 ....43 B4
Meadowsway CH2 ....118 B4
Meadowsweet Rd WA16 ..57 C2
Meadowvale Cl CW5 ....204 C4
Meads Rd ST7 ....193 B2
Meadscroft Dr SK9 ....59 C1
Meadway Bramhall SK7 ...35 C3
Ellesmere Port CH66 ......69 A4
Golborne WA3 ....3 B4
Heswall CH60 ....40 C3
High Lane SK6 ....37 C4
Poynton SK12 ....36 A2
Prestbury SK10 ....87 A3
Runcorn WA7 ....49 C4
Widnes WA8 ....12 A1
Meakin Cl CW12 ....157 A1
Meal St New Mills SK22 ...39 B4
Stockport SK4 ....240 E7
Mealhouse Brow 2
SK1 ....240 F5
Meddings Cl SK9 ....85 A4
Medina Ave CW7 ....126 C1
Medina Way ST7 ....195 A1
Medlar Cl CH4 ....140 C3
Medway Cl Golborne WN7 ..4 B4
Handforth SK9 ....34 B1
Warrington WA2 ....8 C1
Medway Cres WA14 .....238 C6
Medway Dr ST8 ....179 B1
Medway Rd WA3 ....5 A1
Mee St SK11 ....112 C3
Meeanee Dr CW5 ....204 B2
Meerbrook Rd SK3 ......240 A4
Meeting House La WA6 ..74 C1
Meeting La WA5 ....14 C3
Meg La Antrobus CW9 .....53 A2
Macclesfield SK11 ....111 C4
Sutton Lane Ends SK11 ...113 B1
Megacre ST7 ....210 A1
Melbourne Ave M90 ......33 A4
Melbourne Gr CW1 ......191 B3
Melbourne Rd
Blacon CH1 ....117 B2
Bramhall SK7 ....35 C3
Melbourne St SK15 .....242 D1
Melbury Ct WA3 ....9 C3
Melbury Rd SK8 ....35 A3
Melchett Cres CW9 .....104 B4
Melford Cl CW2 ....206 B4
Melford Ct WA1 ....17 B4
Melford Dr
Macclesfield SK10 ....87 B1
Runcorn WA7 ....23 B1
Meliden Gr WA6 ....73 A1
Melkridge Cl CH2 ......119 A2
Melksham Cl SK11 ......112 A4
Mellard St ST7 ....209 B1
Mellington Ave M20 ....239 C8
Mellock Cl CH64 ....66 C3
Mellock La CH64 ....66 C4
Mellor Cl Runcorn WA7 ...24 B1
Stalybridge OL6 ....242 B2
Mellor Cres WA16 ....56 C1
Mellor Rd OL6 ....242 B3
Mellor St Crewe CW1 ...190 B3
Packmoor ST7 ....195 C1
Mellors Bank ST7 ....195 B3
Melrose Ave
Burtonwood WA5 ....6 C4
Cheadle SK3 ....239 F7
Chester CH3 ....119 A1
Sale M33 ....242 B6
Warrington WA4 ....26 B4
Melrose Cres SK12 ......37 B3
Melrose Ct 15 SK9 ....34 C1
Melrose Dr Crewe CW1 ..190 A4
Ellesmere Port CH66 ......94 C4
Melton Ave WA4 ....26 A4
Melton Cl CW12 ....155 C2
Melton Dr CW12 ....155 C2
Melton Rd WA7 ....49 B4
Melton St SK5 ....240 F8
Melverly Dr CH1 ....117 B2
Melville Cl
Warrington WA2 ....16 A4
Widnes WA8 ....13 B1
Melville Rd M44 ....11 B3
Menai Gr SK8 ....240 A2
Menai Rd SK3 ....240 E2
Mendell Cl CH62 ....43 C4
Mendell Prim Sch CH62 ..43 C4
Mendip Ave WA2 ....8 A2
Mendip Cl
Ellesmere Port CH66 ......69 C2
Gatley SK8 ....34 A4
Stockport SK4 ....240 E7
Mendip Ct SK4 ....240 E7
Menin Ave WA4 ....16 B2
Menlow Cl WA4 ....17 B1
Mentmore Gdns WA4 .....26 C3
Mentone Rd SK4 ....240 C7
Meols Cl
Ellesmere Port CH66 ......69 C2
Hale L24 ....21 C1
Mercer Cl SY14 ....213 A2
Mercer Rd WA11 ....1 B3
Mercer St Burtonwood WA5 .6 C3
Newton-le-W WA12 ....2 B2
Mercer Way Chester CH4 .140 C3
Nantwich CW5 ....204 C4
Mercer Wlk CH65 ....70 B2

Mercian Cl CW2 ....206 A2
Mercian Way SK3 ....240 E3
Mercury Ct CH1 ....117 C1
Mere Ave CH63 ....43 A3
Mere Bank CW9 ....127 A4
Mere Brook Wlk CW2 ...190 B1
Mere Cl
Ellesmere Port CH66 ......69 B1
Haslington CW1 ....191 B2
Pickmere WA16 ....80 A4
Sale M33 ....242 F5
Mere Cres CW8 ....123 C3
Mere Ct Alsager ST7 .....193 B2
Chelford SK11 ....83 C2
5 Knutsford WA16 ....57 A1
Mere Home Farm WA16 ..56 A4
Mere La Cuddington CW8 .102 A1
Pickmere WA16 ....79 C4
Mere Rd Marston CW9 .....79 A3
Newton-le-W WA12 ....2 C2
Warrington WA2 ....9 A1
Weston CW2 ....207 A3
Mere Side SK15 ....242 C4
Mere St CW1 ....191 B2
Mere View Gdns WA4 ....26 C3
Merebank Rd CW2 ......190 A1
Merebrook Rd SK11 .....111 C4
Merecroft 3 CH3 ....119 A1
Meredith Ave WA4 ....17 A1
Meredith St CW1 ....190 B3
Merehaven Cl WA16 ......80 A4
Mereheath La WA16 ......56 C3
Mereheath Pk WA16 ......56 C2
Merelake Rd ST7 ....210 A4
Meremore Dr ST5 ....210 B1
Mereside Ave CW12 .....156 A2
Mereside Cl Cheadle SK8 .239 F4
Macclesfield SK10 ....87 A1
Mereside Rd WA16 ....30 B1
Merevale Cl WA7 ....49 C3
Merewood Cl WA2 ....8 B2
Mereworth Dr CW9 .....103 C3
Merganser Cl CW1 ......189 C4
Meriton Rd SK9 ....34 B2
Merlin Ave WA16 ....57 A2
Merlin Cl Runcorn WA7 ...24 A1
Winsford CW7 ....150 A4
Merlin Way Crewe CW1 ..190 A4
Kidsgrove ST7 ....195 B2
Merlyn Ave M33 ....242 C8
Merrick Cl WA2 ....8 C2
Merridale The WA15 ......32 A4
Merriden Rd SK10 ....87 A1
Merrill's Ave CW2 ......190 C3
Merriman Ave WA16 ......57 B2
Merrivale Rd CW2 ......206 A4
Merrydale Cl SK10 ....86 C1
Merryman's La SK9 ......84 A4
Mersey Pl CW7 ....127 A1
Mersey Rd Runcorn WA7 ..23 A2
Sale M33 ....242 B8
Mersey Sq SK1 ....240 E5
Mersey St Runcorn WA7 ..23 A2
St Helens WA9 ....1 A2
Warrington WA1 ....16 A3
Mersey Vale Prim Sch
SK4 ....240 A5
Mersey Valley Visitor Ctr*
M33 ....242 F7
Mersey View WA7 ....48 B4
Mersey View Rd WA8 .....22 A2
Mersey Wlk WA4 ....16 C3
Merseyton Rd CH65 ......70 B4
Merseyton Road Workshops
CH65 ....70 B4
Merseyway SK1 ....240 F6
Mersham Ct WA8 ....12 C2
Merston Dr M20 ....239 C8
Merton Ave
Hazel Grove SK7 ....36 C4
Romiley SK6 ....241 A4
Merton Cl CH64 ....66 C3
Merton Dr CH4 ....141 A2
Merton House Sch CH2 .118 B2
Merton House Sch
(Downswood) CH2 ....237 A4
Merton Rd
Bebington CH65 ....44 A2
Ellesmere Port CH66 ......69 C2
Sale M33 ....242 A8
5 Stockport SK3 ....240 B4
Mertoun Rd WA4 ....16 A1
Mervyn Rd CW8 ....77 C1
Merwood Ave SK8 ....34 B4
Messuage La CW12 .....132 C2
Meteor Cres WA2 ....8 B1
Metron Rd SK12 ....36 A2
Mevagissey Rd WA7 ......50 B3
Mevril Rd SK23 ....65 C3
Mews The Barnton CW8 ...78 A1
Gatley SK8 ....239 B5
Sale M33 ....242 C5
Tarporley CW6 ....168 B4
Wilmslow SK9 ....33 B2
Meyer St SK3 ....240 F2
Meynell Cl CW2 ....190 A1
Meynell Pl CH1 ....118 A3
Meyrick Ct WA12 ....2 A2
Micawber Rd SK12 ....36 C1
Mickle Trafford Village Sch
CH2 ....119 C4
Micklegate WA7 ....50 B4
Micklewright Ave CW1 ..190 B3
Mickley Hall La CW5 ....218 A2
Mid Cheshire Coll (London
Road Studios) CW9 ....103 C3
Mid Cheshire Coll (Verdin
Ctr) CW7 ....126 B1

Mid-Cheshire Coll (Hartford
Campus) CW8 ....103 B3
Middle Hillgate SK1 .....240 F4
Middle La Aldford CH3 ...163 C2
Congleton CW12 ....157 B2
Kingsley WA6 ....74 C1
Middle Wlk
Frodsham WA6 ....74 A4
Knutsford WA16 ....57 A1
Middlecroft CH3 ....119 C3
Middlehills SK11 ....113 A3
Middlehurst Ave CW8 ...102 C4
Middlehurst Rd WA4 .....17 A1
Middlewich High Sch
CW10 ....151 B4
Middlewich Prim Sch
CW10 ....151 A4
Middlewich Rd
Allostock WA16 ....106 B3
Church Minshull CW1,
CW10 ....172 C3
Cranage CW10 ....129 C3
Crewe CW1,CW2 ....189 B2
Holmes Chapel CW4 .....130 A2
Lower Peover WA16 ......81 C1
Nantwich CW5 ....204 C4
Northwich CW9 ....104 B4
Ollerton WA16 ....82 A2
Sandbach CW11 ....174 C4
Winsford CW7,CW10 .....127 C1
Middlewich Road Ind Est
CW10 ....129 A3
Middlewich St CW1 .....190 B3
Middlewood WA3 ....3 C4
Middlewood Dr SK4 .....240 A5
Middlewood Rd
High Lane SK6 ....37 B4
Poynton SK12 ....37 A2
Middlewood Sta SK6 .....37 B3
Middlewood View SK6 ...37 B4
Midfield Cl ST8 ....179 B1
Midgley Cres OL6 ....242 B4
Midhurst Cl SK8 ....34 C4
Midland St WA8 ....13 A1
Midland Terr SK22 ....39 B4
Midland Way WA1,WA5 ...16 A3
Midlothian Ho CH2 .....237 C3
Midpoint 18 Motorway Ind
Est CW10 ....128 C1
Midway SK8 ....35 A3
Milborne Cl CH2 ....118 C3
Mile Bank Rd SY13 .....226 B2
Miles Cl WA3 ....9 C2
Miles St SK14 ....241 F6
Milk St Congleton CW12 ..156 B2
Hyde SK14 ....241 D6
Mill Ave WA5 ....14 C4
Mill Bank CH64 ....67 A3
Mill Bridge Cl CW1 .....190 C2
Mill Brow WA8 ....13 B1
Mill Cl Chester CH2 .....118 B3
Culcheth WA3 ....4 C2
Knutsford WA16 ....57 B2
Warrington WA2 ....8 C2
Mill Cotts SK10 ....88 A4
Mill Ct CH65 ....69 C3
Mill Farm Cl WA2 ....8 C2
Mill Farm Est CW5 ......217 A2
Mill Field Cl CH3 ....180 C1
Mill Gn Congleton CW12 ..156 B2
Willaston CH64 ....67 C4
Mill Gr Bulkeley SY14 ...184 C1
Kidsgrove ST7 ....194 B1
Mill Green La WA8 ....13 C3
Mill Green Specl Sch
WA12 ....2 C2
Mill Hill Ave SK12 ....36 B4
Mill Hill Dr CW11 ....175 A2
Mill Hill Hollow SK12 ....36 B4
Mill Hill La CW11 ....175 A2
Mill La Adlington SK10 ...62 A3
Altrincham WA15 ....32 C2
Audlem, Little Heath CW3 .230 A2
Audlem, Swanbach CW3 ..229 C1
Barthomley CW2 ....208 B4
Blakenhall CW5 ....221 A2
Bold Heath WA8 ....13 B3
Brereton Green CW4 .....153 C4
Burton CH64 ....67 B1
Cheadle SK8 ....239 D6
Chester CH2 ....118 B3
Congleton CW12 ....179 B4
Cronton WA8 ....12 B3
Cuddington CW8 ....101 C3
Denton M34,SK14 ....241 B6
Duddon CW6 ....145 A4
Eaton CW6 ....147 A1
Ellesmere Port CH66 ......69 C3
Frodsham WA6 ....49 C1
Goostrey CW4 ....107 C1
Great Barrow CH3 ....120 C3
Hazel Grove SK7 ....36 C4
Heswall CH60 ....41 A4
Higher Walton WA4 ......25 C4
Huxley CH3 ....144 B1
Kelsall CW6 ....122 B1
Kingsley WA6 ....75 C2
Lindow End SK9 ....84 A4
Little Budworth CW6 ....125 A1
Lymm WA13 ....19 B2
Macclesfield SK11 ....112 B4
Marton CW12 ....132 C1
Middlewich CW10 ....128 A1
Middlewich CW10 ....128 B1
Mobberley WA16 ....58 A2
Mottram St Andrew SK10 ..61 B3
Neston CH64 ....67 B3
Newton-le-W WA12 ....2 C2

Mill La continued
Peover WA16,SK11 ......108 B4
Prestbury SK10 ....61 C3
Sandbach CW11 ....174 B4
Siddington SK11 ....109 C3
Smallwood CW11 ....175 A1
Tarvin CH3 ....121 B2
The Bank ST7 ....195 A4
Warrington WA2 ....7 C2
Warrington, Stockton Heath
WA4 ....16 C1
Weston CW2 ....207 A3
Whitegate CW7 ....126 A3
Willaston CH64 ....42 C1
Mill Lane Cotts CH3 ....120 C3
Mill Mdw WA12 ....2 C2
Mill Park Dr CH62 ....43 C2
Mill Pool La CW5 ....187 B3
Mill Rd Macclesfield SK11 .112 B3
Wilmslow SK9 ....60 A4
Mill Rise ST7 ....195 A1
Mill Row CW11 ....175 B3
Mill St Altrincham WA14 ..238 E5
Chester CH4 ....237 B1
Congleton CW12 ....156 B2
Congleton, Buglawton
CW12 ....156 C2
Crewe CW2 ....190 B2
Golborne WA3 ....3 A4
Macclesfield SK11 ....112 B4
Neston CH64 ....66 B4
Stalybridge SK15 ....242 F1
Warrington WA1 ....16 A3
Wilmslow SK9 ....60 A4
Mill St Mall 11 SK11 .....112 B4
Mill Stream Cl CW4 .....107 C1
Mill View Cl SY14 ....184 C1
Mill View Prim Sch
CH2 ....118 C3
Mill Way CW5 ....204 C1
Mill Wharf CH3 ....143 A3
Millar Cres WA8 ....23 A4
Millbank WA13 ....18 C2
Millbank Cl SK11 ....84 A2
Millbank Ct WA6 ....74 A4
Millbank Dr SK10 ....86 C1
Millbeck Cl CW2 ....207 A3
Millbridge Gdns WA12 ....2 C2
Millbrook Cl Glazebury WA3 .5 B3
Winsford CW7 ....148 C4
Millbrook End CH3 ......166 A1
Millbrook Fold SK7 ......36 C4
Millbrook Gr 10 SK9 .....34 B1
Millbrook St SK1 ....240 F4
Millbuck Way CW11 .....174 B3
Milldale Rd WN7 ....4 A4
Millend La ST7 ....209 B3
Millenium Ct CH64 ....41 C1
Millenium Way ST5 .....210 C1
Miller St WA4 ....16 B2
Millers Croft SK11 ......112 B4
Millers La Lymm WA13 ....19 A3
Waverton CH3 ....143 A2
Millers Mdw SK10 ....88 C3
Millers View ST7 ....195 A1
Millers Wharf ST7 ......193 C4
Millersdale Cl CH62 ......43 C3
Millersdale Gr WA7 ......49 B3
Milley La WA16 ....80 B4
Millfield Bsns Ctr WA11 ...1 C4
Millfield Ct WA15 ....238 F2
Millfield La Haydock WA11 ..1 C4
Saighton CH3 ....142 C1
Tarporley CW6 ....146 B1
Millfield Rd WA8 ....13 B1
Millfield Terr CH66 ....69 B4
Millfields CW5 ....204 B2
Millfields Prim Sch
Bebington CH62 ....43 C2
Nantwich CW5 ....204 B3
Millgate Cuddington CW8 .101 C2
Stockport SK1 ....240 F6
Millgate La M20 ....239 A8
Millhouse Ave WA4 ......16 B1
Millhouse La Croft WA3 ....9 A3
Warrington WA3 ....9 A3
Milling Field The CW4 ...130 B1
Millingford Ind Est WA3 ...3 A4
Millington Cl
Runcorn WA7 ....49 C2
Widnes WA8 ....22 C4
Millington Hall La WA14 ..30 A3
Millington La
Rostherne WA14 ....30 A3
Weaverham CW8 ....102 A3
Millmead ST7 ....193 C4
Millom Pl SK8 ....239 B3
Millrace Dr CW2 ....206 A3
Mills Way CW1 ....173 A1
Millstone Ave ST7 ......194 C1
Millstone Cl SK12 ....36 C3
Millstone La CW5 ....204 C3
Millstone Pas SK11 .....112 C3
Millway Altrincham WA15 ..32 B4
Waverton CH3 ....143 A3
Millway Rd L24 ....21 A2
Millwood WA7 ....24 B1
Millwood Cl 4 SK8 ....34 C4
Millwood Ct L24 ....21 A2
Millwood Cty Prim Sch
L24 ....21 A2
Millwood Terr 2 SK14 ...241 D6
Milne Cl CW2 ....189 C1
Milner Ave WA14 ....238 B7
Milner Cop CH60 ....41 A4

Milner Rd Heswall CH60 ...41 A4
Northwich CW8 ...103 B3
Milner St WA5 ...15 C3
Milnthorpe Rd WA5 ...6 C3
Milton Ave Irlam M44 ...11 C3
Newton-le-W WA12 ...2 A2
Widnes WA8 ...22 C4
Milton Cl
Higher Wincham CW9 ...80 A3
Middlewich CW10 ...151 B3
Milton Cres Cheadle SK8 .239 C5
Talke ST7 ...210 B4
Milton Ct SK7 ...35 C3
Milton Dr Poynton SK12 ...36 B2
Sale M33 ...242 B8
Wistaston CW2 ...206 A4
Milton Gr Helsby WA6 ...73 A1
Sale M33 ...242 A8
Warrington WA4 ...16 B2
Milton Rd Blacon CH1 ...117 C3
Bramhall SK7 ...35 C4
Ellesmere Port CH65 ...70 B2
Golborne WA3 ...3 B4
Widnes WA8 ...23 A4
Milton Rough CW8 ...76 C1
Milton St Chester CH2 ...237 B3
Hyde SK14 ...241 D8
Widnes WA8 ...23 A3
Milton Way CW11 ...174 B3
Milvain Dr WA2 ...8 B1
Milverton Dr SK7,SK8 ...35 A3
Mine Way WA11 ...1 C4
Miners Way Speke L24 ...21 A2
Widnes WA8 ...23 A4
Minerva Ave CH1 ...117 C1
Minerva Cl WA4 ...16 B1
Minerva Ct CH1 ...117 C1
Minister Cl CW7 ...149 B3
Minn-End-La SK11 ...159 A3
Minor Ave SK11 ...112 B2
Minshull La CW5,CW7 ...171 B2
Minshull New Rd CW1 ...189 C4
Minshull St WA16 ...57 A1
Minster Ct Runcorn WA7 ...48 C4
Wistaston CW2 ...205 C4
Minster Dr
Altrincham WA14 ...31 A4
Stockport SK8 ...240 A1
Minton Cl CW12 ...157 A1
Minton Way WA8 ...13 A3
Mirfield Ave SK4 ...240 B6
Mirfield Cl WA3 ...3 B4
Mirion St CW1 ...190 B2
Misty Cl WA8 ...12 B1
Mitchell Ave
Burtonwood WA5 ...6 C3
Kidsgrove ST7 ...194 B1
Mitchell Dr ST7 ...194 B1
Mitchell St Golborne WA3 ...3 A4
Warrington WA4 ...26 B4
Mithril Cl WA8 ...13 C2
Mitton Cl WA3 ...4 C3
Moadlock SK6 ...241 C4
Moat La Audley ST7 ...209 A2
Hollins Green WA3 ...10 C1
Mobberley CE Prim Sch
WA16 ...58 B3
Mobberley Cl WA4 ...17 B2
Mobberley Rd
Ashley WA14,WA15,WA16 ...31 C2
Knutsford WA16 ...57 B2
Wilmslow SK9 ...33 B1
Mobberley Sta WA16 ...57 C4
Moelfre Dr SK8 ...35 B4
Moggie La SK10 ...36 C1
Mold Rd CH4 ...139 A2
Mollington Ct CH1 ...94 C1
Mollington Rd M22 ...33 C4
Molly Pitcher Way WA5 ...15 A3
Molly Potts Cl WA16 ...82 A4
Molyneux Ave WA5 ...15 C4
Mona Ave SK8 ...239 D1
Mona St SK14 ...241 E6
Monarch Cl Crewe CW2 ...189 C2
Irlam M44 ...11 C3
Monarch Dr CW9 ...103 C3
Mond Rd WA8 ...23 A4
Mond St CW8 ...78 A2
Money Ash Rd WA15 ...238 E3
Monica Dr WA8 ...13 A3
Monk St CW1 ...190 A3
Monk's La CW3 ...230 B3
Monks Coppenhall Prim Sch
CW1 ...190 C4
Monks Gr CH65 ...70 A3
Monks La Acton CW5 ...203 C4
Crewe CW1 ...189 C3
Nantwich CW5 ...204 C3
Monks Orch CW5 ...204 C3
Monks St WA5 ...15 C3
Monks Way CW8 ...103 A2
Monksheath Hall Wrkshps
SK10 ...85 A1
Monkswood Cl WA5 ...7 C1
Monmouth Cl WA1 ...17 C4
Monroe Cl WA1 ...17 A4
Monsall Cl SK11 ...112 C4
Monsall Dr SK11 ...112 C4
Montague Ho SK3 ...240 D4
Montague Rd
Ashton-u-Lyne OL6 ...242 A3
Sale M33 ...242 B6
Montague Way SK15 ...242 D2
Montclare Cres WA4 ...16 C1
Montcliffe Cl WA3 ...9 B3
Montgomery Cl WA16 ...57 B2
Montgomery Rd WA8 ...22 B4
Montgomery Way CW7 ...149 A4
Montmorency Rd WA16 ...57 B2
Montpelier Ave WA7 ...48 C3
Montrose Cl
Macclesfield SK10 ...87 A1
Shavington CW2 ...206 A2
Warrington WA2 ...8 C2
Montrose Ct
Chester CH4 ...140 C4
Holmes Chapel CW4 ...130 A1
Monument Rd ST7 ...210 B3
Monument View ST7 ...209 C1
Moody St CW12 ...156 B1
Moon St WA8 ...23 A4
Moor Cl ST8 ...179 C1
Moor Cres CH4 ...139 B1
Moor La Elton WA6 ...72 C1
Frodsham WA6 ...74 A4
Hawarden CH5 ...116 A1
Heswall CH60 ...40 C4
Higher Kinnerton CH4 ...161 B4
Higher Kinnerton, Kinnerton Green
CH4 ...161 B3
Waverton CH3 ...143 A3
Widnes WA8 ...22 C4
Widnes WA8 ...23 A4
Wilmslow SK9 ...59 C3
Woodford SK7 ...35 C2
Moor La S WA8 ...22 C4
Moor Lodge SK4 ...240 B8
Moor Nook M33 ...242 D5
Moor Park Rd M20 ...239 C8
Moor Park Way CW9 ...103 C2
Moor Platt M33 ...242 D5
Moor St CW12 ...156 C1
Moor Top Pl SK4 ...240 B7
Moorcroft WA16 ...80 C2
Moorcroft Ave CH3 ...119 A1
Moorcroft Cres CH3 ...119 B2
Moorcroft Mews CH4 ...140 B3
Moordale Rd WA16 ...57 A1
Moorditch La WA6 ...48 B1
Moore Ave St Helens WA9 ...1 A2
Warrington WA4 ...17 B2
Moore Cl WA8 ...13 B1
Moore Dr WA11 ...1 C3
Moore Gr WA13 ...19 A3
Moore La WA4 ...25 B3
Moore Prim Sch WA4 ...25 A3
Moorfield Ave M34 ...241 A6
Moorfield Cres WA3 ...4 A4
Moorfield Dr Neston CH64 .41 B1
Wilmslow SK9 ...59 C3
Moorfield Gr Sale M33 ...242 D5
Stockport SK4 ...240 B8
Moorfield Prim Sch WA8 .13 B2
Moorfield Rd WA8 ...13 B2
Moorfields
Willaston (nr Nantwich)
CW5 ...205 C3
Wistaston CW5 ...205 C3
Moorhead La CW11 ...154 B2
Moorhill Rd SK11 ...112 B2
Moorhouse Ave ST7 ...193 C2
Moorhouse Cl CH2 ...118 B3
Mooring Cl WA7 ...50 B3
Moorings CW12 ...156 C1
Moorings Cl CH64 ...41 A1
Moorings The
Christleton CH3 ...142 C4
Disley SK12 ...38 C3
Heswall CH60 ...40 B4
Middlewich CW10 ...128 B1
Moorland Ave M33 ...242 C5
Moorland Cl CH60 ...41 A4
Moorland Dr Cheadle SK8 .34 C4
Runcorn WA7 ...50 C4
Moorland Pk CH60 ...41 A4
Moorland Rd
Biddulph ST8 ...179 B1
Ellesmere Port CH66 ...69 C4
Kidsgrove ST7 ...195 B4
Moorlands Ave CW8 ...102 A2
Moorlands Cl SK10 ...87 B2
Moorlands Dr CW5 ...206 A1
Moorlands Jun Sch
M33 ...242 E7
Moorlands Pk CW8 ...102 A2
Moors La CW7 ...149 B3
Moorsbrook Gr 9 SK9 ...34 C1
Moorsfield Ave CW3 ...229 C2
Moorside WA16 ...57 A1
Moorside Ave CH64 ...66 B4
Moorside Ct
Dukinfield M34 ...241 A8
Sale M33 ...242 B6
Widnes WA8 ...22 C4
Moorside La Hyde M34 ...241 A8
Neston CH64 ...66 B4
Pott Shrigley SK10 ...63 C2
Moorside Rd SK4 ...240 A6
Moorson Ave ST7 ...194 C4
Moorview Gdns ST7 ...195 C3
Moorway CH60 ...41 A4
Moran Cl SK9 ...34 C1
Moran Cres SK11 ...112 A4
Moran Rd SK11 ...112 A4
Morcott La L24 ...21 B1
Moresby Cl WA7 ...50 C4
Moresby Dr M20 ...239 B8
Moreton Ave SK7 ...35 C3
Moreton Dr Alsager ST7 ...193 B2
Handforth SK9 ...34 C2
Holmes Chapel CW4 ...130 A2
Poynton SK12 ...36 C2
Sandbach CW11 ...175 B4
Moreton Ho WA14 ...238 B4
Moreton Rd CW2 ...189 C2
Moreton St CW8 ...78 B1
Moreton Terr 1 WA6 ...74 A4
Moreville Cl CW9 ...103 C2
Morgan Ave WA2 ...8 B1
Morgan Cl Blacon CH1 ...117 C3
Crewe CW2 ...190 A2
Morgan Pl SK5 ...240 F8
Morland Ave
Bebington CH62 ...43 B3
Neston CH64 ...66 C4
Morley Cl CH2 ...119 C4
Morley Dr CW12 ...157 A1
Morley Gn SK9 ...33 B1
Morley Rd Runcorn WA7 ...23 A1
Warrington WA4 ...16 A1
Morley St WA1 ...16 B3
Mornant Ave CW8 ...103 A2
Morningside WA14 ...238 B5
Morningside Dr M20 ...239 C8
Mornington Ave
Cheadle SK8 ...239 D4
Ellesmere Port CH65 ...70 B2
Mornington Cl CW11 ...174 B4
Mornington Rd
Cheadle SK8 ...239 D4
Sale M33 ...242 D7
Morphany La WA4 ...51 C3
Morreys La CW6 ...122 C4
Morris Ave WA4 ...16 C2
Morris Cl WA11 ...1 A3
Morris Dr CW8 ...77 B1
Morris Pk CW8 ...103 A2
Morrison Cl WA5 ...15 A3
Mort Ave WA4 ...17 A3
Mortimer Ave WA2 ...16 A4
Mortimer Dr CW11 ...175 B3
Mortlake Cl WA8 ...12 B2
Mortlake Cres CH3 ...119 A1
Morton Ave WA6 ...73 A1
Morton Cl WA5 ...15 B4
Morton Dr SK11 ...112 C2
Morton Rd Blacon CH1 ...117 C2
Runcorn WA7 ...50 B4
Morton St SK4 ...240 E8
Morven Cl WA2 ...8 C2
Moscow Rd SK3 ...240 D3
Moscow Rd E SK3 ...240 D3
Mosedale Gr WA7 ...49 C3
Moseley Ave WA4 ...17 A2
Moseley Grange SK8 ...239 F3
Moseley Rd SK8 ...239 F3
Moseley St 2 SK3 ...240 E4
Moses Ct CH2 ...237 C3
Mosley Cl WA15 ...238 F7
Moss Bank
Bramhall SK7,SK8 ...35 B3
Chester CH2 ...118 B2
Winsford CW7 ...126 B1
Moss Bank Rd WA8 ...23 B4
Moss Bower Rd SK11 ...112 B2
Moss Brow SK10 ...87 C4
Moss Brow La WA16 ...28 B2
Moss Cl Warrington WA4 ...16 C1
Willaston CH64 ...68 A4
Moss Croft CW1 ...190 A4
Moss Dr Manley WA6 ...98 C2
Middlewich CW10 ...151 B3
Moss Farm Recn Ctr
CW8 ...103 B4
Moss Fields Alsager ST7 ...193 A2
Crewe CW1 ...173 A1
Moss Gate WA3 ...10 A3
Moss Gr Broughton CH4 ...140 B3
Lymm WA13 ...19 A2
Newcastle-u-L ST5 ...210 B2
Moss Green Way WA9 ...1 A1
Moss Hey Prim Sch SK7 ...35 B3
Moss La Alderley Edge SK9 .60 A1
Altrincham WA14,WA15 ...238 E4
Altrincham, Timperley
WA15 ...238 F7
Bollington SK10 ...87 C4
Bramhall SK7 ...35 B3
Brereton Green CW12 ...154 C3
Congleton CW12 ...156 C3
Crewe CW1 ...173 A1
Cuddington CW8 ...102 A2
Fowley Common WA3 ...5 B3
Golborne WA3 ...3 A3
High Legh WA16 ...29 C3
High Legh, Sink Moss WA16 .28 B2
Hollins Green WA3 ...10 C3
Irlam M44 ...11 B3
Knutsford WA16 ...56 B3
Lawton-gate ST7 ...194 C2
Lostock Green CW9 ...105 B4
Macclesfield SK11 ...112 B2
Manley WA6 ...99 A2
Middlewich CW10 ...129 A4
Mobberley WA16 ...58 C2
Moore WA4 ...25 A3
Mottram St Andrew SK10 ...61 A1
Norley WA6 ...101 A3
Northwich CW8 ...103 B4
Ollerton WA16 ...83 B2
Partington M31 ...11 C1
Sandbach CW11 ...174 B4
Siddington SK11 ...109 C1
St Helens, Moss Nook WA9 ...1 A1
Styal SK9 ...33 C3
Warmingham CW1 ...173 B2
Moss Lane Bsns Ctr
CW11 ...174 B3
Moss Pl ST7 ...195 A2
Moss Rd Alderley Edge SK9 .60 B1
Congleton CW12 ...178 C4
Moss Rd *continued*
Irlam M44 ...11 B4
Northwich CW8 ...103 B4
Warrington WA4 ...17 A2
Moss Rose SK9 ...60 A1
Moss Rose Football Gnd
SK11 ...112 B2
Moss Side La
Antrobus CW9 ...53 B4
Hollins Green WA3 ...10 C2
Moore WA4 ...24 C4
Moss Side Rd M44 ...11 C3
Moss Sq Crewe CW1 ...190 B2
Macclesfield SK11 ...112 B2
Moss St Weaverham CW8 ...77 B1
Widnes WA8 ...23 B4
Moss Terr Northwich CW8 ...78 B1
Warren SK11 ...112 A3
Wilmslow SK9 ...60 C4
Moss The CW9 ...78 B4
Moss View Rd SK11 ...112 A2
Moss Way ST7 ...193 A2
Mossdale Cl Crewe CW2 .189 C2
Warrington WA5 ...15 A4
Mossfield Cl SK4 ...240 B6
Mossfield Cres 13 ST7 ...195 A1
Mossford Ave CW1 ...190 A4
Mossgrove Rd WA15 ...238 F6
Mosshall La WA4 ...26 C1
Mosslands Cl CH66 ...69 C1
Mossley Ave CH62 ...43 B4
Mossley CE Prim Sch
CW12 ...179 A4
Mossley Ct CW12 ...178 C4
Mossley Rd OL6 ...242 B4
Mossvale CH66 ...69 B4
Mosswood Pk M20 ...239 B8
Mosswood Rd SK9 ...34 C1
Moston Ct 5 CW12 ...156 C2
Moston Gr WA13 ...18 B2
Moston Rd Chester CH2 ...118 B4
Sandbach CW11 ...174 B3
Moston Way CH66 ...69 C2
Mostyn Ave Cheadle SK8 .239 E1
Heswall CH60 ...40 B4
Mostyn Gdns CH64 ...41 A1
Mostyn House Sch CH64 ...66 B4
Mostyn Pl CH1 ...117 C3
Mostyn Sq CH64 ...41 A1
Motcombe Farm Rd
SK8 ...239 B1
Motcombe Gr SK8 ...239 A3
Motcombe Rd SK8 ...239 A2
Motram Cl WA4 ...17 A2
Mottershead Rd WA8 ...23 A4
Mottram Cl
Middlewich CW10 ...151 A4
Stockport SK8 ...240 A1
Mottram Fold SK1 ...240 F4
Mottram Rd
Alderley Edge SK9 ...60 B1
Sale M33 ...242 F5
Mottram St 5 SK1 ...240 F4
Mottram St Andrew Prim Sch
SK10 ...61 A1
Mottram Way SK10 ...87 C1
Moughland La WA7 ...49 A4
Moulders La WA1 ...16 A2
Mouldsworth Cl 2
CW9 ...103 C2
Mouldsworth Motor Mus*
CH3 ...98 C1
Mouldsworth Sta CH3 ...99 A1
Moulton Cl
Davenham CW9 ...103 C2
Knutsford WA16 ...57 B1
Runcorn WA7 ...49 C2
Moulton Sch CW9 ...126 C4
Mount Ave CH60 ...40 C4
Mount Cl CW5 ...204 C3
Mount Ct CH60 ...40 C4
Mount Farm Way CH66 ...69 B1
Mount Mews CH60 ...40 C4
Mount Pl CH2 ...118 C1
Mount Pleasant
Audlem CW3 ...230 A2
Bollington SK10 ...88 A4
Chester CH4 ...140 C4
Congleton CW12 ...156 C1
Crewe CW1 ...190 A3
Elton CH2 ...72 A2
Haslington CW1 ...191 B2
Kidsgrove ST7 ...195 A1
Macclesfield SK10 ...87 A1
Rainow SK10 ...88 B2
Widnes WA8 ...13 A1
Wilmslow SK9 ...60 A4
Mount Pleasant Ave WA9 ...1 A2
Mount Pleasant Dr
CW7 ...149 A4
Mount Pleasant Rd
Davenham CW9 ...103 C1
The Bank ST7 ...195 A4
Mount Pleasant Residential
Pk CW4 ...130 B4
Mount Rd Kidsgrove ST7 ...195 A1
Runcorn WA7 ...49 C4
Stockport SK4 ...240 C6
Mount St Hyde SK14 ...241 E6
Widnes WA8 ...13 A1
Mount Terr SK11 ...112 C4
Mount The
Altrincham WA14 ...238 D5
Altrincham, Halebarns
WA15 ...32 B4
Ashton-u-Lyne OL6 ...242 A3
Chester CH3 ...118 C1
Congleton CW12 ...156 A1
Mount The *continued*
Great Budworth CW9 ...79 A4
Heswall CH60 ...40 C4
Kidsgrove ST7 ...195 A1
Scholar Green ST7 ...194 C4
Mount Way CH3 ...143 A2
Mountain View
Broughton CH4 ...140 C3
Helsby WA6 ...73 A2
Mountbatten Ct CW2 ...190 A2
Mountbatten Way
CW12 ...156 B2
Mountfield Rd
Bramhall SK7 ...35 C
Stockport SK3 ...240 C
Mourne Cl CH66 ...69 A
Mow Cop Rd ST7 ...195 B
Mow La Biddulph ST7,ST8 .179 A
Mount Pleasant ST7 ...195 A
Mowbray Ave M33 ...242 C
Mowbray St 4 SK1 ...240 F
Mowcroft La WA5 ...14 A
Mowpen Brow WA16 ...29 A
Moxon Ave WA4 ...16 C
Moyles Cl WA8 ...12 B
Mudhouse La CH64 ...67 C
Mudhurst La SK12 ...38 C
Muir Rd CH1 ...117 C
Muirfield Ave SK6 ...241 A
Muirfield Cl
Northwich CW9 ...104 A
Warrington WA2 ...9 A
Wilmslow SK9 ...60 B
Muirfield Dr
Macclesfield SK10 ...87 B
Winsford CW7 ...126 B
Muirfield Mews CW7 ...126 B
Mulberry Ave WA3 ...3 C
Mulberry Cl Elton CH2 ...72 B
Gatley SK8 ...34 B
Warrington WA1 ...17 C
Mulberry Ct
Altrincham WA14 ...238 D
Macclesfield SK11 ...112 B
Warrington WA4 ...16 B
Mulberry Gdns CW11 ...174 B
Mulberry Mews SK4 ...240 E
Mulberry Mount St SK3 .240 E
Mulberry Rd CW2 ...189 C
Mulberry Rise CW8 ...103 E
Mulcaster Ct CW1 ...191 E
Mull Cl CH65 ...70 B
Mullein Cl WA3 ...3 B
Mullen Cl WA5 ...7 C
Mullins Ave WA12 ...2 B
Mullion Cl WA7 ...50 A
Mullion Dr WA15 ...238 E
Mullion Gr WA2 ...9 A
Mulsford Ct LL13 ...222 A
Mulsford La LL13,SY14 ...222 A
Murdishaw Ave WA7 ...50 B
Murdishaw West Prim Sch
WA7 ...50 B
Muriel Cl WA5 ...14 B
Murieston Rd WA15 ...238 E
Murray Cl SK10 ...87 A
Murrayfield SK10 ...87 A
Murrayfield Dr CW5 ...205 B
Museum of Hatting Stockport
The* SK1 ...240 E
Museum St WA1 ...16 A
Music Hall Pass CH1 ...237 E
Mustard La WA3 ...4 A
Myddleton La WA2 ...8 E
Myrica Gr CH2 ...119 A
Myrtle Ave Haydock WA11 ...1 A
Higher Kinnerton CH4 ...161 A
Newton-le-W WA12 ...2 E
Myrtle Gr Chester CH2 ...119 A
Warrington WA4 ...16 E
Widnes WA8 ...22 E
Myrtle Rd M31 ...11 E
Myrtle St
Ellesmere Port CH65 ...70 E
Stockport SK3 ...240 E
Mythorne Ave M44 ...11 E

N

Nab Cl SK10 ...63 E
Nab La SK10 ...63 E
Nabbs Cl ST7 ...195 A
Nabbswood Rd ST7 ...195 A
Nairn Ave CW4 ...130 A
Nairn Cl Bebington CH63 ...43 E
Warrington WA2 ...9 A
Nancy View SK10 ...88 A
Nansen Cl WA5 ...15 E
Nansen Rd SK8 ...239 A
Nansmoss La SK9 ...33 E
Nantwich Mus* CW5 ...204 C
Nantwich Rd
Barbridge CW5 ...187
Betley ST7 ...208
Broxton CH3 ...183
Crewe CW2 ...190
Ellesmere Port CH66 ...69
Middlewich CW10 ...151
Sound CW5 ...217
Tarporley CW6 ...168
Wimboldsley CW10 ...150
Woore CW3 ...232
Worleston CW2,CW5 ...189
Wrenbury CW5 ...201
Nantwich Sta CW5 ...204
Nantwich Way 6 SK9 ...34
Naomi Cl CH1 ...117

ier Ct 5 SK4 240 B7
ier Gdns 3 ST7 195 A1
ier Rd Chester CH2 118 B4
ckport SK4 240 B7
ier St Hyde SK14 241 E5
rrington WA1 16 B3
les Rd SK3 240 B3
ley Dr TF9 236 B1
ley Rd TF9 236 B1
es Cl WA5 7 B1
row La SK10 37 A1
rows The WA14 238 C4
eby Rd CW12 156 A2
myth Ave M34 241 A8
La CW7 126 C1
Lane Ret Pk CW7 126 C1
han Dr WA11 1 C3
ghton Lea WA8 12 B2
ghton Rd WA8 23 A4
an Ct CW1 190 A3
igation Cl WA7 50 B3
igation Prim Sch
14 238 D6
igation Rd
rincham WA14,WA15 238 D6
rthwich CW8 103 C4
igation Road Sta
14 238 E6
igation St WA1 16 B3
lor Ave WA3 3 A4
lor Cres CH66 69 C4
lor Ct 12 CW9 103 C4
lor Rd WA8 13 B1
lor St WA1 16 A3
l Ave
ton-u-Lyne OL6 242 A3
ley SK8 239 A1
th Cl SK12 36 B3
dham Cl WA7 23 B1
dham Dr
nage CW4 130 A3
tford CW8 103 A2
dhams Wharf Cl
0 88 A1
St WA8 13 B1
ls Rd WA5 6 A3
son Ave SK12 37 A2
son Bldgs ST7 195 A1
son Cl SK12 37 A2
son Dr M44 11 C3
son Gr ST7 193 C1
son Ind Est ST7 194 B1
son Rd CH65 70 B4
son St Chester CH2 237 C3
ngleton CW12 156 B1
we CW2 190 B1
e SK14 241 E6
cclesfield SK11 112 B4
wton-le-W WA12 2 A2
ncorn WA7 23 A2
dnes WA7 23 A1
nos Cl WA6 73 B1
tune Cl WA7 50 B4
field Cl CW11 191 C4
field Dr CW11 191 C4
s Botanic Gdns*
4 67 A2
sina Gr CW2 205 C4
ton Dr CH2 118 C3
ton Gn CH66 69 B2
ton Gr SK3 240 D1
ton Prim Sch CH64 66 C4
ton Rd
swall CH63,CH64 41 C3
ton CH64 67 A2
aston CH64 67 C4
on St Mary's CE Prim
CH64 41 C1
on Sta CH64 66 C4
on Way SK9 34 B2
on,High Sch CH64 41 C1
er Alderley Mill*
0 85 A3
er Alderley Prim Sch
0 85 A3
er Fold SK10 87 A4
er Lea CW4 130 B4
ercroft Ct WA14 238 C5
erfield WA8 22 C4
erfields SK9 85 A4
erley Rd WA8 12 A1
erlow Ct SK14 241 E6
erpool Rd CH66 69 C4
erton Dr WA6 74 A4
mann St CW9 104 A4
da Cl WA5 15 B4
lle Ave St Helens WA9 1 A1
rington WA2 8 B1
lle Cres WA5 15 A2
lle Dr 9 CH3 119 A1
lle Rd Bebington CH62 43 C4
ster CH3 119 A1
lle St Crewe CW2 190 B1
wton-le-W WA12 2 A2
n Ave SK8 239 E1
n Cl SK7 36 A4
n Rd CH1 117 B2
s Dr CW2 189 B2
Bank Pl WA8 12 A1
Bank Rd WA8 12 A1
Barnet WA8 12 C2
Chester Rd
ington CH62 43 C3
ton CH62,CH66 44 A1
Cotts Hampton SY14 213 C4
ley WA6 99 B4
Crane Bank CH1 118 A1
Crane St CH1 118 A1

New Cut Ind Est WA1 17 B4
New Cut La WA1 17 A4
New Farm Cotts WA3 11 A4
New Farm Ct CH3 120 C3
New Grosvenor Rd CH65 70 A4
New Hall Ave SK8 34 A4
New Hall Cl M33 242 F6
New Hall La Culcheth WA3 4 C1
Culcheth WA3 5 A1
New Hall St SK10 87 B1
New Hey La CH64 68 A3
New Hey Rd SK8 239 E6
New Horwich Rd SK23 65 C4
New Hos CW5 187 B3
New Houses CH3 143 A4
New Inn Cotts WA16 108 B4
New Inn La CW11 176 A1
New King St Audley ST7 209 B1
Middlewich CW10 128 B1
New La
Appleton Thorn WA4 27 A3
Churton CH3 180 C3
Croft WA3 9 A4
Harthill CH3 183 C2
Winsford CW7 149 C2
New Manchester Rd
WA1 17 A4
New Manor Rd WA4 51 A3
New Mills Central Sta
SK22 39 A4
New Mills Newtown Sta
SK22 39 A3
New Mills Prim Sch
SK22 39 A4
New Mills Sch SK22 39 B4
New Moss Rd M44 11 B3
New Pale Rd WA6 99 B3
New Platt La CW4 107 A1
New Rd Anderton CW9 78 B2
Antrobus CW9 27 B1
Astbury CW12 178 A2
Audley ST7 209 C2
Duddon CW6 145 A3
Ellesmere Port CH66 69 A4
Lymm WA13 18 C2
Marton CW12 132 B1
Mere WA16 30 C2
Prestbury SK10 87 A4
Warrington WA4 16 A2
Whaley Bridge SK23 65 C3
Whaley Bridge, Bridgemont
SK23 39 C1
Winsford CW7 126 C1
Wrenbury CW5 216 B2
New School La CH66 44 A1
New St Altrincham WA14 238 D4
Congleton CW12 156 C1
Haslington CW1 191 B3
Neston CH64 66 C3
New Mills SK22 39 B4
Runcorn WA7 23 A1
Sandbach CW11 174 B4
Widnes WA8 23 A4
Wilmslow SK9 59 C3
New St Cotts CW12 157 A2
New Warrington Rd CW9 79 A1
New Wellington Sch
WA15 238 F6
Newall Cl CH3 166 A1
Newall Cres CW7 127 A1
Newberry Gr SK3 240 D1
Newbold Ct 9 CW12 156 C2
Newbold Way CW5 204 C2
Newborough Cl WA5 7 C1
Newboult Rd SK8 239 E6
Newbridge Cl
Runcorn WA7 50 B3
Warrington WA5 7 B1
Newbridge Rd CH65,CH2 70 C2
Newburgh Cl WA7 24 B1
Newbury Ave
Crewe CW1 190 B4
6 Winsford CW7 149 A4
Newbury Cl Cheadle SK8 35 A3
Widnes WA8 13 A2
Newbury Ct SK9 60 A3
Newbury Rd
Chester CH4 140 C3
Gatley SK8 34 B4
Newby Ct CW12 156 A1
Newby Dr
Altrincham WA14 238 D6
Gatley SK8 239 A6
Sale M33 242 E5
Newby Rd SK4 240 C6
Newcastle Rd
Astbury CW12 178 A4
Brereton Green CW11 153 C2
Congleton CW12 156 A1
Hassall Green CW11 176 A2
Haymoor Green CW5 205 B2
Shavington CW2,CW5 206 B2
Smallwood CW11 176 B3
Talke ST7 210 C4
Woore CW3 232 C1
Newcastle Rd N CW11 153 C3
Newcastle Rd S CW11 153 C3
Newcastle St CW1 190 A3
Newchapel Obsy* ST7 195 C1
Newchapel Rd ST7 195 B2
Newchurch Com Prim Sch
WA3 4 C1
Newchurch La WA3 4 C1
Newcombe Ave WA2 16 C4
Newcroft CH1 94 A1
Newcroft Dr SK3 240 D2
Newdigate St
Crewe CW1 190 B2

Newdigate St *continued*
Crewe CW1 190 B3
Newfield Ct WA13 19 A3
Newfield Dr CW1 190 C3
Newfield Rd WA13 18 B2
Newfield St CW11 175 A4
Newfield Terr WA6 73 A1
Newgate
Macclesfield SK11 112 B4
Wilmslow SK9 59 B4
Newgate St CH1 237 B2
Newhall Ave CW11 175 A3
Newhall Ct CH2 118 C3
Newhall Rd CH2 118 C3
Newham Cl SK11 112 C2
Newhaven Rd WA2 8 A2
Newington Ct WA14 238 B3
Newland Cl WA8 12 B2
Newland Mews WA3 4 C3
Newland Way CW5 205 A2
Newlands Ave
Bramhall SK7 35 C4
Cheadle SK8 35 A4
Newlands Cl Cheadle SK8 35 A4
Frodsham WA6 74 B3
Newlands Dr Golborne WA3 3 B4
Manchester M20 239 C8
Wilmslow SK9 59 C3
Newlands Rd
Cheadle SK8 239 D6
Macclesfield SK10 111 C4
Warrington WA4 16 C1
Newlyn Ave
Congleton CW12 178 C4
Macclesfield SK10 86 B1
Newlyn Cl WA7 50 A3
Newlyn Dr SK6 241 A3
Newlyn Gdns WA5 14 B2
Newman Cl CW12 156 A2
Newman RC High Sch
WA4 16 C3
Newman St Hyde SK14 241 E7
Warrington WA4 16 C2
Newman's La CW5 219 B4
Newmarket Cl 1 SK10 87 B2
Newmarket Wlk 12 WA1 16 A3
Newmoore La WA7 24 C2
Newnham Dr CH65 70 B2
Newport Gr ST5 210 C1
Newquay Cl WA7 50 A3
Newquay Ct CW12 178 C4
Newquay Dr Bramhall SK7 35 C4
Macclesfield SK10 111 B4
Newry Ct CH2 118 B2
Newry Pk CH2 118 B2
Newry Pk E CH2 118 B2
Newsham Cl WA8 12 A2
Newsholme Cl WA3 4 C2
Newstead Cl SK12 36 B3
Newstead Terr WA15 238 F7
Newton Ave WA3 9 C3
Newton Bank CW10 128 A1
Newton Bank Prep Sch
WA12 2 C2
Newton Comm Hospl
WA12 2 A1
Newton Cotts CH3 166 B2
Newton for Hyde Sta
SK14 241 F8
Newton Gr WA2 8 C2
Newton Hall Ct CH2 118 C3
Newton Hall Dr CH2 118 C3
Newton Hall La WA16 58 C3
Newton Hall Mews 1
CW10 151 B4
Newton Heath CW10 128 A1
Newton Hollow WA6 74 B1
Newton La Chester CH2 118 C2
Daresbury WA4 51 C4
Golborne WA12 2 C3
Tattenhall CH3 166 B2
Newton Park Dr WA12 2 C2
Newton Park View CH2 118 B2
Newton Pl CW12 156 C1
Newton Prim Sch CH2 118 C2
Newton Rd
Altrincham WA14 238 E7
Ellesmere Port CH65 70 B3
Golborne WA3 3 B3
Handforth SK9 34 A1
St Helens WA9 1 A2
Winwick WA2 8 A3
Newton St Crewe CW1 190 B3
Hyde SK14 241 D8
Macclesfield SK11 112 B4
Stalybridge SK15 242 C2
1 Stockport SK3 240 E4
Newton-le-Willows Com
High Sch WA12 2 B3
Newton-le-Willows Prim Sch
WA12 2 B2
Newton-le-Willows Sta
WA12 2 C2
Newtons Cres CW11 191 C4
Newtons Gr CW11 191 C4
Newtons La CW11 191 C4
Newtown Kidsgrove ST7 195 C1
Neston CH64 66 C4
Newtown Cl CH2 237 B3
Newtown Prim Sch SK22 39 A3
Nicholas Ave CW9 104 B3
Nicholas Ct CH1 237 A2
Nicholas Rd
Weaverham CW8 77 B1
Widnes WA8 22 B4
Nicholas St CH1 237 A2
Nicholas St Mews CH1 237 A2
Nicholls St WA4 17 A1

Nicholson Ave SK10 87 C1
Nicholson Cl SK10 87 C1
Nicholson St
Stockport SK4 240 E6
Warrington WA1 15 C3
Nickleby Rd SK12 36 C2
Nickolson Cl CH2 119 C4
Nicol Ave WA1 17 C4
Nidderdale Cl CW12 157 A3
Niddries Ct CW9 126 C4
Niddries La CW9 126 C4
Nield Ct CH2 118 B4
Nield's Brow WA14 238 C2
Nigel Gresley Cl CW1 191 A2
Nigel Rd CH60 41 B4
Nigel Wlk WA7 24 A1
Nightgale Cl CW1 189 C4
Nightingale Cl
Farndon CH3 180 C1
Middlewich CW10 151 B3
Runcorn WA7 49 C3
Warrington WA3 9 C2
Wilmslow SK9 34 A1
Nightingale Ct 4 CW7 149 B3
Nightingale Way ST7 193 A2
Nile St CW2 190 B1
Nine Hos The CH3 166 A1
Nixon Dr CW7 126 A1
Nixon Rd CW8 101 C2
Nixon St Crewe CW1 189 C3
Macclesfield SK11 112 A4
3 Stockport SK3 240 E4
Nixon's Row CW5 204 B3
No 1 Road N CW2 192 C1
No 1 Road S CW2 192 C1
No 2 Pas SK3 240 D5
No 2 Road N CW2 192 C1
No 2 Road S CW2 192 C1
Noahs Ark La WA16 58 C1
Noble Cl WA3 9 C2
Noel Dr M33 242 D6
Nook La Antrobus CW9 53 C3
Golborne WA3 3 A4
Warrington WA4 17 A2
Warrington, Fearnhead WA2 9 A1
Nook The Bramhall SK7 35 B3
Broughton CH4 140 C3
Chester CH2 118 C2
Guilden Sutton CH3 119 B2
Noon Ct WA12 2 A1
Nora St WA1 16 B3
Norbreck Ave
Crewe CW2 190 A1
Stockport SK8 240 A2
Norbreck Dr WA5 15 A2
Norbury Ave
4 Hyde SK14 241 D6
Warrington WA2 16 B4
Norbury Cl
Hough Common CW2 206 C2
Knutsford WA16 57 B2
Norbury Dr
Congleton CW12 156 C2
Middlewich CW10 151 A4
Norbury Hollow Rd SK7 37 A4
Norbury St
Macclesfield SK11 112 B4
Northwich CW9 104 A4
12 Stockport SK1 240 F5
Norbury Way 9 SK9 34 B3
Norcott Ave WA4 16 C1
Norcott Dr WA5 6 C3
Norden Cl WA3 9 B3
Norfolk Cl M44 11 B3
Norfolk Dr WA5 14 C3
Norfolk Gr ST8 179 B1
Norfolk Ho 1 Sale M33 242 D6
Talke ST7 210 B3
Norfolk Pl WA8 22 B4
Norfolk Rd Chester CH2 118 C2
Congleton CW12 156 C2
Ellesmere Port CH65 70 B3
Kidsgrove ST7 194 C1
Norfolk St Hyde SK14 241 D6
Runcorn WA7 23 A2
Norfolk Wlk SK10 86 C1
Norgrove Cl WA7 50 B4
Norland St WA8 13 B1
Norland's La L35 12 C4
Norleane Cres WA7 49 A4
Norley Ave
Bebington CH62 43 C2
Ellesmere Port CH65 69 C3
Norley CE Prim Sch
WA6 100 C3
Norley Dr Chester CH3 119 B1
Sale M33 242 E6
Norley La Crowton CW8 76 A1
Norley CW8 101 A4
Norley Rd
Cuddington CW8 101 C2
Kingsley WA6 75 A1
Norley WA6 100 B4
Norman Ave Haydock WA11 2 A4
Newton-le-W WA12 2 C2
Norman Cl CH66 94 C4
Norman Dr CW7 149 B3
Norman Rd
Altrincham WA14 238 C6
Runcorn WA7 23 A1
Sale M33 242 B5
Stalybridge SK15 242 C2
Stockport SK4 240 B7
Norman St Hyde SK14 241 E6
Warrington WA2 16 A3
Norman Way CH1 117 C3
Norman's La WA4 52 C2
Norman's Pl WA14 238 D4

Normanby Chase WA14 238 B4
Normanby Cl WA5 15 C4
Normandy Ave 10 CW7 149 B4
Normandy Rd CH2 95 B1
Normans Cotts 9 CH64 66 C4
Normanton Rd SK3 240 A2
Norreys Ave WA5 15 C4
Norris Ave SK4 240 C6
Norris Bank Prim Sch
SK4 240 B7
Norris Bank Terr SK4 240 C5
Norris Hill Dr SK4 240 C6
Norris Rd Blacon CH1 117 C3
Sale M33 242 F5
Norris St WA2 16 B4
North Ave
Stalybridge SK15 242 D3
Warrington WA2 16 A4
North Brook Rd CW6 146 A4
North Cestrian Gram Sch
WA14 238 C5
North Cheshire Hospl
WA4 26 B1
North Cheshire Jewish Prim
Sch SK8 239 C2
North Crofts CW5 204 C3
North Downs WA16 57 B1
North Downs Rd SK8 239 F3
North Dr Heswall CH60 41 A4
High Legh WA16 29 B2
Northwich CW9 104 C4
North Fields WA16 57 B2
North Florida Rd WA11 1 B4
North Gn CH5 116 A3
North Harvey St 8 SK1 240 F5
North Mead SK10 87 A3
North Par CH64 41 A1
North Park Brook Rd WA5 7 C1
North Pl 5 SK1 240 F5
North Rd Altrincham WA15 32 A4
Bebington CH65 44 C2
Ellesmere Port CH65 70 A4
Halewood L26 21 A3
North St Broughton CH4 140 A4
Chester CH3 119 A1
Congleton CW12 156 B2
Crewe CW1 190 B4
Hawarden CH5 116 A2
Haydock WA11 1 C3
Mount Pleasant ST7 195 A3
Newton-le-W WA12 1 C2
North Stafford St CW1 190 B2
North Vale Rd WA15 238 F6
North View Crewe CW1 190 A3
Warrington WA5 14 C4
North Way
Holmes Chapel CW4 130 B2
Hyde SK14 241 E6
Shavington CW2 206 B3
Northbank Ind Pk M44 11 C4
Northbank Wlk CW2 206 B4
Northbury Rd CH66 69 C1
Northcombe Rd SK3 240 E1
Northcote Rd SK7 35 C4
Northdale Rd WA1 17 A4
Northend Rd SK15 242 E2
Northenden Rd
Gatley SK8 239 A6
Sale M33 242 C6
Northern La WA8 12 A2
Northern Pathway CH4 237 C1
Northern Rise CH66 69 C2
Northfield Dr
Biddulph ST8 179 C1
Wilmslow SK9 60 B4
Northfield Pl CW2 206 B3
Northgate CW6 146 A4
Northgate Ave
Chester CH2 237 B4
Macclesfield SK10 87 B1
Northgate Rd SK3 240 C4
Northgate Row CH1 237 B2
Northgate St CH1 237 A3
Northlands CW3 232 B1
Northolt Ct WA2 8 C1
Northstead Ave M34 241 B6
Northumberland Rd M31 11 C1
Northward Rd SK9 59 C3
Northway
Altrincham WA14 238 E6
Chester CH4 141 A4
Lymm WA13 18 B2
Northwich CW8 78 B1
Runcorn WA7 49 C4
Warrington WA2 8 A1
Widnes WA8 12 B1
Northwich Rd
Antrobus CW9,WA4 53 A2
Cranage CW4,WA16 106 C1
Dutton WA4 51 A1
Great Budworth CW9 78 C4
Knutsford WA16 56 B1
Runcorn WA7 50 C2
Runcorn, Brookvale WA7 50 B3
Stretton WA4 52 C4
Weaverham CW8 102 C4
Northwich Sta CW9 104 A4
Northwick Ret Pk CW9 79 B1
Northwood Ave
Middlewich CW10 151 C3
Newton-le-W WA12 2 C2
Northwood Gr M33 242 B6
Northwood La WA16 28 C1
Northwood Rd WA7 23 C1

Norton Ave
Broughton CH4 .140 B3
Warrington WA5 .14 C3
Norton Cotts WA7 .50 C4
Norton Gate WA7 .50 B4
Norton Gr SK4 .240 B5
Norton Hill WA7 .24 B1
Norton La
Runcorn, Norton WA7 .24 B1
Runcorn, Town Park WA7 .50 A4
Norton Priory High Sch
WA7 .24 A1
Norton Priory Mus*
WA7 .24 A2
Norton Priory Walled Gdns*
WA7 .24 A2
Norton Rd CH3 .119 B1
Norton Station Rd WA7 .50 B4
Norton View WA7 .50 A4
Norton Village WA7 .24 B1
Norton Way CW11 .174 B4
Norton's La CH3 .98 A1
Norton-in-Hales CE Prim Sch
TF9 .236 B1
Nortons La CW6 .122 C4
Nortonwood La WA7 .24 B1
Norview Dr M20 .239 B8
Norville CH66 .69 B4
Norway Gr 6 SK5 .240 F8
Norwich Ave WA3 .3 B4
Norwich Dr CH66 .94 C4
Norwood Ave
Bramhall SK7 .35 B3
Golborne WA3 .3 C4
High Lane SK6 .37 B4
Norwood Dr CH4 .141 A3
Norwood Rd SK8 .239 B6
Nottingham Cl WA1 .17 C3
Nun House Cl CW7 .127 A1
Nun House Dr CW7 .127 A1
Nuns Rd CH1 .237 A1
Nunsmere Cl CW7 .127 A1
Nursery Ave WA15 .31 C4
Nursery Cl Kidsgrove ST7 .194 B1
Sale M33 .242 D6
Shavington CW2 .206 B2
Widnes WA8 .13 B2
Nursery Dr Biddulph ST8 .179 B1
Poynton SK12 .36 B2
Nursery Gr M31 .11 C2
Nursery La
Congleton CW12 .156 C1
Nether Alderley SK10 .84 B3
Siddington SK11 .110 A2
Stockport SK3 .240 A3
Wilmslow SK9 .59 C3
Nursery Rd Barnton CW8 .78 A2
Bollington SK10 .87 C4
Haslington CW1,ST7 .192 C2
Scholar Green ST7 .194 C3
Stockport SK4 .240 C6
Nursery The Norley WA6 .100 A4
Northwich CW8 .103 B3
Nutfield Ave CW1 .190 A4
Nuthurst Gdns 17 CW5 .204 C3
Nuttall Ct WA3 .9 B2
Nuttall St M44 .11 C3

O

O'Connell Cl WA11 .1 B3
O'Leary St WA2 .16 B4
Oak Ave Alsager ST7 .193 C1
Disley SK12 .39 A3
Golborne WA3 .3 A4
Haydock WA11 .1 C4
Irlam M44 .11 B3
Macclesfield SK11 .112 A3
Newton-le-W WA12 .2 B2
Romiley SK6 .241 C2
Stockport SK4 .240 B6
Wilmslow SK9 .59 C3
Winsford CW7 .149 B4
Oak Bank SK12 .39 A3
Oak Bank Cl CW5 .205 C2
Oak Bank Dr SK10 .63 A1
Oak Bank La CH2 .119 B3
Oak Brow Cotts SK9 .33 C2
Oak Cl SK9 .59 C3
Oak Cotts Styal SK9 .33 C2
Wrenbury CW5 .216 C2
Oak Dr Bramhall SK7 .35 B4
Higher Kinnerton CH4 .161 A4
Middlewich CW10 .151 B4
Runcorn WA7 .49 B4
Oak Gr Cheadle SK8 .239 E5
Ellesmere Port CH65 .70 A2
Nantwich CW5 .204 C2
Poynton SK12 .36 B2
Oak Ho 7 CW11 .175 A3
Oak House La CW7 .149 A4
Oak La Bollington SK10 .88 A3
Cuddington CW8 .101 C1
Marton SK11 .133 B3
Wilmslow SK9 .59 C3
Oak Lea Ave SK9 .60 A3
Oak Lodge SK7 .35 C4
Oak Mdw CW8 .102 C4
Oak Mews SK9 .34 B1
Oak Rd Altrincham WA15 .238 E3
Cheadle SK8 .239 E5
Chelford SK11 .84 A2
Chester CH4 .140 C3
Hooton CH66 .43 C1
Oak Rd *continued*
Lymm WA13 .18 B2
Mottram St Andrew SK10 .86 A4
Partington M31 .11 B1
Sale M33 .242 D6
Warrington WA5 .14 C2
Oak St Crewe CW2 .190 B2
Croft WA3 .9 A4
Ellesmere Port CH65 .70 B4
Hyde SK14 .241 E8
Northwich CW9 .79 A1
Rode Heath ST7 .193 C4
Sandbach CW11 .174 B4
Stockport SK3 .240 B4
Oak Tree Cl CW1 .190 C3
Oak Tree Dr CW1 .190 C3
Oak Tree Gate CW3 .229 C2
Oak Tree La
Cranage CW10 .129 C4
Newcastle-u-L ST7 .210 B3
Oak View Knutsford WA16 .57 B1
Marton SK11 .133 B3
Speke L24 .21 A2
Oak Villas CW5 .216 C2
Oak Wood Rd WA16 .29 C1
Oakdale Ave
Frodsham WA6 .74 B3
Warrington WA4 .16 B1
Oakdale Cl
Broughton CH4 .139 A2
Chorlton CW2 .207 A2
Oakdale Ct
Altrincham WA14 .238 C5
Stalybridge SK15 .242 E2
Oakdale Dr SK8 .239 B2
Oakdene Ave
Ellesmere Port CH66 .69 B3
Gatley SK8 .34 B4
Warrington WA1 .17 B4
Oakdene Cl CH62 .43 B3
Oakdene Way CW6 .168 B4
Oakenclough Cl SK9 .34 B1
Oakenclough Prim Sch
SK9 .34 B1
Oakes Cnr CW5 .219 C2
Oakfield M33 .242 A7
Oakfield Ave
Cheadle SK8 .239 E6
Chester CH2 .118 C4
Knutsford WA16 .57 B2
Wrenbury CW5 .216 C2
Oakfield Cl
Alderley Edge SK9 .60 A2
Bramhall SK7 .35 C2
Wrenbury CW5 .216 C2
Oakfield Ct WA15 .238 F6
Oakfield Cty Inf Sch
WA8 .22 A4
Oakfield Cty Jun Sch
WA8 .22 A4
Oakfield Dr Chester CH2 .118 C4
Widnes WA8 .22 A4
Oakfield Mews M33 .242 A6
Oakfield Rd
Alderley Edge SK9 .60 A1
Altrincham WA15 .238 E4
Bebington CH62 .43 B4
Blacon CH1 .117 B2
Ellesmere Port CH66 .68 C4
Plumley WA16 .80 C2
Poynton SK12 .36 C2
Stockport SK3 .240 F1
Oakfield Rise CW4 .130 A2
Oakfield St WA15 .238 E5
Oakfield Trad Est WA15 .238 E5
Oakgrove Prim Sch SK8 .34 B4
Oakham Rd M34 .241 A5
Oakhill Cl SK10 .87 A2
Oakhurst Chase SK9 .60 A1
Oakhurst Dr
Stockport SK3 .240 B1
Wistaston CW2 .206 A4
Oakland Ave CW1 .191 B2
Oakland Ct SK12 .36 B2
Oakland St
Warrington WA1 .16 C4
Widnes WA8 .23 A2
Oaklands CH3 .119 C2
Oaklands Ave CH3 .166 A1
Oaklands Cl SK9 .34 C1
Oaklands Com Inf Sch
SK9 .34 C1
Oaklands Cres CH3 .166 A1
Oaklands Dr Lymm WA13 .18 B1
Sale M33 .242 A7
Oaklands Rd Golborne WA3 .3 C4
Ollerton WA16 .82 C3
Oaklands Sch CW7 .149 A4
Oaklea Ave CH2 .118 C2
Oakleaf Lodge SK11 .112 B3
Oakleigh Knutsford WA16 .82 B4
2 Stockport SK4 .240 B7
Oakleigh Ct CW12 .155 C2
Oakleigh Rd SK8 .34 C4
Oakleigh Rise CW8 .78 C1
Oakley Cl CW11 .175 A4
Oakley St CW1 .190 B3
Oakley Villas SK4 .240 B7
Oakmere Cl CW11 .174 C4
Oakmere Dr Chester CH3 .142 A4
Ellesmere Port CH66 .69 C1
Warrington WA5 .14 C2
Oakmere Hall CW8 .101 C1
Oakmere Rd Cheadle SK8 .239 F4
Handforth SK9 .34 B3
Winsford CW7 .125 C1
Oakmere St WA7 .23 A1
Oakmoore WA7 .24 C2
Oaks Dr The CH2 .118 B4
Oaks Pl WA8 .23 A4
Oaks The
Alderley Edge SK9 .60 A1
Bebington CH62 .43 B4
Gatley SK8 .239 A2
Goostrey CW4 .130 B4
Mobberley WA16 .58 C1
Oakside Cl SK8 .239 E6
Oaksway CH60 .41 B3
Oakthorn Gr WA11 .1 B3
Oaktree Cl Barnton CW8 .78 A2
Tarporley CW6 .146 B1
Oaktree Cotts SK8 .239 F3
Oaktree Ct Cheadle SK8 .239 D5
Chester CH2 .119 A2
Oakway M20 .239 C8
Oakways WA4 .26 B3
Oakwood Ave Gatley SK8 .239 B5
Warrington WA1 .16 C4
Wilmslow SK9 .59 C3
Oakwood Avenue Com Prim Sch WA1 .16 B4
Oakwood Cl CH66 .69 B1
Oakwood Com Prim Sch
M31 .11 B2
Oakwood Cres
Crewe CW2 .189 C2
Sandbach CW11 .175 C3
Oakwood Ct WA14 .31 A4
Oakwood Dr SK10 .87 B3
Oakwood Gate WA3 .9 B2
Oakwood La
Altrincham WA14 .238 B1
Barnton CW8 .78 A1
Sandbach CW11 .174 A4
Oakwood Pk CH62 .43 B3
Oakwood Rd Disley SK12 .38 B3
Rode Heath ST7 .193 C4
Romiley SK6 .241 C2
Oat Market 8 CW5 .204 C3
Oathills SY14 .213 A3
Oathills Cl CW6 .146 B1
Oathills Dr CW6 .146 B1
Oatlands SK9 .85 A4
Oban Dr Heswall CH60 .41 A4
Sale M33 .242 E5
Oban Gr WA2 .9 A2
Obelisk Way CW12 .156 B2
Ocean St WA14 .238 B6
Ocean Street Trad Est
WA14 .238 B7
Odeon Bldg CH1 .237 A3
Off Ridge Hill La SK15 .242 C2
Offley Ave CW11 .175 A4
Offley Inf Sch CW11 .175 A4
Offley Jun Sch CW11 .175 A4
Offley Rd CW11 .175 A4
Ogden Ct SK14 .241 E6
Ogden Rd SK7 .35 B3
Oglet La L24 .46 C4
Oil Sites Rd CH65 .71 B3
Okell St WA7 .23 A1
Old Applecroft CW11 .174 B3
Old Bank Cl SK6 .241 A3
Old Bedions Sports Ctr
M20 .239 A8
Old Boston WA11 .2 A4
Old Boston Trad Est WA11 .2 A4
Old Brickworks Ind Est
SK10 .63 C2
Old Butt La ST7 .194 B1
Old Chapel St SK3 .240 D3
Old Cherry La WA13 .28 A4
Old Chester Ct CW5 .187 B3
Old Chester Rd
Barbridge CW5 .187 B3
Ellesmere Port CH66 .69 B2
Helsby WA6 .73 B2
Higher Walton WA4 .25 C4
Old Church Cl CH65 .70 B4
Old Coach Rd
Broxton SY14,CH3 .199 A3
Kelsall CW6 .122 B3
Old Constabulary The
CW5 .204 B3
Old Court Ho The 8
WA16 .57 A1
Old Farm Cl
Macclesfield SK10 .87 A1
Willaston CH64 .68 A4
Old Gardens St 3 SK1 .240 F4
Old Gate Cl CW10 .151 A4
Old George The CH2 .237 B3
Old Gorse Cl CW2 .189 C2
Old Hall Ave SK23 .65 C2
Old Hall Cl WA4 .26 A4
Old Hall Cres SK9 .34 C2
Old Hall Ct Ashton CH3 .121 C4
Malpas SY14 .213 A2
Sale M33 .242 E6
Old Hall Dr CH65 .70 A2
Old Hall Gdns CH2 .237 C4
Old Hall La Elton CH2 .72 A2
Knutsford WA16 .56 A2
Tabley WA16 .55 C2
Woodford SK7 .35 B1
Old Hall Pk CH3 .119 C3
Old Hall Pl CH1 .237 A2
Old Hall Rd Gatley SK8 .239 A6
Northwich CW9 .104 A3
Sale M33 .242 E6
Warrington WA5 .15 B4
Old Hall St SK10 .87 B1
Old Hey Wlk WA12 .2 B1
Old Higher Rd WA8 .21 B3
Old Hutte La L26 .21 A3
Old La Acton Bridge CW8 .76 C2
Old La *continued*
Antrobus CW9 .53 B2
Davenham CW9 .104 B1
Pulford CH4 .162 C1
Heswall CH60 .41 B4
Old Liverpool Rd WA5 .15 C2
Old Man of Mow* ST7 .195 B4
Old Market Pl
4 Altrincham WA14 .238 D5
7 Knutsford WA16 .57 A1
Old Mill Cl Heswall CH60 .41 A4
Lymm WA13 .19 B3
Old Mill Ct CH2 .118 B3
Old Mill La
Hazel Grove SK7 .37 A4
Macclesfield SK11 .112 C3
Whitley WA4 .52 C2
Old Mill Pl CH3 .166 A1
Old Mill Rd CW11 .175 B3
Old Moss La
Fowley Common WA3 .5 C3
Tarvin CH3 .144 B4
Old Oak Dr M34 .241 A7
Old Orchard SK9 .60 A4
Old Orchard The
Antrobus CW9 .53 B2
Cuddington CW8 .101 C2
Old Paddock The CW4 .130 C4
Old Park Rd CW1 .207 B4
Old Pearl La CH3 .119 A1
Old Pewterspear La WA4 .26 C2
Old Pump Ho The CH66 .68 C4
Old Quay Cl CH64 .66 B4
Old Quay La CH64 .66 B4
Old Quay St WA7 .23 A2
Old Rd Anderton CW9 .78 B2
Audley ST7 .209 C2
Cheadle SK8 .239 F6
Handforth SK9 .34 B2
Hyde SK14 .241 D8
Stockport SK4 .240 E7
Warrington WA4 .16 A2
Whaley Bridge SK23 .65 C2
Whaley Bridge, Furness Vale
SK23 .39 B2
Whaley Bridge, New Horwich
SK23 .65 C3
Wilmslow SK9 .60 A4
Old Rectory Gdns SK8 .239 D5
Old School Cl
Farndon CH3 .180 C1
Neston CH64 .66 C3
Old School House La WA2 .8 A4
Old Smithy La WA13 .18 B1
Old St SK15 .242 D2
Old Stack Yd CH3 .120 C3
Old Upton La WA8 .12 C2
Old Vicarage Gdns CW3 .229 C2
Old Vicarage Rd CH64 .68 A4
Old Wargrave Rd WA12 .2 B2
Old Warrington Rd CW9 .79 A1
Old Whint Rd WA11 .1 A3
Old Woman's La CH3 .142 B4
Old Wool La SK8 .239 F4
Old Wrexham Rd CH4 .141 B4
Oldcastle La SY14 .222 C4
Oldfield Brow Prim Sch
WA14 .238 A5
Oldfield Cres CH4 .140 C3
Oldfield Dr
Altrincham WA15 .238 F6
Chester CH3 .119 B1
Mobberley WA16 .58 A2
Oldfield Gr M33 .242 C7
Oldfield La WA14 .20 C2
Oldfield Mews WA14 .238 C5
Oldfield Prim Sch CH3 .119 B2
Oldfield Rd
Altrincham WA14 .238 B5
Ellesmere Port CH65 .70 A3
Lymm WA13 .18 B2
Sale M33 .242 C7
Sandbach CW11 .174 C2
Oldgate WA8 .22 B4
Oldhall St SY14 .213 A2
Oldham Dr SK6 .241 A4
Oldham St Bollington SK10 .88 A4
Hyde SK14 .241 D6
Warrington WA4 .16 B2
Oldham's Rise SK10 .87 B2
Oldhams Hill CW8 .78 C1
Oldhill Cl ST7 .210 C3
Olive Dr CH64 .66 C4
Olive Gr ST5 .210 B1
Olive Rd CH64 .66 C4
Oliver Cl SK10 .87 C4
Oliver La CH66 .69 B4
Oliver St
Stockport SK1,SK3 .240 F4
Warrington WA2 .16 A3
Ollerbarrow Rd WA15 .238 E2
Ollersett Ave SK22 .39 B4
Ollershaw La CW9 .79 B2
Ollerton Cl WA4 .17 A2
Ollerton Rd SK9 .34 C3
Ollier St 21 WA8 .23 A4
Omega Blvd WA5 .6 B1
On The Air', Broadcasting & Sound Shop* CH1 .237 B2
One Oak La SK9 .60 C4
Onneley La CW3 .232 C2
Onslow Rd Blacon CH1 .117 B2
Stockport SK3 .240 C4
Onston La CW8 .101 C4
Onward St SK14 .241 D6
Openshaw La M44 .11 C3
Orange Gr WA2 .8 C1
Orange La CW9 .79 B1
Orchard Ave
Acton Bridge CW8 .76
Lymm WA13 .18
Partington M31 .11
Whaley Bridge SK23 .65
Orchard Brow WA3 .11
Orchard Cl Barnton CW8 .78
Bramhall SK8 .35
Bunbury CW6 .185
Chester CH2 .118
Ellesmere Port CH66 .69
Frodsham WA6 .74
Goostrey CW4 .107
Higher Wincham CW9 .80
Macclesfield SK11 .112
Middlewich CW10 .151
Poynton SK12 .36
Weaverham CW8 .77
Wilmslow SK9 .59
Winsford CW7 .149
Orchard Cotts CW6 .146
Orchard Cres
Kidsgrove ST7 .194
Nantwich CW5 .204
Nether Alderley SK10 .84
Orchard Croft CH3 .119
Orchard Ct Alsager ST7 .193
5 Chester CH3 .119
Haslington CW1 .191
Orchard Dene CW8 .101
Orchard Dr Handforth SK9 .34
Little Leigh CW8 .77
Neston CH64 .66
Orchard Gdns
Congleton CW12 .156
Weaverham CW8 .77
Orchard Gn SK9 .60
Orchard Gr CH3 .180
Orchard Haven CH66 .69
Orchard La CH66 .69
Orchard Park La CH2 .72
Orchard Pl Helsby WA6 .7
Poynton SK12 .3
5 Sale M33 .24
Orchard Rd
Altrincham WA15 .23
Ellesmere Port CH65 .7
Lymm WA13 .1
Whaley Bridge SK23 .6
Orchard Rise CW9 .12
Orchard St Chester CH1 .23
Crewe CW1 .19
Hyde SK14 .24
Northwich CW9 .10
Stockport SK1 .24
Warrington WA1 .1
Warrington, Fearnhead WA2 .
Warrington, Hillcliffe WA4 .2
Willaston (nr Nantwich)
CW5 .20
Orchard The
Alderley Edge SK9 .8
Chester CH3 .14
Disley SK12 .3
Helsby WA6 .7
Orchard Vale SK3 .24
Orchard Way
Congleton CW12 .15
Kelsall CW6 .12
Widnes WA8 .1
Orchards The
Broughton CH4 .14
Pickmere WA16 .7
Shavington CW2 .20
Orchid Cl Huntington CH3 .14
Irlam M44 .1
Orchid Way WA9 .
Orchil Cl CH66 .6
Ordnance Ave WA3 .
Ordsall Cl CW11 .17
Orford Ave
Warrington WA1,WA2 .1
SK12 .3
Orford Cl Hale L24 .2
High Lane SK6 .3
Orford Gn WA2 .
Orford La WA2 .1
Orford Rd WA1,WA2 .1
Orford St WA1 .1
Organsdale Cotts CW6 .12
Orhcards The LL13 .19
Oriel Bank Sch SK3 .24
Oriel Ho CH2 .11
Orion Blvd WA5 .
Orion Bsns Pk SK8 .24
Orkney Cl
7 Ellesmere Port CH65 .7
Widnes WA8 .1
Orme Cl Macclesfield SK10 .8
Prestbury SK10 .8
Orme Cres SK10 .8
Orme St SK9 .6
Ormerod Cl Romiley SK6 .24
Sandbach CW11 .17
Ormesby Gr CH63 .4
Ormond Cl WA8 .1
Ormonde Rd CH2 .11
Ormonde St CH2 .23
Orphanage St SK4 .24
Orrell Cl WA5 .1
Orrishmere Rd SK8 .23
Orton Cl CW7 .12
Ortonbrook Prim Sch
M31 .1
Orwell Cl SK9 .3
Osborne Ave WA2 .
Osborne Gr Gatley SK8 .23
Shavington CW2 .20

orne Rd
incham WA15 238 E5
borne WA3 3 C4
e SK14 241 E5
ckport SK2 240 F3
rrington WA4 16 A1
orne Terr M33 242 B6
ourne Cl
ington CH62 43 C4
dbach CW11 174 B3
mslow SK9 60 B3
ourne Pl 7 WA14 238 D4
r Cl CH2 72 B2
ere Cl SY13 226 A1
rey Ave CW7 149 B3
rey Cl
dlewich CW10 151 B3
corn WA7 49 C3
rrington WA2 8 C2
rey Ct CH2 237 A4
rey Dr SK9 60 B4
rey View ST7 195 B2
ett Cl WA7 50 B4
mere Cl CW11 174 C4
er's La WA16 58 C4
ey Ave CH62 43 B4
rs Bank CW7 126 A1
htrington Cres WA13 19 A2
htrington La WA13 19 A1
htrington Prim Sch
13 19 A2
htrington View
13 19 A2
on Ave Chester CH2 118 C4
e M33 242 E7
on Dr CW12 155 C2
on Mill La CW6 147 A4
on Pl CH1 237 B3
Lady Mother of the
viour RC Prim Sch
7 50 A3
Lady of Lourdes RC Prim
1 M31 11 C2
Lady of Perpetual
ccour RC Inf Sch
8 12 A1
Lady of Perpetual
ccour RC Jun Sch
8 22 A4
Lady's RC Inf & Jun Sch
55 70 A2
Lady's RC Prim Sch
ckport SK3 240 E4
rrington WA4 16 C2
La CH3 184 B3
wood Dr SK8 34 A4
wood La M90 33 B4
wood La W M90 33 A4
wood Prim Sch SK8 34 B4
wood Rd SK8 34 A4
The
smere Port CH65 70 B2
ley SK8 34 A4
nhouse La SK10 87 C4
Hall Com Sch
7 149 A4
r Hill Dr CW7 149 B4
Pl WA16 82 B4
r Rd CW5 172 A4
St John's CE Prim Sch
7 126 A1
rdale WA14 238 B5
rdale La CW8 101 B1
rdale Rd
v Mills SK12 38 C3
aston CH64 43 A1
rdene Rd CW7 149 B4
rfields WA16 57 B2
rhill Dr SK9 60 C4
rhill La SK9 60 C4
rhill Rd SK9 60 B4
rleigh Ct CH4 141 B4
rleigh Rd CH4 141 B4
rleigh St Mary's CE Prim
1 CH4 141 B4
rleigh Terr CH4 141 B4
rpool Gdns CH66 69 C2
rpool Rd CH66 69 C3
rpool Sta CH66 69 C3
rton Cl
ngleton CW12 156 B2
dlewich CW10 151 A4
rton Dr WA6 74 B3
rton Rd ST8 179 C3
rton Way 2 SK9 34 B3
rway CW7 126 C1
rwood Ave CH1 94 C1
rwood La Blacon CH1 117 B2
lington CH1 94 B1
gton Cl WA7 49 C2
n Cl CH1 117 C3
n St Crewe CW2 190 B1
thwich CW9 104 A4
ckport SK3 240 D5
rrington WA2 16 A4
Ind Est The CH5 116 A3
ey Wood Rd CW8 77 C1
sfield WA12 2 C2
Hey Cres ST8 179 B1
Hey Dr ST8 179 B1
orough Cl WA8 12 C2
nham Rd WA2 8 A2
rd Cl CH66 94 C4
rd Ct 1 SK10 112 C4
rd Dr Halewood L26 21 A4
swall CH63 41 C3
miley SK6 241 C4
rd Gr M44 11 B3

Oxford Rd
Altrincham WA14 238 D3
Chester CH4 140 C3
Macclesfield SK11 112 A4
Runcorn WA7 49 A4
Oxford St Crewe CW1 190 A3
Newton-le-W WA12 2 A2
Stalybridge SK15 242 F1
Warrington WA4 16 B2
Widnes WA8 23 A4
Oxford Way SK4 240 D7
Oxhey Fst Sch ST8 179 C1
Oxheys WA7 50 B4
Oxmead Cl WA2 9 A1
Oxmoor Cl WA7 50 A3
Oxney Cl SK11 111 C4
Oxton Cl WA8 12 B2
Oxton Gn CH66 69 B2

P

Pacific Rd WA14 238 A6
Packmoor Prim Sch
ST7 195 C1
Packsaddle Pk SK10 86 C3
Padarn Cl CH4 140 B3
Padden Brook SK6 241 B2
Padden Brook Mews
SK6 241 B2
Paddington Bank WA1 16 C3
Paddock Brow SK10 87 A3
Paddock Chase SK12 36 C3
Paddock Cl SK23 64 C2
Paddock Dr CH64 41 B1
Paddock Hill La WA16 59 A2
Paddock La Audlem CW3 230 A1
Kettleshulme SK23 64 C2
Lymm WA13 19 B4
Partington WA13,WA14 20 A3
Whaley Bridge SK23 65 C3
Paddock Rd CH4 141 C1
Paddock Rise WA7 49 C2
Paddock The
Cheadle SK8 239 E5
Chester CH4 141 A4
Ellesmere Port CH66 69 B2
Elton CH2 72 A2
Handforth SK9 34 B2
Hartford CW8 103 B2
Hassall Green CW11 175 C1
Helsby WA6 73 B1
Heswall CH60 41 B4
Lymm WA13 19 B2
Tarporley CW6 146 B1
Whaley Bridge SK23 65 C3
Willaston (nr Nantwich)
CW5 205 B2
Paddock View CW10 128 B1
Paddock Way CH4 161 A4
Paddock Wlk CW8 101 B3
Paddocks Gn CW12 178 C4
Paddocks The
Prestbury SK10 87 A3
Whitegate CW8 125 A3
Padgate Bsns Ctr WA1 17 A4
Padgate CE Prim Sch
WA2 9 A1
Padgate Com High Sch
WA2 8 C1
Padgate La WA1 16 C4
Padgate Sta WA1 9 A1
Padgbury Cl CW12 156 A1
Padgbury La CW12 156 A1
Padmore Cl CW1 190 A4
Padston Dr ST7 193 A2
Padstow Cl Crewe CW1 190 B4
Macclesfield SK10 111 C4
Warrington WA5 14 C2
Padstow Dr SK7 35 C4
Padstow Sq WA7 50 A3
Padworth Pl CW1 173 A1
Page Gr CW2 206 A2
Page La WA8 13 B1
Paignton Cl WA5 14 C2
Painswick Rd CH66 69 C1
Paisley Ave CH62 43 C2
Palace Fields Ave WA7 50 A4
Palace Fields Local Ctr
WA7 50 A3
Palace Hey CH64 67 A3
Palace Rd M33 242 A7
Palacefields Prim Sch
WA7 50 A3
Palatine Cl CH1 117 B3
Palatine Ind Est WA4 16 B2
Palgrave Cl CH1 118 A3
Palin Dr WA5 14 C3
Pall Mall CW5 204 C3
Pallard Ave WA6 74 B4
Palliser Cl WA3 10 A2
Palm Gr CH66 70 A1
Palma Ave M90 33 A4
Palmer Ave SK8 239 F6
Palmer Cl CW9 103 C3
Palmer Cres WA5 15 B4
Palmer Rd CW11 175 B3
Palmer St M33 242 A6
Palmerston Cl CW1 191 B3
Palmerston Rd SK11 112 A4
Palmerston St SK10 88 A4
Palmerston Way ST8 179 B1
Palmerstone Cl CH1 118 A2
Palmyra Sq N WA1 16 A3
Palmyra Sq S WA1 16 A3
Panda Way CW11 175 A3
Pangbourne Cl
Stockport SK3 240 C2

Pangbourne Cl *continued*
Warrington WA4 26 C3
Panton Pl CH2 118 C2
Panton Rd CH2 118 C2
Parade Rd M90 33 B4
Parade The
1 Alderley Edge SK9 60 A1
Blacon CH1 117 C3
Neston CH64 41 A1
Romiley SK6 241 A1
Paradise CH4 237 B1
Paradise La CW5 171 C4
Paradise Mill (Mus)*
SK11 112 B4
Paradise St SK11 112 B4
Paragon Cl WA8 13 A3
Parbold Ct WA8 22 B4
Parchments The WA12 2 B2
Parish Cl ST7 193 A2
Park Ave
Altrincham, Hale WA15 238 F1
Altrincham, Timperley
WA14 238 E8
Bramhall SK7 35 B3
Broughton CH4 140 C3
Cheadle SK3 239 F7
Cheadle SK8 239 F1
Haydock WA11 1 A3
Hyde SK14 241 D8
Poynton SK12 36 C2
Romiley SK6 241 C2
Sale M33 242 A8
Saughall CH1 94 A1
Talke ST7 210 C4
Tattenhall CH3 166 A1
Warrington WA4 16 B2
Weaverham CW8 77 B1
Whaley Bridge SK23 39 B2
Widnes WA8 13 A1
Wilmslow SK9 60 B4
Winsford CW7 127 A2
Park Ave N WA12 2 B1
Park Ave S WA12 2 B1
Park Bank CW12 156 C1
Park Brook Rd SK11 112 A4
Park Bvd WA1 16 A2
Park Cl Sale WA14 238 F8
Stalybridge SK15 242 C3
Tarvin CH3 121 A1
Park Court Mews SK8 239 E4
Park Cres
Ashton-u-Lyne OL6 242 B2
Cuddington CW8 101 C2
Handforth SK9 34 A1
Warrington WA4 26 B3
Whaley Bridge SK23 39 B2
Park Ct Chester CH2 237 C2
Frodsham WA6 74 A4
Runcorn WA7 49 A4
Sale M33 242 A7
2 Warrington WA1 16 A3
Park Dr Altrincham WA15 238 F1
Chester CH2 119 A2
Ellesmere Port CH65 70 A2
Hyde SK14 241 D8
Stockport SK4 240 B6
Wistaston CW2 205 C4
Park Dr S CH2 119 A2
Park Est CW2 206 B3
Park Gn SK11 112 B4
Park Gr SK4 240 B8
Park House Dr
Prestbury SK10 87 A4
Sandbach CW11 175 B4
Park House La SK10 87 A4
Park House Mews
CW11 175 B4
Park La Audley ST7 209 A2
Congleton CW12 156 C1
Frodsham WA6 74 A4
Hargrave CH3 144 C2
Hartford CW8 103 A2
Hatherton CW5 219 C2
Higher Walton WA4 25 C3
Little Bollington WA14 20 A1
Macclesfield SK11 112 B3
Moulton CW9 126 C4
Pickmere CW9,WA16 79 C4
Poynton SK12 36 C2
Sandbach CW11 174 C3
Park Lane Sch SK11 112 A3
Park Lodge Cl SK8 239 E4
Park Mills Cl CW5 205 B3
Park Mount SK8 239 A5
Park Mount Cl SK11 112 A3
Park Mount Dr SK11 112 A3
Park Prim Sch CH3 166 A1
Park Prim Sch The WA7 24 A1
Park Rd
Altrincham, Bowdon WA14 238 A2
Altrincham, Hale WA15 238 F1
Altrincham, Timperley
WA14,WA15 238 F8
Bebington, Eastham CH62 43 C3
Cheadle SK8 239 E6
Congleton CW12 156 C2
Congleton, North Rode
CW12 134 C1
Ellesmere Port CH65 70 B2
Golborne WA3 3 A4
Haslington CW1 191 B3
Heswall CH60 41 A4
High Lane SK12 37 C3
Hyde SK14 241 D8
Little Budworth CW6 124 C1
Lymm WA13 29 B4
Macclesfield SK11 112 B3
Middlewich CW10 128 B1

Park Rd *continued*
Nantwich CW5 204 C2
New Mills SK22 39 B4
Northwich CW8 78 B1
Partington WA13 19 B4
Romiley SK6 241 C3
Runcorn WA7 49 A4
Sale M33 242 A8
Sandbach CW11 174 B4
Stalybridge SK15,SK16 242 A1
Tarporley CW6 146 B1
Thornton-le-M CH2 71 C1
Warrington WA5 14 C3
Warrington, Orford WA2 8 B1
Whaley Bridge SK23 65 B3
Widnes WA8 13 A1
Willaston CH64 68 A4
Willaston (nr Nantwich)
CW5 205 B3
Wilmslow SK9 59 C4
Park Rd N WA12 2 C2
Park Rd S WA12 2 B1
Park Rd W CH4 141 A4
Park Rise SK6 241 C3
Park Road Com Prim Sch
WA5 14 C3
Park Road Prim Sch
Altrincham WA14 238 E8
Sale M33 242 A8
Park St Bollington SK10 88 A4
Chester CH1 237 B2
Congleton CW12 156 C1
Haydock WA11 1 A3
Macclesfield SK11 112 B4
Neston CH64 66 C4
Northwich CW8 103 C4
Stalybridge SK15 242 E1
6 Stockport SK1 240 F6
Park The Christleton CH3 142 C4
Warrington WA5 14 B2
Park Vale Rd SK11 112 B3
Park View Audlem CW3 230 B4
Bebington CH62 43 B4
Cheadle SK3 239 F7
Congleton CW12 156 C2
Gatley SK8 239 A6
High Lane SK7 37 A4
Little Bollington WA14 20 A1
Nantwich CW5 204 C3
Newton-le-W WA12 2 C2
Park View Ct
Poynton SK12 36 C2
Romiley SK6 241 C2
Park View Rd ST7 195 A2
Park W Blacon CH1 117 C1
Heswall CH60 40 C4
Park Way CH1 94 A1
Park Wlk CH2 118 C2
Parkdale Ind Est WA1 16 B2
Parkdale Rd WA1 17 A4
Parker Ave CW8 103 A3
Parker Dr CH3 180 C1
Parker Dr S CH3 180 C1
Parker St
Macclesfield SK11 112 C4
Runcorn WA7 23 A2
Warrington WA1 16 A3
Parker's Rd CW1 190 A4
Parker's Row CH3 180 C3
Parkers Ct WA7 49 C3
Parkett Heyes Rd SK11 111 C4
Parkfield Crewe CW1 173 A1
Ellesmere Port CH65 70 A1
Parkfield Ave WA4 17 A2
Parkfield Ct WA14 238 C4
Parkfield Dr
Ellesmere Port CH65 70 A2
Helsby WA6 73 A2
Nantwich CW5 204 C2
Parkfield Rd
Altrincham WA14 238 C4
Broughton CH4 139 B2
Cheadle SK8 239 F1
Knutsford WA16 82 A4
Northwich CW9 104 B4
Parkfields La WA2 8 C1
Parkgate
Altrincham WA14 238 B4
Knutsford WA16 57 B2
Parkgate Ave WA16 108 A4
Parkgate Ct CH1 118 A2
Parkgate La Heswall CH64 41 C3
Knutsford WA16 57 B2
Parkgate Prim Sch CH64 41 B1
Parkgate Rd
Chester CH1 118 A2
Macclesfield SK11 112 B2
Mollington CH1 117 C4
Neston CH64 66 B4
Puddington CH66 68 B1
Saughall CH1 94 B2
Shotwick CH1 93 C4
Warrington WA4 16 B1
Parkgate Trad Est WA16 57 B2
Parkgate Way
7 Handforth SK9 34 B2
Runcorn WA7 50 B4
Parkhill Ct WA16 57 A1
Parkhouse Ind Est ST5 210 C1
Parkhouse Rd E ST5 210 C1
Parkhouse Rd W ST5 210 C1
Parkland Cl WA4 27 A2
Parkland Dr CH2 72 A2
Parklands
Ellesmere Port CH66 69 B3
Kidsgrove ST7 195 A1
Sale M33 242 C7
Widnes WA8 12 B2

Parklands Com Prim Sch
CH66 69 B3
Parklands Dr Elton CH2 72 B2
Heswall CH60 41 B3
Parklands Gdns CH66 69 B3
Parklands The
Congleton CW12 157 A1
Stockport SK4 240 E8
Parklands View CH66 69 B3
Parklands Way SK12 36 C2
Parklea CH66 69 B3
Parkleigh CW12 156 C1
Parkroyal Com Sch
SK11 112 B4
Parkside SK6 37 B4
Parkside Bsns Pk WA3 3 A4
Parkside Cl SK6 37 B4
Parkside Ct WA8 13 A1
Parkside Rd
Culcheth WA12,WA2 3 A1
Sale M33 242 D5
Parkstone Dr CW1 190 A4
Parksway WA1 17 B4
Parkview Ct CH60 40 C4
Parkview Pk WA13 29 B4
Parkway Cheadle SK3 239 F7
Connah's Quay CH5 92 C1
Holmes Chapel CW4 130 B2
Wilmslow SK9 60 A3
Parkway Bsns Ctr CH5 92 C1
Parkwood Cl
Bebington CH62 43 C4
Lymm WA13 18 B1
Parliament St 22 CW8 103 C4
Parliament Way CH66 94 C4
Parlington Cl WA8 22 B4
Parnell Sq CW12 157 A1
Parochial CE Prim Sch
OL6 242 A4
Parr Gr WA11 1 A3
Parr St Macclesfield SK11 112 B4
Warrington WA1 16 B2
1 Widnes WA8 13 B1
Parrs Wood Rd M20 239 B8
Parrs Wood View WA4 17 A1
Parry Dr WA4 17 C2
Parry Mead SK6 241 A4
Parry Wlk OL6 242 A4
Parson St CW12 156 B1
Parsonage Ct SK4 240 B8
Parsonage Gn Hale L24 21 C1
Wilmslow SK9 60 A4
Parsonage Rd
Stockport SK4 240 C8
Widnes WA8 23 A2
Parsonage St Hyde SK14 241 D5
Macclesfield SK11 112 B4
Stockport SK4 240 E6
Parsonage Way
Stockport SK8 240 B1
Warrington WA5 15 A3
Parsons La CH2 118 A4
Partington Pl 4 M33 242 B7
Partington Prim Sch
M31 11 C2
Partridge Cl
Congleton CW12 156 C1
Warrington WA3 9 C2
Winsford CW7 149 B3
Partridge Way CW9 79 C3
Parvey La SK11 112 C1
Pasture Cl Kelsall CW6 122 B2
Macclesfield SK10 87 B2
Pasture Dr WA3 9 A4
Pasture La WA2 9 A1
Pasturefield Cl 1 M33 242 F5
Pastures The WA9 6 A4
Patch La SK7 35 B3
Patmos La WA16 105 C4
Patrivale Cl WA1 16 C3
Patten La WA1 16 A3
Patterdale Ave WA2 8 B1
Patterdale Cl
Crewe CW2 189 B2
Stalybridge SK15 242 D3
Patterdale Rd
Partington M31 11 C2
Romiley SK6 241 B4
Patterson Cl WA3 9 C2
Patterson St WA12 2 A2
Paul Cl WA5 14 B3
Paul St WA2 16 A3
Paulden Rd CW9 80 A1
Pavement La WA16 57 C2
Pavilion Way
Congleton CW12 156 B2
Macclesfield SK10 86 C1
Pavilions The
Cheadle SK8 239 D4
Davenham CW9 103 C1
Eccleston CH4 141 A2
Paxford Pl SK9 60 A3
Paxhill Ct SK4 240 A6
Payne Cl WA5 15 B3
Paythorne Cl WA3 4 C2
Peace Dr WA5 15 B3
Peach Field CH3 142 A4
Peach Gr WA11 1 C4
Peach La CW5 189 A1
Peach Tree Cl L24 21 C1
Peacock Ave Gatley SK8 34 A3
Warrington WA1 16 C3
Winsford CW7 149 B3
Peacock Hay Rd ST7 210 C2
Peacock La WA16 29 C3

Peacock Way 5 SK9 34 B3
Peak Bank SK6 241 B3
Peak Rd SK22 39 B4
Peakdale Ave SK8 239 B1
Pear Tree Ave
Crewe CW1 190 A4
Runcorn WA7 49 B4
Pear Tree Cl
Frodsham WA6 49 B1
Hale L24 21 C1
Winsford CW7 149 B4
Pear Tree Dr
Higher Wincham CW9 80 A3
Stalybridge SK15 242 E2
Pear Tree Farm Cotts
CW9 104 C2
Pear Tree Field CW5 205 A2
Pear Tree La
Acton Bridge CW8 76 C2
Whitchurch SY13 225 B1
Pear Tree Rd ST7 209 C1
Pear Tree Way
Chester CH2 118 C3
7 Ellesmere Port CH66 69 C1
Pearl La CH3 119 B1
Pearl St SK10 87 A4
Pearle St SK10 87 B1
Pearlings The CH3 119 A1
Pearson Ave WA4 16 B1
Pearson St
15 Macclesfield SK11 112 C4
Stockport SK5 240 F7
Peartree Cl CW11 175 C3
Peartree La SY14 222 B1
Peartree Pl WA4 16 B2
Pearwood Cl CW6 146 B1
Peaslake Cl SK6 241 D2
Peasley Cl WA2 9 A1
Pebble Brook Prim Sch
CW2 190 B1
Pebble Cl SK15 242 D4
Peck Mill La WA6 98 A4
Peckfield Cl WA7 50 A3
Peckforton Castle*
CW6 167 C1
Peckforton Cl
Gatley SK8 239 A5
Sandbach CW11 174 C4
Peckforton Dr
Ellesmere Port CH66 69 C2
Runcorn WA7 49 C2
Peckforton Hall La
CW6 185 A3
Peckforton Rd CW6 168 A1
Peckforton Way
Chester CH2 118 C3
20 Northwich CW8 103 C4
Peckforton Wlk 11 SK9 34 C1
Peckmill Cl SK9 34 C1
Pedley Hill Adlington SK10 62 C4
Rainow SK10 88 C2
Pedley House La WA16 58 C1
Pedley La Chelford WA16 83 B4
Congleton CW12 157 C2
Pedley St CW2 190 B1
Peebles Cl
Ellesmere Port CH66 68 C3
Holmes Chapel CW4 130 A1
Peel Ave WA14 238 D2
Peel Cl WA1 17 B3
Peel Cres CH3 121 C4
Peel Ct 4 ST7 195 A1
Peel Dr Astbury CW12 178 A4
Sale M33 242 E6
Peel Hall La CH3 121 C4
Peel Hollow ST7 209 A1
Peel House La WA8 13 A1
Peel La CW12 178 B4
Peel Rd WA15 238 E3
Peel Sq CW1 190 A3
Peel St Crewe CW1 190 A3
Hyde SK14 241 F5
Macclesfield SK11 112 B3
Newton-le-W WA12 2 A2
Runcorn WA7 22 C2
Stalybridge SK15 242 C1
Stockport SK2 240 F2
Peel Terr CH2 237 C3
Peelgate Dr SK8 239 A2
Peerglow Park Est
WA14 238 E8
Peerswood Ct CH64 66 C3
Peewit Cl CW7 149 B3
Pegasus Ct M33 242 D7
Peggie's La SK10 62 B1
Pelham Cl CW1 191 B3
Pelham Rd WA4 17 B2
Pelican Cl CW1 191 A3
Pemberton Cl CH64 68 A4
Pemberton Rd CH1 237 A3
Pembridge Ct CH65 70 C2
Pembridge Gdns CH65 70 C2
Pembroke Cl CH4 141 C3
Pembroke Ct WA7 24 B3
Pembroke Dr CH65 70 A2
Pembroke Gdns WA4 26 B2
Pembroke Gr M44 11 B3
Pembroke Rd SK11 111 C4
Pembroke Way CW7 149 A4
Penare WA7 50 B3
Penbrook Cl CW2 189 B2
Pendennis Rd SK4 240 C7
Pendine Cl WA5 7 B1
Pendle Cl Crewe CW1 191 A3
Ellesmere Port CH66 68 C3
Pendle Gdns WA3 4 C1
Pendlebury Rd SK8 239 B6
Pendlebury St WA4 17 A2
Penfold Cl CH1 94 A4
Penfold Hey CH2 118 B4
Penfold Way CH4 162 A4
Penfolds WA7 23 B1
Penhale Mews SK7 35 C4
Peninsula Ho WA2 16 B4
Penistone Dr CH66 69 A3
Penkeith's La WA7 23 A2
Penketh Ave WA5 15 C4
Penketh Bsns Pk WA5 15 A2
Penketh Ct WA7 23 A1
Penketh High Sch WA5 15 A3
Penketh Prim Sch WA5 14 B2
Penketh Rd WA5 15 A2
Penketh South Com Prim Sch
WA5 14 C2
Penkford La WA5 1 B1
Penkford Sch WA12 1 C1
Penkford St WA12 1 C2
Penlington Ct CW5 204 C3
Penmann Cres L26 21 A4
Penmark Cl WA5 7 B1
Penmon Cl CH1 117 B2
Penn Gdns CH65 70 A3
Penn House Cl SK7 35 C4
Penn La WA7 22 C1
Pennant Cl WA3 10 A2
Pennine Ct SK10 87 C1
Pennine Dr
Altrincham WA14 238 B5
Ashton-u-Lyne OL6 242 B4
Pennine Rd WA2 8 C1
Pennine View SK15 242 F4
Pennine Way
Biddulph ST8 179 C1
Winsford CW7 149 A4
Pennine Wlk CH66 69 A3
Pennington Cl WA6 49 B1
Pennington Dr WA12 2 C2
Pennington Gn CH66 69 B2
Pennington La WA5,WA9 1 B1
Penningtons La SK11 111 C3
Penny Bank Cl CH4 139 A2
Penny La Collins Green WA5 1 B1
Cronton WA8,L35 12 A3
Haydock WA11 2 A4
Rainow SK10 88 B2
Stockport SK5 240 F7
Penny's La
Lach Dennis CW9 105 A3
Northwich CW9 104 C4
Pennyfields Rd ST7 195 B1
Pennymoor Dr WA14 238 B6
Pennypleck La CW9 28 A1
Penrhyn Ave SK8 239 E1
Penrhyn Cres
Hazel Grove SK7 36 B4
Runcorn WA7 49 A4
Penrhyn Rd
Northwich CW8 103 C4
Stockport SK3 240 C4
Penrith Ave
Macclesfield SK11 111 C3
Warrington WA2 8 B1
Penrith Cl Frodsham WA6 49 B1
Partington M31 11 C2
Penrose Gdns WA5 14 B2
Penry Ave M44 11 C3
Penryn Cl WA5 14 C2
Pensarn Gdns WA5 7 B1
Pensarn Gr SK5 240 F8
Pensby Ave CH2 118 B3
Pensby Dr CH66 69 B2
Pensby Rd CH60 40 C4
Penshaw Ct WA7 49 C4
Penshurst Wlk 7 M34 241 A5
Pentland Ave WA2 8 A2
Pentland Cl Chester CH3 119 A1
Winsford CW7 149 A4
Pentland Pl WA2 8 A2
Pentre Cl CH3 121 C4
Pentre La CH3 121 C4
Penzance Cl SK10 111 C4
Peony Gdns WA9 6 A4
Peover Ave M33 242 E6
Peover Hall* WA16 107 C4
Peover La Chelford SK11 108 C4
Congleton CW12 157 C3
Peover Prim Sch WA16 108 A4
Peover Rd SK9 34 C3
Pepper Ct SK9 60 A3
Pepper St
Appleton Thorn WA4 27 A2
Ashley WA16 31 C1
Chelford SK11 83 C1
Chester CH1 237 B2
Christleton CH3 142 B4
Hale L24 21 B1
Henbury SK11 111 A4
Lymm WA13 18 C2
Middlewich CW10 128 B1
Nantwich CW5 204 C3
Peppers The WA13 18 C2
Percival Cl CH2 118 B4
Percival La Ollerton WA16 83 A2
Runcorn WA7 22 C1
Percival Rd Chester CH2 118 B4
Ellesmere Port CH65 70 A3
Percival St WA1 16 B3
Percy James Cl ST7 193 C2
Percy Rd CH4 141 B4
Percy St Northwich CW9 104 A4
Stalybridge SK15 242 E2
Stockport SK1 240 F6
Warrington WA5 15 C3
Peregrine Cl CW7 149 B3
Perimeter Rd CH2 72 B3
Perrey St WA7 23 A1
Perrin Ave WA7 48 C4
Perrin St SK14 241 D6
Perrins Rd WA5 6 C3
Perry Fields CW1 173 A1
Perth Cl Bramhall SK7 35 C3
Holmes Chapel CW4 130 A1
Warrington WA2 8 C2
Peter House Rd SK11 112 C2
Peter Pl CW1 190 A3
Peter Salem Dr WA5 15 A3
Peter St
Altrincham WA14 238 D3
Denton M34 241 A7
Golborne WA3 3 A4
Macclesfield SK11 112 B4
Northwich CW9 79 A1
Peter St W SK11 112 B4
Peterborough Cl
Ellesmere Port CH66 94 C4
Macclesfield SK10 87 A1
Peterhouse Gdns SK6 241 C4
Peters Cl SK10 87 A4
Petersburg Rd SK3 240 D2
Petersfield Gdns WA3 4 C2
Petersgate WA7 50 B4
Petersham Dr WA4 26 C3
Peterstone Cl WA5 7 B1
Petham Ct WA8 12 C2
Petrel Ave SK12 36 A2
Petrel Cl Stockport SK3 240 B2
Winsford CW7 149 B3
Petunia Cl
Macclesfield SK11 112 A3
St Helens WA9 6 A4
Petworth Ave WA2 8 A2
Petworth Cl CW2 206 A4
Pevensey Dr WA16 82 A4
Peveril Cl WA4 26 B4
Peveril Dr SK7 36 C4
Peveril Gdns SK12 39 A3
Peveril Mews SK12 39 A3
Peveril Rd WA14 238 C7
Peveril Wlk SK11 111 C4
Pewit La CW5 231 A4
Pewithall Prim Sch WA7 49 A4
Pewterspear Green Rd
WA4 26 C2
Pewterspear La WA4 26 B2
Pexhall Rd CW12,SK11 134 B2
Pexhill Ct SK4 240 A6
Pexhill Dr SK10 111 C4
Pexhill Rd
Macclesfield SK11 111 B3
Siddington SK11 110 B2
Pheasant Cl WA3 9 C2
Pheasant Dr CW9 79 C3
Pheasant Field L24 21 B1
Pheasant Rise WA14 238 D1
Pheasant Way CW7 149 B3
Pheasant Wlk WA16 29 B2
Philip Rd WA8 22 A4
Philip St CH5 116 A1
Philips Dr WA5 14 C4
Philips La CH66 69 B2
Phillip St CH2 118 C2
Phillips Rd CH1 117 B2
Phillips Way CH60 40 C4
Phipps' La WA5 6 C4
Phoenix Ave WA5 7 C1
Phoenix Cl ST7 195 B1
Phoenix St CH5 116 A2
Phythian Cres WA5 14 C2
Piccadilly SK1 240 F5
Pichael Nook WA4 17 A2
Pickenham Cl SK11 111 C3
Pickering Cres WA4 17 B2
Pickering Rd WA8 22 A3
Pickering St CH2 237 C4
Pickering's Pasture (Nature Reserve)* WA8 22 A2
Pickerings Cl WA7 49 B3
Pickford St SK11 112 B4
Pickford's Brow 3 SK1 240 F5
Pickmere Cl
Sandbach CW11 174 C4
Stockport SK3 240 C2
Pickmere Ct 10 SK9 34 B3
Pickmere Dr
Bebington CH62 43 C2
Chester CH3 142 A4
Runcorn WA7 50 B3
Pickmere Gdns SK8 239 F4
Pickmere La
Higher Wincham CW9 79 C3
Pickmere WA16 55 B1
Tabley WA16 55 B1
Pickmere Rd SK9 34 B3
Pickmere St WA5 15 C3
Pickwick Cl CW11 175 B4
Pickwick Pl ST7 194 B1
Pickwick Rd SK12 36 B2
Picow Farm Rd WA7 22 C1
Picow St 1 WA7 22 C1
Picton Ave
Ellesmere Port CH65 70 B3
Runcorn WA7 23 A1
Picton Cl Bebington CH62 43 C2
7 Davenham CW9 103 C2
Warrington WA3 9 B2
Picton Dr Wilmslow SK9 34 C1
Winsford CW7 126 A1
Picton Gorse La CH2 119 A4
Picton La CH2 96 B2
Picton Sq CW4 130 B2
Piele Rd WA11 1 C4
Pierce St SK11 112 B4
Pierpoint La CH1 237 B2
Pierpoint St Golborne WA3 3 A4
Warrington WA5 15 C4
Pigot Pl WA4 16 C3
Pike La WA6 75 A2
Pike Rd SK10 89 A3
Pike St WA4 16 B1
Pike The CW5 204 C2
Pikemere Rd ST7 193 A3
Pikemere Sch ST7 193 A3
Pikenall La CW8 76 B2
Pilgrim Cl WA2 8 A3
Pilgrims Way WA7 24 B1
Pillar Box La CW11 153 A2
Pillmoss La WA4 52 A4
Pillory St CW5 204 C3
Pimblett Rd WA11 1 C4
Pimblett St WA3 3 A4
Pimlico Rd WA7 22 C1
Pincot Rd SK22 39 B4
Pine Ave Newton-le-W WA12 2 B1
Widnes WA8 13 A1
Pine Cl Haydock WA11 1 B3
Macclesfield SK10 87 C1
Talke ST7 210 B4
Pine Ct ST7 193 C2
Pine Gdns CH2 118 B3
Pine Gr Chester CH2 119 A2
Denton M34 241 A7
Ellesmere Port CH66 70 A1
Golborne WA3 3 B4
Sandbach CW11 175 B3
Warrington WA1 17 A4
Winsford CW7 127 A1
Pine Lodge SK7 35 C4
Pine Rd Bramhall SK7 35 C4
Heswall CH60 41 B4
Macclesfield SK10 87 C1
Poynton SK12 36 C2
Runcorn WA7 49 B4
Pine St SK3 240 D4
Pine Tree Cl CH4 139 B2
Pine Trees WA16 57 C4
Pine Wlk Nantwich CW5 204 C2
6 Partington M31 11 C2
Pineapple Pk CW7 127 A1
Pinedale Cl CH1 95 A4
Pinehey CH64 41 B1
Pinehurst SK10 86 C3
Pinellas WA7 23 A2
Pines The WA16 58 C1
Pinetree Cl Barnton CW8 78 A2
Winsford CW7 127 A1
Pineways WA4 26 B3
Pinewood WA14 238 A2
Pinewood Ave WA1 16 C4
Pinewood Cl Elton CH2 72 B2
Stockport SK4 240 A7
Pinewood Ct
Altrincham WA14 238 E1
Sale M33 242 D7
Wistaston CW2 206 A4
Pinewood Dr CH60 41 A4
Pinewood Gr ST5 210 C1
Pinewood Rd
Burtonwood WA5 6 C4
Wilmslow SK9 60 C4
Pinfold Cl WA15 32 B4
Pinfold Craft Ctr* CW5 188 A2
Pinfold Ct CH4 141 C3
Pinfold La Chelford WA16 83 B3
Chester CH4 141 C4
Little Budworth CW6 147 C4
Middlewich CW10 128 A1
Plumley WA16 81 A2
Romiley SK6 241 E4
Wythenshaw M90,WA15 32 C3
Pinfold St 12 SK11 112 B4
Pinfold The LL13 196 B4
Pinfold Way CW8 77 B1
Pingard's La CW8 101 B3
Pingate Dr SK8 35 A3
Pingate La SK8 35 A3
Pingate La S SK8 35 A3
Pingot Croft CH3 142 A4
Pingot La WA6 99 A3
Pinmill Brow WA6 74 A4
Pinmill Cl WA6 74 B4
Pinners Brow WA2 16 A3
Pinners Brow Ret Pk
WA2 16 A3
Pinners Fold WA7 24 A1
Pinsley Green Rd CW5 216 C1
Pinsley View CW5 216 C2
Pintail Ave SK3 240 B2
Pintail Pl CW7 149 B3
Pinwood Ct 18 SK9 34 C1
Piper's Cl CH60 40 B4
Piper's End CH60 40 B4
Piper's La CH60 40 B4
Pipers Ash CW7 126 A1
Pipers Ct CH2 119 A2
Pipers La Chester CH2 119 A2
Puddington CH64 93 A4
Pipers The WA3 3 C4
Pipit Ave WA12 2 B2
Pipit La WA3 9 C2
Pippin Cl CW10 151 B4
Pippits Row WA7 49 C2
Pirie Cl CW12 157 A2
Pirie Rd CW12 157 A2
Pit La
Hough Common CW2 206 C1
Talke ST7 210 B3
Widnes WA8 13 A2
Pitt St Hyde SK14 241 D7
Macclesfield SK11 112 B3
Pitt St *continued*
Stockport SK3 240
Warrington WA5 15
Widnes WA8 23
Pitts Cl CH3 121
Pitts Heath La WA7 24
Pitville Terr WA8 22
Pius XII RC Prim Sch
CH66 69
Place Rd WA14 238
Plaistow Ct WA7 49
Plane Gr ST5 210
Plane Tree Dr CW1 190
Plane Tree Gr WA11 2
Plane Tree Rd M31 11
Plant Cl M33 242
Plant La CW11 174
Plant St CW11 175
Plantagenet Cl 3 CW7 149
Plantation Cl WA7 24
Plantation Dr CH66 69
Plantation Ind Est OL6 242
Plantation St OL6 242
Plas Newton La CH2 118
Platt Ave CW11 175
Platt St SK8 239
Platt's La CH3 164
Platts La Christleton CH3 143
Duddon CH3,CW6 144
Tarvin CH3 121
Tarvin, Broom Bank CH3 144
Tattenhall CH3 183
Platts St WA11 1
Play St SK1 240
Pleasance Way WA12 2
Pleasant St
Macclesfield SK10 87
Northwich CW8 103
Pleasant Way SK7,SK8 35
Pleck Rd CH65 70
Plemstall Cl CH2 119
Plemstall La CH2 97
Plemstall Way CH2 96
Plemston Ct CH66 69
Plex The ST7 19
Plinston Ave WA4 16
Plough Croft ST7 193
Plough La CH3 143
Ploughmans Cl CH66 94
Ploughmans Way
Ellesmere Port CH66 94
Macclesfield SK10 87
Plover Ave CW7 149
Plover Cl Farndon CH3 180
Newton-le-W WA12 2
Plover Dr
Altrincham WA14 238
Runcorn WA7 50
Plover Way WA3 3
Plovers La WA6 7
Plum Terr CH1 237
Plumbs Fold CW8 78
Plumley Cl Chester CH3 11
Stockport SK3 240
Plumley Gdns WA8 12
Plumley Moor Rd WA16 81
Plumley Rd SK9 34
Plumley Sta WA16 81
Plumpstons La WA6 49
Plumtre Ave WA5 15
Plymouth Cl WA7 50
Plymouth Dr SK7 35
Plymouth Gr SK3 240
Plymyard Ave CH62 43
Plymyard Cl CH62 43
Plymyard Copse CH62 43
Poachers La WA4 16
Pochard Ave CW7 14
Pochard Dr
Altrincham WA14 238
Poynton SK12 36
Pochard Rise WA7 50
Pochin Way CW10 128
Pocket Nook La WA3 4
Pocklington Ct WA2 8
Pole La CW9 53
Pole Lane Ends CW9 53
Poleacre Dr WA8 12
Police St 1 WA14 238
Pollard Dr CW5 205
Polldean Ho SK8 239
Pollen Rd WA14 238
Polperro Cl
Macclesfield SK10 86
Warrington WA5 14
Pond Cotts CH2 72
Pond St WA3 4
Pond View Cl CH60 41
Pond Wlk WA9 1
Pool Bank Bsns Pk CH3 12
Pool End Cl SK10 87
Pool End Rd SK10 87
Pool Hall Ind Est CH65,
CH66 70
Pool House Rd SK12 37
Pool La Elton CH2 71
Haslington CW11 192
Lymm WA13 18
Runcorn WA7 23
Tarvin CH3 12
Warrington WA4 16
Pool Meadows Rd CW1 19
Pool Rd WA3 1
Pool Side ST7 194
Pool St Macclesfield SK11 112
Widnes WA8 23
Pool View CW11 19
Poolcroft M33 24

'oole Ave WA2 8 A1
'oole Cres WA2 8 A1
'oole Hall La CH66 69 C4
'oole Hall Rd CH66 69 C4
'oole La CH2 71 C1
'oole Old Hall La CW5 188 B2
'oolford La CW4 129 C1
'ools La CW11 177 A3
'ools Platt La CW9 53 C3
'oolside Ct ST7 193 C2
'oolside Rd WA7 23 A1
'ooltown Com Jun Sch CH65 69 C3
'ooltown Rd CH65 69 C3
'oplar Ave
Altrincham WA14 238 E6
Culcheth WA3 4 C2
Moulton CW9 126 C4
Newton-le-W WA12 2 B2
Runcorn WA7 49 B4
Warrington WA5 14 C2
Wilmslow SK9 59 C3
'oplar Cl
Congleton CW12 156 A2
Cuddington CW8 102 A2
Ellesmere Port CH65 70 A2
Gatley SK8 239 B5
Runcorn WA7 49 B4
Winsford CW7 149 A4
'oplar Dr Alsager ST7 193 C1
Kidsgrove ST7 195 A1
Middlewich CW10 151 B4
'oplar Gr Bollington SK10 88 A4
Crewe CW1 190 C3
Elton CH2 72 A2
Haydock WA11 1 B3
Irlam M44 11 B3
Sale M33 242 B5
'oplar La TF9 236 C3
'oplar Rd Chester CH4 140 C3
Haydock WA11 1 B3
Macclesfield SK11 112 B3
Weaverham CW8 102 B4
'oplar Way SK6 38 A4
'oplar Weint 2 CH64 66 C4
'oplar Wlk M31 11 B2
'oplars Ave WA2 8 B2
'oplars Pl WA2 8 B1
'oplars The Golborne WN7 4 B4
Lymm WA13 18 B2
Wistaston CW2 205 C4
'oppyfields ST7 193 A2
'orlock Cl Heswall CH60 41 A3
Warrington WA5 14 C2
'ort Arcs The CH65 70 B3
'ort St SK1 240 E6
'ortal Gr M34 241 B5
'orter Ave WA12 2 B3
'orter Dr CW9 104 B3
'orter St WA7 23 B1
'orter Way CW9 104 B3
'orters Croft CH3 119 C3
'ortford Cl SK10 86 C1
'orthcawl Cl WA8 12 B2
'ortland Dr Biddulph ST8 179 B1
Scholar Green ST7 194 C3
'ortland Gr
Haslington CW1 191 B3
5 Stockport SK4 240 B8
'ortland Pl WA6 73 B2
'ortland Rd WA14 238 D3
'ortland St
Newton-le-W WA12 1 C2
Runcorn WA7 22 C2
'ortland Wlk SK11 111 C4
'ortleven Rd WA7 50 A3
'ortloe Rd SK8 34 A4
'ortman Pl 4 CW7 149 A4
'ortmarnock Cl SK10 87 A2
'ortola Cl WA4 17 B1
'ortrea Cl SK3 240 F1
'ortree Ave CH63 43 B3
'ortree Dr CW4 130 A1
'ortrush Dr SK10 87 B2
'ortside WA7 50 C4
'ortside Bsns Pk CH65 70 A4
'ortsmouth Pl WA7 50 C3
'ortway M22 33 B4
'ortwood Pl SK1 240 F6
'osnett St SK3 240 C4
'ost Office La
Betley CW2 207 C1
Hampton SY14 213 B4
Norley WA6 100 C3
Runcorn WA7 48 B4
'ost Office Pl 1 CW9 79 A1
'ost Office St WA14 238 D5
'ostles Pl CW9 103 C3
'ott Shrigley Church Sch SK10 63 B2
'otter Cl CW5 205 B2
'otters Barn The* CW11 176 A1
'otters End ST8 179 B1
'otters La WA8 21 C3
'oulton Cres WA1 17 B4
'oulton Dr WA8 22 B4
'oulton Hall Rd CH63 43 A4
'oulton Rd CH63 43 A4
'ound Rd CH66 69 B4
'ovey Rd WA2 8 B1
'owell Ave Hyde SK14 241 E7
Warrington WA3 9 C2
'owell St WA4 16 C2
'owell's Orch CH4 141 B4
'owey La Mollington CH1 94 A3
Saughall CH1 94 A3
'owicke Wlk SK6 241 A1
Pownall Ave SK7 35 C4
Pownall Ct SK9 59 C4
Pownall Green Prim Sch SK7 35 C4
Pownall Hall Sch SK9 59 C4
Pownall Rd
Altrincham WA14 238 D3
Wilmslow SK9 59 C4
Pownall Sq SK11 112 B4
Pownall St SK10 87 B1
Powy Dr ST7 195 A1
Powys St WA5 15 C3
Poynton Cl WA4 17 A2
Poynton High Sch SK12 36 C1
Poynton Ind Est SK10 36 B1
Poynton St 9 SK11 112 B4
Poynton Sta SK12 36 B2
Pratchitts Row CW5 204 C3
Precinct The CW2 189 C1
Preece Cl WA8 12 B2
Preece Ct CW1 190 A3
Preesall Ave SK8 34 A4
Prenton Pl CH4 141 C4
Prescot Rd
Altrincham WA15 238 F2
Widnes WA8 12 B1
Prescot St CH2 118 C2
Prescott Rd SK9 34 A1
Prescott St WA4 16 C2
Prescott Wlk M34 241 B5
Prestbury Ave WA15 238 E6
Prestbury CE Prim Sch SK10 86 C4
Prestbury Cl
13 Northwich CW9 103 C2
Widnes WA8 22 C4
Prestbury Ct SK10 86 C3
Prestbury Dr WA4 17 B2
Prestbury La SK10 87 A4
Prestbury Pk SK10 86 C3
Prestbury Rd
Macclesfield SK10 87 A1
Nether Alderley SK10 86 A3
Nether Alderley, Adder's Moss SK10 85 C3
Wilmslow SK10,SK9 60 C3
Prestbury Sta SK10 87 A4
Preston Ave M44 11 C4
Preston On The Hill WA4 50 C3
Preston St W SK11 112 A3
Prestwich Ave WA3 4 C2
Prestwick Cl
Macclesfield SK10 87 B3
Winsford CW7 126 B1
Prestwood Ct WA3 10 A4
Pretoria St CH4 141 B4
Price Ave CW11 175 A3
Price Gr WA9 1 A1
Pride Cl WA12 2 C1
Priest Ave SK8 239 A4
Priest La SK10 61 A1
Priest St SK1 240 F3
Priestfield Rd CH65 70 B3
Priestley Coll WA1 16 B2
Priestley St WA5 15 C3
Priestner Dr WA6 73 A2
Priestway La CH64 67 C1
Priesty Ct CW12 156 B1
Priesty Fields CW12 156 B1
Primary Cl M44 11 B3
Primitive St ST7 195 B4
Primrose Ave
Haslington CW1 191 B3
Macclesfield SK11 112 A3
Primrose Bank WA14 238 C1
Primrose Chase CW4 130 B4
Primrose Cl
Huntington CH3 142 A3
Runcorn WA7 50 A4
Warrington WA2 8 B1
Widnes WA8 12 C1
Primrose Cotts WA14 238 C1
Primrose Gr WA11 1 C4
Primrose Hill
Crewe CW2 189 C3
Cuddington CW8 101 C2
Kelsall CW6 122 C3
Primrose La WA6 73 A1
Primula Dr WA3 3 B4
Prince Albert St CW1 190 B2
Prince Edward St CW5 204 C3
Prince Henry Sq 10 WA1 16 A3
Prince Rd SK12 37 B3
Prince William Ave CH5 116 A2
Prince's Ave SK6 241 A3
Prince's Rd SK6 241 A3
Prince's St
4 Stockport SK1 240 E6
Widnes WA8 23 A4
Princes Ave
Bebington CH62 43 C3
Chester CH2 237 C3
Northwich CW9 104 A4
Princes Cl WA7 23 C1
Princes Ct CW5 204 C3
Princes Dr M33 242 D5
Princes Pk CW8 78 A1
Princes Pl WA8 12 C1
Princes Rd
Altrincham WA14 238 D6
Ellesmere Port CH65 70 A3
Sale M33 242 D5
Stockport SK4 240 A8
Princes St WA12 2 A2
Princes Way SK11 111 C4
Princess Ave Audley ST7 209 B1
Haydock WA11 2 A4
Warrington WA1 16 C3
Princess Ave *continued*
Warrington, Great Sankey WA5 14 C4
Warrington, Padgate WA1 17 A4
Princess Cl CW2 205 C4
Princess Cres
Middlewich CW10 151 B3
Warrington WA1 16 C3
Princess Ct ST7 210 B3
Princess Dr
Bollington SK10 87 C4
Nantwich CW5 205 A3
Sandbach CW11 175 A4
Wistaston CW2 205 C4
Princess Gr CW2 205 C4
Princess Rd Lymm WA13 18 B2
Wilmslow SK9 59 C3
Princess St
Altrincham WA14 238 C8
Ashton-u-Lyne OL6 242 A4
Bollington SK10 87 C4
Chester CH1 237 A2
Congleton CW12 156 B2
Crewe CW1 190 B3
Hyde SK14 241 E6
Knutsford WA16 57 A1
Northwich CW9 79 C1
Runcorn WA7 23 A2
Talke ST7 210 B3
Warrington WA5 15 B2
Winsford CW7 127 A1
Princess Wlk SK7 36 A4
Princeway WA6 74 A4
Printworks Rd SK15 242 F3
Prior Cl CW2 189 C1
Priory Ave CW9 103 C2
Priory Cl Chester CH2 118 B2
Congleton CW12 179 A4
Crewe CW1 190 A4
Runcorn WA7 24 A1
Sale M33 242 D8
Winsford CW7 126 B2
Priory Ct SK10 86 C1
Priory Dr SK10 86 C1
Priory La SK10 86 C1
Priory Pl Chester CH1 237 B2
Kidsgrove ST7 195 A2
Priory Rd
Altrincham WA14 31 A4
Runcorn WA7 24 B1
Sale M33 242 D7
Stockport SK8 240 A1
Wilmslow SK9 59 C4
Priory Specl Sch M33 242 A6
Priory St
Altrincham WA14 238 C1
Northwich CW9 104 A4
Warrington WA4 16 A2
Priory The Neston CH64 41 C1
Winwick WA2 8 A4
Priory Way CW8 103 A2
Priscilla St CW1 190 C2
Pritchard Dr CW9 103 C1
Probert Cl CW2 190 A2
Proctors Cl WA8 13 B1
Proctors La CW11 174 C3
Proffits La WA6 73 C2
Promised Land La CH3 142 C3
Prospect Ave M44 11 C3
Prospect Dr
Altrincham WA15 32 B4
Davenham CW9 103 C1
Prospect La WA3 10 B2
Prospect Rd M44 11 C3
Prospect Row WA7 48 C4
Prospect St CW12 156 B2
Prospect Vale SK8 239 B1
Prospect Vale Prim Sch SK8 239 B1
Prosperity Way CW10 128 B1
Prosser Rd CH2 95 B1
Protector Way M44 11 C4
Provan Way CH1 117 B3
Providence St OL6 242 A4
Provident St WA9 1 A2
Prunus Rd CW1 190 C3
Pryors The CH3 121 B2
Ptarmigan Pl 7 CW7 149 B3
Public Hall St WA7 23 A2
Pudding La CW6 168 A4
Puddington La
Neston CH64 92 C4
Puddington CH64 93 A4
Puffin Ave SK12 36 A2
Puffin Cl CH65 95 B4
Pulford Cl
Davenham CW9 103 C2
Runcorn WA7 49 C3
Pulford Ct CH4 162 B1
Pulford La CH4 162 A3
Pulford Rd Blacon CH1 117 C3
Ellesmere Port CH65 69 C2
Winsford CW7 126 B1
Pullman Cl CH60 41 B4
Pullman Dr CW9 104 B4
Pump La Churton CH3 181 A3
Runcorn WA7 49 C4
Pumptree Mews SK11 111 C4
Purdy Cl WA5 7 B1
Puritan Bldgs WA7 23 B1
Purley Dr M44 11 B3
Purser La SY14 211 C2
Puss Bank Prim Sch SK10 112 C4
Putney Ct WA7 49 C4
Pye Cl WA11 2 A4
Pye Rd CH60 41 A4
Pyecroft Cl WA5 14 B3
Pyecroft Rd WA5 14 B3
Pyecroft St CH4 141 B4
Pym's La CW1 189 C3
Pymgate Dr SK8 239 A2
Pyrus Ave CW1 190 C3
Pyrus Gr WA6 73 B2
Pytcheley Hollow WA6 100 C3

Q

Quad The CH1 117 C1
Quadrant Cl WA7 50 B3
Quadrant The
Blacon CH1 117 C1
Romiley SK6 241 A2
Warrington WA3 9 C3
Quail Cl WA2 8 B2
Quakers Coppice CW1 191 A1
Quakers Way LL13 180 C1
Quantock Cl
Ellesmere Port CH66 69 A3
Stockport SK4 240 E6
Winsford CW7 149 A4
Quarry Ave CH3 180 C1
Quarry Bank CW6 146 B4
Quarry Bank Mill* SK9 33 C1
Quarry Bank Rd SK9 33 C2
Quarry Cl Chester CH4 141 B4
Runcorn WA7 23 B1
Quarry Ct WA8 12 B1
Quarry Hill CH3 180 C1
Quarry Hts SK15 242 C1
Quarry La
Christleton CH3 142 C4
Kelsall CW6 122 B3
Neston CH64 42 A1
Warrington WA4 26 B3
Quarry Rd Neston CH64 42 B1
New Mills SK22 39 B4
Romiley SK6 241 B2
Quarry Rise SK6 241 B3
Quarry St SK15 242 C1
Quarry Terr ST7 195 A1
Quarrybank CW6 184 C3
Quarrybank Cotts CW6 184 C3
Quay Fold WA5 15 C3
Quay Pl WA7 50 C4
Quay Side WA6 49 B1
Quay The WA6 49 B1
Quayle Cl WA11 1 B3
Quayside
Congleton CW12 156 C1
Neston CH64 66 C3
Quayside Mews WA13 18 C2
Quayside Way SK11 112 C4
Queastybirch La WA4 26 A1
Quebec Rd WA2 16 B4
Queen Anne Ct
1 Macclesfield SK11 112 A3
Wilmslow SK9 60 B3
Queen Sq OL6 242 A4
Queen St Audley ST7 209 B1
Bollington SK10 88 A4
Bunbury CW6 185 C4
Cheadle SK8 239 F6
Chester CH1 237 B2
Congleton CW12 156 B1
Congleton, Buglawton CW12 156 C2
Crewe CW1 190 C3
Ellesmere Port CH65 70 B4
Golborne WA3 3 A4
Hyde SK14 241 E6
Kidsgrove ST7 195 A1
Knutsford WA16 56 C1
Macclesfield SK11 112 B4
Middlewich CW10 128 B1
Nantwich CW5 204 C3
Newton-le-W WA12 2 A2
Northwich CW9 103 C4
Runcorn WA7 23 A2
Shavington CW2 206 B2
Stalybridge SK15 242 D2
Queen Victoria St 26 SK11 112 B4
Queen's Ave Chester CH2 237 C3
Connah's Quay CH5 91 B1
Glazebury WA3 5 B4
Hawarden CH5 116 A2
Macclesfield SK10 87 C1
Romiley SK6 241 A3
Widnes WA8 22 A4
Queen's Cl
Macclesfield SK10 87 C1
Runcorn WA7 22 C1
Queen's Cres CW1 172 C1
Queen's Dr Chester CH4 237 C1
Middlewich CW10 151 B4
Nantwich CW5 204 B2
Sandbach CW11 175 A4
Stockport SK4 240 A6
Queen's Gdns SK8 239 E6
Queen's Par CW7 126 B1
Queen's Park Gdns CW2 189 C2
Queen's Park Ho CH4 237 B1
Queen's Park Rd CH4 237 B1
Queen's Rd
Altrincham WA15 238 F3
Cheadle SK8 239 F4
Chester CH2 237 C3
Romiley SK6 241 A3
Runcorn WA7 22 C1
Wilmslow SK9 60 A3
Queen's Sch CH1 237 A2
Queen's Sch (Jun Dept) CH2 118 B2
Queen's Way CH4 139 A2
Queens Ave
Ellesmere Port CH65 70 A2
Warrington WA1 16 C4
Queens Cl Bollington SK10 87 C3
Stockport SK4 240 A6
Queens Cres
Chester CH2 118 C4
Warrington WA1 17 A4
Queens Ct
1 Stockport SK4 240 A7
Winsford CW7 126 B1
Queens Dr Golborne WA3 3 B4
Helsby WA6 73 A2
Heswall CH60 40 C4
Newton-le-W WA12 2 B3
Warrington WA4 17 A1
Queens Gdns
Ellesmere Port CH65 70 A3
Talke ST7 210 B3
Queens Park Golf Course CW2 189 C2
Queens Park High Sch CH4 237 B1
Queens Pl CH1 237 B3
Queens Rd Chester CH3 119 A2
Ellesmere Port CH66 69 B4
Haydock WA11 2 A4
Queens Terr SK9 34 B2
Queensbury Cl 19 SK9 34 B1
Queensbury Way WA8 12 C2
Queensgate Bramhall SK7 35 C3
Northwich CW8 103 C4
Queensgate Prim Sch SK7 35 C2
Queensway Alsager ST7 193 A3
Chester CH2 118 C3
Crewe CW1 190 B2
Frodsham WA6 74 A4
Gatley SK8 34 B4
Heswall CH60 41 B3
Knutsford WA16 56 C2
Partington M31 11 C2
Poynton SK12 36 B2
Runcorn WA7 22 C2
Widnes WA8 22 C3
Winsford CW7 149 B4
Queensway Trad Est WA8 23 A3
Quill Ct M44 11 C3
Quillet The CH64 66 C4
Quinn St WA8 23 A4
Quinta Prim Sch The CW12 156 A1
Quinta Rd CW12 156 A2

R

Raby Ave CH63 43 A3
Raby Cl Bebington CH63 43 A4
Heswall CH60 40 C4
Widnes WA8 13 C1
Raby Ct CH65 70 B2
Raby Dr CH63 43 A3
Raby Gdns CH64 66 C4
Raby Hall Rd CH63 43 A3
Raby Mere Rd CH63 42 B3
Raby Park Cl CH64 66 C4
Raby Park Rd CH64 41 C1
Raby Rd Neston CH64 66 C4
Thornton Hough CH63 42 A3
Race The SK9 34 B1
Racecourse La CW6 124 A1
Racecourse Pk SK9 59 C3
Racecourse Rd SK9 59 C3
Racefield Cl WA13 18 C2
Racefield Rd
Altrincham WA14 238 C4
Knutsford WA16 56 C1
Radbroke Cl CW11 175 B4
Radcliffe Ave WA3 4 C2
Radcliffe Cl CH3 121 B2
Radcliffe Rd
Sandbach CW11 174 C2
Sutton Lane Ends SK11 135 B4
Raddel La WA4 52 B3
Raddle Wharf CH65 70 B4
Raddon Pl WA4 16 C2
Radford Cl WA8 22 B4
Radlett Cl WA5 14 C2
Radley Dr CH63 41 C3
Radley La WA2 8 C2
Radnor Cl
Congleton CW12 156 A2
Sandbach CW11 174 C4
Radnor Dr Chester CH4 141 A2
Widnes WA8 12 B1
Radnor Park Ind Ctr CW12 156 A2
Radnor Park Trad Est CW12 156 A2
Radnor St WA5 15 C3
Radway Gn CH66 69 C3
Radway Green Rd CW2 208 C4
Rae St SK3 240 C4
Raeburn Ave
Bebington CH62 43 C3
Neston CH64 66 C4
Raeburn Prim Sch CH62 43 B3
Raglan Ct WA3 9 C3
Raglan Dr WA14 238 E8
Raglan Rd
Macclesfield SK10 87 C1
Sale M33 242 A5

Raglan St SK14 241 C6
Ragley Cl SK12 36 C2
Railbrook Ct CW2 190 B1
Railton Ave CW1 190 A4
Railway Age Mus The* CW1 190 B2
Railway Bank SK14 241 C6
Railway Cotts
Congleton CW12 157 A1
Hollinfare WA3 11 A3
Hooton CH66 43 B1
Railway Rd SK1 240 E4
Railway St
Altrincham WA14 238 D4
Crewe CW2 190 B1
Hyde SK14 241 D6
Newton-le-W WA12 2 A2
Stockport SK4 240 E6
Railway Terr Disley SK12 38 B3
Hawarden CH5 116 A2
Railway View WA5 1 B1
Rainbow Cl WA8 12 B2
Rainbow Dr SK12 37 A1
Rainbow St CW1 190 B2
Rainford Cl ST7 195 C1
Rainow Cl CW10 151 A4
Rainow Prim Sch SK10 88 B2
Rainow Rd
Macclesfield SK10 88 A1
Rainow SK10 88 A1
Stockport SK3 240 C2
Rainow View SK10 63 B1
Rainow Way 10 SK9 34 C1
Rajar Cotts WA16 57 C2
Rake House Mews WA6 73 A2
Rake La Backford CH2 95 B3
Christleton CH3 143 A4
Dunham-on-t-H WA6 97 C4
Eccleston CH4 141 B1
Hawarden CH5 139 A4
Helsby WA6 73 B2
Helsby, Helsby Marsh WA6 73 A3
Stoak CH2 95 B2
Rake The Bebington CH62 43 B4
Burton CH64 67 B1
Rake Way CH1 94 A1
Raleigh Cl WA5 7 B1
Raleigh Rd CH64 41 C1
Raleigh St SK5 240 E8
Ramp Rd E M90 33 B4
Ramp Rd S M90 33 B4
Ramp Rd W M90 33 A4
Rampit Cl WA11 1 C4
Ramsbottom St CW1 190 A3
Ramsbrook La L24,WA8 21 B2
Ramsdale Rd SK7 35 C4
Ramsden Ct CH4 140 C2
Ramsey Cl Warrington WA3 9 C2
Widnes WA8 13 C2
Ramsey Rd CH65 70 B1
Ramsfield Rd L24 21 A2
Randall Cl WA12 2 A2
Randle Bennett Cl CW11 174 C4
Randle Mdw CH66 69 C1
Randle Meadow Ct 2 CH66 69 C1
Randolph Pl SK3 240 E3
Range Ct SK10 87 C1
Range Rd SK3 240 E3
Rangemoor Cl WA3 10 A3
Rannoch Cl CH66 69 C2
Ranulph Ct WA6 74 B4
Ranwonath Ct CH2 237 B4
Ranworth Dr WA3 3 C4
Ranworth Rd WA5 14 C3
Rappax Rd WA15 32 A4
Raquets Ct The CW10 127 B3
Rassbottom Brow SK15 242 C2
Rassbottom Ind Est SK15 242 C2
Rassbottom St SK15 242 C2
Ratcliffe St 6 SK1 240 F4
Rathbone Pk CW6 146 B1
Rathlin Cl WA8 13 C2
Rathmell Cl WA3 4 C2
Rathvale Dr M22 33 B4
Raven Cl CW11 175 A4
Raven Cotts TF9 235 A3
Raven's La ST7 209 C2
Ravenbank Com Prim Sch WA13 18 C2
Ravendale Cl CW7 149 C4
Ravenfield Dr WA8 12 B2
Ravenho La SK10 88 B2
Ravenhurst Ct WA3 9 C3
Ravenoak Park Rd SK8 35 A4
Ravenoak Rd SK8 35 A4
Ravens Cl ST7 209 C2
Ravens La CW5 203 C3
Ravenscar Cres M22 33 B4
Ravenscliffe Rd ST7 195 A1
Ravenscroft CW4 130 A2
Ravenscroft Cl CW11 175 B4
Ravenscroft Rd CW2 189 C2
Ravensdale Cl WA2 8 B2
Ravensfield CW8 101 B2
Ravensholme Ct CH3 166 A1
Ravensholme La CH3 166 A1
Ravensmead Prim Sch ST7 209 C2
Ravenstone Dr M33 242 E7
Ravenswood CW8 103 A2
Ravenswood Ave SK4 240 A5
Ravenswood Dr SK8 35 A4
Ravenswood Rd SK9 59 C2
Ravenwood Dr WA15 32 B4
Rawcliffe Cl WA8 12 C2
Rawdon Cl WA7 50 A4
Rawlings Cl WA3 9 C2
Rawlinson Cres L26 21 A4
Rawson Rd CH1 117 C2
Ray Ave CW5 204 C4
Rayleigh Ave CW9 127 A4
Rayleigh Way SK10 86 C1
Raymond Ave WA4 16 B1
Raymond St CH1 237 A3
Raymond Way CH64 67 A4
Rayners Cl SK15 242 C1
Rays Brow CW8 78 A1
Read St SK14 241 C7
Read St W SK14 241 C7
Reades La CW12 179 B4
Readesdale Ave CW2 189 C1
Reading Room La SY14, CH3 199 B4
Rean Mdw CH3 166 A1
Reaper Cl WA5 15 B3
Reaseheath Coll CW5 188 B1
Reay St WA8 13 B1
Record Bsns Pk WA2 16 A4
Rectory Ave WA3 3 B4
Rectory Cl Denton M34 241 A6
Farndon CH3 180 C1
Heswall CH60 40 C4
12 Nantwich CW5 204 C3
Winwick WA2 8 A3
Wistaston CW2 205 C4
Rectory Gdns Lymm WA13 18 C2
Talke ST7 210 B3
Rectory La Adderley TF9 235 A3
Capenhurst CH1 94 A4
Heswall CH60 40 C4
Ledsham CH66 68 C1
Lymm WA13 18 C2
Winwick WA2 8 A3
Rectory View ST7 210 B3
Red Bank Ave WA12 2 C1
Red Brow La WA7,WA4 50 C4
Red Cow Yd 10 WA16 57 A1
Red Ct CH66 69 B4
Red Gables WA4 27 A2
Red Ho SK10 87 C1
Red House La WA14 20 B4
Red La Disley SK12 38 B3
Frodsham WA6 74 B4
Huxley CH3 166 B3
Sandbach CW11 174 B3
Warrington WA4 26 B4
Whitley WA4 52 B1
Red Lion Cl ST7 210 B3
Red Lion La
Ellesmere Port CH66 69 B4
Nantwich CW5 204 B3
Red Pike CH66 69 B4
Red Rose Ct M33 242 B8
Red Row SK7 37 A4
Red Stone Hill WA6 73 B2
Redacre SK12 36 C3
Redacre Cl WA4 51 A2
Redbourne Dr
Chorlton CW2 207 B1
Widnes WA8 12 A2
Redbrook Cl CH62 43 B3
Redbrook Gr 11 SK9 34 B1
Redbrook Rd M31 11 C1
Redbrook Way SK10 62 B3
Redcar Dr CH62 43 B3
Reddish Ave SK23 65 B3
Reddish Cres WA13 18 C2
Reddish La Lymm WA13 19 A3
Whaley Bridge SK23 65 B3
Reddish Rd SK23 65 B3
Reddy La WA14 30 A4
Redesdale Cl
Sandbach CW11 174 C4
Warrington WA2 8 C1
Redesmere Cl
Macclesfield SK10 87 A1
Northwich CW9 104 A3
Redesmere Dr
Alderley Edge SK9 60 A1
Cheadle SK8 239 F4
Redesmere La SK11 110 A2
Redesmere Rd SK9 34 B3
Redfern Ave
Congleton CW12 156 C2
Sale M33 242 E5
Redfern Ho SK6 241 A2
Redgate CW8 103 B4
Redhill Rd Chester CH4 140 C3
Kelsall CW6 122 B3
Redhills Mews CH65 70 A3
Redhouse La Disley SK12 38 C4
Romiley SK6 241 A4
Redhouses SK11 113 B2
Redland Cl CH4 141 A4
Redland Ho CH4 141 A4
Redmain Gr WA3 3 C4
Redmayne Cl WA12 2 A2
Redmere Dr CH60 41 B4
Redmoor La Disley SK12 39 A2
New Mills SK22 39 A3
Redpoll La WA3 9 C2
Redruth Ave SK10 86 C1
Redruth Cl WA7 50 B3
Redshank Ave CW7 149 B3
Redshank Cl WA12 2 B2
Redshank La WA3 9 C2
Redshaw Cl CW10 151 B3
Redstart Cl 4 WA3 3 C4
Redstone Dr CW7 126 A1
Redvales Ct WA3 9 B2
Redvers Ave CH66 44 A1
Redway La SK10 88 A4
Redwood Cl Barnton CW8 78 A2
Broughton CH4 140 C3
Holt LL13 196 B4
Warrington WA1 17 C4
Redwood Ct SK10 87 C3
Redwood Dr
Ellesmere Port CH66 69 C1
Elton CH2 72 B2
Reece Cl CH2 119 C4
Reed La CW9 53 B3
Reedgate La CW9 27 C1
Reedsmere Cl WA4 16 C1
Reedsmere Wlk CW9 78 B4
Reeman Cl SK6 241 A4
Reeman Ct SK9 34 A1
Rees Cres CW4 130 B2
Reeve St WA3 4 A4
Reeves Rd CH3 142 A4
Regal Cl
Ellesmere Port CH66 69 C2
Northwich CW9 103 C2
Regal Cres WA8 22 A4
Regency Cl ST7 210 B3
Regency Ct Chester CH2 119 C4
Winsford CW7 149 B4
Neston CH64 41 A1
Regency Gdns SK8 34 C4
Regency Hospl SK10 112 A4
Regency Pk SK9 59 C3
Regency Prep Sch SK11 112 A4
Regency Way CW9 103 C2
Regent Ave Haydock WA11 1 A4
Macclesfield SK11 112 A3
Warrington WA1 17 A4
Regent Bank SK9 59 C3
Regent Cl Bramhall SK7 35 B2
Shavington CW2 206 A2
Wilmslow SK9 59 C3
Regent Ct
Altrincham WA14 238 D4
Altrincham, Halebarns WA15 32 B4
Regent Rd
Altrincham WA14 238 D4
Widnes WA8 13 A1
Regent St
Ellesmere Port CH65 70 A3
Moulton CW9 126 C4
Newton-le-W WA12 2 A2
Runcorn WA7 23 A2
Warrington WA1 16 A3
Regents Cl CH3 119 A1
Regents Gate CW5 205 A3
Regents Theological Coll CW5 205 A3
Regents Way 5 CW7 149 A4
Regina Ave SK15 242 D2
Reginald Mitchell Prim Sch ST7 194 B1
Registry Cl CW9 103 C2
Reid Ave WA5 15 C4
Reid St CW1 190 B3
Remer St CW1 190 C4
Rena Cl SK4 240 D7
Renaissance Ct CW1 191 A2
Renaissance Way CW1 191 A2
Renbury Pl WA4 51 A2
Rendel Cl WA12 2 B1
Rendlesham Cl WA3 10 A3
Renfrew Ave CH62 43 C3
Renfrew Cl SK10 86 C1
Renown Cl WA3 9 B2
Renshaw Rd CW9 79 B1
Renshaw St WA14 238 E5
Rensherds Pl WA16 29 B3
Renton Ave WA7 23 B1
Repton Ave SK14 241 E7
Repton Cl WA16 29 B2
Repton Dr CW1 191 B3
Repton Rd CH65 70 B2
Reservoir Rd
Stockport SK3 240 D3
Whaley Bridge SK23 65 B4
Reservoir Terr CH2 118 C1
Retreat The Crewe CW1 190 B3
Romiley SK6 241 C1
Reuben St SK4 240 E8
Revesby Cl WA8 12 B1
Rex Bldgs SK9 60 A3
Reynard St SK14 241 D7
Reyner St OL6 242 B2
Reynold St SK14 241 D6
Reynold's La CW11 175 C3
Reynolds Ave
St Helens WA9 1 A1
Warrington WA3 9 C3
Reynolds Mews SK9 60 C4
Reynolds St WA4 16 C2
Rhoden St CW1 191 A3
Rhodes Cl CW1 191 B2
Rhodes St
Dukinfield SK14 241 C7
Warrington WA2 16 B4
Rhodes St N SK14 241 C7
Rhodesway CH60 41 A4
Rhona Cl CH63 43 B2
Rhona Dr WA5 14 C3
Rhone Ct CH3 142 A4
Rhos Ave SK8 239 E1
Rhuddlan Ct CH65 70 B1
Rhuddlan Rd CH1 117 B2
Rhum Cl CH65 70 B1
Rhyl St WA8 22 C4
Ribble Ave CW7 127 A1
Ribble Cl Culcheth WA3 4 C1
Widnes WA8 13 C2
Ribble Dr ST8 179 C1
Ribble Pl CW7 127 A1
Ribblesdale CH65 70 A2
Ribblesdale Ave CW12 157 A3
Ribblesdale Cl CH62 43 C3
Ribchester Gdns WA3 5 A2
Richard Cl WA7 24 A1
Richard Evans Com Prim Sch WA11 1 A3
Richard Moon St CW1 190 A2
Richard Reynolds Ct M44 11 C3
Richard St Crewe CW1 190 A3
Northwich CW9 104 B4
1 Stockport SK1 240 F6
Richards Croft CH3 142 A4
Richardson Cl
4 Sandbach CW11 174 B3
Shavington CW2 206 B3
Richardson St WA2 16 B4
Richbell Cl M44 11 C4
Richmond Ave
Handforth SK9 34 B2
Haydock WA11 1 A4
Runcorn WA7 23 C1
Warrington WA4 17 A2
Warrington, Grappenhall WA4 17 B2
Richmond Care Village CW5 205 A3
Richmond Cl Culcheth WA3 4 B2
Lymm WA13 19 A2
Sale M33 242 F5
Sandbach CW11 174 C4
Stalybridge SK15 242 D1
Richmond Cres CH3 119 B1
Richmond Ct
Altrincham WA14 238 B2
Cheadle SK8 239 C5
Ellesmere Port CH65 70 B2
Richmond Dr Lymm WA13 19 A2
Northwich CW9 104 A2
Richmond Gdns WA12 2 B1
Richmond Gn WA14 238 B2
Richmond Gr SK8 239 F1
Richmond Hill
17 Knutsford WA16 57 A1
Macclesfield SK11 112 C3
Richmond Hill Rd SK8 239 C6
Richmond Ho SK15 242 D1
Richmond Mews CH2 118 C1
Richmond Pl SK11 112 C3
Richmond Rd
Altrincham WA14 238 D5
Altrincham, Bowdon WA14 238 C2
Crewe CW1 190 C3
Romiley SK6 241 C3
Richmond St
2 Hyde SK14 241 E6
Stalybridge SK15 242 F2
Warrington WA4 17 A2
Widnes WA8 13 B1
Rickaby Cl CH63 43 B4
Ridding La WA7 50 A3
Riddings Ct
Altrincham WA15 238 F8
Northwich CW8 103 A2
Riddings La
Hartford CW8 103 A2
Wybunbury CW5 220 A4
Riddings Rd WA15 238 F2
Riddings The CH65 70 A2
Ridge Ave WA15 32 B3
Ridge Cl SK6 241 F2
Ridge Danyers Coll SK8 239 F3
Ridge Hill
Sutton Lane Ends SK11 113 A1
Utkinton CW6 146 A3
Ridge Hill La SK15 242 D3
Ridge Hill Prim Sch SK15 242 C3
Ridge Pk SK7 35 B3
Ridge The CW8 123 B4
Ridge View SK11 112 B3
Ridgeborne Cl WA5 7 B1
Ridgemont Ave SK4 240 B6
Ridgeway Golborne WA3 3 C4
Wilmslow SK9 60 C4
Ridgeway Cl CH66 69 B1
Ridgeway Gdns WA13 18 B2
Ridgeway Ho CH3 121 B2
Ridgeway The
Alvanley WA6 74 A1
Cronton WA8 12 B3
Disley SK12 38 B3
Heswall CH60 41 A4
Runcorn WA7 50 B3
Tarvin CH3 121 B2
Ridgewell Ave 4 WA3 3 B4
Ridgmont Rd SK7 35 C3
Ridgway St Crewe CW1 190 B3
Warrington WA2 16 B4
Ridgway The SK6 241 A1
Ridings Com Inf Sch The CH1 94 A1
Ridings The
Saughall CH1 117 A4
Wilmslow SK9 59 B2
Ridley Cl CW2 206 C1
Ridley Dr WA5 15 B2
Ridley Gr M33 242 F5
Ridley Rd SK10 87 C4
Ridley Wood Rd LL13 196 A2
Ridling La SK14 241 E6
Ridsdale 2 WA8 22 B4
Rifle Rd M21,M33 242 F7
Rigby Ave CW1 190 A4
Rigby Rd ST7 195 A2
Rigby St
Altrincham WA14 238 D
Golborne WA3 3 A
Rigby's Row CW5 204 C
Rigg St CW1 190 A
Riley Bank Mews WA6 74 A
Riley Cl CW11 174 C
Riley Dr WA7 49 A
Rileys Way ST7 209 C
Rilshaw La CW7 150 A
Rilston Ave WA3 4 B
Rimington Cl WA3 4 C
Rimsdale Cl Gatley SK8 239 A
Wistaston CW2 206 A
Ring Rd CH3 119 B
Ring-o-Bells La SK12 38 B
Ringsfield Rd L24 21 A
Ringstead Cl SK9 34 B
Ringstead Dr 15 SK9 34 B
Ringstone Way SK23 65 B
Ringway
Ellesmere Port CH66 69 C
Neston CH64 41 C
Waverton CH3 143 A
Ringway Cl SK10 87 A
Ringway Rd Runcorn WA7 23 B
Wythenshawe M22,M90 33 B
Ringway Rd W M22,M90 33 B
Ringway Trad Est M22 33 C
Ringwood Cl WA3 10 A
Ripley Ave SK8 35 A
Ripley Cl SK7 36 C
Ripley St WA5 15 C
Ripon Ave
Ellesmere Port CH66 69 B
Golborne WA3 3 B
Ripon Cl Macclesfield SK10 87 B
Newton-le-W WA12 2 B
Ripon Dr CW2 206 A
Ripon Row WA7 49 B
Ripon Wlk SK6 241 A
Rise The SK23 65 B
Riseley St SK11 112 B
Riseley's Pas 33 SK11 112 B
Rising Sun Cl SK11 112 A
Rising Sun Rd SK11 112 A
Risley Moss Local Nature Reserve Visitor Ctr* WA3 10 A
Risley Rd WA3 9 C
Rivacre Brow CH66 69 C
Rivacre Bsns Ctr CH66 69 C
Rivacre Rd CH62,CH65, CH66 44 B
Rivacre Valley Ctry Pk* CH66 69 B
Rivacre Valley Prim Sch CH66 69 C
River La Broughton CH4 140 C
Chester CH4 141 B
Farndon CH3 180 C
Partington M31 11 C
River Rd WA4 16 A
River St Congleton CW12 156 B
Macclesfield SK11 112 C
Wilmslow SK9 60 A
River View CW7 126 C
Riverbank Cl
Bollington SK10 87 C
Heswall CH60 40 C
Nantwich CW5 204 C
Riverbank Rd CH60 40 C
Riverdane Rd CW12 156 C
Rivermead Ave WA15 32 B
Riversdale Frodsham WA6 49 B
Warrington WA1 17 C
Riversdale Rd
Cheadle SK8 239 C
Runcorn WA7 49 C
Rivershill M33 242 A
Rivershill Gdns WA15 32 B
Riverside Nantwich CW5 204 B
Northwich CW9 104 A
Riverside Bsns Pk SK9 60 A
Riverside Cl WA1 16 B
Riverside Cres CW4 130 B
Riverside Ct Chester CH4 141 C
Langley SK11 113 B
Riverside Dr
Northwich CW8 103 C
Prestbury SK10 87 A
Riverside Gr CW2 189 B
Riverside Pk CH5 116 A
Riverside Ret Pk WA1 16 B
Riverside Trad Est CW8 103 C
Riverside Wlk CH64 66 B
Riversmead CH3 142 A
Riverton Rd M20 239 B
Riverview Rd CH64 66 C
Rivington Ct WA1 17 C
Rivington Gr M44 11 B
Rivington Rd
Altrincham WA15 238 F
Ellesmere Port CH65 70 B
Runcorn WA7 50 C
Rixton Ave WA5 15 C
Rixton Clay Pits Nature Reserve* WA3 10 C
Roaches The SK11 112 A
Roachill Cl WA14 238 B
Road Beta CW10 151 B
Road Five CW7 127 B
Road Four CW7 127 A
Road One Crewe CW1 207 B
Winsford CW7 127 A
Road St CW6 146 A
Road Three CW7 127 B
Road Two Crewe CW1 207 B

oad Two *continued*
Vinsford CW7 .127 A1
oadside Ct WA3 .3 B4
oan Ct SK11 .112 C4
oan House Way SK11 .112 C4
oan Mews SK11 .112 C4
oan Way SK9 .85 A4
ob La WA12 .3 C3
obert Moffat WA16 .29 B3
obert Salt Ct WA14 .238 E6
obert St Dukinfield SK14 .241 C7
Northwich CW8 .103 C3
Runcorn WA7 .23 B1
Sale M33 .242 E6
Warrington WA5 .15 C3
Widnes WA8 .13 A1
obert's Terr CH1 .118 A1
oberts Ave WA11 .1 A3
oberts Ct WA7 .49 C3
oberts Dr CW9 .104 B3
oberts Rd CW9 .80 A1
obin Cl Rainow SK10 .88 C3
Runcorn WA7 .50 B4
Sandbach CW11 .175 A4
obin Cres SK11 .112 B1
obin Hood Ave SK11 .112 B3
obin Hood La WA6 .73 A1
obin La Chelford SK11 .84 A2
Sutton Lane Ends SK11 .112 B1
obin's La SK7 .35 B4
obins Cft CH66 .69 C1
obins Cl SK7 .35 C4
obins La WA3 .4 B1
obins Way SK10 .88 A4
obinsbay Rd M22 .33 C4
obinson St Hyde SK14 .241 F7
Stockport SK3 .240 D3
obinsons Croft CH3 .142 A4
obinsway WA14 .238 C1
obson St WA1 .16 B3
obson Way 14 WA3 .3 C4
oby Gr WA5 .15 A3
oche Gdns SK8 .35 A3
ochester Cl Golborne WA3 .3 A4
Warrington WA5 .15 B3
ochester Cres CW1 .190 C3
ochester Dr CH65 .70 B2
ochester Ho SK10 .86 C1
ochford Ave M22 .33 B4
ock Bank SK23 .65 C3
ock Cotts CH5 .91 B1
ock Dr WA6 .49 B1
ock Farm Cl CH64 .67 A3
ock Farm Dr CH64 .67 A3
ock Farm Gr CH64 .67 A3
ock La
Burwardsley CW6 .184 B3
Chester CH2 .237 A4
Widnes WA8 .12 C2
ock Rd CH5 .91 C1
ock St SK22 .39 B4
ock The WA6 .73 B1
ockfield Cl WA8 .12 B1
ockfield Dr WA6 .73 B1
ockford Lodge WA16 .57 B1
ockhouse La ST7 .210 B4
ockingham Cl WA3 .10 B3
ocklands La CH63 .42 B4
ocklee Gdns CH64 .67 A3
ocklife La CH6 .91 A2
ocklynes SK6 .241 B2
ocksavage Expressway
WA7 .49 B3
ockside ST7 .195 B3
ockwood Ave CW2 .190 A2
ockwood Cl CW2 .190 A2
ocky La Heswall CH60 .40 C4
Tattenhall CH3 .182 C4
ocky La S CH60 .41 A4
oddy La WA6 .75 C1
ode Ct 7 CW12 .156 C2
ode Hall* ST7 .194 A4
ode Heath Prim Sch
ST7 .193 C4
ode House Cl ST7 .193 C4
ode The ST7 .193 B2
odeheath Cl SK9 .60 B4
odepool Cl SK9 .34 B1
odgers Cl WA6 .49 A1
odmill Dr SK8 .239 A4
odney St
Ashton-u-Lyne OL6 .242 A4
Macclesfield SK11 .112 B4
oe Pk CW12 .178 C1
oe St Congleton CW12 .156 C1
Macclesfield SK11 .112 B4
oebourne Rise CH1 .117 B2
oebuck La M33 .242 A6
oebuck St CW1 .190 B3
oeburn Way WA5 .14 B2
oedean Wlk CW1 .190 B3
oehampton Dr WA7 .49 C4
oehurst La CW7 .126 B1
oemarsh Ct WA7 .49 C3
oewood La
Macclesfield SK10 .88 A1
Macclesfield, Higherfence
SK10 .113 A4
often Ind Est CH66 .43 B1
okeby Ct WA7 .24 B3
okeden WA12 .2 B2
oland Ave WA7 .22 C1
olands Wlk WA7 .23 C1
olleston St WA2 .16 A3
olls Ave CW1 .190 A4
olt Cres CW10 .151 B4
oman Cl
Newton-le-W WA12 .2 B1

Roman Cl *continued*
Runcorn WA7 .23 C1
Roman Ct CH64 .66 C4
Roman Dr CH1 .117 B3
Roman Rd Stockport SK4 .240 E6
Warrington WA4 .16 B1
Roman Rise CW8 .78 A2
Roman Way CW11 .174 C4
Romanes St CW8 .103 C4
Romford Ave M34 .241 A8
Romiley Prec SK6 .241 C2
Romiley Prim Sch SK6 .241 C2
Romiley Rd CH66 .69 C3
Romiley Sta SK6 .241 C2
Romney Cl Neston CH64 .66 C4
Widnes WA8 .13 C1
Romney Croft CH64 .66 C4
Romney Way CH64 .66 C4
Romsey Dr SK8 .35 B3
Rona Ave CH65 .70 B1
Ronald Dr WA2 .9 A1
Ronaldshay WA8 .13 C1
Ronaldsway Halewood L26 .21 A4
Heswall CH60 .40 C3
Ronan Rd WA8 .22 C3
Rood Hill CW12 .156 B2
Rook Rd WA4 .16 C2
Rook St CW2 .190 B1
Rookery Cl
14 Nantwich CW5 .204 C3
Sandbach CW11 .174 B3
Rookery Ct 14 CW11 .174 B3
Rookery Dr
Nantwich CW5 .204 C2
Tattenhall CH3 .166 A1
Rookery Gdns CW9 .103 C2
Rookery Rd
Kidsgrove ST7 .195 B2
Tilston SY14 .198 A2
Rookery Rise CW7 .127 A1
Rookery The
Broughton CH4 .139 A2
Newton-le-W WA12 .2 B2
Rookerypool Cl SK9 .34 B1
Rookfield M33 .242 C7
Rookfield Ave M33 .242 C7
Rooks Way CH60 .40 C4
Roome St WA2 .16 B4
Rooth St SK4 .240 D6
Rope Bank Ave CW2 .206 A4
Rope La CW2 .206 A3
Rope Wlk CW12 .156 B2
Ropewalk The CH64 .41 B1
Rocam Ct WA7 .49 C3
Roscoe Ave
Newton-le-W WA12 .2 C2
Warrington WA2 .16 B4
Roscoe Cres WA7 .48 C4
Roscoe Park Est WA14 .238 E8
Roscoe Rd M44 .11 C4
Roscoe St SK3 .240 D4
Roscoes Yd 3 WA16 .57 A1
Roscote Cl CH60 .40 C4
Roscote The CH60 .40 C4
Rose Ave WA11 .1 C3
Rose Bank WA13 .18 C2
Rose Cl WA7 .50 B3
Rose Cnr CH3 .166 A1
Rose Cotts CW12 .154 C3
Rose Cres WA8 .22 C4
Rose Gdns CH64 .66 C3
Rose Lea Cl WA8 .13 A2
Rose St Stockport SK5 .240 F7
Widnes WA8 .22 C4
Rose Terr Crewe CW1 .190 B3
Stalybridge SK15 .242 D1
Rose Vale SK8 .239 B1
Rose View Ave WA8 .13 A1
Rose Wlk 7 M31 .11 C2
Roseacre Dr SK8 .239 C1
Rosebank Cl CW7 .149 C4
Rosebank Rd M44 .11 B2
Rosebank Sch CW8 .78 A2
Rosebank Wlk CW8 .78 A2
Roseberry Way CW1 .191 B2
Rosecroft CH62 .43 B3
Rosedale Ave
Golborne WA3 .3 B4
Warrington WA1 .17 B4
Rosedale Rd SK4 .240 D8
Rosedene Cl CH2 .118 C4
Rosefield Ave WA13 .18 C2
Rosefield Cl SK3 .240 E1
Roseheath Com Prim Sch
L26 .21 A4
Roseheath Dr L26 .21 A3
Rosehill Ave WA9 .6 A3
Rosehill Rd CW2 .190 A1
Rosemary Ave
Runcorn WA7 .49 C2
Warrington WA4 .16 C1
Rosemary Cl
Broughton CH4 .139 B2
Warrington WA5 .15 B3
Rosemary Dr WA12 .2 C2
Rosemary La LL12 .161 B1
Rosemary Row CH3 .166 A1
Rosemary Wlk M31 .11 C1
Rosemere Dr CH66 .94 C4
Rosemoor Gdns WA4 .26 C3
Rosendale Dr WA3 .10 A3
Rosetree Mdw CW9 .80 A1
Rosevale Rd ST5 .210 C1
Roseville Dr CW12 .179 A4
Roseway SK11 .112 B3
Rosewood Ave
Chester CH2 .118 B3
Frodsham WA6 .74 B4

Rosewood Ave *continued*
Stockport SK4 .240 A5
Warrington WA1 .16 C4
Rosewood Cl CW1 .190 C3
Rosewood Dr CW7 .126 A1
Rosewood Gdns 4 M33 .242 F5
Rosewood Gr CH1 .117 A4
Roslyn Rd SK3 .240 F1
Ross Ave SK3 .240 E1
Ross Cl WA5 .15 B4
Ross Dr CH66 .69 B3
Ross Rd CH65 .70 A3
Ross St WA8 .13 A1
Rossall Cl L24 .21 C1
Rossall Dr SK7 .35 C3
Rossall Gr CH66 .69 B3
Rossall Rd
Warrington WA5 .15 A2
Widnes WA8 .13 B1
Rossbank Rd CH65 .70 A4
Rosscliffe Rd CH65 .70 A3
Rossenclough Rd SK9 .34 B1
Rossendale Rd SK8 .34 B4
Rossett Ave 1 M22 .33 B4
Rossett Bsns Village
LL12 .162 B1
Rossett Cl
Northwich CW9 .103 C2
Warrington WA5 .7 C1
Rossett Pk LL12 .162 B1
Rossfield Rd CH65 .70 A3
Rossfield Rd N CH65 .70 A4
Rosslyn Cl CH5 .116 A1
Rosslyn La CW8 .102 A2
Rosslyn Rd Cheadle SK8 .239 D1
Chester CH3 .119 A2
Rossmill La WA15 .32 A4
Rossmore Bsns Pk CH65 .70 A4
Rossmore Gdns CH66 .69 B3
Rossmore Ind Est CH65 .70 A3
Rossmore Rd E CH65 .69 C4
Rossmore Rd W CH66 .69 B4
Rossmore Sch CH66 .69 B4
Rossmount Rd CH65 .70 A3
Rosswood Rd CH65 .70 A3
Rostherne Ave
Ellesmere Port CH66 .69 C2
Golborne WA3 .3 B4
High Lane SK6 .37 C4
Rostherne Cl WA5 .15 B2
Rostherne Cres WA8 .12 B1
Rostherne Ct WA14 .238 D3
Rostherne Rd Sale M33 .242 F5
Stockport SK3 .240 F1
Wilmslow SK9 .59 C2
Rostherne St 1 WA14 .238 D3
Rostherne Way CW11 .174 C4
Rosthernmere Rd SK8 .239 F4
Rostrevor Rd SK3 .240 E1
Rothay Dr WA5 .14 B2
Rothbury Cl WA7 .49 B3
Rother Dr CH65 .70 A4
Rother Dr Bsns Ctr CH65 .70 A4
Rotherhead Dr SK11 .112 A3
Rotherwood Rd SK9 .59 B3
Rothesay Cl WA7 .23 C1
Rothesay Dr CH62 .43 C2
Rothesay Rd CH4 .141 A4
Rough Bank CW12 .179 C4
Rough Heys La SK11 .111 A4
Roughlea Ave WA3 .4 B2
Roughley Ave WA5 .15 B2
Roughlyn Cres CH4 .140 C1
Roughwood La CW11 .176 A1
Round Gdns SK10 .88 A4
Round Hill Mdw CH3 .142 A4
Round Mdw SK10 .88 C3
Round Thorn WA3 .9 A4
Round Way SK22 .39 B4
Roundabout The WA8 .12 B3
Roundcroft SK6 .241 E3
Roundhey SK8 .34 B4
Roundway SK7 .35 B3
Roundy La SK10 .62 C3
Routledge St WA8 .13 A1
Row The CW7 .126 B1
Rowan Ave WA3 .3 C4
Rowan Cl Alsager ST7 .193 B2
Middlewich CW10 .151 C3
Runcorn WA7 .49 B4
Sandbach CW11 .174 C4
Warrington WA5 .14 C3
Winsford CW7 .126 B2
Rowan Ct 4 Hyde SK14 .241 E5
Wilmslow SK9 .60 A4
Rowan Dr SK8 .35 B4
Rowan Gr CH5 .91 B1
Rowan Lodge SK7 .35 C4
Rowan Pk CH3 .142 C4
Rowan Pl CH2 .119 A2
Rowan Rd CW8 .102 B4
Rowan St SK14 .241 F5
Rowan Way SK10 .87 C1
Rowan Wlk M31 .11 C1
Rowans The CH4 .139 A2
Rowanside SK10 .86 C3
Rowanside Dr SK9 .60 C4
Rowcliffe Ave CH4 .141 A2
Rowena Ct CH2 .118 C2
Rowland Cl WA2 .9 A2
Rowlands View CW6 .146 A4
Rowley Bank La WA16 .29 A1
Rowley Rd SK7 .36 C4
Rowley Way WA16 .82 A4
Rowson Ct 2 M33 .242 D6
Rowson Dr M44 .11 B3
Rowswood Farm WA4 .25 C3
Rowthorn Cl WA8 .22 C4

Rowton Brideg Rd CH3 .142 C4
Rowton Cl 12 CW9 .103 C2
Rowton La CH3 .142 C3
Rowton Rd CW2 .189 B2
Roxborough Cl WA5 .7 A3
Roxburgh Cl SK10 .87 A1
Roxburgh Rd CH66 .68 C3
Roxby Way WA16 .82 A4
Roxholme Wlk M22 .33 B4
Royal Ave WA8 .12 A1
Royal Gdns
Altrincham WA14 .20 C1
Northwich CW9 .103 C2
Royal George St SK1,
SK3 .240 F4
Royal La CW6 .147 A2
Royal Mdws SK10 .87 A1
Royal Mews CW9 .104 B3
Royal Oak Yd 4 SK1 .240 F5
Royal Pl WA8 .22 A4
Royal Rd SK12 .38 B3
Royal Schools for the Deaf
The SK8 .34 B3
Royal Sh Arc The 7
CH64 .66 C4
Royce Ave WA15 .238 E5
Royce Cl CW1 .190 A4
Royce Ct WA16 .56 C1
Royden Ave Irlam M44 .11 C4
Runcorn WA7 .49 A4
Royds Cl CW8 .103 A2
Royds Ct CW11 .174 B3
Roylands Dr CW10 .151 B4
Royle St Congleton CW12 .156 B2
Northwich CW9 .104 A4
Stockport SK1 .240 F3
Winsford CW7 .126 C1
Royle's Pl CW8 .103 B3
Royleen Dr WA6 .74 B3
Royley Carr Flats SK6 .241 A3
Royon Dr SK3 .240 B3
Royston Ave WA1 .17 A4
Royston Cl
Ellesmere Port CH66 .69 C2
2 Golborne WA3 .3 C4
Rozel Cres WA5 .15 A3
Rudd Ave WA9 .1 A1
Rudheath Cl CW2 .189 B3
Rudheath Com Prim Sch
CW9 .104 B3
Rudheath High Sch
CW9 .104 B4
Rudheath Way CW9 .104 C3
Rudloe Ct WA2 .8 C1
Rudstone Cl CH66 .69 A3
Rudyard Cl SK11 .112 A3
Rue De Bohars CW6 .168 B4
Rufford Ave SK14 .241 F6
Rufford Cl Widnes WA8 .12 B1
Wistaston CW2 .206 A4
Rufford Ct WA1 .17 C4
Rufus Ct CH1 .237 A3
Rugby Cl SK10 .87 C2
Rugby Dr SK10 .87 C2
Rugby Ho SK10 .87 B2
Rugby Rd CH65 .70 B2
Ruislip Ct WA2 .8 C1
Runcorn Docks Rd WA7 .22 C1
Runcorn East Sta WA7 .50 B4
Runcorn Rd Barnton CW8 .78 A1
Little Leigh CW8 .77 B3
Moore WA4 .25 B3
Runcorn Spur Rd WA7 .49 B4
Runcorn Sta WA7 .22 C1
Runger La M90,WA15 .32 C4
Runnell The CH64 .41 B2
Runnymede WA1 .17 B4
Runnymede Cl SK3 .240 C2
Runnymede Ct
Stockport SK3 .240 C2
2 Widnes WA8 .13 B1
Runnymede Dr WA11 .1 A3
Runnymede Gdns 5
WA8 .13 B1
Runnymede Wlk 7 WA8 .13 B1
Rupert Row WA7 .50 A4
Ruscoe Ave CW11 .174 C3
Ruscolm Cl WA5 .14 B4
Rush Gdns WA13 .19 A2
Rushes Mdw WA13 .19 A3
Rushey Cl WA15 .32 B4
Rushfield Cres WA7 .50 A3
Rushfield Rd Cheadle SK8 .35 A3
Chester CH4 .141 A3
Rushgreen Rd WA13 .19 A2
Rushmere Cl SK10 .62 C1
Rushmere La CH3 .163 C2
Rushmore Gr WA1 .17 A4
Rusholme Cl L26 .21 A3
Rushside Rd SK8 .35 A3
Rushton Ave WA12 .2 A2
Rushton CE Prim Sch
SK11 .159 A1
Rushton Cl
Northwich CW9 .104 B4
Widnes WA8 .12 C2
Rushton Dr Chester CH2 .118 C4
Hough Common CW2 .206 C1
Middlewich CW10 .151 B4
Romiley SK6 .241 C3
Rushton Fold SK10 .61 A1
Rushton La CW6 .147 B3
Rushton Rd Cheadle SK8 .35 A3
Stockport SK3 .240 B3
Rushy View WA12 .2 A2
Rushyfield Cres SK6 .241 D3
Ruskin Ave
Newton-le-W WA12 .2 B2

Ruskin Ave *continued*
Warrington WA2 .8 B1
Ruskin Ct WA16 .57 A1
Ruskin Dr CH65 .70 B2
Ruskin Gdns SK6 .241 A3
Ruskin Gr SK6 .241 A3
Ruskin Rd
Congleton CW12 .156 B1
Crewe CW2 .190 B1
Ruskin Sch The CW2 .190 B1
Ruskin Way WA16 .57 A2
Rusland Ct M33 .242 A7
Russel Ct WA8 .13 A2
Russell Ave Alsager ST7 .193 B3
High Lane SK6 .37 C4
Sale M33 .242 D7
Russell Cl CW12 .179 A4
Russell Dr CW1 .191 B2
Russell Rd Runcorn WA7 .48 C4
Winsford CW7 .149 B4
Russell St
Ashton-u-Lyne OL6 .242 A4
Chester CH2 .237 C3
Hyde SK14 .241 D7
Russet Cl CW10 .128 A1
Russet Rd CW8 .102 B4
Russett Sch The CW8 .102 C4
Rutherford Cl SK14 .241 D6
Rutherford Dr WA16 .82 B4
Rutherford Way 6
SK14 .241 D6
Ruthin Ave SK8 .239 E2
Ruthin Cl WA5 .7 C2
Ruthin Ct CH65 .70 B2
Ruthin Wlk WA6 .73 A1
Rutland Ave Denton M34 .241 B6
Golborne WA3 .3 B4
Halewood L26 .21 A4
Warrington WA4 .26 A4
Rutland Cl
Ashton-u-Lyne OL6 .242 A2
Congleton CW12 .156 C2
Gatley SK8 .239 B6
Sandbach CW11 .174 B3
Rutland Dr
Middlewich CW10 .151 B4
Weaverham CW8 .77 B1
Rutland La M33 .242 F6
Rutland Pl CH2 .119 A3
Rutland Rd
Altrincham WA14 .238 D6
Hazel Grove SK7 .36 C4
Irlam M44 .11 B3
Kidsgrove ST7 .195 A1
Macclesfield SK11 .112 B2
Partington M31 .11 C1
Rutland St
Ashton-u-Lyne OL6 .242 A2
Runcorn WA7 .22 C1
Rutter Ave WA5 .7 C1
Ryburn Cl CW2 .207 A2
Ryburn Rd SK11 .112 A3
Rydal Ave High Lane SK6 .37 C4
Warrington WA4 .16 A1
Rydal Cl
Ellesmere Port CH65 .70 B1
Gatley SK8 .239 B4
Holmes Chapel CW4 .130 A1
Neston CH64 .66 C3
Winsford CW7 .126 B2
Rydal Ct CW12 .156 A1
Rydal Dr WA15 .32 B4
Rydal Gr Chester CH4 .141 A3
Helsby WA6 .73 A1
Runcorn WA7 .49 A4
Rydal Mount CW1 .173 A1
Rydal Pl SK11 .112 A3
Rydal St WA12 .2 B2
Rydal Way Alsager ST7 .193 B3
Widnes WA8 .12 B1
Rydal Wlk SK15 .242 D3
Ryde Ave SK4 .240 B6
Ryde Cl CW1 .190 A4
Ryder Ave WA14 .238 E7
Ryder Rd Warrington WA1 .17 B4
Widnes WA8 .13 A2
Ryders St CW8 .103 C4
Rye Cl ST7 .193 A2
Ryebank Ave CW1 .190 A4
Ryebank Way SK10 .87 B2
Ryecroft CH2 .72 A2
Ryecroft Cl CW10 .151 A4
Ryecroft La
Duddon CH3,CW6 .144 B3
Mobberley WA16 .57 C2
Ryecroft Rd CH60 .41 B4
Ryedale Cl SK4 .240 B7
Ryedale Way CW12 .179 B4
Ryehills ST7 .209 C1
Rylands Cl SY14 .213 A2
Rylands St
Warrington WA1 .16 A3
5 Widnes WA8 .23 A4
Ryle St SK11 .112 B3
Ryle's Park Rd SK11 .112 B3
Ryles Cl SK11 .112 B3
Ryles Cres SK11 .112 B3
Ryles Ho SK11 .112 B3
Ryles Park High Sch
SK11 .112 B3
Ryleys La SK9 .59 C1
Ryleys Sch The SK9 .59 C1

S

Sabre Cl WA7 50 B4
Sack La CW9 54 C3
Sacred Heart RC Prim Sch
WA5 15 C3
Saddleback Dr SK10 86 C4
Saddlers Rise WA7 50 B4
Sade Ct CW1 190 A3
Sadler Cl CW7 126 B1
Sadler Rd CW7 126 B1
Sadler St WA8 13 B1
Sadler's Cl CW4 130 A2
Sadlers La CW6 124 A1
Sadlers Wells CW6 185 C4
Safferon Cl WA2 9 A1
Saffron Cl WA3 3 C4
Saffron Wlk M31 11 C1
Sagars Rd SK9 34 B2
Sage Cl WA2 9 B1
Saighton CE Prim Sch
CH3 142 C1
Saighton La CH3 142 C1
SS Peter & Paul RC High Sch
WA8 12 C1
St Aelred's RC Tech Coll
WA12 2 B2
St Alban Rd WA5 14 C3
St Alban's RC Prim Sch
SK10 86 C1
St Alban's RC Sch WA5 15 C3
St Albans Cl WA11 2 A4
St Albans Cres WA14 238 C8
St Albans Dr CW5 204 C2
St Albans Pl SK22 39 B4
St Albans St SK22 39 B4
St Ambrose Coll WA15 32 A4
St Ambrose Prim Sch
L24 21 A1
St Ambrose RC Prim Sch
SK3 240 E1
St Ambrose Rd WA8 13 B1
St Andrew's Ave WA15 238 F7
St Andrew's CE Prim Sch
WA2 8 B2
St Andrew's Cl SK6 241 B1
St Andrew's Gdns ST7 193 C1
St Andrew's Rd
Ellesmere Port CH65 70 C2
Macclesfield SK11 112 A4
St Andrews Cl
Northwich CW9 104 C4
Stockport SK4 240 B8
Warrington WA2 9 A2
St Andrews Ct
Altrincham WA15 238 F3
Crewe CW2 190 B1
Ellesmere Port CH65 70 C1
St Andrews Dr
Holmes Chapel CW4 130 A1
Kidsgrove ST7 195 B2
St Andrews Rd
Gatley SK8 239 C1
Stockport SK4 240 B8
St Andrews Sch (Special Needs) CH4 141 B4
St Andrews Wlk
Mickle Trafford CH2 96 C1
New Mills SK22 39 B4
St Ann's Ave CW10 151 B4
St Ann's CE Prim Sch
WA2 16 B4
St Ann's Rd CW10 151 B4
St Ann's Rd N SK8 239 B2
St Ann's Rd S SK8 34 B4
St Ann's Sq SK8 34 B4
St Anne St CH2 237 B3
St Anne's Ct M33 242 C6
St Anne's Dr M34 241 A8
St Anne's Hospl WA14 238 C3
St Anne's La CW5 204 B3
St Anne's Prim Sch
M34 241 A8
St Anne's RC Prim Sch
CW5 204 C2
St Anne's Rd Hyde M34 241 A8
Widnes WA8 13 A1
St Annes Ave WA4 17 A1
St Annes Ave E WA4 17 A1
St Annes CE Prim Sch
M33 242 D6
St Annes RC High Sch
SK4 240 D8
St Anns St M33 242 F5
St Anthony Pl WA2 8 A3
St Anthony's RC Prim Sch
CH4 140 C3
St Asaph Dr WA5 7 C2
St Asaph Rd CH66 94 C4
St Augustine's Ave WA4 16 C2
St Augustine's RC Prim Sch
Runcorn WA7 24 A1
Warrington WA4 16 C2
St Augustine's Rd SK3 240 B4
St Austel Cl WA5 14 C2
St Austell Ave SK10 86 C1
St Austell Cl
Macclesfield SK10 86 C1
Runcorn WA7 50 A3
St Austell Dr SK8 34 A4
St Austins La WA1 16 A2
St Barnabas CE Prim Sch
Macclesfield SK11 112 B3
St Barnabas CE Prim Sch *continued*
Warrington WA5 15 C3
St Barnabas Ct SK11 112 B3
St Barnabas Pl WA5 15 C3
St Basil's RC Prim Sch
WA8 12 A1
St Bede's Ave CW8 77 B1
St Bede's RC Inf Sch
WA8 13 A1
St Bede's RC Jun Sch
WA8 13 A1
St Bede's RC Prim Sch
CW8 102 C4
St Bees Cl SK8 239 B3
St Benedict's RC Prim Sch
Warrington WA2 16 B4
Wilmslow SK9 34 C2
St Benedicts Cl WA2 16 A4
St Bernard's RC Prim Sch
CH65 70 B2
St Berteline's CE Prim Sch
WA7 50 B4
St Brannocks Rd SK8 35 A4
St Brides Cl WA5 14 C2
St Bridget's RC Prim Sch
WA2 8 C2
St Bridgets Cl WA2 8 C2
St Bridgets Ct CH4 141 A3
St Catherine's RC Prim Sch
WA3 3 C4
St Catherines Dr CW8 103 A2
St Chad's Ave SK6 241 C2
St Chad's CE Prim Sch
ST5 210 B1
St Chad's Fields CW7 149 B3
St Chad's Gr SK6 241 C2
St Chad's RC High Sch
WA7 49 B4
St Chad's Rd CH1 117 C2
St Chads Cl CW5 220 A4
St Chads Way TF9 236 B1
St Christopher's Dr SK6 241 A2
St Christopher's RC Prim Sch
SK6 241 A2
St Christophers Cl CH2 118 B4
St Clairs St CW2 190 B1
St Clare's RC Prim Sch
CH4 141 A3
St Clement's RC Prim Sch
WA7 49 A4
St David Rd CH62 44 A3
St David's Ave SK6 241 B2
St David's High Sch
CH4 140 B3
St David's Terr CH4 140 B3
St Davids Cl M33 242 A5
St Davids Dr
Ellesmere Port CH66 94 C4
Warrington WA5 7 C1
St Davids' Ret Pk CH4 140 B4
St Edward's RC Prim Sch
Macclesfield SK11 112 B3
Runcorn WA7 23 A2
St Edwards Cl SK11 112 B3
St Elmo Pk SK12 37 B2
St Elphin's (Fairfield) CE Prim Sch WA1 16 B3
St Elphins Cl WA1 16 B3
St Gabriel's RC Prim Sch
ST7 193 B2
St Gabriels Ct ST7 193 B2
St George's CE Prim Sch
Hyde SK14 241 D5
Stockport SK2 240 F2
St George's Cl WA16 82 B4
St George's Cres
Chester CH4 237 C1
Waverton CH3 143 A3
St George's Ct
Altrincham WA14 238 B7
Widnes WA8 22 B4
St George's Gdns M34 241 A5
St George's Pl SK11 112 B4
St George's Rd CW7 149 B4
St George's St
Macclesfield SK11 112 B3
Stalybridge SK15 242 D3
St George's Way
Northwich CW9 103 C3
Thornton Hough CH63 42 A4
St Georges Ave CH66 94 C4
St Georges Cl WA4 26 C2
St Georges Ct 5 SK14 241 E6
St Georges Dr SK14 241 D5
St Georges Rd SK22 39 B4
St Gerards RC Prim Sch
WA8 23 A4
St Giles Dr SK14 241 F6
St Gregory's RC High Sch
WA5 15 B3
St Gregory's RC Prim Sch
SK10 87 C4
St Helen's Coll (Newton Campus) WA12 2 A2
St Helens CE Prim Sch
WA3 11 A1
St Helens Cl WA3 11 A2
St Helens Rd Golborne WN7 4 A4
5 Northwich CW9 104 A4
St Hilary's Sch
Alderley Edge SK9 60 A1
Alderley Edge SK9 85 A4
St Hilda's Dr WA6 49 B1
St Hugh's Cl WA14 238 E8
St Hugh's RC Prim Sch
WA15 238 F8
St Ives Ave SK8 240 A2
St Ives Cl SK10 86 C1
St Ives Pk CH5 116 A2
St Ives Way CH5 116 A2
St James Ave
Chester CH2 118 C4
Congleton CW12 156 B1
Warren SK11 111 C1
St James CE Prim Sch
Haydock WA11 1 C3
Kettleshulme SK23 64 C2
St James Cl Audlem CW3 230 A2
Frodsham WA6 49 B1
St James Ct
Altrincham WA15 238 E4
Audley ST7 209 B1
Cheadle SK8 34 C3
Connah's Quay CH5 91 B1
Manchester M20 239 B8
St James Dr M33 242 A5
St James St
Ashton-u-Lyne OL6 242 A2
Chester CH2 237 B3
St James Terr 10 CW7 149 A4
St James Wlk 19 CW8 103 C4
St James' CE Prim Sch
CW3 230 A3
St James' Ct ST8 179 C2
St James' Dr SK9 60 A3
St James' RC High Sch
SK8 34 C3
St James' Sq SK22 39 B4
St James' Way SK8 34 C3
St James's CE Jun Sch
CH2 119 A2
St John Ave WA4 16 A1
St John Fisher RC Prim Sch
Denton M34 241 B5
Widnes WA8 13 B1
St John St Chester CH1 237 B2
Newton-le-W WA12 2 A2
St John The Evangelist CE Prim Sch SK11 112 A4
St John The Evangelist RC Prim Sch (Annexe)
ST7 194 C1
St John Vianney Sch
SK4 240 B6
St John's Ave
Knutsford WA16 56 C1
Lostock Gralam CW9 79 C2
St John's CE Prim Sch
Bollington SK10 88 A4
Kingsley WA6 75 B1
Sandbach CW11 175 C3
St John's Cl
Northwich CW9 104 C4
Romiley SK6 241 B2
St John's Ct
Altrincham WA14 238 D3
Hyde SK14 241 F7
Knutsford WA16 57 B1
St John's Dr SK14 241 F7
St John's Rd
Altrincham WA14 238 D3
Bebington CH62 44 A3
Chester CH4 237 C1
Congleton CW12 156 C3
Knutsford WA16 57 A1
19 Macclesfield SK11 112 B4
Wilmslow SK9 59 C2
St John's Rear Rd CH4 237 C1
St John's St WA7 23 A2
St John's Way
Cuddington CW8 102 A1
Sandbach CW11 175 C3
St John's Wood ST7 194 C1
St John's Wood Com Sch
WA16 57 B1
St Johns Dr CW7 149 A4
St Joseph's Cl WA5 14 C3
St Joseph's RC Prim Sch
Sale M33 242 B6
Stockport SK1 240 F5
Warrington WA5 14 C3
Winsford CW7 149 A4
St Josephs Way CW5 205 A3
St Katherines Way WA1 16 B3
St Kilda Cl CH65 70 B1
St Lawrence Ct CW5 204 C3
St Lawrence Rd
Frodsham WA6 74 A4
Hyde M34 241 A7
St Leonard's Way CW3 232 B1
St Leonards Dr WA15 238 F6
St Lesmo Ct SK3 240 C3
St Lesmo Rd SK3 240 C3
St Lewis RC Prim Sch
WA3 4 A1
St Luke's Ave WA3 3 B4
St Luke's CE Prim Sch
WA3 3 C4
St Luke's Cres WA8 13 A2
St Luke's RC Prim Sch
WA6 74 B4
St Luke's Way WA6 49 A1
St Lukes Cl CW4 130 B2
St Margaret's Ave WA2 8 B1
St Margaret's CE Prim Sch
WA2 8 B1
St Margaret's Cl WA14 238 C4
St Margaret's Rd
Altrincham WA14 238 C4
Stockport SK8 240 A2
St Mark's Ave WA14 238 A5
St Mark's CE Prim Sch
CW9 53 B2
St Mark's Prim Sch SK6 241 A4
St Mark's St Haydock WA11 1 A3
St Mark's St *continued*
Romiley SK6 241 A4
St Marks Cres CH66 94 C4
St Marks Rd CH4 140 C3
St Martin's Ave SK4 240 C6
St Martin's Cl SK14 241 F6
St Martin's Rd ST7 210 C3
St Martin's Way CH1 237 A3
St Martins Dr CH66 69 B1
St Martins La WA7 50 B4
St Martins RC Prim Sch
WA7 50 B4
St Mary's Ave CW8 77 B1
St Mary's CE Prim Sch
CW12 178 A4
St Mary's CE Prim Sch
Bebington CH62 44 A3
Bosley SK11 158 B4
Irlam M44 11 B3
Sale M33 242 A6
St Mary's Cl Alsager ST7 193 B3
Hale L24 21 C1
Warrington WA4 26 B3
St Mary's Ct CW12 156 A1
St Mary's Dr Cheadle SK8 239 F6
Whitegate CW7 126 A4
St Mary's Halton CE Prim Sch
WA7 50 A4
St Mary's Hill CH4 237 B1
St Mary's Inf Sch CH1 237 B1
St Mary's RC Inf Sch WA12 2 B2
St Mary's RC Jun Sch
WA12 2 A2
St Mary's RC Prim Sch
Ashton-u-Lyne OL6 242 A4
Congleton CW12 156 B2
Crewe CW2 190 A1
Middlewich CW10 151 B4
New Mills SK22 39 A4
Stockport SK4 240 E6
St Mary's Rd
Altrincham WA14 238 C3
Disley SK12 38 B3
Dodleston CH4 162 A4
Nantwich CW5 204 C4
New Mills SK22 39 A4
Runcorn WA8 23 C1
Warrington WA5 14 C3
Widnes WA7 23 A2
St Mary's St Crewe CW1 190 B2
Warrington WA4 16 B2
St Marys Ct CW5 204 A4
St Matthew's CE Prim Sch
SK3 240 E4
St Matthew's Rd SK3 240 D4
St Matthew's Terr SK3 240 D4
St Matthews CE Prim Sch
WA4 26 C1
St Matthews Cl
Haslington CW1 191 B2
Warrington WA4 26 B4
St Mawes Cl WA8 12 C1
St Mawes Ct SK10 86 C1
St Mawgan Ct WA2 8 C1
St Michael's Ave SK7 35 C4
St Michael's Cl
Little Leigh CW8 77 B3
Widnes WA8 22 B4
St Michael's RC Prim Sch
WA8 22 B4
St Michael's Rd WA8 22 B4
St Michael's Road Ind Est
WA8 22 B3
St Michael's View CW1 190 A3
St Michael's Way CW10 128 B1
St Monica's RC Prim Sch
WA4 26 B4
St Monicas Cl WA4 26 B4
St Nicholas Ct CW5 204 C3
St Nicholas RC High Sch
CW8 103 B3
St Olave St CH4 237 B1
St Oliver Plunkett RC Prim Sch WA3 9 C2
St Oswald's CE Prim Sch
CH1 94 C1
St Oswald's Cres CW11 153 C3
St Oswald's RC Prim Sch
WA1 16 C4
St Oswalds Cl
Malpas SY14 213 A2
Winwick WA2 8 A3
St Oswalds Way CH1 237 B3
St Paul of the Cross RC Prim Sch WA5 6 C3
St Paul's CE Prim Sch
SK15 242 F2
St Paul's CE Prim Sch
CW6 146 A4
St Paul's Cl CW1 190 B2
St Paul's Ct Hyde SK14 241 E7
Warrington WA2 16 A3
St Paul's Hill Rd SK14 241 F6
St Paul's Inf Sch CH2 237 C3
St Paul's Pl 2 CW9 79 A1
St Paul's RC Prim Sch
SK14 241 F8
St Paul's Rd
5 Macclesfield SK11 112 C4
Stockport SK4 240 B8
Widnes WA8 23 A4
St Paul's St Crewe CW1 190 B2
Hyde SK14 241 E7
Stalybridge SK15 242 F2
St Pauls Cl SK15 242 F2
St Pauls Gdns CH66 69 A4
St Pauls RC Prim Sch
SK12 36 C1
St Pauls Trad Est SK15 242
St Peter's Ave WA16 56
St Peter's CE Prim Sch
Duddon CW6 145
Heswall CH60 40
Newton-le-W WA12 2
St Peter's Cl Heswall CH60 40
Lymm WA13 19
St Peter's Ct WA2 16
St Peter's Dr Hyde SK14 241
Little Budworth CW6 147
St Peter's RC Prim Sch
Stalybridge SK15 242
Warrington WA1 17
St Peter's Rise CW11 174
St Peter's Sq SK1 240
St Peter's Way WA2 16
St Peters Rd CW12 156
St Peters Way CH2 119
St Petersgate SK1 240
St Philip (Westbrook) CE Prim Sch WA5 7
St Saviour's CE Prim Sch
ST7 194
St Saviour's RC Inf Sch
CH66 69
St Saviour's RC Jun Sch
CH66 69
St Saviour's St ST7 194
St Stephen Rd WA5 14
St Stephen's Ave WA2 8
St Stephen's RC Prim Sch
WA2 8
St Stephens Cl CH60 41
St Stephens Ct
11 Congleton CW12 156
Sandbach CW11 174
St Teresa's RC Prim Sch
M44 11
St Theresa's Prim Sch
CH1 117
St Thomas CE Prim Sch
ST7 195
St Thomas Ct WA8 12
St Thomas Hospl SK3 240
St Thomas More RC High Sch
CW2 190
St Thomas of Canterbury CE Jun Sch CH2 237
St Thomas St ST7 195
St Thomas' View CH65 70
St Thomas's CE Prim Sch
SK1 240
St Thomas's CE Prim Sch
WA4 16
St Thomas's Pathway
CH1 237
St Thomas's Pl SK1 240
St Vincent Dr CW8 102
St Vincent Rd WA5 14
St Vincent St WA14, WA15 238
St Vincent's RC Inf Sch
WA15 238
St Vincent's RC Jun Sch
WA15 238
St Vincent's RC Prim Sch
Knutsford WA16 57
St Helens WA9 1
Warrington WA5 14
St Wenefredes Gn SY13 214
St Werburgh St CH1 237
St Werburgh's & St Columba's RC Prim Sch
CH2 118
St Werburgh's CE Prim Sch
WA4 16
St Wilfred's Dr WA4 17
St Wilfrid's RC Prim Sch
CW8 103
St Wilfrids Cl CW9 104
St Winefride's RC Prim Sch
Neston CH64 66
Neston CH64 66
St Winifred's Pl SK15 242
St Winifred's RC Prim Sch
SK4 240
Salander Cres CW2 206
Sale Gram Sch M33 242
Sale Sta M33 242
Sale Water Pk* M21 242
Salerno Rd CH2 95
Salesbrook La CW5 228
Salford CW3 230
Salford Pl CW12 156
Salisbury Ave
Broughton CH4 140
Crewe CW2 190
Salisbury Cl Crewe CW2 190
Ellesmere Port CH66 94
Salisbury Pl SK10 87
Salisbury Rd
Altrincham WA14 238
Haydock WA11 1
Salisbury St Blacon CH1 118
Golborne WA3 3
Runcorn WA7 23
Warrington WA1 16
4 Widnes WA8 23
Salkeld St 12 CW9 104
Salop Pl ST7 195
Salop Wlk SK10 86
Salt Line Way CW11 174
Salt Mdws CW5 204
Salt Mus The* CW9 103
Saltash Cl WA7 50
Salter's La
Bickerton SY14 199

tter's La *continued*
roxton CH3 . . . . .183 C1
cton CH2 . . . . .119 B4
tters La
ddington SK11 . . . . .109 C1
ithington SK11 . . . . .132 A4
ttersbrook Gr 12 SK9 . . .34 C1
ttersford Cnr CW4 . . . . .130 C2
ttersgate CH66 . . . . .69 C1
ttney Bsns Ctr CH4 . . .140 C4
ttney Ferry Prim Sch
H4 . . . . .140 A3
ttney Ferry Rd CH4 . . .140 A4
ttney Terr CH4 . . . . .140 A4
tton Gdns WA5 . . . . .15 C4
ttwood Dr WA7 . . . . .50 B3
ttworks Cl WA6 . . . . .49 B1
muel Laycock Specl Sch
K15 . . . . .242 C4
muel St Chester CH2 . .237 C3
rewe CW1 . . . . .190 A3
acclesfield SK11 . . . . . . .112 B4
ackmoor ST7 . . . . .195 C1
tockport SK4 . . . . .240 D7
Varrington WA5 . . . . .15 C2
nbec Gdns WA8 . . . . . . .12 B3
nd La SK10 . . . . .84 C3
ndalwood WA7 . . . . .24 B1
ndalwood Cl WA2 . . . . . . .8 B1
ndbach Com Prim Sch
W11 . . . . .175 A3
ndbach Crosses*
W11 . . . . .175 A3
ndbach High Sch & Sixth
orm Coll CW11 . . . . . . .175 A4
ndbach Rd
ongleton CW12 . . . . .156 A2
ossall Green CW11,ST7 . .176 B1
awton Heath ST7 . . . . . . .193 C3
ode Heath ST7 . . . . .193 C4
ale M33 . . . . .242 F5
ndbach Rd N ST7 . . . . .193 B2
ndbach Rd S ST7 . . . . .193 B2
ndbach Sch CW11 . . . . .175 A3
ndbach Sta CW11 . . . . .174 B4
nderling Rd WA12 . . . . . .2 B2
nders Hey Cl WA7 . . . . .50 A3
nders Sq SK11 . . . . . . .112 B3
nderson Cl
rewe CW2 . . . . .206 B4
Varrington WA5 . . . . .14 B3
ndfield Ave CW5 . . . . .216 C2
ndfield Cl 3 WA3 . . . . . . .3 C4
ndfield Cres WA3 . . . . . . .5 B4
ndfield Ct
3 Frodsham WA6 . . . . .74 A4
Vrenbury CW5 . . . . .216 C2
ndfield La
cton Bridge CW8 . . . . .76 C1
artford CW8 . . . . .103 B2
ndfield Pk CH60 . . . . . . .40 B4
ndfields WA6 . . . . .74 A4
ndford Cres CW2 . . . . .207 B1
ndford Rd
antwich CW5 . . . . .204 C4
ale M33 . . . . .242 F5
ndgate Rd SK10 . . . . . . .87 C1
ndham Gr CH60 . . . . . . .41 B4
ndham Rd L24 . . . . .21 A2
ndheys CH64 . . . . .41 B1
ndhill St SK14 . . . . . . .241 F8
ndhole Cotts 1 CW7 . .149 A4
ndhole La
helford WA16 . . . . .83 B2
rowton CW8 . . . . .101 A4
ndhurst Ave CW2 . . . . .190 A1
ndhurst Dr SK9 . . . . .60 B4
ndhurst Rd L26 . . . . .21 A3
ndhurst St WA4 . . . . .16 C2
ndicroft Cl WA3 . . . . .9 B3
ndiford Rd CW4 . . . . . .130 B2
ndileigh CH2 . . . . .118 C2
ndileigh Ave
ltrincham WA15 . . . . . . .238 F3
nutsford WA16 . . . . .56 C1
tockport SK8 . . . . .240 A2
ndileigh Dr WA15 . . . .238 F3
ndington Dr CW8 . . . . .101 C1
ndiway Bebington CH63 . .43 B3
nutsford WA16 . . . . .57 A1
ndiway Ave WA8 . . . . . . .12 A1
ndiway Cl CW8 . . . . . . .102 A1
ndiway La CW9 . . . . .53 A1
ndiway Pk CW8 . . . . . . .102 C2
ndiway Pl WA14 . . . . . .238 D5
ndiway Prim Sch
W8 . . . . .102 A2
ndiway Rd
ltrincham WA14 . . . . . . .238 D6
rewe CW1 . . . . .190 A4
andforth SK9 . . . . .34 B3
ndle Bridge La WA16,
K9 . . . . .83 C3
ndle Bridge Rise
WA16 . . . . .83 C3
ndon Cres CH64 . . . . . . .66 C3
ndon Park Gdns CW2 . .189 B2
ndon Pl WA8 . . . . .13 B1
ndon Rd CH2 . . . . .118 C2
ndon St CW1 . . . . .190 B2
ndown Cl Culcheth WA3 . . .4 C2
Middlewich CW10 . . . . . . .151 B4
uncorn WA7 . . . . .49 B3
Vilmslow SK9 . . . . .60 B4
ndown Cres CW8 . . . . .102 A2
ndown Dr WA15 . . . . . . .32 B3
ndown Pl SK11 . . . . . . .111 C4
ndown Rd Crewe CW1 . .190 B4

Sandown Rd *continued*
Stockport SK3 . . . . .240 B4
Sandown Terr CH3 . . . . . .118 C1
Sandpiper Cl
Crewe CW1 . . . . .189 C4
Newton-le-W WA12 . . . . . . .2 B2
Sandpiper Ct
Chester CH4 . . . . .141 A1
Kidsgrove ST7 . . . . .195 B1
Sandpiper Dr SK3 . . . . . .240 D2
Sandpiper Way CH4 . . . .141 A2
Sandra Dr WA12 . . . . .2 C2
Sandringham Ave
Chester CH3 . . . . .119 A1
Helsby WA6 . . . . .73 A2
Stalybridge SK15 . . . . . . .242 D3
Sandringham Cl
Altrincham WA14 . . . . .20 C1
Davenham CW9 . . . . .103 C2
Winsford CW7 . . . . .126 B2
Sandringham Ct 5 SK9 . . .60 A3
Sandringham Dr
Poynton SK12 . . . . .36 B2
Stockport SK4 . . . . .240 A5
Warrington WA5 . . . . .15 B2
Wistaston CW2 . . . . .205 C4
Sandringham Gdns 2
CH65 . . . . .70 B1
Sandringham Rd
Macclesfield SK10 . . . . .87 C1
Widnes WA8 . . . . .13 A2
Sandringham Way 4
SK9 . . . . .60 A3
Sandrock Rd CH3 . . . . . . .142 C4
Sands Rd ST7 . . . . .195 C3
Sandsdown Cl ST8 . . . . . .179 B1
Sandside Rd ST7 . . . . . . .193 A2
Sandstone Wlk CH60 . . . . .41 A4
Sandwell Dr M33 . . . . . . .242 B8
Sandwich Dr SK10 . . . . . . .87 B2
Sandwood Ave CH4 . . . . .139 A2
Sandy Brow La WA3 . . . . . . .3 C1
Sandy Cl SK10 . . . . .87 C4
Sandy La Allostock WA16 .106 C3
Astbury CW12 . . . . .177 C3
Aston CW5 . . . . .217 B1
Bold Heath WA8 . . . . .14 A3
Broughton CH4 . . . . .140 B3
Brown Knowl CH3 . . . . . . .199 B4
Bulkeley SY14 . . . . .184 B1
Chester CH3 . . . . .119 A1
Congleton CW12 . . . . .155 B2
Congleton, Astbury Marsh
CW12 . . . . .156 A1
Croft WA3 . . . . .9 A4
Cronton WA8 . . . . .12 B3
Golborne WA3 . . . . .2 C4
Golborne, Lowton WA3 . . . . .4 A4
Goostrey CW4 . . . . .107 B1
Haslington CW11 . . . . . . .192 A4
Hatherton CW5 . . . . .219 C3
Helsby WA6 . . . . .73 A1
Higher Kinnerton CH4 . . . .161 A3
Lymm WA13 . . . . .19 A2
Macclesfield SK10 . . . . .86 B1
Neston CH64 . . . . .67 A4
Romiley SK6 . . . . .241 D3
Runcorn, Preston Brook
WA7 . . . . .50 C3
Runcorn, Weston Point
WA7 . . . . .48 C4
Saighton CH3 . . . . .142 B2
Sandbach CW11 . . . . .174 B3
Stockport SK4,SK5 . . . . . .240 E7
Swettenham CW12 . . . . . .131 C2
Tarvin CH3 . . . . .121 B2
Threapwood SY14 . . . . . . .222 C4
Warrington, Cobbs WA4 . . . .26 B4
Warrington, Longford WA2 . . .8 B1
Warrington, Penketh WA5 . . .15 A2
Weaverham CW8 . . . . .77 B1
Whitegate CW8 . . . . .125 B3
Wilmslow SK9 . . . . .59 C4
Sandy La W WA2 . . . . .8 A2
Sandy Moor La WA7 . . . . . .24 B2
Sandy Rd ST8 . . . . .179 B1
Sandyhill Pl 1 CW7 . . . . .149 B3
Sandyhill Rd CW7 . . . . . . .149 B3
Sandylands Cres ST7 . . . .193 C3
Sandylands Pk CW2 . . . . .205 B4
Sandylane Mews CW12 . .156 B3
Sandymoor La WA7 . . . . . . .24 B2
Sankey Bridges Ind Est
WA5 . . . . .15 B2
Sankey St Golborne WA3 . . . .3 A4
Newton-le-W WA12 . . . . .2 A2
Warrington WA1 . . . . .16 A3
Widnes WA8 . . . . .23 A3
Sankey Sta WA5 . . . . .14 C3
Sankey Valley Ind Est
WA12 . . . . .2 A1
Sankey Valley Pk*
Haydock WA11,WA12 . . . . . .1 B2
* Warrington WA5 . . . . . . .15 B3
Sankey Way WA5 . . . . .15 B3
Sanky La WA4 . . . . .25 C1
Santon Dr WA3 . . . . .3 C4
Sapling La CW6 . . . . .146 C2
Sark Ave CH65 . . . . .95 A4
Sark Ho CH2 . . . . .119 A2
Sarl Williams Ct CH1 . . . .237 A3
Sarn Bank Rd SY14 . . . . .222 C3
Sarn Rd SY14 . . . . .222 B4
Sarra La CH3 . . . . .184 A3
Sarsfield Ave 1 WA3 . . . . . .3 B4
Saughall Cl CW9 . . . . . . .103 C2
Saughall Hey CH1 . . . . . . .94 A1
Saughall Rd CH1 . . . . . . .117 C3

Saunders St CW1 . . . . . . .190 A2
Saundersfoot Cl WA5 . . . . . .7 C1
Saunderton Cl WA11 . . . . . .1 B4
Saville Ave WA5 . . . . .15 C4
Saville Rd SK8 . . . . .239 B6
Saville St SK11 . . . . .112 C3
Savoy Rd CW1 . . . . .207 A4
Sawley Cl Culcheth WA3 . . . .5 A1
Runcorn WA7 . . . . .50 C4
Sawley Dr SK8 . . . . .35 B3
Sawpit St WA13,WA14 . . . .20 A3
Sawyer Brow SK14 . . . . . .241 F8
Sawyer Dr ST8 . . . . .179 B1
Saxon Cl WA4 . . . . .26 B3
Saxon Crossway CW7 . . . .126 A1
Saxon Rd WA7 . . . . .23 B1
Saxon Terr WA8 . . . . .13 A1
Saxon Way Blacon CH1 . . .117 C3
Ellesmere Port CH66 . . . . . .94 C4
Sandbach CW11 . . . . .175 B3
Saxons La
Northwich CW8 . . . . .103 C3
Northwich, Greenbank
CW8 . . . . .103 B4
Sayce St WA8 . . . . .13 A1
Scafell Ave WA2 . . . . .8 B2
Scafell Cl Bebington CH62 . .43 B2
High Lane SK6 . . . . .37 C4
Scaife Rd CW5 . . . . .204 C3
Scaliot Cl SK22 . . . . .39 A4
Scar La SY14 . . . . .198 C1
Sceptre Cl WA12 . . . . .2 A2
Scholar Green Prim Sch
ST7 . . . . .194 C3
Scholar's Ct 3 CH64 . . . . .66 C4
Scholars Cl Chester CH4 . .140 C3
Macclesfield SK10 . . . . . . .111 B4
Scholars Green La WA13 . .18 C1
School Ave CH64 . . . . .66 C3
School Bank WA6 . . . . . . .101 A3
School Brow
Romiley SK6 . . . . .241 A2
Warrington WA1 . . . . .16 B3
School Cl Audley ST7 . . . .210 A1
Knutsford WA16 . . . . .56 C1
Marbury SY13 . . . . .226 C4
Poynton SK12 . . . . .36 C2
School Cres Crewe CW1 . .190 C2
Stalybridge SK15 . . . . .242 D4
School Ct SK3 . . . . .240 F2
School Dr CW8 . . . . .78 A2
School Field Cl CW3 . . . .230 C2
School Gn CH3 . . . . .182 B1
School Hill CH60 . . . . .40 C4
School La Aldford CH3 . . .163 C1
Antrobus CW9 . . . . .53 B2
Astbury CW12 . . . . .178 A4
Audlem CW3 . . . . .230 A2
Bold Heath WA8 . . . . .13 C4
Brereton Green CW11 . . . . .153 C3
Bunbury CW6 . . . . .168 C1
Burwardsley CH3 . . . . .184 A3
Cheadle SK8 . . . . .35 A4
Cuddington CW8 . . . . .102 A1
Eaton (nr Congleton)
CW12 . . . . .156 C4
Ellesmere Port CH66 . . . . . .69 A4
Elton CH2 . . . . .72 A2
Frodsham WA6 . . . . .74 B4
Great Budworth CW9 . . . . . .79 A4
Guilden Sutton CH3 . . . . . .119 C3
Hartford CW8 . . . . .103 B2
Henbury SK11 . . . . .111 A3
Hollinfare WA3 . . . . .11 A1
Hooton CH66 . . . . .43 C1
Irlam M44 . . . . .11 B3
Lostock Gralam CW9 . . . . . .80 A1
Manley WA6 . . . . .99 A3
Marbury SY13 . . . . .215 C1
Marton SK11 . . . . .133 B3
Mickle Trafford CH2 . . . . . .119 C4
Moulton CW9 . . . . .126 C4
5 Nantwich CW5 . . . . .204 C3
Neston CH64 . . . . .42 A1
Neston, Little Neston CH64 . .66 C3
Neston, Parkgate CH64 . . . . .41 A1
Nether Alderley SK10 . . . . . .86 A3
Norley WA6 . . . . .100 B3
Ollerton WA16 . . . . .83 A2
Partington WA14 . . . . .20 B3
Poynton SK12 . . . . .36 C2
Runcorn WA7 . . . . .49 C4
Sandbach, Betchton CW11 . .175 C3
Sandbach, Ettiley Heath
CW11 . . . . .174 B4
Smallwood CW11 . . . . .176 C3
Warmingham CW11 . . . . . .173 C4
Warrington WA3 . . . . .10 B3
Whitley WA4 . . . . .52 C3
School Mews SK7 . . . . .35 C4
School Rd
Altrincham WA15 . . . . .238 F3
Ellesmere Port CH65 . . . . . .70 A3
Handforth SK9 . . . . .34 B2
Lach Dennis CW9 . . . . .104 B3
Sale M33 . . . . .242 B7
Warrington WA2 . . . . .8 B1
Winsford CW7 . . . . .127 A1
Winsford, Meadow Bank
CW7 . . . . .126 C3
School Rd N CW9 . . . . . . .104 C3
School Rd S CW9 . . . . . . .104 C3
School St Chester CH2 . . .118 C2
Golborne WA3 . . . . .3 A4
Haslington CW1 . . . . .191 B3
Newton-le-W WA12 . . . . .2 A2
Warrington WA4 . . . . .16 A2
School Terr WA3 . . . . .3 A4

School Way
Northwich CW9 . . . . .104 A4
Widnes WA8 . . . . .13 B2
Schoolfold La SK10 . . . . . .63 A4
Schools Hill SK8 . . . . . . .239 D3
Schooner Cl WA7 . . . . .50 B3
Scilly Cl CH65 . . . . .70 B1
Scotch Hall La CW9 . . . . . .53 A2
Scotia Wlk 12 WA3 . . . . . . .3 C4
Scotland Rd WA1 . . . . .16 A3
Scott Ave Crewe CW1 . . . .190 C2
Widnes WA8 . . . . .22 C4
Scott Cl
Macclesfield SK10 . . . . . . .113 A4
Rode Heath ST7 . . . . .193 C4
2 Sandbach CW11 . . . . . . .174 B3
Stockport SK5 . . . . .240 F8
Scott Rd SK10 . . . . .87 A4
Scott St WA2 . . . . .16 B3
Scott Wlk WA12 . . . . .2 B1
Scotthorpe Cl SK11 . . . . .111 C3
Scotton Ave CH66 . . . . .69 A3
Scroggins La M31 . . . . .11 C2
Sea Bank CW10 . . . . .128 B1
Sea La WA7 . . . . .23 B1
Sea View CH64 . . . . .66 C2
Seabank Rd CH60 . . . . .40 C3
Seabury St WA4 . . . . .17 A2
Seacombe Dr CH66 . . . . . . .69 C2
Seacombe Gr SK3 . . . . . .240 B4
Seafield Ave CH60 . . . . . . .40 C3
Seaford Cl WA7 . . . . .24 B1
Seaford Pl WA2 . . . . .8 A2
Seagrave Cl CW9 . . . . . . .103 C3
Seagull Cl CW1 . . . . .190 C3
Seahill Rd CH1 . . . . .116 C4
Seal Rd SK7 . . . . .36 A4
Sealand Cl WA2 . . . . .8 C1
Sealand Ind Est CH1 . . . .117 C1
Sealand Rd Blacon CH1 . . .117 B2
Chester CH1 . . . . .118 A1
Sealand CH5 . . . . .116 B3
Sealand Trad Pk CH1 . . . .117 C1
Sealand Way 2 SK9 . . . . . .34 B2
Seamon's Dr WA14 . . . . . .238 A6
Seamon's Rd WA14 . . . . . .238 A6
Seamons Wlk WA14 . . . . .238 B5
Seathwaite Cl WA7 . . . . . . .49 C3
Seaton Cl CW1 . . . . .190 A4
Seaton Pk WA7 . . . . .24 C2
Seaton St CW7 . . . . .127 B1
Seaview Ave CH62 . . . . . . .44 A3
Seaville St CH2 . . . . .237 C3
Secker Ave WA4 . . . . .16 B1
Secker Cl WA4 . . . . .16 B1
Second Ave
Congleton CW12 . . . . .156 A2
Connah's Quay CH5 . . . . . . .92 C2
Crewe CW1 . . . . .190 C1
Kidsgrove ST7 . . . . .194 C1
Poynton SK12 . . . . .36 B1
Runcorn WA7 . . . . .49 C4
Sandbach CW11 . . . . .175 A3
Second Dig La CW5 . . . . .219 B4
Second Wood St CW5 . . . .204 B3
Sedbergh Gr WA7 . . . . .49 C3
Sedburgh Cl CW4 . . . . . . .130 A2
Seddon Rd WA14 . . . . . . .238 D2
Seddon St CW10 . . . . .128 B1
Sedgefield Cl 3 SK10 . . . . .87 B2
Sedgefield Rd CH1 . . . . . .118 A1
Sedgeford Cl SK9 . . . . .34 B1
Sedgewick Cres WA5 . . . . . .6 C3
Sedgmere Ave CW1 . . . . .190 A4
Sedum Cl CH3 . . . . .142 A3
Sefton Ave
Congleton CW12 . . . . .157 A1
Widnes WA8 . . . . .13 A2
Sefton Cres M33 . . . . . . .242 B8
Sefton Dr SK9 . . . . .34 B1
Sefton Rd Chester CH2 . . .119 A2
Sale M33 . . . . .242 B7
Sefton St WA12 . . . . .1 C2
Selby Cl Poynton SK12 . . . .36 B3
Runcorn WA7 . . . . .24 C2
Selby Gdns SK8 . . . . .35 B3
Selby Gn CH66 . . . . .69 A3
Selby St Stockport SK4 . . .240 D8
Warrington WA5 . . . . .15 C3
Selkirk Ave
Bebington CH62 . . . . .43 C2
Warrington WA4 . . . . .17 A2
Selkirk Cl
Ellesmere Port CH66 . . . . . .68 C3
Macclesfield SK10 . . . . .86 C1
Selkirk Dr Chester CH4 . . .141 A4
Holmes Chapel CW4 . . . . . .130 A1
Selkirk Rd CH4 . . . . .141 A4
Seller St CH2 . . . . .237 C3
Selsdon Ct CH4 . . . . .141 B4
Selsey Ave SK3 . . . . .239 F7
Selsey Cl CW1 . . . . .190 A4
Selsey Dr M20 . . . . .239 C8
Selworth Ave M33 . . . . . .242 E6
Selworth Cl 5 WA15 . . . . .238 E6
Selworthy Dr
Crewe CW1 . . . . .190 A4
Warrington WA4 . . . . .17 B2
Selwyn Cl
Newton-le-W WA12 . . . . .2 A3
Widnes WA8 . . . . .13 C2
Selwyn Dr Cheadle SK8 . . . .35 B4
Sutton Lane Ends SK11 . . . .112 C2
Semper Cl CW12 . . . . . . .157 A2
Seneschal Ct WA7 . . . . . . .49 C3
Senna La Antrobus CW9 . . .53 A1
Comberbach CW9 . . . . .78 B4
Sennen Cl WA7 . . . . .50 B3

Sens Cl CH1 . . . . .237 A2
Sephton Ave WA3 . . . . .4 C2
Sergeant York Loop
WA5 . . . . .15 A3
Serin Cl WA12 . . . . .2 B2
Serpentine The CH4 . . . . .141 A4
Service St SK3 . . . . .240 B4
Servite Cl CH65 . . . . .69 C3
Servite Pl 8 CH64 . . . . . . .66 C4
Set St SK15 . . . . .242 C1
Sett Cl SK22 . . . . .39 A4
Seven Sisters La WA16 . . .82 C3
Sevenoaks Cl SK10 . . . . . .87 A1
Sevenoaks Rd SK8 . . . . . .239 B6
Severn Cl
Altrincham WA14 . . . . .238 C6
Biddulph ST8 . . . . .179 C1
Congleton CW12 . . . . .156 C1
Macclesfield SK10 . . . . .86 C1
Warrington WA2 . . . . .8 C1
Widnes WA8 . . . . .13 C2
Severn Dr SK7 . . . . .35 B3
Severn Rd WA3 . . . . .4 C1
Severn Wlk CW7 . . . . .127 A1
Severnvale CH65 . . . . .70 A2
Sewell St WA7 . . . . .23 A1
Sextant Cl WA7 . . . . .50 B3
Sexton Ave WA9 . . . . .1 A1
Seymour Chase WA16 . . . . .82 A4
Seymour Ct WA7 . . . . .24 B2
Seymour Dr
Ellesmere Port CH66 . . . . . .69 C3
Warrington WA1 . . . . .17 A4
Seymour Gr M33 . . . . . . .242 B6
Seymour Ho 16 SK9 . . . . . .34 C1
Seymour Rd SK8 . . . . .35 A4
Shackleton Cl WA5 . . . . . . .15 B4
Shade Terr SK6 . . . . .37 C4
Shadewood Cres WA4 . . . . .17 A1
Shadewood Rd SK11 . . . .112 A3
Shadowmoss Rd M22 . . . . .33 C4
Shady Brook La CW8 . . . . .77 B1
Shady Gr ST7 . . . . .193 B2
Shaftesbury Ave
Chester CH3 . . . . .119 B1
Warrington WA5 . . . . .14 C1
Shaftesbury Rd SK3 . . . . .240 B2
Shaftesbury Way WA5 . . . . .6 C4
Shaftway Cl WA11 . . . . .1 C4
Shakerley Ave CW12 . . . .156 C2
Shakespeare Cl CW9 . . . .104 B4
Shakespeare Dr
Cheadle SK8 . . . . .239 F6
Crewe CW1 . . . . .191 A2
Shakespeare Gr WA2 . . . . . .8 B1
Shakespeare Rd
Neston CH64 . . . . .41 C1
Widnes WA8 . . . . .13 A1
Shalcombe Cl L26 . . . . . . .21 A4
Shalford Dr M22 . . . . .33 B4
Shallacres CH65 . . . . .69 C4
Shallcross Ave SK23 . . . . .65 C2
Shallcross Cres SK23 . . . .65 C2
Shallcross Rd SK23 . . . . . .65 C2
Shambles The WA16 . . . . . .57 A1
Shanklin Cl WA5 . . . . .14 B3
Shannon Cl Chester CH4 . .140 C3
Willaston (nr Nantwich)
CW5 . . . . .205 B3
Shargate Cl SK9 . . . . .34 B1
Sharnbrook Dr CW2 . . . . .189 B2
Sharon Park Cl WA4 . . . . . .17 B1
Sharp St Warrington WA2 . .16 B3
Widnes WA8 . . . . .23 A4
Sharples St SK4 . . . . .240 E7
Sharpley St SK11 . . . . . . .112 B4
Sharston Cres WA16 . . . . . .57 A1
Shavington Ave CH2 . . . . .118 C2
Shavington High Sch
CW2 . . . . .206 A3
Shavington Prim Sch
CW2 . . . . .206 B2
Shavington Sports Ctr
CW2 . . . . .206 A3
Shavington Way CW9 . . . .103 C2
Shaw Dr WA16 . . . . .57 B2
Shaw Entry WA8,L35 . . . . . .12 A4
Shaw Heath SK2 . . . . .240 E3
Shaw Heath View WA16 . . .57 B2
Shaw Moor Ave SK15 . . . .242 F1
Shaw Rd SK4 . . . . .240 B8
Shaw Rd S SK3 . . . . .240 E2
Shaw St
Ashton-u-Lyne OL6 . . . . . .242 A3
Culcheth WA3 . . . . .5 A2
Haydock WA11 . . . . .1 C3
Macclesfield SK11 . . . . . . .112 B4
Runcorn WA7 . . . . .22 C1
Shaw's Rd WA14 . . . . . . .238 D4
Shawbury Gr WA1 . . . . .17 A4
Shawcross Fold 5 SK1 . . .240 F6
Shawell Ct WA8 . . . . .13 C1
Shaws Ave WA2 . . . . .16 B4
Shaws Fold SK9 . . . . .33 C2
Shaws La
Mottram St Andrew SK10 . . .86 B4
Winsford CW7 . . . . .126 C2
Winsford CW7 . . . . .127 A2
Shay La Ashton CH3 . . . . .122 A4
Hampton SY14 . . . . .200 A1
Tarvin CH3 . . . . .121 C2
Shay's La CW6 . . . . .124 C2
Sheaf Cl CH3 . . . . .121 B1
Shearbrook La CW4 . . . . .107 C1
Sheardhall Ave SK12 . . . . .38 C3

Sheath St CW9 .....104 A4
Shed La CH3 .....119 A1
Sheepfield Cl CH66 .....69 B4
Sherwater Cl WA1 .....16 C4
Sheffield Cl WA5 .....15 B3
Sheffield Rd SK14 .....241 F8
Sheffield Row WA12 .....7 B4
Sheffield St SK4 .....240 E7
Sheiling Ct WA14 .....238 C4
Sheilings The WA3 .....3 C4
Shelagh Ave WA8 .....13 A1
Shelbourne Mews 2
SK11 .....111 C4
Shelburne Dr CW1 .....191 B3
Sheldon Ave
Chester CH3 .....119 A1
Congleton CW12 .....157 A1
Sheldon Cl M31 .....11 C2
Sheldon Rd
Hazel Grove SK7 .....36 C4
Poynton SK12 .....37 B1
Sheldrake Dr CH64 .....66 C3
Sheldrake Rd WA14 .....238 B8
Shellbrook Gr 12 SK9 .....34 B1
Shelley Ave CW9 .....80 A3
Shelley Cl Crewe CW1 .....190 C2
Rode Heath ST7 .....193 C4
Shelley Ct 5 CW11 .....174 B3
Shelley Dr CW2 .....189 C1
Shelley Gr WA4 .....16 C2
Shelley Rd Blacon CH1 .....117 C3
Widnes WA8 .....13 A1
Shellow La CW12,SK11 .....134 B3
Shellway Rd CH2 .....71 A2
Shelly Cl CW10 .....151 C3
Shelton Cl WA8 .....13 C2
Shenhurst Cl SK9 .....59 C2
Shenton St SK14 .....241 C8
Shepcroft La WA4 .....26 B1
Shepherd's Brow WA14 .....238 A3
Shepherd's La CH2 .....118 B3
Shepherds Fold Dr
CW7 .....126 B2
Shepherds Row WA7 .....23 C1
Shepley Cl SK7 .....36 B4
Shepley St 1 Hyde SK14 .....241 E6
Stalybridge SK15 .....242 D2
Sheppard Cl CW1 .....190 B3
Sheppenhall Gr CW5 .....217 B1
Sheppenhall La CW5 .....228 B3
Shepperton Cl WA4 .....26 C3
Shepsides Cl CH66 .....69 B2
Shepton Rd CH66 .....69 C1
Sheraton Rd CH3 .....143 A3
Sherborne Cl WA7 .....24 C2
Sherborne Rd
Crewe CW1 .....190 B3
Stockport SK3 .....240 A3
Sherbourne Ave CH4 .....141 A3
Sherbourne Cl SK8 .....35 A3
Sherbourne Rd
Ellesmere Port CH65 .....70 B2
Macclesfield SK11 .....111 C4
Sherbourne Way WA5 .....6 C3
Sherbrook Rise SK9 .....60 B3
Sherbrooke Rd SK12 .....38 B3
Sheri Dr WA12 .....2 C1
Sheridan Ave WA3 .....3 B4
Sheridan Cl CW1 .....173 A1
Sheridan Pl WA2 .....8 A3
Sheridan Way WA7 .....24 B1
Sheringham Cl CH4 .....140 C3
Sheringham Dr CW1 .....190 A4
Sheringham Rd WA5 .....14 C3
Sherlock Ave WA11 .....1 C4
Sherratt Cl CW12 .....156 C1
Sherrington's La CH3 .....199 B4
Sherwin St CW2 .....190 B1
Sherwood Ave
Cheadle SK8 .....239 F2
Sale M33 .....242 D7
Stockport SK4 .....240 A5
Sherwood Cl WA8 .....12 B1
Sherwood Cres WA5 .....6 C3
Sherwood Gr WA6 .....73 A2
Sherwood Rd SK11 .....112 B3
Shetland Cl
Warrington WA2 .....8 C2
Widnes WA8 .....13 C2
Shetland Dr
Bebington CH62 .....43 C4
Ellesmere Port CH65 .....70 B1
Shevington Cl WA8 .....13 C2
Shevington Wlk WA8 .....13 C2
Shield St SK3 .....240 E4
Shiers Dr SK8 .....239 E4
Shiggins Cl WA5 .....15 B3
Shillingford Cl WA4 .....26 C3
Shilton Cl CW10 .....151 C3
Ship St WA6 .....49 B1
Shipbrook Rd
Chester CH2 .....118 C3
Lach Dennis CW9 .....104 B2
Northwich CW9 .....104 B3
Shipgate St CH4 .....237 B1
Shipton Cl
Warrington WA5 .....15 A4
Widnes WA8 .....12 B2
Shirley Ave SK8 .....34 B3
Shirley Ct M33 .....242 C6
Shirley Dr WA4 .....17 A1
Shirley Gr SK3 .....240 E2
Shirleys Cl SK10 .....87 A3
Shirleys Dr SK10 .....87 A3
Shocklach Oviatt CE Prim
Sch SY14 .....211 B4
Shocklach Rd CH2 .....118 C3
Shones Croft CH64 .....67 A3
Shop La Congleton CW12 .....156 C1
Little Budworth CW6 .....124 C1
Shopping Precinct The
CH2 .....72 A2
Shoreham Dr WA5 .....15 A2
Shores Green Dr CW9 .....79 C3
Shores La CW5 .....203 B4
Short Cl WA12 .....1 C2
Short St Haydock WA11 .....1 C3
28 Macclesfield SK11 .....112 B4
Newton-le-W WA12 .....1 C2
Stockport SK4 .....240 E7
Widnes WA8 .....23 A3
Short St E SK4 .....240 E7
Shorthorn Cl CW10 .....128 B1
Shorwell Cl WA5 .....14 B4
Shotwick La CH1 .....93 B3
Shotwick Rd CH5 .....93 A2
Shrewbridge Cres CW5 .....204 C2
Shrewbridge Rd CW5 .....204 B2
Shrewsbury Dr ST5 .....210 C1
Shrewsbury Gdns SK8 .....35 B3
Shrewsbury Rd 11 CH65 .....70 B3
Shrewsbury St WA4 .....16 B2
Shrewsbury Way CH4 .....140 C3
Shrigley Cl SK9 .....34 B1
Shrigley Rd SK10 .....63 A3
Shrigley Rd N SK12 .....37 B2
Shrigley Rise SK10 .....63 B1
Shropshire Cl
Middlewich CW10 .....151 A4
Warrington WA1 .....17 C3
Shropshire La SY13 .....227 C1
Shropshire Rd CH2 .....70 C2
Shropshire St CW3 .....229 C2
Shuldham Cl WA16 .....29 B2
Shurlach Rd CW9 .....104 B3
Shutley La CW8 .....77 B3
Shutlingsloe Way SK11 .....112 A4
Sibbersfield La CH3 .....180 C2
Sibell St CH2 .....237 C3
Sibley Rd SK4 .....240 B7
Sibson Rd M33 .....242 B6
Siddall St 11 CW9 .....104 A4
Siddeley Cl CH4 .....139 B2
Siddeley Dr WA12 .....1 C2
Siddington Ave
Northwich CW9 .....104 A2
Stockport SK3 .....240 D2
Siddington Bank SK11 .....109 C2
Siddington Rd
Handforth SK9 .....34 B3
Poynton SK12 .....36 C1
Siddorn St CW7 .....126 C1
Side Ave WA14 .....238 C1
Side End La SK23 .....64 C2
Side La CW6 .....144 C3
Sidebottom St SK15 .....242 D2
Sidlaw Cl CH66 .....69 A3
Sidley Pl SK14 .....241 F7
Sidley St SK14 .....241 F7
Sidmouth Cl WA5 .....14 C2
Sidmouth Gr SK8 .....34 C4
Sidney Rd CH64 .....41 C1
Siemens Rd M44 .....11 C3
Sienna Cl M44 .....11 C3
Signal Ct CH2 .....118 C1
Silk Hill SK23 .....65 C4
Silk Mill
Macclesfield SK11 .....112 B4
Poynton SK12 .....36 B2
Silk Mill St WA16 .....57 A1
Silk Mus & Heritage Ctr*
SK11 .....112 B4
Silk Rd The
Bollington SK10 .....87 C2
Macclesfield SK10 .....87 C2
Silk St CW12 .....156 B1
Silkstone Cres WA7 .....50 A4
Silsden Ave WA3 .....4 A4
Silvan Ct SK10 .....87 A1
Silver Ave WA11 .....1 A3
Silver Birches M34 .....241 B5
Silver Hill Rd SK14 .....241 E5
Silver La Croft WA3 .....9 C4
Warrington WA3 .....10 B3
Silver St Bollington SK10 .....88 A4
Congleton CW12 .....156 C1
Warrington WA2 .....16 A3
Silver Terr CW11 .....175 B3
Silverbirch Croft CH4 .....139 A2
Silverbirch Way CH66 .....94 C4
Silverdale
Altrincham WA14 .....238 C4
Northwich CW8 .....103 B4
Silverdale Ave M34 .....241 A6
Silverdale Cl
Frodsham WA6 .....74 B4
High Lane SK6 .....37 C4
Silverdale Dr SK9 .....60 A2
Silverdale Rd Gatley SK8 .....239 B4
Newton-le-W WA12 .....2 A2
Stockport SK4 .....240 D8
Warrington WA4 .....16 A1
Silvergate Ct CW12 .....178 C4
Silvermine Cl 17 ST7 .....195 A1
Silvermuir CH1 .....117 C2
Silverne Dr CH65 .....70 A1
Silverthorne Cl SK15 .....242 D1
Silverwood ST7 .....195 A1
Simmonds Cl CW9 .....103 C2
Simms Cross Prim Sch
WA8 .....23 A4
Simon Cl M33 .....242 A5
Simons La WA6 .....74 A3
Simonside WA8 .....12 B1
Simonstone Rd CH4 .....139 B2
Simonswood Cl CW10 .....151 A4
Simpkin Ave WA4 .....16 C2
Simpson Cl CH2 .....95 B1
Simpson Ct CW1 .....173 A1
Simpson La SK10 .....63 B4
Simpson Rd CH2 .....95 B1
Simpson St Hyde SK14 .....241 D6
Wilmslow SK9 .....59 C3
Simpsons Way CH4 .....139 A2
Sinclair Ave Alsager ST7 .....193 A2
Warrington WA2 .....8 A1
Widnes WA8 .....23 A4
Sinderland La WA13 .....20 A4
Sinderland Rd WA14 .....238 C8
Singapore Ave M90 .....33 A4
Singleton Ave CW1 .....190 B3
Singleton Rd
Ellesmere Port CH65 .....69 C2
2 Stockport SK4 .....240 B8
Sir John Deane's Coll
CW9 .....103 C3
Sir Thomas Boteler High Sch
WA4 .....16 C2
Siskin Cl WA12 .....2 B2
Six Acre Gdns WA4 .....25 A3
Six Acre La WA4 .....25 A3
Sixpenny Wlk WA1 .....16 B3
Sixth Ave CH5 .....92 C1
Skaife Rd M33 .....242 E6
Skeath Cl CW11 .....175 C3
Skellern St ST7 .....194 B1
Skellorn Green La SK10 .....62 C4
Skelton Rd WA14 .....238 E7
Skiddaw Cl WA7 .....50 A2
Skip's La CH3 .....142 C4
Skipton Cl SK7 .....36 B4
Skipton Dr CH66 .....69 B3
Skye Cl
Ellesmere Port CH65 .....70 B1
Widnes WA8 .....13 C2
Skye Croft SK6 .....241 D3
Skylark Cl CW1 .....189 C4
Slack St Hyde SK14 .....241 F8
Macclesfield SK11 .....112 C3
Slacken La ST7 .....194 B1
Slade La Mobberley WA16 .....58 A4
Nether Alderley SK10 .....85 C3
Slade St 9 CW9 .....104 A4
Slag La Golborne WA3 .....3 B4
Haydock WA11 .....1 A4
Slater St
Macclesfield SK11 .....112 B3
Warrington WA4 .....16 B2
Slicks Bsns Ctr CW8 .....78 B1
Slindon Cl ST5 .....210 B1
Slutchers La WA1 .....16 A2
Small Ave WA2 .....8 B1
Small Cres WA2 .....8 B1
Small La WA16 .....58 A4
Smallbrook Wlk CW2 .....206 B4
Smallman Rd CW2 .....190 B1
Smallwood CE Prim Sch
CW11 .....176 C3
Smallwood Cl
5 Middlewich CW10 .....151 B4
Newcastle-u-L ST5 .....210 B1
Smallwood Ct 1 CW12 .....156 C2
Smallwood Forge CW11 .....176 B3
Smethwick La CW11,
CW12 .....154 C2
Smith Cl ST7 .....193 A2
Smith Cres WA2 .....16 B4
Smith Dr WA2 .....16 B4
Smith Gr CW1 .....190 A3
Smith La Mobberley WA16 .....57 C3
Rainow SK10 .....89 A3
Smith Rd WA8 .....22 C4
Smith St Cheadle SK8 .....239 F6
Macclesfield SK11 .....112 B3
Warrington WA1 .....16 A3
Smith's La CW8 .....77 B1
Smithfield Dr LL13 .....196 B4
Smithfield La CW11 .....175 B3
Smithfield St LL13 .....196 B3
Smithfields CH3 .....166 B1
Smithills Cl WA3 .....9 B3
Smiths Lawn SK9 .....60 A3
Smithy Bank CW7 .....149 A2
Smithy Brow
Bollington SK10 .....88 B4
Winwick WA3 .....8 C4
Smithy Cl Cronton WA8 .....12 B3
Saughall CH1 .....94 A1
Willaston CH64 .....67 A2
Smithy Ct
Christleton CH3 .....142 C4
5 Ellesmere Port CH66 .....69 B3
Smithy Gn Cheadle SK8 .....35 A4
Milton Green CH3 .....165 C3
Smithy Gr CW11 .....176 A1
Smithy Hill CH63 .....42 A3
Smithy La
Altrincham WA14 .....20 B2
Barthomley CW2 .....208 B3
Barthomley CW2 .....208 B4
Biddulph ST8 .....179 B1
Bosley SK11 .....158 C3
Broxton CH3 .....183 B1
Congleton CW12 .....156 B4
Crewe CW1 .....189 C4
Croft WA3 .....9 A4
Cronton WA8 .....12 B3
Cuddington CW8 .....102 A3
Ellesmere Port CH66 .....69 B3
Great Budworth CW9 .....79 A4
Smithy La *continued*
Helsby WA6 .....73 B3
Hyde SK14 .....241 E5
Kingsley WA6 .....75 A1
Little Leigh CW8 .....77 A3
Lostock Gralam CW9 .....80 A1
Malpas SY14 .....213 A1
Mottram St Andrew SK10 .....61 B1
Mouldsworth CH3 .....98 C1
Partington M31 .....11 C2
Utkinton CW6 .....146 B3
Weston CW2 .....207 B3
Willaston CH64 .....68 A4
Smithy Pathway CH4 .....140 C2
Smithy The CH2 .....118 C4
Smithy Wlk CW11 .....174 C2
Smokehall La CW7,CW9 .....126 C3
Smokehall Lane Ind Est
CW7 .....127 A3
Smokey La SY13 .....224 A1
Smokies Way ST8 .....179 B1
Smyth Rd WA8 .....13 B1
Snab La CH64 .....66 C2
Snabwood Cl CH64 .....66 C3
Snaefell Rise WA4 .....26 B4
Snape Hollow CW2 .....207 C2
Snape La CW2 .....207 C2
Snape Rd Crewe CW2 .....206 B4
Macclesfield SK10 .....87 C1
Snapebrook Wlk 6 SK9 .....34 C1
Snelson La
Chelford SK11 .....108 C4
Chelford, Marthall WA16,
SK9 .....83 B2
Snipe Cl SK12 .....36 A2
Snow Hill SK11 .....112 C3
Snowberry Cl WA8 .....13 C2
Snowberry Wlk M31 .....11 C2
Snowdon Cl
Ellesmere Port CH66 .....69 A3
Warrington WA5 .....14 C3
Snowdon Cres CH4 .....141 A3
Snowdon Dr CW2 .....189 B2
Snowdon St CW8 .....77 C2
Snowdonia Way CW7 .....149 A4
Snowdrop Cl WA7 .....49 C2
Solly Cres CW12 .....156 A1
Solway Cl WA2 .....8 C2
Solway Gr WA7 .....49 B3
Solway Rd CW8 .....78 B1
Somerford Ave CW2 .....190 A2
Somerford Cl CW11 .....175 B4
Somerford Ct 2 CW12 .....156 C2
Somerford Rd CH4 .....139 B2
Somerford Way 3 SK9 .....34 C3
Somerford Wlk WA8 .....13 C2
Somerley Cl CW1 .....190 A4
Somerset Ave ST7 .....194 C1
Somerset Cl
Congleton CW12 .....156 B2
Irlam M44 .....11 B3
Somerset Pl M33 .....242 B8
Somerset Rd
Altrincham WA14 .....238 D6
Chester CH2 .....118 C3
Somerset St CH2 .....237 B4
Somerset Way WA1 .....17 A4
Somerton Ave M33 .....242 C5
Somerton Cl SK11 .....111 C4
Somerton Rd SK11 .....111 C4
Somerville Cl
Bebington CH63 .....43 A3
High Legh WA16 .....29 B2
Neston CH64 .....66 C3
Somerville Cres CH65 .....70 B2
Somerville Gdns WA15 .....238 F7
Somerville Rd WA8 .....22 B4
Somerville St CW2 .....190 A1
Soot Hill CW8,CW9 .....78 B2
Sorbus Cl CH2 .....72 B2
Sorbus Dr CW1 .....190 C3
Sorrel Cl Huntington CH3 .....142 A3
Warrington WA2 .....9 B1
Sossmoss La SK10 .....84 B3
Sound & District Prim Sch
CW5 .....217 C3
Sound La
Ravensmoor CW5 .....203 C1
Sound CW5 .....217 B4
Souracre Fold SK15 .....242 E3
Souter's La CH1 .....237 B2
South Acre Dr
Macclesfield SK11 .....113 A4
Wilmslow SK9 .....34 B2
South Ave Chester CH2 .....237 C4
Haslington CW1 .....191 B2
Warrington WA2 .....16 A4
Warrington, Stockton Heath
WA4 .....16 B1
South Bank CH2 .....118 B2
South Bank Cl SK9 .....60 A1
South Bank Gr CW12 .....156 C1
South Bank Terr WA7 .....22 C2
South Cft CW6 .....185 B4
South Cheshire Coll
CW2 .....190 A1
South Cheshire Coll (Annexe)
CW1 .....190 B2
South Cl Tarporley CW6 .....146 B1
Wilmslow SK9 .....59 C3
South Crescent Rd CH4 .....237 C1
South Crofts CW5 .....204 C3
South Dale WA5 .....14 C3
South Downs WA16 .....57 B1
South Downs Dr WA14 .....238 D1
South Downs Rd WA14 .....238 D1
South Dr Gatley SK8 .....239 A4
Heswall CH60 .....41 A4
South Dr *continued*
Northwich CW9 104
Plumley WA16 80
South Gn CH5 116
South Gr
7 Alderley Edge SK9 60
Sale M33 242
South La
Warrington WA5,WA8 14
Widnes WA8 13
South Lane Entry WA8 13
South Mead SK12 36
South Meadway SK6 37
South Oak La SK9 59
South Par WA7 48
South Park Dr SK12 36
South Park Rd
Gatley SK8 239
Macclesfield SK11 112
South Pier Rd CH65 70
South Rd
Altrincham, Bowdon WA14 238
Altrincham, Hale WA14 31
Ellesmere Port CH65 70
Halewood L24 21
Runcorn WA7 48
Stanlow CH65 70
South St Alderley Edge SK9 60
Chester CH3 119
Congleton CW12 156
Crewe CW2 190
Mount Pleasant ST7 195
3 Widnes WA8 23
South Trafford Coll
WA14 238
South Vale Cres WA15 238
South View Chester CH4 141
Christleton CH3 142
New Mills SK22 39
Withington SK11 132
South View Ave SK11 111
South View Cotts ST7 193
South View Gdns SK8 239
South View La CW7 170
South View Rd CH1 118
South Way CH1 117
South West Ave SK10 87
South Wirral High Sch
CH62 43
Southampton Way WA7 50
Southbank SK9 79
Southbank Ave CW2 206
Southdale Rd WA1 17
Southdown Cl
Macclesfield SK10 87
Stockport SK4 240
Southdown Cres SK8 34
Southern Rd M33 242
Southern St WA4 16
Southey Cl
8 Sandbach CW11 174
Widnes WA8 22
Southfield SK10 87
Southfield Cl SK9 34
Southfield Rd CH66 69
Southfields WA16 57
Southfields Ave WA5 14
Southfields Cl CW5 220
Southgate Ct M33 242
Southlands CW4 130
Southlands Ave WA5 14
Southlands Ct WA7 48
Southlands Mews 6
WA7 22
Southlands Rd CW12 179
Southlands View CW4 107
Southlawn SK9 60
Southport St WA9 1
Southward Rd WA11 2
Southwark Pl CW7 149
Southway
Altrincham WA14 238
Runcorn WA7 49
Widnes WA8 22
Southway Ave WA4 26
Southwell Cl Golborne WA3 3
Romiley SK6 241
Southwood Ave WA7 24
Southworth Ave WA5 15
Southworth La WA2,WA3 8
Southworth Rd WA12 2
Sovereign Cl Golborne WA3 3
Northwich CW9 104
Runcorn WA7 50
Sovereign Ct WA3 9
Sovereign Way CH1 117
Spark Hall Cl WA4 26
Spark La Runcorn WA7 23
Smallwood CW11 154
Sparks Cl CH3 142
Sparrow La WA16 57
Sparrowbutts Gr ST7 195
Sparrowhawk Cl WA7 50
Sparth La SK4 240
Sparthfield Rd SK4 240
Spath La SK8 34
Spath La E SK8 35
Spath Wlk SK8 35
Spawell Cl WA3 3
Speakman Ave WA12 2
Speakman St WA7 22
Speed's Way CH3 180
Speedwell Cl
7 Golborne WA3 3
Heswall CH60 41
Huntington CH3 142
Speedwell Dr CH60 41
Speedwell Rd ST5 210

eke Bvd L24,WA8 ....21 A3
eke Rd WA8 ....22 B3
encer Brook SK10 ....86 C3
encer Cl Alsager ST7 ....192 C2
/idnes WA8 ....12 C1
/istaston CW2 ....206 A4
encer Mews SK10 ....86 C3
encer St Barnton CW8 ....78 A2
orthwich CW8 ....103 C4
enlow Cl SK12 ....36 C1
ennymoor Ct WA7 ....49 C4
enser Rd CH64 ....41 C1
ey Cl Altrincham WA14 ....238 C6
/insford CW7 ....126 C1
ey Dr ST7 ....195 B1
ike Island (Nature
eserve)* WA8 ....23 A3
indle Ave SK15 ....242 F3
indle St CW12 ....156 C1
ink La WA16 ....80 A3
innaker Cl WA7 ....50 B3
inner Cres CW9 ....78 B4
inners La SK12 ....36 B2
inners Way SK10 ....87 C4
inney CW8 ....101 B3
inney Ave
oostrey CW4 ....107 C1
/idnes WA8 ....12 A1
inney Cl Handforth SK9 ....34 B2
/insford CW7 ....150 A4
inney Dr
lesmere Port CH66 ....69 B1
/eston CW2 ....207 A3
inney End CH3 ....166 A1
inney Gdns WA4 ....27 A2
inney La WA16 ....56 C2
inney Mead SK10 ....87 C1
inney The
leadle SK8 ....239 E3
eswall CH60 ....41 B3
awton-gate ST7 ....194 C2
eston CH64 ....41 B1
orley WA6 ....100 C3
andbach CW11 ....175 B3
/illaston (nr Nantwich)
W5 ....205 B3
inney Wlk WA7 ....24 A1
ires Gdns WA2 ....8 A4
irewood Gdns SK6 ....241 A2
ital Wlk CH2 ....118 C1
odegreen La WA14 ....30 B4
out La WA16 ....58 A2
ragg St CW12 ....156 C2
ring Ave 2 CH66 ....69 B3
ring Bank
trincham WA14 ....238 D3
alybridge SK15 ....242 E1
ne Bank ST7 ....195 A4
ring Bank La SK10 ....63 A3
ring Bank Pl SK1 ....240 E4
ring Bank Rd SK22 ....39 B4
ring Cl ST7 ....193 C4
ring Ct WA7 ....23 A1
ring Gdns Crewe CW1 ....190 C3
esmere Port CH66 ....69 B3
yde SK14 ....241 D8
acclesfield SK10 ....87 B1
antwich CW5 ....204 C3
ring Hill CW6 ....168 B4
ring La
oddington CH3 ....181 C3
oft WA3 ....9 A3
mm WA13 ....19 C2
ring Mdw CW8 ....78 C1
ring Mount SK22 ....39 B4
ring Rd
trincham WA14 ....238 D2
oynton SK12 ....36 C1
ring St
alybridge SK15 ....242 D2
idnes WA8 ....23 A3
ilmslow SK9 ....60 A4
ringbank SK10 ....87 C4
ringbank Cl WA7 ....49 A3
ringbank Cres CW7 ....149 B4
ringbourne WA6 ....74 B3
ringburn Gdns WA1 ....17 C4
ringcroft CH64 ....41 B1
ringe La CW5 ....203 A3
ringfield Ave
olborne WA3 ....2 C4
elsby WA6 ....73 A2
mm WA13 ....19 A3
alpas SY14 ....213 B2
arrington, Grappenhall
A4 ....17 A2
arrington, Padgate WA1 ....17 A4
ringfield Cl CH4 ....161 A4
ringfield Cres CW8 ....77 C2
ringfield Ct CH4 ....161 A4
ringfield Dr
hester CH2 ....118 C2
ilmslow SK9 ....59 B3
istaston CW2 ....205 C4
ringfield Pk WA11 ....1 B4
ringfield Prim Sch
33 ....242 B6
ringfield Rd
trincham WA14 ....238 D5
atley SK8 ....239 B5
acclesfield SK11 ....111 C4
alpas SY14 ....213 A2
obberley WA16 ....57 C2
ale M33 ....242 B6
idnes WA8 ....22 A4
ringfield Sch CW1 ....190 C2
ringfield Specl Sch
V1 ....191 A2

Springfield St WA1 ....16 A3
Springfields
Cuddington CW8 ....101 B2
Knutsford WA16 ....57 B2
Mickle Trafford CH2 ....119 C4
Prestbury SK10 ....87 A4
Springfields Dr CW12 ....156 B2
Springhead Cl ST7 ....210 B3
Springhead Prim Sch
ST7 ....210 B3
Springhill SK10 ....88 A1
Springhill Ave CH62 ....43 B3
Springholm Dr WA4 ....26 B2
Springmount WA3 ....3 C4
Springs La SK15 ....242 C3
Springs The WA14 ....238 B2
Springvale Ind Est
CW11 ....174 B3
Springwell Cl CW2 ....206 B4
Springwood Ave WA16 ....57 B2
Springwood Cl
Blacon CH1 ....117 B2
Macclesfield SK10 ....87 B3
Springwood Cres SK6 ....241 E2
Springwood La SK6 ....241 F3
Springwood Prim Sch
SK6 ....241 E3
Springwood Way SK10 ....87 B3
Sprink La CW12 ....157 B3
Sproston Way CW9 ....103 C2
Spruce Ave CW8 ....102 A2
Spruce Cl Golborne WA3 ....3 C4
Warrington WA1 ....17 C4
Spruce Gr ST7 ....193 C4
Spruce Lodge SK8 ....239 D6
Spuley La SK10 ....63 B1
Spunhill Ave CH66 ....69 B1
Spurling Rd WA5 ....6 C3
Spurston Cl WA16 ....29 B2
Square St SK11 ....112 C3
Square The
Altrincham WA15 ....32 B4
Audlem CW3 ....229 C2
Christleton CH3 ....142 C4
Elton CH2 ....71 C3
Holmes Chapel CW4 ....130 B2
Hyde SK14 ....241 D6
6 Lymm WA13 ....18 C2
Stockport SK4 ....240 C7
Woore CW3 ....232 B1
Squires Ave WA8 ....23 A4
Squires Cl WA11 ....1 A3
Squirrel Cl CW8 ....103 B4
Squirrel Dr WA14 ....238 C8
Squirrel's Jump SK9 ....60 B1
Squirrels Chase SK10 ....86 C3
Stable La
Mouldsworth CH3 ....99 A2
Utkinton CW6 ....123 C1
Stables The
Guilden Sutton CH3 ....119 C3
Winsford CW10 ....127 B3
Stablings The SK9 ....60 A3
Stadium Ind Est CH1 ....118 A2
Stadium Way CH1 ....118 A2
Stadmorslow La ST7 ....195 C2
Staffin Ave CH65 ....95 A4
Stafford Cl SK10 ....86 C1
Stafford Gdns CH65 ....70 A3
Stafford Rd WA4 ....16 B1
Stafford St Audlem CW3 ....230 A2
Crewe CW1 ....190 B3
Stafford Way 2 M34 ....241 A5
Stafford Wlk SK10 ....86 C1
Stag Ind Est WA14 ....238 B6
Stage La WA13 ....19 B2
Stainer Cl WA12 ....2 A3
Staines Cl WA4 ....26 C3
Stainforth Cl WA3 ....4 B2
Stainmore Cl WA3 ....10 A3
Staithes Rd M22 ....33 B4
Stalbridge Rd CW2 ....190 B1
Staley Cl SK15 ....242 F2
Staley Hall Cres SK15 ....242 F3
Stallard Way CW10 ....151 B4
Stalmine Ave SK8 ....34 A4
Staly Hall Rd SK15 ....242 F2
Staly Ind Est SK15 ....242 E2
Stalybridge Sta SK15 ....242 C2
Stamford Ave
Altrincham WA14 ....238 A5
Crewe CW2 ....190 B2
Stalybridge SK15 ....242 B2
Stamford Cl
Macclesfield SK11 ....112 B2
Stalybridge SK15 ....242 B2
Stamford Com High Sch
OL6 ....242 B4
Stamford Ct Chester CH3 ....119 B1
7 Lymm WA13 ....18 C2
Macclesfield SK11 ....112 B3
Stalybridge OL6 ....242 A2
Stamford Dr SK15 ....242 C2
Stamford Gr SK15 ....242 C2
Stamford Grange 1
WA14 ....238 C4
Stamford La CH3 ....120 A1
Stamford New Rd
WA14 ....238 D4
Stamford Park Inf Sch
WA15 ....238 E3
Stamford Park Jun Sch
WA15 ....238 E3
Stamford Park Rd
WA15 ....238 E3
Stamford Pl M33 ....242 C6
Stamford Rd
Alderley Edge SK9 ....60 A1

Stamford Rd *continued*
Altrincham WA14 ....238 C2
Blacon CH1 ....117 C3
Handforth SK9 ....34 A1
Little Bollington WA14 ....20 A1
Macclesfield SK11 ....112 B2
Stamford Sq
3 Altrincham WA14 ....238 D5
Ashton-u-Lyne OL6 ....242 A2
Stamford St
Altrincham WA14 ....238 D5
Ellesmere Port CH65 ....70 A3
Sale M33 ....242 A8
Stalybridge SK15 ....242 C2
Stamford St E OL6 ....242 A2
Stamford Way 2 WA14 ....238 D5
Stamore Rd WA7 ....23 B1
Stamp Ave CW1 ....190 B3
Stanbank St SK4 ....240 E8
Stanbridge Ct SK4 ....240 E6
Standford Dr CW9 ....104 A3
Standish Ct WA8 ....22 B4
Stanford Cl CW9 ....103 C3
Stanhope Ave CW1 ....190 C2
Stanhope Cl SK9 ....60 B4
Stanhope Rd WA14 ....238 A2
Stanhope St OL6 ....242 A4
Stanier Cl CW1 ....191 A2
Stanlaw Abbey Prim Sch
CH65 ....70 C1
Stanlaw Rd CH65 ....70 B2
Stanley & Brocklehurst Ct
SK11 ....112 B4
Stanley Ave Hyde SK14 ....241 E8
Warrington, Great Sankey
WA5 ....14 B4
Warrington, Stockton Heath
WA4 ....16 C1
Stanley Bank Rd WA11 ....1 A4
Stanley Cl Hartford CW8 ....103 A2
Widnes WA8 ....13 B1
Stanley Ct ST7 ....193 B2
Stanley Dr Gatley SK8,SK9 ....34 B3
Newcastle-u-L ST5 ....210 B1
Stanley Gr Northwich CW9 ....79 C1
Stockport SK4 ....240 B8
Stanley Green Ind Est
SK8 ....34 C3
Stanley Green Ret Pk
SK8 ....34 C3
Stanley Hall La SK12 ....38 B3
Stanley La CH62 ....43 C2
Stanley Mount M33 ....242 A5
Stanley Park Ct CH4 ....140 C3
Stanley Park Dr CH4 ....140 C3
Stanley Pl Chester CH1 ....237 A2
Warrington WA4 ....16 C1
Stanley Rd Biddulph ST8 ....179 B1
Ellesmere Port CH65 ....70 B4
Handforth SK8,SK9 ....34 C3
Knutsford WA16 ....56 C1
Stockport SK4 ....240 B7
Stanley Rd Ind Est WA16 ....57 A1
Stanley Sq SK15 ....242 C1
Stanley St Chester CH1 ....237 A2
Crewe CW1 ....190 B2
Macclesfield SK11 ....112 B4
Newton-le-W WA12 ....2 A2
Northwich CW9 ....104 B4
Runcorn WA7 ....23 A2
Stalybridge SK15 ....242 C1
Warrington WA1 ....16 A2
Stanley Villas 5 WA7 ....22 C1
Stanley Woods Ave CH2 ....95 B4
Stanlow & Thornton Sta
CH2 ....71 B3
Stanlow Abbey Bsns Ctr
CH65 ....70 B1
Stannage La CH3 ....180 C3
Stanner Cl WA5 ....7 B1
Stannerhouse La CW11 ....175 C2
Stanney Cl
Bebington CH62 ....43 C2
Neston CH64 ....66 C4
Stanney Grange Com Prim
Sch CH65 ....70 B2
Stanney Grange Sports
Complex The CH65 ....70 C2
Stanney High Sch CH65 ....70 B1
Stanney La
Ellesmere Port CH65 ....70 B2
Stoak CH2 ....70 C1
Stanney Mill Ind Est CH2 ....70 C2
Stanney Mill La CH2 ....70 C1
Stanney Mill Rd CH2 ....70 C1
Stanney Ten Ind Est CH2 ....70 C1
Stanney Woods Ave
CH65 ....70 B1
Stanney Woods Ctry Pk*
CH65 ....70 A1
Stanneybrook Cl WA6 ....101 A3
Stanneylands Cl SK9 ....34 B1
Stanneylands Dr SK9 ....34 A1
Stanneylands Rd SK9 ....34 A1
Stansfield Ave WA1 ....16 C3
Stansfield Dr WA4 ....27 A4
Stansfield Rd SK14 ....241 E8
Stanstead Ave WA5 ....14 C2
Stanthorne Ave CW2 ....190 A2
Stanton Cl WA11 ....1 B3
Stanton Ct CH64 ....66 C4
Stanton Dr CH2 ....118 B3
Stanton Rd WA4 ....17 B2
Stanway Dr WA15 ....238 F3
Stapeley Broad Lane CE Prim
Sch CW5 ....205 A1
Stapeley Ct CW1 ....190 A3
Stapeley Gdns L26 ....21 A3

Stapeley Terr CW5 ....205 A2
Stapeley Water Gdns*
CW5 ....205 A2
Stapleford Cl M33 ....242 E7
Stapleford Ct CH66 ....69 C4
Stapleton Ave WA2 ....16 B4
Stapleton Ct WA6 ....74 B4
Stapleton Rd SK10 ....87 A1
Stapleton Way WA8 ....22 A3
Stapley Cl
Northwich CW9 ....103 C2
Runcorn WA7 ....22 C1
Star La Lymm WA13 ....18 B2
Macclesfield SK11 ....112 B2
Starbeck Dr CH66 ....69 A3
Starkey Gr WA4 ....16 C2
Starling Cl Farndon CH3 ....180 C1
Kidsgrove ST7 ....195 B2
Runcorn WA7 ....50 B4
Start La SK23 ....65 A4
Statham Ave Lymm WA13 ....18 B2
Warrington WA2 ....8 B1
Statham Cl Hyde M34 ....241 A7
Lymm WA13 ....18 B2
Statham Com Prim Sch
WA13 ....18 B2
Statham Dr WA13 ....18 B2
Statham La WA13 ....18 A3
Statham St SK11 ....112 B4
Station Ave
Ellesmere Port CH66 ....69 B4
Helsby WA6 ....73 A2
Station Cl Hyde SK14 ....241 D6
Neston CH64 ....66 C4
Station Gn CH66 ....69 B4
Station Hill CW8 ....76 C1
Station La
Guilden Sutton CH2 ....119 C4
Rushton Spencer SK11 ....159 A1
Station Rd Adderley TF9 ....235 A3
Alpraham CW6 ....169 C1
Alsager ST7 ....193 B2
Astbury ST7,CW12 ....178 A1
Backford CH1 ....95 A2
Biddulph ST8 ....179 B1
Bosley SK11 ....135 A1
Chelford SK11 ....84 A1
Chester CH2 ....237 C4
Crowton CW8 ....76 B1
Delamere CW8 ....123 B4
Ellesmere Port CH65 ....70 B3
Ellesmere Port, Little Sutton
CH66 ....69 B3
Elton CH2 ....72 A3
Goostrey CW4 ....131 A4
Hawarden CH5 ....116 A1
Haydock WA11 ....1 B3
Heswall CH60 ....40 C3
Holmes Chapel CW4 ....130 B1
Irlam M44 ....11 C4
Kidsgrove ST7 ....194 C1
Kidsgrove, Newchapel ST7 ....195 C1
Lostock Gralam CW9 ....80 A1
Mobberley WA16 ....57 C4
Mouldsworth CH3 ....99 A1
Mow Cop ST7 ....195 B4
Nantwich CW5 ....204 C3
Neston CH64 ....66 C4
Neston, Burton CH64 ....67 A1
Neston, Parkgate CH64 ....66 B4
New Mills SK22 ....39 A4
4 Northwich CW9 ....79 A1
Partington WA14 ....20 A3
Runcorn WA7 ....22 C1
Sandbach CW11 ....174 B4
Scholar Green ST7 ....195 A4
Stockport SK3 ....240 E4
Sutton WA7 ....50 A2
Warrington WA4 ....16 C1
Warrington, Fearnhead WA2 ....9 A1
Warrington, Great Sankey
WA5 ....14 C3
Warrington, Penketh WA5 ....14 C2
Weaverham CW8 ....77 A1
Whaley Bridge SK23 ....39 B2
Wilmslow SK9 ....60 A4
Wilmslow, Handforth SK9 ....34 B2
Wilmslow, Styal SK9 ....34 A2
Winsford CW7 ....127 A1
Worleston CW5 ....188 C3
Station Rd N WA2 ....9 A1
Station Rd S WA2 ....9 A1
Station St SK10 ....87 B1
Station View
Chester CH2 ....118 C1
Nantwich CW5 ....204 C2
Sandbach CW11 ....174 B4
Staveley Ave SK15 ....242 D3
Staveley Dr CW7 ....126 B1
Stayley Dr SK15 ....242 F2
Steadings The CH3 ....120 A2
Steam Mill St CH2 ....237 C3
Stearns Cl CH1 ....118 A3
Stearns Ho CH1 ....118 A3
Steel St WA1 ....16 C4
Steele Rd CW10 ....151 B3
Steele St CH1 ....237 B2
Steeles Ave SK14 ....241 E7
Steeple Ct CH64 ....66 C4
Steeple St SK10 ....87 C1
Stein Ave WA3 ....3 C4
Stenhills Cres WA7 ....23 B1
Step Hill 30 SK11 ....112 B4
Stephen St WA1 ....16 B3
Stephen's Gr WA6 ....73 A1
Stephens Gdns CH66 ....69 A3
Stephens Rd SK15 ....242 C4
Stephens Terr CH66 ....69 A3

Stephens Way ST7 ....209 C1
Stephenson Dr CW1 ....191 A2
Stephenson Rd WA12 ....2 B1
Stephenson Wlk CW7 ....149 A4
Sterling Cl CW9 ....103 C3
Sterndale Rd
Romiley SK6 ....241 B1
Stockport SK3 ....240 E1
Sterne Cl CW11 ....174 B3
Stetchworth Rd WA4 ....16 A1
Steven Ct CH2 ....237 C3
Stevenage Cl SK11 ....112 A4
Stevenage Dr SK11 ....112 A4
Stevens Rd CH60 ....41 B4
Stevens St SK9 ....60 A1
Steventon WA7 ....24 C2
Steward's Ave WA8 ....22 C4
Stewart St CW2 ....190 A2
Stile End CH2 ....119 C4
Stiles The CW8 ....101 B3
Stiperstones Cl CH66 ....69 A3
Stirling Cl Chester CH3 ....119 A1
Macclesfield SK10 ....86 C1
Stockport SK3 ....240 C2
Warrington WA1 ....17 C4
Winsford CW7 ....127 A2
Stirling Ct
Ellesmere Port CH65 ....70 B2
Holmes Chapel CW4 ....130 A1
Stirling Dr SK15 ....242 D3
Stirrup Cl WA2 ....9 A2
Stitch La SK4 ....240 D7
Stoak Lodge CH65 ....70 B2
Stock La CW2,CW5 ....206 A1
Stockdale Ave SK3 ....240 F1
Stockham Cl WA7 ....50 A4
Stockham La WA7 ....50 A4
Stockholm Rd SK3 ....240 E2
Stockley Farm* CW9 ....54 C4
Stockley La WA4 ....52 C4
Stockport Air Raid Shelters*
SK1 ....240 E5
Stockport Coll of F & H Ed
SK1 ....240 F4
Stockport Rd
Altrincham WA15 ....238 F5
Cheadle SK8 ....239 E6
Romiley SK6 ....241 B2
Stockport SK3 ....240 A3
Warrington WA4 ....17 C2
Stockport Rd E SK6 ....241 A4
Stockport Sta SK3 ....240 E4
Stockport Trad Est SK4 ....240 B4
Stocks Ave 7 CH3 ....119 A1
Stocks Gdns SK15 ....242 F1
Stocks Hill CW7 ....149 C4
Stocks La Chester CH3 ....119 A1
Knutsford WA16 ....82 C1
Rainow SK10 ....88 C3
Stalybridge SK15 ....242 F1
Warrington WA5 ....14 B3
Stockswell Rd WA8 ....12 A2
Stockton Ave 4 SK3 ....240 B4
Stockton Heath Prim Sch
WA4 ....16 B1
Stockton La WA4 ....16 C1
Stockton Rd SK9 ....59 C2
Stoke Abbott Cl SK7 ....35 C4
Stoke Cl CH62 ....43 C2
Stoke Gdns CH65 ....70 B2
Stoke Wlk CH65 ....70 B2
Stokehall La CW5 ....187 C3
Stokes St WA3 ....9 C3
Stokesay Ct CH65 ....70 C2
Stokoe Ave WA14 ....238 A6
Stone Barn La WA7 ....50 A3
Stone Chair La ST7 ....194 C4
Stone Cotts CW12 ....157 C1
Stone Croft CH3 ....142 A4
Stone Cross La N WA3 ....3 B4
Stone Cross La S WA3 ....3 B3
Stone Heyes La CW8,CW9 ....77 C3
Stone House La CW6 ....184 C3
Stone Mead SK6 ....241 E3
Stone Mead Ave WA15 ....32 B4
Stone Pit La WA3 ....3 C1
Stone Pl CH2 ....118 C2
Stoneacre Gdns WA4 ....26 C2
Stonebank Dr CH64 ....67 A3
Stonebridge Rd CW5 ....204 C2
Stonechat Cl
Crewe CW1 ....189 C4
8 Golborne WA3 ....3 C4
Runcorn WA7 ....49 C3
Stonecliffe Ave SK15 ....242 D2
Stonecliffe Terr SK15 ....242 D3
Stonecrop Cl
Runcorn WA7 ....49 C2
Warrington WA3 ....9 B2
Stonehaven Dr WA2 ....9 A2
Stoneheads SK23 ....65 B4
Stoneheads Rise SK23 ....65 B4
Stonehill Cl WA4 ....26 B2
Stonehills Ct WA7 ....23 B1
Stonehills La WA7 ....23 B1
Stonehouse Gn CW12 ....156 B2
Stonelea WA7 ....24 A1
Stoneleigh Cl SK10 ....87 B1
Stoneleigh Gdns WA4 ....17 B1
Stoneley Ave CW1 ....190 B4
Stoneley Rd CW1 ....190 B4
Stonemill Terr SK5 ....240 F7
Stonepail Rd SK8 ....239 A5
Stones Manor La CW8 ....103 B3
Stoney Holt WA7 ....50 B4

Stoney La Delamere CW6 .123 B3
Wilmslow SK9 .59 C3
Stoneyfield SK15 .242 D4
Stoneyfold La SK11 .113 A3
Stoneyford La CW8 .101 B1
Stoneyhurst Cres WA3 .4 B3
Stoneyland Dr SK22 .39 A4
Stony La CW12 .156 B1
Stonyford Rd M33 .242 D6
Stopford St SK3 .240 D4
Stopsley Cl CW12 .155 C2
Stour Cl WA14 .238 C6
Stour Ct CH65 .70 A4
Stourport Cl SK6 .241 A1
Stradbroke Cl WA3 .4 A4
Straight Length WA6 .73 C4
Straight Mile CH4 .162 C3
Straker Ave CH65 .69 C3
Stratford Rd Blacon CH1 .117 C2
Neston CH64 .66 B3
Stratford Sq SK8 .34 B4
Stratford Way SK11 .112 B3
Strathaven Ave CW2 .205 C4
Strathearn Rd CH60 .40 C4
Strathmore Ave M34 .241 B6
Strathmore Cl CW4 .130 A1
Stratton Cl WA7 .50 A3
Stratton Pk WA8 .12 C3
Stratton Rd WA5 .15 A3
Strawberry Cl
Altrincham WA14 .238 B7
Warrington WA3 .9 B2
Strawberry Dr CH1 .95 A4
Strawberry Fields CH3 .142 A4
Strawberry Gn CH1 .95 A4
Strawberry La
Acton Bridge CW8 .76 C2
Mollington CH1 .94 B2
Wilmslow SK9 .59 C3
Street Forest Walks The* SK17 .90 C2
Street Hey La CH64 .43 A1
Street La Adlington SK10 .62 B4
Rode Heath ST7 .176 C1
Whitley WA4 .52 B2
Street The
Mickle Trafford CH2 .119 B4
Whaley Bridge SK10,SK17 .90 B3
Stretton Ave WA3 .3 C4
Stretton Cl CH62 .43 C2
Stretton Hall Mews WA4 .52 C4
Stretton Mill* SY14 .198 A3
Stretton Rd WA4 .26 C1
Stretton Way 3 SK9 .34 B3
Stretton Wlk CW9 .103 C2
Strickland Cl WA4 .27 A4
Strines Ct SK14 .241 E8
Strines Rd SK6 .38 B4
Stringer Ave CW11 .175 B3
Stringer Cres WA4 .16 C2
Stringer's La LL12,CH4 .161 A2
Strumness Cl WA2 .9 A2
Stuart Cl Chester CH3 .119 B2
Winsford CW7 .149 B3
Stuart Ct SK10 .87 A1
Stuart Dr WA4 .16 C1
Stuart Hampson Ct 8 M31 .11 C2
Stuart Pl CH2 .237 B3
Stuart Rd
Altrincham WA14 .238 B7
Runcorn WA7 .24 B2
Stubbs La
Lostock Gralam CW9 .80 A1
Mobberley WA16 .58 C2
Stubbs Pl CH1 .117 C2
Stubbs Terr SK11 .112 C4
Stubby La SK10 .84 C1
Sturgess St WA12 .1 C2
Styal Cl 9 CW9 .103 C2
Styal Ctry Pk* SK9 .33 C2
Styal Gn SK9 .33 C2
Styal Gr SK8 .239 A3
Styal Prim Sch SK9 .33 C2
Styal Rd
Gatley M22,SK8,SK9 .239 A3
Wilmslow SK9 .60 A4
Wythenshawe M22 .33 C4
Styal Sta SK9 .34 A2
Styal View SK9 .34 A1
Styperson Way SK12 .36 C2
Sudbrook Cl WA3 .3 C4
Sudbury Dr SK8 .34 B4
Sudbury Rd SK7 .36 C4
Sudlow La Knutsford WA16 .56 B1
Plumley WA16 .81 B4
Suez St Newton-le-W WA12 .2 A2
Warrington WA1 .16 A3
Suffolk Ave CH65 .69 C3
Suffolk Cl
Congleton CW12 .156 B2
Macclesfield SK10 .86 C1
Warrington WA1 .17 C3
Suffolk Dr SK9 .34 B1
Suffolk Pl WA8 .22 B4
Suffolk Rd WA14 .238 B5
Suffolk St WA7 .22 C2
Sugar La Adlington SK10 .63 A2
Manley WA6 .98 C3
Rainow SK10 .88 B3
Sugar Pit La WA16 .56 C2
Sugden St OL6 .242 A3
Sulby Ave WA4 .16 A2
Sulgrave Ave SK12 .36 C2
Summer Cl WA7 .23 C1
Summer La
Daresbury WA4 .51 B4
Runcorn WA7 .23 C1
Summerfield ST7 .195 A1
Summerfield Ave WA5 .7 C1
Summerfield Cl CH4 .139 A2
Summerfield Dr CW9 .126 C4
Summerfield Pl SK9 .60 A3
Summerfield Rd
Guilden Sutton CH3 .119 C3
Mobberley WA16 .57 C2
Summerfields WA16 .57 B2
Summerfields Ctr SK9 .34 B1
Summerhill Dr ST5 .210 B1
Summerhill Rd SK10 .86 C2
Summerlea SK8 .35 A4
Summerlea Cl SK10 .87 B1
Summers Ave SK15 .242 F2
Summers Cl WA16 .82 A4
Summers Way WA16 .82 A4
Summertrees Rd CH66 .69 C2
Summerville Gdns WA4 .16 C1
Summit Cl WA4 .26 C1
Sumner Rd CH1 .117 C2
Sumner St WA11 .1 A3
Sumpter Pathway CH2 .118 C2
Sunart Cl CW2 .206 A3
Sunbank La WA15 .32 C3
Sunbeam St WA12 .2 B2
Sunbury Cl SK9 .34 C1
Sunbury Cres CH4 .140 C3
Sunbury Gdns WA4 .26 C4
Suncroft Cl WA1 .17 C4
Suncroft Rd CH60 .41 B4
Sundale Dr CW2 .189 B2
Sunderland St SK11 .112 B4
Sundown Cl SK22 .39 A4
Sunfield SK6 .241 C3
Sunfield Cl CH66 .69 B2
Sunningdale Ave
Sale M33 .242 E5
Widnes WA8 .12 A1
Sunningdale Cl
Burtonwood WA5 .6 C3
Northwich CW9 .104 C4
Winsford CW7 .126 A1
Sunningdale Ct M33 .242 E5
Sunningdale Dr
Bebington CH63 .43 A3
Bramhall SK7 .36 A4
Sunningdale Rd
Denton M34 .241 B5
Macclesfield SK11 .112 A3
Sunningdale Way CH64 .66 C2
Sunninghey Ct SK9 .59 C1
Sunny Bank Wilmslow SK9 .59 B2
Wilmslow SK9 .60 A3
Sunny Bank Cl SK11 .112 B3
Sunny Bank Cotts WA8 .14 A2
Sunny Bank Rd WA14 .31 B4
Sunny Lea Mews SK9 .60 A3
Sunnybank Cl WA12 .2 B2
Sunnybank Rd CW1, CW2 .189 C3
Sunnyside Alsager ST7 .193 A2
Malpas SY14 .212 C1
Warrington WA5 .14 C3
Sunnyside Cres OL6 .242 A2
Sunnyside Gr OL6 .242 A2
Sunnyside La WA7 .24 C2
Sunset Cotts CH64 .67 A2
Surrey Dr CW12 .156 C3
Surrey Rd Chester CH2 .119 A3
Kidsgrove ST7 .195 A1
Warren SK11 .112 A2
Surrey St Crewe CW1 .190 C2
Runcorn WA7 .23 A1
Warrington WA4 .16 B2
Surridge WA16 .29 B3
Susan Dr WA5 .14 B3
Susan St WA8 .13 B1
Sussex Ave SK11 .112 A3
Sussex Dr ST7 .194 C1
Sussex Pl CW12 .156 C3
Sussex Rd Chester CH2 .118 C2
Irlam M44 .11 B3
Partington M31 .11 C1
Stockport SK3 .240 B4
Sussex St WA8 .13 B1
Sussex Way CH2 .118 C2
Sutch La WA13 .19 A2
Sutherland Ct WA7 .23 A1
Sutherland Dr
Bebington CH62 .43 B2
Macclesfield SK10 .87 A1
Sutherland St OL6 .242 B3
Sutherland Way CH3 .119 A2
Sutton Ave Culcheth WA3 .4 C2
Neston CH64 .66 C3
Sutton Causeway WA6, WA7 .49 C1
Sutton Cl Bebington CH62 .43 C2
Higher Wincham CW9 .79 C3
Macclesfield SK11 .112 B3
Mickle Trafford CH2 .119 C4
Sutton Dr CH2 .118 C3
Sutton Green Prim Sch CH66 .69 B3
Sutton Hall Dr CH66 .69 A3
Sutton Hall Gdns CH66 .69 A3
Sutton High Sch CH66 .69 C3
Sutton La CW10 .151 B4
Sutton Quays Bsns Pk WA7 .49 C2
Sutton Rd
Alderley Edge SK9 .59 C1
Poynton SK12 .37 A1
Stockport SK4 .240 C7
Sutton St Runcorn WA7 .23 A1
Warrington WA1 .16 B2
Sutton Way
Ellesmere Port CH66 .69 C2
1 Handforth SK9 .34 C3
Sutton's La WA8 .23 A4
Swaine St SK3 .240 E5
Swale Cl SK9 .34 C1
Swale Dr WA14 .238 C6
Swale Rd CH65 .70 A4
Swaledale Ave CW12 .157 A3
Swaledale Cl
Bebington CH62 .43 C3
Warrington WA5 .14 C4
Swallow Cl
9 Kidsgrove ST7 .195 A1
Macclesfield SK10 .113 A4
Warrington WA3 .9 C2
Swallow Ct CW7 .149 B3
Swallow Dr Alsager ST7 .193 A2
Sandbach CW11 .175 A4
Swallow St SK1 .240 F3
Swallowfield Cl CW2 .206 A4
Swallowfield Gdns WA4 .26 C3
Swallowfields CH3 .180 C1
Swallowmore View ST7 .210 B4
Swan Ave WA9 .1 A1
Swan Bank
Congleton CW12 .156 B1
Talke ST7 .210 B4
Swan Cl
Ellesmere Port CH66 .69 C2
Poynton SK12 .36 A2
Talke ST7 .210 B4
Swan Ct CW8 .101 C4
Swan Farm La CW3 .232 A1
Swan Gr WA16 .106 B4
Swan La CW6 .185 C4
Swan Rd WA12 .1 C2
Swan St Congleton CW12 .156 B1
Wilmslow SK9 .60 A4
Swanage Cl WA4 .16 C1
Swanage Ct 6 CW7 .149 B3
Swanbourne Gdns SK3 .240 C2
Swanley La CW5 .203 B2
Swanlow Ave CW7 .149 B3
Swanlow Dr CW7 .149 B3
Swanlow La CW7 .149 C3
Swann La SK8 .35 A4
Swanscoe Av SK10 .88 A4
Swanscoe Cl CW10 .151 A4
Swanscoe La SK10 .88 A2
Swanwick Cl CW4 .107 B1
Sweet Briar Cres CW2 .189 C2
Sweet Brier Cl CW8 .78 A2
Sweetenham Cl ST7 .193 B2
Sweetfield Gdns CH66 .69 B4
Sweetfield Rd CH66 .69 B4
Sweettooth La CW11 .175 A4
Swettenham Cl CW11 .175 B4
Swettenham La CW12 .131 C2
Swettenham Rd
Swettenham CW12 .132 A1
Wilmslow SK9 .34 B3
Swettenham St SK11 .112 C4
Swift Cl Kidsgrove ST7 .195 A1
Warrington WA2 .8 C2
Wistaston CW2 .205 C4
Swinburne Dr CW1 .190 C2
Swindale Ave WA2 .8 A2
Swinden Cl WA7 .24 B1
Swine Market 7 CW5 .204 C3
Swineyard La WA16 .28 B2
Swinford Ave WA8 .13 C1
Swinley Chase SK9 .34 C1
Swinleys Hey CH3 .142 A4
Swinnerton St CW2 .190 B1
Swinton Sq 15 WA16 .57 A1
Swireford Rd WA6 .73 A1
Swiss Cott SK10 .87 A1
Swiss Hill SK9 .60 A1
Swithin Rd M22 .33 C4
Swynnerton Way WA8 .13 A3
Swythamley Cl SK3 .240 A4
Swythamley Rd SK3 .240 A4
Sycamore Ave
Alsager ST7 .193 C1
Altrincham WA14 .238 A5
Congleton CW12 .155 C2
Crewe CW1 .190 B3
Haydock WA11 .1 A3
Newton-le-W WA12 .2 B2
Rode Heath ST7 .193 C4
Widnes WA8 .13 A1
Winsford CW7 .149 B4
Sycamore Cl
Ashton-u-Lyne OL6 .242 B2
Audlem CW3 .230 A2
Biddulph ST8 .179 C1
Handforth SK9 .34 A1
Holmes Chapel CW4 .130 B2
Talke ST7 .210 C4
Sycamore Cres
Barnton CW8 .78 A2
Hollinfare WA3 .11 A1
Macclesfield SK11 .112 A4
Sycamore Ct CW5 .204 C4
Sycamore Dr
Chester CH4 .140 C3
Ellesmere Port CH66 .70 A1
Lymm WA13 .18 B2
Middlewich CW10 .151 C3
Sutton WA7 .50 A2
Sycamore Gr
Broughton CH4 .139 A2
Sandbach CW11 .175 A4
Sycamore La WA5 .15 A3
Sycamore Lane Prim Sch WA5 .15 A3
Sycamore Lodge SK7 .35 C4
Sycamore Rd
Partington M31 .11 C2
Romiley SK6 .241 A4
Runcorn WA7 .49 B4
Sycamore Rise SK11 .112 A3
Sycamore St Sale M33 .242 E6
Stockport SK3 .240 B4
Sycamore Wlk SK8 .239 D6
Sycamores The WA16 .58 C1
Syddal Cl SK7 .35 B3
Syddal Cres SK7 .35 B2
Syddal Gn SK7 .35 B3
Syddal Park Prep Sch SK7 .35 B3
Syddal Park Sch SK7 .35 B3
Syddal Rd SK7 .35 B3
Syddall Ave SK8 .34 B4
Syddall St SK14 .241 D6
Sydney Ave M90 .33 A4
Sydney Rd Blacon CH1 .118 A2
Cheadle SK7 .35 C3
Crewe CW1 .190 C3
Sydney St
Northwich CW8 .103 B4
Runcorn WA7 .48 B4
Syers Ct WA1 .16 C4
Sykes Mdw SK3 .240 D2
Sykes St SK14 .241 F5
Sylvan Ave
Altrincham WA15 .238 F8
Sale M33 .242 C5
Wilmslow SK9 .59 C3
Sylvan Cl CW8 .103 B4
Sylvan Gr WA14 .238 D5
Sylvan Mews CH1 .117 C3
Sylvia Cres WA2 .8 B1
Symondley Rd SK11 .112 C1
Symons Rd M33 .242 B7
Synge St WA2 .16 B4
Sytch Croft CH64 .66 C4

T

Tabley Ave WA8 .12 B1
Tabley Cl Knutsford WA16 .56 C2
Macclesfield SK11 .112 A4
Sandbach CW11 .174 C4
Tabley Gr WA16 .56 C1
Tabley Hill La WA16 .56 A1
Tabley Ho* WA16 .81 A4
Tabley Mere Gdns SK8 .239 F3
Tabley Rd Crewe CW2 .189 C2
Handforth SK9 .34 B3
Knutsford WA16 .56 C2
Tabley St CW9 .79 A1
Tabor St SK11 .112 C3
Tadgers La WA6 .73 B4
Tadman Gr WA14 .238 A6
Tailors View CW5 .204 C3
Talbot Ave CH64 .66 C3
Talbot Cl Neston CH64 .66 C3
Shavington CW2 .206 A2
Warrington WA3 .9 C2
Talbot Gdns CH64 .66 C3
Talbot Rd
Alderley Edge SK9 .60 A1
Altrincham WA14 .238 B2
Dunham-on-t-H WA6 .97 C4
Ellesmere Port CH66 .69 C2
Sale M33 .242 E6
Talbot St Chester CH2 .237 B4
Golborne WA3 .3 A4
Stockport SK1 .240 E5
Talfryn Cl CH5 .91 B1
Talisman Cl WA7 .50 B4
Talke Rd Alsager ST7 .193 C2
Audley ST5 .210 C1
Newcastle-u-L ST7,ST5 .210 B2
Tall Ash Ave CW12 .157 A2
Tall Trees Cl CW8 .103 B3
Tally Ho La CW5 .203 C2
Tamar Cl
Congleton CW12 .156 C1
Macclesfield SK10 .86 C1
Tamar Rd Haydock WA11 .1 B3
Kidsgrove ST7 .195 A1
Tamar Wlk CW7 .127 A1
Tame Cl Biddulph ST8 .179 B1
Sandbach CW11 .174 C4
Stalybridge SK15 .242 F3
Tame St SK15 .242 B1
Tame Wlk 9 SK9 .34 B1
Tameside Coll
Ashton-u-Lyne OL6 .242 A3
Hyde SK14 .241 E6
Tameside General Hospl OL6 .242 B4
Tameside Leisure Pk SK14 .241 F6
Tamworth Cl SK7 .36 B4
Tamworth St WA12 .2 A2
Tan House La
Burtonwood WA5 .7 A3
Widnes WA8 .23 B4
Tanfield Rd M20 .239 B8
Tang The SK6 .241 B1
Tanhouse Ind Est WA8 .23 B4
Tankersley Gr WA5 .15 A3
Tanner St
Congleton CW12 .156 C1
Hyde SK14 .241 D7
Tanner's La WA3 .3 A4
Tanners La WA2 .16 A3
Tanners Way CW5 .204 C2
Tannery La Neston CH64 .66
Warrington WA5 .14
Tannery Way WA14 .238
Tanning Ct 3 WA1 .16
Tanyard Dr WA15 .32
Tanyard La WA15 .32
Tapley Ave SK12 .36
Taplow Cl WA4 .26
Taplow Gr SK8 .239
Taporley War Meml Hospl CW6 .146
Target Cl ST7 .210
Target Rd CH60 .40
Tarn Cl CW7 .126
Tarn Ct WA1 .17
Tarn Mount SK11 .112
Tarnbeck WA7 .50
Tarns The SK8 .239
Tarnway WA3 .3
Tarporley Bsns Ctr CW6 .168
Tarporley CE Prim Sch CW6 .146
Tarporley Cl SK3 .240
Tarporley Com High Sch CW6 .146
Tarporley Rd
Duddon CW6 .145
Ellesmere Port CH66 .69
Little Budworth CW6,CW8 .124
Tarvin CH3 .121
Utkinton CW6 .146
Whitchurch SY13 .225
Whitley WA4 .52
Tarporley Wlk SK9 .34
Tarran Gr M34 .241
Tarran Pl WA14 .238
Tarrant Ct CH1 .94
Tarvin Ave CW2 .189
Tarvin Cl
Ellesmere Port CH65 .70
Golborne WA3 .3
Macclesfield SK11 .112
Middlewich CW10 .151
Runcorn WA7 .49
Tarvin Prim Sch CH3 .121
Tarvin Rd Alvanley WA6 .73
Bebington CH62 .43
Chester, Boughton CH3 .119
Chester, Vicarscross CH3 .119
Christleton CH3 .120
Frodsham WA6 .73
Manley WA6 .99
Tarvin Sands Industries CH3 .121
Tarvin Way 1 SK9 .34
Tasman Cl WA5 .15
Tate Cl WA8 .12
Tate Dr CW1 .191
Tattenhall La
Beeston CW6 .167
Tattenhall CH3 .167
Tattenhall Rd CH3 .166
Tatton Cl Alsager ST7 .193
Chester CH4 .140
Davenham CW9 .103
Winsford CW7 .126
Tatton Ct
4 Handforth SK9 .34
2 Knutsford WA16 .57
Stockport SK4 .240
Tatton Dr CW11 .175
Tatton Hall* WA16 .56
Tatton Lodge 14 WA16 .57
Tatton Pk* WA16 .57
Tatton Pl M33 .242
Tatton Rd Crewe CW2 .189
Denton M34 .241
Handforth SK9 .34
Sale M33 .242
Tatton Rd S SK4 .240
Tatton St Knutsford WA16 .57
Stalybridge SK15 .242
7 Stockport SK1 .240
Tatton Stile WA16 .58
Taunton Wlk 3 M34 .241
Taurus Pk WA5 .7
Tavener Cl CH63 .43
Tavistock Rd WA5 .14
Tavlin Ave WA5 .7
Tawney Cl ST7 .195
Tawny Ct WA7 .49
Taxal & Fernilee CE Prim Sc
SK23 .65
Taxal Ctr The SK23 .65
Taxal Moor Rd SK23 .65
Taxi Rd M90 .33
Taxmere Cl CW11 .174
Tay Cl ST8 .179
Taylor Ind Est WA3 .4
Taylor Rd
Altrincham WA14 .238
Haydock WA11 .1
Taylor St Hyde SK14 .241
Stalybridge SK15 .242
Warrington WA4 .16
Widnes WA8 .13
Taylor's La WA5 .14
Taylors La CW1 .192
Taylors Row WA7 .23
Teal Ave Knutsford WA16 .57
Poynton SK12 .36
Teal Cl Altrincham WA14 .238
Warrington WA2 .8
Warrington, Oakwood WA3 .9
Winsford CW7 .149
Tealby Cl CW9 .104
Teals Way CH60 .40
Tebay Rd CH62 .43

lder Dr M22 33 C4
lder Sq WA8 22 B4
ldington Cl WA4 26 C3
es Ct CH65 70 A4
esdale Cl WA5 14 C4
esdale Rd WA11 1 B4
ler Ct CW10 151 C3
g's Nose Ctry Pk*
11 113 B3
ggsnose La SK11 113 B3
gid Way CH4 140 B3
gsnose Mt SK11 113 B2
egraph Rd CH60 41 A4
ford Cl
ongleton CW12 157 A1
acclesfield SK10 88 A1
lke ST7 210 C4
idnes WA8 12 B2
ford Gdns CW11 174 C2
ford Pl CW5 204 B3
ford Rd CH65 70 C2
ford Way
idlem CW3 229 C2
hester CH4 140 C3
iddlewich CW10 128 C1
ford's Quay CH65 70 B4
mpest Rd SK9 60 B1
mplar Ct SK10 87 A1
mple Ct WA3 9 C3
mple Rd M33 242 D6
mplemoor Inf Sch
33 242 E6
mpleton Cl WA14 238 B6
nbury Cl WA5 15 A4
nby Cl WA5 7 C1
nby Dr WA7 23 B1
nby Rd
acclesfield SK11 111 C3
ockport SK3 240 B3
nchersfield CW5 205 A2
nnyson Ave CW1 190 C2
nnyson Cl
acclesfield SK11 111 C3
orthwich CW9 104 B3
ode Heath ST7 193 C4
ockport SK4 240 B6
istaston CW2 190 A1
nnyson Dr WA2 8 B1
nnyson Rd
eadle SK8 239 F6
lesmere Port CH65 70 A2
idnes WA8 13 A1
nnyson Wlk CH1 118 A3
nsing Cl WA5 15 A4
rence Ave WA1 16 C3
rminal Rd E M90 33 B4
rminal Rd N M90 33 A4
rminal Rd S M90 33 A4
rn Ave ST7 195 B1
rn Cl Altrincham WA14 238 B8
idnes WA8 13 A2
rn Dr SK12 36 A2
rra Nova Sch CW4 108 B1
rrace Rd WA8 23 A3
ick Rd SY13 226 A1
tchill Cl
lesmere Port CH66 69 B1
uncorn WA7 50 B4
tton Cl [8] CW12 156 C2
tton La CW10 151 C2
wkesbury Cl
ramhall SK8 35 A3
hester CH2 118 C4
lesmere Port CH66 94 C4
iddlewich CW10 128 A1
oynton SK12 36 B2
wkesbury Dr SK10 87 C2
wkesbury Rd
olborne WA3 3 A4
tockport SK3 240 B2
ackeray Dr CH3 119 B2
ackery Ct [6] CW11 174 B3
ames Cl
ongleton CW12 156 C1
arrington WA2 8 B1
ames Dr ST8 179 B1
ames Gdns CH65 70 A2
ames Rd WA3 5 A1
ames Side CH65 70 A2
ames Trad Ctr M44 11 C4
amesdale CH65 70 A2
atcher Cl WA14 238 C1
axted Wlk M22 33 B4
e Catholic High Sch
H4 141 B3
e Verdin High Sch
W7 126 B1
eatre Ct CW9 103 C4
elwall Cl [3] WA15 238 E6
elwall Com Inf Sch
A4 17 B2
elwall Com Jun Sch
A4 17 B2
elwall Ind Est WA4 17 B2
elwall La WA4 16 C2
elwall New Rd WA4 17 B2
elwall Rd
lesmere Port CH66 69 C2
ale M33 242 E5
eobald Rd WA14 238 D1
etford Cl SK10 87 B2
etford Rd WA5 14 C3
ewlis St WA5 15 C3
ird Ave
ongleton CW12 156 A2
onnah's Quay CH5 92 C1
rewe CW1 190 C1
idsgrove ST7 194 C1

Third Ave *continued*
Poynton SK12 36 B1
Runcorn WA7 49 C4
Sandbach CW11 175 A3
Thirlmere SK11 111 C3
Thirlmere Ave WA2 8 B2
Thirlmere Cl
Alderley Edge SK9 59 C1
Frodsham WA6 49 B1
Holmes Chapel CW4 130 A2
Stalybridge SK15 242 D4
Winsford CW7 126 C2
Thirlmere Ct CW12 156 A1
Thirlmere Dr WA13 18 C2
Thirlmere Lodge [5]
WA13 18 C2
Thirlmere Rd
Chester CH2 119 A3
Ellesmere Port CH65 70 B1
Neston CH64 66 C3
Partington M31 11 C2
Wistaston CW2 190 A1
Thirlmere Way WA8 22 B4
Thirsk Cl WA7 49 B3
Thirsk Way [6] SK10 87 B2
Thistle Cl WA16 79 C4
Thistle Sq M31 11 C1
Thistle Wlk [4] M31 11 C1
Thistleton Cl SK11 112 B3
Thistlewood Dr SK9 60 B4
Thomas Brassey Cl CH2 237 C4
Thomas Cl Alsager ST7 193 C2
Blacon CH1 117 C3
Ellesmere Port CH65 70 A1
Hyde M34 241 A8
Mickle Trafford CH2 119 C4
Thomas Ct WA7 49 C4
Thomas Ho CH1 118 A3
Thomas Hodges Ct
CW4 130 B2
Thomas Pl CW7 127 A1
Thomas St
Altrincham WA15 238 E4
Biddulph ST8 179 B1
Congleton CW12 156 C2
Crewe CW1 190 B2
Golborne WA3 3 A4
Packmoor ST7 195 C1
Romiley SK6 241 A3
Runcorn WA7 23 A2
Stockport SK1 240 F3
Talke ST7 210 B4
[20] Widnes WA8 23 A4
Thomas St W SK1 240 F3
Thomas Wedge CE Jun Sch
The CH1 94 A1
Thomasons Bridge La
WA4 25 C3
Thompson Ave WA3 4 C2
Thompson Cl WA12 2 B1
Thompson Ct SK15 242 C2
Thompson Fold SK15 242 C2
Thompson St WA3 9 C2
Thomson St SK3 240 E4
Thoresway Rd SK9 59 C3
Thoriby Rd WA3 4 C2
Thorley Gr CW2 190 A1
Thorley La M90 33 A4
Thorley Mews SK7 35 C4
Thorn Cl Runcorn WA7 49 B4
Warrington WA5 14 C2
Thorn Ct SK15 242 D2
Thorn Dr M22 34 A4
Thorn Gr
Altrincham WA15 238 E3
Bramhall SK8 35 A4
Sale M33 242 B6
Thorn Grove Prim Sch
SK8 35 A4
Thorn Ho Chester CH4 141 A3
Stalybridge SK15 242 D2
Thorn La CW8 103 B3
Thorn Rd Bramhall SK7 35 C3
Runcorn WA7 49 B4
Warrington WA1 17 A4
Thorn Tree Cl L24 21 C1
Thorn Tree Dr CW1 173 A1
Thorn Wlk M31 11 C1
Thornberry Cl CH1 117 A4
Thornbury Ave WA3 3 C4
Thorne Cl SK10 87 A3
Thorne Dr CH66 69 A2
Thorney Dr SK7,SK8 35 B3
Thorneyholme Dr WA16 57 A1
Thornfield SK9 60 A2
Thornfield Cl WA3 3 B4
Thornfield Ct [2] SK4 240 A7
Thornfield Hey SK9 60 C4
Thornfield Rd SK4 240 A7
Thornfield Sch SK4 240 A7
Thornfields CW1 173 A1
Thorngrove Dr SK9 60 B3
Thorngrove Hill SK9 60 B3
Thorngrove Rd SK9 60 B3
Thornleigh Ave CH62 43 C2
Thornleigh Dr CH66 69 C3
Thornley Cl [3] WA13 18 B2
Thornley Cres SK6 241 A4
Thornley Rd
Dukinfield M34 241 A8
Lymm WA13 18 B2
Thornley St SK14 241 E5
Thornsgreen Rd M22 33 B4
Thornton WA8 22 C4
Thornton Ave SK11 112 A3
Thornton Bank CW6 169 B2
Thornton Common Rd
CH63 42 B4

Thornton Cres CH60 41 A3
Thornton Dr
Chester CH2 118 B3
Wilmslow SK9 34 B2
Wistaston CW2 206 A4
Thornton Gate SK8 239 A6
Thornton Green La CH2 71 C1
Thornton Ho CH63 42 A3
Thornton Hough Prim Sch
CH63 42 A4
Thornton Mews CH66 69 A4
Thornton Pl [4] SK4 240 B8
Thornton Rd
Ellesmere Port CH65 70 C2
Gatley SK8 34 B4
Warrington WA5 15 A2
Thornton Sq SK11 112 A3
Thorntondale Dr WA5 14 C4
Thorntree Bglws SK11 132 A4
Thorntree Gn WA4 27 A3
Thornway Bollington SK10 88 A4
Bramhall SK7,SK8 35 B4
High Lane SK6 37 C4
Thornwythe Gr CH66 69 C2
Thornycroft CW7 126 A1
Thornycroft Cl SK11 111 C1
Thornycroft St [8] SK11 112 C4
Thorold Gr M33 242 E6
Thorp St SK10 112 B4
Thorpe Cl CW1 189 C4
Thorsby Ave SK14 241 F6
Thorsby Rd WA15 238 E5
Thorsby Way [5] M34 241 A5
Thowler La WA14 30 A3
Threaphurst La SK7 37 B4
Three Fields Cl CW12 156 A2
Threeways CW8 101 B2
Thresher Cl [1] M33 242 F5
Throstle Bank St SK14 241 C8
Thurlestone Rd WA14 238 B6
Thurlow WA3 3 C4
Thursfield Ave ST7 195 B2
Thursfield Prim Sch
ST7 195 C2
Thurstaston Rd CH60 40 C4
Thurston Cl WA5 15 B3
Thurston Gn SK9 60 A1
Thurston Rd CH4 140 C3
Thynne St WA1 16 A2
Tib St M34 241 A6
Tibb St ST7 209 C1
Tibbs Cross La WA8 13 B4
Tidal La WA1 16 C4
Tideswell Cl SK8 34 B4
Tideswell Rd SK7 36 C4
Tidnock Ave CW12 156 C3
Tiffild Ct CW7 127 A2
Tilbury Pl WA7 50 C3
Tildsley Cres WA7 48 C3
Tilestone Paddocks
CW6 168 C3
Tilewright Cl ST7 195 A1
Tillard Ave SK3 240 B4
Tilley St WA1 16 B3
Tilman Cl WA5 15 A4
Tilston Ave WA4 17 A2
Tilston CE Prim Sch
SY14 198 A2
Tilston Rd SY14 213 A3
Tilston Wlk [5] SK9 34 C1
Tilstone Cl
Hough Common CW2 206 C1
Northwich CW9 104 A3
Timber La [2] CW9 103 C4
Timber St SK10 87 C1
Timberfields Rd CH1 117 A4
Timberley Ave WA7 17 A2
Timbersbrook Gr [5] SK9 34 B1
Timberscombe Gdns
WA1 17 C3
Timbrell Ave CW1 190 A3
Timmis Cl WA2 9 A2
Timmis Cres WA8 13 A1
Timperley St WA8 23 A4
Timperley Sta WA15 238 F8
Tinkersfield CW5 205 A2
Tinkwood La SY14 211 C1
Tinsley St WA4 16 C2
Tintagel Cl
Macclesfield SK10 111 C4
Runcorn WA7 50 A3
Tintagel Ct SK15 242 C2
Tintern Ave CH2 118 C3
Tintern Cl Poynton SK12 36 B3
Warrington WA5 7 C1
Tintern Rd SK8 35 A3
Tipping Brow WA16 58 B2
Tipping St WA14 238 D3
Tirley La CW6 123 A1
Tithe Barn Prim Sch
SK4 240 A7
Tithebarn Cl CH60 40 C4
Tithebarn Dr CH64 41 A1
Tithebarn Rd WA15 32 B4
Tithings The WA7 23 C1
Tiverton Cl Chester CH2 118 C3
Sandbach CW11 175 B4
Widnes WA8 12 B2
Tiverton Dr [13] SK9 34 B1
Tiverton Sq WA5 14 C2
Tiveton Ct CW9 103 C3
Tiviot Dale SK1 240 F6
Tiviot Way SK1,SK5 240 F7
Tobermory Cl WA11 1 A3
Tobermory Rd SK8 239 C1
Todbrook Cl SK23 65 B3
Toft Cl Chester CH4 140 C3
Widnes WA8 12 C1

Toft Rd WA16 82 A4
Toft Way SK9 34 C2
Toll Bar Ave SK11 112 C4
Toll Bar Pl WA2 8 A2
Toll Bar Rd
Christleton CH3 142 B4
Macclesfield SK11 111 C4
Warrington WA2 8 A2
Tolland La WA15 31 C4
Tollard Cl SK8 35 A3
Tollbar St SK1 240 F4
Tollemache Dr CW1 190 A4
Tollemache Terr CH2 118 C1
Tollgate Cl ST7 210 B4
Tollgate Dr CW3 229 C2
Tollitt St CW1 190 B2
Tom Brads Croft SK23 65 C4
Tom Fields ST7 209 C1
Tom La WA14 30 C3
Tom Shepley St SK14 241 E6
Tomkinson Cl CW1 189 C4
Tomkinson St CH2 237 C4
Tomlins Terr CH1 117 C3
Tomlinson Ave WA2 16 B4
Tommy's La
Congleton CW12 156 C2
Crewe CW1 190 C1
Tonbridge Cl SK10 87 A1
Toogood Cl CH2 119 C4
Top Farm La CW7 170 C1
Top Rd Frodsham WA6 74 B3
Kingsley WA6 75 A1
Top Station Rd ST7 195 B4
Topgate Cl CH60 41 A4
Topping Ct WA3 9 A2
Toppings The SK6 241 A3
Torbrook Gr [1] SK9 34 B1
Torkington Rd
Gatley SK8 239 B5
Wilmslow SK9 60 B3
Torkington St SK3 240 D4
Toronto Ave M90 33 A4
Torr Rd SK11 112 B2
Torr Rise CW6 146 B1
Torr Top St SK22 39 B4
Torridon Gr CH66 69 C2
Torrin Cl SK3 240 F1
Torrs Valley SK22 39 B4
Torrvale Rd SK22 39 A4
Totland Cl WA5 14 B4
Totland Gr CH2 118 C2
Totton Ct WA1 9 B1
Tourney Gn WA5 7 A1
Tower Hill SK10 88 B2
Tower Hill Rd ST7 195 C4
Tower La Lymm WA13 18 C1
Runcorn WA7 50 B4
Weaverham CW8 77 A1
Tower Rd CH1 118 A1
Tower St SK14 241 D5
Tower Way CW1 190 B2
Towers Cl Poynton SK12 36 C3
Wistaston CW2 206 A4
Towers Ct WA5 15 C4
Towers La WA6 98 B4
Towers Rd SK12 36 C3
Towers The SK10 86 C1
Town Farm La WA6 100 C4
Town Gn The WA4 52 B3
Town Hill WA1 16 A3
Town La Hale L24 21 C1
Mobberley WA16 58 A2
Neston CH64 66 C3
Town Sq
[4] Northwich CW9 103 C4
Runcorn WA7 49 C4
Sale M33 242 B6
Town Well WA6 75 B1
Town's View SK15 242 E1
Towncroft M34 241 A8
Towneley Ct WA8 13 A1
Townend St SK14 241 E6
Townfield Ave CH3 180 C1
Townfield Cl ST7 194 B1
Townfield Ct CW8 78 A2
Townfield Gdns WA14 238 D5
Townfield La
Allostock WA16 106 C3
Barnton CW8 78 A2
Farndon CH3 180 B1
Frodsham WA6 74 B4
Lymm WA13 19 A4
Mollington CH1 94 B1
Tarvin CH3 121 A1
Tiverton CW6 168 B3
Townfield Rd
Altrincham WA14 238 D5
Mobberley WA16 58 A2
Townfield View WA7 24 B1
Townfields
Knutsford WA16 57 B1
Sandbach CW11 175 A3
Townfields Cotts [8]
CW7 149 B4
Townfields Cres CW7 149 B4
Townfields Dr CW7 149 B4
Townfields Gdns [9]
CW7 149 B4
Townfields Rd CW7 149 B4
Townley Pl [23] SK11 112 B4
Townley St SK11 112 B4
Townsend La ST7 194 A4
Townsend Rd CW12 156 C1
Townsfield Dr CW6 147 C4
Townshend Rd CW9 80 A2
Township Cl CH3 182 B1
Townwell Ct CW5 204 B3
Tracy Dr WA12 2 C2

Trafalgar Ave SK12 37 A2
Trafalgar Cl
Northwich CW9 103 C2
Poynton SK12 37 A2
Trafalgar Ct WA8 23 A3
Trafalgar Rd M33 242 C8
Trafford Ave WA5 15 C4
Trafford Cres WA7 49 B3
Trafford Rd
Alderley Edge SK9 60 A1
Handforth SK9 34 A1
Trafford St CH2 237 B3
Tragan Dr WA5 14 B2
Tramway Rd M44 11 C4
Tramway St CH2 237 C3
Tranmere Dr SK9 34 C1
Tranmere Rd [1] SK3 240 B4
Trap Rd CW12 132 B2
Trap St SK11 132 A3
Travers' Entry WA9 6 A4
Travis Brow SK4 240 D5
Travis St Hyde SK14 241 E6
[10] Widnes WA8 23 A4
Treborth Rd CH1 117 B2
Tree Bank Cl WA7 49 A4
Tree Tops CH64 66 C2
Tree Way WA16 82 A4
Treen Cl SK10 86 B1
Treetops Cl WA1 16 C4
Trefoil Cl Huntington CH3 142 A3
Warrington WA3 9 B3
Tregele Cl CH1 117 B2
Trenance Cl WA7 50 B3
Trenchard Dr M22 33 C4
Trent Ave CW7 127 A1
Trent Cl Bramhall SK7 35 B3
Widnes WA8 13 A2
Winsford CW7 127 A1
Trent Way CH60 41 B3
Trentdale CH65 70 A2
Trentham Cl WA8 13 A2
Trentham St WA7 22 C2
Tresham Dr WA4 27 A4
Trevithick Cl CW1 191 A2
Trevone Cl WA16 57 A1
Tribune Ave WA14 238 B7
Tricketts La CW5 205 C3
Tricketts Mews CW5 205 C3
Trident Ind Est WA3 9 C3
Trident Pk WA7 49 C4
Trinity Ave M33 242 D6
Trinity Cl CW2 190 A1
Trinity Ct
[4] Congleton CW12 157 A1
[1] Knutsford WA16 57 A1
Warrington WA3 9 C3
Trinity La SK11 112 C2
Trinity Pl
Congleton CW12 179 A4
[18] Widnes WA8 23 A4
Trinity Rd M33 242 D6
Trinity Sch SK15 242 C1
Trinity Sq SK10 87 C1
Trinity St Chester CH1 237 A2
Runcorn WA7 23 A2
Stalybridge SK15 242 D1
Trinity Terr [15] CW8 103 C4
Troon Cl Bebington CH63 43 B3
Bramhall SK7 36 A4
Haydock WA11 1 A3
Holmes Chapel CW4 130 B1
Troon Dr SK8 239 C1
Trossach Cl WA2 8 C1
Troutbeck Ave
Congleton CW12 156 A1
Newton-le-W WA12 1 C2
Warrington WA5 15 C4
Troutbeck Gr CW7 126 B1
Troutbeck Rd SK8 239 B3
Trouthall La WA16 81 A1
Trowbridge Rd M34 241 A5
Trubshaw Ct ST7 195 B2
Trubshaw Pl ST7 195 A2
Trumans La CH66 69 B4
Truro Cl Bramhall SK7 35 C4
Congleton CW12 178 C4
Ellesmere Port CH66 94 C4
Macclesfield SK10 86 C1
Runcorn WA7 50 B3
Warrington WA1 17 A4
Tudor Cl
Ellesmere Port CH66 94 C4
Northwich CW9 104 C3
Warrington WA4 17 A1
Winsford CW7 149 B3
Tudor Ct [3] WA4 16 C1
Tudor Dr SK10 86 B4
Tudor Gn Blacon CH1 117 C3
Wilmslow SK9 34 C1
Tudor Rd
Altrincham WA14 238 B7
Handforth SK9 34 C1
Runcorn WA7 24 B2
Tudor Way Chester CH3 142 A4
Congleton CW12 156 B1
Nantwich CW5 204 C2
Tudors The SK7 35 B3
Tudorway CH60 41 A4
Tue La WA8 12 A3
Tulip Cl SK3 240 D1
Tulip Dr WA15 238 F6
Tulip Rd Haydock WA11 1 C3
Partington M31 11 C1
Tully Ave WA12 1 C2
Tulworth Rd SK12 36 B2

Tumblewood Dr SK8 239 E4
Tunbridge Cl
Warrington WA5 15 A4
Wistaston CW2 206 A4
Tunnel Rd CW8 78 A1
Tunnicliffe Rd SK11 112 C2
Tunnicliffe St 1 SK11 112 B4
Tunstall Rd Bosley SK11 158 B4
Congleton CW12 157 C1
Tunstall St SK4 240 E6
Turf La SK11 112 B2
Turn St OL6 242 A4
Turnall Rd WA8 22 A4
Turnberry Cl Lymm WA13 18 B2
Macclesfield SK10 87 B2
Northwich CW9 104 C4
Winsford CW7 126 B1
Turnberry Dr SK9 60 B4
Turnberry Rd SK8 239 C1
Turnbury Cl M33 242 B8
Turner Ave ST7 210 A1
Turner Cl Crewe CW1 190 A4
Widnes WA8 12 B2
Turner Gdns SK14 241 E8
Turner La SK14 241 F8
Turner St Bollington SK10 88 A4
Nantwich CW5 204 C3
Turnfield Ho SK8 239 D3
Turnfield Rd SK8 239 D3
Turnhurst Rd ST7 195 C1
Turnock St SK11 112 C4
Turnstone Ave WA12 2 B2
Turret Hall Dr 1 WA3 3 C4
Turriff Dr CH63 43 B2
Turrocks Cl CH64 66 C3
Turrocks Croft CH64 66 C3
Turton Cl Hale L24 21 C1
Warrington WA3 9 B3
Turton St WA3 3 A4
Turves Rd SK8 239 F1
Turville Ho SK9 34 B1
Tuscan Cl WA8 13 A3
Tuscan Rd M20 239 B8
Tushingham Cl CH3 142 A4
Tushingham-with-Grindley CE Prim Sch SY13 214 B1
Tuson Dr WA8 12 C2
Tutor Bank Dr WA12 2 B2
Tweed Cl WA14 238 C6
Tweedsmuir Cl WA2 9 A2
Twemlow Ave CW11 175 A4
Twemlow La CW4 130 B3
Twenty Acre Rd WA5 15 B4
Twinnies Ct SK9 34 A1
Twinnies Rd SK9 34 A1
Twiss Green Com Prim Sch WA3 4 C2
Twiss Green Dr WA3 4 C2
Twiss Green La WA3 4 C2
Twist Ave WA3 3 B4
Two Acre Gr CH66 69 C1
Two Trees Com High Sch M34 241 A5
Two Trees La M34 241 A5
Twyford Cl WA8 13 A3
Twyford La WA8 13 B3
Tyler St SK9 60 A1
Tyler Wlk 13 WA3 3 C4
Tyne Cl WA2 8 C1
Tynedale Ave CW2 190 B1
Tynedale Cl SK11 112 B4
Tynemouth Rd WA7 50 B3
Tynesdale CH65 70 A2
Tynwald Cres WA8 12 C3
Tynwald Dr WA4 26 B4
Tyrer Rd WA12 2 B1
Tytherington Bsns Pk SK10 87 B3
Tytherington Ct SK10 87 B1
Tytherington Dr SK10 87 C2
Tytherington Gn SK10 87 B2
Tytherington High Sch SK10 87 B1
Tytherington La SK10 87 B3
Tytherington Park Rd SK10 87 B2
Tytherington Sh Ctr 8 SK10 87 B2

U

Ullapool Cl CH66 68 C3
Ullswater SK11 111 C3
Ullswater Ave
Crewe CW2 189 C2
Warrington WA2 8 B2
Winsford CW7 126 B1
Ullswater Cres CH2 119 A3
Ullswater Dr SK9 83 C4
Ullswater Gr WA7 49 B3
Ullswater Mans SK11 111 C3
Ullswater Rd
Congleton CW12 156 A1
Ellesmere Port CH65 70 B1
Handforth SK9 34 B2
Ullswater Terr SK15 242 D4
Ulverston Ave WA2 8 A2
Ulverston Cl WA11 1 A3
Ulviet Gate WA16 29 B2
Under Rainow Rd CW12 157 C1
Underbridge La WA4 25 C3
Undercliffe Ho WA4 26 B4
Underhill SK6 241 C2
Underway The WA7 49 C4
Underwood Cl SK10 86 C1
Underwood Dr CH65 70 B1
Underwood Ind Pk CW1 190 A3
Underwood La CW1 190 A3
Underwood Rd SK9 60 B1
Underwood West Inf Sch CW1 190 A3
Underwood West Jun Sch CW1 190 A3
Unicorn Gateway SK11 112 B4
Union Cl CW12 156 B2
Union Ind Est SK11 112 C4
Union Rd
Macclesfield SK11 112 C4
New Mills SK22 39 B4
Union St Chester CH1 237 C2
Congleton CW12 156 B2
Crewe CW2 190 B2
Hyde SK14 241 E6
Macclesfield SK11 112 B4
Runcorn WA7 23 A1
Sandbach CW11 175 A3
Stockport SK1 240 F4
Warrington WA1 16 A3
Union Terr CH1 237 B3
Union Wlk CH1 237 B2
Unity Way ST7 210 B4
Univ of Liverpool (Chester Coll) CH2 237 A4
Univ of Liverpool, Faculty of Veterinary Science (Leahurst) CH64 67 B4
Unsworth Ct WA2 8 C1
Upcast La SK9 59 C2
Uplands CW8 101 B2
Uplands Rd CW9 78 C2
Uplands The
Biddulph ST8 179 C1
Runcorn WA7 50 A4
Upper Cambrian Rd CH1 118 A1
Upper Downs WA14 238 C3
Upper Haigh St CW7 149 B4
Upper Mersey Rd WA8 23 A3
Upper Mersey St CH65 70 B4
Upper Northgate St CH1 237 A3
Upper Raby Rd CH64 42 A1
Upton Ave SK8 35 A4
Upton Bridle Path WA8 12 C2
Upton Cl Golborne WA3 3 B4
Winsford CW7 126 C2
Upton Dr
Altrincham WA14 238 E8
Chester CH2 118 B3
Warrington WA5 14 C3
Upton Grange WA8 12 B2
Upton Heath CE Prim Sch CH2 118 C4
Upton La Chester CH2 118 B4
Widnes WA8 12 C2
Upton Pk CH2 118 B3
Upton Priory Inf Sch SK10 86 C1
Upton Priory Jun Sch SK10 86 C1
Upton Rd CH66 69 B2
Upton Way 12 SK9 34 B3
Upton Westlea Prim Sch CH2 118 C4
Upton-by-Chester High Sch CH2 118 C3
Upwood Rd WA3 3 B4
Urban Ave WA15 238 E4
Urban Dr WA15 238 E4
Urban Rd
Altrincham WA15 238 E4
Sale M33 242 A6
Ure Ct CH65 70 A4
Urmston Ave WA12 2 A3
Urwick Rd SK6 241 B2
Utkinton La CW6 146 C4
Utkinton Rd CW6 146 B3

V

Vahler Terr WA7 23 B1
Vale Ave Sale M33 242 E7
Warrington WA2 16 A4
Vale Cl Broughton CH4 139 B2
Romiley SK6 241 F2
Vale Cotts SK14 241 C8
Vale Cres SK8 239 F2
Vale Ct WA4 51 A2
Vale Gdns Alsager ST7 193 C2
Ellesmere Port CH65 70 A2
Helsby WA6 73 A2
Vale Head SK9 34 B1
Vale Owen Rd WA2 8 B1
Vale Rd Alpraham CW6 169 A2
Altrincham WA14 238 B1
Ellesmere Port CH65 70 A2
Hartford CW8 103 B2
Marston CW9 79 A3
Tiverton CW6 168 C3
Wilmslow SK9 59 C4
Vale Royal Ctyd CW8 126 A4
Vale Royal Dr CW8 126 A4
Vale View CW9 79 B1
Valebrook Dr CW5 220 A4
Valentine Rd
Kidsgrove ST7 195 A1
Newton-le-W WA12 1 C2
Valewood Ave SK4 240 A5
Valiant Cl WA2 8 C1
Valley Brook Bsns Ctr CW2 190 B2
Valley Cl Alsager ST7 192 C2
Cheadle SK8 239 E3
Knutsford WA16 82 A4
Valley Ct WA2 8 C1
Valley Dr Chester CH2 118 B3
Ellesmere Port CH66 69 B3
Wilmslow SK9 34 B2
Valley Gr M34 241 B6
Valley La CW8 101 C2
Valley Rd Bebington CH62 43 B4
Bramhall SK7 35 C4
Cheadle SK8 239 E3
Crewe CW2 190 A1
Macclesfield SK11 112 A3
Stockport SK4 240 A5
Weaverham CW8 77 B1
Wistaston CW2 189 C1
Valley Sch SK7 35 B3
Valley View
Congleton CW12 156 B2
Ellesmere Port CH66 69 B3
Newton-le-W WA12 2 A1
Northwich CW9 104 B4
Valley Way
Knutsford WA16 82 A4
Stalybridge SK15 242 F1
Vanguard Ct WA3 9 B2
Varden Gr SK3 240 D1
Varden Rd SK12 36 C2
Vardon Dr SK9 60 B3
Varey Rd CW12 156 C2
Vaudrey Cres CW12 156 C2
Vaudrey Dr WA1 17 B4
Vaudrey La M34 241 A6
Vaudrey St SK15 242 D1
Vaughan Rd
Stockport SK4 240 D7
Whaley Bridge SK23 65 C3
Vaughans La CH3 142 A4
Vauxhall Cl WA5 14 C2
Vauxhall Rd CW5 204 C4
Vauxhall Way CW7 149 B3
Vearows Pl 13 CW8 103 C4
Venable's Rd CH1 117 C2
Venables Rd CW9 79 A1
Venables Way
High Legh WA16 29 B2
Middlewich CW10 151 C3
Venns Rd WA2 16 B4
Ventnor Ave M33 242 B8
Ventnor Cl
Middlewich CW10 151 B4
Warrington WA5 14 B4
Ventnor Rd SK4 240 A6
Venture Way SK12 36 C2
Verbena Cl M31 11 C2
Verbina Cl WA7 49 C2
Verdin Ave CW8 78 C1
Verdin Cl Moulton CW9 126 C4
Winsford CW7 126 B1
Verdin Ct CW1 190 A4
Verdin St CW9 104 B4
Vere St CW1 190 B3
Verity Cl CW1 191 B2
Vermont Cl WA5 15 B4
Vernay Gn CH4 141 A3
Vernon Ave Audley ST7 209 B1
Congleton CW12 178 C4
Hooton CH66 44 A1
Vernon Cl Audley ST7 209 B1
Cheadle SK8 239 E1
Poynton SK12 36 B1
Saughall CH1 117 A4
Vernon Dr CW3 230 C2
Vernon Gr M33 242 E5
Vernon Jun & Inf Schs SK12 36 C2
Vernon Rd Chester CH1 118 A1
Poynton SK12 36 C1
Vernon St Crewe CW1 190 A3
Hyde SK14 241 E6
Macclesfield SK10 112 C4
4 Stockport SK1 240 F6
Warrington WA1 16 A2
Vernon Way CW1 190 B2
Veronica Way CH66 69 B4
Vetch Cl WA3 11 A3
Vetches The CH3 119 C3
Viaduct Rd WA14 238 D7
Viaduct St
Newton-le-W WA12 2 A2
Stockport SK3 240 E5
Vicar's La CH1 237 B2
Vicarage Ave SK8 35 A4
Vicarage Cl
Guilden Sutton CH3 119 C3
Hale L24 21 C1
Vicarage Ct LL13 196 C4
Vicarage Dr WA11 1 A4
Vicarage Gdns
Hyde SK14 241 F6
Sandbach CW11 174 C4
Vicarage Gr CW7 149 B3
Vicarage Hill WA6 73 B2
Vicarage La
Altrincham WA14 238 C1
Audlem CW3 230 A2
Bunbury CW6 168 C1
Burton CH64 67 B1
Frodsham WA6 74 B4
Hassall Green CW11 175 C3
Helsby WA6 73 B2
Little Budworth CW6 147 C4
Poynton SK12 36 C3
Sandbach CW11 174 C4
Vicarage Rd
Chester CH2 118 C2
Haslington CW1 191 B3
Vicarage Rd *continued*
Haydock WA11 1 A4
Northwich CW9 104 A4
Stockport SK3 240 E2
Widnes WA8 23 A4
Vicarage Row CH62 44 A3
Vicarage Way SK11 111 C4
Vicarage Wlk CW9 104 A4
Vicars Cross Ct 2 CH3 119 A1
Vicars Cross Rd CH3 119 B1
Vicker's Cl CH3 121 C4
Vickers Rd WA8 22 C2
Vickers Way CW9 104 A4
Victoria Ave
Altrincham WA15 238 F7
Crewe CW2 190 A2
Haslington CW1 191 B2
Heswall CH60 41 A3
Holmes Chapel CW4 130 B1
Kidsgrove ST7 194 C1
Warrington, Grappenhall WA4 17 A1
Warrington, Great Sankey WA5 14 B3
Widnes WA8 13 A2
Victoria Cl Bramhall SK7 35 B3
Stockport SK3 240 E3
Victoria Com High Sch CW1 190 B3
Victoria Cres
Chester CH2 237 A4
Chester, Handbridge CH4 237 C1
Victoria Ct Chester CH2 237 A4
Crewe CW1 190 B2
Haslington CW1 191 B2
8 Kidsgrove ST7 195 A1
Victoria Ctr CW1 190 B2
Victoria Dr M33 242 D5
Victoria Gdns SK14 241 F8
Victoria Gr WA8 13 A2
Victoria Inf Sch CH2 237 A4
Victoria Infmy CW8 103 C4
Victoria Mews CH65 70 A3
Victoria Mill Dr CW5 205 B3
Victoria Mkt SK15 242 D1
Victoria Pathway CH4 237 C1
Victoria Pk CW8 78 C1
Victoria Pl Chester CH1 237 B3
Warrington WA4 16 B1
Victoria Rd
Altrincham WA15 238 D3
Broughton CH4 140 B3
Chester CH1 237 A3
Chester CH2 237 A4
Ellesmere Port CH65 70 B3
Macclesfield SK10 87 A1
Neston CH64 67 A3
Newton-le-W WA12 2 B2
Northwich CW9 104 A4
Runcorn WA7 23 A1
Sale M33 242 D5
Warrington, Great Sankey WA5 15 A2
Warrington, Penketh WA5 14 B2
Warrington, Stockton Heath WA4 16 B1
Widnes WA8 23 A3
Wilmslow SK9 60 A3
Victoria Road Prim Sch
Northwich CW9 104 A4
Runcorn WA7 23 A1
Victoria Sq
Warrington WA4 16 B1
Winsford CW7 149 A4
Victoria St
Altrincham WA14 238 D5
Congleton CW12 156 B1
Crewe CW1 190 B2
Knutsford WA16 56 C1
New Mills SK22 39 A3
Northwich CW9 79 C1
Sandbach CW11 175 A4
Stalybridge SK15 242 C2
Warrington WA1 16 B3
Widnes WA8 23 A4
Victoria Trad Ctr WA8 23 A3
Victoria Way SK7 35 B3
Victoria Wlk SK10 112 C4
Victory Rd M44 11 B2
Vienna Rd SK3 240 D2
Vienna Rd E SK3 240 E2
Viewlands Dr SK9 34 B1
Villa Farm CW11 176 A4
Villa Rd CH5 116 A4
Village Cl
Lostock Green CW9 105 A4
Runcorn WA7 50 A4
Warrington WA4 17 C2
Village Ct SK9 34 B1
Village Farm CW5 172 A3
Village La WA4 52 B2
Village Mews SK10 87 A3
Village Rd
Christleton CH3 142 C4
Great Barrow CH3 120 C3
Heswall CH60 40 C4
Waverton CH3 143 B2
Village St WA7 24 C1
Village The
Astbury CW12 178 A4
Burton CH64 67 B1
Prestbury SK10 86 C3
Village Way SK9 34 B1
Villars St WA1 16 B3
Villas The CW4 131 A4
Villiers Russell Cl CW1 190 B3
Villiers St
Ashton-u-Lyne OL6 242 A2
Villiers St *continued*
Hyde SK14 241
Vincent Cl WA5 15
Vincent Dr CH4 141
Vincent St Crewe CW1 190
Macclesfield SK11 112
Vine Bank Rd ST7 195
Vine Cl SK11 112
Vine Cres WA5 14
Vine Rd CH66 69
Vine St Bollington SK10 88
Runcorn WA7 23
Widnes WA8 23
Vine Terr WA8 12
Vine Tree Ave
Crewe CW2 190
Shavington CW2 206
Vine Tree Prim Sch CW2 190
Violet Cl WA3 9
Violet St Stockport SK2 240
Widnes WA8 23
Virginia Chase SK8 34
Virginia Dr CH1 117
Virginia Gdns WA5 15
Virginia Terr CH66 69
Virtual Bsns Ctr CH1 117
Viscount Dr Gatley SK8 34
Wythenshaw M90 32
Viscount Rd WA2 8
Vista Ave WA12 2
Vista Rd
Newton-le-W WA11,WA12 2
Runcorn WA7 49
Vista The M44 11
Vista Way WA12 2
Volunteer Ave 3 CW5 204
Volunteer Fields CW5 204
Volunteer St
Chester CH1 237
Frodsham WA6 49
Vose Cl WA5 15
Vulcan Cl
Newton-le-W WA12 2
Warrington WA2 8
Vulcan Ind Est WA12 2
Vyrnwy Rd CH4 140

W

Waddington Cl
Golborne WA3 3
Warrington WA2 8
Wade Cres CW8 78
Wade Deacon High Sch WA8 13
Wade St CW9 79
Wadebrook Gr 23 SK9 34
Wades La CW7 126
Wadeson Way WA3 9
Wadham Gdns SK6 241
Wadham Way WA15 238
Wadsworth Cl SK9 34
Wagg St CW12 156
Waggs Rd CW12 156
Wagon La WA11 1
Waine St CW1 190
Wainwright Rd WA14 238
Wainwright St SK16 242
Waitney Croft SK10 113
Wakefield Cl CW1 189
Wakefield Cres SK6 241
Wakefield Ho WA5 15
Wakefield Rd
Ellesmere Port CH66 69
Stalybridge SK15 242
Wakefield St WA3 3
Wakefield Wlk M34 241
Wakeham Cl SK11 111
Wakes Mdw CW6 185
Walden Cl WA4 17
Walden Dr CH1 93
Waldon Ave SK8 239
Waldon Rd SK11 112
Waldron Gdns CW2 189
Waldron Rd CW1 191
Waldron's La CW1 173
Walfield Ave CW12 156
Walford Ave CW2 190
Walgrove Cl CW12 156
Walker Ave SK15 242
Walker Cl
Haslington CW1 191
Hyde SK14 241
Walker Dr CW10 151
Walker Fold SK14 241
Walker La Hyde SK14 241
Sutton Lane Ends SK11 112
Walker St Chester CH2 237
Crewe CW1 190
7 Macclesfield SK11 112
Stockport SK1 240
Warrington WA2 16
Walkers La
Ellesmere Port CH66 69
Scholar Green ST7 177
Tarporley CW6 146
Warrington WA5 14
Walkersgreen Rd ST5 210
Wall Fields Rd CW5 204
Wall Hill Way CW8 76
Wall La CW5 204
Wallace Ct CW7 127
Wallace St
Northwich CW8 103
Widnes WA8 23
Wallcroft CH64 68

alled Gdn The CW10 ...127 B3
aller St SK11 ...112 C3
allerscote Cl CW8 ...102 C4
allerscote Com Sch
:W8 ...102 C4
allerscote Rd CW8 ...102 C4
alleys La CW5 ...203 B4
allfields Cl CW5 ...204 C4
allhill La CW11 ...177 B4
allingford Rd SK9 ...34 B3
allis St Crewe CW1 ...190 B2
Varrington WA4 ...16 A2
allrake CH60 ...40 C4
alls Ave CH1 ...118 A1
allsend Ct WA8 ...12 C2
allworth Terr SK9 ...59 C4
allworth's Bank CW12 .156 C1
almer Pl CW7 ...149 B3
almoor Pk CH3 ...119 A1
almsley St
lewton-le-W WA12 ...2 B2
itockport SK5 ...240 F7
Vidnes WA8 ...23 B4
alnut Ave CW8 ...102 B4
alnut Cl Chester CH2 ...118 B4
Varrington WA1 ...17 C4
Vilmslow SK9 ...60 C4
alnut Cotts LL13 ...196 B4
alnut Croft CH3 ...180 C3
alnut Dr CW7 ...127 A1
alnut Gr
llesmere Port CH66 ...70 A1
ale M33 ...242 A6
alnut La CW8 ...103 A3
alnut Rd M31 ...11 B2
alnut Rise CW12 ...156 A1
alnut Tree La
radwall Green CW11 ...153 A2
Varrington WA4 ...26 C2
alnut Tree Rd SK3 ...240 A4
alpole Cl CW1 ...191 B3
alpole Gr WA2 ...8 B1
alpole Rd WA7 ...49 B3
alpole St CH2 ...237 A4
alsh Cl WA12 ...2 B3
alsingham Dr WA7 ...24 B1
alsingham Rd WA5 ...14 C3
alter St Chester CH2 ...237 B4
Varrington WA1 ...16 C4
Vidnes WA8 ...13 B1
althall St CW2 ...190 B1
altham Ave WA3 ...5 B4
altham Ct WA7 ...24 C2
altham Dr SK8 ...35 A3
altham Pl CH4 ...141 A3
alton Ave WA5 ...14 C3
alton Gr ST7 ...210 B4
alton Hall* WA4 ...25 C3
alton Hall Gdns* WA4 ...25 C3
alton Heath Dr SK10 ...87 A2
alton Heath Rd WA4 ...16 A1
alton La WA3 ...9 C3
alton Lea Rd WA4 ...26 A4
alton New Rd WA4 ...26 A4
alton Pl CH1 ...117 C2
alton Rd
ltrincham WA14 ...238 B5
ulcheth WA3 ...4 C2
Varrington WA4 ...26 B4
alton St Runcorn WA7 ...23 A1
Stockport SK1 ...240 F3
alton Way Hyde M34 ...241 B5
alke ST7 ...210 B4
altons The CH4 ...141 C3
andsworth Way WA8 ...22 C3
ansfell Pl WA2 ...8 A2
arbreck Gr M33 ...242 D5
arburton Bridge Rd
VA3 ...11 A1
arburton Cl
ltrincham WA15 ...32 B3
ymm WA13 ...19 A2
omiley SK6 ...241 A1
arburton Dr WA15 ...32 B3
arburton La M31,WA13 ...11 C1
arburton Rd SK9 ...34 B2
arburton St WA4 ...16 B1
arburton View WA3 ...11 A1
ard Ave SK10 ...88 A4
ard Cl WA5 ...7 A1
ard La SK12 ...38 C2
ard St SK14 ...241 E6
ard's La CW11 ...153 B3
ard's Terr CH2 ...118 C2
ardle Ave CW5 ...187 B4
ardle Cotts CW5 ...187 B4
ardle Cres SK11 ...111 C1
ardle Ct M33 ...242 C6
ardle Ind Est CW5 ...187 A4
ardle Mews CW10 ...151 B4
ardle Rd M33 ...242 C6
ardley Rd WA4 ...16 A1
ardour Cl SK11 ...111 C4
ardour St WA5 ...15 C3
ards La CW12 ...179 B4
areham Cl WA1 ...17 B4
areham Dr CW1 ...190 A4
arford Ave SK12 ...37 A1
arford Cres SK9 ...84 A4
arford Hall Dr SK9 ...84 A3
arford La WA16 ...59 A1
arford Pk WA16 ...58 C1
arford Terr WA16 ...59 A1
argrave CE Prim Sch
VA12 ...2 B1
argrave House Sch
VA12 ...2 B1
argrave Mews WA12 ...2 B1

Wargrave Rd WA12 ...2 B1
Warham St SK9 ...60 A4
Waring Ave St Helens WA9 ...1 A1
Warrington WA4 ...16 C3
Warkworth Cl WA8 ...12 B2
Warkworth Ct CH65 ...70 C2
Warley Cl SK8 ...239 E6
Warmingham CE Prim Sch
CW11 ...173 C4
Warmingham Ct 7
CW10 ...151 B4
Warmingham La
Middlewich CW10 ...151 B3
Sandbach CW11 ...174 A4
Warmingham Rd CW1 ...173 B2
Warnley Cl WA8 ...12 B2
Warren Ave Cheadle SK8 .239 D5
Knutsford WA16 ...56 C1
Lostock Gralam CW9 ...80 A2
Warren Cl Knutsford WA16 .56 C1
Middlewich CW10 ...151 A4
Poynton SK12 ...36 A2
Warren Croft WA7 ...50 B4
Warren Ct
Ellesmere Port CH66 ...69 B2
Frodsham WA6 ...74 B3
Warren Dr
Altrincham WA15 ...32 B4
Broughton CH4 ...139 A2
Ellesmere Port CH66 ...69 C4
Newton-le-W WA12 ...2 C2
Warren SK11 ...111 B1
Warrington WA4 ...26 B4
Warren Gr SK11 ...111 B1
Warren Hey SK9 ...60 C4
Warren La Hartford CW8 .103 A2
Warrington WA1 ...17 B4
Warren Lea SK12 ...36 C3
Warren Rd Stockport SK3 .240 E2
Warrington WA2 ...8 B1
Warrington, Appleton WA4 ...26 B4
Warren St SK1 ...240 F6
Warren The CW8 ...101 B3
Warren Way CW6 ...168 B4
Warrener St M33 ...242 D6
Warrilow Heath Rd ST5 .210 B1
Warrington Ave
Crewe CW1 ...190 B3
Ellesmere Port CH65 ...70 A1
Warrington Bank Quay Sta
WA1 ...15 C2
Warrington Bsns Pk WA2 ...8 B1
Warrington Central Sta
WA2 ...16 A3
Warrington Collegiate Inst
WA2 ...8 A1
Warrington District General
Hospl WA5 ...15 C3
Warrington La WA13 ...19 C1
Warrington Mus & Art
Gallery* WA1 ...16 A3
Warrington Rd
Bold Heath L35,WA8 ...13 B4
Comberbach CW9 ...78 B4
Cronton L35 ...12 C4
Cuddington CW8 ...102 A3
Dunham-on-t-H WA6 ...97 B3
Fowley Common WA3,WN7 ...5 B3
Golborne WA12,WA3 ...3 A3
Hatton WA4 ...25 C2
Little Leigh CW8 ...77 A3
Lymm WA13 ...18 A2
Mere WA16 ...56 B4
Mickle Trafford CH2 ...119 C4
Runcorn, Castlefields WA7 ...23 C1
Runcorn, Manor Park WA7 ...24 A2
Warrington, Birchwood WA3 ...9 C4
Warrington, Locking Stumps
WA3 ...9 B2
Widnes WA8 ...13 B1
Warrington St SK15 ...242 E1
Warrington Trad Est
WA2 ...16 A3
Warrington Univ Coll
(Padgate Campus) WA2 ...9 A2
Warton Cl Bramhall SK7 ...36 A4
Warrington WA5 ...15 A2
Warwick Ave
Newton-le-W WA12 ...2 C1
Warrington, Bewsey WA5 ...15 C4
Warrington, Great Sankey
WA5 ...14 B4
Warwick Cl
Kidsgrove ST7 ...195 A2
Knutsford WA16 ...57 B1
Macclesfield SK11 ...111 C3
Neston CH64 ...66 C3
Stockport SK4 ...240 D8
Warwick Com Prim Sch
SK11 ...111 C3
Warwick Ct
Ellesmere Port CH65 ...70 C1
Stockport SK4 ...240 D8
Warwick Dr
Altrincham WA15 ...238 F1
Sale M33 ...242 D6
Warwick Ho 3 M33 ...242 D6
Warwick Mall SK8 ...239 D6
Warwick Pl CW7 ...149 B3
Warwick Rd
Altrincham WA15 ...238 E1
Blacon CH1 ...117 C3
Irlam M44 ...11 B3
Macclesfield SK11 ...111 C3
Romiley SK6 ...241 A2
Stockport SK4 ...240 C7
Warwick Wlk SK11 ...111 C3
Wasdale Dr SK8 ...239 B3

Wasdale Gr CW1 ...173 A1
Wasdale Terr SK15 ...242 D4
Wash La Allostock WA16 ...106 C2
Warrington WA4 ...16 C2
Washington Cl
Biddulph ST8 ...179 B1
Cheadle SK8 ...34 C4
Washington Dr WA5 ...15 B4
Washway Rd M33 ...242 A6
Wasley Cl WA2 ...8 C2
Waste La
Cuddington CW8 ...101 C2
Delamere CW8 ...123 C3
Kelsall CW6 ...122 C2
Watch La CW11 ...174 A3
Water La SK9 ...60 A4
Water Lode CW5 ...204 C3
Water Rd SK15 ...242 C2
Water St Bollington SK10 ...88 A4
Hyde SK14 ...241 D6
Macclesfield SK11 ...112 B4
Newcastle-u-L ST5 ...210 B1
Newton-le-W WA12 ...2 B2
Northwich CW9 ...104 A4
Runcorn WA7 ...23 A2
Stalybridge SK15 ...242 D2
Stockport SK1 ...240 F7
Widnes WA8 ...23 A3
Water's Reach SK6 ...37 C4
Waterbank Row CW9 ...103 C4
Waterbridge Ct
4 Lymm WA13 ...18 B2
Warrington WA4 ...26 B4
Waterfoot La SK23 ...65 B3
Waterford Ave SK6 ...241 F2
Waterford Dr CH64 ...67 A4
Waterford Pl SK8 ...34 A4
Waterford Way WA7 ...50 B3
Waterfront WA7 ...50 C3
Watergate Row CH1 ...237 A2
Watergate Sq CH1 ...237 A2
Watergate St CH1 ...237 A2
Waterhouse Ave SK10 ...87 C4
Waterloo Cl 12 CH65 ...70 B3
Waterloo Gdns OL6 ...242 B4
Waterloo Gr ST7 ...195 A1
Waterloo La WA6 ...74 C1
Waterloo Rd Bramhall SK7 .35 C4
Chester CH2 ...118 B2
Haslington CW1 ...191 B2
Northwich CW8 ...103 C4
Poynton SK12 ...37 A1
Romiley SK6 ...241 E2
Runcorn WA7 ...22 C2
Stalybridge SK15 ...242 D2
Stockport SK1 ...240 F5
Widnes WA8 ...23 A3
Waterloo St
Ashton-u-Lyne OL6 ...242 A4
Macclesfield SK11 ...112 C4
Waterloo St W SK11 ...112 B4
Waterly La WA6 ...74 C3
Watermead Dr WA7 ...50 C3
Watermeetings La SK6 .241 F1
Watermill Dr SK11 ...112 C4
Waters Edge
Anderton CW9 ...78 B2
Chester CH1 ...118 A1
Waters Gn SK11 ...112 B4
Waters Reach SK12 ...36 C3
Waters Reams CH3 ...142 A4
Watersedge WA6 ...49 B1
Watersfield Cl SK8 ...34 C4
Waterside
Macclesfield SK11 ...112 C4
Warrington WA4 ...26 B4
Waterside Cotts CW5 ...216 C3
Waterside Dr WA6 ...49 B1
Waterside La WA8 ...22 B3
Waterside Mews CW11 ...174 C2
Waterside Rd SK12,SK22 ...38 C4
Waterside View CW9 ...104 C3
Waterside Way CW10 ...128 A1
Watertower View CH2 ...118 C1
Waterway CH3 ...143 A3
Waterways WA5 ...15 B3
Waterworks Dr WA12 ...2 C2
Waterworks La
Ellesmere Port CH66 ...68 C4
Winwick WA2 ...8 A4
Watery La Astbury CW12 .178 B3
Winwick WA2 ...7 C3
Watkin St Hawarden CH5 .116 A1
Warrington WA2 ...16 A4
Watkins Ave WA12 ...1 C2
Watkinson Way WA8 ...13 B3
Watlands Rd ST7 ...209 C1
Watling Cres CH4 ...141 C4
Watling Ct CH3 ...119 B1
Watling Dr CW6 ...123 B3
Watling St CW9 ...103 C4
Watson Sq 20 SK1 ...240 F5
Watson St M34 ...241 B7
Watson's Cl CH4 ...139 B2
Watton Cl WA4 ...17 B2
Wavell Ave WA8 ...22 B4
Wavells Way CH3 ...142 A3
Waveney Dr
Altrincham WA14 ...238 C6
Handforth SK9 ...34 B1
Waverley Ave WA4 ...26 B4
Waverley Cl SK10 ...113 A4
Waverley Dr SK8 ...35 A4
Waverley Rd Sale M33 ...242 C8
Stockport SK3 ...240 C3
Waverley Terr CH2 ...118 C2
Waverton Cl
Davenham CW9 ...103 C2

Waverton Cl *continued*
Hough Common CW2 ...206 C1
Waverton Com Prim Sch
CH3 ...143 A3
Waverton Mill Quays
CH3 ...143 A3
Waverton Pk CH3 ...143 A3
Waverton Rd CH66 ...69 C3
Wavertree Ave
Scholar Green ST7 ...194 C4
Widnes WA8 ...23 A4
Wavertree Ct CH66 ...69 C4
Wavertree Dr CW10 ...151 A4
Wavertree Rd CH1 ...117 B3
Way's Gn CW7 ...149 C4
Waybutt La CW2 ...221 B4
Wayfarers Dr WA12 ...2 C1
Wayford Cl WA6 ...49 A1
Wayside ST7 ...193 C1
Wayside Cl WA13 ...18 B1
Wayside Ct CH2 ...119 C4
Wayside Dr SK12 ...36 B2
Wayside Rd SK10 ...112 C4
Waystead Cl CW9 ...103 C2
Waywell Cl WA2 ...8 C2
Weal Stone La CH2 ...118 C3
Weald Dr CH66 ...69 A3
Wealstone Ct CH2 ...118 C3
Wearhead Cl WA3 ...2 C4
Weaste La WA4 ...17 C1
Weates Cl WA8 ...13 C1
Weathercock La CW12 ...157 C2
Weatherstone Cotts
CH64 ...67 B4
Weaver Bank CW5 ...204 B3
Weaver Cl Alsager ST7 ...193 A2
Altrincham WA14 ...238 C1
Biddulph ST8 ...179 B1
Sandbach CW11 ...174 C4
Weaver Cres WA6 ...49 B1
Weaver Ct
Macclesfield SK11 ...112 B4
Northwich CW9 ...103 C4
Weaver Gr
Mickle Trafford CH2 ...119 C4
St Helens WA9 ...1 A2
Weaver Grange CW9 ...126 C4
Weaver La WA6 ...49 A1
Weaver Park Ind Est
WA6 ...49 B1
Weaver Prim Sch CW5 ...204 C2
Weaver Rd Culcheth WA3 ...5 A1
Ellesmere Port CH65 ...70 B1
Frodsham WA6 ...49 B1
Moulton CW9 ...126 C4
Nantwich CW5 ...204 C3
Northwich CW8 ...103 C4
Runcorn WA7 ...49 A3
Weaver St Chester CH1 ...237 A2
Winsford CW7 ...126 C1
Weaver Vale Prim Sch
WA6 ...49 B1
Weaver Valley Rd CW7 ...126 C2
Weaver View
Audlem CW3 ...229 C2
Church Minshull CW5 ...172 A3
Northwich CW8 ...103 C4
Weaverham CW8 ...77 B1
Weaver Way CW9 ...78 C1
Weaverhall La CW7 ...150 A3
Weaverham Forest Prim Sch
CW8 ...77 B1
Weaverham High Sch
CW8 ...102 B4
Weaverham Rd CW8 ...102 A2
Weaverham Way SK9 ...34 C2
Weaverham Wlk M33 ...242 E5
Weavers La SK7 ...35 B3
Weaverside CW5 ...204 C1
Weaverside Ave WA7 ...49 C2
Webb Dr WA5 ...6 C3
Webb's La CW10 ...128 B1
Webbs Orch SK23 ...65 B4
Webster Cl CH4 ...139 B2
Websters La CH66 ...69 C1
Weddell Cl WA5 ...15 B4
Wedge Ave WA11 ...1 A3
Wedgwood Ave ST7 ...210 A1
Wedgwood Dr WA8 ...13 A2
Wedgwood La ST8 ...179 B1
Wedgwood Rd ST7 ...210 B4
Wednesbury Dr WA5 ...14 C3
Weedon Ave WA12 ...2 A3
Weighbridge Rd CH5 ...92 B3
Weint The WA3 ...11 A2
Weir Gr ST7 ...195 A1
Weir La WA1 ...17 C3
Weir St Northwich CW9 ...103 C4
Warrington WA4 ...16 A1
Welbeck Ave WA12 ...2 B1
Welbeck Cl CW10 ...128 A1
Welbeck Rd SK14 ...241 F6
Welch Rd SK14 ...241 F8
Welcroft St 2 SK1 ...240 F4
Weldon Rd WA14 ...238 D6
Welford Ave WA3 ...3 B4
Welford Cl SK9 ...60 C4
Well Ave SY14 ...213 A2
Well Bank CW11 ...175 A3
Well Bank Cotts WA16 ...108 B4
Well Bank La WA16,
SK11 ...108 B4
Well Cl CH64 ...67 A2
Well Farm Cl
Malpas SY14 ...213 A2
Warrington WA1 ...17 B4
Well Field Cl WA16 ...80 A4
Well La Alsager ST7 ...193 B2

Well La *continued*
Antrobus CW9 ...53 A2
Biddulph ST8 ...179 B2
Chester CH2 ...118 C3
Heswall CH60 ...41 A3
Kingsley WA6 ...75 B1
Little Budworth CW6 ...147 C4
Macclesfield SK10 ...88 A1
Manley WA6 ...98 C2
Mollington CH1 ...94 C1
Neston CH64 ...66 C3
Prestbury SK10 ...87 B4
Stretton WA4 ...52 C4
Warrington WA5 ...14 C2
Weaverham CW8 ...77 B1
Well Meadow SK14 ...241 D8
Well Meadow Ct SK14 ...241 D8
Well St Malpas SY14 ...213 A2
Mow Cop ST7 ...195 B4
New Mills SK22 ...39 A4
Winsford CW7 ...126 B1
Welland Cl 13 CW11 ...174 B3
Welland Rd SK9 ...34 C1
Wellbank Ct CW12 ...156 C1
Wellbrook Cl WA7 ...50 B3
Wellcroft Cl CW2 ...206 A4
Weller Ave SK12 ...36 B1
Weller Cl SK12 ...36 B1
Welles St CW11 ...175 A3
Wellesbourne Cl
Macclesfield SK10 ...86 C1
Neston CH64 ...66 B3
Wellesley Ave
Ellesmere Port CH65 ...70 B3
Haslington CW1 ...191 B2
Wellesley Cl WA12 ...2 A3
Wellesley Wlk 13 CH65 ...70 B3
Wellfield
Preston on the Hill WA7 ...50 C3
Romiley SK6 ...241 C4
Widnes WA8 ...13 A2
Winsford CW7 ...127 A1
Wellfield Rd WA3 ...4 C2
Wellfield St WA5 ...15 C3
Wellfield Way SY13 ...225 C1
Wellington Circ SK11 ...112 C4
Wellington Cl
Congleton CW12 ...156 B2
10 Ellesmere Port CH65 ...70 B3
Knutsford WA16 ...57 B2
Newton-le-W WA12 ...2 A2
Sale M33 ...242 C8
Warrington WA2 ...8 C1
Wellington Gate L24 ...21 C1
Wellington Gdns WA12 ...2 A2
Wellington Gr SK2 ...240 F3
Wellington Pl
Altrincham WA14 ...238 D4
Chester CH2 ...237 B3
Wellington Rd
Altrincham WA15 ...238 F6
Bollington SK10 ...87 C4
Broughton CH4 ...139 A2
Ellesmere Port CH65 ...70 B2
Ellesmere Port CH65 ...70 B3
High Lane SK7 ...37 A4
Kidsgrove ST7 ...195 A1
Nantwich CW5 ...204 C2
Wellington Rd N
Ellesmere Port CH65 ...70 B3
Stockport SK4 ...240 D7
Wellington Rd S SK1,
SK2 ...240 F4
Wellington St
Dukinfield SK14 ...241 C7
Macclesfield SK11 ...112 B4
Newton-le-W WA12 ...2 A2
Northwich CW8 ...103 C4
Runcorn WA7 ...23 A2
Stockport SK1 ...240 F5
Warrington WA1 ...16 B3
Widnes WA8 ...23 A3
Wellington St Wrkshps 4
WA1 ...16 B3
Wells Ave CW1 ...191 B3
Wells Cl
Ellesmere Port CH66 ...94 C4
Gatley SK8 ...34 B4
Mickle Trafford CH2 ...119 C4
Warrington WA1 ...17 A4
Wellswood Dr CW2 ...205 C4
Wellswood Rd CH66 ...69 C4
Welsby Cl WA2 ...8 C2
Welsh La CW7 ...149 B3
Welsh Rd
Ellesmere Port CH66 ...68 C2
Shotwick CH1 ...93 B3
Welsh Road Cotts CH1 ...93 B4
Welsh Row
Nantwich CW5 ...204 B3
Nether Alderley SK10 ...84 C3
Welshampton Cl CH66 ...69 B1
Welshmen's La CW5 ...204 B4
Welshpool Cl WA5 ...7 B1
Welton Cl SK9 ...59 C2
Welton Dr SK9 ...59 C2
Welton Gr SK9 ...59 C2
Welwyn Cl WA4 ...17 B2
Wem Gr ST5 ...210 C1
Wemyss Rd CH1 ...117 B2
Wendover Cl WA11 ...1 B4
Wenger Rd WA8 ...13 A3
Wenlock Cl
Macclesfield SK10 ...87 A1
Newcastle-u-L ST5 ...210 C1

Wenlock Cl *continued*
Warrington WA1 17 A4
Wenlock Gdns CH66 69 C1
Wenlock La CH66 69 C1
Wenlock Rd WA7 50 A2
Wenlock Way CH4 140 C3
Wensley Dr SK7 36 B4
Wensley Rd Cheadle SK8 239 C6
Golborne WA3 3 C4
1 Stockport SK5 240 F8
Wensleydale Ave
Bebington CH62 43 C3
Cheadle SK8 239 C6
Congleton CW12 157 A3
Wensleydale Cl WA5 14 C4
Wentworth Ave
Macclesfield SK11 111 C3
Warrington WA1 17 A4
Wentworth Cl
Northwich CW9 104 C4
Widnes WA8 13 A3
Wentworth Dr
Bebington CH63 43 B3
Bramhall SK7 36 A4
Kidsgrove ST7 195 B2
Wentworth Gr CW7 126 A1
Wereton Rd ST7 209 B1
Werneth Low Rd SK6 241 D4
Werneth Rd Hyde SK14 241 F6
Romiley SK6 241 D4
Werneth Sch SK6 241 A2
Wervin Rd CH2 96 A2
Wesley Ave Alsager ST7 193 B2
Haydock WA11 1 C4
2 Sandbach CW11 175 A3
Wesley C CW12 156 B1
Wesley Cl Nantwich CW5 204 C3
Neston CH64 66 B4
Wesley Ct CW7 126 C1
Wesley Gdns 7 ST7 195 A1
Wesley Pl Crewe CW2 190 B1
4 Northwich CW9 104 A4
Wesley St Audley ST7 210 A1
19 Stockport SK1 240 F5
Weson Sq SK11 111 C4
Wessex Cl
Shavington CW2 206 B2
Warrington WA1 17 C4
Wessex Dr CW9 104 B3
West Ave
Altrincham WA14 238 A5
Crewe CW1 190 A2
Gatley SK8 239 C1
Kidsgrove ST7 194 B1
Middlewich CW10 128 B1
Northwich CW9 104 B4
Stalybridge SK15 242 D3
Warrington WA2 16 A4
Warrington, Stockton Heath WA4 16 B1
Weston CW2 207 A3
West Bank
Alderley Edge SK9 85 A4
Chester CH2 118 B2
West Bank Dock Est WA8 22 C3
West Bank Prim Sch WA8 23 A2
West Bank Rd SK10 87 A1
West Bank St WA8 23 A3
West Bond St SK11 112 B4
West Cheshire Coll (Grange Ctr) CH65 70 A3
West Cheshire Coll (Handbridge Ctr) CH4 141 B4
West Cl SK10 87 C4
West Downs Rd SK8 239 F3
West Dr Gatley SK8 239 A4
Heswall CH60 41 A4
Neston CH64 66 C3
Warrington WA5 15 A2
Winsford CW7 127 A1
West Dudley St CW7 126 C1
West End CH3 121 C4
West End Ave SK8 239 A6
West End Cotts CW12 156 B1
West End Gr WA11 1 A3
West End Rd WA11 1 A3
West Gr Alsager ST7 193 C2
Heswall CH60 40 C4
Sale M33 242 B5
West Hall Ct WA16 29 B3
West Heath Gr WA13 18 B2
West Heath Sh Ctr CW12 156 A2
West Hill Cl SK15 242 C2
West Hill Sch SK15 242 C2
West House Ct SK10 86 C1
West Hyde WA13 18 B2
West La Cuddington CW8 101 C2
High Legh WA16 29 B3
Runcorn WA7 49 C4
West Lea M34 241 A6
West Lorne St CH1 237 A3
West Mains L24 21 A2
West Oak Pl SK8 239 F1
West Over SK6 241 A1
West Park Ave
Denton M34 241 B6
Poynton SK12 36 A2
West Park Dr CH66 94 C4
West Park Mus* SK10 87 B1
West Quay Rd WA2 7 C2
West Rd
Altrincham WA14 238 C2
West Rd *continued*
Congleton CW12 156 B2
Ellesmere Port CH65 70 B2
Runcorn WA7 48 B4
Weaverham CW8 77 A1
West Side Ave WA11 1 A3
West St Alderley Edge SK9 60 A1
Chester CH2 237 C4
Congleton CW12 156 B2
Crewe CW1 190 A3
Haslington CW1 191 B3
Macclesfield SK11 112 A4
Middlewich CW10 128 B1
Mount Pleasant ST7 195 A3
Stalybridge SK15 242 C2
Stockport SK3 240 D5
Warrington WA2 16 A4
West Thorpe WA14 238 B2
West Vale CH64 66 C3
West Vale Rd WA15 238 F6
West View
Ellesmere Port CH66 69 A4
Lach Dennis CW9 104 A4
Warrington WA2 9 A1
West View Rd WA6 101 A3
West Way
Holmes Chapel CW4 130 A2
Sandbach CW11 174 C2
Shavington CW2 206 B3
West Wing The CW10 127 B3
Westage La CW9 79 A4
Westbourne Ave CW1 190 A3
Westbourne Gr M33 242 A6
Westbourne Mews CW12 156 A1
Westbourne Rd
Blacon CH1 118 A2
Warrington WA4 26 A4
Westbrook Ave WA4 16 B1
Westbrook Cres WA5 7 A1
Westbrook Ctr WA5 7 B1
Westbrook Dr SK10 87 B1
Westbrook Old Hall Prim Sch WA5 15 B4
Westbrook Rd WA6 75 A1
Westbrook Way WA5 7 A1
Westbury Cl
Middlewich CW10 151 A4
Warrington WA1 17 A4
Wistaston CW2 206 B4
Westbury Ct SK11 112 A4
Westbury Dr SK11 112 A4
Westbury Way CH4 140 C3
Westby Cl SK7 36 A4
Westcliff Gdns WA4 26 C2
Westcourt Rd M33 242 A8
Westdale Rd WA1 17 A4
Westend Ct LL13 196 B4
Westenra Ave CH65 69 C3
Westerham Cl SK10 87 A1
Western App CH2 118 C2
Western Ave Blacon CH1 117 B2
Ellesmere Port CH65 69 C4
Macclesfield SK11 112 B3
Milton Green CH3 165 B1
Nantwich CW5 204 C2
Western Ct CH2 118 C2
Western Dr SK11 112 B3
Western Pk CW11 191 C4
Westfield WA14 238 C3
Westfield Ave
Audley ST7 209 B1
Macclesfield SK10 87 A1
Westfield Cl
Chester CH4 141 A4
Winsford CW7 149 B3
Westfield Cres WA7 22 C1
Westfield Dr
Knutsford WA16 56 C1
Willaston (nr Nantwich) CW2 205 C4
Westfield Gr CW8 77 C2
Westfield Inf Sch CW2 205 C4
Westfield Mews WA7 22 C1
Westfield Prim Sch WA7 22 C1
Westfield Rd Cheadle SK8 34 C4
Mow Cop ST7 195 B4
Northwich CW9 104 A4
Runcorn WA7 22 C1
Westfields WA15 31 C4
Westfields Rise CW3 232 B1
Westford Rd WA4 16 A1
Westgate
Altrincham WA15 238 E2
Sale M33 242 A6
Widnes WA8 22 A4
Wilmslow SK9 60 A3
Westgate Ave CW7 126 A1
Westgate Pk CW2 206 C1
Westholme Cl
Congleton CW12 156 B2
Wistaston CW2 206 B4
Westholme Ct SK9 60 A1
Westhouse Cl CH63 43 B3
Westlands ST7 209 C1
Westlands Cl CH64 41 C1
Westlands Rd CW10 128 A1
Westlands The CW12 156 B1
Westmere Cl CW2 207 A3
Westmere Dr CW1 190 C1
Westminster Ave CH4 141 A3
Westminster Cl
Middlewich CW10 128 A1
Warrington WA4 17 B1
Widnes WA8 22 A4
Westminster Dr
Bebington CH62 43 B4
Bramhall SK8 35 A3
Westminster Dr *continued*
Haydock WA11 1 C4
Wilmslow SK9 60 A2
Westminster Gn CH4 141 B4
Westminster Gr
Ellesmere Port CH65 70 B3
9 Winsford CW7 149 A4
Westminster Ind Pk CH65 69 C3
Westminster Pl 9 WA1 16 A3
Westminster Rd
Broughton CH4 139 A2
Chester CH2 118 C2
Ellesmere Port CH65 70 B3
Macclesfield SK10 87 B1
Westminster St
Crewe CW2 190 B1
5 Macclesfield SK11 112 B4
Westminster Terr CH4 141 B4
Westmoor Gables SK4 240 A8
Westmoreland Cl WA14 31 A4
Westmorland Ave
Talke ST7 210 C4
Widnes WA8 13 A1
Westmorland Cl SK10 86 C1
Westmorland Rd M31 11 C1
Westmorland Terr CW4 130 A2
Weston Cl CW10 151 B4
Weston Cres WA7 49 A3
Weston Ct WA7 48 C4
Weston Dr M34 241 A7
Weston Gr Chester CH2 118 C4
Halewood L26 21 A3
Weston La CW2 206 C3
Weston Point Expressway WA7 49 A3
Weston Point Prim Sch WA7 48 C4
Weston Prim Sch WA7 49 A3
Weston Rd Crewe CW1 207 A4
Runcorn WA7 48 C4
Wilmslow SK9 60 C3
Weston St SK5 240 E8
Weston View WA7 49 B2
Weston Village Prim Sch CW2 207 B3
Westover Rd WA1 16 C4
Westrees CW8 101 B3
Westville Dr CW12 156 A1
Westward Rd
Chester CH3 142 A4
Wilmslow SK9 59 C3
Westway CH60 40 C3
Westway Cres WA3 10 A3
Westwood
Altrincham WA14 238 B4
Runcorn WA7 24 B1
Westwood Ave WA15 238 F7
Westwood Cl CW2 207 A1
Westwood Ct CH64 41 C1
Westwood Lodge WA15 238 F2
Westwood Rd SK8 34 A4
Westy La WA4 16 C2
Wet Gate La WA13 19 C2
Wetheral Rd SK10 87 A1
Wetherby Cl
Chester CH1 118 A1
Newton-le-W WA12 2 B3
Wetherby Way CH66 69 B3
Wetreins La SY14,CH3 197 B3
Wettenhall Rd CW5 188 A2
Wetton La CW8 76 C2
Wexford Ave L24 21 B1
Weybourne Cl CH4 140 C3
Weybridge Cl WA4 26 C4
Weybridge Dr SK10 87 A2
Weygates Dr WA15 32 B4
Weymouth Cl WA7 50 C3
Weymouth Rd WA5 6 C3
Whaddon Dr CH4 140 C2
Whaley Bridge Prim Sch SK23 65 C4
Whaley Bridge Sta SK23 65 C4
Whaley La SK23 65 B4
Whalley Ave Glazebury WA3 5 B4
Sale M33 242 C7
Whalley Cl WA15 238 F8
Whalley Dr CW6 147 A2
Whalley Gr WA8 13 B2
Whalley Hayes SK11 112 B4
Whalley Rd CW9 104 A4
Whalley St WA1 16 B3
Wharams Bank CW11 176 C3
Wharburton Cl CW8 101 C1
Wharf Ct SK23 65 C4
Wharf La CW12 178 A2
Wharf Rd
Altrincham WA14 238 D7
Collins Green WA12 1 C1
Sale M33 242 C7
Whaley Bridge SK23 65 C4
Wharf St Stockport SK4 240 E7
Warrington WA1 16 B2
Wharf The WA7 50 C3
Wharfdale Cl WA5 15 A4
Wharfdale Rd
Congleton CW12 157 A3
Crewe CW1 173 A1
Wharfe Cl CW12 156 C1
Wharfe La CH65 70 A4
Wharfedale WA7 50 A3
Wharfedale Dr CH62 43 C3
Wharford La WA7 24 C2
Wharfside Ct 6 WA4 16 C1
Wharmby Rd WA11 1 C3
Wharton (Donefields) Ind Est CW7 126 C1
Wharton CE Jun Sch CW7 127 A1
Wharton Gdns CW7 127 A2
Wharton Park Rd CW7 126 C1
Wharton Rd CW7 127 A1
Wharton Ret Pk CW7 126 C2
Whatcroft Cl WA7 49 B3
Whatcroft La CW9 104 C1
Wheat Croft SK3 240 F1
Wheat Moss SK11 84 A2
Wheatcroft Cl WA5 15 B3
Wheatfield Cl
Barnton CW8 78 A2
Ellesmere Port CH66 69 B2
Macclesfield SK10 87 B2
Romiley SK6 241 A4
Wheatfield Rd WA8 12 B3
Wheatland Rd CH60 41 B4
Wheatlands WA7 23 C1
Wheatley Ave WA12 2 B3
Wheatley Rd CW1 190 C3
Wheatsheaf La CW9 53 A2
Wheatsheaf Rd SK23 65 C3
Wheelman Rd CW1 190 A4
Wheelock Cl Alsager ST7 193 A2
Wilmslow SK9 34 B1
Wheelock Ct CW11 175 A1
Wheelock Dr CW7 127 A1
Wheelock Prim Sch CW11 175 A2
Wheelock St CW10 128 B1
Wheelock Way 10 ST7 195 A1
Wheldon Cl CH2 118 C4
Wheldrake Cl CH66 69 A3
Whernside WA8 12 B2
Whernside Cl SK4 240 E7
Whetstone Hey CH66 69 B3
Whetstone Rd ST8 179 B1
Whickham Cl WA8 12 C2
Whimbrel Ave WA12 2 B2
Whimbrel Cl WA7 49 C3
Whinberry Rd WA14 238 B7
Whinchat Ave WA12 2 B2
Whinchat Cl WA3 3 C4
Whinchat Dr WA3 9 C2
Whinfell Gr WA7 49 C3
Whipcord La CH1 118 A1
Whirley Cl CW10 151 B4
Whirley La SK10 85 C1
Whirley Prim Sch SK10 86 B1
Whirley Rd SK10 86 B1
Whirlow Rd CW2 206 A4
Whisterfield La SK11 109 C2
Whiston Cl
High Legh WA16 29 B2
Winsford CW7 127 A2
Whiston Mews SK11 113 A2
Whiston St SK11 112 B4
Whitbarrow Rd WA13 18 B2
Whitby Ave Chester CH2 118 B3
Warrington WA2 8 B1
Whitby Cl Cheadle SK8 239 C6
Crewe CW1 190 A4
Poynton SK12 36 B2
Whitby Heath Prim Sch CH65 70 A2
Whitby High Sch The CH66 70 A1
Whitby La CH1 95 A3
Whitby Rd
Ellesmere Port CH65 70 B3
Runcorn WA7 23 A1
Whitby's La CW7 126 A1
Whitchurch Cl WA1 17 A4
Whitchurch Gr ST5 210 C1
Whitchurch Rd
Audlem CW3 229 B2
Broxton CH3 183 A2
Chester CH3 119 A1
Christleton CH3 142 C4
Edge Green SY14,CH3 199 A2
Milton Green CH3 165 B2
Newhall CW3 229 B2
Royal's Green CW3,SY13 228 B1
Sound CW5 217 C2
Waverton CH3 143 A2
Whitchurch Way WA7 49 B4
White Ave CW2 189 C2
White Bear Yd 12 WA16 57 A1
White Broom WA13 19 A2
White Friars CH1 237 A2
White Hall La CW11 173 C4
White Hart Gdns CW8 102 C2
White Hart La CW2 205 C4
White Hart St SK14 241 D8
White House Cl WA11 1 A3
White House Dr WA1 17 C4
White La CH3 142 B4
White Lodge Cl CH62 43 B3
White Lodge Mews CW8 102 A2
White Park Cl CW10 128 B1
White St
Macclesfield SK11 112 B3
Warrington WA1 16 A3
Warrington, Stockton Heath WA4 16 B1
Widnes WA8 23 A3
Whiteacre Rd OL6 242 A4
Whitebarn Rd SK9 85 A4
Whitebeam Ave 13 CH66 69 C1
Whitebeam Cl
Newcastle-u-L ST5 210 B1
Runcorn WA7 24 B1
Whitebeam Row CW8 102 C4
Whitecroft Rd CH66 69 C1
Whitecross Rd WA5 15 C3
Whitefield Lymm WA13 19 A2
Whitefield *continued*
Stockport SK4 240
Whitefield Ave
Newton-le-W WA12 2
Warrington WA1 16
Whitefield Cl
Golborne WA3 3
Lymm WA13 19
Whitefield Ct WA3 4
Whitefield Gr WA13 19
Whitefield Rd Sale M33 242
Warrington WA4 26
Whitefields CH2 72
Whitefriars Wlk 2 M22 33
Whitegate CH3 121
Whitegate Ave WA3 4
Whitegate CE Prim Sch CW8 125
Whitegate Cl CW10 151
Whitegate Fields LL13 180
Whitegate Rd CW7 125
Whitegates SK8 239
Whitegates Cl CH64 42
Whitegates Cres CH64 42
Whitegates Rd SK8 239
Whitehall Ave ST7 194
Whitehall Cl Barnton CW8 78
Wilmslow SK9 60
Whitehall Ct CW5 204
Whitehall Dr
Hartford CW8 103
Shavington CW2 206
Whitehall La CW6 124
Whitehall Pl 6 WA6 74
Whitehall Rd M33 242
Whitehaven La CW5 203
Whitehaven Rd SK7 35
Whitehill Prim Sch SK4 240
Whitehill Rd ST7 195
Whitehill St W SK4 240
Whitehouse Dr WA15 32
Whitehouse Expressway WA7 50
Whitehouse Ind Est WA7 50
Whitehouse La
Nantwich CW5 204
Partington WA14 20
Plumley WA16 80
Whitehouse Rd WA16 30
Whitelands Rd OL6,SK15 242
Whitelea Dr SK3 240
Whiteleas Rd SK23 65
Whiteley Pl WA14 238
Whitelow Rd SK4 240
Whitemere Ct CH65 70
Whitemore Rd CW10 151
Whiteridge Rd ST7 195
Whites La CW2 207
Whites Mdw CH3 142
Whitesands Rd WA13 18
Whiteside Rd WA11 1
Whitesmead Cl SK12 38
Whitethorn Ave WA5 14
Whitethorn Way ST5 210
Whitewell Cl CW5 204
Whitewood La SY14 212
Whitfield Gr WA11 1
Whitfield Rd ST7 195
Whitfields The SK10 87
Whitley Ave Barnton CW8 78
Warrington WA4 17
Whitley Cl
Middlewich CW10 151
Runcorn WA7 48
Whitley Dr CW8 103
Whitley La WA16 55
Whitley Rd SK4 240
Whitley Village Sch WA4 52
Whitlow Ave
Altrincham WA14 238
Nantwich CW5 204
Whitlow La CW9 126
Whitstable Pk WA8 12
Whittaker Ave WA2 8
Whittaker Cl CW1 190
Whittington Gdns CW9 104
Whittle Ave Haydock WA11 1
Warrington WA5 15
Whittle Cl CH5 116
Whittle Hall La WA5 14
Whittles Ave M34 241
Whittles Wlk M34 241
Whittlewood Cl WA3 10
Whitton Dr CH2 118
Whitwell Cl WA5 14
Whitworth Cl WA3 9
Wickenby Dr M33 242
Wicker La
Altrincham WA15 32
Guilden Sutton CH3 120
Wicklow Ave SK3 240
Wicklow Cl CH66 69
Wickson La CH3,CW6 167
Wicksten Dr WA7 23
Widdale Cl WA5 14
Widgeon Cl SK12 36
Widgeon Rd WA14 238
Widgeons Covert CH63 41
Widnes Rd
Warrington WA5 14
Widnes WA8 23
Widnes Sixth Form Coll WA8 12
Widnes Sta WA8 13
Wiend The CH2 118
Wight Cl CH65 70
Wightman Ave WA12 2
Wigmore Cl WA3 10

Wigmore St OL6 242 A4
Wigsey La WA13 19 A4
Wigshaw La WA3 4 B1
Wigwam Cl SK12 36 B2
Wilbraham Cl CW5 204 A4
Wilbraham Rd
Acton CW5 204 A4
Congleton CW12 156 C2
Weaverham CW8 77 C1
Wilbraham's Wlk ST7 209 B1
Wilbrahams Way ST7 193 B2
Wilcock Rd WA11 2 A4
Wilcott Dr SK9 59 C2
Wilcott Rd SK8 239 A5
Wild Arum Cl 6 WA3 3 C4
Wild Clough SK14 241 F5
Wild Goose Ave ST7 195 B2
Wildcote Cl WA8 13 B2
Wilderhope Cl CW2 206 B4
Wilderspool Cres WA4 16 A1
Wilderspool Cswy WA4 16 B2
Wilding Ave WA7 23 A1
Wilding Bsns Pk CH3 119 B2
Wilding St CW1 190 C2
Wildings Old La WA3 9 A4
Wildwood Gr WA1 17 A4
Wilkin Croft SK8 239 E1
Wilkins La SK9 33 C3
Wilkinson Ave WA1 16 C3
Wilkinson Cl WA8 23 A3
Wilkinson Rd SK4 240 E6
Wilkinson St
Ellesmere Port CH65 70 B3
4 Sale M33 242 D6
Warrington WA2 16 B4
Wilkinson St N CH65 70 B3
Willan Rd CH1 117 B2
Willaston CE Prim Sch
CH64 67 C4
Willaston Dr L26 21 A3
Willaston Farm CH64 67 C4
Willaston Green Mews
CH64 67 C4
Willaston Hall Gdns
CW5 205 B3
Willaston Prim Sch
CW5 205 B3
Willaston Rd CH63,CH64 42 B2
Willaston Way 8 SK9 34 B3
Willbank La CW5 202 B3
Willdor Gr SK3 240 B2
Willerby Cl SK11 112 B4
Willeymoor La SY13 225 B4
William Beamont Com High
Sch WA2 8 B1
William Johnson Gdns
CH65 70 B3
William Penn Cl WA5 14 C3
William Rd ST7 195 A1
William St Chester CH1 237 B3
Chester, Hoole Park CH2 118 C2
Congleton CW12 157 A2
Macclesfield SK10 112 C4
10 Northwich CW9 104 A4
Widnes WA8 13 B1
Winsford CW7 126 C1
William Stockton Com Sch
CH65 70 A3
William Wlk 2 WA14 238 D3
Williams Ave WA12 2 B3
Williams Cl CH2 118 B2
Williams Way SK11 111 B4
Williamson Ave SK6 241 A4
Williamson Cres SK23 65 B4
Williamson Rd SK23 65 B4
Willington Ave CH62 43 C2
Willington La
Duddon CW6 145 C4
Kelsall CW6 122 B2
Willington Rd
Duddon CW6 145 A4
Kelsall CW6 122 B2
Tarvin CW6 122 B1
Willis Rd SK3 240 E2
Willis St WA1 16 B3
Willmer Cres ST7 195 A3
Willotts Hill Rd ST5 210 B1
Willoughby Cl Sale M33 242 A7
Warrington WA5 7 B1
Willow Ave Cheadle SK8 239 F2
Newton-le-W WA12 2 C2
Stockport SK5 240 F8
Widnes WA8 13 A1
Willow Bank Bramhall SK8 35 A3
Helsby WA6 73 B1
Willow Bank Ct M20 239 B8
Willow Bank Est WA12 2 C2
Willow Cl Chester CH2 118 B4
Lymm WA13 18 C2
Newcastle-u-L ST5 210 B1
Poynton SK12 36 C2
Runcorn WA7 49 B4
Winsford CW7 126 B2
Willow Cres Chester CH2 119 A2
Warrington WA1 17 A4
Wistaston CW2 189 C1
Willow Ct Alsager ST7 193 C2
Connah's Quay CH5 91 B1
Gatley SK8 239 A6
Higher Kinnerton CH4 161 A4
Macclesfield SK10 87 A1
Middlewich CW10 128 B1
Nantwich CW5 204 C4
Sale M33 242 E7
Willow Dr Blacon CH1 117 B3
Bunbury CW6 185 C4
Handforth SK9 34 B2
Sandbach CW11 175 C4
Willow Dr *continued*
Warrington WA4 16 C1
Willow Gn
Knutsford WA16 56 C2
Weaverham CW8 102 B4
Willow Gr Barnton CW8 78 A2
Chester CH2 119 A2
Ellesmere Port CH1 95 A4
Elton CH2 72 A2
Willow Hayes CH3 121 C4
Willow La Goostrey CW4 107 C1
Thornton Hough CH63,CH64 42 B2
Warrington WA4 26 B2
Willow Lea CH1 94 C1
Willow Rd Chester CH4 140 C3
Haydock WA11 1 C4
High Lane SK6 37 C4
Newton-le-W WA12 2 C2
Partington M31 11 C1
Willow Sq CW7 127 A1
Willow St CW12 156 C2
Willow Tree Gr ST7 193 C4
Willow Tree Mews SK8 239 B1
Willow Tree Rd WA14 238 D3
Willow Way Bramhall SK7 35 B4
Broughton CH4 139 A2
Prestbury SK10 87 A3
Willow Wood Cl OL6 242 B3
Willow Wood Com Jun Sch
CW7 127 A1
Willow Wood Inf Sch
CW7 127 A1
Willoway Rd CH3 119 A1
Willowbank Dr SK10 88 B4
Willowbrow Rd CH63,
CH64 42 B2
Willowcroft Way ST7 195 C2
Willowdale WA12 2 C2
Willowdale Ave SK8 239 B2
Willowdale Way CH66 94 C4
Willowgreen La CW8 77 A3
Willowherb Cl CH3 142 A3
Willowmead Dr SK10 87 A3
Willows SK9 59 C3
Willows Cl CW2 206 A4
Willows The
Frodsham WA6 74 B4
Higher Wincham CW9 79 C3
Partington M31 11 C2
Sandbach CW11 175 A4
5 Stockport SK4 240 A7
Warrington WA5 14 C3
Wilmere La WA8 13 A3
Wilmot Ave WA5 14 C3
Wilmot Dr WA3 2 C4
Wilmslow Ave CH66 69 C3
Wilmslow Cres WA4 17 B2
Wilmslow Dr CH66 69 C3
Wilmslow Grange Sch
SK9 34 B2
Wilmslow High Sch SK9 60 A3
Wilmslow Old Rd
Mottram St Andrew SK10 61 A1
Wythenshawe M90,WA15 33 A3
Wilmslow Park Rd SK9 60 B4
Wilmslow Prep Sch SK9 60 A4
Wilmslow Rd
Alderley Edge SK9 60 A1
Cheadle SK8 239 D5
Gatley SK8,SK9 34 B3
Handforth SK9 34 B2
Mottram St Andrew SK10 61 A2
Mottram St Andrew SK10 61 B3
Mottram St Andrew, Greendale
SK10 86 B4
Woodford SK7 35 B1
Wythenshaw M90,WA15,
SK9 32 C3
Wilmslow Sta SK9 60 B4
Wilmslow Wlk 12 SK11 112 C4
Wilsbury Grange CW8 103 A3
Wilsden Rd WA8 12 A1
Wilson Cl Warrington WA4 17 B2
Widnes WA8 13 B1
Wilson Cres
Lostock Gralam CW9 80 A2
Stalybridge OL6 242 B4
Wilson Dr CW9 126 C4
Wilson La WA3 9 C3
Wilson Patten St WA1 16 A2
Wilson Rd SK4 240 B8
Wilson St Hyde SK14 241 E6
3 Sale M33 242 B7
Warrington WA5 16 A4
Wilsons La CH65 70 A2
Wilton Ave SK8 34 B4
Wilton Cl CW9 103 C2
Wilton Cres
Alderley Edge SK9 59 C1
Macclesfield SK11 111 C3
Wilton Dr WA15 32 B4
Wilton La WA3 4 A3
Wiltshire Cl
Macclesfield SK10 86 C1
Warrington WA1 17 B3
Wiltshire Dr CW12 156 C2
Wiltshire Rd M31 11 C1
Wiltshire Wlk SK10 86 C1
Wilwick La SK11 111 C4
Wimberry Dr ST5 210 B1
Wimbledon Dr SK3 240 C3
Wimboldsley Com Prim Sch
CW10 150 C2
Wincham Ave CW9 79 B2
Wincham Bsns Pk CW9 79 B2
Wincham Com Prim Sch
CW9 79 C3
Wincham La CW9 79 B2
Winchester Ave
Ellesmere Port CH65 70 B2
Warrington WA5 15 B3
Winchester Cl
Shavington CW2 206 A2
Wilmslow SK9 59 C3
Winchester Dr SK4 240 B6
Winchester Pl WA8 22 B4
Winchester Sq CH4 140 C3
Wincle Ave SK12 37 A1
Wincle CE Prim Sch
SK11 136 C1
Windemere Ave CH2 119 A3
Windermere Ave
Warrington WA2 8 B2
Widnes WA8 13 A2
Windermere Cl CH64 66 C4
Windermere Dr
Alderley Edge SK9 59 C1
Congleton CW12 156 A1
Windermere Rd
Ellesmere Port CH65 70 B1
Handforth SK9 34 B2
Haydock WA11 1 A3
High Lane SK6 37 C4
Stalybridge SK15 242 D4
Winsford CW7 126 B1
Wistaston CW2 189 C1
Windermere St WA8 13 A2
Windfield Gdns CH66 69 B4
Windings The CW10 128 A1
Windle Ct Neston CH64 41 C1
Warrington WA3 9 B2
Windlehurst Ct SK6 37 B4
Windlehurst Rd SK6 37 B4
Windmill Cl
Buerton CW3 230 C2
Warrington WA4 26 B3
Windmill Ctr The WA8 23 A4
Windmill Dr CW3 229 C2
Windmill Hill Ave WA7 24 B1
Windmill Hill Ave E WA7 24 B1
Windmill Hill Ave N WA7 24 B2
Windmill Hill Ave S WA7 24 B1
Windmill Hill Ave W
WA7 24 B1
Windmill Hill Prim Sch
WA7 24 B1
Windmill La
Bollington SK10 88 A3
Buerton CW3 230 C2
Christleton CH3 142 B4
Preston on the Hill WA4 51 A3
Warrington, Appleton WA4 26 B3
Warrington, Penketh WA5 14 C3
Windmill Rd M33 242 F5
Windmill Rise CH2 118 B4
Windmill St
Macclesfield SK11 112 C3
Runcorn WA7 23 A1
Windscale Rd WA2 9 A1
Windsor Ave Crewe CW1 190 A3
Gatley SK8 239 A5
Nantwich CW5 204 C2
Newton-le-W WA12 2 B1
Sale M33 242 B8
Stockport SK4 240 A7
Tarporley CW6 146 B1
Wilmslow SK9 59 C4
Windsor Cl
Bollington SK10 87 C3
Cuddington CW8 101 C2
Poynton SK12 36 B2
Windsor Ct Chester CH4 237 B1
1 Warrington WA4 16 C1
Windsor Dr Alsager ST7 192 C2
Altrincham WA14 20 C1
Broughton CH4 139 A2
Ellesmere Port CH65 70 A2
Faddiley CW5 202 C4
Haydock WA11 2 A4
Helsby WA6 73 A1
Sale WA14 238 F8
Stalybridge SK15 242 D3
Warrington WA4 17 A1
Winsford CW7 149 B3
Windsor Gr Cheadle SK8 34 C4
Romiley SK6 241 E2
Runcorn WA7 49 A4
Windsor Ho ST7 210 B3
Windsor Pl CW12 156 C1
Windsor Rd Chester CH4 140 C3
Golborne WA3 3 B4
Widnes WA8 13 A2
Wistaston CW2 205 C4
Windsor Sq SK11 112 B2
Windsor St WA5 15 C3
Windsor Way WA16 56 C1
Windsor Wlk SK2 240 F2
Windways CH66 69 B4
Windy Bank Ave WA3 3 C4
Winfield St SK14 241 F6
Winfield Way WA8 23 A4
Winfrith Rd WA2 9 A1
Wingate Rd
Bebington CH62 43 C3
Stockport SK4 240 C8
Wingfield Ave SK9 59 C3
Wingfield Dr SK9 59 C3
Wingfield Pl CW7 149 A3
Winghay Rd ST7 195 B1
Winifred St WA2 16 B4
Winkwell Dr CH4 141 A3
Winmarith Dr WA15 32 B4
Winmarleigh St WA1 16 A2
Winnington Ave CW8 103 B4
Winnington La CW8 78 B1
Winnington Park Com Prim
Sch CW8 103 B4
Winnington St CW7 126 C1
Winnows The WA7 23 B1
Winscombe Dr CH3 119 B1
Winsfield Rd SK7 36 C4
Winsford Cl WA11 1 C4
Winsford Dr WA5 6 C4
Winsford Gr CH66 69 B2
Winsford High Street Com
Sch CW7 126 B1
Winsford Ind Est CW7 127 B2
Winsford Rd
Cholmondeston CW7 171 A1
Wettenhall CW7 170 C3
Winsford St Chad's CE Prim
Sch CW7 149 C4
Winsford Sta CW7 127 B1
Winsford Way CH1 117 C1
Winsford Wlk M33 242 E5
Winslow Cl WA7 50 B4
Winstanley Cl WA5 15 B3
Winstanley Ind Est WA2 8 A1
Winstanley Rd
Neston CH64 66 C3
Sale M33 242 C7
Winston Ave Alsager ST7 193 B3
Newton-le-W WA12 2 B2
St Helens WA9 1 A1
Winston Ct CH2 119 A3
Winter Gr WA9 1 A2
Winter La SY14 198 A2
Winterbottom La WA16 55 C4
Winterford La CW6 147 A1
Wintergreen Wlk 10 M31 11 C2
Winterlea Dr L26 21 A3
Winterside Cl ST5 210 B1
Winterton Way SK11 112 B2
Winton Ct WA14 238 C2
Winton Gr WA7 24 B1
Winton Rd
Altrincham WA14 238 C2
Golborne WA3 3 C3
Winton St SK15 242 E1
Winwick CE Prim Sch
WA2 8 A3
Winwick La WA3 3 C2
Winwick Link Rd WA2,WA3 8 B3
Winwick Park Ave WA2 8 A3
Winwick Rd
Newton-le-W WA12 2 C1
Warrington WA2 8 A1
Winwick St WA2 16 A3
Winwick View WA5 1 D1
Winwood Rd M20 239 C8
Wirksmoor Rd SK22 39 A4
Wirral Cl WA3 4 C2
Wirral Cres Neston CH64 66 C3
Stockport SK3 240 A4
Wirral Ctry Pk* CH64 67 B4
Wirral Ed Ctr CH62 43 B4
Wirral Met Coll (Carlett Park
Campus) CH62 44 A4
Wirswall Rd SY13 226 B4
Wisenholme Cl WA7 49 C3
Wistaston Ave CW2 189 C1
Wistaston Green Cl
CW2 189 C1
Wistaston Green Inf Sch
CW2 189 C1
Wistaston Green Jun Sch
CW2 189 C1
Wistaston Green Rd
CW2 189 C1
Wistaston Jun Sch CW2 205 C4
Wistaston Pk CW2 189 C1
Wistaston Rd
Crewe CW2 190 B2
Willaston (nr Nantwich)
CW5 205 C3
Wistaston CW5 205 C3
Wistaston Road Bsns Ctr
CW2 190 A2
Wisterdale Cl CW2 206 A4
Witchcroft Heath Rd
SK11 109 A2
Witham Cl CW2 206 A4
Witham St OL6 242 B4
Witham Way ST8 179 C1
Withens Cl CW8 102 B4
Withens La CW8 102 B4
Withenshaw La SK11 136 C3
Wither's La WA16 28 B3
Withers Ave WA2 16 B4
Witherwin Ave WA4 26 C4
Within Way L24 47 C4
Withington Ave WA3 5 A2
Withington Cl
Northwich CW9 104 A3
Sandbach CW11 175 B4
Withinlee Rd SK10 86 B3
Withins Rd Culcheth WA3 4 C2
Haydock WA11 1 C4
Withy Cl WA6 74 B4
Withy Croft CH3 142 A4
Withy Tree Gr 1 M34 241 A6
Withycombe Rd WA5 14 C2
Withyfold Dr SK10 87 C1
Witney Gdns WA4 26 C3
Witney La SY14 213 B4
Witt Rd WA8 23 A4
Wittenbury Rd SK4 240 B6
Wittenham Ho SK9 34 B1
Witter Pl CH2 237 C3
Wittering La CH60 40 B4
Witterings The CH64 41 C1
Witton Church Walk CE Prim
Sch CW9 104 A4
Witton St CW9 79 A1
Witton Wlk 5 CW9 103 C4
Wivern Pl WA7 23 A2
Woburn Ave WA12 2 B1
Woburn Cl Haydock WA11 1 C4
Macclesfield SK10 87 B1
Northwich CW9 103 C3
Woburn Ct SK12 36 C2
Woburn Dr Chester CH2 118 C4
Congleton CW12 179 A4
Cronton WA8 12 B3
Woburn Rd WA2 8 A2
Woking Rd SK8 35 A4
Wolfe Cl
Grappenhall Heys WA4 27 A4
Knutsford WA16 57 B2
Wolseley Ho M33 242 C8
Wolseley Rd M33 242 C8
Wolsey Dr WA14 238 A1
Wolstanholme Cl CW12 156 C1
Wolverham Prim Sch
CH65 70 B2
Wolverham Rd CH65 70 B2
Wolverton Dr
Runcorn WA7 24 B1
Wilmslow SK9 34 B1
Wolvesey Pl CW7 149 A3
Wood Croft CH3 119 C2
Wood Dr ST7 193 A2
Wood End Ct WA8 13 B1
Wood End La CH64 67 C2
Wood Gdns SK9 60 A1
Wood Hey Gr 2 M34 241 A6
Wood La Altrincham WA16 32 B1
Bradwall Green CW10,
CW11 152 C2
Broughton CH4 139 A2
Burton CH64 67 B1
Duddon CW6 145 C4
Goostrey CW4 107 B1
Mobberley WA16 58 A4
Neston CH64 41 B1
Partington M31 11 B2
Runcorn WA7 49 C2
Runcorn, Brookvale WA7 50 B3
Tattenhall CH3 167 A1
Utkinton CW6 146 A3
Warrington WA4 26 C4
Weaverham CW8 102 C4
Wood La E SK10 63 A4
Wood La N SK10 63 A4
Wood La S SK10 63 A4
Wood La W SK10 63 A4
Wood Lane Prim Sch
ST7 210 A1
Wood Meml Sch CH4 140 C3
Wood Orchard La CW3 230 A1
Wood Sorrel Way WA3 3 C4
Wood St
Altrincham WA14 238 D4
Audley ST7 209 C2
Cheadle SK8 239 D6
Congleton CW12 156 B2
Crewe CW2 190 B1
Golborne WA3 3 A4
Hawarden CH5 116 A1
Hyde SK14 241 E6
Macclesfield SK11 112 B4
Mow Cop ST7 195 B4
New Mills SK22 39 A4
Stalybridge SK15 242 D2
Stockport SK3 240 E5
Warrington WA1 16 B3
Widnes WA8 13 B1
Wood View ST7 210 A1
Wood's La CW8 101 B3
Woodacre Gr CH66 69 C4
Woodacre Rd CH66 69 C4
Woodacres Ct SK9 59 C3
Woodale Cl WA5 14 C4
Woodall Cl M33 242 D6
Woodall Dr WA7 23 A1
Woodavens Gr CW3 229 A1
Woodbank Cl CW2 206 A4
Woodbank La CH1 93 B3
Woodbank Rd
Ellesmere Port CH65 70 A1
Warrington WA5 15 A2
Woodbine Ave M44 11 B2
Woodbine Cres SK2 240 F3
Woodbine Rd WA13 19 A2
Woodbourne Rd SK22 39 A3
Woodbridge Cl WA4 26 C2
Woodbrook SK23 65 C4
Woodbrook Ave SK14 241 F6
Woodbrook Ct SK23 65 C4
Woodbrook Rd SK9 60 B1
Woodburn Dr CH60 40 C3
Woodbury Rd SK3 240 B3
Woodchurch La CH66 69 C3
Woodchurch Wlk 5
M33 242 F5
Woodclose CH66 44 A1
Woodcock La ST7 195 B3
Woodcocks' Well CE Prim
Sch ST7 195 B3
Woodcote Ave CH65 70 A1
Woodcote Cl WA2 8 B1
Woodcote Pl CW11 191 C4
Woodcote View SK9 34 C1
Woodcotes The CH62 43 B3
Woodcott Ave CW7 126 A1
Woodcott Cl CW2 206 C1
Woodcott Gr 3 SK9 34 C1
Woodcotthill La CW5 217 A2

Woodcroft ST7 210 A1
Woodend WA7 50 C4
Woodend Cl CW10 151 B3
Woodend La
Altrincham WA16 32 C1
Hollins Green WA3 10 B1
Hyde SK14 241 D5
Mobberley WA16 58 C4
Woodend Rd CH65 69 C3
Woodfall Cl CH64 67 A3
Woodfall Gr CH64 67 A3
Woodfall Inf Sch CH64 67 A3
Woodfall Jun Sch CH64 67 A3
Woodfall La CH64 67 A3
Woodfield Ave SK6 241 A4
Woodfield Cl CH4 139 A2
Woodfield Gr
Chester CH2 119 A3
Sale M33 242 A8
Woodfield Ho CH2 119 A3
Woodfield Prim Sch
CH2 119 A3
Woodfield Rd
Altrincham WA14 238 C6
Bramhall SK8 35 A4
Ellesmere Port CH65 70 B3
Woodfield Rd N 9 CH65 70 B3
Woodfields CH3 142 C4
Woodfin Croft SK11 84 A2
Woodford Ave
Dukinfield M34 241 A8
Golborne WA3 3 B4
Woodford Cl Crewe CW2 189 C1
Helsby WA6 73 A1
Runcorn WA7 49 A3
Warrington WA4 17 B2
Woodford Court Ind Est
CW7 149 A4
Woodford La
Prestbury SK10 61 B4
Winsford CW7 149 A4
Woodford La W CW7 149 A4
Woodford Lodge High Sch
CW7 149 A4
Woodford Park Ind Est
CW7 148 C4
Woodford Prep Sch SK7 35 B1
Woodford Rd
Bramhall SK7 35 C2
Poynton SK12 36 A3
Wilmslow SK9 61 A4
Woodgate Ave ST7 194 A3
Woodgreen La CW5 171 B3
Woodhall Cl
Warrington WA5 15 A4
Woodford SK7 35 C2
Woodhall Rd
Kidsgrove ST7 195 B2
Stockport SK5 240 F8
Woodham Cl CW8 103 B3
Woodham Gr CH64 66 C3
Woodhatch Rd WA7 50 A3
Woodhead Dr WA15 238 F1
Woodhead Rd WA15 238 F1
Woodhey Hall La CW5 202 A3
Woodhey La CW5 202 B3
Woodhill Ave CH4 140 C3
Woodhouse Cl WA3 9 C2
Woodhouse End Rd
SK11 135 A4
Woodhouse La
Biddulph ST8 179 C1
Buerton CW3 235 B4
Partington WA14 20 B2
Warren SK11 111 C1
Wythenshawe M22 33 B4
Woodhouse Mid Sch
ST8 179 C1
Woodhouse Park Prim Sch
M22 33 B4
Woodhouse Rd M22 33 B4
Woodland Ave
Crewe CW1 190 C2
Lymm WA13 19 A1
Nantwich CW5 205 A3
Newton-le-W WA12 2 C2
Widnes WA8 12 C1
Woodland Bank CH2 96 C1
Woodland Cl SK11 84 A2
Woodland Ct ST7 193 B2
Woodland Dr WA13 19 A1
Woodland End SK11 84 A2
Woodland Gdns CW1 190 B3
Woodland Rd
Ellesmere Port CH65 70 A1
Rode Heath ST7 193 C4
Woodland View
Ellesmere Port CH66 69 A4
Whaley Bridge SK23 65 C1
Woodland Wlk
Bebington CH62 43 B4
Runcorn WA7 24 A1
Woodlands Ave
Chester CH1 118 A2
Congleton CW12 156 B2
Kidsgrove ST7 194 B1
Woodlands Cl
Cheadle SK8 35 A4
Eaton CW6 147 A4
Neston CH64 66 B4
Woodlands Cres WA16 29 B2
Woodlands Ct
Altrincham WA15 238 E5
18 Knutsford WA16 57 A1
Woodlands Dr
Chester CH2 118 C2
Goostrey CW4 107 C1
Knutsford WA16 57 A1
Warrington WA4 17 B2
Woodlands Gr CW8 77 C2
Woodlands Ind Est WA12 2 B3
Woodlands Inf Sch CH66 69 C1
Woodlands Jun Sch
CH66 69 C1
Woodlands La
Altrincham WA15 238 E5
Chester CH3 119 A1
Woodlands Parkway
WA15 238 E6
Woodlands Pk CW12 156 B2
Woodlands Rd
Altrincham WA14,WA15 238 E5
Handforth SK9 34 C2
Hartford CW8 103 B3
High Lane SK12 38 A3
Huntington CH3 142 A3
Macclesfield SK11 112 B3
Neston CH64 66 B4
New Mills SK22 39 A4
Sale M33 242 C6
Wilmslow SK9 33 C1
Woodlands Rd E CW8 103 B3
Woodlands The
Higher Wincham CW9 80 A3
Northwich CW8 78 C1
Woodlands Way CW6 146 B1
Woodlark Cl CW7 150 A4
Woodlea Ave CH2 118 C4
Woodlea Cl CH62 43 B3
Woodlea Ct CW8 103 B4
Woodlea Dr SK10 87 C4
Woodleigh WA14 238 A5
Woodleigh Ct SK9 60 A1
Woodley Fold WA5 14 C2
Woodman St 2 SK1 240 E6
Woodmount Cl SK6 241 F2
Woodnoth Dr CW2 206 B3
Woodpecker Cl WA3 9 C2
Woodpecker Dr CW9 103 C2
Woodridge WA7 24 B1
Woodridings WA14 238 B3
Woodrow Way M44 11 C4
Woodruff Cl ST7 195 C1
Woodruff Wlk 14 M31 11 C2
Woods Ct WA12 2 A2
Woods Gr SK8 35 A4
Woods La SK8 35 A4
Woods Rd M44 11 C4
Woods The 4 WA14 238 E6
Woodsfin La CH3 183 C4
Woodshutt's St ST7 194 C1
Woodside
Ellesmere Port CH65 70 B1
Knutsford WA16 57 A1
Lawton-gate ST7 194 C2
Siddington SK11 110 A2
Woodside Ave
Alsager ST7 193 C2
Frodsham WA6 74 B4
Kidsgrove ST7 195 A1
Wistaston CW2 189 C1
Woodside Ct CH2 118 B2
Woodside Dr
High Lane SK6 37 C4
Sandbach CW11 175 B3
Woodside La Lymm WA13 19 A1
Poynton SK12 36 C2
Wistaston CW2 189 C1
Woodside Prim Sch WA7 49 B4
Woodside Rd
Blacon CH1 117 B3
Haydock WA11 1 C4
Warrington WA5 14 C3
Woodside St SK22 39 A3
Woodside Terr CW9 104 A2
Woodslands Rd CH4 141 A4
Woodsome Cl CH65 70 A1
Woodsome Dr CH65 70 A1
Woodstock Ave
Bramhall SK8 35 A4
Newton-le-W WA12 2 B1
Woodstock Cl SK10 87 A1
Woodstock Dr CW10 151 C3
Woodstock Gdns WA4 26 C3
Woodstock Gr WA8 12 B1
Woodstock Rd WA14 238 C8
Woodthorn Cl WA4 24 C2
Woodvale WA14 238 C2
Woodvale Cl WA2 8 C1
Woodvale Rd
Ellesmere Port CH66 69 B3
Knutsford WA16 82 A4
Woodview Cres WA8 22 A4
Woodview Rd WA8 22 A4
Woodville Dr M33 242 A7
Woodville Pl WA8 12 B1
Woodville Rd
Altrincham WA14 238 C3
Sale M33 242 A7
Woodward St CW8 77 B1
Woodward Wlk CH3 121 B2
Woodyear Rd CH62 43 C4
Woolacombe Cl WA4 16 B1
Woolaston Dr ST7 193 B2
Woolden Rd M44 11 A4
Woollam Dr CH66 69 B4
Woolley Ave SK12 36 B1
Woolley Cl WA6 49 B1
Woolmer Cl WA3 10 A3
Woolston Ave CW12 157 A1
Woolston CE Prim Sch
WA1 17 B4
Woolston Com High Sch
WA1 17 A4
Woolston Com Prim Sch
WA1 17 B4
Woolston Dr CW2 206 C1
Woolston Grange Ave
WA1 9 B1
Woolston Rd WA11 1 B4
Woolton Ct CH66 69 C4
Woore Prim Sch CW3 232 A1
Woore Rd Audlem CW3 230 B2
Buerton CW3 230 B2
Wootton St SK14 241 D8
Worcester Ave
Denton M34 241 A5
3 Golborne WA3 3 A4
Worcester Cl
Romiley SK6 241 A1
Talke ST7 210 B4
Warrington WA5 15 B3
Worcester Pl CH1 118 A2
Worcester St CH65 70 B3
Worcester Wlk 3 CH65 70 B3
Wordsworth Ave
Warrington WA4 16 A1
Widnes WA8 22 C4
Wordsworth Cl
7 Sandbach CW11 174 B3
Wistaston CW2 189 C1
Wordsworth Cres CH1 118 A3
Wordsworth Dr CW1 190 C2
Wordsworth Ho SK10 86 C1
Wordsworth Mews CH1 118 A3
Wordsworth Sq CH1 118 A3
Wordsworth Way
Alsager ST7 193 B2
Ellesmere Port CH66 69 C1
Works La CW9 79 C1
World Way M90 33 A4
Worleston CE Prim Sch
CW5 188 C3
Worleston Cl CW10 151 B3
Wornish Nook CW11 154 C1
Worrall St
Congleton CW12 156 C2
Stockport SK3 240 E3
Worsborough Ave WA5 15 A3
Worsley Ave
Saughall CH1 117 A4
Warrington WA4 16 C2
Worsley Dr CW12 157 A1
Worsley Rd WA4 16 A1
Worsley St Golborne WA3 3 A4
Warrington WA5 15 C4
Worth Prim Sch SK12 36 C1
Worthing St CW9 104 B4
Worthington Ave 16 M31 11 C2
Worthington Cl
Henbury SK11 111 B4
Nantwich CW5 205 A3
Runcorn WA7 50 A4
Worthington Ct
Chester CH2 118 B2
Sale M33 242 E6
Worthington Prim Sch
M33 242 F6
Worthington Rd
Denton M34 241 B5
Sale M33 242 F6
Worthington St SK15 242 C1
Wr Twr (Mus)* CH1 118 A1
Wr Twr Rd CH64 41 C1
Wr Twr St CH1 237 A3
Wrayton Lodge M33 242 B5
Wrekin Way CH4 140 C3
Wren Ave CW4 129 B1
Wren Cl Crewe CW1 189 C4
Macclesfield SK10 87 A1
Runcorn WA7 50 A3
Warrington WA3 9 C2
Wrenburry Cl ST5 210 B1
Wrenbury Cres SK3 240 C2
Wrenbury Dr SK8 239 E6
Wrenbury Hall Dr CW5 217 A3
Wrenbury Heath Rd
CW5 217 B3
Wrenbury Ind Est CW5 217 A2
Wrenbury Prim Sch
CW5 216 C2
Wrenbury Rd Aston CW5 217 A2
Marbury SY14 201 B1
Wrenbury Sta CW5 217 A2
Wrenbury Wlk M33 242 E5
Wrenmere Cl CW11 174 C4
Wrenshot La WA16 29 B3
Wrexham Cl
Biddulph ST8 179 B1
Warrington WA5 7 C1
Wrexham Ind Est (Ystad Ddiwdiannol Wrecsam)
LL13 196 A1
Wrexham Rd
Bickerton SY14 200 A4
Bulkeley SY14,CW6 184 C1
Burland CW5 203 B4
Chester CH4 141 A2
Faddiley CW5,CW6 202 B3
Holt LL13 196 A4
Malpas SY14 212 C1
Pulford CH4 162 C3
Wright Ave CW9 104 B3
Wright Cres WA8 23 A3
Wright St
Ashton-u-Lyne OL6 242 A4
Kidsgrove ST7 194 B1
Wright Tree Villas M44 11 B3
Wright's La
Burtonwood WA5 6 C2
Sandbach CW11 175 B3
Wrights La WA5 13 C1
Wrigley La SK10 86 A2
Wrigley Rd WA11 1 C3
Wrinehill Rd CW5 220 C4
Wroxham Cl Chester CH2 237 B4
Helsby WA6 73 A2
Wroxham Rd WA5 14 C3
Wrynose Rd CH62 43 C4
Wyatt St SK4 240 E6
Wybersley Rd SK6 38 A4
Wybunbury Delves CE Prim Sch CW5 220 A4
Wybunbury La CW5 205 C2
Wybunbury Rd
Willaston (nr Nantwich) CW5 205 B3
Wybunbury CW5 220 A4
Wych House Bank CW5 204 B3
Wych House La CW10 128 B1
Wych La SK10 62 B3
Wyche Ave CW5 204 B3
Wyche Cl CW9 104 C3
Wyche La CW6 185 C4
Wyche Prim Sch CW5 204 C3
Wyche Rd CW6 185 C4
Wychelm Rd M31 11 C2
Wychwood WA14 238 B1
Wychwood Ave WA13 18 B2
Wychwood Pk CW2 207 A1
Wycliffe Ave SK9 60 A4
Wycliffe Ct CH2 119 A1
Wycliffe Rd
Ellesmere Port CH65 69 C2
Haydock WA11 1 C4
Wycliffe St SK4 240 D6
Wyedale CH65 70 A2
Wyedale Rd WA11 1 B3
Wyncroft Cl
Ellesmere Port CH65 70 A2
Widnes WA8 22 B4
Wyncroft Ct CW8 77 B1
Wyncroft Rd WA8 22 B4
Wynd The CW6 122 B2
Wyndham Cl Bramhall SK7 35 C4
Northwich CW9 103 C3
Wyndham Cres CH66 69 C1
Wyndham Rd CH1 117 B2
Wynfield Ave M22 33 C4
Wyngate Rd
Altrincham WA15 31 C4
Cheadle SK8 239 F1
Wynnstay Rd
Broughton CH4 139 B2
Sale M33 242 B7
Wynter Cl SY14 198 A2
Wythburn Gr WA7 49 C3
Wythens Rd SK8 34 A4
Wythenshawe Rd M33 242 F6

Y

Yagol Gynradd Holt Com Prim Sch LL13 196 B4
Yardley Ave WA5 15 C4
Yarmouth Rd WA5 14 C3
Yarrow Cl CH4 139 B2
Yarwood Cl CW8 103 C4
Yarwood St WA14 238 D3
Yarwoodheath La WA14 30 C4
Yatehouse La CW10 128 B4
Yates Cl WA5 15 B3
Yates Rd New Mills SK22 39 B4
Thornton-le-M CH2 71 C1
Yates St CW2 190 B1
Yealand Ave SK4 240 D7
Yeald Brow WA13 18 A2
Yeardsley Ave SK23 39 B2
Yeardsley Gn SK23 65 B4
Yeardsley La SK23 39 B2
Yearsleys La WA6 101 A3
Yeld La CW6 122 C4
Yeoford Dr WA14 238 B6
Yeoman Way CH66 69 C1
Yeovil Cl WA1 17 B4
Yerburgh St CH2 118 B2
Yew St SK4 240 C5
Yew Tree Ave WA12 2 A2
Yew Tree Bank CW6 145 A3
Yew Tree Cl
Broughton CH4 139 B2
Bulkeley SY14 184 B1
Little Budworth CW6 147 C4
Lymm WA13 18 C2
Macclesfield SK11 112 A3
Middlewich CW10 128 A1
Prestbury SK10 87 A4
Thornton-le-M CH2 71 C1
Wilmslow SK9 60 B4
Yew Tree Ct Alsager ST7 193 C1
Wimboldsley CW10 150 C2
Yew Tree Dr Barnton CW8 78 A2
Nantwich CW5 204 B3
Sale M33 242 E6
Yew Tree Farm Trad Est
WA11 2 A4
Yew Tree Gr SK8 239 A3
Yew Tree La
Appleton Thorn WA4 27 B3
Astbury CW12 178 B2
Bridgemere CW5 232 A3
Yew Tree Park Rd SK8 35 A3
Yew Tree Rd
Poynton SK10 37 A1
Wistaston CW2 206 A4
Yew Tree Way
Golborne WA3 3 A4
Prestbury SK10 87 B3
Yew Wlk 1 M31 11 C1
Yewdale Dr CH66 69 C1
Yewlands CW8 101 B3
Yewlands Dr WA16 57 B1
Yewtree Cl CH64 66 C4
Yewtree La SK12 36 C2
Yewtree Rd WA16 80 C2
Yonne The CH1 237 A2
York Ave Culcheth WA3 4 C1
Sale M33 242 B7
Warrington WA5 14 C4
York Cl Biddulph ST8 179 B1
Stockport SK8 240 A1
Talke ST7 210 B4
York Cres SK9 60 B4
York Ct 2 WA4 16 C1
York Dr Altrincham WA14 238 D1
Mickle Trafford CH2 96 C1
Warrington WA4 17 A1
Winsford CW7 149 B3
Wythenshaw M90 32 C4
York Ho 1 M33 242 B7
York Pl WA7 23 A1
York Rd Altrincham WA14 238 C1
Connah's Quay CH5 91 B1
Ellesmere Port CH65 70 B3
Irlam M44 11 B3
Sale M33 242 A7
Warrington WA4 17 A1
Widnes WA8 22 B4
York St Altrincham WA15 238 E3
Chester CH1 237 B3
Macclesfield SK10 112 C4
Stockport SK3 240 E4
Warrington WA4 16 B2
York Terr M33 242 A6
Yorkshire Rd M31 11 C1
Yorston Lodge Sch
WA16 56 C1
Yule St SK3 240 D4

Z

Zan Dr CW11 175 A2
Zan Ind Pk CW11 175 A2
Zara Ct WA11 1 B4
Zinnia Dr M44 11 C4
Zion St 21 CW8 103 C4

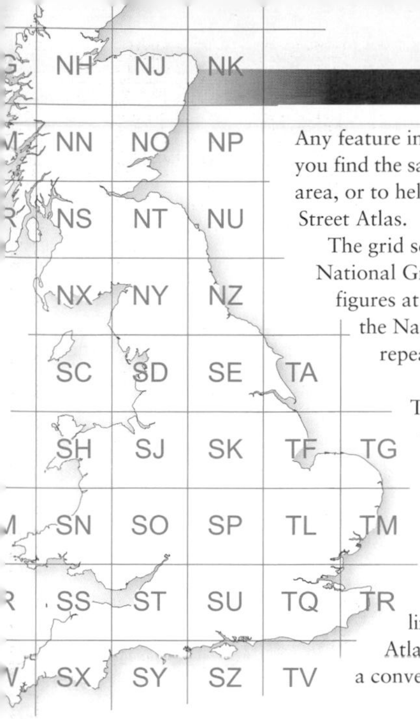
NH NJ NK
NN NO NP
NS NT NU
NX NY NZ
SC SD SE TA
SH SJ SK TF TG
SN SO SP TL TM
SS ST SU TQ TR
SX SY SZ TV

Using the Ordnance Survey National Grid

Any feature in this atlas can be given a unique reference to help you find the same feature on other Ordnance Survey maps of the area, or to help someone else locate you if they do not have a Street Atlas.

The grid squares in this atlas match the Ordnance Survey National Grid and are at 1 kilometre intervals. The small figures at the bottom and sides of every other grid line are the National Grid kilometre values (**00** to **99** km) and are repeated across the country every 100 km (see left).

To give a unique National Grid reference you need to locate where in the country you are. The country is divided into 100 km squares with each square given a unique two-letter reference. Use the administrative map to determine in which 100 km square a particular page of this atlas falls.

The bold letters and numbers between each grid line (**A** to **C**, **1** to **4**) are for use within a specific Street Atlas only, and when used with the page number, are a convenient way of referencing these grid squares.

Example *The railway bridge over DARLEY GREEN RD in grid square A1*

Step 1: Identify the two-letter reference, in this example the page is in **SP**

Step 2: Identify the 1 km square in which the railway bridge falls. Use the figures in the southwest corner of this square: Eastings **17**, Northings **74**. This gives a unique reference: **SP 17 74**, accurate to 1 km.

Step 3: To give a more precise reference accurate to 100 m you need to estimate how many tenths along and how many tenths up this 1 km square the feature is. This makes the bridge about **8** tenths along and about **1** tenth up from the southwest corner.

This gives a unique reference: **SP 178 741**, accurate to 100 m.

Eastings (read from left to right along the bottom) come before Northings (read from bottom to top). If you have trouble remembering say to yourself "Along the hall, THEN up the stairs"!

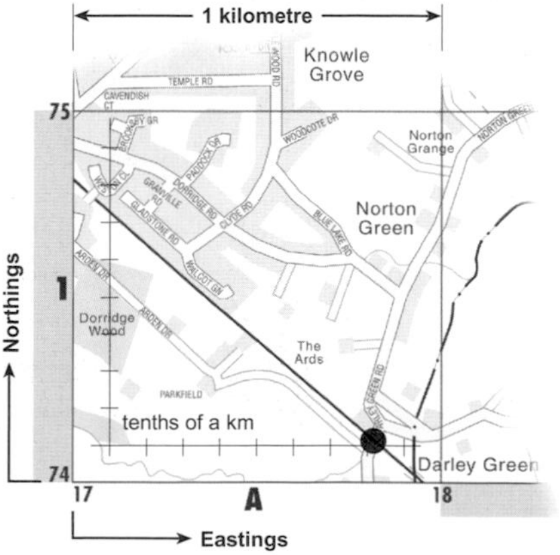
1 kilometre
Knowle Grove
TEMPLE RD
CAVENDISH CT
75
WOODCOTE DR
Norton Grange
Norton Green
BLUE LAKE RD
1
Northings
Dorridge Wood
ARDEN DR
The Ards
PARKFIELD
tenths of a km
74
Darley Green
17
A
18
Eastings

Notes

Addresses

Name and Address	Telephone	Page	Grid reference